W9-CKT-704

The Broadway Design Roster

The Broadway Design Roster

Designers and Their Credits

Bobbi Owen

Bibliographies and Indexes in the Performing Arts, Number 27

GREENWOOD PRESS
Westport, Connecticut • London

Library of Congress Cataloging-in-Publication Data

Owen, Bobbi.
  The broadway design roster : designers and their credits / Bobbi Owen.
      p. cm.—(Bibliographies and indexes in the performing arts, ISSN 0742–6933 ; no. 27)
  Includes bibliographical references and index.
  ISBN 0–313–31915–4 (alk. paper)
    1. Set designers—New York (State)—New York—Biography—Dictionaries. 2. Costume
  designers—New York (State)—New York—Biography—Dictionaries. 3. Stage lighting
  designers—New York (State)—New York—Biography—Dictionaries. I. Title. II. Series.
  PN2096.A1 O93 2002
  792′.025′09227471—dc21
  [B]   2002069612

British Library Cataloguing in Publication Data is available.

Library of Congress Catalog Card Number: 2002069612
ISBN: 0–313–31915–4
ISSN: 0742–6933

First published in 2003

Greenwood Press, 88 Post Road West, Westport, CT 06881
An imprint of Greenwood Publishing Group, Inc.
www.greenwood.com

Printed in the United States of America

The paper used in this book complies with the
Permanent Paper Standard issued by the National
Information Standards Organization (Z39.48–1984).

10 9 8 7 6 5 4 3 2 1

792.025
Owe

Contents

List of Illustrations

Preface

Nearly twenty years ago, I set out to write a book about the small group of designers who, I felt certain, established the field of American costume design. During a semester of supported research leave in fall 1983, I intended to write profiles of the ones I already knew were important, among them Irene Sharaff, Patricia Zipprodt, Lucinda Ballard, Miles White, Theoni V. Aldredge, and Raoul Pène du Bois. I also decided to identify major designers active earlier in the century and write profiles of them as well. And, I planned to see lots of plays and identify designers with developing careers. So I went to New York City, planning to stay as long as my friends Judy and David Adamson would have me; I confidently introduced myself to Dorothy Swerdlove at the New York Public Library for the Performing Arts with a couple of legal pads in hand. Reality struck quickly. Not only were there more important designers than I had realized, it was almost impossible to find out what they had designed, much less examine their aesthetic. I have now written four books and numerous articles, not just about costume designers, but scenery designers, lighting designers, and designers who work in multiple areas and am starting to think that I'm finally in control of the background information needed for the book I originally intended to write. I would not trade the time spent studying the nearly 2400 designers included in this book for anything, and hope I have provided a basis for further research for others as well as for myself.

Reference books are not written in isolation and I received assistance in many ways. At The University of North Carolina at Chapel Hill, my research was supported by the Institute for the Arts and Humanities, the Pogue Endowment, the Scholarly Publications Fund administered by The College of Arts and Sciences, and the Department of Dramatic Art. Several undergraduate and graduate students at UNC worked as my assistants, making copies in the library, surfing the web, filing, making phone calls, and generally being useful. They include Stacy Brackman, Regina Blanding, Jacqueline Brown, Jamie Linens, Shavonnie Ray, David Syracuse, Lisa Tice, Wes Walker and Tony Young. Regina Sullivan worked with me for several semesters while in graduate school and was especially helpful. Every time I opened folders containing information discovered when working on my previous books and saw familiar hand-writing, I was grateful once again for the assistance provided by Lynn Roundtree and Becket Royce. Suzanne Schultz Reed was helpful yet again finding leads to pursue on the West Coast as was Cynthia Stewart on the computer and Jennifer Cole in New York City. I also had help from Phyllis Ryan, Betty Futrell, Harriet Siler, Linwood Futrelle, and Karen McCullough.

The research for this book could not have been completed without the resources of several libraries. I was assisted by the helpful staff at The Billy Rose Theatre Collection in the New York Public Library for the Performing Arts, especially by Olive Wong and Christopher Frith. I want to thank in particular the tireless pages, notably Nailah Holmes, and their supervisor, Louise Martzinek. While using that archive, I had valuable conversations about American designers with Barbara Cohen-Stratyner, curator of exhibitions. I also found useful information at the British Library, the Museum of the City of New York, the Shubert Archive, and in the libraries of The University of North Carolina at Chapel Hill, particularly the Roland Holt Collection of theatre playbills and memorabilia from the first decades of the twentieth century in the Rare Book Collection.

When I did *Costume Design on Broadway, Designers and their Credits, 1915-1985* (Greenwood Press, 1987), Lexus-Nexus was not yet widely available and InfoTrac mainly indexed popular periodicals. Today there are indispensable electronic research tools, including Academic Universe, the Biography and Genealogy Master Index, the Social Security Database on Ancestry.com, the on-line London Times index, and even City Directories on-line. However, some of the best information I found, particularly about designers at the beginning of the twentieth century, remains available only by paging through dusty volumes and looking at microfilms.

My research benefitted most of all from personal contacts. I have corresponded with hundreds of designers through the years and find them always to be generous with time and information. In many cases, family members and colleagues of designers have been equally helpful. I hope I have summarized their work effectively and that the admiration I have for their creativity is evident in these pages. This book is dedicated to them all, but especially to the ones I couldn't identify or find much about. Designers don't thrive on being recognized, but their contribution deserves to be remembered.

Finally, I thank my husband, Gordon Ferguson, for his expertise with computers of course, but mostly for his love. It's not just when I'm writing books that I rely on him.

Introduction

Ferdinand.   *This is a most majestic vision, and*
                  Harmonious charmingly. May I be bold
                  To think these spirits?
Prospero.   *Spirits, which by mine art*
                  I have from their confines call'd to enact
                  My present fancies.
Ferdinand.   *Let me live here ever...*
                    —The Tempest: *Act IV, Scene 1, 117-122*

Many people identify the theater with performers, directors and plays. For them, going to the theater means watching a favorite actor, admiring a new interpretation of a classic, or being among the first to attend a new play. For others, however, going to the theatre means an opportunity to see how the designers provide a visual interpretation to support the text, the acting, and the directing. As long as plays have been presented, choices have been made about the environment in which they occur, the garments the performers wear, and how to focus the audience's attention.

This book contains brief biographies of the 2,372 scenery, costume and lighting designers who worked on Broadway in the twentieth century, beginning with the 1899-1900 season and ending with the 2000-2001 season. The biographies are followed by a list of each designer's credits. The book contains appendices that list the winners of major design awards and some original renderings to illustrate the range of twentieth century Broadway productions. A selected bibliography and an index of plays are also included.

The emphasis is on individuals rather than companies, but some small businesses formed by designers have been retained as examples. As with modern playbills, suppliers of theatrical scenery, lighting instruments and garments are included with the acknowledgements. The entries for designers who work in groups and some whose names have changed or who use pseudonyms have been consolidated into one entry. In these instances, the reader is referred to another heading. For example the three designers who collaborated as "Motley" are all represented in that entry rather than under their individual names. Aliases have been cross-referenced whenever possible.

This book does not simply compile information available in theater programs, but represents the best judgement currently available about design credits. It usually contains the same information that can be found by reading a program, but before designers names were routinely included in playbills, they could only be identified via other sources, including press releases, reviews, news articles, contracts, personal papers, and through research done by scholars.

The list of credits below the designer's name contains notes set in parentheses when the program stated that a designer contributed specific elements to a production, such as a gown for a particular performer or the scenery for one scene rather than an entire production. It uses a dagger symbol (†) to indicate collaborations with other designers. This symbol also refers the reader to the index which lists all the credits together. It is necessary to read both citations for a comprehensive summary.

The index, containing the nearly 10,000 plays produced on Broadway in the twentieth century, is presented in strict alphabetical order by the designers' last names, rather than by area of design. The reader is urged to review the entry for the entire production because many times more than one designer was involved with the scenery, costumes, and/or lights.

What qualifies as a Broadway play is the subject of considerable discussion. The annual editions of *Best Plays* and *Theatre World* do not always agree. These discrepancies are further complicated because the definitions of eligibility for Tony Award nominations and the designation of theater spaces change. In an attempt to be inclusive, the categorization of productions made by the curators in the New York Public Library for the Performing Arts and by the American Theatre Wing have been used. The new "Internet Broadway Database" may help resolve the problem, but the information contained in it is still in the process of being verified. Therefore, the nature and definition of Broadway plays and theaters which has changed considerably during the twentieth century remains in flux.

In most cases, playbills were reviewed to obtain the names of designers, particularly during those times when they were included among the acknowledgements, if published at all. Unfortunately, it was impossible to find programs for 62 plays produced between 1900 and 1914, and so a few designers from those years may have been inadvertently omitted.

Searching through playbills for designers makes fascinating reading. The playbill from *The Man in the Moon* performed in the New York The-

atre during the last season of the nineteenth century contains two long
sections of acknowledgements at the very back. The first is called "The
Scenery" and tells the reader that D. Frank Dodge designed Act I, Scene
1 and Act II, Scenes 1 and 3. Henry E. Hoyt designed Act I, Scenes 2
and 3 and St. John Lewis designed Act II, Scene 2. Act III was designed
and painted by Ernest Albert. These citations, clearly presented, suggest
collaboration and an intricate production. These credits are followed by
additional ones:

THE APPOINTMENTS:

Costumes from designs of Mme. Seidle, executed by Mesdames Ripley and Caughley.
Costumes of the "Orchid Ballet" designed and hand-painted by Mme. Seidle and executed
by F. H. McCoun.
Scenery constructed by Messrs. George Williams and John Cunningham.
Construction of "The Halls of Columbia" by Mr. John Cunningham.
Properties by Mr. Edward Seidle.
Electrical Effects by Messrs. Jos. Lee and J. Whalen
Illuminating Effects by The New York Calcium Light Company.
Artificial Vegetables and Fruit by The Theatrical Flower Decorating Company.
Perruquiers, Messrs. Gluth & Coyle.
Shoes by A. J. Cammeyer.
Tights by the Brooklyn Knitting Co.
Uniforms executed by Messrs. Warnock & Co. and Smith, Gray & Co.
Draperies, Carpets, etc., from the establishment of Mr. John Wanamaker.
Leather Furniture in the Promenade de Luxe from the Pierce Manufacturing Co.
Gas and Electrical Fixtures from the establishment of Black, Boyd & Co.
The American Watchman's Time Detecter Electric Clock used in this establishment.
Messrs. Hardman, Peck & Co.'s Piano used in this establishment exclusively.
The Gram-o-phones operated between acts in the Main Corridor are furnished by
The National Gram-o-phone Corporation.

Playbill: *The Man in the Moon* by Louis Harrison and Stanislaus Stange.
From the copy in the Roland Holt Collection in the Rare Book Collection,
The University of North Carolina at Chapel Hill. By permission.

This book is not a *history* of theatrical design on Broadway, but it does
present one basis for such a study: all the scenic, costume and lighting
designers who worked on Broadway during the twentieth century, together
with their credits. It is intended to be a record of the contributions made
by designers to productions. The biographies are meant to provide an
introduction to the designers' careers and some context, however brief, in
which to view their credits amassed on Broadway.

THE BROADWAY DESIGN ROSTER:

Designers and Their Credits

Designers and Their Credits

Eleanor Plaisted Abbott

Eleanor Plaisted Abbott an illustrator and artist who contributed costume designs to a 1909 Broadway production, was born in Lincoln, Maine in 1875. She studied at the Philadelphia School of Design, in Paris, and at the Drexel Institute with Howard Pyle. She contributed regularly to *Scribner's Magazine* and other periodicals, as well as illustrating books including *Treasure Island*. Widely exhibited during her lifetime, she died in 1935.

Costumes: 1909 *The Barber of New Orleans*

Franklin Abbott

Franklin Abbott designed the settings for one production on Broadway in 1924. An architect, he was associated with Peabody, Wilson and Brown at 389 Fifth Avenue, New York City in 1918 and resided in Philadelphia. In the early 1930s, he established his own firm at 420 Lexington Avenue.

Sets: 1924 *The Way Things Happen*

Harry L. Abbott

Harry L. Abbott was set designer for a single Broadway production in 1938. As early as 1918 he was president and treasurer of Abbott Scrim Profile Company, remaining in that position through the early 1930s. The company was located at 539 West 46th Street in 1918 and at 266 West 44th Street, New York City in 1932.

Sets: 1938 *The Wild Duck*†

James Acheson

James Acheson has won Academy Awards for best costume design for *The Last Emperor, Dangerous Liaisons* and *Restoration*. Born in Leicester, England, he studied at the Wimbledor School of Art, where he received a B.A. degree in 1968. Known primarily as a film designer (*Monty Python's The Meaning of Life* and *Little Buddha* among many others), he has also done costumes for plays, operas including *Le Nozze di Figaro* at the Metropolitan Opera and for television, notably *Dr. Who* from 1973-1976 and 1978-1989.

Costumes: 1995 *His Excellency the Governor*

Lowell Achziger

Lowell Achziger was born in 1949 in Denver, Colorado and received a B.F.A. at Carnegie Mellon University. A specialist in lighting for film and television, he designed lights for the original off-Broadway production of *Godspell*. His credits include designs for the McCarter Theater Center in Princeton, New Jersey and the Academy Theatre in Lake Forest, Illinois.

Lights: **1982** *Eminent Domain*

Mitch Acker

Mitch Acker first designed lighting on Broadway in 1981. He has designed lights for rock concerts, night clubs in Atlantic City, New Jersey, and for the Yarmouth Playhouse in Yarmouth, Massachusetts and the Hollywood Playhouse in Ft. Lauderdale, Florida. Off-Broadway he designed lights for plays including *Live at Crystal Six*. In 1989 he formed TTE Scenic Studio in Atlanta, Georgia, specializing in exhibits, industry shows and theater construction. TTE became part of Production Resource Group L.L.C. in the late 1990s.

Lights: 1981 *Marlowe*

P. Dodd Ackerman

Philip Dodd Ackerman, Sr. (also known as Ackermann) initially received credit for the scene designs of a Broadway show in 1904, after which time his name appeared in numerous playbills until he retired in 1938. Originally from Florida where he was born in 1876, he studied art in Paris and Germany before beginning his career. His design expertise was generally used for scenery, although he contributed lighting designs to two productions in the late 1920s. He was the principal designer of P. Dodd Ackerman Scenic Studio and occasionally collaborated on designs for large productions. Ackerman died on January 5, 1963.

Sets: 1904 *Paris by Night* **1906** *The Greater Love*† (Act II); *The Three of Us* **1909** *A Citizen's Home*; *The Newlyweds and Their Baby*; *The Only Law*; *A Woman of Impulse*† **1911** *Dr. De Luxe*† (Acts I, II); *The Lily and the Prince*† (Act II); *Thais*† (Act I, II, IV) **1912** *The Firefly*† (Act II, III) **1913** *The Purple Road*† (Act III) **1914** *Dancing Around*† **1915** *A World of Pleasure*† **1916** *Any House*; *Her Soldier Boy*†; *The Passing Show of 1916*†; *Pay-Day*; *Robinson Crusoe, Jr.*† **1917** *De Luxe Annie*†; *Furs and Frills*; *The Grass Widow* **1918** *The Passing Show of 1918*† **1919** *Carnival*; *A Lonely Romeo*; *Take It from Me* **1920** *The Broken Wing*; *The Guest of Honor*; *Her Family Tree*†; *Little Miss Charity*; *The Passion Flower*; *Three Live Ghosts* **1921** *Danger*; *The Ghost Between*; *The Nightcap*; *Nobody's Money*; *The Skirt*; *The Title* **1922** *The Advertising of Kate*; *For Goodness Sake*; *Frank Fay's Fables*; *Go Easy, Mabel*; *Kempy*; *The Rotters* **1923** *Chicken Feed*; *Ginger*; *Little Jessie James*; *Magnolia*; *Polly Preferred*; *Stepping Stones*†; *Thumbs Down*; *The Wasp* **1924** *Alloy*; *Betty Lee*; *Conscience*; *The Lady Killer*; *My Girl*; *Pigs*; *Sitting Pretty*; *Stepping Stones*† **1925** *Alias the Deacon*; *All Dressed Up*; *The Green Hat*; *A Kiss in a Taxi*; *Merry, Merry*; *No, No Nanette*; *The Pelican*; *The Piker* **1926** *2 Girls Wanted*†; *Castles in the Air*†; *The Climax*; *The Ghost Train*; *The Girl Friend*; *Twinkle, Twinkle*; *Up the Line*; *A Weak Woman*; *What's the Big Idea*; *The Woman Disputed* **1927** *The Barker*; *Crime*; *Excess Baggage*; *Half a Widow*; *Honor Be Damned*; *It Is to Laugh*; *Just Fancy*; *Kempy*; *Lady Alone*; *Lost*; *Madame X*; *My Princess*; *Sinner*; *The Spring Board*; *Trial of Mary Dugan*; *Window Panes* **1928** *Caravan*; *Crashing Through*; *Cross My Heart*; *The Father*; *Jealousy*; *Just a Minute*; *La Gringa*; *The Lady of the Orchids*; *Marriage on Approval*; *Relations* **1929** *Conflict*; *Freddy*; *Headquarters*; *The Humbug*; *Mountain Fury*; *Murder on the Second Floor* **1930** *The Challenge of Youth*; *Courtesan*; *Dear Old England*; *A Farewell to Arms*; *Frankie and Johnnie*; *The Long Road*; *The Ninth Guest*; *Phantoms*; *Recapture*; *The Tyrant* **1931** *Cold in Sables*; *It Never Rains*; *Nikki*†; *Steel* **1932** *The Budget*; *The Devil Passes*; *East of Broadway*; *The Girl Outside*; *The Inside Story*; *Life Begins*; *Nona* **1933** *Marathon*; *Move On, Sister*; *Sailor, Beware*; *Strange Gods*; *An Undesirable Lady* **1934** *Birthday*; *Brittle Heaven*; *A Divine Moment*; *Hotel Alimony*; *No Questions Asked*; *Picnic*; *Queer People*; *The Red Cat*; *Richard of Bordeaux*; *Strangers at Home*; *Yesterday's Orchids* **1935** *Abide with Me*; *How Beautiful with Shoes*; *Little Shop*; *Macbeth*; *Othello*; *Sailor, Beware*; *Stick-in-the-Mud*; *A Touch of Brimstone* **1936** *Among Those Sailing*; *In the Bag* **1937** *A House in the Country* **1938** *The Happiest Days*; *Time and the Conways*

Lights: 1927 *Honor Be Damned* **1929** *Hot Chocolates*†

P. Dodd Ackerman Studio

P. Dodd Ackerman was the principal designer at the P. Dodd Ackerman Scenic Studio, located at 140 West 39th Street, New York City. Ackerman worked in creative association with Ben Glick and D. Frank Dodge. Members of the Board of Directors were Charles Chapman, Vice-President and Louis Ehrenberg, Secretary. The scenic studio produced designs for many productions between 1915 and 1934 and also painted productions for other designers. For additional information, see "P. Dodd Ackerman."

Sets: **1909** *Idols* **1910** *Bright Eyes* **1911** *The Girl of My Dreams* **1913** *What Happened to Mary* **1915** *The Peasant Girl* (as: Ackerman Brothers) **1916** *If I Were King*† **1917** *Barbara* **1918** *The Riddle: Woman* **1919** *Our Pleasant Sins* **1920** *Betty Be Good* **1921** *The Six-Fifty* **1923** *Aren't We All?*; *If Winter Comes*; *Not So Fast*†; *What's Your Wife Doing* **1924** *Shipwrecked*; *Sweet Seventeen* **1925** *Aren't We All?*; *Patsy* **1926** *Head or Tail*; *The Noose*; *Treat 'Em Rough* **1927** *Blood Money*; *Merry-Go-Round*; *Yes, Yes, Yevette* **1928** *Hello, Yourself* **1929** *Be Your Age*; *Her Friend, the King* **1930** *Five Star Final*; *I Want My Wife* **1931** *Divorce Me, Dear* **1932** *Troilus and Cressida* **1934** *Every Thursday* **1935** *A Lady Detained*

Costume Acknowledgments

Costume Acknowledgments have been an important component of theatrical playbills since the first performances on Broadway stages. The index of this book lists "ACKS" for hundreds of productions where no credit to an individual was to be found but mention of some entity that provided costumes was recorded. The credits in this category come from many areas of costume, including department stores, construction houses, rental houses, dyers and painters, embroiderers, fabric shops, as well as sources for wigs, hosiery, and shoes. The category also includes numerous small custom shops, tailors, fashion houses and occasionally theaters, which supplied either raw materials or costumes to a production without naming an individual as costume designer.

Lighting Acknowledgments

Even in the days before producers acknowledged the need for lighting designers, they were aware of the need to illuminate actors. When electricity became generally available producers employed electricians and rented or purchased lighting equipment. Playbills in the early years of the twentieth century occasionally mention the name of an electrician and his staff, an "electrical engineer," or some other individual, often a playwright or director, who created critical lighting effects. More often credit was given to an equipment company, some of which specialized in theatrical lighting. The plays in the index of this volume that make no reference to a lighting designer had no designer cited. "ACKS" means a company provided lighting equipment to a production and was acknowledged for that contribution.

Scenery Acknowledgments

Scenic designers were the first designers to consistently receive credit for their contributions to theatrical productions. The index of this book uses the citation "ACKS" when no designer is listed, but acknowledgements exist for scenic elements or properties. Quite often there are references to scenic studios, some of which remain active today. Scenic studios have been part of theater production since the nineteenth century, when firms such as Joseph and Phil Harker in London and Cirker and Robbins in the United States supplied standard settings for plays in the repertoire of a company and to those requiring contemporary furniture. Collaborations between designers, studios, interior decorators, and properties were often acknowledged in the back of playbills as the profession of scenic designer developed.

Daniel Adams

Daniel Adams created the lighting design for numerous tours, concerts and appearances by stars of the entertainment business. His credits include David Bowie's 1974 tour, Diana Ross' return engagement at Caesar's Palace, and the 1977 United States tour *Evening with Diana Ross*.

Lights: 1977 *Lily Tomlin in "Appearing Nightly"*

Eugene V. Adams

The scenery for a 1912 production was designed by Eugene V. Adams. His home in New York was at 47 West 106th Street.

Sets: 1912 *Our Wives*† (Acts I, II)

John Wolcott Adams

John Wolcott Adams, who died in New York City on June 23, 1925, was born in Worcester, Massachusetts in 1874, the descendant of two presidents of the United States. He was a popular magazine illustrator and artist whose choice of favorite subject matter and style was influenced by his teacher, Howard Pyle. His theatrical experience was mainly as an actor. In addition to designing a set on Broadway for Walter Hampden he appeared in the 1913 film, *Saved by Parcel Post*.

Sets: 1923 *The Jolly Roger*†

Kevin Adams

Kevin Adams was born in Texas in the 1960s and received his undergraduate education at the University of Texas at Austin. His M.F.A. is from the California Institute of the Arts where he studied with Michael Devine. His training and early professional experience, mainly on the West Coast, was as a scenic designer, but gradually he started lighting his own sets and now works primarily as a lighting designer. His credits include numerous productions for performance artists, and plays at the Williamstown Theatre Festival notably *Camino Real*, the Steppenwolf Theatre, the Huntington Theatre, Manhattan Theatre Club and the Public Theatre, including Anna Deavere Smith's *House Arrest*. The recipient of an NEA/TCG Design Fellowship, Adams has also received a Lucille Lortel Award for *The Mineola Twins*, among many Drama Desk,

Drama Logue and LA Weekly nominations and awards for his designs. He has also worked as a video artist and created photo-based art which has been featured in exhibitions and is represented in the permanent photography collection of the Los Angeles County Museum of Art. Twenty-first century designs include *Hedda Gabler* with Kate Burton and *Sexaholix - A Love Story* written by and starring John Leguizamo in the 2001-2001 Broadway season. Other recent productions include *Hedwig and the Angry Inch, And God Created Great Whales* and *Betty's Summer Vacation.*

Lights: 1998 *Getting and Spending* 2001 *A Class Act*

Eric Adeney

Eric Adeney (also known as Eric Ardenay) was an artist and actor who collaborated with Donald Wolfitt on the designs for the 1947 production of *Hamlet* on Broadway. He also appeared with Wolfitt in *As You Like It, Richard III, Othello* and *A Midsummer Night's Dream*, all in London. He appeared in the silent film version of *Hamlet* as Francisco and Reynoldo. Throughout the 1940s, he designed scenery for many productions in which he also performed, including *King Lear* and *The Romance of David Garrick*. In 1950 his studio was located on Albert Street in London.

Sets: 1947 *Hamlet*†
Costumes: 1947 *Hamlet*†

William Adler

A credit line reading "The All-Nation costumes designed and made by William Adler, New York" appeared above the cast list with the Broadway debut he made in 1906, a remarkable accomplishment in a time when costume designers were rarely cited, much less acknowledged on the first page of a theater program. His costume house was located at 105 West 39th Street and he lived at 840 228th Street, New York City during the first decade of the twentieth century.

Costumes: 1906 *Seeing New York* 1913 *Somewhere Else*† (The "Lord Fauntleroy" costume)

Stephen Adnitt

Stephen Adnitt, a British costume designer has been creating the wardrobe and accessories for Dame Edna when she appears on television and in theaters since the mid-1980s, including the 2001 production *Dame Edna: The Royal Tour*. He has designed extensively for other television programs and stars, including Cila Black for whom he has created costumes since the mid-1980s. He has done costumes for the *U.K. Gladiators*, dance, plays, and for *Fire and Ice*, an ice ballet for Torvill and Dean. His costumes for Barry Humphries' creation Dame Edna reflect changing contemporary fashions in an especially clever way. His designs have been exhibited in the Royal Gallery in Worcester, England and at the Victoria Arts Center in Melbourne, Australia.

Costumes: 1999 *Dame Edna*

Gilbert Adrian

Gilbert Adrian, known for most of his career simply as "Adrian" was born in Naugatuck, Connecticut in 1903 as Adrian Dolph Greenburg. Before he moved to Hollywood initially to design for Rudolf Valentino, he created costumes for musical revues. He spent the majority of his career designing costumes for the movies, and created many styles which werevery popular, including the "Letty Lynton" gown. This success led him to open his own custom design business in Beverly Hills after designing for M-G-M from 1925 to 1939. Married to Janet Gaynor and the father of one son, Robin, he retired to Brazil in 1952 to paint landscapes. He returned to Hollywood in 1958 and died a year later while beginning to design *Camelot* for which he posthumously received a Tony Award. The award was shared with Tony Duquette who, at the request of the producers, completed the designs after Adrian's death.

Costumes: 1921 *George White's Scandals*† (Women's costumes) **1923** *Fashions of 1924* ("Indu-Chi"); *Nifties of 1923*† **1944** *In Bed We Cry* (Miss Chase's gowns); *Mrs. January and Mr. X*; *Slightly Scandalous* **1946** *Obsession* (Gowns) **1960** *Camelot*†

Joan Adrian

Joan Adrian served as costume supervisor for one production on Broadway during the 1933-34 season. She also played the role of "A Guest" in the same play. She left the show in late 1934 to move to Hollywood for a career acting in films.

Costumes: 1934 *Are You Decent?* (Costume Supervisor)

Patricia Adshead

Patricia Adshead, a native of Cheshire, England designed two shows in the 1970s. Educated in England and the United States, she has designed costumes in regional theaters, for film and daytime television. Her off-Broadway credits in the 1970s include, *Ionescopades*, *The Two Orphans* and *Why Hannah's Skirt Won't Stay Down* and in the 1980s *The Gay Divorcee*, *The Hired Man*, and *The Phantom Lady*.

Costumes: 1975 *Angel Street* **1979** *Once a Catholic*

Nanzi Adzima

The daughter of George and Rita Edgerton Adzima, Nanzi Adzima was born on March 9, 1949 in Westfield, Massachusetts. She received a B.F.A. in 1971 from the New York University School of the Arts where she designed her first play, *The Relapse*. Her professional debut occurred in 1973 at the New York Shakespeare Festival's Public Theatre with the opening of *Siamese Connection*. She has numerous commercial and public television credits, and received two Emmy Awards for the daytime drama *Guiding Light* and a nomination for *Square One TV*. Her costume designs have been seen in many regional theaters, including the Milwaukee Repertory, the Indiana Repertory Theatre, Actors Theatre of Louisville, the McCarter Theater Center, PlayMakers Repertory Company and Syracuse Stage.

Costumes: 1981 *The Five O'clock Girl* **1987** *Safe Sex*

Argemira Affonso

Affonso Argemire designed costumes for a 1997 Broadway production.

Costumes: 1997 *Forever Tango*

Raymond Aghayan

Ray Aghayan, the son of an Iranian couturier was born Reymond G. Aghayan in Tehran in 1927 (some sources suggest 1934) and originally moved to California to study architecture. Although he has designed occasionally in New York, the majority of his creative activity has been on the West Coast where he works extensively in television and film. In addition he has created costumes for nightclub performers and revues. Mr. Aghayan has had a long term association with Bob Mackie with whom he's created costumes for many of Hollywood's most glamorous stars. They collaborated on the designs for the long-running Carol Burnett Show and created ready-to-wear collections which featured evening clothes. His numerous awards include two Emmy's for costume design for the *Annual Academy Awards Presentations*, one in 1988 and the other in 1992.

Costumes: **1960** *Vintage '60*† **1962** *The Egg* **1970** *Applause* **1971** *On the Town*† **1974** *Lorelei*† (Miss Channing's costumes)

David Agress

The many and varied lighting design credits for David Agress include the *World Figure Skating Championships* and the *Super Bowl 2000 Half-Time Show, Lulie*, a musical for children by Yo Yo Ma, concerts for Liza Minnelli, Chita Rivera and Bette Midler, and projects for IBM, Reebok, Cadillac, and Wal-Mart among others. He has designed lights for operas in the United States and Europe, ballets including *But Not For Me* for the Martha Graham Company as well as plays. Honors include two Ace Awards.

Lights: **1990** *Michael Feinstein in Concert* **1991** *Liza Minnelli: Stepping Out at Radio City* **1997** *King David*

Paul Aimes

Paul Aimes designed costumes for one show in 1927.

Costumes: **1927** *Polly of Hollywood*

Christopher Akerlind

Christopher Akerlind, who designed lights for the first time on Broadway in 1990 was born in Hartford, Connecticut on May 1, 1962, the son of Raymond and Gail Akerlind. He received a B.A. from Boston University where he launched his design career with *Hamlet*. His M.F.A. is from the Yale University School of Drama. A busy, prolific designer for theater, dance and opera, he worked extensively as an assistant to Jennifer Tipton; he credits her as an influential force in his career along with Mark Lamos. A nomination for a Maharam Award (subsequently renamed an American Theatre Wing Design Award) accompanied his Broadway debut with *The Piano Lesson*. He spent two years as co-artistic director of the Portland Stage Company where he also designed lights for many productions and is the resident lighting designer at Opera Theatre of St. Louis. Credits in other regional theaters include the Guthrie Theatre, La Jolla Playhouse, the McCarter Theater Center, the Huntington Theatre, Opera Theatre of Saint Louis, Chicago's Court Theatre, and the Dallas Theatre Center. In New York his many designs include *The Skriker, Silence*, and *Troilus and Cressida* for the Public Theatre, and productions at C.S.C., New York Theatre Workshop, Lincoln Center, the American Jewish Theatre, and Playwrights Horizons.

Lights: **1990** *The Piano Lesson* **1994** *Philadelphia, Here I Come!* **1996** *Seven Guitars* **2000** *The Tale of the Allergist's Wife*

D. M. Akin

D.M. Akin (also known as D. M. Aiken) created settings for two Broadway productions, one in 1908 and the other in 1917.

Sets: **1908** *Three Twins*† (as: D.M. Aiken) **1917** *Oh Boy!*

Ernest Albert

Ernest Albert was known primarily as a landscape artist although he contributed scenic designs and paintings to nearly 100 Broadway productions between the 1899-1900 season and 1918. He was born in Brooklyn, New York, and studied in New York City, learning scene painting under Harley Merry. In 1880 he became art and scenic director at Pope's Theatre in St. Louis, Missouri. He helped design color schemes for buildings at the 1893 World's Fair in Chicago. In 1894 he returned to New York where he did settings for numerous Shakespearean plays, often working in collaboration with other noted scene painters of his time, including D. Frank Dodge, Homer Emens and John C. Young. He continued to collaborate with other artists, as well as designing productions entirely by himself. In 1919 he was elected president of the Allied Artists of America. As a fine art painter he began to exhibit oils and watercolors at the turn of the twentieth century and devoted his talents to landscapes for the last twenty years of his life. Albert died at the age of 88 in New Canaan, Connecticut on March 26, 1946.

Sets: 1899 Ben Hur†; A Greek Slave† 1900 The Belle of Bohemia†; The Bostonians† (Act II); Broadway to Tokio†; The Casino Girl†; In the Palace of the King; The Moment of Death; Sag Harbor† (Act I); Sapho 1901 The Climbers†; The Girl from Up There†; The Liberty Belles; The Little Duchess; The New Yorkers†; Vienna Life† (Act II); When Knighthood Was in Flower† 1902 An American Invasion; Ben Hur†; The Billionaire; When Johnny Comes Marching Home† (Act III) 1903 The Fisher Maiden; A Japanese Nightingale† (Act I, III); The Jewel of Asia (Designed and painted); Mam'selle Napoleon; A Midsummer Night's Dream; Mr. Bluebeard†; Red Feather; The Rogers Brothers in London† (Act II) 1904 In Newport†; The Man from China; The Triumph of Love; The Usurper; The Virginian†; The Winter's Tale† 1905 The Earl and the Girl†; Happyland; The Money Makers; Once upon a Time; The Prodigal Son† 1906 The Blue Moon†; Brewster's Millions†; Forty-five Minutes from Broadway†; Gallops†; George Washington, Jr.†; Lincoln; The Parisian Model; The Tourists; Twiddle-Twaddle 1907 The Grand Mogul; The Rogers Brothers in Panama†; The Shoo-Fly Regiment; The White Hen† (Act I) 1908 Algeria; The Chaperons (Designed and painted); Fifty Miles from Boston†; The Gay Musician†; Golden Butterfly† (Act II); Little Nemo†; The Soul Kiss† 1909 Antony and Cleopatra†; The Barber of New Orleans; Herod; The House Next Door† (Design and painting); The Man Who Owns Broadway† (Act I, III); The Rose of Algeria†; The Silver Star; The Writing on the Wall 1910 The Inferior Sex (Designed and painted); Madame Sherry; Twelfth Night† 1911 The Faun (Act II); Gaby; Gypsy Love; The Happiest Night of His Life† (Act I); Hell; Hello, Paris; The Pink Lady; Temptations; The Triumph of an Empress; Winter Garden†; Ziegfeld Follies of 1911† 1912 The Count of Luxembourg; The Indiscretion of Truth† (Act I); Ziegfeld Follies of 1912 1913 Half an Hour; Iole; The Sunshine Girl† (Act I); The Younger Generation; Ziegfeld Follies of 1913† 1914 Papa's Darling†; Ziegfeld Follies of 1914† 1917 Jack O'Lantern† 1918 The Better 'Ole

Kurd Albrecht

Kurd (or Kurt) Albrecht, the German painter and scenic designer, lived in Berlin. In 1909 and 1910 his paintings, "Dans le Port" and "La Premiere Neige" were shown in a major exhibition in Berlin. In November 1930 he arrived in New York to make preparations for the German Opera Company 1931 tour of the United States. He was stage manager of the company at that time.

Sets: 1929 The Freiburg Passion Play

Theoni V. Aldredge

Born in Greece on August 22, 1932, educated at the American School in Athens and at the Goodman School of Drama in Chicago, Theoni Vachliotis Aldredge has designed extensively for stage and film. Her first professional designs were for the Goodman Theatre in 1950. In 1957 she moved to New York City and began a long association with Joseph Papp and the New York Shakespeare Festival. Well known for quality design with attention to period detail and heightened theatricality, she has won three Tony Awards (Annie 1977, Barnum 1980, La Cage Aux Follies 1984) garnered from 11 nominations. In 1969 she was presented the Maharam Award for her designs for Peer Gynt. Miss Aldredge has also designed several films, most notably The Great Gatsby for which she received an

Academy Award. Inducted into membership of The Players Club in 1989, she has also been honored with an Obie Award for Distinguished Service to off-Broadway Theatre, a Career Achievement Award by the Costume Designers' Guild and is on the roster of the Theatre Hall of Fame. She is married to the actor, Tom Aldredge. Twenty-first century credits include *The Spitfire Grill* at Playwrights Horizons.

Costumes: 1959 *Flowering Cherry*; *The Nervous Set*; *Silent Night, Lonely Night*; *Sweet Bird of Youth*† (Miss Geraldine Page's clothes) 1960 *The Best Man*; *A Distant Bell* 1961 *The Devil's Advocate*; *First Love*; *I Can Get It for You Wholesale*; *Mary, Mary* 1962 *Mr. President*; *Tchin-Tchin* 1963 *Strange Interlude*† (Miss Geraldine Page's costumes) 1964 *Any Wednesday*; *Anyone Can Whistle*; *Luv*; *Poor Richard*; *Ready When You Are*; *The Three Sisters*† 1965 *Cactus Flower*; *Minor Miracle*; *The Playroom*; *Skyscraper* 1966 *A Delicate Balance*; *First One Asleep, Whistle*; *A Time for Singing* 1967 *Daphne in Cottage D*; *Illya Darling*; *Little Murders*; *That Summer-That Fall*; *The Trial of Lee Harvey Oswald*; *You Know I Can't Hear You When the Water's Running* 1968 *Before You Go*; *I Never Sang for My Father*; *The Only Game in Town*; *Portrait of a Queen*; *Weekend* 1969 *Billy*; *The Gingham Dog*; *No Place to Be Somebody*; *Zelda* 1971 *The Incomparable Max* 1972 *Much Ado About Nothing*; *The Sign in Sidney Brustein's Window*; *Sticks and Bones*; *That Championship Season*; *Two Gentlemen of Verona*; *Voices* 1973 *The Au Pair Man*; *Boom Boom Room*; *Nash at Nine*; *No Hard Feelings* 1974 *An American Millionaire*; *Find Your Way Home*; *In Praise of Love* 1975 *A Chorus Line* 1976 *The Belle of Amherst*; *The Eccentricities of a Nightingale* 1977 *Annie*; *The Threepenny Opera* 1978 *Ballroom* 1979 *Break a Leg*; *The Grand Tour*; *I Remember Mama*; *The Madwoman of Central Park West* 1980 *42nd Street*; *Barnum*; *Clothes for a Summer Hotel*; *Onward Victoria* 1981 *Dreamgirls*; *Woman of the Year* 1982 *Ghosts*; *A Little Family Business* 1983 *The Corn Is Green*; *La Cage Aux Folles*; *Merlin*; *Private Lives* 1984 *The Rink* 1987 *Blithe Spirit*; *Dreamgirls*;

Teddy and Alice 1988 *Chess* 1989 *Gypsy* 1990 *Oh, Kay!* 1991 *Gypsy*; *Nick & Nora*; *The Secret Garden* 1992 *High Rollers Social and Pleasure Club* 1994 *The Flowering Peach* 1995 *The School for Scandal* 1996 *Taking Sides* 1997 *Annie*; *Three Sisters* 2000 *The Best Man* 2001 *Follies*

John Alexander

Like many designers in the first decades of the twentieth century, John W. Alexander was a scenic designer who occasionally created costumes as well. He was married to costume designer Elizabeth Alexander, and together they designed many of Maude Adams' productions. He was born in Allegheny, Pennsylvania and showed an ability to draw at a young age. He first worked as an illustrator for periodicals. Mr. Alexander traveled widely in Europe, but spent most of his life in New York City. He was an early advocate of hanging black back drops, and he experimented with lighting techniques. Active in many societies, he served as President of the National Academy of Design. Mr. Anderson was also a prolific portrait painter of academic, literary, and theatrical personalities. He died on May 31, 1915. In the following Broadway season, *The Birthday of the Infanta* was revived at Stuart Walker's Portmanteau Theatre, using his costume designs.

Sets: 1911 *Chanticler*† 1914 *The Legend of Leonora*
Costumes: 1905 *Peter Pan* (*Maude Adams*) 1916 *The Birthday of the Infanta*

Mrs. John Alexander

Elizabeth Alexander (also known as Mrs. John Alexander) is most often remembered as the creator of costumes for *Peter Pan* for Maude Adams. A native of New York City, she was born in 1867 and married John W. Alexander in 1887 (no relation though they shared the same last name). Mrs. Alexander received no formal training in the arts or theater prior to her successful career designing sets and costumes. Shortly after the death of her husband in 1915, she retired from theatrical design and helped establish the Arden Galleries in New York. Until her death at the age of 80 in 1947 in Princeton, New Jersey, she was an active and enthusiastic patron of the arts. She served at various times with the School Art League and the Arts Council of New York. She was on the executive committee in the United States which helped raise funds for the construction of the Shakespeare Memorial Theatre in Stratford-upon-Avon. Mr. and Mrs. Alexander had one son, James W. Alexander, named for her father.

Sets: 1916 *A Kiss for Cinderella*
Costumes: 1912 *Peter Pan* 1916 *A Kiss for Cinderella* (Costume Supervisor) 1917 *The Imaginary Invalid*

Selma Alexander

Selma Alexander designed costumes for many shows in the 1930s. She worked in the early 1930s at Lillian Sloane, Inc. and was later employed by the costume department at Saks-Fifth Avenue where her expertise in choosing contemporary fashions led to her theatrical credits.

Costumes: 1932 *Bulls, Bears, and Asses* (Costume Supervisor) 1933 *The Blue Widow*; *Far-Away Horses*; *Hilda Cassidy*† (Women's costumes); *The Sophisticrats* (Costume Supervisor) 1934 *False Dreams, Farewell* (Costume Supervisor); *The Wind and the Rain* (Costume Supervisor) 1935 *Moon over Mulberry Street* (Costume supervisor); *Petticoat Fever* (Costume Supervisor)

Charles Alias

The credit line for Charles Alias, costume designer, in the 1902 production of *The Silver Slipper* reads "costumes by Charles Alias, London." He is also referred to as simply "Alias, London." His career was spent mainly as a "costumier," or costume maker, for other designers. Alias died in Great Britain on May 11, 1921.

Costumes: 1902 *The Silver Slipper*† 1903 *A Princess of Kensington*†

Barbara Allen

Barbara Allen was an actress who appeared on Broadway during the 1920s. She achieved success portraying dizzy brunette man-chasers in film, on radio and television. She adopted the stage name "Vera Vague" for her appearances on the Bob Hope radio shows. Miss Allen, who died in 1974, was married to Norman Morrell, a television producer.

Costumes: 1927 *The Stairs* (Miss Sand's costumes)

Fred Allen

A partner in a company using new technology to create lighting design templates, Field Template, Fred Allen works mainly on the West Coast. He also designs lights for national and international tours, as well as productions in theaters around the world. He was production manager at the UCLA Center for the Performing Arts during the 1984 Olympics and has also participated in the renovation of historic theaters. Involved with theater lighting since the early 1960s, he has designed for Shari Lewis, the Paris Opera Ballet and the Los Angeles productions of *Catskills on Broadway* and *Blown Sideways Through Life*.

Lights: 1991 *Christmas Carol, A (Stewart)* 1992 *Christmas Carol, A (Stewart)* 1994 *Christmas Carol, A (Stewart)*

J. P. Allen

When George Bernard Shaw's play *The Philanderer* was produced by Winthrop Ames on Broadway in 1913, it featured men's garments designed by J. P. Allen. Proprietor of a ready-to-wear shop at 1225 Broadway, Allen also supplied custom-made garments through the teens and twenties.

Costumes: 1913 *The Philanderer*† (Men's costumes)

Leigh Allen

Leigh Allen designed settings for a production in 1934 on Broadway.

Sets: 1934 *Mother Lode*

Paul Allen

In 1923 Paul N. Allen created settings for a Broadway play. He was associated with Harry Greene in Allen & Greene, a theatrical business at 1493 Broadway in the late teens, while residing at 501 West 15th Street, New York City. He later moved to the West Coast where he worked as a cinematographer until retiring in 1930 with credits including *Broken Blossoms* for D.W. Griffith. Mr. Allen, who was born in 1895, died in Hollywood, California on August 15, 1956 at age 61.

Sets: 1923 *The Alarm Clock*

George Allgier

The settings for a Broadway play in 1933 were designed by George J. Allgier. He was born on October 10, 1889 in Glen Hazel, Pennsylvania and appears on the list of men who registered for the draft at the beginning of World War I. During the 1930s he resided at 301 West 24th Street in New York City and taught at Textile High School,

Sets: 1933 *A Church Mouse*

Fred Allison

Lighting designer Fred Allison studied at Southern Methodist University and at Lester Polakov's Studio with Jean Rosenthal. Among his many off-Broadway credits in the 1960s and 1970s were productions at Sheridan Square Playhouse, Actor's Playhouse, Equity Library Theatre, the Astor Hotel, the Midway Theatre, and the IASTA Theatre. He also designed for the Metropolitan Opera Ballet. He designed in regional theaters including the Margo Jones Theatre in Dallas and the Repertory Theatre of New Orleans, and for both the Dallas Civic Opera and the Boston Opera. Allison, who designed lights for many industrial shows and for *The Milliken Breakfast Show* for seventeen years, died at age 42 on November 3, 1985 in Long Beach, California.

Lights: 1969 *Three Men on a Horse* **1970** *Norman, Is That You?*

Madame Allouise

Madame Allouise designed a gown worn by Isabella Lee who appeared opposite John Barrymore in a 1912 Broadway production. The firm of Allouise Milliners was located at 271 West 33rd Street in New York and was run by Barbara Allouise. She was born on September 21, 1889 and died in January 1971. At the time of her death she was living in Suffolk, Mas-

sachusetts with her son Peter Allouise (1918-1985).

Costumes: 1912 *The Affairs of Anatol*† (Miss Lee's dress)

Al Alloy

Although you will find his name only rarely in playbills, Al Alloy was involved with the lighting for over two hundred productions during his Broadway career, including many directed and produced by David Merrick, Brady and Wyman, and Max Gordon, and many designed by Jo Mielziner. He was born Oscar Alloy in 1887 in New Orleans to a Spanish family recently emigrated from Gibraltar. At age seventeen he ran away from home, joining a brother in Philadelphia who worked as a theater electrician. Alloy soon became involved with the theater and quickly surpassed his brother with his expertise and flair with lighting effects. He met his wife, actress Barbara Grace, while creating lights for *Most Immoral Lady* starring Alice Brady, in which she played a small part. They were married on November 27, 1928 and had two children, including a son, Anthony Alloy, who followed his father into the theater business, initially as a lighting designer. Al Alloy developed from electrician to lighting designer at the same time the field was evolving. He did his job, professionally andcreatively, and did not care about receiving credit or seeing his name in playbills. His influence remains evident however, not only in the productions he lit but with the colleagues he influenced. Among his honors is a 1960 Tony Award given in the Stage Technician category. During his association with the annual "Festival of Music" in Philadelphia from 1948 to 1960 he created the 'dancing waters' lighting effect. He also designed numerous industrial and Las Vegas shows during his remarkable career which occurred as lighting design was becoming a profession. Al Alloy died in Sunrise, Florida in 1976.

Lights: 1936 *The Women*† **1943** *Bright Lights of 1943* **1944** *The Late George Apley* **1957** *Good As Gold* **1960** *The Good Soup* **1961** *Ross*

Sir Laurence Alma-Tadema

Sir Lawrence (Laurens) Alma-Tadema was born January 8, 1836 in Dronkyp in the Netherlands and by the age of 16 was painting in the classical tradition, revealing an amazing talent and an eye for period detail. He studied and worked in Belgium before relocating to London in the early 1870s. His wide knowledge of architecture and antiquities allowed him to tell stories in paintings like *Egyptians Three Thousand Years Ago, The Education of the Children of Clovis* and *Tarquinius Superbus*. When these and other works came to the attention of Herbert Beerbohm Tree and Henry Irving among others, he was commissioned to provide paintings as backdrops for plays with classical settings. His designs included *Cymbeline, Hypatia,* and Irving's last production *Coriolanus.* He was a member of the Royal Academy of Antwerp, the Royal Academy of London, and the Royal Society of Painters in Water Colors. Knighted in 1899, he received the Order of Merit in 1903 from King Edward VII. Alma-Tadema died on June 25, 1912 in Wiesbaden, Germany at age 77.

Sets: 1902 *Julius Caesar (Richard Mansfield)* **1912** *Julius Caesar*†

Ralph Alswang

Ralph Alswang made his debut on Broadway as a set designer for *Comes the Revelation* in 1942, as a lighting designer for *Home of the Brave* in 1945, and as a costume designer for *Beggars Are Coming to Town* in 1945. He was born in 1916 and raised in Chicago where he attended classes at the Chicago Art Institute and the Goodman Theatre. He also studied with Robert Edmond Jones. For the majority of his distinguished career Mr. Alswang concentrated on scenery and lighting, but he also designed costumes occasionally. In addition he designed theaters (including the Uris in New York City), guided restorations of theaters (including the Palace Theatre in New York City), directed and produced. He developed a theater technique called "Living Screen" which integrated live action and motion pictures, and produced *Is There Intelligent Life on Earth?* using the method, for which he held three patents. Ralph Alswang was married in 1944 to Betty Taylor, an interior designer, and they had three children. He died in New York City on February 15, 1979 at age 62.

Sets: 1942 *Comes the Revelation* **1945** *Home of the Brave* **1946** *I Like It Here; Lysistrata; Swan Song* **1947** *The Gentlemen from Athens; Our Lan'; The Whole World Over; A Young Man's Fancy* **1948** *Jenny Kissed Me; The Last Dance; Seeds in the Wind; Set My People Free; Small Wonder; A Story for Strangers; Strange Bedfellows; Trial by Jury* **1949** *How Long Till Summer; The Mikado; The Pirates of Penzance; Trial by Jury* **1950** *Julius Caesar; Kathryn Dunham and Her Company; King Lear; Legend of Sarah; Let's Make an Opera; Peter Pan; Pride's Crossing; Tickets, Please* **1951** *Courtin' Time; Love and Let Love; The Number; Out West of Eighth* **1952** *Conscience; Iolanthe; The Mikado; The Pirates of Penzance; Trial by Jury/ H.M.S. Pinafore; Two's Company* **1953** *The Bat; Be Your Age; The Ladies of the Corridor; The Pink Elephant; Sing Till Tomorrow* **1954** *Fragile Fox; The Magic and the Loss; The Rainmaker* **1955** *Catch a Star; Deadfall; The Southwest Corner* **1956** *Affair of Honor; The Best House in Naples; The Hot Corner; Time Limit; Uncle Willie* **1957** *The First Gentleman; Hide and Seek; The Tunnel of Love* **1958** *Love Me Little; Sunrise at Campobello* **1959** *The Girls Against the Boys; Hostile Witness; A Raisin in the Sun* **1961** *Come Blow Your Horn* **1963** *The Advocate* **1964** *Comedy in Music Opus 2; Fair Games for Lovers* **1965** *Ken Murray's Hollywood; World of Charles Aznavour* **1966** *At the Drop of Another Hat; The Committee* **1967** *Halfway Up the Tree* **1972** *Fun City*

Costumes: 1945 *Beggars Are Coming to Town*†; *Home of the Brave* **1947** *The Whole World Over* **1948** *The Happy Journey/ The Respectful Prostitute* (Costume Supervisor); *The Last Dance* **1955** *Deadfall* **1964** *Comedy in Music Opus 2; Fair Games for Lovers* **1965** *Ken Murray's Hollywood* **1966** *At the Drop of An-*

other Hat

Lights: 1945 *Home of the Brave* **1946** *Lysistrata; Swan Song* **1947** *The Gentlemen from Athens; Our Lan'; A Young Man's Fancy* **1948** *The Play's the Thing; Small Wonder; A Story for Strangers; Strange Bedfellows; Trial by Jury* **1949** *How Long Till Summer; The Mikado; The Pirates of Penzance; Trial by Jury* **1950** *Daphne Laureola; Julius Caesar; King Lear; Let's Make an Opera; Peter Pan; Pride's Crossing* **1953** *Anna Russell and Her Little Show; The Bat; The Ladies of the Corridor; The Pink Elephant; Sing Till Tomorrow* **1954** *Fragile Fox; The Rainmaker* **1955** *Deadfall; The Southwest Corner* **1956** *Affair of Honor; The Best House in Naples; The Hot Corner; Time Limit; Uncle Willie* **1957** *The First Gentleman; Hide and Seek; The Tunnel of Love* **1958** *Epitaph for George Dillon; Sunrise at Campobello* **1959** *At the Drop of a Hat; The Girls Against the Boys; Hostile Witness; A Raisin in the Sun* **1961** *Come Blow Your Horn* **1963** *The Advocate; The School for Scandal* **1964** *Comedy in Music Opus 2; Fair Games for Lovers* **1965** *Beyond the Fringe†; Ken Murray's Hollywood; World of Charles Aznavour* **1966** *At the Drop of Another Hat; The Committee* **1967** *Halfway Up the Tree*

Nathan Altman

Nathan Altman was a Russian painter, book, scenic and graphic designer, and member of the Russian avant-garde art community. He was born on December 10, 1889 and died on December 12, 1970 in Leningrad where he resided most of his life. He lived in Paris during the 1920s and 1930s and while there received a gold medal for scene design in the 1925 International Exhibit for the Decorative Arts and Industry. Marc Chagall and Nathan Altman were the principal designers for the Moscow State Jewish Theatre, which opened in 1919 and was closed by an edict of Stalin in 1948.

Sets: 1926 *The Dybbuck†* **1948** *The Dybbuck*

Franklyn Ambrose

Franklyn Geramia Ambrose designed settings for Broadway plays during the 1930s. In 1920 he worked as a clerk and resided at 246 East 120th Street, New York City. In the mid-1930s he worked in collaboration with Stephen Golding who was the proprietor of a scenic studio.

Sets: 1934 *The Drunkard* **1935** *Mulatto†* **1936** *The Pirates of Penzance*

John Ambrosone

Although John Ambrosone made his Broadway debut in 1997, this prolific lighting designer amassed numerous credits throughout the world prior to that time. He is Resident Lighting Designer for the American Repertory Theatre, in residence at Harvard University, where he has designed lights for many plays, including *Mother Courage, Man and Superman*, and The *Doctor's Dilemma*. His work has also been seen at the Alley Theatre, the Long Wharf Theatre and Arena Stage among other regional theaters. Off-Broadway credits include *Nocturne* by Adam Rapp.

Lights: 1997 *The Old Neighborhood*

Karle O. Amend

Karle Otto Amend was born in Columbus, Ohio on January 15, 1889. Although his first job in the theater was as a paint boy for Schell Scenic Studios in Columbus, he initially intended to be an actor and performed with both vaudeville and stock companies. His first credit as a scenic artist was for a 1912 production of *East Lynne* in Ohio, after which he devoted his talents to creating and painting scenery. He became a member of United Scenic Artists in 1918 and established the Karle O. Amend Scenic Studio in the early 1920s. He designed settings for numerous productions under his own name and others for which his studio received design credit. Karle O. Amend died on January 2, 1944 at the age of 54.

Sets: 1925 *The Dagger; Earl Carroll's Vanities†; Florida Girl†; Mercenary Mary* **1926** *Potash and Perlmutter, Detectives* **1927** *Tommy* **1928** *Keep Shufflin'; Sh! the Octopus; We Never Learn* **1929** *Town Boy* **1931** *Coastwise; The Devil's Host; Nikki†; School for Virtue* **1932** *Angeline Moves in; Border Land; Broadway Boy; A Few Wild Oats; Shuffle Along of 1933*

1933 *Before Morning*; *The Locked Room*; *Under Glass* 1934 *Broadway Interlude*; *Gypsy Blonde*; *Her Majesty, the Widow*; *Slightly Delirious*; *Too Much Party* 1935 *Nowhere Bound*; *One Good Year*; *Potash and Perlmutter*; *Smile at Me*; *Them's the Reporters* 1936 *The Devil of Pei-Ling*; *The Sap Runs High* 1937 *Cross-Town*; *Howdy Stranger* 1939 *I Must Love Someone*; *When We Are Married* 1942 *The Time, the Place, and the Girl* 1944 *Right Next to Broadway*

Karle O. Amend Studio

Karle O. Amend established the Karle O. Amend Scenic Studio in the early 1920s, an enterprise which remained in operation until the early 1940s in various New Jersey locations. Unlike many other scene shops the studio stayed open during the Depression, due mainly to Amend's persistence. The Karle O. Amend Scenic Studios also produced and painted scenery for other designers including Albert R. Johnson and Hugh Willoughby.

Sets: 1923 *The Newcomers* 1926 *The Love City* 1929 *Nice Women* 1930 *Spook House* 1931 *Ebb Tide*; *The Wooden Soldier* 1932 *The Man Who Changed His Name* 1933 *Crucible*; *Tommy* 1934 *One More Honeymoon* 1937 *Work Is for Horses*

Harriet Ames

Harriet Ames supervised the costumes for one production on Broadway in 1950. She was born in Milwaukee, Wisconsin and studied in Philadelphia and New York City, graduating from the Calhoun School in 1931. In 1935 she married Paul A. Ames, a securities analyst, and together they backed many Broadway productions, including *Brigadoon, Guys and Dolls,* and *Silk Stockings*. Mrs. Ames died on July 27, 1976 at age 62.

Costumes: 1950 *Hilda Crane*† (Costume Supervisor)

E. Amies

E. Amies collaborated with several other designers to create costumes for a revue in 1922.

Costumes: 1922 *Greenwich Village Follies*† (Jenny Lind, Widow Brown, Miss Heath's Speciality Gown.)

Michael Anania

Michael Anania is a native of Brockton, Massachusetts where he was born on October 1, 1951. After receiving a B.F.A. at Boston University, he became designer in residence at Tufts University, subsequently spending ten years on the faculty of Emerson College. He was resident scenic designer at the Paper Mill Playhouse for many years, beginning in 1985, where he designed numerous productions. His designs for opera include *H.M.S. Pinafore, La Boheme, The Merry Widow,* and *Pajama Game* at the New York City Opera, *Desire under the Elms* at the New York Opera Repertory Theatre at City Center Theatre, and several productions for the Lake George Opera Festival. His sets for the North Shore Music Theatre, include *Children of Eden*. In April 2001, his scenery was featured in *Leader of the Pack* in Boston, a production focusing on 1960s popular music and starring Mary Wilson, one of the original Supremes. Additional twenty-first century credits include *The Spitfire Grill* at Playwrights Horizons.

Sets: 1980 *Canterbury Tales* 1989 *Run for Your Wife* 1990 *Change in the Heir*; *A Little Night Music* 1991 *The Most Happy Fella* 1992 *110 in the Shade* 1994 *Wonderful Town* 1995 *The Merry Widow* 1997 *The Wizard of Oz* 1998 *The Wizard of Oz* 1999 *The Wizard of Oz* 2001 *The Gathering*

F. Richards Anderson

F. Richards (Richard) Anderson was 60 years old when he died in 1935. Trained as an architect, he decorated and designed many theaters. With Abraham L. Erlanger he helped plan the New Amsterdam Theatre and then worked closely with Henry Beaumont Herts and Hugh Tallent, the primary architects. He was also responsible for the auditorium and boxes. As head of the Schneider-Anderson Costume Company he was well known in theatrical circles as a costume designer. Mr. Anderson was associated for 35 years with Florenz Ziegfeld and A.L. Erlanger, designing many of the shows produced by Erlanger Amusement Enterprises. After the death of Mr. Erlanger, he served as general manager of his producing organization. F. Richards Anderson had many credits for designing costumes on Broadway prior to the twentieth century, including *The Bride Elect* in 1898.

Costumes: 1899 *Ben Hur*†; *Ben Hur*†; *A Greek Slave*; *Rogers Brothers in Wall Street* **1900** *Chris and the Wonderful Lamp*; *Foxy Quiller*; *Marcelle*; *The Rogers Brothers in Central Park*; *Star and Garter*; *Sweet Anne Page* **1902** *Ben Hur*; *The Billionaire*; *Maid Marian*; *The Rogers Brothers in Harvard*; *The Toreador*† **1903** *Babette*†; *A Japanese Nightingale*; *A Midsummer Night's Dream*; *The Rogers Brothers in London* **1904** *Babette*†; *The Rogers Brothers in Paris* **1905** *Fritz in Tammany Hall*; *The Ham Tree*; *Lifting the Lid*; *The Rogers Brothers in Ireland*; *The White Cat*† **1906** *Forty-five Minutes from Broadway*; *The Free Lance*; *The Prince of India* **1907** *The Grand Mogul*; *Lola from Berlin*; *The Talk of New York* **1908** *Little Nemo*; *The Soul Kiss*†; *A Waltz Dream*; *Ziegfeld Follies of 1908*† **1909** *The Silver Star* **1910** *The Bachelor Belles*† **1911** *The Pink Lady* **1912** *Eva*; *The Man from Cook's*; *Oh! Oh! Delphine*; *She Stoops to Conquer*† **1913** *The Little Café* **1914** *The Dragon's Claw* **1915** *Around the Map*†; *Fads and Fancies*†; *Fads and Fancies*† **1916** *Ben-Hur*; *Miss Springtime*†

John Murray Anderson

John Murray Anderson, a native of St. John's, Newfoundland, was born on September 20, 1886 and died at the age of 67 on January 30, 1954. He came to the United States in 1910 after studying in Lausanne, Switzerland and Edinburgh. He served the theater in a variety of functions: dancer, producer, writer, director, and lyricist. He devised six *Greenwich Village Follies*, also serving as a costume designer on one of the productions and a set designer on another. He occasionally also designed lights. In fact in all of the productions for which he received credit as a designer he had an additional role, often as director. "Murray" also worked as a producer for Radio

City Music Hall, the New York Hippodrome, and Metro-Goldwyn-Mayer as well as on Broadway, and encouraged the talents of young theater aspirants, including E. Carleton Winckler.

Sets: 1923 *Greenwich Village Follies*†
Costumes: 1924 *Greenwich Village Follies*† ("The Happy Prince")
Lights: 1939 *One for the Money*† **1940** *Two for the Show* **1948** *Heaven on Earth*

Keith Anderson

Keith Anderson calls Siesta Key, Florida home and designed the 1990-1991 edition of Ringling Bros. and Barnum & Bailey Circus and subsequently a television special featuring the Circus. He is also a writer and teaches trapeze, serving as the aerial coordinator for *King Solomon's Mines*. He designed costumes for *Walt Disney's World on Ice: Mickey Mouse Diamond Jubilee* and was production designer for *Disney's World on Ice starring Peter Pan.*

Sets: 1989 *Meet Me in Saint Louis*
Costumes: 1989 *Meet Me in Saint Louis*

Paul Anderson

The British lighting designer Paul Anderson designs lights and serves as production electrician for a variety of venues, including industrial and fashion shows. He studied at the Mountview Theatre School and at the York College of Arts and Technology before serving as the resident designer of the Joseph Rowntree Theatre from 1982 until 1987. His designs for lights have been seen at Théâtre de Complicité, the Young Vic, and in the West End. Anderson's lighting designs for *The Chairs* were nominated for a Laurence Olivier Award in London and a Drama Desk Award in New York. Other New York credits include *Mnemonic* in 2001 and *The Noise of Time* in 2000 presented by Théâtre de Complicité at Lincoln Center. He should not be confused with Paul Thomas Anderson, the American director, writer, and producer.

Lights: 1998 *The Chairs*

Percy Anderson

Percy Anderson, born in 1851, died in London on October 10, 1928 at the age

Figure 2: Percy Anderson: "MacDuff" in Act II of *Macbeth*, 1916.
Reprinted by permission, The Museum of the City of New York

of 77 after a long and distinguished career designing costumes (and occasionally sets) in the United States and Great Britain. At a period in theatrical history when little credit was extended to costume designers, Mr. Anderson's name appeared in playbills and his contribution was acknowledged in reviews. He was instrumental in laying the groundwork for the costume designers working as professionals today, blending theatrical necessity with historical period without following the pedantic modes common at the end of the nineteenth century. He was both well known and respected by the public and his contemporaries. In England Mr. Anderson was known for his work with the producer Sir Herbert Beerbohm Tree and for the original productions of the Gilbert and Sullivan operettas. Beginning with *The Yeoman of the Guard*, he was responsible for all the D'Oyly Carte productions at the Savoy. The majority of his design assignments on Broadway occurred prior to 1900 and included: 1894: *The Devil's Advocate*; 1895: *His Excellency*; 1896: *The Geisha, Half A King*; 1897: *The Tempest*; and 1898: *Trelawny of the "Wells"*. Mr. Anderson also painted watercolor portraits of many distinguished people and exhibited with the New Water Colour Society in London. See Figure 2: Percy Anderson: *Macbeth*

Sets: 1906 *The Light Eternal*† (Design and properties) 1912 *Tantalizing Tommy*† (Designed) 1916 *Macbeth*†; *The Merry Wives of Windsor*†

Costumes: 1899 *Becky Sharp*† 1900 *The Rose of Persia*; *San Toy* 1901 *Captain Jinks of the Horse Marines*; *Quality Street* 1902 *A Country Girl*; *The Emerald Isle*†; *Mary of Magdala* 1903 *Sweet Kitty Bellairs*; *Ulysses* 1904 *Becky Sharp*; *The Cingalee*; *Fatinitza*; *Girofle-Girofla* 1905 *Adrea*† (other costumes); *The Toast of the Town*; *Veronique* 1907 *The Merry Widow*†; *Miss Hook of Holland*; *Sappho and Phaon* 1908 *The Girls of Gottenburg* 1909 *Herod* 1910 *The Lucky Star* 1911 *Kismet*; *The Slim Princess*† (Costumes) 1913 *Good Little Devil* 1916 *Macbeth*; *The Merry Wives of Windsor* (Also accessories) 1917 *Chu Chin Chow* 1919

Aphrodite†; *Monsieur Beaucaire* **1920** *Mecca*† (Men's and Women's costumes) **1924** *Macbeth* **1936** *Princess Ida*

Richard Anderson

Richard Anderson designed costumes for a play on Broadway, in 1970.

Costumes: 1970 *Charley's Aunt*

Mariano Andreu

Mariano Andreu was a Catalan artist and illustrator, born in Barcelona in 1888, near the Circo Barceloné theater. His graphic talent led him from illustrating books to sketching sets and costumes. He spent much of his life in London, after studying at the school of Arts and Crafts in Barcelona, where he continued to paint and draw, but also designed often for Michel Fokine, including the world premier of *Don Juan* at the Alhambra. His theatricalwork was seen in New York for the Ballet Russe de Monte Carlo in their appearances at the Metropolitan Opera. The production he designed on Broadway, *Much Ado About Nothing*, starred John Gielgud and Margaret Leighton and was originally produced in London. He did sets and costumes for productions at Stratford-upon-Avon, at Covent Garden and in Paris where he lived for most of his life. His paintings and designs are in the permanent collection of the Institut del Teatre in Barcelona. Andreu died in Biarritz in 1976.

Sets: 1959 *Much Ado About Nothing*

Costumes: 1959 *Much Ado About Nothing*

Herbert Andrews

Herbert Garnet Andrews, born in New York City in 1909, studied at the Pratt Institute and the Berkshire School of Design. Mr. Andrews was well known as a scenic designer for the theater and for NBC-TV where he designed over ten thousand sets between 1960 and 1990. Mr. Andrews began his career as a designer in summer stock and with the Group Theatre. After that time he designed extensively for stage, television, and motion pictures. In addition to his credits on Broadway for costume design, he created clothes for many television productions, including twenty *Miss America Pageants.* He became a member of United Scenic Artists in 1934 and a life member in 1985. Mr. Andrews died in September 1990.

Sets: **1938** *My Heart's in the Highlands;* *Sing for Your Supper* **1939** *Swingin' the Dream†* **1940** *Cue for Passion* **1942** *Let Freedom Sing; Porgy and Bess* **1943** *Porgy and Bess* **1944** *Porgy and Bess* Costumes: **1936** *Battle Hymn* **1938** *My Heart's in the Highlands* **1939** *Swingin' the Dream*

Martha Andrews

Martha Andrews designed the women's costumes for one production on Broadway during the 1928-1929 season.

Costumes: **1929** *S.S. Glencairn* (Women's costumes)

Angel

Beginning in the late nineteenth century, Angel provided costumes for hundreds of productions, mainly in and around London, for theater, opera and dance. Morris Angel was a costume designer, but mainly through Morris Angel and Company, Morris Angel and Sons, Ltd., and other variations, he made costumes for other designers. His name appeared in playbills with increasing frequency from the 1890s through the 1950s. After his death in 1941, his costume business was managed by others. His Broadway during the first two decades of the twentieth century, both as a designer in his own right and through his business, were for productions that were transferred to Broadway after successful London runs.

Costumes: **1901** *A Message from Mars†* **1902** *A Cigarette Maker's Romance†* **1910** *Get-Rich-Quick Wallingford†* (Costumes) **1911** *Bunty Pulls the Strings†* **1913** *General John Regan* (Uniforms)

Waldo Angelo

Waldo Angelo was born on August 26, 1920 in New Jersey and received his formal education at Seton Hall in South Orange, New Jersey. He studied with DeChirico and at the Art Students League in New York City. Mr. Angelo, who taught at Chouinard Art Institute, had one-person exhibits

of his creative work in New York, Toronto, Capri and Santa Barbara. A long time associate of and assistant to Raoul Pène Du Bois and Willia Kim, his contribution to costumes and sets on the Broadway stage was extensive in that capacity. Mr. Angelo died on March 8, 1992.

Costumes: **1952** *Shuffle Along*

Boris Anisfield

Boris Anisfield (also known as Boris (Ber) Izrailevich Anisfeldt), a painter whose works are in the permanent collections of the Hermitage, Chicago Art Institute and the Brooklyn Museum was born in Beltsy, Bessarabia, Russia on October 2, 1879. His works have been widely exhibited. He came to the United States in 1918 and became a naturalized citizen in 1924. He spent several years in New York painting scenery and designing costumes and scenery for opera, ballet and one Broadway production. In 1928, he was appointed Professor of Advanced Drawing and Painting at the Chicago Art Institute and held that position until retiring in 1968. He died in Waterford, Connecticut on December 4, 1973 at age 94.

Sets: **1926** *Schweiger* Costumes: **1926** *Schweiger*

S. Anisfield

S. Anisfield designed costumes for one play during the 1934-35 season on Broadway.

Costumes: **1935** *Recruits*

Kathleen Ankers

Kathleen Ankers was widely known as an art director and production designer on television, with credits including *Late Night with David Letterman, The Rosie O'Donnell Show, The Late Show with Tom Snyder,* and *F.Y.I.* on ABC-TV, and numerous specials and series. Born in London, she designed for the Old Vic in Bristol, London and Liverpool, the Citizen's Theatre in Glasgow, and in London's West End. She began her career in the theater in her teens with a repertory company in Farnham, where she went hoping to work on scenery and costumes but was assigned to work in the box office. When the designer came down with the mumps, she got her start creating sets and costumes. In addition to her designs on Broadway she has designed sets and costumes off-Broadway and for regional theaters, including the Hartford Stage. She died on October 24, 2001. Some of her designs are in the permanent collection of the Museum of the City of New York.

Sets: 1952 *Mr. Pickwick*
Costumes: 1952 *Fancy Meeting You Again*; *Mr. Pickwick* 1974 *My Sister, My Sister*
Lights: 1952 *Mr. Pickwick*

Michael Annals

Michael Annals, a British designer, was born on April 21, 1938 and attended the Hornsey College of Art. He designed sets and costumes for many companies around the world, including the Royal Shakespeare Company, the Stratford (Ontario) Festival, The National Theatre, Covent Garden, American Ballet Theatre, and the Royal Ballet. His career began at the Old Vic in 1961 when he designed *Macbeth*. Designs in London's West End included sets and costumes for *Design for Living*, *Privates on Parade*, and *Noises Off*. He also designed for film, notably *Joseph Andrews*. During the 1966-1967 academic year he was an Associate Professor of Scenic Design at Yale University. Mr. Annals always preferred to design both sets and costumes for a production, as was the case with most of his credits on Broadway. Annals died in London on June 1, 1990.

Sets: 1965 *Royal Hunt of the Sun* 1966 *Those That Play the Clowns* 1968 *Her First Roman*; *Morning Noon and Night*; *Staircase* 1972 *Captain Brassbound's Conversion* 1983 *Noises Off* 1985 *Benefactors*
Costumes: 1965 *Royal Hunt of the Sun* 1966 *Those That Play the Clowns* 1968 *Her First Roman*; *Morning Noon and Night*; *Staircase* 1983 *Noises Off*

Yury Annyenkov

Yury Pavlovich Annyenkov (also known as Jurij Annyenkoff, Georges Annenkopf, George Annet, George Annenkov, etc.), the Russian designer,

artist and art critic was born in Petropavlosk, Russia on June 1, 1889. He studied at St. Petersburg University and with Savelii Zeidenberg. His creative and innovative designs were seen in St. Petersburg at the Bat and Kholmskaya's Crooked Mirror Theatre and in Petrograd for Tolstoy's *The First Distiller*, among many theaters. He emigrated to Germany in 1924 and then to France, continuing to design for theater and films. He also painted portraits which are collected in museums around the world, and wrote essays on art. In 1965, he published his memoirs, *Diary of My Acquaintances*. Annyenkov died on July 18, 1974 in Paris.

Sets: 1931 *New Chauve-Souris*† 1935 *Revisor*
Costumes: 1931 *New Chauve-Souris*†

Sal Anthony

Sal Anthony, born Sal Anthon Cocuzza on July 8, 1925, died on June 12, 1991. A prolific costume designer, he designed on Broadway during the 1950s, but mainly designed for television, working extensively on specials during its' Golden Age. He appeared in *Black Elk Lives* in the early 1980s.

Costumes: 1952 *Buttrio Square* (Costume Supervisor) 1954 *The Bad Seed* 1959 *The Girls Against the Boys*

Robert Anton

Robert (Robbie) Anton, a native of Fort Worth, Texas studied set design at Carnegie Institute of Technology and Lester Polakov's Studio and Forum of Stage Design. Known primarily as a puppet designer, his Anton Theatre toured throughout the United States and Europe. He died a suicide on August 29, 1984 in Los Angeles at age 35.

Sets: 1972 *Elizabeth I*

Loy Arcenas

Loy Arcenas was born on March 3, 1953 in the Philippines and was a pre-med student at the University of the Philippines prior to taking a design course at the English National Opera. His first scenic designs were for *Antigone* in the Philippines. He has extensive credits in regional theaters, off-Broadway and in his native land.

Notable productions include *The Pinter Plays* at Classic Stage Company, *Nebraska* at La Jolla Playhouse, *The Glass Menagerie* at Arena Stage and *Life is a Dream* at American Repertory Theatre. He has designed for many theaters on the West Coast and in 1987 received the Los Angeles Critics Circle Award for *Three Postcards* at South Coast Repertory Theatre. His scenery in 2001 for *O Pioneers!* was featured in the collaboration between the Women's Project Theatre and the Acting Company. He has worked several times with George C. Wolfe, on *Caucasian Chalk Circle* for the New York Shakespeare Festival, and *Spunk*. Interested in directing as well as design, Arcenas did both for *Flipzoids* at Theatre for a New City in 1996.

Sets: 1990 *Once on This Island*; *Prelude to a Kiss*; *Spunk* **1994** *The Glass Menagerie* **1995** *Love! Valour! Compassion!* **1996** *The Night of the Iguana* **1998** *High Society*

Julie Archer

Julie Archer, a designer of lights and sets, was born on May 5, 1957 in Minneapolis, Minnesota. She studied at the School of Visual Arts at the University of Minnesota before moving to New York City at age 18. She quickly found work (in various capacities) with Mabou Mines and since the mid-1970s has designed sets, lights and puppets for numerous productions with the company, including *Peter & Wendy* for which she received an American Theatre Wing, OBIE and Dramalogue Awards, and *An Epidog* for which she won another American Theatre Wing Award. Her career has been influenced by Ruth Malaczeck, one of the founding members, with whom she has often collaborated. In 1980 she designed the settings for *Vanishing Pictures* with Ruth Malaczeck and received an Obie Award. Her set and lighting designs for *Hajj*, also for Mabou Mines, won the Joseph Maharam Award in 1983. *Vanishing Pictures* at Theatre for a New City for which she designed the scenery, also garnered her an OBIE award. She has designed for the International Puppetry Festival at The Public Theatre,

for the Geffen Playhouse, and *Las Horas de Belén - A Book of Hours* set in a 17th century Mexican women's prison. That production opened the Brava Theatre Center in San Francisco in 2000.

Lights: 1988 *The Gospel at Colonus*

Madame Arlington

Madame Arlington created costumes for two revues, one in 1918 and the other in 1926. From 1900, her business, the Arlington Cloak and Suit Company, was located at 55 Walker Street in New York.

Costumes: 1918 *Hitchy Koo 1918*† **1926** *Earl Carroll's Vanities*†

Paul Arlington

Paul Arlington, Inc. was a costume house located at 118 West 48th Street in New York City. In 1921, Kathryn A. Arlington served as president and Mary Silverstein was secretary and treasurer.

Costumes: 1912 *The Girl from Brighton* **1923** *The Passing Show of 1923*

Mathias Armbruster

Mathias (Matt) Armbruster (sometimes Ambruster) collaborated on the scenic designs for a musical production in 1905, produced by Klaw and Erlanger at the New Amsterdam Theatre. Born in Wurttenburg, Germany in 1839, he studied painting and came to Cincinnati, Ohio by way of Paris, He was the proprietor of the Armbruster Scenic Studio where he created backdrops for many touring companies and minstrel shows, although his contribution was rarely acknowledged in theater playbills. The studio provided scenery for Sarah Bernhardt, Robert Mantell, Helen Modjeska, and Al Field among many others. Together with his sons, Otto, Albert and Emil, he operated one of the largest scene painting studios in the United States. Otto Armbruster moved to New York in 1891 where he worked often at the Broadway Theatre, and undoubtedly deserves credit for scenic designs, although his name does not appear in any extant playbills. After the death of Mathias Armbruster in 1920, his son Albert ran the studio until 1958 when he retired and the business closed. The Armbruster

Collection at The Ohio State University contains their archives, including many original scenic designs.

Sets: **1899** *The School for Scandal* **1902** *The School for Scandal* **1904** *The School for Scandal* **1905** *The Dagger and the Cross*; *Othello* (With sons); *The White Cat*† **1910** *Sarah Bernhardt in Rep*

Horace Armistead

Horace Armistead was born in 1898 in England where he got his start in theater as a studio paint boy. He moved to the United States in 1924 and worked initially as a charge man for Cleon Throckmorton, the designer and producer. He later opened his own shop. He won the Tony Award in 1948 for the sets for Gian Carlo Menotti's *The Medium*, for which he also created the costumes. He also designed sets and costumes for the Metropolitan Opera and the New York City Ballet. Mr. Armistead died in 1980 at the age of 82.

Sets: **1936** *The Fields Beyond* **1942** *What Big Ears* **1947** *The Telephone/The Medium* **1949** *Regina* **1950** *Arms and the Girl*; *The Consul*

Costumes: **1947** *The Telephone/The Medium*

Alice Armstrong

Alice Armstrong was costume supervisor for one show in 1930. An artist, Miss Armstrong studied with George Bridgman, George Luks, and Jonas Lie among others. She was born in Elma, New York on April 8, 1906 and died in June 1995. Numerous exhibits of her paintings were held between 1931 and 1946 at the Anderson Gallery, the Florence Tricker Gallery, the National Academy of Design and the Bronx Museum among others. In private life, she was known as Mrs. A. Washington Pezet.

Costumes: **1930** *Schoolgirl* (Costume Supervisor)

Betty Coe Armstrong

Betty Coe Armstrong designed the costumes for two Broadway productions in the late 1950s. She died in New York in 1989.

Costumes: **1958** *The Day the Money Stopped* **1959** *God and Kate Murphy*

Dorothy Armstrong

As a child, Dorothy Armstrong performed in vaudeville with her brother, Ellis Armstrong. They toured in *The Man from Mexico* and Rutan's *Song Birds*. She later worked as an interior decorator with Pieter Myer through their business, Armstrong & Myer, Inc., 200 West 10th Street in New York City. Myer was president and she was secretary and treasurer. For additional information, see the entry for "Pieter Myer."

Sets: **1922** *Greenwich Village Follies*†

Costumes: **1921** *Tangerine*† ("Tangerine Island")

Will Steven Armstrong

Will Steven Armstrong specialized in scenic design during his career in theater although he also designed lights and costumes. He was awarded the Tony for outstanding scene design in 1962 for *Carnival* and an Obie for *Ivanov* in 1959. Mr. Armstrong was born in New Orleans in 1930 and died August 12, 1969. He studied both at Louisiana State and Yale Universities and worked as an assistant to Jo Mielziner, Donald Oenslanger and Boris Aronson. Mr. Armstrong designed the stage of the American Shakespeare Festival in Stratford, Connecticut as well as sets, lights and costumes for that company.

Sets: **1959** *The Andersonville Trial* **1960** *Caligula* **1961** *Carnival*; *A Cook for Mr. General*; *I Can Get It for You Wholesale*; *Kwamina*; *Subways Are for Sleeping* **1962** *Tchin-Tchin* **1963** *Dear Me, the Sky Is Falling*; *Nobody Loves an Albatross*; *One Flew over the Cuckoo's Nest* **1964** *I Had a Ball*; *The Passion of Joseph D*; *Ready When You Are*; *The Three Sisters* **1966** *The Lion in Winter*; *Pousse-Cafe*; *Three Bags Full*; *Wayward Stork* **1967** *The Imaginary Invalid*; *Something Different*; *Tonight at 8:30*; *A Touch of the Poet* **1968** *Forty Carats* **1969** *The Front Page*; *Zelda*

Costumes: **1959** *The Andersonville Trial* **1960** *Caligula* **1964** *A Girl Could Get Lucky* **1966** *The Lion in Winter*

Lights: 1959 *The Andersonville Trial* 1961 *Carnival*; *A Cook for Mr. General*; *I Can Get It for You Wholesale*; *Kwamina*; *Subways Are for Sleeping* 1962 *Tchin-Tchin* 1963 *Dear Me, the Sky Is Falling*; *Nobody Loves an Albatross*; *One Flew over the Cuckoo's Nest*; *The Rehearsal*; *Semi-Detached* 1964 *The International Cup/The Battle of Niagara and the Ear*; *The Passion of Joseph D*; *Ready When You Are* 1966 *Three Bags Full* 1967 *Something Different* 1969 *The Front Page*; *Zelda*

William Armstrong

William Armstrong graduated from the Yale School of Drama. In addition to credits as a lighting designer on Broadway, he has contributed designs to the Williamstown Theatre Festival, the American Repertory Theatre and the Indiana Repertory Theatre. Credits for lighting designs include *Hedda Gabbler* and *'Night, Mother* at The Guthrie Theatre and *The Mother of Us All* at the Lenox Arts Center. He served as a scenic artist for the 1993 film *Carlito's Way*.

Lights: 1980 *A Lesson from Aloes* 1981 *Scenes and Revelations* 1982 *Macbeth*

Peter Arno

Born on January 8, 1904, Curtis Arnoux Peters was known through his professional life as Peter Arno. He launched his career as a cartoonist with a sale to *The New Yorker* in 1925, where he became a regular contributor. His cartoons, featuring bold lines and satirizing society, were collected in several books. Mr. Arno wrote revues to which he also contributed costume and scenic designs. He also wrote one-man shows in which he performed. Peter Arno died in 1968.

Sets: 1930 *The New Yorkers†* 1931 *Here Goes the Bride†*
Costumes: 1927 *The New Yorkers†* 1929 *Murray Anderson's Almanac†* 1930 *The New Yorkers†*

Barry Arnold

Barry Arnold, a native of New York City, first worked on Broadway as production designer for a show in 1970. He started designing in summer stock at Eagles Mere Playhouse and initially worked in New York at the Equity Library Theatre. Off-Broadway designs include *Curley McDimple*, *The Millionairess*, *To be Young Gifted and Black*, *Love and Maple Syrup*, and *Smile Smile Smile*. He has designed lights for many productions at the Roundabout Theatre, including *The Waltz of the Toreadors*, *Room Service*, *The Entertainer*, and *Springtime for Henry*.

Sets: 1970 *The President's Daughter*
Costumes: 1970 *The President's Daughter*
Lights: 1970 *The President's Daughter* 1976 *Bubbling Brown Sugar* 1982 *Joseph and the Amazing Technicolor Dreamcoat*

John Arnone

Born January 12, 1949 in Dallas, Texas, John Arnone studied at Southern Methodist University and received an M.F.A. at the University of Michigan. With extensive credits in regional theaters, including La Jolla Playhouse, Arena Stage, the Guthrie Theatre, Hartford Stage and the Huntington Theatre among others, he has also designed *Cutting Up* for Twyla Tharp and Baryshnikov, for television and for film (*Sex, Drugs, Rock & Roll* and *Me and Veronica* among others). Honors include an Obie Award in 1992 for Sustained Excellence and the Tony, Outer Critics Circle, Dora Mavor Moore, LA Drama Critics Circle, and Drama Desk Awards for *The Who's Tommy*. A long time collaborator with directors Des McAnuff, Len Jenkin, Garland Wright and Keith Reddin, Arnone is known for his creative use of technology, powerful visualizations and creativity with both small and large budgets.

Sets: 1991 *The Homecoming* 1993 *The Who's Tommy* 1994 *Best Little Whorehouse Goes Public, The*; *Grease*; *Twilight: Los Angeles*, 1992 1995 *How to Succeed in Business Without Really Trying*; *Sacrilege* 1996 *Sex and Longing* 1998 *The Deep Blue Sea* 1999 *Marlene* 2000 *The Best Man*; *The Full Monty*; *Ride Down Mt. Morgan*

Boris Aronson

Boris Aronson, painter, scenic designer and occasionally a costume and lighting designer, was born in Kiev, Russia in 1900 and studied at the State Art School, the School of Modern Painting, and with Alexandra Exter at the School of Theatre. He created sets and costumes in the United States for the first time at the New York City Yiddish Theatre in 1924, beginning a career of outstanding design. Among the many prizes won by Mr. Aronson were Tony Awards for outstanding scenic design for *The Rose Tattoo, Follies, Company, Zorba, Cabaret* and *Pacific Overtures.* He designed extensively for the theater, ballet and film. The breadth and creativity of his work has received belated recognition since his death on November 16, 1980. The lavishly illustrated *The Theatre Art of Boris Aronson* by Frank Rich was published by Knopf in 1987, and his designs continue to be collected and featured in exhibitions.

Sets: 1927 *2x2=5* 1930 *Josef Suss* 1932 *Walk a Little Faster* 1934 *Ladies' Money; Small Miracle* 1935 *Awake and Sing; Battleship Gertie; The Body Beautiful; Paradise Lost; Three Men on a Horse; Weep for the Virgins* 1937 *Western Waters* 1938 *The Merchant of Yonkers* 1939 *Awake and Sing; The Gentle People; Ladies and Gentlemen* 1940 *Cabin in the Sky; Heavenly Express; The Unconquered* 1941 *Clash by Night; The Night before Christmas* 1942 *Cafe Crown; R.U.R.; The Russian People* 1943 *The Family; South Pacific by Rigsby; What's Up* 1944 *Sadie Thompson* 1945 *The Assassin; The Stranger* 1946 *Gypsy Lady; Truckline Cafe* 1948 *Love Life; Skipper Next to God; The Survivors* 1949 *Detective Story* 1950 *The Bird Cage; The Country Girl; Season in the Sun* 1951 *Barefoot in Athens; I Am a Camera; The Rose Tattoo* 1952 *I've Got Sixpence* 1953 *The Crucible; The Frogs of Spring; My Three Angels* 1954 *Mademoiselle Colombe* 1955 *Bus Stop; The Diary of Anne Frank; Once upon a Tailor; A View from the Bridge* 1956 *Girls of Summer* 1957 *A Hole in the Head; Orpheus Descending; The Rope Dancers; Small War on Murray Hill* 1958 *The Cold Wind and the Warm; The Firstborn; J.B.* 1959 *Flowering Cherry; A Loss of Roses* 1960 *Do Re Mi; Semi-Detached* 1961 *The Garden of Secrets; A Gift of Time* 1963 *Andorra* 1964 *Fiddler on the Roof* 1966 *Cabaret* 1968 *The*

Price; *Zorba* 1970 *Company* 1971 *Follies* 1972 *The Creation of the World and Other Business; The Great God Brown* 1973 *A Little Night Music* 1976 *Fiddler on the Roof; Pacific Overtures* 1981 *Fiddler on the Roof* 1989 *Jerome Robbins' Broadway†* 1990 *Fiddler on the Roof*

Costumes: 1927 *2x2=5* 1937 *Western Waters* 1938 *The Merchant of Yonkers* 1940 *Cabin in the Sky; Heavenly Express* 1968 *The Price*

Lights: 1945 *The Stranger* 1948 *The Survivors* 1950 *The Country Girl; Season in the Sun* 1952 *I've Got Sixpence* 1953 *The Frogs of Spring* 1957 *The Rope Dancers; Small War on Murray Hill*

Frances Aronson

Frances Aronson regularly creates lighting designs for the Huntington Theatre, at the Williamstown Theatre Festival, at the Long Wharf Theatre and at the American Repertory Theatre among other regional theaters. A native of Texas, she has designed lights for many off-Broadway productions as well, including *More Lies About Jerzy* (Vineyard Theatre), *Entertaining Mr. Sloane* (Classic Stage Company), and *Arts and Leisure* (Playwrights Horizons). She is a frequent collaborator with James Lapine, Ben Levit, Barnet Kellman, and Garland Wright. Honors include an Obie Award for Sustained Excellence in Lighting Design. Twenty-first century designs include *Psych* the Signature Theatre.

Lights: 1992 *Falsettos*

Irene Aronson

Irene Aronson, known for her work as a printmaker and painter was born in Dresden, Germany on March 8, 1918. She received B.A. and M.A. degrees from Columbia University (1960; 1962) after studying art in various schools, including the Slade School of Fine Arts in London and the Art Students League in New York. She has worked in the print departments of major museums in the U.S. and England and has had her own prints exhibited around the world. Miss Aronson has also written and illustrated magazine articles. In the mid-1940s she was assistant costume designer for the Barnum and Bailey Circus as well as contributed costume designs to a Broadway production. Her works are in the permanent collections of the Metropolitan Museum of Art, the Victoria and Albert Museum and the National Collection of Fine Arts (Washington, D.C.) among others.

Costumes: 1946 *The Front Page*

Ruth Kanin Aronson

See Ruth Kanin.

Martin Aronstein

Martin Aronstein was born on November 2, 1936 in Pittsfield, Massachusetts and studied at Queens College of the City of New York. In 1960 he became lighting designer for the New York Shakespeare Festival where his talent for subtle, evocative lighting became apparent, leading to numerous productions for that company and others. His list of lighting credits is long and includes productions in New York both on and off-Broadway, in regional theaters, for dance companies, as American lighting supervisor for foreign companies at the Kennedy Center in Washington, D.C., and on the West Coast. His designs were nominated for five Tony Awards and he also received awards for lighting from the Los Angeles Drama Critics Circle, including the Angstrom Lighting Award for Lifetime Achievement in 1997, which honors a lighting designer whose career was established in the small theaters of Los Angeles. Aronstein, who died on May 3, 2002 in Van Nuys, California, taught at Columbia University, the University of California at Davis, and the University of Southern California.

Lights: 1964 *I Was Dancing; The Milk Train Doesn't Stop Here Anymore; A Severed Head; Tiny Alice* **1965** *Cactus Flower; The Impossible Years; Royal Hunt of the Sun* **1966** *The Investigation; Slapstick Tragedy; Those That Play the Clowns* **1967** *The Astrakhan Coat; How Now Dow Jones; Marat/Sade; Song of the Grasshopper* **1968** *The Education of H.Y.M.A.N. K.A.P.L.A.N.; Forty Carats; George M!; The Guide; Her First Roman; I'm Solomon; Morning Noon and Night; Promises, Promises* **1969** *Billy; Buck White; The Dozens; The Law of*

the Land; The Penny Wars; Play It Again, Sam* **1970** *Chinese, The/ Dr. Fish; The Gingerbread Lady; Grin and Bare It!/ Postcards; Paris Is Out; Park* **1971** *Ain't Supposed to Die a Natural Death; And Miss Reardon Drinks a Little; Four in a Garden; The Incomparable Max* **1972** *Ambassador; Different Times; Don't Play Us Cheap; Hurry, Harry; The Little Black Book; Moonchildren; Much Ado About Nothing; Promenade, All!; Sugar* **1973** *The Au Pair Man; The Beggar's Opera; Boom Boom Room; Measure for Measure; Nash at Nine; Scapin; Tricks* **1974** *An American Millionaire; Fame; My Fat Friend; Next Time I'll Sing to You* **1975** *Kennedy's Children; The Ritz* **1976** *I Have a Dream; The Poison Tree* **1977** *Dirty Linen/ New Found Land* **1978** *Hello, Dolly!; Players* **1979** *The Grand Tour* **1980** *Blackstone!; Division Street; Home; Mixed Couples* **1982** *Ghosts; Medea; Whodunnit* **1983** *Noises Off* **1984** *Beethoven's Tenth; A Woman of Independent Means* **1985** *Benefactors* **1986** *Wild Honey* **1987** *Pygmalion* **1990** *Accomplice* **1993** *The Twilight of the Golds* **1998** *Peter Pan*

John L. Arthur

The author of the play, *What Would You Do?*, John L. Arthur also designed the set. Principally an actor, stage manager, and song writer, he was born John Arthur Gillespie about 1868 and died in New York City on May 11, 1914 at age 46. "Absence Makes the Heart Grow Fonder" was among his most popular songs.

Sets: 1914 *What Would You Do?†* (Also directed)

Mason Arvold

In September 1967 Mason Arvold, a painter and scenic designer, exhibited his paintings and collages in a one-man show at the Morris A. Mechanic Theatre Lounge in Baltimore, Maryland, and subsequently at both the Galerie Internationale and Parke Bernet in New York City. He was born in Fargo, North Dakota in 1920 and learned to design while working with his father who ran the Little Country Theatre at North Dakota State University. After moving to New York City he also assisted A.A. Ostrander with the development of lighting and projection techniques for fashion shows. He died on July 1, 2000.

Lights: 1950 *Alive and Kicking*

Setsu Asakura

Setsu Asakura, one of the major theatrical designers in Japan, made her New York debut in 1978 when she directed and designed *The Dolls Sisters*, a production that toured to locations including La Mama E.T.C. She was born in Japan in 1922, the daughter of a famous Japanese sculptor and is both a set designer and painter, but has concentrated her creative energies on the theater since the mid-1960s, after breaking the gender barrier in Kabuki theater. The winner of two Japanese Academy Awards for film design, she is actively involved with the Japan Art, Stage, and Television Association and the Japanese section of the International Organization of Scenographers and Theatre Technicians. She designs regularly for Yukio Ninagawa creating new versions of Western and Japanese classics, including *Romeo and Juliet, Macbeth* and *Nigorie*. Her book *All About Theatrical Space* was published in 1986 and in 1988, an exhibition of her designs *The Scenic Art of Setsu Asakura* toured the United States. Recent designs include an opera version of *The Tale of Genji* in 2000.

Sets: 1993 *Yabuhara Kengyo*

William F. Ash

William F. Ash (or Ashe) was lighting designer for a show on Broadway in the 1920s. Initially he worked as a scenic and panoramic artist from a studio at 158 West 23rd Street In New York. As an electrician, he was later associated with Illo Equipment Company and Illo Frank Theatrical Supplies, both located on West 47th Street in 1932.

Lights: 1924 *Badges*

Don Ashton

Don Ashton designed sets for one show on Broadway in 1963. A British interior designer, he has designed hotels throughout the Far East, including the Holiday Inn Harbour View, the Mandarin Hotel and the Shangri-La, all in Hong Kong, and the China World in Beijing. The hotel in Beijing, on Jiangoumenwai is part of the China World Trade Center. Don Ashton was the Art director for the films *The Bridge on the River Kwai* and *Indiscreet*, among others. He has also taught and mentored young theater and interior designers, including Alan Roderick-Jones, a scenic designer who works on the West Coast. He is proprietor of a fine art gallery, Impressions, in Scunthorpe, Norfolk, England.

Sets: 1963 *Photo Finish*

G. Bradford Ashworth

George Bradford Ashworth was born on February 4,1892 in Fall River, Massachusetts and studied painting with George Bellows and Kenneth Hayes Miller. He founded Studio Alliance in 1936 with Arthur Segal and Robert Barnhart to supply all details to a production. The first production mounted by Studio Alliance was *Dead End* in 1936, designed by Norman Bel Geddes. In addition, he designed sets for plays and U.S.O. camp shows. Bradford Ashworth, who died in 1951. wrote *Notes on Scene Painting*. The book, edited by Donald Oenslager and first published in 1952, remains in print. Studio Alliance was closed in 1953 by Arthur Segal, who had become president of the organization.

Sets: 1934 *Lost Horizons; Tight Britches* **1935** *On Stage; Whatever Goes Up*

Nils Asther

Nils Asther, a star of silent films in his native Sweden and later in Germany, made a successful transition to talkies in Hollywood after taking a hiatus from movies to study voice and diction in England. While there, he acted in productions and contributed scenery to a show which subsequently moved to New York. He starred in many movies, including *The Single Standard* with Greta Garbo and *The Bitter Tea of General Yen* with Barbara Stanwyck. His infrequent appearances on Broadway included *Flight into Egypt* directed by Elia Kazan and *The Strong and Lonely* directed by Margaret Webster.

Born in Hellerup, Denmark to Swedish parents on January 17, 1897, he was raised in Malmö, Sweden and attended the Royal Danish Theatre School. He died at age 84 in 1981.

Sets: **1936** *The Lights o' London†*

David Atchison

David Atchison was a lighting designer who devised electrical effects that were then created in association with New York Calcium Company, located at 410 Bleeker Street. New York Calcium Lighting Company had general illumination as its primary purpose but also worked with theaters.

Lights: **1911** *The Never Homes* **1912** *Hokey-Pokey and Bunty, Bulls and Strings; Roly Poly and Without the Law* **1913** *All Aboard*

Joe Atkins

British lighting designer Joe Atkins works extensively throughout the United Kingdom and has Broadway credits for plays that have transferred from London's West End. Credits include *School for Wives* at the Cork Opera House and *Elvis the Musical* in Dublin, as well as *Abroad Lysistrata* at the Old Vic and *Robin - Prince of Sherwood*, both in London. His designs have also been seen in Liverpool, Birmingham, Cardiff and Paris. He was born in Sutton Coldfield and studied at Liverpool and Cardiff Universities. The acclaimed production of *An Ideal Husband* was directed by Peter Hall and presented initially at the Globe in London before being produced in New York. In addition to creating lighting designs, he has credits as a video lighting cameraman and for fashion shows. Atkins is married to the actress Amanda Garwood and has a son, Luke.

Lights: **1993** *Blood Brothers* **1996** *An Ideal Husband†*

Laura Sawyer Atkinson

Laura Sawyer Atkinson was an actress who appeared as Laura Sawyer in early movies, with Otis Skinner's Stage Company, and as leading lady of the Edison Company. She was born in 1885 and died at age 85 on September 7, 1970 in Matawan, New Jersey, the widow of Charles Frederick Wolff. She appeared in the 1912 film *The Lighthouse Keeper's Daughter* and the 1913 films *The Daughter of the Hills, Three of a Kind, Leaves of a Romance,* and *The Battle of Trafalgar.*

Sets: **1921** *The Survival of the Fittest*

Charles J. Auburn

Charles J. Auburn designed settings on Broadway in the 1920s. In addition, the Charles J. Auburn Scenic Studio received credit for additional productions between 1925 and 1932. In 1932 he worked as an electrician and resided at 242 East 19th Street in New York City. His widow, Mrs. Virginia Dodge Auburn died in 1957.

Sets: **1923** *For Value Received; Go West, Young Man; The Love Set; My Aunt from Ypsilanti* **1924** *Shooting Shadows; The Strong* **1925** *The Four Flusher†* (as: Charles J. Auburn Scenic Studio); *The Gorilla; Two by Two* (as: Charles J. Auburn Scenic Studio) **1930** *The Traitor* (as: Charles J. Auburn Scenic Studio) **1932** *Air Minded* (as: Charles J. Auburn Scenic Studio)

Audré

Audré studied at both the Traphagen School of Fashion and Syracuse University. Since 1946 she has designed costumes in N.Y.C. and around the country for plays, operas, industrial shows, and television. For ten years, she was the costume designer for the St. Louis Municipal Opera Company amassing credits for over 100 musicals and during eighteen years did nearly 200 musicals for the Starlight Theatre in Kansas City, Missouri. She has also designed uniforms and executed them through her shop, the Studio of Audré. In 1964 she wrote a pamphlet about costume design as a career, *To Take a Giant Step up a Glass Ladder.*

Costumes: **1946** *Three to Make Ready* **1947** *Topaz* **1950** *Arms and the Girl* **1954** *The Starcross Story* (Costume Supervisor) **1955** *The Righteous Are Bold; A Roomful of Roses* (Costume Supervisor); *The Wayward Saint* **1956** *The Happiest Millionaire* **1957** *Miss Isobel* **1960** *Cut of the Axe* **1963** *Hidden Stranger; Once for the Asking* **1965** *A Very Rich Woman*

Vilma Auld

Vilma Auld, a ballerina and choreographer designed costumes on Broadway for one show in 1963. She was born in Germany and raised in Tacoma, Washington, studying ballet with Nico Charisse and Ivan Novikoff. Vilma Auld appeared in the musical revue *Vintage '60* and *The Egg*. Both plays were produced by Zev Bufman, whom she married in 1962. Since then she has concentrated her talent and energy on costume design and producing plays.

Costumes: 1963 *Pajama Tops*

Joseph G. Aulisi

Joseph G. Aulisi made his debut on Broadway in 1968 with the opening of *Man in the Glass Booth* but his designs have been seen off-Broadway since *The Ox Cart* in 1966. Mr. Aulisi has designed costumes for numerous films including *Night Falls on Manhattan, Shaft* (1971), *Three Days of the Condor, The Pope of Greenwich Village, On Deadly Ground, Charlie's Angels: The Movie,* and *Brighton Beach Memoirs.* For television, Mr. Aulisi has designed costumes for the series *Beacon Hill* and made-for-T.V. movies, including *Gore Vidal's Lincoln* for which he was nominated for an Emmy Award.

Costumes: 1968 *The Man in the Glass Booth* **1970** *Happy Birthday, Wanda June* **1972** *All the Girls Come Out to Play; An Evening with Richard Nixon; Inner City; Ring Round the Bathtub; Tough to Get Help* **1974** *God's Favorite; Thieves* **1975** *Murder among Friends* **1976** *Rockabye Hamlet* **1977** *Unexpected Guests* **1978** *The November People* **1983** *Marilyn* **1986** *Broadway Bound; Precious Sons* **1987** *Barbara Cook: A Concert for the Theatre; A Month of Sundays* **1988** *Rumors* **1989** *Artist Descending a Staircase; Jerome Robbins' Broadway*† (Supervising designer); *Jerome Robbins' Broadway*†; *Run for Your Wife*

Avril

The costumes for a 1911 Broadway play were designed by Avril.

Costumes: 1911 *Youth* (Gowns)

Adrian Awan

Adrian Awan spent the majority of his professional life on the West Coast. At the time of his death on June 10, 1968, he had recently retired from 20th Century Fox where he had been employed as exploitation manager. He also supervised the technical aspects of productions for the Hollywood Bowl and musicals for the Los Angeles and San Francisco Civic Light Opera Associations.

Sets: 1945 *The Red Mill*
Lights: 1945 *The Red Mill* **1946** *Gypsy Lady*

Elizabeth Axtman

Elizabeth Axtman was active on Broadway from 1915 to 1917 during which time she designed costumes for the actress Grace George for all the productions in which she appeared. For one production, *The Claim,* she also designed the set. As a young woman, she worked primarily as a dressmaker through her business located at 25 West 21st Street in New York, while residing at 55 East 55th Street. A native of North Dakota, Elizabeth Axtman was born September 20, 1892 and died in August 1981.

Sets: 1917 *The Claim*†
Costumes: 1913 *Half an Hour* (Miss George's gowns); *The Younger Generation* (Miss George's gowns) **1914** *The Truth*† (Miss George's gowns) **1915** *Captain Brassbound's Conversion* (Miss George's gowns); *The Earth* (Miss George's gowns); *The Liars* (Miss George's gowns); *Major Barbara* (Miss George's gowns); *The New York Idea* (Miss George's gowns) **1917** *The Claim*† (Miss George's gowns); *L'Elevation* (Miss George's gowns)

Lemuel Ayers

Lemuel Ayers was both a designer of sets, lights and costumes and a theatrical producer. He was born in New York City on January 22, 1915. He earned a degree in architecture from Princeton University and one in drama from the University of Iowa. Mr. Ayers received the Donaldson Award for both sets and costumes for *Kiss Me Kate* in 1943 and for *Camino Real* in 1952. He also received the Donaldson Award for *My Darlin' Aida* in 1952 and *Kismet* in 1953. He was married in 1939 and had two children. Mr. Ayers died in 1955 after a brief but brilliant career. He served as art director for the film *Meet Me in St. Louis.*

Sets: 1939 *Journey's End; They Knew What They Wanted* 1941 *Angel Street; As You Like It; Eight O'clock Tuesday; They Walk Alone* 1942 *Autumn Hill; The Pirate; Plan M; The Willow and I*† 1943 *Harriet; Oklahoma!* 1944 *Bloomer Girl; Peepshow; Song of Norway* 1946 *Cyrano De Bergerac; St. Louis Woman* 1948 *Inside U.S.A.; Kiss Me Kate* 1950 *Out of This World* 1951 *Music in the Air; Oklahoma!* 1952 *Kiss Me Kate; My Darlin' Aida; See the Jaguar* 1953 *Camino Real; Kismet* 1954 *The Pajama Game*

Costumes: 1941 *Angel Street; As You Like It; Macbeth* 1946 *Cyrano De Bergerac; St. Louis Woman* 1948 *Kiss Me Kate* 1950 *Out of This World* 1951 *Music in the Air* 1952 *Kiss Me Kate; My Darlin' Aida; See the Jaguar* 1953 *Camino Real; Kismet* 1954 *The Pajama Game*

Lights: 1944 *Bloomer Girl* 1952 *My Darlin' Aida* 1953 *Camino Real*

Mrs. Julia Bacon

Mrs. Julia Bacon created gowns for the Russian émigré and actress Alla Nazimova (1879-1945) for three of her Broadway appearances.

Costumes: 1902 *A Doll's House* (Miss Nazimova's gowns) 1908 *A Doll's House* (Miss Nazimova's gowns) 1910 *Little Eyolf* (Miss Nazimova's gowns)

James Bailey

James Bailey was a British designer and painter. He designed the 1949 production of *A Midsummer Night's Dream* at Stratford-upon-Avon, ballets including *Giselle* and the operas *Manon Lescault* and *Rigoletto* at Covent Garden. He was also associated with Sadler's Wells Ballet. Bailey studied at the Byam School of Art, the Slade School, and with European stage designers Randolphe Schwabe and Vladimir Polunin. His paintings, to which he devoted most of his time after 1960, were exhibited in London and Monte Carlo. He lived from March 7, 1921 (or 1922, as is sometimes published) until July 2, 1980.

Sets: 1950 *As You Like It* 1952 *The Millionairess*

Costumes: 1950 *As you Like It*

Léon Bakst

Léon Bakst, after a fortunate meeting with Diaghilev, designed many works for the Ballets Russe. He was a major influence on both fashion and costume during his lifetime. Bakst was born in Grodno, Russia in 1866 and studied in St. Petersburg but spent most of his life in Paris where he died in 1924. In addition to his designs for the stage he created clothes for couture houses, including Worth and Paquin. An artist of great originality, Léon Bakst used strong colors and bold geometric forms. His designs graced the Broadway stage during the late teens and early twenties.

Sets: 1916 *The Big Show*† 1922 *Revue Russe*†

Costumes: 1916 *The Big Show*† (Costumes for "The Sleeping Beauty") 1919 *Aphrodite*† (Additional costumes) 1920 *Mecca*† (Additional costumes) 1922 *Revue Russe*†

Mike Baldassari

Mike Baldassari, the lighting designer, was born May 2, 1965 in Atlantic City, New Jersey, son of Vincent and Claire Baldassari, an electrical engineer and homemaker/librarian. He grew up in Parsippany, New Jersey where he studied with the Big Band drummer Vincent Mizzoni and played professionally. Technical theater captured his interest however, when he not only used his drums musically but to create sound effects. He graduated from the University of Connecticut in 1987; after college he participated in the United Scenic Artists' Lighting Design Internship program. In the early 1990s, he began a long-term association with Jules Fisher and Peggy Eisenhauer. For *Cabaret*, he and Peggy Eisenhauer as co-designers received nominations for the Tony and Drama Desk Awards and won an *Entertainment Design Award* (EDDY). Additional theater credits include *Tenderloin* directed by Walter Bobbie, *Savion Glover - Footnotes* (lighting and scenic design) and Yeston's *Phantom*. Baldassari has been the American Associate Lighting Designer for numerous productions transferred from the U.K. to Broadway, such as *Racing Demon*, *An Inspector Calls* and *Dancing at Lughnasa*. His television credits include *Garth Brooks Live from Central Park* for which he received an Emmy Award nomination. He was the director of lighting for Neil Young's *Harvest Moon* tour and the lighting consultant to Vice President Al Gore during the 2000 Presidential Debates.

Lights: 1996 *An Ideal Husband*† **1998** *Cabaret*†

Gail Baldoni

Gail Baldoni is production coordinator for Dodger Costumes, the largest costume house in the United States. She started working for the costume company in 1990 when it was known as Eaves-Brooks and has held increasingly important positions, all the while maintaining her career as a costume designer. Off-Broadway credits include *The Yiddish Trojan Women*, *Jolson & Co.*, *Kander and Ebb: A Celebration*, and *Home of the Brave* at the Jewish Repertory Theatre. For the Ogunquit Playhouse she has designed costumes for productions including *A Majority or One* and *Dial M for Murder* and at the Helen Hayes Performing Arts Center in Nyack, New York, she created costume designs for *A Tale of Two Cities*. Television designs include the daytime drama *Another World* for which she was nominated for an Emmy Award. Among her twenty-first century designs is *Zorba* at the North Shore Music Theatre.

Costumes: 1994 *Wonderful Town*

Frances H. Ball

Frances H. Ball designed scenery for one play on Broadway in 1927. She resided at 147 West 74th Street in New York City in the 1920s.

Sets: 1927 *The Wandering Jew*

Robert Ballagh

Robert Ballagh was born in Dublin on September 22, 1943. He studied at St. Michael's College and architecture at the College of Technology in Dublin. A painter, printmaker and theatrical designer, he had his first one-man show in Dublin in 1969. Since that time, his work has been often exhibited and he has received many awards, including an ICAD in 1980 for illustration and the Martin Toonder Award in 1981. His paintings are in the permanent collection of the National Gallery of Ireland, on stamps for the Irish Postal Service, and on the currency issued by the Central Bank of Ireland. In addition to all the iterations of *Riverdance* from its beginning on *Eurovision* into New York by way of London, he has designed scenery at the Gate Theatre in Dublin for *I'll Go On* (professional debut as a scenic designer), *Salomé*, *The Importance of Being Earnest* and *Endgame*.

Sets: 1996 *Riverdance*†; *Riverdance - The Show* (Also projections) **1997** *Riverdance* (Also painted images) **1998** *Riverdance* **2000** *Riverdance on Broadway*

Lucinda Ballard

Lucinda Ballard was born Lucinda Davis Goldsborough in New Orleans on April 3, 1908. Her father was a lawyer and her mother the political cartoonist Doré. Trained as an artist in New York City and Paris, she married William F. R. Ballard in 1930. That marriage ended in 1938 and in 1951 she married lyricist Howard Dietz. Miss Ballard began her active career in theater as an assistant to the scenic designers Norman Bel Geddes and Claude Bragdon, and made her professional debut in 1937. In 1947 she received the first Antoinette Perry Award for Costume Design for five plays: *Happy Birthday*, *Another Part of the Forest*, *Street Scene*, *John Loves Mary* and *The Chocolate Soldier*. She won a second Tony Award in 1962 for *The Gay Life*, received the Donaldson Award for *The Glass Menagerie* in 1945 and was nominated for an Academy Award for *A Streetcar Named Desire*. Her career designing costumes encompassed theater, film and ballet as well as revivals of productions that she originally designed. She died on August 19, 1993.

Sets: 1937 *As You Like It*† **1943** *The Moon Vine* **1948** *Make Way for Lucia*

Costumes: **1937** *As You Like It*† **1938** *Great Lady* **1939** *Morning's at Seven; The Three Sisters* **1940** *Higher and Higher* **1942** *Solitaire* (Costume Supervisor); *Stars on Ice* **1943** *The Moon Vine; My Dear Public* **1944** *I Remember Mama; Listen Professor; Sing Out, Sweet Land* **1945** *Memphis Bound; A Place of Our Own* **1946** *Annie Get Your Gun; Another Part of the Forest; Happy Birthday; Show Boat* **1947** *Allegro; The Chocolate Soldier; John Loves Mary; Street Scene; A Streetcar Named Desire* **1948** *Love Life; Make Way for Lucia* **1949** *The Rat Race*† (Miss Field's costumes) **1950** *The Wisteria Trees* **1951** *The Fourposter* **1952** *Mrs. McThing* **1953** *Carnival in Flanders; My Three Angels* **1955** *Cat on a Hot Tin Roof; Silk Stockings*† **1957** *A Clearing in the Woods; The Dark at the Top of the Stairs; Orpheus Descending* **1958** *The Girls in 509; Handful of Fire; J.B.* **1959** *A Loss of Roses; The Sound of Music*† **1960** *Invitation to a March* **1961** *The Gay Life* **1962** *Lord Pengo; Romulus; Tiger Tiger Burning Bright*

Ariel Ballif

Ariel Ballif was born in Rexburg, Idaho on May 29, 1926 and received a B.A. in art and theater from Brigham Young University in 1947. After a brief stay in New York City taking theater design courses at the New School for Social Research and creating displays for Macy's, he studied with Donald Oenslager and Frank Poole Bevan at Yale, receiving an M.F.A. His New York and Broadway debut occurred in 1953, shortly after completing graduate school. He was resident designer for the Virginia Museum Theatre when it opened and subsequently founded The Renaissance, a dinner theater in Virginia. Upon returning to Utah in 1962, he taught at the University of Utah until shortly after founding Theatre 138 with Tom Carlin and Stewart Falconer in 1966. The following year he joined the faculty at Yale University, where his students included John Lee Beatty and Santo Loquasto. In 1972 he returned to Utah, resumed designing and directing for Theatre 138 and in 1987, resumed teaching at the University of Utah. His credits include

scenery for *Big River, The Miser, Driving Miss Daisy, The Three Musketeers* and *Chicago* for the Pioneer Memorial Theatre at the University of Utah and the 1991/1992 production of *The Nutcracker* at BalletWest. Ballif died on April 21, 1994. Four days later, he was posthumously awarded the 1994 Madeleine Award for distinguished service in the arts by the Madeleine Arts and Humanities Council.

Sets: **1953** *A Pin to See the Peepshow*

Noël Ballif

Noël Ballif is a French director who works primarily in television, movies and radio. He participated in a mid-1950s production on Broadway as the designer of sets and costumes and is listed in the 1957 edition of the *Annuaire biographique du cinéma et de la télévision en France, en Belgique et en Afrique du Nord.*

Sets: **1955** *Dancers of God*
Costumes: **1955** *Dancers of God*

Ballou

David R. (Tex) Ballou was born in Manila, The Philippines in 1925, the son of Charles Nicholas Senn Ballou and Emily Barnes Smith Ballou and a family that includes the portrait artist Bertha Ballou. Ballou received an M.F.A. at the Goodman Art Institute where he later spent six years as head of the costume program, teaching among others Theoni V. Aldredge. Ballou credits Mordecai Gorelik as a major influence on his career, along with Richard Whorf and his other teachers while studying at Biarritz. His debut was for *Bachelor Born* for the Lynchburg (Virginia) Little Theatre. Ballou, who designs scenery, lights and costumes, has been awarded almost every professional prize in the New York theater, including a Tony nomination for the scenic design for *The Legend of Lizzie* in 1959, the Vernon Rice Award for *Machinal*, and Obie awards for *Machinal, A Doll's House* and the design of the off-Broadway Theatre Four. He has over three hundred credits for industrial productions for Coca-Cola, I.B.M., Chevrolet, McDonald's, Charles of the Ritz and many others. Active in the profession, he has served as Vice President and on various committees for United Scenic Artists. His son Mark Ballou is an actor who recently appeared in *Dreamers* among other films and television shows.

Sets: 1956 *Wake Up, Darling* 1959 *Legend of Lizzie*

Costumes: 1954 *The Flowering Peach* 1955 *Red Roses for Me* 1959 *Legend of Lizzie*

Lights: 1956 *Wake Up, Darling*

Bill Ballou

Bill Ballou has designed sets, sound, and lights and worked as a technician throughout New England, beginning with musicals in high school and followed by productions at the Rockland County Community Theatre. His credits include productions at Hartford Stage Company, American Place Theatre, Smith College, StageWest and Shakespeare and Company. His credits also include sound design off-Broadway and in regional theaters. He was born in Manhattan on April 26, 1950 and received a B.A. in theater from Hampshire College in 1978. His mother, Billie Ballou, is a storyteller. He maintains a shop specializing in metal work and woodwork for theaters and also consults on the conception and coordination of feature films. Bill Ballou has created and engineered scenery for Elizabeth Streb and her performance company Ringside, for appearances in New York and California.

Sets: 1981 *Heartland*

Lights: 1981 *Heartland*

Pierre Balmain

Pierre Alexander Claudius Balmain originally intended to be an architect, but his fondness for sketching dresses led him to a position in 1934 with Molyneux who advised him to devote himself to dress design. After service with the French army during World War II, he worked briefly for Lucien LeLong and then opened his own couture house. Balmain specialized in feminine, elegant clothes and was an influential part of the "New Look" which revolutionized fashion in the late 1940s. He not only designed clothes for a loyal and elegant clientele that included royalty and film stars, but maintained ready-to-wear operations in New York and Paris, created perfumes, and designed costumes for films, theater and ballets. Pierre Balmain received a Tony Award in 1980 for outstanding costume design for *Happy New Year*. He was born in St.-Jean-de-Maurienne on May 18, 1914 and died in Paris June 29, 1982.

Costumes: 1952 *The Millionairess* (Miss Hepburn's dresses) 1960 *Rape of the Belt*† (Miss Cummings' and Redman's gowns) 1980 *Happy New Year*

E. G. Banks

E. G. Banks, generally known as Harry Banks, was a British scene painter who worked with W. B. Spong and Bruce Smith primarily in London. His credits in the 1880s and 1890s include productions at the London Gaiety Theatre and at the Theatre Royal Globe. All of the productions for which he designed and painted the back drops were imported to New York from London for a run on Broadway.

Sets: 1899 *Little Ray of Sunshine, A* 1902 *The Cross-ways*†; *The Happy Hypocrite*† (Acts I and III) 1910 *Mr. and Mrs. Daventry*† (Acts I and III)

Leslie Banks

Leslie Banks was an actor in movies and the theater in both New York and England who also directed and produced during a career lasting forty years. He was born in Liverpool, England on June 8, 1890 and died in London on April 21, 1952. As a young man he considered the priesthood, then painting, before appearing on stage at the Town Hall, Brechin as Old Gobbo in *The Merchant of Venice*. His New York debut on stage was in 1914 in *Eliza Comes to Stay*. In 1930 he not only designed the set, but also directed and starred in *The Infinite Shoeblack*. He was honored as a Commander of the British Empire in 1950.

Sets: 1930 *The Infinite Shoeblack*†

Travis Banton

Travis Banton moved to New York City from Waco, Texas where he was born in 1894, to study at Columbia. He took courses in painting at the Art Students League where his gift for painting fabrics was rewarded with a scholarship and led him to positions with the New York fashion salons of Madame Frances and Lucile. After designing costumes for two shows on Broadway in the early 1920s, Mr. Banton moved to Hollywood where he spent the majority of his career designing glamorous costumes for numerous movies such as *A Farewell to Arms, A Song to Remember, How Green Was My Valley*, and *Shanghai Express*. He held positions in the major movie studios and also designed for private customers. In 1956, he returned to New York to create costumes for Rosalind Russell in *Auntie Mame*. One of the great Hollywood costume designers, Mr. Banton died in 1958.

Costumes: 1922 *The Fool* (Gowns) **1924** *My Girl* **1956** *Auntie Mame*† (Miss Russell's clothes)

Vicki Baral

Vicki Baral works primarily with her husband Gerry Hariton creating sets and lights for plays and television on the East and West Coasts. Designs for television include the setting for Joan Rivers' *The Late Show*. She was born in Baltimore in 1951 and graduated from Brandeis University. Baral and Hariton work extensively in California on scenic and lighting designs and as art directors and/or production designers. They have collaborated on *Miss Universe Pageants, The Mickey Mouse Club, Funhouse* and *Wild West Showdown* for which they received an Emmy Award nomination. From 1974 to 1978 they were resident designers at the University of California at Riverside and have also served as resident designers for the Matrix Theatre. Their designs for the setting and lighting of *Betrayal* for the Matrix Theatre won two Los Angeles Critics Awards in 1982. Theatre credits include many productions at the Pasadena Playhouse and various projects that feature multimedia projections. Together they have also begun to work as producers.

Sets: 1986 *Raggedy Ann*† **1988** *Mail*†

Edith Barber

Edith Barber designed the dresses for one show in 1930. She spent the majority of her career in the theater in the wardrobe department of the Kingsway Theatre.

Costumes: 1930 *Marigold*† (Dresses)

Georges Barbier

Georges Barbier is most often remembered as an illustrator who contributed to *Gazette du Bon Ton, Femina, Journal des Dames et des Modes, Vogue* and many others. He spent his life painting, illustrating and designing after studying at the Academie des Beaux-Arts in Paris. Georges Barbier, a disciple of Léon Bakst and Paul Poiret, was born in Nantes, France in 1882 and died in Paris in 1932 and is not to be mistaken for the American stage and screen actor George W. Barbier (1865-1945.) The French artist received credits for many individual costumes or gowns for productions and once in his career also contributed scenic designs to a Broadway show. His credits in France include scenery and costumes for the Folies Bergère often in collaboration with Erté, *Amarilla* for Anna Pavlova's company, *Coeurs en Folie* for the John Tiller Girls, and *Monsieur Baucaire* for the Marigny Company.

Sets: 1923 *Casanova*
Costumes: 1922 *The Bunch and Judy*† (Costumes in Act I, Scene II) **1923** *Casanova* **1928** *The Age of Innocence*† (Miss Cornell's Act I, II, III costumes); *Angela*†; *The Red Robe*†; *White Lilacs*† **1929** *Boom Boom*†; *Broadway Nights*†; *Pleasure Bound*†

Randy Barcelo

Both of Randy Barcelo's parents were trained as architects. He was born in Cuba in 1946 and attended the University of Puerto Rico before moving to New York and studying with Lester Polakov. He later taught occasionally at the Studio and Forum of Stage Design. His designs were often seen both on and off-Broadway in New York and also on the West Coast. Mr. Barcelo received two Tony nominations for his designs, the first for *Jesus Christ Superstar* directed by Tom O'Horgan with whom he often worked and the second for *Ain't Misbehavin'*. Additional credits include Hector Berlioz's *Les Troyens* in Vienna, Leonard Bernstein's *Mass* in Washington, D.C. and costumes for the New York Shakespeare Festival. Shortly before he died on December 6, 1994, he designed costumes for *Si Señor! Es Mi Son!* for Ballet Hispánico.

Costumes: 1971 *Jesus Christ Superstar*; *Lenny* **1972** *Dude* **1974** *Leaf People* (Also make-up); *The Magic Show* **1975** *The Night That Made America Famous* **1978** *Ain't Misbehavin'*; *A Broadway Musical* **1988** *Ain't Misbehavin'*

William Barclay

Since William Barclay graduated from Ohio State University in 1976 he has amassed numerous credits (as both William and Bill Barclay) for scenic design for theatrical productions and set decoration, scenic design, production design and art direction for movies. Among his first New York credits were the scenery for *Grace* at the American Place Theatre in 1981 and *The Butter and Egg Man* at the Manhattan Punch Line Theatre the following year. His scenery has been featured at the Folger Theatre in Washington, D.C., often at the Vineyard Theatre off-Broadway, and at the Circle Repertory Company, among others. Movies include *She's the One, A Brooklyn State of Mind, Beaches* and *Glengarry, Glen Ross.* His designs are in the permanent collection of the Lawrence and Lee Theatre Research Institute at Ohio State University. Twenty-first century designs include *Hello Muddah, Hello Fadduh!* at the Triad Theatre.

Sets: 1992 *Solitary Confinement* (Scenery and art direction) **1994** *Sally Marr...and Her Escorts*

Henry Bardon

Henry Bardon was born in Czechoslovakia on June 19, 1923 and moved to England in the 1930s and studied at the Dundee College of Art in Scotland where he began to paint scenery. Early in his career he designed for the theater, before concentrating on opera and ballet. His professional de-but was *The Firstborn* in Perth, Australia and his initial production in London was *Everything in the Garden* in the West End in 1962 but *The Dream* for Frederick Ashton in 1964 helped establish his brilliant reputation for romantic and decorative scenery. He designed scenery for many productions for which the costumes were designed by David Walker, during a long-term and successful collaboration. Credits include *Lucia de Lammermoor* for Joan Sutherland in Australia, *I Puritani* for Federico Fellini, and *Così Fan Tutte* at Covent Garden. Henry Bardon died in July 1991.

Sets: 1993 *Cinderella* **1995** *Cinderella*

A. R. Barker

Adella Barker was a character actress who made her stage debut in 1881 in *Around the World in Eighty Days*. She toured with Lillian Russell, performed in many Gilbert and Sullivan operettas, and appeared in early films, including one with Francis X. Bushman. Known to be especially interested in her own stage presence, she also contributed costumes to a 1909 production in which she did not appear. Miss Barker, who retired from the stage in 1919 after appearing in *The Little Teacher*, died on September 29, 1930 in Amityville, Long Island, New York.

Costumes: 1909 *Two Women and That Man*

Corinne Barker

Corinne Barker was an actress who appeared on Broadway in plays including *Shirley Kaye, Abe and Mawruss* and *The Squab Farm*. She also performed in early movies while under contract to Cosmopolitan Productions. She occasionally modeled hats and gowns for advertisements and appeared on the cover of the January 1918 issue of *Theatre Magazine*. Her contribution to costume design was as supervisor for one production in 1925. Victim of heart disease, she died at age 35 on August 6, 1928.

Costumes: 1925 *No, No Nanette* (Costume Supervisor)

Shirley Barker

Shirley Barker created costumes both

on Broadway and for movies. In New York she was associated with the couture house founded by Lady Duff Gordon known as Lucile, Ltd. During the 1940s she worked as an assistant to the film designer, Irene. Movie credits, in collaboration with Irene, include *Living in a Big Way* and *Three Darling Daughters.*

Costumes: **1919** *Greenwich Village Follies*† **1920** *Genius and the Crowd* (Gowns); *Her Family Tree* **1921** *Two Little Girls* **1922** *The Blue Kitten*† **1923** *Go-Go*; *Lady Butterfly*

Alan Barlow

Alan Barlow, a native of England was born in Coventry and began designing at the Bristol Old Vic when he was 19 years old. His London debut was *She Stoops to Conquer* for the Old Vic, directed by Michael Redgrave. Since that time he has designed numerous productions for the Stratford (Ontario) Festival, Dublin's Abbey Theatre, Covent Garden, and the Old Vic. Specializing in theater and opera, Mr. Barlow has also taught at the National Theatre School in London and been resident designer for a number of companies. His credits include directing plays for which he has also been much honored, and occasionally conducting. His scenic and costume designs are in the permanent collection of the Victoria and Albert Museum.

Sets: **1972** *There's One in Every Marriage*

Costumes: **1972** *There's One in Every Marriage*

Gregg Barnes

Gregg Barnes is an especially busy costume designer of plays, musicals, extravaganzas and revues. In addition to designing regularly for Radio City Music Hall where he has been Resident Costume designer since 1995, his costumes are often seen off-Broadway, including *Disappearing Act* and *Zombie Prom* among others. He designed a wide variety of productions during his six season tenure as Resident Costume Designer at the Paper Mill Playhouse from *Death of a Salesman, You Never Know, Gigi,* to *Call Me Madam.*

Among his many credits are costume designs for the Old Globe, Arena Stage, Glimmerglass Opera, the Alvin Ailey Company, the Moscow Children's Musical Theatre, and the world premiere of the opera *Desire under the Elms* at City Center. An instructor in Technical Theatre at New York University, he earned his B.A. at the University of California, San Diego and his M.F.A. at New York University in 1983.

Costumes: **1993** *Cinderella* **1994** *Radio City Christmas Spectacular*† **1995** *Cinderella; The Merry Widow; Radio City Christmas Spectacular* **1996** *Radio City Christmas Spectacular* **1997** *Radio City Christmas Spectacular*†; *Side Show; The Wizard of Oz* **1998** *Radio City Christmas Spectacular*† (Santa's Gonna Rock and Roll, etc.); *The Wizard of Oz* **1999** *The Wizard of Oz*

Will R. Barnes

Will R. Barnes, who died on November 27, 1939, was a stage costume designer and an artist specializing in water-color landscapes. Born in Australia, he worked in London before emigrating to New York in the late 1890s where he was soon designing costumes. He contributed costume designs to several plays and musical revues in London beginning with *An Arabian Girl and Forty Thieves* in 1899 for which he was co-costume designer with the British designer Howell Russell. During an era when many productions arrived in New York after playing in London, both *The Prince of Pilsen* and *The College Widow* were seen in New York before the moving to London. In the mid-1920s, he stopped designing for the theater in order to concentrate on painting. He often worked in collaboration with Charles LeMaire, Archie Gunn, and Cora MacGeachy. Many of his charming sketches for chorus girls in musical comedies are in the Billy Rose Theatre Collection, housed in the New York Public Library for the Performing Arts at Lincoln Center.

Costumes: **1900** *Arizona; Fiddle-Dee-Dee; Hodge, Podge, & Co.; Woman and Wine* **1901** *Hoity Toity* (Costumes and gowns); *The Little Duchess*† **1902** *The Mocking Bird; Twirly Whirly* **1903**

The Prince of Pilsen† **1904** *The College Widow; The Sho-gun†; The Yankee Consul* **1905** *The Duke of Duluth; The Gingerbread Man†* **1906** *Dream City; The Student King* **1907** *The Rogers Brothers in Panama†* (Costumes); *The Time, the Place and the Girl; A Yankee Tourist†* **1908** *The Queen of the Moulin Rouge* **1910** *Naughty Marietta; The Old Town†; The Spring Maid†* **1912** *Robin Hood; The Rose Maid* **1913** *Rachel; Rob Roy* **1914** *The Dancing Duchess†* **1917** *Cheer-up (Hippodrome)†; Eyes of Youth†* **1918** *Everything†* **1919** *Elsie Janis and Her Gang†; Happy Days†* **1920** *Good Times* **1921** *Get Together†* (Ice Ballet) **1922** *Better Times†* (Other costumes); *Elsie Janis and Her Gang†* **1923** *Stepping Stones†* **1924** *Stepping Stones†*

Robert Barnhart

Robert Barnhart both created sets and acted in Broadway shows. He was a partner with G. Bradford Ashworth and Arthur Segal in Studio Alliance, a scenery construction business, when it was founded in 1936. He also designed the set for a 1938 production of *The Two Bouquets.* He joined the Broadway cast of *Tobacco Road* in 1940, replacing Del Hughes in a role he had played previously with the Boston Company.

Sets: **1934** *Invitation to Murder; Too Many Boats; While Parents Sleep* **1935** *Petticoat Fever* **1944** *Good Morning Corporal*

Kenn Barr

Kenn Barr was active on Broadway during the 1940s and 1950s. During the early 1950s he had a shop, "The Sand Barr" on Fire Island and designed many of the clothes sold there, as well as through the department store Russeks. Mr. Barr taught fashion and costume design at the University of Minnesota. A regular collaborator with lighting designer Peggy Clark and director Margo Jones, he designed costumes for several seasons at the Dallas Theatre Center.

Costumes: **1941** *Gabrielle* **1942** *The Sun Field; What Big Ears* **1946** *Toplitzky of Notre Dame* **1950** *Southern Exposure* **1951** *Angels Kiss Me; Darkness at Noon*

1952 *The Climate of Eden* **1956** *Girls of Summer* **1959** *The Warm Peninsula*

Watson Barratt

Watson Barratt was a prolific scenic designer who occasionally designed costumes and lights. He was born in Salt Lake City, Utah, on June 27, 1884 and studied in New York and Wilmington, Delaware. He began professional life as an illustrator, specializing in magazine covers. He entered the theater as a scenic artist, later becoming the chief scenic designer for the Shuberts. His first scene designs on Broadway were seen in 1917 and he debuted as a costume designer on Broadway in 1926, after which he did numerous productions, including lighting for one in 1950. Mr. Barratt, who also served as director of the St. Louis Municipal Opera for several years, died in 1962.

Sets: **1917** *A Night in Spain* **1918** *Girl o' Mine; An Ideal Husband; A Little Journey; Little Simplicity; The Melting of Molly; The Passing Show of 1918†; Sinbad; Sleeping Partners* **1919** *The Dancer; Monte Cristo, Jr.; Oh, What a Girl; The Passing Show of 1919; Shubert Gaieties of 1919; A Sleepless Night* **1920** *Cinderella on Broadway†; Floradora; The Outrageous Mrs. Palmer; Tick-Tack-Toe* **1921** *Blossom Time; Bombo; In the Night Watch†; The Last Waltz; The Mimic World; The Silver Fox; The Whirl of New York* **1922** *The Goldfish; The Hotel Mouse; The Lady in Ermine; Make It Snappy†; The Passing Show of 1922; The Rose of Stamboul; Springtime of Youth†; Thin Ice* **1923** *Artists and Models; Caroline; The Dancing Girl; Dew Drop Inn; For All of Us; The Passing Show of 1923; Topics of 1923* **1924** *Artists and Models; Blossom Time; The Dream Girl; The Farmer's Wife; Innocent Eyes; The Passing Show of 1924; The Student Prince; Vogues of 1924; The Werewolf* **1925** *Artists and Models; Big Boy; Gay Paree; June Days; A Lady's Virtue; The Love Song; Mayflowers; Princess Flavia; The Virgin of Bethulia* **1926** *Blossom Time; Countess Maritza; First Love; Gay Paree; Great Temptations; Katja; The Merry World; A Night in Paris; The Padre; The Pearl of Great Price* **1927** *Artists and Models; Cherry Blossoms; The Circus Princess;*

The Crown Prince; Immortal Isabella?; The Love Call; Mixed Doubles; My Maryland; A Night in Spain; The Nightingale; The Scarlet Lily **1928** *12,000; Angela; Countess Maritza; Greenwich Village Follies; The Kingdom of God; Luckee Girl; The Red Robe; The Silent House; Sunny Days; Young Love* **1929** *Boom Boom; Broadway Nights; The Lady from the Sea; The Love Duel; Music in May; A Night in Venice; Pleasure Bound; Street Singer; A Wonderful Night*† **1930** *Artists and Models; Lost Sheep; Meet My Sister; Nina Rosa; The Royal Virgin; Scarlet Sister Mary; Three Little Girls* **1931** *As You Desire Me; Blossom Time; Cynara; Experience Unnecessary; If I Were You; Peter Ibbetson; The School for Scandal; The Student Prince; The Wonder Bar* **1932** *A Little Rocketeer; Marching By; Smiling Faces* **1933** *The Mikado; Ten Minute Alibi* **1934** *Music Hath Charms; No More Ladies; The Perfumed Lady; A Roman Servant; The Shatter'd Lamp; So Many Paths; Ziegfeld Follies: 1934*† **1935** *Knock on Wood; Laburnum Grove; Living Dangerously* **1936** *Black Limelight; The Case of Clyde Griffiths; Come Angel Band; The Golden Journey; Green Waters; Lady Precious Stream; The Laughing Woman; Mid-West* **1937** *Frederika; Hitch Your Wagon; The Lady Has a Heart*†; *Merely Murder; Tell Me, Pretty Maiden; Three Waltzes; Wise Tomorrow* **1938** *Bachelor Born; Blossom Time; Come Across; Madame Capet; Outward Bound; You Never Know*† **1939** *Billy Draws a Horse; Clean Beds; Close Quarters; Foreigners; The Importance of Being Earnest; The Time of Your Life; The White Steed* **1940** *Kind Lady; Leave Her to Heaven; Love's Old Sweet Song; Romantic Mr. Dickens; The Time of Your Life; Walk with Music* **1941** *Ah, Wilderness!; Golden Wings; Hope for a Harvest; My Fair Ladies; Night of Love* **1942** *Little Darling; Magic/ Hello, Out There*†; *The Rivals; Yesterday's Magic* **1943** *Artists and Models; Ask My Friend Sandy; Blossom Time; The Student Prince; This Rock; Ziegfeld Follies: 1943* **1944** *Bright Boy; Pick-Up Girl; Sheppy* **1945** *Happily Ever After; A Lady Says Yes; Rebecca* **1946** *Flamingo Road; January Thaw* **1947** *Heads or Tails; Little A; Louisiana Lady* **1948** *Ghosts; Hedda Gabler; My Romance* **1950** *With a Silk Thread* **1954** *The Starcross Story* **1955** *The Righteous Are Bold*

Costumes: **1926** *The Pearl of Great Price*† (Court of Luxury, Love, Vanity, Wanton) **1930** *Hello, Paris*† **1935** *Living Dangerously* **1939** *The Importance of Being Earnest* (Costumes Supervised) **1942** *Magic/ Hello, Out There*; *The Rivals* **1950** *With a Silk Thread*

Lights: **1950** *With a Silk Thread*

Christopher Barreca

Christopher Barreca was born on March 1, 1957 in Pittsfield, Massachusetts. His B.F.A. in music and drama is from the University of Connecticut, followed by an M.F.A. from Yale University, where he made his professional debut with the scenic design for *The Philanderer* starring Christopher Walken and Brook Adams. After completing graduate school he assisted Jerry Rojo from 1978 to 1979 and then Ming Cho Lee from 1982 and 1987 while also working at Atlas Scenic Studio. At the American Ibsen Theatre in Pittsburgh, Pennsylvania, which he helped found in the early 1980s, he received experience designing a wide variety of productions, working with directors ranging from Charles Ludlum to Travis Preston, after which he began working more extensively in regional theaters. He has designed scenery for many productions at the Mark Taper Forum, the South Coast Repertory, Berkeley Repertory, and at ACT in San Francisco, among other theaters on the West Coast; at the Dallas Theatre Center and the Indiana Repertory Theatre in the middle of the country; and at Center Stage in Baltimore and Hartford Stage. His recent design activity has been centered in and around New York. He designs not only for theater, but for dance and opera. After four years on the faculty of Southern Methodist University, he was appointed Head of Production and Design at the California Institute of the Arts in 1996. Honors include many Drama Logue and Back Stage West Garland Awards, and an American Theatre Wing Award for *Chronicle of a Death Foretold*.

Sets: **1991** *Our Country's Good* **1992**

Hamlet; *Hamlet (Roundabout)*; *Search and Destroy* **1995** *Chronicle of a Death Foretold* **1999** *Marie Christine*

Lewis Barrington

Lewis Barrington designed sets on Broadway in the mid-1920s. An artist, his studios and home were located at 220 West 14th Street in New York City in 1925.

Sets: 1925 *The Book of Charm* **1927** *Big Lake*

John Barrymore

John Barrymore, a member of one of the most respected American theatrical families, was interested in painting early in his life and studied art in Europe. A position as a cartoonist for the *New York Journal* ended soon after it began and he turned to acting at age twenty-one, finding enormous success on stage and in movies. Known as "The Great Profile," he had a flair for comedy and was known as a great lover on stage and off. John Barrymore, who used his artistic training to occasionally offer designs for settings, died on May 29, 1942 at age 60.

Sets: 1921 *Clair De Lune*†

Natalie Barth

See Natalie Barth Walker.

Ralph Barton

Ralph Barton was born in Kansas City, Missouri on August 14, 1891 and studied in Paris. He was a skilled cartoonist and caricaturist whose work appeared in *Vanity Fair, Judge, Life* and *Smart Set.* He illustrated books, designed the theater curtain of caricatures for the 1922 *Chauve Souris*, and created sets for one Broadway show. Ralph Barton died a suicide on May 20, 1931.

Sets: 1923 *Poppy*

Hugo Baruch

Credits for scenery for Hugo Baruch and for Hugo Baruch & Cie. appear as early as 1898 in Germany, for a production of *Don Juan in der Hölle* at the Apollo Theatre in Berlin. The original family business was related to creating objects and curiosities from plastic and with crafts before it specialized in theatrical sets, costumes, accessories, and properties. The New York branch of Hugo Baruch and Company was located at 915 Broadway in the early years of the twentieth century. In 1910, there were studios in London, New York, Vienna, and Berlin. Hugo Baruch, Sr. died in 1904. Hugo Baruch, Jr. who succeeded his father in the family business and wrote under the pseudonym Jack Bilbo, died in 1967.

Sets: 1908 *Fluffy Ruffles*† **1909** *The Chocolate Soldier*† (Act I) **1910** *The Girl in the Taxi* (Also properties) **1912** *Baron Trenck* (Properties and furniture) **1913** *The Five Frankforters* **1914** *The Queen of the Movies*

Costumes: 1909 *On the Eve*† (Uniforms); *Ziegfeld Follies of 1909*† (Lyre bird costume, armor, and properties) **1910** *The Girl in the Taxi*; *Ziegfeld Follies of 1910*† (Speciality costumes, armor, properties) **1912** *Baron Trenck* **1914** *The Queen of the Movies*

Charles Basing

Charles Basing, an American painter of murals, was born on July 23, 1865 in Victoria, Australia. He painted among other projects, the ceiling in Grand Central Station and also designed museum interiors in New York City for Columbia University and in Pittsburgh for the Carnegie Institute. He died on February 3, 1933 in Marrakech, Morocco. He worked in collaboration with brothers Arthur T. and J. Monroe Hewlett on stage settings and murals. For credits and additional information see the entry "Hewlett and Basing."

Sets: 1912 *Peter Pan*†

William H. Batchelder

William H. Batchelder studied stagecraft with Harry Feldman and at the Yale School of Drama after receiving a B.A. at Harvard in 1958. Early in his career, he worked as an assistant to Jean Rosenthal. Born on June 27, 1937 in New York City, he is known primarily as a lighting designer and a production manager. He has served as stage manager for productions New York City Center Light Opera Company at the New York City Center and on Broadway starting with *The Right Honorable Gentleman* in 1965. He has

also worked as production manager and lighting designer for Elliot Feld, as well as stage manager and lighting designer for the Martha Graham Dance Company.
Lights: 1972 *Captain Brassbound's Conversion*

Alfred Bauer

Alfred Bauer designed sets in 1935 on Broadway. It is unlikely that the designer is the same Alfred Bauer (1906-1974) who founded and was the long-time director of the Berlin Film Festival.
Sets: 1935 *Few Are Chosen*

Laura Bauer

Costume designer Laura Bauer made her Broadway debut in 2001. Since 1989 she has designed costumes for the Steppenwolf Ensemble in Chicago, including *A Clockwork Orange*. She also designs regularly for the Atlantic Theatre Company in New York, including *American Buffalo*, *Mojo* and *Dangerous Corner*. Her costumes have been featured at the Williamstown Theatre Festival and in London's West End. Films include *The Story of a Bad Boy*, *Sweet and Lowdown* for Woody Allen, and *High Fidelity* which received a Costume Designers Guild Award nomination for best costume design. Twenty-first century designs include *Hobson's Choice* at Atlantic Theatre Company directed by David Warren, *Further from the Furthest Thing* at Manhattan Theatre Club directed by Neil Pepe, and *The Underpants* by Steve Martin at the Classic Stage Company, directed by Barry Edelstein.
Costumes: 2001 *One Flew over the Cuckoo's Nest*

Greta Baum

Greta Baum served as costume designer for one production in 1935.
Costumes: 1935 *Few Are Chosen*

Peter Bax

Peter Bax designed sets in the early 1930s on Broadway. He was the assistant stage manager for numerous productions in London directed by William Abingdon, including *The Forest*, *London Life*, *A Midsummer Night's Dream* and *The Claimant* in 1924, *Rose Marie* in 1925, *The Desert Song* and *The Wandering Jew* in 1927, *Show Boat* and *London Pride* in 1928, and *The New May* in 1929. As was the practice in the theater of the time, he very likely contributed designs to these productions and others, particularly contemporary pieces or those in the standard repertory, in his capacity as assistant stage manager.
Sets: 1931 *The Venetian*†

John W. Baxter

John W. Baxter, a British director of plays and movies, lived and worked primarily in England. He directed Deborah Kerr in the film *Love on the Dole* and was active directing and producing films between 1933 and 1959, after which he was named managing director of a television studio. He died in February 1975.
Sets: 1925 *The Fall of Eve*†

Howard Bay

Howard Bay, widely known as a scenery and lighting designer, was involved with nearly two hundred productions during his career. Originally from Centralia, Washington where he was born on May 3, 1912, he directed and taught as well as designed for the theater after his professional debut in 1933 with *There's a Moon Tonight*. Mr. Bay also designed for television, film, and industrial shows. He lectured, wrote books about design and was active in professional associations, serving as President of United Scenic Artists. Occasionally during his long, prolific career Mr. Bay also contributed costume designs to a production in addition to the sets and lights, including *Man of La Mancha* which he designed with Patton Campbell, and with whom he shared a Tony nomination. He won a Tony Award for *Toys in the Attic*, a Maharam Award for *Man of La Mancha* and Donaldson Awards for *Carmen Jones* and *Up in Central Park*. Mr. Bay died on November 21, 1986 at age 74 while working on a production of *The Music Man* to be presented at the Peking Opera House.
Sets: 1936 *Battle Hymn*; *Chalk Dust* **1937** *Marching Song*; *Native Ground*;

One Third of a Nation; Power **1938** Life and Death of an American; The Merry Wives of Windsor; Sunup to Sundown; Trojan Incident **1939** The Little Foxes **1940** The Corn Is Green; The Fifth Column; Morning Star **1941** Brooklyn, U.S.A.; The Man with Blond Hair **1942** Count Me in; The Eve of Saint Mark; The Great Big Doorstop; Johnny 2x4; The Moon Is Down; The Strings, My Lord, Are False; Uncle Harry **1943** Carmen Jones; The Corn Is Green; The Merry Widow; A New Life; One Touch of Venus; The Patriots[t]; Something for the Boys **1944** Catherine Was Great; Chicken Every Sunday; Follow the Girls; Listen Professor; Men to the Sea; The Searching Wind; Storm Operation; Ten Little Indians; Violet; The Visitor **1945** Deep Are the Roots; Devil's Galore; Marinka; Polonaise; Up in Central Park **1946** Show Boat; Woman Bites Dog; The Would-Be Gentleman **1948** As the Girls Go; Magdalena **1949** The Big Knife; Magnolia Alley; Montserrat **1950** Come Back, Little Sheba; Hilda Crane; Michael Todd's Peep Show; Parisienne **1951** The Autumn Garden; Flahooey; The Grand Tour; Two on the Aisle **1952** The Shrike **1953** The Children's Hour; Mid-summer **1955** The Desperate Hours; Red Roses for Me **1956** Night of the Auk; A Very Special Baby **1957** The Music Man **1958** Interlock **1959** A Desert Incident **1960** The Cool World; Cut of the Axe; Toys in the Attic; The Wall **1961** Isle of Children; Milk and Honey **1963** Bicycle Ride to Nevada; My Mother, My Father and Me **1964** Never Live over a Pretzel Factory **1969** Fire! **1970** Cry for Us All **1976** Home Sweet Homer; Poor Murderer **1977** Man of La Mancha **1979** The Utter Glory of Morrissey Hale **1992** Man of La Mancha
Costumes: **1938** The Merry Wives of Windsor; Sunup to Sundown; Trojan Incident **1950** Hilda Crane[t] **1957** Look Back in Anger (Costume Supervisor) **1976** Home Sweet Homer[t] **1977** Man of La Mancha[t] **1992** Man of La Mancha[t]
Lights: **1944** Chicken Every Sunday; Follow the Girls; Men to the Sea **1945** Up in Central Park **1948** Magdalena **1949** Magnolia Alley **1951** The Autumn Garden; Flahooey **1953** Mid-summer **1955** The Desperate Hours; Red Roses for Me

1956 Night of the Auk; A Very Special Baby **1957** Look Back in Anger; The Music Man; Romanoff and Juliet **1958** Interlock **1959** A Desert Incident; The Fighting Cock **1960** The Cool World; Cut of the Axe; Toys in the Attic; The Wall **1961** Isle of Children; Milk and Honey **1963** Bicycle Ride to Nevada; My Mother, My Father and Me **1964** Never Live over a Pretzel Factory **1969** Fire! **1970** Cry for Us All **1976** Home Sweet Homer; Poor Murderer **1977** Man of La Mancha **1979** The Utter Glory of Morrissey Hale

Elizabeth Beard
In 1937, Elizabeth Beard served as costume supervisor for one production.
Costumes: **1937** Tide Rising (Women's Costume Supervisor)

Mr. Beardsley
Mr. Rudolph Beardsley, partner with Alexander Grinager in the scenic studio Grinager and Beardsley, was a painter and illustrator. He was born in 1875 in New York City and died there on August 15, 1921. In addition to the productions he worked on in collaboration with Alexander Grinager, he also designed lighting for a production in 1914. For additional information, see the entry for Grinager and Beardsley and the one for Alexander Grinager.
Lights: **1914** The Silent Voice[t]

Cecil Beaton
Cecil Beaton designed many handsome costumes and sets during his lifetime and will always be remembered for his contribution to both the stage and film versions of My Fair Lady. Cecil Walter Hardy Beaton was born in London on January 14, 1902 (1904 is sometimes cited) and began sketching costumes at a very young age, dressing himself and his family for playlets which he also staged. Cecil Beaton's designs for opera, stage and film were regularly seen in the United States and England. He specialized in settings and costumes and for one production on Broadway in 1946 also designed the lighting. Details of his life as a photographer and designer have been well documented through publications of his diaries, reminiscences, and photographs. He selected an official bi-

ographer, Hugo Vickers, shortly before his death in 1980 at the age of 76. The book, *Cecil Beaton, A Biography* was published in 1986. He was nominated for six Tony Awards and received four: *Quadrille* in 1955, *My Fair Lady* in 1957, *Saratoga* in 1960, and *Coco* in 1970.

Sets: 1946 *Lady Windermere's Fan* 1950 *Cry of the Peacock* 1952 *The Grass Harp* 1954 *Quadrille* 1955 *The Chalk Garden; The Little Glass Clock* 1956 *The Glass Clock* 1959 *Look after Lulu; Saratoga* 1960 *Tenderloin* 1969 *Coco*

Costumes: 1946 *Lady Windermere's Fan* 1950 *Cry of the Peacock* 1952 *The Grass Harp* 1954 *Portrait of a Lady; Quadrille* 1955 *The Chalk Garden; The Little Glass Clock* 1956 *My Fair Lady* 1959 *Look after Lulu; Saratoga* 1960 *Dear Liar; Tenderloin* 1969 *Coco* 1976 *My Fair Lady* 1981 *My Fair Lady†*

Lights: 1946 *Lady Windermere's Fan*

John Lee Beatty

John Lee Beatty was born on April 4, 1948 in Palo Alto, California. He attended Brown University, graduating cum laude with a B.A. in English literature in 1970. He attended Yale and received an M.F.A. in design in 1973. At the beginning of his career, he was influenced by Ming Cho Lee, Arnold Abramson, and Douglas W. Schmidt and is now in turn influencing a new generation of designers. His first designs were for *The Jenkins Red Carriage* in the fourth grade and since that time he has designed for television, opera, extensively on and off-Broadway and in most of the major regional theaters. He has received numerous honors including the Tony, Obie, Drama Desk, Outer Critics Circle, Maharam, Jefferson (Chicago), and Los Angeles Drama Critics awards. Whether impressionistic or realistic, his scenic designs are noted for their evocative theatricality, as seen in designs for productions as diverse as *The Mystery of Irma Vep, Most Happy Fella, the Road to Mecca,* and *Lips Together, Teeth Apart.* Twenty-first century designs include *Major Barbara* in the 2001-2002 Broadway season.

Sets: 1976 *The Innocents; Knock Knock*

1978 *Ain't Misbehavin'; Water Engine, The/ Mr. Happiness* 1979 *Faith Healer; Whoopee* 1980 *Fifth of July; Hide and Seek; Talley's Folly* 1981 *Crimes of the Heart; Duet for One; The Five O'clock Girl; Fools* 1982 *Alice in Wonderland; The Curse of an Aching Heart; Is There Life after High School; Monday after the Miracle* 1983 *Angels Fall; Baby; Passion* 1985 *The Octette Bridge Club* 1986 *Loot* 1987 *Burn This; The Nerd; Penn & Teller* 1988 *Ain't Misbehavin'* 1990 *The Cemetery Club* 1991 *Penn & Teller: The Refrigerator Tour* 1992 *The Fifteen Minute Hamlet; The Most Happy Fella; The Price; The Real Inspector Hound; A Small Family Business* 1993 *Abe Lincoln in Illinois; Anna Christie; Redwood Curtain; The Sisters Rosensweig; White Liars & Black Comedy* 1994 *Philadelphia, Here I Come!* 1995 *A Delicate Balance; The Heiress; My Thing of Love* 1996 *Chicago; A Delicate Balance; The Father; Once upon a Mattress* 1997 *An American Daughter; Ivanov; The Lily and the Prince; The Little Foxes; Proposals* 1998 *Footloose* 1999 *Ring 'Round the Moon* 2000 *Proof* 2001 *The Dinner Party*

Thomas Becher

Thomas Becher was born in Ireland and educated in England. He first began designing costumes in London for revues. His credits in the United States include shows on Broadway and designs for Ringling Bros. and Barnum & Bailey Circus. The costume designer should not be confused with the architect, educator, and designer in Vancouver, British Columbia who has the same name.

Costumes: 1952 *New Faces of 1952* 1953 *John Murray Anderson's Almanac* 1955 *Catch a Star* 1956 *New Faces of '56* 1961 *New Faces of '62* 1965 *The Family Way*

Jeffrey Beecroft

Jeffrey Beecroft was born on April 1, 1956 in Sacramento, California, the son of M.T. and Judith Beecroft. He received an M.F.A. at New York University's Tisch School of the Arts. His influences have been John Gleason, Dean Tavolaris, and Ridley Scott. He works extensively in the United Kingdom where he debuted with *The Playboy of the Western World* and *We Won't Pay! We Won't Pay!* in London's West End. He has also designed *Cherry Orchard, Oedipus Rex,* and *Three Sisters* at the Royal Exchange, and *Three Sisters* in London. He designed *Troilus and Cressida, Hamlet, Cyrano de Bergerac* and *Much Ado about Nothing* for the Royal Shakespeare Company, and *After Aida* at the Old Vic. He has taught seminars in design atthe University of Southern California, and as a fellow at Oxford University, where he designed for the Oxford Playhouse. Prizes for theater design include the Evening Standard Award in the United Kingdom, two Tony Award nominations, Outer Drama Critics Award, and two San Francisco Drama Critics Awards. Off-Broadway he has designed productions such as *The Transfiguration of Benno Blimpie* at Playwrights Horizon. Increasingly, he is using his creativity on screen, as production designer for commercials, music videos, and films including *Dances with Wolves* (Oscar Award nomination), *The Game, The Bodyguard, Message in a Bottle,* and *12 Monkeys* for which he received a BAFTA Award nomination. In both 1993 and 1995, he was designated Designer of the Year by the Museum of Modern Art.

Lights: 1984 *Cyrano De Bergerac*†; *Much Ado About Nothing*†

Geoffrey Beene

Geoffrey Beene is one of America's top fashion designers. Before studying fashion in New York and Paris, he contemplated a career in medicine, studying at Tulane University. After working for several fashion houses (including Molyneux and Teal Trania), he launched his own line with his first collection in 1963, quickly winning recognition for his innovative choice of fabric and details that retain simplicity while evoking quality. He specializes in both attractive and comfortable clothes and is the recipient, so far, of eight Coty American Fashion Awards, among numerous other honors. Occasionally Mr. Beene contributes designs to film, ballet and theater. Mr. Beene was born in Haynesville, Louisiana on August 30, 1927. His designs have been featured in exhibitions in Los Angeles, Tokyo, and at the Fashion Institute of Technology in New York and are in numerous permanent collections.

Costumes: 1968 *Avanti!*† (Fashion consultant)

Ben Beerwald

Benjamin Beerwald (Bierwald) was chief electrician of the Century Theatre in New York City and as such was responsible for the illumination of many productions, although he did not officially receive design credit nor function as a designer in the same sense as contemporary lighting designers. The September 1913 issue of *Theatre Magazine* featured "Benny" in an article entitled "A Maker of Moons" recounting his creation of moonlight and moonrise for the 1912 Broadway production of *Joseph and his Brethren.*

Lights: 1911 *The Allah* **1912** *The Daughter of Heaven; Joseph and His Bretheren; Racketty-Packetty House* **1916** *Miss Springtime* **1917** *Ziegfeld Follies: 1917*

Edith Lutyens Bel Geddes

Edith Lutyens Bel Geddes was born Edith Adams de Habbelinck on August. 1, 1916 (1917 is sometimes cited) and studied at the University of Brussels. Her first marriage was to British architect Archibald Charles Lutyens, and her third was to designer Norman Bel Geddes in 1954. She was active in the theater in various capacities: producer, writer, editor of *Theatre Arts,* and costume designer. Mrs. Lutyens Bel Geddes also executed costumes for other designers. In addition to her Broadway credits she designed costumes for Ballet Hispánico, the Joffrey Ballet, Alvin Ailey, Ringling Bros. and Barnum & Bailey Circus, and for films. As co-costume designer for *Ondine,* she shared a Tony Award with Richard Whorf in 1954. She died at age 95 in Hudson, New York on August 16, 2002.

Costumes: 1948 *Ghosts*† **1951** *Not for Children*† (Other costumes) **1952** *The Shrike* **1953** *The Crucible; A Girl Can*

Tell 1954 *Wedding Breakfast* 1961 *Do You Know the Milky Way?*; *A Gift of Time* 1962 *Giants, Sons of Giants* 1963 *Bicycle Ride to Nevada; Dear Me, the Sky Is Falling; Too True to Be Good* 1964 *The Deputy*

Norman Bel Geddes

Norman Bel Geddes was a designer of sets, lights and costumes, a producer and an industrial designer. He was born Norman Melancton Geddes in 1893 in Adrian, Michigan and died in 1958. His first designs for the theater, in 1916 in Los Angeles were followed by his New York debut at the Metropolitan Opera. Bel Geddes never created costumes unless he also designed the sets for a production, and he was interested in their illumination as well. He is credited with incorporating lenses into theater lighting. His career was remarkable, and although his list of credits on Broadway is not long, he was involved in well over two hundred productions during his lifetime, designing, writing about design and producing. His creativity was well used in the theater where he designed such innovative productions as *The Miracle* for Max Reinhardt and was important in the development of the New American Stagecraft movement. He also designed and consulted on the design of theaters around the world. Norman Bel Geddes was married five times; his wives included costume designers Frances Resor Waite in 1933 and Edith Lutyens in 1954. The actress Barbara Bel Geddes is his daughter. See Figure 3: Norman Bel Geddes: *The Patriot*
Sets: 1917 *I.O.U.* 1918 *I.O.U.* 1921 *Ermine* 1922 *Orange Blossoms*; *The Truth about Blayds* 1923 *Will Shakespeare* 1924 *Lady, Be Good*; *The Miracle*; *Quarantine*; *She Stoops to Conquer* 1925 *Arabesque* 1926 *Devil in the Cheese* 1927 *Creoles*; *Damn the Tears*; *Five O'clock Girl*; *John*; *Julius Caesar*; *Spread Eagle* 1928 *The Patriot*; *She Stoops to Conquer* 1929 *Fifty Million Frenchmen* 1930 *Change Your Luck* 1931 *Hamlet* 1932 *Flying Colors* 1935 *Dead End* 1936 *Iron Men* 1937 *The Eternal Road*; *Seige* 1940 *It Happens on Ice* 1941 *It Happens on Ice* 1943 *Sons and Soldiers*

1944 *Seven Lively Arts*
Costumes: 1921 *Ermine* 1923 *Will Shakespeare* 1924 *The Miracle* 1925 *Arabesque* 1926 *Devil in the Cheese* 1930 *Change Your Luck†* 1931 *Hamlet†* (Also directed and adapted) 1935 *Dead End* 1936 *Iron Men* 1937 *The Eternal Road* 1940 *It Happens on Ice* 1941 *It Happens on Ice* 1943 *Sons and Soldiers*
Lights: 1917 *I.O.U.* 1918 *I.O.U.* 1924 *The Miracle* 1931 *Hamlet* 1932 *Flying Colors* 1937 *The Eternal Road* 1940 *It Happens on Ice*

Dolaro Belasco

Dolaro Belasco designed costumes for one play in 1939. A second cousin of David Belasco, she was born Genevieve Belasco in London, the daughter of Selina Dolaro, an actress and writer, and Benjamin Belasco, who operated a night club. As an actress on stage, in film, and on radio, she used the name Genevieve Dolaro. She worked on stage with Lillian Russell and Otis Skinner and in film with Rudolph Valentino, among others. She died in New York City in 1956 at the age on 85.
Costumes: 1939 *Cure for Matrimony*

Ursula Belden

Born in Germany on September 27, 1947, Ursula Belden, the daughter of Edith and Ernest Mugdan came to the United States as a young child. She attended the University of Michigan and was in the class of 1976 at the Yale University School of Drama where she studied with Ming Cho Lee. Since making her professional debut with *Sleuth* at the Indiana Repertory Theatre in 1978, she has designed over 150 productions in regional theaters including the Mark Taper Forum, Pasadena Playhouse, Kennedy Center, Cleveland Playhouse, Denver Theatre Center, Walnut Street Theatre, Cincinnati Playhouse, Pittsburgh Public Theatre, and many others. Off-Broadway credits include more than two dozen plays, among them American and/or New York premieres and classics, including Strindberg's *A Dream Play*. She also designs throughout the world, including recent productions in Berlin, Prague and Canada. Credits for film include production design for Rajko

Figure 3: Norman Bel Geddes: *The Patriot:* 1928. Courtesy of Norman Bel Geddes Collection, Theatre Arts Library, Harry Ransom Humanities Research Center, The University of Texas at Austin.

Grlik's video-film *Pasta Paollo*. Head of the design program at Ohio University's School of Theater, her designs are regularly included in the Prague Quadrennial Design Exhibition.

Sets: **1984** *Quilters*

E. Hamilton Bell

Edward Hamilton Bell was trained as a painter and worked as an actor before designing sets and costumes for productions, originally in his native England. He appeared in operas and musicals at the Savoy Theatre and initially came to the United States to appear in the 1909 production of *The Magistrate*. His designs however, preceded him, arriving in New York with touring productions. As early as 1891, his name appears in playbills such as the one for *Twelfth Night* for Marie Wainwright for which he designed "all the scenery, costumes, furniture and appointments." Other nineteenth century credits include *Richard III* for Henry Irving, *As You Like It* and *Love's Labor's Lost* for Augustin Daly, and *Henry IV* and *For Bonnie Prince Charlie* for Julia Marlowe. When the New Theatre opened, he was appointed Art Director and as such was involved with all their productions. Bell, who also maintained an interior design studio for private customers at 18 East 41st Street in New York City, is believed to have died in 1929.

Sets: **1908** *Sister Beatrice†* **1909** *Cottage in the Air†*; *The School for Scandal*; *Strife†* **1910** *Beethoven*; *The Bluebird*; *Brand*; *Liz the Mother*; *Merry Wives of Windsor†*; *Old Heidelberg*; *Sister Beatrice†*; *A Son of the People*; *The Thunderbolt*; *Turning Point*; *Twelfth Night†*; *The Winter's Tale†*; *The Witch*; *Your Humble Servant* **1911** *The Arrow Maker*; *The Blue Bird†*; *Nice Wanton*; *Nobody's Daughter†*; *The Piper*; *Vanity Fair* **1912** *The Flower of the Palace of Han†*; *The Terrible Meek†*

Costumes: **1908** *Sister Beatrice* **1909** *Antony and Cleopatra*; *The School for Scandal*; *Strife* **1910** *Beethoven*; *The Bluebird*; *Brand*; *Liz the Mother*; *Merry Wives of Windsor*; *Old Heidelberg*; *Sister Beatrice*; *A Son of the People*; *The Thunderbolt*; *Twelfth Night*; *The Winter's Tale*; *The Witch*; *Your Humble Servant* **1911** *The Arrow Maker*; *The Blue Bird*; *Nobody's Daughter*; *The Piper*; *Vanity Fair* **1912** *The Flower of the Palace of Han*; *The Terrible Meek* **1913** *Much Ado About Nothing†* (Mr. Drew's costumes)

Stanley Bell

Stanley Bell, a British director, producer and scenic designer, worked occasionally in New York in 1930 and 1931 designing plays for Gilbert Miller and the Charles Frohman Company. He was born in North Hingham, England on October 8, 1881 and studied at the Leeds School of Science for a career as an analytical chemist. In 1897 he began painting scenery and in 1900 began acting. As a member of Sir Herbert Beerbohm Tree's Company he performed, designed sets, and stage managed from 1906 to 1914, after which he entered military service. Throughout the 1920s and 1930s he produced and designed numerous plays and ice spectacles in the United States and Great Britain. During World War II he organized Garrison and Station Theatres. He was honored with a Commander of the British Empire (C.B.E.) in 1946. Stanley Bell died on January 4, 1952 at age 70.

Sets: **1930** *Dishonored Lady*; *Marseilles*; *One, Two, Three/ The Violet*; *Petticoat Influence†*; *Stepdaughters of War* **1931** *Company's Coming*

Joseph F. Bella

Joseph F. Bella was born in Greensburg, Pennsylvania on August 12, 1940 and studied at Carnegie Mellon University and Catholic University of America. While a student at Catholic University he designed costumes for several productions, including *Medea*. In the late 1960s he returned to Carnegie Mellon as an instructor in costume design, subsequently serving on the faculties of Hunter College in New York City and Montclair State College in New Jersey. Mr. Bella's costume designs have been seen at many theaters, including the Great Lakes Shakespeare Festival, the Baltimore Opera Company, the Opera Society of Washington, the Walnut Street Theatre in Philadelphia, and off-Broadway. Mr. Bella concentrates his design activity on costumes, but also occasionally creates sets and lights. Prior to working in the professional theater, Mr. Bella worked as a dress designer and pattern maker.

Costumes: 1973 *The Waltz of the Toreadors*

Constance Bellamy

Constance T. Bellamy designed scenery on Broadway in the mid-1920s. In addition, she was associated with the McIlroy Studios and also worked as a decorator from an office on 57th Street. In 1932 she was a member of the decorating firm Frances White, at 821 Madison Avenue, New York City.

Sets: 1924 *The Red Falcon*

Adolphe Bellotte

Playwright Adolphe Bellotte (Belot) was born in Pointe-à-Pitre, Guadeloupe on November 6, 1829. He wrote nearly 100 plays and short romantic novels, often in collaboration. He was co-author of *Sapho* with Madame Alphone Daudet with which Olga Nethersole created a bit of a scandal in 1900. Only one of his plays, *Le Testament de César Girodot*, produced at the Paris Odéon in 1859, became part of the repertory of the Comédie Française. Interested in the appearance of his characters, he often selected gowns for them to wear. As he wrote a play about Madame DuBarry, it is likely that gowns from an earlier production that he designed, as "Adolphe Bellotte, of Paris" were subsequently used for David Belasco's production of *Du Barry*. He died in 1890, making his Broadway credit posthumous.

Costumes: 1901 *Du Barry†*

Rick Belzer

Rick Belzer made his Broadway debut as a lighting designer in 1995, but his association with lights on the Broadway stage date to *Cats* in 1982 when he assisted David Hersey, after which he reproduced the lights for numerous productions of that musical during its' national tours. During a ten year period, he produced 80 musicals at the Candlewood Playhouse in New Fairfield, Connecticut while continuing to design lights. In 1992, shortly after *The New York Times* named Candlewood Playhouse as "the state's premier show place for popular musicals" he left to start Belzer Design International. Since then he has designed lights for tours of *Godspell, Joseph and the Amazing Technicolor Dreamcoat, Starlight Express*, and *Annie Get Your Gun* as well as productions in Las Vegas and Europe.

Lights: 1995 *Jesus Christ Superstar*

Ludwig Bemelmans

Ludwig Bemelmans, a painter and writer was born in Meran, in the Austrian state of Tirol, on April 27, 1898 and died on October 1, 1962. He came to the United States in 1914, attaining citizenship in 1918. He wrote and illustrated many books and also articles for magazines that included *Vogue* and *Town and Country* and in 1935 he served as costume supervisor for one production. In 1957 he was awarded the Children's Spring Book Award by *The New York Herald Tribune* for the first of a series of books about a little girl. The popular volumes that he wrote and illustrated have remained in print since publication. They include *Madeline, Madeline's Rescue* and *Madeline in London*.

Costumes: 1935 *Noah* (Costume Supervisor)

G. K. Benda

G.K. Benda (Georges K. Benda), who designed costumes for television and movies in France, London and the United States. was born in Paris. He studied at the Beaux Arts and contributed costumes to a musical revue on Broadway in 1924. Movies for which he received screen credit include *Knight Without Armour* in 1937 and *Bonnie Prince Charlie* in 1947. He is also cited in the 1955 edition of the *Annuaire biographique du cinéma et de la télévision en France, en Belgique et en Afrique du Nord* as a costume designer.

Costumes: 1924 *Andre Charlot's Revue of 1924†*

Henri Bendel

In an article in *Theatre Magazine* in 1925, Henri Bendel wrote, "In all my years of importing and originating women's gowns, furs and millinery, I have found nothing to compare with the fascination of equipping a play with costumes, especially those for the women in it." Born in Lafayette, Louisiana, Henri Bendel arrived in New York in 1899 and opened a small millinery shop. His business soon expanded into broader merchandise, and he emerged as one of the fashion leaders of the city, with a keen sense of what appealed to women's tastes of the time. The shop which he started has had changes of location and of owners, but continues under his name to be responsive to contemporary tastes. Mr. Bendel personally designed gowns for numerous productions on Broadway during his career in fashion. He died in 1936 at the age of 69.

Costumes: 1907 *The Lancers†* 1910 *The Upstart†* (Miss Cowl's motor apparel) 1912 *The Affairs of Anatol†* (Miss Lee's costumes); *The Explorer†* (Gowns for Miss Lane and Miss Sheldon); *She Stoops to Conquer†* (Miss Russell's costumes) 1913 *All Star Gambol†* (Miss Dressler's gowns); *The Amazons†* (Miss Burke's gowns) 1914 *The Girl from Utah†* (Miss Sanderson's gowns); *The Laughing Husband†*; *The Rule of Three* 1915 *The Boomerang* (Miss Hedman's gowns); *A Celebrated Case†* (Gowns); *The Duke of Killicrankie* (Hats); *Mr. Pim Passes By*; *The Natural Law†* (Gowns); *The Natural Law†*; *The Unchastened Woman†* (Miss Stevens' gowns in Third Act) 1916 *The Blue Envelope* (Miss Reynolds' dresses and millinery); *The Great Pursuit* (Hats); *Our Little Wife†* (Miss Illington's gowns); *Sybil* (Miss Sanderson's gowns) 1917 *Blind Youth*; *Broken Threads†* (Gowns); *The Case of Lady Camber* (Gowns); *Her Regiment* (Ladies dresses); *If* (Gowns for Miss Bensen and Shields); *Odds and Ends of 1917†* (Miss Lorraine's gowns); *On with the Dance†* (Miss Dean's gowns); *Rambler Rose* (Miss Sanderson's gowns) 1918 *Experience*; *Forever After* (Miss Brady's gowns); *Girl o' Mine* (Miss Harper's gowns and hats); *He Didn't Want to Do It* (Hats, gowns, and costumes); *Humpty Dumpty* (Gowns); *The Invisible Foe* (Miss McDonald's gowns); *Lightnin'*; *Nancy Lee* (Miss Walker's dresses);

Nothing But Lies (Miss Olive Wyndham's costumes); *The Off Chance* (Miss Barrymore's cowns); *Remnant†* (Miss Cheston's costumes); *The Saving Grace* (Gowns); *She Walked in Her Sleep* (Gowns and hats); *The Woman on the Index* (Gowns, hats, and wraps) 1919 *Adam and Eva†* (Miss Shepley's gowns); *Carnival* (Miss Ferguson's gowns); *The Challenge* (Miss Macintosh's gowns); *The Crimson Alibi* (Miss Lawton's and James's gowns); *Déclassé* (Gowns and hats); *First Is Last†* (Gowns); *Forbidden* (Miss Herman's gowns); *The Gold Diggers*; *His Honor, Abe Potash* (Miss English's gowns); *The Little Blue Devil†* (Miss Lorraine's gowns); *Miss Millions*; *Smilin' Through* (Miss Cowl's gowns); *Tumble in* (Lingerie and costumes); *The Unknown Woman* (Miss Rambeau's gowns and millinery); *A Voice in the Dark* (Miss Wyndham's gowns); *The Woman in Room 13* (Miss Beecher's gowns) 1920 *Call the Doctor* (Dresses); *A Hole in the Wall†* (Miss Hedman's gowns); *One* (Dresses); *Scrambled Wives* (Gowns); *Seeing Things* (Gowns) 1921 *A Bill of Divorcement*; *Captain Applejack†* (Modern dresses); *The Elton Case* (Gowns); *The Grand Duke* (Dresses); *Music Box Revue†* (Miss Bennett's costumes); *Nice People†* (Miss Maddern's gowns); *The Squaw Man†* (Miss Lydia Hoyt's gowns); *Tangerine†* (Miss Sanderson's gowns); *Tarzan of the Apes* (Gowns); *Ziegfeld Follies: 1921†* (Mary Eaton's silver dress) 1922 *The Charlatan*; *The Czarina* (Miss Keane's gowns); *Shore Leave* (Gowns) 1923 *Kid Boots†*; *Laugh, Clown, Laugh†* (Gowns and hats); *The Laughing Lady* (Ladies gowns); *Mary, Mary, Quite Contrary*; *Romeo and Juliet†* (Miss Cowl's costumes) 1924 *The Fake*; *The Farmer's Wife*; *The Moon Flower* 1925 *Accused*; *Hamlet†* (Miss Morrison's gowns); *Oh! Mama†* 1927 *Caste* (Gowns and hats); *Mariners†* (Miss Wright's gowns) 1928 *The Unknown Warrior* ("Audes" costumes) 1930 *Dancing Partner* (Hats and gowns)

Isaac Benesch

Issac Benesch designed three sets on Broadway, one each in 1931, 1932 and 1933. He also lectured at the Neighborhood Playhouse on theatrical design. Born on March 10, 1910, Benesch lived for most of his life in Baltimore, Maryland where he died in November 1973. The "Great House of Isaac Benesch" was a furniture company with stores in Baltimore and Annapolis, Maryland, and Pottsville and Wilkes-Barre, Pennsylvania. The Baltimore store was the largest of the four. It was located on Mulberry Street near the intersection with Howard, in what was once a thriving business district and in the mid-1990s redevelopment to provide residential housing and studios for artists began. His father, the senior Isaac Benesch, was a merchant who immigrated from Germany in 1883, arriving aboard the JJ Nurnberg, of Bremen.

Sets: 1931 *People on the Hill* **1932** *Merry-Go-Round* **1933** *The Sophisticrats*

Earl Benham

Earl Benham began his career in the theater as a minstrel singer, and performer in musical revues, including *Hitchy Koo of 1918, Very Good, Eddie,* and *The Little Millionaire.* He is remembered, however, not for his performances, but in the costume field. After giving up acting, he became a well known theatrical tailor, serving performers and private customers. The individual garments he created were occasionally acknowledged in playbills. Mr. Benham died in 1976 at the age of 89.

Costumes: 1921 *Good Morning, Dearie†* (Men's costumes)

Evan Bennett

Evan Bennett designed the clothes for a show in 1936.

Costumes: 1936 *Spring Dance* (Clothes designed and assembled)

Harry Gordon Bennett

Harry Gordon Bennett designed sets on Broadway between 1935 and 1946 as H. Gordon Bennett. He also designed plays for Theatre 4, including *Dracula* in 1943, and *Cap and Gown* in 1941 while on assignment from the Special Services Office during World War II. He studied at the Art Institute of Chicago and the American Academy ofArt, also in Chicago and exhibited his painting and illustrations both in one-man and group shows. He created the

illustrations of an edition of *La Divina Commedia: III Paradiso* published by Washington Square Press in 1966.

Sets: 1911 *The Price* **1935** *Mother Sings* **1942** *All Comforts of Home; Oy Is Dus a Leben!* **1944** *According to Law; A Strange Play* **1945** *Lady in Danger* **1946** *Duchess of Malfi*

Alexander Benois

Alexander Benois (Alexandre, Aleksandr) created the costumes with his son, Nicholas Benois, for the *Chauve Souris* revue in 1925. Alexander Benois was born in St. Petersburg on May 4, 1870 and began his design activity there in 1901 with *Sylvia.* He moved to Paris in 1905 and was important in the resurgence of Russian Ballet. With Diaghlev and Léon Bakst, he formed a society of painters and musicians called "The World of Art." A painter with an excellent reputation he was credited in his own time with elevating the scene designer to a position of importance. Alexander Benois, who died in 1960 at the age of 90 is remembered in particular for his designs for ballets, and his collaboration with Diaghlev. His son, Nicholas (1901-1988) and niece, Nadia (1896-1975) had careers as theatrical designers. A museum in Leningrad, opened in 1988, contains many paintings and designs by this family of theatrical designers.

Costumes: 1925 *Chauve Souris†*

Nicholas Benois

Nicholas (Nichola) Alexandrovich Benois created costumes in collaboration with his father, Alexander Benois, for a revue in 1925. Born in 1901, he decided at age 15 to have a career in the theater and received his training at the Academy of Fine Arts in St. Petersburg. His first designs were for the ballet *Seasons* at the age of 18. In 1925 he moved to Paris to design for Nikita Balieff's theater but was soon invited by Alexander Sanin to design *Khovanshchina* at La Scala. These successful designs led to a position at Teatro Reale in Rome for five years, and in 1935, Nicholas Benois was offered the post of scenery director at La Scala where he later invited his father to design. An prolific designer, creating sets and costumes mainly for opera companies around the world, he created a cultural link in 1965 between Italy and what was then known as USSR, arranging for productions to travel between La Scala and the Bolshoi. Subsequently he designed productions at the Bolshoi, including Benjamin Britten's *A Midsummer Night's Dream* and *Un Ballo In Maschera*. An honorary member of the Academy of Arts of the USSR, he died on March 30, 1988.

Costumes: **1925** *Chauve Souris*†

Benrimo

J. Harry Benrimo was an actor, playwright, and producer who was active in the theater in California, London and New York. His acting career began in California, but he soon moved to New York where he first appeared in *The First Born* in 1897, later performing the same role in London. He coauthored several plays, including *The Yellow Jacket* with George C. Hazelton, which he also designed. Born in San Francisco on June 21, 1874, he died on May 26, 1942.

Sets: **1917** *The Willow Tree* **1928** *The Yellow Jacket*
Costumes: **1917** *The Willow Tree* **1928** *The Yellow Jacket*
Lights: **1928** *The Yellow Jacket*

Thomas D. Benrimo

Thomas D. Benrimo, a surrealist painter, was the brother of J. Harry Benrimo, who was also active in the theater. Thomas Benrimo worked at one time for the scenic studio Gates and Morange. He was a member of the Taos (New Mexico) Art Colony, living and painting in residence for the twenty years prior to his death in May 1958. Prior to moving to Taos he taught at Brooklyn's Pratt Institute in the Department of Advertising and Design from 1936 to 1939.

Sets: **1916** *The Tempest*
Costumes: **1916** *The Tempest*

Ben Benson

Ben Benson, who is sometimes cited as Bensen, designed only one play on Broadway but was a prolific costume designer for ballet. He designed numerous productions for the New York City Ballet throughout the 1980s and in 1993 designed a new production of *Cinderella* for the Fort Worth Ballet Company what toured widely and was always enthusiastically received. In 1988 he moved to England where he designed for the English National Ballet, including *Les Sylphides*, *Encounters* and a revival of Balanchine's *Who Cares?* in 1997. Benson died on September 12, 1998.

Costumes: **1976** *Kings*

Susan Benson

Susan Benson was born on April 22, 1942 in Bexley Heath, Kent, England. She studied at the West of England College of Art in Bristol. She moved to Canada in 1966 and designed for the Vancouver Playhouse and at the Manitoba Theatre Center. She is most widely known for her numerous designs at the Stratford (Ontario) Festival where she has been designing steadily since *The Medium* opened in 1974. Her early designs were mainly for costumes, but for the most part she designs both sets and costumes for productions with which she is involved. She also designs sets and costumes for the Canadian Opera Company, including the world premiere of *The Golden Ass* in 1999, the National Ballet of Canada, including *The Taming of the Shrew* and *Romeo and Juliet*, at the National Arts Center, the Guthrie Theatre, and for the National Ballet of Finland. Her many awards include six Dora Mavor Moore Awards, one Jessie and one Ace. She was elected to the Royal Canadian Academy in 1988. In addition to being a theatrical designer she is a portrait painter. Her solo painting exhibitions have featured portraits of the prominent Stratford (Ontario) Festival actors William Hutt and Nicholas Pennel. Susan Benson often collaborates on productions with her husband, lighting designer Michael Whitfield.

Sets: **1987** *The Mikado*
Costumes: **1987** *The Mikado*

Frederick Bentley

Frederick Bentley designed one set on Broadway in 1926. A British actor and singer, he was understudy to Robert Blythe in the role of Peregrine Smith in *Wild Geese* in London in the 1920s. He also performed with Mohawk Minstrels in London as a child. At the time of his death on November 12, 1939 in London, he was a music publisher, working as an editor for the Lawrence Wright Music Company.

Sets: 1926 *The Great Adventure*

Suzy Benzinger

In March 1999, Suzy Benzinger received the Irene Sharaff Young Master Award from the Theatre Development Fund, a tribute to her quickly developing career as a costume designer. She attended the State University of New York at Stony Brook and worked in the costume shop at Studio Arena Theatre in Buffalo, where she first worked with Theoni V. Aldredge, Florence Klotz and Jane Greenwood - all of whom had an impact. Jane Greenwood helped her obtain a position as shopper at Brooks Van Horn Costume Company and by the mid-1980s she was assisting Theoni Aldredge on Broadway shows including *Dreamgirls*, *La Cage aux Folles* and *42nd Street* as well as on movies, including *Ghostbusters*. Although she began to design productions herself, her first major New York production was *Miss Saigon* and since that time she has been needing assistants of her own. She has designed costumes at the Goodspeed Opera House, for television, films including three Woody Allen movies: *Don't Drink the Water*, *Deconstructing Harry* and *Celebrity*. Off-Broadway credits include *You Should Be So Lucky*, *The Boys in the Band*, and *The Show Goes On*. Among her twenty-first century designs is *Roadside* for the York Theatre Company.

Costumes: 1991 *Miss Saigon*† 1993 *Ain't Broadway Grand* 1999 *Saturday Night Fever*†

Christian Bérard

Christian-Jacques Bérard, born in France in 1902, died at the age of 47 in 1949. During his short but productive life he painted, illustrated books, sketched fashions, created advertisements, and designed costumes

and scenery. He designed for the theater, ballet, and film, mainly in France. His designs were marked by a love of fantasy and baroque decoration which he used with considerable style. Noteworthy designs include the Cocteau film *Beauty and the Beast* and a production of *Clock Symphony* by Massine at Sadler's Wells.

Sets: 1948 *Madwoman of Chaillot* 1952 *Amphitryon*; *Les Fourberies de Scapin*†
Costumes: 1948 *Madwoman of Chaillot* 1952 *Amphitryon*; *Les Fourberies de Scapin*

Bertha Beres

Bertha Beres created costumes for the featured dancers in one play in 1932.
Costumes: 1932 *There You Are*† (Mexican Dancer's costumes)

Miss Ouida Bergere

Ouida Bergere, a film actress, talent agent and playwright for stage and screen, made her Broadway debut in *The Stranger* in 1911. She wrote many plays including *Bella Donna*, *That Woman*, *The Vicious Circle*, *Suburbia Comes to Paradise* and *Kick In* and also wrote silent film scripts. She was the widow of Basil Rathbone and a famous hostess in Hollywood. At the time of her death in New York City on November 29, 1974 at age 88 she was working on her memoirs.

Sets: 1927 *The Command to Love* 1928 *The Wrecker*

Joan Bergin

The Irish designer Joan Bergin designs costumes mainly for movies, and sometimes for plays. Movie credits include *My Left Foot*, *In the Name of the Father*, *Dancing at Lughnasa*, *Art*, *David Copperfield*, *The Boxer*, and *An Awfully Big Adventure*. Her connection with Gate Theatre in Dublin is long standing, and she has created costumes for *Long Day's Journey into Night*, *Betrayal* and *Stella by Starlight* among many others. For television she designed a special starring the magician David Copperfield for Hallmark Classic Presentations, and *An Everlasting Piece*.

Costumes: 1995 *Translations* 2000 *Riverdance on Broadway*†

Robert W. Bergman Studio

Robert W. Bergman was Vice President of the Art Students League of New York in 1916 and worked as a scenic artist at Lee Lash Studios in 1918. "Berg" had a reputation as a perfectionist and painted scenery for the Washington Player's shops. He also painted for Robert Edmond Jones and Norman Bel Geddes, who subsequently arranged for him to set up his own studio. In 1922 he was President of Bergman, Nayan Studios, Inc. and resided in Jamaica, Queens. The scenic design credit for *Spanish Love* in 1920 cited Nayan Bergman, a variation of that name. Robert W. Bergman Studio, Inc. was located at 142 West 49th Street in New York City in 1931, an address shared with designer Robert Edmond Jones.

Sets: 1920 *Spanish Love* **1922** *The Charlatan* **1924** *Old English* **1927** *Spellbound*

Emanuel Berian

Emanuel Berian (also known as Emil František Burian) designed lighting for one production on Broadway in 1936. He lived from 1904 to 1959 and founded his own theater in 1933 in his native Czechoslovakia, the "D34" he created sophisticated theatrical effects some by combining live action and projection. He was deported from Czechoslovakia in 1941 but subsequently returned to restore the avant-garde theater after World War II.

Lights: 1936 *Battle Hymn*

Oliver P. Bernard

Oliver Percy Bernard was born April 8, 1881 in Camberwell, London, son of a theater manager and an actress, and performed on stage when young. He studied stage design and architecture and gained experience at the Royal Opera as an assistant scenic artist. After service in World War I which included surviving the sinking of the Lusitania he returned to the theater working in various capacities. He spent time in New York as principal scenic artist for Klaw and Erlanger, was technical director to the Boston Opera Company and artist-in-residence at Covent Garden for the Grand Opera Syndicate. He designed in the West End, worked on the British Empire exhibition at Wembly in 1924, created entrances for hotels and interiors, and also designed industrial buildings. Honors include the Military Cross and O.B.E. for Bernard who died in London on April 12, 1939.

Sets: 1907 *The Hurdy-Gurdy Girl* **1909** *The Sins of Society†*; *The Widow's Might*

Aline Bernstein

Aline Bernstein had a distinguished career as the first prominent female scenic and costume designer. She was born on December 22, 1882, the daughter of actor Joseph Frankau, and originally hoped to follow in his footsteps. However, she began designing dresses for the Neighborhood Playhouse and soon left behind all thoughts of performing. In addition to designing on Broadway for thirty-four years, she helped found the Museum of Costume Art at Rockefeller Center (now at the Metropolitan Museum of Art). In 1926 she became the first woman to attain membership as a scenic designer in the Brotherhood of Painters, Decorators and Paperhangers of the American Federation of Labor, the union which at that time represented designers. In 1950 she received a Tony Award for the costumes for *Regina*. Mrs. Bernstein, in addition to a busy career designing, also wrote two novels, *Three Blue Suits* and *The Journey Down*. Her relationship with novelist Thomas Wolfe was recorded by Wolfe in many of his books. Their correspondence was collected in *My Other Loneliness*, edited by Suzanne Stutman and published in 1983 by the University of North Carolina Press. Married to Theodore Bernstein and the mother of two children, Aline Frankau Bernstein died in 1955 at the age of 72.

Sets: 1924 *The Little Clay Cart* **1925** *The Critic*; *The Dybbuck*; *The Legend of the Dance* **1926** *The Apothecary*; *The Dybbuck†*; *Grand Street Follies*; *The Lion Tamer*; *The Little Clay Cart*; *Ned McCobb's Daughter*; *The Romantic Young Lady* **1927** *Commedia del'Arte*; *Grand Street Follies*; *If*; *The Love Nest*; *Lovers* and Enemies; Tone Pictures/The White Peacock **1928** Caprice; The Cherry Orchard[†]; The First Stone; Grand Street Follies; Hedda Gabler; Improvisations in June; L'Invitation Au Voyage; Maya; Peter Pan; The Would-Be Gentleman **1929** The Cherry Orchard; The Game of Love and Death; Grand Street Follies; Katerina; The Lady from Alfaqueque; The Living Corpse; Mademoiselle Bourrat; On the High Road; The Seagull **1930** Alison's House; Grand Hotel; The Green Cockatoo; The Lady from Alfaqueque; Romeo and Juliet; Siegfried; Women Have Their Way/ The Open Door[†] **1931** Getting Married; Reunion in Vienna; Tomorrow and Tomorrow **1932** The Animal Kingdom; Clear All Wires; Firebird; Jewel Robbery; Lenin's Dowry; Liliom; The Lion and the Mouse **1933** The Cherry Orchard; A Good Woman, Poor Thing; Thunder on the Left; We, the People **1934** Between Two Worlds; Children's Hour; Judgement Day; L'Aiglon; Mackerel Skies **1935** Camille; Night in the House; Sunny Morning, A/ The Women Have Their Way/ etc. **1936** And Stars Remain; Days to Come **1937** Storm over Patsy; To Quito and Back **1938** American Landscape **1940** The Male Animal **1950** The Happy Time

Costumes: **1916** The Inca of Jerusalem; The Queen's Enemies **1921** The Great Broxopp **1922** Fashions for Men (Costume Supervisor) **1924** The Little Clay Cart; She Stoops to Conquer (Costume Supervisor) **1925** Caesar and Cleopatra; The Dybbuck; Grand Street Follies[†]; Hamlet[†]; The Legend of the Dance **1926** The Apothecary; The Dybbuck[†]; Grand Street Follies; The Lion Tamer; The Little Clay Cart; Ned Mc Cobb's Daughter; The Romantic Young Lady; White Wings (Women's dresses) **1927** Commedia del'Arte; The Doctor's Dilemma[†] (Miss Fontanne's dresses); Grand Street Follies[†]; If; The Love Nest; Lovers and Enemies; Tone Pictures/The White Peacock **1928** The Cherry Orchard; The First Stone; Grand Street Follies; Hedda Gabler; Improvisations in June; Maya; Peter Pan; The Would-Be Gentleman **1929** The Game of Love and Death; Grand Street Follies; The Lady from Alfaqueque; The Living Corpse; On the High Road[†]; The Seagull[†] **1930** Alison's House; Grand Hotel (Miss

Leontovich's costumes); The Green Cockatoo[†]; The Lady from Alfaqueque[†]; Romeo and Juliet; Siegfried[†]; Women Have Their Way/ The Open Door **1932** Clear All Wires; Liliom **1933** The Cherry Orchard **1934** L'Aiglon **1935** Camille; Night in the House; Sunny Morning, A/ The Women Have Their Way/ etc. **1937** To Quito and Back **1938** American Landscape **1939** The Little Foxes **1942** The Willow and I **1943** Harriet; The Innocent Voyage **1944** Feathers in a Gale; The Searching Wind **1947** The Eagle Has Two Heads **1949** Regina **1950** Burning Bright; An Enemy of the People; The Happy Time; Let's Make an Opera

Lights: **1924** The Little Clay Cart

Melville Bernstein

Melville Bernstein designed two sets in 1939 on Broadway.

Sets: **1939** Cure for Matrimony; Steel

Gabriel Berry

Gabriel Berry became the first American to receive an individual medal from the International Design Quadrennial in Prague when she was awarded a Silver Medal in 1995 for her contributions to experimental theater. Much honored for her costume designs for theater, dance and opera, she has received an Obie Award for sustained excellence as well as a Bessie Award for her work in dance. Since beginning her professional career in 1979, she has worked closely with theater artists ranging from Charles Ludlam to JoAnne Akalaitis and Peter Sellars. Known for her ability to work, always hands-on, in many different formats, she moves easily from experimental works to interdisciplinary projects to the classics. Resident costume designer at La MaMa E.T.C. she has also served as an associate at the New York Shakespeare Festival and the New York Theatre Workshop. Twenty-first century designs include Mercy for Meredith Monk and Ann Hamilton at the Brooklyn Academy of Music, The Mother of Us All at the San Francisco Opera, and Yoshiko Chuma's 10,000 Steps at the Dublin Dance Festival.

Costumes: **1986** Cuba & His Teddy Bear

Emile Bertin

Emile Bertin, who designed under the name "Bertin," was a painter, illustrator and scenic designer. He was born on January 29, 1878 in Surenes (Seine), France and lived and worked in Paris. He received a diploma in 1915 from the School of Decorative Arts and studied with Eugène Carrière. He participated in exhibitions at Salon d'Automne, Artistes Indépendants, and the Salon des Humanistes. At one time, he served as president of the union of scenic designers and scenic painters in France. He designed occasionally for the Comédie Française, where he mainly painted scenery, and also for the Champs-Elysees Theatre, Theatre des Arts, and Theatre du Gymnase in Paris. In London he designed *Mozart* in 1926, (revived in 1929), and *Mariette* in 1929. Emile Bertin died in Paris in 1957.

Sets: 1939 *Folies Bergère†* **1955** *Arlequin Poli Par 'Amour*; *Le Barbier de Seville*

Robert Bessoir

In 1992, Robert (Bob) Bessoir created lights for a Broadway show. Co-Lighting Director of the daytime drama *One Life to Live* with Stephen Reid, he was nominated for a Daytime Emmy Award in 1999. His numerous television credits also include *All My Children*, *Good Morning, America* and *ABC News and Sports*. Off-Broadway and regional credits include *Iolanthe* for the New York Gilbert & Sullivan Players, *Talking Things Over with Chekhov*, *Race* and *Buya Africa* at the John Houseman Studio Theatre, *Mort Sahl's America* at Theatre Four, *Yiddle with a Fiddle* at Town Hall and *The Paper Bag Players and You*.

Lights: 1992 *The Sheik of Avenue B*

M. Betout

M. Charles Betout designed a repertory of seven French plays in 1924. His credits as a designer in France of both sets and costumes date from 1905.

Costumes: 1924 *7 French Plays (Including l'Avare)*

Frank Bevan

Frank Bevan, the son of a lawyer, was born in Scranton, Pennsylvania in 1903. He did his undergraduate study at Lafayette College and received an M.F.A. from the Yale School of Drama in 1929 after studying with George Pierce Baker. That same year, he joined the faculty at Yale to teach theatrical design. He remained on the Yale faculty until his retirement in 1971 except for the years between 1934 and 1944 when he designed costumes for the Metropolitan Opera and theaters in New York City. Frank Bevan, who occasionally acted, worked as a design assistant to David Belasco and Robert Edmond Jones. In addition to his own design work, his contribution to the theater has been through fostering the talents of the many students who studied with him. Mr. Bevan died November 22, 1976.

Costumes: 1938 *The Greatest Show on Earth*; *Knickerbocker Holiday* **1944** *Rhapsody*

Andre Bicat

Andre Reginald Bicat was born on December 27, 1909 in Southend-on-Sea, England and successfully painted in oil and watercolor, as well as created textile designs, ceramics, sculpture, etchings and lithographs, without any formal training. At the time of his death in December, 1996 his works were in the permanent collections of the National Gallery of Wales, the British Museum, the Dallas Museum of Fine Art and the Victoria & Albert Museum. During World War Two, he worked in an intelligence unit located in New Delhi where he devised and produced a variety of airborne deceptions, such as dummy paratroopers and "paraflexes" that were actually fireworks that gave the impression of advanced weaponry. His stage designs were primarily in the 1930s when he designed scenery for Marie Rambert's ballet company, the film *Rob Roy* and plays. His Broadway credit was for the premiere of T. S. Eliot's play *Murder in the Cathedral* in the United States. Honors included the OBE.

Sets: 1938 *Murder in the Cathedral*

Stephen Bickford

Stephen Bickford was production and lighting designer for a 1991 Broadway show, for which he created a series of metal chambers containing musicians, properties for the various acts, and the featured animals. His career in lighting has ranged from industrial promotions and concerts to theme parks, as well as theater, film and television.

Sets: 1991 *Moscow Circus*
Lights: 1991 *Moscow Circus*

Jean Bilibine

Jean Bilibine (also known as Ivan Yakovlevich Bilibin, Iwan-Jakowlewitsch Bilibine), a painter and theatrical designer, was born in St. Petersburg, Russia on August 4, 1876. He studied with Repin and created illustrations for Russian stories, recorded the designs of Russian peasant costumes, and worked in a museum in Moscow. A member of the Academie des Beaux Arts in St. Petersburg, he also designed sets and costumes for *Tzar Saltan* for the Opera Prive de Paris in 1929 and productions at other locations, including Broadway. His designs in London included costumes for the 1923 ballet *An Old Russian Folk Lore*, and scenery and costumes for the 1925 ballet *The Romance of a Mummy* at Covent Garden. He died in Leningrad on February 7, 1942.

Sets: 1930 *A Glass of Water*
Costumes: 1930 *A Glass of Water*

Jef Billings

In 1984, Jef Billings created the costumes for a Broadway production featuring the magician Doug Hemming. He graduated from Oswego State University in 1970 and received his M.F.A. from the Tisch School of the Arts at New York University in 1977. In 1999, he received an Emmy Award for *The Snowden Raggedy Ann and Andy Holiday Show*, one of his many designs for performers on ice. He designs regularly for Scott Hamilton, Jayne Torvill and Christopher Dean, and for Nancy Kerrigan. He also designed Kerrigan's wedding gown. He has designed costumes for Cher and Carol Burnett as well as for *South Pacific* but is most widely known for his designs for Tom Scallen's Ice Capades at Madison

Square Garden, Champions on Ice, and *Beauty and Beast: A Concert on Ice.*

Costumes: 1984 *Doug Henning and His World of Magic*

Ken Billington

Ken Billington learned the craft of lighting design through study at the Lester Polakov Studio and Forum of Stage Design and by assisting Tharon Musser, Thomas Skelton, William Rittman, and Pat Collins. His first designs in New York were for *Fortune and Men's Eyes* off-Broadway in 1969. He was born on December 29, 1946 in White Plains, New York. He has been honored with numerous awards, including a Tony Award for *Chicago* among many nominations, and honors from the Los Angeles Drama Critics, the Boston Drama Critics Association, and the New York Drama Desk, He also received a Lumen Award for lighting the Red Parrot nightclub and an Ace Award. Just as he learned through being an assistant, he hires assistants, among them Clifton Taylor, John McKernon and Jason Kantrowitz to work with him as he designs projects around the country. When his assistants move on into their own careers, he continues to support their work while he trains new ones. Recent designs include many projects for major opera companies, industrial promotions, interiors, and extravaganzas. He has designed the Radio City Music Hall Christmas Show every year since 1979. Twenty-first century designs include *If You Ever Leave Me...I'm Going With You* written, directed, and starring Renée Taylor and Joe Bologna.

Lights: 1973 *Chemin De Fer; Holiday; The Visit* **1974** *Bad Habits; Love for Love; The Rules of the Game* **1975** *The Member of the Wedding; Rogers and Hart; The Skin of Our Teeth; Sweet Bird of Youth* **1976** *Checking Out; Fiddler on the Roof* **1977** *Knickerbocker Holiday; She Loves Me; Side by Side by Sondheim; Some of My Best Friends* **1978** *Do You Turn Somersaults?; On the Twentieth Century; Working* **1979** *The Madwoman of Central Park West; The Magnificent Christmas Spectacular; Snow White and the Seven Dwarfs; Sweeney Todd* **1980**

Happy New Year; *It's Spring*; *The Magnificent Christmas Spectacular*; *Perfectly Frank*; *A Rockette Spectacular with Ginger Rogers* **1981** *America*; *Copperfield*; *Fiddler on the Roof*; *Foxfire*; *My Fair Lady*; *A Talent for Murder*; *Wally's Cafe* **1982** *Blues in the Night*; *A Doll's Life* **1984** *End of the World*; *Play Memory*; *Shirley Maclaine on Broadway*; *The Three Musketeers* **1985** *Grind*; *Home Front* **1986** *Jerome Kern Goes to Hollywood*; *A Little Like Magic* **1987** *Late Nite Comic*; *Roza*; *Stardust*; *Sweet Sue* **1988** *The Christmas Spectacular* **1989** *Meet Me in Saint Louis*; *Tru*† **1990** *The Christmas Spectacular*; *Fiddler on the Roof*; *Lettice & Lovage* **1991** *The Big Love*; *Christmas Spectacular* **1992** *Metro*; *Radio City Christmas Spectacular* **1993** *Ain't Broadway Grand*; *Radio City Christmas Spectacular*; *Radio City Easter Show*†; *The Red Shoes* **1994** *A Little More Magic*; *Radio City Christmas Spectacular*; *Radio City Easter Show*† **1995** *Buttons on Broadway*; *Hello, Dolly!*; *Moon over Buffalo*; *Radio City Christmas Spectacular*†; *Radio City Easter Show*† **1996** *The Apple Doesn't Fall*; *Chicago*; *Inherit the Wind*; *Radio City Christmas Spectacular*†; *Radio City Spring Spectacular*† **1997** *Annie*; *Candide*; *Dream*; *Radio City Christmas Spectacular*†; *Radio City Spring Spectacular*† **1998** *An Evening with Jerry Herman*; *Footloose*; *Radio City Christmas Spectacular*† **1999** *Waiting in the Wings* **2000** *The Search for Signs of Intelligent Life in the Universe*

Charles Bingham

Charles Bingham created lighting designs for a production on Broadway during the 1899-1900 season. An electrician, he resided at 104 West 89th Street in New York, according to an 1899 New York City directory.

Lights: 1899 *Children of the Ghetto*

Howell Binkley

A native of Winston-Salem, North Carolina, Howell Binkley received his B.F.A. from East Carolina University. He then assisted lighting designers Tharon Musser, Jennifer Tipton and Dennis Parichy and spent three years as the lighting supervisor for the Acting Company in the late 1970s and early 1980s, after which he designed lights for Paul Taylor and American Ballet Theatre. He designs often for Parsons Dance Company which he co-founded, for the Peter Pucci Plus Dancers and recently *The Pied Piper* for American Ballet Theatre. In 1990 his long-term collaboration with Michael Kahn began at the Shakespeare Theatre in Washington, D.C. with plays including *Hamlet* and *Richard III* and subsequently continued with the London and New York productions of *Kiss of the Spider Woman*. His extensive credits in regional theaters include productions at Hartford Stage (*The Glass Menagerie*), the George Street Playhouse, the Guthrie Theatre, Berkshire Theatre Festival (*Toys in the Attic*) and the Dallas Theatre Center. Honors include a Helen Hayes Award and a Tony Award nomination for *Kiss of the Spider Woman*. Twenty-first century credits include *The Spitfire Grill* at Playwrights Horizons.

Lights: 1993 *Kiss of the Spider Woman* **1994** *Grease* **1995** *How to Succeed in Business Without Really Trying*; *My Thing of Love*; *Sacrilege* **1996** *Taking Sides* **1998** *High Society*; *Parade* **2000** *The Best Man*; *The Full Monty*

Mary Binning

Mary Binning designed costumes for a Broadway play in 1937.

Costumes: 1937 *Many Mansions*† (Costumes selected)

The Birdie Sisters

The Birdie Sisters designed a play in 1970 in collaboration with Ella Luxembourg and Peter Harvey.

Costumes: 1970 *Gloria and Esperanza*†

Judy Birdwood

Judy Birdwood, a British designer, created costumes in 1964 for a revue. The production started as the 1963 undergraduate revue at Cambridge University, where producer Michael White saw it, and subsequently moved it to London's West End. In 1964 the show moved to New York City.

Costumes: 1964 *Cambridge Circus*

William Birns

William Birns worked in collaboration with other theater artists on each of his Broadway credits, mainly providing interior designs. In 1931 he also contributed furniture, paintings and art objects from the Galleries of William Birns to *Joy of Living*. Although he received an acknowledgement in the playbill, by that time he was considered to be a valuable source for period furniture. An antique dealer who specialized in renting furniture and properties for plays and movies, his business was located in 1919 at 103 West 37th Street prior to moving to 307 West 37th Street in New York City. Born in Germany, he moved to New York City in 1888 where he quickly established his business. His shop suffered when the movie industry left New York for the West Coast, and he relocated his shop to Third Avenue at 55th Street. William Birns died at age 77 on January 9, 1948.

Sets: 1912 *His Wife by His Side* (Furniture and furnishings) **1915** *Taking Chances* (Decorations and hangings) **1927** *One Glorious Hour* (Interior decoration) **1928** *That Ferguson Family* (Properties)

Paul Bismarck

Paul Bismarck designed lighting for two productions on Broadway in the late teens. He was an electrician, residing at 328 West 44th Street in New York City.

Lights: 1917 *Chu Chin Chow* **1919** *Aphrodite*†

Henry Bissing

Known as Henry, Harry, and H. Harry Bissing, Trow's 1907-08 New York City Directory identifies him as an engineer, living at 419 West 42nd Street.

Lights: 1900 *Marcelle* **1903** *A Japanese Nightingale*; *The Rogers Brothers in London* **1904** *A Venetian Romance* **1905** *Fritz in Tammany Hall* (With assistants); *The Mayor of Tokio*†; *The Rogers Brothers in Ireland*

Jonathan Bixby

Jonathan Bixby was born in Media, Pennsylvania, a suburb of Philadelphia. After moving to New York, he worked in wardrobe while studying at the Lester Polakov's Studio and Forum of Stage Design. Together with playwright Douglas Carter Beane and actress Cynthia Nixon he founded the Drama Dept., where he designed costumes for numerous productions including *June Moon*, *The Torch Bearers* and *As Bees in Honey Drown*. Additional off-Broadway credits include *Urinetown*, *Man is Man*, *Advice From a Caterpillar*, *The Coconuts* (Art Deco Society 1996 Award), and *the Comedy of Errors* for the Acting Company. Regional theater credits were amassed at the Geffen Playhouse, Berkshire Theatre Festival and the McCarter Theater Center. He worked with two longterm collaborators: Carol Luiken on the daytime drama *All My Children* with whom he also received an Emmy Award and Gregory Gale who began as his assistant and became his co-designer. *Urinetown: The Musical*, which he designed with Gregory Gale, opened in the 2001-2002 Broadway season on September 20, 2001 after a successful off-Broadway run. Jonathan Bixby died on April 29, 2001 at age 41 due to complications from colon cancer.

Costumes: 1995 *Hello, Dolly!* **1997** *Street Corner Symphony* **1999** *Band in Berlin*†

Maria Bjørnson

Maria Bjørnson received Tony Award nominations for both the scenery and costumes of *Phantom of the Opera* and received Drama Desk Awards for each. Other honors include the Prague Biennale in 1982. She designs regularly for the Royal Shakespeare Company, Glasgow Citizens' Theatre (where her career began), and the English National Opera. Her opera designs are known throughout Europe and the United States and include *Die Meistersinger*, *Don Giovanni* and *Katya Kabanova* for the Scottish Opera, *Jenufa* in Houston, and *Ernani*, *From the House of the Dead*, *Toussaint L'Ouverture*, *Rigoletto* and Wagner's *Ring Cycle* for the English National Opera. Ballet designs include the 1998 production of *The Sleeping Beauty*. She was born in Paris in 1949 of Norwegian and Rumanian parents, and raised in England where she studied at the Central School of Art and Design.

Sets: **1988** *The Phantom of the Opera* **1990** *Aspects of Love*
Costumes: **1988** *The Phantom of the Opera* **1990** *Aspects of Love*

Mary Blackburn

Mary Blackburn was costume designer for several productions in the late teens. A dressmaker, she ran a small shop at 43 West 56th Street in New York City in the late teens and early twenties.

Costumes: **1917** *Art and Opportunity* (Miss Painter's dresses) **1918** *East Is West* (Modern gowns); *Fiddler's Three* (All except Act One); *Glorianna* (Miss Painter's costumes); *Hitchy Koo 1918*† **1919** *Five O'clock* (Gowns); *La, La, Lucille* (All Gowns); *The Little Blue Devil*† (Costumes); *The Velvet Lady* (Wedding Gown, Bridesmaids, Miss Marbe's cloak)

Jean Blackburne

In 1929, Jean Blackburne designed costumes for one play.

Costumes: **1929** *A Ledge*

Jack Blackman

Jack Blackman studied at Columbia University and with Lester Polakov at the Studio and Forum of Stage Design. Mr. Blackman is known as a set and lighting designer who works in theater, film and television, especially for ABC-TV. He designed the off-Broadway theater Stage 73 and was art director for the 1985 film *The Ultimate Solution of Grace Quigley* and the 1992 film *House Sitter*.

Sets: **1964** *The Sign in Sidney Brustein's Window* **1965** *Postmark Zero*
Costumes: **1965** *Postmark Zero* (Production design)
Lights: **1965** *Postmark Zero*

Robert Blackman

Robert Blackman is primarily a set designer who got interested in theater while attending High School in Houston, Texas. He studied at the University of Texas and at Yale. His designs are often seen on the West Coast, including the Seattle Repertory, Oregon Shakespeare Festival, and in 35 productions at PCPA. Mr. Blackman works

regularly at A.C.T. in San Francisco where he is credited with designing 25 plays, including *Division Street* which moved to Broadway. Mr. Blackman occasionally designs costumes for plays generally when also designing the sets.

Costumes: **1980** *Division Street*

Judith Bland

Judith Bland is based in London, where she has designed costumes for numerous plays and is also the director and founder of the independent distribution company, Eaton Films. Founded in 1989, Eaton Films concentrates on distributing family movies to cinemas around the world. Her designs for the Royal Shakespeare Company include the mini-company tour of *The Beaux Stratagem* in 1989. The production she designed on Broadway, *Aren't We All?* was imported after a successful run in London's West End.

Costumes: **1985** *Aren't We All?*

Sue Blane

After studying at London's Central School with Ralph Koltai in 1968, Sue Blane, who was born in 1950, spent her first two years of professional life as the resident designer with the Citizens' Theatre in Glasgow, Scotland. She has also designed for the Glyndbourne Opera Festival (*Porgy and Bess*, Opera North (*The Love For Three Oranges*, the English National Opera (*Der Rosenkavalier, Carmen, Kønigskinder*), the Royal Shakespeare Company (*A Midsummer Night's Dream*, the English National Ballet (*Alice in Wonderland*, at La Scala and in Berlin. *The Rocky Horror Show* premiered at the Royal Court Theatre in London, and did not achieve much success in the U.S. until made into the film, *The Rocky Horror Picture Show*. This enormous success, with its particularly wacky sensibility led to other films for Sue Blane, including *Shock Treatment*, but she primarily designs for theater, opera and ballet. A frequent collaborator of Richard Eyre, Sam Mendes, John Caird, and Jonathan Miller, she is known for her flamboyant, theatrical designs.

Costumes: **1975** *The Rocky Horror Show*†

John E. Blankenchip

John E. Blankenchip was born in Independence, Kansas on November 14, 1919. He received a B.F.A. in scene design and directing from the Carnegie Institute of Technology in 1941, where he studied with Lloyd Weninger and Bess Schraeder Kimberly. In 1943 he received an M.F.A. from Yale University after studying with Donald Oenslager, Frank Bevan, George Eisenhower and Stanley McCandless. Mr. Blankenchip worked as assistant designer under Harry Horner for shows including *Winged Victory*. He always preferred to design all elements of a production when possible, and in his debut on Broadway created sets, lights and costumes. Mr. Blankenchip, who is now an Emeritus Professor, taught design and directing at the University of Southern California.

Sets: 1951 *Angel in the Pawnshop* **1952** *The Long Watch*
Costumes: 1951 *Angel in the Pawnshop* **1952** *The Long Watch*
Lights: 1951 *Angel in the Pawnshop*

Whitney Blausen

Whitney Blausen was born on January 21, 1943 in Oceanside, Long Island, New York, the daughter of Martha and Bernard Blausen. She received a B.A. from Sarah Lawrence and studied with Betty Edwards, at the Lester Polakov Studio, and the Fashion Institute of Technology where she received an M.A. in Museum Studies in 1989. *The Changing Room* in 1973 marked her debut on Broadway, but a production of *Edward II* at the Clark Center in 1965 was her professional debut as a costume designer. Active in both the Costume Society of America and the United States Institute for Theatre Technology, Blausen has a particular interest in vernacular costume. From 1977-81 she was on the faculty of Parsons School of Design and has also taught at the Universities of Rhode Island and Georgia, F.I.T., New York University, and The Cooper Hewitt Museum. A prolific writer about theatrical and fashion designers, she was the head of the Costume Collection in New York City from 1974 until 1993.

Costumes: 1973 *The Changing Room* 1974 *Mourning Pictures*; *The National Health* 1975 *Don't Call Back*†

Marilyn Bligh-White

Marilyn Bligh-White designed costumes for a Broadway show in 1981. She was born in Parametta, Australia and worked originally for the couturier Chris Jacovides, before joining the Elizabethan Theatre Trust. In addition to credits in film and television, she has designed for the Royal Ballet, the Shakespearean Company and the Cellblock Theatre, all in Sydney. After moving from Australia to the United Kingdom, she served as a member of Queen Elizabeth's personal staff in London for a time before returning to costume design.

Costumes: 1981 *Animals*

Albert Bliss

James Albert Bliss was born in Abington, Massachusetts and attended Parsons School of Design, Columbia University, and the Art Students League where he studied painting with John Sloan. He was best known as a window display designer, a field in which he succeeded because of his ability as a scene painter. In 1924 he created window settings for Lord & Taylor using the windows as a form of proscenium arch through which passers-by could look. The enormous success of the window displays for that Christmas season led to additional commissions. In 1929 he formed his own business, the Bliss Display Company, through which he created window designs for all the major department stores in New York and many others throughout North and South America. Albert Bliss died on May 12, 1988 at age 85.

Sets: 1925 *The Little Poor Man*† 1926 *Easter*; *Kept* 1927 *Ink* 1928 *Meek Mouse*

Norman Blumenfield

Norman Blumenfield designed lights for a play in 1957 on Broadway.
Lights: 1957 *Simply Heavenly*

Arthur Boccia

The short list of credits for costumes designed by Arthur Boccia on Broadway in the mid-1970s are only a small portion of his design activity. Mr. Boccia has designed numerous costumes for television and film, and after serving as an assistant to Don Foote on the design and execution of costumes for the Ringling Bros. and Barnum & Bailey Circus, began to design for the circus himself. His costume designs are often seen for ice shows, including Walt Disney's World on Ice productions of *Aladdin*, *Peter Pan*, *Happily Ever After*, and *Snow White and the Seven Dwarves*. His designs for the theater have been seen in the national tours of *Gigi*, *Music Man*, and in *Porgy and Bess* on the West Coast. He received a Tony nomination in 1975 for *Where's Charley?*

Costumes: **1974** *Where's Charley?* **1975** *Death of a Salesman* **1976** *Pal Joey*

George Bockman

George Bockman started professional life as a dancer, appearing in shows such as *High Button Shoes* and *Up in Central Park*. He spent many years as a leading dancer with the Humphrey-Weideman Company and began his involvement with costumes by designing for that company. These early designs led to costumes for solo concerts by Doris Humphrey and other dancers, and then to television. Mr. Bockman spent the majority of his career as staff scenic designer for NBC-TV. He also created interior designs for private clients. He died on November 11, 1979 at age 70.

Costumes: 1952 *The Chase*

Rose Bogdanoff

Rose Bogdanoff designed costumes on Broadway as well as for off-Broadway experimental theater organizations for fifteen years before becoming one of television's first costume designers. She only rarely designed scenery. At the time of her death in 1957 at the age of 53, she was the senior costume designer for NBC-TV which she joined in 1948. Miss Bogdanoff was born in Philadelphia and studied at the Art Institute of Chicago and the San Francisco Art School. She then worked with Jo Mielziner, as his assistant for costumes, for productions including *Merrily We Roll Along* and *Romeo and Juliet* in 1934 and *Saint Joan*, *Hamlet* and *The Wingless Victory* in 1936. Considered to be an expert on color, she often lectured at universities and for the Free Lecture Series at the New York Public Library.

Sets: 1944 *War President*

Costumes: **1938** *Abe Lincoln in Illinois* **1940** *The Man Who Killed Lincoln* (Costume Supervisor) **1941** *Cream in the Well*; *Junior Miss* (Costume Supervisor) **1942** *The Moon Is Down*; *Nathan the Wise* **1943** *I'll Take the High Road*; *The Patriots*† **1944** *Chicken Every Sunday*; *Last Stop*; *Sophie*; *War President* **1945** *It's a Gift*; *The Rugged Path*†; *The Stranger* **1946** *Lysistrata* **1948** *Bravo*; *Kathleen*; *Me and Molly*; *Summer and Smoke*; *The Survivors* **1951** *The Rose Tattoo* **1953** *The Trip to Bountiful*

Edgar Bohlman

Edgar Bohlman was born in Cottage Grove, Oregon on January 1, 1902 and studied architecture at the University of Oregon. He designed sets and costumes in New York between 1928 and 1931, and also for the American Opera Company and the Theatre Assembly. He then turned his attention to painting and illustrating, often on ballet and theater subjects. His paintings were exhibited in New York and Europe. Other projects included documenting clothing worn in the Moroccan Sahara and illustrating *Moroccan Marriage*. Edgar Bohlman died in San Francisco on September 18, 1953.

Sets: 1929 *A Ledge*; *Lolly*; *The Novice and the Duke* **1930** *Everything's Joke*; *They Never Grow Up* **1931** *The Venetian Glass Nephew*

Costumes: **1929** *Lolly* **1930** *They Never Grow Up* **1931** *The Venetian Glass Nephew*† (Costume Supervisor)

Aloys Bohnen

Aloys L. Bohnen, originally from Minneapolis, Minnesota was born September 30, 1880, He designed costumes for one show in 1916, but was mainly known as a fine art painter. Bohnen was a resident of California at the time of his death in May 1967.

Costumes: 1916 *Robinson Crusoe, Jr.*

Bill Bohnert

Bill Bohnert, son of the professional artists Herbert and Margaret Bohnert, was born on March 3, 1932. He received a B.A. in architecture at the Massachusetts Institute of Technology and an M.F.A. in stage design at Yale, where he studied with Donald Oenslager. He is primarily an art director for television, and for ten years designed *The Ed Sullivan Show*. Television designs include *America's Funniest Home Videos*, *Comic Relief* (Ace Award for *Comic Relief V*), *Everyday* for Joan Lunden, award shows including the *1989 Emmy Awards*, *The Country Music Association Awards*, *Grammy Awards*, specials, and sitcoms. He also designs children's shows, including the series *Mathnet* for Children's Television Workshop, *The Electric Company*, and *Kids Are People Too*, telethons, game shows, live casino shows in Las Vegas, and many, many more. In addition, he has developed ways to incorporate computer imaging into this designs and works with real-time animation.
Sets: *1984 Doug Henning and His World of Magic*

Saul Bolasni

Saul Bolasni, originally from Cleveland, Ohio, started out as a dancer and then used his background to design costumes for dance companies in the United States and Europe. Among his many credits for dance is *Streetcar Named Desire* for the Dance Theatre of Harlem in 1994. He has also designed numerous plays and television shows, including the daytime drama *Ryan's Hope* for many years. Mr. Bolasni paints portraits and has created art work for magazines and businesses.
Costumes: 1951 *Courtin' Time* 1954 *The Rainmaker* 1967 *A Minor Adjustment*; *Of Love Remembered*

Richard Boleslavski

Richard Boleslavski (Boleslawsky), an actor and director, was born in Warsaw, Poland in 1887 (some sources state 1889) and first appeared on the stage in 1906. He performed with the Moscow Art Theatre as a member of the first Studio, before moving to New York in 1922, where he continued to act. He also began to direct and produce plays, and founded the American Laboratory Theatre, which operated from 1923 until 1930, with Maria Ouspenskaya. In 1929, he directed a production of *Judas* and, as was common at the time, also designed the costumes. Mr. Boleslavski, the author of three books also directed and produced films. He died in Los Angeles, California on January 17, 1937.
Costumes: 1929 *Judas* (Also directed)

Madame Sara Bolwell

Madame Sara (Sarah) Bolwell collaborated on the costume designs for two 1911 Broadway productions. Originally an employee of Maurice Hermann in his costume house, she spent most of her career as wardrobe mistress for Liebler and Company, maintaining their stock of costumes, executing designs, supervising the staff of permanent and seasonal labor, and occasionally designing. Liebler and Company, formed by partners George C. Tyler (1867-1946) and Theodore Liebler (1852-1941), was a prominent New York theatrical producing organization from 1897 until the end of World War I. Madame Bolwell's death, on December 18, 1911 at age 54 in New York City was reported in the December 29, 1911 issue of *The New York Dramatic Mirror*, accompanied by no further information.
Costumes: 1911 *The Allah*; *The Garden of Allah*†

Frederica Bond

Frederica Bond created the women's costumes for a show in 1937.
Costumes: 1937 *Work Is for Horses* (Women's clothes)

Kirk Bookman

Lighting designer Kirk Bookman has amassed extensive credits since the early 1980s for dance companies, in regional theaters, and off-Broadway, in addition to his growing list of designs on Broadway. His designs at the Goodspeed Opera House include *Pal Joey*, *Strike Up the Band*, and *It's a Bird, It's a Plane, It's Superman*. At the

Manhattan Theatre Club he designed lights for *The Green Heart*, for the Public Theatre he has done *?De Donde?*, as well as productions including *Havana is Waiting*, *As Thousands Cheer*, *June Moon*, *Exactly Like You*, *Les MIZrahi*, and others in a variety of New York venues. Twenty-first century credits include *Rude Entertainment* for the Drama Dept.

Lights: 1995 *Gentlemen Prefer Blondes* 1997 *The Gin Game*; *The Sunshine Boys* 1999 *Band in Berlin*

Franklin Booth

Franklin Booth, a pen-and-ink illustrator and charcoal artist, was born July 8, 1874 in Indiana. After brief periods studying art technique he worked as an illustrator for various newspapers and magazines, with illustrations appearing in *Harper's Monthly*, *Collier's* and *Scribner's Magazine* when he was quite young. The first book for which he provided illustrations, *The House of a Thousand Candles* was followed by dozens more. The illustrations for which he is best remembered were created for Theodore Dreiser's *A Hoosier Holiday*. The two men shared an Indiana heritage and became friends when Booth studied at the Art Students League in New York in the early 1900s. His realistic style and ability to draw people, interiors, and landscapes was much in demand for books, periodicals, and advertisements. Booth died on August 28, 1948.

Sets: 1915 *Children of Earth*†

John N. Booth, Jr.

John Newton Booth, Jr. designed several shows between 1923 and 1941. Little is known of his personal history beyond his creative credits. He collaborated with Hugh Willoughby (1891-1973) and became his partner in Booth-Willoughby, Inc., in the mid-1920s, later joining Frederick Jones III in Booth, Willoughby & Jones, Inc. For additional information, see these entries. John N. Booth, Jr.'s father, for whom he was named, was a piece dyeing expert. Both men, residents of Englewood, New Jersey, died in 1943.

Sets: 1924 *The Chocolate Dandies*†

Costumes: 1923 *Helen of Troy, New York*† (Men's modern clothes) 1924 *Merry Wives of Gotham*† (Other costumes); *Sweet Little Devil*† (South American costumes) 1926 *Castles in the Air*† (Men's costumes) 1928 *Chee-Chee*†; *Houseboat on the Styx* 1929 *The Silver Swan*† 1931 *The Great Man*† (Other costumes) 1932 *Through the Years* 1933 *Murder at the Vanities*† (Mr. Lugosi's costume) 1934 *All the King's Horses*†; *Saluta* 1941 *Viva O'Brien*

Booth-Willoughby

After John Newton Booth (d. 1943) and Hugh Willoughby (1891-1973) collaborated on the scenery for *The Chocolate Dandies* in 1924, they became partners in Booth-Willoughby, Inc., through which they designed additional shows. They later joined forces with Frederick Jones III in Booth, Willoughby & Jones, Inc. For additional information, see the entries under each of their names.

Sets: 1924 *The Chocolate Dandies*†

Costumes: 1926 *Earl Carroll's Vanities*† 1927 *The Wild Man of Borneo*†

Noël Borden

Noël Borden designed *K2* in 1983 on Broadway, after designing the costumes originally for a production of the play at the Arena Stage in Washington, D.C. in 1982. The play was revived as part of Arena Stage's 50th anniversary season in January 2001 with the original design team. She graduated from the School of Fine Arts at the University of Wisconsin in Milwaukee. She has both designed and assisted other designers at Arena Stage and at PCPA in Santa Monica, California. Additional credits at Arena Stage include costumes for *Checkmates*, *American Splendor*, and *Born Guilty*.

Costumes: 1983 *K2*

Frank J. Boros

Frank J. Boros was born in Bridgeport, Connecticut on March 4, 1943. He attended the University of Connecticut and began designing there, starting with costumes for *Don Giovanni*. He received an M.F.A. at Yale in 1969 where he studied with Frank Poole Bevan. In 1975 he made his debut on

Broadway with the openings of two plays at the same time. Besides designing costumes and scenery for the theater, Mr. Boros is an art director in the film business. Recent designs include *A Naughty Knight* with director William Martin presented by the Jewish Repertory Theatre in 2001.

Sets: 1975 *The Lieutenant* 1981 *Shakespeare's Cabaret* 1985 *Home Front*† (Adapted original design)

Costumes: 1975 *The Lieutenant; P.S. Your Cat Is Dead* 1981 *Shakespeare's Cabaret*

Thierry Bosquet

Thierry Bosquet was born on May 2, 1947 in Brussels where he continues to make his home although his busy schedule as a scenery costume designer for opera, ballet, theater, film and television means he is often away. His mother, Denise Thoran Bosquet was a painter who taught him to draw when he was very young, and he received further exposure to the arts from her father, an opera director and conductor, and his paternal grandfather, a concert pianist. Immediately after completing study at the National School of Architecture, Art and Design in Brussels in 1958 he began working in the theater, principally with Maurice Béjart doing designs for ballet, beginning with *Mathilde, Capriccio* and *The Merry Widow*. His designs have been seen at all the major opera venues throughout the world, including Company Toronto, the San Francisco Opera, the New York City Opera in North America. The subject of a Belgian television film by Jean Antoine, his numerous paintings, murals, and frescos can be seen in various chateaus in Belgium and France. He recreated some of the rooms in the Palace of Versailles in miniature, and his drawings of Versailles as it was in the time of Louis XIV were published in Spring 2001. Twenty-first century credits include costumes for *Merry Widow* at the San Francisco Opera and *La Renie Margot* at the Festival de Villers in Belgium, and sets and costumes for *Cyrano de Bergerac* at Théâtre Royal du Parc in Brussels and for *Les Fourberies de Scapin* at Théâtre Pont Neuf in Nantes.

Sets: 1993 *The Mikado*

Costumes: 1993 *The Mikado*

Boss and Ormston

Charles E. Boss and George W. Ormston worked together through Boss and Ormston in the early teens. Ormston constructed scenery for many designers, being particularly in demand as the style of design changed from painted back drops to realistic settings. The Ormston Construction Company, later known as Boss and Ormston, was located at 306 11th Avenue. Playbills acknowledge his contribution for set construction for *Septimus* in 1909, and both *Never So Blind* and *The Yankee Girl* in 1910. Charles E. Boss (c.1875-1940), designed and painted scenery, working under his own name, through Boss and Ormston, and through Young Brothers and Boss. Additional information can be found under each of those headings.

Sets: 1911 *Speed* 1912 *The Marriage-Not*

Charles E. Boss

Charles E. Boss died at age 65 on March 17, 1940 in Mount Vernon, New York. He was a scenic artist active in early films, including D.W. Griffith's *Way Down East*. He also built displays for the New York World's Fair for General Motors Corporation, and designed and painted scenery for summer stock, municipal stock companies and theater chains. For additional information and credits, see the entries for "Boss and Ormston" and "Young Brothers and Boss."

Sets: 1904 *The Fortunes of the King* 1906 *The Greater Love*† (Act I) 1915 *Arms and the Man; You Never Can Tell*† (Act III) 1932 *Carrie Nation*

Michael Bottari

Michael Bottari is from Philadelphia where he was born October 14, 1948, the son of Guido and Malvina Bottari. He studied for two years at Temple University and two years at New York University School of the Arts. His career in the theater has been influenced by high school drama coach Francis A.

Perri, apprentice leader Jack Batman, art teacher Robert Rabinowitz and designer Robert Green. He has been designing in collaboration with Ronald Case for more than thirty years. Together they have created sets and/or costumes for numerous touring productions, off-Broadway shows, productions in regional theaters, television and industrial promotions. Honors include two nominations for the Carbonnell Award in south Florida, the Barrymore Award in Philadelphia for *Cabaret* in 1994, the 1998 Dean Goodman Choice Award for *Dames at Sea*, and nominations for the National Touring Awards for Best Costume Design for both *Fiddler on the Roof* and *Man of La Mancha* in 2001. In addition to theatrical design, Michael Bottari taught design at Marymount College, St. John's University and for American Ballet Theatre.

Sets: 1989 *Prince of Central Park*†
Costumes: **1989** *Prince of Central Park*† **1996** *State Fair*†

Dimitri Bouchène

Dimitri Bouchène, a painter, was born in St. Tropez, France, in 1893 (1898 is generally cited) of Russian heritage, raised in Russia, and studied at the School for the Advancement of Fine Art in St. Petersburg, and at the Académie Ransom in Paris. His first exhibition of paintings took place in Paris in 1928, after which they were shown in London, Brussels, Antwerp, and the United States. In addition to his designs on Broadway, he created sets and costumes for Louis Jouvet and Michel Fokine among others at the Ballets de Monte Carlo, La Scala, and for Paris Opera ballet productions. Bouchène, whose paintings are in several museums and private collections, also painted murals, including some in Windsor Castle. He died in Paris in February 1993, reportedly at age 99.

Sets: 1942 *The Prodigal Son*
Costumes: 1942 *The Prodigal Son*

Boué Soeurs

Boué Soeurs was a high fashion house operating in two locations in 1921, one at 9 Rue de la Paix in Paris, and other at 13 West 56th Street in New York City. In 1925 an additional salon was opened in the Mayfair area of London. Two sisters, Madame Sylvie Boué Montegut and Baronne Jeanne Boué d'Etrellis established the haute couture house in 1899 and were immediately successful, as they already had a reputation among their friends, who soon became their clients, for dressing in a decidedly romantic and feminine way. Their lightweight, pastel-colored frocks featured lace and were trimmed with rosettes made from folded silk ribbons as well as with embroidery enhanced with silver and gold threads. Especially successful in New York, they advertised themselves as "The Only Rue de la Paix House in America" and flourished until the early 1930s. Although they are only included here as having credits for two Broadway productions in the 1920, they also provided numerous additional gowns, frocks and lingerie items that were credited in playbills at the time with acknowledgements.

Costumes: 1921 *The Scarlet Man* **1923** *Little Miss Bluebeard*† (Miss Bordoni's Act III evening gown)

Mel Bourne

Mel Bourne was born on November 22, 1923 in Newark, New Jersey and grew up in Chicago. After pursuing a degree in electrical and chemical engineering at Purdue and LeHigh Universities and service in World War II, he turned his attention to design. He studied with Frank Bevan at the Yale University School of Drama and worked as an assistant to Robert Edmond Jones for four years. He made his New York debut with the Theatre Guild's production of *Seagulls over Sorento*. He spent most of the 1950s and 1960s as a television designer working on series such as *Kojak, Hallmark Hall of Fame, Goodyear-Philco Playhouse* and *Howdy Doody*. In the 1970s, however he began to design movies, and since the premiere of *Annie Hall* in 1977 has spent most of his time designing films. His credits as art director include several films with Woody Allen in addition to *Annie Hall: Interiors, Manhat-*

tan, *A Midsummer Night's Sex Comedy, Zelig.* Films for other directors are numerous: *Indecent Proposal, the Fisher King, Striptease, Something to Talk About, The Natural, Fatal Attraction* and *Reversal of Fortune,* among many others. His designs are regularly honored with Academy Award nominations for Art Direction and Production Design and many of them, such as the pilot for *Miami Vice* on television and *Interiors* on film have started trends.

Sets: 1952 *The Male Animal; Seagulls over Sorrento* 1953 *End As a Man*
Costumes: 1953 *End As a Man*
Lights: 1952 *Seagulls over Sorrento*

H. M. Bowdoin

Harold M. Bowdoin, who designed the Soldiers' and Sailors' Monument on Riverside Drive in New York City, spent most of his professional life as an architect. He mainly designed residences for clients in the greater New York area and in Florida but also contributed to designs to theater buildings, through his association with designer and architect Joseph Urban. Only rarely did he use his expertise to design for the stage, but in 1906 he collaborated on the scenery for a Broadway show. In the late 1920s he retired and moved to Newtown, Connecticut where he died at age 80 on November 29,1949.

Sets: 1906 *Neptune's Daughter†* (Diving bells for the mermaids) 1909 *A Trip to Japan†* (Mermaid effects)

Will Bowen

Will Bowen co-founded the Almeida Theatre in Islington with Chris Naylor and Pierre Audi and worked there as production coordinator and designer until 1982 when he started free-lancing. His credits as a production manager are extensive and he occasionally designs sets and or costumes as well A native of England, he studied at Oxford where he initially met and became associated with Rowan Atkinson. Since then he has been involved with all of Atkinson's shows, including the one marking his debut on Broadway.

Sets: 1986 *Rowan Atkinson at the Atkinson*

Costumes: 1986 *Rowan Atkinson at the Atkinson*

John Boxer

John Boxer was born in New York City, the son of Isidore and Jenny Boxer. He studied at New York University, at Parson's School of Design and with Charles James. In addition to his credits on the Broadway stage, he designs costumes for films and television, including *Raging Bull* and *See You in the Morning.* He is not to be confused with the British character actor who has the same name.

Costumes: 1956 *A Very Special Baby* 1957 *Compulsion* 1960 *Advise and Consent*

Jerry Boxhorn

Jerry Boxhorn designed numerous costumes for television, and was a consultant for the first color broadcast from WNBT-TV. Series on which he worked include the soap operas *The Guiding Light* and *All My Children.* He also designed variety shows for Martha Raye, Danny Thomas and Jackie Gleason. His costume designs were used on Broadway in the 1950s, early in career. Mr. Boxhorn died September 11, 1975 at the age of 55.

Costumes: 1952 *Hook 'n Ladder* 1956 *The Best House in Naples*

Consolata Boyle

Irish costume designer Consolata Boyle made her Broadway debut in 1988. Film credits for this Dublin-based designer are extensive, and include *The Secret of Roan Inish, The Snapper, This is My Father, Nora, The Serpent's Kiss, Nothing Personal,* and *Angela's Ashes.* She has collaborated with movie directors David Mamet, Stephen Frears and John Sayles, among others. She also designs costumes for the theater in Ireland.

Costumes: 1988 *Juno and the Paycock*

John Boyt

John Boyt has designed sets, costumes and/or lights for numerous productions in New York since 1946. Besides his designs for the theater, he created costumes and scenery for ballets, operas, and television. He designed the world premier of Aaron Copeland's *The Tender Land* and many other productions at the New York City Center. John Boyt was born in Newark, New Jersey on April 19, 1921 and graduated from the University of Iowa in 1942. He also attended Northwestern University and studied at the Mohawk Drama Festival in Schenectady, New York. Credits include numerous productions for Ballet West, the Houston Ballet, and for the Miami City Ballet. His designs for the Balanchine ballet "Western Symphony" continue to be used, most recently seen as part of the television special *Ballanchine Celebration* in 1993 and in the production by the Miami City Ballet in 1995. John Boyt died in November 1986.

Sets: **1946** *The Playboy of the Western World* **1956** *Debut*

Costumes: **1946** *A Flag Is Born*; *The Playboy of the Western World*; *Years Ago†* **1947** *Anthony and Cleopatra†* (Men's costumes) **1955** *The Wooden Dish* **1956** *Debut*; *The Lovers*

Lights: 1956 *Debut*

John Braden

John Braden was born on January 20, 1935 in Frederick, Colorado and attended the California College of Arts and Crafts, Chicago Art Institute, Goodman Theatre School and the Art Students League. He first worked in New York as a paint boy at the Metropolitan Opera before assisting a stellar list of designers: Eldon Elder, Robert Randolph, William and Jean Eckart, Miles White, and Karinska, to name only a few. His New York debut was *Single Man at a Party* which opened in 1959 off-Broadway. In 1964 he designed *Shadow Ground* for the New York City Ballet, after which he ran the New York City Ballet shop for several years, also working on three worlds fair pavilions. He joined ABC-TV in 1970 as staff designer, creating sets for shows including *Charlie Rose* and *Good Morning, America*. He received an Emmy Award for an ABC network news special and has many, many credits for art direction, scenic design and directing on television John Braden has a twin brother, Herb, who

designs for television and movies in California.

Sets: 1970 *Candida*

Mrs. Lillian Trimble Bradley

Mrs. Lillian Trimble Bradley was a playwright and director. She wrote some of her plays in collaboration with her husband, George H. Broadhurst, including *The Red Falcon* in 1923 and *Izzy*, first produced in 1924. Born in Milton, Kentucky in 1875, she was educated in Kentucky and France. The playbill for *Keep it to Yourself* in 1918 recorded her contribution to the play as: "Scenery designed and color schemes selected by Mrs. Lillian Trimble Bradley, decorations and furnishings selected by Mrs. Lillian Trimble Bradley." She both directed and designed scenery for *The Wonderful Thing*. She also directed and produced plays, including those written by herself, her husband and others in New York and London and is generally considered to be the first woman to direct a play in New York. Mrs. Bradley died in 1959.

Sets: 1918 *Keep It to Yourself* **1919** *The Crimson Alibi* **1920** *The Wonderful Thing*

Scott Bradley

Scott Bradley was born on September 5, 1961 in St. Louis, Missouri into a family of commercial artists. He received a B.A. in stage design at the University of Illinois in 1983, studying Kabuki design and painting with Shozo Sato and an M.F.A. at Yale in 1986. He has studied with and been influenced by Ming Cho Lee, Jane Greenwood, Michael Yeargan and Dunya Ramicova. Related training includes a 1978 painting internship in St. Louis and a 1979 internship at the International Arts Conference in Lucerne, Switzerland. His first design was *The Birthday Party* in 1977. Scenic designs include *Picasso at the Lapin Agile, Late Night with David Letterman, The Lost Boys,* and *A Midsummer Night's Dream* and *Ah, Wilderness!* at the Huntington Theatre. He has also designed *Road to Nirvana* for the American Repertory Theatre, *The Island of Anyplace*

at the Loeb Drama Center, and *The Hostage* for Portland Stage. Honors includea Drama Desk Nomination for *Joe Turner's Come and Gone*, a Jefferson Award for *The Notebooks of Leonardo da Vinci* and numerous American Watercolor Society purchase prizes.
Sets: 1988 *Joe Turner's Come and Gone* 1996 *Seven Guitars*

Thomas Bradley
Thomas Bradley collaborated on the sets for a 1905 production on Broadway.
Sets: 1905 *The Mayor of Tokio*†

William Bradley Studio
William Bradley began his career in theater as a singer and dancer, appearing in 1885 in *The Little Tycoon* at the Old Standard Theatre. He left New York City to work in Ohio theaters but returned in 1908 to work for Henry B. Harris. While supplying properties for productions he decided to open his own studio. William Bradley Studios specialized in properties and was located at 318 West 43rd Street, New York City. Through this business he supplied properties for numerous productions of George C. Tyler and others. He served on the staff of the Hudson Theatre as Master of Properties in 1924. He was also author of *The American Stage of Today* (1910) which contained photographs of leading performers of the day.
Sets: 1929 *The Guinea Pig*

Grace E. Brady
Mrs. Grace E. Brady, a dressmaker, lived and worked from her residence at 36 West 50th Street in New York in 1908. She resided at 29 West 57th Street in New York in 1910.
Costumes: 1913 *Tante*† (Miss Barrymore's gowns)

Claude Bragdon
Claude Bragdon was a practicing architect for most of his life, specializing in railroad stations. He was born in Oberlin, Ohio on August 1, 1866 and received his education at the University of Michigan. He first designed buildings in Rochester, New York, and later in New York City. A prolific author and translator, Mr. Bragdon wrote twenty books on architecture and related topics. He served as art director for Walter Hampden's productions during the 1920s and 1930s, designing scenery and costumes for some of the shows. Mr. Bragdon died on September 17, 1946.
Sets: 1918 *Hamlet* 1923 *Cyrano De Bergerac* 1925 *The Merchant of Venice*; *Othello* 1926 *Caponsacchi*; *Cyrano De Bergerac*; *The Immortal Thief*; *The Servant in the House* 1927 *An Enemy of the People* 1928 *Caponsacchi*; *Cyrano De Bergerac*; *An Enemy of the People*; *King Henry V*; *The Light of Asia* 1929 *Bond of Interest*; *Caponsacchi*; *Richelieu* 1932 *Cyrano De Bergerac* 1934 *Hamlet* 1935 *Achilles had a Heel* 1936 *Cyrano De Bergerac* 1937 *An Enemy ofthe People*
Costumes: 1923 *Cyrano De Bergerac* 1925 *The Merchant of Venice*; *Othello* 1926 *Caponsacchi* 1927 *An Enemy of the People* 1928 *Caponsacchi*; *Cyrano De Bergerac*; *An Enemy of the People*; *King Henry V*; *The Light of Asia* 1929 *Caponsacchi*; *Richelieu* 1935 *Achilles had a Heel* (Entire Scenic Production Design) 1936 *Cyrano De Bergerac* (Entire Scenic Production Design) 1937 *An Enemy of the People* (Entire Scenic Production Design)

Charles Brandon
After graduating from the University of Iowa in 1953, as a major in communication and theater, Charles A. Brandon was staff designer for the Cleveland Playhouse for the 1957-58 season, and later resident designer for the Falmouth Playhouse. He designed productions in New York at the Cherry Lane Theatre, Actor's Playhouse, and Equity Library Theatre and also designed *The Smokeweaver's Daughter* in 1959.
Sets: 1957 *Simply Heavenly* 1963 *The Heroine*

H. George Brandt
H. George Brandt designed three productions on Broadway in the early 1920s. On one occasion he designed both sets and costumes for the production. He is not to be confused with

George W. Brandt (1916-1963) a producer who was successful on the so-called Subway Circuit.

Sets: 1920 *Ladies Night*† 1921 *The Demi-Virgin; Getting Gertie's Garter*
Costumes: 1921 *The Demi-Virgin* (Acts II and III)

Bob Brannigan

Bob (Robert P.) Brannigan, who designed lighting for a production in 1962 also worked as a Broadway stage manager. This experience led him to managing large-scale events, including the 1962 Seattle World's Fair and positions as director of operations at Lincoln Center and the New York City Center. In 1975, he formed Brannigan-Lorelli Associates, Inc., an independent theater consulting service with Robert A. Lorelli. Clients included the renovation of City Center in the mid-1980s, the New Play House Theatre in Cleveland, Ohio and St. Peter's Church Theatre in New York City.

Lights: 1962 *The Egg*

Gail Brassard

The costume designer Gail Brassard works extensively in regional theaters (Goodspeed Opera House, Indiana Repertory Theatre, Studio Arena Theatre, McCarter Theater Center, The Shakespeare Theatre, among others), off-Broadway, and in television. In addition she created over 300 costumes for performers and animals featured in the 124th edition of the Ringling Bros. and Barnum & Bailey Circus in 1994. Born in Leominster, Massachusetts in 1953, she received a B.A. from the University of Massachusetts, Amherst and an M.F.A. from Brandeis University. Other New York credits include *Visiting Mr. Green, The Rothschilds,* and *Songs for a New World* at W.P.A. Theatre, *Pal Joey* at Encores!, and *Juno, The Waiting Room,* and *Christina Alberta's Father* at the Vineyard Theatre. For PBS-TV she designed *Sweeney Todd in Concert.* Honors include American Theatre Wing Design Award nominations for *The Matchmaker* at the Roundabout Theatre and *The American Clock* at Signature Theatre.

Costumes: 1990 *The Miser* 1991 *Taking Steps*

Eugene Braun

Eugene Braun was born in Tisza-Ujlak, Hungary and studied electricity in a Budapest technical school prior to emigrating to New York City at age sixteen. At the time of his death on April 9, 1965 at age 77 he was head electrician at Radio City Music Hall. He was on the electrics staff at Radio City in various capacities from the time it opened in 1932. Earlier he was an electrician for New York Calcium Company, on the electrical staff of Lew Fields' Theatre, and had also worked an assistant electrician at the Winter Garden and Roxy Theatres. The 1918 playbill for *Oh, Lady! Lady!* credits him as a member of the Princess Theatre Studios.

Lights: 1918 *Oh, Lady! Lady!; Oh, My Dear* 1942 *Stars on Ice* 1944 *Hats Off to Ice* 1946 *Icetime* 1947 *Icetime of 1948* 1948 *Howdy, Mr Ice* 1949 *Howdy Mr. Ice of 1950*

Luis Bravo

Luis Bravo, born in Añatuya, Santiago del Estero, Argentina, was raised in Buenos Aires where he lived from the age of eight. Primarily a musician, he studied cello at the Municipal Conservatory of Music with Manuel de Fallas and the University of Buenos Aires. and in the United States with Ronald Leonard. He has performed chamber music, recitals and with many orchestras, including the Los Angeles Philharmonic Institute Orchestra and the Buenos Aires Philharmonic. Recently, he has devoted his creativity to Argentine culture, through documentary film, recordings and in the theater. He created and directed *Forever Tango* as well as designing the lights. He won the Simpatia Prize for his production in 1996 at the Spoleto (Italy) Festival.

Lights: 1997 *Forever Tango*

Ruth Brenner

Ruth Brenner contributed designs to two shows on Broadway in the 1920s.

Sets: 1925 *Starlight*†
Costumes: 1925 *Starlight* (Some designs) 1929 *The Little Show*

Maurice Brianchon

Maurice Brianchon, a painter, designed scenery and/or costumes for two shows on Broadway in the early 1950s. He was born in 1899 at Fresnay-sur-Sarthe, France and studied at the Academy of Decorative Art. In 1937 he joined the faculty at the National Academy of Fine Arts in Paris continuing in that position until 1949. As a young man in France he designed sets and costumes for plays and operas, including *La Seconde Surprise de l'Amour* and *Sylvia*, before concentrating on painting and teaching. Although he died in 1979, his works, mainly landscapes and portraits, continue to be featured in New York, as they were in 1986 in an exhibit of paintings depicting dogs at An American Gallery and in 1994 in an exhibit of 19th and 20th century European paintings at the David Findlay Galleries.

Sets: 1952 *Les Fausses Confidences*; *Les Fourberies de Scapin*†
Costumes: 1952 *Les Fausses Confidences*

Fanny Brice

The comic actress and singer Fanny Brice was born Fanny Borach in New York in 1891 and performed in amateur contests, at benefits, in her parents' saloon, and in a burlesque show before appearing in the Ziegfeld Follies of 1910, after which she regularly starred in musical reviews and comedies. She was married to Billy Rose at the time *Crazy Quilt* was produced and not only appeared in the production in which she sang "I Found a Million Dollar Baby" but also designed the costumes. Miss Brice, who died in 1951, was also married at one time to Nicky Arnstein, a gangster. Their relationship is at the center of the musical and subsequent film *Funny Girl*.

Costumes: 1931 *Billy Rose's Crazy Quilt*

Andrew Bridge

Andrew Bridge was born on July 21, 1952 in England, the son of Peter Bridge, a theatrical producer, and his wife Roslyn. He studied at Port Regis and Bryanston Schools, as well as the London Academy of Music and Drama, and counts Richard Pilbrow among those who have influenced him. He won Tony, Drama Desk and Outer Circle Critics Awards for *The Phantom of the Opera*, Tony Awards for *Sunset Boulevard*, *Fosse*, and a Lighting Industry Federation Award for architectural lighting for the Lloyd's of London Headquarters. His designs include the *Siegfried and Roy* spectacular in Las Vegas and *Shirley Bassey in Concert*. West End credits include *Saturday Night Fever*, *Time*, *Billy Bishop Goes to War*, *Canterbury Tales*, *The Boyfriend*, and *Little Me*. In London where he designed *Madam Butterfly* at Albert Hall in 1998, he is a consultant for commercial presentations, industrial promotions, and architectural projects through a design company, "Imagination." He lives in London with wife, Susan and son, Oliver.

Lights: 1984 *Oliver!* 1988 *The Phantom of the Opera* 1990 *Aspects of Love* 1992 *Five Guys Named Moe* 1993 *Joseph and the Amazing Technicolor Dreamcoat* 1994 *Sunset Boulevard* 1999 *Fosse*; *Saturday Night Fever*

Kenneth Bridgeman

Kenneth Bridgeman designed scenery and costumes for a 1963 Broadway production. He studied at the West of England College of Art and first worked professionally in advertising. Mr. Bridgeman was resident designer for the Belgrade Theatre, Coventry in the 1960s and as a freelance designer for many repertory theaters in England. He has worked as set decorator for several feature films and for the British television series *The Prisoner*. He was also the art director for the 1985 film *Ordeal by Innocence*.

Sets: 1963 *Semi-Detached*
Costumes: 1963 *Semi-Detached*

Rose T. Briggs

Rose T. Briggs spent her career as a museum curator in Plymouth, Massachusetts, the town where she was born May 26, 1893. She studied at Radcliffe, the New York School of Fine and Applied Arts, in Paris, and at Harvard. She went from holding the position of curator of costumes for the Plymouth Antiquarian Society in 1929 to becoming it's director in 1958. The author of a dozen books, Miss Briggs was active in many New England Preservation Societies. Her publications include *Plymouth Rock: Its History and its Significance*, *Picture Guide to Historic Plymouth*, and *Notes on Vegetable Dyeing*. Some of her books were co-authored by Helen T. Briggs, her sister. Rose T. Briggs lent her expertise in costume to one production in 1926.

Costumes: 1926 *The Moon Is a Gong*

Robert Brill

A native of Salinas, California, the scenic designer Robert Brill attended Hartnell Community College but became compelled by theatrical design during an internship at the Oregon Shakespeare Festival where he worked with designers Bill Bloodgood and Richard Hay in 1983. He has since returned to design. While completing his undergraduate education at the University of California at San Diego where he studied with Robert Israel, he co-founded the Sledgehammer Theatre with Ethan Feerst and Scott Feldsher designing sets and lights for many of their productions. The active San Diego theater community provided further exposure, and he gained experience designing for the Old Globe and the San Diego Repertory Theatre, and as production designer for San Diego-based low budget films. By 1994 he was designing in major regional theaters throughout the country with many productions in New York and Chicago. Designs for the Steppenwolf Company include *A Streetcar Named Design* and for the Goodman Theatre, *The Return of Martin Guerre*. Among his many honors are Joseph Jefferson Awards and a Drama Desk Award for *The Rehearsal*.

Sets: 1996 *Buried Child*; *The Rehearsal* **1997** *God's Heart* **1998** *Cabaret* **2001** *Design for Living*; *One Flew over the Cuckoo's Nest*

Pat Britten

Pat Britten served as costume coordinator for the 50 year celebration of the Neighborhood Playhouse.

Costumes: 1978 *Neighborhood Playhouse at 50–A Celebration*† (Costume Coordinator)

Gertha Brock

Gertha Brock designed costumes for a Broadway play in 1968. She was among those mentioned in "Scenes in New York Drama" in the April 1973 issue of *Ebony*, as a black designer active in New York. She was born on March 23, 1922 and died in Los Angeles, California in October 1974.

Costumes: 1968 *Summer of the 17th Doll*

Annette Brod

Annette Brod was president of Annette Brod, Inc., a firm of dressmakers located on the third floor at 37 West 57th Street in New York in the 1930s. At the time she contributed gowns to a Broadway production, she resided at 300 Central Park West. Janet Cohen was vice-president and secretary of the company.

Costumes: 1932 *Belmont Varieties* (Miss Astaire's costume)

Herbert Brodkin

Herbert Brodkin, who died at age 77 on October 31, 1990, received an M.F.A. from Yale University in 1940. He was born on November 9, 1921 in New York City and studied at the University of Michigan, receiving a B.A. there in 1934. He designed scenery and lights for theater and Hollywood studios prior to focusing on television, initially as a set designer but primarily as a producer in a career lasting some forty years. He was responsible for *The Defenders* as well as shows for *Playhouse '90*, *The Elgin Hour*, and *Studio One*. With Robert Berger he formed Titus Productions in the 1960s and continued producing provocative productions, including *Skokie*, *Mandela*, *Sakarov* and *Pueblo* until dissolving the company in 1989. A retrospective show in 1985 at the Museum of Broadcasting featured productions from his television career.

Sets: 1947 *Caribbean Carnival*; *This Time Tomorrow* **1948** *The Silver Whistle*

Lights: 1947 *Volpone* **1948** *The Silver Whistle*

Tom Broecker

Tom Broeker designed costumes on Broadway for a 1998 production. A graduate of the Yale School of Drama, he is an active designer for television, including *Saturday Night Live* and the series *House Party*. He has numerous regional credits at Hartford Stage, Portland Stage, the Oregon Shakespeare Festival, and for the Williamstown Theatre Festival among others. He often designs costumes for the Shakespeare Theatre in Washington, D.C. where he did *Henry IV* in 1994, and *Henry V* in 2001. Off-Broadway credits include *Never the Sinner* at the Houseman Theatre, *First Lady Suite* at the Public Theatre and many productions including *Arabian Nights* at Manhattan Theatre Club for which he received an American Theatre Wing nomination.

Costumes: 1998 *Side Man*

Carol Brolaski

Carol Brolaski designs costumes for movies and plays. Films include *Honey, I Shrunk the Kids.* She designed *Stand-up Tragedy* initially at Hartford Stage and subsequently at the Criterion Center Stage Right in New York. She also designed *In the Belly of the Beast* at the Joyce Theatre and both *In the Hands of It's Enemy* and *The Traveler* in Los Angeles.

Costumes: 1990 *Stand Up Tragedy*; *Stand-Up Tragedy*

Louis Bromberg

Louis Bromberg designed sets on Broadway between 1925 and 1940. An artist, his studio was located at 9 East 14th Street in New York City in the mid-1920s. In addition, he illustrated *The Outline of Man's Knowledge* by Clement Wood in 1925.

Sets: 1925 *Flesh* **1927** *The Field God* **1929** *The Broken Chair*; *Cortez* **1930** *The Noble Experiment* **1932** *Blue Monday*; *Intimate Relations* **1934** *Hipper's Holiday* **1936** *Truly Valiant* **1937** *Thirsty Soil* **1940** *Russian Bank*

Lou Bromley

Lou Bromley was the son of Walter Lewis Bromley, a painter who exhibited in London between 1866 and 1892

at the Suffolk State Gallery. He worked with the Federal Theatre Project in one of twenty-two marionette units. One of his marionette productions, a variety show based on *Don Quixote*, toured Los Angeles parks in a van that contained a puppet stage.

Sets: 1936 *Don't Look Now*

Cleveland Bronner

Cleveland Bronner not only contributed special effects, costume and scenic designs to a 1922 Broadway production, he choreographed the ballet sequences. Born c.1875 in Detroit, Michigan, he was primarily a dancer and choreographer, but also performed in vaudeville. Together with his wife, dancer Ingrid Solfeng, he worked often for J. J. Shubert appearing in *Passing Show of 1920* and *Midnight Rounders*, among others and provided choreography for ballet sequences. Bronner died November 9, 1968 in Norwalk, Connecticut.

Sets: 1922 *Make It Snappy*† (Also effects)

Costumes: 1922 *Make It Snappy*†

Sara Brook

Sara Brook made her debut in New York as a costume designer in 1966 with *A Whitman Portrait* at the Gramercy Arts and on Broadway in 1969 with the opening of *The Front Page*. She graduated from Brooklyn College where she began designing costumes. Off-Broadway credits include *The Effect of Gamma Rays on Man-in-the-Moon Marigolds*. Sara Brook, who has designed costumes for two major summer musical theater circuits, Music Fair and Oakdale Music Tents, has extensive credits in the theater, film, television and for industrial shows.

Costumes: 1969 *The Front Page* **1970** *Child's Play*; *Chinese, The/ Dr. Fish*; *Inquest* **1971** *And Miss Reardon Drinks a Little*; *Ari*; *The Philanthropist*; *Twigs* **1972** *Captain Brassbound's Conversion*; *Hurry, Harry*; *The Little Black Book* **1973** *Children of the Wind* **1974** *My Fat Friend* **1979** *Murder at the Howard Johnson's*

Arthur D. Brooks

Arthur D. Brooks who collaborated on the costume designs for a 1914 Broadway production spent his career as an industrial designer. He worked for the Brooks Company in New York City, specialists in printing, stationary and producing lithographs from 1900 to 1932, rising through the ranks to become the company president in 1925. He left Brooks Company to become head of design for the Eaton Manufacturing Company in Cleveland, Ohio, a position he held until 1948. An expert in decorative and graphic arts, Brooks died on August 8, 1951.

Sets: 1903 *Mr. Bluebeard*†
Costumes: 1914 *The Dancing Duchess*†

Bernard Brooks

Bernard S. Brooks, who designed sets for three Broadway productions in the early 1930s, was president and treasurer of the Fulton Shirt Company in New York City. He lived with his wife Viola at 2980 Valentine Avenue.

Sets: 1932 *Moral Fabric* 1933 *Fantasia/ A Temporary Husband/ Crescendo*; *One Wife or Another*

Donald Brooks

Donald Brooks, a native of New York, has achieved success both as a costume designer for stage and film, and as a fashion designer. He studied at Parsons School of Design where he later taught, and at Syracuse University. Focusing on excellent materials and elegant lines, Mr. Brooks received many awards, particularly during the 1960s and 1970s when he was especially influential in the fashion industry. For fashion design, he has been honored with three "Coty" Awards, a "Winnie" in 1962, a "Return Award" in 1967, and Parsons Medal for Design. In the theater, he received a Drama Critic's Award for *No Strings*, and a Tony nomination for the same production. In film, he was nominated for an Oscar for *The Cardinal* in 1964, and for television he won an Emmy Award for *The Letter* starring Lee Remick. In 1995 was named as a consultant to the Ann Taylor specialty chain.

Costumes: 1961 *No Strings* 1963 *Barefoot in the Park* 1964 *Fade Out-Fade In*; *Poor Bitos* 1965 *Diamond Orchid*; *Fade Out-Fade In*; *Flora, the Red Menace* 1968 *Promises, Promises* 1969 *Last of the Red Hot Lovers* 1970 *Minnie's Boys* 1972 *Night Watch* 1974 *Good News*; *Summer Brave* 1975 *The Member of the Wedding*; *A Musical Jubilee* 1977 *Knickerbocker Holiday* (Gowns); *Party with Betty Comden and Adolph Green* (Miss Comden's downs); *She Loves Me* (Gowns) 1979 *Carmelina*; *Monteith and Rand* 1983 *Dance a Little Closer*

Sydney Brooks

Sydney Lee Brooks attended the University of Utah and started her involvement with costumes through designing and doing wardrobe for summer stock companies. Her costume designs have been seen at the Provincetown Playhouse, AMAS Repertory, Lion Theatre, Circle Repertory Theatre, New Federal Theatre, and Masterworks Theatre among others. Her film credits include *Eischeid*. In addition to designing costumes, Sydney Brooks designs hair, acts, and collects antique clothes.

Costumes: 1975 *The Glass Menagerie*

Lez Brotherston

Lez Brotherston graduated from the Central School of Art and Design in London in 1984, after which he immediately designed the film *Letter to Brezhnev*, the start of a busy career designing sets and costumes for dance, opera, theater and film. He has designed for the Royal Danish Opera, Opera Zuid, Welsh National Opera, and the Hong Kong Arts Festival among others, working often with directors Aidan Lang and Malcolm Fraser. Designs for dance include productions for Sadler's Wells, the Northern Ballet Theatre, Scottish Ballet and Norwegian National Ballet, collaborating often with directors and choreographers Matthew Bourne and Christopher Gable. He frequently designs for the Manchester Royal Exchange and the Greenwich Theatres, as well as in London's West End. Much honored for his designs, he won Tony, Drama Desk, and Los Angeles Outer Critics Circle Awards for the costume design for his Broadway debut *Swan Lake*, and Drama Desk and Drama-Logue Critics Awards for the set. His designs for *Cinderella* won Laurence Olivier Awards for both sets and costumes.

Sets: 1998 *Swan Lake*
Costumes: 1998 *Swan Lake*

Charles E. Brown

As a young man, Charles E. Brown designed scenery and created mechanical effects. He spent the majority of his professional life in advertising in increasingly important positions, serving as advertising director for the Radio Corporation of America as well as for the National Broadcasting Company. NBC-TV relocated him from the East Coast to West Coast, where he worked for them in San Francisco and Hollywood. In 1948 he was elected as the second president of the Television Academy of Arts and Sciences, and from 1949 until 1957 was vice president of Bing Crosby Enterprises. He died in Los Angeles at age 62 in October 1958.

Sets: 1908 *Mary Jane's Pa*† (Mechanical effects) **1909** *The Florist Shop*† (Mechanical effects) **1911** *Little Boy Blue*†; *Miss Jack*† (Mechanical effects)

Georgianna Brown

Georgianna S. Brown, in private life Mrs. Charles H. Brown, was active on Broadway in the 1920s. In 1922 she resided at 100 West 85th Street in New York, and in 1932 at 4428 Carpenter Avenue.

Sets: 1922 *Greenwich Village Follies*†
Costumes: 1922 *Greenwich Village Follies*† ("Chauve Souris")

Gertrude Brown

Gertrude G. Brown designed costumes for one show in 1927. She was born in Maldern, West Virginia and studied at the Maryland Art Institute, at Columbia University and in Europe. A private pupil of Henry B. Snell, she spent her professional career as a painter, and a painting instructor mainly in and around Washington, D.C.

Costumes: 1927 *Big Lake*

Jack Brown

Jack O. Brown was born April 30, 1934 and spent his career working as a lighting and scenic designer, and as a scene painter, amassing credits with the Opera Society of Washington and Boston Arts, among other locations. Off-Broadway designs included *Stephen D*, *Dylan* and *Slow Dance on the Killing Ground*. After graduating from what was then Carnegie Institute of Technology with a major in acting, he operated the White Barn Theatre near Pittsburgh in 1963 and then began a long association as assistant to Oliver Smith. He also assisted William Pitkin, serving in that capacity for the Broadway production of *Invitation to a March*. Jack Brown, who worked as a scenic artist at the Metropolitan Opera for many years died on January 13, 1993.

Sets: 1972 *Heathen!*
Lights: 1963 *Natural Affection* **1964** *Beeckman Place*; *Ben Franklin in Paris*; *Dylan*; *Slow Dance on the Killing Ground*

Larry W. Brown

Larry W. Brown designed scenery for his first Broadway show in 1999 shortly after receiving his M.F.A. from Rutgers University. He has designed numerous sets for the New Jersey Shakespeare Festival, the George Street Playhouse and productions for children, including *The Lion King of Mali* produced by Theatreworks USA.

Sets: 1999 *Rollin' on the T.O.B.A.*

Lewis Brown

Lewis (Lew) Brown is from California, where he was born in 1928. He graduated from the University of California, Los Angeles 1951 and has designed extensively for the theater and ballet companies in the U.S. His first costume designs were for *Pride and Prejudice* at UCLA in 1947. He debuted in New York at the City Ballet with *Medea* in 1958. Mr. Brown has received several Critics Awards in Los Angeles and San Diego for his costumes in those two cities. A specialist in historical plays, Mr. Brown is known for his skill with strong characterization. His costumes were an integral part of the

1994 Los Angeles Music Center Opera Company's production of *Faust* that was revived in 2000 at the Chicago Lyric Opera. He also designed the costumes when Gordon Davidson restaged *Candide* at the Ahmanson Theatre in the mid-1990s, and regularly creates costumes at the Old Globe, including *Henry IV* and *Way of the World*, both with director Jack O'Brien, a frequent collaborator.

Costumes: 1967 *Marat/Sade* **1968** *Jimmy Shine* **1969** *Fire!*; *A Flea in Her Ear* **1991** *Mule Bone* **1994** *The Government Inspector*

Michael Brown

Michael Brown, who made his Broadway debut in 1999, received his B.A. from Brown University where he majored in art history, and his M.F.A. in scenic and lighting design from Brandeis University. He has designed numerous productions at the Williamstown Theatre Festival and off-Broadway at theaters including Minetta Lane, New York Performance Works, Raw Space and the Signature Theatre. His lights for *Bedfellows*, directed by Jim Simpson with whom he often works, won the 1998 Obie Award. Twenty-first century credits include scenery for *Unwrap Your Candy* for the Vineyard Theatre and *Tintypes* at the McGinn Cazale Theatre.

Sets: 1999 *The Price*

Patrika Brown

Patrika Brown designed lights for a play on Broadway in 1975. With dancer Karin Dwyer she opened three retail food shops in New York City, including The Erotic Baker at 73 West 83rd Street. They also published *The Erotic Baker Cookbook* in 1983.

Lights: 1975 *Boccaccio*

Paul Brown

Paul Brown mainly designs costumes and occasionally sets for opera. He has collaborated three times with movie director Philip Haas for the films *Up at the Villa*, *The Blood Oranges*, and *Angels and Insects*, his first film, for which he was nominated for an Academy Award for costume design. Designs for opera include *Lady Macbeth of Mtsensk* at the Metropolitan Opera, *Parsifal* at the Paris Opera, *Fidelio* at the English National Opera, *The Midsummer Marriage* at the Royal Opera, and *Lulu* at Glyndbourne. Paul Brown, the British costume designer is not to be confused with the American screenwriter, producer and director, or the American music engineer, all of whom have the same name.

Costumes: 1994 *Medea*

Ralph Brown

Ralph Brown collaborated on the scenic designs on Broadway in 1946. It is unlikely that the scenic designer was also the noted tap dancer (d. 1990) who appeared in films or is the actor of the same name currently appearing in movies.

Sets: 1946 *Song of Bernadette†*

Zack Brown

Zack Brown, a designer of sets and costumes, was born on July 10, 1949 in Honolulu. He received a B.F.A. from Notre Dame in 1968 where he began designing, and an M.F.A. from Yale. His New York debut came in 1977 with the opening of *Tartuffe* at Circle in the Square, for which he received a Drama Desk nomination for Best Costumes. With his Broadway debut, *The Importance of Being Earnest*, also in 1977, he received a Tony Award nomination for the setting. His designs for the settings and costumes for *La Gioconda* earned him two Emmy Awards when the opera, performed by the San Francisco Opera, was broadcast. These honors are only a few of the numerous ones he has received. Among the regional theaters for which he has designed are the Williamstown Theatre Festival, the Guthrie Theatre, Arena Stage and the Yale Repertory Theatre. Opera designs include *Die Fledermaus* at the Houston Grand Opera, *Rigoletto* at the Metropolitan Opera, and *Otello* for the Washington Opera. His designs for the sets and costumes for the Kevin McKenzie's production of *Swan Lake* for the American Ballet Theatre continue to receive excellent notices for the atmosphere they evoke and the contrasts they create.

Sets: 1977 *The Importance of Being Earnest*; *Tartuffe* 1978 *13 Rue De l'Amour*; *Man and Superman* 1979 *Loose Ends* 1980 *Major Barbara*; *The Man Who Came to Dinner*; *Past Tense* 1983 *On Your Toes* 1988 *The Devil's Disciple*; *The Night of the Iguana* 1992 *Chinese Coffee*; *Salome* 1995 *Garden District*
Costumes: 1977 *Saint Joan*; *Tartuffe* 1978 *13 Rue De l'Amour*; *Man and Superman* 1980 *Major Barbara*; *The Man Who Came to Dinner* 1983 *On Your Toes* 1988 *The Devil's c* 1992 *Chinese Coffee*; *Salome* 1995 *Garden District*

Mr. Bothwell Browne

Mr. Bothwell Browne designed costumes on Broadway in 1911. A successful female impersonator in vaudeville, he lived from 1877 until 1947. One of the highlights of his career was Mack Sennett's 1917 film *Yankee Doodle in Berlin* about an American pilot who obtains German military secrets by masquerading as a woman. He played the leading role in *Miss Jack* in 1911 on Broadway, and also designed the costumes.
Costumes: 1911 *Miss Jack*

Catherine Browne

Catherine Browne designed sets, lights and costumes for a 1966 production which originated in London's West End and subsequently moved to Broadway.
Sets: 1966 *The Killing of Sister George*
Costumes: 1966 *The Killing of Sister George*†
Lights: 1966 *The Killing of Sister George*

H. K. Browne

H. K. Browne (Halbot Knight Browne) signed most of the illustrations he created for serials and novels "Phiz" beginning with *Pickwick Papers* although he signed the first two plates for that book "Nemo" He did the illustrations for many of Charles Dickens' works as well as those of other nineteenth century British fiction writers. As a young painting student he won the Silver Isis medal from the Society of Arts for the best illustration of an historical subject. His style, developed through training painting with watercolor, was also appropriate for theatrical backdrops used at the time. Although his success as an illustrator prevented him from amassing too many credits in the theater, he did occasionally design, using his own name rather than his pseudonym. His Broadway scene design credit was for a production initially staged in London, that arrived in New York ten years after his death in London on July 9, 1892.
Sets: 1902 *The Cross-ways*†

Andrew and Margaret Brownfoot

Andrew and Margaret Brownfoot collaborated on the settings and costumes for a Broadway show in 1970. They were married after meeting as students at the Central School of Arts and Crafts. After completing school Andrew became the resident designer for the Puppet Theatre on BBC Television. The Brownfoots have designed numerous plays at Stratford East's Stage 60 Company where they have worked as resident designers. Designs include *Widower's Houses*, *Saint's Day* and *Little Winter Love*. Their designs have also been seen at the Palace Theatre in Watford and include a production of *As Dorothy Parker Once Said*.
Sets: 1970 *The Boy Friend*
Costumes: 1970 *The Boy Friend*

Brownie

Brownie, born Helaine L. Brown, died in New York City on April 21, 1942. She was an actress, and appeared in the chorus of many Broadway musicals including *Anything Goes* and *Earl Carroll's Vanities*. She also designed the costumes for a show in 1932.
Costumes: 1932 *Dangerous Corner*

Bruck-Weiss

Bruck-Weiss, located at 6-8 West 57th Street in New York City during much of the 1920s was a custom shop that specialized in clothing that was considered theatrical even when worn on the street. The shop catered to customers, including actresses who desired "the Mode Individual" which meant a complete ensemble: garments, accessories and underpinnings - all but the shoes. Olga Petrova's entire costume (except footwear) were specially created by Bruck-Weiss for a 1927 Broadway production. In the late 1920s, the shop relocated to 20-22 West 57th Street.

Costumes: 1927 *What Do We Know?*† (Olga Petrova's gown)

Adrienne Brugard

Adrienne Brugard designed costumes for a 1914 production on Broadway.

Costumes: 1914 *Kitty Mackay*

John Brunton

John C. Brunton, who died at age 74 on February 15, 1951 in Yonkers, New York was a set designer and builder of sets and properties. He designed plays under his own name and through John Brunton Studios, which he operated in Atlantic City and at 226 West 41st Street in New York City. Floats and parade decorations were also created in his studios. He came to the United States from London when young and progressed from properties builder to scene designer. Undoubtedly he designed more productions than those for which he received credit, as he was on the staffs of Klaw & Erlanger and Florenz Ziegfeld. At the time of his death he was working for NBC-TV.

Sets: 1909 *The House Next Door*† (Design and properties) **1910** *Rebecca of Sunnybrook Farm*† (Design and properties) **1911** *The Senator Keeps House*† (Design and properties) **1919** *A Burgomaster of Belgium* (as: John Brunton Studio) **1920** *Her Family Tree*† (as: John Brunton Studio) **1922** *Montmartre; The Night Call*

Robert Brunton

Robert F. Brunton first designed sets and ran a scenic studio in Boston, Massachusetts before relocating to New York in the early 1920s where he constructed and painted sets for many Broadway designers. He operated the New Amsterdam Studio during the 1920s and a theatrical supply business on West 49th Street in the 1930s, residing in Long Island City, Queens, New York. Also employed as a theatrical manager, his portrait appeared in the December 4, 1919 issue of *Dramatic Mirror*. He should not be confused

with Robert A. Brunton (d. 1923) a Scottish film director and producer.

Sets: 1915 *Around the Map*† **1934** *Another Love*

Robert Bryan

Robert Bryan created lighting for a production in 1983 for the Broadway stage, with which he was originally involved in London. For the Broadway production he worked in collaboration with an American designer, as was common at the time. He has extensive credits in the United Kingdom including productions in the West End (*Night and Day, Separate Tables, A Murder is Announced*), for the Royal Shakespeare Company (*Poppy, Privates on Parade, Once in a Lifetime*), and for the Royal National Theatre (*Measure for Measure, A Long Day's Journey into Night, On the Razzle, Jumpers*). He has served as lighting consultant for the Glyndebourne Festival Opera. A protégé of Richard Pilbrow at Theatre Projects, he helped establish the profession of lighting design in Great Britain.

Lights: 1983 *All's Well That Ends Well*†

Hope Bryce

(Patricia) Hope Bryce was born in San Francisco and received her education at Smith College. A summer job with Hattie Carnegie led to a modeling career. After marriage to Otto Preminger (she was his third wife), and the birth of twins in 1960, she put her fashion knowledge to use as costume co-ordinator on the films her husband produced and directed, beginning with *Bonjour Tristesse*. She designed costumes on Broadway in 1973.

Costumes: 1973 *Full Circle*

Brymer

Brymer collaborated on the designs for Broadway productions during the 1920s and 1930s. He was one of the house designers at Manning, Inc., a small fashion and costume construction concern run by Mildred and Maybelle Manning in 1933-1934, and certainly provided costumes for more plays than his list of credits suggests. Brymer also designed for the movies, working at Universal Studios in the mid-1930s.

As an assistant to movie designer Vera West, he provided costumes for *The Great Impersonation* and *Magnificent Obsession*. He collaborated with Travis Banton on *Crash Donovan* and *My Man Godfrey*.

Costumes: 1923 *Vanities of 1923*† 1933 *Murder at the Vanities*† 1934 *Mahogony Hall*† (Other costumes); *The Milky Way* (Gowns); *No Questions Asked* (Gowns); *Whatever Possessed Her* (Gowns)

Fred Buchholz

Fred Buchholz was drawn to the theater at an early age. Right out of high school he served on the staff of Arena Stage and then moved to New York city to work for the New York Shakespeare Festival. Influenced by Jennifer Tipton and Bill Mintzer, he studied lighting design at studied at SUNY-Purchase. His New York debut came with *Frimbo* at the Grand Central Terminal. Other off-Broadway credits include *Mary Stuart* and *How It All Began* for Des McAnuff, and *Maybe I'm Doing It Wrong* for Joan Micklin Silver. Buchholz currently creates properties and special effects for film, television, and theater, and is particularly adept at those incorporating light, working through Acme Special Effects. Projects include work for Laurie Anderson, Peter Brook, James Ivory, and Robert Wilson. He has received three Emmy Awards for his television designs.

Lights: 1982 *Pump Boys and Dinettes*

Wilfred Buckland

Wilfred Buckland's first experiences with the theater were as an actor with the Daly Company. His appearance with Maude Adams in *The Little Minister* in 1897 was among his roles before he became David Belasco's art director and a busy designer of sets and stage properties. Late nineteenth century credits for scenic design include *Apples of Eden, Rain Clouds*, and *In Old New Amsterdam*, in 1898 at the Empire Theatre. Given the many plays and revues produced by David Belasco, Buckland's list of credits for which he received acknowledgement in the playbill only represent the shows with which he

was involved in New York. In the late teens, he moved to California, where he worked as an art director for movies. He was born January 1, 1866 and died a suicide, in Los Angeles on July 7, 1946.

Sets: 1902 *The Darling of the Gods*† (Stage decorations and accessories) 1903 *Darling of the Gallery Gods, The* and *The Dress Parade*† (Stage decorations and accessories); *Sweet Kitty Bellairs*† (Stage decorations and accessories) 1904 *The Music Master*† (Stage decoration); *Pillars of Society*† (Properties and furnishings); *Zaza* 1905 *Adrea*† 1906 *The Rose of the Rancho*† 1907 *A Grand Army Man*† 1909 *The Lily*† (Stage decorations) 1910 *Pillars of Society* 1911 *The Boss*† 1914 *Omar, the Tentmaker*† (Also director and producer)

Sam'l B. Budd

Samuel Budd who was born in New Paltz, New York in 1835, was a descendant of an old English family. In 1861 at age 26, he moved to New York City and opened a men's furnishing store at the corner of Fifth Avenue and 24th Street, which was thriving at the time of his death in July 1912. It is likely that his eldest son was involved with the 1903 Broadway production that cites Sam'l B. Budd in the credits as responsible for the lights.

Lights: 1903 *The County Chairman*

Mabel A. Buell

Mabel A. Buell designed sets on Broadway under her own name between 1917 and 1939 as well as through a scenic studio, originally knownas the Buell Scenic Studio. In the late teens the studio was renamed the "Mabel A. Buell Scenic Studio." Mabel Buell, who was born on August 16, 1875 and died in April 1968, was married to Herbert Schulze, a scenic designer who also worked through the studio. Her daughter Joy Buell (d. 1999) was also active in the New York theater as a scenic artist.

Sets: 1917 *Good Morning, Rosamond* 1919 *Love Laughs* 1921 *The Triumph of X* 1922 *The Bronx Express* 1924 *Plain Jane* 1926 *The Judge's Husband* 1932 *Cradle Snatchers* 1933 *Blackbirds of 1933* 1937 *Sea Legs* 1939 *Lew Leslies' Blackbirds of 1939*

Mabel A. Buell Scenic Studio

The Mabel A. Buell Scenic Studio, originally known as the Buell Scenic Studio, was located at 1402 Broadway and was active from the teens until 1937. The business, initially managed by Nina Giles Buell who retired in 1926, then passed to her daughter, Mabel. Both Mabel Buell and her husband, scenic designer Herbert Schulze worked through the studio, although only Mabel Buell garnered credits under her own name. Nina Buell died in Palm Beach, Florida on December 30, 1947.
Sets: 1921 *The Squaw Man* 1928 *Straight through the Door* 1932 *Blackberries of 1932*† 1936 *Summer Wives* 1937 *Straw Hat*

Henry Buhler

Henry Buhler collaborated on the scenic designs for one Broadway production and was a scenic painter and designer for another. He resided at 1410 Prospect Avenue in New York in 1910.
Sets: 1900 *Prince Otto*† 1906 *Bedford's Hope*† (Scenes painted)

Cora Bulger

Cora Bulger collaborated on the designs for a show in 1921.
Costumes: 1921 *The Fan*† (Hats and gowns)

W. H. Bull

W. H. (William Howell) Bull was an illustrator and painter. He was born in Buffalo, New York in 1861 and spent most of his professional life in California. In additional to his one known credit as a scenic designer, he worked as an illustrator for *Sunset* magazine, the Southern Pacific Railroad, and Stanford University, among others. A founding member of the California Society of Artists, he died in San Mateo, California in 1940.
Sets: 1907 *Dr. Wake's Patient*

Blake Burba

A native of St Louis, Missouri, where he was born on March 30, 1970, Blake Burba was nominated for a Tony Award for the lighting design of his very first Broadway show. He graduated from Webster University in 1992 and then spent six years at the Opera Theatre of St. Louis, four of them as resident assistant lighting designer, working with Christopher Akerlind (whom he identifies as a mentor) and Robert Wierzel, among others. He has designed lights for the Cherry Lane Theatre, the Coronet Theatre, *Quills* and *Bright Lights, Big City* at the New York Theatre Workshop and *Too Many Clothes* at the Kitchen, among others. He also designed *Not Suitable for Children* at the McCarter Theatre and *Triptych* for Merce Cunningham Studio. Recent designs include the New York Theatre Workshop benefit at Studio 54, reuniting the original *Rent* cast.
Lights: 1996 *Rent* 1997 *London Assurance*

Edward Burbridge

Edward Burbridge has designed many off-Broadway productions, operas, ballets, national tours, television and regional theater productions. He was born in New Orleans on May 23, 1933 and studied at Pratt Institute and the Lester Polakov Studio and Forum of Stage Design. The recipient of the John Hay Whitney Fellowship to study European theaters, his career has been influenced by Boris Aronson. Among his many productions for The Negro Ensemble Company are *Summer of the Seventeenth Doll, Daddy Goddess* and *The First Breeze of Summer.* In addition, he was art director for the television series *Kojak*, has numerous credits in regional theaters and for television. He served as production designer for the 1990 TV special *Martin* and was designer for the television special *A Renaissance Revisited.* His designs for the Metropolitan Opera featured in the 1995 exhibition, "Onstage: A Century of African-American Stage Design" at the New York Public Library for the Performing Arts at Lincoln Center.
Sets: 1967 *Marat/Sade* 1968 *Jimmy Shine; Mike Downstairs; Summer of the 17th Doll* 1969 *Buck White; Does a Tiger Wear a Necktie?; Our Town* 1973 *Chemin De Fer; Holiday; Status Quo Vadis; The Visit* 1974 *Absurd Person*

Singular 1975 *The First Breeze of Summer* 1980 *Reggae* 1988 *Checkmates* 1991 *Mule Bone*

Saul F. Burger

Saul (Paul) F. Burger created costumes for a production during the 1928-29 season. He was born in 1891 and spent the majority of his professional life as a screenwriter for movies. He died in Los Angeles, California on June 16, 1937.
Costumes: 1928 *Straight through the Door* (Miss Lee's and Gate's gowns)

Everett Burgess

Everett Burgess designed one set in 1940 on Broadway.
Sets: 1940 *Quiet Please*

Hermann Burghart

Hermann Burghart (Burghardt) collaborated on the scenic designs for a 1907 production. His design for *Salome* and sketches for Acts II and II of *Tales of Hoffman* both produced by the Metropolitan Opera Company were included in "The Art of the Theatre." The exhibition of original designs for the stage was held at 714 Fifth Avenue in November, 1914 by the Stage Society of New York.
Sets: 1907 *The Christian Pilgrim†* (Act I, Scene 1; Act IV, Scene 2)

Deidre Burke

Deidre Burke designed costumes for a 1992 production on Broadway. She also designed the feature garden for the New Zealand Home and Interiors Exhibition in Wellington in 1997, collaborating with landscape architect Tim Hobbs.
Costumes: 1992 *The Sheik of Avenue B*

Lloyd Burlingame

Lloyd Lamson Burlingame has been production designer for plays both on and off-Broadway since he debuted in New York City with the opening of *Leave It to Jane*. Born in Washington, D.C. on December 31, 1934, the son of Harry and Estelle Burlingame, he had an early introduction to the arts by his uncle, Lloyd Embry, a portrait painter. After study at Carnegie Mellon University he spent a year at La Scala on a Fulbright Scholarship initiating his

study of opera, which has remained of particular interest. Mr. Burlingame prefers to have responsibility for all of the design elements for a production, after the example set by Robert Edmond Jones, and has had that responsibility with most of his Broadway credits. Mr. Burlingame, is emeritus professor of the Department of Design at New York University, where he served as chair from 1972-1997. In 1985 a retrospective show of his scenic designs and touchable art was held in New York City, and a one-man show of recent work, "Once More with Feeling," was held at the Wadsworth Atheneum in Hartford, Connecticut in 1988. At work on a book of memoirs, *My Days in the Theatre* and one about the collaboration between Gustav Mahler and painter Alfred Roller in the early 20th century, he continues to teach, design and mentor young designers. In 1997, he was honored with a *Theatre Crafts International* (now *Entertainment Design*) Award.
Sets: 1964 *Alfie* 1966 *First One Asleep, Whistle*; *The Loves of Cass Mc Guire*; *Philadelphia, Here I Come* 1967 *The Astrakhan Coat*; *Keep It in the Family* 1968 *Woman Is My Idea* 1969 *Love Is a Time of Day* 1970 *Not Now, Darling*
Costumes: 1964 *Alfie* 1966 *Philadelphia, Here I Come* 1967 *The Astrakhan Coat* 1968 *Woman Is My Idea* 1969 *Love Is a Time of Day* 1970 *Not Now, Darling*
Lights: 1963 *The Lady of the Camellias* 1965 *Boeing-Boeing*; *Inadmissable Evidence*; *The Right Honorable Gentleman* 1966 *First One Asleep, Whistle*; *Help Stamp Out Marriage*; *The Loves of Cass Mc Guire*; *Philadelphia, Here I Come* 1967 *Brief Lives*; *There's a Girl in My Soup* 1968 *A Day in the Death of Joe Egg*; *The Flip Side*; *Rockefeller and the Red Indians*; *Woman Is My Idea* 1969 *Hadrian VII*; *Love Is a Time of Day* 1970 *Not Now, Darling* 1971 *A Midsummer Night's Dream*; *The Philanthropist* 1972 *Via Galactica*; *Vivat! Vivat Regina!*

Walter W. Burridge

Walter W. Burridge was a scene designer and painter with credits for productions appearing as early as 1884. A native of Chicago, he often collaborated with Edward Morange, Frank E. Gates, Richard Marston, John H. Young, Edward Albert, Ernest M. Gros, Hughson Hawley and Homer Emens. These scenic artists were all active in that same era and often worked together in small groups. His program credit for *The Harvester* in 1904 reads: "All the scenes from the brush of Walter Burridge." Nineteenth century credits include *The Count of Monte Cristo* at the Grand Opera House in 1884, *Dorothy* in New Haven and several productions in Boston. Burridge was also a fine art painter. He died in Albuquerque, New Mexico in June 1913 of an apparent heart attack, after spending the two months immediately prior to his death painting scenes of the Grand Canyon.

Sets: 1900 *Arizona†*; *The Bostonians†* (Act I); *The Devil's Disciple*; *Prince Otto†* 1901 *Up York State* 1902 *A Country Girl†*; *King Dodo*; *The Sultan of Sulu* 1903 *The County Chairman*; *Peggy from Paris†*; *The Prince of Pilsen*; *The Wizard of Oz†* (Act I, Scene I; Act II) 1904 *The College Widow*; *Common Sense Bracket*; *The Harvester*; *The Sho-gun*; *Woodland*; *The Yankee Consul†* 1906 *The Galloper*; *The Man from Now*; *The Stolen Story*; *The Student King* 1907 *The Merry Widow*; *The Ranger†*; *The Rogers Brothers in Panama†*; *Tom Jones*; *A Yankee Tourist* 1908 *Devil, The (Adapted by Herford)*; *Mary Jane's Pa†* 1909 *The Florist Shop†*; *The Gay Hussars*; *The Love Cure* 1910 *The Little Damozel*; *Madame X*; *Miss Patsy* 1911 *Everywoman*; *Excuse Me*; *Kismet†*; *Mrs. Avery* 1912 *A Fool of Fortune*; *The Man from Cook's†*; *The Trail of the Lonesome Pine†*; *The Woman-Haters†* (Act III) 1913 *Arizona†* (Acts I, IV)

Ann Burrows

Ann Burrows designed costumes on Broadway in 1922. She resided at 2444 Morris Avenue in Queens, New York in the mid-1920s.

Costumes: 1922 *Frank Fay's Fables†*

John Bury

John Bury was born in Aberystwyth, Wales on January 27, 1925. Origi-

nally an actor, he progressed to design work through various technical positions. His design career began in 1946 at Joan Littlewood's Theatre Workshop and designed for many productions between 1954 and 1964. His first designs for the Royal Shakespeare Company in Stratford-upon-Avon were sets and costumes for *Julius Caesar* in 1963, and from 1964 until 1968 he was head of design for the RSC. At the RSC he also began his long and bountiful collaboration with Peter Hall. Mr. Bury was appointed Head of Design at the Royal National Theatre of Great Britain in 1973 and remains the only artist to ever serve as head of design in both of England's major theaters. Mr. Bury's work was first seen in New York City in 1974 when he designed the sets and lights for *Oh, What a Lovely War*. Mr. Bury also designed for films and opera and consulted on the design of theaters. In 1975 he received a Gold Medal for design in Prague which was followed by a Golden Troika in Prague, in 1979. He was elected a fellow of the Royal Society of the Arts in England in 1968 and also was honored with the Order of the British Empire (O.B.E.). *Amadeus* brought Mr. Bury a Tony nomination for outstanding costume design, and Tony Awards for both the set and lights in 1981. When John Bury died at age 75 on November 12, 2000, although ill and semi-retired, he was working on the revival of *A Midsummer Night's Dream* for the Glyndebourne Festival.

Sets: 1964 *Oh What a Lovely War*; *The Physicists* 1967 *The Homecoming* 1970 *The Rothschilds* 1971 *Old Times* 1972 *Via Galactica* 1976 *No Man's Land* 1980 *Amadeus*; *Betrayal* 1986 *The Petition*

Costumes: 1964 *The Physicists* 1967 *The Homecoming* 1970 *The Rothschilds†* 1972 *Via Galactica* 1976 *No Man's Land* 1980 *Amadeus*; *Betrayal* 1986 *The Petition*

Lights: 1964 *Oh What a Lovely War*; *The Physicists* 1967 *The Homecoming* 1971 *Old Times* 1976 *No Man's Land* 1980 *Amadeus*; *Betrayal* 1986 *The Petition*

Margaret Bury

Margaret Greenwood Bury, a British designer, created the costumes for a production on Broadway in 1960 that was imported after a successful run in London's West End. She was the first wife of designer John Bury.

Costumes: 1960 *The Hostage*

Scott Bushnell

Scott Bushnell has designed costumes in many regional theaters, including Center Stage and A.C.T. She is a long time associate of Robert Altman, and has worked on most of his films and theater productions, including the off-Broadway production at St. Clement's Theatre of *2 By South*. Beginning with the film *Thieves Like Us* she has worked for him in various capacities: costume designer, casting director, associate producer, producer and more recently executive producer. In addition to designing costumes for a show on Broadway she was casting director and assistant to Altman, consistent with other projects for which she had multiple functions. Increasingly she is involved almost exclusively in film, retaining her interest in costumes with designs for the film *Streamers* in 1983 (also co-producer), *Vincent & Theo* in 1990 and the women's wardrobe for *The Player* in 1992. She served as executive producer for both *Mrs. Parker and the Vicious Circle* and *Short Cuts*.

Costumes: 1982 *Come Back to the 5 & Dime, Jimmy Dean, Jimmy Dean*

Bill Butler

The British costume designer Bill Butler studied at the Wimbledon School or Art. He works throughout the United Kingdom and has designed numerous shows in London, including *Absurd Person Singular, Charley's Aunt* and *Outside Edge*. The production that marked his Broadway debut transferred to New York from London's West End.

Costumes: 1990 *Buddy: The Buddy Holly Story*†

Clara Butler

Clara Butler, known in private life as Mrs. Frank I. Frayne, was at one time the champion lady rifle shot of the world. Her husband was Frank Ives Frayne (1836-1891), an actor and champion short-range rifle shot of the world. They toured with Otis Skinner and performed an act in which Mr. Frayne shot an apple off Clara Butler's head. She was also a sculptor, and exhibited at the Royal Academy in London in 1881 and 1883. Born Miss Clehorow Caroline Butler, she resided at 224 Brooklyn Avenue in Valley Stream, Long Island in 1932. She is referred to as the late Mrs. Clara Butler Frayne in the obituary of her son, also named Frank I. Frayne, in 1938.

Sets: 1925 *The Handy Man*

Jeanne Button

Jeanne Button was born May 8, 1930 and received her training at Carnegie Institute of Technology (B.S.) and at the Yale School of Drama (M.F.A.) She has designed costumes for television, many regional theaters, and has extensive credits off-Broadway. Honors include a Maharam Award for *MacBird*. She taught costume design at Yale, New York University and Tulane University (1990-2000) where she is now Professor Emerita. Jeanne Button was appointed principal costume designer for the Great Lakes Theatre Festival in summer 1985 and since 1995 has been co-artistic director of the Tulane Summer Shakespeare Festival where she has designed *The Big Shot of Africa, The Merry Wives of Windsor, As You Like It* and *Much Ado About Nothing*, among many others.

Costumes: 1969 *The Watering Place* 1970 *Henry V* 1976 *The Robber Bridegroom* 1979 *Richard III; Wings* 1986 *Arsenic and Old Lace* 1993 *The Twilight of the Golds*

Alexandra Byrne

Alexandra Byrne designed scenery and costumes for a play on Broadway in 1990. A noted British designer, she is active in regional theaters throughout the United Kingdom and as a costume and scenic designer, and art director for British television and for movies. She has designed *Hamlet, Temptation,* and many other productions for the

Royal Shakespeare Company. Productions in London also include numerous plays at the Soho Poly Theatre and *Life of Napoleon*, the theatrical directing debut for Kenneth Branagh with whom she often works. She received an Academy Award nomination for the costume design for *Hamlet* starring and directed by Branagh, and a Golden Satellite Award for Outstanding Costume Design for *Elizabeth*. Another frequent collaborator at the RSC is director Roger Mitchell, who also did Richard's Nelson's play *Some American's Abroad* which transferred to Broadway. .

Sets: 1990 *Some Americans Abroad*

Costumes: 1990 *Some Americans Abroad*

Robert Byrne

Robert Byrne designed costumes for a show in 1937. A native of Washington, D.C., he was born on December 10, 1902 and studied in the U.S. at George Washington University and the Corcoran Art School, and in Paris at the Grande Chaumière. A painter and lecturer, his specialty is Mediaeval Art. From 1939 to 1942, he worked as Docent at the Cloisters for the Metropolitan Museum of Art. Mr. Byrne served as President of the Theatrical Costume Designers Union, a division of United Scenic Artists in the late 1930s and early 1940s.

Costumes: 1937 *London Assurance* (Men's costumes)

Dave Caddy

Dave Caddy designed costumes for two shows in the 1930s.

Costumes: 1931 *Fata Morgana†* 1935 *Strip Girl*

Giles Cadle

The British scenic designer Giles Cadle occasionally creates costume designs as well for plays and operas. He studied at architecture at Kingston Polytechnic and then stage design at Notttingham Polytechnic. His sets for Opera North include *Eugene Onegin* and his designs for the Almeida Opera's production of *Siren Song* were seen at Glyndebourne in 1999. He has designed at the Young

Vic (*Six Characters Looking for an Author*) and the Almeida Theatre (*Gangster No. 1*). Additional designs in New York include the Samuel Beckett Festival at Lincoln Center in 1996.

Sets: 2000 *Wrong Mountain*

Costumes: 2000 *Wrong Mountain*

Ian Calderon

Ian Calderon was born on July 20, 1948. He received a B.A. from Hunter College in 1970 and an M.F.A. from the Yale University School of Drama in 1973 after studying with Donald Oenslager and Ming Cho Lee. His involvement with lights began when he was in high school and has continued ever since. He has numerous credits off-Broadway, in regional theaters, and for rock concerts. He is also a production supervisor, producer and lighting consultant. Two Tony Award nominations, for *That Championship Season* in 1973 and *Trelawney of the "Wells"* in 1976, are among his many honors. In 1980 he co-founded, along with partner Robert Redford, the Sundance Institute where he serves a Director of Digital Initiatives.

Lights: 1972 *Sticks and Bones*; *That Championship Season* 1975 *The Lieutenant* 1976 *Trelawney of the "Wells"* 1978 *Cheaters*; *The Effect of Gamma Rays on Man-in-the-Moon Marigolds*; *Paul Robeson*; *Timbuktu* 1983 *Breakfast with Les and Bess*

Anne Caldwell

Anne Caldwell, a playwright and lyricist also composed music for some of the musical revues she created. Often collaborating with R. H. Burnside, Victor Herbert, Jerome Kern, and Vincent Youmans, her music and lyrics for the stage appeared as early as 1906. In the teens and twenties they include *Chin-Chin, The Lady In Red, Stepping Stones* and *Three Cheers*. She was born in Boston, Massachusetts in 1867 and died on October 22, 1936 at the age of 60. Caldwell contributed costume designs to one play in 1928.

Costumes: 1928 *The High Hatters*

M. J. Caldwell

M. J. Caldwell contributed an electrical effect to a 1910 Broadway production.

A scenic studio, "Rough & Caldwell" was located at 122 West 29th Street, New York City during the beginning of the twentieth century. In 1906, the studio relocated to 156 West 29th Street.
Lights: 1910 *The Spring Maid*† (Electric fountain)

Frank Callaghan

Frank Callaghan specialized in electrical fixtures, according to a 1901-1902 New York City directory. He resided at that time at 133 West 113th Street.
Lights: 1910 *Bright Eyes*†

Herbert Callister

Herbert Callister created costumes for one production in 1937.
Costumes: 1937 *Arms for Venus*

Callot Soeurs

Three sisters, daughters of an antique dealer, founded Callot Soeurs in 1895 at 9 Avenue Matignon in Paris. The eldest sister, Madame Gerber, was the principle designer. For a time Vionnet worked as a pattern maker in the couture house. Their romantic, feminine dresses were all made from high quality materials combining originality with exceptionally good taste. Until the house closed in 1937 (some sources suggest 1935) it was frequented by rich society matrons, including an American, Mrs. De Acosta Lydig, and actresses who desired gowns from Callot Soeurs to wear both on and off stage.
Costumes: 1907 *All-of-a-Sudden Peggy*† (Miss Tempest's costumes) 1910 *The Girl with the Whooping Cough* (Miss Suratt's gowns) 1911 *Macbeth (Kellerd)*† (Miss Marlowe's costumes); *The Red Rose*† (Miss Surratt's black spangled gown) 1912 *Whirl of Society*† (Mlle. Desly's gowns); *Ziegfeld Follies of 1912*† (Dresses and gowns for Miss Lorraine) 1913 *High Jinks* (Miss Mayhew's gowns); *The Honeymoon Express*† (Miss Desly's gowns); *Much Ado About Nothing*† (Miss Marlowe's costumes) 1914 *What It Means to a Woman*† (Miss Jolivet's gowns) 1917 *Ziegfeld Follies: 1917*†

Gladys E. Calthrop

Gladys E. Calthrop (often G. E. Calthrop) was born in Ashton, Devonshire, England in 1900, the daughter of Frederick and Mabel Treeby. After receiving her education in England, she married Major Everard Calthrop and spent her professional career designing sets and costumes both in England and the United States. Beginning with *Vortex* in London in 1925, she designed the original productions for most of Noel Coward's plays until she retired from the theater in the late 1940s to pursue her interest in decorating. She returned to the theater in the late 1950s to design a production of *The Edwardians* in London, set in a period which she had always found compelling. Gladys Calthrop, who died on March 7, 1980, also wrote fiction and was a fine art painter.
Sets: 1925 *Beware of Widows*; *Hay Fever*; *Master Builder*; *The Vortex*; *Young Woodley* 1926 *John Gabriel Borkman*; *The Master Builder*; *Red Blinds*; *This Was a Man*†; *The Three Sisters*; *Twelfth Night* 1927 *The Cradle Song* 1928 *This Year of Grace*† 1929 *Bitter Sweet*† 1930 *The Cradle Song* 1931 *Private Lives* 1933 *Design for Living* 1934 *Conversation Piece* 1935 *Point Valaine* 1936 *Tonight at 8:30* 1937 *Excursion* 1939 *Dear Octopus*; *Set to Music*
Costumes: 1925 *Hay Fever*; *Master Builder*; *The Vortex*; *Young Woodley* 1926 *John Gabriel Borkman*; *The Master Builder*; *Saturday Night*; *The Three Sisters* 1927 *The Cradle Song*; *Inheritors* 1928 *This Year of Grace*† 1929 *Bitter Sweet*† 1930 *The Cradle Song* 1934 *Conversation Piece* 1939 *Set to Music*

Colin Campbell

Colin Campbell, known as Royce Carleton during his acting career, was born in Edinburgh in 1859 and began acting in plays as early as 1875. He made his debut in London in 1882 in *Far From the Madding Crowd* after which he appeared in numerous plays on both sides of the Atlantic until his death on January 14, 1895. For a play written by Edward E. Rose, he contributed designs for the lights, receiving posthumous credit when the play was performed in New York as part of the 1899-1900 Broadway season.
Lights: 1899 *The Gadfly*

Irma Campbell

Irma Campbell contributed designs to two productions in 1920.

Costumes: 1920 *French Leave†* (Act III); *Three Showers* (All frocks and women's costumes)

John P. Campbell

John P. Campbell, son of Bartley Campbell, a playwright, designed both sets and costumes for a production in 1919. He worked with producers, including Henry Miller and Oliver Morosco before joining a stock brokerage firm in New York as a secretary. Mr. Campbell died at the age of 67 on October 15, 1938.

Sets: 1919 *Dark Rosaleen*
Costumes: 1919 *Dark Rosaleen*

Patton Campbell

Born in Omaha, Nebraska on September 10, 1926, Patton Campbell received both a B.A. and an M.F.A. at Yale. His career has been principally as a costume designer, but he began as a scenic, lighting and costume designer in various summer stock theaters and as an assistant to Rouben Ter-Arutunian. He has designed for many companies, including the New York City Opera, the Santa Fe Opera and the Opera Company of Boston. He has also designed national tours and productions at the New York City Center. His list of extensive costume and scenery credits includes many operas, both world premieres and works from the standard repertory. His designs for opera have been broadcast on television, principally by WNET. Mr. Campbell was nominated for a Tony Award in 1977 for *Man of La Mancha*, which he designed with Howard Bay. In addition to his design activity, Mr. Campbell is an educator, having taught at Barnard College, Juilliard, New York University, Columbia University, SUNY-Purchase, and Southern Methodist University.

Sets: 1955 *The Grand Prize*
Costumes: 1955 *All in One, Trouble in Tahiti*; *Twenty Seven Wagons Full of Cotton* 1956 *Fallen Angels* 1957 *A Hole in the Head*; *The Makropoulos Secret* 1958 *Howie* 1960 *There Was a Little*

Girl 1961 *All American*; *The Conquering Hero* 1965 *The Glass Menagerie* 1966 *Agatha Sue, I Love You* 1967 *Come Live with Me*; *The Natural Look* 1968 *Loot* 1977 *Man of La Mancha†* 1992 *Man of La Mancha†* 1993 *The Student Prince†*
Lights: 1955 *The Grand Prize*

William Camph

William Camph, also known simply as "Camph" collaborated on the scenic designs for Broadway productions beginning in 1902. As early as 1900, New York City directories identify him as a property man, residing at 200 East 27th Street in 1900 and at 204 West 83rd Street in 1910. In 1916 he worked as a contractor from 227 West 50th Street in New York, and in 1917 was associated with the Astor Theatre. He amassed numerous credits for properties, including *The Boys of Company "B"* in 1907 and *A Rose o' Plymouth Town* in 1902. William Camph and his contemporaries John Brunton, Gus Weidhaas, and Thomas Mangan were often the only individuals responsible for any scenic element to be identified in a program, in particular for productions that relied on painted backdrops, making the properties an especially important design element.

Sets: 1902 *The Crisis†* 1907 *On Parole†* (Also properties) 1908 *The Prisoner of Zenda†* (Also properties) 1909 *The Fair Co-Ed†* (Also properties) 1911 *The Enchantress* (Also properties)

Robert Caney

Scenic artist Robert Caney, known as Caney and R. Caney, lived from 1847 to 1911. A British scenic painter and designer, he was active in London from 1866 through the first decade of the twentieth century. He contributed to many productions at Covent Garden, Drury Lane and the Grand National Amphitheater, often in collaboration with other active scenic artists of that time, such as Joseph Harker, Bruce Smith, and Walter Spong. His designs for the pantomimes held during the holiday season at the Theatre Royal in Drury Lane were widely regarded as wonderful. One of the scenic designs he created for *Jack and the Beanstalk*

in 1899 is reproduced in *Theatre on Paper* by Alexander Schouvaloff.
Sets: 1901 *The Price of Peace†*; *The Sleeping Beauty and the Beast†* (as: R. Caney) 1903 *Mother Goose†* (as: R. Caney) 1905 *The White Cat†* (as: R. Caney)
Costumes: 1900 *Mrs. Dane's Defense* (as: Caney: Miss Millward's gowns)

Clifford Capone

A native of New York City, Clifford Capone studied at the Traphagen School of Fashion, the Art Students League, Pratt, and Parsons. His career has been spent principally designing costumes for films, including eight movies with Dino de Laurentis. He has designed over 50 shows off-Broadway, including many at the APA-Phoenix Theatre, beginning with *The Witch Finders* in 1956. His credits in regional theaters include costume designs at the Goodman Theatre, American Shakespeare Festival, Hartman Theatre, San Diego Shakespeare Festival, Buffalo's Studio Arena Theatre and Stage/West. His costumes have also been seen on the television series, *Nurse* and in numerous variety specials. Twenty-first century credits include *Family Week* by Beth Henley in 2000.
Costumes: 1976 *Something's Afoot†*

Caramba

Signor Luigi Sapelli of Milan, Italy, used the pseudonym Caramba (occasionally Carramba) in his professional life as a theatrical and fashion designer. He lived from 1865 (some sources state 1867) until 1936 and maintained couture houses called either Caramba, or A. Sapelli and Co., in Vienna, London, Buenos Aires, New York and Milan during the height of his career. Caramba also published *Corriere de Teatro*, a periodical about the theater, in Italy. He designed scenery and costumes for the Teatro d'Arte in Turin, at La Scala, Carama Opera, and for the Marchetti Opera Company. He came from a family of artists and actors, although his father, Luigi Sapelli di Capriglio had a career in the Italian Army. Allesandro Sapelli, possibly a brother or son, also participated in the couture house.

Costumes: 1912 *The Daughter of Heaven†* 1914 *The Garden of Paradise†* (as: A. Sapelli); *Twelfth Night*

Emilio Carcano

Emilio Carcano began his career as an assistant to Renzo Mongiardino and Franco Zeffirelli for both films and theaters in his native Italy. He designed sets for Bertucelli's film *Paulina 1800*. His first production in Paris for "Group TSE," who produced *Heartaches of a Pussycat* on Broadway, was *24 Heures*. He has also designed Herb Gardner's *La Fraîcher de l'Aube* and *L'Etoile du Nord* in Paris and the 1994 production of *Rondine* at La Scala. Several productions for which he created the scenery at the Spoleto Festival in Italy for Giancarlo Menotti, have also been seen at the Spoleto Festival in Charleston, South Carolina, including the 1996 production of *Eugene Onegin*. In addition to scenic design, Emilio Carcano is an interior decorator with Rudolf Nureyev's Paris home among his projects.
Sets: 1980 *Heartaches of a Pussycat*

Daniel J. Carey

Daniel J. Carey (also known as D. J. Carey) was staff electrician for Equity Players, Inc. in the 1920s. In the mid-1920s he also designed lights for two productions on Broadway. *Cole's New York City Directory* lists him as an electrician as early as 1915, when he resided at 272 West 154th Street. In 1932 he remained employed as an electrician and lived with his wife Odette at 69 Tiemann Place in New York City.
Lights: 1925 *Brother Elks*; *Candida*

Julia Carlisle

Mrs. Julia Carlisle spent her career in the theater as a wardrobe mistress. She contributed costume designs to one show in 1932.
Costumes: 1932 *Never No More*

Charles Carmello, Jr. Jr.

A playwright and scenic designer, Charles Carmello, Jr. has worked in summer stock and regional theaters. He is the author of the play *Saints Alive* which was performed in New York in

1979, and *La Mattanza* performed in 1986.

Sets: **1976** *Wheelbarrow Closers*

Hattie Carnegie

Hattie Carnegie (Henrietta Kanengeiser) was born in Vienna, Austria in 1886 and died in New York City in 1956. She was a powerful force in the world of fashion, adapting Parisian models to American tastes. At the age of eleven she moved to the U.S. with her family and went to work for a milliner. She progressed rapidly to running her own business, transforming the freelance hat designs she originally created late at night into a multi-million dollar business. Miss Carnegie contributed designs to Broadway shows, and was in particular demand for those requiring contemporary gowns. See Figure 4: Hattie Carnegie: *Lady in the Dark*

Costumes: **1927** *The Command to Love*† (Miss Cooper's gowns); *The Second Man* (Gowns) **1928** *Holiday*† (Gowns) **1930** *Rebound*† (Gowns) **1931** *Perfectly Scandalous*† (Miss Schafer's gowns) **1933** *Forsaking All Others*†; *A Good Woman, Poor Thing*† (Miss Purcell's Act III gown); *The Locked Room* (Gowns); *Under Glass* (Gowns) **1934** *Slightly Delirious* **1935** *Triumph* (Miss Matteson's gowns) **1936** *Alice Takat*† (Miss Christian's gowns); *The Promise* (Ladies dresses); *Three Wise Fools* (Miss Love's costume) **1938** *All That Glitters*; *The Circle* **1939** *The Philadelphia Story*† (Miss Allen's and Miss Booth's gowns); *Ring Two*† (Miss Walker's clothes, Miss Van Cleve's Act I costume); *Skylark* **1941** *Lady in the Dark*† (Gowns) **1942** *Morning Star*† (Clothes) **1943** *Another Love Story*; *Lady in the Dark*† **1945** *The Overtons*; *The Ryan Girl* (Miss Havoc's gowns); *State of the Union*† (Gowns) **1948** *Tonight at 8:30*† (Miss Lawrence's gowns)

Ruth Carnegie

Ruth Carnegie designed costumes and accessories for plays in 1915 and 1916. A dressmaker, she lived and worked at 2542 Broadway during the teens.

Costumes: **1915** *When the Young Vine Blooms* (Hats) **1916** *Our Little Wife*† (Other gowns)

Carns and Williams

Carns and Williams collaborated on the scenic designs for a Broadway production in 1906 from a studio located at 518 West 22nd Street in New York City. It is likely that Williams refers to George Williams, a scenic designer, painter and builder also active at that time.

Sets: **1906** *The Girl Patsy*

Michael Carr

Michael Carr, born Michael Cohen on March 17, 1900 in Leeds, Yorkshire, England, appeared in the 1937 film *Let's Make a Night of It*. He also designed sets on Broadway, but should not be confused with the American actor of the same name who performed on Broadway. In 1922 he was associated with Blanding Sloan and Peter Larsen in an artists' studio called "Wits & Fingers Studio" at 17 East 14th Street in New York City. He died on September 16, 1968.

Sets: **1923** *Uptown West*†

Edward Carrick

Known for much of his life as Edward Carrick, Edward Anthony Craig was the son of Edward Gordon Craig and grandson of Ellen Terry. He was born in London on January 3, 1905 and studied painting in Italy from 1917 to 1926. His first exhibition in London was in 1928 where he signed his works "Edward Carrick." Undoubtedly influenced by his father's design activity, he was art director for Associated Radio Productions in 1932 and art director for Associated Talking Pictures in London from 1931 to 1935. He worked in New York City in the 1930s as a painter, producer, and decorator. He then worked with other film companies such as Ealing Films, and as an independent producer and stage director. In 1938 he founded the first school specializing in film studies in England. He also wrote widely on the subject of film design, including "Moving Picture Sets, A Medium for the Architect" in *Architectural Record*, "Designing for the Motion Pictures" in *Design* in 1950. Notably, he wrote an analysis of his fathers life and career,

Figure 4: Hattie Carnegie: *Lady in the Dark*: "Dream Sequence" gown for Miss Gertrude Lawrence, 1941. Reprinted by permission, The Museum of the City of New York.

Gordon Craig: The Story of His Life, published in 1968 and helped establish the Craig Archive at Eton College. His theatrical designs were not often seen in the U.S., but in addition to his 1936 New York credit, he designed *Macbeth* at Stratford-upon-Avon, which later toured the United States. Edward Anthony Craig died on January 21, 1998 in Thame, Oxfordshire, England.

Sets: 1936 *Night Must Fall*

Frank Carrington

Frank Carrington was an actor who appeared on stage and screen. He contributed the lighting designs to one production on Broadway in the mid-1920s. He was widely known however, as the co-founder, producer and director of the Paper Mill Playhouse in Millburn, New Jersey which he began in 1938 with Antoinette Scudder. In 1972 the Paper Mill Playhouse was named the State Theatre of New Jersey. Mr. Carrington died on July 3, 1975 at age 73.

Lights: 1925 *Wild Birds*

Earl Carroll

Earl Carroll is perhaps best remembered as a creator of musicals and revues, including several editions of *Earl Carroll's Vanities* from 1923 to 1936 for which he was the major writer and composer. Many of his productions were performed in the Broadway theater named for him located at 755 Seventh Avenue. He was born on September 16, 1893 in Pittsburgh and began his career in theater selling programs. He moved to New York in 1912, after traveling in Asia and serving as a pilot in the Army Air Service in World War I, to become a songwriter for a music publisher. After an appearance in vaudeville in 1917 he worked steadily in New York until 1938, when he moved to Hollywood to become an associate producer for 20th Century Fox Film Corporation. He contributed set designs to two plays, including *The Lady of the Lamp* in 1920, the first production which he managed. Mr. Carroll died in a plane crash on June 17, 1948 near Mt. Carmel, Pennsylvania at age 56.

Sets: 1916 *A Lady's Name* **1920** *The Lady of the Lamp*

Julia Carroll

Julia Carroll (also known as Miss Carroll) collaborated on designs for two shows on Broadway, one in the early years of the century and the other in the mid-1920s. She spent most of her professional life as the manager of a fashionable Madison Avenue dress shop. Miss Carroll died at age 92 on October 20, 1959.

Costumes: 1902 *Mrs. Jack* (as: Miss Carroll: gowns) **1917** *Losing Eloise* (as: Miss Carroll: Miss Watson's gowns) **1924** *In His Arms†*

Audrey Carter

Audrey Carter designs costumes for plays, film, music videos, and has also created a ready-to-wear collection. She has designed for Kiss, Motley Crüe, Joan Jett (including her concerts in a Broadway theater), and Duran Duran, among others. Her designs for the *Moscow Circus* include both the 1991 Broadway version and the subsequent *Moscow Circus - Cirk Valentin* for producer Steven E. Leber.

Costumes: 1991 *Moscow Circus*

Lincoln J. Carter

Lincoln J. Carter, a playwright and scenic designer, was born in Rochester, New York on April 14, 1865 and spent much of his life in the Midwest, primarily in Indiana and Chicago, although his acting company toured as far as Alaska. He wrote melodramas, a genre that lost popularity during his lifetime, and extended his activities to encompass scenic design for his own productions and for those of others. He designed scenery, directed and acted in many of his own. plays The programs in New York as well as on tour that contain an acknowledgement of his scenic designs for *Bedford's Hope* include this note: "The panoramic effects used in this production are covered by United States patents, and any infringement will be prosecuted to the fullest extent of the law, by Lincoln J. Carter, patentee." His play, *An American Ace* for which he also did the scenery was not a success, and after it closed he concentrated on scenic design, writing for motion pictures, and traveling. He was 61 years old when he died on July 13, 1926.

Sets: 1906 *Bedford's Hope†* (Scenic effects design) **1918** *An American Ace*

Deirdre Cartier

Deirdre Cartier designed costumes on Broadway in 1971, although her costumes were seen before then off-Broadway, in plays including *The Iceman Cometh* directed by Jose Quintero, and in several productions for the Lincoln Center Repertory Theatre. She has designed numerous shows at the American Shakespeare Festival in Stratford, Connecticut.

Costumes: 1970 *Blood Red Roses*

Ronald Case

Ronald Case was born in Los Angeles on July 30, 1950, the son of Almon and Lois Case. He studied for two years at Rio Hondo Junior College in California and for two years at New York University School of the Arts. Influences on his career include an acting teacher in high school, Squire Freidel, and designers Eoin Sprott and Robin Wagner. He assisted properties designer Eoin Sprott for several Broadway shows, including *Pippin, The Wise Child, Jesus Christ Superstar, Sgt. Pepper's on the Road* and *Antony and Cleopatra.* With Michael Bottari, his collaborator for more than thirty years, he designs sets and/or costumes for a variety of productions: tours, such as *Fiddler on the Roof, Man of La Mancha, Ballroom, The King and I, Showboat,* and *The Pirates of Penzance*; off-Broadway plays including *431 of My Closest Friends, Living Proof, The Man Who Shot Lincoln, After the Fair,* and *Opal*; and for regional theaters and industrial promotions. Much honored for their designs, they have also created puppets for the Disney workshop production of *Carnival* and taught scenic and costume design for American Ballet Theatre's "Make a Ballet" program.

Sets: 1989 *Prince of Central Park†*
Costumes: 1989 *Prince of Central Park†* **1996** *State Fair†*

Don Casey

Don Casey was lighting designer for a Broadway play in the early 1920s. In 1919 he maintained an office at 1493 Broadway in New York City.

Lights: 1923 *The Lullaby*

Michael Casey

A native of Austin, Texas, Michael Casey graduated from the University of Texas in 1977, after taking a year off to study at the Traphagen School of Fashion. He worked on the staff of New York costume shops and designed in regional theaters before making his New York debut with designs for Ginger Rogers at Radio City Music Hall. After designing seven productions for the Rockettes, he relocated to the West Coast in 1981 and designed for four seasons at the American Conservatory Theatre. In 1984 he opened Michael Casey Couture in San Francisco, specializing in gowns for evening and special occasions. His fashion designs include the inaugural ball gown for Texas Governor Ann Richards. His collections have been shown at Nieman Marcus and Esther Wolf. Additional costume design credits include productions for the San Francisco Ballet. The couture designer should not be confused with architectural restoration specialist Michael H. Casey.

Costumes: 1981 *America*

Richard Casler

Richard Casler not only worked as an assistant to many outstanding American designers including Jo Mielziner, Rouben Ter-Arutunian, Russel Wright, William and Jean Eckart, Donald Oenslager, Boris Aronson and George Jenkins, he was a prolific designer himself. Born in Oakland, California, he received his undergraduate education at Stanford University and an M.F.A. from Yale in 1958. While still in graduate school, he began designing religious dramas for Union Theological Seminary. After completing his degree he later taught at Union, and designed scenery, costumes and lights for numerous productions, including the American premiere of Benjamin Britten's *Noah's Flood.* Among his off-Broadway designs were *The Saving Grace, Love in Buffalo* and *Thistle in My Bed.* In 1970, he relocated to Dallas, Texas with his wife, Sami Casler, a theater technician he met at Yale, and their thee children. As Vice-president of Robert Young, Associates, he became involved in display design. When William and Jean Eckart moved to Dallas in 1971 as members of the faculty at Southern Methodist University, he joined them, to teach design as a part-time adjunct professor. He died in November 1986.

Lights: 1965 *Anya* 1969 *Red White and Maddox*

Cassidy and Sons

Cassidy and Sons were responsible for the lighting for two 1912 productions. The family specialized in electrical fixtures from a shop at 133 West 23rd Street in New York in 1908. The business expanded, and in 1917 Cassidy and Sons Manufacturing Company, Lighting Fixtures, was located at 101 Park Avenue. Jonathan G. Cassidy served as president, Albert Wahle, Vice-president, George W. Cassidy, Secretary, and F. W. Cassidy was treasurer. At the time of his death on June 19, 1955 at age 73, George W. Cassidy was the retired president of Cassidy Company, located in Long Island City, Queens, New York. Cassidy Co. manufactured lighting fixtures.

Lights: 1912 *Broadway Jones*; *Ready Money*

Oleg Cassini

Oleg Cassini, born Oleg Loiewski in Paris in 1913, grew up in Italy where he studied at the Academia Belle Arti. His earliest work in fashion was as a sketch artist. He had a small shop in Rome before moving to New York in 1936 where he started using his mothers maiden name, Cassini. A naturalized citizen, Cassini spent several years in California designing costumes for the movies, and has occasionally contributed designs to theatrical productions. Cassini is widely known for the designs he created for Jacqueline Kennedy Onassis while she was in the White House; many of the gowns he

designed for her were featured in a 2001 exhibition at the Metropolitan Museum of Art. Cassini is the author of two books about his life and career: *Pay the Price* and *In My Own Fashion.* His numerous awards include five first prizes at Mostra della Moda in Turin.

Costumes: 1948 *As the Girls Go* 1960 *Critics' Choice* (Clothes) 1962 *Come on Strong*† (Miss Baker's costumes)

Julio Castellanos

The painter Julio Castellanos designed sets for many theatrical and ballet productions in Mexico, and in the 1930s contributed designs for scenery to a Broadway play. Born in Mexico City in 1905, he studied art and traveled through the Americas and Europe before devoting himself to painting, both murals and figures. He was the director of the Federal Department of Plastic Arts in the early 1940s in Mexico City, where he died in 1947.

Sets: 1938 *Mexicana*

Castillo

Castillo (Antonio Canovas de Castillo) was born in Spain in 1908 where he originally studied to be an architect. He moved to France during the Spanish Civil War and got his start as a fashion designer creating women's accessories and gowns. After designing for Parisian houses, he moved to New York initially to work with Elizabeth Arden, but soon established his own reputation. During this period in his career, between 1945 and 1950, he also began designing costumes for plays and at the Metropolitan Opera. He returned to Paris in 1950 to design for Lanvin and in 1964 started showing his own collections, while continuing to design occasionally for the theater and films, including in 1971 *Nicholas and Alexandra.* Castillo, who died in 1984, closed his couture business in 1970.

Costumes: 1946 *Present Laughter*† (Costumes for Miss Dalton and Miss Linden) 1947 *Medea* 1948 *Inside U.S.A.*† (Miss Lillie's gowns); *The Play's the Thing*† (Miss Emerson's gowns) 1950 *Ring 'Round the Moon* 1958 *Goldilocks*; *The Marriage-Go-Round*† (as: Lanvin-Castillo: Miss Colbert's dresses); *The Visit*† (Miss Fontanne's clothes)

Castle and Harvey

Castle and Harvey was a scenic studio run by William E. Castle and Walter Harvey. They collaborated on several productions early in their careers, as well as painting scenery for many additional productions individually and through their associations with other scenic studios. From 1914 until the late 1930s, William E. Castle was a partner in the scenic design studio Dodge and Castle which he formed with D. Frank Dodge. Walter M. Harvey was principally a scene painter and during the 1930s was a partner in Wood and Harvey Studios, New Jersey. For additional credits, see individual entries for William E. Castle, Walter Harvey, Dodge and Castle, and Wood and Harvey.

Sets: 1904 *The Shepherd King*; *The Winter's Tale*† 1905 *Lifting the Lid*† 1906 *The Greater Love*† (Act III) 1907 *The Man on the Case* 1911 *Dr. De Luxe*† (Act III); *Thais*† (Act III); *Winter Garden*†

William E. Castle

William E. Castle designed sets for several productions in the 1920s under his own name. He began his career as a paint boy for Gates and Morange in their scenic studio. Early in his career he formed a partnership with Walter Harvey, the Castle and Harvey Scenic Studio, before designing and painting on his own. In the 1920s the scenic design studio Dodge and Castle was formed by D. Frank Dodge and William E. Castle and operated at 241 West 62nd Street in New York City. They collaborated on several productions between 1914 and 1934 and painted the scenery for many additional productions. For additional credits, see the entry "Dodge and Castle" and the one for "Castle and Harvey."

Sets: 1922 *The Clinging Vine* 1923 *Battling Buckler*; *A Love Scandal*; *The Magic Ring* 1924 *Lollipops*†; *The Magnolia Lady*; *The Man in Evening Clothes*; *Merry Wives of Gotham* 1926 *The Captive*; *Honest Liars*; *The Square* 1927 *Celebrity*; *Interference*; *Love Is Like That*; *Pickwick*; *That French Lady* 1928 *Our Betters*; *Paris*

E. Castle-Bert

Eugene Castle-Bert, occasionally referred to as E. Castlebert, an artist and designer resided at 214 West 42nd Street in New York City in 1901. His wife, known as Madame or Mrs. Castle-Bert was a prolific producer of stage costumes. He should not be confused with Eugene Castle (1897-1960), founder of Castle Films.

Sets: 1900 *The Princess Chic*

Madame Castle-Bert

Known as Madame or Mrs. Castle-Bert, and as Mathilde Castelbert, she was active in the area of stage costumes during the first decade of the twentieth century, designing, but mainly executing them for many of the active designers. In this way, she contributed to the success of many Broadway productions, for example, *Babette* where the playbill states: "Miss (Fritzi) Scheff's gowns designed by Mrs. Siedel (sic) and executed by Mrs. Castlebert." The costume business was initially located at 312 West 41st Street in New York City, and later at 316 West 42nd Street. Her husband, Eugene Castle-Bert (occasionally Castlebert), was an artist and designer.

Costumes: 1902 *Miss Simplicity*† 1906 *The Crossing* 1908 *School Days* 1909 *Old Dutch*† (Gowns and accessories) 1910 *The Yankee Girl*†

Virginia Estes Cates

Virginia Estes Cates designed and supervised costumes for several shows in the 1930s.

Costumes: 1933 *All Good Americans* (Costume Supervisor); *Sailor, Beware* 1934 *Ladies' Money* (Costume Supervisor); *Small Miracle* (Costume Supervisor) 1935 *Battleship Gertie* (Costume Supervisor); *Sailor, Beware*

Julia Cerrell

Julia Cerrell, president and treasurer of Julia, Inc., a firm of dressmakers located on the ninth floor at 32 East 57th Street, collaborated on the costumes for a 1937 Broadway production. Anna J. Caesar was vice-president and secretary of Julia, Inc. Julia Cerrell resided at 77 Park Avenue.

Costumes: **1937** *Many Mansions†* (Miss Campbell's and Miss Davidson's costumes)

Michael J. Cesario

Michael J. Cesario designs costumes regularly for regional theaters throughout the United States. Born July 16, 1948 in Kenosha, Wisconsin, Mr. Cesario received a B.A. from the University of Wisconsin at Whitewater and an M.F.A. from Ohio University. In addition to his costumes for the theater, he has also designed television, industrial promotions, and musical revues, including *I Love New York, Salute to Cy Coleman* and at Disney World. He heads the graduate design program at Purchase College - State University of New York and is the leading designer of uniforms for marching bands and drum and bugle corps.

Costumes: **1980** *Musical Chairs*

Lydia Chaliapine

The daughter of the Russian basso Feodor Ivanovitch Chaliapine, Lydia Chaliapine was an actress and singer in Russia before leaving in the early 1920s to live in Berlin and Paris. She performed in Paris in 1924 with the Russian *Theatre du Coq d'Or* and came to the U.S. in the early 1930s. She acted in plays, and also occasionally designed costumes, usually for herself. She was most widely known as a vocal coach. She assisted many well-known singers at the Metropolitan Opera with their preparation for Russian roles. Miss Chaliapin died at age 74 in December 1975.

Costumes: **1934** *Continental Varieties* (Mlle. Chaliapine's and Madame Runitch's Costumes)

Cary Chalmers

Cary Chalmers first designed on Broadway in 1981 and has numerous credits in television and theaters. His 'stage design' for his own SoHo apartment was featured in a Cooper-Hewitt Museum exhibit in 1983 called "Design for Theatre" that examined the way architecture and theater connect.

Sets: **1981** *Marlowe*

Ida Hoyt Chamberlain

Miss Ida Hoyt Chamberlain, the sister of Neville Chamberlain, contributed sets to a 1923 production on Broadway. Her musical comedy *Enchanted Isle* was performed at the Lyric Theatre in New York in 1927, starring Greek Evans and Madeline Grey. Miss Chamberlain alsoperformed recitals of her compositions at the Hotel Biltmore. She died in her home in Odiham, Hampshire, England in 1943 at age 72.

Sets: **1927** *Enchanted Isle*

C. Haddon Chambers

The playwright Charles Haddon Chambers was born in Stanmore, New South Wales in 1860 to British parents who were serving in the Colonial Civil Service. After completing his education, he worked for the civil government before moving to London to pursue a career as a journalist. He wrote numerous plays beginning with *One of Them* in 1886, that were performed in Australia, England and the U.S. Other works include *The Tyranny of Tears*, *The Golden Silence* and *The Queen of Manoa*. On two occasions in the teens, he contributed scenic designs to productions of his own plays. Chambers died on March 28, 1921 at age 60.

Sets: **1911** *Passers-By†* (Also wrote) **1913** *Tante* (Also adapted)

Russell H. Champa

Russell H. Champa is a busy lighting designer, mainly for the theater. His designs include productions for Circle Repertory Company, the Barrow Group, and the Perry Street Theatre in New York, and the Williamstown Theatre Festival, the Dallas Theatre Center, the McCarter Theater Center, and at Trinity Repertory Theatre. He is a frequent collaborator with directors Beth Milles, Richard Jenkins, and Oskar Eustis. Twenty-first century credits include *Love* at the East 13th Street Theatre.

Lights: **1996** *God Said Ha!*

Chanel

Gabrielle Chanel, generally referred to as Coco Chanel has one of the best known fashion names associated with the 20th century. Chanel created several designs and perfumes that have become classics. While building her own niche in the world of fashion, she also designed ballets, films, and in 1929 created gowns for Miss Gertrude Lawrence on Broadway. Chanel was born in 1883 in France and died there in 1972. Her personal life was filled with adventure, which contributed to her success. After incredible successes in the 1920s and 1930s she closed her couture house with the beginning of World War II, only to re-enter the business at the age of 70, several years later. *Coco*, a musical which opened in 1969 on Broadway and starred Katherine Hepburn, was based on the story of her life.

Costumes: 1925 *The Last of Mrs. Cheyney* (Gowns) 1929 *Candle-Light*† (Dresses for Miss Lawrence)

Stewart Chaney

Stewart Chaney was born in Kansas City, Missouri, and studied at Yale University with George Pierce Baker and also in Paris with André L'Hote. He began his career as a designer in summer stock and made his Broadway debut in 1934. For the following thirty years his designs for scenery, costumes and occasionally lights were seen regularly in plays, operas and ballets. During the 1940s Mr. Chaney designed two films, *Up in Arms* and *The Kid From Brooklyn*. He also worked in television during its early years. Mr. Chaney, born in 1910, died on November 9, 1969 at the age of 59. His designs appeared in several issues of *Theatre Arts Magazine* often coinciding with opening nights and are included in the collections of the Smithsonian Institution in Washington, D.C.

Sets: 1934 *The Bride of Torozko*; *Dream Child*; *Kill That Story* 1935 *Ghosts*; *The Old Maid*; *On to Fortune*; *Parnell*; *Times Have Changed* 1936 *Aged 26*; *Hamlet*†; *Hedda Gabler*; *New Faces of 1936*; *O Evening Star*; *Parnell*; *Spring Dance* 1937 *But for the Grace of God*; *Having Wonderful Time* 1938 *Wuthering Heights* 1939 *Life with Father* 1940 *Joan o' the Shoals*; *Suzanna and the Elders*; *Twelfth Night* 1941 *Blithe Spirit*; *The More the Merrier*; *Sunny River* 1942

The Lady Comes Across; *Morning Star* 1943 *Blythe Spirit*; *Dark Eyes*; *The Innocent Voyage*; *Three's a Family*; *The Voice of the Turtle*; *The World's Full of Girls* 1944 *Down to Miami*; *Dream with Music*; *The Duke in Darkness*; *Embezzled Heaven*; *The House in Paris*; *Jacobowsky and the Colonel*; *Laffing Room Only*; *The Late George Apley*; *Pretty Little Parlor*; *Public Relations*; *Trio* 1945 *Dunnigan's Daughter*; *Many Happy Returns*; *Mr. Strauss Goes to Boston*; *One Man Show*; *Signature* 1946 *A Joy Forever*; *Obsession*; *The Winter's Tale* 1947 *Bathsheba*; *Craig's Wife*; *The Druid Circle*; *An Inspector Calls*; *Laura* 1948 *Doctor Social*; *Life with Mother*†; *Red Gloves*; *You Never Can Tell* 1949 *I Know My Love*; *The Ivy Green*; *My Name Is Aquilon* 1950 *Design for a Stained Glass Window*; *Great to Be Alive* 1951 *The King of Friday's Men*; *Lo and Behold!*; *The Moon Is Blue*; *Seventeen* 1952 *Much Ado About Nothing* 1953 *A Girl Can Tell*; *Late Love*; *Sherlock Holmes* 1957 *The Hidden River* 1960 *The Forty-ninth Cousin* 1964 *A Severed Head*

Costumes: 1935 *Ghosts*; *The Old Maid*; *Parnell* 1936 *Aged 26*; *Hamlet*; *Hedda Gabler*; *New Faces of 1936*; *Parnell* 1938 *Wuthering Heights* (Also directed) 1939 *Life with Father* 1940 *Twelfth Night* 1942 *The Lady Comes Across* 1944 *The Duke in Darkness*; *Embezzled Heaven*; *Jackpot*; *The Late George Apley* 1945 *Dunnigan's Daughter* 1946 *A Joy Forever*; *The Winter's Tale* 1947 *Bathsheba*; *An Inspector Calls* 1948 *Doctor Social*; *You Never Can Tell* 1949 *I Know My Love*; *The Ivy Green* 1950 *Design for a Stained Glass Window*; *Great to Be Alive* 1951 *The King of Friday's Men*; *Lo and Behold!* 1952 *Much Ado About Nothing* 1953 *Sherlock Holmes* 1964 *A Severed Head*

Lights: 1944 *Down to Miami* 1946 *Obsession* 1947 *Bathsheba*; *The Druid Circle*; *An Inspector Calls* 1948 *Doctor Social* 1949 *I Know My Love* 1950 *Design for a Stained Glass Window* 1951 *The King of Friday's Men*; *Lo and Behold!*; *The Moon Is Blue* 1953 *Late Love*; *Sherlock Holmes* 1957 *The Hidden River* 1960 *The Forty-ninth Cousin*

David Chapman

David Chapman is an architect who studied architecture at the Georgia Institute of Technology. He was born in Atlanta, Georgia on November 11, 1938 and is principally known as a scenic designer, though he occasionally creates both sets and costumes for a production. Mr. Chapman, who received the Maharam Award for his set design for *The First*, includes designers Boris Aronson and Robin Wagner and the sculptor Steffan Thomas as major influences on his career. His film work includes art direction for *The Cotton Club*, *Legal Eagles* (New York locale) and production design for *Dirty Dancing*, *Mystic Pizza*, *Grumpy Old Men*, *Lost in Yonkers*, *This is My Life*, and *High Fidelity*, among many others.

Sets: 1969 *Red White and Maddox* **1972** *Promenade, All!* **1973** *Nash at Nine* **1974** *The Magic Show* **1981** *The First* **1982** *Othello* **1983** *Zorba* **1987** *Cabaret*
Costumes: 1969 *Red White and Maddox*

David Charles

David Charles has a long list of credits as a costume designer in regional theaters and an even longer one as assistant to and co-designer with Jane Greenwood. The designs they created together for *She Loves Me* were rewarded with nominations for both Tony and Olivier Awards. Working not only in theater, but for opera, movies and television, he has served as costume designer assistant for *Sense and Sensibility*, *Arthur*, *Sweet Liberty* and the *Kennedy* miniseries. He is not to be confused with the sound designer and audio engineer who has the same name.
Costumes: 1992 *The Show-Off* **1993** *She Loves Me*†

Michael Chekhov

Michael Alexandrovich Chekhov began his career in the theater in Russia, where he was a founding member of the Studio One Group at the Moscow Art Theatre and later its director. A nephew of the playwright Anton Chekhov, he was born in St. Petersburg, Russia in 1891. He left Russia in 1927, traveling throughout Europe and acting with various companies including Max Reinhardt's. He settled in England for a short time, beginning a school for training actors. He moved to the United States in 1927 and taught acting in his own studio, continuing to act and direct and also occasionally design. Michael Chekhov spent the last fifteen years of his life in California, appearing in numerous films and coaching actors. He died September 30, 1955.
Sets: 1941 *Twelfth Night*
Costumes: 1941 *Twelfth Night*

Nick Chelton

Nick Chelton was born in the Paddington area of London on June 18, 1946 and learned lighting design through training at Theatre Projects, where he served as lighting designer from 1971 to 1975. *Hamlet*, starring Alan Bates, was his London debut in 1971. His designs are often seen throughout England in plays and operas. He has designed lighting for the Greenwich and Royal Court Theatres, the Royal Shakespeare Company and in the West End. His designs for opera have been seen at the Kent Opera, Opera North, Scottish Opera, English National Opera, Royal Opera, Covent Garden, and the Metropolitan Opera among others.
Lights: 1989 *Shirley Valentine*

Alexander Chertov

Alexander Chertov was born in Minsk, Russia and as a youth emigrated to the United States. He began his career as a scenic artist in movies and worked in film studios in both Ft. Lee, New Jersey and Hollywood. He designed settings in New York mainly for Jewish plays and for the Yiddish Art Theatre. He died in Hollywood, California at age 79 on October 22, 1961.
Sets: 1933 *Yoshe Kalb* **1935** *Waiting for Lefty*

Dawn Chiang

Dawn Chiang was born in Palo Alto, California, on July 19, 1953, the daughter of Franklin Chiang and Julienne Lau. She received a Bachelor of Arts at Oberlin College in 1975. She began her career in southern California, assisting lighting designers Tharon Musser, John Gleason, and designing for the Mark Taper Forum, the Ahmanson Theatre and South Coast Repertory. She was resident lighting designer for the New York City Opera and has co-designed with Richard Pilbrow. She received Drama Logue Critics Awards for her lighting designs at South Coast Repertory in 1978 and 1980. In New York, her design for *A Man for All Seasons* at the Roundabout Theatre was nominated for a 1987 American Theatre Wing Award. She designs for many regional theaters, opera and concert presentations. She also designed the theatrical and architectural lighting for an immersion exhibit for the New York Fire Department, *The Fire Zone*, that teaches visitors about fire prevention and safety through imaginative use of multimedia and theatrical effects.

Lights: 1979 *Zoot Suit* **1990** *A Little Night Music* **1993** *Tango Pasion*†

Madame Chilek

Madame Chilek designed a show on Broadway in the late 1940s.

Costumes: 1948 *David's Crown*

Marie Anne Chiment

Marie Anne Chiment, daughter of Dr. John A. and Fides Chiment was born in Albuquerque, New Mexico in 1954. She received a B.A. in drama from the University of California at San Diego, Maxima Cum Laude in 1976, and an M.F.A. in theater design from New York University in 1981. A designer of both sets and costumes she has more than 100 productions to her credit for theaters, and dance and opera companies throughout the United States. Her first significant design was *A Midsummer Night's Dream*, directed by David Chambers at Arena Stage. She was nominated for the 2000 Barrymore Award for Excellence in Theatre for her set designs for *Born Yesterday* at the Delaware Theatre Company, where she often works. Other credits include many American and world premieres such as *Patience & Sarah* at the Lincoln Center Festival, *Orpheus Descending* in 1994 and *The Song of Magnun* in 1992, both for the Lyric Opera of Chicago, and *Loss of Eden*

at the Opera Theatre of St. Louis in 2002. Her designs have been published in *Costume Designer's Handbook* and *Fabric Painting for the Stage* as well as in various issues of *Opera News, Stage Directions*, and *Theatre Crafts International* (now *Entertainment Design.*

Costumes: 1992 *Metro*†

Chipmonck

E.H. Beresford Monck uses "Chipmonck" as his professional name. Additional credits for this California-based designer include designs for Delores Del Lago. He received a nomination for a Tony Award for the lighting design of *The Rocky Horror Show*.

Lights: 1975 *The Rocky Horror Show*

Alison Chitty

Alison Chitty, a British designer of sets and costumes, was born in 1948 and trained at St. Martin's School of Art and at Central School of Art and Design. From 1971 until 1974 she was assistant designer at Victoria Theatre, Stoke-on-Trent, serving as head of design from 1974 until 1977. She has designed for theaters throughout the United Kingdom, including productions for the Riverside Studios, the Royal Shakespeare Company, the Crucible Theatre in Sheffield, Theatre Royal, and Hampstead Theatre. As resident designer at the Royal National Theatre she designed *A Month in the Country, Don Juan, Danton's Death, Tales from Hollywood, Venice Preserv'd*, and many others, as well as *Orpheus Descending* for Peter Hall in 1988 and the 2000 premiere of *Remembrance of Things Past* adapted by Harold Pinter for which she won an Olivier Award. Her opera designs, seen around the world have been much honored: *Billy Budd* and *Khovvanschina* both received Olivier Awards. Alison Chitty is also committed to training new designers and serves as Director of the Motley Theatre Design Course.

Sets: 1989 *Orpheus Descending*
Costumes: 1989 *Orpheus Descending*†

André Chotin

André-Marcel Chotin was born in Paris on April 24, 1888 and died in Boulogne-Billancourt, France on December 20,

1969. He was a painter of still lifes and maritime scenes who exhibited regularly at the Salon des Indépéndants, the Salon d'Automne and Galeries Zak in Paris. He was also a pantomimist and dancer, and in the early 1920s appeared in and contributed scenic designs to a Broadway production.
Sets: 1922 *A Fantastic Fricassee*

Charles Chrisdie

Charles H. Chrisdie designed costumes for several shows on Broadway between 1928 and 1934. In addition, he participated in the production of thousands of additional costumes through his theatrical costume house, Charles Chrisdie and Co., Inc. which he operated with his wife, Alice Chrisdie, beginning in 1872 at 41 W. 47th Street in New York City. The business later relocated to 294 Bowery. Mr. Chrisdie died in London on January 3, 1934.
Costumes: 1900 *The Rebel*[†] 1901 *The Red Kloof* 1928 *The Golden Age* 1929 *The Octoroon* 1930 *The Traitor* 1931 *Little Women; Miracle at Verdun*[†] 1932 *Troilus and Cressida* 1933 *The World Waits* 1934 *When in Rome*

Robert Christen

Robert (Bob) Christen, son of Clarence and Wilma Christen, was born in Appleton, Wisconsin on October 6, 1949. He received his B.A. in theater from the University of Wisconsin at Madison in 1971 where he studied with and was influenced by Gilbert V. Hemsley, Jr. He also acknowledges lighting designer Jennifer Tipton as important to his career. Resident Lighting designer for the Goodman Theatre in Chicago since 1975, his professional debut was the premiere of David Mamet's *American Buffalo* at Goodman Stage 2 in 1975. His numerous credits are mainly in the Chicago area, although he has occasionally designed in other places, including the New York companies Hubbard Street Dance, Apple Corps Theatre, Second Stage and the Joseph Papp Public Theatre, where his designs for *Wings* were nominated for a Drama Desk Award. He received the Joseph Jefferson Award for Best Lighting Design for *Boseman and*

Lena, produced by the Northlight Theatre, in 1986, among many nominations. Twenty-first century designs include *Pacific Overtures* at the Chicago Shakespeare Festival. The lighting designer is not to be confused with historian Robert J. Christen (1928–1981) an American scholar and author.
Lights: 1993 *The Song of Jacob Zulu*

Roy Christopher

As a prolific set and production designer for television for more than thirty years, Roy Christopher has been nominated for numerous Emmy Awards and received many, including those for his designs for several editions of the *Academy Awards Show, The Richard Pryor Show, Murphy Brown*, and *Frasier*. He is production designer for series' including the current *Becker* and *Just Shoot Me!*, and others such as *My Sister Sam, Chico and the Man, Valerie, Wings, Welcome Back, Kotter* and *Growing Pains*. He received an M.A. at California State University at Fresno, where he subsequently taught. He was also artistic director at Cahuenga Playhouse in Los Angeles and worked as a scene painter for NBC-TV. His theater designs, mainly on the West Coast, include *Peculiar Pastimes, The Boys from Syracuse, Jane Heights, Come Back Little Sheba* and the 1999 production of *Light Up the Sky* at the Pasadena Playhouse, his first design for the theater since 1987.
Sets: 1984 *A Woman of Independent Means*

Laurie A. Churba

Laurie A. Churba has designed costumes for many productions at the Blue Light Theatre Company, where she serves on the Associate Artists Committee, for director Joanne Woodward, including *Waiting for Lefty* and director Austin Pendleton including *The Seagull*. Among her television credits are *Saturday Night Live* for which she has been costume design assistant as well as stylist for parodies of commercials. Her costumes have also been featured at the Williamstown Theatre Festival and the Rorschach Theatre Company,
Costumes: 1999 *The Price*

Howard Church

An engineer with the American Telephone and Telegraph Company when it's emphasis was still on serving telegraph customers, Howard Church collaborated on the scenic elements for a 1911 Broadway production. He lived at 456 West 159th Street in New York in 1917.

Sets: 1911 *The Lily and the Prince*† (Act III, Scene 2)

Nan Cibula-Jenkins

Nancy Cibula-Jenkins has designed costumes in many of the prominent regional theaters in the U.S. including the Goodman, Hartford Stage, Arena Stage, Alliance Theatre Company, and the American Repertory Theatre. Her designs are also seen often off-Broadway. She studied at Syracuse University and the Fashion Institute of Technology, and in 1981 received an M.F.A. from the Yale School of Drama. Her designs for the Pulitzer Prize winning play, *GlenGarry Glen Ross* won the Los Angeles Dramalogue Critics Award in 1985. She has also received the Michael Merritt Award for Design and Collaboration and a Jefferson Award for the costume designs for *Much Ado about Nothing*. Committed to education as well as to design, she is chair of the design/technical department in the theater school of DePaul University. Twenty-first century designs include *Boy Gets Girl* at the Manhattan Theatre Club, *Anthony and Cleopatra* at Chicago Shakespeare Theatre and *Wit* at the Goodman Theatre.

Costumes: 1984 *Glengarry Glen Ross* (as: Nan Cibula) **1987** *Speed-the-Plow* (as: Nan Cibula)

Cirker and Robbins

The partnership between Mitchell Cirker and Robert Nelson Robbins produced designs for numerous Broadway shows between 1919 and 1944 under the name of Cirker and Robbins Scenic Studios. As with most scenic studios of the era, the designs credited to Cirker and Robbins Scenic Studio were often for contemporary plays which required a simple single set. Within the firm,

Mitchell Cirker was the business manager and Robert Robbins the creative and technical partner. Mitchell Cirker was born in New York City and studied painting at the National Academy of Design. He worked as a stage hand, electrician, and scene painter before joining R. N. Robbins. Throughout his life he continued to exhibit landscapes and seascapes but never received individual credit for the scenic design of a Broadway show. He died at age 70 on February 4, 1953. Robert N. Robbins also designed sets using his own name and additional information is available under his entry in this book.

Sets: 1919 *Penny Wise* **1920** *An Innocent Idea* **1926** *The Jay Walker*; *Little Spitfire* **1927** *Four Walls*; *The Gossipy Sex*; *Out of the Night* **1928** *Eva the Fifth*; *The Skull* **1929** *All the King's Men*; *Borrowed Love*; *Diana*; *Family Affairs*; *How's Your Health*; *Let Us Be Gay*; *Mendel, Inc*; *Nice Women*†; *Seven*; *Subway Express*; *Zeppelin* **1930** *Ada Beats the Drum*; *Ballyhoo*; *The Blue Ghost*; *London Calling*; *Luana*; *Many a Slip*; *Oh, Promise Me*; *Once in a Lifetime*; *Penal Law 2010*; *Pressing Business*; *Ritzy*; *This Man's Town*; *Who Cares?* **1931** *As Husbands Go*; *Caught Wet*; *Fast and Furious*; *The Great Barrington*; *Miss Gulliver's Travels*; *She Lived Next to the Firehouse*; *Society Girl*; *A Woman Denied* **1932** *20th Century*; *Black Tower*; *On the Make*; *The Passionate Pilgrim*; *Take My Tip*; *That's Gratitude* **1933** *The Drums Begin*; *Four O'clock*; *Ghost Writer*; *Heat Lightning*; *The Party's Over* **1934** *John Brown* **1935** *Loose Moments*; *Play, Genius, Play*; *Squaring the Circle*; *Strip Girl* **1936** *All Editions*; *Brother Rat*; *Lend Me Your Ears*; *Mimie Scheller*; *Pre-Honeymoon* **1937** *Abie's Irish Rose*; *Blow Ye Winds*; *Brown Sugar*; *Penny Wise*; *Room Service* **1938** *Lightnin'*; *What a Life* **1939** *Farm of Three Echoes*; *Once upon a Time*; *The Primrose Path*; *See My Lawyer* **1940** *Goodbye in the Night*; *Scene of the Crime* **1941** *Out of the Frying Pan* **1942** *Sweet Charity* **1943** *The Army Play by Play*; *Boy Meets Girl*; *The Milky Way* **1944** *Mrs. Kimball Presents*

Joseph A. Citarella

Costume designer Joseph A. Citarella

has been associated with New York City Opera since 1980, as director of wardrobe and as a costume designer. Beginning with *Regina* in 1992, the same year he made his Broadway debut, his designs for New York City Opera include *La Bohème*, *H.M.S. Pinafore* and several NYCO National Company tours. He has also designed costumes in regional theaters and off-Broadway. Committed to teaching subsequent generations of designers, he has taught costume design at Fashion Institute of Technology in New York since the mid-1980s.

Costumes: 1992 *Regina*

Deirdre Clancy

Deirdre Clancy is one of the most distinguished British designers for theater, film, television, and opera. She concentrates mainly on costumes, but occasionally designs scenery as well. Her debut in 1965 was for a Christmas pantomime at Lincoln Theatre Royal. She has worked extensively for the Royal National Theatre in London, the English National Opera, the Metropolitan Opera in New York, and the Stratford (Ontario) Shakespeare Festival. She was born in Paddington, London, England on March 31, 1943 and studied at the Birmingham College of Art. Among her many films is *Mrs. Brown* for which she won a BAFTA Award. Clancy is also a portrait painter and has had exhibits with the Royal Society of Portrait Painters. In 1980 she designed a set of stamps for the Royal Mail to celebrate British Theatre. Her costumes designs for the 1990 Royal Opera House production of *Prince Igor* were displayed at the Music Theatre Gallery in London in that same year and are in the permanent collection at Louisiana State University.

Sets: 1997 *A Doll's House*
Costumes: 1976 *The Innocents†* **1985** *Strange Interlude* **1986** *Wild Honey* **1997** *A Doll's House*

Elizabeth Hope Clancy

The costume designer Elizabeth Hope Clancy was born in Forest Hills, New York on August 26, 1964, daughter of Paul and Barbara Clancy. Her earliest training came from a stylish New

York grandmother who taught her how to shop and a creative Virginia grandmother who taught her how to make things by hand. She attended the College of William and Mary (B.A. 1986) as an undergraduate, studying with Patricia Wesp and Jerry Bledsoe. After additional training from Lester Polakov at his Studio and Forum of Stage Design she did her graduate work with Jane Greenwood and Ming Cho Lee at the Yale School of Drama (M.F.A. 1991). Clancy's New York credits include shows at Playwrights Horizons, the Vineyard Theatre, Classic Stage Company, the Signature Theatre, and the Joseph Papp Public Theatre where she designed *In the Blood*, by Suzan-Lori Parks. *In the Blood* was directed by David Esbjornson with whom she often collaborates. She has also designed in many regional theaters: The Shakespeare Theatre, the Guthrie Theatre, Mark Taper Forum, Hartford Stage, Cincinnati Playhouse, and the Long Wharf Theatre, among others.

Costumes: 2000 *Ride Down Mt. Morgan*

Howard Claney

Howard Claney designed the set for a Broadway production in 1925. An actor, he appeared in many plays between 1921 and 1929, such as *Don Juan*, *Voltaire* and *The Little Poor Man*. Between acting assignments he worked as a radio announcer and in 1932 was associated with the National Broadcasting Company. He returned to the New York stage in 1959 in *An Evening with George Bernard Shaw*, and appeared in both *Romeo and Juliet* and *Figuro in the Night* in 1962. Claney was born in Pittsburgh, Pennsylvania on April 17, 1898 and died in Charlotte, North Carolina in April 1980.

Sets: 1925 *The Little Poor Man†*

Joseph Clare

Joseph Clare learned to be a scene painter as a 14-year-old apprentice to William Bronson at the Theatre Royal in Liverpool, England, where he was born in 1846. In 1871 he emigrated to New York to work with Lester Wallack (1818-1888) at the theater established by Wallack's father James William Wallack, Jr. (1818-1873). For many years, Joseph Clare supervised the scenic requirements for productions at Wallack's Theatre in New York including those that went on tour from that location, although he received program credit for only two. After Wallack's Theatre closed, he continued to paint scenery through other theaters and scenic studios until his death at age 71 on June 3, 1917 at Central Islip, Long Island, New York.

Sets: 1904 *Fatinitza†*; *Girofle-Girofla†* (Act III)

Clarise

A dressmaker, Clara Clarise provided gowns for a featured performer in a 1914 Broadway production using "Clarise" as her professional name. Clara Clarise was Clara Skolnik in private life, partner in a firm of dress manufacturers located at 141 West 36th Street in New York City during the teens and twenties. Born April 20, 1885, she died in Chicago, Illinois in April 1973.

Costumes: 1914 *Pretty Mrs. Smith†* (Miss Greenwood's gowns)

Gilbert Clark

A. Gilbert Clark designed costumes on Broadway in 1923. He was president of Gilbert, Inc., a firm of dressmakers located at 7 East 55th Street at that same time. A man of many interests, he also starred in one of the productions, *Jack and Jill* for which he provided costume designs. His residence was located at 116 West 11th Street in 1920, and then at 828 Seventh Avenue for the remainder of the 1920s.

Costumes: 1923 *In Love with Love*; *Jack and Jill†* (Also played principal role)

Jane Clark

Jane Clark has served as assistant art director for many commercials, as an illustrator of magazines, books and newspapers, and as a scenic and/or costume designer in regional theaters, on, off and off-off-Broadway. She graduated from the Yale School of Drama and has served as storyboard artist,

sketch artist and story board illustrator for numerous movies, including *Madness of King George, A League of Their Own, Last Exit to Brooklyn* and *Prizzi's Honor.* Additional theater designs include costumes for *The Knack* at the Roundabout Theatre, *Phantom Limbs* at the Theatre of the Open Eyes, and sets for *Mirage* at the Hudson Guild.

Sets: 1982 *Master Harold...and the Boys*

Peggy Clark

As with many designers of her generation, Peggy Clark's initial exposure to the theater was as a performer. She gave up acting, however, and became a major force in the establishment of theatrical lighting design as an independent profession. Born Margaret Bronson Clark in Baltimore, she graduated from Smith College and in 1938 received an M.F.A. at Yale University, where she was introduced to all areas of design. Only three months after graduation Peggy Clark made her debut on Broadway, designing the costumes for *The Girl From Wyoming.* Although she continued to design costumes for a time, she also served in various technical positions and designed scenery while developing an expertise in stage lighting. During her career she lit over one hundred productions on Broadway. Teaching was also part of her life: at her alma mater Smith College, at Yale, and at Lester Polakov's Studio and Forum of Stage Design. Peggy Clark was the first woman elected President of United Scenic Artists Local 829, in 1968. She was named a fellow of the United States Institute for Theatre Technology in 1978. Married to Lloyd R. Kelley, a theatrical electrician from 1960 until his death in 1972, she was also known as Peggy Clark Kelley. She died at age 80 on June 18, 1996.

Sets: 1941 *Gabrielle* 1951 *The High Ground*

Costumes: 1942 *The Great Big Doorstop* (Costume Supervisor); *Uncle Harry* 1944 *Ramshackle Inn* 1945 *Dark of the Moon; Devil's Galore* 1951 *The High Ground*

Lights: 1926 *Gentlemen Prefer Blondes* 1941 *Gabrielle* 1946 *Beggar's Holi-*

day 1947 *Brigadoon; High Button Shoes; Medea; Topaz* 1948 *Love Life; The Rape of Lucretia* 1949 *Along Fifth Avenue; Gentlemen Prefer Blondes; Touch and Go* 1950 *All You Need Is One Good Break; Bless You All* 1951 *The High Ground; Paint Your Wagon* 1952 *Kiss Me Kate; Of Thee I Sing; Pal Joey* 1953 *In the Summer House; Kismet; Maggie; The Trip to Bountiful; Wonderful Town* 1954 *On Your Toes; Peter Pan* 1955 *No Time for Sergeants; Plain and Fancy; The Righteous Are Bold; Will Success Spoil Rock Hunter?* 1956 *Auntie Mame; Bells Are Ringing; Mr. Wonderful; New Faces of '56* 1957 *Eugenia; Nude with Violin; The Potting Shed* 1958 *Flower Drum Song; Present Laughter; Say, Darling* 1959 *Billy Barnes Revue; Cheri; Goodbye Charlie; Juno* 1960 *Bye, Bye, Birdie; A Distant Bell; Under the Yum-Yum Tree; The Unsinkable Molly Brown* 1961 *Mary, Mary; Sail Away; Show Girl* 1962 *Romulus* 1963 *The Girl Who Came to Supper* 1964 *Bajour; Poor Richard* 1966 *The Best Laid Plans* 1968 *Darling of the Day* 1969 *Jimmy; Last of the Red Hot Lovers* 1971 *How the Other Half Loves* 1980 *Musical Chairs*

Rose Clark

Rose Clark was an actress who performed on Broadway and in films. She was part of a popular vaudeville act, Adler and Clark, teamed with her husband, Jeffrey Adler. In the late 1920s she also designed gowns on Broadway. Miss Clark died at the age of 80 in Hollywood in 1962.
Costumes: 1927 *We All Do* (Gowns for Misses Shoemaker, Givney, and Williams) 1928 *Tonight at 12* (Gowns)

Agnes Clarke

Agnes Clarke designed costumes for a show in 1929.
Costumes: 1929 *Young Alexander*

Bill Clarke

Bill Clarke was born on October 9, 1958 in Landstuhl, Germany, where his father was serving in the military, and was raised in Raleigh, North Carolina and Oxon Hill, Maryland. He attended the University of Virginia, where he received a B.A. in 1980, and the Yale School of Drama where he received an M.F.A. in 1987. Related training includes courses at the Art Students League and the School of Visual Arts. The design for *A Walk in the Woods*, which premiered at the La Jolla Playhouse, was honored with a Drama Logue Award and the San Diego Theatre Critics Circle Award. Bill Clarke designs sets and occasionally costumes in New York for the New York Shakespeare Festival, W.P.A., and Manhattan Theatre Club, among others. He also designed *Abby's Song* at City Center. His regional theater credits include productions at the Milwaukee Repertory Theatre, McCarter Theater Center, the Old Globe, Cincinnati Playhouse, PlayMakers Repertory Company, and others.
Sets: 1988 *A Walk in the Woods*

Grace O. Clarke

Grace Omstead Clarke designed costumes for a show in 1918. An artist and teacher, she was associated with the Peabody Institute in Brooklyn and the Metropolitan Museum of Art in New York for most of her professional life. Miss Clarke died on June 24, 1924 at age 75.
Sets: 1912 *Much Ado About Nothing; The Rivals*
Costumes: 1918 *The Army with Banners* 1923 *The Chastening* 1924 *The Admiral*

Rufus Clarke

Rufus Clarke designed costumes for a 1914 Broadway production. Two men with that name lived and worked from Brooklyn, New York during the early decades of the twentieth century. One was born on August 2, 1895 and died December 6, 1997 and the other lived from 1892 until 1990.
Costumes: 1914 *The Marriage of Columbine*†

Paul Clay

While Paul Clay has some credits as a theatrical designer, it is as a visual artist that he is best known. In 1991, he was honored at the Eighth Annual "Bessie" Award Ceremony for his on-going contributions in the non-mainstream dance and experimental theater venues in New York City. He shared the award with Lora Nelson and Cydney Wilkes, his collaborators on *A Window on the Nether Sea* at the Downtown Art Company. He has designed for Mabou Mines, lights for Susan Marshal's *Walter's Finest Hours*, and the set for *Skin* at Soho Repertory, among others in New York, as well as with members of experimental companies in London. Contributions to film include the video for *It's a Man's World* at Apple Corps Theatre and his position as visual advisor for *What Happened Was...* which won the 1994 Grand Jury Prize at Sundance. He should not be confused with the sound editor for stage and film who has the same name.

Sets: 1996 *Rent*

T. M. Cleland

T. M. Cleland was born Thomas Maitland Cleland in Brooklyn, New York in 1880 and studied at the Artist-Artisan Institute in New York City. A painter and illustrator, he spent most of his life working as a graphic artist designing books, brochures, and magazines. He worked as art editor for *Fortune* and *McClures*. Mr. Cleland, who received a gold medal from the American Institute of Graphic Arts in 1940, died at age 84 on November 9, 1964.

Sets: 1923 *Scaramouche*
Costumes: 1923 *Scaramouche*

Thomas J. Cleland

Thomas J. Cleland received program credit for the lighting designs for two Broadway productions. Although *The Earl and the Girl* in 1905 originated in New York, the playbill identifies him as "Thomas J. Cleland, Chicago."

Lights: 1905 *The Earl and the Girl*
1906 *The Love Route*

Clemons

Clemons Inc. consisted of two clothing salons, one at 1409 Broadway and the other at Sixth Avenue and 64 Nassau Street. Oscar Oestreicher was president of the family business, with Carl and Isaac Oestreicher serving as vice-presidents, William Oestreicher as secretary and Morris Oestreicher as treasurer.

Costumes: 1927 *The Wild Man of Borneo*[†]

Evelyn T. Clifton

Evelyn T. Clifton, who designed costumes for several shows in the late 1920s, lived at 22 East 15th Street in Manhattan in 1920.

Costumes: 1927 *The Belt*; *Earth*; *In Abraham's Bosom*; *Rapid Transit* **1928** *Box Seats*[†]; *Hoboken Blues*

George Clisbee

George Clisbee was born in Chicago and studied in Paris at Julien's Studio. During World War I he served with the French ambulance service and the United States Army. From 1919 to 1926 he worked as art editor for *The Cleveland Daily News*. A prolific writer of short stories, mainly about cats, he was also a magazine illustrator. Mr. Clisbee died at age 41 on December 5, 1936.

Sets: 1923 *Salome*
Costumes: 1923 *Salome*

Hallye Clogg

Hallye Clogg performed in the chorus of musical comedies in the last decade of the nineteenth century. She retired from life on the stage to begin life back stage as a wardrobe mistress. For 30 years, she was head of the costume department and wardrobe mistress at the Theatre Guild. In 1963 she dressed her final production, *Tovarich*. Mrs. Haritte (Hallye) Clogg Cannon died in 1965 in Bay Shore, Long Island at the age of 86.

Costumes: 1942 *Yesterday's Magic* (Costumes assembled)

C. Clonis

Cleovulos Clonis was born in Greece in 1907. He studied at the University of Athens and has designed scenery not only in Greece but throughout Europe, including London and Frankfurt. Between 1932 and 1945 he designed numerous settings for the National Theatre in Greece, including *Agamemnon*, *Hamlet* and *Oedipus Rex*.

Sets: 1952 *Electra*; *Oedipus Tyrannus*

Elizabeth Stuart Close

In 1925, Elizabeth Stuart Close, an American fashion designer active in the 1920s and 1930s, created costumes for a play on Broadway. Beginning in the early 1920s, she was manager of P. Clement Brown, a costume house located at 620 Fifth Avenue, and resided in Brooklyn.

Costumes: 1925 *Cain†*; *White Gold*

Warren Clymer

Warren Clymer first became involved with stage design as an undergraduate at the University of Iowa where he earned a B.A. He also attended Indiana University where he received an M.A. He was born on December 29, 1922 in Davenport, Iowa. In the early 1950s he worked for three years with Jo Mielziner and Howard Bay. Since then he has spent very little time working on stage productions, devoting his talents instead to design for television and feature films. His television designs have been honored with two Emmy Awards for Art Direction/Set Design.

Sets: 1961 *Write Me a Murder*

Frances Clyne

Frances Clyne, who was known for her designs for women's fashions owned a retail shop that featured hats and gowns on Fifth Avenue in New York City. She was occasionally invited to contribute her design ability to the Broadway stage for shows requiring smart contemporary fashions. Miss Clyne died in 1944 at the age of 63.

Costumes: 1925 *All Dressed Up*; *Jane, Our Stranger* 1927 *Fallen Angels* (Gowns); *Mariners†* (Miss Kennedy's, Miss Hall's dresses) 1933 *The Drums Begin* (Women's costumes); *The Mask and the Face* (Gowns and hats)

Scott Clyve

Scott Clyve graduated from State University of New York at Purchase and has a rapidly growing list of credits as a lighting designer. He has worked extensively as resident lighting designer for Rude Mechanicals, and the Chain Lightning Theatre where his designs include *Woman of Paris*, *To Moscow*, and *Edward II*. Additional productions include designs for the Connecticut Ballet Company, the Broward Center for the Performing Arts, and the national tours of *Your Arms Too Short to Box with God*, *Song of Singapore*, and *Dance Across America*. Twenty-first century credits include the New York Dance Alliance Finale 2000 at the Waldorf Astoria.

Lights: 2001 *The Gathering*

Norman Coates [American]

The lighting designer named Norman Coates (as distinguished from the British designer of sets and costumes with the same name) was born in Norristown, Pennsylvania on January 25, 1952 and received his B.A. at Temple University. He began designing at Temple with a production of *Pale Horse, Pale Rider*. Since then he has designed lights for dance, regional theaters and off-Broadway, and national tours. His lighting designs for *Limbo Tales* were honored with a Villager Award. Director of the lighting design program at the North Carolina School of the Arts in Winston-Salem since 1990, he has also been resident lighting designer for the North Carolina Theatre in Raleigh, North Carolina, where he has designed numerous productions, and spent two seasons at PlayMakers Repertory Company in Chapel Hill.

Lights: 1985 *The News* 1989 *Prince of Central Park*

Norman Coates [British]

The British designer Norman Coates, not to be confused with the American lighting designer of the same name, has been associated with Inter-Action and The Almost Free Theatre in England for the past several years. He has designed sets and costumes for the world premieres of many plays by Edward Bond, Robert Patrick, Heathcote Williams and James Saunders.

Sets: 1979 *Dogg's Hamlet, Cahoot's Macbeth*

Costumes: 1979 *Dogg's Hamlet, Cahoot's Macbeth*

Henry Ives Cobb, Jr.

Henry Ives Cobb, Jr., the American architect who created the master plan for the University of Chicago and was one of the designers of the Chicago World's Fair, designed settings for a Broadway play in the late teens. He was born in Brookline, Massachusetts in 1859 and studied at the Massachusetts Institute of Technology and Harvard University. One of the first architects to use steel in tall buildings, he also designed the Fashion Center Building at 575 Seventh Avenue (at 38th Street), restored by George Ranalli in the mid-1990s and the Newberry Library. He died in 1931.

Sets: 1917 *Have a Heart*

Gladys Cobb

Gladys Cobb contributed designs for the ladies clothes to a play on Broadway in 1947. This British costume designer was born in 1892 and first worked as a volunteer assistant for sets an properties for theaters in England, including the Old Vic. She worked as Cecil Beaton's assistant for many years when he designed costumes for plays and films. She often designed sets an costumes for plays in London, including the 1951 production of *The Three Sisters* at the Sandwich and *Waters of the Moon* at Theatre Royal, Haymarket.

Costumes: **1947** *The Druid Circle* (Ladies clothes)

James Cochran

James Cochran designed costumes on Broadway in the late 1930s.

Costumes: 1938 *Haiti; Pinocchio*

Jeanetta Cochrane

A British Costume Designer, Jeanetta Cochrane was born in 1883 and studied at the Slade School of Art and the Regent Street Polytechnic. For 50 years she taught courses on scenery and costumes at the Central School of Arts and Crafts in London. Her specialty was costume history, and she was instrumental in training designers to use a unified method to assemble sets, costumes and properties for each production. Her book *Costume Colour and Cut*, was published in 1955. As a designer, she worked extensively in England and Western Europe creating costumes for some of the most famous performers of the twentieth century, including Ellen Terry, Mrs. Patrick Campbell and John Gielgud for whom she designed *Hamlet, Love for Love* and *The Relapse*. The Cochrane Theatre in London is named for this designer and educator who died in 1957.

Costumes: 1947 *Love for Love*

Steve Cochrane

Steve Cochrane made his Broadway debut in the late 1980s. He designs lights for theaters throughout the United States, including *Dial 'M' for Murder* at the Denver Theatre Center and *Evita* in Boston. He also designed the national tour of *Fiddler on the Roof* which was performed at the Wang Center in Boston and at the Shubert Theatre in New Haven, Connecticut among many other locations. The lighting designer should not be confused with the contemporary musician with the same name.

Lights: 1987 *Oba Oba* **1999** *The Wizard of Oz*

Felix E. Cochren

Felix E. Cochren has designed not only settings but also costumes on Broadway. He studied art and theater at Carnegie Mellon University and spent five years as resident costume designer and graphic artist at Brooklyn's Billie Holiday Theatre. His many sets for the Negro Ensemble Company include *A Soldier's Play*. Among his Audelco Awards for stage design is one for his costumes for *Lotto* at the Billie Holiday Theatre in 1992. Recent costume designs include *Lost Creek Township* for the Crossroads Theatre.

Sets: 1980 *Home* **1981** *Inacent Black*
Costumes: 1983 *Amen Corner*

Gene Coffin

Gene Coffin was a costume designer who worked on Broadway as well as in films and television. From 1953 to 1963 he designed the clothes for the Theatre Guild's "U.S. Steel Hour." His films include the 1961 version of *Lolita* as well as *Goodbye, Columbus* and *Act One*. Mr. Coffin, who was born in 1905, died on October 17, 1977 at the age of 72 in New York City.

Costumes: 1954 *Dear Charles* (Miss Tallulah Bankhead's gowns) **1956** *Affair of Honor*; *Someone Waiting* **1959** *Jolly's Progress* **1960** *The Forty-ninth Cousin*

Max Cohen

Max A. Cohen designed costumes for a show on Broadway in 1923. Early in his professional life he was involved with the theater, collaborating with Helen Mahieu through the costume business Max & Mahieu from 1911 to 1914 as well as designing costumes under his own name. He spent the majority of his career in the movie business. In 1925 he opened the first movie house on 42nd Street, by converting a legitimate stage house, Wallack's Theatre, into a movie showplace named Anco for his wife, Anne Cohen. For the following 50 years he operated movie theaters, as owner and president of Cinema Circuit, including the New Amsterdam Theatre which was converted to a movie house in 1937. Max Cohen, a long time resident of the Sherry-Netherland Hotel, died in 1971 at the age of 75. For additional credits see "Max & Mahieu."

Costumes: 1923 *Ginger*

Viola Cohn

Viola Cohn is credited with the design for the costumes for a show in 1934.

Costumes: 1934 *Too Much Party*

Franco Colavecchia

Franco Colavecchia is from Cham County, Durham, England where he was born in 1937. He was educated at London University and received specialized training in painting at the Lincoln School of the Arts and St. Martin's School in London. He studied set design at the Wimbledon Theatre School and at the Slade School. His professional debut occurred in two locations at the same time, with the opening of *The Homecoming* at the Oxford Playhouse and of *Cellini* at the Edinburgh Festival. Mr. Colavecchia designs both sets and costumes and has received awards in England and the United States, including a shared Emmy for the set design for "Pavarotti

in Philadelphia: *La Boehme*," broadcast by PBS. Additional scenery in the United States include *Carmen* and *Madama Butterfly* for the New York City Opera where he has designed more than forty productions. Honors in England include an award by the British Arts Council and the Royal Society Award for Art and Industry. Since 1996 he has been on the faculty of the North Carolina School of the Arts, having taught previously at Harvard, State University of New York at Purchase, Carnegie Mellon and as head of scenic design at DePaul University..

Sets: 1974 *Treemonisha*

Costumes: 1974 *Treemonisha*

Sandy Cole

Born in Chicago, Sandy Cole attended Northwestern University. When she became interested in fashion, she moved to New York and joined a Seventh Avenue dress house, working in publicity and public relations. She then worked for the Tapplinger Organization in public relations, and in 1963 began her own business, Allen and Cole. This venture led to a boutique in South Hampton where she also designed for private customers. In addition to her costume designs for the theater, Sandy Cole designed the film *Doc* starring Faye Dunaway and Stacy Keach.

Costumes: 1973 *Out Cry*

Paul Colin

Paul Colin, who died in Noigent-sur-Marne at age 92 on June 18, 1985, was a famous French posterist and theatrical designer. Born in France in 1892, he designed over twelve thousand posters during his career, beginning in the early 1920s with commissions from the Theatre des Champs-Elysées, where he later designed scenery. Among the hundreds of settings he designed were those for the films *Lilliom* directed by Fritz Lang and *Carnet de Bal* directed by Julien Duvivier. He painted the setting for *La Revue Nègre* in 1925 which introduced Josephine Baker to Paris. His designs have been exhibited often, most recently in a retrospective at the Sorbonne in 1982.

Sets: 1929 *Wake Up and Dream*†
Costumes: 1929 *Wake Up and Dream*†

John Collette

John Collette was well known on the West Coast as a scenic artist. He was also a long time associate of Oliver Morosco, for whom he did numerous settings. He died in the great influenza epidemic of 1918, on November 19, 1918 in Los Angeles.
Sets: 1911 *A Man of Honor* (Designed and executed) 1914 *Help Wanted*; *The Miracle Man*; *So Much for So Much* 1917 *Lombardi, Ltd.*

Harry Collins

Harry Collins, proprietor of a successful dress salon, designed costumes for numerous productions on Broadway between 1916 and 1921. In addition he also designed scenery for one production. Harry, Inc. and Harry Collins, Inc. were both located at 9 East 57th Street in New York from the mid-teens until 1923. In addition to his own involvement with costumes, Harry Collins employed a supervisor of costumes, Bert French, who was probably responsible for designs as well, although his name does not appear in any Broadway theater programs.
Sets: 1919 *First Is Last*†
Costumes: 1916 *The Co-Respondent* (Gowns for Miss Chambers) 1917 *De Luxe Annie* (Miss Grey's and Hall's gowns); *Furs and Frills*†; *Going Up* (Act I and III gowns); *Hitchy Koo* (Miss La Rue's gowns); *On with the Dance*† (Miss Moorfields' gowns); *Over the 'Phone* (Miss Belwin's and Valentine's gowns); *A Tailor-Made Man*† (Gowns) 1918 *Oh, Lady! Lady!* (Gowns); *Oh, My Dear* (Gowns); 1919 *Adam and Eva*† (Miss Arnold's and Prince's gowns); *An Exchange of Wives* (Gowns for Miss Herne and Miss Dab); *First Is Last*† (Gowns); *The Little Whopper*; *Too Many Husbands* (Miss Winwood's gowns) 1920 *Anna Ascends* (Gowns worn by Miss Brady and Ladies Chorus); *An Innocent Idea* (Gowns) 1921 *Dear Me* (Miss La Rue's gowns); *Wait till We're Married* (Miss Coakley's Act I costumes)

Pat Collins

Pat Collins, born in 1932, has been de-signing lights on Broadway regularly since her debut in 1977. Credits off-Broadway include *How I Got that Story* and *A Life in the Theatre*. Her designs have been honored with a Tony Award for *I'm Not Rappaport* in 1986, a Drama Desk Award for *Execution of Justice* in 1986, a Los Angeles Drama Critics Award for *The Dybbuck*, and a Maharam Award nomination for *A Life in the Theatre*. Since studying at Brown University (B.A. 1954 in Spanish Literature) and the Yale University School of Drama, she has worked extensively in opera and dance as well as theater. She should not be confused with the television and movie actress (1935-1997) with the same name.
Lights: 1977 *The Threepenny Opera* 1978 *Ain't Misbehavin'*; *King of Hearts*; *Stages* 1980 *The Bacchae*; *Charlotte* 1981 *The Floating Light Bulb* 1982 *Steaming* 1983 *Baby*; *Moose Murders* 1985 *The Boys of Winter*; *I'm Not Rappaport* 1986 *Arsenic and Old Lace*; *Execution of Justice*, 1987 *Death and the King's Horseman*; *Sherlock's Last Case* 1988 *Ain't Misbehavin'* 1989 *The Heidi Chronicles* 1991 *Lucifer's Child* 1992 *Conversations with My Father*; *The Fifteen Minute Hamlet*; *The Real Inspector Hound* 1993 *The Sisters Rosensweig* 1995 *A Delicate Balance* 1996 *A Delicate Balance*; *Once upon a Mattress* 1997 *An American Daughter* 2000 *A Moon for the Misbegotten*; *Proof*

Una Collins

Una Collins died June 1, 1964 in Dublin, Ireland at the age of 64. An actress and singer she was often cast in the plays of Sean O'Casey, and was considered to have given the definitive performance to those roles. She appeared with the Radio Eireann Repertory Company and was married to the script writer Dominic O'Riordan. The play she designed was first produced in London in 1963.
Costumes: 1964 *Oh What a Lovely War*

Vincent Collins

In 1919 Vincent Collins designed sets for a show on Broadway. In 1920 he was President of Vincent Collins, Inc., Decorators, 749 Fifth Avenue, New York City.

Sets: 1919 *Nothing But Love*†

Alvin Colt

Alvin Colt has been designing costumes steadily for the theater and ballet since 1940. His costume designs have been seen on Broadway since *On the Town* opened at the Adelphi Theatre in 1944. Born in Louisville, Kentucky on July 15, 1916, he attended Yale, studying with Donald Oenslager, Frank Bevan and Pavel Tchlitchev. He has designed for television, most notably *The Adams Chronicles* series for WNET in 1976 for which he received two Emmy Award nominations. Since 1994 he has been designing costumes for *Forbidden Broadway* including the spin-off *Forbidden Hollywood* and the recent *Forbidden Broadway 2001: A Spoof Odyssey*. Additional twenty-first century designs include *If You Ever Leave Me...I'm Going With You* written, directed and starring Renée Taylor and Joe Bologna. Mr. Colt received the Tony Award for his costume designs in 1957 for *Pipe Dream* and has been nominated five additional times. In 1996, he was honored with the Irene Sharaff Lifetime Achievement Award and in 2001 he became a member of the Theater Hall of Fame.

Sets: 1947 *Music in My Heart*
Costumes: 1944 *On the Town* 1946 *Around the World in Eighty Days* 1947 *Barefoot Boy with Cheek*; *Music in My Heart* 1949 *Clutterbuck* (Costume Supervisor) 1950 *Guys and Dolls* 1951 *Top Banana* 1953 *The Frogs of Spring* 1954 *Fanny*; *The Golden Apple* 1955 *The Lark*; *Phoenix '55*; *Pipe Dream* 1956 *Li'l Abner*; *The Sleeping Prince* 1957 *Copper and Brass*; *Rumple* 1958 *Blue Denim*; *Say, Darling* 1959 *Destry Rides Again*; *First Impressions* 1960 *Christine*; *Greenwillow*; *Wildcat* 1961 *The Aspern Papers*; *Thirteen Daughters* 1962 *The Beauty Part* 1963 *Here's Love* 1964 *The Crucible*; *The Seagull*; *Something More!* 1967 *Henry, Sweet Henry*; *The Imaginary Invalid*; *The Paisley Convertible*; *Tonight at 8:30*; *A Touch of the Poet* 1968 *Golden Rainbow*; *The Goodbye People* 1972 *Sugar* 1974 *Lorelei*† 1980 *The Roast* 1981 *Broadway Follies* 1989 *Jerome Robbins' Broadway*† 1990 *Accom-* *plice*; *Night of 100 Stars III* 1994 *Comedy Tonight* 1995 *Sacrilege* 1998 *The Herbal Bed* 1999 *Waiting in the Wings*

Giulio Coltellacci

Born in Rome on April 12, 1916, Giulio Coltellacci was one of that city's foremost men of the theater. He originally studied sculpture and design before enrolling at the Academia de Belle Arti to study stage and costume design with V. Grassi. After serving as an assistant to the Italian designer Aldo Calvo in the early 1940s, he made his debut in 1945 with the set and costume designs for *Rebecca*. Living alternately in Paris and Rome, he designed numerous operas and plays in each city, in addition to designs in London and New York. His stage designs won many Passerelle d' Argento Awards in Rome. As a painter and illustrator he contributed regularly to the Paris edition of *Vogue*, and *Rivista Teatro*, Rome and in 1958 his paintings were exhibited in a New York gallery. Giulio Coltellacci died in 1983.

Sets: 1964 *Rugantino*
Costumes: 1964 *Rugantino*

Comelli

Attilio Comelli, a costume designer, who was known throughout his career simply as "Comelli" worked mainly in London, but between 1904 and 1913, his designs were featured in Broadway productions. He had a brother, E. Comelli, who was also a costume designer. They both worked often at Drury Lane, the Alhambra, and other London theaters. Attilio Comelli's costume designs are in the permanent collection of the Victoria and Albert Museum, and are also reproduced in Schouvaloff's *Theatre on Paper* and in *Drama: It's Costume and Decor* by James Laver. He was born c.1858 and died on September 3, 1925.

Costumes: 1904 *The Medal and the Maid* 1905 *The Prodigal Son*; *The White Cat*† 1912 *The Count of Luxembourg* 1913 *The Girl on the Film*†; *The Marriage Market*

Homer Conant

For most of his years in the theater Homer B. Conant worked for the Shubert Organization. He was born in Nebraska in 1887 and died in New York in 1927. Mr. Conant primarily painted stage scenery but was also a mural designer and painter. Between 1916 and 1920 he contributed costume designs to fifteen productions and settings to four productions on Broadway, generally in collaboration with other designers employed by the Shubert Organization.

Sets: 1916 *The Girl from Brazil* 1917 *Maytime* 1920 *The Century Revue*; *Cinderella on Broadway*†

Costumes: 1916 *Follow Me*; *The Girl from Brazil* (All gowns); *The Passing Show of 1916* (Dresses) 1917 *Barbara*; *Doing Our Bit*; *Maytime*; *Over the Top* 1918 *Sinbad*†; *Somebody's Sweetheart* (Gowns) 1919 *Nothing But Love*† (Gowns); *The Passing Show of 1919*† 1920 *As You Were*; *The Century Revue*; *Cinderella on Broadway*†; *Tick-Tack-Toe*

H. A. Condell

Born in Berlin, Germany in 1905, H. A. Condell studied there with Ernest Stern. Between 1925 and 1930 he designed for various theaters in Berlin and for films, before accepting a position as the chief stage and costume designer at the Mellini Theatre Hannover, and subsequently at the Civic Opera in Berlin. In 1933 he helped found the Culture Group Opera and Playhouse in Berlin, traveling when possible to the United States to design for the American League for Opera in New York. In 1940 Mr. Condell relocated to New York where he primarily designed operas and taught scene design at both the Dramatic Workshop and the New School for Social Research. A prolific designer, he created sets and occasionally costumes for many American opera companies, and designed regularly in New York City at City Opera and City Center. Mr. Condell died on November 6, 1951.

Sets: 1942 *Winter Soldiers* 1946 *Yours Is My Heart* 1950 *The Barrier* 1951 *Springtime for Henry*†

Costumes: 1946 *Yours Is My Heart*

Anne Cone

Anne Cone designed gowns for a show in 1929.

Costumes: 1929   *Deep   Channels* (Gowns)

John Conklin

John Conklin was born on June 22, 1937 in Hartford, Connecticut, the son of William Palmer Conklin and Anne Marshall Conklin. He received both a B.A. and an M.F.A. at Yale University where he studied with and was influenced by Donald Oenslager. As an undergraduate at Yale he began his career as a designer with a production of *Tom Jones*. Mr. Conklin, who prefers to design both sets and costumes for productions, works regularly for the major opera companies and regional theaters throughout the United States. His designs have been seen at Hartford Stage (where he collaborated for many years with former Artistic Director Mark Lamos and lighting designer Pat Collins), the Guthrie Theatre, Seattle Repertory Theatre, San Diego Shakespeare Theatre, Williamstown Theatre Festival, and Pennsylvania Ballet, among many others. Increasingly he designs (and occasionally directs) opera, including productions at the Santa Fe Opera, Houston Grand Opera, the Opera Company of St. Louis, Glimmerglass, and the New York City Opera, where he is director of production. On the faculty at New York University, he teaches Conceptual Foundations of Design.

Sets: 1963 *Tambourines to Glory* 1971 *Scratch* 1973 *The Au Pair Man* 1974 *Cat on a Hot Tin Roof*; *Leaf People*; *Lorelei* 1976 *Rex* 1977 *Bully* 1980 *The Bacchae*; *The Philadelphia Story* 1984 *Awake and Sing* 1988 *A Streetcar Named Desire*

Costumes: 1963 *Tambourines to Glory* 1976 *Rex* 1977 *Bully*; *Romeo and Juliet* 1980 *The Bacchae*

Anna Conkwright

Anna Conkwright, of New York, according to the playbill for *The Girl in the Train* collaborated with Wilhelm, of London, on a 1910 Broadway production.

Costumes: 1910 *The Girl in the Train*†

Connors and Bennett

Connors and Bennett received credit

for a single Broadway production in 1926. James Connors, who was identified as 'theatrical' in Trow's 1922 New York City Directory resided at 133 West 67th Street in 1922. It is likely that Bennett is H. Gordon Bennett about whom additional information can be found in this volume.

Sets: 1926 *The Half-Caste*

Paule Constable

The British lighting designer Paule Constable was born November 9, 1966, daughter of Wing Commander Paul Constable and Evelyn Rose Hadley. She studied English and drama at Goldsmiths' College, and trained further in the music industry. She began her career as an electrician and production manager, but since 1993 has mainly been designing lights. She has numerous credits for theater and opera throughout the United Kingdom, for companies including the Royal Shakespeare Company, Royal National Theatre (first woman to design lights), Royal Court Theatre, Royal Opera House, Théâtre de Complicité, Lyric Hammersmith, English National Opera, and Donmar Warehouse. Her design for *The Street of Crocodiles* was nominated for an Olivier Award, as were *Uncle Vanya* and *Amadeus*. In addition to her active career, Paule Constable is mother of Bram and Morgan Richards. Twenty-first century designs include *Mountain Language* and *Ashes to Ashes* as part of the Pinter Festival at Lincoln Center 2001, originally produced at the Royal Court Theatre and *Rigoletto* at the Royal Opera House, also broadcast on BBC-TV.

Lights: 1999 *Amadeus*; *The Weir*

Continer and Golding

The team of Continer and Golding collaborated on the designs for a Broadway show in 1932. Both Anthony Continer and Stephen Golding designed productions individually. Anthony Continer (also known as Antonio Contineri) designed sets for four productions on Broadway between 1929 and 1934 and was associated at one time with scene designer Homer F.

Emens. Stephen Golding was president of Golding Scenic Studios in 1919.

Sets: 1932 *'Ol Man Satan*

Anthony Continer

Anthony Continer designed sets for four productions on Broadway between 1929 and 1934. In addition, he collaborated with Stephen Golding on a set design. Antonio Contineri was associated with the scenic design firm Homer F. Emens, Artists, at 533 West 43rd Street in 1915 and resided in Union Hill, New Jersey.

Sets: 1929 *Decision*; *Great Scott*; *Uncle Vanya* 1934 *Africana*

Gordon Conway

Gordon Conway designed costumes for films in England and the U.S. and for plays during the 1920s and 1930s. She was born in Cleburne, Texas in December 1894 and began professional life designing playbills and theatrical posters for New York and London theaters. In 1921 she designed costumes for the first time, in London. She then worked steadily in the theater, but also devoted much time and energy to illustrating fashion magazines, including *Eve* and *The Tatler*. She lived much of her life abroad, maintaining a studio in Paris. Miss Conway, who died in 1956, was the subject of exhibits at the American Institute of Architects Foundation in Washington, D.C., "That Red Head Gal: Fashions and Designs of Gordon Conway, 1916-1936" and "Red, Hot & Southern: The International Fashions and Designs of Gordon Conway, 1916-1936" in Fredericksburg, Virginia.

Costumes: 1920 *The Charm School* 1932 *There's Always Juliet†* (Miss Best's Dresses)

William Conway

William Conway died at age 36 on February 10, 1950 in London where he was general manager of a theatrical production company, H. M. Tennent, Ltd. From 1930 to 1939 he was theater correspondent for *The London Daily Mail*, a position he left to become business manager and director for John Gielgud. In 1947 he directed and designed lights for two productions on

Broadway in which John Gielgud appeared.
Lights: 1947 *The Importance of Being Earnest*; *Love for Love*

O'Kane Conwell

Margaret O'Kane Conwell designed costumes on Broadway between 1913 and 1924. In 1915, she designed the program for the 225th anniversary of the founding of the town of Caldwell, New Jersey. An artist, she maintained a studio as a dressmaker at 132 Madison Avenue in New York City in 1916, commuting from her home in New Jersey. By 1922 she had relocated her home and studio to 27 Beekman Place.
Sets: 1914 *A Pair of Silk Stockings*† (Act II)
Costumes: 1913 *Prunella* 1914 *A Pair of Silk Stockings*† (Act II) 1915 *Around the Map*†; *Maternity*† (Miss Savage's gowns) 1916 *The Guilty Man* (Miss Fenwick's gowns); *Hush!* (Miss Frazier's and Miss Winwood's dresses) 1917 *The Fugitive* (Miss Stevens' gowns); *The Lady of the Camellias*† 1918 *The Betrothal* 1919 *Angel Face* 1920 *The Girl from Home*; *Hitchy Koo 1920* (Gowns and costumes for Act I and finale); *The Night Boat* (Dresses) 1921 *Romance* (Miss Keane's costume) 1924 *In His Arms*† (Miss Shannon's dresses); *The Way Things Happen* (Some designs)

Marie Cooke

Marie Cooke contributed costumes to productions between 1916 and 1920.
Costumes: 1916 *The Century Girl*† 1917 *Ziegfeld Follies: 1917*† 1919 *Happy Days*†; *Ziegfeld Midnight Frolic*† 1920 *Ziegfeld Girls: 1920*†

John Marshall Coombs

John Marshall Coombs designed the sets and lights for a production on Broadway in 1930.
Sets: 1931 *No More Frontier*
Lights: 1931 *No More Frontier*

Pamela Cooper

The daughter of the prominent Hollywood agent Frank Cooper, Pamela Cooper literally grew up in the theater. She was born in Los Angeles, California on March 25, 1952 and received a Bachelor of Arts from Ithaca College.

After receiving her Master of Fine Arts in 1976 at the University of California at Los Angeles, she worked as an assistant lighting designer at the Mark Taper Forum. She acknowledges Gordon Davidson (who gave her a start in the business) as a mentor along with Jean Rosenthal and Tharon Musser. With extensive experience designing for rock concerts and pop artists, she also has numerous credits in Las Vegas and Atlantic City, for dance companies, and for regional theaters including the Denver Theatre Center. Her Broadway debut was directed and choreographed by Michael Peters, a frequent collaborator. She also designed lights for dances which Michael Peters choreographed for the Royal Winnipeg Ballet and the National Ballet of Canada. While continuing to design occasionally, she is currently a personal manager for performers including Ben Vereen, writers and choreographers.
Lights: 1985 *Leader of the Pack*

Theodore Cooper

Theodore (also known as Edward and Ted) Cooper created sets and lights for two productions on Broadway, and for dozens in other locations. He amassed credits in summer stock, regional theaters, and off-Broadway. He was born in 1920 and retired after a long career in 1998. He died on December 5, 1999.
Sets: 1949 *Texas, Li'l Darlin'* 1950 *A Story for Sunday Evening*
Lights: 1949 *Texas, Li'l Darlin'* 1950 *A Story for Sunday Evening*

Gail Cooper-Hecht

Costume designer Gail Cooper-Hecht has created costumes for numerous off-Broadway productions, for theaters in the New York area and in the regional theaters, in addition to her credits on-Broadway. She has designed several national and international tours, with *The Sound of Music*, *Camelot*, *Woman of the Year* and *The Odd Couple* among them. Her costumes are often seen at the American Jewish Theatre, the Jewish Repertory Theatre, the Folksbiene Yiddish Theatre, and at the Mirror Repertory. Television credits include the CBS-TV series *The Recovery Room*, *Purlie* for "Great Performances" (Emmy Award nomination), *Glenn Miller* for PBS and *Plaza Suite* for Home Box Office. Recent credits include *The Gardens of Frau Hess*, *Love in a Thirsty Land*, *Our Place in Time*, *Names*, *Bermuda Avenue Triangle*, and *Songs of Paradise* at Theatre Four.

Costumes: 1987 *Late Nite Comic* **1990** *Those Were the Days* **1996** *The Apple Doesn't Fall*

Arthur Corbault

In 1906, Arthur Corbault collaborated on a scenic design for a Broadway production.

Sets: 1906 *Gallops†*

Alexander Corbett

Alexander B. Corbett was an American scenic artist who was on the staff of the Los Angeles Theatre in the late nineteenth century. He collaborated with another painter, Bradley, on a production of *The Winter's Tale* that subsequently toured to Dallas, Texas. Between 1899 and 1907, he was active on the Broadway stage, designing and presumably painting scenery.

Sets: 1899 *Macbeth* **1900** *Macbeth* **1901** *Richard Savage* **1903** *The Taming of Helen* **1907** *The Ambitious Mrs. Alcott*; *The Straight Road†*

Daniel Cordoba

Daniel Cordoba, a producer, director, choreographer and costume designer was born in Valencia, Spain and received a law degree from the University of Madrid. At the age of 28, he became the Governor of Andalucia, and subsequently a representative in the Spanish Congress. While holding these positions, he developed an interest in the folklore of his native country. During the process of studying songs and dances dating back to the Eighth Century he accumulated more than 9,000 melodies and lyrics from which *Cabalgata* was created. The show originated in Spain where it played for three years, before opening in South America, Cuba, Mexico, and in the U.S.

Costumes: 1949 *Cabalagata (a.k.a. A Night in Spain)*

Edward B. Corey

Edward B. Corey designed sets on Broadway in 1921. In 1925 Edward B. Corey was president of William A. Taylor, Inc., security brokers and insurance at 205 Columbus Avenue in New York.

Sets: 1921 *Only 38*

Sol Cornberg

Sol Cornberg, who was born June 22, 1910, began an apprenticeship at the Cleveland Playhouse in 1926 while in high school, becoming technical director of the theater in 1930. While retaining this position in Ohio he was also a theater consultant, lighting consultant and technical director for other theaters. He also served as technical advisor for the Federal Theatre in Ohio, Michigan and Kentucky and taught at Case Western Reserve University. Sol Cornberg published *A Stage Crew Handbook* (in collaboration with Emanuel L. Gebauer) in the late 1930s and became Director of Studio and Play Planning for the National Broadcasting Company in New York City in the early 1940s. After serving in World War II he resumed his career in television production. In 1954 Sol Cornberg revised *Television Techniques*, originally published by Hoyland Bettinger in 1947. Married to author Catherine Gaskin, Sol Cornberg died on October 2, 1999.

Lights: 1933 *Growing Pains*

Eric Cornwell

Eric Cornwell designs lights for concerts, opera, theater, and dance. In addition to working with Mandy Patinkin for his Broadway appearance in *Mamloshen*, he designed Patinkin's concerts on Broadway and his tours. He has also designed lights for the Brooklyn Academy of Music, the Berkshire Opera Company, and Il Piccolo Teatro del 'Opera. Designs for dance include productions for the Lucinda Childs Dance Company and the Joffrey II Dancers. Among his honors is a Maharam Award nomination for designs for Mabou Mines.

Lights: 1998 *Mamaloshen*

Corrigan and DeSoria

Twice Corrigan and DeSoria collaborated on designs for a Broadway production, initially for scenery and then for lights. Corrigan refers to Emmett Corrigan (1871-1932), an actor who was born Antoine Zilles, in Amsterdam, Holland. He immigrated to the United States with his family in the mid-1880s and made his acting debut at age 14, in Baltimore, Maryland in *Esmeralda, The Cigar Girl of Cuba*. His subsequent roles were frequent, on tours and in New York. Between 1902 and 1910 he was active back stage, rather than on stage. After 1925 he appeared mainly in films. DeSoria refers either to Charles DeSoria, an artisan who lived at 373 Bleeker Street, or to the Spanish painter and caricaturist, Cipriano Duque DeSoria (1850-1924).
Sets: 1908 *Three Twins*†
Lights: 1910 *Bright Eyes*†

E. David Cosier, Jr.

E. David Cosier, Jr. was born in San Francisco on June 23, 1958. He received a B.A. in theater from Santa Clara University and an M.F.A. from the Yale University School of Drama in 1988. Working primarily as a scenic designer, he has designed off-Broadway at the American Jewish Theatre and the Theatre for the New City, among others. Regional theater credits include *Social Security* for the Indiana Repertory Theatre, *Billy Bishop Goes to War* for the Missouri Repertory Theatre and *A Christmas Carol* and *As You Like It* for the Arts District Theatre of the Dallas Theatre Center. Television designs include *Saturday Night Live* for NBC-TV and *House Party*. He acknowledges both Eugene Lee and Ming Cho Lee as mentors. E. David Cosier is married to scenic designer Deb Booth.
Sets: 1990 *The Piano Lesson*

Peter Cotes

Peter Cotes, an actor, director, author, and occasional designer of sets and lights, was born Sydney Boulting in Maidenhead, England on March 19, 1912. He appeared on stage for the first time when he was four years old, as a page in *Henry V*. His credits as a director and adaptor of plays in England in the 1940s and 1950s are lengthy, notably the first stage production of *The Mousetrap*. In addition he directed *A Pin to See the Peepshow* and *Hidden Stranger* in New York. In the 1950s and 1960s he worked more often in television and film. His autobiography, *Thinking Aloud*, was published in 1993. He died on November 10, 1998 in Chipping Norton, England.
Sets: 1963 *Hidden Stranger*
Lights: 1963 *Hidden Stranger*

Robert Cothran

Robert M. Cothran was born in Detroit on May 9, 1930 and designed his first sets for *Antigone* at the Vanderbilt University Theatre in Nashville, Tennessee in 1949. He studied at Vanderbilt, the University of Tennessee and at Yale University with Donald Oenslager. He designs principally in regional theaters and served for many years as resident designer for the Clarence Brown Company at the University of Tennessee. Robert Cothran is also a graphic artist and designs industrial exhibits.
Sets: 1986 *Honky Tonk Nights*

Derek Cousins

A freelance graphic designer in England, Derek Cousins works mainly in television and film. He studied at the Royal College of Art where he illustrated an edition of *Canterbury Tales*. He subsequently made his debut as a stage designer with a production of the play, *Canterbury Tales*. In 1951 his business, D. Cousins, Costumiers, was located at 172 Railway Approach in London.
Sets: 1969 *Canterbury Tales*

Jennie Covan

Jennie Covan designed costumes for one show in 1930. The 1925 Manhattan City Directory identifies her as an author, residing as 25 West 16th Street.
Costumes: 1930 *General John Regan*

Miguel Covarrubias

Miguel Covarrubias, a painter, illustrator and caricaturist was born in Mexico City in 1902 and died there in 1957. He came to New York in 1923 and with the support of the Mexican Government quickly established himself as an enterprising and creative force. Within a short time of his arrival he published books of caricatures, contributed regularly to *Vanity Fair* and *The New Yorker*, and designed ballets and one play on Broadway. During his lifetime he also wrote and illustrated ethnological studies.

Sets: 1925 *Androcles and the Lion*; *Garrick Gaieties†*; *Man of Destiny†* 1926 *Garrick Gaieties†*

Costumes: 1925 *Androcles and the Lion* 1926 *Garrick Gaieties†*

Eugene Cox

Eugene Cox designed settings for a Broadway play in 1924. An artist, he lived in New York City in the early 1920s, but resided in London at 36 Great James Street by 1925.

Sets: 1924 *Easy Street*

Tom Adrian Cracraft

A set designer, Tom Adrain Cracraft (occasionally Crascraft) designed scenery for many plays on Broadway and contributed costumes to one. An especially active designer with the Federal Theatre Project, he designed sets for many of the new plays produced between 1935 and 1939, including the New York versions of *It Can't Happen Here*, which opened in twenty-one theaters simultaneously on October 27, 1936. He spent the last ten years of his life in Hollywood designing for film and television studios, and the Hilton Hotel chain. Mr. Cracraft died on October 8, 1963 at the age of 58.

Sets: 1932 *Goodbye Again* 1933 *Hilda Cassidy*; *Kultur*; *Love and Babies*; *Shady Lady*; *They All Come to Moscow* 1934 *All Rights Reserved*; *Broomsticks, Amen!*; *I, Myself*; *Roll Sweet Chariot*; *Wednesday's Child* 1935 *Black Pit*; *Symphony* 1936 *American Holiday*; *Class of '29*; *Help Yourself*; *It Can't Happen Here*; *Murder in the Cathedral* 1937 *A Hero Is Born* 1938 *The Hill Between*; *Window Shopping* 1941 *Popsy* 1943 *Goodbye Again*; *The Petrified Forest*

Costumes: 1936 *Murder in the Cathedral* (Costume Supervisor)

Benjamin Craig

Benjamin Craig designed a set for a Broadway production in 1907 that he also built.

Sets: 1907 *The Builders†* (Designed and constructed)

Edith Craig

Edith Craig, a member of a distinguished British theatrical family, spent her career as an actress, producer and designer. Born Edith Geraldine Wardell in 1869, her mother was Dame Ellen Terry, her father Edward William Godwin, an architect and theatrical designer, and her brother Edward Gordon Craig. She first appeared on stage, using the name Ailsa Craig, at age nine in *Olivia* together with her mother, brother, and step-father Charles Wardel. She acted with and designed many costumes for Henry Irving, including *Faust* in 1901. She appeared in *Alice-Sit-by-the Fire* in New York with her mother in 1905. By 1911, she was working mainly as a director for the Pioneers (a theater society in London), and for the Everyman Theatre in Hampstead. After Ellen Terry died in 1928, she assisted with the publication of biographies and memoirs, as well as Terry's correspondence with George Bernard Shaw. Edith Craig died on March 27, 1947 in Small Hythe, Kent, England. In 1987, *Ellen and Edy: A Biography of Ellen Terry and Her Daughter, Edith Craig* by Joy Melville, was published.

Sets: 1903 *Man Who Stole the Castle*

Costumes: 1900 *Prince Otto†*

Gordon Craig

Although his name does not appear often in playbills documenting credits of designers and directors on the Broadway stage, Edward Henry Gordon Craig's influence and presence was important. He was born in 1872 in Stevenage, Hertfordshire, England, the son of architect and theatrical designer Edward William Godwin and the actress Ellen Terry. He trained as an actor and joined Henry Irving's company in 1889, gaining experience with that company and with his mother's productions in all aspects of the theater as he began formulating theories about production. His first scenic designs were for *For Sword or Song* for Fred Terry and *Much Ado About Nothing* for his mother in 1903, after which he moved to the continent, wrote, founded a theater journal, ran a school of acting and contributed designs to productions. His final designs were for *Macbeth* in New York in 1928. The author of many books on various aspects of the theater, including acting, directing, and design, he was regarded by many as a twentieth century theater prophet. His papers and library were obtained by the Rondel Collection in Paris shortly before his death on July 29, 1966 in Vence, France.

Sets: 1928 *Macbeth*
Costumes: 1928 *Macbeth*†

Ned Crane

In 1932 Ned Crane, who resided at the Hotel Fulton, designed the settings for a Broadway play. As an actor, he appeared in the 1958 production *The Confederacy*.

Sets: 1932 *Triplets*

David Craven

David Craven supervised the costumes for a production on Broadway in 1962. It is unlikely that he is the Canadian abstract painter, born in 1947, who has the same name.

Costumes: 1962 *Moby Dick* (Costume Supervisor)

Hawes Craven

Hawes Craven, best known as Henry Irving's scene painter, was born Henry Hawes Craven Green on July 3, 1837 in Kirkgate, Leeds, England. He performed on stage as a child, but then turned his talents to painting through study at Marlborough House School of Design and as an apprentice to John Gray, scene painter at the Britannia Theatre in Hoxton and William Roxby Beverley at Drury Lane and Covent Garden. When Henry Irving became manager of the Lyceum Theatre in 1878, Craven had been on the staff for some years. When *Hamlet* opened later that year, it was the start of a very successful collaboration between an actor/director and a designer.

Widely regarded as one of the finest scene painters of the late nineteenth and early twentieth century due to the quality and innovation in his designs, he was one of the first scene painters to use "electrical effects" to enhance his backdrops. For many years after his death on July 22, 1922 in London, his scenic designs and paintings remained in use, including productions on Broadway.

Sets: 1899 *The Merchant of Venice*†; *Robespierre*† 1903 *Ulysses* 1906 *The Lyons Mail*; *Markheim*† (Acts I, III) 1907 *The Merchant of Venice*† 1912 *His Excellency the Governor* 1913 *Hamlet*†

Crayon

Hermann Křehan's (also known as Crayon-Křehan) debut in New York was as scenic and costume designer for *Manon Lescaut* in 1949, the first new production at the Metropolitan Opera of *Manon Lescaut* in twenty years. He trained as an architect in Zurich, graduating from the Darmstadt School and designed his first settings for Max Reinhardt in Berlin in the late teens, later designing for the Theatre an der Wien in Vienna. He came to the United States initially to design *l'Bohème* and *Old Maid and the Thief* for television. He also designed *Wieder Metropol* in 1926, and *At Heidelberg* in 1932.

Sets: 1948 *Morey Amsterdam's Hilarities*

Larry Crimmins

As resident lighting designer at Hartford Stage in Connecticut, Larry Crimmins designed numerous plays in the early 1970s. His work was seen on the Broadway stage, beginning in 1974.

Lights: 1974 *My Sister, My Sister* 1977 *Gemini*

Marie Crisp

Marie Crisp designed costumes for a play in the mid-1930s while residing at 189 St. Nicholas Street, New York City. She was also an actress who appeared in early films,

Costumes: 1934 *Big Hearted Herbert*

Frederick Crooke

Born in Guilford, Surrey, England on October 27, 1908, Frederick Crooke (also known as Croake) was a painter and scene designer. He studied at the Heatherley School of Art in London and began designing for the theater in the 1930s, starting with sets and costumes for *Primrose Time* at the Royal Theatre in Brighton. Additional designs appeared at Sadler's Wells, the Old Vic, Stratford-upon-Avon, and the Svenska Theatre in Finland throughout the 1940s and 1950s. The production he designed on Broadway in 1956 originated at the Old Vic in London. He died in 1991.

Sets: 1956 *Troilus and Cressida*
Costumes: 1956 *Troilus and Cressida*

Margaret Crosse

Margaret Crosse was the original costume designer for *Riverdance*, as acknowledged in the playbill of the 1998 version which was co-designed by Jen Kelly.

Costumes: 1998 *Riverdance*† (Original design)

Laura Crow

Laura Crow, professor at the University of Connecticut, was born on September 29, 1945 in Hanover, New Hampshire, daughter of James F. Crow a noted geneticist. After receiving a B.F.A. from Boston University and M.F.A. at the University of Wisconsin, she attended the Courthauld Institute of Art, University of London. Her professional career began in London, where two of the productions she designed, as resident designer for the Greenwich Theatre Company, transferred to the West End. She has designed over 300 productions, in regional theaters throughout the United States, off and on Broadway, and in Japan and Europe. She was resident designer for New York's Circle Repertory Company for thirteen years. Honors include Drama Desk, OBIE, Maharam, and American Theatre Wing Awards in New York City, a Joseph Jefferson Award in Chicago, and Drama-Logues, Back Stage West Garland Awards, and a Bay Area Critics Award on the West

Coast. Her designs have been included in three United States' Exhibitions at the Prague Quadrennial. Recipient of a 2002 Fulbright Scholar Fellowship for study of ritual dress in Southeast Asia, she is the Head of the Costume Working Group for the Scenography Commission of OISTAT, the International Organization of Scenographers, Theatre Architects and Technicians.

Costumes: 1973 *Warp*† 1975 *Sweet Bird of Youth* 1978 *Water Engine, The/ Mr. Happiness* 1980 *Fifth of July* 1987 *Burn This* 1992 *The Seagull* 1993 *Redwood Curtain*

Edward Crowe

Edward Crowe designed costumes for one show in 1922. Mr. Crowe, who was born in Meadville, Pennsylvania, attended Allegheny College. President of Cordeau et Cie., a small couture house located at 1 West 47th Street in New York City, he died in 1925 at age 37.

Costumes: 1922 *The Advertising of Kate*

Bob Crowley

Bob Crowley, originally from County Cork, Ireland, is a designer of sets and costumes for plays, operas, ballets, and film and an occasional director who has been working steadily since his professional debut in 1975 with *A Midsummer Night's Dream* at the Bristol and subsequently London Old Vic. He has had productive long-term collaborations with Adrian Noble, Nicholas Hytner, and Richard Eyre, during which he has created many fresh approaches to classics and compelling designs for new plays. He is an Associate Artist at both the Royal National Theatre and for the Royal Shakespeare Company. His list of credits and awards is lengthy, including Laurence Olivier Awards for *Ghetto* at RNT and *The Plantagenets* for RSC. He won Tony Awards for the sets for *Carousel* and *Aida*, among many nominations in both the set and costume categories. Twenty-first century designs include scenery and costumes for *The Seagull* at the Delacorte Theatre.

Sets: 1987 *Les Liaisons Dangereuses* 1994 *Carousel* 1995 *Racing Demon* 1998 *The Capeman; The Judas Kiss; Twelfth Night* 1999 *Amy's View; The*

Iceman Cometh; Putting It Together 2000 *Aida* 2001 *The Invention of Love*
Costumes: 1987 *Les Liaisons Dangereuses* 1994 *Carousel* 1995 *Racing Demon* 1998 *The Capeman; The Judas Kiss* 1999 *Amy's View; The Iceman Cometh; Putting It Together* 2000 *Aida* 2001 *The Invention of Love*

Herbert Crowley

Herbert E. Crowley designed costumes for a play in 1916. A British artist, Mr. Crowley married costume designer Alice Lewisohn (died 1972) in 1924. From October 24 to November 14, 1914 an exhibition of his drawings, paintings and grotesques was held at the Berlin Photographic Company in New York City. A catalog, with an introduction by Martin Birnbaum, was subsequently published. He later participated in an exhibition called "Speak Their Language." Some of his papers are in the collections of Metropolitan Museum of Art.
Costumes: 1916 *The Kairn of Koridwen*

Audrey Cruddas

Audrey Cruddas was born in Johannesburg, South Africa on November 16, 1914, moved to England as a young child, and studied at the St. John's Wood School of Art. Her first professional designs were the sets for *The White Devil* in 1948. Shortly after the opening of that production she was invited to design *King John* for the Royal Shakespeare Festival in Stratford-upon-Avon, which led to numerous additional designs. Audrey Cruddas usually designed both sets and costumes for productions, and occasionally designed lights. Her designs for the opera, ballet and theater were seen around the world. The recipient of the Donaldson Award for *Caesar and Cleopatra* in the 1951-52 season, Audrey Cruddas died in 1979.
Sets: 1956 *Macbeth* 1958 *Hamlet; Henry V*
Costumes: 1951 *Antony and Cleopatra; Caesar and Cleopatra* 1956 *Macbeth* 1958 *Hamlet; Henry V*
Lights: 1958 *Hamlet; Henry V*

Keith Cuerden

Keith Cuerden designed sets and cos-

tumes for many plays at Circle in the Square, including *Plays for Bleeker Street* and *The Grass Harp.* He was born January 14, 1930 and died in New York City on June 15, 1997.
Sets: 1954 *The Girl on the Via Flamina*
Costumes: 1954 *The Girl on the Via Flamina*

Marie Cummings

Madame Marie Cummings designed costumes for a 1903 production.
Costumes: 1903 *My Lady Peggy Goes to Town*[†] (Women's costumes)

Gwendolyn Cumnor

Gwendolyn Cumnor contributed costume designs to a play in 1928.
Costumes: 1928 *Parisiana* ("Galliwog, Paris Green")

Miss Bessie B. Cunningham

Miss Bessie B. Cunningham was costume supervisor for a show in 1931. She worked in the wardrobe department of the Theatre Guild for many years and resided at 509 West 121st Street, New York City.
Costumes: 1931 *Green Grow the Lilacs* (Costume Supervisor)

John Cunningham

John Cunnningham designed scenery for Broadway productions at the beginning of the twentieth century and is not to be confused with the actor working at its' end. Trow's 1898 New York City Directory lists him as being in the furniture business at 22 New Bowery and residing at 15 Madison Avenue.
Sets: 1899 *Why Smith Left Home*[†] 1902 *The Mocking Bird*

Brian Currah

Brian Mason Currah is from Plymouth, Devonshire, England where he was born on August 19, 1929. He is both a stage designer and teacher of design, having served of the faculty at the Croydon College of Art, Worthing College of Art, Theatre Clwd and the University of Alberta. His debut in theater was in 1951 at the Hippodrome in Stockton, England and since then his sets have been seen throughout the British Isles, in Canada, and the United States.

Sets: **1964** *The Caretaker* **1967** *After the Rain*

Ann Curtis

Costume designer Ann Curtis was born on May 19, 1937 in London. She studied at Central St. Martin's College of Art and Design from 1955-1959 and from 1979-1997 was Lecturer in the history of costumes. Her professional debut was with *The Government Inspector* for the Royal Shakespeare Company in 1965, directed by Peter Hall. Early in her career she worked in a partnership with John Bury, codesigning numerous plays and operas, as was the case with her Broadway debut *The Rothschilds* in 1970. She has also designed costumes for numerous productions at the Stratford (Ontario) Festival. In addition to John Bury and Peter Hall, she includes Tanya Moiseiwitsch, Desmond Heeley, John Barton, and Robin Phillips among major influences and mentors. Her designs have been much honored, with New York Drama Desk and Tony nominations for *Me and My Girl*, a Tony nomination for *Jekyll & Hyde*, a Dora Mavor Moore nomination (Toronto) for *Aspects of Love*. In addition, she received an Elizabeth Sterling Haynes Award (Edmonton, Alberta) for *The Crucible*, and two additional Haynes nominations for *Aspects of Love* and *Cyrano De Bergerac*. In 1999, her costume designs were featured in the United Kingdom presentation at the Prague Quadrennial.

Costumes: **1970** *The Rothschilds*† **1986** *Me and My Girl* **1997** *Jekyll & Hyde*

Marianne Custer

Originally from Minneapolis, Minnesota, Marianne Custer was born on July 12, 1947. She received a B.A. from the University of Minnesota in 1970 and her M.F.A. from the University of Wisconsin at Madison in 1973. She has been on the faculties of Southern Illinois University, the University of Colorado, and the University of Tennessee. She has been Resident Costume Designer of the Clarence Brown Theatre in Knoxville, Tennessee since

1974 where her designs include *Rip Van Winkle* directed by Anthony Quayle, who also played the title role, and the *Oresteia*. Besides costume designs on Broadway, her credits include The National Theatre of Germany in Weimar, The National Theatre of Hungary in Pecs, the Municipal Theatre of Istanbul, PlayMakers Repertory Company, and Seven Stages in Atlanta.

Costumes: **1979** *A Meeting in the Air*

Ladislas Czettel

Ladislas Czettel, a costume and fashion designer was born in Budapest, Hungary on March 12, 1894. Before he came to the United States in 1934 to design costumes for the Metropolitan Opera, he spent twelve years as head of design at the Vienna State Opera. He studied at Max Reinhardt's Dramatic School and with León Bakst in Paris. In addition to theater designs, Mr. Czettel designed haute couture fashions for Henri Bendel, Jay-Thorpe, and private customers. His films include *Pygmalion*. Mr. Czettel died at the age of 55 on March 5, 1949.

Costumes: **1942** *Rosalinda* **1944** *Helen Goes to Troy*

Liz da Costa

Liz da Costa, born in London on January 28, 1955, designed for the Royal Exchange Theatre in Manchester upon winning an Arts Council Bursary, after studying at the Central School of Art and Design. Her first London production was *The Changeling* at Riverside Studios, followed by numerous productions in the West End and for the Royal Shakespeare Company. Also a designer of dance costumes, she met choreographer Micha Bergere at Riverside Studios, which led to collaborations including *Solo Ride* at Contemporary Dance Theatre and Ballet Rambert. As associate designer to John Napier, she contributed to *Starlight Express* in London and the U.S. She has taught theater design at Hounslow Borough College.

Sets: **1987** *Breaking the Code*
Costumes: **1987** *Breaking the Code*

Daffi

In 1970 Daffi created sets as well as

appeared in the production asSolange, the eight-foot tall chicken, and St. Bernard, a schizophrenic. *Gloria and Esperanza* transferred to Broadway after a successful run at La MaMa E.T.C.
Sets: 1970 *Gloria and Esperanza*

Asadata Dafora

John Warner Dafora Horton, who was known professionally as Asadata Dafora, was born in Freetown, Sierra Leone on August 4, 1890. Primarily a dancer, choreographer, and composer, he wrote, choreographed, provided the music, and designed the costumes and scenery for *Kykunkor, or Witch Woman* in the mid-1930s, which became his best known work. He was the first African choreographer to present African dances on the American stage. Between 1930 and his death in New York on March 4, 1965 he created and staged many works based on African traditions. In 1979 the Charles Moore Dancers and Drums of Africa honored his memory with a program of dances at the Marymount Manhattan Theatre.
Sets: 1934 *Kykunkor*
Costumes: 1934 *Kykunkor* (Music, choreography, author)

Warren Dahler

Warren Dahler, a painter and designer who was born in New York City on October 12, 1897, attended the University of Chicago and studied with George Grey Barnard. He designed murals, including one for the Missouri State Capitol, and many sets for Broadway plays early in his career, from his studio at 611 West 127th Street in New York City, often working collaboration with Lois Phipps. He also participated in exhibits at the National Academy of Design and occasionally designed costumes. Mr. Dahler died in 1961.
Sets: 1913 *The Things That Count*† (Act I portrait) 1915 *The Glittering Gate*†; *Tethered Sheep*† 1916 *Great Katherine*; *The Inca of Perusalem*; *The Queen's Enemies*† 1922 *The Czarina*
Costumes: 1916 *Great Katherine*

Marjorie Dalmain

Marjorie Dalmain created sets for two plays on Broadway in 1922.

Sets: 1922 *Manhattan*; *Up the Ladder*

F. Mitchell Dana

Lighting designer F. Mitchell Dana was born Frank Livingston Mitchell, II on November 14, 1942. He was educated at Utah State University where he received a B.F.A. in 1964 and the Yale School of Drama where he received an M.F.A. in 1967. His credits in regional theater in the United States read like a who's who of regional theaters, including fifty productions at A.C.T. between 1972 and 1980, the 1972 Stratford (Ontario) Festival and productions at the Goodman Theatre among many, many others. Off-Broadway he has designed at the Manhattan Theatre Club and the Brooklyn Academy of Music. In addition he has designed lights for television and industrials and has lectured on lighting design at many universities.
Lights: 1970 *Charley's Aunt* 1974 *The Freedom of the City* 1978 *The Inspector General*; *Man and Superman*; *Once in a Lifetime* 1980 *The Suicide* 1981 *Mass Appeal* 1982 *Monday after the Miracle* 1984 *The Babe* 1986 *Oh Coward!*

David Dangle

David Dangle first designed costumes on Broadway in 1994. In the same year, he designed costumes for the made-for-television movie *Tears and Laughter: The Joan and Melissa Rivers Story.*
Costumes: 1994 *Sally Marr...and Her Escorts*† (Joan Rivers' costumes)

Jack Daniels

Jack Daniels was the lighting designer for a play on Broadway in 1944.
Lights: 1944 *Dark Hammock*

Jacques Darcy

Jacques Darcy (or D'Arcy) collaborated on the costumes for a show in 1929. He was also a painter, who worked mainly in gouache, and exhibited in New York galleries, including the Reinhardt.
Costumes: 1929 *Murray Anderson's Almanac*†

C. Tomlinson Dare

C. Tomlinson Dare shared credit for the costume designs for a show in 1915.
Costumes: 1915 *The Clever Ones*†

Daphne Dare

Daphne Dare, who was named Head of Design at the Stratford (Ontario) Festival in 1975, designed costumes for dozens of shows there and in her native England. She was born in Yeovil, Somerset, England in 1929 and attended the Bath Academy of Art and London University. Her first position in the theater was as a scene painter at the Birmingham Repertory Theatre. She began to design costumes and sets in 1958, starting with *Amphitryon 38* at the Bristol Old Vic, and after that time while continuing to design settings concentrated on costumes. At Bristol she first encountered Robin Phillips, then a young actor who became her long-term collaborator, both in England and in Canada. She also designed costumes for television, notably *Dr. Who* and *Fall of Eagles*, and for motion pictures including *Carla's Song*. In the mid-1980s she retired to Roehampton, England although she continued to work occasionally, including *London Assurance* with Sam Mendes. On September 27, 2000, Daphne Dare died in London.
Sets: 1988 *Macbeth*
Costumes: 1971 *Abelard and Heloise*

Robert Darling

Robert Darling is from Oakland, California where he was born on October 1, 1937. He received a B.A. from San Francisco State University and in 1973 an M.F.A. from the Yale School of Drama. He worked as an assistant to Will Steven Armstrong and Ming Cho Lee, and studied with and was influenced by Robert Edmond Jones, Donald Oenslager and the opera producer Kurt Herbert Adler. His New York debut occurred with the opening of *Another Evening with Harry Stoones* in 1962. He also has extensive credits lighting ballet, opera and musical theater for companies such as the San Francisco, New York City, Houston and Santa Fe Operas, as well as directing. He has served as producer and artistic director for the Central City Opera House, on the opera-musical theater policy panel of the National Endowment for the Arts and is a founding member of the Alliance for New Mu-

sic Theatre. His designs are in the permanent collections of the Smithsonian Museum and the Museum of the City of New York, and were exhibited at the Prague Quadrennial in 1975 and 1987.
Lights: 1964 *Cambridge Circus*

Don Darnutzer

Don Darnutzer designs lights for theater, opera, children's theater, national tours, and dance. He was born in Sparta, Wisconsin on May 10, 1951 and received a B.A. in theater in 1979 from the University of Wisconsin at Madison, where he studied with Gilbert V. Hemsley, Jr. He then assisted Hemsley on Broadway shows including *Comin' Uptown* and *Your Arms Too Short to Box With God*, and at the New York City Opera and the Opera Company of Boston. He was the lighting coordinator for the national tour of *Sugar Babies* and for Ballet Folklorico de Mexico. In addition to designs for the Denver Center Theatre Company, Mark Taper Forum, Cleveland Playhouse, Arena Stage, Alley Theatre and the Milwaukee Repertory Theatre, he has designed for La Societe Lyrique d'Aubigny in Quebec City and Fundacion Teres Careno in Caracas, Venezuela. Darnutzer is married to theatrical set designer Vicki Smith.
Lights: 1999 *It Ain't Nothing But the Blues*

Jean Dary

Jean Dary designed one play on Broadway in 1926.
Sets: 1926 *The Play's the Thing*

Marie-Hélène Dasté

Marie-Hélène Dasté was born December 2, 1902 in Lyngby, Denmark, daughter of Jacques Copeau who founded Vieux-Columbier in Paris. After completing her studies, she worked as a costume designer in her fathers theater, beginning at age 18. There she met Jacques Copeau with whom she continued to collaborate throughout much of her career, notably at the Comédie Française, Théâtre Montparnasse and the Compagnie Renaud-Barrault. Both she and her husband, actor and director Jean Dasté (1904-1994), were founding members of the

"Compagnie des Quinze" with whom she also performed. All the company members participated in every aspect of production to conserve funds so Madame Dasté sketched costumes. In 1957, she joined the company of Jean-Louis Barrault, performing and continuing to collaborate on costume designs for the company. Marie-Hélène Dasté died in Beaune, France on August 28, 1994.

Costumes: 1946 *Oedipus* **1948** *Oedipus Rex*

Millia Davenport

Millia Davenport was born March 30, 1895 in Cambridge, Massachusetts. After attending Barnard College she studied in Paris and in New York at the School of Fine and Applied Arts. Between 1918 and 1920 she designed sets and costumes for the Wits and Fingers Studio in New York City, after which she concentrated costumes, often working on productions with Jo Mielziner and Robert Edmond Jones. She designed costumes for the Greenwich Village Theatre and the Provincetown Playhouse in addition to her credits on Broadway. In 1948, she wrote a book that remains a standard costume history reference, *The Book of Costume*. The recipient of an honorary degree from Parsons School of Design in New York City in 1981, she died on January 18, 1992 at age 96.

Costumes: 1923 *Helen of Troy, New York*† (Russian Boys and Girls) **1924** *Desire under the Elms*; *George Dandin, or the Husband Confounded*† **1925** *Last Night of Don Juan, The/ The Pilgrimage*; *Love for Love*† **1926** *East Lynne*; *The Square* **1927** *The Good Hope* **1928** *Falstaff* **1938** *Heartbreak House*; *The Shoemaker's Holiday* **1940** *Journey to Jerusalem*; *Love for Love* **1946** *Truckline Cafe*

Leon Davey

Leon G. Davey was born in London on August 6, 1904. His career began in the early 1920s with productions at the Glasgow Royal Theatre, the Lyceum Theatre in Edinburgh, and for the Oxford Players. He made his London debut in 1930 with the scenery for *Land of*

the *Christmas Stocking* at the Hampstead Everyman Theatre. His production credits, extending into the 1950s in London are extensive and include *The Man of Yesterday, The Two Mrs. Carrolls, A Woman Passed By, Sitting Pretty, The School for Spinsters, The Kid from Stratford, Miss Mabel, Two Dozen Roses, Top Secret*, and *The Green Bay Tree*. He also designed for the Kingsway Theatre, Blackpool's Grand Theatre, and Brighton's Theatre Royal. During World War II he was active with the Entertainment National Service Association.

Sets: 1948 *Don't Listen Ladies*

Michael Davidson

Throughout the 1960s Michael C. Davidson was an active scenery and lighting designer. In addition to designing lighting and scenery for a production on Broadway in 1969, he lit off-Broadway productions such as *Adaptation-Next, Collision Course, Get Thee to Canterbury* and *3 from Column A*. He designed lights for the Berkshire Theatre Festival in 1967 and 1968. As a technical and lighting consultant, he also lit displays, industrial promotions, residences, building interiors, and sculptures. Originally from Portland, Oregon, he studied anthropology in Mexico and Southern California.

Sets: 1969 *No Place to Be Somebody*
Lights: 1969 *No Place to Be Somebody*

Spencer Davies

Spencer Davies designed numerous productions for the Goodman Theatre in Chicago in the 1940s, including *Family Portrait* and *The Merry Wives of Windsor*. Two renderings, one for each play were reproduced in the July 1940 issue of *Theatre Arts Magazine*. He served as both art director and set designer for the 1975 television series *Give-n-Take*.

Sets: 1961 *The Billy Barnes People*

Benjamin C. Davis

Benjamin C. Davis designed costumes in 1925 for a Broadway play. He was the co-owner with Max Silverstein of the Central Neckwear Company located at 104 Fifth Avenue and also operated Benjamin Davis, Costumes at 1890 Park Avenue. Davis resided at 1102 Simpson Street in New York during the 1920s.

Costumes: 1925 *Bringing Up Father*

Bob Davis

Bob Davis, a resident of Elizabeth New Jersey, had a jewelry business in the early years of the twentieth century at 3A Maiden Lane in New York City. He collaborated on the costume designs, providing gowns and accessories for a 1914 Broadway production. The costume designer is not to be confused with the tap dancer who has the same name.

Costumes: 1914 *Twin Beds*† (Gowns and accessories)

Charles Davis

Mr. Charles T. Davis created lights for a Broadway production in 1921. Born in 1892, he spent the majority of his career as a cinematographer. He died in Washington, D.C. on October 3, 1936.

Lights: 1921 *In the Night Watch*

Fiona Davis

Fiona Davis studied in the two-year program at Circle in the Square. She not only collaborated on the costumes for *Wilder, Wilder, Wilder*, she appeared in the production. A frequent co-designer with Dede Pochas in the early 1990s, they also worked together on *Who Will Carry the World?* at the Anderson Theatre and *Four Plays of the Sea* for the Willow Cabin Theatre Company. Davis appeared in *Three Tall Women* at the Arizona Theatre Company and *A Child's Christmas in Wales* at the Harold Clurman Theatre.

Costumes: 1993 *Wilder, Wilder, Wilder*†

Hubert Davis

Hubert Davis designed costumes in the 1920s on Broadway. He was born in Milton, Pennsylvania on March 15, 1902 and studied at the Julian Academy in Paris. He painted many pictures of the contrast between beauty and ugliness in coal mining regions from his studio at 405 Carnegie Hall. His works, mainly lithographs, were widely exhibited in the United States

and Europe, and are part of the permanent collection of the Museum of Modern Art. Mr. Davis also wrote, illustrated and published "Symbolic Drawings of Hubert Davis for An American Tragedy by Theodore Dreiser" in 1930. He died on October 22, 1981.

Costumes: 1925 *Dearest Enemy*† (Act I) **1928** *Hot Pan*

Jeff Davis

Born on April 14, 1950 in Philadelphia, Jeff Davis received a Bachelor of Arts in 1972 from Northwestern University. He worked as an associate designer to Jo Mielziner and as an assistant to Tharon Musser, both of whom he credits with influencing his career (along with Delbort Unruh). In 1975 he designed *Ride the Winds*, his New York debut. With extensive credits in regional theaters, national tours, industrial shows, film, and television, Jeff Davis is principally a lighting designer who occasionally designs settings. He is also actively involved with United Scenic Artists, the union governing theatrical designers.

Lights: 1980 *The Man Who Came to Dinner* **1983** *The Man Who Had Three Arms* **1987** *The Musical Comedy Murders* **1989** *Born Yesterday* **1990** *Change in the Heir* **1992** *110 in the Shade*; *Regina* **1993** *Cinderella* **1994** *Wonderful Town* **1995** *Cinderella* **1996** *Tartuffe: Born Again* **1997** *Play On!*

Joe Davis

A British lighting designer, Joe Davis was born in London on December 19, 1912. He became associated with H. M. Tennent, Ltd. when the production company was formed in 1936, and as their lighting designer created lighting effects for over five hundred productions during a career lasting fifty years. Earlier he had worked for Strand Electric (beginning in 1926), and as production electrician for Charles B. Cochran and Julian Wylie. As lighting designer for Marlene Dietrich for twenty-two years he worked in the United States, Vienna and Moscow. A founding member of the Society of British Theatre Lighting Designers, he also served that organization as President

and Life President. He died at age 72 on July 5, 1984.
Lights: 1960 *Irma La Douce*

John Davis

John William Davis worked as head of light crews for the Shubert Organization andSidney Kingsley. He won a Tony Award in the "Stage Technician Category" for *Picnic* in 1954; the lights for the production were designed by Jo Mielziner. The citation read in part: "For constant good work as a theater electrician." He was probably responsible for the lighting design for many more productions than those for which he received credit, because he worked at a time when lighting designers were regarded primarily as electricians. At the time of his death on May 27, 1960 in Westport, Connecticut, he was an electrician for NBC-TV.
Lights: 1945 *The Wind is Ninety* 1954 *The Burning Glass*

Lindsay W. Davis

Born in St. John, Washington on February 12, 1953, Lindsay W. Davis first began designing for the theater in summer stock. He graduated from Harvard in 1975 and received an M.F.A. in 1978 in theatrical design from the New York University School of the Arts where he studied with Fred Voelpel. After completing his formal schooling, he worked as a costume assistant to Patricia Zipprodt for three years, and for Theoni V. Aldredge for two years, working in that time on numerous Broadway shows. His first professional credits as a costume designer in New York were at Radio City Music Hall. A designer of both sets and costumes, he specializes in costumes. He works mainly in New York and Los Angeles, and as time allows in the regional theaters, including the Huntington Theatre in Boston, the New Hampshire Stage Festival, Arena Stage, Cleveland Playhouse, and Goodspeed Opera House. With films including *Zeisters*, Davis is Visiting Associate Professor in academic year 2001-2002, and head of the costume program at the University of Missouri at Kansas City.
Sets: 1983 *Five-Six-Seven-Eight... Dance!*†

Costumes: 1983 *Five-Six-Seven-Eight... Dance!* 1985 *The Mystery of Edwin Drood* 1990 *The Cemetery Club*; *A Little Night Music* 1992 *110 in the Shade*

Richard Davis

Richard C. Davis designed sets in 1970 for a production on Broadway. His recent activity is with the television and movie industry, as producer and location manager.
Sets: 1970 *The Cherry Orchard*

Robert Peter Davis

In 1923 Robert Peter Davis was designer of the settings for a play on Broadway. He was president of the Brotherhood of Painters, Decorators & Paper Hangers of America in 1915, and resided at 216 East 59th Street, New York City.
Sets: 1923 *Roseanne*

Peter J. Davison

The British designer of sets and costumes, Peter J. Davison, was born in Darbyshire, England in 1955. He originally intended to teach drama, but after completing his studies began professional life as an electrician until 1977 when he became an assistant designer for opera at the Royal Opera House. He remained there until 1986, learning about designing as he assisted the designers who came through the shops and studios with productions. He designs plays (Royal National Theatre, Royal Shakespeare Company, Theatre Clwyd, etc.), operas (English National Opera, Deutshe Staatsoper, Bayerishe Staatsoper, New York's Metropolitan Opera, Opernhaus Zurich, etc.), and dance (Stuttgart Ballet, Birmingham Royal Ballet, etc.), and frequently collaborates with directors Jonathan Miller and Jonathan Kent, co-artistic director of the Almeida Theatre.
Sets: 1994 *Medea* 1995 *His Excellency the Governor* 2000 *Copenhagen*; *Jesus Christ Superstar*
Costumes: 2000 *Copenhagen*

Robert Davison

Robert Davison, scenic and costume designer, was born in Long Beach, California on July 17, 1922. After study at Los Angeles City College he moved to New York where he was influenced by the Russian Constructivists and the Neo-Romantics. Although he made his debut on Broadway as a costume designer in 1944, Mr. Davison did not design his first set on Broadway until 1945. Notable designs include sets and costumes for *Galileo* for Brecht in Los Angeles in 1947, *La Barca di Venezia per Padova* in Spoleto, Italy in 1963, and many productions for the Ballets Russe de Monte Carlo. He also exhibited three duco paintings at the E.B. Dunkel Scenic Studio, with the American Watercolor Society, and at the Eastern States Exhibition.

Sets: 1945 *The Day before Spring* 1946 *Around the World in Eighty Days*; *A Flag Is Born*; *O Mistress Mine* 1947 *Galileo*; *Miracle in the Mountains*
Costumes: 1944 *Hand in Glove*; *Song of Norway*† 1947 *Miracle in the Mountains*

S. J. Dawkins

Steven J. Dawkins designed lighting for two 1916 Broadway productions. An electrician, he resided at 408 West 19th Street, New York City.

Lights: 1916 *Six Who Passed while the Lentils Boiled*; *The Trimplet*

Beatrice Dawson

Beatrice "Bumble" Dawson was born in Lincoln, England on January 26, 1908 and died on April 16, 1976. She designed costumes for numerous movies and was nominated for an Academy Award in 1955 for *Pickwick Papers*. She studied at the Slade School of Art and the Chelsea Polytechnic, and made her debut as a costume designer in 1945 at the Haymarket Theatre in London with *The Duchess of Malfi*.

Costumes: 1971 *Old Times*

Trevor Dawson

British lighting designer Trevor Dawson has worked in the theater as a stage manager, lighting designer and production manager. He was in residence at the Lyric Theatre, Belfast and currently serves as production manager at the Abbey Theatre, while continuing his design career. His designs have been seen throughout the U.K.

but primarily in Dublin where he has designed for all the major theaters. His lights have been seen in the Abbey Theatre productions of *The Plough and the Stars, Silver Tassie* and *You Can't Take It with You*, etc. and for the Gate Theatre they include *A Woman of No Importance* and *Salome*, directed by Stephen Berkoff, which was also part of the 1989 Edinburgh Festival.

Lights: 1991 *Dancing at Lughnasa*

Marie Day

Marie Day was born in Toronto, Canada in 1933 and studied at the Ontario College of Art afar which she worked at the Mermaid Theatre in England. In 1954 she served as design assistant to Tanya Moiseiwitsch at the Stratford (Ontario) Festival. When she designed *Henry IV, Part I* in 1958 with Moiseiwitsch, she became the first Canadian to design on the Festival's main stage. Her first solo design at Stratford, Ontario was Benjamin Britten's opera, *The Rape of Lucretia* for which she was won a Guthrie Award. She has designed often for the Canadian Opera Company, the Shaw Festival and the Charlottetown Festival. Marie Day has also written and illustrated two books for children about early times: *Dragon in the Rocks* (1995) and *Quennu and the Cave Bear* (1999).

Costumes: 1960 *Love and Libel*

William H. Day

William H. Day, who was credited in programs as Wm. H. and as W.H. Day, was the art director for the Lyceum Theatre in New York during the last decade of the nineteenth century. In that capacity, he was surely responsible for numerous scenic designs but few were recorded. The twentieth century credit that does appear was posthumous however, because his designs remained available for use, generally in productions that were revived or on tour. Born c.1834, he died in Glasgow Scotland on December 13, 1898. His scenic designs prior to 1900 include a Philadelphia production of *The Prince and the Pauper* in 1889 which played at the Lyceum Theatre in 1890. He also

designed *Frou-Frou* in 1886, *The Wife* in 1889, and *Don Caesar* in 1891.
Sets: **1910** *The Private Secretary* (Art and scenic director)

Henry Dazian

Dazians Theatrical Emporium was located at 142 West 44th Street in New York City beginning in 1906. The business was begun by Wolf Dazian (c.1815-1902) at $4\frac{1}{2}$ Marion Street, later Lafayette Street, selling dry and fancy goods, attracting customers including P. T. Barnum. The business was passed on to his eldest son, Henry (1854-1937) in 1878, who became an expert on period costumes and expanded the business beyond dry goods, although keeping it related to fabric. Later the business was managed by Emil Friedlander who began as an errand boy in 1900. He expanded the company's rental business when he purchased thousands of uniforms throughout Europe after World War I and continued to add to the inventory of garments whenever an opportunity presented itself. The business also made the curtains for Radio City Music Hall when it opened. Today Dazians is associated principally with fabrics and has branches in New York, Miami, Chicago, Dallas, and Beverly Hills. The credits listed below are only a small portion of the Broadway productions with costumes by Dazians, but are those with which Henry Dazian was personally involved. The list includes *l'Aiglon* for which the original costume for Maude Adams was reported to cost $1350, and *DuBarry*. The garment worn by Mrs. Leslie Carter as Madame Du Barry, designed by Worth and executed by Dazians for that play, was said to use 55 yards of fabric costing $45 per yard.
Costumes: **1899** *My Lady's Lord*†; *The Only Way* **1900** *L'Aiglon*† (Costumes) **1901** *Alice of Old Vincennes*; *Du Barry*† (Design and execution); *A Royal Rival*; *The Second in Command* **1902** *Hon. John Grigsby*†; *The Twin Sister*† **1903** *The Fisher Maiden*†; *Miss Elizabeth's Prisoner*†; *The Pretty Sister of José*† **1905** *La Belle Marseillaise*; *A Yankee Circus on Mars*† **1906** *Brigadier Ger-*

ard; *Mizpah* **1908** *The Jesters* **1909** *Flag Lieutenant* (Uniforms) **1910** *The Brass Bottle*; *Our Miss Gibbs*† (Japanese costumes) **1911** *The Siren*† (Uniforms) **1913** *Iole*† (Costumes); *Mlle. Modiste*† (Uniforms) **1915** *Rosemary*† (Costumes)

Mercedes de Acosta

Mercedes de Acosta was a playwright and well-known screen writer in the 1920s and 1930s. She was born in Paris, raised in New York and educated at several schools in Europe. Eva Le Gallienne starred in two of her plays that were produced in New York, *Sandro Borrecelli* and *Jeanne d'Arc*. She also wrote books of poetry. Mercedes de Acosta, who was born in New York City in 1893, died there on May 9, 1968.
Sets: **1924** *The Assumption of Hannele*
Costumes: **1924** *The Assumption of Hannele*

Judy Dearing

Judy Dearing began her life in the theater as a dancer and choreographer, and as an actress. Because she had learned to sew as a child and often made her own costumes for dancing, the transition to costume designer was an easy one to make. She designed numerous shows in New York for companies including the Negro Ensemble Company, the New York Shakespeare Festival, and Alvin Ailey. She designed for the American Place Theatre, including *Do Lord Remember Me, The Dream Team* and *Celebrations*, for the Goodspeed Opera House, the Goodman Theatre in Chicago, and the New Federal Theatre. For her costume designs, Judy Dearing received four Audelco Awards, an Obie for *A Soldier's Play* in 1985, and a Tony Award nomination for *Once on This Island*. Raised in Manhattan, she graduated from City College, where she majored in math and science. At the time of her death on September 30, 1995, at age 55, she was a professor of design at Howard University, had two shows running on Broadway, and a production of *Porgy and Bess* on tour.
Costumes: **1974** *Lamppost Reunion* **1976** *For Colored Girls Who Have Considered Suicide*; *The Poison Tree* **1978**

The Mighty Gents **1984** *The Babe* **1987**
Death and the King's Horseman **1988**
Checkmates **1990** *Once on This Island*
1992 *Shimada* **1995** *Having Our Say;*
Swinging on a Star

Jean Fournier deBelleval

Jean Fournier de Belleval designed sets
and costumes for a play in 1951 on
Broadway.
Sets: **1951** *Ti-Coq*
Costumes: **1951** *Ti-Coq*

Joan and David deBethel

British designers Joan and David de-
Bethel collaborated on the designs for
a Broadway production in 1955. David
deBethel was also an author, with
books including *The Tyrolese Cookery
Book* in 1937 and *Bouquet Garni* in
1939 and again in 1945, both published
by the Medici Society in London. They
co-authored a play, *Ring for Catty* that
opened at London's Lyric Theatre in
February 1956, starring Patrick Mc-
Goohan and Mary Mackenzie. An article in "The Independent" on October
17, 1993 about the difficulties faced by
elderly self-employed individuals without health insurance identified Joan de
Bethel is a painter, and a decorator of
pottery cats. The article also refers to
her as a widow of almost-70.
Sets: **1955** *Joyce Grenfell Requests the
Pleasure†*

John Decker

John Decker was a successful caricaturist of New York and Hollywood personalities and had a brief career as an
actor. He worked for the newspaper
The Evening World in New York City,
but after it closed in 1928 moved to
California where he was employed as a
stand-in for actors playing artists. He
painted and drew but found his greatest popular success transposing famous
faces onto copies of famous paintings,
such as Greta Garbo masquerading as
Mona Lisa and W. C. Fields as Victoria
Regina. His serious paintings were also
successful and widely exhibited, bringing him honors including the John Barton Payne Medal for American paint-

ing. Born in San Francisco, he died
June 8, 1947 at age 52 in Hollywood.
Sets: **1929** *Top o' the Hill*

Marie Decker

Marie Decker collaborated on gowns
for a show on Broadway in 1917. A
dressmaker, she resided at 903 Sixth
Avenue, New York City in 1915 and
moved to 46 West 66th Street the fol-
lowing year. In 1920 she lived at 132
East 47th Street.
Costumes: **1917** *Lord and Lady Algy†*
(Miss Fenwick's gowns, after drawings by
Ben Ali Haggin)

J. Michael Deegan

Born on June 12, 1951 in Ridgeway,
Pennsylvania, John Michael Deegan
earned a B.F.A. at Carnegie Mellon
University. He began designing while
in high school, where he first created
sets for *You Can't Take It with You.*
His designs have been seen in productions by many organizations, including
the Cape Playhouse, The Acting Company, Houston Ballet, and the opera
companies of Boston, Atlanta, Columbus and Portland among others. He
credits his experience working with Helen Pond and Herbert Senn with his
success as a lighting designer. He is
married to Sarah G. Conley, a costume
designer and scene painter with whom
he often collaborates, especially on operas.
Lights: **1989** *The Circle* **1990** *Shadowlands*

William De Forest

William De Forest was responsible for
the design of the sets, lights and costumes for a play in 1948, and sets for
an additional production in 1949. At
the time of his death at age 67 in 1956,
he resided in Wiscasset, Maine.
Sets: **1948** *The Rats of Norway* **1949**
Diamond Lil†
Costumes: **1948** *The Rats of Norway*
Lights: **1948** *The Rats of Norway*

Edward DeForrest

Edward DeForrest designed costumes
for one play and sets for another in the
1940s.
Sets: **1943** *Victory Belles*
Costumes: **1946** *Apple of His Eye*

Guy DeGerald

Guy DeGerald designed costumes on Broadway in the 1920s.

Costumes: 1924 *Andre Charlot's Revue of 1924*† **1925** *By the Way*

De Guary

B. De Guary, who worked at one time as a designer on the staff of Eaves Costume Company, designed costumes for a Broadway play in the 1930s. The designers' home was located at 233 East 46th Street in the mid-1930s.

Costumes: 1930 *The Tyrant* (Miss Sinclair's and Mr. Cahern's costumes) **1931** *The Admirable Crichton* (Miss Bainter's gown); *Colonel Satan*† (Miss Landi's costumes); *The Great Barrington*† (Miss Cayube's gowns)

Ruth Deike

Ruth Deike collaborated on the costume designs for a show in 1916.

Costumes: 1916 *The Inca of Perusalem*

Edward Demmler

Edward Demmler designed lights for a Broadway production in 1922. He later worked at Radio City Music Hall where he was responsible for the hydraulics.

Lights: 1922 *Better Times*

Robert DeMora

Robert (Bob) DeMora studied in Connecticut at the Whitney School of Art and in New York at the Cooper Union School of Art. He is best known as a scenic designer, and has over 300 shows to his credit. His first assignment in the theater was at the Gretna Playhouse in Pennsylvania. He has designed both on and off Broadway, for stock companies, and at the Festival of Two Worlds in Spoleto. Additional designs include the 1988 production of *The Last Musical Comedy*.

Costumes: 1973 *Bette Midler* **1985** *Leader of the Pack*

Laurie Dennett

Laurie Dennett, a British designer of sets, studied at the Wimbledon School of Art and has designed many West End productions. In 1964 she was awarded the Royal Society of Arts Bursary for theatrical design. Credits include scenery and/or costumes for nu-merous plays at the Hampstead Theatre such as the 2000 production *The Good Samaritan*, and many designs in Manchester. She served as the theater designer for an arts complex in Chester, England created by architect Terry Farrell and Company in 1994.

Sets: 1981 *The Dresser*

W. W. Denslow

Although William Wallace Denslow illustrated many books during his career, he is best known for the original illustrations for *The Wonderful Wizard of Oz*, published in 1901. He was born in Philadelphia in 1858 and studied at Copper Institute and the National Academy of Design. He started his career in 1872 drawing illustrations for newspapers. He gradually worked more often as a book illustrator, mainly for children's books some of which he wrote or co-authored. His realistic yet fanciful style was equally well suited to theatrical design which he contributed to two Broadway productions. He collaborated on the stage version of *The Wizard of Oz* and had illustrated *The Pearl and the Pumpkin* when it was published in 1904, co-written with Paul West. W. W. Denslow, as he was known, died in 1915.

Sets: 1905 *The Pearl and the Pumpkin* **Costumes: 1903** *The Wizard of Oz*† (Character costumes) **1905** *The Pearl and the Pumpkin*

Jeanne Denson

JeanneDenson designed costumes on Broadway in the late 1920s.

Costumes: 1928 *Atlas and Eva*

Paul de Pass

Paul de Pass has used his artistry in a wide range of design activity including corporate presentations, museum exhibit design, scenery design for Broadway shows, regional theaters, opera, television, film, and commercial art direction. Among his work for industrials are those for Merck, Pfizer, Novartis and Miles Pharmaceuticals, BMW, Mercedes-Benz and Lincoln-Mercury. He designed IBM's Technology Center at the Atlanta Olympics and the Louis Vuitton Classic at Rockefeller Center's antique auto exhibit. Television projects include the re-design of QVC's facilities and the new BBC/Discovery Channel's *People & Arts* Network, for which he won the Broadcast Designers Association's International Gold Medallion Award. His museum work includes the design of *The Endurance* (1999 SEGD Award) and *Body Art: Marks of Identity*, both at the American Museum of Natural History. His theater and film designs are represented in the permanent collections of the McNay Museum in San Antonio, Texas and the Museum of the Moving Image in New York City. Over 100 television commercials include those for IBM, for which he won a CLIO Award for production design. He studied at the High School of Music and Art, Cooper Union, at Carnegie Mellon University (B.F.A. 1972), and Sarah Lawrence College.

Sets: 1979 *Oklahoma!*† 1980 *Brigadoon*† 1981 *Oh, Brother*† 1983 *The Tapdance Kid*† 1991 *Peter Pan*† **Lights:** 1982 *Cleavage*†

Anne De Paur

Anne DePaur designed costumes for one play in 1940.
Costumes: 1940 *Big White Fog*

Marion De Peu

Marion De Peu (De Pew) created costumes on Broadway in the mid-1920s. At that time she lived at 20 Charlton Street in New York City.
Costumes: 1925 *The Little Poor Man*

Connie DePinna

Artist Connie (Constance Gordon) De-Pinna, the daughter of Leo S. and Vivian DePinna, designed costumes for a play in 1937. Some of her original designs are in the Shubert Archive.
Costumes: 1935 *Jubilee*† 1937 *Three Waltzes*

Jane Derby

Jane Derby, a fashion designer, was born Jeanette Barr on May 17, 1895 in Rockymount, Virginia. She specialized in designs for petite women, and was president of her own firm, Jane Derby Inc., on 7th Avenue for 35 years. She occasionally contributed her designs to stage and films. Mrs. Derby died in 1965 at the age of 70.
Costumes: 1955 *Janus* (Miss Margaret Sullivan's clothes by)

Jack Derrenberger

Jack Derrenberger designed sets for one show in 1954.
Sets: 1954 *Hayride*

John Derro

John Derro began his involvement with costumes at the age of 17, working with the film designer Irene in Hollywood. He was born in 1926, and was active on Broadway in the late 1940s and the early 1950s. Additional designs include the road company for Sylvia Sidney's tour in *O Mistress Mine*.
Costumes: 1948 *Small Wonder*; *Town House* 1950 *Now I Lay Me Down to Sleep* 1951 *Glad Tidings* (Costume Supervisor)

Zoe de Salle

Zoe de Salle created gowns for a production in 1939. Madame de Salle was a fashion designer who exhibited small, but elegant collections of clothes. She concentrated on workmanship and simple sleek lines in her garments, through the 1940s.
Costumes: 1939 *Straw Hat Revue* (Miss Coca's gown)

John De Santis

An art director, production manager, scenic and lighting designer, John De Santis has worked extensively on the West Coast. He was Production Manager from 1968 to 1978 at the Mark Taper Forum, and has also worked for the Dallas Civic Opera and as art director for HBO. In 1984 he was Production Manager for the Olympic Arts Festival. Recent designs include scenery and lights for *Viva Vittorio!*, and lights for *Stand-Up Opera* at the Tiffany Theatre. He should not be confused with John Eugene DeSantis, the interior designer and magazine editor.
Lights: 1978 *A Broadway Musical*

Raymond Deshays

Raymond Deshays (Deshayes) was responsible for one set design on Broadway in 1939. In collaboration with Marc Henri, Laverdet, Jean Gabriel

Domergue and Arnaud he also created scenery for a revue on the London stage in 1921, *Fun of the Fayre*. His credits in France begin in 1910 with a production of *Faust* at the Odéon and continued with many productions for Opéra Comique through the 1920s, 1930s, 1940s, and 1950s, including *Le Jongleur de Notre Dame*, *Gargantua*, *George Dandin* and *Pelléas et Mélisande*. He also designed for le Chatelet and the Folies Bergère.

Sets: 1939 *Folies Bergère*†

Leopold De Sola

Leopold De Sola designed the ladies costumes for a play in 1931.

Costumes: **1931** *The Great Man*† (Ladies, Act II)

Frank Detering

Frank Detering was a lighting designer, active between 1911 and the early 1930s who had his own stage electrical business, where he created lights and mechanical effects. Just before his death in March 1939 he was working on the stage crew of *The Boys from Syracuse*, handling spotlights.

Lights: 1911 *The Pink Lady* **1912** *Oh! Oh! Delphine* **1913** *The New Henrietta*; *Ziegfeld Follies of 1913* **1920** *What's in a Name* **1927** *Romancing 'Round*; *Show Boat* **1931** *The Laugh Parade*

Kathleen Detoro

Kathleen Detoro was born in Norwalk, Connecticut, daughter of Dr. and Mrs. Fredric Detoro. She received a B.A. in design from the Pratt Institute and also trained at the Metropolitan Museum of Art in New York. While she has created costumes for plays, primarily on the West Coast, for A.C.T., the Pasadena Playhouse, and other theaters, it is as a designer for feature films and television that she is best known. Among the television series she has designed are *Get Real*, *The Boys are Back*, and *Ally McBeal*, among others. She was nominated for the Costume Designer's Guild 2000-2001 Award for Best Costume Design in a Contemporary Television Series, for Calista Flockhart's costumes in *Ally McBeal*. Movies include *Zelly & Me*, *Dead Man on Campus*, *Hard Rain*, and *Scream II*.

Costumes: 1992 *Solitary Confinement*

Lowell Detweiler

Lowell Detweiler was born on June 29, 1947 in Bucks County, Pennsylvania. He received an M.F.A. from New York University in 1973 and spent a season at the Guthrie Theatre as Resident Assistant, working with Desmond Heeley, John Jensen, Hal George and Carl Toms. In addition he assisted John Conkin for two years. His professional design debut occurred during the first season of Syracuse Stage with a production of *An Enemy of the People*. Mr. Detweiler, who designs sets in addition to costumes, is also a painter, and teaches on the faculty of the Tisch School of the Arts at New York University. He received a Daytime Emmy Award for his costume designs for *Square One TV* for the Children's Television Workshop in 1988, and has designed for the Houston Opera, Goodspeed Opera, American Stage Festival, the Criterion Theatre, Alabama Shakespeare Festival, Minneapolis Children's Theatre and the Moscow Central Theatre, among others.

Sets: 1989 *Starmites*

Costumes: 1978 *Tribute* **1986** *Corpse!*

A. Deutsch

Alexander Deutsch maintained a small costume house at 13 West 28th Street in New York City, as early as 1909. He resided at 344 West 88th Street.

Costumes: 1916 *The Yellow Jacket*

Michael Devine

Michael Devine, son of playwright Jerry Devine is Director of Exhibits and Creative Director of the Museum of Science and Industry in Chicago. He attended the School of Theatre at San Francisco State College where he majored in scene design. He has extensive credits for scenic design for film, theater, and television, principally on the West Coast, for theaters including the Mark Taper Forum, the Los Angeles Music Center, and South Coast Repertory. He has also designed at La MaMa E.T.C. and New Theatre For Now in New York City, the Cincinnati

Playhouse, Milwaukee Repertory Theatre, and for Théâtre du Soleil in Paris, among others. While working for Disney Imagineering, he was involved with projects throughout the United States.
Sets: 1970 *Paul Sills' Story Theatre*

Sophia Harris Devine
See Motley.

Ernest de Weerth
Ernest de Weerth began his career in the theater as an assistant stage manager at the Neighborhood Playhouse, and within six months was designing sets and costumes for the theater. He was born in Paris on August 21, 1894 to an American mother, Helene Baltzell, and a German father, for whom he was named. He studied at Eton and Oxford. During the rehearsals for *The Miracle* he was personal assistant to Max Reinhardt and continued to work with Reinhardt following that opening. Mr. de Weerth designed costumes for theater and film and wrote many articles on stage design. He died in Rome on March 29, 1967.
Sets: 1921 *The Great Way*; *The Trial of Joan of Arc* 1923 *Sandro Botticelli* 1926 *Kwan Yin* 1928 *'T Is to Blame for Everything*
Costumes: 1921 *The Great Way* 1923 *Sandro Botticelli* 1926 *Kwan Yin* 1927 *Grand Street Follies†* (Finale costumes); *A Midsummer Night's Dream* 1928 *'T Is to Blame for Everything*; *Peripherie* 1931 *Thais* (Miss Garden's costumes)

Frederica DeWolfe
Frederica DeWolfe designed costumes for plays during the first decade of the twentieth century. She designed contemporary garments for use as theatrical costumes and gowns for private customers, from a small custom shop called DeWolfe, Wachner and Company, Dressmakers. Her partner in the shop located at 23 West 45th Street in New York City, was Sophia Wachner. DeWolfe, who was born in Europe in August 1866, later worked from her home at 169 Claremont Avenue where she resided until the early 1920s. Referred to in playbills as both Mademoiselle Frederica DeWolfe and Madame

F. DeWolfe, she died in Los Angeles, California on February 27, 1955.
Sets: 1912 *Over the River* (as: DeWolfe, Wachner and Co.)
Costumes: 1907 *Comtesse Coquette* (as: Mlle. F. DeWolfe: Miss Nazimova's gowns); *The Lady from Lane's* (as: Mlle. Frederica DeWolfe) 1908 *The Prima Donna* (as: DeWolfe, Wachner and Co.: Dresses) 1909 *The Debtors†* (as: DeWolfe, Wachner and Co.: Gowns); *Old Dutch†* (as: DeWolfe, Wachner and Co.: Six sister's gowns) 1910 *A Skylark†* (as: DeWolfe and Co.) 1911 *Little Boy Blue* (as: DeWolfe, Wachner and Co.); *The Slim Princess†* (as: DeWolfe, Wachner and Co.: Gowns) 1913 *The American Maid* (as: DeWolfe, Wachner and Co.); *Iole†* (as: DeWolfe, Wachner and Co.: Gowns)

Elsie de Wolfe
Born Ella Anderson de Wolfe in New York on December 20, 1865, Miss Elsie de Wolfe was an actress, author, and interior decorator. As Lady Mendl (after marriage to Sir Charles Mendl in 1926) she was also a society leader. She was educated in Scotland after which she returned to the United States where she participated in amateur theatricals. Her professional debut was in 1891 with an appearance in Sardou's play *Thermidor*. Believing herself to be a mediocre performer, she left the stage in 1905 to become America's first female decorator and led a rebellion against drabness. In 1906 she established her reputation when she decorated the Colony Club, the first social club for women in New York City. She moved to France at the beginning of World War I and served at the Ambrine Mission caring for gas burn victims. When the war ended, she returned to New York, where her decorating business was located on 5th Avenue while she resided on Sutton Place, but then settled in Versailles. When World War II began, she moved to California. She returned to Versailles after the war, living there until her death on July 12, 1950 at the age of 84.
Sets: 1915 *Common Clay*; *Nobody Home*; *Very Good, Eddie* 1917 *Polly with a Past†* 1918 *Daddies*

Ray Diffen

Ray Diffen was born in Brighton, Sussex, England on February 28, 1922 and is known both as a costume designer and as a costumer. Head of his own costume house, Ray Diffen Stage Clothes, Inc. in New York he turned thousands of designs into reality. Prior to the opening of his costume house he was costumer for the Royal Shakespeare Company, the Old Vic, the Stratford (Ontario) Festival (from its opening in 1953 until 1959), and at the Guthrie Theatre in Minneapolis. He has also been influential in training others who create costumes from costume designs and served as mentor to numerous designers. At the 1999 Irene Sharaff Award presentations, he was honored by the Theatre Development Fund with their first-ever Benchmark Award, for contributions in costume technology.

Costumes: 1959 *Five Finger Exercise*† (Miss Tandy's clothes) 1960 *Under the Yum-Yum Tree* 1962 *The Fun Couple* 1963 *Andorra* 1964 *The Three Sisters*† 1966 *Dinner at Eight* 1974 *Noel Coward in Two Keys* 1976 *Home Sweet Homer*†

T. J. Digby

Thomas J., or T. J. Digby, who worked extensively in Great Britain initially worked with limelight before becoming an electrician. The term electrician remained common in the U.K. until the 1960s when it was slowly replaced with lighting designer. However, the functions of the electrician usually also included responsibilities for design. His credits in London, between 1910 and 1930. include *The Chocolate Soldier, A Pageant of Great Women, The Bird of Paradise* and *Let Us Be Gay*. On three occasions, productions he designed in England were transferred to Broadway, complete with his designs.

Lights: 1906 *Mauricette* 1910 *The Girl in the Taxi* 1927 *The Wandering Jew*

Leon Di Leone

Leon Di Leone, a scenic and lighting designer, was resident designer for Playhouse on the Mall, Paramus, New Jersey from 1969 to 1972 and from 1974 to 1976. He also designed the first national tour of *Jesus Christ Superstar*.

Lights: 1975 *Angel Street* 1976 *Wheelbarrow Closers*

Eileen Diss

Eileen Diss is a British designer of theater, film and television. She was born on May 13, 1931 and studied at the Central School of Art and Design. She designed for the British Broadcasting Corporation from 1952 to 1959 including series, operas adapted for television, and films. Other television credits include all the episodes of *Jeeves and Wooster* for Masterpiece Theatre. At the Royal National Theatre in London her credits begin with the 1976 production of *Blithe Spirit* and have continued regularly since then. She has designed most of Harold Pinter's plays, beginning with *Exiles* in 1969 in the West End and at the Gate Theatre, and the Pinter Festival at Lincoln Center in summer 2001. Feature films include *Secret Places*, Pinter's *Betrayal* in 1982, *84 Charing Cross Road*, and *A Handful of Dust*. She has been much honored for television design, winning the BAFTA in 1962, 1965, 1974, and 1992. In private life she is known as Mrs. Raymond Everett.

Sets: 1972 *Butley* 1977 *Otherwise Engaged*

M. Dobuzhinsky

Mstislav Valerianovich Dobuzhinsky (Dobujinsky) was born in St. Petersburg in 1875 and studied at the Imperial Russian Academy of Fine Arts before beginning his career as a designer of sets and costumes with Meyerhold in 1907. He designed ballets produced by Diaghilev, including *The Fairy Doll* for Anna Pavlova. With the onset of the Russian Revolution he left Russia for Lithuania and began working for theaters in Dresden, Prague, Brussels, and London. In 1939 he joined Michael Chekhov's Theatre in New York. He also designed sets and costumes for other companies in the United States and Canada, for the Metropolitan Opera Company in the 1940s and 1950s, including *Boris Gudonov* and *Un Ballo in Maschera*, and productions for the New York City Opera, such as *The Love for Three*

Oranges. Mr. Dobuzhinsky died on November 21, 1957 at age 82 in New York City.

Sets: 1927 *Chauve Souris*† 1930 *A Month in the Country* 1939 *The Possessed* 1941 *Anne of England*
Costumes: 1930 *A Month in the Country* 1941 *Anne of England*
Lights: 1941 *Anne of England*

Peter Docherty

Peter Docherty, a British designer of sets and costumes, was born on June 21, 1944 in Blackpool, England. He trained at the Central School of Art and Design and at the Slade School of Fine Art, after which he specialized in dance (especially ballet), collaborating regularly with the choreographers Peter Darrell and Eric Hynd. He has also designed operas and concert shows. He has taught at the Wimbledon School of Art and at Central Saint Martins College of Art and Design and exhibited his paintings and designs in many locations. He is the author of the profusely illustrated *Design for Performance.*
Sets: 1977 *Side by Side by Sondheim*

John Dodd

John P. Dodd was a lighting designer with many credits for dance companies, rock bands and theaters. He designed for the Harkness Ballet Company, La MaMa E.T.C., Theatre Genesis and was lighting director of the Living Theatre in the 1980s. Founder and president of 14th Street Stage Lighting, Inc. in New York, his off-Broadway credits included *Buried Child* in 1979. John Dodd died on July 14, 1991 in New York City.
Lights: 1972 *Inner City*

Dodge and Castle

The scenic design studio Dodge and Castle was formed by D. Frank Dodge and William E. Castle and operated at 241 West 62nd Street in New York City. They collaborated on several productions between 1911 and 1921, and then again in 1934 as well as painting the scenery for many additional productions for other designers. Both D. Frank Dodge and William E. Castle also designed scenery under their own names.

Sets: 1911 *The Littlest Rebel* 1912 *Bachelors and Benedicts*; *Elevating A Husband*; *Freckles*; *The Master of the House*†; *Modest Suzanne*; *The Opera Ball*; *Ready Money*; *The Rose Maid*; *The Woman-Haters*† (Acts I, II) 1913 *Her Little Highness*; *The Madcap Duchess*; *The Master Mind*† (Act I); *Rachel*† (Painted); *Sweethearts* 1914 *The Crinoline Girl*; *The Governor's Boss*; *Maria Rosa*; *A Mix-Up*†; *A Pair of Sixes* 1915 *90 in the Shade*; *A Full House*† 1916 *The Co-Respondent*; *Fast and Grow Fat*; *Getting Married* 1917 *Broken Threads*; *Friend Martha*; *Her Regiment*; *His Little Widows*†; *The Lodger*; *Over the 'Phone*; *When Johnny Comes Marching Home*† 1918 *Another Man's Shoes*; *Daddy Long Legs*; *Ladies First*† 1919 *An Exchange of Wives*†; *Good Morning, Judge*; *She's a Good Fellow* 1920 *French Leave*; *Frivolities of 1920*; *Kissing Time*; *The Night Boat*; *Oh, Henry*; *Tip Top*† 1921 *Transplanting Jean* 1934 *The Only Girl*

D. Frank Dodge

D. Frank Dodge designed numerous productions under his own name (as D. Frank Dodge and simply as Dodge) between 1900 and 1911, and then was partner with William E. Castle in the scenic studio Dodge and Castle, which was active between 1914 and 1934. He also had scenic design credits prior to 1900, including *Rob Roy* in 1894, *An American Beauty* in 1896, and *The Belle of New York* in 1897 (in collaboration with Ernest Albert) which was also successful in London the following year. He died in Burlingame, California in April, 1952.

Sets: 1899 *Papa's Wife*† (Acts I, III) 1900 *The Belle of Bohemia*†; *Broadway to Tokio*†; *The Cadet Girl* (Acts I, II, Scenes 1,2 and III, Scenes 1,2); *The Casino Girl*†; *Her Majesty, the Girl Queen of Nordenmark*†; *A Million Dollars*† (Act I, Scenes 2, 3); *Quo Vadis*; *Sweet Anne Page*; *Woman and Wine*† 1901 *Lovers' Lane*†; *The New Yorkers*†; *The Strollers*; *Vienna Life*† (Act I) 1902 *A Chinese Honeymoon*; *The Defender*; *Fad and Folly*† (Act II); *Heidelberg*; *Sally in Our Alley*†; *Tommy Rot*† (Act II); *When Johnny Comes Marching Home*† (Act I); *The Wild Rose* 1903 *Blonde in Black*; *Cynthia*;

The Runaways; *There and Back* **1904** *In Newport†*; *Lady Teazle†* (Act I); *The Maid and the Mummy*; *Olympe†*; *Sergeant Kitty*; *Taps* **1905** *The Duke of Duluth†* (Act I); *The Earl and the Girl†*; *Fantana†*; *The Mayor of Tokio†* **1907** *Genesee of the Hills*; *A Knight For A Day*; *The Lady from Lane's†*; *The Top o' th' World†* **1908** *Salvation Nell†*; *School Days* **1909** *A Broken Idol*; *The Debtors* **1910** *The Deacon and the Lady*; *The Other Fellow*; *The Spring Maid* **1911** *Jumping Jupiter†* (Act III); *Little Miss Fix-It†* (Act I); *Mrs. Bumpstead-Leigh*

M. Paul Dodge

M. Paul (Michael Paul) Dodge designed scenery for a production on Broadway in 1927. An artist, he resided at 2441 Seventh Avenue, New York City in the teens and twenties. In the early 1930s, he relocated to California where he designed sets for Metro-Goldwyn-Mayer for eighteen years. He died on September 16, 1953 at the Motion Picture Country Home in California.

Sets: 1927 *The Comic*

Peter Dohanos

S. Peter Dohanos was a scenic designer for television, film, and theater and a watercolor painter. He was born in Cleveland, Ohio in 1930, the son of the artist Steve Dohanos. He grew up in Westport, Connecticut and graduated from Dartmouth. He designed many films including *Diary of a Mad Housewife*, and was active in television, notably as art director for *The Kraft Television Theatre* and as production designer for the *Bell Telephone Hour*. Dohanos died in East Hampton, New York on December 26, 1988.

Sets: 1959 *Kataki* **1980** *Tricks of the Trade*
Lights: 1980 *Tricks of the Trade*

Judith Dolan

Judith Dolan was born in Baltimore, Maryland and attended Towson State College where she considered a career in acting and Stanford University where she received an M.F.A. and studied with Douglas Russell. After finishing graduate school, she moved abroad and for five years was head of the costume department at the Abbey Theatre in Dublin. In the United States she has designed costumes for television, and film, as well as numerous productions for theaters including The Acting Company, American Repertory Theatre, the New York City Opera, The Shakespeare Theatre, and off-Broadway. Honors include a Tony Award for *Candide* and a Lucille Lortel Award for *The Petrified Prince*. In addition to her prolific career as a costume designer, she is Professor of Design, University of California, San Diego. She also continues her own training, receiving a PhD from Stanford in 1996 in Directing/Design, studying directing with Carl Weber.

Costumes: 1981 *Merrily We Roll Along* **1982** *Joseph and the Amazing Technicolor Dreamcoat* **1997** *Candide* **1998** *Parade*

Robin Don

Robin Don, originally from Fife, Scotland, studied engineering and sculpture in Edinburgh before becoming a design assistant to Ralph Koltai with whom he worked for ten years. Since his professional debut with *Four Little Girls* at Open Space in the late 1960s, he has designed sets and costumes for numerous plays throughout the U.K., operas throughout the world, and ballets, notably in London, Scotland, and Chile. His set for *The Winter Guest* was much honored receiving the London Critics' Circle Award. When the British entry won the Golden Troika Award at the Prague Quadrennial in 1979 and again in 1983, his designs for opera were included.

Sets: 1992 *Someone Who'll Watch over Me*
Costumes: 1992 *Someone Who'll Watch over Me*

Stephen Doncaster

Stephen Doncaster, a British designer who trained at the Old Vic School, has worked for many theaters including the Royal Shakespeare Company, the Royal Court and the English Stage Company. He has designed sets and supervised costumes for commercial television in England for series such as

The Avengers, Private Eye and Red-cap. Additional designs by Mr. Don-caster have been seen at the Notting-ham Players, Glasgow Citizens' The-atre, the Actor's Company, the Royal Exchange Theatre, and in London's West End. For many years, he was head of design training at Nottingham College of Art and Design, which he co-founded with Patrick Robertson.

Sets: 1958 *Epitaph for George Dillon*
Costumes: 1981 *The Dresser*

Mary Jo Dondlinger

Mary Jo Dondlinger, who earned her undergraduate degree at Berra Col-lege in Lake Forest, Illinois, where she studied with Craig Miller, made her Broadway debut in 1989. Her credits off-Broadway and in regional theaters are extensive, and include productions at the Goodspeed Opera House, the York Theatre Company, the Great Lakes Shakespeare Festival, the Amer-ican Shakespeare Theatre and Lamb's Theatre. She also designed the na-tional tour of *The Fantasticks* star-ring Robert Goulet, *Sleeping Beauty* for Boston Ballet, and *The Nutcracker* at the Wang Center. Among her twenty-first century designs is light-ing for *Roadside* for the York Theatre Company.

Lights: 1989 *Sweeney Todd* 1990 *The Miser*; *Zoya's Apartment* 1991 *Get-ting Married*; *On Borrowed Time*; *Taking Steps* 1992 *Anna Karenina* 1995 *The School for Scandal*

Captain Cushing Donnell

Captain Cushing Donnell wrote a play that was produced on Broadway in 1929 for which he also designed the sets and costumes. Captain Donnell was said to be the first American to discharge a firearm in the First World War. He also wrote *Shadows of the Cross* which was produced in Dublin. He was born Murray Cushing Donnell in Maine on July 7, 1886 and died in Orange County, California on May 31, 1951.

Sets: 1929 *Chinese O'Neill*
Costumes: 1929 *Chinese O'Neill*

Candice Donnelly

Candice Donnelly received her M.F.A. from the Yale School of Drama in 1985, where one of her classmates was direc-tor Michael Engler, who has become a frequent collaborator. Her profes-sional debut with the Yale Repertory with costumes for *Fences* and *What the Butler Saw*. Since then she has been especially busy designing in re-gional theaters (Berkeley Repertory, Center Stage, Williamstown Theatre Festival, American Repertory Theatre, McCarter Theater Center, City Center Stage I, etc.), off-Broadway (Gramercy Theatre, Vineyard Theatre, Public Theatre, Playwrights Horizons, Classic Stage Company) and for films (*Frogs for Snakes, Alchemy*). As Artist-in-Residence, she teaches costume design and rendering at Brandies University.

Costumes: 1987 *Fences* 1989 *Master-gate* 1991 *Our Country's Good* 1992 *Search and Destroy* 1996 *Hughie*

Vyvian Donner

Vyvian Donner was an authority on women's fashion and wrote a monthly column for the Washington D.C. mag-azine, *The Diplomat*. Between 1932 and 1962 she created one minute fash-ion commentaries on newsreels for the Fox Movietone News. Ethel Trapha-gen, whom she met while studying art at Cooper Union, encouraged her to consider a career in fashion. One of the early female members of United Scenic Artists, she occasionally designed sets as well as costumes, and generally worked in collaboration with other de-signers. The program for *Ned Way-burn's Town Topics* in 1915 states that she designed "A Number of Effective Principal and Chorus Costumes" read-ing more like a review than playbill copy. Miss Donner, who died in 1965 at the age of 65 also designed theatrical posters.

Costumes: 1915 *Ned Wayburn's Town Topics*† (Some principals, and chorus cos-tumes) 1916 *Ziegfeld Follies: 1916*† 1926 *The Desert Song*†

Richard Dorfman

Richard Dorfman was born in Colorado Springs, Colorado on February 2, 1955.

He received a Bachelor of Arts in theater arts at Drew University in 1978 and a Master of Fine Arts at New York University in 1981. Richard Dorfman's first professional design was for *'Cause Maggie's Afraid of the Dark*, written and directed by Howard Ashman for the WPA Theatre in New York City in February 1978. Off-Broadway credits include designs for the Irondale Ensemble Project where he was Resident Designer from 1983 to 1986. From 1980 to 1986 he designed thirty-one productions as Resident Lighting Designer for the New Jersey Shakespeare Festival. He was nominated for an American Theatre Wing Design Award in 1987 for *The Life of the Land*, produced at the Pan Asian Repertory Theatre. He is not to be confused with the sports and business executive who has the same name.
Lights: 1980 *Of the Fields, Lately*

John Dos Passos

Novelist John Dos Passos also wrote and designed plays. He was born on January 14, 1896 in Chicago and died on September 28, 1970. He received a Bachelor of Arts degree from Harvard in 1916. In the 1920s he was very active, traveling, painting with watercolors, writing plays, novels, poetry, and pamphlets and even designing scenery. Most of his talents, however, were devoted to writing, producing thirty books including *District of Columbia* and the acclaimed trilogy *U.S.A.* Interestingly his scenic designs were not limited to his own plays, although he did design scenery for all of his own plays that were produced in New York during his lifetime.
Sets: 1926 *The Moon Is a Gong*† **1927** *The Belt; Centuries* **1928** *The International* **1929** *Airways, Inc.*

Jay Doten

Jay Doten was the playwright and scene designer for a play produced at the Provincetown Playhouse in 1934.
Sets: 1934 *Green Stick*†

Cynthia Doty

Costume designer Cynthia Doty who earned her B.F.A. degree at Emerson College, started her association with Zack Brown in 1980, assisting him on over forty productions, mainly operas, around the world. During that same time, she also developed her own career, designing costumes for productions at Circle in the Square (*Ghetto*, *The Devil's Disciple*, etc), for Washington Opera, including *Goya*, and in film. She has designed for the Santa Fe Opera, Barter Theatre, and the Chelsea Theatre Company.
Costumes: 1990 *Zoya's Apartment*†

Gladys Douglas

Gladys Douglas designed the gowns for a show in 1932. Two women with that name resided in New York City in the mid-1930s, according to the 1933-1934 Manhattan and Bronx City Directory. One lived at 140 West 103rd Street and the other at 217 West 129th Street.
Costumes: 1932 *Blackberries of 1932* (Gowns)

Wade Douglas

Wade Douglas was a scenic designer in the teens and twenties. He was associated with the Joseph Physioc Studios. He should not be mistaken for the writer D. Elaine Hall who uses the name as one of her pseudonyms.
Sets: 1919 *Thunder* **1921** *Thank You; The Wheel*

Wayne Dowdeswell

British lighting designer Wayne Dowdeswell has designed many productions for the Royal Shakespeare Company, both in Stratford-upon-Avon and in London at the Barbican. He has worked often with Terry Hands, as director and co-designer, including *The Seagull* and *Tamburlaine the Great*. Widely known as a pyrotechnic expert, he has also designed for the Tricycle Theatre in London and the Newcastle Playhouse. His lighting designs for *Medea* were nominated for a Laurence Olivier Award when the production was performed in London before being brought to New York.
Lights: 1994 *Medea*

Julius F. Dowe

Julius F. Dowe, a painter, worked on a Broadway production in 1910. He maintained a studio and residence at

213 E. 59th Street in New York. With Theodore Reisig, he ran the scene shop at the Manhattan Opera House at the time the play was produced.

Sets: 1910 *Naughty Mariettat*

Edward Duryea Dowling

Edward Duryea Dowling was a lighting, costume and scenic designer as well as a director and producer for the Shubert Organization. For the Federal Theatre Project he served for a short time as director of vaudeville, with headquarters in New York City and responsibility for touring companies of comedy, vaudeville and circus performers. During World War II he was a Sergeant Major in change of theater activities in London for the Special Services Division, and also directed a show for the United Service Organizations to entertain troops in Iceland. Prior to directing plays he was a dialogue director for Paramount Pictures in the early days of talking movies. He died on December 18, 1967 at age 63.

Lights: **1939** *Streets of Paris* **1941** *Sons o' Fun*

Madame Dowling

The theatrical designer Madame Mary L. Dowling, was known in private life as Mrs. Burt Haverly. She was the proprietor of a small costume business located at 154 West 44th Street in New York City where she mainly executed costumes for other designers. She died in 1916.

Costumes: **1904** *Paris by Night* **1905** *A Yankee Circus on Marst*

Hans Dreier

Hans Dreier was a prolific art director for motion pictures. He won three Academy Awards, in 1950 for *Sunset Boulevard* in the black and white category and *Samson and Delilah* in the color category, and in 1945 for *Frenchman's Creek* among many nominations. At Paramount Studios he was supervising art director from 1927 to 1950, working often with Rouben Mamoulian and Cecil B. DeMille. A native of Germany, he was born on August 21, 1885 in Bremen and studied architecture and engineering at Munich University. He served in the German Army

during World War I, beginning his film career in Berlin prior to coming to the United States in 1921. He died on October 24, 1966 in Bernardsville, New Jersey at the age of 71.

Sets: **1929** *The Marriage Bed*

Marie Dressler

Marie Dressler was born Leila Marie Koerber on November 9, 1969 in Cobourg, Ontario, Canada and began her career on stage in 1886, appearing in *Under Two Flags*, adopting as her stage name that of a German aunt. She made her New York debut in 1892 in *The Robber of the Rhine* quickly becoming one of the best known stage actresses in America. Although successful in London and New York, she had problems with her health and didn't pursue her desire to manage her own theater, moving instead to California where she met Mack Sennet and began to appear in films. With the advent of talking pictures she became a star, appearing in *Anna Christie* in 1930, winning an Academy Award in 1931 for *Min and Bill*, followed by many more. The author of an autobiography, *The Life Story of an Ugly Duckling*, published in 1924, she was known in private life as Mrs. J. H. Dalton. She died on July 28, 1934 in Santa Monica, California.

Sets: **1913** *All Star Gambol* (Also starred) **1914** *A Mix-Upt* (Also starred and directed)

Costumes: **1913** *All Star Gambolt* (Also starred)

Henry Dreyfuss

Henry Dreyfuss was a set designer who also designed theater interiors. Born in New York City in 1904 he designed numerous sets for plays on Broadway, occasionally also designing the costumes and lights as well as the interiors of theaters. He also worked as art director for companies which presented films. As an industrial designer, he formed Henry Dreyfuss and Associates to manufacture and merchandise products. He died a suicide with his wife, Mrs. Doris Marks Dreyfuss, on October 5, 1972. He was 68.

Sets: 1912 *The Talker* 1924 *Two Strangers from Nowhere* 1926 *Beau Gallant*; *Beau-Strings* 1927 *The Manhatters* 1928 *Hold Everything* 1929 *Remote Control* 1930 *An Affair of State*; *Blind Mice*; *The Boundary Line*; *Fine and Dandy*; *A Kiss of Importance*; *The Lily and the Prince*; *Pagan Lady*; *Sweet Stranger*; *This Is New York* 1931 *The Cat and the Fiddle*; *The Gang's All Here*; *The Man on Stilts*; *Philip Goes Forth*; *Shoot the Works* 1933 *Strike Me Pink* 1934 *Continental Varieties* 1935 *Continental Varieties*; *Paths of Glory*
Costumes: 1912 *The Talker* 1927 *The Manhatters* 1928 *The Merry Wives of Windsor* 1930 *An Affair of State*†
Lights: 1931 *Shoot the Works*

Joseph F. Driscoll

Joseph F. Driscoll was born in Pennsylvania and lived at 27 Watts Avenue in New York City in 1901 and at 578 East 163rd Street in 1909. He worked as a clerk when he was in his teens, before joining the executive staff at Wallack's Theatre as an electrician. Driscoll migrated to California to work in the movie industry, and died in Los Angeles on September 23, 1962.
Lights: 1910 *Getting a Polish* 1911 *Disraeli* 1912 *Disraeli*

Helen Dryden

Helen Dryden was born in Baltimore, Maryland on November 26, 1887 and studied with Ethel Traphagen and at the Pennsylvania Academy of Fine Arts. She was known for magazine illustrations, covers, and posters, as well as stage designs. She designed costumes on Broadway between 1917 and 1921, and also did automobile designing. Some of the covers she did for *Vogue*, *Vanity Fair* and *The Delineator* were included in the 1984 exhibit "The Feminine Gaze: Women Depicted by Women, 1900-1930" at the Whitney Museum of American Art in Stamford, Connecticut. Helen Dryden died in 1934.
Sets: 1914 *Watch Your Step*†
Costumes: 1917 *Jack O'Lantern*† (Costumes) 1919 *The Rose of China*† (Miss Richardson's costumes) 1920 *Sophie* 1921 *Captain Applejack*† (Miss Nash's Act II costume)

Pierre Du Bois

Pierre Du Bois created costumes for a featured player in a 1936 Broadway show.
Costumes: 1936 *The Case of Clyde Griffiths* (Miss Barker's clothes)

Raoul Pène Du Bois

Raoul Pène Du Bois launched his career on Broadway in 1930 with the design of one costume for *Garrick Gaieties*. This design was the beginning of fifty years creating creative and colorful costumes, imaginative sets, and occasional lighting designs. He trained briefly at the Grand Central Art School, but coming from a family rich in artistic heritage his natural talents found ready employment in theater and films. His grandfather, Henri Pène Du Bois, was an art and music critic; his uncle, Guy Pène Du Bois, a painter; and cousin, William Pène Du Bois, a book illustrator. He received a Tony Award for the costumes for *No, No, Nanette* in 1973 and a Tony Award for set design in 1953 for *Wonderful Town*. In addition to his Broadway credits he designed in London and Paris. Raoul Pène Du Bois' costumes and scenery graced films, ice shows, ballets, night clubs, aquacades, the Rockettes, and commercial illustrations. He was born in November 29, 1914 on Staten Island and died in New York on January 1, 1985 at age 72. In 1999, Theatre Development Fund honored his achievements as a designer with its' Irene Sharaff Posthumous Award.
Sets: 1934 *Thumbs Up*† 1939 *Du Barry Was a Lady*; *One for the Money* 1940 *Hold onto Your Hats*; *Panama Hattie*; *Two for the Show* 1941 *Liz the Mother*; *Sons o' Fun* 1948 *Heaven on Earth*; *Lend an Ear* 1950 *Alive and Kicking*; *Call Me Madam* 1951 *Make a Wish* 1952 *In Any Language*; *New Faces of 1952* 1953 *John Murray Anderson's Almanac*; *Maggie*; *Wonderful Town* 1954 *Mrs. Patterson* 1955 *Plain and Fancy*; *The Vamp* 1956 *Bells Are Ringing* 1957 *Ziegfeld Follies* 1963 *Student Gypsy, or The Prince of Liederkrantz* 1964 *P.S. I Love You* 1971 *No, No, Nanette* 1973

Irene 1975 *Doctor Jazz* 1979 *Sugar Babies*

Costumes: 1930 *Garrick Gaieties*† 1934 *Keep Moving*†; *Life Begins at 8:40*†; *Ziegfeld Follies: 1934*† 1935 *Jumbo*† 1936 *Ziegfeld Follies: 1936*† (Costumes for 'Red Letter Day" and "Of Thee I Spend") 1937 *Hooray for What!* 1938 *Leave It to Me!* 1939 *Du Barry Was a Lady*; *Leave It to Me!*; *One for the Money*; *Too Many Girls* 1940 *Hold onto Your Hats*; *Panama Hattie*†; *Two for the Show* 1941 *Liberty Jones*; *Sons o' Fun* 1943 *Carmen Jones* 1945 *Are You with It?*; *The Firebrand of Florence* 1948 *Heaven on Earth*; *Lend an Ear* 1950 *Alive and Kicking*; *Call Me Madam*† 1951 *Make a Wish* 1952 *In Any Language* 1953 *Maggie*; *Wonderful Town* 1954 *Mrs. Patterson* 1955 *Plain and Fancy*; *The Vamp* 1956 *Bells Are Ringing* 1957 *The Music Man*; *Ziegfeld Follies* 1959 *Gypsy* 1963 *Student Gypsy, or The Prince of Liederkrantz* 1964 *P.S. I Love You* 1968 *Darling of the Day* 1971 *No, No, Nanette* 1973 *Irene*† 1974 *Gypsy* 1975 *Doctor Jazz* 1979 *Sugar Babies* 1980 *Reggae* 1989 *Jerome Robbins' Broadway*†

Lights: 1948 *Lend an Ear*

Madame Dubosc

Madame Dubosc designed costumes for Miss Ellen Terry in a production that originated in London and then was performed in 1905 on Broadway. The name Dubosc was a common one among performers in movies at the beginning of the twentieth century. Both Andre Dubosc (1865-1935) and Gaston Dubosc (1860-1941), originally from France, appeared in many films.

Costumes: 1905 *Alice Sit-by-The-Fire*† (Miss Terry's costumes)

Caroline Dudley

Caroline Louise Carter Dudley was born in Lexington, Kentucky on June 10, 1862 and reared in Ohio. After nine years of marriage and the birth of one son she divorced Leslie Carter, became an actress and retained his name for stage use, appearing as Mrs. Leslie Carter. David Belasco created *The Heart of Maryland* and other plays for her which proved to be great successes. After losing Belasco's support

she moved to England for a time, returning occasionally to the New York stage. Her career never regained the level of success achieved under Belasco and they did not work together again. She died in Santa Monica, California on November 13, 1937. Caroline Louise Carter Dudley should not be confused with Gertrude Lady Dudley (1879-1952), a British actress who used the stage name Gertie Millar.

Sets: 1917 *The Claim*†; *Peter Ibbetson*†

Costumes: 1917 *The Claim*† (Also accessories); *Hamilton*† (Costume Supervisor); *Peter Ibbetson*†

John H. M. Dudley

Retired army officer Colonel John H.M. Dudley died at the age of 77 on August 25, 1954 in Elizabeth, New Jersey. He was born Henry Carter in Bristol, England, the son of two musicians. He came to Boston in 1895, becoming a citizen in 1901. Beginning in theater as an actor, he established a business in Elizabeth, New Jersey for architecture, theatrical scene painting and clay modeling in 1902, one of many varied activities in his life. From 1932 to 1954, he served as director of the Board of Freeholders of Union County, New Jersey.

Sets: 1910 *Tillie's Nightmare* 1919 *Nothing But Love*† 1922 *The Monster*

William Dudley

William Dudley, a British painter and designer of sets and costumes, has credits for a wide range of theater and opera pieces, beginning with *Hamlet* for the Nottingham Playhouse in 1970 and including five years in residence with the Royal Court Theatre in London. He was born on March 4, 1947 in London and studied marine painting at St. Martin's School of Art, the Slade School of Art and with Nicholas Georgiadis. He first worked in amateur theater as a scene painter and actor. He gradually began designing and working with professional theaters in the West End, for the Royal National Theatre and the Royal Shakespeare Company. He designed a new production of *Der Ring der Nibelungen*, directed by Peter Hall in 1984 at Bayreuth, the set-

ting for *Billy Budd* at the Metropolitan Opera, and *Dance of the Vampires* for Roman Polanski in Vienna. Other credits in the United States include sets and costumes for *Lucia Di Lammermoor* at the Lyric Opera of Chicago. His seven Olivier Awards (to date) are for the sets of *The Merry Wives of Windsor*, *The Mysteries*, *The Rise and Fall of Little Voice*, *Dispatches*, *Mary Stuart*, and *All My Sons*, and the costumes for *Amadeus*.
Sets: 1990 *Cat on a Hot Tin Roof* **1999** *Amadeus*
Costumes: 1999 *Amadeus*

Lady Duff Gordon

See Lucile.

C. B. DuMoulin

C. B. DuMoulin designed sets for a Broadway play in the mid-1920s.
Sets: 1925 *The Fall of Eve*†

Boyd Dumrose

Boyd Dumrose designed the scenery for the long-running daytime drama *Loving*, which required eighty-five working sets. He received his degree in theater arts from the University of California, Los Angeles and began in the theater as an actor. He moved to New York City in 1957 and subsequently served as a design assistant to George Jenkins and Robert Randolph. Among his honors is a 1984 design award from the Broadcast Designers Association for the television movie that launched *Loving*.
Sets: 1969 *Three Men on a Horse*

Clarke Dunham

Clarke Dunham is a prolific designer of both sets and lighting, with more than three hundred productions to his credit. He received a Marharam Award for *The Me Nobody Knows*, Tony nominations for the settings for *End of the World* and *Grind* and has worked often with Harold Prince. He designs extensively in regional theaters such as the Goodman. Awards include a Jefferson Award for *Twentieth Century*. Additional credits include numerous operas, such as the New York City Opera production of *Candide*, *Madame Butterfly* at the Lyric Opera of Chicago, and design and direction of *Das Liebesverbot*

at the 1983 Waterloo Festival. In the early 1990s his designs for model railroads were featured in an exhibit at the Barnum Museum in Bridgeport, Connecticut, and since then at The Station at Citicorp Center. Raised on Philadelphia's Main Line, he is married to the poet, playwright, and lyricist Barbara Tumarkin Dunham.
Sets: 1970 *The Me Nobody Knows*; *A Place for Polly* **1973** *The Iceman Cometh*; *The Waltz of the Toreadors* **1976** *Bubbling Brown Sugar* **1984** *End of the World*; *Play Memory* **1985** *Grind* **1987** *Late Nite Comic* **1997** *Candide*
Lights: 1967 *The Girl in the Freudian Slip*; *The Ninety-Day Mistress* **1970** *The Me Nobody Knows*; *A Place for Polly* **1977** *Something Old, Something New*

Eugene Dunkel

Eugene B. Dunkel (also known as Evgenii Borisovich Dunkel) was a set designer and mural painter born on April 30, 1890 in Verny (Alma-Ata), Russian Turkestan. He studied painting in Moscow, and in St. Petersburg and Vilna, where he also worked in the theater. After leaving Russia he came to the United States where he designed sets and built and painted the scenery for the Ballet Russe de Monte Carlo from 1930 to 1940. He had his own studio, E.B. Dunkel Studios, where he executed his own work and that of other designers. He designed and executed sets for many designers and companies, including the American Ballet and the Ballet Moderne and also for television and opera. He died in Pelham, New York at age 81 in April 1972.
Sets: 1933 *One Sunday Afternoon*; *The Scorpion* **1934** *Fools Rush in*† **1937** *The Fireman's Flame*; *Naughty Naught '00* **1938** *Bridal Crown*; *The Girl from Wyoming* **1940** *The Man Who Killed Lincoln* **1942** *The Chocolate Soldier* (as: E.B. Dunkel Studios)

Timothy Dunleavy

Timothy Dunleavy graduated from the North Carolina School of the Arts, and started his career as a fashion designer creating children's clothes for Bloomingdale's, Bergdorf Goodman, and Bonwit Teller. He has created collections for fashion magazines, including Seventeen and Glamour, and a "Barbie Fashion Show." His off-Broadway credits include *Veronica's Room* and *Livin' Dolls*. In the early 1990s, he began designing children's clothing.

Costumes: 1983 *Breakfast with Les and Bess*

John Dunn

Costume designer John Dunn was born in 1953. He studied at the University of Illinois where he majored in theater and the Art Students League where he took courses in drawing. He counts Rita Ryack, with whom he co-designed the film *Casino* as well as Santo Loquasto and William Ivey Long among his mentors. His list of credits for made-for-television movies and major motion pictures is long and includes *City of Hope, Basquiat, Mr. Wonderful, Whispers in the Dark, The Object of My Affection* and *Ghost Dog: The Way of the Samurai*. Twenty-first century credits include Todd Solondz's *Storytelling* which was first shown at the 2000 Cannes and New York Film Festivals. He is not to be confused with the sound editor who has the same name.

Costumes: 1985 *Benefactors*

Thomas F. Dunn

Thomas F. Dunn designed sets in 1920 for a production on Broadway. In 1924 he designed *Bunty Pulls the Strings* with Sydney Cook in London. An architect, he had studios in New York City in 1922. He is not to be confused with the vaudeville actor (1850-1914) who had the same name.

Sets: 1920 *Don't Tell*

Jacques Dupont

Jacques Dupont designed sets and costumes for ballets, operas and plays in the United States, France and England. He was born in Charou, France on January 16, 1909 and died in Paris on April 21, 1978. His debut in Paris was scenery for *La Sonate des Spectres* in 1934 at the Rideau de Paris where he subsequently designed many more productions. He also designed for the Opéra Comique, Théâtre de

la Reine (Versailles), Festival d'Aix-en-Provence, Théâtre Hébertot and the Festival de Bordeaux. Additional New York productions include *Faust* and *Carmen*, directed by Jean-Louis Barrault at the Metropolitan Opera.

Sets: 1963 *Phaedre* 1965 *La Grasse Valise*

Costumes: 1963 *Phaedre* 1965 *La Grasse Valise*†

Paul du Pont

Paul du Pont was born in Bradford, Pennsylvania, the son of an opera singer and a chemist. Originally trained to be a singer, he changed to painting and then to ballet. A serious fall through an open trap door while on tour with a ballet troupe cut short his dancing career. His first costume designs were for ballet, after which he designed for the Group Theatre and the Theatre Guild. In addition to the theater, he designed extensively for television, including the Sid Caesar–Imogene Coca Variety series. Mr. du Pont died on April 20, 1957 at age 51.

Sets: 1951 *Diamond Lil*

Costumes: 1936 *Johnny Johnson* 1939 *The Time of Your Life* 1940 *Another Sun; The Fifth Column; Retreat to Pleasure; The Time of Your Life* 1942 *All Comforts of Home; The Chocolate Soldier; A Kiss for Cinderella; Let Freedom Sing; Porgy and Bess; The Strings, My Lord, Are False; The Time, the Place, and the Girl* 1943 *The First Million; One Touch of Venus; Porgy and Bess* 1944 *Anna Lucasta; Porgy and Bess; Pretty Little Parlor* 1949 *Diamond Lil* 1950 *All You Need Is One Good Break; Parisienne* 1951 *Diamond Lil* 1953 *Oh, Men! Oh, Women!* (Costume Supervisor)

Lights: 1951 *Diamond Lil*

Eugene Dupuis

Eugene Dupuis collaborated on a lighting design in 1905.

Lights: 1905 *The Mayor of Tokio*†

Tony Duquette

Tony Duquette was born Anthony Michael Duquette in Los Angeles on June 11, 1914 and designed for the most part on the West Coast. He created costumes for numerous plays, operas and ballets. His extensive involvement with films was in many areas, including sets, costumes, and properties, including sculptures. Other areas of design included interiors, furniture, stage curtains, and jewelry. His paintings were exhibited in one-man shows in California, and he also created so-called 'celebrational environments.' When Gilbert Adrian died at the beginning of the production process of *Camelot* he had done preliminary costume designs for the play. Tony Duquette, one of Adrian's close friends, accepted the challenge and responsibility for completing the costume designs for that show at the request of the producers. His efforts were rewarded with a Tony Award for outstanding costume design, shared posthumously with Adrian. He died September 9, 1999 at age 85 in Los Angeles.

Costumes: **1960** *Camelot†*

Duke Durfee

Duke Durfee was born on September 9, 1952 in Wheaton, Illinois and received a B.A. degree from Mankato State College, as well as an M.F.A. from Pennsylvania State University where he studied with Anne A. Gibson. After completing college he held an his internship at The Guthrie Theatre although his first design was *The Tempest* at Mankato State. He moved to New York in 1981 to assist Karl Eigsti and Lawrence Miller and has worked since then on Broadway and in regional theaters. He designs videos, industrial promotions, commercials and films such as *The Flamingo Kid* for which he was art director.

Sets: **1989** *Metamorphosis*

DuWico

DuWico Lighting Equipment Company was formed by Gus Durkin and Harol Williams and operated at 313 West 41st Street. The name DuWico was prevalent in hundreds of Broadway playbills and is included in this volume as an example of suppliers of equipment also supplying aesthetic values.

Lights: **1919** *Penny Wise* **1923** *In the Palace of the King* **1925** *Don't Bother*

Mother; *Easy Terms*; *Fool's Bells*; *Kosher Kitty Kelly* **1926** *Castles in the Air*; *Chicago*; *The Half-Caste†*; *Head or Tail*; *The Matinee Girl*; *Old Bill, M.P.*; *Sunshine*; *Wooden Kimono* **1927** *10 Per Cent*; *Excess Baggage*; *Judy*; *Madame X*; *Off-Key*; *The Spider*; *Talk about Girls* **1928** *The Clutching Claw*; *Divorce a La Carte*; *Present Arms*; *Skidding*; *The Spider*; *Spring 3100*; *The Street Wolf*; *Veils* **1929** *Dinner Is Served*; *Messin' 'Round*; *The Silver Swan* **1930** *Light Wines and Beer*; *So Was Napoleon* **1931** *Here Goes the Bride* **1933** *Humming Sam*; *The Lady Refuses*; *The World Waits* **1936** *All Editions*; *Victoria Regina†* **1938** *Spring Thaw* **1939** *George White's Scandals* **1940** *Separate Rooms* **1942** *Janie*; *A Kiss for Cinderella*; *You'll See the Stars* **1943** *Try and Get It* **1947** *For Love or Money*; *I Gotta Get Out*; *The Magic Touch* **1948** *Don't Listen Ladies*; *The Hallams* **1949** *Diamond Lil*; *Gayden*; *The Ivy Green*; *Love Me Long*; *Metropole*

Harry Dworkin

Harry Dworkin designed sets in 1944 for a single production on Broadway.

Sets: **1944** *Slightly Scandalous*

John Dwyer

John T. Dwyer was an actor who occasionally contributed set designs while appearing in roles in the 1920s. Off-Broadway stage appearances included parts in *Over the Hill to the Poor House* in 1920 and *Jack O'Hearts* and *The Man in the Shadow* in 1926. Dwyer was born in 1877 and died on December 7, 1936.

Sets: **1922** *Billeted* **1926** *Nic Nax of 1926*

Chris Dyer

Christopher (Chris) Dyer is a British designer of scenery and costumes, who was born February 2, 1947. After attending the Ravensbourne College of Art and Design in Bromley he worked as a scene painter at the Bristol Old Vic from 1971 to 1973, and subsequently worked at Stratford-upon Avon with Hayden Griffin, Abd'el Farrah and John Napier. Since 1975, as Associate Designer for the Royal Shakespeare Company, he has designed numerous productions including new plays such as *The Bundle* and classic works such as *The Roaring Girl, The Winter's Tale* and *Macbeth*. Designs for opera include productions at La Scala, the Scottish Opera, and the Royal Opera House. He has also designed at the Stratford (Ontario) Festival and for the English Shakespeare Festival.

Sets: 1989 *The Merchant of Venice*
Costumes: 1989 *The Merchant of Venice*†

Michael Eagan

Michael Eagan is a Canadian set designer who occasionally designs costumes. He was born in St. Stephen, New Brunswick in 1942 and studied at the University of New Brunswick and at the National Theatre School where he taught scenography from 1987 to 1998. His designs have been seen in all the major Canadian theaters (Shaw Festival, Stratford Festival, etc.), all as well as in and around New York City. He was nominated for Dora Mavor Moore Awards for set design for *Albertine, En Cinq Temps,* and for costume design for *The Mystery of Irma Vep.* His designs have been exhibited in Toronto and Montreal.

Sets: 1980 *Happy New Year*

Holmes Easley

Holmes Easley is a set designer with credits at the Roundabout, the GEVA Theatre, the Asolo Theatre and many other off-Broadway and regional theaters. He was born September 24, 1934, in San Saba, Texas, and studied with Freda Powell at Sul Ross College in Texas and with Donald Oenslager at the Yale Drama School. His initial professional design was the set for *Anastasia* at the Alley Theatre in Houston in 1957. He taught stage design at Stanford University and at Colgate University after completing his own degree at Yale. For the past twenty years he has been set decorator for *The Guiding Light* and *As the World Turns* as well as for many other productions at CBS-TV.

Sets: 1973 *The Play's the Thing*

Howard Eaton

Howard Eaton is a British lighting designer, whose work appeared on Broadway in 1979. As the owner of Howard Eaton Lighting Ltd., he provides technological advances to theaters, including radio remote modules at the Guildhall School of Music and Drama. While designing lights for numerous productions in London's West End and Britain's regional theaters, he devised technical solutions that he now provides to others as a consultant. He used this expertise to help create the specialized lighting for *Sunset Boulevard* in London in 1994. He lectures frequently, including seminars sponsored by the Association of British Theatre Technicians.

Lights: 1979 *Dogg's Hamlet, Cahoot's Macbeth*

Arthur Ebbetts

Arthur Ebbetts (Ebbets) designed lighting on Broadway between 1917 and 1918 and sets on Broadway in 1924. He worked as a stage director in the late teens, and in the early 1930s worked as a stage manager, residing at 4611 Spuyten Duyvil Parkway in New York City.

Sets: 1924 *The Main Line*
Lights: 1917 *Why Marry?*† 1918 *Why Marry?*†

Marsha L. Eck

Marsha L. Eck works mainly as a set designer for opera, often in collaboration with Tito Capobianco. Their joint work includes *Manon* and *Lucia di Lammermoor* at the New York City Opera and *Falstaff* at the Chilean National Opera. Her designs have been seen at Circle in the Square, at the New York Shakespeare Festival for *The Corner* and *The Children,* and at the Juilliard School of Music and Drama Theatre. Married to costume designer Joseph G. Aulisi, she participated in the 1994 Mount Holyoke College Symposium, "Women in Design."

Sets: 1969 *Trumpets of the Lord* 1972 *Mourning Becomes Electra* 1973 *Molly*

William and Jean Eckart

Beginning with sets and lights for *Glad Tidings* and *To Dorothy a Son* in 1951,

William and Jean Eckart provided designs for some of Broadway's most popular shows. William Eckart was born in 1920 in New Iberia, Louisiana and received a B.S. in architecture from Tulane University in 1942 and an M.F.A. in stage design at Yale in 1949. He married Jean Levy in 1943 and they had two children. Jean Eckart was born in Chicago on August 18, 1921 and received a B.F.A. at Newcomb College and an M.F.A. at Yale. Most of their design work for theater, film, television and industrial productions was done jointly. Their design credits were generally for scenery and lighting, but occasionally they also contributed costumes to productions. In 1954 they received the Donaldson Award for *The Golden Apple* for their scenery. They relocated to Texas in 1971 to join the faculty at Southern Methodist University. In 1976 Jean Eckart returned to school herself, receiving an M.S.W.S. from the University of Texas at Arlington. From 1978 to 1986 she worked in the mental health field at the Community Psychotherapy Center in Dallas, as well as in private practice, but continued as well to give lectures on theatrical design. Jean Eckart died on September 6, 1993. William Eckart continued to teach at S.M.U. until 1991 when he retired, although he continued to design occasionally, including a production for the Colorado Shakespeare Festival and one for *The Illusion* in 1999. He died on January 23, 2000 in Dallas.

Sets: 1951 *Glad Tidings*; *To Dorothy, a Son* 1952 *Gertie* 1953 *Dead Pigeon*; *Oh, Men! Oh, Women!* 1954 *The Golden Apple*; *Portrait of a Lady*; *Wedding Breakfast* 1955 *Damn Yankees* 1956 *Li'l Abner*; *Mister Johnson* 1957 *Copper and Brass* 1958 *The Body Beautiful* 1959 *Fiorello* 1960 *Viva Madison Avenue* 1961 *The Happiest Girl in the World*; *Let It Ride!*; *Take Her, She's Mine* 1962 *Never Too Late* 1963 *Here's Love*; *Oh Dad, Poor Dad, Mamma's Hung You...*; *She Loves Me* 1964 *Anyone Can Whistle*; *Fade Out-Fade In* 1965 *Fade Out-Fade In*; *Flora, the Red Menace*; *The Zulu and the Zayda* 1966 *Agatha Sue, I Love You*; *Mame* 1967

Hallelujah, Baby! 1968 *The Education of H.Y.M.A.N. K.A.P.L.A.N.*; *Maggie Flynn* 1969 *The Fig Leaves Are Falling* 1970 *Norman, Is That You?* 1974 *Of Mice and Men*

Costumes: 1955 *Damn Yankees* 1956 *Mister Johnson* 1959 *Fiorello* 1974 *Of Mice and Men*

Lights: 1954 *Portrait of a Lady*; *Wedding Breakfast* 1956 *Li'l Abner* 1957 *Copper and Brass* 1958 *The Body Beautiful* 1959 *Fiorello* 1960 *Viva Madison Avenue* 1961 *The Happiest Girl in the World*; *Let It Ride!*; *Take Her, She's Mine* 1962 *Never Too Late* 1963 *She Loves Me* 1964 *Fade Out-Fade In* 1965 *Fade Out-Fade In*; *The Zulu and the Zayda* 1966 *Agatha Sue, I Love You* 1974 *Of Mice and Men*

Eddie Eddy

Edward J. Eddy was a set designer on Broadway in the 1920s and 1930s. He worked as a laborer in the teens and resided at 1267 Park Avenue in 1915.

Sets: 1927 *Love in the Tropics* 1928 *Potiphar's Wife* 1929 *Broken Dishes*; *The Come-on Man*; *A Comedy of Women*; *Indiscretion*; *The Patriarch*; *The Town's Woman* 1930 *Nancy's Private Affair*; *Room 349*; *Room of Dreams*; *Troyka* 1931 *Privilege Car* 1932 *Singapore* 1933 *Late One Evening* 1934 *The First Legion* 1935 *This Our House*

Alfredo Edel

Before designing costumes, mainly for musical revues on the Broadway stage, Alfredo Edel designed productions at La Scala, for theaters in London and at the Paris Opera and Comédie Française. The first costumes he designed in the United States were for a pageant, *America*, at the Chicago World's Fair in 1893, and those in the early years of the twentieth century were generally acknowledged in playbills as coming from "M. Alfredo Edel, 10 Avenue des Tilleuls, Villa Montmorency, Paris" which added to their glamour. He designed many productions at the New York Hippodrome, including *Romance of a Hindoo Princess*, the *Four Seasons*, *The Land of the Birds*, and *The Ballet of the Butterflys*. He also designed for the Metropolitan

Opera. He occasionally worked in collaboration with his wife, a portrait and miniature painter. The July 4, 1944 New York Times obituary for Mrs. Florence Atherton Edel, refers to her as his widow.

Costumes: 1905 *A Society Circus*†; *A Yankee Circus on Mars*† 1908 *Algeria*; *The Land of the Birds*; *Ziegfeld Follies of 1908*† 1909 *Ziegfeld Follies of 1909*† 1910 *Ziegfeld Follies of 1910*† 1911 *Around the World*

Ruth Edell

Ruth Edell supervised the costumes for a Broadway production in 1934. She was an actress who appeared in *Smile at Me* on Broadway in 1935, and at the Brighton Theatre, Brighton Beach in 1937 in *Behind Redlights.*

Costumes: 1934 *Piper Paid*† (Costume Supervisor)

Serge Edgerly

Serge Edgerly designed one set on Broadway in 1932.

Sets: 1932 *The Tree*

Kate Edmunds

Kate Edmunds was born in Detroit, Michigan on March 20, 1952. She received a B.F.A. from Wayne State University where she studied drawing, painting and printmaking, and received an M.F.A. from the Yale School of Drama. An admirer of the work of Boris Aronson, she continued her study of design through an apprenticeship with Tony Straiges and then designed scenery on the regional theater circuit, with additional credits off and off-off Broadway. In the mid-1990s, she relocated to California where she has been in residence at both the Berkeley Repertory Theatre and American Conservatory Theatre and also teaches at the University of California at Berkeley. A frequent collaborator with Sharon Ott and Carey Perloff, her designs have been much honored, primarily with Drama Logues on the West Coast.

Sets: 1980 *Charlie and Algernon*

Andy Edwards

British costume designer Andy Edwards, who has designed extensively in the United Kingdom, is also amassing credits in the United States. His designs in the West End include productions for the Reduced Shakespeare Company, *Side by Side by Sondheim* and *Saturday Night Fever* which originated at the London Palladium. He designed costumes for the extravaganza *EFX* at the M-G-M Grand in Las Vegas and the twenty-first century television series *The Vice*. He should not be confused with American arts administrator Andrew Edwards.

Costumes: 1999 *Saturday Night Fever*†

Ben Edwards

Ben Edwards, born George Benjamin Edwards in Union Springs, Alabama on July 5, 1916, studied in New York City at the Feagin School of Dramatic Arts, the Kane School of Art, and through association with Gordon Craig, Robert Edmond Jones and Jo Mielziner. He first designed sets and lights at the Barter Theatre in Abingdon, Virginia and first designed on Broadway in 1938. One of the most active Broadway designers of the twentieth century, his credits for settings, lighting design, and occasionally costumes were extensive in the theater, for television and feature films. Mr. Edwards also produced plays. Married to the costume designer Jane Greenwood, one of his two daughters is Sarah Edwards, also a costume designer. Ben Edwards, who was awarded the Tony Lifetime Achievement Award in 1998 died on February 12, 1999.

Sets: 1938 *Cap't Jinks of the Horse Marines*; *Coriolanus*; *Diff'rent*; *No More Peace*; *Pygmalion* 1940 *Another Sun* 1947 *Medea* 1948 *Sundown Beach* 1949 *Diamond Lil*† 1950 *Captain Brassbound's Conversion* 1952 *Sunday Breakfast*; *The Time of the Cuckoo* 1953 *The Remarkable Mr. Pennypacker* 1954 *Anastasia*; *Lullaby*; *The Traveling Lady* 1955 *The Honeys*; *Tonight on Samarkind* 1956 *The Ponder Heart*; *Someone Waiting* 1957 *The Dark at the Top of the Stairs*; *The Waltz of the Toreadors* 1958 *The Disenchanted*; *Jane Eyre*; *A Touch of the Poet*; *The Waltz of the Toreadors* 1959 *God and Kate Murphy*; *Heartbreak House* 1960 *Face of a Hero*; *A Second String*

1961 *The Aspern Papers*; *Big Fish, Little Fish*; *Midgie Purvis*; *Purlie Victorious*; *A Shot in the Dark* 1962 *Harold* 1963 *The Ballad of the Sad Cafe* 1964 *Hamlet* 1965 *The Family Way*; *A Race of Hairy Men* 1966 *How's the World Treating You?*; *Nathan Weinstein, Mystic, Connecticut*; *Where's Daddy* 1967 *More Stately Mansions* 1969 *The Mother Lover* 1970 *Hay Fever*; *Purlie* 1972 *Purlie* 1973 *Finishing Touches*; *A Moon for the Misbegotten* 1976 *A Matter of Gravity*; *A Texas Trilogy* 1977 *An Almost Perfect Person*; *Anna Christie*; *A Touch of the Poet* 1981 *To Grandmother's House We Go*; *The West Side Waltz* 1982 *Medea* 1984 *Death of a Salesman* 1985 *The Iceman Cometh* 1988 *Long Day's Journey into Night* 1989 *A Few Good Men* 1990 *A Christmas Carol* 1991 *Park Your Car in Harvard Yard* 1992 *The Show-Off*; *A Streetcar Named Desire* 1996 *A Thousand Clowns*

Costumes: 1938 *Cap't Jinks of the Horse Marines*; *Coriolanus*; *Diff'rent*; *No More Peace*; *Pygmalion* 1950 *The Bird Cage*; *Legend of Sarah* 1952 *Desire under the Elms*; *Sunday Breakfast* 1953 *The Emperor's Clothes*; *The Remarkable Mr. Pennypacker* 1954 *Anastasia*; *The Traveling Lady* 1957 *The Waltz of the Toreadors* 1958 *A Touch of the Poet*; *The Waltz of the Toreadors*

Lights: 1950 *Captain Brassbound's Conversion* 1952 *The Time of the Cuckoo* 1954 *Anastasia*; *Lullaby*; *The Traveling Lady* 1955 *Tonight on Samarkind* 1956 *The Ponder Heart*; *Someone Waiting* 1957 *The Waltz of the Toreadors* 1958 *Ages of Man*; *A Touch of the Poet*; *The Waltz of the Toreadors* 1959 *God and Kate Murphy*; *Heartbreak House* 1960 *Face of a Hero*; *A Second String* 1961 *The Aspern Papers*; *Big Fish, Little Fish*; *Midgie Purvis*; *Purlie Victorious*; *A Shot in the Dark* 1962 *Harold* 1965 *The Family Way*; *A Race of Hairy Men* 1966 *How's the World Treating You?*; *Nathan Weinstein, Mystic, Connecticut*; *Where's Daddy* 1969 *The Mother Lover* 1970 *Hay Fever* 1973 *Finishing Touches*; *A Moon for the Misbegotten* 1976 *A Texas Trilogy* 1977 *An Almost Perfect Person*; *Anna Christie*; *A Touch of the Poet*

Hilton Edwards

Hilton Edwards, actor and director, was born in London on February 2, 1903 and is best known for founding (with Michael MacLiammoir) the Dublin Gate Theatre in 1928, where he produced and directed over three hundred plays. His first stage appearance was with the Charles Doran Shakespeare Company in 1920, after which he joined the Old Vic in London. He came to the United States in 1948 and designed lighting for two plays which he directed and in which he also appeared. While in America he was involved in additional productions and worked in television. Hilton Edwards died on November 18, 1982 in Dublin.
Lights: 1948 *The Old Lady Says "No"*; *Where Stars Walk*

Jack Edwards

Jack Edwards was born in Easton, Pennsylvania, on December 29, 1934 and studied at Pennsylvania State University and Ithaca College. Theatre design training was received at Lester Polakov's Studio and Forum of Stage Design. His first costume designs were for a play which he also wrote, *Queen Wilheminia's Lover* produced in Stockerton Junction, Pennsylvania. He was costume director at the Guthrie Theatre for eighteen years, during which time he also designed costumes in New York and other locations around the U.S. His designs for *A Christmas Carol* were used for a remarkable twenty-one seasons at the Guthrie Theatre, from 1975 through 1995. Since 1991, he has been the costume designer for Dayton Department Store's annual holiday auditorium show, creating productions of *The Adventures of Pinocchio*, *Beauty and the Beast* and *Puss in Boots* among others, using three-dimensional figures, many of them animated. He also directs for the Boston Early Music Festival, including *Ercole Amante* and *L'Orfeo*.
Costumes: 1967 *What Did We Do Wrong?*

Norman Edwards

At age 15, Norman Edwards began making and sketching clothes while attending art school and by age 17 was designing professionally in New York City. He had couture businesses in New York and London where he designed gowns for film, stage and private customers, including Myrna Loy and Ginger Rogers. A four time winner of the American Fashion Competition, he also designed cars, jewelry and furs.

Costumes: 1943 *Try and Get It*

Sarah Edwards

Costume designer Sarah Josephine Edwards, daughter of costume designer Jane Greenwood and scenic designer Ben Edwards (1916-1999), received her B.A. Degree from Sarah Lawrence College in 1986, after which she studied at Lester Polakov's Studio and Forum of Stage Design. While beginning her own career as a designer, she served as an assistant. She has designed off-Broadway and for television.

Costumes: 1989 *Tru*

Larry Eggleton

William Lawrence Eggleton was born in 1920 and became a member of United Scenic Artists in 1949. He died on September 16, 1990. While he sometimes designed for theater, he devoted his talents to commercials and television, working at one time for the Columbia Broadcasting System.

Sets: 1950 *Black Chiffon*

Peter M. Ehrhardt

Peter M. Ehrhardt has designed lights for numerous productions at the Goodspeed Opera House, including plays that later transferred to Broadway. He was born in Elizabeth, New Jersey on February 21, 1950, the son of Peter L. and Ardel Leimbach Ehrhardt. Although he began designing in high school with *West Side Story*, he studied engineering in college. He received design training through courses at the Lester Polakov Studio and Forum of Stage Design, and by association with Jean Rosenthal and Thomas Skelton. He has also designed at the Juilliard School, the New Jersey Shakespeare Festival, the New Jersey Institute of Technology and at the Hartt School of Music. The recipient of the Carbonel Award from the Southern Florida Critics Association, in addition to being a freelance designer, he is a full-time electrician at NBC-TV, where his assignments include *Late Night with Conan O'Brien*.

Lights: 1975 *Very Good, Eddie* **1976** *Going Up* **1979** *Whoopee* **1987** *Sally*

Karen Eifert

Karen Eifert was born March 25, 1950 in Pittsburgh, Pennsylvania, and received a B.A. from Miami University in 1972, where she studied with Jean L. Druesedow who later became head of the Costume Institute at the Metropolitan Museum of Art. She then moved to New York and in 1972 designed *The Maid's Tragedie* at Equity Library Theatre. Although Karen Eifert continues to design, mainly off-off-Broadway and for industrials, she has been wardrobe supervisor for several Broadway productions, including the *Best Little Whorehouse in Texas, Joseph and the Amazing Technicolor Dreamcoat, She Loves Me,* and *Ipi Tombi*.

Costumes: 1981 *Hey, Look Me Over!* (Costume Coordinator)

Karl Eigsti

Karl Eigsti was born on September 19, 1938 in Goshen, Indiana and studied at Indiana and American Universities and at the School of Visual Arts in New York City. In 1964 he received an M.A. from Bristol University in England while on a Fulbright Award. He first designed sets professionally for *Billy Budd* at Arena Stage in 1964 and first designed costumes professionally at the Guthrie Theatre in 1968 for *Sgt. Musgrave's Dance*. He has designed sets for over two hundred productions on and off-Broadway and in regional theaters, worked as an art director for television productions and taught design at New York University, SUNY-Purchase and Brandeis University where he is head of the design. Awards include the Maharam Award and a Tony nomination for *Knock-Out* in 1979, a Los Angeles Drama Critics Award in 1986 for *Tartuffe* and a Helen Hayes in 1988 for *Les Blancs*. Recent credits include *Collected Stories* at the Huntington Theatre, *The*

Taming of the Shrew at the Delacorte Theatre, and *Valparaiso* in Cambridge, Massachusetts.

Sets: 1970 *Henry V*; *Inquest*; *Othello* 1974 *Yentl* 1975 *Sweet Bird of Youth* 1977 *Cold Storage* 1978 *Eubie*; *Once in a Lifetime* 1979 *Knockout*; *Murder at the Howard Johnson's* 1980 *The American Clock* 1982 *Almost an Eagle*; *Joseph and the Amazing Technicolor Dreamcoat*; *The World of Shalom Aleichem* 1983 *Amen Corner* 1984 *Accidental Death of an Anarchist*; *Alone Together*

Costumes: 1977 *Cold Storage* 1982 *Almost an Eagle*

Lou Eisele

Lou Eisele has worked both as a costume designer and as an assistant to costume designers for plays and circus shows. He was born in 1912 in New York City and studied at the Art Students League and at the Art Institute of California and with many individual instructors. Mr. Eisele has taught design courses, and written books about drawing and design. His extensive credits as a costume designer include operettas, operas, ice shows, night clubs, television, the theater and the circus.

Costumes: 1944 *Follow the Girls* 1945 *The Girl from Nantucket*; *A Lady Says Yes*; *Star Spangled Family*; *Too Hot for Maneuvers* 1947 *Caribbean Carnival*; *Icetime of 1948*†; *A Young Man's Fancy* (Costume Supervisor) 1948 *My Romance*

Peggy Eisenhauer

Peggy Eisenhauer was born in New York City on April 24, 1962, the daughter of Ray and Bebe Eisenhauer. She has a sister, Lyn, who is an architect. She received a B.F.A. from Carnegie Mellon University in drama and counts Bob Olson, Jules Fisher and Stephen Bickford as mentors. She began designing at age fifteen with *American Hurrah* for the Elmwood Playhouse in Nyack, New York and has designed lighting for many productions, including tours for the Cars, Billy Ocean, Lisa Lisa and other performers; the *New Chita Rivera Cabaret-Revue*; and the concert films *Cyndi Lauper in Paris* for Home Box Office, *Hearts of Fire* starring Bob Dylan, and *Michael Jackson*

for Pepsi-Cola. She is perhaps best known, however for her work collaborating, both with Jules Fisher (through Third Eye Studio) with whom she has been co-designing for several years, and with whom she shares a Tony Award for *Bring in 'da Noise, Bring in 'da Funk* among many nominations, and with Mike Baldassari.

Lights: 1989 *Dangerous Games* 1991 *Catskills on Broadway* 1992 *Tommy Tune Tonite! A Song and Dance Act*† 1993 *Angels in America, Part II: Perestroika*†; *Angels in America: Millennium Approaches*† 1994 *Best Little Whorehouse Goes Public, The*†; *A Christmas Carol*† 1996 *Bring in 'da Noise, Bring in 'da Funk*†; *A Christmas Carol*† 1997 *A Christmas Carol*†; *Street Corner Symphony*† 1998 *Cabaret*†; *A Christmas Carol*†; *Ragtime*† 1999 *The Gershwins' Fascinating Rhythm*; *Marie Christine*† 2000 *Jane Eyre*†; *The Wild Party*†

Vasser Elam

Vasser Elam created one lighting design on Broadway in 1929.

Lights: 1929 *White Flame*

Eldon Elder

Eldon Elder, a setting and lighting designer who occasionally contributed costumes to plays and operas, was born on March 17, 1921 in Atchison, Kansas. He studied at Kansas State Teachers College (now Emporia State College) with Professor R. Russell Porter and at the University of Denver. After receiving an M.F.A. from Yale in 1950, he assisted one of his mentors in New Haven, Donald Oenslager, for a year. His first professional designs were for the Provincetown Playhouse in 1949 with his first designs on Broadway following soon after. He designed sets, costumes and lights for many of the New York Shakespeare Festival's productions in the Belvedere Lake Theatre in the late 1950s and early 1960s. Mr. Elder also consulted on the design of theaters. At the invitation of the Chinese Stage Decoration Institute he toured China and lectured while on a Guggenheim Foundation grant. Mr. Elder, who died on December 11, 2000 in New York City was the author of

Will It Make a Theatre? and *Eldon Elder: Designs for the Theatre.*

Sets: 1951 *Legend of Lovers*; *The Long Days* 1952 *The Grey Eyed People*; *Hook 'n Ladder*; *Time Out for Ginger* 1953 *Take a Giant Step* 1954 *The Girl in Pink Tights*; *One Eye Closed* 1955 *All in One*, *Trouble in Tahiti*; *The Heavenly Twins*; *Phoenix '55*; *Twenty Seven Wagons Full of Cotton*; *The Young and Beautiful* 1956 *Fallen Angels* 1957 *Shinbone Alley* 1962 *The Affair*; *The Fun Couple* 1965 *Mating Dance* 1967 *Of Love Remembered* 1974 *James Whitmore in Will Rogers' U.S.A.* 1976 *Music Is* 1989 *Hizzoner*

Costumes: 1974 *James Whitmore in Will Rogers' U.S.A.*

Lights: 1951 *The Long Days* 1952 *The Grey Eyed People*; *Time Out for Ginger* 1953 *Take a Giant Step* 1954 *The Girl in Pink Tights*; *One Eye Closed* 1955 *All in One*, *Trouble in Tahiti*; *The Heavenly Twins*; *Twenty Seven Wagons Full of Cotton* 1956 *Fallen Angels* 1962 *The Affair*; *The Fun Couple* 1967 *Of Love Remembered* 1974 *James Whitmore in Will Rogers' U.S.A.*

Marianna Elliott

Marianna Elliott has many credits for costume design in the leading regional theaters throughout the U.S., including the Mark Taper Forum, and Arena Stage where she is resident designer. A graduate of Parsons School of Design, her film designs include *Whose Life Is It Anyway?*, *American Flyer*, and *Ballad of a Sad Cafe*. Much honored for her designs she received two Los Angeles Drama Critics Circle Awards, a Distinguished Artist Award from the Los Angeles Music Center 100, and several Drama-Logue Awards among others. Twenty-first century designs include *QED* in the Vivian Beaumont Theatre, Lincoln Center.

Costumes: 1997 *Play On!*

Charles Ellis

Charles Ellis started his career as a scenic artist for Provincetown Playhouse but soon turned his attention to acting. He appeared in *Ambush*, *Diff'rent*, *Valley Forge*, *Key Largo*, and the 1932 production of *Showboat* among others. After a career on the stage, he became an abstractionist painter. An exhibit of his paintings in 1935 in New York featured still lifes, watercolors and portraits. Charles Ellis was married to the actress Norma Millay, a sister of Edna St. Vincent Millay. He died on March 11, 1976 at age 83.

Costumes: 1919 *Greenwich Village Follies*† (Javanes and batik)

Chris Ellis

Chris Ellis, a British lighting designer, has long been associated with the Leicester Theatre Trust as lighting designer and production manager, even serving a year's term as acting theater director. He has lit many productions in the West End, for the Royal Shakespeare Company, the Royal National Theatre, the Hong Kong Arts Festival, the Netherlands Opera, the Scottish Opera, and the Welsh National Opera. A member of the Society of British Designers, he designed the lighting installation for the new Haymarket Theatre. Additional credits in the United States include *H.M.S. Pinafore* at the Shubert Performing Arts Center in New Haven, Connecticut. He should not be confused with the American actor who has the same name.

Lights: 1986 *Me and My Girl*

Melville Ellis

Melville Ellis was born in San Francisco and worked in the theater in many capacities. He performed in vaudeville, was an accomplished pianist and had an act that he performed with Irene Bordoni. He occasionally put his artistic talents to work for the Shubert Organization designing entire productions for them, including the costumes, and occasionally also writing music and lyrics. An energetic and creative force, he was generally acknowledged in playbills as "Mr. Melville Ellis" along with a statement that he had designed and personally overseen the execution of the design elements. The 1915 playbill for *Maid in America* states that he designed the costumes and scenery, but that they were "Borrowed from Everybody." Illness forced Mr. Ellis to leave the Palace Theatre on March 27, 1917 during a performance. He died less than a week later of typhoid fever on April 4, 1917, at about 41 years of age.

Costumes: 1908 *Marcelle*; *Mlle. Mischief*; *Mr. Hamlet of Broadway* 1909 *Belle of Brittany*; *The Girl and the Wizard* 1910 *The Girl and the Kaiser*†; *The Jolly Bachelors*; *The Prince of Bohemia*; *Tillie's Nightmare*; *Up and Down Broadway* 1911 *The Balkan Princess*†; *The Duchess*; *The Kiss Waltz*; *Vera Violetta* 1912 *All for the Ladies*; *Broadway to Paris*†; *The Passing Show of 1912*; *Patience* 1913 *All Aboard*; *The Beggar Student*†; *The Geisha*; *Iolanthe*; *Joseph and His Brethren*; *Lieber Augustin*; *The Man with Three Wives*; *The Passing Show of 1913* 1914 *Dancing Around*; *Experience*†; *The Midnight Girl*; *The Passing Show of 1914*†; *Pretty Mrs. Smith*† (Other gowns); *The Whirl of the World* 1915 *Cousin Lucy*; *Maid in America*†; *Maid in America*†; *Miss Information*; *Very Good, Eddie* (Costume Supervisor)

Todd Elmer

Todd Elmer was born in Staten Island, New York on November 21, 1956 and received an M.F.A. at Boston University in 1978. He spent several years in New York as a lighting designer working off-Broadway at the Juilliard School, the Manhattan School of Music, the School of American Ballet, the Harold Clurman Theatre and the Astor Place Theatre, among others. He assisted designers such as Thomas Skelton, Craig Miller, Richard Nelson, and Paul Gallo on Broadway shows. After touring with various productions he became lighting supervisor for the American Ballet Theatre in 1988. He also spent three years a production stage manager for an ice skating company and designed lights for the 1983 Bermuda Festival.

Lights: 1979 *The Price*

Elsie and Camille

Elsie Winch and Camille Gabrielson were dressmakers who worked from a small salon on the third floor at 47 West 5th Street in the mid-1930s. In addition to serving private customers, in 1931 they collaborated on the costume designs for a Broadway play.

Elsie Winch lived at 47 West 56th Street.

Costumes: 1931 *After All*

Joseph Elsner

Joseph Elsner (also known as Ellsner) was active on Broadway in the teens and twenties. An electrician, he resided at 140 West 109th Street, New York, New York.

Lights: 1907 *Hip! Hip! Hooray!* 1908 *The Battle in the Skies* 1909 *A Trip to Japan* 1914 *Wars of the World* 1915 *Hip-Hip-Hooray* 1917 *Cheer-up (Hippodrome)* 1918 *Everything* 1920 *Good Times*

Charles Elson

Charles Elson was born on September 5, 1909 in Chicago and received degrees at the University of Illinois, the University of Chicago, and Yale University. He designed numerous settings, often designing the lighting for those same productions and occasionally contributing costume designs as well. He worked regularly as an assistant to Donald Oenslager. An author as well as a committed educator, Mr. Elson taught at Hunter College of the City University of New York from 1948 to 1974, when he became Professor Emeritus. While on the Hunter College faculty he designed forty-eight productions for their theater. He also served on the design faculties of the University of Iowa, Yale, and the University of Oklahoma. He died in Armonk, New York on March 30, 2000.

Sets: 1946 *Hidden Horizon* 1947 *Duet for Two Hands*; *The First Mrs. Fraser* 1948 *Cup of Trembling*; *Kathleen*; *Power without Glory*; *Private Lives* 1950 *An Enemy of the People* 1951 *Borscht Capades*; *Nina* 1952 *Collector's Item*; *The Deep Blue Sea* 1954 *His and Hers* 1955 *Champagne Complex* 1956 *The Lovers*

Costumes: 1951 *Nina*† (Production Designer) 1955 *Champagne Complex*

Lights: 1945 *Pygmalion* 1946 *Born Yesterday*; *Hidden Horizon*; *Land's End*; *Loco*; *Present Laughter*; *Three to Make Ready*; *Years Ago* 1947 *As You Like It*; *Duet for Two Hands*; *The First Mrs. Fraser*; *Message for Margaret* 1948 *Cup of Trembling*; *Kathleen*; *Power without Glory*; *Private Lives* 1949 *Regina* 1950

An Enemy of the People; The Lady's Not for Burning; Out of This World **1951** Borscht Capades; Music in the Air; Nina; The Rose Tattoo **1952** Collector's Item; The Deep Blue Sea **1953** The Little Hut **1954** His and Hers **1955** Champagne Complex **1956** The Lovers **1957** Compulsion **1958** Blue Denim; Maria Golovin **1959** First Impressions **1960** Wildcat **1962** The Perfect Setup **1963** Photo Finish **1967** Mother Courage

Julian Eltinge

Julian Eltinge was born William Dalton on May 14, 1883 in Newtonville, Massachusetts. His first stage appearance was in Boston when he appeared at age ten, as a little girl. This began a career as one of the United States' most successful female impersonators. A serious actor, he never exaggerated female traits as was common at the time, but rather used costumes (which he often designed), make-and talent to portray beautiful women in comic situations. Producer Al Woods named a theater in his honor after the enormous success of The Fascinating Widow in the 1911-1912 Broadway season. He died in New York on March 7, 1941.

Costumes: 1914 The Crinoline Girl (Designed gowns and starred)

Henry Emden

A British artist, Henry Emden (sometimes Harry) was a prolific scene painter who worked mainly at Drury Lane in London. Born in 1852, he is acknowledged in playbills as early as 1870 when he assisted F. Fenton on Link by Link. His credits continue into the teens. Additional designs include Whittington and His Cat, Patience and Jack and the Beanstalk. All of the productions for which he received credit on Broadway were imported, together with his scenery, from London. Because it was generally more expensive to transport complete stage settings than to commission new ones, his designs were clearly considered integral to the productions. Just as he had initially worked as an apprentice to scene painters, his apprentices included Robert M. McCleery. Emden died in 1930, at age 78.

Sets: 1901 The Price of Peace[†]; The Sleeping Beauty and the Beast[†] **1903** Mother Goose[†]; Mr. Bluebeard[†] **1905** The White Cat[†] **1913** Hop o' My Thumb[†]

Emens and Unitt

Homer Emens (1862-1930) and Edward G. Unitt collaborated on many productions and received playbill credits as a team. Their studio was located at 152 West 46th Street in New York City, the same location as Unitt and Wickes (Joseph E. Wickes) another prolific painting duo. As was common at that time, all three scene painters worked together on some occasions, known as "Emens, Unitt and Wickes." For additional information and credits, see that entry, as well as "Homer Emens" and "Edward G. Unitt."

Sets: 1903 Babette **1904** Babette; The Serio-Comic Governess; The Two Roses; A Wife without a Smile **1905** Jinny, the Carrier; The Lady Shore; Miss Dolly Dollars; Nancy Stair **1906** Cousin Louisa (as: Emmons and Unitt) **1907** The Boys of Company "B"; Much Ado About Nothing **1911** Winter Garden[†] **1913** Beauty and the Barge; The Spiritualist[†] (Designed and painted)

Homer Emens

Homer Farnham Emens (sometimes Emmons or Emmens) was born on May 9, 1862 in Volney, New York and died on September 15, 1930. He was known as a scene painter and watercolorist and often designed one or two sets within multi-set plays, specializing in outdoor scenes. He started as an apprentice to Philip Goatcher at Madison Square Garden and worked for the American Opera Company. In 1893 he opened his own paint studio at 533 West 43rd Street, while continuing to design, notably the Metropolitan Opera's production of Parsifal, the first performance of the opera in the United States. Some of the productions Homer Emens designed before 1900 included Blue Jeans in 1890, Mavourneen and Alabama in 1891 and Three Musketeers in 1899.

Sets: 1899 More Than Queen; Peter Stuyvesant[†]; Peter Stuyvesant[†] **1900** Chris and the Wonderful Lamp[†]; In a Balcony; The Land of Heart's Desire;

Lost River[†]; *Monte Cristo*[†]; *The Village Postmaster* **1901** *New England Folks* **1902** *Dolly Varden*[†] (as: Homer Emmons); *Her Lord and Master*; *Mary of Magdala*[†] (Act III); *When Johnny Comes Marching Home*[†] (Act II) **1903** *Babes in Toyland*[†]; *Captain Dieppe*[†]; *The Proud Prince*[†]; *The Vinegar Buyer*[†] (Act I) **1904** *Granny*[†]; *A Madcap Princess*[†]; *The Old Homestead*; *Piff! Paff! Pouf!*[†]; *That Man and I*[†]; *Twelfth Night*; *The Winter's Tale*[†] **1905** *Beauty and the Barge*[†]; *Cousin Billy*[†]; *Just Out of College*[†]; *Mlle. Modiste*; *The School for Husbands*[†] **1906** *About Town*[†]; *The Blue Moon*[†]; *Cymbeline*[†]; *Eileen Asthore*[†]; *The Great Divide*[†]; *His House in Order*[†]; *The Mountain Climber*[†]; *Pippa Passes*[†]; *The Red Mill*[†] **1907** *Artie*; *The Christian Pilgrim*[†] (Acts III, IV 3); *Hip! Hip! Hooray!*[†]; *His Excellency the Governor*[†]; *The Hoyden*; *Jeanne d'Arc*[†]; *O'Neill of Derry*[†] (Acts I, IV); *The Right of Way*[†]; *The Rogers Brothers in Panama*[†]; *The Rose of Alhambra*[†]; *The Secret Orchard*[†]; *The Spoilers*[†]; *The Step-Sister*; *The Straight Road*[†]; *The Sunken Bell*[†]; *Twelfth Night*[†] **1908** *Funabashi*[†]; *Lonesome Town*; *The Prima Donna*; *A Waltz Dream* **1909** *The Candy Shop*[†] (Act I); *The Fair Co-Ed*[†]; *The Nigger* **1910** *The Arcadians*; *Electricity*; *The Merry Whirl*[†] (Act II); *The Old Town*; *The Speckled Band*; *Twelfth Night*[†]; *Two Women* **1911** *Kismet*[†]; *The Lily and the Prince*[†] (Act IV); *The Marionettes*[†]; *Nobody's Daughter*[†]; *The Siren*; *The Twelve Pound Look*; *The Zebra* **1912** *The Girl from Montmartre*; *The High Road*[†]; *The Lady of the Slipper*; *Oh! Oh! Delphine*[†]; *Robin Hood*[†]; *The Truth Wagon* **1913** *The American Maid*; *The Land of Promise*; *The Marriage Market*; *Mlle. Modiste*; *The Sunshine Girl*[†] (Act II) **1914** *The Prodigal Husband*; *Ziegfeld Follies of 1914*[†] **1915** *A Celebrated Case*; *The Chief*; *Cock O' the Walk*; *The Duke of Killicrankie*; *The Natural Law*; *Our Mrs. McChesney* **1916** *Betty*; *Margaret Schiller*; *The Merchant of Venice*; *Sybil* **1917** *The Belinda/New Word/ Old Friends/Old Lady*; *The Case of Lady Camber*; *Jack O'Lantern*[†]; *The Lady of the Camellias*; *Rambler Rose*; *Seremonda*; *The Three Bears* **1918** *Belinda*; *Dear Brutus*; *Humpty Dumpty*; *The Off Chance*; *The Saving Grace* **1919**

Come Along[†]; *Déclassé*; *Mis' Nelly of N'Orleans* **1920** *Mary Rose*; *Pietro*; *Sacred and Profane Love*

Emens, Unitt and Wickes

Homer Emens (1862-1930), Edward G. Unitt, and Joseph E. Wickes (d. 1950) were all active scenic designers and painters in their own right, but also collaborated on some productions and received playbill credits as a group, "Emens, Unitt and Wickes." For additional information and credits, see their individual and studio entries.

Sets: **1902** *A Doll's House* **1906** *The Light Eternal*[†] (Act II) **1907** *The Tattooed Man* **1908** *A Doll's House*

Terence Emery

British designer Terence Emery creates sets and costumes for plays and operas. At the Royal Opera House, his designs include *re d'Inghilterra*, *Alceste*, *Castor et Pollux* and *Oresteia*. He designed costumes for *Teseo* at Sadler's Wells, scenery for *Orfeo* at Royal Albert Hall, and both sets and costumes for *Riccardo Primo* for the Handel Opera Society in Covent Garden. Emery has also designed productions for Anthony Rooley's Consort of Musiche.

Costumes: **1987** *Pygmalion*

Beverly Emmons

Lighting designer Beverly Emmons was born on December 12, 1943. She studied dance at Sarah Lawrence College where she received a B.A. degree. As an apprentice at the American Dance Festival at Connecticut College she was influenced by the creative work of Jean Rosenthal and Thomas Skelton. This introduction to lighting design led to study with Tom Skelton at Lester Polalov'sStudio and Forum of Stage Design and a career in lighting. On Broadway her designs have been honored with nominations for several Tony Awards, an Obie Award for distinguished lighting design, and a Bessie Award. She won Maharam awards for *The Elephant Man* and *The Life and Adventures of Nicholas Nickleby* and American Theatre Wing Awards for *Passion*, *The Heiress* and *Jekyll*

& *Hyde*. Emmons has also designed for dance including pieces by Meredith Monk and the Martha Graham Dance Company. In collaboration with Robert Wilson she has lit *Einstein on the Beach* at the Metropolitan Opera and the Brooklyn Academy of Music, and also *CIVIL warS*.
Lights: 1975 *Bette Midler's Clams on the Half Shell Revue*; *A Letter for Queen Victoria* 1979 *The Elephant Man* 1980 *A Day in Hollywood/A Night in the Ukraine*; *Heartaches of a Pussycat*; *Reggae* 1981 *The Dresser*; *Life and Adventures of Nicholas Nickleby*,† *Piaf* 1982 *Good*; *Is There Life after High School?*; *Little Me* 1983 *All's Well That Ends Well*†; *Doonesbury*; *Total Abandon* 1986 *Mummenschanz* 1987 *Stepping Out* 1988 *Michael Feinstein in Concert* 1992 *High Rollers Social and Pleasure Club* 1993 *Abe Lincoln in Illinois* 1994 *Passion* 1995 *Chronicle of a Death Foretold*†; *The Heiress* 1997 *Jekyll & Hyde* 1998 *The Herbal Bed* 1999 *Annie Get Your Gun*

Ann Emonts

Ann Emonts was born in Fresno, California on June 23, 1951 and received a B.A. from the University of California-Santa Barbara, and an M.F.A. from New York University where she studied with Carrie Robbins. Her first costume designs were at the University of California for a production of *The Tempest* and her Broadway debut occurred in 1979. She has designed numerous productions at Playwrights Horizons and other off-Broadway theaters and is active in regional theaters as well, particularly on the West Coast.
Costumes: 1979 *Comin' Uptown* 1981 *Oh, Brother* 1983 *The Tapdance Kid*

Victor En Yu Tan

See Tan, Victor En Yu.

Jeff Engel

Lighting designer Jeff Engel is mainly known for his designs for television. Among his credits for specials are *Quincy Jones: The First 50 Years* and *Penn &Teller's Home Invasion Magic*. He is lighting director for the Nicoledeon series *Global Guts* and in 1996 received a nomination for a Daytime Emmy Award for lighting design for that show.
Lights: 1990 *Night of 100 Stars III*

Johan Engels

Scenic and costume designer Johan Engels has numerous credits for ballet, opera and theater. He studied at the University of Pretoria in South Africa. He designs for the Royal Shakespeare Company, the Donmar Warehouse, the Chichester Festival, and the National Theatre of Norway, among others and often collaborates with director Sam Mendes. The costume designs for *Tamburlaine* for RSC were nominated for an Olivier Award. In addition to *The Return of Ulysses* at Glimmerglass, he designed sets and costumes for *Il Ritorno d'Ulysse in Patria* for the New York City Opera's 2001-2002 season.
Sets: 1998 *Electra*
Costumes: 1998 *Electra*

George Enright

George Enright was a theatrical manager, and in this capacity supplied a variety of elements to productions. He mainly booked theaters, hired performers and musicians, and arranged for technical support. In addition, in 1902 he collaborated on the lighting designs for a show. His office was located at 112 West 31st Street in New York City.
Lights: 1902 *Ben Hur*†

Entwistle

"Entwisle" designed scenery for one production in 1924 on Broadway. Robert C. Entwistle, a painter and an electrician, was associated with Charles Schmitz and the Rialto Stage Lighting Company, located in 1925 at 304 West 52nd Street in New York City. Born October 1, 1892, he resided at 1425 Amsterdam Avenue until moving to the Bronx, where he died in December 1981. He also designed scenery and lights for productions in collaboration with Louis Kennel between 1919 and 1931. For additional credits see the entry "Kennel and Entwistle."
Sets: 1924 *Leah Kleschna*†

Erté

Erté (born Romain de Tirtoff) had a

long, varied career designing costumes and fashions under the name derived from the French pronunciation of his initials. He was born in St. Petersburg, Russia on November 10, 1892 and after studying painting in Russia went to Paris. He worked originally for an undistinguished fashion designer, Caroline, but quickly joined Paul Poiret as a sketch artist. His first designs for the theater were produced in 1914, although he worked primarily as a fashion designer prior to World War I. In the early 1920s he came to the United States to design for Florenz Ziegfield and other producers, finding success as a stage designer throughout the 1920s and 1930s. In 1967 many of his drawings, paintings, sculptures, decorative arts, and designs were exhibited in New York and later purchased by the Metropolitan Museum of Art. His creative works are widely collected in museums and books, such as *Erté at Ninety-Five*, published in 1987. He died in Paris at age 97 on April 21, 1990.

Sets: 1922 *Greenwich Village Follies*[†] **1993** *Radio City Easter Show*[†] **1994** *Radio City Easter Show*[†] **1995** *Radio City Easter Show*[†] **1996** *Radio City Spring Spectacular*[†] (Gershwin number) **1997** *Radio City Spring Spectacular*[†] (Gershwin number)

Costumes: 1922 *George White's Scandals*[†] (Seas costumes) **1923** *George White's Scandals*[†] (Additional costume designs); *Topics of 1923*[†] **1924** *George White's Scandals* **1925** *Artists and Models*; *George White's Scandals*[†] **1926** *George White's Scandals*[†] (Additional sketches); *A Night in Paris*[†] **1927** *Manhattan Mary* **1928** *George White's Scandals*[†] **1929** *George White's Scandals*[†] (Parisian costumes) **1993** *Radio City Easter Show*[†] **1994** *Radio City Easter Show*[†] **1996** *Radio City Spring Spectacular*[†] (Gershwin number) **1997** *Radio City Spring Spectacular*[†] (Gershwin number)

Marcel Escoffier

French designer Marcel Escoffier designed costumes for a play on Broadway in the early 1960s. Born in Monte Carlo on November 29, 1910, he has designed costumes, lights and sets for the opera and theater, and directed plays. His opera designs have been seen around the world, including the 1994 *La Fille du Tegiment* at the Metropolitan Opera. M. Escoffier has also designed films, including *Carmen* (1945), *Mayerling* (1968) and *Blood and Roses* (1960).

Costumes: 1963 *The Lady of the Camellias*

Diane Esmond

Diane Esmond contributed sets and costumes to a Broadway play in 1963.

Sets: 1963 *Berenice*
Costumes: 1963 *Berenice*

Manuel Essman

Manuel Essman (also known as Easman, Essmann), born in 1898 died in April 1967 at age 68. He worked on Broadway, at the Federal Theatre, the Provincetown Playhouse, and for the New Playwrights Theatre. He studied at the Carnegie Institute of Technology and designed the film *Rhapsody in Steel* for the Ford Motor Company. He was a set designer for the Columbia Broadcasting System with numerous television designs to his credit including *The Ed Sullivan Show*. During World War II he was a photographer and writer for *Stars and Stripes*. At the time of his death he was devoting his energies to sculpture.

Sets: 1928 *Singing Jailbirds* **1936** *The Conjur Man Dies*; *Walk Together Chillun* **1937** *Processional* **1938** *Androcles and the Lion* **1939** *Coggerers, The/Mr. Banks of Birmin/The Red Velvet Coat*

Heidi Ettinger

Heidi Prentice Ettinger was born on August 16, 1951 in San Francisco to Richard Prentice Ettinger and Barbara Lynn Ettinger. She received a B.F.A. at Occidental College in Los Angeles where her first design assignment was *King David*. She designs both sets and costumes for plays when possible, but has additional credits for set design. She is also a successful producer. Productions include *A Midsummer Nights' Dream* at the Delacorte Theatre, and *Painting Churches,*

American Passion and many other productions off-Broadway and in regional theaters, notably La Jolla Playhouse where she often collaborates with Des McAnuff. She received an Obie Award for the sets for *Painting Churches* and Drama Desk, Maharam and Tony Awards for the sets for *Big River* and a Tony Award for *The Secret Garden*. Married at one time to producer Rocco Landesman, she is the mother of three sons who are invariably mentioned in her program biographies.

Sets: 1983 *'night Mother* (as: Heidi Landesman) 1985 *Big River* (as: Heidi Landesman) 1991 *The Secret Garden* (as: Heidi Landesman) 1993 *The Red Shoes* (as: Heidi Landesman) 1995 *Moon over Buffalo* (as: Heidi Landesman); *Smokey Joe's Cafe* (as: Heidi Landesman) 1997 *Triumph of Love* 1998 *The Sound of Music* 2001 *The Adventures of Tom Sawyer* **Costumes:** 1983 *'night Mother* (as: Heidi Landesman)

Joe Eula

Joe Eula was born January 16, 1925 in Connecticut and studied at the Art Students League in New York City. His considerable talent for drawing led to a career in fashion illustration. Joe Eula spent much of his professional career as the main fashion illustrator for *Harper's Bazaar*, Italy and France on whose pages his expressive watercolors recorded contemporary fashion. He also drew many design sketches for Geoffrey Beene. In addition, he has contributed costumes to plays and ballets, including *Dances at a Gathering* for Jerome Robbins in 1968. Twenty-first century illustrations include "The Real Studio 54" in *The New York Times Magazine* by Bob Colacello in 2001.
Costumes: 1969 *Private Lives*† 1979 *Got Tu Go Disco*

Eleanor Eustis

Eleanor Eustis designed one set in 1929 on Broadway.
Sets: 1929 *Paolo and Francesca*

Charles Evans

Charles Evans began professional life as an artist but changed to scene design, beginning with productions at the Playhouse in the Park in Philadelphia. Mr. Evans also had his own company, Design Associates, in Lambertville, New Jersey where sets for shows were built. He has served as designer and artistic director at the Vancouver Playhouse Theatre Company in British Columbia. During his career he has occasionally provided costume designs to productions for which he has also designed scenery. He should not be confused with Charles E. Evans the performer, Charles Evans, 2nd, the painter, nor Charles Evans, the co-founder of Evan-Picone. He is the brother of Hollywood personality Robert Evans.
Sets: 1965 *Me and Thee*
Costumes: 1965 *Me and Thee*†

James B. Fagan

James Bernard Fagan made his first stage appearance in 1895 as an actor in Sir Frank R. Benson's Company, and while he continued to act off and on throughout his life, he is remembered principally as a producer and playwright. He was born in Belfast, Ireland on May 18, 1873 and attended Clongowes Wood College and Trinity College, where he considered a career in law. J. B. Fagan acquired the Big Game Museum in Oxford and converted it into the Oxford Playhouse, giving John Gielgud, Tyrone Guthrie, Raymond Massey and other young actors their start and developing a reputation as a Shakespearean director. *And So to Bed* and *The Improper Duchess* are among the plays he wrote. He died on February 17, 1933 in Hollywood, California at age 59 shortly after adapting *Smilin' Through* for Norma Shearer.
Sets: 1927 *And So to Bed* 1928 *The Cherry Orchard*†

Sven Fahlstedt

Sven Fahlstelt designed a production on Broadway in 1962.
Sets: 1962 *The Father*

John Falabella

John Falabella was born in New York City on October 9, 1952. At the age of ten he began designing fashions, and received his formal training at New York University, earning a B.F.A. in 1974. He worked as an assistant to Oliver Smith for four years and made his Broadway debut as a set designer in 1976 for *Kings* and as a costume designer in 1980 for *The Lady from Dubuque*. His designs were seen at the American Stage Festival in New Hampshire, Candlewood Playhouse, the Huntington Theatre Company, Goodspeed Opera, and the Walnut Street Playhouse, among other theaters. He was production designer for *TAD* for Great Performances/Dance in America and art director for *Happy New Year USA* on PBS. Mr. Falabella taught scene design at Boston University from 1986 until his death, from AIDS, on July 6, 1993 in New York.

Sets: 1976 *Kings* 1980 *Perfectly Frank* 1982 *Blues in the Night* 1983 *The Caine Mutiny Court Martial*; *The Guys in the Truck* 1987 *Barbara Cook: A Concert for the Theatre*; *Safe Sex* 1990 *An Evening with Harry Connick, Jr. and His Orchestra* 1993 *Tango Pasion* (Artistic supervisor)

Costumes: 1980 *The Lady from Dubuque*; *Perfectly Frank* 1983 *The Guys in the Truck*; *The Man Who Had Three Arms* 1985 *Home Front* 1993 *Tango Pasion*

Gabriella Falk

In addition to designing scenery and costumes for the theater, Gabriella Falk, a native of Great Britain, has film credits including *In Search of Gregory* and *The Adding Machine* and in regional theaters throughout the United Kingdom. From 1971 to 1973 she was a design consultant for Inter-Action Productions in London's West End. Also a textile designer, she works from her home in Exton, England.

Sets: 1977 *Dirty Linen/ New Found Land*

Costumes: 1977 *Dirty Linen/ New Found Land*

Charles B. Falls

Charles B. Falls (C. B. Falls), a graphic artist, occasionally designed sets and costumes on Broadway between 1919 and 1935. He designed posters for "Victory" book campaigns in World War I and World War II. He was born in Ft. Wayne, Indiana in 1874 and died on April 15, 1960 at age 85. At age twenty-one he moved to Chicago and worked for an architect before joining the art staff at the *Chicago Tribune*. Mr. Falls specialized in illustrations, posters (including show posters) and large-scale murals. A writer and book illustrator, he also designed fabrics and furniture. In 1922 he served as president of the Guild of Free Lance Artists in New York City. During the last years of his life he worked to develop art talent in disabled veterans.

Sets: 1919 *Greenwich Village Follies* 1926 *Henry IV, Part I†*

Costumes: 1926 *Henry IV, Part I†* 1935 *Macbeth*; *Othello*

Miss Fanchon

Miss Fanchon, born Fanny Wolff, c.1890 in Los Angeles was trained in ballet and both taught and did solo performances as "Fanchon" during her dance career. She was also partner in the Fanchon and Marco (her brother Michael Marco Wolff) stage revues, creating as well as performing in them. Fanchon and Marco also produced prologues called "Ideas" for the Fox Theatre Chain, and films. In the 1940s she owned and managed a popular restaurant in New York City, the "Fanchon and Arnold Park Avenue Restaurant" with her husband Arnold Michelman (1907-1982). Together they also produced shows on Broadway, including *On with the Dance, Summer Romance* and *Turn off the Moon*, and films including *Books are Lighter than Rifles* in 1947. No death date is known.

Costumes: 1921 *Sun-kist†* (All other designs)

Tony Fanning

A graduate of the North Carolina School of the Arts, scenic designer and art director Tony Fanning did his graduate work at Yale University School of Drama. Although he continues to design for the theater, often at the South Coast Repertory, Seattle Repertory, and the Geffen Playhouse among others, he works primarily in film. Beginning with stints as an assistant on the HBO series *Tales From the Crypt*, his responsibilities have increased through set design for *The Hudsucker Proxy, Wild Hearts Can't Be Broken,* etc., to art direction for *The Indian in the Cupboard, Jingle All the Way, Amistad* and *Rocket Boys.* His design for the scenery of *Two Trains Running* was nominated for an NAACP Theatre Award.

Sets: 1992 *Two Trains Running*

Hilda Farnham

Hilda Farnham designed costumes for one Broadway show.

Costumes: 1930 *Change Your Luck†*

Abd'el Farrah

Abd'el (Abdelkader) Elkader Farrah was born in Boghari, Algeria on March 28, 1926 and designed his first production in 1953 in Amsterdam. A designer of both sets and costumes, he has had a long association with the Royal Shakespeare Company in London and at Stratford-upon-Avon. A prolific designer with over three hundred productions to his credit, he has taught design in France and Canada. His designs are in the permanent collections of the Victoria and Albert Museum and have been reproduced in many books on stage design, including *Stage Design Throughout the World Since 1950, Stage Design Throughout the World Since 1960,* and *Lights of the Western Theatre* by Alfred Farag.

Sets: 1973 *Emperor Henry IV*
Costumes: 1973 *Emperor Henry IV*

Thomas Farrar

Thomas Prince Farrar was born in New Orleans. He studied architecture at Tulane University and in Europe prior to becoming a set designer. He was, at one time, art director for Ringling Bros. and Barnum & Bailey Circus, where he was associated with costume designer Miles White. Also an industrial designer, he was a member of the firm Van Doren, Nowland and Schladermundt. Thomas Farrar died at age 50 on June 11, 1951.

Sets: 1928 *The Perfect Alibi* **1929** *Michael and Mary* **1930** *Mrs. Moonlight* **1931** *Give Me Yesterday; The Roof* **1934** *Mahogony Hall*

Eleanor Farrington

Eleanor Farrington, known primarily as a set designer, created sets, costumes and lights for a Broadway show in 1945, a remarkable accomplishment for a woman at that time. She was active beginning in 1938.

Sets: 1938 *Michael Drops In* **1945** *The Deep Mrs. Sykes*

Costumes: 1945 *The Deep Mrs. Sykes*

Lights: 1945 *The Deep Mrs. Sykes*

A. H. Feder

A. H. (Abe) Feder was well-known as a lighting and scenery designer throughout a career which began in 1932 with the lighting design for *Trick or Trick* and eventually encompassed more than 300 productions. He was born in Milwaukee, Wisconsin on June 27, 1909 and studied at the Carnegie Institute of Technology with Woodman Thompson and Alexander Wykcoff. Mr. Feder designed the lighting for plays, ballets and operas throughout the United States and lectured extensively. He created lights for most of the Federal Theatre projects and was closely associated with *The Cradle Will Rock* and *Macbeth* directed by Orson Welles. He was also consultant for the lighting of interiors of theaters, museums, galleries, and buildings, including the Kennedy Center in Washington, D.C., the Israel National Museum in Jerusalem and Rockefeller Plaza in New York City. He was instrumental in the development of the profession of lighting design as it progressed from relying on electricians for the presence of light on stage to relying on designers for the quality of light on stage. To honor his memory, the lights at Rockefeller Center and the Empire State Building were turned off for one hour, on the Monday night following his death at age 87 on April 24, 1997.

Sets: 1950 *The Gioconda Smile* **1963** *Once for the Asking* **1964** *Blues for Mr. Charley*

Costumes: 1964 *Blues for Mr. Charley*

Lights: 1933 *One Sunday Afternoon* **1934** *Calling All Stars; Four Saints in Three Acts* **1935** *Ghosts; The Hook-Up* **1936** *The Conjur Man Dies; Hedda Gabler; Macbeth; New Faces of 1936* **1937** *I'd Rather Be Right; Native Ground;*

Without Warning **1938** *Androcles and the Lion*; *The Big Blow*; *Cap't Jinks of the Horse Marines*; *Coriolanus*; *The Cradle Will Rock*; *Diff'rent*; *Here Come the Clowns*; *No More Peace*; *Prologue to Glory*; *Pygmalion*; *Sing for Your Supper* **1940** *Hold onto Your Hats*; *Johnny Belinda*; *A Passenger to Bali* **1941** *Angel Street* **1942** *Autumn Hill*; *Magic/ Hello, Out There*; *Walking Gentleman* **1943** *Winged Victory* **1950** *The Gioconda Smile* **1951** *A Sleep of Prisoners* **1952** *Dear Barbarians*; *Three Wishes for Jamie* **1953** *A Pin to See the Peepshow* **1954** *The Boyfriend*; *The Flowering Peach*; *The Immoralist* **1955** *Inherit the Wind*; *Seventh Heaven*; *The Skin of Our Teeth*; *The Young and Beautiful* **1956** *My Fair Lady* **1957** *A Clearing in the Woods*; *Orpheus Descending*; *Time Remembered*; *A Visit to a Small Planet* **1958** *The Cold Wind and the Warm*; *Goldilocks* **1959** *A Loss of Roses* **1960** *Camelot*; *Greenwillow* **1962** *Tiger Tiger Burning Bright* **1963** *Once for the Asking* **1964** *Blues for Mr. Charley*; *The Three Sisters* **1965** *On a Clear Day You Can See Forever* **1971** *Scratch* **1975** *Doctor Jazz*; *Goodtime Charley* **1979** *Carmelina*

Gerald Feil

Gerald Feil, who designed lights on Broadway in the mid-1960s, works primarily in the film industry. His assignments as a photographer, cameraman, and producer have taken him on location to several continents. Perhaps best known for his camera work and editing for *Lord of the Flies* in 1963, Gerald Feil was also director of photography for *He Knows You're Alone* and *Friday the 13th, Part III*. His 1972 documentary *The Empty Space* about Peter Brook was included in the 2000 DVD release of *Lord of the Flies*.

Lights: 1964 *Traveler without Luggage*

Frances Feist

Frances Feist was an artist who had exhibits of her work all over the world. She studied at George Washington University in Paris, and with Winold Reiss and Tony Nell. Born in Newark, New Jersey. on April 10, 1910, Frances Feist came from a family of artists including an uncle, Max Weyl whose

paintings are in many major museums. Her aunt, Margery Weyl Feist often collaborated with her on designs. Miss Feist's career began when she won a contest sponsored by the Cotton Club to find a costume designer, leading to eight productions at the Cotton Club in addition to her Broadway credits. Her husband, Gustav A. Weidhaas (d. 1938) provided properties, mechanical devises and illusions for theatrical productions through Weidhaas Studios, and her son Francis (Ted) Weidhaas was also a scenic designer. At the time of her son's death on December 19, 1986, she was referred to as deceased.

Costumes: 1938 *Good Hunting* (Miss Winwood's costume and Miss Lanner's Act III dress) **1939** *Lew Leslies' Blackbirds of 1939*; *Yokel Boy*†

Félix

Félix, in rue du Faubourg Saint-Honoré, Paris was a small exclusive haute couture salon that provided gowns for private and theatrical customers at the beginning of the twentieth century.

Costumes: 1904 *The Pit*†

Richard Ferrer

Richard Ferrer designed sets for a Broadway play in 1974. A native of Louisiana, he studied at Tulane University and received a B.A. in architecture from the University of Southwestern Louisiana. He began his professional career as an architect for the Vieux Carre Commission of the City of New Orleans, renovating and restoring historic structures in the French Quarter. He has designed scenery for theater, television and the ballet in New Orleans, and for the American Theatre in Washington, D.C. in addition to other locations. Additional productions include *The Nutcracker* for the Washington Ballet.

Sets: 1974 *Rainbow Jones*

David Ffolkes

David Ffolkes was born October 12, 1912 in Hagley, Worchestershire, England. He began to study architecture in Birmingham but left to pursue a career in theater. His first designs were for the

Cambridge Arts Theatre. He spent a year in residence at the Old Vic where he met and often designed for Maurice Evans. In 1936 Mr. Ffolkes arrived in New York with the Evans Company and stayed in the United States to design sets and costumes for additional productions, as well as to teach for a time at Boston University. In addition to numerous plays and ballets, David Ffolkes designed films including *Journey to the Center of the Earth, Alexander The Great, Darling,* and *You Only Live Twice* which was being completed at the time of his death in 1966. His designs for *Henry VIII* were honored with the first ever Tony Award for outstanding set design in 1947.

Sets: 1937 *King Richard II*; *Young Mr. Disraeli* **1938** *Hamlet* **1939** *Hamlet*; *Henry IV, Part I* **1940** *King Richard II* **1946** *Henry VIII* **1948** *Where's Charley* **1951** *Where's Charley* **1953** *Men of Distinction*

Costumes: 1937 *King Richard II*; *Young Mr. Disraeli* **1938** *Hamlet* **1939** *Hamlet*; *Henry IV, Part I* **1940** *King Richard II* **1943** *Richard III* **1946** *Henry VIII*; *What Every Woman Knows* **1947** *Brigadoon*; *Man and Superman* **1948** *Sleepy Hollow*; *Where's Charley* **1949** *Along Fifth Avenue*; *Browning Version, The and A Harlequinade* **1951** *Flahooey*; *Seventeen*; *Springtime for Henry*; *Where's Charley* **1953** *Men of Distinction*

Ada B. Fields

Ada B. Fields (also known as Bertha A. Field) was owner of the Fields Costume Company, 398 Fifth Avenue, fourth floor, in the early 1920s when she designed plays on Broadway. Prior to that she was on the design staff of the Schneider-Anderson Costume Company.

Costumes: 1921 *George White's Scandals*† (Women's costumes); *June Love* (as: Bertha A. Field); *The Perfect Fool*† **1922** *Ziegfeld Follies: 1922*† (Country Girls, Etc.) **1923** *The Rise of Rosie O'Reilly*†

Miss Finch

Miss Flora Finch, an actress on stage and in early movies, was born in England. She began her career with the Ben Greet Players. A tall, thin, angular woman, she was a very popular comic actress who often appeared opposite the short and round John Bunny. Her movie debut occurred in two Vitagraph Pictures *A Night Out* and *The New Secretary* released in 1910. Always conscious of her appearance, she paid much attention to her own costumes, and in 1907 designed them for others as well. At the time of her death on January 4, 1940 in Hollywood, she was a stock player at Metro-Goldwyn-Mayer.

Costumes: 1907 *The Lancers*† (Ensemble ladies in Acts II, III)

Arden Fingerhut

Arden Fingerhut, one of the foremost contemporary lighting designers, studied chemistry at New York University and received a graduate degree in scene design from Columbia University before turning her attention and talents to lighting design. She worked for several years honing her skills at the O'Neill Theatre Center under the tutelage of John Gleason, who encouraged her innovative and abstract approach to lighting. Her early association with Joseph Chaikin at the Open Theatre influenced her style, as did her long term relationship with Elizabeth Swados. She taught lighting design for twelve years at New York University and in 1987 joined the theater department at Williams College, initially as chair. She designed lights in most of the regional theaters in the United States, on and off-Broadway, and for dance and opera and was awarded an Obie in 1982 for sustained excellence. Born in Minneapolis in 1946, she died on May 13, 1994.

Lights: 1978 *Da* **1979** *Bent* **1980** *Hide and Seek* **1981** *Einstein and the Polar Bear*; *The Father* **1983** *Plenty*; *Slab Boys*; *Teaneck Tanzi: The Venus Flytrap* **1984** *Alone Together* **1985** *Hay Fever* **1992** *Chinese Coffee*; *Salome*

Alicia Finkel

Alicia Finkel was born in Buenos Aires, Argentina on November 17, 1934 and received both B.F.A. and M.F.A. degrees from the National School of Fine Arts in Buenos Aires where she studied with Rodolfo Franco. Her first costume designs were for *The Dinner of Three Kings* at the Teatro Nathanael in 1957. From 1968 to 1976, she served as the principal costume designer at the Goodman Theatre in Chicago, and then was head of the Costume Design Program at the University of Connecticut until retiring. Her costume designs were honored with two Joseph Jefferson Awards in Chicago for *The Lady's Not for Burning* (1973) and *A Doll's House* (1974). In 1996, her book, *Romantic Stages: Set and Costume Design in Victorian England*, was published by McFarland Press.

Costumes: 1974 *The Freedom of the City*

Imero Fiorentino

Born on July 12, 1928 in New York City, Imero Ovidio Fiorentino has been instrumental in developing the art of lighting design for television, elevating design for the small screen from its origins in engineering. After graduating with a Bachelor of Fine Arts from Carnegie Mellon University in 1950, he served as lighting director for ABC-TV from 1950 to 1960. In 1960 he formed Imero Fiorentino Associates, a consulting company specializing in lighting for special events and television. His credits on television range from Miss Piggy to Miss America, and since 1960 (when he first lit the Nixon-Kennedy debates) he has been lighting political conventions, including the 1988 Republican National Convention in the Louisiana Superdome. He was honored with a Merit Award from his alma mater in 1974, nominations for Emmy Awards in lighting and scenic design, and an Excellence in Design Award and an Award of Excellence from the Illuminating Engineering Society.

Lights: 1975 *The NightThat Made America Famous*

Tazeena Firth

Tazeena Firth is a British designer of both sets and costumes who works primarily in Europe. From 1954 to 1957 she designed for the Theatre Royal, Windsor, England before working for other theaters including the Royal Shakespeare Company and the English Stage Company. From 1961 to 1979 she designed in partnership with Timothy O'Brien. She has designed numerous operas and plays for most of the major companies in the world. She was born in Southampton, England on November 1, 1935 and educated at St. Mary's, Wantage and the Chatelard School. Honors include the Gold Medal for set design at the 1975 Prague Quadriennale, shared with Timothy O'Brien, Ralph Koltai and John Bury. Timothy O'Brien and Tazeena Firth received Tony Award nominations for both scenery and costumes for *Evita*.

Sets: 1979 *Bedroom Farce*†; *Evita*† **1982** *A Doll's Life*†
Costumes: 1979 *Evita*†

Joseph C. Fischer

A costumer with his own business, Joseph C. Fischer designed costumes for plays as well as executing them for other designers. His shop was at 123 West 37th Street in New York City during the first decade of the twentieth century. The theater program for *His Honor the Mayor* in 1907 lists his name above that of the cast. At that time if information about costume designers was included, it was usually found in the back of playbills.

Costumes: 1906 *His Honor the Mayor*
1910 *The Deacon and the Lady*†

A. S. Fishback

Alexander Sigmund Fishback (also A. S. Fishbach) died August 11, 1952 at the age of 69 after working in the costume business for most of his life. In addition to his design credit, he executed the costumes for many plays including *Abie's Irish Rose, The Vagabond King* and *Beggar on Horseback*.

Costumes: 1928 *Cock Robin*

Jules Fisher

Jules Edward Fisher is a lighting designer of considerable renown with design experience dating back to his high school days when he designed *January Thaw*. He was born in Norristown, Pennsylvania on November 12, 1937 and attended Pennsylvania State

University before receiving a B.F.A. from the Carnegie Institute of Technology. After working as a carpenter, stage manager and lighting designer in Pennsylvania, he arrived in New York in October 1959 to become lighting director at the 74th Street Theatre, and has been designing lights in New York City steadily ever since. He frequently designs in collaboration with Peggy Eisenhauer. He has received several Tony Awards: for *Pippin* (1972), *Ulysses in Nighttown* (1974), *Dancin'* (1978), *Grand Hotel, The Musical* (1990), *Will Rogers Follies* (1991), *Jely's Last Jam* (1992), and *Bring in 'da Noise, Bring in 'da Funk* (with Peggy Eisenhauer), among numerous nominations. In addition to being an active designer, Fisher is a consultant through Jules Fisher Associates, Inc., (a theater consulting group), Jules Fisher Enterprises, Inc., (a production company) and Jules Fisher & Paul Marantz Inc. (architectural lighting design specialists) and regularly participates in The Broadway Lighting Master Classes. In 1994, he was inducted into the Theatre Hall of Fame.

Lights: 1964 *Anyone Can Whistle*; *A Girl Could Get Lucky*; *High Spirits*; *P.S. I Love You*; *The Sign in Sidney Brustein's Window*; *The Subject Was Roses*; *The White House* 1965 *And Things That Go Bump in the Night*; *The Devils*; *Do I Hear a Waltz?*; *Half a Sixpence*; *Pickwick*; *The Yearling* 1966 *Hail Scrawdyke!* 1967 *Black Comedy*; *Little Murders*; *A Minor Adjustment*; *The Natural Look*; *The Trial of Lee Harvey Oswald*; *You Know I Can't Hear You When the Water's Running* 1968 *Before You Go*; *The Cuban Thing*; *The Grand Music Hall of Israel*; *Hair*; *Here's Where I Belong*; *The Man in the Glass Booth*; *The Only Game in Town* 1969 *But, Seriously*; *Butterflies Are Free*; *Canterbury Tales*; *Trumpets of the Lord*; *The Watering Place* 1970 *The Engagement Baby*; *Gantry*; *Home*; *Inquest*; *Minnie's Boys*; *Sheep of the Runway* 1971 *Jesus Christ Superstar*; *Lenny*; *No, No, Nanette*; *You're a Good Man, Charlie Brown* 1972 *Fun City*; *Lysistrata*; *Mourning Becomes Electra*; *Pippin* 1973 *Full Circle*; *The Iceman Cometh*;

Molly; *Seesaw*; *Uncle Vanya* 1974 *Thieves*; *Ulysses in Nighttown* 1975 *Chicago* 1976 *Rockabye Hamlet* 1977 *American Buffalo*; *Golda*; *Hair* 1978 *Dancin'* 1981 *Frankenstein* 1982 *Rock 'n Roll! The First 5,000 Years* 1983 *La Cage Aux Folles* 1985 *Song & Dance* 1986 *Big Deal*; *Rags* 1988 *Legs Diamond* 1989 *Grand Hotel, The Musical* 1991 *Nick & Nora*; *Will Rogers Follies* 1992 *Death and the Maiden*; *Jelly's Last Jam*; *My Favorite Year*; *Tommy Tune Tonite! A Song and Dance Act*[†]; *Two Shakespearean Actors* 1993 *Angels in America, Part II: Perestroika*[†]; *Angels in America: Millennium Approaches*[†] 1994 *Best Little Whorehouse Goes Public, The*[†]; *A Christmas Carol*[†]; *Twilight: Los Angeles, 1992* 1995 *A Christmas Carol*; *Chronicle of a Death Foretold*[†]; *Victor/Victoria* 1996 *Bring in 'da Noise, Bring in 'da Funk*[†]; *A Christmas Carol*[†] 1997 *A Christmas Carol*[†]; *Street Corner Symphony*[†] 1998 *A Christmas Carol*[†]; *Ragtime*[†] 1999 *Marie Christine*[†] 2000 *Jane Eyre*[†]; *The Wild Party*[†]

Linda Fisher

Linda Fisher was born September 30, 1943 in Lindsay, California, the daughter of Doris and Lt. Colonel James Howard Fisher. After receiving a B.F.A. at the University of Texas where she studied with Paul Rinehardt, she earned her M.F.A. at Yale. Her first professional costume design was for *The Three Sisters* at the Yale Repertory Theatre. In 1970, her costumes were seen in New York for the first time in *The Brass Butterfly* at the Chelsea Theatre Center. She received several honors for the costume designs for *Mornings at Seven* including the Maharam Award. Linda Fisher also designs for film, television, and in the regional theaters. Her twenty-first century costume designs include *The Hostage* and *A Life* at the Irish Repertory Theatre, *Modern Orthodox* and *The Bungler* at Long Wharf Theatre and *The Streets of New York* for the Irish Repertory Theatre.

Costumes: 1975 *Boccaccio* 1980 *Morning's at Seven* 1981 *Foxfire*; *Rose* 1982 *Good* 1994 *A Tuna Christmas* 1996 *Bus Stop*

Mary Fisher

A British costume designer, Mary Fisher provided costumes on Broadway between 1907 and 1911 from her establishment at 26 Bedford Street, London. Her credits in London began in 1890 when she made costumes for Percy Anderson's designs for *Carmen up to Date*. Mainly a costumer, she occasionally contributed original designs to productions, amassing over 100 program credits between 1900 and 1931.

Costumes: 1907 *The Little Michus†* **1911** *Bunty Pulls the Strings†*

Rick Fisher

Rick Fisher was born in Philadelphia on October 19, 1954. He received a B.A. from Dickenson College in Carlisle, Pennsylvania in 1976 where he learned the art and craft of theater. He also served as an apprentice at the Viking Theatre in Atlantic City and as an apprentice and later master carpenter at the Playhouse in the Park in Philadelphia. His lighting designs have been seen mainly throughout the United Kingdom and London, where he has lived since 1976. His design has been influenced by associations in London with Tom Donnellan and Steve Whitson. He frequently designs for director Stephen Daldry, in collaboration with designer Ian Mac-Neil. Design credits include the lighting for numerous fringe shows, regional theaters, opera companies, productions for the Royal Shakespeare Company, and the Royal National Theatre. Shows in London's West End include *Serious Money, J.J. Farr, A Walk in the Woods, Marya* and *Hidden Laughter*. He won the 1994 Laurence Olivier Award for lighting design for three productions: *Machinal, Hysteria,* and *Moonlight* and both a Drama Desk and Tony Award for *An Inspector Calls*.

Lights: 1988 *Serious Money* **1990** *Some Americans Abroad* **1994** *An Inspector Calls* **1998** *Swan Lake* **1999** *Via Dolorosa*

Clyde Fitch

Playwright William Clyde Fitch was born on May 2, 1865 in Elmira, New York and died on Chalons-sur-Marne, France on September 4, 1909, a few days after an operation for appendicitis. After completing his education at Amherst College, he abandoned his plans for a career in architecture, due in part to the success of a short play *Betty's Finish* at the Boston Museum, which he wrote while searching for a job. An adaptation of *Beau Brumell* for Richard Mansfield in 1890 established his reputation. His best known plays include *Barbara Fretchie, Captain Jinks of the Horse Marines* and *The Girl with the Green Eyes*. For the productions of two of his plays on Broadway, he also contributed set designs.

Sets: 1905 *Her Great Match* (Also wrote) **1907** *The Truth* (Also wrote)

Eugene Fitsch

Eugene Camille Fitsch (also known as Eugene C. Fritsch) was born December 11, 1892 in Alsace-Lorraine, France and came to American to work as a bookbinder. He studied at the Albright Art School and with Mahonri Young, Frank V. DuMond and Joseph Pennell. He joined the faculty of the Art Students League of New York where he had studied in 1942, teaching graphic arts. He was a painter, graphic artist and set designer who occasionally also designed costumes. In 1932 he maintained a studio at 5 East 14th Street in New York City and in 1936 founded the American Artists School at that location. In addition to teaching and lithography, he designed scenery, costumes and lights for theatrical productions, which in turn became subjects of his lithographs, which are widely collected. The "Shared Perspectives: The Printmaker and Photographer in New York, 1900-1950" exhibition at the Museum of the City of New York in 1993 included his lithographs. Eugene Fitsch died in 1972.

Sets: 1928 *Him* **1929** *Winter Bound* **1931** *Ladies of Creation* **1932** *When Ladies Meet* **1934** *Whatever Possessed Her*

Costumes: 1928 *Him*

Edward Fitzgerald

Edward Fitzgerald was born in Dublin,

Ireland in 1876 and spent his career in the theater as an actor and business manager. He was educated at Uppingham School and Dublin University. As an actor, he appeared in New York with the Richard Mansfield Company from 1902 to 1905. He went back to England in 1905 but quickly returned to New York, staying until called to military service for World War I. Having a relatively common name, his later history is not clear. He should not be confused however with the Duke of Leinster (c.1893-1976) who was married at one time to actress May Etheridge, the American radio broadcaster Ed Fitzgerald (c.1893-1982) nor the American cinematographer (1901-1996).

Sets: 1937 *Wall Street Scene*

Edward Fitzpatrick

As a lighting designer Edward Fitzpatrick created effects for one production in 1939. It is unlikely that he was the band leader and radio personality (d. 1960) who shared the same name.

Lights: 1939 *Steel*

Robert Fletcher

Robert Fletcher was born Robert Fletcher Wyckoff on August 23, 1923 (1922 is sometimes cited) in Cedar Rapids, Iowa and studied at Harvard and the University of Iowa. He entered the theater as a director and designer for the Council Bluffs (Iowa) Little Theatre. After service in World War II he appeared on Broadway as an actor before concentrating his talents on designing sets and costumes. His credits are extensive and varied. He has designed for the Stratford (Ontario) Festival, the Brattle Theatre in Cambridge, Massachusetts (which he helped found), the Spoleto Festival, San Francisco Ballet, Boston Opera, and many others. Robert Fletcher has designed regularly for television since the late 1950s when he was a staff designer for NBC-TV. He is perhaps best known for the *Star Trek: The Motion Picture, Star Trek II: The Wrath of Kahn, Star Trek III: The Search for Spock* and *Star Trek IV: The Voyage Home* although he has designed many films set in a variety of eras.

Sets: 1960 *Farewell, Farewell, Eugene* **1964** *High Spirits* **1969** *Hadrian VII* **1980** *A Life* **1985** *Doubles*
Costumes: 1958 *The Firstborn* **1960** *Farewell, Farewell, Eugene* **1961** *The Happiest Girl in the World; How to Succeed in Business Without Really Trying* **1962** *A Family Affair; Little Me; The Moon Besieged; Nowhere to Go But Up* **1964** *Foxy; High Spirits* (Miss Tammy Grimes' gowns) **1966** *Walking Happy* **1969** *Hadrian VII* **1970** *Cry for Us All* **1980** *A Life* **1982** *Othello; Seven Brides for Seven Brothers* **1985** *Doubles*

Frank Hallinan Flood

Frank Hallinan Flood, originally from Ireland, graduated from the National College of Art and Design in 1978 and held the Robert Smithson Memorial Scholarship at the Brooklyn Museum of Art from 1978 to 1979. He worked as a design assistant at the Abbey Theatre in Dublin, Ireland for a year and as assistant to Hayden Griffen at Covent Garden and was art director for the film *Da*. He was resident designer at the National Opera in the 1980-81 season but since the mid-1990s has amassed numerous credits in regional theaters throughout the United States including the Long Wharf. He received a Helen Hayes Award for *Juno and the Paycock* at Arena Stage, where he also designed *The Price*.

Sets: 1988 *Juno and the Paycock*

Walter Florell

Walter Florell, son of a German father and an Austrian duchess was born in Hamburg in 1911 and raised in Berlin. He gave up a career in ballroom dancing when the hats his partner wore attracted the attention of the Duchess of Kent in London. A milliner for theatrical shows, actresses and private customers, he contributed hats to several Broadway shows as well as designing all the costumes for three. He also provided hats for movies including *Easter Parade, Harvey,* and *Sunset Boulevard.* He moved to New York in the late 1930s and worked for Lily Dache before opening his own salon on 57th Street in 1939. Throughout his career he steadfastly refused to reveal details of his personal life and background, putting the focus instead on making his clients more glamorous. He retired in 1963 and settled in Wilton, Connecticut, planning to paint and write, but returned to Seventh Avenue for a short time in the late 1970s. Walter Florell died on October 6, 1986 at age 75.

Costumes: **1943** *The Merry Widow* **1945** *Mr. Strauss Goes to Boston* **1946** *Beggar's Holliday*

Chris Flower

Chris Flower designed the settings for a show on Broadway in 1980.

Sets: **1980** *Quick Change*†

Frederick Foord

See Frederick Ford.

Donald Foote

Donald Foote spent much of his career designing costumes for the circus and ice shows. He studied at Chounard Art Institute and first worked with costumes in a movie studio. He was associated with Theoni V. Aldridge at the New York Public Theatre, assisted Motley on Broadway, and Billy Livingston with the Ice Capades and Ice Follies. He designed costumes for Ringling Bros. and Barnum & Bailey Circus from 1970 until his death in 1984 at the age of 52.

Costumes: **1964** *The Subject Was Roses*

Barbara Forbes

Barbara Forbes designs costumes for theater and dance in and around New York. Off-Broadway productions include *Remembrance, Handy Dandy,* and *Home Games* at the John Houseman Theatre and *The Tavern* at the Equity Library Theatre. Among her many designs for American Stage Company in Teaneck, New Jersey is *The Art of Murder*. At the George Street Playhouse in New Brunswick, New Jersey where she is resident designer *Relativity, David's Mother, Near the End of the Century,* and *Ed Linderman's Broadway Jukebox* are a small portion of her many designs. For the Dance Theatre of Harlem she designed costumes for *Ginastera*.

Costumes: **1989** *The Merchant of Venice*†

Frederick Ford

In the early 1920s Frederick Leslie Ford designed scenery for a show produced on Broadway; his surname was spelled incorrectly in the playbill, as Foord. He was born in New Bedford, Massachusetts in 1894 and received as B.S. in architecture from the Massachusetts Institute of Technology in 1924. He began professional life as a draftsman for other architects, but ultimately established his own firm, F. Leslie Ford. A specialist in residences and public and commercial buildings, he designed many churches (principally in Massachusetts) including the Weymouth Universalist Church, the Auburndale Congregational Church, and the Wollaston Methodist Church. He died on January 5, 1984 in Marion, Massachusetts.

Sets: **1923** *Time*

R. Forester

R. Forester created sets for a show on Broadway in the mid-1920s. He appeared in *The Whirl of the World* at the London Palladium in 1925.

Sets: **1925** *Chivalry*

C. Formilli

C. Formilli contributed scenic designs to two Broadway productions. It is likely that he was Italian painter, Cesare Formilli, who exhibited two landscapes in Rome in 1887, and was author and illustrator of *The Castles of Italy*, published in London by A. & C. Black in 1933. C. Formilli is also mentioned as a graphic artist and watercolorist in the 1934 edition of *Dizionario Illustrato Dei Pittori, Disegnatori e Incisori Italiani Moderni e Contemporanie*.

Sets: **1903** *Mother Goose*† **1913** *Hop o' My Thumb*†

Stanley Fort

In 1933 Stanley Fort designed sets on Broadway for one production. In 1925 he worked as a plasterer from his residence at 2658 Eighth Avenue in New York City.

Sets: **1933** *The Mountain*†

Thomas Fowler

Thomas Fowler received credit as the scenic designer for a Broadway show in 1934. He was proprietor of Fowler's Scenic Studios, located at 261 West 54th Street in New York City in 1932, a supplier of "theatrical supplies and equipment."

Sets: 1934 *Legal Murder*

Fox and Vincent

Fox and Vincent collaborated on the scenery for a Broadway production in 1902. James A. Fox (c. 1868-1922) was a scene designer and painter who headed the scenic department at the Metropolitan Opera House. H. A. Vincent (1864-1931) designed a production in 1915. Additional information and credits can be found under each of their names.

Sets: 1900 *The Belle of Bridgeport†*

Frederick Fox

Frederick Fox was a scenic and lighting designer who occasionally contributed costume designs to a production as well. Born on July 10, 1910 in New York City, he studied at Yale after graduating from Phillips Exeter Academy and worked initially as an architect. Before his New York debut, *Farewell Summer* in 1937, he designed many summer stock productions. A prolific designer of plays and operas, Mr. Fox also designed television specials and shows, and was among the first designers to successfully make the transition when color replaced black and white. He designed numerous films between 1936 and 1961 as a scenic designer and lighting director, and received additional credits as a producer and costume designer. The setting for *Darkness At Noon* won him a Donaldson Award in 1951. He died in Englewood, New Jersey on September 11, 1991 at age 81.

Sets: 1937 *The Bat; Farewell Summer; Orchids Preferred* 1938 *The Man from Cairo; There's Always a Breeze* 1940 *Blind Alley; Johnny Belinda; The Strangler Fig* 1941 *All Men Are True; Brooklyn Biarritz; Good Neighbor; Junior Miss; Snookie* 1942 *The Doughgirls; Johnny on a Spot; Magic/ Hello, Out There†; Wine,* *Women and Song; Yankee Point* 1943 *Lady, Behave; Land of Fame; Men in Shadow; The Naked Genius; The Snark Was a Boojum; Those Endearing Young Charms; The Two Mrs. Carrolls* 1944 *Anna Lucasta; The Day Will Come; Dear Ruth; Decision; Hickory Stick; The Man Who Had All the Luck; The Odds on Mrs. Oakley; Only the Heart; Ramshackle Inn* 1945 *Alice in Arms; Calico Wedding; Good Night Ladies; A Goose for the Gander; Kiss Them for Me; Marriage is for Single People; The Wind is Ninety* 1946 *Little Brown Jug; Mr. Peebles and Mr. Hooker* 1947 *John Loves Mary* 1948 *Light Up the Sky; Make Mine Manhattan* 1949 *They Knew What They Wanted* 1950 *Southern Exposure* 1951 *Angels Kiss Me; Darkness at Noon; Never Say Never* 1952 *The Climate of Eden; The Seven Year Itch* 1953 *Room Service* 1954 *Anniversary Waltz; King of Hearts; Lunatics and Lovers; Reclining Figure* 1955 *The Wayward Saint* 1956 *Speaking of Murder* 1957 *Fair Game; The Greatest Man Alive* 1958 *Howie* 1959 *Golden Fleecing; The Warm Peninsula* 1960 *The Hostage; A Mighty Man Is He; Send Me No Flowers* 1961 *From the Second City; Mandingo*

Costumes: 1942 *Johnny on a Spot* 1944 *Only the Heart* 1945 *Alice in Arms* 1949 *They Knew What They Wanted* 1952 *The Seven Year Itch* 1954 *King of Hearts; Lunatics and Lovers; Reclining Figure* 1957 *The Greatest Man Alive* 1959 *Golden Fleecing* 1960 *Send Me No Flowers* 1961 *Mandingo* 1965 *La Grasse Valise†* (Costume Supervisor)

Lights: 1943 *Men in Shadow* 1944 *Career Angel* 1945 *Alice in Arms; Good Night Ladies; The Secret Room* 1946 *Little Brown Jug* 1947 *John Loves Mary* 1950 *Southern Exposure* 1951 *Angels Kiss Me; Darkness at Noon* 1952 *The Seven Year Itch* 1953 *Room Service* 1954 *Anniversary Waltz; King of Hearts; Lunatics and Lovers; Reclining Figure* 1955 *The Wayward Saint* 1956 *Speaking of Murder* 1957 *The Greatest Man Alive* 1958 *Howie* 1959 *Golden Fleecing; The Warm Peninsula* 1960 *The Hostage; A Mighty Man Is He; Send Me No Flowers* 1961 *From the Second City; Mandingo*

James Fox

James A. Fox was a scene designer and painter. For more than twenty years he worked in the scenic department of the Metropolitan Opera House, where he was involved with productions including *Tosca*, *Carmen* and *the Girl of the Golden West*. At the time of his death on November 23, 1922, he was its' head. In addition to designing sets under his own name, Fox also collaborated with H.A. Vincent as "Fox and Vincent." See that entry for additional credits.

Sets: 1900 *A Million Dollars*† (Act II, 3) **1905** *Fedora* **1908** *The Gay Musician*†

Miss Mary Fox

Miss Mary Fox designed the settings for a single Broadway show in 1925 and appeared in the film with that title in the same year. Also known as Mary Foy, she appeared with family in the popular vaudeville act, Eddie Foy and the Seven Little Foys, beginning in 1910. She then appeared in films between the early 1920s and 1935 when she married actor Lyle Latell. In two films, *Don't Bother Mother* and *Gambling* she used the name Mary Foy, after which she appeared as Mary Fox. She died in 1987 at age 84.

Sets: 1925 *Don't Bother Mother*

Kenneth Foy

Kenneth Foy was born on July 22, 1950 in New York City and received a B.F.A. at Cooper Union. He first became involved with theater while attending summer camp, where he created sets for *The Mikado*. He has served as resident designer for the Kenyon (Ohio) Festival and the Berkshire Theatre Festival, and beginning in 1988 was on the staff at the Metropolitan Opera. He also designed for the Manhattan Theatre Club, Juilliard, Studio Arena Theatre, Long Wharf Theatre and the Lyric Opera of Chicago among others, and designed the world premiere of Thomas Passatiere's opera *The Three Sisters*. Designs in the twenty-first century include scenery for *Syringa Tree*, *Say Yes!*, *Dame Edna: The Royal Tour*, *The New Red Hot and Blue* and *If You Ever Leave Me...I'm Going With You*.

Sets: 1981 *Candida* **1982** *Macbeth* **1989** *Gypsy* **1990** *Oh, Kay!* **1991** *Gypsy* **1996** *The Apple Doesn't Fall* (Also projections) **1997** *Annie* **1998** *An Evening with Jerry Herman* **1999** *Dame Edna*

Mrs. Lulu Fralik

Between 1904 and 1911 Lulu Fralik designed costumes that were worn on the Broadway stage. She was credited in playbills with several variations of her name, appearing as both Mrs. and Madame. Her surname was spelled as Fralik, Fralick, and Frallik.

Costumes: 1904 *Richelieu*†; *The Taming of the Shrew*† (All other costumes) **1905** *Richelieu*† **1907** *Richelieu*† **1908** *Don Quixote*† **1909** *Richelieu*† **1911** *Macbeth (Kellerd)*† (Costumes, weapons, and jewelry)

Millard France

Millard H. France (occasionally Willard France) designed sets for four shows between 1915 and 1927. He operated a scenic studio, Millard H. France Company, at 504 West 38th Street, with his son, Chester A. France. The business initially provided storage for stage settings, but subsequently became a scene painting studio and ultimately a scenic construction business. In 1931 the company became known as Millard H. France Sons, Inc., and was operated at the same location by Chester, Edward and Raymond France, continuing to provide theatrical scenery. In 1925 Millard France resided at 461 Fort Washington Avenue in New York City.

Sets: 1915 *The Critic* **1918** *The Awakening*† **1924** *The Fatal Wedding* **1927** *One for All*

Wesley France

Wesley France is a lighting designer who also works as production manager and tour manager for the Market Theatre Company of Johannesburg, South Africa. His first production was *Sweeney Todd* in the Laager. Additional credits in New York include lighting supervision of *Woza Africa!* at Lincoln Center, and lighting designs for *Born in the RSA*, *Bohpa* and *Asinamali*.

Lights: 1987 *Asinamali!*

Madame Frances

Madame Frances owned and operated a dress salon, Frances, in New York City from the teens until the early 1930s, located initially at 1764 Broadway and then at 10 West 56th Street. The shop, similar to that headed by Lucile, provided both custom-made gowns and Paris imports, making it popular with private customers and theatrical clients. It is likely that this is a different designer than Madame Francis, of London, who was active on Broadway during the first years of the twentieth century. Given the overlap of dates, it is possible that some of the credits attributed to Madame Frances belong to Frances Cline, who was active during the twenties and thirties.

Costumes: 1911 *The Fascinating Widow†* (Gowns, hats and riding habits); *Gypsy Love†* (Act II company); *The Red Rose†* (Other gowns) 1912 *Modest Suzanne; Tantalizing Tommy; The Truth Wagon; The Typhoon; The Woman-Haters* 1913 *The Second Mrs. Tanqueray* 1920 *The Mirage* 1923 *Ziegfeld Follies: 1923†* (Gowns) 1925 *American Born* 1929 *Family Affairs†* (Miss Burke's costumes) 1931 *Right of Happiness†* (Ladies gowns)

Kay Francis

Kay Francis was an actress who as a young girl abandoned a business career for the stage. She was quite successful in Hollywood making over 50 films. She first appeared on Broadway in the 1920s and returned from California in 1946 for additional roles. She was born in Oklahoma City on January 13, 1899 (some sources state1903) and died in August of 1968. Miss Francis' mother was also an actress. Together they moved to New York City where her mother gave up her stage career and opened the Katherine Gibbs Secretarial School. The first professional role played by Kay Francis was as "Player Queen" in *Hamlet* in 1925. She continued to play small roles, and assist with costumes until her first film, *Gentleman of the Press* in 1929.

Costumes: 1927 *Damn the Tears†*

Madame Francis

Madame Francis, of 6, Orchard Street, London, designed costumes for many productions in London in the first two decades of the twentieth century. Two of them were brought to Broadway after successful London runs. Among her other credits are *Miss Cinderella, Mary Goes First, The Mysterious Mr. Bugle* and *The Dangerous Age*. It is likely that she is a different designer than Madame Frances, sometimes cited as Madame Francis, the American couturier, active from the teens into the thirties.

Costumes: 1901 *A Message from Mars†* 1903 *Facing the Music†*

Richard Francis

Richard Francis, an electrician, lived at 108 West 15th Street in New York City in 1901. In 1907 the New York City Directory identifies him as a foreman, residing at 720 Cauldwell Avenue.

Lights: 1900 *The Village Postmaster*

Erle Payne Franke

Erle Payne Franke (also known as Earl and Erl Franke) designed sets and costumes for one show in 1922 and costumes for an additional production in 1924. In 1925 Erle Studios, Inc., a firm of decorators, was located at 161 East 60th Street in New York City, with Erle Franke as President. He was born in New York on June 26, 1897 and died in Los Angeles, California on October 4, 1961.

Sets: 1922 *Greenwich Village Follies†*
Costumes: 1922 *Greenwich Village Follies†* (Gowns, "Village Workshop, Spanish Dancer") 1924 *No Other Girl* (Miss Eaton's and Miss Carroll's costumes)

Beulah Frankel

Beulah Frankel received her first credit on Broadway as technical director for *Me, the Sleeper* in 1949. A native of New York City, she studied at the Carnegie Institute of Technology and the New School for Social Research. As a child she took dance and acting classes at the Neighborhood Playhouse but began her professional career in lighting assisting Bill Richardson. Her first designs in New York were costumes for *Show-Off* and *Julius*

Caesar at the Arena Theatre in the Edison Hotel. She became an independent producer after initially working in New York and Hollywood as a scenic designer and art director. The first woman member of the Motion Picture Art Directors Society, her designs for commercials were awarded fifteen Clios. She is associated with the following companies: Beulah Frankel Productions, Inc., Los Angeles (producing plays, films and television); Eastern Scenic Backdrops, Inc. (renting painted backdrops); and D'Arcy Design, Ltd. (designing restaurant interiors). She is married to William Stokes Tillisch.

Costumes: 1950 *Julius Caesar* (Costume Supervisor); *The Show-Off*
Lights: 1950 *The Show-Off*

P. T. Frankl

Paul T. Frankl, a native of Vienna emigrated to the United States in 1914 after studying at the University of Vienna, the University of Munich and art schools in Paris and Munich. In addition to working as an interior decorator he created modern settings for plays and designed modern furniture for the Johnson Company of Grand Rapids, Michigan. He was president of a Madison Avenue art gallery and interior design studio (the Frankl Galleries), lectured at the Metropolitan Museum of Art, New York University, and the University of Southern California, and wrote books on contemporary design. Prior to World War I, he was important in the modern art movement. He died on March 21, 1958, at age 71 in Palos Verdes Estates, California.

Sets: 1911 *Helena's Husband* **1915** *A Bear* **1921** *Sonya*

C. Lovat Fraser

C. Lovat Fraser was a British graphic artist and theatrical designer. He was born Lovat Claud Fraser on May 15, 1890 and died suddenly in 1921 at thirty-one years of age. A talent for drawing and a fondness for bright colors made him an influential designer early in this century. He designed for the Lyric Theatre, Hammersmith where he collaborated with

actor-manager Nigel Playfair. He carried his pencils along while serving in World War I and recorded battle scenes at Ypres, France. Both an illustrator and an artist, Mr. Fraser, who loved the eighteenth century, was a book illustrator and wrote poetry under the pen name "Honeywood." A book chronicling his life and art, *The Book of Lovat* by Haldane MacFall, was published in 1923. His designs and drawings have been the subject of exhibits at Middleton hall, University of Hull, the Ashmolean Museum at Oxford, and at the Victoria and Albert Museum.

Sets: 1908 *Agnes* **1920** *The Beggar's Opera* **1928** *The Beggar's Opera*
Costumes: 1920 *The Beggar's Opera* **1928** *The Beggar's Opera*

Miriam Frazer

Miriam Frazer designed costumes for one show on Broadway in the late 1920s. A dressmaker she lived and worked from 188 West 185th Street in New York City.

Costumes: 1927 *What Do We Know?*†

Karl R. Free

Karl R. Free contributed designs for costumes to a play on Broadway in 1938. He was a watercolorist; his paintings are in the major New York museums. He was born in Davenport, Iowa and was an associate curator at the Whitney Museum of American Art. Mr. Free died on February 16, 1947, New York City.

Costumes: 1938 *Pocahontas*

Pat Freeborn

Pat Freeborn designed costumes for a play in 1955.

Costumes: 1955 *Iolanthe*

Madame Freisinger

Madame Elise Seeger Freisinger (Friesinger) provided costumes for many Broadway shows, sometimes as costume designer but even more often by executing the designs of others. For example, she made the costumes for *The Prince of Pilsen* from the designs of Will R. Barnes and Archie Gunn with whom she frequently worked. In the last decade of the nineteenth century, Elise Seeger moved from her native Bremen, Germany where she was born on November 10, 1855, to New York City to become head of the costume department of the Metropolitan Opera House. She often claimed to have been born with a pair of scissors in her hands with which she could work magic. She married Mr. Freisinger at the end of the first of her six seasons creating opera costumes. Madame Freisinger then opened her own business on East Eighteenth Street, later relocating to 127 West 41st Street, executing costumes for musicals, plays, and operas working often for David Belasco. Remarkably, she even had a telephone number in 1906. An account of her life, experiences with costumes, and memories of the stars who wore them, "Stars and Scissors," was published in *Good Housekeeping Magazine* in February 1930. She died in Los Angeles, California on September 5, 1945.

Costumes: **1899** *Becky Sharp*† **1900** *Trilby* **1902** *The Darling of the Gods*†; *Robin Hood* **1903** *Darling of the Gallery Gods, The and The Dress Parade*†; *Hedda Gabler* (Mrs. Fiske's gowns); *A Princess of Kensington*† **1904** *Leah Kleschna* (Mrs. Fiske's costumes); *Richelieu*†; *Sergeant Kitty*† **1905** *The Mayor of Tokio*† (as: E.S. Freisinger); *Richelieu*† **1906** *The Kreutzer Sonata*† **1907** *Richelieu*†; *Ziegfeld Follies of 1907*† **1908** *Don Quixote*†; *The Fool Hath Said: 'There Is No God'*†; *Our American Cousin*; *Salvation Nell*; *Ziegfeld Follies of 1908*† **1909** *Richelieu*† **1910** *The Green Cockatoo*; *Hannele*; *Turning Point* **1911** *Love among the Lions* (Little Boy Blue's costume); *The Red Rose*† (Men's costumes) **1913** *Much Ado About Nothing*†; *The Poor Little Rich Girl*; *Somewhere Else*† (Principal women's costumes) **1915** *Trilby*† (Gowns) **1917** *When Johnny Comes Marching Home* **1923** *Romeo and Juliet*† (Miss Cowl's costumes) **1926** *The Ladder* (Period costumes) **1928** *The Royal Box*

Jesse Fremont

Jesse Fremont contributed designs for dresses to a Broadway show in 1922. He resided at 73 Perry Street and worked as treasurer of the Picture Pocket Company, an accessories business at 509 Fifth Avenue in New York City.

Costumes: **1922** *Manhattan* (Dresses)

Carroll French

Carroll French, a sculptor, designed costumes for a play in the mid-1930s. He was born in Michigan and learned sculpture in foundries, and also on board wooden ships in Lake Michigan. The winner of several gallery awards for his art, he died on November 11, 1971 in New York City at age 82.

Costumes: **1934** *Valley Forge*

Jared French

Jared French was a painter and sculptor who also did many murals, beginning his career as a young participant in the Federal Arts Project in the 1930s. He was born in Ossining, New York on February 4, 1905, and studied at the Art Students League at Thomas Hart Benton and at Amherst College (B.A. 1925). His works in tempera, cast metal and stone have been widely collected by museums and individuals. Included in several of the Biennial exhibitions at the Whitney Museum, his work was displayed in the Museum of Modern Art's "Americans, 1943: Realists and Magic Realists" exhibit, among others. In the late 1930s he applied his considerable talents to the costume designs for a Broadway show. French died on January 15, 1988 in Rome where he spent most of the last twenty years of his life, although he also had a home in Hartland, Vermont.

Costumes: **1938** *Billy the Kid*

Michael Frenkel

Michael (Mikhail) Frenkel was born in Kiev, Ukraine and received an M.A. in stage design and scenography at the Moscow Art Theatre drama school in 1972, after studying at the School of Fine Arts and the College of Theatrical and Design Arts in Kiev. His first designs were for *Cat's House* at the Kiev Operetta Theatre in 1964. In 1965 he joined the staff at the Young People's Theatre in Kiev as chief scenic designer with productions including *My Poor*

Marat. In 1968 he began an association with the Lesya Ukrainka Academic Drama Theatre when *Look Back in Anger* opened. He amassed numerous credits for scenery, costume and lighting design in many theaters throughout the former Soviet Union, as well as in Greece, Germany, and Bulgaria. His designs for *King Matiush I* and *The Piper From Strakonici* won two Soviet Union Ministry of Culture Awards (equivalent to a Tony Award) and his designs for *Into the Whirlwind* were honored with a Drama Desk Award. Since relocating to the United States in the mid-1990s, due in part to the devastation in the Ukraine following the nuclear reactor accident in Chernobyl, he has designed in regional theaters, including the Milwaukee Repertory Theatre, the Milwaukee Chamber Theatre, and the Broadway Theatre Center.
Sets: 1996 *Into the Whirlwind*
Costumes: 1996 *Into the Whirlwind*
Lights: 1996 *Into the Whirlwind*

Joseph Fretwell III

Joseph Fretwell III was born in Anderson, South Carolina on September 19, 1915 to a talented family of painters and musicians. He attended Duke University where he was active with the Duke Players and Yale University where he studied with Frank Bevan and Donald Oenslager. His interest in costume design began in his grammar school days. Upon arriving in New York he worked with Raoul Pène du Bois, making his own Broadway debut in 1942. Additional costume designs include *This is The Army* with Irving Berlin. He died on September 5, 1992.
Costumes: 1942 *The Flowers of Virtue* **1949** *The Rat Race*† (Other costumes); *The Traitor*; *The Velvet Glove* (Costume Consultant)

Sylvia Friedlander

Sylvia Friedlander spent most of her career in the theater as an actress and producer. The daughter of Max Friedlander, at one time Chairman of the Board of Dazians, she was a student at Smith College and the New York School of the Theatre. She designed costumes for the Ida Kaminska Company at the Roosevelt Auditorium, and

Yoshe Kalb for the Habimah Troupe's Tour of the U.S. She worked on television programs with producer David Susskind including *The Kay Kyser Show*, featuring the big-band leader. In addition, she produced plays for the Equity Library Theatre and other theaters, including those on Broadway. Sylvia Friedlander Robins was born in New York City in 1918 and died there on November 6, 1992 at age 74.
Costumes: 1970 *Light, Lively, and Yiddish*

Charles Friedman

Born in Poland on September 20, 1902, Charles Friedman was raised on the Lower East Side of New York City, where he died on July 18, 1984. He directed plays wherever he found the opportunity, in settlement houses and small theaters. Representative productions include *Pins and Needles, Carmen Jones, Street Scene* and the Federal Theatre production of *Sing for Your Supper* in 1939. He wrote the script and lyrics for *My Darlin' Aida.* Charles Friedman was also a director, producer and writer for television.
Sets: 1927 *Rutherford and Son* **1928** *Waltz of the Dogs* **1929** *The Silver Tassie*
Lights: 1935 *Mother*

Mary E. Friedman

Mary E. Friedman designed costumes for a play in the mid-1920s. Born in Wisconsin on August 15, 1882, she attended Smith College and graduated from New York University. A dressmaker, her salon, "Mary R." provided gowns to private and theatrical customers from Rooms 1-2 at 2853 Broadway. She resided at 643 Lafayette Avenue in Mt. Vernon, New York. She later relocated her salon to Los Angeles, California and died there on April 5, 1950.
Costumes: 1926 *Magda* (Character costumes)

Samuel J. Friedman

Samuel J. Friedman spent the majority of his career in the garment trade in Yonkers, New York. The 1909-1910 New York City directory lists him as a designer, residing at 125

West 146th Street, and in 1913, he designed scenery for a Broadway production. Born in New York, he moved to Yonkers as a young child. He died in Miami, Florida at the age of 58 on March 15, 1941.
Sets: 1913 *Rachel*†

Frisbie & Mayerhofer

Frisbie & Mayerhofer "invented and prepared" the lights for a 1900 production of *Caleb West* at the Manhattan Theatre according to the production program.
Lights: 1900 *Caleb West* (Invented and prepared)

Florence Froelich

Florence Froelich designed plays in 1909 and 1925 on Broadway.
Costumes: 1909 *The Goddess of Reason*
1925 *Gypsy Fires*

Miriam Frone

Miriam Frone supervised the women's costumes for a play on Broadway in the mid 1930s.
Costumes: 1934 *Strangers at Home* (Women's Costume Supervisor)

Norma Fuller

Norma Fuller collaborated on the costume designs for a play in 1937.
Costumes: 1937 *Pins and Needles*†

Ralph Funicello

Scenic designer Ralph Funicello, born in Mamaroneck, New York on September 5, 1947, has designed over two hundred productions throughout the United States and Canada. He attended Boston University and graduated from New York University in 1970, studying with Ming Cho Lee and Wolfgang Roth. He designed the first two productions at the Denver Theatre Center in 1980 and designs extensively at the Old Globe (Associate Artist), Mark Taper Forum, the South Coast Repertory, the Seattle Repertory, and the American Conservatory Theatre (Director of Design 1988-1990). He has also designed for the Pacific Conservatory, the Guthrie Theatre, the New York Shakespeare Festival, Manhattan Theatre Club, the New York City Opera, the McCarter Theater Center,

and at Lincoln Center, among many others. Active in professional circles, he has served on the Theatre Panel of the National Endowment for the Arts, as a Director at Large for USITT, and holds the Powell Chair in Set Design at San Diego State University. His designs which are widely exhibited have also received many honors, including Los Angeles Drama Critics Circle Awards, Back Stage West Garland Awards, Dramalogue Awards, a Bay Area Theatre Critics Circle Award, and the 1998 Michael Merritt Award for Excellence in Design and Collaboration, Twenty-first century designs include *Mary Stuart, Enrico IV, The Education of Randy Newman, the Circle, Master Harold and the Boys*, and *QED*.
Sets: 1980 *Division Street*

V. C. Fuqua

In addition to his credits as a lighting designer on Broadway in the mid-1960s, V. C. Fuqua has designed in regional theaters including the Cape Playhouse, Playhouse-in-the-Park in Philadelphia, the McCarter Theater Center and off-Broadway. He received a B.A. in technical writing at the Massachusetts Institute of Technology and an M.A. from the University of Texas in lighting design.
Lights: 1965 *The Glass Menagerie; Me and Thee* **1966** *Pousse-Cafe*

Lydia Furbush

Lydia Furbush designed costumes for two plays in the mid-1930s. The daughter of Dr. Charles Lincoln Furbush, a physician in the medical corps who did research on the causes and cures of yellow fever, she attended the Academy of Fine Arts in Philadelphia and the Nixon School in Florence, Italy. Her fashion and costume designs were seen in New York, London and Paris. In 1937, she married architect Lancelot F. Sims.
Costumes: 1933 *Men in White* **1934** *Gentlewoman* (Women's clothes) **1935** *The Dominant Sex*

Roger Furse

Roger Kemble Furse, a British designer and painter was born September 11, 1903 in Ightham, Kent, England. He designed scenery and costumes in England for numerous plays at the Old Vic and in London's West End. He began professional life as a portraitist in Paris and in New York. In 1931 he became associated with Laurence Olivier and thereafter devoted his talents to theatrical design. He designed several films, including *Ivanhoe, The Road to Hong Kong* and *The Prince and the Show Girl*, winning an Oscar for the design of Laurence Olivier's *Hamlet* in 1948. In 1951 his business, W. J. Furse and Company, Limited, supplied "Cinema and Theatre Lighting" from its location at 7 Carteret Street, Westminster, England. Roger Furse died on August 19, 1972 on the island of Corfu, Greece.

Sets: **1938** *Spring Meeting*† **1950** *Daphne Laureola*† **1951** *Antony and Cleopatra*; *Caesar and Cleopatra* **1952** *Venus Observed* **1960** *Duel of Angels*; *The Tumbler*

Costumes: **1946** *Henry IV, Part I*; *Henry IV, Part II* **1965** *Pickwick*†

Yukio Furukawa

In 1993, Yukio Furukawa designed lights for a Broadway play.

Lights: **1993** *Yabuhara Kengyo*

Madame Gabbetio

The *Fascinating Mr. Vanderveldt* playbill credits one of the collaborating costume designers as Madame L. Gabbetio, Manchester Street, London. As Madame Gabbetti, she contributed designs to *Merely Mary Ann* in London in 1904.

Costumes: **1906** *Fascinating Mr. Vanderveldt*† (Other gowns)

Donna Gabriel

Donna Gabriel supervised the costumes for a production in the late 1930s

Costumes: **1939** *Where There's a Will*† (Costumes Supervised)

Lillian Gaertner

Lillian Gaertner designed scenery and costumes for many operas and plays in addition to her work as an illustrator and painter. Her designs for *Egyptian Helen* by Richard Strauss were seen at the Metropolitan Opera House in 1928. The settings for that production were

designed by Joseph Urban, with whom she often worked. She also designed murals, including those decorating the lobby of the New Ziegfeld Theatre at its opening in 1928. Born in New York City on July 5, 1906, she studied painting with Joseph Hoffman and Ferdinand Schmutzer. She married Harold Palmedo on January 19, 1930.

Sets: **1926** *The Straw Hat*

Costumes: **1926** *The Straw Hat*

Raimonda Gaetani

Raimonda Gaetani was born in Naples, Italy in 1942 and studied at the Architecture University there, where she became interested in theater. Her film designs include Federico Fellini's *Casanova* (with fellow Italian designer Danilo Donati), G. Ferrara's *Un Coeur Simple*, and the 1996 *Jane Eyre*. She has additional credits for productions at the Teatro Alla Scala in Milan, the Quirius Theatre in Rome, Covent Garden (*Cavalleria Rusticana, I Pagliacci*), and the Metropolitan Opera *La Traviata* in 1998. She frequently collaborates with Eduardo de Filippo, author of *Filumena*.

Sets: **1980** *Filumena*

Costumes: **1974** *Saturday Sunday Monday* **1980** *Filumena*

David S. Gaither

David S. Gaither was principally a set designer who also created lights and costumes on Broadway between 1922 and 1933. He served as President of United Scenic Artists in the late 1930s. Also a painter, in 1932 he resided at 29 Perry Street in New York City.

Sets: **1923** *The Rivals* **1924** *The Wonderful Visit* **1925** *Episode*; *Nocturne* **1926** *Ghosts*; *Old Bill, M.P.* **1927** *Ghosts* **1929** *Queen Bee* **1930** *Gold Braid* **1932** *Riddle Me This* **1933** *Foolscap*; *Riddle Me This*; *Two Strange Women*

Costumes: **1927** *Ghosts* **1930** *Gold Braid* (Production design)

Lights: **1927** *Ghosts*

Galanos

James Galanos was born in Philadelphia, Pennsylvania on September 30, 1924. After studying fashion design in New York at the Traphagen School of Fashion, he moved to California and worked for a short time with the film costume designer, Jean Louis. In 1951, he showed his first collection and has been successfully designing fashion ever since. Known for the beauty of line and quality craftsmanship, Galanos is one of the premier American fashion designers, creating many of the gowns worn by First Lady Nancy Reagan, including both inaugural dresses. Based in California he occasionally contributes designs to plays and films.

Costumes: 1968 *The Flip Side†* (Gowns)

Gregory Gale

Costume designer Gregory Gale's designs for *Mary Stuart* and *The Infernal Machine* at the Jean Cocteau Repertory are among his many credits. He worked with costume designer Jonathan Bixby (d. 2001), initially as an assistant, then as an associate, and subsequently as a co-designer on productions such as *Hello, Dolly!*, *Street Corner Symphony*, and *As Bees in Honey Drown*. Other designs include productions at Goodspeed Opera House and with the Drama Dept. Twenty-first century credits include *Rude Entertainment* for the Drama Dept. and *Urinetown: The Musical* in the 2001-2002 Broadway season.

Costumes: 1999 *Band in Berlin†*

J. F. Gallagher

J. F. Gallagher designed one set in 1928 on Broadway. In 1925 he resided at 50 Union Avenue in New York City.

Sets: 1928 *The Age of Innocence†*

Fannie Gallent

Fannie Gallent created costumes for a Broadway show in 1933.

Costumes: 1933 *They All Come to Moscow* (Costumes executed)

Paul Gallis

Scenic designer Paul Gallis who was born in 1943 is a self-taught designer. He has designed theater, opera and ballet throughout The Netherlands, Germany and France since making his debut in 1974 at The Holland Festival. He serves on the artistic board of Theatre Group Amsterdam, and in 1992 won the Dutch Proscenium

Award for his theatrical designs. Additional designs in the United States include *the Barber of Seville* for Long Beach Opera.

Sets: 1993 *Cyrano: The Musical*

David Gallo

Scenic designer David Gallo was born in 1966 and attended SUNY-Purchase, where although he didn't graduate he studied with and was inspired by John Boyt and learned many of the technical elements needed by a successful designer. His long list of off-Broadway credits began with a collaboration with Chris Ashley, for whom he would later design *Bunny Bunny* and *Machinal* written by Sophie Treadwell and directed by Michael Grief. Other off-Broadway productions include *The Wild Party*, *Jar the Floor*, *The Bubbly Black Girl* and pieces for Blue Man Group. His designs in regional theaters include Keith Glover's *Thunder Knocking on the Door*, *Golden Boy*, *Dark Paradise* and a new production of *Sweeney Todd* in Cincinnati, among others. Much honored for his striking, original designs, honors include two American Theatre Wing Awards (*The Wild Party*, *Jitney*) among many nominations, Lucille Lortel Awards, Outer Critics Circle Awards, Drama Desk Awards, and the 2000 Obie Award for Sustained Excellence. Twenty-first century designs include *Wonder of the World* in the 2001-2002 Broadway season.

Sets: 1996 *Hughie* 1997 *Jackie*; *View from the Bridge, A* 1998 *Little Me*; *More to Love* 1999 *Epic Proportions*; *The Lion in Winter*; *Voices in the Dark†*; *You're a Good Man, Charlie Brown* 2001 *King Hedley II*

Paul Gallo

Lighting designer Paul Gallo first studied music, art, and dance at Ithaca College (B.F.A. 1974), but became interested in stage design, changing his major to theater and art. Born on February 24, 1953, he studied at Yale University with Ming Cho Lee and received an M.F.A. there in 1977. From 1979 to

1981 he was resident designer at Juilliard, from 1981 to 1983 resident designer at the American Repertory Theatre, and in 1984 was named Associate Lighting Designer at Arena Stage. He has also designed at Playwrights Horizons, the New York Shakespeare Festival, the Westside Theatre, and all of the other major venues in and around New York. Paul Gallo's collaborations with Martha Clarke include *The Garden of Earthly Delights* (for which he received a Maharam Award), *Vienna: Lusthaus* (for which he received an American Theatre Wing Award), and *The Hunger Artist* (for which he received an American Theatre Wing Award). In 1986 his lighting designs were honored with an Obie Award for sustained excellence for work that season: *The House of Blue Leaves, Smile, The Front Page,* and *Drood*. Other honors include six Tony Award nominations and the Outer Critics Circle Award for *The Civil War* in 1999. His credits in the twenty-first century include *Hans Christian Anderson* at San Francisco's Geary Theatre, *Family Week* in New York, and *45 Seconds From Broadway* in the 2001-2002 Broadway season.

Lights: **1980** *John Gabriel Borkman; Passione; Tintypes* **1981** *Candida; Grown-ups; Kingdoms; The Little Foxes* **1982** *Beyond Therapy; Come Back to the 5 & Dime, Jimmy Dean, Jimmy Dean* **1983** *Heartbreak House* **1985** *The Mystery of Edwin Drood* **1986** *The House of Blue Leaves; Smile* **1987** *The Front Page* **1988** *Spoils of War* **1989** *Anything Goes; City of Angels; Lend Me a Tenor* **1990** *Six Degrees of Separation* **1991** *I Hate Hamlet* **1992** *Crazy for You; Guys and Dolls* **1995** *The Tempest* **1996** *Big; A Funny Thing Happened on the Way to the Forum; Skylight*† **1997** *Titanic; Triumph of Love* **1998** *On the Town; The Soundof Music* **1999** *The Civil War; Epic Proportions* **2000** *The Man Who Came to Dinner; The Rocky Horror Show* **2001** *42nd Street*

Dolores Gamba

Dolores Gamba was born in Brooklyn on May 7, 1952 and received a B.A. from Ramapo College in Mahway, New Jersey. She considered a career in acting, but turned her attention to costumes. Her first costume designs were for summer stock and between 1976 and 1981 she designed many shows off-off-Broadway. *Of the Fields, Lately* was originally produced at Theatre Off-Park and later moved to Broadway. A long time wardrobe supervisor at Radio City Music Hall, she has also been involved with wardrobe for films.

Costumes: **1980** *Of the Fields, Lately*

Leo Gambacorta

Leo Gambacorta designed a show on Broadway in 1980. He has designed sets for Playwrights Horizons, the Separate Theatre Company and in regional theaters, as well as working as a scenic artist and lighting designer for the Laura Dean Dancers. He has also served as an adjunct professor of speech and theater at John Jay College and is well known as a road manager for musicians, including J. J. Johnson, George Benson, VSOP, and the JVC Grande Parade du Jazz festival.

Sets: **1980** *Black Broadway*
Costumes: **1980** *Black Broadway*
Lights: **1980** *Black Broadway*

Arline Gardiner

Arline Gardiner created dance costumes for a play in 1919 in collaboration with another designer. Miss Gardiner was mainly a dancer, who performed with the Gardiner Trio in the early teens and in the Richard Herndon revue *Americana* in 1927 and 1928.

Costumes: **1919** *Take It from Me*†
(Dance costumes)

Barry Garlinger

Barry Garlinger was lighting designer for a Broadway show in 1964.

Lights: **1964** *Conversation at Midnight*

Frank Garrison

Frank Garrison designed sets on Broadway between 1924 and 1927. He was primarily a producer who worked with Al G. Fields, John W. Vogel, and others on various minstrel shows. He died on April 11, 1933 in Columbus, Ohio at age 50.

Sets: **1924** *Blind Alleys* **1927** *The Banshee*

Daisy Garson

In 1927, Daisy Garson designed costumes on Broadway. She resided at 411 West End Avenue, New York City in the mid-1920s.

Costumes: 1927 *Merry-Go-Round*† (Costumes for Tampa and Park Avenue)

William Gaskin

William George Gaskin designed sets and costumes on Broadway in 1930. He was also a much exhibited watercolorist and oil painter in the late 1920s, who worked mainly on the West Coast. He was born in San Francisco on December 12, 1892 and died there on June 25, 1968. His painting, "San Francisco Scene," is in the collection of the San Francisco Art Commission.

Sets: 1928 *Hoboken Blues* 1930 *General John Regan*; *The Playboy of the Western World*

Costumes: 1930 *The Playboy of the Western World*

Mordecai Gassner

Mordecai (Mordi) Gassner contributed the designs for sets and costumes for a play in 1948. He was principally a scenic designer, beginning his career at the Westchester Playhouse in Mt. Kisco, New York. He was also art director for films produced by Douglas Fairbanks, Sr. Mr. Gassner received two Guggenheim Fellowships to study painting in Europe, and often had his own paintings and murals exhibited. Born in April 1899, he died in January 1995.

Sets: 1948 *Gone Tomorrow/ Home Life of a Buffalo/Hope is the Thing*; *Minnie and Mr. Williams*

Costumes: 1948 *Minnie and Mr. Williams*

Claudie Gastine

Claudie Gastine, born in Marseille, France began her career as an assistant to Lila deNobili and Rostislav Dobujinsky. She often designs sets and costumes for Gian Carlo Menotti, the Groupe TSE L'Étoile du Nord and the Groupe TSE Theatre Moderne. Film designs include *Jane Eyre, Sense and Sensibility* and *The Nutcracker* both with Rudolf Nureyev and for IMAX.

Her costumes and scenery for opera at Opéra de la Bastille include *Un Ballo in Maschera* and *Dialogues des Carmelites*. In 1998 she recreated and updated the 1924 designs by Alexander Benois for the ballet *Giselle* at Ballet de l'Opéra in Paris.

Costumes: 1980 *Heartaches of a Pussycat*

Gates and Morange

Gates and Morange were active on Broadway for four decades. In 1894 Frank E. Gates, a native of Chicago, and Edward A. Morange from Cold Springs, New York painted a curtain, "Leaving for the Masked Ball" at the Court Square Theatre in Springfield, Massachusetts, which led to their partnership. Their first stage set was *Off the Earth* in 1894 for the American Travesty Company. Frank Gates' brother Richard later joined the firm. Scenic artists (and scenic designers) Alexander Grinager, Arne Lundborg, William E. Castle, Orestes Raineri, and Thomas Benrimo were employed at Gates and Morange, among others. In 1919 Gates and Morange was located at 155 West 29th Street. By 1931 it had relocated to 220 West 42nd Street, and later operated at 530 W. 47th Street. This active studio supplied the designs for settings for numerous productions and painted additional productions, such as *The Garden of Allah, Citizen Pierre, The Daughter of Hearn,* and *Joseph and His Brother.* Frank E. Gates and Edward A. Morange also designed settings under their own names. Additional information may be found under those entries.

Sets: 1899 *The Ameer*† (Act II); *The Gadfly*; *Rogers Brothers in Wall Street*† (Act I) 1900 *Chris and the Wonderful Lamp*†; *The Greatest Thing in the World*; *Sag Harbor*† (Acts II, III, IV) 1901 *The Night of the 4th*† 1902 *Captain Molly*; *Divorcons*; *Mary of Magdala* †(Acts I, II, V) 1903 *Her Own Way*; *Marta of the Lowlands*; *Raffles, the Amateur Cracksman*; *Under Cover*; *The Vinegar Buyer*† (Acts II, III) 1904 *Judith of Bethulia*†; *Lady Teazle*† (Act II); *The Pit*† 1905 *The Duke of Duluth*† (Act II); *The Firm of Cunningham*; *The Mayor of Tokio*†; *Monna*

Vanna; The Squaw Man 1906 Cape Cod Folks; The Kreutzer Sonata; The Love Letter† (Act III); Marrying Mary; The New York Idea 1907 The Christian Pilgrim† (Act V 1, 2); Hip! Hip! Hooray!†; In the Bishop's Carriage; The Rogers Brothers in Panama† 1908 Devil, The (Adapted by Konta and Trowbridge); The Flower of Yamato; Golden Butterfly† (Act I) 1909 The Bridge† (Acts I, III, IV); The Dawn of a Tomorrow; The Fortune Hunter; The Fourth Estate; The Gay Life; His Name on the Door; The Melting Pot; The White Sister; A Woman of Impulse† 1910 The Barrier; Getting a Polish; The Jolly Bachelors†; Mary Magdalene† (Act I, III); Merry Wives of Windsor†; None So Blind; Pomander Walk; Twelfth Night†; The Yankee Girl 1911 Becky Sharp; The Garden of Allah; Green Stockings† (Act I, II); Kismet†; Little Miss Fix-It† (Act II); Passers-By†; The Sign of the Rose; The Silent Call; The Squaw Man; The Thunderbolt 1912 The Blindness of Virtue (Act II); The Daughter of Heaven†; Frou-Frou; The High Road†; The Lady of Dreams; Oliver Twist; Racketty-Packetty House; Robin Hood†; The Typhoon 1913 General John Regan; A Man's Friends; Mrs. Peckham's Carouse; Rob Roy; The Strange Woman†; When Dreams Come True; Widow by Proxy; Ziegfeld Follies of 1913† 1914 The Dickey Bird; The Marriage of Columbine; Polygamy† (Act II); Pygmalion; Rio Grande; Under Cover 1915 Inside the Lines†; Treasure Island 1916 The 13th Chair; Rio Grande; See America First; Turn to the Right† 1917 Colonel Newcome†; Disraeli; The Gay Lord Quex; Our Betters 1918 April; The Garden of Allah; Head over Heels†; Her Country†; Service; Success 1919 Come Along†; Forbidden 1920 The Bat; Daddy Dumplins; The First Year; Genius and the Crowd†; Three Showers 1921 Alias Jimmy Valentine; A Bill of Divorcement; Good Morning, Dearie; The Straw; Wake Up, Jonathan 1922 The Bunch and Judy; A Pinch Hitter; To the Ladies 1923 Cymbeline†; The Dice of the Gods; The Exile; The Mad Honeymoon; Mary Jane McKane; Wildflower 1924 New Brooms; Paradise Alley; Rose-Marie 1926 Betsy† 1927 Behold This Dreamer; Jimmie's Women; Money from Home; Much Ado About Nothing 1928

Diplomacy; The Merry Wives of Windsor; Rainbow; Sherlock Holmes 1929 Among the Married; Great Day; Houseparty; Ladies of the Jury; Mrs. Bumpstead-Leigh; Sherlock Holmes; Sweet Adeline; Your Uncle Dudley 1930 Mr. Samuel; The Rivals; The Well of Romance 1931 The Admirable Crichton; Colonel Satan

Frank E. Gates

Frank E. Gates is perhaps best known as partner with Edward A. Morange in the scenic studio Gates and Morange. He studied at the School of Fine Arts at Washington University in St. Louis, Missouri. Frank Gates' brother Richard was also involved with the firm. He also exhibited paintings in the mid-1930s. Little additional personal information is known about Frank E. Gates who also designed under his own name. He is usually thought to be from the Chicago area, but it is likely that he is the same Frank E. Gates who was born in Ohio on September 20, 1882 and died in Los Angeles on October 14, 1959.

Sets: 1899 Becky Sharp†; Children of the Ghetto† 1900 Lost River†; Monte Cristo† 1901 A Gentleman of France†; Miranda of the Balcony†; Unleavened Bread†; The Unwelcome Mrs. Hatch†; When Knighthood Was in Flower† 1902 The Cavalier†; Little Italy† 1903 Merely Mary Ann†; Nancy Brown†; Romeo and Juliet† 1904 Becky Sharp†; Bird Center†; Leah Kleschna† 1905 Fantana†; The Toast of the Town† 1906 Fascinating Mr. Vanderveldt†; The Red Mill† 1907 Fascinating Flora†; The Lady from Lane's†; The Ranger†; The Rose of Alhambra†; Salomy Jane†; Sappho and Phaon† 1908 The Battle†; The Boys and Betty†; His Wife's Family†; The Man from Home†; Marta of the Lowlands†; The Soul Kiss† 1909 The Conflict†

F. G. Gaus

F. G. Gaus was lighting designer for a 1905 production. Two men with that last name worked as electricians in New York at the beginning of the twentieth century, so it is possible that either of them was responsible for the electrical effects for Fedora. Fred Gaus was born January 8, 1882 and emigrated to the United States as a young man. He died in Fresno, California on October 13, 1975. Frederick Gaus, born January 8, 1880, lived most of his life in New York City. He retired to Florida, where he died in November 1962.

Lights: 1905 *Fedora*

Henry L. Gebhardt

Henry L. Gebhardt, a theatrical properties maker in New York City, also designed a set on Broadway in 1918. He supplied "theatrical properties, papier maché and advertising novelties" from 433-5 West 42nd Street, and "theatrical supplies and equipment" from 523 West 45th Street in New York City from the 1920s through the early 1950s, as Wilfred and Henry L. Gebhardt, Inc. He was born in Germany and moved to the United States as a young man. He served two terms on the Board of Education in Cliffside Park, New Jersey, where he resided at the time of his death on September 29, 1942 at the age of seventy-six. The studio continued under his son, Wilfred Gebhardt, and provided properties for *Mr. Roberts* in 1948, among other productions.

Lights: 1918 *The Garden of Allah*

Larry Gebhardt

Larry Gebhardt created one lighting design on Broadway in 1949.

Lights: 1949 *All for Love*

Philip Gelb

Philip Gelb, a producer, set designer and illustrator, produced plays on Broadway such as *A-Hunting We Will Go* in 1940, and *Honky Tonk - L'Historie de la Burlesque* in 1941. He also produced *Swing Chamber Music* at the Hotel Times Square Grill and *Who Do* at the 1939 World's Fair. Born October 16, 1909, he illustrated *The Merry Gentleman of Japan* a children's story published in 1935 that H. W. Reiter and Shepard Chartoc adapted from *The Mikado*. A play he co-authored with Cyril Heiman, *House in a Sea* was produced by Campus Theatre 170 at the University of California, Los Angeles in 1951. Philip Gelb died on July 31, 1991 in Bronx, New York. He should not be confused with the musician and composer who has the same name.

Sets: 1930 *Life Is Like That* 1932 *Anybody's Game; Jamboree* 1933 *Come Easy* 1934 *Geraniums in My Window; Halfway to Hell; The Wind and the Rain* 1935 *Triumph*

Gunnar Gelbort

Gunnar Gelbort designed costumes for three plays on Broadway in 1962. The productions were all part of world tour of the Royal Dramatic Theatre of Sweden.

Costumes: 1962 *The Father*[†]; *Long Day's Journey into Night; Miss Julie*

Guy Geoly

Guy Geoly made his Broadway debut with the costume designs for a 1989 production. Between 1982 and 1990 he designed numerous productions at the Paper Mill Playhouse, including *Suite in Two Keys, Inherit the Wind, Windy City, Barnum, My One and Only*, and *Shenandoah*.

Costumes: 1989 *Shenandoah*

Hal George

Costume designer Hal George was born January 24, 1937 in Santa Ana, California and received his B.A. at the University of Southern California where he studied with John Blakenchip and became the first undergraduate to design a major production, *A Midsummer Night's Dream*. He has designed for major theaters and opera houses throughout the country. As resident costume designer for the Juilliard School, his designs include *Elegy for Young Lovers, L'Ormindo, The Mines of Sulphur* and the Michael Caccoyannis' *La Boheme*. Designs for the New York City Opera include *Mefistofele*, for the San Francisco Opera they include *Manon*, and for the Lyric Opera of Chicago, *Attila*. He has also designed productions at the American Shakespeare Festival, the Guthrie Theatre, the San Diego Shakespeare Festival, the Pennsylvania Ballet. The Santa Fe Opera, the Kansas City Opera, the Washington Opera, and the Netherlands Opera in Amsterdam.

Costumes: 1968 *Mike Downstairs* 1972 *The Creation of the World and Other Business* 1983 *Zorba*

Joseph George

Joseph George designed lights for three productions in the first decade of the twentieth century on Broadway. An electrician, he worked from 321 West 43rd Street in 1903 and later from 1441 Broadway, New York City.

Lights: 1903 *The Jersey Lily*; *The Jewel of Asia* 1905 *The Duke of Duluth*

Madame Georgette

Madame Georgette designed costumes for a play in 1935.

Costumes: 1935 *Times Have Changed*

Rolf Gérard

Rolf Gérard, a set designer who also designs costumes, was born in Berlin on August 9, 1909. His mother was the famous Italian soprano, Mafalder Salvatini, and his father, Dr. Walter Gérard, a German scientist of French descent. He attended school in Germany and studied medicine in Heidelberg and Paris, receiving his M.D. in Switzerland in 1937. He practiced medicine in England where he moved in 1936. His London debut was in 1944 for *Awake and Sing*, soon after designing *Romeo and Juliet* at Stratford-upon-Avon directed by Peter Brook. He has since designed extensively for theater, ballet and opera in Europe and the United States, including twenty productions for the Metropolitan Opera. In 2001, the Musee Epper in Ascona, Switzerland displayed several of his designs in the exhibit *Rolf Gerard: Homage to Giuseppe Verdi*. An officer of the French Legion of Honor and a British subject, Mr. Gérard resides in Switzerland where he continues to paint. He should not be confused with opera singer and voice teacher, James Rolf Gerard (1894-1978).

Sets: 1949 *Caesar and Cleopatra*; *That Lady* 1952 *Evening with Beatrice Lillie, An* 1953 *The Love of Four Colonels*; *The Strong Are Lonely* 1959 *The Fighting Cock* 1960 *Irma La Douce* 1963 *Tovarich*

Costumes: 1949 *Caesar and Cleopatra*; *That Lady* 1953 *The Love of Four Colonels*; *The Strong Are Lonely* 1959 *The Fighting Cock* 1960 *Irma La Douce*

Charles German

Charles German designed costumes for featured players in a show on Broadway in 1924.

Costumes: 1924 *Innocent Eyes†* (Mlle. Mistinguette's costumes)

Virginia Gerson

Active as a costume designer at the very beginning of the twentieth century, Virginia Gerson was 87 years old when she died on August 3, 1951. She often worked with an old friend, playwright Clyde Fitch, beginning with *Barbara Fretchie* in the 1898-1899 Broadway season. An author and illustrator of books for children, her best known works were *Happy Heart Family* published in 1904 and *Little Miss Dignity* which she wrote when she was nineteen.

Costumes: 1900 *In a Balcony*; *The Land of Heart's Desire*

Zvi Geyra

Zvi Geyra, born in Jerusalem in 1927, was raised in Kibbutz Mishmar Ha'Emek and studied at the Bezalel School of Art in Israel. After military service, he moved to New York City in 1950 to study at the Dramatic Workshop with Mordecai Gorelik. While there he designed for Irving Piscator. His designs for theater include productions at La Jolla Playhouse during a summer season residency, plays in Los Angeles, at the Fred Miller Theatre in Milwaukee, in Israel, off-Broadway, and on. He has designed extensively for television, both in the United States, as art director for WNTA, WCBS, New York's Channel 5, and for the M-G-M television Studios and Videotape Center, and in Israel. After returning to Israel he continued designing for theater, television and several movies, including *Kuni Lemel* and *Adam and Eve*. At the beginning of the twenty-first century he created 25 paintings for the Museum of the Diaspora: "Sabbath Traditions throughout the Ages" which are on permanent display. Other paintings can be found in private collections throughout the United States and Israel. His son, Don Geyra, is a scenic artist who works in the New York area, and a fine art painter.

Sets: 1958 *Edwin Booth* 1960 *The Long Dream*

Lights: 1958 *Edwin Booth*

A. Christina Giannini

A. Christina (Stia) Giannini, who is from Philadelphia, Pennsylvania was born into a family of singers and musicians. She studied at Douglas College of Rutgers and the Birmingham, England College of Arts and Crafts, and also held a study grant at the Opern Studio in Zurich to study design in conjunction with the Zurich Opera. Although she designs costumes for theater and opera, she is most widely known as a ballet designer, using costumes to create moving sculpture, collaborating with choreographers including Robert Lindgrim, Alvin Ailey, Gerald Arpino, Heinz Poll, and Chiang Ching among others, for productions in the United States, Europe, South America, Canada, Israel, and the Far East. Her costume designs have been featured on the cover of *Dance* magazine. Among her honors are two Venezuelan Oscar Awards for Design, in 1995 for *Don Quixote* and in 1996 for *The Nutcracker* both at the Ballet National de Caracas. Designs in the twenty-first century include *Romeo and Juliet* for the Washington Ballet, *La Lupe: My Life, My Destiny* for the Puerto Rican Traveling Theatre, *Cinderella* for North Carolina Dance Theatre, and both *Carmen* and *Lucia de Lammermoor* in Santa Barbara.

Costumes: 1965 *Me and Thee†* (Fashion coordinator) 1969 *Three Men on a Horse* 1981 *A Taste of Honey*

Michael Giannitti

Michael Giannitti was born in Stamford, Connecticut on July 27, 1962, the son of Joseph and Marie Giannitti. He attended Bates College, where he began designing and received a Bachelor of Arts in 1984. After attending the Yale University School of Drama, where he received an M.F.A. in 1987, he assisted Jennifer Tipton. His first professional design in New York City was *Soft Sell* at La MaMa E.T.C. in 1986, choreographed by Marta Renzi. He has designed several productions for Shakespeare & Company, including *Richard III, Love's Labor's Lost, The Lear Project, Romeo and Juliet* all in the company's original home at Edith Wharton's Mount and *Coriolanus* in the new Founders' Theatre in 2001. He has also designed dance for choreographer Susan Rethort, and both scenery and lighting for *Rhinoceros* at the Kirby Shakespeare Theatre in Madison, New Jersey.

Lights: 1988 *Joe Turner's Come and Gone*

Alice Gibson

Alice Gibson (Mrs. Alice Berliner Greenbaum) designed numerous costumes both on and off Broadway. Married to Carl Greenbaum, she died in New York on September 17, 1963 at the age of 63.

Costumes: 1947 *Heads or Tails* 1951 *Never Say Never; The Small Hours* 1953 *The Bat* 1956 *Speaking of Murder* 1958 *Cloud 7* 1962 *Night Life*

Frederick Gibson

Frederick J. Gibson, originally from Whitby, Ontario designed scenery for two productions early in the twentieth century on Broadway. He spent most of his professional career working in graphic design, both for A. A. Vantine & Co. and as advertising manager of *The Evening Telegram*. Founder of the Sphinx Club, as association for men involved with advertising, he was blind for the last fifteen years of his life. At the time of his death in New York City at age 66 on February 21, 1925, he was general manager of the *Bronx Home News*.

Sets: 1900 *Prince Otto†* 1903 *The Wizard of Oz†* (Act I, Scene 3)

Marguerite Gidden

Marguerite Gidden, a dressmaker, designed gowns for a show in 1935. She catered to private and theatrical customers from a small salon at 379 Fifth Avenue and resided at 301 East 38th Street, Apt. 8E, New York City.

Costumes: 1935 *Creeping Fire* (Miss Paterson's gowns)

Edward Gilbert

Edward Gilbert is a native of New

York City who studied at the Parsons School and the Art Students League. His first professional designs were costumes for his sister, the actress Ruth Gilbert (who appeared on the *Milton Berle Show*) in the original production of *The Iceman Cometh*. His career as a scenic and occasional costume designer, developed through his association with fellow designer Stuart Chaney, and George S. Kaufman who wrote *The Solid Gold Cadillac*. Additional designs include *New Faces* and *Correspondent Unknown*. He should not be confused with the author Edward M. Gilbert (1875-1956) nor the theater director associated with Long Wharf and the Pittsburgh Public Theatre.

Sets: 1939 *Straw Hat Revue* **1940** *All in Fun* **1942** *New Faces of 1943* **1944** *No Way Out; While the Sun Shines* **1945** *The Next Half Hour; The Overtons; Star Spangled Family* **1946** *Icetime; If the Shoe Fits; Toplitzky of Notre Dame* **1947** *Icetime of 1948*† **1948** *Hold It* **1949** *All for Love; Metropole; Yes, M' Lord* **1950** *The Day after Tomorrow* **1953** *The Solid Gold Cadillac*

Costumes: 1942 *New Faces of 1943* **1949** *Yes, M' Lord*

Enid Gilbert

Enid Gilbert designed scenery, costumes and lights for plays on Broadway in the mid-1940s.

Sets: 1946 *The Bees and the Flowers*
Costumes: 1945 *The Assassin* **1946** *The Bees and the Flowers*
Lights: 1946 *The Bees and the Flowers*

Edythe Gilfond

Edythe Gilfond was for many years Martha Graham's costume designer. She studied at Hunter College, F.I.T. and in Paris. During the early 1930s she designed fashions on Seventh Avenue and in the late 1930s designed Anna Sokolow's costumes for the Bennington Dance Festival. Martha Graham admired the designs and Edythe Gilfond became her first costume designer with the opening of *American Document* in 1938. Other pieces for Martha Graham included *Dark Meadow*, and *Letter to the World*. She

also designed for Merce Cunningham and for Aaron Copeland's *Appalachian Spring*. In the early 1950s, Edythe Gilfond turned her talents to television, designing numerous variety, dramatic shows and soap operas, including *Edge of Night*. Her designs for dance and theater have been widely exhibited. Married to the dance writer and critic Henry Gilfond, she died on August 21,1989 in Southampton, Long Island at age 79.

Costumes: 1953 *The Fifth Season* (Costumes Supervised)

William Gill

A painter, playwright and actor, William Gill wrote *Our Goblins*, 1880 (in which he also appeared), *Adonis*, 1886 (produced in Boston), *My Boys*, 1897, and *Mrs. Mac, the Mayor*, 1904. He maintained a studio at his home on Longwood Avenue in the Bronx and also contributed scene designs to two Broadway productions, neither of which he wrote.

Sets: 1900 *Little Nell and the Marchioness* **1901** *My Lady*

Michael Gilliam

Most of lighting designer Michael Gilliam's credits are on the West Coast, although he has designed throughout the United States. He began designing at the University of Southern California in the mid-1980s, and since then has designed often at the Pasadena Playhouse, the Mark Taper Forum, the Old Globe, and the Coast Playhouse in Hollywood, among other theaters. Designs at the North Shore Music Theatre in Massachusetts include *Oliver!* and at the Denver Theatre Center include *Joseph and His Technicolor Dreamcoat*, for which he was nominated for a Denver Drama Critics Award. In 1999 he was awarded the Career Achievement Award from the Los Angeles Drama Critics Circle. Off-Broadway credits include *Zooman and the Sign* at the Second Stage Theatre and *The View from Here* at Lamb's Little Theatre. Twenty-first century credits include *Blue* at the Gramercy Theatre, directed by Sheldon Epps.

Lights: 1990 *Stand Up Tragedy*

Nina Gilman

Nina Gilman designed costumes for the ladies in a play in 1922.

Costumes: 1922 *Liza* (Ladies costumes)

Léon Gischia

Léon Gischia, the French painter and stage designer was born in Dax, Lourdes in 1902. He studied archeology, literature and painting with Othon Friesz and Fernand Léger. He collaborated on the Pavillion of Modern Times at the Paris World Exposition in 1937. He became a stage designer in 1945, initially designing *Murder in the Cathedral* for Vilar and helping create the style of the Théâtre National Populaire - simple, evocative stage settings and elaborate costumes. He remained associated with that company for many years. During the 1920s he traveled throughout the United States painting, and in the 1950s he returned to the U.S. as a theatrical designer. M. Gischia, who also edited several textbooks, died in May 1991 in France.

Costumes: 1958 *Théâtre National Populaire* ("Le Triomphe De L'Amour," Etc.)

John Gleason

John James Gleason was born on April 10, 1941 in Brooklyn, New York, and attended Hunter College where he received a Bachelor of Arts degree. He was the resident lighting designer from 1967 to 1972 for the Repertory Theatre of Lincoln Center, where he designed twenty-one productions. His first professional design was *Tartuffe* in January, 1965 at the ANTA Washington Square Theatre. Influenced by his mentor, Charles Elson, he is not only a designer of lights but also was a master teacher on the faculty of the Tisch School of the Arts at New York University from 1972-1997. With numerous shows on Broadway to his credit including Nicol Williamson's *Hamlet, The Great White Hope, My Fair Lady,* and *The Royal Family,* he has also designed extensively off-Broadway, in regional theaters, at the National Theatre of the Deaf, and for opera, including *Live from Lincoln Center.* A man of diverse talents, he has also written screenplays and been contributing editor for *Lighting Dimensions.* In 1975 he won a Los Angeles Drama Critics Circle Award for *Savages.*

Lights: 1965 *La Grasse Valise* **1968** *A Cry of Players*; *The Great White Hope*; *Lovers and Other Strangers*; *We Bombed in New Haven* **1969** *Hamlet (starring Nichol Williamson)*; *Home Fires/Cop Out*; *The National Theatre of the Deaf* **1970** *Brightower*; *Candida*; *Othello*; *Sganarelle*; *Songs from Milkwood*; *Two by Two* **1971** *Frank Merriwell (or Honor Changed)* **1972** *The Love Suicide at Schofield Barracks*; *Tough to Get Help* **1973** *The Pajama Game*; *A Streetcar Named Desire*; *Veronica's Room*; *The Women* **1974** *All over Town*; *Flowers†*; *Lorelei*; *Over Here*; *Who's Who in Hell* **1975** *Don't Call Back*; *Hello, Dolly! (Starring Pearl Bailey)*; *The Royal Family* **1976** *Herzl*; *My Fair Lady* **1978** *Angel*; *Platinum* **1980** *The Philadelphia Story* **1981** *Macbeth*; *The Survivor* **1983** *The Guys in the Truck* **1993** *The Mikado*

Tatiana Gleboya

Costume designer Tatiana Gleboya has designed numerous productions for the Pushkin, Stanislavsky, and Ermolova Theatres as well as for the Theatre of the Soviet Army and for Central Television of the USSR. Her debut in the United States was with a 1990 production on Broadway. The winner of numerous awards in her native Russia, her designs have also been widely exhibited.

Costumes: 1990 *Zoya's Apartment†* (Original designs)

Ivan Glidden

Ivan (Isador) Glidden designed costumes for a play on Broadway in the mid-1930s. He lived and worked from 81 Ridge in 1931, according to the Manhattan and Bronx City Directory published that year.

Costumes: 1936 *Jefferson Davis*

Ernest Glover

Ernest Glover designed settings for five productions on Broadway in the early 1940s.

Sets: 1940 *Every Man for Himself*; *Suspect* **1942** *The Sun Field*; *Vickie* **1944** *School for Brides*

Cookie Gluck

Cookie (Carolyn) Gluck, who is also known as Carolyn O'Neal, collaborated on the designs for a Broadway play in 1973. She was born in Brooklyn and received a B.A. in 1968 and an M.A. in 1971 from the University of Wisconsin at Madison. Primarily a graphic artist, she has designed *The Porter* and *The Women of Baghdad* for Story Theatre, *Orphans* for the Steppenwolf Company, and costumes (with Julie Nagel) for Hubbard Street Dance Company, all in Chicago. She has also done costumes for commercials and in 1990 designed a new wardrobe for the Chicago Bulls' mascot, Benny.

Costumes: 1973 *Warp†*

Englebert Gminska

Englebert Gminska was a New York City interior decorator who lived at 2342 Ryer Avenue in 1917. City directories of the time included a listing of "Artistic Decorators" for individuals who specialized in interior designs for private customers as well as for theatrical settings.

Sets: 1915 *Eugenically Speaking†* (Decorations)

Edwin William Godwin

Edward William Godwin, a theatrical designer and architect who also adapted literary works for performance, was born on May 26, 1833 in Bristol, England and died in London on October 6, 1886. He designed many productions for Henry Irving and Elen Terry, with whom he had two famous children, Edward Gordon Craig and Edith Craig. Godwin's designs for the theater included *Rouge et Noir, Helena in Troas, The Faithful Shepherdess, Fair Rosamund* and *The Fool's Revenge* as well as many Shakespeare plays. In addition to *The Merchant of Venice* which ran on Broadway during the 1899-1900 season, *Claudian* at the Park Theatre in Brooklyn in 1887 was designed by Godwin. Neither production was seen in America until after his death.

Costumes: 1899 *The Merchant of Venice*

Peter Goffin

Peter Goffin, a British stage designer and director, began professional life as an interior decorator and mural painter. He was born February 28, 1906 in Plymouth, Devonshire, England. Employment in various theaters, including the Barn Theatre, Chesham Bois, England in the 1935-36 season, led him to design for the D'Oyly Carte Opera Company in 1949. He remained as resident designer until being appointed Artistic Director in 1961. An author and educator, Mr. Goffin lectured widely on theater design and theater education before his death in 1974.

Sets: 1948 *Yeomen of the Guard* 1955 *The Mikado; Ruddigore; Yeomen of the Guard*

Costumes: 1948 *Yeomen of the Guard* 1955 *Ruddigore; Yeomen of the Guard*

Stephen Golding

Stephen Golding designed one set in 1935 on Broadway. In 1919 he was president of Golding Scenic Studios, Inc., 1493 Broadway in New York City with William Golding, Vice President and Bert LaMont, Secretary. His designs for *Mulatto* were done in collaboration with Franklyn Ambrose.

Sets: 1935 *Mulatto†*

Ellen Goldsborough

Ellen Goldsborough designed costumes on Broadway in the early 1930s.

Costumes: 1930 *Mrs. Moonlight* 1931 *Give Me Yesterday* (Designed and selected); *The Roof* 1951 *I Am a Camera*

Eleanor Goldsmith

Eleanor Goldsmith, born in 1923, received her training at the Juilliard School, Syracuse University and the Hobbard School of Painting in Massachusetts. After working at Eaves Costume Company, and Brooks Costume Company, she served as an assistant for costumes to Lemuel Ayers, Paul duPont and Nat Karson. She made her Broadway debut as a costume designer in 1945.

Costumes: 1946 *Mr. Peebles and Mr. Hooker* 1947 *Finian's Rainbow; Lovely Me* (Costumes Supervised) 1948 *Inside U.S.A.†; Jenny Kissed Me; The Young and the Fair* **1949** *The Biggest Thief in Town*; *The Father*; *Texas, Li'l Darlin'*

Jess Goldstein

Jess Goldstein has a B.F.A. from Boston University and an M.F.A. from Yale where he studied with Ming Cho Lee and Jane Greenwood. He was born in New York City on March 30, 1949. In addition to his many Broadway productions, he designs extensively in the regional theaters and off-Broadway, since he first designed costumes at Boston University for a production of *J.B.* He has designed costumes for the Mark Taper Forum, Long Wharf Theatre, Roundabout Theatre Company, Guthrie Theatre, Acting Company, Hartford Stage, and the Williamstown Theatre Festival, among others. Mr. Goldstein taught costume design part-time at Rutgers University before joining the faculty at Yale University. Much honored for his costumes, twenty-first century designs include *Black Forest* and *Enchanted April* at Long Wharf, *Stranger* for the Vineyard Theatre, and *Spinning into Butter* and *Ten Unknowns* at the Mitzi E. Newhouse Theatre.

Costumes: 1980 *Charlie and Algernon*; *Tintypes* **1987** *Sweet Sue* **1988** *A Streetcar Named Desire* **1992** *The Fifteen Minute Hamlet*; *The Most Happy Fella*; *The Real Inspector Hound* **1993** *Candida*; *White Liars & Black Comedy* **1995** *Love! Valour! Compassion!*; *The Play's the Thing* **1996** *Inherit the Wind*; *Tartuffe: Born Again* **1999** *Night Must Fall*; *The Rainmaker* **2000** *Proof* **2001** *Judgment at Nuremberg*

Lawrence L. Goldwasser

As a partner in Televideo Productions in New York City, Lawrence L. (Larry) Goldwasser designed, directed and produced hundreds of television commercials. He was born on August 4, 1916 in Yonkers, New York, the son of Ida L. and Ben Goldwasser, and studied at Yale University with Donald Oenslager. While at Yale he was the official designer for the WPA in Connecticut. His credits also include interiors, summer stock, and productions for the 1939 World's Fair. His career as a scenic designer for the theater was just beginning when interrupted by World War II. After the war he became involved in television and gradually began directing. He designed and directed live television at ABC-TV and directed live and filmed productions for the J. Walter Thompson Agency. He also taught design at Marymount College, Tarrytown, New York. Mr. Goldwasser who retired to North Carolina in 1990, died in Chapel Hill on January 20, 2001.

Sets: 1938 *The Devil Takes a Bride*; *Ringside Seat*; *Washington Jitters* **1939** *Streets of Paris* **1940** *At the Stroke of Eight*; *A Passenger to Bali* **1946** *Made in Heaven*

Costumes: 1946 *Made in Heaven*

Natalia Gontcharova

Natalia Gontcharova, a Russian-French artist, was born in Ladyzhino, Tonla, Russia on June 4, 1881. She studied at the School of Painting, Sculpture and Architecture in Moscow. Early in her career she met the painter Mikhail Larinov. They later married and together led the Primitive Movement in Moscow. Her first stage designs were produced in Moscow in 1909. She designed for Diaghilev and the Russian Ballet and also produced marionettes. Her productions of *Le Coq d'Or* (1914), *Les Noces d'Aurore* (1922) and *Nuit sur le Mond Chauve* (1923) for the Ballets Russes were widely admired. She spent much of her life in Paris where she moved with Larinov in 1917, becoming a French citizen in 1938. A much honored painter and stage designer, her creative works, paintings, sculptures and designs are widely exhibited and collected. She died in Paris on October 17, 1962.

Sets: 1931 *New Chauve-Souris*[†]

Costumes: 1931 *New Chauve-Souris*[†]

Tim Goodchild

British designer Tim Goodchild has been creating sets and costumes for operas and play houses throughout the United Kingdom since the early 1980s. He has extensive credits in London's West End, for the Royal Shakespeare Company, the Royal National Theatre and the New Shakespeare Company in Regents Park. He has designed operas for the Royal Danish Opera, the English National Opera, the Australian Opera, and the Edinburgh Festival, among others. His designs have been honored with Laurence Olivier Awards for the costumes for *The Relapse* in 1997 and the sets and costumes for *Three Hours After Marriage* in 1998. Twenty-first century credits include sets and costumes for *The Seven Year Itch* and *The Mikado*, both in the West End.

Sets: 1992 *Five Guys Named Moe*

Ruby Ross Goodnow

Ruby Ross Goodnow designed a set on Broadway in 1922. In the mid-1920s she resided at 160 East 38th Street, New York City. Born on December 24, 1910, she was a long time resident of Onondaga, New York and died in February 1972.

Sets: 1922 *The Plot Thickens*†

Bruce Goodrich

Bruce Goodrich has designed many productions off-Broadway, including costumes and scenery for *Jest a Second* at the Jewish Repertory Theatre, costumes for *Marathon '97* at Ensemble Studio Theatre, *Rendez-Vous with Marlene* at the 47th Street Playhouse, and scenery and costumes for *Greetings!* at the Houseman Theatre. Among his many designs at Primary Stages Company are scenery and lighting for *Laughing Matters*, scenery for *Washington Square Moves*, and scenery and costumes for *Bargains*. His degrees are from Carnegie Mellon University and the University of Wisconsin at Milwaukee. He is Professor of Costume Design at California State University, Fullerton.

Sets: 1992 *The Sheik of Avenue B*

Laura Gordon

Laura Gordon designed gowns for a Broadway show in 1939. She was president of Laura, Inc., a shop that provided women's clothing from two locations in the mid-1930s, 44 East 46th Street and 439 Madison Avenue. Murray Gordon was vice-president and Ida B. Gordon was the secretary of the business.

Costumes: 1939 *Where There's a Will*† (Miss Landis' gowns)

Michael Gordon

Michael Gordon, a lighting designer, director, and actor, was born on September 6, 1909 in Baltimore. He attended the John Hopkins University and received a Bachelor of Arts degree in 1929, after which he studied at Yale University under George Pierce Baker, earning a Master of Fine Arts degree in 1932. He went to New York, acted and also worked as a stage manager for the Group Theatre among other locations. He directed many films including *Cyrano de Bergerac, For Love of Money, Another Part of the Forest,* and *Pillow Talk.* In the latter he pioneered the split screen technique. There is a gap between his movies, from 1951 to 1957, because he was blacklisted in Hollywood for refusing to testify before the House Un-American Activities Committee. During that time he directed Broadway plays, including *The Tender Trap* which later provided his re-entry into the movie business. For television he directed *Room 222* (among other series) and various special programs. He taught at the University of California, Los Angeles from 1971-1990 and died on April 29, 1993 in Los Angeles.

Lights: 1938 *Casey Jones*; *My Heart's in the Highlands*; *Rocket to the Moon* 1939 *The Gentle People*; *Thunder Rock* 1940 *Heavenly Express*; *Night Music*

Stephen Gordon

Steven R. Gordon was a set designer active in 1932 who resided at 333 Central Park West, New York City, with his wife. He was the owner and operator of a scenic studio, Stephen Gordon Scenic Studio, located at 650 Broadway. In 1934, the studio was known as "Stephen & Staff" was located at 456 Fourth Avenue and operated by Stephen R. and William S. Gordon.

Sets: 1932 *New York to Cherbourg*

Mordecai Gorelik

Mordecai (Max) Gorelik, a scenic designer, director, author and educator, also occasionally designed costumes and lights during his long, distinguished career. He attended the Pratt Institute and studied with Norman Bel Geddes, Robert Edmond Jones and Serge Soudeikine. He was born on August 25, 1899 in Shchedrin, Russia. His family emigrated to New York in 1905 and as a youth Max worked in his father's newsstand. His first professional production was *King Hunger* at the Hedgerow Theatre in Moylan, Pennsylvania in 1924. He made his Broadway debut with designs for *Processional* in 1925, after working at the Neighborhood Playhouse as a scene painter and technician and at the Provincetown Playhouse. He served as principal designer for The Group Theatre from 1937 to 1940. The author of over one hundred articles and the books *New Theatres for Old* and *Toward a Larger Theatre*, he taught design and lectured widely. From 1960 to 1972 he was on the faculty of Southern Illinois University, which awarded him an honorary degree in 1988. Mordecai Gorelik died on March 23, 1990 at age 90 in Sarasota, Florida.

Sets: 1925 *Processional* **1926** *The Moon Is a Gong*† **1927** *Loud Speaker* **1928** *The Final Balance* **1931** *1931–* **1932** *Success Story* **1933** *All Good Americans; Big Night; Little Ol' Boy; Men in White* **1934** *Gentlewoman; Sailors of Cattaro* **1935** *Let Freedom Ring; Mother; The Young Go First* **1938** *Casey Jones; Rocket to the Moon; Tortilla Flat* **1939** *Thunder Rock* **1940** *Night Music* **1947** *All My Sons* **1952** *Desire under the Elms* **1954** *The Flowering Peach* **1955** *A Hatful of Rain* **1957** *The Sin of Pat Muldoon* **1960** *A Distant Bell*

Costumes: 1925 *Processional* **1929** *Fiesta*† (Original Costumes Procurred in Mexico) **1955** *A Hatful of Rain* (Production design by)

Lights: 1947 *All My Sons* **1955** *A Hatful of Rain*

Edward Gorey

Edward Gorey was an author and artist. He applied his considerable talents to designing sets and costumes for a Broadway show in 1977, and won a Tony Award for the costumes. The following year, he returned to Broadway with another show. A native of Chicago, he was born there on February 22, 1925, studied at the Art Institute of Chicago and graduated from Harvard with a degree in French. His many books attracted a loyal and devoted following, due mainly to his unique view of the world. He also designed for Les Ballets Trocadero de Monte Carlo and created the opening segment for the *Mystery* series on PBS. Author of 90 books and illustrator of nearly 60 more, he died on April 15, 2000 in Massachusetts.

Sets: 1977 *Dracula* **1978** *Gorey Stories*

Costumes: 1977 *Dracula*

Maria Gortinskaya

Maria Gortinskaya, a native of Russia, lived from 1883 to 1973. She designed many productions for the Moscow Art Theatre and in the mid-1920s, her designs for costumes and scenery were used in a Broadway production. Examples of her designs for scenery were included in Oliver Sayler's book, *Inside the Moscow Art Theatre*, published in 1925.

Sets: 1925 *The Daughter of Madame Angot*

Costumes: 1925 *The Daughter of Madame Angot*

David Graden

David Graden designed costumes for a Broadway show in 1979. He worked mainly on the West Coast in theater, television and film, with stage designs including *Snoopy* and *P.S. Your cat is Dead*. For two years, he was design assistant for the Center Theatre Group at the Mark Taper Forum, and was assistant designer on the film *The Bell Jar*. He was born in Washington state on September 17, 1955 and died in San Francisco on November 28, 1989.

Costumes: 1979 *The Utter Glory of Morrissey Hale*

Anne Graham

Anne Graham designed costumes on Broadway for a play in 1959. She also designed costumes for television and fashion.

Costumes: 1959 *Kataki*

Jane Graham

Jane Graham was the scenic designer for a 1963 Broadway production.

Sets: 1963 *The Rehearsal*

Madeline Ann Graneto

Madeline Ann Graneto is from Harlingen, Texas where she was born on December 1, 1944. She received a B.F.A. from Ohio University at Athens, and an M.F.A. from Brandeis University. As a young girl, she won a prize for a Halloween costume which led her ultimately to a career in costume design. She designs mainly for television and film, and received an Emmy Award for her costumes for *Pryor's Place*. Her designs on the West Coast have been rewarded with at least eight Drama Logues. She is also the founder and president of Pearl Buttons & Co.

Costumes: 1984 *Beethoven's Tenth*

Mary Grant

Mary Grant designed costumes on Broadway between 1942 and 1946, returning in 1961 for another production. During the interval, she designed films at Paramount, Universal and RKO Studios in Hollywood, including *The Vagabond King*, *We're No Angels*, *Sweet Smell of Success* and *The Bachelor Party*. Her move to Hollywood was due in part to her marriage to actor Vincent Price.

Costumes: 1942 *The Cat Screams* 1944 *Mexican Hayride*; *Seven Lively Arts*† 1945 *Marinka*; *Polonaise* 1946 *Woman Bites Dog* 1961 *Big Fish, Little Fish*

Helen Grayson

Helen Grayson designed costumes for two plays on Broadway in the 1930s. After graduating from Bryn Mawr College she worked in New York as a dress designer. During World War II she directed documentary films for the Office of War Information, and later created films for the State Department. During the Depression she served as advisor of the Federal Theatre Costume Workshop. Helen Grayson died on May 16, 1962.

Costumes: 1933 *Little Ol' Boy* (Clothes by) 1934 *Jayhawker* (Miss Stone's costumes)

Victor Graziano

Victor Graziano designed one set in 1934 on Broadway. Born in New York on October 19, 1887, in 1915 he worked as a shoemaker on St. Nicholas Avenue in New York City. He spent the majority of career as a scenic artist and resided at 1824 Barnes Avenue in the mid-1930s. He died in New York City in July 1965.

Sets: 1934 *Errant Lady*

Lillian Greenfield

Lillian Greenfield designed costumes on Broadway in 1922. She aspired to a career as a soprano and debuted at Carnegie Chamber Music Hall in October 1928. She was born in New York on May 24, 1902 and died in Los Angeles on November 3, 1989.

Costumes: 1922 *Raymond Hitchcock's Pinwheel*†

Andrew Greenhut

Andrew Jay Greenhut was born on June 15, 1935 in Philadelphia. He received both Bachelor of Arts and Master of Arts degrees at the University of Miami, where he began designing. Among his numerous off-Broadway productions are *A Day in the Life of Just About Everyone*, *The Wedding of the Siamese Twins*, *Naomi Court*, and the revival of *Dylan*. Although his list of credits includes many theatrical productions, he is best known for his designs for television. He designed over 1,000 television commercials for major projects between 1970 and 1990, winning a CLIO Award for his design for a Minnesota Mining and Manufacturing Company (3M) advertisement. He also designed many syndicated television shows, among them *For You Black Woman* and *That Talk Show*, and sets for beauty pageants, including the *Miss World America Pageant*. He taught at the University of Miami, Southwest Missouri State University and the University of Delaware. Since 1990 he has lived in Pennsylvania where he continues to design, for the Pennsylvania Youth Theatre and at Moravian College, and serves the professional theater community as a Distinguished Member of The League of American Theatre Owners and Producers.

Sets: 1976 *Best Friend*

Howard Greenley

Howard Greenley designed galleries, residences and hotels during his career as an architect. He was born in Ithaca, New York on May 14, 1874 and died in Middlebury, Vermont on November 24, 1963. After studying at Trinity College in Hartford, Connecticut, he attended the École des Beaux Arts in Paris and the American School of Fine Arts in Fontainebleu, France. Before entering private practice, he worked as a draftsman, and designed scenery.

Sets: 1917 *Lord and Lady Algy*

Jane Greenwood

Jane Greenwood was born in Liverpool, England on April 30, 1934 and studied at London's Central School of Arts and Crafts. She designed her first professional costumes at the Oxford Playhouse in 1958. She moved to Canada to work as a draper at the invitation of Tanya Moiseiwitsch and after three seasons at the Stratford (Ontario) Festival moved to New York City to work with Ray Diffen. Her Broadway debut as a costume designer occurred in 1963 with the opening of *Ballard of The Sad Cafe*. Since that time she has been a busy designer in the theater and has also done costumes for films, operas and television. In addition, Jane Greenwood teaches costume design at Yale, and has taught at the Juilliard School and for Lester Polakov at the Studio and Forum of Stage Design. Married to set designer Ben Edwards (1916-1999), one of their two daughters, Sarah, is a costume designer. Highly regarded for her elegant and beautiful costumes, she was honored by Theatre Development Fund with the 1998 Irene Sharaff Lifetime Achievement Award. Recent designs include *Major Barbara* in the 2001-2002 Broadway season.

Costumes: 1963 *The Ballad of the Sad Cafe* 1964 *Hamlet* (Clothes) 1965 *Half a Sixpence†* (Costume Supervisor); *A Race of Hairy Men* 1966 *How's the World Treating You?*; *The Killing of Sister George†* (Costume Supervisor); *Nathan Weinstein, Mystic, Connecticut*;

Where's Daddy (Clothes) 1967 *More Stately Mansions* 1968 *I'm Solomon; The Prime of Miss Jean Brodie; The Seven Descents of Myrtle* 1969 *Angela; The Mother Lover; The Penny Wars; The Wrong Way Light Bulb* 1970 *Hay Fever; Les Blancs; Othello; Sheep of the Runway* 1971 *70, Girls, 70* 1972 *That's Entertainment; Wise Child* 1973 *Finishing Touches; A Moon for the Misbegotten* 1974 *Cat on a Hot Tin Roof* 1976 *California Suite; A Matter of Gravity; A Texas Trilogy; Who's Afraid of Virginia Woolf?* 1977 *An Almost Perfect Person; Anna Christie; Caesar and Cleopatra; The Night of the Tribades; Otherwise Engaged; A Touch of the Poet; Vieux Carre* 1978 *Cheaters; The Kingfisher* 1979 *Faith Healer; Knockout; Romantic Comedy* 1981 *Duet for One; The Supporting Cast; To Grandmother's House We Go; The West Side Waltz* 1982 *Medea; The Queen and the Rebels* 1983 *Heartbreak House; Plenty* 1984 *Alone Together* 1985 *The Iceman Cometh* 1986 *Lillian* 1988 *Ah, Wilderness!; Long Day's Journey into Night; Our Town* 1989 *The Circle; The Secret Rapture; The Tenth Man* 1990 *A Christmas Carol* 1991 *The Big Love; An International Marriage; Park Your Car in Harvard Yard* 1992 *The Price; A Streetcar Named Desire; Two Shakespearean Actors* 1993 *Abe Lincoln in Illinois; She Loves Me†; The Sisters Rosensweig* 1994 *No Man's Land; Passion* 1995 *A Delicate Balance; The Heiress; Master Class; A Month in the Country* 1996 *A Delicate Balance; Once upon a Mattress* 1997 *An American Daughter; The Lily and the Prince; The Little Foxes; Proposals; The Scarlet Pimpernel* 1998 *The Deep Blue Sea; High Society; Honour; The Scarlet Pimpernel* 2000 *James Joyce's The Dead; A Moon for the Misbegotten* 2001 *The Dinner Party*

Howard Greer

Howard Greer was born in Nebraska in 1886 and died in Los Angeles in 1964. He started his career working for the haute couture designer Lucile. After service in World War I worked in Paris for Paul Poiret and Molyneux. It was during this time in Europe that he began designing theatrical costumes in addition to fashion. When he returned to the United States he contributed designs to Broadway shows and worked again for Lucile for a short time. His designs for *Greenwich Village Follies* led to a position as Chief Designer at the West Coast Studios of Famous Players-Lasky (later Paramount Pictures Corporation). His film credits are extensive between the years 1923 and 1953. He also had his own couture house, Greer, Inc. which catered to movie stars and private customers. Mr. Greer retired in 1962. His autobiography, *Designing Male* chronicles his career.

Sets: 1922 *Greenwich Village Follies*† **Costumes: 1921** *Ziegfeld Midnight Follies*† **1922** *Greenwich Village Follies*† ("Red Headed, The Nights") **1923** *Jack and Jill*† (Act I, also performed) **1933** *The Lake* (Miss Hepburn's costume) **1936** *Reflected Glory* (Miss Bankhead's gowns) **1940** *Quiet Please* (Miss Wyatt's gown)

Ivan Gremislavsky

Ivan Iakovlevich Gremislavsky was born in 1886 in Moscow. His parents were Iakov Ivanovich and Maria Alekseevna Gremislavski, make-up artists for the Moscow Little Theatre and later for the Moscow Art Theatre. He studied at the Artists-Industrial School, the School of Painting, Sculpture and Architecture, and with Konstantin A. Korovin. He was influenced by his family and Alexander N. Benois, although Stanislavski was his great mentor. His first designs were for *World Holiday* and *Burial of Hope* at the Moscow Art Theatre in 1913. From 1922 to 1924 he toured Europe and America with the Moscow Art Theatre, and between 1926 and 1930 designed sets and costumes for two major works in conjunction with A. Golovin, *Marriage of Figaro* and *Othello*. He also worked for many years in the technical departments of the Moscow Art Theatre Musical Studio. In 1967 a collection of articles, illustrations, essays and additional materials about Ivan Gremislavsky, who died in 1954, was published in Moscow.

Sets: 1923 *The Lower Depths*† **1925**

Love and Death/ Aleko/ Fountain of Bakkchi Sarai/ etc.† **Costumes: 1925** *Love and Death/ Aleko/ Fountain of Bakkchi Sarai/ etc.*†

Bruce Gresham

Bruce Gresham designed scenery for a 1903 production.
Sets: 1903 *Mr. Bluebeard*†

Anthony Greshoff

Anthony Greshoff (also known as Tony Greshoff, A. Greshoff) was active on Broadway from 1902 to 1931 as a lighting designer. Few clues to his background are available in any of the standard (or unusual) sources, although the 1899 New York City directory identifies him as an electrician, residing at 348 West 21st Street. The playbill for *The Modern Magdalen* reports the following technical and design elements: "Set Painted by Joseph Physioc, Electrical Effects by A. Greshoff."
Lights: 1902 *The Modern Magdalen* **1908** *Ziegfeld Follies of 1908* **1912** *Ziegfeld Follies of 1912* **1915** *Fads and Fancies* **1919** *Angel Face; Clarence; On the Hiring Line* **1920** *Bab; The Girl in the Spotlight; Poldekin* **1921** *Alias Jimmy Valentine; Dulcy; Golden Days; The Intimate Strangers; The Perfect Fool; Two Little Girls; The Wren; Ziegfeld Midnight Follies* **1922** *The Drums of Jeopardy; Listening In* **1923** *Adrienne; The Rivals* **1924** *The Chocolate Dandies* **1927** *The Adventurous Age; Behold This Dreamer; Spellbound* **1928** *Diplomacy; Sherlock Holmes* **1929** *Houseparty; Sherlock Holmes; Your Uncle Dudley* **1930** *It's a Grand Life; Mr. Samuel; The Rivals* **1931** *The Admirable Crichton*

Madame Mary Grey

The actress known as (Madame) Mary Grey was born Ada Bevan ap Rees Bryant in Wales in c.1878 and performed as a young girl with her brother Charles Bryant, and in Frank Benson's Shakespeare Company. She was featured in many productions directed by her husband James B. Fagan in London and on tour throughout the world. Her roles were numerous, ranging through the classics and new plays, with Madame Ranevsky in *The Cherry Orchard* at the Lyric, Hammersmith in a cast including John Gielgud, often mentioned as a highlight. She occasionally designed her own gowns. Mary Grey died at age 97 in London in October of 1974.

Costumes: 1913 *The Philanderer†* (Ladies)

Hayden Griffin

Hayden Griffin has designed professionally since 1967 after taking a design course at Sadler's Wells. He was born January 23, 1943 in Pietermaritzburg, South Africa. His credits range throughoutthe United States, in Europe and England from the Royal Court, the Metropolitan Opera, the Royal National Theatre, Chichester, the Aarhus Theatre in Denmark, York, Stratford-upon-Avon and Edinburgh to the West End and Vienna. In addition to earning extensive credits designing operas, plays and ballets, he teaches design to students and design assistants who often credit him as a valued mentor. A frequent collaborator with director Michael Blakemore, they have worked together on *Money & Friends, The Crucible* and *After the Fall*. Production designs for films include *Painted Angels, Conquest,* and *Intimacy* which premiered at the 2001 Sundance Film Festival.

Sets: 1968 *Rockefeller and the Red Indians* 1978 *Players*
Costumes: 1968 *Rockefeller and the Red Indians* 1978 *Players*

Peter V. Griffin

Peter V. Griffin, who designed scenery for a 1907 musical revue, lived at 594 St. Ann's Avenue in the Bronx in 1910.

Sets: 1907 *Ziegfeld Follies of 1907†*

Grinager and Beardsley

Grinager and Beardsley, a scenery studio owned by Alexander Grinager and Rudolph Beardsley, was active on Broadway in 1914 and 1915. For additional information see the entries under their respective names.

Sets: 1914 *The Dragon's Claw; The Silent Voice†* 1915 *Just Outside the Door*

Alexander Grinager

Alexander Grinager studied painting at the Royal Academy in Copenhagen,

Denmark for four years and in Paris at the Julien Academy, as well as in Norway, Italy and Sicily. He was born in Albert Lea, Minnesota on January 26, 1865. A member of the Allied Artists of America, Artists League of Minneapolis and the American Federation of the Arts, his murals adorned many buildings, including the United States Department of Commerce, the New York Central Rail Road and Grand Central Palace. He designed and painted many productions during his long association with David Belasco, receiving program credit for only a few. He worked as a head designer and scene painter for Gates and Morange, Ernest Albert, Castle and Harvey, and also in collaboration with Rudolph Beardsley in 1914 and 1915. He died March 8, 1949 at age 84. For additional information see the entries "Beardsley" and "Grinager and Beardsley."

Sets: 1899 *Ben Hur†* 1911 *Chantecler†* 1920 *Call the Doctor†; One†*

Ricki Grisman

Ricki Grisman designed costumes on Broadway in 1946.

Costumes: 1946 *On Whitman Avenue*

William Grogan

William Grogran designed lights on Broadway beginning in the 1899-1900 season.

Lights: 1899 *Becky Sharp* 1904 *Becky Sharp*

Jerry Grollnek

Jerry Grollnek, a lighting designer, did one show in 1976 on Broadway.

Lights: 1976 *Debbie Reynolds Show*

David Gropman

David Gropman has designed sets on Broadway and in Europe for the theater and dance, beginning with *The Nutcracker* in the second grade. More importantly, he has designed sets for David Henry Hwang's *Family Emotions,* and *Danbury Mix* for the Paul Taylor Dance Company. He was born June 16, 1952 in Los Angeles to Helen and Paul Gropman, who worked in advertising and public relations. He attended San Francisco State University where he studied with Eric Sinkonnen and received a B.A. He studied with Ming Cho Lee at the Yale School of Drama, which he attended as a recipient of the Donald Oenslager Scholarship, and earned an M.F.A. He is a prolific production designer of films that include James Ivory's *Mr. and Mrs. Bridge* starring Paul Newman and Joanne Woodward, with the set design by his wife, scenic designer Karen Schultz. Other films are *Chocolat, The Shipping New, A Civil Action, Waiting to Exhale, Searching for Bobby Fischer, Slaves of New York, Key Exchange, Sweet Lorraine, Come Back to the Five and Dime, Jimmy Dean, Jimmy Dean* and *The Cider House Rules* for which he received a 2000 Oscar Award nomination.

Sets: 1979 *The 1940s Radio Hour* 1980 *Passione* 1981 *Mass Appeal* 1982 *Come Back to the 5 & Dime, Jimmy Dean, Jimmy Dean*; *A Little Family Business* 1984 *Open Admissions* 1987 *Death and the King's Horseman*

William Gropper

William Gropper and Jacob Meth collaborated on the costumes for four Broadway shows in the early 1920s. William H. Gropper, a costume maker, painter, and illustrator was born in New York City on December 3, 1897 and died in Manhasset on June 6, 1977. He worked initially in the garment district before his love of drawing led him to study and then to work as a cartoonist. His drawings and paintings have been collected in several books and also exhibited. He also created murals, including one for the Department of Interior building in Washington, D.C. For additional information about Jacob Meth, see his entry.

Costumes: 1921 *The Idle Inn*[†] 1923 *Anathema*[†]; *The Inspector General*[†]; *The Shame Woman*[†]

Ernest Gros

Ernest M. Gros designed settings for numerous productions for David Belasco, who admired his realistic painting style. Some of the nearly 200 productions he designed were produced prior to 1900 and included *The Strange Adventure of Miss Brown, The Shop Girl,* and *Princess Bonnie* in 1895, and *El Capitan* and *The Shepherd Girl* in 1896. Ernest Gros was born in Paris and emigrated to New York City late in the nineteenth century. He also painted murals of panoramic views, a popular art form in the 1880s and 1890s.

Sets: 1899 *The Ameer*[†] (Act III); *Ben Hur*[†]; *A Greek Slave*[†]; *Make Way for the Ladies*; *My Lady's Lord*[†]; *The Only Way*; *Sherlock Holmes*; *Three Little Lambs*[†] 1900 *Chris and the Wonderful Lamp*[†]; *Foxy Quiller*; *The Husbands of Leontine*; *Ib and Little Christina*; *Janice Meredith*[†]; *L'Aiglon*[†] (Acts II, IV, V); *Marcelle*; *Naughty Anthony*; *The Rogers Brothers in Central Park*; *Self and Lady*; *Sweet Nell of Old Drury*; *Zaza* 1901 *Alice of Old Vincennes*; *The Auctioneer*[†]; *Du Barry*; *Eben Holden*; *The Girl from Up There*[†]; *The Rogers Brothers in Washington*; *To Have and to Hold*; *Under Two Flags* 1902 *Aunt Jeannie*; *Ben Hur*[†]; *The Darling of the Gods*[†]; *The Eternal City*[†]; *Hearts Aflame*[†]; *Imprudence*; *The Joy of Living*; *Maid Marian*; *Robin Hood*; *The Rogers Brothers in Harvard*; *There's Many a Slip*; *The Toreador*; *The Two Schools* 1903 *The Admirable Crichton*; *Darling of the Gallery Gods, The* and *The Dress Parade*[†]; *A Japanese Nightingale*[†] (Acts II, IV); *The Rogers Brothers in London*[†] (Acts I and III); *Sweet Kitty Bellairs*[†]; *The Unforeseen* 1904 *Brother Jacques*; *Business Is Business*; *Duke of Killcrankie*; *The Music Master*[†] (Designed and painted); *Pillars of Society*[†] (Designed and painted); *The Rogers Brothers in Paris*; *The Ruling Power*[†] (Act III); *The School Girl*; *The Sorceress*; *That Man and I*[†]; *Yvette* 1905 *Adrea*[†]; *La Belle Marseillaise*; *The Catch of the Season*; *Cousin Billy*[†]; *De Lancy*; *Friquet*; *The Girl of the Golden West*; *The Ham Tree*[†]; *Peter Pan* (Maude Adams); *The Rogers Brothers in Ireland*; *The Rollicking Girl* 1906 *The American Lord*; *Brigadier Gerard*; *Clarice*; *The Duel*; *The Free Lance*; *The Judge and the Jury*; *The Light Eternal*[†] (Acts I, III, IV); *The Little Cherub*; *Mizpah*; *The Rich Mr. Hoggenheimer*; *The Rose of the Rancho*[†] 1907 *The Christian Pilgrim*[†] (Acts I, 4; II 1, 2); *Comtesse Coquette*; *The Dairymaids*; *A*

Grand Army Man†; *The Marriage of Reason*†; *The Morals of Marcus*; *The Movers*; *The Thief*; *The Toymaker of Nuremberg*; *The Warrens of Virginia*; *When Knights Were Bold* 1908 *The Fighting Hope*; *The Honor of the Family*; *The Jesters*; *Love Watches*; *Salvation Nell*†; *Twenty Days in the Shade* 1909 *Arsene Lupin*; *The Dollar Princess*; *The Easiest Way*; *The Fires of Fate*†; *Flag Lieutenant*; *Is Matrimony A Failure?*; *Israel*; *The Lily*†; *The Richest Girl*; *Septimus* 1910 *The Concert*; *Decorating Clementine*; *The Foolish Virgin*; *Hannele*; *Just A Wife*; *Nobody's Widow*; *Olive Latimer's Husband*† (Designed); *Sherlock Holmes* 1911 *Little Boy Blue*†; *The Return of Peter Grimm*; *The Runaway*† (Act IV); *Sire*; *The Thief*; *The Woman* 1912 *The Bird of Paradise*; *The Case of Becky*; *The Governor's Lady*; *The Man from Cook's*†; *Peter Pan*† (Act I); *What Ails You?* 1913 *The Man Inside*; *The New Secretary*; *The Poor Little Rich Girl*†; *Somewhere Else*; *The Temperamental Journey* 1914 *The Phantom Rival*; *Sari*† 1915 *The Boomerang*; *Marie Odile*; *Marie-Odile*; *Peter Pan* 1916 *The Heart of Wetona*; *Little Lady in Blue*; *The Music Master*; *Seven Chances* 1917 *Polly with a Past*†; *Tiger Rose*; *The Very Minute* 1918 *The Auctioneer*; *Remnant* 1919 *The Gold Diggers*; *The Son-Daughter* 1920 *Deburau*; *One*† 1921 *The Easiest Way*; *The Grand Duke*; *The Return of Peter Grimm* 1922 *The Merchant of Venice*; *Shore Leave*; *Spite Corner* 1923 *The Comedian*; *Mary, Mary, Quite Contrary*; *Nifties of 1923*†; *One Kiss* 1925 *The Grand Duchess/ The Waiter*

Grosvois and Lambert

In 1939 Grosvois and Lambert collaborated on scenic designs for a Broadway play.

Sets: 1939 *Folies Bergère*†

Anton Grot

Anton Grot, an art director for films, created the first practical stairway used in motion pictures. His prolific movie career began in 1913 with *The Mouse and the Lion*, included *Mildred Pierce* and *The Private Lives of Elizabeth and Essex* in 1939, and culminated in 1950 with the release of *Backfire*. He retired in 1947, ending a career in which he designed over one hundred films, most of them for Warner Brothers and many of them directed by Cecil B. DeMille. Born Antocz Franciszek Grosvewski on January 18, 1884 in Kelbasin, Poland he came to the United States in 1909 at the age of 25. He studied at the Cracow Academy of Arts and at the Technical College in Koenigsberg, Germany. He was hired in 1913 by Sigmund Lubin to design sets for the Lubin Company in Philadelphia, which led to assignments for additional movies and to Hollywood in 1922, where he designed Douglas Fairbanks' and Mary Pickford's films. Unlike many of the scenic designers and art directors of his era, he was trained as an artist and had no background in construction. Before starting to build a set, he created designs, rendering them in charcoal or pen and ink before construction. He received a special Academy Award for a "ripple machine" in 1940. Anton Grot died in 1974 at age 90.

Sets: 1920 *A Hole in the Wall*

Barbara Guerdon

Barbara Guerdon supervised costumes for a play in 1938.

Costumes: 1938 *Tortilla Flat* (Costumes Supervised)

Jules Guérin

Jules Guérin, an artist, was born in St. Louis, Missouri in 1866. The winner of many prizes and awards, he specialized in decoration for buildings, banks, opera houses, state capitol buildings and theaters, including the Lincoln Memorial in Washington, D.C. and the original Pennsylvania Railroad Station in New York City. His paintings received the Silver Medal at the 1904 St. Louis Exhibition and the Gold Medal at the 1915 Panama Exposition. In 1928 he contributed designs to a play on Broadway and in 1931 was elected to the National Academy of Design. Jules Guérin died in Neptune, New Jersey on June 13, 1946.

Sets: 1909 *Antony and Cleopatra*† 1928 *The Beaux Stratagem*

Costumes: 1928 *The Beaux Stratagem*

Robert Guerra

Robert Guerra is mainly known as an art director and production designer for films that include *The Last of the Mohicans, The Pelican Brief, Family Business, See You in the Morning, Annie* and *Heaven Help Us.* His designs for settings on Broadway were first seen in 1973, followed by additional productions in the 1980s.

Sets: 1973 *Warp* **1980** *Manhattan Showboat* **1981** *America*

Robert Gundlach

Robert Gundlach graduated from the Art School of The Cooper Union in 1937. Except for a brief stint as a commercial artist and service in World War II, he has been working as a designer ever since. His work in theater, television and film is extensive, although he has only a single Broadway credit. Early in his career he was scenic designer and technician for the Chekhov Theatre Studio. In the late 1940s he designed the stage and auditorium to convert an old theater on Bleeker Street from motion picture usage to legitimate stage productions for NEW STAGES, INC. For ANTA Experimental Theatre at NEW STAGES, he designed *The Four Horsemen of the Apocalypse.* He served as staff designer for NBC-TV in the late 1940s and early 1950s and for CBS-TV from 1954 to 1958. The majority of his career has been as an art director and production designer, principally for feature films and made-for-television movies. Productions include: *Married to It; Rachel, Rachel; Bang the Drum Slowly; Oliver's Story; Eyes of Laura Mars; See No Evil, Hear No Evil; Fighting Back; I, The Jury; Hero at Large;* and *Firepower.* He has also designed countless commercials.

Sets: 1948 *The Happy Journey/ The Respectful Prostitute*

Archie Gunn

Archie Gunn, one of the earliest costume designers to receive playbill credit, was also a magazine illustrator, and painter. He was born in Taunton, Somerset, England, on October 11, 1863 and studied at Tettenham College in Staffordshire and the Calderon Art Academy in London. His first drawing lessons were from his father, portrait painter Archibald Gunn. After some success painting portraits, he began designing theater posters and at age 25 emigrated to the United States. He illustrated covers and articles for *The New York World* and the magazine *Truth* from his studio at 120 West 49th Street in New York. In addition, he designed costumes for plays and created a popular series of pastel sketches of beautiful girls that where widely reproduced and known as the "Archie Gunn Girl' series. He died in New York on January 16, 1930 at age 66.

Costumes: 1899 *The Ameer* **1900** *The Cadet Girl* **1901** *Du Barry*[†]; *The Little Duchess*[†] **1902** *The Chaperons; The Defender* **1903** *Blonde in Black; The Jersey Lily; The Prince of Pilsen*[†] **1904** *The Maid and the Mummy; Sergeant Kitty*[†]; *Woodland* **1905** *The Gingerbread Man*[†]; *A Society Circus*[†] **1906** *The Man from Now* **1907** *The Top o' th' World*

John Gunter

The noted British designer of sets and costumes, John Forsyth Gunter has extensive credits for the Royal Shakespeare Company, the Royal Court Theatre, in London's West End and other theaters in England and on the continent. Born in Billericay, Essex, England on October 31, 1938, he studied at the Central School of Art and Design, and then spent three years as resident designer for the Schauspiel Haus, Zurich. Mr. Gunter served as the Head of the Theatre Design Department at the Central School of Art and Designin London from 1974 to 1982. Noted productions in London include *The Rivals* and *The Government Inspector.* For the Royal Shakespeare Company he has designed *Love's Labor Lost, Twelfth Night, Julius Caesar, Juno and the Paycock,* and *Jingo* among many others. His opera credits include the 1998 Glyndebourne production of *Simon Boccanegra, Don Quichotte* at the English National Opera in 1994, *Peter Grimes* in Buenos Aires, *Andrea Chenier* for the Welsh National Opera, *The Turn of the Screw* for the

Munich State Opera and *Die Meistersinger* in Cologne. His designs have been honored with numerous prizes, including West End Theatre and Laurence Olivier awards. Twenty-first century designs include Peter Hall's production of *Otello* at the Chicago Lyric Opera, that opened in September 2001.

Sets: 1971 *The Philanthropist* **1976** *Comedians†* **1981** *Rose* **1983** *All's Well That Ends Well†*; *Plenty* **1986** *Wild Honey* **1996** *Skylight*
Costumes: 1976 *Comedians* **1996** *Skylight*

David Guthrie

David F. Guthrie, who specializes in ballet design, was born in Glasgow, Scotland on May 18, 1922. Between 1958 and 1976 he worked primarily as Oliver Smith's assistant. He also worked for and trained under William and Jean Eckart, Boris Aronson and Jo Mielziner. His first professional costume designs were for the American Ballet Theatre. David Guthrie also has over one hundred commercials and industrial shows to his credit, including the design for the theater for the Du Pont Pavilion at the 1965 New York World's Fair. He has created numerous sets and costumes for the Cleveland San Jose Ballet Company, as resident designer. Recent designs include costumes in 1988 for the Limon Troupe and the set for *Coppelia* at the 1990 Edinburgh Festival.

Sets: 1972 *Different Times* **1973** *The Pajama Game*
Costumes: 1972 *Different Times* **1973** *The Pajama Game* (Designed by)

Michel Gyarmathy

Michel Gyarmathy was born in Budapest, Hungary and went to Paris in 1929, by way of Vienna, as a young artist to study and paint. In 1964 he not only designed settings and costumes for the *Folies Bergère* on Broadway, but also produced and directed the production. He was associated with the *Folies Bergère* beginning in the late 1930s after Paul Derval, director of the Folies Bergère, saw his drawings on the pavement near the theater. After World War II, he was named Artis-

tic Director, remaining in that position until 1992 when the theater closed for a time. The theater re-opened in 1993 under the leadership of Argentinean Alfredo Arias and changed considerably from Gyarmathy's trademark 'le music-hall' style that featured plumassieres and elaborate sets. Awarded the Prix de Rome for design and décor, his life and career during World War II was the inspiration for the French film *The Last Metro*. He died in Paris on October 30, 1996 at age 88.

Sets: 1964 *Folies Bergère*
Costumes: 1964 *Folies Bergère*

Morton Haack

Morton Haack, best known as a film designer, was born in Los Angeles on June 26, 1924 and lived for a time with his family in Mexico City, where he studied with Diego Rivera. After returning to the United States, he worked as in industrial designer, for Lockheed in California where he helped design airplane interiors, and in New York City at Grand Central Palace on expositions. His initial experience with movies was on Edith Head's staff, before he starting designing at Paramount Studios. His film credits include *Jumbo, Please Don't Eat the Daisies, Make Mine Manhattan* and *Games*. He received Oscar nominations for costume design for *The Unsinkable Molly Brown, Planet of the Apes* and *What's The Matter With Helen*. In addition to his Broadway costumes, he also designed for leading ladies at La Scala. Morton Haack died on March 22, 1987.

Costumes: 1948 *Make Mine Manhattan*; *Strange Bedfellows*

Helen A. Haas

Helen A. Haas designed costumes for a play on Broadway in 1922. She was born in Brooklyn on September 20, 1899, and studied with Emile Antoine Bourdell fora career as a sculptor. Her portrait heads of prominent historical figures were commissioned around the world, and are collected in many museums including the Museum of the City of New York (Dorothy Gish), the Museum of Natural History (General

Theodore Roosevelt), and the Luxembourg Museum in Paris. In private life she was Mrs. Ruffin de Langley. Helen Haas de Langley died in March 1987.

Costumes: 1922 *Frank Fay's Fables*†

Moe Hack

Moe Hack (also known as Monroe B. Hack, Mac Hack) was a director and lighting specialist. His parents were co-owners and managers of the Thalia and Atlantic Theatres in the Bowery in New York City, and although they encouraged their son to study law he pursued a career in theater. David Belasco arranged for a scholarship for Hack to attend Carnegie Institute of Technology. After service in World War II he returned to New York and in 1945 he directed *Winterset* at Equity Library Theatre. He gradually specialized in lights and became known as a lighting technical director around the country. He served as a design and lighting expert on the staff of the Federal Theatre where he worked with Howard Bay and others to develop *The Living Newspaper, One Third of A Nation, Power,* and *Pinocchio.* He toured with Gertrude Lawrence providing technical support for *Pygmalion.* However, he never entirely gave up directing and directed plays including *Phantoms* (1930), *Blue Holiday* (1945) and *E=MC2* (1948) on Broadway. He also produced *Seeds in the Wind* (1948), the Old Vic tour to New York City in 1948 (with Howard Newman), and *Talent '49* in 1949. He produced over 100 shows at the Tamiment (Pennsylvania) Playhouse, notably *The Princess and the Pea* which became *Once Upon a Mattress,* and a hit on Broadway.

Lights: 1937 *One Third of a Nation* **1938** *Life and Death of an American;* *Pinocchio* **1941** *Brooklyn, U.S.A.* **1942** *The Eve of Saint Mark;* *Proof through the Night* **1943** *The Family;* *The Patriots* **1944** *Storm Operation;* *Thank You, Svoboda* **1945** *The Tempest* **1948** *Gone Tomorrow/ Home Life of a Buffalo/Hope is the Thing*

Jeanette Hackett

Jeanne (Janette, Jeanette) Hackett, an actress and dancer in musical revues,

was born in 1898 in New York City and died there on August 16, 1979. She first performed in vaudeville in 1907, touring until her eighteenth birthday when she could legally perform in New York, and remained active until the 1940s. She initially performed with her brother Albert before forming her own company, the Jeannette Hackett Chorus, performing, choreographing and also designing settings, lights and costumes. She later teamed up with Harry Delmar whom she subsequently married. They separated both professionally and personally in the late 1920s. In 1930 she married the singer John Steel and staged productions for her husband while continuing to perform and choreograph.

Costumes: 1927 *Delmar's Revels*
Lights: 1943 *Hairpin Harmony*

George Haddon

George Haddon (Hadden) was active on Broadway between 1923 and 1930 as a setting and costume designer. "George Haddon, Theatricals," was located at 675 Madison Avenue in the mid-1920s. He appeared in the 1920 film *Beyond the Horizon* and in 1933 was dialogue director for *Cavalcade.*

Sets: 1923 *The Other Rose*
Costumes: 1923 *Laugh, Clown, Laugh*†
1926 *Lulu Belle* **1928** *Minna* **1930** *Tonight or Never* (Supervising Art Director)

Rose Hagan

Rose Hagan designed costumes, hats and gowns, on Broadway in 1921. For the majority of her career, she operated millinery shops, one on 57th Street and one in the Drake Hotel. She died on July 29, 1948.

Costumes: 1921 *The Fan*† (Hats and gowns)

Claude Hagen

Claude L. Hagen was acknowledged for contributions to two Broadway productions in the early years of the twentieth century. Given the nature of his credits, it is likely that he participated in more than are known. Trow's 1898 Manhattan and Bronx Directory identifies him as a contractor working from 28 West 29th Street and residing at 169

West 35th Street. At the beginning of the twentieth century, he is identified as an artisan, living and working from 520-542 West 26th Street in New York City.

Sets: 1902 *Dolly Varden†* (Mechanical effects) 1903 *The Jersey Lily†* (Designed and built)

Mrs. Louise Haggeman

Mrs. Louise Haggeman designed costumes for a production on Broadway in 1905.

Costumes: 1905 *The Dagger and the Cross*

Ben Ali Haggin

Ben Ali Haggin, portrait painter and stage designer, was a native of New York City. He was born in 1882 and died September 2, 1951. He received his art training in Munich and at the Art Students League, first exhibiting his paintings in 1908. He had numerous one-man shows around the world. He was an impresario, creating balls and pageants. He directed the Beaux Arts Balls from 1927 to 1933 and balls for the Metropolitan Opera in the mid-1930s.

Costumes: 1917 *Lord and Lady Algy†* (Drawings) 1922 *Rose Briar* (Louis VII Tableau, Costumes in the Cabaret) 1924 *Ziegfeld Follies: 1924†* 1927 *The Marquise* (Costume Supervisor)

H. P. Hall

H. P. Hall collaborated on the scenery for a 1908 production.

Sets: 1908 *The Second Mrs. Tanqueray†*

Peter J. Hall

The theatrical designer, Peter J. Hall was born in Bristol, England to Scottish parents. He works often on the West Coast, where he was resident stage and costume designer for the Mark Taper Forum in the mid-1960s. His designs for opera companies throughout the world include *Aida*, *I Puritani*, *Lohengrin*, *La Forza del Destino*, and *Boris Godunov* in 1974, at the Metropolitan Opera, *L'Isle des Fous* in Spoleto, Italy in 1961, *Don Giovanni* for the Chicago Lyric Opera in 1964, *Samson et Dalila* in Dallas in 1964, and many, many more. He is,

in addition, a fashion designer, an interior decorator, and a painter. Credits for designing sets and costumes include *Romeo and Juliet* and *Much Ado About Nothing* for the in the early 1960s and Royal National Theatre of Great Britain and *Giselle* for the American Ballet Theatre. His article about designing for the opera, "Living Figures," appeared in the November 14, 1964 issue of *Opera News*. The theatrical designer is not to be confused with the British director and theater manager, Sir Peter Hall, nor Peter Ruthven Hall whose designs for *Vinegar Tom* and *The House of Bernarda Alba* both produced in Oxford, were part of the were part of the British exhibit at the 1987 Prague Quadrienale.

Costumes: 1979 *Zoot Suit*

Stafford Hall

Stafford Hall, who was born in Derbyshire, England in 1853 (some sources state 1858), collaborated on the sets for a 1905 Broadway production. The playbill stages that his scenic artistry could be seen in London regularly at Drury Lane, the Royal Court Theatre, and the Princess Theatre. His designs and scene paintings were used in London, Leeds and Liverpool as early as 1877 and he often collaborated with the leading scenic artists of the day, Walter Hann, William Telbin, and Bruce Smith, among others. Additional nineteenth century credits in America include *Clito* in Boston in 1886 and *Claudian* in 1887 in Brooklyn. *Claudian* was originally performed in London's Princess Theatre in 1883. Representative drawings are in the permanent collection of the Victoria and Albert Museum. Hall died in 1922.

Sets: 1905 *The Babes and the Baron†*

Halston

Halston, the fashion designer was born Roy Halston Frowlick in Des Moines, Iowa on April 23, 1932 and studied at the Chicago Art Institute. He began his career in fashion as a custom milliner in Chicago, moved to New York and worked for Lily Dache in 1958, and became fashion designer at Bergdorf Goodman in 1959. He remained at Bergdorf's until the late

1960s when he opened his own couture house, becoming one of the most important American voices of the early 1970s. In addition to fashion, he designed costumes for Broadway, film, and television, including Lauren Bacall's costumes for *Applause* on CBS-TV in 1973. He also designed for Martha Graham's company and for the Dance Theatre of Harlem. His business lost its' caché when he agreed to design lower-priced clothes for J. C. Penny in 1982. His 1984 attempt to buy his business back failed. Halston died in San Francisco ion March 1990.

Costumes: 1977 *The Act*

John Hambleton

John Hambleton graduated from the University of Kentucky in 1923 and taught at the New York School of Fine and Applied Art in New York and in Paris. He worked mainly in the areas of graphic art and fashion illustration. He has also advised fashion houses about promotion and advertising and in 1930 was appointed director of publicity for the James A. Hearn and Son Department Store. His costume designs were seen on Broadway between 1934 and 1940. He should not be confused with the Canadian author (1901-1961) with the same name.

Costumes: 1934 *Merrily We Roll Along* (Costumes Supervised) **1935** *First Lady*; *Tomorrow's a Holiday* **1936** *Stage Door*; *The Women*; *You Can't Take It with You* **1937** *Fulton of Oak Falls*† (Character Costumes for Miss Newcombe and Miss Faust); *The Ghost of Yankee Doodle*; *I'd Rather Be Right*† (Modern clothes) **1938** *Fabulous Invalid*; *I Married an Angel*; *Save Me the Waltz*; *Sing Out the News* **1939** *Stars in Your Eyes* **1940** *John Henry*

James Hamilton

James Hamilton has designed lighting and settings for many productions in and around New York and for tours. He earned his undergraduate degree from the Rhode Island School of Design and graduate degree from Yale University. Among his credits are the national tours of *Oliver* and *The World of Suzy Wong*. He has also designed for La Mama E.T.C.

Sets: 1969 *The New Music Hall of Israel* **1979** *Got Tu Go Disco*
Lights: 1969 *The New Music Hall of Israel*

W. Franklin Hamilton

W. Franklin Hamilton designed scenery for two productions in 1904. A decorator, his studio was located at 1004 Times Building in 1910 in New York City. His residence was 1 West 104th Street. He was also partner with Thomas G. Moses in Moses and Hamilton, which was active between 1900 and 1904. For additional information and credits see the "Moses and Hamilton" entry.

Sets: 1904 *The Isle of Spice*; *Little Johnny Jones*

Aubrey Hammond

Aubrey Hammond designed sets for two productions on Broadway in 1934. He was born in Folkestone, England on September 18, 1893, studied at Bradfield College and also studied art in Paris and London. His first design in 1913 led to numerous productions in London, plays and operas in New York, and films. After service in World War I, when he assisted in developing camouflage and illustrated military publications, he resumed his design career. He also created theatrical posters. He was scenic supervisor for the opening of the Shakespeare Memorial Theatre in Stratford-upon-Avon. In 1936 he became an art director for films and joined the faculty of the Westminster School of Art. He died on March 19, 1940 at age 46.

Sets: 1934 *The Shining Hour*; *A Successful Calamity*

J. G. Hammond

As a young man, James G. Hammond worked as an artisan in the theater, as well as designing scenery. In 1903, he married Clara Turner and they created two vaudeville acts, "The Constant Couple" and "Aunt Clare and Uncle Jim." The acts were successful enough that by the end of the first decade of the twentieth century, they were on tour throughout the United States and Europe. After retiring from the stage, they moved to Waterford, Connecticut where he became the state representative from that district. He died at age 83 on January 6, 1962 in New London, Connecticut.

Sets: 1904 *Judith of Bethulia†* 1907 *Miss Pocahontas* (Designed and painted)

Natalie Hays Hammond

Natalie Hays Hammond, a painter, inventor, theatrical designer and museum director studied with Sergi Soudeikine. Born in Lakewood, New Jersey on January 6, 1905, she designed sets and costumes in the mid-1930s for theatrical productions, after winning a contest at the Laboratory Theatre in New York to design a production for Alla Nazimova. In the 1930s she developed a method to adhere metal to other surfaces. She had numerous one-woman shows, and in 1957 founded the Hammond Museum in North Salem, New York where she also created elaborate gardens. An author and illustrator, she wrote *Elizabeth of England*, *Anthology of Pattern* and *New Adventure in Needlepoint Design*. Miss Hammond, who died at age 81 on June 30, 1985, was the subject of a retrospective in 1994.

Sets: 1931 *The Social Register†*
Costumes: 1933 *La Nativite*

Carolyn Hancock

Carolyn Hancock, a designer of scenery and costumes, started her career as technical director for the Theatre Guild in its early days. She not only designed the sets and costumes for the Garrick Gaieties in 1925 but also appeared in the show. She was active in developing the Costume Institute at the Metropolitan Museum of Art. Carolyn Hancock, who died on April 19, 1951, was married to scene designer Lee Simonson.

Sets: 1923 *The Devil's Disciple*; *The Race with the Shadow*; *Windows* 1924 *The Locked Door*; *They Knew What They Wanted* 1925 *Ariadne*; *Garrick Gaieties†*; *Man of Destiny†* 1926 *An American Tragedy*; *At Mrs. Beam's*; *Garrick Gaieties†* 1935 *The Taming of the Shrew* 1940 *The Taming of the Shrew†* 1945 *The Secret Room*
Costumes: 1923 *The Devil's Disciple*; *The Race with the Shadow* 1924 *They Knew What They Wanted* 1925 *Ariadne*; *Garrick Gaieties*; *Man of Destiny* 1926 *At Mrs. Beam's*; *Garrick Gaieties†* 1943 *The Family*

Terry Hands

Terrence David Hands started his career in theater as founder/director of the Everyman Theatre in Liverpool, England where he worked from 1964 to 1966. He is known in the United States primarily for his association with the Royal Shakespeare Company which he joined in 1966 as artistic director of Theatre-Go-Round (for touring productions). From 1967 to 1977 he was Associate Director of the Royal Shakespeare Company, and in 1978 became Co-Artistic Director with Trevor Nunn. From 1986 until 1989 he was Artistic Director of RSC; he now holds the title of Director Emeritus. From 1975 to 1977 he was also Consultant Director of the Comédie Française in Paris. His directorial debut on Broadway was *All's Well That Ends Well* in 1984. He was born on January 9, 1941 in Aldershot, Hampshire, England and attended Birmingham University (Bachelor of Arts, English language and literature with honors) and the Royal Academy of Dramatic Art. His directing, as well as his lighting designs have been much honored in Europe as well as in the United States, including a Tony Award nomination for best lighting design for *Much Ado About Nothing*.

Lights: 1984 *Cyrano De Bergerac†* (Also directed); *Much Ado About Nothing†* (Also directed) 1988 *Carrie* (Also directed) 2000 *Macbeth* (Also directed)

Walter Hann

Walter (W.) Hann, one of the best known British scenic artists was born January 11, 1837 (perhaps 1838) in London, youngest of nineteen children, and died there on July 16, 1922 at age 84. He apprenticed under J. W. Callcott, and also studied with William Roxby Beverley, Charles Marshall, and John Coleman. He was associated with several London theaters, but mainly worked from his own studio in Murphy Street where he designed and painted many sets for the actor/managers Dion Boucicault, Wilson Barrett, Henry Irving and Herbert Beerbohm Tree, among others. His assistants included Joseph Harker and his only apprentice was Bruce Smith, both of whom became equally successful. The list of productions he designed and painted is long and includes the original production of *Peter Pan* in 1904.

Sets: 1899 *The Merchant of Venice*† **1900** *The Bugle Call* **1901** *The Merchant of Venice*†; *A Message from Mars* **1902** *The Happy Hypocrite*† (Acts II and IV) **1903** *The Light That Failed*† **1905** *Alice Sit-by-The-Fire*; *The Freedom of Suzanne* **1907** *The Merchant of Venice*† **1908** *The Second Mrs. Tanqueray*† **1910** *Mr. and Mrs. Daventry*† (Acts II and IV); *Smith* **1913** *The Light That Failed*†; *Mice and Men*†

William Hanna

William J. Hanna was responsible for one set design in 1916 on Broadway. Born in Belfast, Ireland, he emigrated to the United States in 1896 and worked as a builder. During the first decade of the twentieth century he formed a series of partnerships with others in the construction trades including Timothy O'Connell and Alfred Frymier. When his brother T. A. Hanna joined them, the business became Hanna Brothers. Although he spent most of his professional career building schools, hospitals, and apartment buildings, he also did some work for theaters, and in 1916 designed sets. William J. Hanna died August 2, 1946 at age 63. He should not be confused with William Denby Hanna (1910-2001) of Hanna-Barbera, nor his father, William John Hanna who built early Santa Fe railway stations.

Sets: 1916 *Turn to the Right*†

Mrs. Ingeborg Hansell

Mrs. Ingeborg Hansell, who studied painting in Stockholm and at the Art Students League, designed sets and costumes on Broadway in the 1920s. An exhibit of her designs for stage curtains and plays including the 1922 *Greenwich Village Follies* was held in 1923 at the Art Center. Her husband

Nils Hansell was a civil engineer and they resided at 5012 Waldo Avenue with their son, Nils, Hansell, Jr. in 1932. They later resided in Malvern, New York. Born September 19, 1883, she died in June 1978 in Honolulu, Hawaii.

Sets: 1922 *Greenwich Village Follies*† **1924** *Greenwich Village Follies*† **Costumes: 1922** *Greenwich Village Follies*† **1924** *Greenwich Village Follies*†

Joseph Hansen

Joseph Hansen was set designer for one production in 1933 on Broadway. In 1930 he was associated with Ernot Blitzen in Hansen & Blitzen, purveyors of theatrical goods. The business continued in 1932 from his residence at 423 West 43rd Street in New York City where he lived with his wife, Mercy Hansen.

Sets: 1933 *Fly by Night*

Emilie Hapgood

Emilie Bigelow Hapgood was president of the New York Stage Society in 1914 when she invited Harley Granville-Barker to direct a play in New York. He chose *Androcles and the Lion* with sets and costumes by his English designer, Norman Wilkinson. Soon after arriving in New York, Granville-Barker met Robert Edmond Jones at an exhibition of theatrical designs sponsored by the New York Stage Society, where his scenic designs for *The Man Who Married A Dumb Wife* were on display. The play was added as a curtain raiser to the production of *Androcles and the Lion* and the two plays opened on January 27, 1915. The production of *The Man Who Married a Dumb Wife* is generally regarded as the beginning of the modern Broadway era, and the designs by Robert Edmond Jones the introduction of the New American Stagecraft. Emilie Bigelow married critic and playwright Norman Hapgood (1868-1937) on June 17, 1896 and divorced him in Paris in spring 1915. Together with his brother (Emory) Hutchins Hapgood, they were active members of the Greenwich Village arts community.

Sets: 1917 *The Magic*

Cyril Harcourt

The British actor and playwright Cyril Harcourt was born Cyril Perkins circa 1872 and adopted the name Harcourt for his appearances on stage. He wrote many plays, mainly melodramas and light comedies, beginning with *The Axis* in 1904, and often performed in them. *A Pair of Silk Stockings* was a modest hit in London before opening in New York where it was a great success. His other plays include *A Place in the Sun*, *A Lady's Name* and *The Recompense*. His interest in describing location when writing plays was also useful for creating stage settings. Also an author of novels and for newspapers, he died in Menton, Alpes-Maritimes, France, on March 4, 1924 at age 52.

Sets: 1914 *A Pair of Silk Stockings*† (Also wrote)

William Harford

William Harford was a British scenic artist who also painted watercolor landscapes that were exhibited at the Royal Academy. His first theatrical credit was at the Theatre Royal, Bristol in 1870 where he collaborated with George Gordon, Frank Jones and others. Between 1870 and 1876, he mostly worked as an assistant to George Gordon in London, after which he designed and painted scenery for numerous London theaters, often working with other scenic artists, including Walter Hann, Bruce Smith, and Stafford Hall. Both of his Broadway credits were for productions imported after successful runs in London. Born in 1842, he died in 1919.

Sets: 1900 *The Gay Lord Quex* **1903** *The Marriage of Kitty*

Bill Hargate

Bill Hargate, a native of St. Louis, Missouri was born on May 6, 1935. He studied at the Art Institute of Chicago and the Goodman Theatre, receiving a B.F.A. His many costume designs have been seen in a variety of locations, including both on and off-Broadway, and at the St. Louis Municipal Opera where he has designed costumes for approximately 50 productions. The majority of his design work has been in

television where he has over 500 credits, among them the series' *Murphy Brown, My Sister Sam, Ink, Love and War*, and numerous specials. The proprietor of Bill Hargate Costumes since 1985 where costumes for movies, plays, television and theater are executed and rented, he has also designed costumes and gowns for Candice Bergen, Geena Davis, Barbara Mandrell and others. His television designs have been honored with four Emmy Awards, for *Murphy Brown, Musical Comedy Tonight III, Pinocchio* and *Once Upon a Brothers Grimm*. In 2001 the Costume Designers Guild honored him with its' career achievement award.

Costumes: 1979 *Oklahoma!*; *Peter Pan*

Roy Hargrave

Roy Hargrave was the lighting designer for a Broadway production in 1944 which he also directed. He first appeared on stage as Alexander in a 1927 production of *The Spider* in New Haven which subsequently moved into New York City. He worked steadily thereafter, acting, writing and directing plays into the late 1940s. Roy Hargrave was born in New York City in 1908 and was educated at the Barnard and McKenzie Schools.

Lights: 1944 *Pick-Up Girl*

Gerry Hariton

Gerry Hariton was born August 1, 1951 in New York City, the son of Lucie and Harry Hariton. He attended Brandeis University and received a Bachelor of Arts degree summa cum laude in 1973. He subsequently received an M.F.A. from Brandeis University under Howard Bay, where he met Vicki Baral. Based in Los Angeles, he has worked almost exclusively with Vicki Baral since 1978. Together they have received five Los Angeles Drama Critics Circle Awards, including one for *Mail*, which later played on Broadway. This husband and wife design team have extensive production design credits for series, specials and movies on television and for commercials, while continuing to design for the theater.

Sets: 1986 *Raggedy Ann*† **1988** *Mail*†

Joseph Harker

Joseph Cunningham Harker was born in Levenshulme, Manchester, England on October 17, 1855. His first production was *Hamlet* with the Theatre Royal, Glasgow in 1881. In 1888 he designed and painted *Macbeth* for Henry Irving in London followed by several more productions for Irving at the Lyceum Theatre. He also worked for Herbert Beerbohm-Tree as a designer and scenic painter. Joseph C. Harker helped established his family as the stars of the English school of scenic artists. Author of *Studio and Stage*, he had four sons, Joseph, Roland, Colin and Phil who joined him as scene painters. Joseph C. Harker died at age 71 on April 15, 1927, but his descendants continued the family association with scenery.

Sets: **1899** *Robespierre†*; *Waterloo* **1901** *The Messenger Boy†* **1902** *The Importance of Being Earnest* **1903** *The Light That Failed†* **1905** *Love and the Man*; *Veronique†* (Acts I, II) **1906** *Caesar and Cleopatra†*; *Markheim†* (Acts II, IV) **1908** *Irene Wycherley* **1912** *Hamlet*; *Julius Caesar†* (Design and painting) **1913** *Hamlet†*; *Hop o' My Thumb†*; *The Light That Failed†*; *The Merchant of Venice†* **1917** *Colonel Newcome†*

Joseph and Phil Harker

Joseph C. Harker and son Phil Harker worked together as scene painters and designers in London. Between 1915 and 1922 four productions designed and painted by Joseph C. and Phil Harker were transferred from London to New York. Phil Harker traveled with the set, and because he was responsible for the necessary alterations to the scenery received co-design credit with his father. After the death of Joseph C. Harker in 1927, Phil Harker and his brothers Joseph, Colin and Roland continued the family business. After Phil died in 1933, Joseph became head of the company. In 1951 Harker Brothers, Scenic Artists still operated in London from a shop on Horsely Street, almost seventy-five years after the family entered the theater business. With descendants of Joseph and Phil Harker, scenic designer David Homan formed

Harker, Homan and Bravery Limited in 1953. Both Joseph C. and Phil Harker designed independently as well as in collaboration in England. Their designs, particularly for the D'Oyly Carte Opera, continued in use after their deaths, which accounts for the posthumous credits listed below.

Sets: **1915** *Quinneys* **1917** *Chu Chin Chow* **1919** *Aphrodite* **1920** *Mecca* **1922** *The Voice from the Minaret* **1938** *The Flashing Stream* **1948** *H.M.S. Pinafore* **1951** *Trial by Jury/ H.M.S. Pinafore* **1955** *H.M.S. Pinafore*; *Trial by Jury*

John W. Harkrider

John W. Harkrider was born in Abilene, Texas in November 1891 (1900 is sometimes cited) and when young appeared in silent movies. He was active on Broadway beginning in 1925, and for many years was associated with Florenz Ziegfeld for whom he directed, designed, and created spectacles. He also designed costumes for film beginning in 1929 when he went to Hollywood with Ziegfeld initially to design costumes for a *Follies* sequence in *Glorifying the American Girl*. After that film, although he continued to design in New York, he continued to designs settings and costumes for movies and became an art director at M-G-M. Additional films include *Whoopee, Three Smart Girls, Roman Scandals, Merry-Go-Round of 1938* and *My Man Godfrey*. In the 1940s, he also was a talent scout and casting director. He died in 1954.

Costumes: **1926** *No Foolin'†* **1927** *Rio Rita*; *Show Boat*; *Ziegfeld Follies: 1927†* **1928** *Rosalie*; *The Three Musketeers*; *Whoopee* **1929** *Midnite Frolics†*; *Show Girl* **1930** *Simple Simon*; *Smiles* **1931** *Ziegfeld Follies: 1931* **1932** *Hot-Cha!†*; *Music in the Air*; *Show Boat* **1941** *Let's Face It* **1942** *Let's Face It*

H. Harndin

H. (Herbert) Harndin was an electrician who worked from 49 West 28th Street and resided at 50 West 26th Street in New York City at as early as 1898. He was active in the Broadway theater from the 1899-1900 through the 1902-1903 season.

Lights: 1899 *Ben Hur*†; *Ben Hur*† 1900 *Chris and the Wonderful Lamp* (Electric butterfly dance invented and patented) 1902 *Ben Hur*†

Donald Harris

Donald Harris designed settings on Broadway in the mid-1970s. He has designed in regional theaters including the Mark Taper Forum, Ahmanson Theatre, Westwood Playhouse, StageWest, and the Company Stage. He received the Los Angeles Drama Critics Circle Award for *Cyrano de Bergerac*. In 1974, he was resident lighting designer for the Old Globe Shakespeare Festival. He was art director the television show *On the Rocks* and the 1979 film *Swap Meet*.

Sets: 1974 *Me and Bessie* 1976 *I Have a Dream*

George W. Harris

George W. Harris was a painter, etcher and scenic designer who developed new techniques for scenic painting. He was born in 1876 (some sources say 1878) and died on February 14, 1929. He was credited with scenic design, costume design, properties, and/or scene painting for more than fifty plays in London in the 1920s, many for Basil Dean. One of the productions he designed on Broadway, *Hassan*, was featured in the 1990 exhibit "Theatre on Paper" at The Drawing Center in New York City.

Sets: 1924 *Hassan*; *Peter Pan* 1925 *Easy Virtue* 1926 *The Constant Nymph*; *This Was a Man*†

Costumes: 1924 *Hassan*; *Peter Pan*

James Berton Harris

James Berton Harris was born in Traverse City, Michigan in September 1940. He received a B.A. at the University of Michigan where he was the first undergraduate to design a major production. He studied at Yale with Frank Poole Bevan and received an M.F.A. His costume designs are seen both in New York and around the United States in regional theaters.

Costumes: 1972 *Promenade, All!* 1974 *Rainbow Jones* 1976 *The Runner Stumbles*

Margaret Harris

See Motley.

Mrs. Sidney Harris

Mrs. Sidney Harris, (also known as Miriam Cole Harris) died in 1925 in Pau, France at age 92. She was born on the Island of Dosoris near Hen Cove, New York, and was a direct descendant of early American settlers. She was a prolific writer whose work included the books *The Sutherlands* and *Rutledge*.

Sets: 1919 *Toby's Bow*; *Up from Nowhere*

Sophia Harris

See Motley.

Howard Harrison

British lighting designer Howard Harrison made his Broadway debut with two productions that opened in 1999. Born in London, he studied at the Central School of Speech and Drama. His many lighting designs include productions in the West End and for the Royal Shakespeare Company, the Royal National Theatre, Donmar Warehouse, Royal Opera House, and English National Opera. He has also designed operas and ballets for many companies. Additional credits in the U.S. include *Martin Guerre* at the Guthrie Theatre, and *Nabucco* for the Metropolitan Opera. Twenty-first century designs include *The Witches of Eastwick* in London's Royal Drury Lane Theatre and *Mamma Mia!* in the 2001-2002 Broadway season.

Lights: 1999 *Kat and the Kings*; *Putting It Together*

Llewellyn Harrison

Llewellyn Harrison, a set designer, created scenery for the Negro Ensemble Company, and for the New Federal Theatre among other theaters in New York City. He also designed sets in London for the American Arts Festival, in Washington, D.C. for Ford's Theatre, and in Rome for Teatro Umberto. His credits as an art director include *Fly By Night* and *Rain Without Thunder* and as lead scenic artist include *Twin Peaks*. He also owned and operated Techprops, a theatrical properties business. He died on November 14,

1994, in Richmond, Virginia, at age 47, shortly before some of his designs went on display in "ONSTAGE: A Century of African American Stage Design" at the New York Public Library for the Performing Arts at Lincoln Center in 1995.

Sets: 1987 *Don't Get God Started*

Marcus Harrison

Marcus Harrison created costumes on Broadway in 1927. Harry and Marcus Harrison were the principles of the Harrison Company, which sold dry goods and novelties, at 741 East Ninth Street in New York City in the mid-1920s. His residence was 1595 Maccombs Road.

Costumes: 1927 *Tommy*† (Miss Entwhistle's gowns)

Mrs. Marcus Harrison

Mrs. Marcus Harrison designed costumes on Broadway in 1925. Her husband was one of the proprietors of New York's Harrison Company.

Costumes: 1925 *The Book of Charm*

Bruce Harrow

Bruce Harrow, who also design as "Shadow," a native of Lakeview, Oregon was born on July 31, 1940. He majored in art as an undergraduate at San Francisco State College and in theater design as a graduate student. On a McKnight Fellowship, he apprenticed at the Guthrie Theatre through the doctoral program at the University of Minnesota and was influenced there by the designs of Tanya Moiseiwitsch and Desmond Heeley. He first designed costumes for the Actors Workshop in San Francisco and made his New York debut with a production of *The Bacchants* at the Lincoln Center Library Theatre. A costume designer for television, dance, and movies as well as theater, Harrow won a Golden Globe for the costume design of *I Never Promised You a Rose Garden*, and shares an Emmy for the design of *Betcha Don't Know* produced by the Children's Television Workshop. Recent theater designs include productions for Theatre Under the Stars, *Joseph and the Amazing Technicolor Dreamcoat* in San Francisco and *Jolson: The Musical* in Toronto. His art

work has been exhibited in New York and London.

Costumes: 1972 *Heathen!*

Edward Hartford

Edward Hartford, an actor, stage manager, and lighting designer, began professional life as stage manager for the Theatre Guild's production of *The Guardsman*, followed by *Porgy* in New York and London. He has also toured throughout the Orient as a stage manager. He performed in *The Second Man* with Lynn Fontanne and Alfred Lunt. His father, Michael Hartford, helped build the Boston Opera House. Edward Hartford, who originated a method to handle film in early movies, died on May 29, 1942 at age 53 in New York City.

Lights: 1925 *Love's Call*

Edna Hartman

Edna (Eda) Hartman, who designed costumes on Broadway between 1917 and 1920, was a costumer. She worked from a shall shop at 49 East 10th Street in New York City.

Costumes: 1917 *Tiger Rose*† (Miss Ulric's dresses) 1918 *Remnant*† (Miss Nash and Miss Baker's costumes) 1920 *Thy Name Is Woman* (Miss Nash's costume)

Hartmann and Fantana

Hartmann and Fantana, also known as Fantana & Hartmann was a partnership between Louis Hartmann and Martin Fantana that mainly provided properties for theatrical productions. Their business was located at 518 West 30th Street in New York through the early 1930s. In addition, they collaborated on the scenery for a production in 1926 Louis Hartmann was known primarily as a lighting designer although he also designed sets. Additional information about his career can be found under his name.

Sets: 1926 *Not Herbert*

Louis Hartmann

Louis Hartmann (also known as Hartman) started in theater in the 1890s as a properties boy at Hammerstein's Harlem Opera House. He became David Belasco's chief electrician in

1901 and worked with him until Belasco's death in 1931. An innovative stage electrician, he was one of the first lighting designers and readily transferred his expertise from gas lighting systems to electrical systems. He developed many techniques including the first incandescent spotlights, indirect overhead lighting, and silvered reflectors. Together Belasco and Hartmann banished footlights for the 1915 production of *The Return of Peter Grimm*. At the time of his death at age 64 on February 9, 1941, Hartmann was on the sound staff at Radio City Music Hall. He was the author of *Theatre Lighting: A Manual of the Stage Switchboard*, a work which documented some of the developments he pioneered.

Lights: 1902 *The Darling of the Gods*† **1903** *Darling of the Gallery Gods, The and The Dress Parade*†; *Sweet Kitty Bellairs* **1904** *The Music Master*; *Zaza* **1906** *The Rose of the Rancho* **1909** *The Lily* **1910** *The Concert*; *Just A Wife* **1912** *The Case of Becky* **1913** *Good Little Devil*; *The Temperamental Journey* **1917** *Tiger Rose* **1918** *The Auctioneer* **1919** *The Son-Daughter* **1920** *Deburau* **1921** *The Easiest Way*; *The Return of Peter Grimm* **1923** *Mary, Mary, Quite Contrary* **1924** *Ladies of the Evening*; *Tiger Cats* **1925** *Accused*; *Canary Dutch*; *The Dove* **1926** *What Never Dies* **1928** *The Bachelor Father* **1929** *It's a Wise Child* **1930** *Dancing Partner*

Peter Hartwell

Peter Hartwell was born in Canada. After completing training at Sadler's Wells Theatre Design School, he worked with Hayden Griffen as an assistant and then co-designer, and designed scenery and costumes for Caryl Churchill's plays in London including *Top Girls, Serious Money* and the original production of *Cloud 9*. He designed productions at the New York Shakespeare Festival as part of an exchange with the Royal Court Theatre, and has off-Broadway credits including *Aunt Dan and Lemon*. Among the many productions he has designed at the Shaw Festival are *Village Wooing, the Madras House, Six Characters in Search of an Author* and *A Foggy Day*.

His designs are also often seen at the Stratford (Ontario) Festival, and the Ford Center's Studio Theatre, and the CanStage Berkeley Street Theatre in Toronto.

Sets: 1988 *Serious Money*
Costumes: 1988 *Serious Money*

John Harvey

John Harvey, who was born in 1915, was active as a Broadway lighting designer between 1961 and 1973. A native of Philadelphia, he founded the Philadelphia Opera Company and headed the production department for seven years. He worked as an assistant to Jo Mielziner for sixteen years, from 1945 to 1961, on more than forty Broadway productions and on the design of the Vivian Beaumont Theatre. He also designed lights for the Opera Company of Boston. Harvey, who retired in 1980, died on April 4, 1994.

Lights: 1961 *Kean* **1962** *Come on Strong*; *A Passage to India* **1963** *110 Degrees in the Shade*; *Tovarich* **1964** *The Deputy* **1965** *Mating Dance*; *A Very Rich Woman* **1967** *More Stately Mansions* **1968** *Happiness Is Just a Little Thing Called a Rolls Royce* **1969** *My Daughter, Your Son* **1973** *No Sex Please, We're British*

Peter Harvey

Peter Harvey was born January 2, 1933 in Quiriqua, Guatemala, a descendant of British colonials. He studied in Central America, North America and Europe and moved to the United States in 1956, settled in New York City in 1958, and became a United States citizen in 1961. A set and costume designer, he designed numerous ballets for companies including the New York City Ballet, the Washington National Ballet and the Metropolitan Opera Ballet. Influenced by the work of Léon Bakst, Christian Bérard, Oliver Messel and Cecil Beaton, his mentor was Rouben Ter-Arutunian. His first production was *Pantomime for Lovers* for the Miami Ballet in 1954, and he also designed summer stock for companies in Maine, Rhode Island, Connecticut and Florida. He taught set design, costume design, scene painting and costume history at Pratt Institute in Brooklyn from 1970 to 1987. While he has credits in various milieu, his most important work was for the New York City Ballet, including the original designs for Balanchine's *Jewels*, and off-Broadway for productions including *Boys in the Band*, *Dames at Sea*, and *Black Picture Show*. He is not to be confused with the cameraman who has the same name.

Sets: 1964 *Baby Wants a Kiss* **1970** *Park*; *Water Color/ Criss Crossing* **1975** *A Letter for Queen Victoria* (Set supervisor) **1978** *The Effect of Gamma Rays on Man-in-the-Moon Marigolds*

Costumes: 1964 *Baby Wants a Kiss* **1965** *All in Good Time* **1970** *Gloria and Esperanza*† (Costume Supervisor); *Park*; *Water Color/ Criss Crossing* **1975** *A Letter for Queen Victoria* (Costume Supervisor); *The Rocky Horror Show*† (Costume Supervisor); *The Rocky Horror Show*† (Set supervisor) **1978** *The Effect of Gamma Rays on Man-in-the-Moon Marigolds*

Walter Harvey

Walter M. Harvey attended the Cincinnati Art School in his hometown of Cincinnati, Ohio. He was principally a scene painter and was a partner in Ward and Harvey Studios, Inc., 502 West 38th Street, New York, with Herbert Ward. There he painted *Irene*, *Tobacco Road*, and *Earl Carroll's Vanities* among other productions. Examples of his work as a mural painter adorn the walls of the Polyclinic Hospital in New York City. Walter M. Harvey died on October 27, 1945 in Englewood, New Jersey.

Sets: 1912 *Our Wives*† (Act III) **1913** *The Purple Road*† (Acts I, II) **1930** *First Night*† **1931** *Papavert*†; *Unexpected Husband*† **1932** *Through the Years*†; *Trick for Trick*† **1933** *It Happened Tomorrow*† **1934** *A Ship Comes in*†

Tim Hatley

The British designer Tim Hatley was born in Luton, England and graduated with honors in 1989 from the Central Saint Martins College of Art. He has designed productions for Théâtre de Complicité, the Almeida Theatre, the Gate, the Royal National Theatre (including *Hamlet* starring Simon Russell

Beale in 2000), the Royal Shakespeare Company, and in the West End. Additional New York credits include *Traverse* off-Broadway and the Gate Theatre production of *Happy Days* at Lincoln Center. His designs have been much honored, including the Linbury Prize for Stage Design, Plays and Players Critics Awards, Time Out Awards, Evening Standard Awards, and a Laurence Olivier Award for *Stanley* in 1997.

Sets: 1997 *Stanley*

Costumes: 1997 *Stanley*

Madame Haverstick

Madame Haverstick designed costumes on Broadway in the early 1920s. The 1922-1923 New Trow's York City Directory suggests that Marie Track was known professionally as Madame Haverstick. However, the subsequent directory, published in 1924, identifies Anna T. Haverstick as the president and treasurer of Haverstick Studios, Inc, The small custom salon which provided gowns for private and theatrical customers was located at 146 West 44th Street in New York in both volumes. That same directory states that Anna T. Haverstick resided at 143 Hancock Street in Brooklyn, New York.

Costumes: 1920 *Cinderella on Broadway*† **1921** *The Squaw Man*† (Gowns)

Elizabeth Hawes

Elizabeth Hawes was a fashion designer, who contributed costume designs to the theater. She was born in New Jersey in 1903 and died in 1971. After study at Vassar, she took classes at Parson's School of Design and in Paris before becoming the Paris stylist for Lord and Taylor and Macy's. In the U.S. in the late 1920s she opened her own fashion house. She also designed for various manufacturers. Her autobiography, *Fashion is Spinach* relates the story of her years in the fashion business.

Costumes: 1928 *Paris* **1929** *Meteor*† (Gowns) **1934** *The Perfumed Lady* **1935** *A Touch of Brimstone*† (Miss Philip's gowns) **1936** *A Room in Red and White* (Gowns)

Charles Hawkins

Charles Hawkins designed costumes on Broadway in 1936. The Manhattan City Directory in 1933-1934 lists two men with that time. One was an artist who lived and worked from 20 East 35 Street. The second Charles Hawkins was a painter who resided at 100 Carroll, City Island.

Costumes: 1936 *It Can't Happen Here*

John Hawkins

John F. Hawkins designed sets and costumes on Broadway in the late 1920s. An artist, Mr. Hawkins paintings were exhibited posthumously at the Argent Galleries in New York in 1940. At the time of his death on May 22, 1939 in Santa Monica, California, he worked in the drafting department of Metro Studios.

Sets: 1927 *A Connecticut Yankee* **1928** *Chee-Chee*

Costumes: 1927 *A Connecticut Yankee*

William Hawley

William Hawley was a scenic artist and designer who worked primarily in England, at the Theatre Royal, Bristol and the Lyceum Theatre in London. He has credits as early as 1871 as an assistant to G. Gordon and William Harford on *Mary Warner*. He also painted scenery, including *The Victoria Cross* in 1894, which played in New York, and for *The Case of The Rebellious Susan* in London in 1895. *The Prisoner of Zenda* for which he received credit as "Art and Scenic Director" in New York was originally performed in London in 1895 and his contribution was acknowledged in the same way. Given the range of dates, from 1871 to 1930, it is possible that *Jonica* was designed by another man with the same name. The scenic artist, however, should not be confused with the American actor, William E. Hawley (1910-1976).

Sets: 1908 *The Prisoner of Zenda†* **1914** *What Would You Do?†* (Also painted) **1930** *Jonica*

Irene Hawthorne

Irene Hawthorne designed the costumes and properties, wrote, choreographed, and starred in a Broadway play in 1956. She had been a premiere danseuse at the Metropolitan Opera and the Opera National in Mexico City before creating performances that integrated dance, theater, music and mime. After retiring from the stage in 1958, she taught and choreographed. A degree in dramatic literature in 1939 from the University of California was her educational background. Born in San Francisco, she died on October 24, 1986 in New York City.

Costumes: 1957 *Autobiography*

Richard L. Hay

Richard Laurence Hay was born May 28, 1929, in Wichita, Kansas, and has a B.A. in architecture and an M.A. in theater arts from Stanford University. He has designed nearly two hundred productions at the Oregon Shakespeare Festival since his association began in 1953, including the entire Shakespeare canon. His first position was as technical director and in 1970 he became the principal scenic designer. He also has designed over one hundred additional productions in many regional theaters around the United States, notably the Denver Theatre Center where he was Associate Artistic Director for design from 1984 to 1991. In addition to his stage designs he designed three theaters for the Ashland Festival, two theaters for the Old Globe and two theater spaces for the Denver Center Theatre. His designs have been much honored, with prizes including five Hollywood Drama Logue Critics Awards and the 1989 Oregon Governor's Award for the Arts. The author of *A Space for Magic: Stage Settings by Richard L. Hay* (1979), his designs were also exhibited in "Scenic Design of Richard L. Hay" at the Schneider Museum of Art in Ashland, Oregon in 2001.

Sets: 1968 *The Resistible Rise of Arturo Ui*

Costumes: 1968 *The Resistible Rise of Arturo Ui*

Dermot Hayes

British set designer Dermot Hayes has been designing throughout the United Kingdom since the early 1980s when he frequently created scenery at the Lyric Studio, Hammersmith. He has also

done many productions at the Royal Lyceum Theatre in Edinburgh, including *Gaslight, Mother Courage and Her Children,* and *Dancing at Lugnasa.* His designs for *Agrippina* for the Buxton Festival, *Seven Lears* at the Royal Court, *Heartbreak House* at the Derby Playhouse and *The Debutante Ball* at the Hampstead Theatre are among his other credits.
Sets: **1981** *Life and Adventures of Nicholas Nickleby,*†

Edward Haynes
Edward Haynes, a native of Burleson, Texas attended the University of Texas where he received both bachelor and master's degrees in fine arts. He also studied at Yale University and at Lester Polakov's Studio and Forum of Stage Design. He has assisted on Broadway shows, including *Anya, The Royal Hunt of the Sun,* and *Fiddler on the Roof.* He is, in addition, a draftsman at Feller Scenery Studios.
Sets: **1976** *Going Up*

Blanche Hays
Blanche Hays designed costumes for two plays on Broadway in the 1920s. She was associated with Elsa Schiaparelli in Paris at that same time.
Costumes: **1921** *The Verge* (Costume Supervisor) **1925** *Adam Solitaire*

David Hays
David Arthur Hays (sometimes Hayes), a scenic and lighting designer and producer, was born on June 2, 1930 in New York City. During his career he has worked with many great designers, actors and directors, including Roger Furse, Leslie Hurry, Oliver Gielgud and Peter Brook. He received a Bachelor of Arts at Harvard University in 1952 and began a Fulbright Fellowship to the Old Vic in the same year. He attended the Yale University School of Drama from 1953 to 1954 and then Boston University, where he earned an M.F.A. in 1955 under Raymond Sovey and Horace Armistead. He was an apprentice at the Brattle Theatre in Cambridge, Massachusetts from 1949 to 1952 where he worked with Robert O'Hearn. His first design, *Hay Fever* in 1951, was at the Brattle Theatre. With over

sixty Broadway plays and thirty ballets for George Balanchine to his credit, it is little wonder he has received two Obie Awards (for *The Quare Fellow* and *The Balcony*), several Tony nominations, two honorary doctorates, and the New York Drama Critics Award for *No Strings.* His book, *Light on the Subject,* was published by Limelight Editions in 1990.
Sets: **1956** *The Innkeeper; Long Day's Journey into Night* **1958** *The Night Circus* **1959** *The Rivalry; The Tenth Man; Triple Play* **1960** *All the Way Home; Love and Libel; Roman Candle* **1961** *Gideon; Look: We've Come Through; No Strings; Sunday in New York* **1962** *A Family Affair; In the Counting House* **1963** *Lorenzo; Strange Interlude* **1964** *Hughie; The Last Analysis; Marco Millions; A Murderer among Us* **1965** *Diamond Orchid; Drat! the Cat!; Mrs. Dally; Peterpat* **1966** *Dinner at Eight; We Have Always Lived in the Castle* **1967** *Dr. Cook's Garden* **1968** *A Cry of Players; The Goodbye People* **1969** *The National Theatre of the Deaf* **1970** *The Gingerbread Lady; Songs from Milkwood; Two by Two* **1978** *Platinum* **1981** *Kingdoms*
Lights: **1956** *The Innkeeper* **1959** *The Tenth Man; Triple Play* **1960** *All the Way Home; Love and Libel; Roman Candle* **1961** *Gideon; Look: We've Come Through; No Strings; Sunday in New York* **1962** *A Family Affair; In the Counting-House* **1963** *Lorenzo; Strange Interlude* **1964** *Baby Wants a Kiss; Hughie; The Last Analysis; Marco Millions; A Murderer among Us* **1965** *Diamond Orchid; Drat! the Cat!; Mrs. Dally; Peterpat* **1966** *Dinner at Eight; We Have Always Lived in the Castle* **1967** *Dr. Cook's Garden* **1968** *The Goodbye People* **1981** *Bring Back Birdie*

Madame Hayward
Madame Hayward, New Bond Street, London, according to *The Fascinating Mr. Vanderveldt* playbill, designed gowns and costumes for productions on Broadway during the first decade of the twentieth century. All the productions were performed in New York after successful London runs. In addition, she designed for Ethel Barrymore and Billie Burke, among others, for many of

their stage appearances.
Costumes: 1900 *The Bugle Call*† 1905 *Alice Sit-by-The-Fire*† (Miss VanBrugh's gowns) 1906 *Fascinating Mr. Vanderveldt*† (Miss Jeffrey's gowns) 1907 *All-of-a-Sudden Peggy*† (Miss Matthew's and Miss Beckley's gowns) 1909 *Penelope* (Miss Tempest's costumes) 1910 *Smith*†

Edith Head

Edith Head was one of Hollywood's best known costume designers. Born in San Bernadino, California on October 28, 1898, she attended the Otis and Chouinard Art Schools taking fashion design courses at night while teaching languages during the day. Her first contact with the movies was in 1933 when she joined Paramount Studios to work as a sketch artist for Howard Greer and Travis Banton. By 1938 she had become head of design. Edith Head, who won eight Oscars for movie costume design, had considerable influence on American fashions. In the late 1950s she contributed costume designs to two Broadway plays. Edith Head, who died October 24, 1981, was married to the set designer Wiard Ihnen. For professional use she retained the name of her first husband, Charles Head.
Costumes: 1958 *Edwin Booth*; *The Pleasure of His Company*

Thyza Head

Thyza Head designed costumes for a featured player in a 1922 Broadway show.
Costumes: 1922 *Billeted*† (Miss Bolton's Act II costume)

Timothy Heale

Timothy Heale was lighting designer on Broadway in 1977 for one production.
Lights: 1977 *Ipi Tombi*†

Douglas Heap

Douglas Heap was appointed head of design at the Royal Academy of Dramatic Art in 1969. He was born in London on August 7, 1934, the son of Clifford Vernon and Alexandra Jessica Heap, who entertained audiences with miniature theaters. He studied at the Byam Shaw School of Drawing and Painting and initially designed professionally for *Bid Time Return* in 1958.

Beginning with *Boesman and Lena* in 1971 he has designed all of Athol Fugard's plays in London. He has numerous additional credits in London and throughout the United Kingdom. Opera designs include productions in Wexford, for the Kent Opera, and at the Coliseum. He also designed *Pygmalion* for the Theatre of Comedy, *For Your Wife*, *The Canterbury Tales*, and *Barnaby and the Old Boys*.
Sets: 1974 *Sizwe Banzi is Dead*† 1987 *Pygmalion*

Miss Sarah Hecht

Miss Sarah Hecht contributed designs to a Broadway show in 1920. An illustrator, she resided at 560 West 149th Street in New York City.
Costumes: 1920 *The Light of the World*†

H. Heckroth

Hein Heckroth was a German painter and stage and film designer born in Giessen, Germany on April 14, 1897 (some sources state 1898 and 1901). After meeting with success in Germany in the early 1930s as a scenic designer, he traveled throughout the world concentrating on designing film settings. He won two Academy Awards for sets: for *The Red Shoes* in 1943 and *Tales of Hoffman* in 1951. His paintings and designs have been widely exhibited and collected and have been the subject of numerous books and articles. He was director of settings for the Frankfurt City Stage for the thirteen years prior to his death on July 6, 1970 in Amsterdam.
Sets: 1942 *The Big City*; *The Green Table*
Costumes: 1942 *The Big City*; *The Green Table*

Desmond Heeley

A noted designer, Desmond Heeley's designs for both sets and costumes have been widely seen in his native England, in Canada, and in the United States. He was born in West Bromwich, Staffordshire, England, on June 1, 1931 and trained at the Ryland School of Art, drawn to the theater in part because of his admiration for the work of Oliver Messell. His first

Figure 5: Desmond Heeley: *Rosencrantz and Guildenstern Are Dead*: "Musician" (Flute, Horn Player), 1967. Courtesy of Desmond Heeley. Photograph by Jan Juracek.

professional designs were for the Birmingham Repertory Theatre. He then proceeded to design for all the major theater companies in England, beginning with the Royal Shakespeare Company in 1948. He has had a long association with the director Michael Langham, and designed thirty-four productions both for Mr. Langham and others at the Stratford (Ontario) Festival as well as numerous productions at The Guthrie Theatre in Minneapolis. He has designed for the American Ballet Theatre, the Australian Ballet, the Houston Ballet, the London Festival Ballet, the National Ballet of Canada, Sadler's Wells Royal Ballet and the Stuttgart Ballet Companies among others. His opera credits in England and in the United States include the much praised production of *Brigadoon* at the New York City Opera in 1985 and *Manon Lescaut, Don Pasquale, Pelleas and Melisande* and *Norma* for the Metropolitan Opera, as well as productions at Covent Garden, the Vienna State Opera and the English National Opera. Mr. Heeley won two Tony awards in 1967, one for the costumes and another for the scenery of *Rosencrantz and Guildenstern are Dead*. Although semi-retired, he none-the-less continues to design, including the world premiere of *The Snow Maiden* for the Houston Ballet in 1998 and a line of greeting cards at the beginning of the twenty-first century. See Figure 5: Desmond Heeley: *Rosencrantz and Guildenstern are Dead*

Sets: **1958** *Twelfth Night* **1967** *Rosencrantz and Guildenstern Are Dead* **1979** *Teibele and Her Demon* **1980** *Camelot* **1981** *Camelot* **1987** *South Pacific* **1989** *The Circle* **1991** *Brigadoon* **1996** *Brigadoon*

Costumes: **1958** *Twelfth Night* **1967** *Rosencrantz and Guildenstern Are Dead* **1973** *Cyrano* **1979** *Teibele and Her Demon* **1980** *Camelot* **1981** *Camelot* **1987** *South Pacific* **1991** *Brigadoon* **1996** *Brigadoon*

J Hegeman

In 1903, J. Hegeman contributed costumes to a Broadway production.

Costumes: **1905** *The Gingerbread Man*†

Hildegart Heitland

Mrs. Hildegart Heitland designed costumes for a play in 1944, for which her husband, W. Emerton Heitland designed the scenery. A portrait painter, she exhibited in London.

Costumes: **1944** *Earth Journey*

W. Emerton Heitland

Wilmont Emerton Heitland designed costumes for a play on Broadway in 1916 and scenery for a play in 1944. A painter and illustrator, he was born in Superior, Wisconsin on July 5, 1893. For most of his career he worked as an illustrator of magazines, including *Delineator* and *Harper's Bazaar*. He also taught at the Art Students League. Mr. Heitland was widely exhibited and the winner of many awards for his paintings and illustrations. He died in 1969.

Sets: **1944** *Earth Journey*
Costumes: **1916** *Six Who Passed while the Lentils Boiled*

John Held, Jr.

John Held, Jr., an author and illustrator, used his considerable talents to record the Jazz Age. His woodcuts and cartoons published in *The New Yorker, Life,* and *College Humor* captured the spirit of the age. Author of short stories and novels as well as a comic strip, he was born in Salt Lake City, Utah, on January 10, 1889, and died in Belmar, New Jersey on March 2, 1958. In the early 1940s he was artist in residence at Harvard University and the University of Georgia before serving in the Army Signal Corps.

Sets: **1926** *American* **1928** *Americana*†
Costumes: **1926** *American* **1928** *Americana*

Andre Heller

The Viennese multi-media artist Andre Heller has produced films, including *Driving Me Crazy*, created Luna Luna in Hamburg, Germany, an installation of fine art that's also known as Heller's Fairground of the Visual Arts, organized a variety show, *Flic Flac*, exhibited flying sculpture, and designed Swarovski Crystal World, a high-tech theme park near Innsbruck, Austria. He spent the early part of his professional life as a writer, but in 1976 created *Circus Roncalli*, a combination of animal acts, poetry readings and modern music, after which he continued to create similar events. In 1991, one of his productions was presented on Broadway, for which he also designed the scenery. A book about an installation he created in Berlin, *Die Zaubergaerten des Andre Heller* won two international prizes for printing in 1996.

Sets: **1991** *Andre Heller's Wonderhouse*

Robert Heller

Robert P. Heller designed one set on Broadway in 1930. During the 1940s he was director of radio programming for CBS-TV. He assisted Frank Capra during World War II with *Why We Fight*, an army orientation film. After the war he returned to CBS and from 1946 to 1948 was head of the documentary unit. In 1954 he moved to Great Britain and began working in television. At his death at age 60 in London in 1975 he was head of documentary and factual programming for the Associated Television Corporation of Britain.

Sets: **1930** *Petticoat Influence*†

Lauren Helpern

Lauren Helpern, a native New Yorker who studied at New York University, is a scenic designer, set decorator, and interior decorator for private homes and commercial spaces. She assisted Robin Wagner and Loren Sherman as she was establishing her own career, and has many credits off-Broadway including productions at the Apollo Theatre, McGinn/Cazale Theatre, Raw Space, and New Georges, as well as for corporate events, commercials and videos. As a member of the Luce Group she designs special events in partnership with lighting designers Traci Klainer, Frank DenDanto III, and Chuck Cameron, including hospital fundraisers, benefits, and launch parties. She often designs in collaboration with David Gallo, including all the productions of the Blue Man Group, *A History of the American Film* at Juilliard, and

her Broadway debut. She also designed *Always...Patsy Cline* in Las Vegas. Twenty-first century designs include *Underneath the Lintel* for the SoHo Playhouse and *Dragapella!* at Upstairs.

Sets: **1999** *Voices in the Dark*†

Lindy Hemming

Lindy Hemming was born on August 21, 1948 in Haverfordwest, Wales and studied in London at the Royal Academy of Dramatic Art. In the 1970s she joined the Hampstead Theatre Club where director Michael Rudman gave her the opportunity to design numerous shows. The experience gained there led to many additional productions. Her designs have been seen at the Royal National Theatre, at the Royal Shakespeare Company, off-Broadway, and in the West End. She has designed many feature films, including *Topsy-Turvy, Goldeneye, Blood and Wine, Tomorrow Never Dies, The World is Not Enough, Lara Croft: Tomb Raider* Her costume designs for *All's Well That Ends Well* here honored with a Tony Award nomination, the film *Porterhouse Blue* received a British Academy of Film and Television Sciences Award nomination, and *Topsy-Turvy* won the Academy Award.

Costumes: **1983** *All's Well That Ends Well*

Gilbert V. Hemsley, Jr.

Gilbert V. Hemsley, Jr. was born in Bridgeport, Connecticut in 1936. He debuted in New York with the lighting designs at the New York City Opera in 1978 for *Andrea Chenier*. This production was the first of thirty-five operas for the New York City Opera and the Metropolitan Opera, with many other productions for major opera companies. In addition, he designed numerous productions for dance companies such as the American Ballet Company, Alvin Alley, Martha Graham, and the Bolshoi Opera and Ballet. He was also a noted production manager who managed the opening of the Kennedy Center for the Performing Arts in Washington, D.C., and national tours of European and Asian companies around the

United States. He did his undergraduate and graduate work at Yale University, completing an M.F.A. in 1960, after which he joined the faculty at Princeton. Later he became an assistant to Jean Rosenthal. After several very busy seasons, he looked for a respite and joined the faculty at the University of Wisconsin, where his "retirement" lasted only a brief time. Using his students as assistants he resumed an active career, teaching students in the same way he had learned from Jean Rosenthal. When he died on September 5, 1983 his family, friends, colleagues and students established a lighting internship in his honor at the New York City Opera. Some of his original lighting designs continue to be used, and so he has received posthumous credits.

Lights: 1966 *Right You Are If You Think You Are*; *The School for Scandal*; *We, Comrades Three* **1967** *War and Peace*; *The Wild Duck*; *You Can't Take It with You* **1973** *Cyrano* **1974** *Jumpers* **1976** *Porgy and Bess*; *Your Arms Too Short to Box with God* **1977** *I Love My Wife* **1978** *The Mighty Gents* **1979** *Comin' Uptown*; *Monteith and Rand*; *The Most Happy Fella*; *Sugar Babies* **1983** *Porgy and Bess* **1990** *Street Scene* **1993** *The Student Prince†*

W. T. Hemsley

W. T. Hemsley was born in Newcastle-on-Tyne on June 2, 1850 and trained to be an engineer. While attending the Mechanics' Institute in Swindon, he painted scenery for a production and decided to change careers. He was an assistant to Augustus Harris and William Roxby Beverley and in 1880 made his own debut with *The Eviction* at the Olympic Theatre. The production was followed by many, many more in the major London theaters including Sadler's Wells, the St. James and the Adelphi. He occasionally contributed costume designs to productions as well. All of the productions for which he received credit as a scenic designer, artist and painter, were brought to New York after successful London runs. He died on February 8, 1918 at age 68.

Sets: 1900 *The Degenerates* **1903** *The*

Light That Failed† **1905** *Carmen* **1908** *Carmen* **1910** *Get-Rich-Quick Wallingford†* **1913** *The Light That Failed†*; *The Merchant of Venice†*; *Mice and Men†* **Costumes: 1905** *Carmen†* (Other costumes) **1908** *Carmen†* (Other costumes)

Mark Henderson

Mark Henderson is a British lighting designer. He has designed operas throughout Europe and the United Kingdom, dance for Sadler's Wells Ballet and Ballet Rambert, fashion shows for Zandra Rhodes and Laura Ashley, and numerous plays for the Royal Shakespeare Festival. In the West End he has more that fifty credits, including *Caine Mutiny Court Martial, A Patriot for Me* with Alan Bates (both in London and Los Angeles), *Figaro, Pump Boys and Dinettes,* and *Scarlet Pimpernel* among others. His honors include Laurence Olivier Awards in 1992 and 1994 for Best Lighting Design, the 1993 prize from the Lighting Industry Federation, and two nominations for Tony Awards. Twenty-first century designs include *Lulu* at the Kennedy Center in Washington, D. C., originally produced by the Almeida Theatre.

Lights: 1986 *Rowan Atkinson at the Atkinson* **1990** *Cat on a Hot Tin Roof* **1995** *His Excellency the Governor*; *Indiscretions (Les Parents Terribles)*; *Racing Demon* **1998** *The Judas Kiss* **1999** *Amy's View†*; *The Iceman Cometh* **2000** *Copenhagen†*; *The Real Thing†*

William Penhallow Henderson

William Penhallow Henderson, an architect and painter, was born in Medford, Massachusetts in 1877 and studied at the Massachusetts Normal Art School and at the Boston Museum of Fine Arts. He painted portraits, landscapes, and murals, and occasionally designed for the theater. His exhibitions included one in the Museum of Navajo Ceremonial Art in Santa Fe, New Mexico. Mr. Henderson died on October 15, 1943.

Sets: 1915 *Alice in Wonderland*
Costumes: 1915 *Alice in Wonderland*

Stephen Hendrickson

Stephen Hendrickson is a set designer

who has also taught at New York University. He trained as a theater designer but works mainly in television and film. He has been art director for films including *The Boys From Brazil*, *Live and Let Die* and *Fletch Lives*, and production designer for *Eye for Eye*, *For Richer or Poorer*, *Annie* (1999), *Diary of a Hit Man*, *Major League II*, *Arthur* and the third "Muppet" movie.
Sets: 1972 *Wild and Wonderful*

Marc Henri

Marc Henri, a prolific British designer, was active on Broadway in the 1920s. He has extensive credits on the London stage for scene design between 1915 and 1919, including *Samples!* (1915), *Look Who's Here!*, *The Best of Luck* (1916), *Suzette*, *Cheep*, *Bubbly* (1917), *Flora*, *The Beauty Spot*, *The Officer's Mess* (1918), *The Very Idea*, *Kissing Time*, *Cinderella*, *The Kiss Call* and *Baby Bunting* (1919) among many others. His name also appeared in playbills for over seventy productions in London in the 1920s, with credits such as scenic painter, scenic designer, scene builder and costume designer. The 1930 interior decorations that he did with Laverdet at the Whitehall Theatre in London were restored in 1986 by Felicity Youett.
Sets: 1924 *Andre Charlot's Revue of 1924*† **1925** *Charlot Revue*† **1928** *This Year of Grace*† **1929** *Wake Up and Dream*†
Costumes: 1929 *Wake Up and Dream*†

Henry Herbert

Henry Herbert, an actor from England, was known for portrayals of roles in Shakespearean plays. He first appeared with the Ben Greet Company and subsequently appeared with F.R. Benson's Company in England. He also managed Benson's companies. He first appeared in New York City in 1912 in *The 'Mind-the-Paint' Girl* after which he remained in the United States appearing in additional plays and occasionally designing. One of the original members of The Elizabethan Stage Society, he was Associate Director of Stratford-upon-Avon for a time. He died on February 20, 1947.
Sets: 1922 *Bavu*

Jocelyn Herbert

Jocelyn Herbert, the distinguished British designer of sets and costumes, was born on February 22, 1917. She studied in England and France with George Devine and Michel St. Denis, who both were influential during her career. She did not begin to design until the age of forty, with *The Chairs* for the English Stage Company at the Royal Court Theatre. Since that time she has designed countless productions, working extensively in theater and opera. Companies for which she has designed include the Royal National Theatre, Royal Shakespeare Company, Metropolitan Opera, Paris Opera, and Sadler's Wells in addition to productions in London's West End and on Broadway. While Jocelyn Herbert's film designs have been few they have been notable, including *Tom Jones*, *Hamlet*, *If...*, and *The Hotel New Hampshire*. *Jocelyn Herbert: A Theatre Workbook* edited by Cathy Courtney was published in 1993. Her birthday is among those acknowledged annually in the *London Times* and *The Guardian*, most recently when she turned 84 in February 2001.
Sets: 1963 *Chips with Everything*; *Luther* **1965** *Inadmissable Evidence* **1969** *Hamlet (starring Nichol Williamson)* **1970** *Home* **1977** *The Merchant* **1989** *3Penny Opera*
Costumes: 1963 *Chips with Everything*; *Luther* **1965** *Inadmissable Evidence* **1969** *Hamlet (starring Nichol Williamson)* **1970** *Home* **1977** *The Merchant* **1989** *3Penny Opera*
Lights: 1963 *Chips with Everything*; *Luther*

Leo Herbert

Leo Herbert, who began his career as an actor and occasional lighting designer, spent the majority of it working with stage properties. Most of his performances were before he served in World War II. After being discharged in 1944, he designed lights for a production in which he also appeared, and in 1945 he performed in *Seven Mirrors* and was also on the stage crew. He continued to perform small roles and work as a stagehand until 1954 when he became production property-man for David Merrick's *Fanny.* In all, he worked on properties for 250 Broadway productions, including all 88 of David Merrick's shows, and in 1984 was appointed the house propertyman at the Booth Theatre. At the time of his death in August 1993, he had just completed ten seasons as property master for *Sesame Street* on PBS-TV.

Lights: 1944 *Earth Journey*

Madame Hermann

Madame Louisa Hermann worked with Maurice Hermann (1866-1921) executing costumes for many designers. Occasionally, she also designed them. Maurice and Louisa Hermann (also known as Herrman and Herrmann) resided at 345 East 72nd Street in New York City. The 1890 New York City Census lists a Louisa Hermann, age 55. If the census refers to the costumer, then Maurice was most likely her son. For additional information see the entry for Maurice Hermann.

Costumes: 1904 *Zaza* **1907** *A Yankee Tourist*†

Maurice Hermann

Maurice Herrmann, who was born in 1866, began supplying and designing costumes to Broadway shows in 1880 from an establishment on Grand Street at the time when Miner's Theatre, Tony Pastor's Theatre and the old London Theatre were at the height of their success. He moved gradually uptown along with the theaters and when he died on June 29, 1921, at age 66, had his costume business on West 48th Street. Mr. Herrmann, whose name was spelled in all possible variations, had several late nineteenth century credits for costume design on Broadway, including *Apples of Eden, Rain Clouds,* and *In Old New Amsterdam,* in 1898 and *At the White Horse Tavern* in 1899. In the twentieth century, he continued to design, but also increased the number of costumes he executed for other designers, including Percy Anderson. The costume house was started by his father, Samuel Hermann (c.1826-1903) who emigrated to New

York from Berlin, Germany, where he had been a successful costumer, circa 1868. Madame Louisa Hermann, either his wife or mother, also designed costumes as well as worked with him in costume house.

Costumes: 1899 *Macbeth; The Song of the Sword*† **1900** *Henry V*† (Mr. Mansfield's costume); *Macbeth; The Pride of Jennico; The Rebel*†; *The Sunken Bell* **1901** *If I Were King*†; *The Merchant of Venice* (Also executed); *Miranda of the Balcony*† (Moorish and Arabian costumes); *Richard Savage; Tom Moore* **1902** *As You Like It*† (Miss Gallatin's costumes); *Captain Molly*† **1903** *The Proud Prince*† **1904** *The Fortunes of the King; The Taming of the Shrew*† (Mr. Sothern's and Miss Marlowe's costumes) **1905** *Monna Vanna; Othello* **1907** *Twelfth Night* (Costumes for Miss Sothern and Mr. Marlowe) **1908** *Hamlet*† **1909** *Cameo Kirby* **1911** *Macbeth (Kellerd)*† (Mr. Sothern's costumes) **1913** *Much Ado About Nothing*†; *Much Ado About Nothing*† (Mr. Sothern's costumes) **1914** *Secret Strings*† **1916** *David Garrick* (Mr. Sothern's and Miss Carlisle's costumes) **1918** *Hamlet* (Mr. Hampden's Hamlet costume) **1919** *The Jest* **1920** *Rollo's Wild Oat* (Hamlet costume and Miss Kummer's prologue costume)

Hjalmar Hermanson

Hjalmar Hermanson was known principally as an art director and designer for NBC-TV where he created sets for news anchors, among other designs, beginning in 1951. He was born in Finland on January 20, 1907, and as a youth washed paint brushes for a scenic artist. He studied at the National Academy of Design, the Grand Central Art School and Columbia University. He had hoped to be a commercial artist, but a broken right index finger limited his ability to do fine work. He turned to scene painting for theatrical productions and gradually began to design. As designer for the Works Progress Administration's Federal Theatre Unit, he designed *The Living Newspaper, Triple A Plowed Under* and *Injunction Granted.* After service as an anti-aircraft sergeant during World War II he worked for CBS-TV, where his designs included the sets for the second Nixon-Kennedy debate. He died in December 1994.

Sets: 1936 *The Living Newspaper*

Riccardo Hernández

Riccardo Hernández made his professional debut at the Yale Repertory Theatre in 1992 with the scenic design for *The Death of the Last Black Man in the Whole Entire World.* After completing his M.F.A. at the Yale School of Drama in 1992, he began designing scenery for productions in and around New York, at the Joseph Papp Public Theatre, the Manhattan Theatre Club, and Playwrights Horizons, among many others. He has also designed in regional theaters including Arena Stage and the Goodman Theatre. His designs for opera include *Amistad* for the Chicago Lyric Opera. He won an Audelco Award in 1995 for the scenic design for *Blade to the Heart.* Twenty-first century designs include *Togpdog/Underdog* and *Elaine Stritch at Liberty* at the Joseph Papp Public Theatre.

Sets: 1995 *The Tempest* **1996** *Bring in 'da Noise, Bring in 'da Funk* **1998** *Parade* **2001** *Bells Are Ringing*

E.J. Herrett

E. J. (Emery J.) Herrett designed costumes on Broadway in the late 1920s. He studied at Cooper Union, Chicago Art Institute and Pratt Institute before beginning a career designing sets and/or costumes for films and theater. Prior to retirement to the Virgin Islands, he owned and operated an Inn in Dover Furnace, New York. Mr. Herrett died in December of 1955 at the age of 62.

Costumes: 1927 *Just Fancy*; *Merry Malones*† (Men's clothes) **1928** *Jarnegan*

David Hersey

Although David Kenneth Hersey began his career in theater as an actor, he promptly became one of Europe's leading lighting designers upon moving to London in 1968. His work in opera, ballet and with major theater companies comprise over two hundred productions. The list of his awards is almost as long as the list

of his credits: three Tony Awards, for *Evita, Les Miserables* and *Cats*; a Maharam Award for *Nicholas Nickleby*; a Dora Mavor Moore Award for *Les Miserables* and *Cats*; and also Drama Logue Critic's Awards, Los Angeles Drama Critics Awards, Civil Trust Awards, Drama Desk Awards, and a 1996 Olivier Award. He was born in Rochester, New York on November 30, 1939 and was educated at Oberlin College. In 1971 he founded David Hersey Associates, Limited which specializes in the design and manufacture of specialist lighting equipment and effects for theater and also architectural lighting.

Lights: 1981 *Life and Adventures of Nicholas Nickleby*,† ; *The Life and Adventures of Nicholas Nickleby*; *Merrily We Roll Along* **1982** *Cats* **1986** *The Life and Adventures of Nicholas Nickleby* **1987** *Les Miserables*; *Starlight Express* **1988** *Chess* **1991** *Miss Saigon*

Mr. Albert Herter

The artist Albert Herter was born in New York City and studied with Carroll Beckwith in New York and J. P. Laurens in Paris. Known for his portraits and as a mural painter, he won the Lipincott Prize in 1897, among many other awards for his paintings. He exhibited widely and was active in professional societies. Early in the teens he contributed costume designs to a Broadway production, his only known theatrical credit. After one of his sons, Everit, was killed at Chateau-Thierry in 1918, he painted a mural for the Gare de l'Est in Paris as a memorial to all those who served in the war, and was subsequently awarded a Chevalier of the Legion of the Honor of France. He died at age 78 in Santa Barbara, California on February 15, 1950.

Costumes: 1912 *Much Ado About Nothing*

B. Russell Herts

Benjamin Russell Herts lived from May 27, 1908 until November 3, 1954. He created set designs for five shows in 1915 and was scenic and costume designer for an additional show in 1916. He spent his life mainly as an interior decorator and was president of Herts Brothers Co., Inc., Interior Decorators at 37 West 57th Street in New York City in 1919, moving in 1931 to 20 West 57th Street. Both locations were popular with theatrical designers due to the variety and quality he could invariably provide. He also wrote books including *A Female of the Species*, *The Son of Man* and *Grand Slam*. In addition, he edited the magazine *Moods* from 1908 to 1909 and *Forum* from 1909 to 1910.

Sets: 1915 *Eugenically Speaking*† (Furnishings); *Husband and Wife*; *The Liars*; *My Lady's Honor*† (Furnishings); *The New York Idea* 1916 *Merry Christmas, Daddy*

Costumes: 1916 *Merry Christmas, Daddy*

Mr. Tom Heslewood

An actor and costume designer, Tom Heslewood was born in in 1868 in Hessle, Yorks, England and made his acting debut in *Haste to the Wedding* in 1892 in London. In addition to acting, he designed costumes for many productions, most of them in London, including *A Lady of Quality*, *Bonnie Dundee*, *Queen's Romance*, *His Majesty's Servant*, and in 1905, *Hamlet* for Henry Irving. He designed costumes for and appeared in *King Richard the Second* for the Stratford-upon-Avon Festival Company in 1926. To facilitate construction of the costumes he designed, he maintained a business that also executed costumes for other designers. A costume design for the "Dragon King" in *Where the Rainbow Ends* (Savoy Theatre, 1911) was included in the 1991 exhibit and published in the accompanying book *Design on Paper*. Heslewood died on April 28, 1959.

Costumes: 1909 *The Noble Spaniard*

Hewlett & Basing

Brothers Arthur T. and J. Monroe Hewlett and associate Charles Basing formed the scenic studio Hewlett & Basing. Between 1919 and 1920 they collaborated on the designs for three productions on Broadway. Charles Basing was a mural painter who also designed plays under his own name. Arthur T. Hewlett, a mural painter, worked with his brother J. Monroe Hewlett, an architect, on the scenery for many productions by Maude Adams. For additional credits and information, see the entries "Charles Basing," "A.T Hewlett," and "J. Monroe Hewlett."

Sets: 1919 *For the Defense* 1920 *Beyond the Horizon*; *A Little Water on the Side*

Arthur T. Hewlett

Arthur Thomas Hewlett died at age 81 on November 11, 1951. He was principally a fine art painter who created murals at the Eastman School of Music in Rochester, New York, in the main office of the Bank of New York, and on the ceiling of the Grand Central Station, featuring signs of the Zodiac. He collaborated with his brother J. Monroe Hewlett on the scenery for many productions starring Maude Adams. An 1892 graduate of Columbia College, he was a descendant of the family for whom the village of Hewlett on Long Island was named. His family imported tea and sugar, and Arthur Hewlett was involved with their business, Hewlett & Co., 79 Wall Street throughout his life.

Sets: 1912 *Peter Pan*† 1920 *All Soul's Eve*†

J. Monroe Hewlett

J. Monroe Hewlett was born in the family home at Lawrence, Long Island on August 1, 1868. He graduated from Columbia University in 1890 and joined the architectural firm of McKim, Mead and White. After further study in Paris he founded Lord & Hewlett, Architects at 2 West 45th Street in New York City. From 1932 to 1935 he was resident director of the American Academy in Rome. He designed hospitals in Brooklyn, New York and Danbury, Connecticut as well as libraries, churches, houses and country estates. As a member of the committee for the Beaux Arts Ball in New York he designed settings for their events, and with brother A.T. Hewlett designed for Maude Adams. With Bassett Jones, who supervised lights for Maude Adams, he developed a technique to create depth by using light

zones between gauze drops and a black
velvet backdrop. This technique was
first used in *Chantecler*, designed by
John W. Alexander. J. M. Hewlett
died in 1941.

Sets: 1911 *Chantecler*† 1912 *Peter Pan*†
1918 *Freedom* 1920 *All Soul's Eve*†

Walker Hicklin

Costume designer Walker Hicklin has
worked in regional theater throughout the United States (Trinity Repertory Company, South Coast Repertory, American Conservatory Theatre,
etc.), off-Broadway (Manhattan Theatre Club, Playwrights Horizons, etc.)
His films include *Reckless*, *Longtime
Companion*, and *Prelude to a Kiss*.
Twenty-first century designs include
The Bard of Avon by Amy Freed at the
South Coast Repertory.

Costumes: 1990 *Prelude to a Kiss*

Ami Mali Hicks

Ami Mali Hicks, an artist and writer,
was born in Brooklyn, New York on
January 3, 1876, and died in 1955. She
studied art in New York and Paris. She
founded the Guild of Arts and Crafts
in New York in the 1890s and was
a pioneer in the American arts and
crafts movement. An author of articles
on interior decoration, she contributed
to *Ladies Home Journal,* and *The
Woman's Home Companion*. She also
collaborated with and assisted Robert
Edmond Jones.

Costumes: 1921 *Macbeth*† 1926 *The
Immortal Thief* (Costumes Supervised
and painted)

Julian Hicks

The British scenic artist Julian Hicks
was born in London on December 1,
1858 and studied at St. Mary's College.
He made his professional debut designing and painting a ballet, *Enchantment*
at the Alhambra in 1887, after which
he did numerous productions, mainly
in London. He never limited himself to
one kind of production nor venue during his long and distinguished career,
designing scenes for plays, musicals,
operas, and dance. Some of his scenes
were transported to New York where
they were also enjoyed by Broadway

audiences. Additional productions include *Floradora*, *The Belle of Brittany*
and *His Highness, My Husband*. He
died in 1941. His father, who worked as
a scenic artist as well, was also named
Julian Hicks. Productions before 1887
credited to their name were done by the
senior Hicks.

Sets: 1901 *The Price of Peace*†; *The
Sleeping Beauty and the Beast*† 1903
Mr. Bluebeard† 1905 *Veronique*† (Act III)
1906 *Mr. Hopkinson*

Hickson

Richard J. Hickson was the creative
force behind Hickson, Inc, which provided gowns, and accessories to private
and theatrical customers. There were
two shops, at 657 Fifth Avenue and at
One East 52nd Street during the teens
and twenties. Both provided custom
tailored frocks and as well as imported
designs. Hickson specially designed
gowns for numerous shows set in the
contemporary time, between 1913 and
1925. According to Caroline Milbank
in *New York Fashion*, he also started a
trend when he introduced bustle-back
frocks in 1917. Born in 1884, he died
in Florida in February 1979.

Costumes: 1913 *The Fight* (Gowns and
hats for Miss Wood and Miss Wycher-
ley); *Shadowed* 1915 *Cock O' the Walk*
(Gowns) 1917 *Broken Threads*†; *Busi-
ness before Pleasure* (Miss Joe's gowns);
In for the Night (Gowns, coats, and hats
Especially Designed); *The Knife* (Miss
Olive Wyndham's gowns); *On with the
Dance*† (Miss Huban's gowns); *Our Bet-
ters* (Gowns and hats); *A Tailor-Made
Man*† (Miss Kingsley's gowns); *The Very
Minute* (Gowns) 1918 *The Crowded
Hour* (Miss Cowl's uniforms); *Daddies*
(Dresses); *The Indestructible Wife*† (Miss
Gombel's Gowns); *The Love Mill* (Miss
Fischer's Gowns); *Madonna of the Future*
(All Gowns, wraps, and hats); *The Man
Who Stayed at Home* (Miss Kaelred's
gowns); *Roads of Destiny* (Miss Reed
and Miss Belwin's gowns); *The Unknown
Purple*† (Miss MacKellar's gowns) 1919
Cappy Ricks (Miss Crawley's Second and
Third Act gowns); *The Lady in Red*† (Miss
Rowland's gowns); *Nothing But Love*†
(Miss Sunshine's costume); *Up in Ma-
bel's Room* (Gowns) 1920 *The Acquittal*

(Miss Herne's gowns); *The Blue Flame†* (Miss Theda Bara's gown); *Mamma's Affair* (Miss Shannon and Miss Kaelred's gowns); *The Outrageous Mrs. Palmer†* (Miss Young's tailoring) **1921** *The Broadway Whirl* (Miss Ring's first gown) **1922** *So This Is London* (Miss Carroll's gowns) **1925** *The Four Flusher* (Gowns)

Douglas Higgins

Douglas Higgins, a native of Canada, attended the University of British Columbia and Yale University. He has designed off-Broadway at the American Place Theatre and the Chelsea Theatre among others, and in regional theaters as well as for commercials. He was art director for the 1984 film *Runaway*, the first of many credits in film that also include production design for the made-for-television movies: *Generation X, How Doc Waddems Finally Broke 100,* and *Max Q,* among others and for major motion pictures: *Masterminds, Crying Freeman, The Color of Courage, Navigating the Heart* and *USFS: The Ranger, the Cook, and a Hole in the Sky.* Many of the films were made in British Columbia.

Sets: 1974 *Love for Love*; *The Rules of the Game* **1975** *The Member of the Wedding*

Girvan Higginson

Girvan Higginson was a lighting designer, scenic designer and director who was active on Broadway in the 1940s. Born in California on November 2, 1910, he graduated from Yale University where he specialized in stage lighting. His father was the architect Augustus Higginson, who worked in Chicago and Santa Barbara, California. He was the nephew of John Higginson, founder of the Boston Symphony. Girvan Higginson also directed *Speak of the Devil* and produced *Eye on the Sparrow* and *The Nightingale* in New York City. He appeared in *1776* and *Gentlemen, the Queen* in the mid-1920s as a juvenile lead. He died in Santa Barbara on November 1, 1968.

Sets: 1942 *The Willow and I†*

Lights: 1942 *The Willow and I* **1947** *The Story of Mary Surratt*

John A. Higham

John A. Higham, who designed lights on Broadway between 1905 and 1915, was President of Display Stage Lighting Company. In 1919, the business was renamed Display & Stage Lighting Company and located at 266 West 44th Street, New York. The treasurer of the firm, William E. Price, was also a Broadway lighting designer.

Lights: 1905 *Monna Vanna* **1906** *The Kreutzer Sonata* **1910** *Pillars of Society* **1915** *Children of Earth†*

J. Allen Highfill

J. Allen Highfill, who was born July 5, 1947 and died on July 5, 1989, designed costumes for a Broadway show in 1977. He amassed many credits as a costume designer for television specials and in 1984 was honored with an award for "Excellence in National Performance and Craft" for art direction. His television designs include the series *Davy Crockett* and the specials *Casey at the Bat, Darlin' Clementine,* and *The Legend of Sleepy Hollow.* He designed costumes for movies including *Breathless* and *Men Don't Leave.*

Costumes: 1977 *Lily Tomlin in "Appearing Nightly"*

Susan Hilferty

Susan Hilferty, who first designed costumes at the Berkshire Theatre Festival, received a B.F.A. in painting from Syracuse University and an M.F.A. in theater design at Yale. Born in Arlington, Massachusetts on January 23, 1953, she also studied at St. Martin's School of Art in London. She designs regularly in regional theaters, won the Bay Area Theatre Circle Award for the costumes in *Tooth of Crime,* and received the 2000 Obie Award for Sustained Excellence in Costume Design. In addition to a busy career as a costume designer she has taught at Parsons School of Design and in 1993 joined the faculty at NYU's Tisch School of the Arts. In 1997, she was named chair, succeeding Lloyd Burlingame, bringing the program her creative energy, talent and devotion to training students. Twenty-first century designs include *In the Penal Colony* at

Classic Stage, and *Sorrows and Rejoicings* at the McCarter Theater Center.
Costumes: 1980 *A Lesson from Aloes* 1985 *Blood Knot* 1987 *Coastal Disturbances* 1995 *How to Succeed in Business Without Really Trying* 1996 *The Night of the Iguana*; *Sex and Longing* 2000 *Dirty Blonde*

Linda Lee Hill

Linda Lee Hill supervised the costumes for a play on Broadway in 1937.
Costumes: 1937 *Farewell Summer* (Costume Supervisor)

Gregory Allen Hirsch

A native of Los Angeles, lighting designer Gregory Allen Hirsch was born in 1946. He has designed new productions of the *The Magic Flute* and *Aida* for Portland Opera, and many productions for the opera companies of Palm Beach, Pittsburgh, Tulsa, Utah and Fort Worth, among others. He received the Bay Area Theatre Critics' Circle Award and his second Hollywood Drama-Logue award for his design for the original San Francisco production of *The Phantom of the Opera*. His first Hollywood Drama-Logue was for *Fiddler on the Roof* at the San Diego Civic Light Opera. He also designs live television broadcasts.
Lights: 1992 *Man of La Mancha*

Susan Hirschfield

Susan Hirschfield is an active designer in regional theaters, for television and off-Broadway. She has designed costumes at Goodspeed Opera, The Walnut Street Theatre, Portland Stage Company, Pennsylvania Stage Company, and numerous productions for the Alliance Theatre. Among her off-Broadway credits is *The Legend of Sharon Shashanovah*. At the Juilliard School she has designed both *Othello* and *The School for Scandal*. As an associate designer she has worked on the daytime dramas *One Life to Live* and *All My Children*.
Costumes: 1989 *Starmites*

Mrs. Raymond Hitchcock

Mrs. Raymond Hitchcock was a singer and actress who used the name Flora Zabelle. She was the daughter of the Rev. Dr. M. M. Mangasarian of Philadelphia and appeared on the stage initially in Chicago in 1900. She was married to the stage and silent screen star Raymond Hitchcock and often appeared on stage with him. After his death in 1929, she became a costume designer and partner in Jacques Bodart, Inc. Undoubtedly, many shows in the 1920s were costumed by her, but not credited in the playbills of the time. Her sister was the wife of Earl Benham, the theatrical tailor. Mrs. Hitchcock died October 7, 1968 at the age of 88.
Costumes: 1924 *New Brooms*

Hitchins & Balcom

Hitchins & Balcom (Balkum) collaborated on costume designs for two Broadway productions in 1904. Owen C. Hitchins (1885-1964) and William Balcom were dressmakers, with a small custom studio located at 108 West 48th Street in New York City between 1904 and 1910. Hitchins also designed costumes under his own name during that time.
Costumes: 1904 *Brother Jacques*; *The Pit*†

Owen Hitchins

Owen C. Hitchins, born on October 14, 1885, was a dry goods buyer at the beginning of the twentieth century and resided at 219 West 34th Street in New York. By 1904, at age nineteen, he was providing gowns to private and theatrical customers through a small shop at 108 West 48th Street, while living at 650 West 85th Street. He was also associated with another dressmaker, William Balcom, through Hitchins & Balcom. Hitchins died in September 1964.
Costumes: 1910 *The Spring Maid*† (Miss Macdonald's gowns) 1911 *A Certain Party*†

Charles E. Hoefler

Charles E. Hoefler, who has designed sets on and off-Broadway and for stock companies, makes his living designing industrial promotions. He was born on May 25, 1930 in Detroit and attended the University of Michigan, where he received a B.A. in 1952 and an M.F.A.

in 1953. He served an apprenticeship with Tobins Lake Studios, South Lyon, Michigan when it was a design and construction shop. His first Broadway experience was with projections for the Oliver Smith design for *Jimmy* in 1970. His designs have been honored with the Drama Critics Award and Bronze, Silver and Gold Awards at the New York International Film and Television Festival.

Sets: 1980 *It's So Nice to Be Civilized*
Lights: 1980 *It's So Nice to Be Civilized*

Constance Hoffman

Costume designer Constance Hoffman did her undergraduate study at the University of California at Davis and received her M.F.A from Yale University in 1991. She has designed extensively in regional theaters, including Center Stage, Hartford Stage, and the Alley Theatre, among others, as well as off-Broadway at the Theatre for a New Audience. She also collaborated with Julie Taymor on *Titus*. *The Green Bird*, her Broadway debut was nominated for a Tony award, and in 2001 she was honored by Theatre Development Fund with the Young Master Award at the annual Irene Sharaff Costume Design awards.

Costumes: 2000 *The Green Bird*

Sydne Hoffman

Sydne Hoffman designed costumes on Broadway in 1935.

Costumes: 1935 *The Hook-Up* (Costume Supervisor)

Jack Hofsiss

Jack Hofsiss was born in New York City on September 28, 1950 and studied at Georgetown, George Washington, and Catholic universities. Known primarily as a director, his professional debut was *Rebel Women* for the New York Shakespeare Festival at the Public Theatre in 1976. Among his extensive theater credits is the Broadway production of *The Elephant Man* for which he received the Tony Award for Best Direction. Television credits includes the daytime drama *Another World*. He not only directed the 1993 revival of *The Student Prince*, originally staged at the

New York City Opera, but also received design credit, supervising among other elements the reconstruction of the original lighting design by the late Gilbert V. Hemsley, Jr.

Sets: 1993 *The Student Prince†* (Supervisor)
Costumes: 1993 *The Student Prince†* (Supervisor)
Lights: 1993 *The Student Prince†* (Supervisor)

Sybyl Nash Hogan

Sybil Nash Hogan designed gowns for a Broadway play in 1935. She mainly provided knit goods from a small shop at 38 East 57th Street in New York City, and resided at 1230 Park Avenue.

Costumes: 1935 *Cross Ruff* (Gowns)

Emil Holak

Before coming to the United States, Emil Holak designed with Ernst Stern and Oscar Strnad for Max Reinhardt in Berlin. Along with George H. Holak he was proprietor of Holak Studios, Theatrical Supplies at 451 First Avenue in New York.

Sets: 1942 *I Killed the Count*

Donald Holder

Donald Holder, a native of New York City, was born on May 12, 1958 and received a B.S. degree in forestry at the University of Maine in 1980, and an M.F.A. in Technical Design at Yale in 1986, where he received the Edward C. Cole Award for Excellence. His career has been influenced by the lighting designs of Jennifer Tipton. His first professional design, *The Water Engine*, was performed for the Muhlenberg Theatre Program in 1981. He has served as resident designer for the SoHo Repertory Theatre, the George Street Playhouse and Ballet Hispánico of New York, and as a facilities design consultant with Imero Fiorentino Associates. Donald Holder, who is married to director Evan Yinoulis, received a 1999 American Theatre Wing Design Award. Twenty-first century credits include *Chaucer in Rome* at the Mitzi E. Newhouse Theatre, Lincoln Center, *Glimmer, Glimmer and Shine* at City Center Stage I, and *Once Around the City* at Second Stage Theatre.

Lights: 1989 *Eastern Standard* 1990 *Spunk* 1992 *Solitary Confinement* 1995 *Holiday* 1996 *Hughie*; *Juan Darién: A Carnival Mass* 1997 *All My Sons*; *The Lion King* 1999 *Voices in the Dark* 2000 *The Green Bird* 2001 *Bells Are Ringing*; *King Hedley II*

Geoffrey Holder

A man of many talents, Geoffrey Lamont Holder was born in Port-of-Spain, Trinidad on August 1, 1930 and studied there at Queens Royal College. His involvement in the theater began in 1950 when he appeared with his brother Boscoe Holder's dance company in Trinidad, after which he performed extensively. He led his own dance company in the late 1950s. Besides being a dancer, Mr. Holder is an actor, director, choreographer, drama critic, author, painter, and costume designer. He first designed costumes professionally for the John Butler Dance Theatre in 1958. Since then, he has regularly contributed to productions in multiple ways, often including costume designs. Among them is *Dougla* for the Dance Theatre of Harlem. In 1975, he won two Tony Awards, one for directing and one for costume design for *The Wiz*. He was nominated again in 1978 for the costume design for *Timbuktu*. Mr. Holder is married to the dancer, Carmen De Lavallade.

Costumes: 1975 *The Wiz* (Also directed) 1978 *Timbuktu* (Also directed and choreographed) 1984 *The Wiz*

Hollander

Louis P. Hollander provided costumes from two locations, one on Boylston Park Square in Boston and the other at 290 Fifth Avenue in New York City. His company, L. P. Hollander & Co. was an importer. It also executed costumes for productions including those at Boston's Toy Theatre and for many designers who worked on Broadway. For at least one production, Louis Hollander himself contributed specially designed costumes. His son Louis P. Hollander, Jr. (1893-1980) was a union organizer and labor leader who worked in the garment industry beginning at age 14, and in 1912 helped organize the United Brotherhood of Tailors.

Costumes: 1902 *Little Italy*

Klaus Holm

Klaus Holm was both a scenic and lighting designer, although the majority of his Broadway credits are for lighting. He was also an educator and theater consultant. He was on the faculty at Colorado College and from 1970 until 1985, at Wilkes College (now University) in Wilkes-Barre, Pennsylvania. He was born Klaus Kuntze in Dresden, Germany on June 27, 1920, the son of sculptor and painter Martin Kuntze and dancer and choreographer Hanya Holm. He attended New York University, receiving a B.S. in 1948, and then went to graduate school of Yale University, earning an M.F.A. in 1951. He designed scenery for many productions off-Broadway at the Phoenix Theatre and Circle in the Square, New York City Center, Goodspeed Opera House, New York City Opera, and Central City Opera, among others. Between 1961 and 1962 he was lighting design consultant at the New York State Theatre and at Lincoln Philharmonic Hall at Lincoln Center. His designs for television included the set for *The Kate Smith Show* in 1951 for NBC. He shared the 1956 Obie Award for design and lights with Alvin Colt. Holm died on October 8, 1994.

Sets: 1962 *Moby Dick*; *Private Ear, The/ The Public Eye*

Lights: 1954 *The Girl on the Via Flamina*; *The Golden Apple* 1955 *Phoenix '55* 1960 *Advise and Consent*; *Semi-Detached* 1961 *Donnybrook!*; *Once There Was a Russian* 1962 *Private Ear, The/ The Public Eye*; *Something about a Soldier* 1963 *The Heroine*

Ralph Holmes

Ralph Holmes is a lighting designer who works in theater, opera, ballet and modern dance. He also has extensive credits for television design and was associated with CBS-TV beginning in 1949. He served as lighting and art director for *Dance in America* on PBS and as lighting designer for the daytime television drama *The Guiding Light*.

Lights: 1961 *General Seeger*

Roy Holmes

Roy Holmes designed lighting for one show in 1940 on Broadway.

Lights: 1940 *Meet the People*

T. Holmes

T. (Theodore) Holmes was an architect with offices at 562 East 156th Street in New York at the beginning of the twentieth century. He resided at 15 West 106th Street at the time he designed scenery for a Broadway production.

Sets: 1905 *The Babes and the Baron†*

Glen Holse

Glen Holse was born in Beresford, South Dakota and graduated from Washington University in St. Louis, Missouri. His early designs were for a wallpaper firm and as a network television staff designer creating sets for shows featuring Eddie Fisher and Steve Allen. He designed in Las Vegas as art director for revues at the Tropicana, the Thunderbird Hotel, Aladdin Hotel and for Liberace. International credits include sets in Korea, Puerto Rico and Rio de Janeiro. He also designed settings for wax museums in Buena Park, California, Tokyo and Osaka, Japan. Glen Holse died on February 14, 1983 in Bakersfield, California at the age of 52.

Sets: 1959 *Billy Barnes Revue*

Mrs.Robert L. Holt

Mrs. Robert L. Holt designed costumes for a featured player in a 1935 Broadway play.

Costumes: 1935 *Point Valaine* (Miss Fontanne's dresses)

David Homan

David Homan was born in Christiana, Norway on September 10, 1907 and studied at the Glasgow Art School, in Cornwall and in Rome. He first worked as a scene painter in the early 1930s and subsequently as set designer for many productions before service in World War II. In the late 1940s he became managing director of Ambassador's Scenic Studios, a company that supplied sets for productions throughout the United Kingdom. With descendants of Joseph and Phil Harker he formed Harker, Homan and Bravery

Limited in 1953, serving as the firm's director and secretary.

Sets: 1934 *And Be My Love*

Mrs. Charles Hone

Mrs. Josephine Hoey Hone was the daughter of John Hoey, an official with the Adams Express Company, and Josephine Shaw Hoey (1822-1896) an actress who performed as Mrs. Russell. When her husband, Charles Russell Hone died, she found it necessary to work. After an attempt as a horticulturist, she became a dressmaker from 1 East 39th Street, New York City. She made gowns for private customers and for theatrical designers, and in 1901 contributed costume designs to two productions. She also appeared in *The Stubbornness of Geraldine*, receiving good notices. Ill health forced her to give up her dressmaking business and potential career as an actress, shortly before she died on June 5, 1905 in New York City.

Sets: 1901 *The Shades of Night* (Miss DeWolfe's costumes)

Costumes: 1901 *When Knighthood Was in Flower†*

Frances Hooper

Frances Hooper graduated from Smith College in 1917, and spent most of her career in journalism and as head of the Frances Hooper Advertising Agency. An outspoken advocate for women's rights, she was also an avid book collector and active in the theater, mainly in Chicago. She designed costumes for one Broadway production, in 1936. Miss Hooper died in May 1986 in Kenilworth, Illinois, a suburb of Chicago.

Costumes: 1936 *Love on the Dole* (Women's character costumes)

Hiram Hoover

Hiram Hoover, a scenic artist and craftsman, designed one set in 1932 for the Broadway stage. Born in Arkansas on February 14, 1878, he spent the majority of life in Los Angeles, California, where he died on May 15, 1967.

Sets: 1932 *The Devil's Little Game*

Richard Hoover

Richard Hoover is widely known as a production designer for films, including *Cradle Will Rock*, *Dead Man Walking*, *Bob Roberts*, *Payback*, and *Girl, Interrupted* and for television including the series *Twin Peaks*. His credits as a set designer are numerous, and include productions at Playwrights Horizons, Circle Repertory Company, New York Theatre Workshop, the Guthrie Theatre, the Milwaukee Repertory Theatre and the Old Globe. The scenic design for *Not About Nightingales* won many accolades, including the Tony, Evening Standard, London Critics Circle, Drama Desk, and New York Outer Critics Circle Awards, and a Laurence Olivier nomination. Twenty-first century designs include *Speaking in Tongues* at the Grammercy Theatre.

Sets: 1999 *Not about Nightingales*

William Hoover

William Hoover designed scenery for four productions at the beginning of the twentieth century and most likely constructed scenery for many more. He was associated with Boston's Park Theatre, as John H. Young's assistant painter, in the 1890s. His credits suggest some skill with mechanical devices. An architect named William H. Hoover, Jr. lived at 176 Broadway in New York City in 1898.

Sets: 1904 *Girofle-Girofla†* (Design and construction); *Home Folks†* **1905** *The Ham Tree†* (Mechanical design and construction) **1906** *Forty-five Minutes from Broadway†*

Arthur Hopkins

The producer and director Arthur Hopkins was born in Cleveland, Ohio, on October 4, 1878. After a brief career in journalism, in 1905 he opened a nickelodeon, the first one in New York. In 1912 he produced his first big success, *The Poor Little Rich Girl*. During the next thirty years he produced many new plays, becoming a major force in the American theater. His productions included *Anna Christie* in 1921, *The Hairy Ape* with the Provincetown Players, *Machinal* featuring Clark Gable, and *The Petrified Forest* starring Leslie Howard and

Humphrey Bogart. At the time of his death on March 22, 1950, he was preparing to produce a new play by Thornton Wilder.

Sets: 1913 *Evangeline* (Also producer)

George Hopkins

George James Hopkins was born on March 23, 1896 in Pasadena, California and designed scenery for the theater before becoming a set designer and art director for the movies. Between 1917 and 1919 he worked for Realart Studio and Famous Players-Lasky, after which he worked as art director for George Fitzmaurice, and then joined Warner Brothers where he remained for most of the rest of his career. He won Academy Awards for *A Streetcar Named Desire*, *My Fair Lady*, *Who's Afraid of Virginia Woolf?* and *Hello, Dolly*, receiving seven additional nominations. Hopkins, who early in his career occasionally used the pseudonym "Neje" died on Hollywood on February 11, 1985 at age 88.

Costumes: 1915 *The Unchastened Woman†* (Miss Stevens' gowns in Act I and II)

Harry Horner

Harry Horner worked as an architect before devoting his talents to the theater. Known primarily as a scenic designer and director, he was born on July 24, 1910 in Holic, Czechoslovakia and studied acting and directing with Max Reinhardt. In the early 1930s he acted, directed and occasionally designed settings, lighting and costumes. After coming to the United States in 1935 he assisted Max Reinhardt and Norman Bel Geddes in New York. His credits for set design in theater and opera are numerous as were his directing credits for theater and television. His film designs garnered him Academy Awards for the art direction of *The Hustler*, *The Heiress* and a nomination for *They Shoot Horses, Don't They?* He died on December 5, 1994 in Pacific Palisades, California.

Sets: 1938 *All the Living*; *Escape This Night* **1939** *Family Portrait*; *Jeremiah*; *The World We Make* **1940** *The Burning Deck*; *Reunion in New York*; *The*

Weak Link 1941 *Banjo Eyes*; *Five Alarm Waltz*; *In Time to Come*; *Lady in the Dark*; *Let's Face It* 1942 *A Kiss for Cinderella*; *Let's Face It*; *Lily of the Valley*; *Star and Garter*; *Under this Roof*; *Walking Gentleman* 1943 *Lady in the Dark*; *Winged Victory* 1946 *Christopher Blake* 1948 *Joy to the World*; *Me and Molly* 1953 *Hazel Flagg* 1961 *How to Make a Man*

Costumes: 1939 *Family Portrait*; *Jeremiah*

Lights: 1942 *Lily of the Valley* 1946 *Christopher Blake*† 1953 *Hazel Flagg* 1961 *How to Make a Man*

Richard Hornung

Richard Hornung was born in Allentown, Pennsylvania on February 16, 1950 and attended Kutsztown State College in Pennsylvania, where he designed costumes for the first time for *Salome* which he also directed. He received an M.F.A. from the University of Illinois at Champagne/Urbana. He assisted costume designers on numerous Broadway shows and worked as a dyer/painter for costume shops in New York, as well as designing in regional theaters. His Broadway costume debut occurred in 1981 at Circle in the Square. In the mid-1980s he began designing costumes for the movies, including *Raising Arizona*, *Barton Fink*, *Doc Hollywood*, *The Grifters* and *The Hudsucker Proxy*. He died in Los Angeles on December 30, 1995, at age 45, a victim of AIDS.

Costumes: 1981 *Candida* 1985 *The News*

Michael J. Hotopp

Michael J. Hotopp, scenic and lighting designer for theater and television, studied at Carnegie Mellon and New York Universities. He created the environments for *CBS This Morning*, *Fox News Channel*, *The Oprah Winfrey Show*, music and drama specials on PBS-TV, and music videos. Hotopp has won Emmy Awards for the CBS-TV Studio Sets for both the 1994 and 1998 Winter Olympic Games (Production Design and Art Direction) and a third Emmy for *Sports Illustrated 40 for the Ages*. Other awards include a Clio for an IBM commercial. He has also amassed many credits for productions on and off-Broadway, international theater projects, fashion shows, industrial promotions and television commercials. The national tours of *Evita* and *Annie* are among touring credits, as well as designs in regional theaters such as the Goodspeed Opera House, the Baltimore Opera, and Pittsburgh Playhouse. Since 1994, he has been the President of Hotopp Associates Limited, a scenic design firm in New York City that provides scenic designs and services for television, theatrical and corporate clients.

Sets: 1979 *Oklahoma!*† 1980 *Brigadoon*† 1981 *Oh, Brother*† 1983 *The Tapdance Kid*† 1991 *Liza Minnelli: Stepping Out at Radio City*; *Peter Pan*† 1992 *Radio City Christmas Spectacular*† 1993 *Radio City Christmas Spectacular*† 1994 *Radio City Christmas Spectacular*† 1995 *Radio City Christmas Spectacular* 1996 *Radio City Christmas Spectacular*†; *Radio City Spring Spectacular*† 1997 *Radio City Christmas Spectacular*†; *Radio City Spring Spectacular*† 1998 *Radio City Christmas Spectacular*† (Santa's Gonna Rock and Roll, etc.)

Lights: 1982 *Cleavage*†

Norris Houghton

Norris Houghton was born Charles Norris Houghton on December 26, 1909 in Indianapolis, Indiana. He attended Princeton University where he received a Bachelor of Arts degree, Phi Beta Kappa in 1931 and designed sets at the Triangle Club. He was assistant to Robert Edmond Jones at Radio City Music Hall in 1932 and in 1934 went to the Soviet Union on a Guggenheim Fellowship, leading to expertise on Russian Theatre. After serving in the United States Naval Reserve from 1942 to 1945 he began directing. In September 1953 he founded the Phoenix Theatre with T. Edward Hambleton and became co-managing director. The first production at the Phoenix, *Madame, Will You Walk*, opened on December 1, 1953. In 1963 he resigned as managing director but remained on the Board of Directors and as Vice-President of the Phoenix Corporation. Having served onthe faculty of Columbia University and Vassar College, in 1967 he was appointed professor and Dean, Division of Theatre Arts, State University of New York at Purchase, where he remained until retiring in 1980. Lee Simonson was his mentor and he often acknowledged Gordon Craig and Robert Edmond Jones as major influences. His memoirs, *Entrances and Exits*, were published by New York Limelight Editions in 1991. Norris Houghton died in New York City on October 9, 2001 at age 92.

Sets: 1937 *In Clover* **1938** *Dame Nature; Good Hunting; How to Get Tough About It; Stop-Over; Waltz in Goose Steps; White Oaks* **1956** *The Sleeping Prince* **1957** *The Makropoulos Secret*

Ann Hould-Ward

Ann Hould-Ward was born in Glasgow, Montana on April 5, 1951, the daughter of Stanley and Beverly Hould. She studied art and theatrical design at Mills College in Oakland, California and at the University of Virginia. Additional study was done at the Art Students League in New York City. Her first costumes appeared on the stage at Mills College in a production of *The Lesson*. As an assistant to costume designer Patricia Zipprodt, Ann Hould-Ward worked on many Broadway shows prior to her own debut. She received a Tony Award nomination for her first Broadway play, *Sunday in the Park with George*, which she co-designed with Patricia Zipprodt, and won the Tony Award in 1994 for *Beauty and the Beast*. Her beautiful renderings, often referred to as illustrations, reveal a gift with color and texture that is in demand on and off-Broadway, in the top regional theaters, and for dance. Twenty-first century designs include American Ballet Theatre's *The Pied Piper, The New Red Hot and Blue* at Goodspeed Opera House, the premiere of *Say Yes!* at the Berkshire Theatre Festival and *Aeros* in Los Angeles.

Costumes: 1984 *Sunday in the Park with George*† **1985** *Harrigan 'n Hart* **1987** *Into the Woods* **1992** *Falsettos* **1993** *In the Summer House; Saint Joan;*

Three Men on a Horse; Timon of Athens **1994** *Beauty and the Beast* **1995** *The Molière Comedies; On the Waterfront* **1997** *Dream* **1998** *Little Me; More to Love*

Ena Hourwich

Ena Hourwich designed costumes on Broadway in the late 1920s. Born July 23, 1906, she attended Antioch College and did graduate study at New York University and the New York School of Social Work. In 1938 she married Edward Kunzer, later residing in Jefferson, Colorado. Ena Hourwich Kunzer died on May 8, 1989.

Costumes: 1929 *The Silver Tassie*

Grace Houston

Grace Houston was born in New Bedford, Massachusetts on October 25, 1916. She performed in Radio City Music Hall as a Rockette, but gave up dancing to become a costume designer. After working as an assistant to Irene Sharaff and Billy Livingston she debuted on Broadway as the costume designer for *The Two Mrs. Carrolls*. In the 1940s and 1950s she designed costumes for films, including *Abbott and Costello Meet Frankenstein* and *Crime of Passion*.

Costumes: 1943 *Land of Fame; The Two Mrs. Carrolls; What's Up* **1944** *Hats Off to Ice*†; *Men to the Sea; Violet* **1945** *Live Life Again; Up in Central Park*† **1946** *Burlesque; Call Me Mister; Icetime*† **1949** *Howdy Mr. Ice of 1950*† **1950** *The Consul; The Golden State*

Charles Howard

Charles Howard was an actor in vaudeville, burlesque and musical comedies. He contributed costumes to two plays in the early 1920s. He died at age 65 on July 2, 1947. His final Broadway role was the Sheriff in *Bloomer Girl*.

Costumes: 1920 *The Cave Girl* **1921** *The Triumph of X*† (Mrs. Herbert Gresham's gowns)

Noel Howard

Costume designer Noel James Howard made his Broadway debut in 1992, but had experience with costumes on Broadway long before then. He has worked for many years as an assistant

to costume designer Andreane Neofitou, supervising most of the 30 international productions of *Les Miserables*. He should not be confused with the screenwriter and director (1920-1987) with the same name.
Costumes: 1992 *Five Guys Named Moe*

Pamela Howard

Pamela Howard, a British designer, was born in Birmingham, England on January 5, 1939 and studied at the Slade School of Fine Art and University College, London. She began designing in 1959 and has designed for many theaters in the United Kingdom, including the Royal Shakespeare Company, the Old Vic, the Royal National Theatre, Theatre Clywyd, and Lyric Hammersmith. With Peter Gill she helped create the Riverside Studios where she designed *The Cherry Orchard* and *Tree Tops*. She has taught design, and founded a graduate degree program in scenography that uses resources in Prague, Barcelona, Utrecht and the Central Saint Martins College of Art and Design in London. When Great Britain won the Golden Triga at the 1991 Prague Quadrennial, her designs for *John Brown's Body* were part of the exhibit. Her book, *What Is Scenography?*, published by Routledge in 2001, is part of the *Theatre in Context* series.
Sets: 1984 *Kipling*
Costumes: 1984 *Kipling*

Phillip Howden

Phillip Howden was one of the British scenic artists who flourished at the turn of the twentieth century. His one credit in New York is among dozens in London, where he designed and painted in many of the theaters. He was associated with the Alhambra Palace Theatre in 1899 where he assisted Shallud with the settings for *Red Shoes*.
Sets: 1905 *The Babes and the Baron†*

George W. Howe

George W. Howe was born George Hauthalen in Salzburg, Austria in 1896 and ran away to America when he was fourteen. He was known primarily as an illustrator for *Collier's, American, Good Housekeeping, Women's Home*

Companion and other magazines. He studied art in Paris and worked in various positions before devoting himself to serial illustrations. He also designed and painted scenery for motion picture studios. Just before his death in 1941 he executed a series of paintings which were subsequently used as posters for the Barnum and Bailey Circus.
Sets: 1923 *White Cargo* **1924** *Garden of Weeds* **1926** *White Cargo*

Rob Howell

British designer Rob Howell creates scenery and costumes for productions throughout the United Kingdom and on the European continent. He has designed many plays in the West End, as well as for the Royal Shakespeare Company and the Royal National Theatre. For Eddie Izzard, he did both the *Glorious Tour* and his *UK Tour 1999/2000*. His scenic designs for *The Glass Menagerie* performed at the Donmar Warehouse and the Comedy Theatre, and for *Chips with Everything* at RNT were nominated for Olivier Awards in 1996 and 1997 respectively. Twenty-first century designs include *Lulu* produced by the Almeida Theatre Company and performed at the Kennedy Center in Washington, D.C.
Sets: 2000 *Betrayal*; *True West*
Costumes: 2000 *Betrayal*; *True West*

Henry E. Hoyt

Many of the scenic artists active during the turn of the twentieth century were British, but Henry E. Hoyt was American. He was born c.1835 in New Hampshire and first worked as a scenic artist in Philadelphia, where his credits included *The Isle of Delos* in the 1870s. He relocated to New York in the early 1880s where he designed and painted at the Park Theatre, the Grand Opera House, the Fourteenth Street Theatre, and the Casino. For many years he was the head scenic artist at the Metropolitan Opera House, but old and new. Late nineteenth century credits include *The Gypsy Baron, King Arthur*, and *Half a King*. The 1886 playbill for *Ermine* at the Casino Theatre had the statement: "Second scene copyrighted." Elected president of the

American Society of Scenic Painters in 1896, he died in Germantown, Pennsylvania on January 19, 1907 at age 77. His posthumous credit was for a play he originally designed for William Gillette in 1896 at the Garrick Theatre.
Sets: 1899 *My Lady's Lord*[†]; *Sister Mary*; *Three Little Lambs*[†]; *Why Smith Left Home*[†] 1900 *Broadway to Tokio*[†]; *The Monks of Malabar* 1901 *The Merchant of Venice*[†] 1902 *A Country Girl*[†] 1904 *Fatinitza*[†]; *Girofle-Giroflа*[†] (Act I) 1906 *Country, Girl, The and Lilli Tse* 1910 *Secret Service*

Julia Hoyt

Julia Hoyt was an actress on stage and screen, beginning her career in 1921 in the film *The Wonderful Thing* with Norma Talmadge. She was part of trend in the early 1920s for young members of high society to perform in movies so as to escape the endless circuit of teas and balls. Her many acting credits on Broadway include roles in *Anatomy of Love* and *The Rhapsody*. Miss Hoyt died on October 31, 1955 at the age of 58. In 1927 she collaborated with another actress, Kay Francis, on the costume designs for a Broadway play.
Costumes: 1927 *Damn the Tears*[†] (Miss Griffith's costumes)

Peggy Hoyt

American fashion designer Peggy Hoyt was born in Saginaw, Michigan in November 1893 and spent seven months as an apprentice in a Fifth Avenue millinery shop before opening her own establishment at 516 Fifth Avenue in 1917. Instead of importing hats, or copying styles from Paris, she created her own and quickly became a success. After designing the costumes for *The Merry Widow* she expanded her shop to include gowns, which were equally successful. Regarded as one of America's first fashion designers, preceding Elizabeth Hawes and Claire Potter, she created original, feminine clothes, and continued to design gowns and costumes for theatrical productions along with those for her private costumes. Known in private life as Mrs. Aubrey L. Eads, she died on October 26, 1937 in New York City.

Costumes: 1920 *The Outrageous Mrs. Palmer*[†] (Hats) 1921 *Danger*; *The Merry Widow*; *Nice People*[†] (Hats); *The Skirt* (Miss Barriscales' gowns); *Two Blocks Away* (Miss Carroll's Act II costume and cape) 1922 *The Clinging Vine* 1924 *Cobra*[†] (Miss Anderson's gowns) 1927 *The Royal Family*[†] (Miss Andrews' gowns) 1933 *Her Master's Voice*[†] (Miss Crew's clothes)

René Hubert

René Hubert was born in France in 1899 and designed costumes throughout Europe and in the U.S. He created designs for plays, and beginning in 1927 for numerous films. His costume designs for film received two Academy Award nominations, one for *Desirée* and one for *The Visit*. The gown he designed for Julia (Jeanne Crain) in *Centennial Summer* in 1946, and one for Julie (Jean Simmons) in *Desirée* in 1954 were part of the "Hollywood and History: Costume Design in Film" exhibition at the Los Angeles County Museum of Art and published in the book with the same name. His designs for several of his films, *Wintertime*, *Sweet Rosie O'Grady*, *The Lodger*, *Wilson* and others were featured in the 1989 exhibit "Dressing the Part" at the Brooklyn Museum. He died in 1973.
Costumes: 1923 *The Mountebank* (Miss Ravine's Act II and IV gowns and hats)

Richard Hudson

Born on September 6, 1954 in Harare, Zimbabwe, Richard Hudson attended the Peterhouse School in Marondera, Zimbabwe and then earned his B.A., with honors, from the Wimbledon School of Art. He has since designed many productions in Europe and the United States, mainly operas and plays. His designs for *The Rake's Progress* originally staged at the Lyric Opera of Chicago, was also performed at the Saito Kinen Festival in Japan. He has designed numerous productions for the Royal Shakespeare Company, and in 1988 received the Laurence Olivier award for his designs at the Old Vic. His designs for *La Bête* won the 1991 American Theatre Wing Design

Award. They were also nominated for a Tony Award and those for *The Lion King* won one. In 1999 Richard Hudson became a Fellow of the Royal Society of Arts and Royal Designer for Industry (R.D.I.)

Sets: 1991 *La Bête* **1997** *The Lion King*
Costumes: 1991 *La Bête*

Allen Lee Hughes

Lighting designer Allen Lee Hughes, a native of Washington, D.C., was born on December 29, 1949, began designing in high school while working with the Garrick Players in Middleton, Virginia and as a lighting assistant at Arena Stage. He received a B.A. from Catholic University in 1972 and an M.F.A. from New York University in 1979, where he studied with John Gleason. His first main stage design at Arena Stage was *Once In A Lifetime* in 1976. He debuted off-Broadway in 1979 with *Bebop, the Hip Musical*. From 1979 to 1981 he assisted Jennifer Tipton and Arden Fingerhut, while continuing to design at Arena Stage and for small opera and dance companies. He became resident lighting designer for Eliot Feld in 1985. Since then his designs have been seen throughout the U.S. for dance companies and regional theaters. His designs have been honored many times and include nominations for Tony Awards for *K-2, Strange Interlude* and *Once on This Island*, a Maharam and an Outer Circle Critics Award for *K-2*, a Hollywood Drama Logue Critics Award for *Quilters*, and a Boston Theatre Critics Circle Award for *A Soldier's Story*. He has also won two Helen Hayes Awards for designs at Arena Stage, and in 1994 he received the Michael Merritt Award for Excellence in Design and Collaboration. Arena Stage created the Allen Lee Hughes Fellows Program, an annual competition to increase the participation of ethnic minorities in professional theater, in 1990. Twenty-first century designs include *Pacific dances* for Eliot Feld Ballet Tech.

Lights: 1983 *K-2* **1984** *Accidental Death of an Anarchist*; *Quilters* **1985** *Strange Interlude* **1990** *Once on This Island* **1991** *Mule Bone* **1995** *Having Our Say*

Mick Hughes

Mick Hughes, who was born in 1938 in London, worked as a television cameraman for the British Broadcasting Company and as an electrician for the Margate Stage Company before beginning his career as a lighting designer. In 1961, he lit *Gaslight* at Theatre Royal, Margate, and in 1966 made his West End debut with *The Fighting Cock*. Since then he has designed numerous productions for the English National Opera, the Royal Shakespeare Company, and in the West End. He has also directed a long list of plays at the Swan Theatre in Worcester and taught lighting design at the Birmingham Polytechnic. Twenty-first century credits include *A Kind of Alaska, Monologue*, and *One for the Road*, produced by the Gate Theatre, Dublin and presented as part of the Harold Pinter Festival at Lincoln Center in summer 2001, and *By Jeeves* in the 2001-2002 Broadway season.

Lights: 1993 *Wonderful Tennessee*

Marie Humans

Marie Humans designed costumes for a play on Broadway in 1947 in collaboration with another designer.

Costumes: 1941 *Crazy with the Heat*[†]

Edna Hume

Edna Hume designed gowns for a featured player in a 1937 Broadway show.

Costumes: 1937 *The Lady Has a Heart*[†] (Miss Spongs' gowns)

Wilson Hungate

Wilson Hungate designed one set on Broadway in 1924. He resided at 325 East 57th Street in Manhattan. A member of the Lotus Club, he died in April 1943 in New York City.

Sets: 1924 *The Fake*[†]

Grady Hunt

Grady Hunt, who designed costumes for a Broadway show in 1961, is mainly known for his prolific designs for television, including series, mini-series, made-for-TV movies, and specials. His career began with early television programs, including the variety shows that featured Berle and Steve Allen. Costume design for series include *Quark, Fantasy Island, Starman, The Six Million Dollar Man, Police Woman, Wonder Woman,* and *The New Mike Hammer,* to name only a few. He was the costume supervisor on *Torn Curtain* and designed costumes for *The Perils of Pauline.* Hunt was born in Texas in 1921 and attended Southern Methodist University and the University of Houston.

Costumes: 1961 *The Billy Barnes People*

Olga Hunt

Olga B. Hunt was the proprietor of a small gown shop at 13 East 8th Street in the early 1930s. She resided at 56 West 9th Street at that same time, and also designed the women's costumes for a 1934 Broadway show.

Costumes: 1934 *Hipper's Holiday* (Women's costumes)

Peter Hunt

Peter Hunt, a director and lighting designer, was born in Pasadena, California on December 16, 1938. He attended The Hotchkiss School, where he first designed lights, and Yale University where he received both a B.A and an M.F.A. His first production in New York where he spent nearly ten years as a free-lance lighting designer was the 1961 off-Broadway show, *The Sap of Life.* From 1964 to 1968 he designed for Richard Rogers at Lincoln Center and at the New York State Theatre. He also designed in London and for the film *1776.* In the late 1960s he began directing more frequently, and since then has designed lights only occasionally. His directorial debut in New York City was *Book* in 1968, and in 1972 he won the Tony Award for directing *1776.* Since 1989 he has been artistic director of the Williamstown Theatre Festival, the same theater where he directed his first play and where in 1957, he started to design lights.

Lights: 1963 *Tambourines to Glory* **1966** *Annie Get Your Gun; Wayward Stork* **1968** *Noel Coward's Sweet Potato* **1977** *Bully*

Allison McLellan Hunter

Alison McLellan Hunter, a noted interior designer on the West Coast was a native of Bristol, England. After moving to New York she worked for Hattie Carnegie and designed Broadway shows before relocating to California in the 1940s to design costumes for film stars. She left the costume business and became a leading interior designer in Hollywood, as well as a painter with several exhibits of her work. Her brother is the television and film writer Ian McLellan. She died on June 10, 1979 at age 67.

Costumes: 1931 *Everybody's Welcome†; Experience Unnecessary†* **1932** *Great Magoo; A Little Rocketeer†* **1935** *Scoundrel*

Timothy Hunter

Lighting designer Timothy Hunter has had a long association with Alvin Ailey's Dance Theatre where he has lit many productions. Other dance credits include designs for the Dance Theatre of Harlem, Houston Ballet, Pittsburgh Ballet, Boston Ballet, and solo performances by his wife, dancer Maxine Sherman, among others. Theater designs include *Mirette* at the Goodspeed Opera House and *Peter Pan* for the St. Louis Municipal Opera. Twenty-first century designs include *Summer of '42* at the Variety Arts Theatre.

Lights: 1995 *Smokey Joe's Cafe* **1997** *The Wizard of Oz* **1998** *The Wizard of Oz*

Rex Huntington

When Rex Huntington designed costumes on Broadway in 1965 and again in 1981 he was simply continuing what he spent his entire professional life doing. He was making strippers and dancers, in his words "look good." Originally from Richmond, Indiana, he moved to Detroit, Michigan at age 17 to work in an automobile factory, but soon found his way into show business, initially as a way to occupy his free time. With partner Bob Greenwood, he opened a shop, Rex Costumes, where he produced amazing and functional creations for Ann Corio, Georgia Southern, Chesty Morgan, Toots Bronner, Carrie Fennill, Charmaine, Ann

Perri, and others. The business was later relocated to Chicago. He was interviewed for a story for the September 5, 1991 issue of the *The Wall Street Journal*, and at the age of 84 was still making costumes for striper Tempest Storm. Born on March 25, 1907, he died on September 13, 1992.

Costumes: 1965 *This Was Burlesque*† **1981** *This Was Burlesque*

Leslie Hurry

Leslie Hurry, one of Britain's foremost designers, was born in London on February 10, 1909, and attended St. John's Wood Art School. He designed the ballet *Hamlet* in 1942, the first of numerous plays, ballets and operas for the major companies of Great Britain. He went to Canada to design sets and costumes in 1955 for the Stratford (Ontario) Festival and returned many times to design additional productions. His designs were well known for their lyrical quality of line and color. His theatrical designs and costumes have been exhibited often, most recently at the Royal Festival Hall in London. His final realized design was *Caesar and Cleopatra* at the Shaw Festival, Niagara-on-the-Lake, Ontario in 1975. At the time of his death on November 20, 1978, he was working on designs for *Mazeppa* for the Boston Opera, which were never produced.

Sets: 1956 *Richard III*; *Tamburlaine the Great*
Costumes: 1956 *Richard III*; *Tamburlaine the Great*

Raymond Newton Hyde

Raymond Newton Hyde, who designed costumes for a play in 1917 was born in Boston in 1863. He studied couture in Paris but was better known as a landscape painter than for his costume designs. His professional life was mainly in journalism. He first worked as assistant art director for *The World* and later as art director for the *New York Herald*, retiring from that position in 1915. Mr. Hyde died on May 28, 1933 at the age of 68.

Costumes: 1917 *Eileen*

Ghretta Hynd

Ghretta Hynd, who made her Broad-way debut in 1988, uses her creativity for theater, film and video as well as with computer graphics. She has also collaborated with Lee Breuer, who wrote and directed *The Gospel at Colonus*, on *Sister Suzie Cinema*, *Lear* and *The Warrior Ant*. She assisted Lindsay Kemp on the costumes for *Flowers*, a play which Breuer devised, directed and designed, initially at Edinburgh's Traverse Theatre before it was seen in London and New York.

Costumes: 1988 *The Gospel at Colonus*

Holly Hynes

Costume designer Holly Hynes has been with the New York City Ballet since 1985 and since 1989 has been Director of Costumes. A prolific and accomplished designer, she has designed more than seventy ballets for companies including New York City Ballet as well as the Pennsylvania Ballet, Royal Ballet at Covent Garden, San Francisco Ballet, Koninklijk Ballet van Vlaanderen (Belgium), Suzanne Farrell Ballet, and the Joffrey Ballet, among others. Born in Des Moines, Iowa on December 7, 1955, daughter of William J. Hynes and Phyllis Barnhart, she graduated from Coe College in 1978 after which she spent two years as project manager at Brooks Van Horn and five years as Barbara Matera's assistant for dance. Her association with Barbara Matera, John David Ridge, Desmond Heeley, Rouben Ter-Arutunian, and Santo Loquasto has also been valuable. Her designs are in the permanent collection of the Museum of the City of New York and will be in the President William J. Clinton Library in Little Rock, Arkansas. They have also have been exhibited at Lincoln Center and the Marvin Cone Galleries in Cedar Rapids, and those for Balanchine's *Divertimento #15* were published on the coverof *Dance Magazine* in September 2000.

Costumes: 1991 *Getting Married; On Borrowed Time*

John Iacovelli

Scenic and production designer John Iacovelli works mainly in Southern California, partly because of his position

as head of design at the University of California, Riverside. He was production designer for five seasons of *Babylon 5*, winning two Hugo awards, the Sci-Fi Universe Award and the Space Frontier Foundation Award. Credits as art director include episodes of *A Different World*, *Santa Barbara* and *The Cosby Show*, among others. His film credits include *Honey, I Shrunk the Kids*, *Ruby in Paradise*, and *Public Enemy #2*. He designs regularly for the Mark Taper Forum, the South Coast Repertory, the Old Globe, Pasadena Playhouse, and the Los Angeles Theatre Center. His scenic designs have also been seen at the Dallas Theatre Center, the Utah Shakespeare Festival, and the Oregon Shakespeare Festival. Son of an artist father, he was born on February 25, 1959 in Reno, Nevada, and after graduating from the University of Nevada, Las Vegas earned his M.F.A. at New York University in 1984. Among his many honors is an Emmy Award for Art Direction and the 2001 Lifetime Achievement Award from the Los Angeles Drama Critics Circle.
Sets: 1993 *The Twilight of the Golds* **1998** *Peter Pan*

Wiard Ihnen

Wiard "Bill" Boppo Ihnen, a film art director, was born in Jersey City, New Jersey on August 5, 1897 and joined the East Coast art department of Famous Players-Lasky in 1919. He soon moved to California and his first movie, *Idols of Clay*, was produced in 1920. It was followed by many others, notably *Becky Sharp* in 1935 which he designed with Robert Edmond Jones, *Stagecoach* in 1939, and his final movie *The Gallant Hours* in 1960. He won Academy Awards for Art Direction for *Wilson* and *Blood on the Sun* while working for Twentieth Century Fox. During World War I and World War II he served in the army as a camouflage expert. He was also a painter and an authority on early California architecture, and served a term as president of the Art Directors Guild. He met costume designer Edith Head while working on *Cradle Song* in 1933 and they were married in 1940, although she re-

tained the name of her first husband for professional use. Bill Ihnen died in June 1979 at age 91.
Sets: 1925 *Hell's Bells* **1928** *Bottled*

Joseph Ijaky

Josef Ijaky designed one set on Broadway in 1970.
Sets: 1970 *Light, Lively, and Yiddish*

George Illian

George Illian, an artist and illustrator, designed the setting and collaborated on the costume design for a Broadway play in 1926. He was born in Milwaukee in 1894 and studied at the Art Institute of Chicago and the Royal Academy in Munich. One of the organizers of the Artist's Guild, he taught art to disabled veterans after World War I. He spent most of his life in New York City and Mt. Vernon, New York, where he lived with his wife Margaret. George Illian died in 1932.
Sets: 1926 *Henry IV, Part I*†
Costumes: 1926 *Henry IV, Part I*†

Ilmar and Tames

Ilmar and Tames together designed the setting and costumes for a single Broadway production in 1935. Samuel Tames (1888-1970) was a painter who resided at 241 Madison Avenue in New York City in 1932.
Sets: 1935 *Bertha, the Sewing Machine Girl*
Costumes: 1935 *Bertha, the Sewing Machine Girl*

James F. Ingalls

James F. Ingalls studied at the University of North Carolina at Chapel Hill, received his undergraduate degree from the University of Connecticut, and took his M.F.A. from the Yale University School of Drama in stage management. He served as stage manager at Yale for three seasons prior to moving to New York City and spending two years as production stage manager for Twyla Tharp. His first New York production as lighting designer was *96A* for Eccentric Circles Theatre at St. Malachy's Church. When Paul Gallo left Amen Repertory Theatre, Jim Ingalls was named lighting designer and spent three years with the company.

He has also been principal lighting designer for the American Repertory Theatre. His credits include numerous productions in regional theaters and collaborations with Peter Sellars, Adrianne Lobel, George Tsypin, and Stanley Wojewodski. Jennifer Tipton has been instrumental in shaping his career (in part because he studied her original designs for Twyla Tharp while re-creating them on the road), as has Thomas Skelton, with whom he worked while a stage manager at Yale. In 1985 Ingalls received the first of his two Helen Hayes Awards in Washington D.C. for *The Count of Monte Cristo*. He has also received an Obie Award for sustained excellence in lighting. Additional credits include *Passageio* and *Il Combatimento di Tancredi e Clorinda* in Aix-en-Provence, *Lohengrin* for the Brussels National Opera, *The Rake's Progress* at the Théâtre du Chatelet in Paris, and *Theodora* at the Glyndebourne Opera. Twenty-first century designs includes lighting for *The Gambler* at the Metropolitan Opera.

Lights: 1983 *'night Mother* **1984** *The Human Comedy* **1996** *The Night of the Iguana* **1997** *Ivanov; The Young Man from Atlanta* **2000** *George Gershwin Alone*

Sigrid Insull

Sigrid Insull, a native of Indianapolis, Indiana, was born on December 12, 1941 and did both her graduate and undergraduate work at Indiana University. Her first costume designs were for a presentation of two operas by Benjamin Britten in a cathedral in Indianapolis. She has designed many films, television productions (*I Feel A Song Coming On* for PBS) and plays (*Ellen Terry/Shakespeare's Heroines*) starring Trish Van Devere. She teaches design at Stony Brook University in Long Island, New York.

Costumes: 1980 *Canterbury Tales*

Paul Iribe

Paul Iribe (sometimes Fribe), born Paul Iribarnegaray in Angoulême, France in 1883, was primarily a fashion illustrator. He was responsible for the 1908 catalog, *Les Robes de*

Paul Poiret which brought attention to Poiret's fashions and an original style of illustration that focused on garments rather than settings. He created illustrations and designed advertisements for Paquin, Callot Soeurs, *Vogue*, *Femina*, and satirical newspapers in France, among others. He spent most of the 1920s in America, where he designed costumes and interior settings, primarily for Paramount Pictures. Iribe died in France in 1935.

Costumes: 1920 *French Leave†* (Mrs. Coburn's Act I, II gowns)

Christopher Ironside

Christopher Ironside, a British artist and designer, was born on July 11, 1913 and trained at London's Central School of Arts and Crafts. He designed many medals, coins, reverses and coats-of-arms, and the obverse side of Britain's first six decimal coins. He co-founded the Society of Numismatic Artists and Designers with Philip Nathan in 1990. His paintings and drawings are in many public and private collections and he exhibited widely in one-man shows. In collaboration with his brother, Robin C. Ironside, he also designed for the theater. Awarded the Order of the British Empire in 1971, Christopher Ironside died in 1992 at age 79 in Winchester, England.

Sets: 1954 *A Midsummer Night's Dream†*

Costumes: 1954 *A Midsummer Night's Dream†*

Robin Ironside

Robin C. Ironside was born on July 10, 1912 and studied at the Courtauld Institute and on the continent. He spent the majority of his professional career working at the Tate Gallery and writing. In addition, he was active with the Contemporary Art Society. He published several books in the 1940s, including *British Painting Since 1939* and *The Pre-Raphaelites*. In collaboration, brothers Christopher and Robin Ironside designed sets and costumes for many productions, beginning with *Der Rosenkavalier* at Covent Garden in 1948. Robin Ironside died on November 2, 1965.

Sets: 1954 *A Midsummer Night's Dream*†
Costumes: 1954 *A Midsummer Night's Dream*†

Laurence Irving

Laurence Henry Foster Irving, painter, illustrator, and designer of scenery and costumes for the theater and films, was born on April 11, 1897 in London. He studied at the Byam Shaw School and began designing with the sets and costumes for *Vaudeville Vanities* in London in 1926. He was in the service in World War I and World War II. He was art director in Hollywood for Douglas Fairbanks' films *The Man in the Iron Mask* (1928) and *The Taming of the Shrew* (1929) as well as other films. A governor of Stratford Memorial Theatre, Stratford-upon-Avon and the Royal Academy of Dramatic Art, he was awarded an Order of the British Empire in 1944. He was the biographer of his grandfather, Sir Henry Irving and helped inspire the formation of the Theatre Museum in London. Laurence Irving died in 1988.

Sets: 1932 *There's Always Juliet* 1933 *Evensong* 1938 *I Have Been Here Before*

Eiko Ishioka

Eiko Ishioka is a graphic and theatrical designer from Japan. She initially studied industrial design at Tokyo National University of Fine Arts and Music and then changed to graphic and commercial design. While Art Director for the fashionable Parco department stores in Japan in the 1970s she created displays that are still considered extraordinary. Her first film was *Mishima*, an American film directed by Francis Ford Coppola, which won a special jury prize for artistic achievement at the Cannes Film Festival in 1985. Her other film work includes *The Cell* and Coppola's *Bram Stoker's Dracula* for which she won an Academy Award for Costume Design. In 1986 she was production designer for the Faerie Tale Theatre's *Rip Van Winkle*. A book about her designs, *Eiko by Eiko* was published in 1982 and a second book *Eiko on Stage* in 2000. Eiko Ishioka received nominations for Tony

Awards for both the sets and costumes for *M. Butterfly* in 1988.

Sets: 1988 *M. Butterfly* 1996 *Dreams & Nightmares* (Visual Artistic Director)
Costumes: 1988 *M. Butterfly* 1996 *Dreams & Nightmares* (Visual Artistic Director)
Lights: 1996 *Dreams & Nightmares*† (Visual Artistic Director)

Walter J. Israel

Walter J. Israel designed costumes on Broadway in the mid-1940s. He worked for many years on the West Coast in costume houses with his wife Ethel, and as head designer for film studios, particularly Schenck and United Studios. Mr. Israel, who was born August 4, 1882 in California, also designed costumes for the Los Angeles Light Opera Association. Films include *Oliver Twist* (1922), *Ashes of Vengeance* (1923), and *The Seahawk* (1924). The Israel's also executed hundreds of gowns for *The Eternal Flame* in 1922, produced by Norma Talmadge. Israel died on January 6, 1970 in Los Angeles.

Costumes: 1944 *Song of Norway*† 1945 *The Red Mill*

Nikolai Iznar

Nikolai Iznar designed scenery and costumes on Broadway in 1925 with Ivan Gremislavsky. He and Natal'ya Sergeevna Iznar (1893-1967) often collaborated with Ivan Gremislavsky. Natives of Russia, they spent the majority of their careers designing sets and costumes for the Moscow Art Theatre. Some of Natal'ya Sergeevna Iznar's designs were published in the volume *Inside the Moscow Art Theatre* in 1923.

Sets: 1925 *Love and Death/ Aleko/ Fountain of Bakkchi Sarai/ etc.*†
Costumes: 1925 *Love and Death/ Aleko/ Fountain of Bakkchi Sarai/ etc.*†

Andrew Jackness

Andrew Jackness received an M.F.A. from the Yale University School of Drama in 1979 after studying with Ming Cho Lee. He also studied at the Pratt Institute and Lester Polakov's Studio and Forum of Stage Design. Andrew Jackness was born in New York City on September 27,

1952, the son of Jack and Meredith Jackness. His designs have been seen on and off-Broadway, at the Schiller Theatre in Berlin, the Royal National Theatre in London, in major regional theaters in the United States, and at the Williamstown Theatre Festival. As a production designer he worked on the feature films *Longtime Companion*, *The Imposters*, *Big Night* and *The Love Letter* among others, *Blue Window* for American Playhouse and *Grownups* for Great Performances. Much honored for his designs, he often works with costume designers Juliet Polsca and Jane Greenwood. He also illustrated *Pamela's First Musical* a book for children by playwright Wendy Wasserstein. On the faculty at New York University, he teaches design for film.

Sets: 1979 *Wings* **1980** *John Gabriel Borkman* **1981** *Grown-ups*; *The Little Foxes* **1982** *Beyond Therapy*; *Whodunnit* **1986** *Precious Sons* **1988** *Michael Feinstein in Concert*; *Spoils of War* **1997** *The Scarlet Pimpernel* **1998** *The Scarlet Pimpernel*

Sheila Jackson

Shelia Jackson designed costumes for a Broadway in the late 1940s.

Costumes: **1947** *The Merchant of Venice*

Edward Jacobi

Edward J. Jacobi designed lighting for one production on Broadway in 1927. An electrician, he resided at 230 West 149th Street in 1922 and at 317 West 58th Street in New York City in 1925.

Lights: 1927 *Love in the Tropics*

Sally Jacobs

Sally Rich Jacobs, a British designer of sets and costumes, works frequently in the United States and the United Kingdom. She was born in London on November 5, 1932 and studied at Saint Martin's School of Art and the Central School of Arts and Crafts. She began her career working in the film industry, specializing in continuity. Her first professional design was *Five Plus One* at the Edinburgh Festival in 1961. Additional credits include many collaborations with director Peter Brook including the still remarkable 1970 *A Midsummer Night's Dream*. She has also designed for the Royal Shakespeare Company in London and Stratford-upon-Avon, and in London's West End. Films include *Nothing But the Best*, *Marat/Sade* and *Catch Us If You Can*. While designing in Los Angeles, mainly with Gordon Davidson at the Mark Taper Forum in the late 1960s, she lectured on theater design at the California Institute of the Arts in Los Angeles. In the 1990s, she designed many operas, including *Turandot* at the Royal Opera, as well as *Three Birds Alighting on a Field* at the Royal Court and *A Scot's Quare* in Glasgow, among others productions.

Sets: 1965 *Marat/Sade* **1971** *A Midsummer Night's Dream*

Costumes: 1971 *A Midsummer Night's Dream*

John Jacobsen

John W. Jacobsen was born in Bronxville, New York on October 8, 1945 to Eric and Mary Jacobsen. He received a B.A. in art history at Yale University in 1967 and two years later an M.F.A. in stage design after studying with Donald Oenslager. His first design, *Breaking Point* (1964), was at Yale, where he also won a national award for best undergraduate scenic design for de Ghelderode's *Dr. Faustus*. He has over sixty productions to his credit in regional and New York theaters, and extensive credits in Boston for companies including the Charles Playhouse, Goldovsky Opera, Opera Company of Boston and Boston Ballet. Since the mid-1970s he has been producing shows using advanced media technologies such as lasers and IMAX/OMNIMAX© film, primarily for museums. His company, White Oak Associates is an established museum planning and production firm with new museum projects across America. For example, his company was the executive producer of all the exhibits and theaters in Exploration Place (2000), a new creative learning center in Wichita, Kansas, for *The Living Sea*, an

IMAX© film by MacGillivray Freeman Films that was nominated for an
Academy Award in 1995, and of THE
WORKS for the Carnegie Science Center in Pittsburgh.

Sets: 1974 *Mourning Pictures*

Jacques

Actress Lillian Lorraine was born Eu-
lallean de Jacques on January 1, 1892
in San Francisco and baptized Mary
Ann Brennan. Her Broadway debut
was in the chorus of *The Gay White
Way* and in 1907 and in 1909 joined
the *Ziegfeld Follies* becoming a star
and appearing in the revues through
1918, as well as being featured in other
productions. In 1921, she slipped on
the ice and broke her back, was par-
alyzed, but recovered. She returned
to the stage although she was never
again as successful as she was before
her accident. In 1934 she designed
costumes for a production using the
name Jacques. Mary Ann Brennan,
also known as Lillian Lorraine and as
Jacques died on April 17, 1955 in New
York City.

Costumes: 1934 *Broadway Interlude*

Walter Jagemann

Walter Jagemann, originally from Vienna, began his professional career
building and painting scenery at the
Metropolitan Opera and in Joseph Urban's studio. He worked as an assistant to Jo Mielziner for scenery on productions including *On Borrowed Time,
Save Me the Waltz, I Married an Angel, Annie Get Your Gun, Dream Girl,*
and *Knickerbocker Holiday* in the 1930s
and 1940s while also working as a set
designer. He often worked in collaboration with designers Russell Patterson and Herbert Andrews. In the early
1950s, he became foreman at the National Scenery Studio, owned in part
by Jo Mielziner. Born on May 24, 1903,
Jageman died in March 1960.

Sets: 1935 *George White's Scandals*†
1939 *Swingin' the Dream*†; *Yokel Boy*

Charles James

Charles James, son of an English father and American mother, grew up,
studied and designed fashion on both
sides of the Atlantic. He was born

in London in 1905 and first worked
there as a milliner, calling himself
"BOUCHERON," but he soon moved
to New York and began designing for
private costumers. In the ensuing years
he held positions in various fashion
houses, including Elizabeth Arden in
New York and with Hardy Amies in
London. His peers considered him a
genius for his imagination. James also
taught fashion, notably at the Rhode
Island School of Design and at Pratt.
He occasionally contributed designs for
featured actresses in Broadway shows.
He died in New York on September 23,
1978.

Costumes: 1945 *Beggars Are Coming to
Town*† (Miss Comingore's and Miss Ame's
dresses)

Finlay James

Finlay James gave up a career in law
to design for the theater. He was
born in Angus, Scotland and received
a Diploma of Art in Dundee, Scotland.
He has designed sets and costumes in
Glasgow, Rome, Amsterdam, London
(including the Old Vic and in the West
End), and in Edinburgh among many
other locations. His first designs on
Broadway were seen in 1971. A teacher
as well as a designer, he spent fourteen years as head of the School of
Design in the College of Art and Design in Birmingham, England and has
also been head of design at the City of
Birmingham Polytechnic. In 1974 his
costume designs for *Crown Matrimonial* were nominated for a Tony Award.

Sets: 1970 *Conduct Unbecoming* **1973**
Crown Matrimonial **1985** *Aren't We All?*
1987 *Blithe Spirit*
Costumes: 1970 *Conduct Unbecoming*
1973 *Crown Matrimonial*
Lights: 1970 *Conduct Unbecoming*

Toni-Leslie James

Costume designer Toni-Leslie James
received much attention for her strikingly fresh designs with her Broadway
debut, *Jelly's Last Jam* in 1992, receiving Tony and Drama Desk nominations and an American Theatre
Wing Award. Her credits as a costume designer in New York began
in 1980, when she spent a year as

wardrobe assistant for the Dance Theatre of Harlem, and then three years a resident designer for the Alvin Ailey American Dance Theatre, amassing credits as well for Circle Repertory Company, Royal Court Theatre (London), Berkeley Repertory Theatre, the Pan Asian Repertory, and the Ensemble Studio Theatre, among others. Born and raised in 1957 in Clairton (near Pittsburgh), Pennsylvania, she received her B.F.A. at Ohio State University. Married to lighting designer David Higham, she designs costumes for the daytime drama *As the World Turns* and has also designed may productions for the Public Theatre, and in collaboration with George C. Wolfe and Graciella Danielle. Among her honors is the 1996 Irene Sharaff Young Master Award, from Theatre Development Fund. Twenty-first century credits include costumes for *The Philadelphia Story* at Hartford Stage and *A raisin in the Sun* at Center Stage in Baltimore.

Costumes: 1990 *Spunk* 1992 *Jelly's Last Jam* 1993 *Angels in America, Part II: Perestroika; Angels in America: Millennium Approaches* 1994 *Twilight: Los Angeles, 1992* 1995 *Chronicle of a Death Foretold; The Tempest* 1997 *God's Heart* 1998 *Footloose* 1999 *Marie Christine* 2000 *The Wild Party* 2001 *King Hedley II*

Neil Peter Jampolis

Neil Peter Jampolis has numerous credits for designing lighting and sets on Broadway, and for opera and dance companies in the United States. He was born in Brooklyn on March 14, 1943, attended Arizona State University, and received a B.F.A. from the Art Institute of Chicago in 1971. He occasionally designs costumes for plays and operas. His designs for opera include over 200 productions at companies such as the Santa Fe Opera, Houston Grand Opera, Metropolitan Opera, La Scala, and the Netherlands Opera. Mr. Jampolis received a Tony Award for *Sherlock Holmes*, amid four nominations, with the one for *Black and Blue* shared with his wife and co-designer Jane Reisman. On the faculty of the University of California, Los Angeles, he also directs plays.

Sets: 1970 *Borstal Boy* 1971 *Earl of Ruston; To Live Another Summer* 1985 *The Search for Signs of Intelligent Life in the Universe* 1986 *The World According to Me* 1988 *The World According to Me* 1989 *Sid Caesar and Company* 1990 *Jackie Mason: Brand New; The Sound of Music* 1993 *Camelot* (Scenery supervision); *Mixed Emotions* 1994 *Jackie Mason: Politically Incorrect* (Production design and lights) 1996 *Love They Neighbor* (Production design/lighting) 1997 *Street Corner Symphony*

Costumes: 1971 *Earl of Ruston* 1972 *Butley* 1986 *Into the Light* 1994 *Jackie Mason: Politically Incorrect* 1996 *Love They Neighbor* (Production design/lighting)

Lights: 1970 *Borstal Boy; Les Blancs* 1971 *Earl of Ruston; To Live Another Summer* 1972 *Butley; Wild and Wonderful; Wise Child* 1973 *Crown Matrimonial; Emperor Henry IV; Let Me Hear You Smile* 1974 *Sherlock Holmes* 1976 *The Innocents* 1977 *Otherwise Engaged* 1979 *Knockout; Night and Day* 1980 *The American Clock; Harold and Maude* 1981 *Life and Adventures of Nicholas Nickleby,†* 1984 *Kipling* 1985 *The Search for Signs of Intelligent Life in the Universe* 1986 *Into the Light; The World According to Me* 1988 *The World According to Me* 1989 *Black and Blue†; The Merchant of Venice; Orpheus Descending†; Sid Caesar and Company* 1990 *Jackie Mason: Brand New; The Sound of Music* 1993 *Camelot; Mixed Emotions* 1994 *Jackie Mason: Politically Incorrect* 1996 *Love They Neighbor* (Production design/lighting)

Dorothy Jeakins

Dorothy Jeakins was a stage and film costume designer. She was born on January 11, 1914 in San Diego, California, and studied in Los Angeles at the Otis Art Institute. Her first costume designs were for *The Taming of the Shrew* at the American Shakespeare Festival in 1946, and she made her Broadway debut in 1950. In addition to theatrical costume designs in New York she designed for many California theaters. Much of Miss Jeakins' career as a costume designer was spent in film. She designed over 50 films and won three Academy Awards for outstanding costume design, among twelve nominations. Her first movie was *Joan of Arc* in 1948 (Academy Award) and her last was John Huston's *The Dead* in 1987. Her other Academy awards were for *Samson and Delilah* (1950) and *The Night of the Iguana* (1962). *Major Barbara*, (1957), *Too Late the Phalarope*(1957), and *The World of Suzy Wong*(1959) were all nominated for Tony Awards in the outstanding costume design category. Miss Jeakins died in Santa Barbara, California on November 21, 1995

Costumes: 1950 *Affairs of State*; *King Lear* **1956** *Major Barbara*; *Too Late the Phalarope* **1958** *Cue for Passion*; *Winesburg, Ohio*; *The World of Suzie Wong* **1960** *A Taste of Honey* **1963** *My Mother, My Father and Me*

Jean

A successful fashion instigator during the early decades of the twentieth century, "Jean" was actually the name of a sample dress shop with two locations, one at 500 Fifth Avenue and the other at One West 42nd Street, both owned by Arthur Lindau. He was born on April 22, 1889 and died in Miami, Florida, in March 1973. The shops were frequented by prominent society matrons and actresses because they featured one-of-a-kind gowns.

Costumes: 1912 *Bella Donna* (Miss Nazimova's gowns) **1913** *The Misleading Lady* (Miss Buck's gowns) **1914** *That Sort* (Miss Nazimova's gowns)

Clare Jeffrey

Clare Jeffrey, born in Dorset, England studied in art schools in Hornset and Willesden, and at the Old Vic Theatre School where she later taught. Her designs were seen in many theaters in England, including Stratford-upon-Avon, the Marlowe Theatre in Canterbury, and for the Nottingham Playhouse beginning in the early 1950s with the costumes for *The Country Wife*. In 1957 she became co-designer at the Crest Theatre in Canada and in 1958 designed costumes for a Broadway play.

Costumes: 1958 *The Entertainer*

David Jenkins

David Jenkins has designed settings for major regional theaters and worked as an art director for the television productions *American Playhouse* and *Theatre in America*. Educated at Earlham College, Indiana University and the Yale School of Drama, he is married to stage designer Leigh Rand, who often works as his assistant. Jenkins was born on July 30, 1937 in Hampton, Virginia. He has many credits an art director for television commercials, through Wieden & Kennedy, where he has designed spots including the Bo Jackson and Spike Lee campaigns for Nike, and at the Mark Taper Forum where he frequently collaborates with director Robert Egan. Twenty-first century designs include *My Fair Lady*, *Who's Afraid of Virginia Woolf?* and *The New England Sonata Play* at Trinity Repertory Company where he often designs scenery.

Sets: 1973 *The Changing Room* **1974** *The Freedom of the City* **1975** *Rogers and Hart* **1976** *Checking Out* **1977** *Saint Joan* **1979** *The Elephant Man*; *Strangers* **1980** *I Ought to Be in Pictures* **1981** *Piaf* **1982** *The Queen and the Rebels*; *Special Occasions* **1983** *Total Abandon* **1987** *Sherlock's Last Case*; *Stardust*; *Stepping Out* **1989** *Welcome to the Club* **1990** *Accomplice* **1991** *The Crucible* **1992** *A Little Hotel on the Side*; *The Master Builder*; *Two Shakespearean Actors* **1993** *Candida*; *The Student Prince*† **1994** *Hedda Gabler*; *No Man's Land*; *The Shadow Box* **1996** *Taking Sides* **1998** *The Herbal Bed* **2000** *James Joyce's The Dead*

George Jenkins

George Clarke Jenkins is a well-known scenery and lighting designer and art director for films. Occasionally during his career he also contributed costume designs to a production. He was born in Baltimore on November 19, 1908 (1911 is also cited) and studied architecture at the University of Pennsylvania. He worked as an architect and interior designer before assisting Jo Mielziner from 1937 to 1941, while also beginning his own career as a designer. including productions for the San Francisco Opera Association. As an art director for films, he is known for his detailed and realistic sets, as evidenced in movies such as *All the President's Men* (Academy Award), *The Miracle Worker, The China Syndrome, The Subject Was Roses, Sophie's Choice, The Dollmaker* and *Presumed Innocent.* He received the Donaldson Award for his settings for *I Remember Mama* in 1945. From 1985 to 1988 he was Professor of Motion Picture Design at the University of California at Los Angeles.

Sets: 1943 *Early to Bed* 1944 *Allah Be Praised; I Remember Mama; Mexican Hayride* 1945 *Are You with It?; Common Ground; Dark of the Moon; The French Touch; Memphis Bound; Strange Fruit* 1948 *Time for Elizabeth; Tonight at 8:30* 1949 *Lost in the Stars* 1950 *Bell, Book and Candle; The Curious Savage* 1952 *Three Wishes for Jamie* 1953 *Gently Does It; Touchstone* 1954 *The Bad Seed; The Immoralist* 1955 *Ankles Aweigh; The Desk Set* 1956 *The Happiest Millionaire; Too Late the Phalarope* 1957 *Rumple* 1958 *Cue for Passion; Once More, with Feeling; Two for the Seesaw* 1959 *Jolly's Progress; The Miracle Worker; Tall Story* 1960 *Critics' Choice; One More River* 1961 *Thirteen Daughters* 1962 *Step on a Crack; A Thousand Clowns* 1963 *Jennie* 1965 *Catch Me If You Can; Generation* 1966 *Wait until Dark* 1968 *The Only Game in Town* 1972 *Night Watch* 1976 *Sly Fox*

Costumes: 1929 *Gambling* 1930 *So Was Napoleon* (Gowns and hats) 1934 *Anything Goes* (Gowns) 1945 *Common Ground; The French Touch* 1950 *The Curious Savage†* 1955 *The Desk Set*

Lights: 1943 *Early to Bed* 1944 *Allah Be Praised; I Remember Mama* 1945 *Are You with It?; Common Ground; Dark of the Moon; The French Touch; Memphis Bound; Strange Fruit* 1950 *Bell, Book and Candle; The Curious Savage†* 1953 *Gently Does It; Touchstone* 1954 *The Bad Seed* 1955 *Ankles Aweigh; The Desk Set* 1956 *The Happiest Millionaire; Too Late the Phalarope* 1957 *Rumple* 1958 *Cue for Passion; Once More, with Feeling; Two for the Seesaw* 1959 *The Miracle Worker; Tall Story* 1960 *Critics'Choice; One More River* 1961 *Thirteen Daughters* 1962 *Step on a Crack; A*

Thousand Clowns 1965 *Catch Me If You Can; Generation* 1966 *Wait until Dark* 1976 *Sly Fox*

Donald F. Jensen

Donald (Don) F. Jensen, the son of Ernest and Margaret O'Conner Jensen, was born in Emporia, Kansas on October 2, 1931. He received a B.F.A. in the School of Drawing and Painting at the University of Kansas in 1953, and studied set design with Lester Polakov and under Milton Smith at Columbia University. Principally a set designer, his first designs were for *Gallantry* at Columbia University and in 1957 he designed costumes for *Winkelburg* at the Renata Theatre in New York City. For the next forty years his designs included *Family Business* at the Astor Place (1977), *Jacques Brel* 25th Anniversary at the Village Gate (1995), *2 by N. Richard Nash, Life Anonymous* (1996) and *Loss of D Natural* (1998). He has assisted Desmond Heeley, Franco Zeffirelli, and Theoni Aldredge in addition to his own designing.

Sets: 1964 *The Sunday Man*
Costumes: 1964 *The Sunday Man*
Lights: 1964 *The Sunday Man*

John Jensen

John Jensen is a set and costume designer active in regional repertory theater and opera companies. From 1982 through 1991 he was head of the design/tech program at Rutgers University. He was born on December 20, 1933 in Weiser, Idaho. After graduating from Hillsboro High School he attended the University of Oregon, graduating in 1953 with a B.S. degree. Design and fine art studies continued at Pratt Institute, Lester Polakov's Studio and Forum of Stage Design, and other New York schools. He assisted Jo Mielziner for two years. For eight years he had a close association with The Guthrie Theatre where he was resident designer sharing production design with Tanya Moiseiwitsch and Desmond Heeley among others. His first professional design was *Ardele* at the Guthrie Theatre in 1969.

Sets: 1973 *Cyrano* 1980 *Watch on the Rhine* 1983 *The Man Who Had Three*

Arms

Jimnolds

Jimnolds collaborated on a set on Broadway in 1923.

Sets: 1923 *Helen of Troy, New York*†

Jocelyn

Jocelyn designed costumes on Broadway in the early 1950s.

Costumes: 1951 *The Number*; *Out West of Eighth* **1953** *Be Your Age* **1954** *The Magic and the Loss* (Clothes)

Joel

Joel was responsible for the interiors of a 1936 Broadway production in collaboration with Lucile who designed the exterior settings.

Sets: 1936 *The Life and Loves of Dorian Gray*† (Interiors)

Tom John

Tom H. John is an art director and production designer for television, and a scenic designer for theater and dance. He has won five Emmy Awards, including one each for *My Name is Barbra* in 1965, *Much Ado About Nothing* in 1973 and *Beacon Hill* in 1976. He is the only art director to receive television's Peabody Award for Special Achievement, awarded in 1966 for art direction of *Death of a Salesman, Color Me Barbra* and *The Strollin' Twenties*. Television designs include the series *Tattinger's* and *Kate and Allie*, and the 1998 NBC-TV movie *The Long Island Incident*. He has also designed for Radio City Music Hall, Alvin Ailey, Dance Theatre of Harlem and the San Francisco Ballet among other companies. His film work includes art direction for *Zoot Suit, Thank God It's Friday* and production design for *The Mirror Has Two Faces*.

Sets: 1968 *George M!* **1971** *Frank Merriwell (or Honor Changed)* **1972** *The Selling of the President* **1975** *The Wiz* **1976** *Guys and Dolls* **1983** *Five-Six-Seven-Eight... Dance!*†; *Marilyn*; *Peg*

Martin Johns

Early in his career, British designer Martin Johns designed scenery at Belgrade Theatre in Coventry, for the Tyneside Theatre Company and at

Theatre Royal in York. He is head of design at the Leicester Haymarket Theatre and has also held that position at theaters in Newcastle and York. Production credits in London's West End include *Merrily We Roll Along, Lady Audley's Secret, Rolls Hyphen Royce* and *Let the Good Times Roll*. In addition, he has designed productions for the Royal National Theatre, Watford Palace, the Birmingham Repertory Theatre, the English Touring Opera, and the Cleveland (England) Theatre Company where he is on the board. *Me and My Girl*, for which he received a Tony Award nomination, started at the Leicester Haymarket, moved to the West End and later opened in New York City.

Sets: 1986 *Me and My Girl*

Albert R. Johnson

Albert Richard Johnson was primarily a set designer who also occasionally designed lights. He began designing in 1929 and his final production opened in October 1967, just prior to his death on December 21, 1967. He was born in La Crosse, Wisconsin on February 1, 1910 and began working in theater at the age of fifteen as a scene painter for the Farmington, Long Island Opera House. His first New York design was *The Criminal Code* in 1929 at the age of nineteen, after which he studied with Norman Bel Geddes. During his busy career he was a consultant on productions and designs for the New York World's Fair, Radio City Music Hall, Ringling Bros. and Barnum & Bailey Circus, and Jones Beach. He also directed and designed lights for industrial promotions.

Sets: 1929 *The Criminal Code*; *Half Gods* **1930** *Three's a Crowd* **1931** *The Band Wagon* **1932** *Americana*; *Face the Music*; *Foreign Affairs*; *The Mad Hopes* **1933** *As Thousands Cheer*; *Face the Music*; *Let 'em Eat Cake* **1934** *The Great Waltz*; *Life Begins at 8:40*; *Revenge with Music*; *Union Pacific*; *Ziegfeld Follies: 1934*† **1935** *The Great Waltz*; *Jumbo* **1937** *Between the Devil* **1938** *Great Lady*; *Leave It to Me!*; *You Never Know*† **1939** *George White's Scandals*; *Leave It to Me!* **1940** *John Henry* **1941** *Crazy*

with the Heat **1942** *Proof through the Night*; *The Skin of Our Teeth* **1943** *My Dear Public* **1944** *Sing Out, Sweet Land* **1945** *The Girl from Nantucket*; *Live Life Again* **1947** *Dear Judas* **1949** *Two Blind Mice* **1950** *Pardon Our French* **1952** *The Chase*; *Fancy Meeting You Again*; *Of Thee I Sing*; *Shuffle Along* **1958** *Cloud 7* **1962** *Night Life* **1967** *What Did We Do Wrong?*
Lights: 1932 *Americana* **1941** *Crazy with the Heat* **1945** *The Girl from Nantucket*; *Live Life Again* **1947** *Dear Judas* **1958** *Cloud 7* **1962** *Night Life*

Bernard Johnson

Choreographer, dancer, costume and fashion designer Bernard Johnson was born on December 12, 1936 in Detroit, Michigan. He studied at the Detroit Art Institute and the Detroit School of Arts and Crafts, and in New York at the Fashion Institute of Technology. His first costume design was a "Gypsy" gown for Josephine Baker in 1957, after which this multi-talented man designed films, shows on and off-Broadway, television, musical revues and commercials. He designed stage wardrobes for Melba Moore, Diana Ross, the Temptations, Lena Horne and Martha Reeves and the Vandellas, among many others. He often cited Edith Head and Vincent Dee, both at Universal Studios, and the fashion illustrator and teacher of fine and commercial artists, Bernadine Sether, as mentors and career influences. As a dancer he appeared in musicals on Broadway. From 1989 to 1992 he was on the American Dance Festival faculty, teaching jazz dance in the U.S. as well as in Moscow. At the time of his death in New York City on January 22, 1997, he was also teaching dance and costume design at the University of California, Irvine. See Figure 6: Bernard Johnson: *Eubie*
Costumes: 1971 *Ain't Supposed to Die a Natural Death* **1972** *Don't Play Us Cheap* **1973** *Raisin* **1976** *Bubbling Brown Sugar*; *Guys and Dolls* **1978** *Eubie* **1982** *Waltz of the Stork*

Doug Johnson

Doug Johnson, a painter, illustrator, theatrical designer, and producer was born in Toronto, Canada in 1940 and studied painting in Europe after attending the Ontario College of Art. He moved to New York City in 1968 to work with advertising agencies and for magazines including *Sports Illustrated, Look* and *Playboy*. His advertising consulting firm, Performing Dogs, was involved with several Broadway shows, and as a partner in Dodger Productions, he has produced them as well. Doug Johnson has exhibited widely in both group and individual shows and has taught at the School of Visual Arts. He was art director for the 1979 film *Take Down* and in 1992 designed costumes for the Hartel and Dalton dancers.
Sets: 1982 *Pump Boys and Dinettes*†

Gertrude Johnson

Gertrude Johnson designed costumes for a revue on Broadway in 1922. The 1920 Manhattan Directory identifies her as a designer with a studio at 149 West 46th Street. She resided at 1760 Topping Avenue at least through 1923.
Costumes: 1922 *Plantation Revue*

Helen Johnson

Helen Johnson, born August 1, 1906 in New York City made movies using both her given name and Judith Wood. As Helen Johnson, she appeared in *Sin Takes a Holiday, It Pays to Advertise* and *Children of Pleasure* among others. As Judith Wood, mainly after 1930, she appeared in *The Road to Reno, Girls about Town, Looking for Trouble* and others. She also designed costumes under both names. Married at one time to P. C. Wren, a British diplomat, she spent the majority of her life and career in Hollywood.
Costumes: 1928 *The International*

Alfred Cheney Johnston

As a lighting designer, Alfred Cheney Johnston was active on Broadway in the late 1930s. He was the official photographer for Florenz Ziegfeld, Jr. from 1917 to 1931 and is best known for his photos of various editions of *Ziegfeld Follies*, especially studio shots of showgirls. He also photographed advertising and industrial layouts and

Figure 6: Bernard Johnson: *Eubie*: Costume rendering for Act I finale: "Jazz." By permission, Billy Rose Theatre Collection, The New York Public Library for the Performing Arts, Astor, Lenox and Tilden Foundations. Photograph by Jan Juracek.

published *Enchanting Beauty*, a 1937 photographic study of the human figure, issued by Swan Publications in New York. Alfred Cheney Johnston, Inc., a commercial photography studio, was located at 114 E. 47th Street City. Johnston also had a studio at his home in Oxford, Connecticut. Born in 1884, he died in Ansonia, Connecticut on April 19, 1971 at age 87.

Lights: 1937 *Sea Legs*

Mabel E. Johnston

Mabel E. Johnston was active on Broadway during the 1920s. In 1940 she was elected Vice President of the Theatrical Costume Designers Union division of United Scenic Artists.

Costumes: 1923 *Little Jessie James*; *Sun Showers*; *Vanities of 1923*†; *White Cargo* (Miss Pierce's costumes) **1924** *The Grab Bag*†; *Moonlight*; *Music Box Revue*† ("Rock-a-Bye-Baby") **1925** *Puzzles of 1925*† **1926** *Criss Cross*† (Cinderella, Etc.) **1927** *Allez-Oop*; *Lucky*; *Merry Malones*† (Women's costumes); *Yours Truly* **1928** *Animal Crackers*; *Box Seats*†; *Cross My Heart*; *Earl Carroll's Vanities*†; *Veils*; *Yours Truly* **1929** *Great Day*; *Woof, Woof* **1933** *Murder at the Vanities*† (Miss Baclanova's Gown and last costume) **1941** *My Fair Ladies* (Costume Supervisor)

Virginia Johnston

Virginia Johnston supervised the set design for a 1960 Broadway production.

Sets: 1960 *The World of Carl Sandburg*

Anna Hill Johnstone

Anna Hill (Johnnie) Johnstone was born April 7, 1913 in Greenville, South Carolina, daughter of Albert S. and Anna Watkins Johnstone. She began designing costumes in the mid-1930s while at Columbia University and in the following years designed numerous plays on Broadway and on the East Coast. In the late 1940s she began designing movies and did several, including *On the Waterfront*, *Splendor in the Grass*, *The Verdict*, *Seprico*, *The Last Tycoon* and *East of Eden*. She was nominated for Academy Awards for *The Godfather* in 1972 and *Ragtime* in 1981. Known in private life as Mrs.

Anna Johnstone Robinson, she died on October 16, 1992 at age 79 in Lenox, Massachusetts.

Costumes: 1934 *And Be My Love*† (as: Johnnis Johnstone: Costumes supervised) **1944** *That Old Devil* (as: Johnnie Johnstone) **1945** *And Be My Love* (as: Johnnie Johnstone) **1946** *Temper the Wind* **1947** *For Love or Money* **1949** *Lost in the Stars* **1950** *Bell, Book and Candle*†; *The Country Girl*; *The Curious Savage*† **1951** *The Autumn Garden* **1952** *Flight into Egypt* **1953** *The Children's Hour*; *Tea and Sympathy* (Clothes) **1954** *All Summer Long* (Clothes); *The Tender Trap* **1957** *The Egghead*; *The Hidden River*; *The Sin of Pat Muldoon* **1958** *The Man in the Dog Suit*; *Whoop-Up* **1959** *Sweet Bird of Youth*†; *Triple Play* **1960** *One More River* **1964** *After the Fall* **1966** *The Investigation* **1967** *A Warm Body*

Johnnie Johnstone

See Anna Hill Johnstone.

Edouard Jonas

Edouard (Edovard) Léon Jonas, who designed the set in 1926 for a Broadway show, was born in France in 1883. After studying painting and working for a time in the theater, his career was devoted to art and antiques, mainly in France. In the early 1930s, he maintained an American location to display and sell his acquisitions, "Edouard Jonas of Paris, Inc.," devoted to pictures and engraving, located at 9 East 56th Street in New York City. As the curator, he wrote the catalogue copy for a 1930 exhibition of the collection at the Museum Cognacq-Jay in Paris. Jonas died in France in 1961

Sets: 1926 *Mozart*

Mark Jonathan

Mark Jonathan was born in London. He has been designing lighting for plays, operas, ballets, and musicals since 1973. He was based at Glyndebourne Opera beginning in 1978 and since 1993 has been head of lighting at the Royal National Theatre in London. At the RNT his designs include *Honk!*, *Skylight*, *The Waiting Room* and *Titus Andronicus*. His designs include the musicals *Peggy Sue Got Married*, *Sweet Charity* and *Marlene* in London's West

End, and many plays for British theater companies. Designs for ballet include extensive work for the Birmingham Royal Ballet including the world premieres of *Far From the Madding Crowd, The Protecting Veil, The Season,* and *Power.* At Stuttgart Ballet, he designed *Landschaft und Errinerung* and *Exilium.* His opera designs have been seen at Los Angeles Opera, as well as in Britain, France, Italy, Belgium, and Israel. His designs were part of the British entry at the 1999 Prague Quadrennial.
Lights: 1999 *Marlene*

Jones and Erwin

Jones and Erwin collaborated on the set design for a Broadway play in 1928. Frederick W. Jones III and Hobart S. Erwin were partners in Jones & Erwin, interior decorators located at 729 Madison Avenue in 1927. In 1931 the directors of the company (which had moved to 15 East 57th Street) were Hobart S. Erwin, William J. Muldowney and Adolph M. Dick. As was common in the era, interior decorators sometimes supplied settings for contemporary productions and received credit in the playbill. Frederick W. Jones III also designed productions under his own name and additional information is available under his entry in this book.
Sets: 1928 *The Phantom Lover*

Alexander Jones

Alexander Jones designed costumes on Broadway between 1937 and 1940. A graduate of the Yale School of Drama, he was involved with the W.P.A. Federal Theatre Project from 1936-1938.
Costumes: 1937 *Swing It†* **1938** *Life and Death of an American; On the Rocks* (Gowns for "Lady in Grey") **1940** *Morning Star*

Bassett Jones

Bassett Jones was born in New Brighton, Staten Island on February 6, 1877 and died at the age of 82 on January 25, 1960. He studied engineering at the Stevens and Massachusetts Institutes of Technology and spent his life principally designing elevators and architectural lighting systems. He designed lights for the New York World's Fair, the Empire State Building, the Chrysler Building, and the Irving Trust Company. Bassett Jones also made several contributions to stage lighting, creating the first floodlight units and devising other special equipment. He supervised stage lighting for many of Maude Adams' plays including *Peter Pan* in 1912.
Sets: 1925 *Cain†*
Costumes: 1925 *Cain†*
Lights: 1912 *Peter Pan* **1925** *Cain*

Captain H. Oaks Jones

Captain H. Oaks Jones designed a Broadway play in 1930.
Costumes: 1930 *Marigold†*

Christine Jones

Scenic and costume designer Christine Jones graduated from Concordia University in Montreal and received her M.F.A. from New York University in 1992. Her credits for theater and opera are extensive and include productions at Glimmerglass Opera, the New York Shakespeare Festival, American Repertory Theatre, Williamstown Theatre Festival and the Jean Cocteau Repertory. Scenic designs at Hartford Stage include *Tartuffe* and *King Richard III.* Twenty-first century productions include *Nocturne* presented by New York Theatre Workshop together with American Repertory Theatre and *Bitterroot* at La MaMa, E.T.C.
Sets: 2000 *The Green Bird†*

Frederick W. Jones III

Frederick W. Jones III was active as a setting and occasional costume designer on Broadway throughout the 1920s. His sets were featured in the September 1923 issue of *Theatre Magazine.* He was, in addition, an interior decorator, associated with National Interior Decorators located at 2575 Broadway in New York City in 1922, and an actor. In 1927 he was associated with Jones & Erwin, interior decorators at 729 Madison Avenue. Jones occasionally designed in collaboration with Hobart S. Erwin.
Sets: 1923 *Dagmar; Jack and Jill* **1924** *The Man Who Ate the Popomack; Paolo*

and *Francesca* **1925** *Caesar and Cleopatra*; *Captain Jinks*; *Hamlet*; *Starlight*†
1926 *Shanghai* **1928** *Shanghai Gesture*; *The Unknown Warrior*
Costumes: **1923** *Jack and Jill*† (Colonial costumes and principal role)

Gary Jones

Gary Jones was born in Toledo, Ohio on February 24, 1947 and studied at Ohio University, the Fashion Institute of Technology and for one year at Hunter College. He worked at the New York Shakespeare Festival with Theoni V. Aldredge and Milo Morrow for ten years, beginning when he was nineteen. *Fashion*, which he designed at Ohio University was his debut as a costume designer. A busy and dedicated costume designer, Mr. Jones is a particularly active in film. He has been collaborating with Ann Roth since the late 1970s beginning as her assistant for the film *Hair*, followed by *Working Girl*, *Postcards from the Edge*, *Dave*, *The Bonfire of the Vanities* and many others. His responsibilities continued to increase, as did his delight in their work, and he became her partner. Working out of offices at the Costume Depot, together they designed *The Talented Mr. Ripley*, receiving nominations for both Academy Award and Costume Designers' Guild Awards. They also co-designed designed *The English Patient* among other films. Twenty-first century designs include costumes for the films *Heartbreakers* and *The Princess Diaries*.
Costumes: **1984** *Open Admissions*†

Maxine Jones

Maxine and Alexander Jones collaborated on the designs for a 1937 Broadway show.
Costumes: **1937** *Swing It*†

Robert Edmond Jones

Robert Edmond Jones, designer and producer, was born in Milton, New Hampshire on December 12, 1887 and began designing for the theater in 1911. He studied at Harvard and brought great originality of design and color to the theater, perhaps influenced by his admiration for Max Reinhardt.

While working on a pageant in Madison Square Garden he became acquainted with one of Reinhardt's artists, who invited him to Germany to see the producer's methods. The outbreak of war forced his return to America in 1915. Jones' designs for *The Man Who Married A Dumb Wife*, included at the last moment as a curtain raiser for *Androcles and the Lion*, are generally regarded as marking the beginning of the "New American Stagecraft." He was associated with Kenneth Macgowan and Eugene O'Neill in the production of many plays at the Greenwich Village Playhouse, where he directed and designed many of O'Neill's plays. A prolific designer, he had many productions to his credit, well beyond the list included here, especially in the areas of costumes and lights. He often controlled or supervised those elements without receiving credit for their actual design. He was art director for the opening production at Radio City Music Hall. His book, *The Dramatic Imagination*, is a classic. Robert Edmond Jones died on November 26, 1954. See Figure 7: Robert Edmond Jones: *The Jest*

Sets: **1915** *The Devil's Garden*; *Interior*; *The Man Who Married a Dumb Wife*; *Trilby* **1916** *Caliban by the Yellow Sands*; *Good Gracious, Annabelle*; *The Happy Ending* **1917** *The Deluge*; *Granny Maumee* (Also directed); *The Rescuing Angel*; *Rider of Dreams, The/ Granny Maumee/ Simon*; *A Successful Calamity* **1918** *Be Calm, Camilla*; *The Gentile Wife*; *Hedda Gabler*; *Redemption*; *The Wild Duck* **1919** *The Jest* **1920** *George Washington*†; *Samson and Delilah*; *The Tragedy of Richard III* **1921** *Anna Christie*; *The Claw*; *Daddy's Gone A-Hunting*; *The Idle Inn*; *Macbeth*; *The Mountain Man*; *Swords* **1922** *The Deluge*; *The Hairy Ape*†; *Hamlet*; *Romeo and Juliet*; *Rose Bernd*; *The S.S. Tenacity*; *Voltaire* **1923** *Hamlet*; *The Laughing Lady*; *Launzi*; *A Royal Fandango* **1924** *Desire under the Elms*; *Fashion*†; *George Dandin, or the Husband Confounded*†; *The Living Mask*; *The Saint*; *The Spook Sonata*†; *Welded* **1925** *Beyond*; *The Buccaneer*; *The Fountain*; *In a Garden*; *Love for Love*; *Michel Auclair*; *Trelawney*

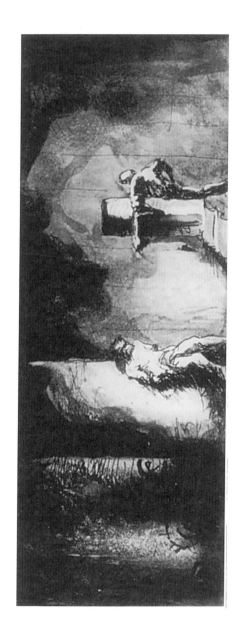

Figure 7: Robert Edmond Jones: *The Jest:* Set rendering, 1919. By permission, Billy Rose Theatre Collection, The New York Public Library for the Performing Arts, Astor, Lenox and Tilden Foundations. Photograph by Jan Juracek.

of the "Wells" 1926 The Great God Brown; The Jest; Love 'em and Leave 'em 1927 The Claw; The House of Women; Paris Bound; Trelawney of the "Wells" 1928 Holiday; Machinal; Martine; The Money Lender; Mr. Moneypenny; Salvation; These Days 1929 Becky Sharpe; The Channel Road; The Commodore Marries; Cross Roads; Ladies Leave; See Naples and Die; Serena Blandish; Week-End 1930 Children of Darkness; The Green Pastures; Rebound; Roadside 1931 Camille; The Lady with a Lamp; Mourning Becomes Electra; The Passing Present 1932 Camille; Lucrece; Mourning Becomes Electra; Night over Taos 1933 Ah, Wilderness!; The Green Bay Tree; Mary of Scotland; Nine Pine Street 1934 Dark Victory; Joyous Season 1935 Green Pastures 1937 Othello 1938 The Devil and Daniel Webster; Everywhere I Roam; The Seagull; Susanna, Don't You Cry 1939 Kindred; The Philadelphia Story; Summer Night 1940 Juno and the Paycock; Love for Love 1942 Without Love 1943 Othello 1944 Helen Goes to Troy; Jackpot† 1946 The Iceman Cometh; Lute Song 1950 The Enchanted 1951 Green Pastures

Costumes: 1915 The Devil's Garden; The Man Who Married a Dumb Wife 1916 Caliban by the Yellow Sands (Also properties) 1917 Granny Maumee (Also directed); Rider of Dreams, The/ Granny Maumee/ Simon 1920 George Washington†; The Tragedy of Richard III 1921 Macbeth†; Swords 1922 Hamlet; Romeo and Juliet; Voltaire (Women's costumes) 1923 Hamlet; Launzi 1924 Fashion†; George Dandin, or the Husband Confounded†; The Living Mask; The Spook Sonata; Welded 1925 Beyond; The Buccaneer; The Fountain; Love for Love†; Trelawney of the "Wells" 1926 The Great God Brown; The Jest; Little Eyolf (Miss Eames' and Miss Gilmore's costumes) 1927 The House of Women (Gowns) 1928 Martine; Mr. Moneypenny† 1929 Becky Sharpe (Gowns); The Channel Road; See Naples and Die† 1930 Children of Darkness 1931 Camille; Mourning Becomes Electra; The Passing Present 1932 Lucrece; Mourning Becomes Electra; Night over Taos 1933 Mary of Scotland; Nine Pine Street 1935 Green Pastures 1937 Othello 1938 The Devil and

Daniel Webster; Everywhere I Roam; The Seagull; Susanna, Don't You Cry 1939 Summer Night 1942 Without Love 1943 Othello 1946 The Iceman Cometh; Lute Song† 1950 The Enchanted 1951 Green Pastures

Lights: 1922 His Honor the Mayor 1924 The Spook Sonata; Welded 1925 Beyond; The Buccaneer; Trelawney of the "Wells" 1926 The Jest 1931 Camille; The Passing Present 1933 Mary of Scotland 1935 Green Pastures 1938 The Devil and Daniel Webster; Susanna, Don't You Cry 1939 Summer Night 1940 Romeo and Juliet 1942 Without Love 1943 Othello 1944 Helen Goes to Troy 1946 The Iceman Cometh; Lute Song

Steven Jones

During Steven Jones' brief life he was involved with costumes for many different forms of entertainment, including ice capades, the circus, New York musicals, and film. He was born January 9, 1962 and studied at New York University. While there, he designed a children's show, Starblast that toured to locations including the White House. Design credits include costumes for Olympus on my Mind off-Broadway, the film Marionettes, Incorporated and musicals at the Playhouse in the Park in Cincinnati and Music Theatre in Wichita, Kansas. He was an assistant designer for Ringling Bros. and Barnum & Bailey Circus, Walt Disney's World on Ice, and also for Starlight Express and My One and Only on Broadway. Steven Jones died in New York City at age 28, on April 28, 1991, a victim of AIDS.

Costumes: 1988 Romance/Romance

Gerard Jongerius

Gerald Jongerius designed one set in 1982 on Broadway. The production, a one-man-show performed by Dutch theater-artist Herman van Veen, was successful in Europe and the United Kingdom before transferring to New York. It was directed by Michel Lafaille who conceived it with the Mr. van Veen.

Sets: 1982 Herman Van Veen: All of Him

Jonel Jorgulesco

Jonel Jorgulesco designed costumes and sets on Broadway in 1932. He was born in Berlin on August 18, 1904 and studied stage design in Berlin and Frankfurt. During the 1920s he was resident designer for the Boston Repertory Theatre, and in the 1930s he designed for the Broadway stage and created many settings for the Metropolitan Opera including *Don Pasquale, Die Walküre, La Traviata* and *La Nozze di Figaro*. A contributor to several books about scenic design, Mr. Jorgulesco served as art director for the Young & Rubicon advertising agency and design consultant for various companies. In 1960 he moved to St. Thomas, Virgin Islands to pursue a career in architectural design. He died in St. Thomas on November 7, 1966.
Sets: 1932 *Child of Manhattan; Too True to Be Good*
Costumes: 1932 *Too True to Be Good*

Joseph

Joseph was a small exclusive shop that initially provided costumers with accessories, mainly custom-made or ready-to-wear hats. Located at 632 Fifth Avenue, New York, the advertisements in playbills of the time invariably began with a cursive "Joseph, Fifth Avenue" signature and made much of being opposite St. Patrick's Cathedral. By 1910, Joseph was offering gowns to walk-in, private and theatrical customers and in the mid-teens, the shop relocated to 2 West 57th Street. In the early 1920s, Paul Poiret's designs were available through Joseph.
Sets: 1911 *Marriage a La Carte* (Miss Ryan's hats and gowns)
Costumes: 1900 *Florodora* **1901** *The Brixton Burglary* **1902** *The Silver Slipper*† (Hats) **1906** *The Social Whirl*† (Hats) **1910** *The Girl and the Kaiser*†; *Keeping Up Appearances; We Can't Be As Bad As All That* **1911** *The Balkan Princess*† (Miss Gunning's and Miss Whitmore's Act II gowns); *The Enchantress*† (Miss Gordon's Act II dresses); *Gaby* (Miss Clifford's gowns); *Hell* (Miss Clifford's gowns); *Over Night; Temptations* (Miss Clifford's gowns) **1913** *The Family Cupboard; Mlle. Modiste*† (Miss Scheff's

hats and dresses) **1914** *Apartment 12-K* (Gowns); *Experience*†; *The Passing Show of 1914*† **1921** *March Hares*

Peter Joseph

Peter Joseph designed costumes and sets on Broadway in 1965 and 1966. His credits include many summer musicals for the producers Guber, Ford and Gross, and headliners' costumes in clubs. Mr. Joseph has designed the national tours of *Fiorello!* and *I Married an Angel* and for television, including *The Hollywood Palace*. He should not be confused with the British painter nor the businessman and gallery owner who have the same name.
Costumes: 1965 *Catch Me If You Can* **1966** *A Joyful Noise*

James Leonard Joy

James Leonard Joy was born in Detroit, Michigan in 1949 and received a B.A. in theater from the University of Michigan. Instead of attending law school as he originally planned, he received an M.F.A. at Carnegie Mellon University in theatrical design. He spent three years as an assistant to Ben Edwards and three years as an assistant to José Varona. His professional career began at the Chautauqua Opera. He has extensive regional theater experience, including productions during lengthy associations with the Goodspeed Opera, Huntington Theatre, Missouri Repertory Theatre, Kansas City Lyric Opera, Cincinnati Playhouse, Arena Stage. and Alliance Theatre. He has designed extensively for the Disney theme parks in Orlando, Florida and Paris. Honors include the 1995 Lucille Lortel Award, and 1996 Theatre L.A. Ovation Awards for *Camping with Henry and Tom*. Twenty-first century scenic designs include *Blue* at the Gramercy Theatre.
Sets: 1981 *Ned and Jack* **1985** *Take Me Along* **1990** *Peter Pan* **1991** *Peter Pan*† (Neverland scenery) **1992** *Regina* **1996** *State Fair* **1997** *Play On!*

Emmett Joyce

Emmett Joyce, a fashion designer and retailer, designed costumes on Broadway in the 1930s. He operated his own business, Emmett Joyce, Inc., and designed for many department stores and costume houses, including Hattie Carnegie and Saks Fifth Avenue. He died at age 72 in 1972.

Costumes: **1918** *Someone in the House*† **1930** *Pagan Lady* (Miss Ulric's costumes) **1933** *Forsaking All Others*† (Miss Hanley's clothes); *A Good Woman, Poor Thing*† (Miss Purcell's and Miss Hanley's costumes)

Judith

Judith designed costumes for a play in 1967.

Costumes: **1967** *Sing, Israel, Sing*

Alexander Julian

Fashion, furniture and costume designer Alexander Julian, born February 8, 1948 is a native of North Carolina, who graduated from the University of North Carolina at Chapel Hill. Known for his use of color and creative ways of updating traditional styles, he won the first of five Coty Awards in 1977, two years after moving to New York. He is the youngest designer to ever win that honor and be named to the Coty Hall of Fame. Additional theater-related designs include costumes for the leading men in Robert Altman's *The Player* in 1992. He has designed uniforms for sports teams, including the uniforms for the men's basketball team at UNC-Chapel Hill, the Charlotte Hornets, and the Newman Haas car racing team.

Costumes: **1990** *An Evening with Harry Connick, Jr. and His Orchestra* (Wardrobe)

Madame Julie

Madame Julie was the name used by Louis M. Julie, the proprietor of a custom shop, when he furnished gowns and cloaks to theatrical and private customers during the first two decades of the twentieth century. Julie's retail shop, at 261 Greene Street in New York, was popular because of its' unique styles.

Costumes: **1912** *Bachelors and Benedicts*; *The Trial Marriage* (Miss Ware's gowns); *The Wall Street Girl*† (Show girl gowns) **1913** *The Ghost Breaker*; *The Girl and the Pennant*; *Nearly Married* (Miss Grey's gowns) **1914** *Kick In* (Miss Grey's gowns); *Twin Beds*† (Gowns); *Under Cover* (Gowns); *What Would You Do?* (Miss Barriscale's gowns) **1915** *Common Clay*

Juliet

Juliet (Juliet Delf) was a comedienne and mimic who was adept at satirizing her fellow performers, including Nazimova. She appeared in musical revues in the 1920s and 1930s and died in New York on March 24, 1962 at the age of 74.

Costumes: **1925** *George White's Scandals*† (Additional costumes)

Philipp Jung

Philipp Jung was born on June 10, 1949 in Cleveland, Ohio and studied at Ohio University, the Yale School of Drama (M.F.A. 1983) and in the English National Opera Design Program. An admirer of the creativity of Boris Aronson, his own designs were honored with the English Arts Council Design Bursary. Off-Broadway credits included *The Lisbon Traviata*, *Closer Than Ever*, *It's a Man's World* and *The Dark at the Top of the Stairs*. Jung, who was on the faculty of California Polytechnic Institute in San Luis Obispo from 1990 to 1992, died on December 10, 1992, at age 43.

Sets: **1979** *The Madwoman of Central Park West* **1989** *Eastern Standard*; *Mastergate*

Madame Valentina Kachouba

Madame Valentina Kachouba designed costumes for a play in 1933.

Costumes: **1933** *Saint Wench*

Peter Kaczorowski

Lighting designer Peter Kaczorowski was born in Buffalo, New York on September 22, 1956 and earned his undergraduate degree Magna Cum Laude (Theatre/English) from the State University of New York at Geneseo in 1978 after which he assisted designers including John Bury, Beverly Emmons, Craig Miller, Tom Skelton, Neil Peter Jampolis and Andy Phillips. He designs regularly on Broadway and off, for resident companies such as the Roundabout Theatre, Lincoln Center Theatre, Encores!, and Manhattan Theatre Club, as well as for most leading regional theaters and opera companies in the United States. European credits include productions at Royal Opera Covent Garden, Scottish Opera, Bonn State Opera, Opera North, and the Edinburgh Festival. Among the productions that established his career are *La Clemenza di Tito* for the Houston Grand Opera, *The Loman Family Picnic* at Manhattan Theatre Club, *Grandchild of Kings* at the Irish Repertory Theatre, and *Lohengrin* for the Seattle Opera. He is the recipient of the Tony, Drama Desk, Outer Critics Circle, and Hewes Design Awards. Twenty-first century credits include *Thou Shalt Not* in the 2001-2002 Broadway season and *Kiss Me, Kate* in London's West End.

Lights: **1991** *The Homecoming* **1992** *The Show-Off*; *A Small Family Business* **1993** *Candida*; *She Loves Me* **1994** *Picnic* **1995** *Company*; *On the Waterfront*; *The Play's the Thing* **1997** *Jackie*; *Steel Pier*; *Three Sisters* **1998** *Ah, Wilderness!*; *Honour* **1999** *Kiss Me Kate*; *The Rainmaker* **2000** *Contact*; *The Music Man* **2001** *The Producers*

Melanie Kahane

Melanie Kahane, an interior and industrial designer, was born in New York on November 26, 1910. Her father, an architect and engineer, introduced her to architecture and as a child she made clothing and furniture for her dolls. She studied costume design and commercial illustration at Parsons School of Design, and did some theatrical designing. After a year in Paris, she worked as an illustrator, Broadway costume designer and sketch artist before opening her own business in 1936, and devoting herself to interior decoration and design. An author and lecturer she was active in many organizations related to interior design, and entered the Interior Design Hall of Fame in 1985. Married to Ben Grauer, an NBC-TV news broadcaster, she died at age 78 in December 1988 in New York City.

Costumes: **1934** *A Roman Servant*†

Theodore Kahn

Theodore Kahn was a set designer who received credit for five plays between 1928 and 1934 on the Broadway stage. The Theodore Kahn Scenic Studio was located at 155 West 29th Street, New York City in 1927.

Sets: **1928** *The K Guy* **1930** *Brown Buddies*† **1931** *Sugar Hill* **1932** *The Barrister* **1934** *Good-Bye Please*†

Robert Kalloch

Robert Kalloch (Kallick) was born on January 13, 1893 in New York City and studied at the New York School of Fine and Applied Art. He worked for Lucile, Ltd. as a sketch artist in the early teens and while there began designing gowns for Irene Castle, Marie Dressler and Anna Pavlova. In the early 1930s he moved to California to work for Columbia Pictures where his contemporary designs were in demand by stars including Irene Dunne, Fay Wray and Grace Moore among others. His many films include *It Happened One Night*, *Mr. Smith Goes to Washington*, *Blondie*, *His Girl Friday*, *Panama Hattie*, and *Mrs. Miniver* which he co-designed with Gile Steele. He died in Hollywood, California on October 19, 1947.

Costumes: **1914** *A Mix-Up* (Miss Dressler's costumes)

Myer Kanin

Myer Kanin received credit for a scenic design on Broadway in 1932 through his scenic studio. An artist, his studio was located at 1236 Boynton Avenue in New York in the early 1930s. His play, *The Willoughbys*, written in collaboration with Harry Ingram, was published in 1938.

Sets: **1932** *Blackberries of 1932*†

Ruth Kanin

Ruth Kanin (Ruth Kanin Aronson) was born January 5, 1920 in Detroit, Michigan. She attended Immaculate Heart College and worked in New York City as a costume designer between 1946 and 1960. She is the sister of writer/producer Garson Kanin. She left the theater business to pursue other interests, including family therapy and teaching psychology, in Los

Angeles. Ruth Kanin is also the author of *Write the Story of Your Life*. a how-to book which grew out of her doctoral research and of *Eat! Eat!* a cookbook containing recopies for European/Jewish cuisines.

Costumes: 1946 *Born Yesterday*; *Years Ago*† (as: Ruth Kanin Aronson: Costume Supervisor)

George Kanlan

George Kanlan designed scenery on Broadway in 1911.

Sets: 1911 *The Three Lights*

Jason Kantrowitz

Jason Kantrowitz made his New York debut as a lighting designer with the opening of *Irene Worth: Letters of Love* at the Roundabout Theatre in 1979. He attended Carnegie Mellon University and held an apprenticeship at the National Opera Institute from 1979 to 1980. He was born on May 31, 1957 in Glens Falls, New York and has accumulated many credits off-Broadway, in regional theaters and for national tours. Since 1980 he has been associated with lighting designer Ken Billington, initially as an assistant, then as an associate and subsequently as co-designer. He has many credits as an industrial and architectural lighting designer, and also produces live special events, including *2001: An Opera Odyssey*, a fund raiser for Opera Pacific, and events for The National Geographic Society, Alta Vista, Maryland Public Television, and others. Twenty-first century designs include *The Syringa Tree*.

Lights: 1989 *Starmites*; *Tru*† **1993** *Radio City Easter Show*† **1994** *Radio City Easter Show*† **1995** *Radio City Christmas Spectacular*†; *Radio City Easter Show*† **1996** *Radio City Christmas Spectacular*†; *Radio City Spring Spectacular*† **1997** *Radio City Christmas Spectacular*†; *Radio City Spring Spectacular*† **1998** *Radio City Christmas Spectacular*† **1999** *Dame Edna*

Pavel Kaplevich

Russian designer Pavel Kaplevich collaborated with Peter Kirilov on the scenery for a Broadway show in 1997. Produced by the Sovremennik Theatre, this new version of *The Cherry Orchard* had an American debut in 1997 and was subsequently performed in Moscow the following year. Among Kaplevich's credits for movies are production design *Limita* and costumes for *Mama*, both filmed in Russia. Twenty-first century designs in Moscow include sets and costumes for *Collection* by Harold Pinter and sets and costumes for *Wit Works Woe* by Oleg Menshikov, which was also performed in Riga.

Sets: 1997 *The Cherry Orchard*†

C. Karl

British costume and scenic designer C. (Charles) Karl, also known as C. Carl, flourished from 1885 to 1934. His designs, for costumes only, were seen in New York during the first decade of the twentieth century. Remarkably, he occasionally received program credit between the title and the cast list. His designs and models are the permanent collection of the University of Bristol and some of his creative work was published in the catalog *University of Bristol Theatre Collection, Part I* (1988).

Costumes: 1900 *Hamlet* **1903** *Dante* **1904** *Hamlet*; *Much Ado About Nothing*; *Romeo and Juliet* **1905** *The Merchant of Venice*; *Romeo and Juliet*; *The Taming of the Shrew*; *Twelfth Night* **1907** *The Merchant of Venice*; *Romeo and Juliet*

Margaret Karns

Margaret Karns designed costumes for a Broadway play in 1939. She was part of a group of students from Antioch College in Ohio who moved to New York in 1939 to attempt to reopen the old Provincetown Playhouse.

Costumes: 1939 *Steel*

Nat Karson

Nat Karson, a scenic designer and television producer, was Art Director at Radio City Music Hall from 1936 to 1943. He was born circa 1908 in Zurich, Switzerland, the son of an architect who was a refugee from Russia. At a young age he moved with his family to Chicago where he won an art prize in high school and a scholarship to the Art Institute of Chicago. His debut in the theater as a designer occurred with *Hamlet* as conceived by John Houseman and Orson Welles. In addition he designed the so-called "voodoo" *Macbeth* for Houseman and Welles for the Federal Theatre Project. He considered his design for the *Hamlet* produced in Elsinore, Denmark in 1949 a great personal success. His credits as a set designer were numerous and he occasionally contributed costumes and lighting as well. Mr. Karson also spent several years designing in London. He died at age 46 on September 29, 1954.

Sets: **1934** *Calling All Stars* **1935** *The Hook-Up* **1936** *Macbeth*; *White Man* **1937** *Arms for Venus* **1938** *Journeyman*; *Right This Way*; *Roosty* **1939** *The Hot Mikado* **1940** *Keep Off the Grass*; *Liliom* **1941** *High Kickers* **1943** *A Connecticut Yankee* **1946** *The Front Page*; *Nellie Bly* **1948** *Ballet Ballads*

Costumes: **1936** *Macbeth*; *White Man* **1939** *The Hot Mikado* **1940** *Keep Off the Grass*; *Liliom* **1946** *Nellie Bly* **1948** *Ballet Ballads*

Lights: **1943** *A Connecticut Yankee* **1946** *Nellie Bly* **1948** *Ballet Ballads*

Chrisi Karvonides

Chrisi Karvonides, also known as Chrisi Karvonides-Dushenko, received her B.F.A. from Emerson College where she began designing costumes, and her M.F.A. from Yale University. While at Yale, she designed *Sweeney Todd*, *The Cherry Orchard*, *Man Is Man* and other plays. The Fox-TV series *Circus* featured her designs as did *If Memory Serves* at the Pasadena Playhouse. She served as an assistant designer for major motion pictures including *A River Runs Through It* and *Batman II* while establishing her career as a costume designer for film. Her movie credits include *The One*, *The Glass House*, and *Beautiful*, all recent releases.

Costumes: **1992** *Two Trains Running*

John Kasarda

John Kasarda has numerous credits as a scenic designer in regional theaters such as The Philadelphia Drama Guild, where he has been resident designer; the American StageFestival in New Hampshire; the Goodman Theatre, and Center Stage. Off-Broadway credits include productions at The Public

Theatre and Manhattan Theatre Club. He has designed for opera, television, and the 1984 Louisiana World Exposition in New Orleans. His most extensive credits are as an assistant designer and assistant art director. He has worked on Broadway shows including *Chicago*, *Mack & Mabel*, *The Good Doctor*, *The Mooney Shapiro Songbook*, *Good* and *Seesaw*. He was art director for *The Verdict*, *Sabrina*, *Ransom*, *The Hard Way*, and *Great Expectations*. Born June 8, 1943 in Chicago, Illinois, he received his B.A. from the University of Iowa and his M.F.A. from Carnegie Institute of Technology. Honors include an Emmy Award in 1986 for art direction for *Death of a Salesman*.

Sets: **1983** *All's Well That Ends Well*† **1984** *Cyrano De Bergerac*†; *Much Ado About Nothing*†

Natasha Katz

Natasha Katz was born in New York City and attended Oberlin College where she studied set and lighting design and held an internship with Roger Morgan. While at Oberlin she began designing lights, starting with *Otherwise Engaged*, and later spent two summer seasons as the resident lighting designer for the Pittsburgh Civic Light Opera. She was associate to Jules Fisher for the national and world tours of *La Cage aux Folles* and has also assisted Marcia Madeira, Ken Billington, and David Segal. She has designed in regional theaters such as the Mark Taper Forum, the Great Lakes Shakespeare Festival, the Dallas Theatre Center, Trinity Repertory, and the Spoleto Festival, as well as in Australia and Europe, and designed lights for many off-Broadway theaters. Additional credits include concert acts for Shirley MacLaine, and others, as well as Tommy Tune's nightclub and concert act and the 1988 *Tommy Tune and the Manhattan Rhythm Kings* tour of Russia. She also designs architectural lighting, including projects for *EFX!* and for Niketown. Honors include the Tony Award for *Aida* and nominations for *Beauty and the Beast* and *Twelfth Night*. Twenty-first century credits include *Dance of Death* in the 2001-2001

Broadway season.

Lights: 1985 *Aren't We All?*; *Pack of Lies* 1986 *Honky Tonk Nights* 1987 *Breaking the Code* 1989 *Gypsy* 1990 *The Cemetery Club*; *Peter Pan*; *Shogun: The Musical* 1991 *Gypsy*; *Peter Pan* 1992 *Hamlet (Roundabout)*; *Someone Who'll Watch over Me* 1993 *A Grand Night for Singing*; *My Fair Lady* 1994 *Beauty and the Beast* 1996 *State Fair* 1997 *Barrymore*; *The Scarlet Pimpernel* 1998 *The Capeman*; *The Scarlet Pimpernel*; *Twelfth Night* 1999 *Ring 'Round the Moon* 2000 *Aida*; *Seussical the Musical*

Alice Kauser

Alice Kauser, theatrical agent and play broker, and sometimes a scenic designer, was born in the American consulate in Budapest where her father, Joseph Kauser, was a consular representative from the United States. Her mother was the opera singer Berta Gerster. She was educated in Europe and lived in Pensacola, Florida with her family before moving to New York City. Miss Kauser was a strong advocate to have plays written by American playwrights produced abroad, in part because she was able to draw upon her mother's contacts and those of her godfather, Franz Liszt. Alice Kauser, who maintained offices at 1432 Broadway, died at age 73 on September 9, 1945.

Sets: 1912 *The High Road*† (Interior decoration)

Ulla Kazanova

Ulla Kazanova, an actress born in Stockholm, Sweden supervised the costumes for a play on Broadway in 1935. Her first appearance on stage in the U.S. was as the Baroness in *First Lady* by George S. Kaufman. She died on March 22, 1985 at age 83.

Costumes: 1935 *If a Body* (Miss Locke's costumes, supervisor)

Rose Keane

Rose Keane, an actress originally from Kansas City, studied at the American Academy of Art and supervised costumes for Broadway shows between 1927 and 1930. She appeared on stage in a number of shows including *Celebrity*, *The Monkey Talks*, and *Red Rust*. In 1930, she became the first

of theatrical producer Herman Shumlin's three wives. Shumlin (1898-1979) directed most of the original productions of Lillian Hellman's plays, including *Watch on the Rhine* and *The Little Foxes* as well as many hits, among them *The Corn is Green*, *Inherit the Wind*, *The Deputy* and *The Male Animal*.

Costumes: 1927 *Celebrity* (Costume Supervisor) 1930 *Blind Mice* (Costume Supervisor)

Frances Keating

Frances Keating, an interior decorator, designed one set in 1929 on Broadway. She resided at 215 West 51st Street in 1924 and at 150 East 54th Street in 1932.

Sets: 1929 *The Dragon*

John William Keck

World Wide Christmas was John William Keck's debut as Art Director at Radio City Music Hall in 1973. He subsequently designed numerous productions at Radio City including rock concerts for major performers. He was born in New York City on December 4, 1929, son of Charles Keck, a sculptor, and studied at the High School of Music and Art and the Pratt Institute. He began his career in the theater as a scenic artist for McDonald-Stevens and Nolan Scenery Studios. His first position after joining United Scenic Artists was as a scenic artist for a production at Radio City Music Hall in 1954, after which he joined Nolan Brothers Scenic Studios where he remained until 1973. Between 1973 and 1980, he was Art Director for Radio City Music Hall, and from 1980 until 1997, was a scene painter and sculptor at the Metropolitan Opera. One of the publishers of the *New York Theatrical Sourcebook* from 1995 to 2000, he died on April 3, 2001.

Sets: 1979 *Snow White and the Seven Dwarfs* 1980 *It's Spring*; *A Rockette Spectacular with Ginger Rogers*

Madame Keeler

Katherine Southwick Keeler designed costumes for two Broadway plays, one in 1917 and another in 1924, as Madame Keeler. An artist, illustrator, and author of children's books, she was born Katherine Southwick on January 9, 1887 in Buxton, Maine. After study at the Chicago Academy of Fine Art and the Art Institute of Chicago, she opened a studio at 221 West 11th Street in New York City. Married to painter R. Burton Keeler, she exhibited widely. Her books include *Children's Zoo, Dog Days* and between 1946 and 1949, a series about Meadow Brook Farm. She died in 1968, a resident of Fairfield, Connecticut.

Costumes: 1917 *Canary Cottage*† **1924** *Topsy and Eva*

M. L. Keen

M.L. Keen was costume designer for a play on Broadway in 1931.

Costumes: 1931 *Tom Sawyer/ Treasure Island*

William Kellam

William Kellam founded a scenic studio in 1890, the William Kellam Company at 35 New Chambers Street which executed scenery for many designers. He also designed under his own name, and resided at 412 Pearl Street His son, William Kellam, Jr., who succeeded him in the family business in 1934, also designed scenery for Broadway shows.

Sets: 1900 *Caleb West*† (Design and construction) **1903** *The Jersey Lily*† (Designed and built) **1908** *Three Twins*† **1913** *The Spiritualist*† (Designed and built)

William Kellam, Jr.

William Kellam, Jr. began working at age fourteen building stage scenery for the company his father founded in 1890, the William Kellam Company. He left the business only once (for service in World War I) and took over the company in 1934 when his father retired. The William Kellam Company built sets for Group Theatre productions, *Life With Father*, and many productions designed by Howard Bay. When he died on April 22, 1944, several of the productions running on Broadway had been constructed by his scenic studio: *Twentieth Century, Subway Express, Room Service*, and *Earl Carroll's Vanities*.

Sets: 1943 *The Patriots*†

Bill Kellard

Costume designer Bill Kellard has received two Daytime Emmy Awards for his designs for *Sesame Street* during his long association with the series. His other television credits include the daytime dramas *Ryan's Hope* and *Search for Tomorrow* for which he has also been honored with Emmy nominations and awards. He designed national tours of *Show Boat, Guys and Dolls*, and *Shenandoah* among others. His collaborations with Bill Irwin, who created *Fool Moon*, also include *A Flea in Her Ear*.

Costumes: 1993 *Fool Moon* **1995** *Fool Moon* **1998** *Fool Moon*

Marjorie Bradley Kellogg

Marjorie Bradley Kellogg is a creative, prolific designer of sets whose credits include productions for major regional theaters, on and off-Broadway, films, and television. She has received numerous honors: the Los Angeles Drama Logue Award in 1988 for *Babbitt* and in 1991 for *Pirates*, the Boston Theatre Critics Circle Best Design Award, the 1983 American Council on the Arts Young Artists Award, the 1994 Michael Merritt Award for Excellence in Design and Collaboration, and the 1995 Mary L. Murphy Award, among others. She was born in Cambridge, Massachusetts on August 30, 1946, the daughter of Jarvis Phillips and Bradley Langdon Kellogg. After receiving a Bachelor of Arts degree at Vassar College in 1967 and half a year in graduate school, she left formal education behind to learn design by assisting Ming Cho Lee. Since 1995 she has been on the faculty at Colgate University; before then she taught at Columbia and Princeton Universities. In addition to designing she has written several science fiction novels, including *Lear's Daughters* and *A Rumor of Angels*. Twenty-first century designs include *Thief River* for the Signature Theatre Company, *An Infinite Ache* at the Long Wharf Theatre, and *Two Sisters and a Piano* for the Oregon Shakespeare Festival.

Sets: 1974 *Where's Charley?* **1975** *Death of a Salesman* **1976** *The Poison*

Tree **1978** *The Best Little Whorehouse in Texas*; *Da* **1979** *Spokesong* **1981** *The Father* **1982** *The Best Little Whorehouse in Texas*; *Present Laughter*; *Solomon's Child*; *Steaming* **1983** *American Buffalo*; *Heartbreak House*; *The Misanthrope*; *Moose Murders* **1985** *Joe Egg*; *Requiem for a Heavyweight* **1986** *Arsenic and Old Lace* **1987** *A Month of Sundays* **1991** *Lucifer's Child*; *On Borrowed Time* **1992** *The Seagull* **1993** *Any Given Day*; *Saint Joan*; *Three Men on a Horse*

Robert Kellogg

Robert Kellogg designed the lighting for a Broadway production in 1973. In the early 1970s he worked as an assistant to Martin Aronstein at the New York Shakespeare Festival and has also worked as an actor.

Lights: 1973 *Here Are Ladies†*

Jen Kelly

Jen Kelly, who was born in 1960 in Derry, Ireland, is both a costume and fashion designer. He studied at the College of Design and Marketing and then majored in theater design at the National College of Art and Design, where he graduated. He has designed extensively for theater, opera and television in the United Kingdom, and in 1995 showed his first collection of haute couture. His line of clothing, displayed originally in a studio in Molesworth Street and later from 50 North Great George Street in Dublin, is available to private and retail clients in Dublin, New York, and Japan. Among his customers are Jean Kennedy Smith, Enya, Roma Downey, and former Irish President Mary Robinson.

Costumes: 1996 *Riverdance*; *Riverdance - The Show* **1997** *Riverdance* **1998** *Riverdance†* **2000** *Riverdance on Broadway†*

Lloyd Kelly

Lloyd Kelly created lighting designs for a Broadway production in the mid-1920s. He should not be confused with the portrait and landscape artist.

Lights: 1925 *Princess Ida*

Robert Kelly

Robert Kelly was a lighting designer in 1962 on Broadway. He has also worked as an art director for television, including the series *Laugh-In* and specials for Shirley MacLaine and Goldie Hawn. He was unit manager for broadcasts of the 1988 Summer Olympics.

Sets: 1962 *The Egg*

Lindsay Kemp

Lindsay Kemp, who was born and raised in Bradford, England, studied art, mime, and ballet in London, and also studied mime with Marcel Marceau. He appeared with the Charles Weidman Dance Company and in 1964 formed the Dance Mime Company. *Flowers* – a play which he devised, directed and designed – was originally done at Edinburgh's Traverse Theatre, later moving to the Regent Theatre in London before arriving in New York City in 1974. He has spent most of his life away from his native England, living and working for long periods in Rome, Jerusalem, and California while creating imaginative interpretations of classics and inventing new works. Recent credits include his versions of *Alice* (after Lewis Carroll) in Jerusalem in 1989, *A Midsummer Night's Dream* at the Beersheba Municipal Theatre in 1995, *Cinderella: A Gothic Operetta* at Sadler's Wells as part of the London International Mime Festival in 1995, and *Variete* which toured England in 1996.

Sets: 1974 *Flowers*

Costumes: 1974 *Flowers* (Also directed)

Kennel and Entwistle

Louis Kennel and Robert C. Entwistle designed settings for productions on Broadway between 1919 and 1931. Entwistle worked primarily as a painter and as an electrician and Louis Kennel as a scenic designer and builder. For additional information and individual credits see the entries under their names.

Sets: 1919 *The Phantom Legion* **1920** *The Skin Game* **1922** *The Nest*; *Swifty* **1927** *Lady Do* **1931** *Savage Rhythm*

Lights: 1920 *The Skin Game* **1922** *The Nest* **1927** *Lady Do*

Louis Kennel

Louis Kennel had Broadway credits as a costume and lighting designer, but his major activity in the theater was as a scenic designer. He was born in North Bergen, New Jersey on May 7, 1886 and studied painting with George Bridgman, Charles Graham, Ernest Gros, and William Lippincott. In 1940 he brought together theater technicians and director Royce Emerson into Louis Kennel, Inc. to produce and support play production by other producers. His primary business, however, was Louis Kennel Scenic Studios, 1427 44th Street in North Bergen, New Jersey, specializing in "Designing, Building and Painting for Theatre and T.V." His solo credits range from the twenties through the fifties. He also designed in collaboration with Robert C. Entwistle through "Kennel and Entwistle" from 1919 to 1931, and in collaboration with Rollo Peters through "Peters and Kennel" in 1918. Louis Kennel died in September 1975.

Sets: 1924 *Leah Kleschna*† 1926 *Hangman's House*; *One Man's Woman* 1928 *Falstaff* 1930 *Apron Strings*; *The Plutocrat*; *That's Gratitude*; *Those We Love* 1932 *The Little Black Book* 1934 *Moor Born*; *Order Please*; *Re-Echo* 1935 *Moon over Mulberry Street* 1936 *Black Widow*; *Halloween* 1937 *London Assurance* 1938 *Day in the Sun*; *Don't Throw Glass Houses* 1940 *Horse Fever* 1941 *Brother Cain*; *First Stop to Heaven* 1947 *The Magic Touch* 1949 *Anybody Home*; *Twelfth Night* 1951 *Springtime Folly*; *Springtime for Henry*† 1957 *Waiting for Godot*

Costumes: 1934 *Re-Echo* (Production design) 1949 *Anybody Home* (Costume Supervisor); *Twelfth Night*

Lights: 1949 *Anybody Home*

Frances Kenny

Frances Kenny has designed costumes for many theaters on the West Coast, including the Intiman Theatre, the Oregon Shakespeare Festival, San Jose and Berkeley Repertory Theatres, A.C.T., and the Mark Taper Forum. She has also designed dance for the Pat Graney Company. Twenty-first century credits include *New Patagonia* at the Leo K. Theatre in Seattle, and *The Mandrake Root* at Long Wharf Theatre.

Costumes: 1993 *The Kentucky Cycle*

Sean Kenny

Sean Kenny was an Irish designer and architect. He was born in Portoe, Tipperary, Ireland on December 23, 1932 and studied architecture in Dublin and with Frank Lloyd Wright. He designed settings for the first time in Hammersmith, England, but it was *The Hostage* in London which gave him his real entrance into the theater – thanks to the offer of work from an old Irish friend, Brendan Behan. His credits for settings, and occasionally costumes, were extensive in England. He also designed for film, television and night clubs. He continued to practice as an architect when his schedule allowed, especially for new theaters and theater renovations. Mr. Kenny, who received a Tony Award for the sets for *Oliver!* in 1963, died on June 11, 1973.

Sets: 1962 *Stop the World, I Want to Get Off* 1963 *Oliver!* 1965 *Oliver!*; *Pickwick*; *Roar of the Greasepaint – The Smell of the Crowd* 1973 *Here Are Ladies* 1984 *Oliver!*

Costumes: 1963 *Oliver!* (Designed by) 1965 *Oliver!* (Designed by) 1973 *Here Are Ladies* (Designed by) 1984 *Oliver!* (Designed by)

Lights: 1962 *Stop the World, I Want to Get Off* 1965 *Roar of the Greasepaint – The Smell of the Crowd* 1973 *Here Are Ladies*†

Carl Kent

Carl Kent, a set, lighting and costume designer and a native of New York City, was born on January 28, 1918. He studied at the Art Students League and the National Academy of Design. Also well known as a jazz pianist, he entered theater as a technical supervisor and assistant to scenic designer Harry Horner. Mr. Kent also designed sets for NBC-TV and CBS-TV and for ballet, including *The New Yorker* for Ballet Russe in 1940. Mr. Kent died in New York City on December 13, 1959.

Sets: 1940 *'Tis of Thee* 1944 *Career Angel* 1945 *Concert Varieties* 1949 *The Little Father of the Wilderness*

Costumes: 1945 *Concert Varieties*
Lights: 1944 *Peepshow*

Guy Kent

Guy Kent has designed costumes extensively for NBC-TV, including specials, plays, series, and variety shows as well as commercials. He was born in Ft. Leavenworth, Kansas on May 4, 1922 and attended West Point and American University in Washington, D.C. He studied design at the Corcoran Museum, Boston Museum of Fine Arts, Parsons School of Design, and the Art Students League. During service in World War II, he was costume director at the Weisbaden Opera House in Germany. He designed costumes on Broadway between 1949 and 1961. Guy Kent died on February 3, 1985
Costumes: 1949 *Magnolia Alley* 1953 *The Pink Elephant* 1956 *The Innkeeper*; *Uncle Willie*; *Wake Up, Darling* 1961 *Let It Ride!*; *Midgie Purvis*

Mrs. R. Kerner

Mrs. R. (Laura) Kerner contributed costume designs to Broadway shows in the teens. She sometimes designed costumes as Madame Kerner. A dressmaker, she lived at and worked from 1746 Bathgate Avenue in New York City.
Costumes: 1916 *FloraBella* 1917 *Flo-Flo* (Act I costumes and lingerie)

Leo Kerz

Leo Kerz was a scenic, lighting, and costume designer, as well as a producer and director. He was born on November 1, 1912 in Berlin, and studied there with Bertolt Brecht, Erwin Piscator and Laszlo Moholy-Nagy. His first settings were produced in Berlin in 1932, after which he designed throughout Europe and in South Africa. He came to the United States in 1942 and assisted Jo Mielziner, Watson Barratt and Stewart Chaney. He also designed sets for numerous operas, including *The Magic Flute* and *Parsifal* for the Metropolitan Opera, and the premieres of *The Moon* by Carl Orff and *The Tempest* by Frank Marin at New York City Opera in collaboration with Erich Leinsdorf. He also designed for films and television, includ-

ing a stint as a CBS-TV staff designer between 1949 and 1954. Mr. Kerz, who lectured widely and wrote on trends in design, died on November 4, 1976 in New York City.
Sets: 1947 *Anthony and Cleopatra*; *Open House* 1948 *Bravo*; *For Heaven's Sake, Mother* 1949 *The Biggest Thief in Town* 1950 *Edwina Black* 1952 *The Sacred Flame*; *Whistler's Grandmother* 1954 *Hit the Trail* 1959 *Moonbirds* 1961 *Rhinoceros* 1973 *Children of the Wind*
Costumes: 1947 *Open House*
Lights: 1944 *According to Law*; *A Strange Play* 1946 *Christopher Blake*[†]; *Flamingo Road* 1947 *Heads or Tails*; *Little A*; *Louisiana Lady*; *Open House* 1948 *For Heaven's Sake, Mother*; *Me and Molly* 1949 *The Biggest Thief in Town* 1950 *Edwina Black* 1951 *Ti-Coq* 1952 *The Sacred Flame*; *Whistler's Grandmother* 1954 *Hit the Trail* 1959 *Moonbirds* 1961 *Rhinoceros* 1973 *Children of the Wind*

Philip Kessler

Philip Kessler designed sets and costumes for a Broadway play in 1947.
Sets: 1947 *Trial Honeymoon*
Costumes: 1947 *Trial Honeymoon*

Omar Kiam

Omar Kiam, a fashion designer, was born in Monterey, Mexico in 1894, son of parents from Houston, Texas who were operating a hotel. He changed his name from Alexander to Omar upon reading *The Rubaiyat*. He worked in the fashion business as a milliner and later for a retail fur company, where his enterprising manner and skill as a designer led to great success. He left the fur business to open his own dress shop, but was soon enticed to Hollywood by Samuel Goldwyn to design for film stars in 1935. His movies included *A Star is Born*, *The Adventures of Marco Polo*, *Dodsworth* and *Wuthering Heights*. The wedding dress he designed for Merle Oberon in that movie was much admired and copied. He returned to New York as chief designer for Ben Reig Corporation and developed a trim called cord eyelet as a response to the shortage of laces during World War II. He occasionally contributed costume designs to Broadway shows and had two exhibitions of his designs at the Metropolitan Museum of Art. Omar Kiam died in New York City on March 28, 1954.

Costumes: 1928 *A Play without Name* (Miss Wood's and Miss Wilson's costumes) **1930** *Dishonored Lady* (Miss Cornell's Act I, Scene I costumes); *His Majesty's Car*† (Act II, III) **1932** *Dinner at Eight* (Costumes for Lynn Fontanne and Ina Claire) **1933** *For Services Rendered* (Miss Risdom's gown) **1934** *Oliver! Oliver!* (Miss Anderson's Clothes) **1939** *The Man Who Came to Dinner* (Costumes for Lynn Fontanne and Ina Claire)

Garland Kiddle

Garland Kiddle designed costumes on Broadway for the first time in 1984. His work is seen regularly on the West Coast, in particular in Los Angeles and Orange County. He has won numerous prizes, including ten Drama-Logue Awards, and in 1981, a Career Achievement Award for Continued Excellence in Costume Design. His television credits are also extensive and include *The Young and the Restless*, *Perfectly Frank* for Home Box Office and *Crazy Nights* for MGM-TV.

Costumes: 1984 *A Woman of Independent Means*

Frederick Kiesler

Frederick John Kiesler lived from September 22, 1892 to December 27, 1965 and worked as an architect and scenic designer. He was born in Vienna and came to the United States in 1926. He was head of set design at the Juilliard School of Music from 1933 to 1957 and then director of the Laboratory at the Columbia University School of Architecture. His first set was for *R.U.R.* in 1922 in Berlin. He received credit for numerous designs at Juilliard, exhibited architectural and theatrical designs, and influenced the emerging environmental theater with plans and design for "Endless Theatre." He also designed the first projected scenery at the Metropolitan Opera, for *In the Pasha's Garden* in 1935. He was a member of United Scenic Artists from 1934 to 1965.

Sets: 1946 *No Exit*
Lights: 1946 *No Exit*

Willa Kim

Willa Kim is from Los Angeles, California. After an initial Broadway production when she was very young, she studied at the Chouinard Institute of Art as a scholarship student, and then began her professional career in earnest with the *Red Eye of Love* in 1961. She has designed costumes both on and off Broadway, throughout the U.S., in Europe and Asia. A designer with an excellent sense of color and line, she has also designed operas, over 125 ballets, and television, winning two Emmy Awards for *The Tempest* and *A Song for Dead Warriors* when the ballets were broadcast. The recipient of many honors, Willa Kim has an Obie (*The Old Glory* in 1964), a Drama Desk Award for *Promenade* (1969) and *Operation Sidewinder* (1970), the Maharam, Drama Desk and Variety New York Drama Critics Poll awards for *The Screens* in 1971, among many, many others. She has received two Tony Awards for *Sophisticated Ladies* and for *Will Rogers Follies* out of six nominations. Theatre Development Fund honored her in 1999 with the Irene Sharaff Lifetime Achievement Award and in 2001, she was presented the Ruth Morley Designing Woman Award by the League of Professional Theatre Women. Both were testimony to her incomparable artistry. Twenty-first century designs include *Eyes of the Soul* and *Bésame Mucho* for Ballet Hispánico.

Costumes: 1946 *The Duchess Misbehaves* **1963** *Have I Got a Girl for You* **1966** *Hail Scrawdyke!*; *Malcolm* **1972** *Lysistrata* **1974** *Jumpers* **1975** *Goodtime Charley* **1978** *Dancin'* **1979** *Bosoms and Neglect* **1981** *Sophisticated Ladies* **1985** *Song & Dance* **1986** *Long Day's Journey into Night* **1987** *The Front Page* **1988** *Legs Diamond* **1991** *Will Rogers Follies* **1992** *Four Baboons Adoring the Sun*; *Tommy Tune Tonite! A Song and Dance Act* **1994** *Grease* **1995** *Victor/Victoria*

Alan Kimmel

A scene designer for stage and television, Alan Kimmel designed his first production in New York City the year before he received a B.F.A. in Scene Design from the Carnegie Institute of Technology in June 1959. His debut production, *Sweeney Todd* (the melodrama) in September 1958, opened the Sullivan Street Playhouse, which shortly after became the home of the *Fantasticks*. From 1972 to 1982 he was staff designer for ABC-TV. In 1983 he won an Emmy Award for the set design of *The Morning Show* on ABC-TV, and in 1992 another, for the ABC-TV news special *A Line in the Sand*. Additional television designs include *Eye to Eye with Connie Chung*. A dedicated teacher as well, he received a grant from the state of New York to implement a practical internship program allowing senior design majors from the State University of New York at Fredonia to spend a resident semester in New York City. Kimmel, who has lectured at Fordham University on "Language and Knowing," was born on April 9, 1938 in Cedarhurst, New York. Recent designs include *At Wit's End* and *Carnal Knowledge* in New York, and *Funny Girl* at the North Shore Music Theatre.

Sets: 1971 *You're a Good Man, Charlie Brown* 1972 *Mother Earth*
Costumes: 1971 *You're a Good Man, Charlie Brown*

Adrienne King

Adrienne King contributed costume designs to a 1908 production.
Costumes: 1908 *Toddles* (Gowns)

Alexander King, Jr.

Alexander King, Jr. designed interiors for a Broadway show in collaboration with Joseph Physioc. He was born Alexander Konig in Vienna on November 13, 1899 and came to the United States with his parents prior to World War I, becoming a citizen in 1920. He studied painting and began illustrating magazines and books, including a special edition of Eugene O'Neill's plays. Between 1930 and 1955 he stopped painting, became an editor, was associated with *Americana, Stage, Life* and *Vanity Fair*. In 1959 he appeared on the Jack Parr television show and was a big success with his witty, irreverent commentary, which he used

to a good effect on many subsequent television appearances until his death on November 17, 1965. Volumes in his memoirs include *Mine Enemy Grows Older, May this House Be Safe from Tigers* and *Rich Man, Poor Man*, and *Freud and Fruit*.

Sets: 1920 *Scrambled Wives*†

Lawrence King

Lawrence S. King has designed sets and costumes on Broadway since 1974. A native of Wichita, Kansas, he received a B.A. at Wichita State University and his M.F.A at Yale. *The Rivals* for the Yale Repertory Theatre was his first professional design assignment. He has designed many productions for regional theaters, off-Broadway theaters, and opera companies. Recent credits include *Hothouse* and *The Contractor* at the Chelsea Theatre Company. Mr. King often works in collaboration with designer Michael Yeargan and director Robert Drivas.

Sets: 1974 *My Sister, My Sister* 1975 *The Ritz*† 1976 *Me Jack, You Jill* 1977 *The Night of the Tribades; Something Old, Something New* 1978 *Cheaters* 1981 *It Had to Be You*†
Costumes: 1975 *The Ritz* 1976 *Me Jack, You Jill*† 1977 *Something Old, Something New*†

Muriel King

Muriel King was an American fashion designer who created original fashions for department stores including Lord & Taylor, as well as in her own East 61st Street salon, also designed costumes for plays and films between 1935 and 1945. Born in Bayview, Washington, she studied painting at the University of Washington and the New York School of Fine Arts. In the late 1920s, she worked in Paris as a sketch artist for magazines including *Vogue, Manners* and *Modes*. Her films include *Stage Door, Appointment for Love*, and *Casanova Brown*. She retired in 1957, and resumed painting with watercolors, residing in Bethel, Connecticut. She died on March 21, 1977 at age 76.

Costumes: 1934 *Joyous Season* 1935 *There's Wisdom in Women* (Miss Weston's, Miss Lawford's, and Miss Maddeux's gowns)

Peter W. King

Peter W. King designed lights for Broadway shows between 1900 and 1912 under his full name, and also as "King." An electrician, he lived at 234 East 118th Street in New York City in 1900. By 1903 he was an electrical contractor, with a business located at 1370 Broadway and lived at 447 East 119th Street.

Lights: 1900 *Cashel Byron's Profession*; *Star and Garter* **1904** *Ransom's Folly* **1905** *The Lion and the Mouse* **1907** *The Struggle Everlasting* **1908** *Pierre of the Plains* (as: King) **1909** *On the Eve* **1910** *A Skylark* **1912** *The Typhoon*† (as: King)

Raphael Kirchner

Raphael Kirchner was a native of Vienna, Austria who spent much of his life in London. In 1915, he came to the U.S. and in 1916 designed costumes on Broadway. He also designed theatrical posters. A mural painter and interior designer, Mr. Kirchner created the interior of the Century Theatre in New York City. He died on August 2, 1917.

Costumes: 1916 *The Century Girl*†

Peter Kirillov

Peter Kirillov designed scenery on Broadway in 1997.

Sets: 1997 *The Cherry Orchard*†

Roger Kirk

Well-known in his native Australia as a costume (and occasional set) designer, Roger Kirk first designed in the United States in the mid-1990s. His first job was as a stagehand in television studios in Sydney, after which he spent three years in London's West End mainly working on stage properties. When he returned to Australia, he began designing for ABC television, with variety shows, and in 1981 designed for the theater for the first time, making his debut with *Chicago* for the Sydney Theatre Company. Since then he has designed numerous plays, operas, and musicals, in addition to continuing to design television specials, series, and films. His designs in London's West End include *Whistle Down the Wind*. He has received two Australian Film Institute Awards, for *Blood Oath* and

Rebel, and a Tony Award for *The King and I*.

Costumes: 1995 *The King and I* **1996** *The King and I* **2000** *Jesus Christ Superstar* **2001** *42nd Street*

Sam Kirkpatrick

Sam Kirkpatrick was born on October 25, 1940 in County Fermanagh, Ireland. After completing his "A" level exams he studied at the Belfast College of Art for two years, and in 1962 received a diploma with distinction from the Central School of Arts and Crafts. *Philoctetes* in 1964 at the Royal National Theatre in London was his professional debut. His designs for costumes and scenery were seen in Japan, Great Britain, Canada and throughout the United States. He designed costumes for films including Orson Welles' *Chimes at Midnight*, and productions such as *Rip Van Winkle* and *The Dancing Princess* for Faerie Tale Theatre. The recipient of two Los Angeles Drama Logues for costume design, for *The Misanthrope* in 1982 and *Undiscovered Country* in 1985, he designed sets and costumes for many productions at the Alabama Shakespeare Festival, The Old Globe, New York City Opera, The Guthrie Theatre and the Stratford (Ontario) Festival. He died on March 1, 1994 at age 53, a victim of AIDS.

Sets: 1985 *Wind in the Willows*

Jack Kirwan

Irish landscape artist and designer Jack Kirwan has designed scenery and costumes for many productions. A resident of Dublin, he has designed many productions with Robert Ballagh for the Gate Theatre, including *Riverdance* and a festival of Samuel Beckett's plays. He also designed *A Couple of Blackguards*, a play by Frank McCourt.

Sets: 2001 *Stones in His Pockets*
Costumes: 2001 *Stones in His Pockets*

Yetta Kiviette

Yetta Kiviette (also known as Kiviette, Yvette Kiviat, Mrs. Michael Kalette, etc.) was born on Staten Island and after graduating from high school attended art school. She entered the theater as a sketch artist first for the Mahieu Costume Company, and later for Brooks Costume Company. She subsequently opened her own shop from which she designed and executed costumes for plays, with musicals as her specialty, especially those that required lots of feathers. She first designed on Broadway in 1917 and was active until 1948 using variations on her name. She often worked with Cora MacGeachy and Will R. Barnes.

Sets: 1932 *Ballyhoo of 1932†* (Act II finale)

Costumes: 1917 *Odds and Ends of 1917†* 1920 *Betty Be Good* (Gowns and hats); *Silks and Satins* 1921 *Love Dreams* (Miss Michelena's gowns) 1923 *Battling Buckler* (Gowns and costumes); *Helen of Troy, New York†* (Russian principals, Act II designs); *Nifties of 1923†* (Opening Number costumes) 1924 *The Chocolate Dandies*; *Dear Sir†*; *Greenwich Village Follies†* ("West of the Moon," Happy Melody, Pipes of Pan"); *Merry Wives of Gotham†* (Other costumes); *Sweet Little Devil†* 1925 *Captain Jinks*; *Tip Toes* (Gowns and costumes) 1927 *Funny Face*; *Good News* (Frocks) 1928 *Anna*; *Blackbirds of 1928* (Costumes and gowns); *Congai†* (Miss Gerald's modern gowns); *The Great Necker*; *Here's Howe*; *Hold Everything*; *A Lady for a Night*; *Mrs. Dane's Defense* (Miss Heming's, Miss Martin's and Miss Hoyt's gowns); *Sherlock Holmes†* (Miss Martin's, Miss Hoyt's and Miss Scheff's gowns); *Treasure Girl* 1929 *Cross Roads*; *Follow Through†* (Ladies costumes); *Heads Up*; *Lady Fingers* (Frocks); *See Naples and Die†* (Miss Sear's costumes); *Seven†* (Miss Caugaye's gowns); *Spring Is Here*; *Top Speed* 1930 *Girl Crazy*; *The International Review†* (Miss Lawrence's finale gown); *Lost Sheep†* (Ladies apparel); *Nine-Fifteen Revue*; *Three's a Crowd†* 1931 *America's Sweetheart†* (Miss Lake's frocks); *The Band Wagon†* (Modern gowns and costumes); *The Cat and the Fiddle†* (Gowns); *Free for All* (Gowns); *George White's Scandals†* (Miss Merman's gowns); *Here Goes the Bride*; *Shoot the Works†* (Principal's costumes); *Singin' in the Rain* ("The Blues"); *The Wonder Bar†* (Albertina Rasch Dancers); *You Said It* 1932 *Bal-*
lyhoo of 1932† (Roulette number, Act II Finale); *Face the Music†*; *George White's Music Hall Varieties†* (Gowns for featured actresses); *Take My Tip* (Gowns); *Take a Chance†* (Frocks); *Walk a Little Faster* 1933 *Design for Living†* (Most gowns); *Let 'em Eat Cake* (Women's costumes); *Roberta*; *Strike Me Pink*; *$25.00 an Hour* (Gowns) 1934 *Life Begins at 8:40†*; *No More Ladies†* (Miss Swanson's gowns); *Ziegfeld Follies: 1934†* 1937 *Between the Devil* 1942 *Janie* (Miss Watkins, Miss Cushman's costumes, Miss Anderson's gowns) 1948 *Light Up the Sky*

Harriet Klamroth

Harriet Klamroth, later Harriet Klamroth Morse, designed a set in 1918 on Broadway. She was one of the American designers, together with Norman Bel Geddes, Robert Edmond Jones, Willy Pogany, Lee Simonson, and others, who embraced European developments in stagecraft during the teens. Her designs were included in an exhibit of American designers of the "New Stagecraft" at the Bourgeois Galleries in New York in 1919. Born February 16, 1891, she died in New York City on February 26, 1988.

Sets: 1918 *Crops and Croppers* 1921 *The Playboy of the Western World*

Ray Klausen

Ray Klausen has designed over 250 shows for theater and television. His stage credits include *Jubilee!* at Bally's Grand in Las Vegas, *Hello Hollywood* at the MGM Grand in Reno, and productions for the Mark Taper Forum and the Loretto Hilton Theatre. His credits include sets for Cher, Diana Ross, Martha Graham, Michael Jackson, Bea Arthur, Liza Minnelli, Ann-Margaret, Elton John, Princess Grace, Barbra Streisand, Madonna, and Elvis. He created set designs for all the *American Music Awards* shows, eleven American Film Institute Salutes, six Academy Award shows, ten Kennedy Center Honors, two Tony Awards, and a *Night of 1000 Stars*. He is the recipient of three Emmy Awards and eleven nominations, and the Hoffman Scholar Chair at Florida State University. He was born on May 29, 1939 in Jamaica,

New York and received a B.A. at Hofstra, an M.A. at New York University in 1963, and an M.F.A. at Yale University in 1967. Twenty-first century designs include *Pete 'n' Keely* at the John Houseman Theatre, *Call Me Madam* for the Reprise Series in Los Angeles, and *My Favorite Broadway*.

Sets: 1990 *Night of 100 Stars III* 1994 *Comedy Tonight* 1999 *Waiting in the Wings*

Klaw & Erlanger

Klaw & Erlanger was a partnership between Marc Klaw (1858-1936) and A.L. (Abraham Lincoln) Erlanger (1860-1930) that produced hundreds of productions in New York. They started in 1888 booking theaters and within ten years were a powerful theatrical force. Initially they sent established companies of actors, such as the Augustin Daly Company, on tours, but then they started producing their own show, beginning with *The Great Metropolis* in 1890. With hundreds of productions, many of them musicals to their credit, they were successful until the partnership was dissolved in 1919. After that time, both Klaw and Erlanger continued to produce show individually. The theaters in which they produced shows usually had studios for scenic artists, or they contracted for scenery with an existing studio. For some of their productions, a costume designer was cited, often with an accompanying reference to execution of the costumes by Klaw & Erlanger, but for at least three productions, they also received design credit. The costume workroom was located at 152 West 34th Street, and later at 120 West 31st Street.

Costumes: 1901 *The Governor's Son* 1907 *The Round Up* 1911 *Ziegfeld Follies of 1911*†

Alonzo Klaw

Alonzo Klaw, son of Marc Klaw of the producing firm Klaw & Erlanger, was himself a theatrical producer. He was born on April 15, 1885 in Louisville, Kentucky and studied at the New York School of Art and the Art Students League. He designed a single set on Broadway in 1924. He died on January 12, 1944 in Winter Park, Florida at age 58.

Sets: 1924 *Hell Bent*

Debra J. Kletter

Debra Kletter has designed lighting for many off-Broadway theaters including Playwrights Horizons, Manhattan Theatre Club, WPA, and Circle Repertory Company. She has also designed for numerous regional theaters including Berkeley Repertory, the Long Wharf Theatre, South Coast Repertory and Hartford Stage. She received a Drama-Logue Award for lighting design for work at South Coast Repertory and has more than forty productions to her credit as resident designer for the Production Company. Her Broadway debut, *Prelude to a Kiss*, was designed for playwright Craig Lucas and director Norman René, a team with whom she has also designed *Reckless*, *Three Postcards*, *Missing Persons*, and *Marry Me a Little*.

Lights: 1990 *Prelude to a Kiss*

Kliegl Brothers

Kliegl Brothers Universal Electric Stage Lighting Company, Inc., founded in 1896, was the first American company to specialize in manufacturing equipment for stage lighting. Brothers John H. Kliegl and Anton T. Kliegl devised a light that projected a powerful beam by means of carbons, making indoor motion pictures more practical. That light became known as the "Klieg light." In 1903 Kliegl Brothers installed the first incandescent lighting system at the Metropolitan Opera House. They also supplied lighting equipment and effects to producers including David Belasco, George M. Cohan, Charles Frohman and William A. Brady. John and Anton Kliegl were born in Bad Kissingen, Bavaria, Germany and attended school in Munich. They emigrated to the United States in 1918, arriving during the blizzard of that year. John Kliegl died at age 89 on September 30, 1959. (Anton Kliegl had died earlier.) While the company continues its specialty in theatrical lighting, it has also pioneered electric lighting systems in schools, museums, golf driving ranges, auditoriums, arenas and offices. Devices developed by the company included footlights with special features, remote systems, pinhole dimlights, and projection equipment. Kliegl Brothers has supplied lighting instruments for thousands of productions on the Broadway stage, but Kliegl Brothers and Henry Kliegl received design credit for only a few.

Lights: 1902 *The Darling of the Gods*†; *The Ninety and Nine* 1903 *Babes in Toyland*; *Darling of the Gallery Gods, The and The Dress Parade*†; *The Proud Prince*; *The Wizard of Oz* 1905 *As Ye Sow*; *At the Threshold*; *The System of Dr. Tarr* 1906 *Cousin Louisa*; *The Light Eternal* 1907 *The Christian Pilgrim*; *The Ranger*; *The Rogers Brothers in Panama*; *Salomy Jane* 1908 *Algeria*; *Don Quixote*†; *Electra*; *The Flower of Yamato*; *The Yankee Prince* (as: Kliegl Illuminating Co.) 1910 *Bright Eyes*†; *Drifting*; *The Merry Whirl*; *Two Women* 1911 *The Garden of Allah*; *Miss Jack*; *Thais* 1912 *The Bird of Paradise* (Electrical lighting and storm effect); *The Typhoon*† 1913 *The Love Leash*; *The Poor Little Rich Girl*; *Rachel* 1914 *Maria Rosa*; *Omar, the Tentmaker*; *The Rule of Three* 1915 *A Miracle of St. Anthony* 1917 *Eileen*; *Seremonda* 1921 *The Wandering Jew* 1923 *The Exile* 1926 *The Half-Caste*†

Henry Kliegl

Herbert A. (Henry) Kliegl was the son of John H. Kliegl who founded Kliegl Brothers with his brother Anton. Henry joined his father in the theatrical lighting business and also designed the lighting for a Broadway production in 1919, although as a member off Kliegl Brothers he was certainly responsible for additional productions in the format generally followed before lighting designers emerged in their own right. Herbert Kliegl died at age 64 on October 3, 1968.

Lights: 1919 *Aphrodite*†

Stephanie Kline

Stephanie Kline received an M.A. at the University of California, Los Angeles and initially worked as a curatorial assistant in the Costume and Textiles Section of the Los Angeles Museum of Art. While there, she met Dorothy Jeakins, and became her assistant for films, including *Catch 22* and *Little Big Man*. Her professional debut as a costume designer occurred at the Mark Taper Forum where she first designed *Story Theatre* for Paul Sills.

Costumes: 1970 *Paul Sills' Story Theatre*

William Kline

William Kline was the set designer for the Abbey Theatre Players performances in New York City in the late 1930s. An artist, he resided and had a studio at 244 West 14th Street, New York City in 1920.

Sets: 1927 *The Good Hope*† 1937 *Honor Bright*

Florence Klotz

Florence Klotz, who is from New York, attended the Parsons School of Design. Upon completion of her studies she went to work at Brooks Costume Company painting and distressing fabrics, a position she held until Irene Sharaff asked her to assist on *The King and I*. During the 1950s she worked as an assistant to many costume designers including Irene Sharaff, Miles White and Lucinda Ballard. After the opening of *The Gay Life*, Lucinda Ballard encouraged Florence Klotz to stop assisting and begin designing herself – which she did. In 1961, she designed her first Broadway show and since that time has designed some of Broadway's most successful plays and musicals, along with ballets and films. Nominated for seven Tony Awards, she has won six times: *Follies* (1972), *A Little Night Music* (1973), *Pacific Overtures* (1976), *Grind* (1985), *Kiss of the Spider Woman* (1989) and *Show Boat* (1995). She specializes in costumes that are clothes for real people. The costumes for *Follies* are a perfect example, because they were not just a chorus line of costumes. Each individual design expresses each individual character. Inducted into the Theatre Hall of Fame in 1997, she was nominated for an Academy Award for *A Little Night Music*.

Costumes: **1961** *A Call on Kuprin*;
Take Her, She's Mine **1962** *Never Too
Late* **1963** *Nobody Loves an Albatross*;
On an Open Roof **1964** *One by One*†;
The Owl and the Pussycat **1965** *Mating Dance* **1966** *The Best Laid Plans*;
It's a Bird...It's a Plane...It's Superman
1970 *Norman, Is That You?*; *Paris Is
Out* **1971** *Follies* **1973** *A Little Night
Music* **1976** *Legend*; *Pacific Overtures*
1977 *Side by Side by Sondheim* **1978**
On the Twentieth Century **1980** *Goodbye Fidel*; *Harold and Maude* **1981** *The
Little Foxes* **1982** *A Doll's Life* **1983**
Peg **1985** *Grind*; *Jerry's Girls* **1986**
Rags **1987** *Roza* **1989** *City of Angels*
1993 *Kiss of the Spider Woman* **1994**
Show Boat

Clayton Knight

Clayton Knight, an illustrator, contributed costume and scenic designs to
a Broadway play in 1925. He illustrated several books on aviation and
others based on his experiences as an
American aviator in World War I. He
also illustrated adventure books for
boys. He died July 17, 1969 at age 78
in Danbury, Connecticut.
Sets: **1926** *Henry IV, Part I*†
Costumes: **1926** *Henry IV, Part I*†

H. P. Scenic Studio Knight

The H.P. Knight Scenic Studio received
credit for scenic design of Broadway
plays between 1909 and 1918. The studio was located at the corner of Walton Avenue and East 140th Street in
1908 and at 123 East 138th Street in
1919. Directors of the scenic studio
were Harry P. Knight, Clara Kurtz,
and Jacob Plate. In 1927, the studio
relocated to 334 Walton Avenue.
Sets: **1909** *Meyer & Son* **1915** *John
Gabriel Borkman*†; *When the Young Vine
Blooms* **1918** *The Awakening*†

Willis Knighton

Willis Knighton, who was born on December 25, 1906 in Oregon, was active
on Broadway between 1944 and 1949.
He first worked in the theater as a technical director. A teacher of design,
Mr. Knighton was associated with the
University of Utah and the Dramatic
Workshop at the New School for Social

Research. In the 1940s he also held the
position of summer art director at the
Chapel Theatre at Great Neck, Long
Island. His company, Knighton Studios, was located at 157 Houndsditch,
London, England in 1951. He died in
Los Angeles on June 20, 1971.
Sets: **1944** *Meet a Body* **1945** *Brighten
the Corner* **1946** *Song of Bernadette*†
1949 *Gayden*; *The Shop at Sly Corner*
Costumes: **1944** *Meet a Body* **1949** *The
Shop at Sly Corner*

Edward Knoblock

Edward Knoblock was a playwright
and novelist. The first successful show
he wrote was *Kismet*, originally produced in 1911. He also wrote scenarios
for films and collaborated with Arnold
Bennett and J. B. Priestley among others. He occasionally contributed costume designs to his own plays. Mr.
Knoblock was born April 7, 1874 in the
U. S. and graduated from Harvard, although he spent the majority of his life
in Great Britain, became a British subject. He performed on the stage for the
first time in England. His autobiography, *Round the Room*, was published
in 1939. He died July 20, 1945, in London.
Costumes: **1927** *The Mulberry Bush*
(Also Author)

John Koenig

John Koenig was born in Berlin in 1911
and brought to the United States as a
toddler. He studied at the University of
Pennsylvania, Grand Central School of
the Arts and the Yale Drama School.
He designed sets and/or costumes for
shows in New York, Pasadena, California and for Orson Welles' Mercury
Theatre. As Private John Koenig he
designed *This is the Army* for Irving
Berlin. He served as designer at the
Virginia Museum of Fine Arts between
1956 and his death on February 1,
1963.
Sets: **1937** *Many Mansions* **1938**
Gloriana; *Glorious Morning*; *Heartbreak
House*; *Here Come the Clowns*; *Missouri
Legend* **1940** *Charley's Aunt* **1941** *Little
Dark Horse* **1942** *This Is the Army*
Costumes: **1938** *Missouri Legend* (Production design) **1940** *Charley's Aunt*; *Pal*

Joey 1941 *In Time to Come; Pal Joey* 1942 *This Is the Army*

Norbert U. Kolb

Norbert U. Kolb graduated from the Tisch School of the Arts at New York University. He has designed scenery and lighting for many regional theaters and opera companies including the Cleveland Playhouse, Kentucky Opera and Virginia Opera. He also designs industrial promotions and trade shows. Designs for television include *Sarah, Plain and Tall, Sarah: Skylark* and for CBS Sports, the *1997 Winter Olympic Games.* Among his twenty-first century credits is *Fame: The Musical* in Pasadena.

Sets: 1994 *Ian McKellen: A Knight Out at the Lyceum*

Fred Kolo

Fred Kolo was born on September 27, 1942 in Columbus, Nebraska, the son of Fred T. and Helen Paulson Kolouch. He received a B.A. at Dartmouth College and attended the Yale University School of Drama, Lester Polakov's Studio and Forum of Stage Design and the Art Students League. He worked as an assistant at the Metropolitan Opera and for Raoul Pène Du Bois, and made his New York debut with Robert Sealy's *Meat and Potatoes* at La Mama E.T.C. He has received two Joseph Jefferson Award nominations in Chicago for productions at the Academy Festival Theatre and three Carbonell Awards in Miami. A designer of scenery, costumes and lights for theater, television, industrial promotions and film, he also directs, produces and writes. Fred Kolo is also known for his collaborations with Robert Wilson: *The Life and Times of Sigmund Freud* at the Brooklyn Academy of Music; *Deafman Glance* at the Brooklyn Academy of Music, the University of Iowa, the Nancy Festival, Holland Festival and in Paris; and scenery for *The Life and Times of Joseph Stalin* at the Brooklyn Academy of Music and the Teatro Municipal, São Paulo, Brazil.

Sets: 1990 *Truly Blessed*
Lights: 1990 *Truly Blessed*

Ralph Koltai

Ralph Koltai, a designer of Hungarian-German descent, was born in Berlin on July 31, 1924 and studied there and at London's Central School of Arts and Crafts, where he was head of theater design from 1965 to 1973. His first design assignment was the opera *Angelique* in 1950 and since that time he has designed sets and costumes for nearly two hundred plays, operas and ballets around the world. An Associate Designer of the Royal Shakespeare Company from 1965 to 1987 he designed numerous productions, and has also designed for the Royal National Theatre, Royal OperaHouse, and English National Opera, among other organizations. He directed and designed *The Flying Dutchman* in Hong Kong in 1987 and *Metropolis* in 1988. The recipient of numerous awards, he was co-winner of an Individual Gold Medal for Stage Design and co-winner of the Golden Troika National Award at the 1975 Prague Quadriennale, and won an Individual Silver Medal in 1987. He was recipient of the 1979 Designer of the Year Award from the Society of the West End Theatres for *Brand.* In 1983, he was honored with Commander of the British Empire and in 1997, *Ralph Koltai, Designer for Stage* was published.

Sets: 1968 *Soldiers* 1974 *As You Like It* 1984 *Cyrano De Bergerac*†; *Much Ado About Nothing*† 1985 *Pack of Lies* 1988 *Carrie* 1993 *My Fair Lady* (Based on original designs)
Costumes: 1968 *Soldiers* 1974 *As You Like It* 1985 *Pack of Lies*
Lights: 1968 *Soldiers*

Theodore Komisarjevsky

Theodore Komisarjevsky, born Fyodor Fyodorovich Komissarzhevsky, began his theater career in czarist Russia where his sister Vera was one of the great Russian actresses and his father a noted tenor. He was born in Venice on May 23, 1882 and began professional life as an architect, leaving his practice to manage his sister's theater and gradually directing more and more plays. In 1918 he moved to England, became

a British subject, and directed, designed, choreographed, and produced plays with great success at Stratford-upon-Avon and in London. The Theatre Guild initially brought him to New York to stage productions in 1922, and he subsequently returned to the United States to design plays including *Russian Bank* in 1940, *Crime and Punishment* in 1947 and *Love for Three Oranges* at the City Center, leaving only when ill health forced his withdrawal. He was the second husband of British actress Peggy Ashcroft and exerted considerable influence on twentieth century theater interpretations of classical repertory. He died on April 17, 1954 in Darien, Connecticut.
Sets: **1922** *The Tidings Brought to Mary*† **1935** *Escape Me Never*

Charles Kondazian

Charles H. Kondazian designed on Broadway between 1928 and 1930. He was president of Charles Kondazian, Inc., Women's Apparel, at 112 Madison Avenue, New York City.
Costumes: **1928** *Holiday*† (Gowns) **1930** *Rebound*† (Gowns)

Pierre Kontchalovsky

Pierre Kontchalovsky designed sets and costumes for a Broadway play in 1925. A major Russian Impressionist painter, he was born Pyotr Pyotrovich Konchalovsky in 1876 and died in 1956. His grandson, Andrei Kontchalovsky emigrated to the United States in 1980 and has directed the films *Duet for One, Runaway Train, Maria's Lovers* and *Shy People.*
Sets: **1925** *La Perichale; The Law and the Man*
Costumes: **1925** *La Perichale*

Geoff Korff

Geoff Korff is a lighting designer who has numerous credits in regional theaters, off-Broadway, and on the West Coast. He graduated from California State University, Chico and received his M.F.A. from the Yale School of Drama. Twenty-first century designs include *The Body of Bourne, For Here or To Go?* (Mark Taper Forum), *The Cosmonaut's Last Message to the Woman he Once Loved in the Former Soviet Union* (La Jolla Playhouse), and *Mizlansky/Zilinsky* at the Geffen Playhouse.
Lights: **1992** *Two Trains Running*

Michael Krass

Costume designer Michael Krass began designing on Broadway in 1996, receiving Drama Desk and American Theatre Wing nominations for his debut. His credits off-Broadway are extensive, and include many seasons at the Hangar Theatre. He has designed costumes for the Goodman Theatre, Chicago Shakespeare Festival, and in Dublin and Japan. He heads the design program for Playwrights Horizons at NYU. Twenty-first century designs include *Chaucer in Rome* at the Mitzi E. Newhouse Theatre, *The Credeaux Canvas* at Playwrights Horizons' Wilder Theatre, *The Right Way to Sue* presented by New Georges and Here, *Lobby Hero* at Playwrights Horizons, and *The Man Who Had all the Luck* at the Williamstown Theatre Festival. He also designed *Hedda Gabler* in the 2001-2001 Broadway season.
Costumes: **1996** *The Rehearsal* **1997** *View from the Bridge, A* **1998** *Getting and Spending* **1999** *The Lion in Winter; You're a Good Man, Charlie Brown*

Jay Krause

Jay Krause designed sets, lights and costumes for a production on Broadway in 1955. He also designed the stage décor for "Baile de Colores," a gala for the Los Angeles Chamber Orchestra. Owner of Omega Cinema Props in Los Angeles he is involved with many productions for other designers as well.
Sets: **1955** *A Day by the Sea*
Costumes: **1955** *A Day by the Sea*
Lights: **1955** *A Day by the Sea*

Arnold A. Kraushaar

Arnold A. Kraushaar designed one set on Broadway in 1920. In the late teens he was a musician, and then operated an art gallery at 680 Fifth Avenue in New York City in 1922. In the mid-1920s he worked as an engineer and resided at 11 Vermilye Avenue in New York City.
Sets: **1920** *Lady Billy*

Hermann Křehan

See Crayon.

Frank Krenz

Frank Krenz has designed costumes for major motion pictures, ice shows, magic acts, for dance and for the theater. He was associate designer for Theoni V. Aldredge for movies including *Ghostbusters* and Broadway shows including *Dreamgirls* while his own career was beginning. His designs at the Pubic Theatre include *A Midsummer Night's Dream* directed by A.J. Antoon, and at the Roundabout Theatre include *The Visit*. During the mid-1990s he began designing ice musicals for producer Kenneth Feld, and has done *The Wizard of Oz on Ice*, *Troy Story on Ice*, and the on-ice version of *Starlight Express*. Born and raised near Grand Rapids, Michigan, he graduated from Michigan State University. Twenty-first century credits include Janet Jackson's *All for You* tour.
Costumes: 1990 *Lettice & Lovage*† **1992** *The Visit* **1996** *Radio City Spring Spectacular*† **1997** *Radio City Spring Spectacular*†

Howard Kretz

Howard Kretz designed one set on Broadway in 1916 in collaboration with Warren Dahler.
Sets: 1916 *The Queen's Enemies*†

Jan Kroeze

Jan Kroeze, who designed lights on Broadway initially in 1998, has extensive credits in theater and fashion. His business, jkld, has offices in America and Europe and is the leading company in the world of fashion. He has designed lights for Seventh on Sixth, Donna Karan, Gucci, Ralph Lauren, Helmut Lang and others in the fashion industry for showrooms, fashion shows, and special events for media, private customers, and the public. His lights have been seen in the Minetta Lane, Atlantic Theatre, Playwrights Horizons, and other off-Broadway theaters, as well as for the New York Shakespeare Festival.
Lights: 1998 *Freak*

Nick Kronyack

Nick (Nicholas S.) Kronyack (Croniac), who was active on Broadway between 1912 and 1915 as a lighting designer, spent ten years as head electrician of the Winter Garden Theatre beginning with its opening. For nineteen years he was Chief of Electrical Maintenance at Radio City Music Hall. Most likely, he was responsible for additional designs at both locations than those with which he is credited. Kronyack, who resided at 987 2nd Avenue in New York City, died at the age of 74 on May 12, 1952, in Passaic, New Jersey.
Lights: 1912 *The Passing Show of 1912*† **1913** *The Honeymoon Express* (as: Kronyah); *The Passing Show of 1913* **1914** *Dancing Around*; *The Passing Show of 1914* **1915** *Maid in America*

Hovav Kruvi

Hovav Kruvi designed a Broadway show in 1968.
Costumes: 1968 *The Grand Music Hall of Israel*

Kathryn Kuhn

Kathryn Kuhn, who designed costumes mainly for Florenz Ziegfeld and Mike Todd, started her career as a dressmaker in 1911. She also designed for Sonja Henie and her ice shows. Mrs. Kuhn, wife of publicist Robert Kuhn, was an active costume designer until 1950 when she began to design only for private customers, including Sophie Tucker. She died on September 15, 1979 at the age of 84 in New York City.
Costumes: 1942 *Priorities of 1942* (Luba Malina's gown) **1943** *Artists and Models*; *For Your Pleasure* (Gowns for Yolanda and Miss Miller) **1945** *Hollywood Pinafore*† (Modern clothes) **1946** *If the Shoe Fits* **1947** *Icetime of 1948*† **1948** *Howdy, Mr. Ice*† **1949** *Howdy Mr. Ice of 1950*†

Walt Kuhn

Walt Kuhn, an artist, was born in New York City in 1880 and after studying art in Europe worked as a cartoonist and instructor of drawing and painting. His paintings are in the permanent collections of many museums in the U. S. He also designed ballets, pantomimes and plays, and wrote and produced films about his art. He died in New York City on July 13, 1948.

Costumes: 1927 *Merry-Go-Round*†

Kurzman

Kurzman Waist and Dress Company was located at 141 West 36th Street in New York during the 1930s. Israel Kurzman, who resided with his wife at 1947 80th Street in Brooklyn, New York was the proprietor. Alexander Kurzman was the business bookkeeper, and resided with his wife Rose at 8301 Bay Parkway, Brooklyn, New York. Kurzman provided gowns for a featured player on Broadway in 1931.

Costumes: 1931 *Wonder Boy*† (Miss Dawn's gown)

Jon Kusner

Lighting designer Jon Kusner, who made his Broadway debut in 1999, was Ken Billington's associate lighting designer for *Footloose* both in New York and on the national tour as well as for the International Tour of *Chicago*. While being part of the Billington Design Studio, he has also amassed credits of his own in off- and off-off-Broadway theaters, and for industrial promotions.

Lights: 1999 *Rollin' on the T.O.B.A.*

Lucien Labaudt

Lucien Labaudt was born in Paris on May 14, 1880, and after living in London for several years, moved to the U.S., becoming an American citizen in 1906. He worked as an artist and correspondent for *Life Magazine* during World War II, and died in a plane crash in Assam, India in 1943 while on assignment. Largely self-taught, he created many mural paintings that won prizes and were widely exhibited and collected. In 1928 he contributed costume designs to a Broadway show.

Costumes: 1928 *Lady Dedlock*

Félix Labisse

Félix Louis Victor Léon Labisse was a painter and scenic designer who founded the Club du Cinema in Ostend, Belgium. He served as editor-in-chief for *Tribord* in Ostend from 1927 to 1931 after which he settled in Paris. Born in Marchiennes, France on March 9, 1905, of Belgian descent, he exhibited paintings widely in Europe, South America, the Far East and the United States. His works are in the permanent collections of New York City's Museum of Modern Art, Paris' Musée d'Art Moderne, and the Musée de Lille. In addition to scenic design on Broadway he created theatrical settings for the Comédie Française, the Ballets de Monte-Carlo, and for theater companies in Lyon, Geneva and Lausanne. He began designing in Paris in 1935 and designed numerous productions through the thirties, forties and fifties. He died in 1982.

Sets: 1952 *Le Process*; *Occupe Toi d'Amelie*

Lights: 1952 *Le Process*

Bernice Ladd

Bernice (Mrs. Adolphe) Ladd designed costumes for a Broadway show in 1932. During that same time she was an assistant to Jo Mielziner for costumes, and resided at 2095 Grand Boulevard.

Costumes: 1932 *Distant Drums*

Paul Laighton

Paul Laighton was responsible for a scenic design in 1915 on Broadway. New York City directories in 1907 and 1918 identify him as the manager of the Bramhall Playhouse, 138 East 27th Street, New York City. He resided at 156 East 93rd Street.

Sets: 1915 *The Importance of Coming and Going*†

Stewart Laing

Scottish designer Stewart Laing won a Tony Award for the scenic designs for his first Broadway play. Born in 1961 in Blairgowrie and raised in East Kilbride, he began his career designing in Glasgow for the Citizens and Tramway Theatres and at the Derby Playhouse, after graduating from the Central School of Art and Design in London in 1983 and assisting Phillip Prowse. Additional credits in the United Kingdom include productions at the Scottish Opera, Opera North, the Royal Court Theatre, the Royal Shakespeare Company, and for the Royal National Theatre. He often collaborates with directors Tim Albery and Richard Jones, although increasingly he has also been directing. Directorial credits include *Dance of Death* at the Citizens' Theatre and three one-acts by J. G. Ballard at the Tramway Theatre, both in 2000, and *Happy Days* performed at the Tramway and Traverse Theatres in 2001. Twenty-first century design credits include the premiere of David Sawer's *From Morning to Midnight* at the English National Opera and *La Boheme* at the Motherwell Theatre in Glasgow.

Sets: 1997 *Titanic*
Costumes: 1997 *Titanic*

Suzanne Lalique

Suzanne Lalique designed two shows on Broadway in 1955. Born in 1892, she was the daughter of the French glass artist and worked initially in haute couture. She made her theater debut in Paris with 1936 at Charles Dulin's Atelier Theatre, and the following year designed sets and costumes for *Chacun Sa Vérité*, the first of numerous productions for the Comédie Française where she was head of design from 1937 to 1971. Her film work includes *Le Bourgeois Gentilhomme* (1958) and *Le Marriage de Figaro* (1959) with director Jean Meyer. Her exotic still-lifes were displayed at Bergdorf Goodman in 1933, and her designs for glass continue to be widely exhibited. She died in Paris at age 97 in 1989.

Sets: 1955 *Le Bourgeois Gentilhomme*
Costumes: 1955 *Le Bourgeois Gentilhomme*; *Le Jeu De l'Amour et Du Hasard*

Carmen Lamola

Carmen Lamola designed costumes on Broadway in the 1970s. A fashion designer, she also created clothing for private customers in the 1970s and early 1980s, including John Travolta.

Costumes: 1974 *Henry Fonda As Clarence Darrow* (Mr. Fonda's wardrobe) **1975** *Henry Fonda As Clarence Darrow*

Edward La Moss

Scenic artist and designer Edward La Moss was associated with the Boston Museum Theatre as early as 1877, and was head painter from 1884 to 1889. He initially assisted T. B. Glesing and later collaborated for some projects with William Gill. Credits prior to 1900 include *The Beggar Student* in 1882 and *A Trip to Africa* in 1884. During the first few years of the twentieth century, his scenery was seen in New York. In 1905, Edward Moss was listed in the Trow Business Directory of Greater New York as a costumer, with a studio at 956 Third Avenue.

Sets: 1900 *The Cadet Girl*† (Act II, Scene 3) **1903** *Peggy from Paris*† **1904** *The Yankee Consul*†

Osbert Lancaster

Sir Osbert Lancaster became a cartoonist for the *Daily Express* in 1939. He was born in London on August 4, 1908, and after studying law and English literature attended the Slade School of Art. He also created illustrations for book jackets, large murals, and posters for the London Transport System. He was a member of the editorial board of the *Architectural Review* and also wrote on architecture. Beginning in the early 1950s Sir Osbert Lancaster designed sets and costumes for many companiesincluding the Royal Ballet at Covent Garden, the Glyndebourne Opera, the D'Oyly Carte Opera, and for ballets such as *Pineapple Poll*, *Bonne Bouche*, *Coppélia* and *La Fille Mal Gardée*. Sir Osbert Lancaster, who was knighted in 1975, died in 1986.

Sets: 1957 *Hotel Paradiso*†
Costumes: 1957 *Hotel Paradiso*

Jack Landau

Jack Landau, a director and producer, was born on January 5, 1925 in Braddock, Pennsylvania and studied in the United States and England, including a year at the Old Vic in London. During the 1940s and 1950s while designing sets, costumes, and occasionally lights for plays, he gradually began directing. In 1956 he joined the American Shakespeare Festival Theatre and Academy as associate director and directed numerous plays for the company. He also designed, produced and directed for television. Mr. Landau died on March 16, 1967 in Boston at 42 years of age.

Sets: 1950 *A Phoenix Too Frequent*
1951 *Buy Me Blue Ribbons* 1952 *Dear Barbarians*
Costumes: 1950 *A Phoenix Too Frequent* 1951 *Buy Me Blue Ribbons* 1952 *Dear Barbarians*
Lights: 1944 *War President*

David J. Lander

David J. Lander has many credits in and around New York City as well as in regional theaters. From 1994 until 1998 he was the resident lighting designer for H. T. Chen and Dancers. Off- Broadway credits include productions at the New York Theatre Workshop, Soho Playhouse, the New Victory Theatre and the Joseph Papp Public Theatre. His lighting designs for *Fiddler on the Roof* were seen at the Sundance Theatre Festival, for *Grandma Sylvia's Funeral* on Vandam Street, and those for *Golden Child* at South Coast Repertory received a Drama-Logue Award.
Lights: 1998 *Golden Child* 2000 *Dirty Blonde*

Heidi Landesman

See Heidi Ettinger.

Henry Landish

Henry Landish (Landishman) created one scenic design on Broadway in 1932. During the 1920s, he was associated with Apex Theatrical Curtain Company, located at 4 West 26th Street in New York City. Originally from Russia where he was born on July 22, 1884, he later lived in Los Angeles, where he died on November 22, 1965.
Sets: 1932 *The House of Doom*

Landolff of Paris

Monsieur E. Landolff was the proprietor of a haute couture salon, E. Landolff & Cie., at 8 Chaussée d'Antin, Paris where he designed and supervised the creation of gowns for private and theatrical customers at the beginning of the twentieth century. The salon also executed the costumes for *The Bird Ballet* designed by Alfredo Edel at the New York Hippodrome in 1908. He retired from the salon (although it continued under the same name) in 1910 but in 1914 worked from 18 rue Lafitte

in Paris, again executing costumes for Alfredo and later Florence Edel.
Costumes: 1899 *Papa's Wife* (Mlle. Held's gown) 1906 *The Parisian Model*† 1907 *The Merry Widow*† (as: Landoff) 1909 *The Gay Hussars*; *A Trip to Japan*† (Ballet costumes)

Hugh Landwehr

Hugh Landwehr is a scenic designer who studied at Yale College, where he received a B.A. in 1972. For five years he was an assistant designer for the Hartford Stage Company. Although based in New York City, he has had long term relationships with Center Stage in Baltimore beginning with *The Runner Stumbles* in 1977, and with the Williamstown Theatre Festival. He has designed many off-Broadway productions such as *Snow Orchid* at Circle Repertory Company, *Lady House Blues*, *Chekov Sketchbook*, *Taxi Tales* at the Century Theatre and *Marion* at the Juilliard School. Regional theater credits include productions at the Guthrie Theatre, Long Wharf, Alley Theatre, Seattle Repertory Theatre, Milwaukee Repertory Theatre, Alaska Repertory Theatre, and the Santa Fe Festival. He has taught at the University of Wisconsinat Madison, Williams College and the North Carolina School of the Arts. Twenty-first century designs include *The Streets of New York* for the Irish Repertory Theatre.
Sets: 1983 *A View from the Bridge* 1987 *All My Sons* 1996 *Bus Stop*

William T. Lane

William T. Lane is a native of St. Louis, Missouri. He received his B.S. and M.F.A. in theater design from Northwestern University. For the following eight years he was a free lance designer in Chicago and the Head of Design for the Department of Theater and Dance at Barat College in Lake Forest, Illinois. In 1979 he moved to Providence, Rhode Island and became the resident costume designer at Trinity Repertory Company. Since then he has designed over 200 productions with the Tony Award winning company and formed long term collaborations with all its' Artistic Directors: founder Adrian Hall, Anne Bogart, Richard Jenkins and currently Oskar Eustis. Twenty-first century designs include costumes for Peter Parnell's two part epic *The Cider House Rules* directed by Mr. Eustis. The costume designer should not be confused with the Canadian director who has the same name.

Costumes: 1982 *The Hothouse*

Edgar Lansbury

Edgar George McIldowie Lansbury was born in London on January 12, 1930 and came to the United States in 1941, becoming a naturalized citizen in 1953. His mother was the actress Moyna MacGill, and his sister is actress Angela Lansbury. Known primarily as a film producer and art director, he began in theater as an apprentice at the Windham (New Hampshire) Playhouse in 1947, where he returned to design in 1953-54. His New York debut was *The Wise have not Spoken* at the Cherry Lane Theatre in 1954. He served as art director for ABC-TV in 1955, and CBS-TV from 1955 to 1962, and in 1964 formed Edgar Lansbury Productions, a motion picture and theater production company. He has subsequently produced many shows on Broadway, including *Gypsy* (1974), *American Buffalo* (1977), and *Broadway Follies* (1981). Films include *Godspell* (1973), *The Subject Was Roses* (1968), and *The Clairvoyant* (1982). *The Subject Was Roses*, which he produced, won a Tony Award as Best Play in 1963. Recent productions include *All The Queen's Men* at the Westport Country Playhouse in 1989, *Advice from a Caterpillar* in 1990, and *The Country Club* in 1992.

Sets: 1964 *The Subject Was Roses*

Lanvin

Jeanne Lanvin, a French couturier entered the fashion business as an apprentice at age 13 to a dressmaker. Her successful House of Lanvin, Faubourg St. Honoré was begun by creating dresses for children, who requested her designs when they grew up. Shortly before World War I she introduced gowns, and later wedding dresses. Her elegant *robes de style* were much in demand by private customers, and in 1926 she started to offer men's wear. Her distinctive embroideries and delicate use of sequins made her popular with actresses as well. She died on July 6, 1946 in Paris; the House of Lanvin continued.

Costumes: 1922 *The Awful Truth*† (Ina Clair's gowns)

Robert Lanza

Robert Lanza designed costumes for a play in 1947.

Costumes: 1947 *Laura*

Roy LaPaugh

Roy LaPaugh designed one set on Broadway in 1933.

Sets: 1933 *The Mountain*†

Peter Larkin

Peter Larkin, a designer of sets, lights and sometimes costumes, was born in Boston on August 26, 1926. He studied at Yale University and with Oliver Larkin, his father. His Broadway debut as a scenic designer was in 1952 but he made his New York debut a year earlier with *The Wild Duck* at City Center. He has been honored for outstanding set design with Tony Awards for *Teahouse of the August Moon* and *Ondine* in 1954, and *Inherit the Wind* and *No Time for Sergeants* in 1956, as well as a Maharam Award for *Les Blancs* (1970). Additional credits include production design for the films *Tootsie*, *Compromising Positions*, *get Shorty*, and *Three Men and a Baby*, and art direction for *Reuben, Reuben* among others. Twenty-first century production designs include *Miss Congeniality* and *The Crew*.

Sets: 1952 *Dial "M" for Murder* **1953** *The Teahouse of the August Moon* **1954** *Ondine*; *Peter Pan* **1955** *Inherit the Wind*; *No Time for Sergeants* **1956** *New Faces of '56*; *Protective Custody*; *Shangri-La* **1957** *Compulsion*; *Good As Gold*; *Miss Isobel* **1958** *Blue Denim*; *Goldilocks*; *The Shadow of a Gunman* **1959** *First Impressions*; *Only in America* **1960** *Greenwillow*; *Wildcat* **1962** *Giants, Sons of Giants*; *Nowhere to Go But Up* **1963** *Marathon '33* **1964** *The Crucible*; *The Seagull* **1966** *The Great In-*

doors; *Hail Scrawdyke!* 1970 *Les Blancs;*
Sheep of the Runway 1971 *Twigs* 1972
Wise Child 1973 *Let Me Hear You Smile*
1974 *Thieves* 1977 *Ladies at the Alamo*
1978 *Dancin'* 1979 *Break a Leg* 1981
Broadway Follies 1983 *Doonesbury* 1984
The Rink 1986 *Big Deal*
Costumes: 1956 *Protective Custody*
Lights: 1952 *Dial "M" for Murder* 1953
The Teahouse of the August Moon 1955
Damn Yankees 1956 *Shangri-La*

Robert Larkin

Robert E. Larkin worked primarily as
an electrician during a 55-year span.
At the beginning of his career he was
associated with David Belasco and at
the end of it was working in television.
It is likely that he was responsible for
more designs, especially for lights, than
those credited to him. A long time resident of New York, he lived at 601 West
113th Street and died in April 1963 in
Fort Lauderdale, Florida at age 75.
Sets: 1915 *Maternity*
Lights: 1917 *Maytime*

Johannes Larsen

An art director and scenic designer,
Johannes Larsen was born in Banga-
lore, India, the son of Lutheran missionaries from Denmark. He immigrated to the United States in 1934
and studied at the Yale Drama School
with Donald Oenslager after which he
worked in theaters around America,
including the Dock Street Theatre in
Charleston, South Carolina and the
Civic Theatre in Fort Wayne, Indiana.
He also worked for Universal Pictures
making scale models. He designed the
1942 summer season at the McCarter
Theatre before spending the rest of
World War II in London, broadcasting for Voice of America. He moved
to California in 1946, began working
for Paramount Studios, quickly moving
through the ranks to become an art director. His first movie as art director
was *The Secret of the Incas* in 1953, followed by many, many more. He won an
Academy Award for *The Rose Tattoo*
and received nominations for *Hud, The
Spy Who Came In from the Cold, The
Molly Maguires,* and *Heaven's Gate.*
He died in North Hollywood on March
24, 2001.

Sets: 1939 *The Three Sisters* 1940
Boyd's Daughter; Return Engagement
1942 *The First Crocus*
Lights: 1940 *Boyd's Daughter*

Yngve Larson

Yngve Larson, who was born February 11, 1913 in Gothenburg, Sweden,
designed often at the Royal Dramatic
Theatre in Stockholm in the 1940s and
1950s. His design for *Modell Beatrice* done in collaboration with As-
mund Arle is included in René Hainaux and Yves-Bonnat's *Stage Designers Throughout the World Since 1950.*
They credit him with about 120 productions.
Sets: 1962 *Miss Julie*

Miss Grace LaRue

Grace LaRue Hamilton was an actress, born in 1882 in Kansas City,
who appeared on the Broadway stage,
mainly in musical revues including editions of *The Ziegfeld Follies.* The 1910
Madame Troubadour playbill states:
"Gowns and hats worn by Miss La
Rue designed by her and executed by
Madame Frances of Paris, France."
The widow of film actor Hale Hamilton, her first marriage to actor Byron
D. Chandler ended in divorce. She died
in Burlingame, California on March 12,
1956 at age 75.
Costumes: 1910 *Madame Troubadour*

Lee Lash Studios

Through the Lee Lash Studios, Lee
and Samuel Lash designed theatrical
productions and constructed those designed by others. The studio was located in Mt. Vernon, New York in the
late twenties and at 1476 Broadway in
1931. Lee Lash was born in San Francisco in 1864 and was active as a scenic
artist in New York City at the turn of
the century. He studied in Paris at the
Académie Julian, and with Boulanger
and Lefebvre between 1880 and 1886.
He participated in a painting exhibition in 1891 in California, in 1893 in
New York City and in 1899 at the Paris
salon.
Sets: 1905 *The Gingerbread Man* 1909
The Goddess of Liberty; The Motor Girl
1910 *Olive Latimer's Husband*† (Painted);

Up and Down Broadway **1911** *Jumping Jupiter*[†] (Acts I, II); *Modern Marriage* **1912** *The Trail of the Lonesome Pine*[†] **1913** *Lieber Augustin*[†] (Act II); *Oh, I Say*[†] **1934** *Tomorrow's Harvest*

Oscar Laske

Oscar Laske designed Broadway costumes in 1928.

Costumes: 1928 *Servant of Two Masters*

Margaret Lathem

Margaret Lathem was active on Broadway as a scenic designer in the mid-1920s.

Sets: 1924 *Try It with Alice*

Alice Laughlin

Alice Denniston Laughlin designed one set in 1933 on Broadway. A painter, muralist, designer of stained glass and woodcuts, and an expert on medieval art, she was born on October 19, 1895 in New York City and died on July 30, 1952 in Pittsburgh, Pennsylvania. She studied with Vassily Shoukhoeff in Paris and at the New York Art Students League and participated in many exhibitions of stained glass and woodcuts.

Sets: 1933 *La Nativite*

Madame Laurent

Madame Laurent designed costumes in 1907.

Costumes: 1907 *The Coming of Mrs. Patrick*

Jules Laurentz

Jules Laurentz designed one set in 1936 on Broadway. His scenery construction business, J. Laurentz Studios, was active in New York before World War II.

Sets: 1936 *To My Husband*

Laverdet

Laverdet (also known as London Laverdet) was a French set designer who worked as a scenic artist and occasionally designed for the Comédie Française. He designed scenery and/or costumes for some thirty-six productions on the London stage during the 1920s, and designed scenery for *Mieux que Nue!* with Deshayes and Arnaud, Ronsin, Roger and Durand, and Canut at the Moulin Rouge Music Hall in Paris in 1925. The 1930 interior decorations that he did with Marc Henri at the Whitehall Theatre in London were restored in 1986 by Felicity Youett. The two designers worked together through Marc Henri and Laverdet, Ltd. in London, until it closed for business in October 1934.

Sets: 1924 *Andre Charlot's Revue of 1924*[†] **1925** *Charlot Revue*[†] **1928** *This Year of Grace*[†] **1929** *Wake Up and Dream*[†]

Costumes: 1929 *Wake Up and Dream*[†]

Lavignac & Pellegry

Lavignac & Pellegry (Pelegry) collaborated on the design for a Broadway set in 1939. The production originated in France. André Emile Gustave Pelegry (1894-1969) was responsible for the décor of a number of productions in Paris in the mid and late 1940s, including *Trois Garçons, Une Fille* at the Châtelet and *Les Héritiers Bouchard* at Porte Saint-Martin. Later in life, he was a camera man in the French film industry.

Sets: 1939 *Folies Bergère*[†]

W. Robert La Vine

W. Robert La Vine, a costume designer and the author of a book on film costume design, *In A Glamorous Fashion*, studied at the Art Institute of Chicago. During his career he served as assistant to Cecil Beaton and headed the re-production of *My Fair Lady* in 1976. He worked for Paramount Pictures Corporation as archivist and assisted planning for the exhibition, *The Glamour of Hollywood Design* at the Metropolitan Museum of Art. Mr. La Vine died in August 1979.

Costumes: 1968 *Maggie Flynn* **1969** *Jimmy*

Roger LaVoie

Roger LaVoie designed scenery for the concert version of *Sally* performed on Broadway at the Academy Theatre. He was born on December 12, 1947 in Fitchburg, Massachusetts, the son of John J. LaVoie and Dorothy E. LeGére. He received a B.A. at Emerson College and an M.F.A. at the Yale University

School of Drama. Roger LaVoie includes director Tom Haas and designer John Conklin as influential figures in his life and on his designs. His career began at Emerson College in 1967 with a production of *Peer Gynt*. He designs for ballet companies through the world, and did sets and costumes for the Ballet Theatre of Boston's production of *The Nutcracker*.

Sets: 1987 *Sally*

Arthur Law

Playwright and actor Arthur Law was born on March 22, 1844 in Northrepps, Norfolk, England and after service with the Royal Scots Fusiliers started performing. He wrote more than 60 pays, with *The New Boy*, *The Mystery of a Hansom Cab* and *The Magic Opal* among the most successful. He died in Parkstone, Dorset, England on March 2, 1913. Arthur Law is credited with the scenic design for a 1909 Clyde Fitch play in at Maxine Elliott's Theatre.

Sets: 1909 *The Bachelor*

H. Robert Law

H. Robert Law was one of the busiest scenic artists and designers in New York, beginning in 1905. He worked alone, but also in collaboration with others, including P. Dodd Ackerman. For example, for *World of Pleasure* he designed Act I, Scenes 1, 3, 4 and Act II, Scene 2, with Ackerman doing Act I, Scene 2 and Act II, Scenes 1, 3, and 4. He maintained an active studio where his own designs and those of others were executed. Among his credits in London is scenery for the two-part revue *The Rainbow* in 1923 in London, in collaboration with Marc Henri and Oliver Bernard. He also produced vaudeville shows. H. Robert Law died on October 20, 1925 at age 49, although the studio bearing his name remained active through 1931.

Sets: 1905 *As Ye Sow*; *King Lear†* (Designed and painted); *Macbeth*; *The Marriage of William Ashe†* 1906 *Clothes†*; *Hamlet (Mantell)*; *The Law and the Man*; *The Love Route*; *The Man of the Hour*; *The Redskin* (as: R.A. Law) 1907 *Anna Karenina*; *The Comet*; *Divorcons*; *King Lear†*; *Macbeth* 1908 *The Blue Mouse* (as: Law); *The Gentleman from Mississippi*; *Girls*; *Glorious Betsy*; *The Man Who Stood Still*; *The Mimic World†* (All but last act); *The Servant in the House*; *The Wolf* (as: Robert Law) 1909 *An American Widow*; *The Beauty Spot†*; *The City* (as: Law); *The Dollar Mark†* (Designed and painted); *The Girl and the Wizard*; *The Goddess of Reason*; *The Great John Ganton*; *The Lottery Man*; *The Return of Eve*; *Such a Little Queen*; *A Woman's Way* 1910 *Bobby Burnit*; *Children of Destiny*; *The Commuters*; *The Country Boy* (Designed and painted); *The Deserters*; *He Came from Milwaukee*; *The Heights*; *A Man's World*; *A Skylark* 1911 *As a Man Thinks*; *The Balkan Princess*; *The Boss†*; *Bought and Paid For*; *Bunty Pulls the Strings†* (Painted); *The First Lady in the Land* (as: H. Robert Low); *H.M.S. Pinafore*; *Kindling*; *The Kiss Waltz*; *The Lights o' London†*; *The Little Millionaire†*; *Maggie Pepper*; *An Old New Yorker†*; *Over Night*; *The Rack†* (Designed and painted); *The Revue of Revues†*; *The Scarcrow*; *The Wedding Trip†* (Painted); *When Sweet Sixteen†* (Painted) 1912 *The Argyle Case†*; *H.M.S. Pinafore*; *The Indiscretion of Truth†* (Act II); *Little Miss Brown*; *Little Women†* (Designed and painted); *Making Good†*; *Mere Man*; *My Best Girl†*; *Patience*; *The Right to Be Happy*; *The Trial Marriage*; *Within the Law*; *The Yellow Jacket* 1913 *All Aboard†*; *The Beggar Student*; *Divorcons†*; *The Fight*; *H.M.S. Pinafore*; *John the Baptist*; *Lieber Augustin†* (Acts I, III); *The Lure*; *The Master Mind†* (Act II); *The Misleading Lady*; *The Passing Show of 1913†*; *The Princess Players*; *Shadowed*; *The Things That Count†* 1914 *The Charm of Isabel†* (Painted); *Dancing Around†*; *Don't Weaken†* (Designed and painted); *Life†* (All other scenery); *The Passing Show of 1914†*; *A Thousand Years Ago*; *When Claudia Smiles*; *The Yellow Ticket* 1915 *The Earth†* (Painted); *Maid in America*; *Three of Hearts†*; *The Ware Case†*; *The White Feather†*; *A World of Pleasure†* 1916 *David Garrick*; *Fixing Sister*; *The Man Who Came Back*; *Robinson Crusoe, Jr.†* 1917 *Cheer-up (Hippodrome)†* (Scenes 5-8 (Sc. 5 together)); *Out There*; *When Johnny Comes Marching Home†* 1918 *Her Country†*; *Hitchy Koo 1918*; *Oh,*

Look! **1919** *At 9:45* **1921** *The Intimate Strangers†* **1923** *Sun Showers†* **1924** *Keep Kool*

H. Robert Studio Law

H. Robert Law began his Broadway career in 1915 and designed both under his own name and through a scenic studio. The H. Robert Law Studio was located at 502 West 138th Street in New York City and continued in operation until 1931.

Sets: **1900** *Trilby* **1911** *Miss Jack†* **1912** *The Point of View†*; *The Wall Street Girl* **1914** *The Midnight Girl*; *A Perfect Lady†* (Act III) **1915** *Mr. Myd's Mystery* **1916** *His Majesty Bunker Bean*; *The Master* **1917** *Eileen* **1918** *Listen Lester*; *A Stitch in Time* **1919** *Hitchy Koo 1919†*; *Luck in Pawn*; *The Velvet Lady* **1920** *As You Were*; *Hitchy Koo 1920*; *Look Who's Here*; *Poldekin†*; *Scandals of 1920* **1921** *Dulcy*; *Golden Days*; *Peg o' My Heart*; *Two Little Girls* **1922** *The Endless Chain*; *The French Doll*; *Just Because*; *Molly Darling*; *Our Nell*; *Persons Unknown*; *Queen o' Hearts* **1923** *Runnin' Wild* **1924** *Be Yourself*; *Dawn*; *I'll Say She Is*; *The New Poor* **1925** *Kosher Kitty Kelly*; *Tell Me More†* **1931** *Little Women*

Joseph Law

Joseph Law designed one set in 1922 on Broadway. A carpenter, he resided at 1018 Avenue A in New York City in 1916.

Sets: **1922** *Spice of 1922*

Al. Lawrence

Al. Lawrence, perhaps Alexander or Albert, collaborated on the scenery for a 1901 production. His name occasionally appeared in playbills of that era for constructing scenery with P. J. McDonald

Sets: **1901** *The Night of the 4th†*

Les Lawrence

Les Lawrence, a sculptor and ceramist, was born Edwin Lawrence in Corpus Christi, Texas on December 17, 1940. He attended Southwestern State College in Weatherford, Oklahoma where he received a B.A. He also attended Arizona State University where he received an M.F.A. in ceramics in 1970 and served on the faculty as a guest artist. He has exhibited in numerous art shows receiving many prizes and awards.

Sets: **1972** *Jacques Brel Is Alive and Living in Paris*

Miss Margaret Lawrence

Miss Margaret Lawrence was an actress who performed many roles on Broadway during the teens and twenties. For one of the plays in which she starred she also designed the costumes. Her first role was *Peter Pan* in summer stock and she first appeared on Broadway in *Over Night*. In private life she was married to Orson D. Munn and the mother of two children. During her husband's service in World War I as a Lieutenant Commander she performed in many comedies. She was born August 2, 1889 in Trenton, New Jersey, and died in New York City on June 9, 1929.

Costumes: **1922** *Secrets*

Pauline Lawrence

Pauline Lawrence designed costumes on Broadway in 1933. Born in Los Angeles, she worked mainly as a pianist and accompanist. She joined the Denishawn Company at age 17 as a pianist, also doing some dancing in minor roles. At a later date she also worked as a pianist for Martha Graham. She designed costumes mainly for the dance productions of her husband José Limon, for whom she also worked as pianist and agent. Pauline Lawrence died July 16, 1971 in Stockton, New Jersey at the age of 70.

Costumes: **1933** *As Thousands Cheer†* (Lonely Hearts); *Candide* **1934** *Life Begins at 8:40†*

Kate Drain Lawson

Kate Drain Lawson, a scenic designer, actress, theater executive and costume designer, was born Kate Drain in Spokane, Washington on July 27, 1894. She attended art school in Paris and first appeared on stage as a dancer in Paris in 1921. She was married to playwright John Howard Lawson from 1918 to 1924. She began on Broadway as an assistant stage manager and during

her career served in various capacities such as assistant to the designer, technical director, musical director and designer. During World War I she served with the Ambulance Americaine and in World War II served with the Red Cross in India. This multi-talented artist appeared in numerous films, designed for television and organized the costume department on the West Coast for NBC-TV, retiring in 1976. She died at age 83 on November 14, 1977.
Sets: **1926** *The Chief Thing*† **1927** *Mr. Pim Passes By*† **1930** *Garrick Gaieties* **1934** *Four Saints in Three Acts*†; *Valley Forge* **1935** *Eden End*; *A Slight Case of Murder*; *To See Ourselves* **1936** *The Holmses of Baker Street*; *Love from a Stranger* **1937** *A Point of Honor*
Costumes: **1923** *Roger Bloomer* **1930** *Garrick Gaieties*† **1934** *Four Saints in Three Acts* **1935** *A Slight Case of Murder*; *Stick-in-the-Mud* (Costume Supervisor) **1937** *A Point of Honor* **1938** *Knights of Song* **1940** *Meet the People*†

Mark Lawson

Mark Lawson was born in Stockholm, Sweden, but came to Chicago with his parents when he was six months old. He later lived in St. Paul and Minneapolis, Minnesota where he learned to paint scenery from Paul Clausen, at that time the region's premier scenic artist. He subsequently worked in Boston at Stetson's Globe Theatre before moving to New York City. He joined the staff of the New York Hippodrome when it opened and spent fourteen years working there, initially with art director Arthur Voegtlin and later as head scenic artist. He was also on the staff of the Ernest Grau Studio and the Oden Waller Studio. Mark Lawson died in New York City at age 62 in May 1928.
Sets: **1907** *Hip! Hip! Hooray!*† **1917** *Cheer-up (Hippodrome)*† (Scenes 1-5, 9-11; Sc. 5 together) **1919** *Miss Millions* **1922** *Better Times*†

H. B. Layman

H. Bernard Layman was active on Broadway in the mid-1920s. In 1921 he was manager of the exposition department of John H. French Co., general building contractors, in New York

City. By the mid-1920s he had joined Rothe & Co., Inc. at 222 West 46th Street.
Sets: **1926** *Sure Fire*

Augustín Lazo

Augustín Lazo was a well-known Mexican surrealist painter who studied at the Academy of San Carlos, and in Europe. He designed numerous settings for plays in his native country, being especially active in the 1940s and collaborating often with Xavier Vilaurrutia. Mr. Lazo, who started in the theater translating plays by Shakespeare and Pirandello into Spanish, also wrote plays. In 1947 the Teatro Mexicano presented his plays *La Huella* and *El Case de Don Juan Manuel* which he also designed. Born in 1898 (some sources say 1900) in Mexico City, he died there in 1971.
Costumes: **1938** *Mexicana*

Wilford Leach

Born Carson Wilford Leach on August 26, 1929 in Petersburg, Virginia, Wilford Leach was the principal director of the New York Shakespeare Festival from 1977 until his death on June 18, 1988 at age 59. He taught at Sarah Lawrence College and was "artistic director" at La Mama E.T.C. where he created many projects for Ellen Stewart, though always crediting her as artistic director. He attended the College of William and Mary (A.B., 1949) and the University of Illinois (M.A., 1954, Ph.D., 1957). A workshop production at the Public Theatre of *The Mandrake* led to his initial New York Shakespeare Festival in the Park productions, *All's Well That Ends Well* and *The Taming of the Shrew*. In the fall of 1979 he gave up teaching and joined the Public Theatre full-time. He received Tony Awards for directing for *The Pirates of Penzance* and *The Mystery of Edwin Drood*.
Sets: **1981** *The Pirates of Penzance*†

Jean-Guy Lecat

Jean-Guy Lecat has been technical director for Peter Brook since 1976, in charge of adapting the many different spaces where Brook's company has performed around the world. He entered theater in 1967 as assistant set designer at the Théâtre du Vieux Colombier and the Avingon Festival. An experienced stage manager, scenographer, lighting and scenic designer, he has worked at La Mama E.T.C. and The Living Theatre and designed productions for Jean-Louis Barrault, Jean-Pierre Vincent, Dario Fo, Jean Vilar and others. Recent U.S. credits include *The Man Who*, adapted by Peter Brook and performed by his "Centre Internationale de Creations Theatrales," at the Brooklyn Academy of Music in 1995.

Sets: 1983 *La Tragedie de Carmen*

Ellen Lee

Ellen Lee designed costumes for the first time on Broadway in 1986. Additional designs include costumes for Alaina Reed, Roz Ryan and Terry Burrell for their club acts. Ellen Lee also works as a wardrobe supervisor for Broadway shows, including *Woman of the Year*, *Bubbling Brown Sugar*, *Ain't Misbehavin'*, *Night of the Iguana*, and *Eubie*.

Costumes: 1986 *Uptown...It's Hot*

Eugene Lee

Eugene Lee has many design credits for television including *Night Music, Kids in the Hall*, and *House Party*. He is a proponent of real items instead of façades and of environmental settings which encompass not only the stage but the entire theater space, including the relationship between actor and audience. Eugene Lee is well known as the original designer of *Saturday Night Live*, which he initially designed in collaboration with his former wife, Franne Lee. He has been principal designer at Trinity Repertory Theatre since 1968 and with David Rotundo is co-owner of Scenic Services, a lighting and design company located in Providence, Rhode Island. His first professional designs were *A Dream of Love* and *Belch* at the Theatre of the Living Arts in Philadelphia in 1966. Eugene and Franne Lee received the "most promising designers" Drama Desk Award in 1970-71 and each received a Tony, Maharam and Drama Desk Award for *Candide*. Their

scenic design for *Sweeney Todd* also garnered a Tony Award. He won an American Theatre Wing Design Award in 1999. Born on March 9, 1939 in Beloit, Wisconsin, he studied at Carnegie Mellon and Yale and has been married to Brooke Lutz since 1981. He teaches at Brown and Carnegie Mellon Universities and at the Rhode Island School of Design. Carnegie Institute of Technology.

Sets: 1970 *Wilson in the Promise Land* 1972 *Dude*† 1974 *Candide* 1975 *The Skin of Our Teeth* 1977 *Some of My Best Friends* 1979 *Gilda Radner Live from N.Y.*†; *Sweeney Todd* 1981 *Merrily We Roll Along* 1982 *Agnes of God*; *The Hothouse* 1994 *Show Boat* 1995 *On the Waterfront* 1998 *Colin Quinn - An Irish Wake*; *Ragtime* 2000 *A Moon for the Misbegotten*; *Seussical the Musical*

Costumes: 1998 *Colin Quinn - An Irish Wake*

Lights: 1982 *The Hothouse*

Franne Lee

Franne Lee has designed many productions both on and off-Broadway, concentrating mainly on costumes. She began her career with the Theatre of the Living Arts in Philadelphia, and since then has designed throughout the United States and in Europe for Peter Brook's International Center for Theatre Research. Franne Lee received two Tony awards, for *Candide* in 1974 and for *Sweeney Todd* in 1979. Born Franne Newman on December 30, 1941 in the Bronx she received an M.F.A. from the University of Wisconsin at Madison. She went to Madison intending to study art, but while assisting an art instructor paint a set, discovered the theater. Her first design was *Oh Dad, Poor Dad, Mama's Hung You in the Closet and I'm Feeling So Bad*. She has designed costumes for films, including *One Trick Pony, Dead Ringer, The Local Stigmatic, Sweet Nothing*, and *Baby, It's You*. Television credits include *The Scarlet Letter* on PBS and the first five years of *Saturday Night Live* on NBC-TV, designed in conjunction with her former husband, Eugene Lee. Twenty-first century designs include costumes for the film *Chinese*

Coffee directed by Al Pacino.
Sets: 1972 *Dude*†
Costumes: 1974 *Candide; Love for Love*
1975 *The Skin of Our Teeth* 1977 *Some
of My Best Friends* 1979 *Gilda Radner
Live from N.Y.*†; *Sweeney Todd* 1981 *The
Moony Shapiro Song Book* 1982 *Rock
'n Roll! The First 5,000 Years* 1993
Camelot (Costume Supervision and additional designs)

Ming Cho Lee

Master designer Ming Cho Lee began designing in New York City in 1958 with *The Infernal Machine* at the Phoenix Theatre. He was born in Shanghai on October 3, 1930 and received a B.A. at Occidental College. He attended the University of California at Los Angeles from 1953 to 1954. He studied with Chinese watercolorist Kuo-Nyen Chang and spent five years working as assistant to Jo Mielziner. Ming Cho Lee's productions on Broadway barely represent the designs he has created for opera, dance and theater in major companies around the country. His originality is remarkable and he has influenced countless students at New York University and at the Yale University School of Drama, where he is Co-Chair of Design. He likes to work with students that he has trained and regularly hires them as assistants, often commenting that his teaching makes him a better designer and designing makes him a more effective teacher. All of his students agree. His list of awards is also long and includes a 1990 Distinguished Career Achievement Award from the National Endowment for the Arts, the Peter Zeisler Award at Arena Stage in 1987, Maharam Awards for *Electra* in 1965 and *Ergo* in 1968, a Tony Award for *K-2* in 1983, a Guggenheim in 1988, Los Angeles Drama Critics and Hollywood Drama Logue Critics Awards for *Traveler in the Dark* in 1985, Maharam Awards, and many more. His wife, the former Betsy Rapport, works as his assistant and they have three sons.
Sets: 1962 *The Moon Besieged* 1963
Mother Courage and Her Children 1966
Slapstick Tragedy; A Time for Singing
1967 *Little Murders* 1968 *Here's Where*

I Belong 1969 *Billy; La Strada* 1972
Much Ado About Nothing; Two Gentlemen of Verona 1975 *All God's Chillun
Got Wings; The Glass Menagerie* 1976
*For Colored Girls Who Have Considered
Suicide* 1977 *Caesar and Cleopatra;
Romeo and Juliet; The Shadow Box* 1978
Angel 1979 *The Grand Tour* 1983 *The
Glass Menagerie; K2* 1986 *Execution of
Justice,*
Lights: 1962 *The Moon Besieged*

Tom Lee

Thomas Bailey Lee, an interior and industrial designer, was born in Costa Rica. He studied at the Traphagen School and the National Academy. In the late 1930s he was display director at Bonwit Teller, and at the same time a set and costume designer for the American Ballet Company. After service in World War II he formed his own firm and designed exhibitions for the Metropolitan Museum of Art, the Smithsonian Museum and other museums, and showrooms for fashion designers. This experience led to hotel design, beginning with Colonial Williamsburg's first motor lodge, and then for hotels all over the world. He completed the design for the interior of the Park-Lane Hotel in New York shortly before his death in July 1971.
Sets: 1940 *Louisiana Purchase*
Costumes: 1940 *Louisiana Purchase;
Walk with Music*

Honor Leeming

Honor Leeming supervised the setting for a Broadway play in 1930. She resided at 123 West 57th Street in 1932.
Sets: 1930 *Out of a Blue Sky*

Benjamin Leffler

Ben Leffler spent eighteen years as master electrician at the Hudson Theatre, 141 West 44th Street in New York City. He designed lighting for many productions on Broadway in the 1920s, and as staff electrician was certainly responsible for additional productions during those years when lighting designers were seldom credited. He died at age 76 in 1949 in New York City.
Costumes: 1907 *The Christian Pilgrim*
Lights: 1922 *The Lion and the Mouse*
1924 *Flossie* 1926 *The Climax; The*

Man from Toronto 1927 *The Banshee; The Lady Screams; The Love Thief* 1928 *Gods of the Lightning* 1929 *The Octoroon; Pansy*

John Lehmeyer

John Lehmeyer, a costume designer and director for opera and theater, has spent much of his career in Baltimore designing for Center Stage and the Baltimore Opera Company, where he has served as Resident Designer and Assistant General Manager since 1975. He has designed for the Boston Opera Company and for regional theaters including Trinity Repertory Theatre and the Milwaukee Repertory Theatre. Mr. Lehmeyer, was born in Baltimore on February 10, 1940. Twenty-first century credits include direction and costume design for *Faust* for the Baltimore Opera Company.

Costumes: 1970 *Wilson in the Promise Land*

Maxine Leigh

Maxine Leigh supervised the costumes for a play in 1937.

Costumes: 1937 *Blow Ye Winds* (Costume Supervisor)

D. Lellouch

D. Lellouch collaborated on the costumes for *The Garden of Allah* in 1911. A note in the 1911 playbill states: "D. Lellouch of the Yeldez Palace, Tunis."

Costumes: 1911 *The Garden of Allah*†

Charles LeMaire

Charles LeMaire, known primarily as a costume and fashion designer, was born in Chicago in 1896 and entered the theater as a vaudeville actor. He became interested in costume design through shopping for and painting fabrics. Known for the glitter and extravagance of his costumes, he first designed costumes in 1919 on Broadway. He made his Broadway debut as a scenic designer as "Sergeant Charles LeMaire" during World War I in the previous year, but all subsequent scenic designs were in combination with costume designs. In addition to his Broadway credits he designed costumes for Brooks Costume

Company and headed its costume department until 1929, when he organized his own firm. After service in World War II he settled in Hollywood and from 1943 to 1960 was Executive Director of Wardrobe at 20th Century Fox Studios. He won three Academy Awards for film designs. Mr. LeMaire died on June 8, 1985 in Palm Springs, California.

Sets: 1918 *Atta Boy* 1923 *Hammerstein's Nine O'clock Revue* 1932 *Ballyhoo of 1932*† (Act II finale)

Costumes: 1919 *Elsie Janis and Her Gang*† 1920 *Broadway Brevities of 1920* 1922 *Daffy Dill; Elsie Janis and Her Gang*†; *Ziegfeld Follies: 1922*† (Blunder Land, Etc.) 1923 *Hammerstein's Nine O'clock Revue; Mary Jane McKane* (Gowns and costumes); *Poppy; Wildflower* 1924 *Artists and Models*† (Dresses); *Be Yourself*† (Dresses); *Betty Lee; The Grab Bag*†; *Hassard Short's Ritz Revue* ("Monsieur Beaucair"); *The Magnolia Lady*† (All Principals except Miss Chatterton; Female chorus); *Rose-Marie; Sitting Pretty*† (Act I); *Vogues of 1924; Ziegfeld Follies: 1924*† 1925 *The Cocoanuts; Earl Carroll's Vanities; Greenwich Village Follies*†; *Merry, Merry; Tell Me More* (Costumes and gowns) 1926 *Betsy; Earl Carroll's Vanities*†; *Hello, Lola*† (Miss Fuller's costumes); *The Ramblers; Twinkle, Twinkle* 1927 *Africana; Five O'clock Girl; The Love Call*† (Act III); *My Princess; The New Yorkers*† (Additional dresses); *Rufus LeMaire's Affairs; Take the Air*† 1928 *George White's Scandals*†; *Get Me in the Movies*† (Miss Baxter's Cleopatra costume); *Hello, Daddy; Hello, Yourself; The New Moon; Rain or Shine; Rainbow; Three Cheers* (Miss Stone's costumes) 1929 *Fioretta*†; *George White's Scandals*† (American costumes); *Midnite Frolics*†; *Murray Anderson's Almanac*†; *Ned Wayburn's Gambols; Sons o' Guns; Sweet Adeline* 1930 *Ballyhoo; Earl Carroll's Vanities*†; *Fine and Dandy; Flying High; Luana; The New Yorkers*† (Special costumes); *Princess Charming; Ripples; Strike Up the Band* 1931 *America's Sweetheart*†; *Earl Carroll's Vanities*†; *East Wind; George White's Scandals*†; *Of Thee I Sing*†; *Shoot the Works*† (Costume Director); *The Wonder Bar*† 1932 *Ballyhoo of 1932*† (Roulette number, Act II Finale); *George White's Music Hall Varieties*[†]; *Hot-Cha!*[†]; *Take a Chance*[†] (Frocks) **1933** *Blackbirds of 1933*; *Both Your Houses*[†]; *Melody*; *Of Thee I Sing*[†] (Dresses) **1934** *Say When*; *Ziegfeld Follies: 1934*[†] **1935** *George White's Scandals* **1936** *Mainly for Lovers* (Miss Gish's and Miss Hartzell's gowns)

Jacques Le Marquet

Jacques Le Marquet designed one setting on Broadway in 1958. He is also the author of *Jardins à la Française*, published in 1972 by Gallimard.

Sets: 1958 *Théâtre National Populaire*

Lucy L'Engle

Lucy B. L'Engle, a painter born in New York City on Sept. 28, 1889 studied at the Art Students League and in Paris. She had exhibitions of her paintings from the 1950s in several locations in the eastern U.S., including three solo showings in Provincetown, Massachusetts. Also known as a crafts worker, she painted murals for buildings and in 1922 she designed costumes on Broadway. She died in Truro, Massachusetts in 1978.

Costumes: 1922 *Mr. Faust*

Jose Lengson

Costume designer Jose Lengson was born on August 28, 1954. He designed costumes for numerous productions at Radio City Music Hall, as well as for Disney on Ice and in regional theaters. He died on May 9, 1991.

Costumes: 1990 *The Christmas Spectacular*[†] **1991** *Christmas Spectacular*[†] (Additional costumes) **1992** *Radio City Christmas Spectacular*[†] (Additional designs) **1993** *Radio City Easter Show*[†] **1994** *Radio City Easter Show*[†] **1995** *Radio City Easter Show*[†] **1996** *Radio City Spring Spectacular*[†] **1997** *Radio City Spring Spectacular*[†]

Agnes Lenners

Agnes Lenners designed gowns and hats for a Broadway show in 1921.

Costumes: 1921 *The Fan*[†] (Hats and gowns)

Gertrude Lennox

Actress Gertrude Best Lewin was known during her stage career as Gertrude Lennox. She received credit for a single scenic design on Broadway in 1923 and died on July 11, 1940.

Sets: 1923 *Meet the Wife*[†]

Frank Lentz

Franklin A. Lentz created scenery in 1903. He lived at 1 West 97th Street in New York, according to the New York City directory of 1901. He later worked as a performer and was known to his friends as "Fuzzy."

Sets: 1903 *Erminie*

Tina Leser

Tina Leser was born Christine Wetherill Shillard-Smith in Philadelphia in 1911. After study at the Philadelphia Academy of Art and the Sorbonne in Paris, she opened a shop in Honolulu in 1935, selling imported Chinese brocades and garments she designed. After Pearl Harbor was attacked and the United States entered the Second World War, she moved to New York where beginning in 1943 she designed sportswear that was carried by Saks Fifth Avenue and other department stores. Occasionally, she also designed costumes for the theater. In the early 1950s, fashion designer Liz Clairborne began her career in the fashion industry as a sketch artist for Tina Leser. Honored with both a Coty Fashion Critics' Award and a Neiman-Marcus Award in 1945 and a U.S. Department of Commerce Citation in 1957, Tina Leser died in 1986.

Costumes: 1946 *Park Avenue*[†]

Jean le Seyeux

Jean le Seyeux, born in 1894, wrote musical revues and designed settings in Europe and the United States for productions such as *Femmes en Folie* at the Folies Bergère in the 1935-36 season. Occasionally he designed costumes and scenery as well. Beginning in 1945 he wrote revues for the Casino de Paris in Monte Carlo, continuing there until his death in 1957. He spent the years during World War II in New York writing and designing.

Sets: 1940 *Earl Carroll's Vanities*
Costumes: 1940 *Earl Carroll's Vanities*

Lew Leslie

The producer Lew Leslie was born Lewis Lessinsky in Orangeburg, New York in 1886 and started in show business as a vaudeville performer. Beginning in the early 1920s he produced a series of successful revues on Broadway featuring black performers: *Blackbirds*, *Rhapsody in Black* and subsequent editions in following seasons. Lew Leslie introduced future stars Ethel Waters, Lena Horne, Bill Robinson, Aida Ward, Billie Cortez and others though these productions, beginning with the hit 1922 *Plantation Revue* starring Florence Mills, which he later produced in London. He died on March 11, 1963 at age 73.

Sets: 1922 *Plantation Revue*

Hugh Lester

Hugh Lester designed the lighting for a Broadway production in 1980. He has worked as lighting consultant for the National Air and Space Museum in Washington, D.C. and designed the lighting for an exhibition hall at the Folger Shakespeare Library. As lighting designer at Arena Stage in the late 1960s and early 1970s he designed many productions. He was also tour director for *Gin Game* starring Jessica Tandy and Hume Cronyn.

Lights: 1980 *Charlie and Algernon*

Samuel Leve

Samuel (Sam) Leve, a scenic designer who has also occasionally designed costumes and lighting, was born on December 7, 1910 near Pinsk, Russia. He came to the United States in 1920 and studied at Yale University and art schools in New York before beginning his career in theater designing summer stock. He designed sets for over one hundred productions, on Broadway and at the Metropolitan Opera, the Mercury Theatre, and the Theatre Guild, among others. He designed throughout the world as well, including productions in Rio de Janeiro, Canada, Israel, and London. He also designed spectacles and two synagogues; lectured at Yale, New York University, and Florida State University, and wrote books, including *On Jewish Art*.

Samuel Leve's many awards include the 1985 Goldie, named for Abraham Goldfadn, the father of Yiddish Theatre. He died in New York City at age 91 on December 6, 1999.

Sets: 1937 *Cherokee Night*; *Julius Caesar*; *The Miser/ The Great Cat/ Snickering Horses*; *Tobias and the Angel* 1938 *The Big Blow*; *The Shoemaker's Holiday* 1940 *Medicine Show* 1941 *The Beautiful People*; *The Distant City*; *Macbeth* 1942 *All in Favor*; *Beat the Band*; *The Life of Reilly*; *Mr. Sycamore*; *They Should Have Stood in Bed* 1943 *Apology* 1944 *Dark Hammock*; *Hand in Glove*; *Last Stop*; *Sophie*; *Thank You, Svoboda*; *Wallflower* 1945 *It's a Gift*; *Oh, Brother*; *Round Trip*; *A Sound of Hunting* 1946 *A Family Affair* 1947 *The Story of Mary Surratt* 1949 *Clutterbuck* 1950 *All You Need Is One Good Break* 1951 *Dinosaur Wharf*; *Lace on Her Petticoat* 1952 *Buttrio Square* 1953 *The Fifth Season* 1955 *Hear! Hear!* 1956 *Double in Hearts*; *Goodbye Again* 1963 *Have I Got a Girl for You* 1964 *Cafe Crown* 1982 *The Dybbuck*

Costumes: 1951 *Dinosaur Wharf* (Production design)

Lights: 1937 *Julius Caesar* 1938 *The Shoemaker's Holiday* 1940 *Medicine Show* 1943 *Apology* 1944 *Hand in Glove* 1948 *Madwoman of Chaillot* 1951 *Dinosaur Wharf* 1952 *Buttrio Square* 1963 *Cafe Crown*; *Have I Got a Girl for You* 1982 *The Dybbuck*

Madame Julie Levick

Madame Julie Levick designed costumes on Broadway in 1921.

Costumes: 1921 *The Married Woman*

Michael Levine

Canadian designer Michael Levine was born in Toronto in 1960 and studied at the Ontario College of Art and the Central School of Art and Design in London. From 1981 to 1983 he assisted Philip Prowse at Glasgow Citizens' Theatre and then, at the age of 24 designed *Strange Interlude* for which he received both Laurence Olivier and Tony Award nominations. Based in Canada since the late 1980s, he often designs for the Canadian Opera House, the Shaw Festival, the Tarragon Theatre, and CenterStage in Toronto. He continues to design in the U.K. as well, for the Welsh National Opera and the English National Opera, among others. His set for the 1992 production of *A Midsummer Night's Dream* at RNT, directed by Robert Lepage, was set in a pond of mud and is still being discussed.

Sets: 1985 *Strange Interlude†*

Nigel Levings

Lighting designer Nigel Levings has extensive credits for theater and opera in his native Australia. He has also amassed numerous credits in the U.K., for companies including the English National Opera, Welsh National Opera, Royal Shakespeare Company, Royal Opera House, and at the Edinburgh Festival. He began study for a career in law, but instead turned to stage lighting in the 1960s. At the time there was little opportunity in Australia for lighting designers, so he traveled to Europe and America where he was further inspired toward his career choice by Jules Fisher. For the last thirty years, he has been an important force in the development of the field in Australia. Honors include a Tony Award nomination and an Outer Critics Circle Award for *The King and I*.

Lights: 1995 *The King and I* **1996** *The King and I*

Norman Levinson

Norman Levinson designed costumes for a musical revue in 1923. During the 1920s he was president and treasurer of Levinson Textiles Company, Inc., 621 Broadway. A family business, Benjamin Levinson was vice-president and Leo Levinson was secretary. In 1921, the business was devoted to *waists*, and by 1925 to dresses, from a small salon at 500 Seventh Avenue. He should not be confused with Norm Levinson (1925-), a theater executive, manager and press agent.

Costumes: 1923 *Greenwich Village Follies†* ("Rooster Show" Girls, etc.)

Maxine Levy

Maxine Levy designed costumes on Broadway in 1931.

Costumes: 1931 *People on the Hill*

Ted Levy

Irving (Ted) Levy designed lights for a production on Broadway in 1928. He is known primarily as a partner with Ed Kook in Century Lighting Company, founded in 1929. The "leko," a compact ellipsoidal spotlight, was developed by and named after Levy and Kook. Century Lighting has supplied lighting equipment for thousands of Broadway shows and other productions.

Lights: 1928 *The Wrecker*

Nat Lewis

Nat Lewis, for 47 years a haberdasher in New York City, was originally from Selma, Alabama. He catered to the theatrical trade and his contribution of garments and accessories to shows was often acknowledged in playbills, but he only received design credit once. Mr. Lewis died at age 74 on January 26, 1956. He shouldn't be confused with the painter who has the same name.

Costumes: 1937 *Hitch Your Wagon†* (Mr. Curzon's costume) **1941** *Native Son* (Miss Burr's robe, Miss Harrison's gowns)

Pamela Lewis

Pamela Lewis designed one set on Broadway in 1964. She has also designed scenery for two touring productions in Capetown, South Africa: *The Birthday Party* and *Night of the Iguana.*

Sets: 1964 *Sponomo*

St. John Lewis

At the age of twelve, St. John Lewis exhibited a portrait in the Academy of Art in London. When he was nineteen, he moved to the United States where he worked as a painter and scenic artist. He was born in France circa 1867 to Welsh parents. He worked with John H. Young, D. Frank Dodge, MacCoughtry, and was a partner in H. Robert Law's studio. His relatively brief list of credits includes *The Hall of Fame* for which he received credit above the cast list, remarkable in 1902. Late-nineteenth century credits include *Way Down East, The Last Chapter,* and *Man in the Moon.* Lewis died on August 21, 1915 in New York City at age 48.

Sets: 1900 *The Belle of Bridgeport†*; *The Giddy Thing†*; *Madge Smith, Attorney†*; *A Million Dollars†* (Act I, 1; Act II, 1; Act III) 1901 *The King's Carnival*; *The Widow Jones* (Designed and painted) 1902 *The Hall of Fame* 1904 *The Ruling Power†* (Acts I, II and IV)

Stephen Brimson Lewis

Stephen Brimson Lewis was born in 1964 in Hertfordshire, England and studied at the Central School of Art and Design. He has designed costumes and scenery for plays and operas throughout the world, and been honored with several honors, among them a Laurence Olivier Award in 1995. His long term collaboration with director Sean Mathias has resulted in the movie *Bent, Design for Living* which originated at the Donmar Warehouse and then played in the West End, *Indiscretions* (a.k.a. *Les Parents Terribles/Parents From Hell*, and *A Little Night Music* at the Royal National Theatre, among others. Designs for opera include productions at the Dallas Opera, the Royal Opera House, Australian Opera, and the Monte Carlo Opera.

Sets: 1995 *Indiscretions (Les Parents Terribles)* 2000 *Rose*
Costumes: 1995 *Indiscretions (Les Parents Terribles)* 2000 *Rose*

Walter Lewis

Walter S. Lewis designed scenery in 1927 on Broadway. He was a partner with James Van Sickler in Manhattan Scenic Studios, located at 260 West 10th Street, New York City in the early 1920s. His residence was 28 West 63rd Street in the mid-1920s.

Sets: 1927 *Africana†*

Alice and Irene Lewisohn

Sisters and collaborators Alice and Irene Lewisohn founded the Neighborhood Playhouse, where they directed, designed, adapted and performed numerous plays. Together they also nurtured the talents of countless other designers and performers. They not only designed but directed *Jephthah's Daughter* on Broadway in 1915. Irene,

who was active in the Museum of Costume Art and served as its president, died on April 4, 1944. Alice Lewisohn Crowley, who married the artist (and occasional costume designer) Herbert E. Crowley in 1924, lived in Switzerland after the Neighborhood Playhouse closed. She published the chronicle *The Neighborhood Playhouse* in 1959 and died in Switzerland on January 6, 1972 at age 88.

Sets: 1915 *Jephthah's Daughter* 1916 *Thanksgiving*
Costumes: 1915 *Jephthah's Daughter†* 1916 *Thanksgiving*

Hervig Libowitzky

Hervig Libowitzky, a scene designer and art director, works primarily in Europe. He was born in Vienna and studied at the Vienna Academy of Fine Art. He has been art director for the films *The Prisoner of Zenda, The Girl From Petrovka, The Fifth Musketeer* and *Permission to Kill*. For his Broadway debut, *Into the Light*, he designed the scenery and projections in collaboration with Neil Peter Jampolis.

Sets: 1986 *Into the Light†*

Todd Lichtenstein

Todd Lichtenstein designed lighting for one production on Broadway in 1983. He has designed in numerous regional theaters, including the Capital Repertory Company, Albany, New York and the Pennsylvania Stage Company. Credits in off-Broadway theaters include productions at the Equity Library Theatre, Phoenix Theatre, La Mama E.T.C., and Playwrights Horizons. He has also assisted lighting designer Dennis Parichy. Television experience includes lighting design for the ABC-TV program *Daytime*.

Lights: 1983 *The Ritz*

Oscar Liebetrau

Oscar Liebetrau, who was born on October 20, 1889, designed scenery for three plays in the 1920s. He was associated with Cleon Throckmorton, Inc., 102 West 3rd Street, New York City in the early 1930s.

Sets: 1923 *Sun-Up*; *Sylvia* 1928 *Sun-Up*

James Light

James "Jimmy" Light was born in Pittsburgh, Pennsylvania where his father, a British contractor, was constructing a building. Raised in England, he returned to the United States at age fourteen, later studying painting and architecture at the Carnegie Institute of Technology and Ohio State University. He moved to New York to attend Columbia University and shared a room over the Neighborhood Playhouse in Greenwich Village with designer Charles Ellis. A chance encounter with Eugene O'Neill at a public swimming pool led to continued interaction and to Light's involvement with the theater, initially as an actor. In the early 1920s he began directing the plays of August Strindberg and O'Neill, including the first production of *S.S. Glencairn* and a controversial production of *All God's Chillun Got Wings* starring Paul Robeson. He was director of the Experimental Unit of the New York Federal Theatre Project and directed plays including *Chalk Dust*. He served as Dean of the Drama faculty at the New School for Social Research from 1939 to 1942 where he continued to direct. The founder of Reader's Theatre, Jimmy Light died on February 10, 1964 at the age of 69.

Sets: 1929 *Earth Between, The/ Before Breakfast*

Edward Clarke Lilley

Edward Clarke Lilley was an actor and director. He began his career in Salt Lake City, Utah with the Leighton Players Stock Company before forming his own company as actor, director and manager. He debuted as a Broadway director with *Ziegfeld Follies* in 1931, which was followed by editions of *Ziegfeld Follies* in 1934 and 1935, *Hot Cha, The Show Is On* and others. He also directed for films and musical stock companies. Edward Lilley died at age 86 on April 3, 1974.

Lights: 1939 *One for the Money†*

Michael Lincoln

Born on March 21, 1953 in Scottsbluff, Nebraska, lighting designer Michael Lincoln grew up in Alliance. He attended Knox College where he received a B.A. with Honors in 1975, and Brandeis University (M.F.A., 1979). His contacts with Craig Miller, Jim Ingalls and Paul Gallo provided further valuable education. From 1979 until 1983, he designed most of the productions of the Los Angeles Ballet, including *The Nutcracker* as well as shows for other West Coast theaters, receiving Los Angeles Drama Critics Circle and Drama Logue Awards. His designs have been seen in regional theaters from Hartford Stage and the Indiana Repertory Theatre, to the Alley Theatre, among others, and in many off-Broadway houses, notably Playwrights Horizons, the Vineyard Theatre, and Primary Stages. Twenty-first century credits include the national tour of *Copenhagen* and *Looking for Normal* by Jane Anderson.

Lights: 1996 *Skylight†* **1998** *More to Love* **2000** *Copenhagen†*

D. Scott Linder

D. Scott Linder was born on August 6, 1948 in Tulsa, Oklahoma. He attended the University of Texas and began designing for opera, theater, and ballet groups in Tulsa. He assisted Gilbert V. Hemsley, Jr. on a couple of productions, receiving additional training and mentoring. He spent six years as lighting director for *Holiday on Ice*, and five years as technical director for Madison Square Garden. He also served as master electrician and assistant designer for over thirty road companies, ballets and Broadway plays. Scott Linder is also a theater, broadcast and media designer/consultant.

Lights: 1977 *Toller Cranston's Ice Show*

Jack Martin Lindsay

Jack Martin Lindsay designed costumes for a Broadway play in 1966. He was born in Tacoma, Washington and studied at Whitman College, Tulane University and Carnegie Institute. After moving to New York City in 1962, he assisted designers, including Oliver Smith, Boris Aronson and Tony Walton.

Costumes: 1966 *My Sweet Charley*

Richard T. Lingley

Richard T. Lingley designed scenery for the Broadway stage in 1913. He maintained a studio at 527 Fifth Avenue, Room 501 in 1909 and resided in Yonkers, New York.

Sets: 1913 *The Family Cupboard*

Margaret Linley

Margaret Linley graduated from Smith College. She began her career as an actress at the Pasadena Playhouse and became a casting agent in California. She moved to New York to become casting director for the Theatre Guild, subsequently joined A.&.S Lyons Theatrical Agency and designed one set on Broadway in 1931. Margaret Linley Delima died at age 67 on May 27, 1969 in Altadena, California.

Sets: 1931 *Jack and the Beanstalk*

Charles Lisanby

Charles Lisanby has created lighting and scenic designs on Broadway since 1955. His television credits are extensive and include *The Garry Moore, Red Skelton,* and *Jack Benny* shows and more than one hundred specials. He has been nominated for nine Emmy Awards and won two, including one for *Baryshnikov on Broadway.* He has designed productions at Radio City Music Hall (including the 1984 *MTV Awards*), *Night of 100 Stars,* television commercials, and the *Folies Bergère* in Las Vegas. He has also designed the interior of a Hilton Hotel in Australia.

Sets: 1957 *Hotel Paradiso†* 1979 *The Magnificent Christmas Spectacular* 1980 *The Magnificent Christmas Spectacular* 1988 *Christmas Spectacular* 1990 *The Christmas Spectacular* 1991 *Christmas Spectacular* 1992 *Radio City Christmas Spectacular†* 1993 *Radio City Christmas Spectacular†* 1994 *Radio City Christmas Spectacular†* 1996 *Radio City Christmas Spectacular†* 1997 *Radio City Christmas Spectacular†* 1998 *Radio City Christmas Spectacular†* (The Parade of the Wooden Soldiers)

Lights: 1955 *The Little Glass Clock* 1956 *The Glass Clock*

Lucille Little

Lucille Little was active on Broadway between 1948 and 1950.

Costumes: 1948 *Oh, Mr. Meadowbrook* (Costume Supervisor) 1949 *The Big Knife* 1950 *Come Back, Little Sheba*

Mr. Owen Little

Mr. Owen Lewis Little designed scenery for a 1913 Broadway production. The playbill credit reads "architect." He spent the majority of his life and career in California, where he was born on July 26, 1891 and died on April 2, 1955.

Sets: 1913 *The Philanderer†*

Billy Livingston

Billy (Billi) Livingston designed numerous plays on Broadway between 1934 and 1950. She also created costumes for many additional shows performed by ice skaters.

Costumes: 1934 *Calling All Stars; Life Begins at 8:40†; Ziegfeld Follies: 1934†* 1935 *Parade†* (Ain't So Hot, Etc.) 1936 *The Pirates of Penzance* 1938 *Who's Who* 1940 *Panama Hattie†* (Modern gowns) 1943 *The Naked Genius; Something for the Boys* 1944 *Hats Off to Ice†; Laffing Room Only* 1945 *Good Night Ladies* 1946 *Icetime†* 1948 *Howdy, Mr. Ice†* 1949 *All for Love; Howdy Mr. Ice of 1950†*

Lester M. Livingston

Lester M. Livingston designed gowns for a featured player in 1924 and costumes for a production the following year. Lester Livingston, Ltd., a custom shop for gowns, was located at 7 East 46th Street in New York City in the mid-1920s. He resided at 420 Riverside Drive at that time.

Costumes: 1924 *Sweet Seventeen* (Miss Drake's Act I gowns) 1925 *The Backslapper*

John Robert Lloyd

John Robert Lloyd, a scenic and sometimes costume and lighting designer, began his career in the theater as an actor performing in Italian productions. Born in St. Louis on August 4, 1920, he studied at the Art Students League, the Hadley Art School, Washington University and the University of Missouri. He assisted Robert Edmond Jones, Lemuel Ayers and Nat Karson and developed an early specialization in masks, make-up and sculptural stage elements. After working as a designer in summer stock he made his New York debut in 1948 off-Broadway with *The Duenna* at the Greenwich Mews Theatre. His Broadway debut was in 1949, after which he designed numerous industrials, exhibits, films and television shows, both freelance and as staff designer for NBC-TV. Work on television included *The Aldrich Family*, *Chrysler Medallion Theatre* and *Ellery Queen*. John Robert Lloyd was production designer for the films *The Boys in the Band*, *The Owl and the Pussycat*, and *The Exorcist*, among others. He died on December 17, 1998.

Sets: **1949** *Touch and Go* **1951** *Stalag 17* **1952** *Bernadine* **1955** *Almost Crazy* **1957** *Holiday for Lovers*; *Monique* **1958** *Drink to Me Only* **1960** *Laughs and Other Events*

Costumes: **1949** *Mrs. Gibbon's Boys*; *Touch and Go* **1960** *Laughs and Other Events*

Lights: **1951** *Stalag 17* **1952** *Bernadine* **1955** *Almost Crazy* **1957** *Holiday for Lovers* **1958** *Drink to Me Only* **1960** *Laughs and Other Events*

Adrianne Lobel

Adrianne Lobel was educated at the Yale University School of Drama and has worked as a scenic artist at Chicago's Goodman Theatre and Lyric Opera. She has designed scenery for the American Repertory Theatre, the Juilliard School of Music, the La Jolla Playhouse, Arena Stage, Hartford Stage, the Manhattan Theatre Club, the American Place Theatre and many other off-Broadway and regional theaters. Her awards include the Joseph Jefferson Award for *Play Mas* at the Goodman Theatre. She has often collaborated with Peter Sellars and together they have done *The Government Inspector* at Yale, *The Mikado* for the Chicago Lyric Opera, *The Visions of Simone Machard*, at La Jolla and *Nixon in China* which premiered at the Houston Grand Opera. She has also worked with directors Andrei Serban, Lee Breuer, and Andrei Belgrader and with choreographer Mark Morris, most recently on a produc-

tion of *The Nutcracker* in Brussels. In 1977 her book, *A Small Sheep in a Pear Tree*, was published by Harper and Row. Twenty-first century designs include *The Three Sisters* at the McCarter Theater Center and *Once Around the City* at Second Stage Theatre.

Sets: **1983** *My One and Only* **1994** *Passion* **1997** *The Diary of Anne Frank* **1998** *On the Town*

Robert E. Locher

Robert Evans Locher (Locker), architect and interior designer, was born on November 1, 1888 in Lancaster, Pennsylvania. He designed interiors of public buildings in New York City, Washington, D.C. and other cities, and was associate editor for *House and Garden* at one time. He also created illustrations for *Vogue* and *Vanity Fair*, designed book jackets, and produced industrial designs for Lunt Silversmiths, Sargent Hardware, and Imperial Paper & Color Corporation. He also designed costumes and scenery on Broadway during the 1920s. His work is in the collection of the Whitney Museum of American Art. Robert Locher died on June 18, 1956.

Sets: **1915** *Forbidden Fruit* (as: Robert Locker); *In April*; *Saviors*†; *The Shepherd in the Distance* **1920** *Greenwich Village Follies* **1921** *Greenwich Village Follies*† **1923** *Greenwich Village Follies*†

Costumes: **1911** *Helena's Husband* **1915** *Forbidden Fruit* (as: Robert Locker); *In April*; *Saviors*; *The Shepherd in the Distance* **1920** *What's in a Name*† (Bridal veil dresses, etc.) **1921** *Greenwich Village Follies* **1923** *Greenwich Village Follies*†; *Jack and Jill*† (Costumes and principal role) **1929** *Murray Anderson's Almanac*†

Bernard Lohmuller

Bernard Lohmuller, who was born in Texas on April 27, 1876, designed a set on Broadway in 1927. He resided at 123 West 57th Street in the early 1930s but then moved to California where he spent the majority of his career. He died in Los Angeles on November 12, 1955.

Sets: **1927** *Allez-Oop*

Figure 8: William Ivey Long: *The Producers*: "Roger DeBris" as the Chrysler Building, 2001. Courtesy of William Ivey Long.

William Ivey Long

William Ivey Long, from Seaboard, North Carolina, was born August 30, 1947. He studied history at William and Mary College (A.B. 1969), studied art history as a Kress fellow at the University of North Carolina at Chapel Hill (1969-1972) and received his M.F.A. at Yale in 1975. The theater tradition in his family is strong – both parents were long-time Carolina Playmakers and his brother Robert is a theater consultant. His designs are seen in opera (including *A Quiet Place* and *Trouble in Tahiti* in Houston and Vienna), and dance for choreographers including Twyla Tharp, Peter Martins, Paul Taylor, and Garth Fagan. Additional designs include Mick Jagger/The Rolling Stones' "Steel Wheels" Tour, the Pointer Sisters, Miss Universe Pageants, and the movies *The Cutting Edge*, *Life with Mikey*, and *Curtain Call*. He spent over thirty seasons with *The Lost Colony* outdoor drama, as an actor, prop master and technical director, and production designer. For the costume designs for *Nine* he was awarded the Maharam and Drama Desk Awards, and his first Tony. He also received Tony Awards for *Crazy for You* and *The Producers*, from seven nominations. With six shows running on Broadway at the same time at the beginning of the twenty-first century, his lively imagination and creativity is matched by his success and willingness to mentor others.   See Figure 8: William Ivey Long: *The Producers*

Costumes: **1978** *The Inspector General* **1979** *The 1940s Radio Hour* **1980** *Passione* **1981** *Mass Appeal* **1982** *Nine* **1984** *End of the World*; *Play Memory* **1986** *Smile* **1987** *Sleight of Hand* **1988** *Mail* **1989** *Eastern Standard*; *Lend Me a Tenor*; *Welcome to the Club* **1990** *Six Degrees of Separation* **1991** *The Homecoming* **1992** *Crazy for You*; *Guys and Dolls*; *Private Lives* **1993** *Laughter on the 23rd Floor* **1994** *A Christmas Carol*; *Picnic* **1995** *A Christmas Carol*; *Company*; *Smokey Joe's Cafe* **1996** *Big*; *Chicago*; *A Christmas Carol* **1997** *1776*; *A Christmas Carol*; *King David*; *Steel Pier* **1998** *Cabaret*; *A Christmas Carol* **1999** *Annie Get Your Gun*; *The Civil War*; *Epic*

Proportions; *Swing!* **2000** *Contact*; *The Man Who Came to Dinner*; *The Music Man*; *Seussical the Musical* **2001** *The Producers*

Miguel Lopez-Castillo

Scenic designer Jose Miguel Lopez-Castillo, originally from Mexico City, is the son of Graciela Castillo del Valle, a costume designer for movies and theater, and Miguel Lopez Somera, a television producer. He received his M.F.A. from the Tisch School of the Arts at New York University in 1989 and designs for theater and film. He has designed scenery at Once Dream Theatre, Circle in the Square, Theatre Row Theatre, and the Harold Clurman Theatre, all in New York. Films include *Addicted to Love*.

Sets: **1993** *Wilder, Wilder, Wilder*

Santo Loquasto

Santo Loquasto received a Liberal Arts degree at King's College and an M.F.A. from Yale. A designer of plays, ballets and operas, he designs both sets and costumes for many of his productions. A native of Wilkes-Barre, Pennsylvania, he was born July 26, 1944. He began designing professionally with *Cat on a Hot Tin Roof* at the Williamstown Theatre Festival in 1965 and designed in New York for the first time in 1970 at Astor Place. He is a busy, prolific designer, well-known for the wide range of his talents and his designs for modern playwrights, including Sam Shepard, David Rabe and David Mamet, and modern choreographers such as Twyla Tharp, Paul Taylor and James Kudelka. Often acknowledged as an influence on an emerging generation of designers, he credits Michael Annals and John Conklin as his own mentors. His work in film includes: production design for *Desperately Seeking Susan*, *Big*, and *Bright Lights, Big City*; costumes for *Zelig* and *A Midsummer Night's Sex Comedy*; and art direction for *Crimes and Misdemeanors*, *New York Stories* and *She-Devil*. He is the recipient of numerous honors, including Tony Awards for both scenic and costume design, Maharam, Drama Desk, American Theatre Wing, Obie, and Outer

Critics Circle Awards, and a British Academy Award for the production design of the film *Radio Days*. Twenty-first century designs include costumes for *Westerly Round* for Twyla Tharp, and sets and costumes for *Dance of Death* in the 2001-2002 Broadway season.

Sets: 1972 *Miss Margarida's Way*; *Sticks and Bones*; *That Championship Season* 1973 *Boom Boom Room* 1975 *Kennedy's Children*; *Murder among Friends* 1976 *Legend* 1977 *American Buffalo*; *The Cherry Orchard*; *Golda*; *Miss Margarida's Way* 1978 *King of Hearts*; *The Mighty Gents* 1979 *Bent*; *The Goodbye People*; *Sarava* 1980 *The Suicide* 1981 *The Floating Light Bulb* 1982 *The Wake of Jamie Foster* 1985 *Singin' in the Rain* 1987 *Sweet Sue* 1989 *Cafe Crown*; *The Secret Rapture*; *The Tenth Man* 1991 *Lost in Yonkers* 1992 *Jake's Women*; *Juno and the Paycock* 1993 *The Goodbye Girl* 1994 *Broken Glass* 1995 *A Month in the Country*; *The Rose Tattoo* 1997 *Barrymore* 1999 *Fosse* 2000 *The Tale of the Allergist's Wife*

Costumes: 1975 *Kennedy's Children* 1977 *American Buffalo*; *The Cherry Orchard*; *Golda*; *Miss Margarida's Way* 1979 *Sarava* 1980 *The Suicide* 1981 *The Floating Light Bulb* 1989 *Cafe Crown*; *Grand Hotel, The Musical*; *Miss Margarida's Way* 1991 *Lost in Yonkers* 1992 *Juno and the Paycock* 1993 *The Goodbye Girl* 1994 *Broken Glass* 1997 *Barrymore* 1998 *Ragtime* 1999 *Fosse*

Samuel Lorber

Samuel Lorber designed costumes for a featured player in 1921. He was multi-talented and led a varied career – dentist, radio commentator on WSBC in Chicago, costume designer, and editorial writer for *The Jewish Daily Forward*. He died March 6, 1951, age 65.

Costumes: 1921 *Captain Applejack*† (Miss Foster's Act I dress)

Jean Louis

Jean Louis, best known for his glamorous, high-fashion designs for films, was born Louis Berthault in Paris in 1907. After studying in an art school he went to work for Drecoll, and in 1935 he moved to New York to work for Hattie Carnegie. His career in the movies, including *The Solid Gold Cadillac* for which he won an Oscar, began in 1943. He was nominated for fourteen Academy Awards and designed costumes for over 60 movies, mainly for glamorous stars including Rita Hayworth, Marilyn Monroe, Judy Garland and Julie Andrews. He returned to New York briefly in 1951 to design a Broadway show, and in the early 1960s left the film industry to open a salon in Beverly Hills. He died on April 20, 1997 in Los Angeles, at age 89.

Costumes: 1951 *Love and Let Love*

Kermit Love

Puppeteer and costume designer Kermit Love was born in in 1920 in New Jersey. After making his Broadway debut at age 17, he designed many different kinds of costumes for dance, television, theater. He designed the original *Rodeo* and *One Touch of Venus* for Agnes De Mille, *Fancy Free* for Jerome Robbins, numerous pieces for George Balanchine at the New York City Ballet, including *The Spellbound Child* and *Don Quixote*, and *The Nutcracker* for the Joffrey Ballet. He also designed "Big Bird" and the other characters for *Sesame Street* for which he won an Emmy Award, and in the early 1990s created another children's television program, *Whirligig*. In addition to designing costumes for the theater, he has written and directed plays. A painter, working mainly in oils, he has taught mask and puppet designing and construction at Pratt Institute.

Costumes: 1937 *The Fireman's Flame*; *Naughty Naught '00* (Girls bathing costumes) 1944 *Dark Hammock*; *Suds in Your Eye*

Katherine H. Lovell

Katherine Adams Lovell was born in Brooklyn, New York, and designed costumes on Broadway in 1917. She also studied painting at Pratt Institute and privately, and in 1938 an exhibit of her landscapes was held at the Studio Guild Gallery in New York.

Costumes: 1917 *Cheer-up (Hippodrome)*†; *Eyes of Youth*†

David L. Lovett

David L. Lovett has designed scenery and costumes for many theaters in Canada, including the Citadel, Rice Theatre and Edmonton Opera. Designs include *Most Happy Fella*, *Komagata Maru Incident*, and *Bedroom Farce*. He is the Theatre Design Program Coordinator at the Wimbledon School of Art at the University of Alberta. Twenty-first century designs include costumes for *The Importance of Being Earnest* at the Stratford (Ontario) Festival.

Sets: 1980 *Mister Lincoln*
Costumes: 1980 *Mister Lincoln*

Colin Low

Colin Archibald Low, a documentary director and animator, was born in 1926 in Cardston, Alberta, Canada. He studied at the Calgary School of Fine Arts and worked initially as a graphic artist for the National Film Board of Canada, gradually changing his focus to animation and directing. He has been with the National Film Board since 1945 in a variety of capacities. He has won numerous awards for his films, many of the them documentaries or educational, which include *The Age of the Beaver*, *Days of Whiskey Gap* and *The Winds of Fogo*.

Sets: 1961 *Do You Know the Milky Way?*

Milton Lowe

Milton Lowe, who designed lighting for a Broadway production in 1946, worked for the Shubert Producing Organization as an electrician. He died at age 59 on March 8, 1947 in New York City.

Lights: 1946 *Yours Is My Heart*

Marilyn Lowey

Lighting designer Marilyn Lowey is a native New Yorker who studied acting and theatrical design at Emerson College and earned her M.F.A. from Carnegie Mellon University in 1976. She has designed many industrial promotions, television productions, and concert performances for Neil Diamond, Liza Minnelli, Johnny Mathis, Diana Ross, Bette Midler, and others. Since 1985, she has designed the *Champions on Ice* productions and beginning in 1996 many dance pieces for the Cleveland San Jose Ballet. Honors include an Emmy Award for the lighting design for *Neil Diamond: Hello Again* on CBS-TV in 1986, when she became the first woman to receive an Emmy Award for lighting design.

Lights: 1990 *An Evening with Harry Connick, Jr. and His Orchestra*

Mina Loy

Mina Loy was a modernist poet who first published her poems in 1914. She was part of the New York avant-garde from 1916 until about 1925, deriving words and images from a search for new poetic forms. She was born in London, England on December 27, 1882, and died in Aspen, Colorado in 1966.

Costumes: 1918 *Karen* (Miss Marinoff's dress and hat)

Lucile

Lucile (also known as Lady Duff Gordon) was born Lucy Kennedy in London in 1862 and ran an influential fashion house in London, with branches in New York (opened in 1909) and Paris (opened in 1911). Married to Sir Cosmo Duff Gordon, she had fashion knowledge and insight which she made into an even more successful business venture using her title, Lady Duff Gordon. This pioneering woman designer created gowns that were flamboyant, but were also softly colored and romantic. She often dressed dancers and actresses for Broadway productions, including Irene Castle, and worked regularly for Florenz Ziegfeld. In 1932 she published her autobiography, *Discretions and Indiscretions*, but died in relative obscurity in 1936 in London. At the end of her career she collaborated on scenery for a production. Lucile was often actively involved in designing gowns and costumes for theatrical productions, but sometimes received credit when garments were obtained from her couture house. The last production on Broadway for which she received posthumous credit, was clearly for gowns from her salon.

Sets: 1936 *The Life and Loves of Dorian Gray*† (Exteriors)

Costumes: 1905 *Alice Sit-by-The-Fire*†
(Miss Terry's gowns); *Beauty and the
Barge*† 1910 *Baby Mine* (Miss Clark's
and Miss Troutman's gowns); *He Came
from Milwaukee* 1911 *A Certain Party*†;
The Enchantress† (Miss Gordon's Act I
dresses); *Jumping Jupiter*† (Miss Hop-
per's gowns); *A Single Man* (Gowns);
The Three Romeos 1912 *The Affairs of
Anatol*† (Miss Kane's, Keane's and Em-
met's gowns); *A Butterfly on the Wheel*
(Miss Titheradge's gowns); *The Explorer*†
(Gowns for Miss Collier); *The Return from
Jerusalem* (Madame Simone's gowns);
Whirl of Society† (Mlle. Desly's costumes)
1913 *Beauty and the Barge*†; *The Girl
on the Film*† (Miss Seymour's dresses in
II, III); *The Honeymoon Express*† (Miss
Desly's costumes); *Iole*† (Miss Rogers'
gown); *The Master Mind*† (Liss LaSalle's
gowns) 1914 *The Beautiful Adventure*†
(Gowns for Miss Murdock); *Marrying
Money*; *My Lady's Dress*† (Gowns); *A
Pair of Silk Stockings*† (Gowns); *A Pair of
Sixes*; *Pretty Mrs. Smith*† (Miss Scheff's
hats and gowns); *Twin Beds*† (Gowns);
Watch Your Step† 1915 *The Doctor's
Dilemma*† (Miss McCarthy's gowns); *The
Great Lover* (Miss Kalick's gowns); *Ma-
ternity*† (Miss Morrison's gowns); *Ned
Wayburn's Town Topics*† (Miss Molyneux
Act I, Sc 3 and Subway); *The Shadow*†;
The Shadow† (Gowns); *Ziegfeld Follies:
1915*† 1916 *Bunny* (Miss O'Brien's
gowns); *The Cohan Revue*† (Miss Valli's
gowns and headdresses); *The Fear Market*
(Gowns); *His Bridal Night* (The Dolly
Sisters' gowns); *Ziegfeld Follies: 1916*†
1917 *Furs and Frills*†; *The Gypsy Trail*
(Miss Cahill's gowns); *Her Husband's Wife*
(Miss Laura Hope Crews' gowns); *Lord
and Lady Algy*† (Miss Elliott's gowns);
Miss 1917; *Why Marry?*; *Ziegfeld Follies:
1917*† 1918 *An Ideal Husband* (Miss Ju-
lia Arthur's dresses); *The Riddle: Woman*
(Miss Kalich's gowns); *Three Faces East*;
Why Marry?; *Ziegfeld Follies: 1918*†
1919 *Curiosity* (Miss Fenwick's gowns);
First Is Last† (Gowns); *The Lady in
Red*† (Miss MacTammany's gown); *Scan-
dal* (Miss Larrimore's and Miss Hast's
gowns) 1920 *The Broken Wing* (Last
Act evening gowns); *The Outrageous Mrs.
Palmer*† (Miss Young's gowns); *Sally*†
(Dolores' gowns in Act I and Last Scene);
Ziegfeld Follies: 1920† (Gowns) 1921

The Circle (Mrs. Carter's, Miss Winwood's II, III, Miss Mac's dresses); *Nice
People*† (Miss Larrimore's gowns); *The
White Peacock* (Madame Petrova's Act I
gown); *Ziegfeld's 9 O'clock Frolic*† ("Gondoliers" costumes) 1927 *Ziegfeld Follies:
1927*† 1938 *No Time for Comedy*† (Miss
Fontanne's gowns)

Lucinda

Lucinda Reichenbach was the president
of a small dress salon at 501 Madison Avenue, called Lucinda's Shop, Inc.
during the 1930s. Her husband, Harry
L. Reichenbach (1882-1931), was one of
the first press agents for actors and producers of motion pictures.

Costumes: 1931 *Fast Service* (Gowns
and Lingerie)

Michael Lucyk

Michael Lucyk was born February 14,
1920 in Mahanoy City, Pennsylvania,
and studied in Paris at the École de
Louvre and with Charles James. He
worked for Pierre Balmain in Paris and
also for Karinska. As an assistant to
Miles White, he worked on *Gentlemen
Prefer Blondes*. He died in December
1986.

Costumes: 1947 *Sweethearts*

John Plummer Ludlum

John Plummer (Plumer) Ludlum, an
artist, designed one set in 1935 on
Broadway. He lived with his wife Rose
at 214 West 96th Street in New York
City during the mid-1930s. Born in
New York on September 12, 1906, he
died on August 30, 1993 in Orange
County, California.

Sets: 1935 *Provincetown Follies*

Carol Luiken

Carol Luiken (sometimes recorded as
Lunken) designs both sets and costumes, but specializes in costumes. She
was born September 6, 1945 in Paterson, New Jersey. After studying at
Columbia University she worked as an
assistant at the Santa Fe Opera. Her
opera designs include productions in
Santa Fe as well as in Spoleto, Italy,
and for the Baltimore Opera Company. Her designs have been seen off-
Broadway sine she debuted there in

1970. She has also designed and illustrated fashion, and taught design, but recently has concentrated on designing for television where she designs the daytime drama *All My Children*. She received an Emmy Award for the show in 1990 with her co-designer at that time, Jonathan Bixby.

Costumes: **1976** *Checking Out* **1978** *Once in a Lifetime*

A. J. Lundborg

A. J. (Arne Jansteen) Lundborg designed sets for eight Broadway productions between 1928 and 1938. He worked at one time for Gates and Morange, and maintained a studio for painting at 326 West 55st Street in 1932.

Sets: **1928** *The Big Pond* **1929** *The Nut Farm* **1933** *The World Waits* **1934** *False Dreams, Farewell*; *Page Miss Glory* **1935** *Boy Meets Girl* **1936** *The Illustrator's Show* **1938** *School Houses on the Lot*

Kert Lundell

Kert Fritjof Lundell was born in Malmö, Sweden on June 17, 1936, and moved to Laguna Beach, California with his family when he was 15. Mr. Lundell, who studied at Yale, moved to New York after study at the Goodman School of Drama. He was a scenic designer who occasionally also contributed costume and lighting designs to productions. His sets for theater were seen throughout the United States and in Europe. He served as consultant to the American Place Theatre in 1971 when its new space was built. He also taught, designed films (including *They All Laughed* in 1981) and designed for television. Through his career he designed more than 75 productions culminating with *Contact with the Enemy* for the Ensemble Studio Theatre in 1999. Kurt Lundell died at age 64 on September 11, 2000 in New York.

Sets: **1966** *The Investigation*; *Under the Weather* **1968** *Carry Me Back to Morningside Heights* **1971** *Ain't Supposed to Die a Natural Death*; *Solitaire/ Double Solitaire* **1972** *Don't Play Us Cheap*; *The Lincoln Mask*; *The Sunshine Boys* **1975** *Hughey/ Duet*; *The Night That Made*

America Famous **1976** *1600 Pennsylvania Avenue*†; *Rockabye Hamlet* **1978** *The November People* **1982** *Waltz of the Stork* **1989** *Shenandoah*

Costumes: **1966** *Under the Weather* **1968** *Carry Me Back to Morningside Heights*

Lights: **1968** *Carry Me Back to Morningside Heights*

Sir Edwin Lutyens

Sir Edwin Lutyens, a British architect, designed a set on Broadway in 1929. He is best known in theater circles as the architect of the Royal National Theatre complex in London, which he designed with Cecil Massey. He is also credited with scenic design for such London productions as *Quality Street* (1921) and *Berkeley Square* (1929). Known for his wide range of talents, he was born in London in March 1869, studied at the Royal College of Art and was influenced early in his career by landscape gardener Gertrude Jekyll. He died on January 1, 1944.

Sets: **1929** *Berkeley Square*

Ella Luxembourg

Ella Luxembourg designed costumes for a play in collaboration with other designers in 1970. In the mid-1970s she was a member of Bergenstage Inc., a repertory theater in Bergen County, New Jersey.

Costumes: **1970** *Gloria and Esperanza*†

Thomas Lynch

Thomas Michael Lynch was born in Asheville, North Carolina on February 19, 1953 and received B.A. and M.F.A. degrees at Yale University. Influenced by Ming Cho Lee and Robin Wagner, he has also studied painting and print-making. Honors for his scenic designs include Joseph Jefferson Awards for *Pal Joey* (1988) and *The Time of Your Life* (1989), Tony Award nominations for *The Heidi Chronicles* (1989) and *The Music Man* (2000), and an Applause Award in New Jersey (1991). His designs for *A Quiet Place*, which he created for the Vienna State Opera, were included in the 1987 Prague Quadrennial Scenography Exhibition. His designs for opera have also been seen in the United States. Austria, and the Netherlands. He has designed the off-Broadway production and national tour of *Driving Miss Daisy*, the musical version of *Kiss of the Spiderwoman* directed by Hal Prince at the State University of New York at Purchase, and for the New York Shakespeare Festival. Sets: 1980 *Tintypes* 1984 *Design for Living* 1985 *Arms and the Man* 1986 *You Can Never Tell* 1989 *The Heidi Chronicles* 1991 *The Speed of Darkness* 1992 *My Favorite Year; The Visit* 1994 *The Rise and Fall of Little Voice* 1995 *Having Our Say* 1997 *The Young Man from Atlanta* 1998 *Ah, Wilderness!* 1999 *Swing!* 2000 *Contact; The Music Man*

Tomas MacAnna

Tomas MacAnna, the Irish director, started his career as a writer, with many radio plays produced on Irish Radio and by the BBC. He joined the Abbey Theatre in 1947, the youngest director ever hired by the company and became Artistic Director of the New Abbey Theatre in 1966. In addition to directing at the Abbey and in theaters around the world, he also designed settings and occasionally costumes for many productions. Mr. MacAnna commissioned *Borstal Boy* from Brendan Behan which he directed and designed at the Abbey Theatre in 1968, before bringing the play to Broadway. In July 2000, the National Theatre in Dublin held a tribute in honor of his contributions featuring a performance of Hugh Leonard's *A Life* and reminiscences about and from Mr. MacAnna. Costumes: 1970 *Borstal Boy*

MacCoughtry

MacCoughtry collaborated with St. John Lewis, as Lewis and MacCoughtry, on four productions at the beginning of the twentieth century. Sets: 1900 *The Belle of Bridgeport*†; *The Giddy Thing*†; *Madge Smith, Attorney*†; *A Million Dollars*† (Acts I, 1; II, 1, III)

Brian MacDevitt

Lighting designer Brian MacDevitt was born October 6, 1956 and earned his B.F.A. from the State University of New York, Purchase. After additional

study with Bill Mintzer, he began designing lights, initially at the Woodstock Playhouse in the late 1970s and then gradually worked his way from summer stock to off-Broadway to regional theaters and national tours. By the late 1980s he was designing in the major regional theaters and off-Broadway houses including Manhattan Theatre Club, Steppenwolf Theatre, Playwrights Horizons, and the Brooklyn Academy of Music. He is on the faculty of SUNY-Purchase and New York University. Among his many honors is the 1994 Obie Award for Sustained excellence. Twenty-first century designs include the 2001-2002 season Broadway shows *A Thousand Clowns*, *Urinetown* and *Major Barbara*. Lights: 1994 *What's Wrong with this Picture?* 1995 *Love! Valour! Compassion!; Master Class* 1996 *Present Laughter; Sex and Longing; Summer and Smoke* 1997 *The Diary of Anne Frank; God's Heart; Proposals; Side Show* 1998 *Wait until Dark* 1999 *Night Must Fall* 2000 *Ride Down Mt. Morgan; True West* 2001 *The Dinner Party; The Invention of Love; Judgment at Nuremberg*

Phil MacDonald

Phil (Phyllis P.) MacDonald was active on Broadway between 1933 and 1937. She worked as a scenic artist at Fulton Studios, and resided at 15 West 25th Street in New York City during the mid-1930s. She should not be confused with the minimalist painter (1927-1983) nor the actress (1905-1995), all of whom share the same name. Costumes: 1933 *It Happened Tomorrow* (Gowns) 1934 *Hotel Alimony* 1937 *One Thing after Another* (Gowns)

Heather MacDonald

An actress, documentary director, and costume designer, Heather MacDonald has had a varied career in theater and film. Stage appearances include *American Music* in Los Angeles and productions with the California Shakespeare Festival. She designed hair and make-up for *A Child's Christmas in Wales* and *The Taffetas* in Phoenix in the mid-1990s, and won a 1995 Sundance

Film Festival Award for *Ballot Measure 9* about Oregon's 1992 anti-gay ballot initiative. As Heather MacDonald-Rouse, she created costumes for a production on Broadway in the mid-1960s.
Costumes: 1966 *Wait a Minim!* (as: Healther MacDonald-Rouse)

Jed Mace

Jed Mace, born in Texas in 1917, studied at Southern Methodist University with Dr. Edyth Renshaw. His first costume designs were at Southern Methodist University for a group of plays including *Mary Tudor* and *Would-be Gentleman.* In 1950, he designed *Hamlet* at Elsinore, and in 1952 received a special award for his costume designs at the Berlin Festival and in London. His credits were many and varied, including work with Ira and Lee Gershwin and Robert Breen, all of whom he acknowledged as influential. For most of his career he was based in Dallas, Texas, where he operated Jed Mace Interiors, Inc. from the early 1950s until the mid-1980s. He designed productions throughout the greater-Dallas area, as well as for galas and charity events. In 1960, Mr. Mace designed Harold Arlen's *Blues Opera,* which opened in Amsterdam. He died on June 15, 1994 in Terrell, Texas.
Costumes: 1953 *Porgy and Bess*

Molly MacEwan

Molly MacEwan designed sets for two Broadway plays in 1948.
Sets: 1948 *John Bull's Other Island; Where Stars Walk*

Cora MacGeachy

Cora MacGeachy designed numerous costumes on Broadway between her debut with the *Hip! Hip! Hooray!* in 1907 and *George White's Scandals* in 1929. She also worked for costume houses, including the Schneider-Anderson Costume Company and Max & Mahieu. Her specialty was musical revues and she often worked in collaboration with other designers. Little is known of the life or background of this prolific and talented designer. She was born in Illinois on August 4, 1894 and in the late 1920s relocated to Hollywood where she worked for the

First National Studios, mainly as a song writer. Shortly before her death in Los Angeles on June 23, 1960, she composed the music for "Hymn to the United Nations." Many of her original designs are in the Shubert Archive, the Museum of the City of New York, and the Billy Rose Theatre Collection in New York Public Library for the Performing Arts at Lincoln Center.

Costumes: 1907 *Hip! Hip! Hooray!*† **1910** *Bright Eyes* **1911** *The Hen-Pecks* (as: Cora McGeechey); *La Belle Paree*†; *The Never Homes; The Wedding Trip; Winter Garden*† **1912** *Hanky Panky; Hokey-Pokey and Bunty, Bulls and Strings; Roly Poly and Without the Law; The Sun Dodgers; The Wall Street Girl*† **1913** *The Pleasure Seekers*† **1914** *The Debutante*†; *Hello Broadway; Ziegfeld Follies of 1914* (as: Cora MacGeahy) **1915** *Around the Map*†; *Fads and Fancies*†; *Fads and Fancies*†; *Hip-Hip-Hooray*†; *Ned Wayburn's Town Topics*† (Nearly every principal and chorus costume); *Ziegfeld Follies: 1915*†; *Ziegfeld Midnight Frolic; Ziegfeld's Midnight Frolics* **1916** *The Century Girl*†; *The Cohan Revue*†; *Ziegfeld Follies: 1916*† **1917** *Ziegfeld Follies: 1917*† **1918** *The Passing Show of 1918*†; *Sinbad*† **1919** *A Lonely Romeo; The Passing Show of 1919*† **1920** *Cinderella on Broadway*†; *Floradora; The Passing Show of 1921; Poor Little Ritz Girl*† **1921** *Music Box Revue*† (Additional costumes); *The Perfect Fool*†; *Ziegfeld Midnight Follies*† **1922** *Better Times*† ("The Story of a Fan"); *Make It Snappy*† (Dresses); *Ziegfeld Follies: 1922*† ("Black Crook Amazons, Fencing Girls, Palm Beach") **1923** *George White's Scandals*†; *One Kiss* (Miss Groody's gowns); *The Rise of Rosie O'Reilly*†; *Stepping Stones*† **1924** *Stepping Stones*† **1927** *Merry Malones*† (Women's costumes); *Take the Air*†; *Ziegfeld Follies: 1927*† **1929** *George White's Scandals*† (American costumes)

Ian Lloyd MacKenzie

In 1930 Ian Lloyd MacKenzie designed sets for a Broadway play. An actor, he appeared in London in *The Witch of Edmonton* in 1936 and in *The Melody That Got Lost* in 1938. He returned to New York in 1940 to appear in

King Lear and *Macbeth*, after which he planned to make a film of *Richard III*.
Sets: 1930 *Marigold*

Bob Mackie

Bob (Robert Gordon) Mackie is widely known for his flamboyant designs on television for Judy Garland, Cher, Carol Burnett, and others and for his Las Vegas shows. He was born in Los Angeles on March 24, 1940 and studied art and theatrical design at the Chouinard Art Institute from 1958 to 1961. He worked as an assistant for Jean Louis and Edith Head before teaming up with Ray Aghayan, with whom he designed for many years. He also has designed lines of glamorous evening clothes and furs. Much honored, he won nine Emmy Awards out of nineteen nominations, the Costume Designers Guild Award in 1968, and the Fashion Achievement Award from Otis/Parsons School of Design in 1987. His designs for *Pennies from Heaven* in 1981 were nominated for an Academy Award. A retrospective of his designs, "Unmistakably Mackie" was held at the Museum of the Fashion Institute of Technology in 1999.
Costumes: 1971 *On the Town†* **1974** *Lorelei†* (Miss Channing's costumes) **1976** *Debbie Reynolds Show* (Gowns) **1978** *Platinum* **1994** *Best Little Whorehouse Goes Public, The* **1995** *Moon over Buffalo*; *Radio City Easter Show†* (Dancing in Diamonds, additional costumes) **1996** *Radio City Spring Spectacular†* **1997** *Radio City Spring Spectacular†*

Mary MacKinnon

Mary MacKinnon, a fashion magazine illustrator, designed costumes on Broadway in 1930. Born in New York City, she studied at the Art Students League with Robert Henri. She began her career as an illustrator for Sears, Roebuck and Company during the 1920s before she was hired by Edna Chase at *Vogue*. She married Frederick Johnson in 1930 and stopped working for magazines, but began painting portraits with subjects including the Duchess of Windsor. She died September 22, 1962 at the age of 72.
Costumes: 1930 *Made in France* (Gowns and Miss Blair's Costumes)

Robert Mackintosh

Robert Mackintosh was born May 26, 1925 and attended Pratt Institute and Parsons School of Design. In addition to the theater he designed for *Holiday on Ice, The Garry Moore Show* on television from 1960 to 1964, numerous off-Broadway shows, and costumes for drag performer Charles Busch in *Green Heart* that he based on an earlier design for a gown for Lena Horne. Author of two novels, *Silk* and *A Heritage of Lies* he also co-wrote *The Life and Times of a Saloon Singer* about Bobby Short. He designed Ruby Dee's one-woman show, *My One Good Nerve* which opened the day he died, February 13, 1998.
Costumes: 1952 *The Gambler*; *Wish You Were Here* **1954** *Anniversary Waltz* **1955** *Silk Stockings†* **1956** *Mr. Wonderful* **1957** *Fair Game* **1958** *Interlock*; *Third Best Sport†* (Miss Holm's clothes) **1959** *Masquerade* **1960** *A Second String* **1966** *Mame* **1967** *How Now Dow Jones*; *Sherry!* **1969** *Butterflies Are Free*; *The Fig Leaves Are Falling* **1983** *Mame*

Woods Mackintosh

In addition to his credits on-Broadway, William Woods Mackintosh has designed scenery off-Broadway at the New York Shakespeare Festival, American Place Theatre, Proposition and the Hudson Guild. He has been art director for numerous films, including *Remo Williams: The Adventure Begins, Jaws 3-D, The World According to Garp, Heaven and Earth, Die Hard with a Vengeance*, and *One Trick Pony*.
Sets: 1978 *Runaways†*

Elizabeth MacLeish

Elizabeth MacLeish designed one set in 1977 on Broadway.
Sets: 1977 *Ipi Tombi†*

Jack Maclennan

Jack Maclennan designed sets and lights for one play in 1935. An electrician, he resided at 4523 Barnes Avenue in New York City with his wife Mary in 1932. He died in Seattle, Washington in June 1987.
Sets: 1935 *Something More Important/The Old Woman/etc.*

Lights: 1935 *Something More Important/The Old Woman/etc.*

Micheal MacLiammoir

Micheal MacLiammoir, also known as Micheál M'Liammóir, was an actor and director. He was born on October 24, 1899 in County Cork, Ireland. He studied painting at the Slade Art School in London. His credits at Dublin's Gate Theatre, which he founded with Hilton Edwards, were extensive, and he occasionally designed sets and costumes for plays in which he acted or directed. He performed onstage as a child as early as 1911 and on Broadway in 1948 when the Gate Theatre Company toured America, in a play he also designed. He appeared often in London and Ireland in films and on television. Additional American performances include *The Importance of Being Oscar* in 1961 and *I Must be Talking to My Friends* in 1967. An author of poems, plays and short stories, usually in Gaelic, he died on March 6, 1978 in Dublin.

Sets: 1948 *The Old Lady Says "No"*
Costumes: 1948 *The Old Lady Says "No"*

Ian MacNeil

Stage designer Ian MacNeil was born in London on February 5, 1960 and raised in New York. He is the son of Robert B. W. MacNeil, former PBS news reporter (MacNeil/Lehrer Newshour), and Rosemarie Copland MacNeil. Both of his parents worked in the theater before his father became a journalist. After receiving his B.A. at Trinity College in Connecticut, he moved to London in mid-1980s and studied at the Croydon School of Art. He then worked for small theater companies including the Derby Playhouse, Contact Theatre Manchester, Cheltenham Everyman, and the Gate Theatre where he began collaborating with director Stephen Daldry. Since then he has designed for major companies throughout the U.K. and in 1994 was named one of Britain's Top Ten designers by *The Guardian.* His design for *An Inspector Calls* won the 1992 Laurence Olivier Award, and when it arrived in New York, won Critics' Circle and Drama Desk Awards. The production of *Tristan and Isolde* he designed at the English National Opera won the 1997 Olivier Award for Best Opera Production, and *Machinal* for Royal National Theatre was named one of the 1990s most remarkable productions. Twenty-first century credits include *Albert Speer* directed by Trevor Nunn and Caryl Churchill's *Far Away* at the Royal Court, both in London.

Sets: 1994 *An Inspector Calls* 1999 *Via Dolorosa*
Costumes: 1994 *An Inspector Calls* 1999 *Via Dolorosa*

Percy Macquoid

Percy Macquoid, R.I., a British artist and designer, created numerous sets and costumes for Sir Herbert Beerbohm Tree's productions in London. He was born in 1852 and studied in Marlborough, England and at the Royal Academy. His many books include *A History of English Furniture.* The initials after his name indicate that he was a member of the Royal Institute of Painters in Watercolours. He died in 1925 at age 73.

Sets: 1901 *D'Arcy of the Guards*
Costumes: 1901 *D'Arcy of the Guards* 1906 *Paolo and Francesca* 1916 *King Henry VIII*†; *The Merchant of Venice* (Some designs and Costume Supervisor) 1917 *Colonel Newcome*

Marcia Madeira

Marcia Madeira won a Drama Desk Award and a Tony nomination for the lighting design for *Nine.* She was born in Boston on January 25, 1945 and graduated from Bradford College in 1965. She studied for two years at Yale and received a B.F.A. from Carnegie Mellon University in 1969. Her design debut was at the Kennebunkport Playhouse with a production of *My Fair Lady* in 1964. Her many credits off-Broadway include *Cloud Nine, Privates on Parade* and *Here's Love.* She has also designed lights in regional theaters (often for the Huntington Theatre Company), for opera, for national tours, and *Ice Capades: On Top of the World.* Twenty-first century designs

include *The Will Rogers Follies* at the Gateway Playhouse.
Lights: 1980 *The Music Man* 1982 *Nine* 1983 *Marilyn*; *My One and Only*

Molly Maginnis

Molly Maginnis was born in Washington, D.C. on December 24, 1951. She received a B.F.A. in painting from Washington University in St. Louis in 1973 and in 1976 an M.F.A. in Costume Design from Carnegie Mellon University, where she now serves on the faculty as Adjunct Professor of Costume Design. She enjoyed acting as a child and this, along with her interests in fashion and art, led her to costume design. Her professional debut as a costume designer occurred in 1975 at the North Shore Music Theatre with the production of *Come and Be Killed*. She has designed numerous films including *Town and Country*, *In a Shallow Grave*, *Broadcast News*, *As Good As It Gets*, *Look Who's Talking Now*, *Mr. Jekyl & Ms. Hyde*, *Home Front*, and *Life as a House*. Among her many honors are an ACE Award nomination for the film *Billy the Kid*, a BAFTA nomination for the PBS television series *Tales of the City*, and a Drama Logue Award for the play *Sherlock's Last Case*.
Costumes: 1983 *Show Boat*

Georg Magnusson

Georg Magnusson designed sets for a production on Broadway in the early 1960s presented by the Royal Dramatic Theatre of Sweden.
Sets: 1962 *Long Day's Journey into Night*

Helen Mahieu

Helen Mahieu designed costumes on Broadway between 1927 and 1943. Max Cohen and Helen Mahieu designed together through the costume business, Max & Mahieu where they also executed costumes for other designers. For additional credits and information, see the entries "Max Cohen" and "Max & Mahieu."
Costumes: 1927 *Bye, Bye, Bonnie*; *Footlights* 1928 *Just a Minute*; *Keep Shufflin'* 1931 *Sugar Hill* 1932 *Shuffle Along of 1933*† (Butterfly Ensemble)

1942 *New Priorities of 1943* 1943 *Hairpin Harmony*

Mainbocher

Mainbocher (Main Bocher) was born Main Rousseau Bocher in Chicago on October 24, 1890. He went to Europe as a young man to study piano and voice, but soon became a sketch artist for designers. Credited with the development of the basic black dress, he also designed for the Girl Scouts and the WAVES. One of the last couturier designers who specialized in made-to-order clothes, his fashion designs were never mass-marketed or mass-produced. He often designed gowns for actresses in plays in addition to those for his private customers. Mainbocher died December 27, 1976 at the age of 85 in Munich.
Costumes: 1941 *Blithe Spirit* 1945 *Dream Girl*† (Miss Betty Fields costumes); *Foolish Notion* 1946 *Park Avenue*† (Miss Corbett's gowns) 1948 *The Leading Lady* 1949 *The Smile of the World*† (Miss Gordon's clothes) 1950 *Call Me Madam*† (Miss Merman's dresses) 1951 *Not for Children*† (Miss Betty Field's costumes); *Point of No Return* 1953 *Kind Sir*; *The Prescott Proposals* 1956 *The Great Sebastian* (Miss Fontanne's dresses) 1959 *The Sound of Music*† (Miss Mary Martin's clothes) 1964 *Tiny Alice*† (Gowns)

Bruno Maine

Bruno Jalmar Manninen was born in Finland and came to the United States at age thirteen, changing his name when he became a citizen in 1923. He apprenticed at a scenic studio and subsequently designed for John Murray Anderson. In 1933 he succeeded Vincent Minnelli as Art Director at Radio City Music Hall, where he remained for eighteen years. His Christmas and Easter Pageants were widely admired, as were the ice shows he designed for Sonja Henie and the inaugural balls he created for Dwight D. Eisenhower in 1953 and 1957. Bruno Maine died at age 65 on July 30, 1962.
Sets: 1942 *Stars on Ice* 1944 *Hats Off to Ice* 1947 *Icetime of 1948*† 1948 *Howdy, Mr. Ice* 1949 *Howdy Mr. Ice of 1950*
Lights: 1951 *Bagels and Yox*

Alexander Maissel

Alexander Maissel directed musicals including *Trial by Jury* and *Iolanthe* at the Cherry Lane Theatre. In the early 1960s he was musical director of *Pirates of Penzance* at the Light Opera of the Provincetown Playhouse, where he also directed *Ruddigore*. In the 1930s he was a partner with Aida Maissel and John F. Grahame in Theatre Art Productions, theatrical producers, located at 147 West 46th Street in New York City.

Sets: **1934** *Wrong Number*

Jean-Denis Malclès

Born in Paris on May 15, 1912, the son of a sculptor, Jean-Denis Malclès is a painter, lithographer and theatrical designer. He studied with Louis Gognot and Rulhmann and has exhibited at Salon d'Automne and the Salon des Artistes Décorateurs. In collaboration with Andre Beaurepaire, he designed the background for "Théâtre de la Mode," the miniature display of haute couture that helped restore France as a center of fashion after the Second WorldWar. He has designed for many theaters, including the Opéra de Paris, Comédie Française, La Scala, Covent Garden, Le Théâtre de Jean Anouilh, and Cie Renaud-Barrault. Honors include the Chevalier de la Légion d'Honneur.

Sets: **1952** *La Repetition Ou l'Amour Puni* **1957** *Romanoff and Juliet*
Costumes: **1952** *La Repetition Ou l'Amour Puni*; *Occupe Toi d'Amelie*

Miss Dora Malet

Miss Dora Malet designed the ladies' costumes in a 1926 Broadway play.

Costumes: **1926** *Nica* (Ladies costumes)

John Malkovich

John Malkovich, known for his performances on stage and in films, has occasionally designed costumes, scenery, and sound as well. Originally from Benton, Illinois, where he was born December 9, 1953, he attended Eastern Illinois and Illinois State Universities before moving to Chicago with a group of friends who formed the Steppenwolf Company. He has also directed plays, including *Balm in Gilead* for

which he received an Obie in 1985, and *The Caretaker* for which he also designed the costumes. He won an Obie Award for his New York debut performance in *True West*, and a Drama Desk Award for his Broadway debut as "Biff" in *Death of a Salesman*. Widely regarded as one of the finest American actors, twenty-first century credits include performances in the films *Shadow of the Vampire, Knockabout Guys*, and *Ghost World* which he produced.

Costumes: **1986** *The Caretaker*

Vincent Mallory

Vincent Mallory designed sets on Broadway in the mid-1930s. He wrote *Sound in the Theatre* in collaboration with Harold Burris-Meyer and Lewis S. Goodfriend. Mallory died shortly after the first edition was published in 1959 by Theatre Arts Books.

Sets: **1934** *Green Stick*†

Philip Maltese

Philip Maltese designed one set in 1932 on Broadway.

Sets: **1932** *The Show-Off*

Rouben Mamoulian

Rouben Mamoulian, an innovative director of theater and films, was a founding member of the Directors' Guild of America. He was born on October 8, 1897 in Tiflis, Georgia, Russia and studied law at the University of Moscow and then theater at the Vakhtangov Studio of the Moscow Art Theatre. He began directing in London in 1922 and came to New York in 1923 to direct several landmark musicals, including *Oklahoma!* and *Carousel*. A versatile and creative designer, he won numerous prizes throughout his distinguished career, including a Donaldson Award in 1945 for *Carousel*. He also received first prize at the Venice International Film Festival in 1931 for *Dr. Jekyll and Mr. Hyde* and for *Queen Christina* in 1934 for film direction. Occasionally Mr. Mamoulian designed scenery, lights and/or costumes for productions which he directed. He died on December 4, 1987 in Los Angeles.

Sets: **1927** *Porgy*†
Costumes: **1927** *Porgy*
Lights: **1949** *Leaf and Bough*

Thomas Mangan

Thomas Mangan designed scenery on Broadway at the beginning of the twentieth century. Mainly a carpenter, he resided at 132 West 62nd Street in New York City in 1910.

Sets: **1904** *Home Folks*† **1905** *The Duchess of Dantzic*

Mannie Manim

Mannie Manim was born on July 10, 1941 in South Africa. Over the past forty years he has designed, directed and/or produced over three hundred productions in South Africa and abroad. He is producing director of the Johannesburg Market Theatre Company, which he co-founded with Barney Simon in 1976, and Managing Trustee of the Market Theatre Foundation. His designs have been influenced by Frank Staff, Meshak Mosia, and Jean Rosenthal and been informed by practical experience. He is the recipient of several awards: AA Life Vita Award for Best Original Lighting Design (1985 through 1988); The Shirley Moss Award for Greatest Practical and Technical Contribution to Theatre in South Africa (1980); the South African Institute for Theatre Technology Award for Outstanding Achievement as a Theatre Technician, Administrator and Lighting Designer (1981); and the AA Life Award for Most Enterprising Producer (1984). Recent productions include *Sacrifice of Mmbatho (Daughter of Nebo)* which toured to the Brooklyn Academy of Music in 1994, and serving as producer for the Handspring Puppet Company of Johannesburg.

Lights: **1988** *Sarafina!*

Maybelle Manning

Mrs.Maybelle Manning was an active designer in the teens and twenties, creating costumes for Florenz Ziegfeld and the Ringling Brothers Circus, as well as for two Broadway shows. Before working as a costume designer she created clothes for wholesale houses in New York, and with her sister Mildred, was the proprietor of Manning, Inc. In private life, she was the wife of Lee E. Olwell, at one time the publisher of the *New York Journal.* Maybelle Manning, who was named the "World's Best Dressed Woman" in 1920, died at age 74 on January 1, 1967.

Costumes: **1926** *Daisy Mayme* **1927** *Sidewalks of New York*†

Mildred Manning

Mildred Manning, a native of New York City, began her career as an actress, appearing onstage in chorus roles in *Oh! Delphine* and *Little Nemo Over the River*, and in many films for Biograph, Vitagraph, and D.W. Griffith. Between 1929 and 1940 she designed costumes for many Broadway shows. With her sister Maybelle, she was the proprietor of Manning, Inc., founded in 1927, employing Brymer (who was also a costume designer on Broadway) as a house designer. The September 1917 issue of *Photoplay* feature an interview with her, "An Ingénue Who Won't Ingénue" concerning the roles she preferred to play in movies.

Costumes: **1929** *Diana; Family Affairs*†; *Salt Water* **1931** *She Lived Next to the Firehouse* **1932** *The Budget* (Gowns) **1933** *Birthright* (Gowns); *Heat Lightning* (Dresses) **1934** *Come What May*† (Women's costumes); *Too Many Boats*† (Costumes) **1935** *Lady of Letters; Loose Moments* (Women's costumes); *A Touch of Brimstone*† (Miss Castle's gowns) **1936** *Mimie Scheller* (Miss Gerald's costume) **1937** *Abie's Irish Rose* (Stylist); *Hitch Your Wagon*† (Miss Moore's evening gown) **1938** *Casey Jones* (Miss Conklin's dresses) **1940** *My Sister Eileen; The Old Foolishness* **1941** *Mr. and Mrs. North*

Lawrence Mansfield

Lawrence Mansfield designed one set in 1951 on Broadway.

Sets: **1951** *Springtime for Henry*†

Peter Maradudin

Peter Maradudin, a lighting designer, was born on February 16, 1959 in Washington, D.C. to Alexi and Margaret Maradudin. He did his undergraduate work at Stanford University and received his M.F.A. from the Yale University School of Drama. Jennifer Tipton has been his major career influence and mentor. His first professional job after school was also his first Broadway production, *Ma Rainey's Black Bottom*. It opened in October of 1984 at the Cort Theatre after a trial run in Philadelphia. Since that time he has designed numerous shows around the country, primarily on the West Coast in regional theaters, designing often at the South Coast Repertory, A.C.T. and Seattle Repertory Theatre. He has won many Los Angeles Drama Critics Circle Awards, Theatre Critics Awards in San Diego and Portland, numerous Drama Logue Awards, and a 2000 Dean Goodman Choice Award (formerly Drama Logue) for his lighting designs for *Juno and the Paycock* and *Tartuffe*.

Lights: **1984** *Ma Rainey's Black Bottom* **1993** *The Kentucky Cycle*

Marvin March

Marvin March, who began his career in television specializing in properties and lighting, designed sets and lights for a production on Broadway in 1964. He is primarily a set designer and an art director for films, with *Lethal Weapon 2*, *Skin Deep*, *Ghostbusters*, *Flashdance*, *Tango & Cash*, *How to Make An American Quilt*, *The Out-of-Towners*, and *The General's Daughter* among his many credits. In 1995, he was elected as a governor for the art director's section of the Academy of Motion Picture Arts and Sciences. Honors include an Oscar nomination, with Ken Adam, for set decoration for *Addams Family Values*.

Lights: **1964** *The Caretaker*

Larry J. Margulies

Larry J. Margulies collaborated on the costumes for a play in 1924. Long affiliated with the dress trade, in 1932 he advocated the five-day work week and hourly wages for an eight-hour day.

Costumes: **1924** *Innocent Eyes*†

Maritza

Sari Maritza was an actress who mainly appeared in films in Europe and for Paramount Pictures, using her Austrian mother's maiden name. Born Patricia Detering Nathan in Tientsin, China on March 17, 1910 to a British officer and his wife, she studied in Europe and first performed in Vienna. Her film appearances included *Forgotten Commandments, International House* and *A Lady's Profession*. She stopped acting in the mid-1930s when she realized her striking beauty could not overcome her inability to act. According to Jack D. Hamilton in *They Had Faces Then*, while working for a lens maker during World War Two, she developed an effective way to polish plastic gun sights. Sari Maritza died at age 77 in 1987.

Costumes: **1931** *Right of Happiness*† (Miss Nicoll's costumes; Mr. DuRoy's pj's and loungers)

Georges Marix

Georges Marix designed costumes for a play in 1936.

Costumes: **1936** *Granite*

Kirah Markham

Kirah (Kyra) Markham was born Elaine Hyman in Chicago, Illinois on August 18, 1891. She studied at the Art Institute of Chicago, but gave up painting in 1919 to perform with the Chicago Little Theatre. Her relationship with novelist Theodore Drieser during that time has been well documented. In 1916, she performed with the Provincetown Players and supported herself by doing illustrations. She took classes at the Art Students League with Alexander Abels, and in the 1930s worked with the New York City Federal Arts Project. Her art work, mainly etchings and lithographs is in many museums and collections, including the Museum of Modern Art, the Smithsonian Institution, and the New York Public Library. Later married to set designer, David S. Gaither, she died in 1967.

Costumes: **1924** *Fashion*† **1933** *Foolscap*

Andrew B. Marlay

Andrew B. Marlay was born in Dayton, Ohio on May 20, 1956. In 1978 he received a B.F.A. from the New York University School of the Arts. After making his Broadway debut at age 23, he went on to design the costumes for numerous plays, musicals, operas and ballets. In addition to Broadway, his designs have been seen at Lincoln Center, off-Broadway and in many regional theaters. In 1986, he co-founded Penn and Fletcher, Inc., with Ernest A. Smith. Their company began as a resource for custom embroideries needed by the theatrical costume, fashion and bridal industries and in 1996, was expanded to include interior design. Their unique embroidery work for interiors has been featured regularly in *House Beautiful, Elle Décor, House & Garden* and *Martha Stewart Living*. In Spring 1998, Penn and Fletcher, Inc., opened a Design Services division through which Mr. Marlay now designs custom residential interiors for a wide range of private clients.

Costumes: 1979 *Strider* **1990** *Truly Blessed*

James Maronek

James Maronek is from Milwaukee, Wisconsin where he was born on December 4, 1931. He studied at the Layton School of Art in Milwaukee and earned both a B.F.A. and an M.F.A. at the Art Institute of Chicago. He has received Chicago's Joseph Jefferson Award for Best Scenic Design for *Guys and Dolls* at the Goodman Theatre, and another Jefferson for Best Lighting Design for *Beckoning Fair One* at the Organic Theatre. He was resident designer at the First Chicago Center and written and edited for *Chicago Guide*. On the faculty at DePaul University, he has also been active as a member and officer of United Scenic Artists. His designs have been included in exhibitions and United States entries in the Prague Quadrennial.

Sets: 1982 *Do Black Patent Leather Shoes Really Reflect Up?*

Luis Márquez

Luis Márquez, a photographer, cinematographer and designer, was born in Mexico in 1899. In the mid-1930s he experimented with hand-tinting his black and white photographs that were then published as postcards. He often photographed people and paid particular attention to their clothing and environment, dressing them in garments and surrounding them with objects from his personal collection. In May 1937, *National Geographic Magazine* published four of his photographs, bring him recognition beyond Mexico. *Mexico in Pictures* contains his photographs, as does *Mexican Folklore: 100 Photographs by Luis Márquez* published in 1954. The subject of "El imaginario de Luis Márquez" in the journal *Alquimia*, September-December 2000, he died in 1978. The artist should not be confused with baseball player Luis Angel Marquez (1925-1988).

Sets: 1949 *Cabalagata (a.k.a. A Night in Spain)*

Gregg Marriner

Gregg Marriner designed lights for regional theaters such as the Indiana Repertory Theatre, the Portland Stage Company, Paper Mill Playhouse, Ogunquit Playhouse and the Poinciana Playhouse. He also designed off-Broadway productions at the Equity Library Theatre and the Actor's Studio. He designed club acts for performers Tammy Grimes and Lee Roy Reams, and the 1983 production of *The Buck Stops Here* off-Broadway. Assistant to Tharon Musser for *42nd Street* and *Dreamgirls*, Gregg Marriner, who was born April 25, 1953, died at age 33 in August 1987, a victim of AIDS.

Lights: 1980 *Canterbury Tales*

Frank Marsden

Frank Marsden collaborated on the scenery of two Broadway productions during the first decade of the twentieth century.

Sets: 1906 *Forty-five Minutes from Broadway†* **1907** *Polly of the Circus*

Reginald Marsh

Reginald Marsh, a painter of realistic scenes of New York life, was the son of artists. His paintings hang in the Metropolitan Museum of Modern Art and the Whitney Museum, among others. He was born in Paris on March 14, 1898 and moved with his family to Nutley, New Jersey when he was two. He graduated from Yale in 1920 and studied at the Art Students League. In the early 1920s he drew illustrations for magazines and "cartoonicle chronicles" of the vaudeville circuit. In the mid-twenties he began illustrating in *The New Yorker* and continued to contribute to the magazine throughout his life. He also designed sets while beginning to seriously paint and develop his artistic style. In addition to the scenery he designed in the mid-1920s on Broadway, he also created productions for movie houses, dance centers, and the curtain for Otis Skinner's *Sancho Panza*. Marsh died in Vermont on July 3, 1954 at age 56.

Sets: **1922** *Greenwich Village Follies†* **1924** *Fashion†*

Richard Marston

Scenic designer and artist Richard Marston was born in England, son of Henry Marston, a Shakespearean actor. He initially followed his father onto the stage, but found stage design more appealing and apprenticed at the Drury Lane Theatre. The majority of his credits were prior to the twentieth century, and began in America with *The Black Crook* in 1866 at Niblo's Garden Theatre in New York. Among his other nineteenth century credits are *Two Orphans, Two Men of Sandy Bar, False Friend, Lights o' London* and *Dakolar*. During his fifty year career, he painted many productions for Richard Mansfield, David Belasco, and through the painting studio of Dodge and Castle. The productions listed below represent only a small proportion of his contributions to early stage design, especially exterior scenes. When the Protective Alliance of Scenic Painters was formed in 1885, he served as the chairman. Marston died in New York City on February 16, 1917 at age 75.

Sets: **1899** *The Ameer†* (Act I); *Cyrano De Bergerac†*; *Papa's Wife†* (Acts II) **1900** *Henry V*; *The Middleman* **1901** *Beaucaire*; *The Marriage Game* **1904** *Fatinitza†*; *Girofle-Girofla†* (Act II); *Home Folks†*; *In Newport†*; *A Little Bit of Everything*; *The Two Orphans* **1905** *At the Threshold*; *Lifting the Lid†*; *The Prodigal Son†*; *Sergeant Brue* **1907** *The Marriage of Reason†*; *The Right of Way†* **1912** *She Stoops to Conquer* **1913** *The Marriage Game*

Madame Marte

Madame Marte designed costumes for a 1906 Broadway play.

Costumes: **1906** *Mr. Hopkinson†*

Martin

Martin designed sets for one Broadway show in 1933.

Sets: **1933** *Tattle Tales*

Connie Martin

Fashion and costume designer Connie Martin made her Broadway debut in 1996. As a stylist, she has designed films, covers for publications, personal appearances, and music tours. Her fashion experience includes work with Charivari.

Costumes: **1996** *God Said Ha!*

Daisy Martin

Daisy Martin designed costumes on Broadway in 1923. Her small shop for "modes" was located at 3 West 108 Street in New York City during the 1920s.

Costumes: **1923** *Roseanne*

Henry Martin

Henry Martin, a landscape painter, also contributed scenery to a 1900 production on Broadway. He exhibited at the Royal Academy in London beginning in 1874. His paintings of the Cornwall coast were included in a 1958 exhibition at the Newlyn (England) Art Gallery. He was born circa 1840 and died in 1908.

Sets: **1900** *Prince Otto†*

Ashley Martin-Davis

Ashley Martin-Davis, who studied at the Central School of Art and Design and the Motley Theatre Design program at Riverside Studios, has been designing through the United Kingdom since the mid-1980s. She has designed numerous productions for the Royal Shakespeare Company as well as for the Royal National Theatre. Her designs for scenery have also been seen at the Theatre Royal in York, the Almeida Theatre, the Crucible Theatre in Sheffield, Manchester Royal Exchange, and the Donmar Warehouse. Opera designs include *Don Giovanni* for Opera North and *I Due Foscari* for the Scottish Opera. Twenty-first century designs include *The Winter's Tale* at RNT, *The Critic* at the Royal Exchange, Manchester, and *The Rivals* for RSC.

Sets: **1995** *Translations*

Hugh Mason

Hugh Mason designed a set on Broadway in the mid-1930s. He resided with his wife Elizabeth at 3120 Bainbridge Avenue in New York City in 1932.

Sets: **1933** *Raw Meat*

Richard Mason

Richard G. Mason was born in New York City in 1929, the son of Dr. and Mrs. G. R. Mason. He received a B.A. from Swarthmore College in 1950 and an M.F.A. from the Yale University School of Drama. His teachers and mentors include Donald Oenslager, Frank Poole Bevan, H. A. Condell, and Mordecai Gorelik who he also assisted. He designed costumes for *Uncle Vanya* at the Fourth Street Theatre in the mid-1950s, and scenery and costumes for several productions for the Columbia Players, Falmouth Playhouse, Allenberry Playhouse, Ivoryton and Tamiment. He also has taught and worked as an interior decorator.

Sets: **1973** *Bette Midler*

Michael Massee

Michael D. Massee was born on December 2, 1937 in Corvallis, Oregon, graduated from Portland State University in 1960 and received an M.F.A. from the Mason Gross School of the Arts at Rutgers University in 1984. He acknowledges John Jensen and Charles Gauup as major influences. His career as a scenic designer began in 1959 with *Man and Superman* at Portland State University. Since then he has designed opera, film, television and theater. Off-Broadway credits include the sets and costumes for *The End of All Things Natural, Piano Bar, Dolores,* and *Sexual Perversity in Chicago,* among others. Among his film credits are *Love Song for Miss Lydia* (PBS) and *Tomorrow is Monday.* From 1985 to 1988 he was the principal designer at William Paterson College, and since 1989 has been Head of the Design Program at Fordham University at Lincoln Center.

Sets: **1988** *Paul Robeson*
Costumes: **1988** *Paul Robeson*

André Masson

André Masson, one of the major French surrealist painters, was born in Balagny-sur-Therain, France on January 4, 1896. He studied at the Academie Royale des Beaux-Arts in Brussels, and at the École des Beaux Arts in Paris. Also a stage designer, he made his professional debut with *Les Présages* for the Ballets de Monte Carlo in 1933 and collaborated often with Jean Louis Barrault in France. His paintings are widely collected and exhibited in Europe and the United States. The themes of his paintings are echoed in books he wrote, including *Mythology of Nature, Mythology of Being* and *Nocturnal Notebook.* Shortly before his death on October 28, 1987 in Paris at age 91, an exhibition of his drawings was presented at the Hayward Gallery in London. A major retrospective was held at the Museum of Modern Art in New York in 1976.

Sets: **1952** *Hamlet*
Costumes: **1952** *Hamlet*

Barbara Matera

Barbara Gray Matera, a native of Hythe, Kent, England, studied painting and drawing at St. Martin's School of Art in London. Although her school offered no course in theater design at that time, she was placed for an internship as student designer with the Adelphi Players, a repertory company in Cheshire, England, run by Jack Boyd. This position led in turn to wardrobe work with the Ballet Rambert. While at Ballet Rambert she had the opportunity to assist with the construction of costumes for new ballets. Seasonal positions in the costume shops of the Old Vic and Stratford-upon-Avon led her to start her own business, after which she was invited to the Stratford (Ontario) Festival. In 1962 she moved to New York City, initially to work with Ray Diffen, and then at Van Horn's just prior to its merger with Brook's, where she remained for six years and met her husband, Arthur Matera. In 1967, she formed her own

business, Barbara Matera, Ltd., known around the world for its quality costumes. In addition to creating costumes for plays, operas and ballets, films and television from designers' renderings, she occasionally designed, notably for diva Joan Sutherland and for New York City Ballet. An exhibition, "Inside and Out: The Costumes of Barbara Matera, Ltd.," was held at the New York Public Library for the Performing Arts at Lincoln Center in 1996, and reprised for the 2001 Smithsonian Folklife Festival in Washington, D.C. in July 2001. Honors for this talented costume maker and designer include the 2001 Artisan Award from Theatre Development Fund. She died on September 13, 2001 in New York City.
Costumes: **1969** *Private Lives†* (Miss Tammy Grimes costumes)

Mrs. A. E. Mathieson

Mrs. A. E. Mathieson (Irmgard Knopf Mathieson), originally from Denmark, was married to the soloist and conductor Aksel Helge Mathieson. She often traveled with her husband, and designed costumes for a play in 1925. She also worked as a wardrobe mistress.
Costumes: **1925** *Lucky Sambo*

William Henry Matthews

William Henry Matthews designed costumes for numerous Broadway shows, beginning in 1907. He was the son of a Presbyterian minister who was pastor at the Greenwich Church in New York City in the early years of this century. Mr. Matthews often worked in collaboration with Cora MacGeachy, Gladys Monkhouse and Will R. Barnes. In 1923 he designed sets as well as costumes for a Broadway production. William Henry Matthews lived from 1873 to 1946. He should not be confused with theater manager William H. Matthews (d. 1917).
Sets: **1923** *The Deep Tangled Wildwood*
Costumes: **1907** *Hip! Hip! Hooray!†* (All other costumes); *Ziegfeld Follies of 1907†*; *Ziegfeld Follies of 1907†* **1908** *Golden Butterfly*; *Ziegfeld Follies of 1908†* **1909** *Ziegfeld Follies of 1909†* **1910** *The Deacon and the Lady†*; *A Skylark†*;

Ziegfeld Follies of 1910† **1911** *The Enchantress†*; *La Belle Paree†*; *Thais*; *Winter Garden†*; *Ziegfeld Follies of 1911†* **1912** *The Firefly* (Costumes and dresses) **1913** *Her Little Highness*; *The Madcap Duchess*; *The Pleasure Seekers†* **1914** *The Debutante†*; *Wars of the World†* **1915** *Arms and the Man†*; *Arms and the Man†*; *Hip-Hip-Hooray†*; *A Modern Eve*; *The Modern Eve* **1916** *The Century Girl†* **1917** *Cheer-up (Hippodrome)†*; *Eyes of Youth†* **1918** *Everything†*; *The Kiss Burglar* **1919** *A Young Man's Fancy* **1920** *The Girl in the Spotlight*; *The Lady of the Lamp*; *Respect for Riches* **1922** *Better Times†*; *Frank Fay's Fables†*; *Marjolaine* **1923** *The Deep Tangled Wildwood* **1924** *The Magnolia Lady†*; *Merry Wives of Gotham†* **1926** *Slaves All* **1928** *Earl Carroll's Vanities†*; *Elmer Gantry†* **1929** *Fioretta†*; *The Silver Swan†* **1930** *King Lear* **1931** *Hamlet†*; *Julius Caesar†*; *The Merchant of Venice†*

Beatrice Maude

Beatrice Maude designed costumes for a play in 1931. A native of New York City, where she was born on July 22, 1892, she was also an actress and appeared on the Broadway stage in 1918 in *Seven Up*. She died in Los Angeles, California in October 1984.
Costumes: **1931** *In the Best of Families*

Max & Mahieu

Max Cohen and Helen Mahieu collaborated on designs through their costume business, Max & Mahieu, where they also executed costumes for other designers. At one time, Broadway costume designer Cora MacGeachy worked in their studio. For additional credits and information, see the entries "Max Cohen" and "Helen Mahieu."
Costumes: **1911** *A Certain Party†*; *The Revue of Revues* **1912** *Broadway to Paris†* (Chorus costumes) **1913** *The Master Mind†* (Miss Rossmore's gowns) **1914** *The Passing Show of 1914†*

Mimi Maxmen

Costume and scenic designer Mimi (Mary Elizabeth Berman) Maxmen studied at the University of Michigan with Zelma Weisfeld, at Yale University, and Lester Polakov's Studio and the Forum of Stage Design. She was born May 12, 1945 in Minneapolis, Minnesota, daughter of Shirley Aronson and Edward J. Berman. Films include *Tumbleweeds, The Mesmerist, Spent,* and *Turn of Faith.* Her first New York theater work was as resident costume designer for the Roundabout Theatre. Other New York credits include *Uncle Vanya,* the original productions of *A Shayna Maidel* and *A...My Name Is Alice,* and productions for Second Stage, Playwrights Horizons, and American Place Theatre. She has also designed in regional theaters, including the Pittsburgh Public Theatre, Mark Taper Forum and Cleveland Playhouse. In addition she has designed costumes and scenery for the New York City, Joffrey and Metropolitan Opera Ballet Companies. She teaches and lectures widely on the subject of costume design for dance, and teaches "A New York and Los Angeles Practical Guide for Film and Theatrical Costume Designers" at Parson's School of Design, a course she developed. Among her honors is an Obie Award.

Costumes: 1973 *The Play's the Thing* **1995** *Uncle Vanya*

Mr. Maxwell

Mr. Maxwell designed lighting for one play on Broadway in 1914. He also designed costumes for the 1923 London production of *If Winter Comes* by A. S. M. Hutchinson and B. Macdonald Hastings.

Lights: 1914 *The Silent Voice†*

Murray Mayer

Murray Mayer was active on Broadway between 1929 and 1934. His residence was at 313 West 121st Street in New York City in the late 1920s and at 322 West 72nd Street in the early 1930s.

Costumes: 1929 *City Haul* (Costume Supervisor) **1934** *A Roman Servant†*

Mayo

Paul Mayo, a British designer, was born in Bristol, England on December 13, 1908. His designs in London's West End include *The Cherry Orchard* and the *Silver Curlew.* In the late 1940s and throughout the 1950s he designed productions for the London Masque

Theatre, Westminster Theatre and the New Theatre. He has also designed for television. His credits in Paris include *Orpheus* at the Ballets des Champs Élysées and *La Bonne Compagnie* and *L'Homme Qui a Perdu Son Ombre,* both at Mathurins.

Sets: 1952 *Baptiste*

Duane F. Mazey

Duane F. Mazey designed scenery and lighting for a play in 1976. He served as production stage manager for *Staggerlee* in New York in 1987 and for *Sid Caesar and Company: The Legendary Genius of Comedy* in 1989.

Sets: 1976 *Let My People Come†*
Lights: 1976 *Let My People Come*

Stanley R. McCandless

Stanley McCandless, co-founder of the graduate theater program at Yale University, spent forty years teaching lighting design at Yale. He was born on May 9, 1897 in Chicago and received a B.A. from the University of Wisconsin in 1920 and an M.A. in architecture from Harvard University in 1923. In addition to teaching at Yale he was associated with Century Lighting from 1944 to 1964, and was a consultant for Radio City Music Hall, the United Nations Assembly Hall, and the National Gallery of Art. He wrote *Methods of Lighting the Stage, Syllabus of Stage Lighting* and many articles. His few credits on the Broadway stage do not begin to measure the influence he had on generations of students and colleagues. He devoted his ingenuity and technical skills to developing the field of lighting design. Stanley McCandless died in 1967.

Lights: 1937 *The Lady Has a Heart; Many Mansions* **1944** *Rhapsody*

Charles McCarry

Art director and designer Charles Eugene McCarry was born in Philadelphia on November 23, 1957. After earning his M.F.A. at Yale University in 1986, he worked as an assistant designer in New York and taught at Carnegie Mellon University from 1990 to 1992, while establishing his career. Designs in regional theaters include productions at

the Indiana Repertory Theatre, Portland Stage, Philadelphia Drama Guild, Hartford Stage, and the Pennsylvania Opera Theatre. He has designed for television and film, serving as set designer for the daytime drama *Another World* and art director for the feature film *Wall Street*, among others. He also designs business interiors.
Sets: 1992 *3 from Brooklyn*

Ellen V. McCartney

While Ellen V. McCartney was studying for her M.F.A. in costume design at Yale University she designed *Neapolitan Ghosts* and the premiere of *A Walk in the Woods*. Her designs for the Boston Shakespeare Company with director Peter Sellars include *Lighthouse, Mother Courage* and *Macbeth*. She has designed in regional theaters including Portland Stage Company, and the Camden Shakespeare Company, and off-Broadway.
Costumes: 1988 *A Walk in the Woods*

R. McCleery

Robert Charles McCleery (McCleere) was a British designer and painter who regularly created settings for the Theatre Royal, Drury Lane. He often worked in collaboration with other designers including Bruce Smith, Robert Caney, Harry Emden, and Harry Brooke, among others. *Jack and the Beanstalk* (1899) and *Babes in the Wood* were among the pantomimes he designed. He was especially active in London during the 1920s, although the majority of his New York credits were before that time. Before concentrating on scenic art, he was a fine art painter, and had his landscapes exhibited between 1887 and 1892. He died in London in 1927.
Sets: 1901 *The Price of Peace†*; *The Sleeping Beauty and the Beast†* 1903 *Mother Goose†*; *Mr. Bluebeard†* 1905 *The Babes and the Baron†*; *The White Cat†* 1910 *Henry of Navarre*; *The Scarlet Pimpernel* 1913 *Hop o' My Thumb†* 1915 *Stolen Orders†*

Charles Henry McClennahan

Charles Henry McClennahan graduated in 1984 from Yale University

where he was the recipient of the Donald Oenslager Scholarship. At Yale he also received a Graduate Commitment Award from the Afro-American Cultural Center for his contribution to the Center and the black community at Yale. Founder of MINDTECK (Minority Designers and Technicians Network), a placement service for minorities in media and theater, he has designed many productions in New York and the surrounding area for film, theater and video. Off-Broadway productions include *A Tribute to Harry Chapin, Degga, Further Mo'*, and *East Texas Hot Links* for which he won an Audelco Award in 1994. He also designed the set for *Shelia's Day* at the Kennedy Center in Washington, D.C.
Sets: 1984 *Ma Rainey's Black Bottom*

Langdon McCormick

Playwright Langdon McCormick was born in Port Huron, Michigan and studied at Albion College. An actor, he appeared with Otis Skinner in the late 1890s and in his own plays. The scenery and lights he designed were always for plays he wrote. His many plays included *How Hearts Are Broken, The Life of an Actress, Wanted by the Police* and *Toll Gate Inn*. For *The Honeymoon Express* he created, built, and patented an effect of an automobile racing a train, together with a magician named Howard Thurston. McCormick died in June 1954.
Sets: 1913 *The Honeymoon Express†* 1919 *The Storm*
Lights: 1919 *The Storm* 1926 *The Ghost Train*

MarjorieMcCown

Costume designer and novelist Marjorie McCown, who was born in 1955, received her undergraduate degree from New York's Fashion Institute of Technology. She has designed many musical and operas, working at the Goodspeed Opera House and San Diego Opera among other locations. Additional credits include *The Turn of the Screw* in 1988, and the 1989 revival of *The Pajama Game* at New York City Opera. Her novel, *Death by Design*, about a costume designer who is killed with her Emmy Award statuette, was published in 2000.

Costumes: 1990 *Street Scene*

J. McCreery

James Lindsay McCreery (McCleary), originally from Berkeley, California, was the proprietor of a dry goods store at the corner of Broadway and 11th Street in New York City. He contributed designs, as well as fabrics and furnishings, to Broadway productions at the end of the nineteenth and beginning of the twentieth century. Occasionally James McCreery & Company would advertise in theater playbills. When Ada Rehan appeared at Daly's Theatre in *Twelfth Night* in 1898, the program contained a full page advertisement for James McCreery & Company's Upholstery Department. It claimed to be a source for "Repps, Damasks, Felts, Plushes, Velours, Velveteen" with "Estimates and Designs Furnished." J. McCreery, who was also a painter, maintained a studio at 411 Hudson Street. He exhibited at the Brooklyn Museum in the mid-1930s and painted murals for the Works Project Administration including one in the United States Post Office in Monett, Missouri.

Sets: 1906 *Caesar and Cleopatra*† (as: J. McCleary)
Costumes: 1901 *The Auctioneer*

Jack McCullagh

Jack McCullagh, a scenic artist and art director, designed sets for one Broadway show in 1962.

Sets: 1962 *The Perfect Setup*

Mark McCullough

Mark McCullough is a lighting designer with numerous credits throughout the United States and the United Kingdom. He has designed many operas, including *Le Nozze di Figaro* at the Metropolitan Opera House, and *The Beggar's Opera* at Opéra du Rhin, among others. He designed *Whistle Down the Wind* in London's West End and many productions for the Royal Shakespeare Company, among them *The White Devil* and *The Duchess of Malfi*. Twenty-first century productions include *Old Money* at the Mitzi E. Newhouse Theatre, *Agrippina* at Glimmerglass Opera, *Thérèse Raquin* for the Dallas Opera, *Lobby Hero* at Playwrights Horizons, and *The Queen of Spades* in Covent Garden. He also designed lights for *Il Ritorno d'Ulysse in Patria* for the New York City Opera's 2001-2002 season.

Lights: 2000 *Jesus Christ Superstar*

George McCurdy

George A. McCurdy was an electrician who worked in Broadway theaters during the first two decades of the twentieth century. In 1902, he also received credit for a lighting design. He worked from 397 Eighth Avenue, and resided at 8 West 66th Street in 1916. In 1922, he lived at 201 East 126th Street.

Lights: 1902 *A Country Girl*

John T. McCutcheon

John Tinney McCutcheon was a staff cartoonist for the *Chicago Tribune* for 43 years. He was born in 1870 in South Raub, Indiana and graduated from Purdue University, where he studied with Ernest Knaufft, in 1889. He also traveled as a correspondent for the *Tribune* during the Spanish and Boer Wars, and World War I. He won a Pulitzer Prize in 1931 for a cartoon, "A Wise Economist Asks a Question." He wrote articles and drew illustrations for magazines including *Saturday Evening Post* and was the author of *Stories of Filipino Warfare, Bird Center Cartoons* and *In Africa*. In 1902, he collaborated on the costume designs for a Broadway play, written by George Ade, a newspaper columnist with whom he had worked. John T. McCutcheon died on June 10, 1949 in Lake Forest, Illinois.

Costumes: 1902 *The Sultan of Sulu*

P. J. McDonald

Patrick J. McDonald specialized in "Scenery and Stage Construction, Mechanical Effects and Intricate Devices" from his studio at 320 West 24 street in New York City. He mainly constructed scenery, which he did for many designers, and for productions at the Grand Opera House at 265 Eighth Avenue. Occasionally he also designed scenery and mechanical devices. He should not be confused with the 1920 Olympic shot put champion with the same name.

Sets: 1901 *The Night of the 4th†* 1902 *Joan o' the Shoals†*; *The Sword of the King†* 1903 *Babes in Toyland†* 1904 *Ransom's Folly†* (Designed and built) 1907 *The Rogers Brothers in Panama†*; *The Struggle Everlasting†*

T. Bernard McDonald

Thomas Bernard McDonald built many sets at the beginning of the twentieth century, and occasionally designed them as well. Born in Ludlow, Vermont, he had no formal training when at age twenty he began designing and building scenery. He specialized in productions that needed realistic settings rather than painted backdrops through his company, the T. B. McDonald Construction Company, Inc. located at 534 West 30th Street. He established the business with his father, T. J. McDonald in 1898 and together they created scenery for producers including Charles Frohman, Klaw & Erlanger, David Belasco, George S. Kaufman, Moss Hart, and many others. He retired in 1946 and died in Katonah, New York on March 29, 1954 at age 78.

Sets: 1900 *Florodora†* (Design and construction) 1905 *Mary, Mary, Quite Contrary†* 1907 *O'Neill of Derry†* (Design and construction); *Ziegfeld Follies of 1907†* 1908 *Miss Innocence*; *The Queen of the Moulin Rouge†* (Designed and built); *Wildfire*; *Ziegfeld Follies of 1908†* (Designed and built) 1909 *The Fair Co-Ed†* (Also construction); *A Fool There Was†*; *The House Next Door†* (Design and construction); *The Rose of Algeria†* 1910 *The Bachelor Belles*; *Rebecca of Sunnybrook Farm†* 1911 *The Senator Keeps House†*; *When Sweet Sixteen†* (as: Bernard MacDonald: designed and built) 1913 *The Ghost Breaker†*; *The New Henrietta†* (Design and construction); *The Strange Woman†* (Designed and built)

John F. McEvoy

John F. McEvoy designed costumes for one play on Broadway in 1934.

Costumes: 1934 *The First Legion*

Alice McFadden

Alice McFadden designed costumes for a Broadway show in 1934.

Costumes: 1934 *Roll Sweet Chariot†*

James McFetridge

James C. McFetridge has designed the lights for five productions of *Stones in His Pockets*, at the Lyric Theatre in Belfast where it originated, in Dublin, in London's West End, on Broadway and in Toronto. He is the Technical Stage Manager at the Lyric Theatre where he often designs lights. His designs have also been seen at the Gaiety Theatre, Dublin, the Millennium Dome in London, Playhouse Theatre in Derry, and the Tinderbox Theatre Company.

Lights: 2001 *Stones in His Pockets*

Michael McGarty

Set designer Michael McGarty has designed in many off-Broadway houses and regional theaters. Manhattan Theatre Club, Circle in the Square, the Living Theatre, Trinity Repertory Theatre and the Dallas Theatre Center are among the theaters where he has worked with directors Jack Hofsiss, Lawrence Kasdan, Julie Taymor and Adrian Hall, among others. Designs for television include *Fools Fire* for American Playhouse and the 1997 Council of Fashion Design Awards for the E! Entertainment Television. Twenty-first century credits include *Power Plays* directed by Alan Arkin.

Sets: 1995 *Master Class* 1996 *God Said Ha!* 1998 *Wait until Dark*

Michael McGiveney

Michael McGiveney, who produces shows for Walt Disney Imagineering, including *Honey, I Shrunk the Kids Movie Set Adventure* and *Pocahontas Animation Discovery Adventure*, has had a varied career. He was born in 1941 and raised in Los Angeles, the son of Owen McGiveney (1884-1967), a British vaudeville performer who brought the "Bill Sikes Act" to the United States. He succeeded his father as a fast change artist in *Quick Change*, a 90-minute stage show that features one actor, fifty-seven costume changes

and twenty-four characters. He also appeared in the long-running *It's Magic* in 1976. That show closed in 1984 after 31 consecutive years, and when it was revived in 1994 it he directed it. He has also designed lights and worked as a production manager for performers Vikki Carr and Johnny Mathis, as well as for the productions *Ice Follies* and *Concert on Ice* with Peggy Fleming.
Lights: 1984 *Doug Henning and His World of Magic*

Patricia McGourty

Born in Chicago, Illinois, on March 12, 1947, Patricia McGourty studied art and scenic design at the University of Iowa. *The Madwoman of Chaillot* at the University of Iowa was her first major design project. Upon moving to New York City in 1970, she focused on costume, studying at the Fashion Institute of Technology. She served as assistant to Willa Kim, Jeanne Button and Ruth Morley and was resident costume designer for the off-off-Broadway Shade Company. After that beginning she designed over 20 shows for the New York Shakespeare Festival, including *The Pirates of Penzance,* shows for regional theaters and Broadway plays. Honors include a Tony Award nomination for the costumes for *Big River.* In 1985, she left New York City to marry and live in the Middle East.
Costumes: 1981 *Crimes of the Heart; The Pirates of Penzance* **1982** *Pump Boys and Dinettes* **1983** *Doonesbury* **1985** *Big River; Dancing in the End Zone*

Paul McGuire

Paul C. McGuire designed costumes for a play in 1955 and scenery for a production in 1966. Known primarily as a set designer and scenic artist, he occasionally designs costumes for plays. He assisted Howard Bay, Motley, and Rolf Gérard at the Metropolitan Opera. He has many summer stock credits, including *Carousel* in 1965.
Sets: 1966 *Annie Get Your Gun*
Costumes: 1955 *The Southwest Corner*

Reid McGuire

R. Reid McGuire (MacGuire) designed sets in 1923 for two shows on Broad-

way. An artist, he lived at 55 West 183rd Street in 1925.
Sets: 1923 *Sharlee; Vanities of 1923*

Mercie McHardy

Mercie McHardy designed costumes on Broadway in 1930.
Costumes: 1930 *Nine Till Six* (Women's costumes)

William McHone

William McHone was active on Broadway between 1968 and 1971. He has designed many productions for television, including *Studio One*, the *Omnibus* series, and specials. Prior to designing *Forty Carats* on Broadway, he created costumes for the original French production *Quarante Carats*.
Costumes: 1968 *Forty Carats* **1971** *Four in a Garden*

Evelyn McHorter

Evelyn McHorter began her career working with Lucile, Ltd. in London. When she came to America, she worked for J. M. Gidding as his in-house designer and designed costumes for many shows on Broadway. The J. M. Gidding Co. was located on Fifth Avenue between 56th and 57th Streets in the 1920s.
Costumes: 1922 *Ziegfeld Follies: 1922*† (Flappers gowns, etc.) **1923** *Aren't We All?* (Miss Beatty's gowns); *Cinders*† (Other gowns); *Kid Boots*†; *Ziegfeld Follies: 1923*† **1924** *Plain Jane* (Miss Manville's costumes); *Ziegfeld Follies: 1924*† (Additional costumes) **1925** *Cradle Snatchers* **1926** *The Captive*† (Miss Menkins's gowns) **1927** *Take the Air*†; *Venus*† (Miss Collings' gowns) **1929** *Fiesta*† (Additional costumes); *Houseparty* (Act II and III dresses); *Ladies of the Jury* (Miss Fiske's dresses); *Your Uncle Dudley* (Dresses) **1930** *It's a Grand Life*; *Mr. Samuel* (Dresses)

Robert T. McKee

Robert Tittle McKee was active on Broadway between 1917 and 1920. An architect, he resided at 42 East 78th Street in 1922 and at 225 East 79th Street in 1932.
Sets: 1904 *Camille; Joseph Entangled; Man Proposes* **1906** *Clothes*†; *Grierson's*

Way **1917** *L'Elevation* **1918** *The Indestructible Wife* **1920** *The "Ruined" Lady*

Mary McKinley

Mary McKinley-Haas was born in St. Louis, daughter of Lee Carrington and Florence Dowden McKinley and received a B. A. at Smith College. She studied at the National Academy of Design from 1965 to 1966, the Art Student's League from 1973 to 1974, and at Lester Polakov's Studio and Forum of Stage Design. It was at Smith College that she first designed costumes, for a production of *Ah, Wilderness!* She worked often with Freddy Wittop as an assistant, associate and co-designer, and with Robert Fletcher. Off-Broadway productions include *Dear Oscar* and *The Bed Before Yesterday.* From 1968 until 1973, she was head of the costume design department at ABC-TV and from 1975 to 1978 designed costumes for CBS-TV, both in New York. Also an artist, she has exhibited widely, including one-person and group shows.

Costumes: 1962 *Calculated Risk* **1963** *The Heroine* **1967** *Keep It in the Family* **1972** *Dear Oscar; Mother Earth* **1976** *The Innocents†* (Costume Supervisor)

John McLain

John McLain attended the College of William and Mary and Carnegie Mellon University. He has designed lights throughout the United States for most major regional theaters and many opera companies. Designs include: *Peter Allen and the Rockettes,* the international tour of *Porgy and Bess, The Golden Land* off-Broadway, and *Falstaff* to open the new Opera House in Amsterdam. He has also designed lights for television, movies, and for *Tom Scallen's Ice Capades.* Twenty-first century designs include *The Women* for the Roundabout Theatre Company.

Lights: 1969 *A Flea in Her Ear; The Three Sisters; Tiny Alice* **1974** *Leaf People* **1977** *The Importance of Being Earnest; The Night of the Tribades; Saint Joan; Tartuffe* **1978** *13 Rue De l'Amour* **1979** *Spokesong* **1980** *Major Barbara; Past Tense* **1982** *The Queen and the*

Rebels **1983** *On Your Toes* **1989** *Hizzoner*

Sheila McLamb

Shelia McLamb (also known as Shelia McLamb-Wilcox) was born January 8, 1955 in Morehead City, N.C. and attended college at North Carolina School of the Arts and Eastern Carolina University. She did graduate work at Yale, where she studied with Ming Cho Lee. Her first design assignment was *I Am A Camera* at the School of the Arts.

Costumes: 1982 *Master Harold...and the Boys*

Derek McLane

As an undergraduate at Harvard University, Derek McLamb designed student productions and collaborated with fellow student Peter Sellars, gaining experience that allowed him to develop an eclectic style that he honed during graduate study at Yale University (M.F.A. 1984). From the notorious *King Lear* he did with Sellars, to the festival stage at the St. Louis Opera and the jigsaw puzzle show curtain for *Present Laughter* on Broadway, he has extensive credits in a wide variety of projects. He has designed in most of the major regional theaters, but his most important work has been off-Broadway at Playwrights Horizons (*The Monogamist*) and the Roundabout (*Three Sisters*), both directed by Scott Elliott. Twenty-first century designs include *Time and Again* at City Center Stage II and *The Credeaux Canvas* at Playwrights Horizons' Wilder Theatre.

Sets: 1994 *What's Wrong with this Picture?* **1995** *Holiday* **1996** *Present Laughter; Summer and Smoke* **1997** *London Assurance; Three Sisters* **1998** *Honour*

Graham McLusky

The British lighting designer Graham McLusky has been designing productions throughout the United Kingdom since the late 1970s. His extensive credits encompass productions for tours, in fringe theaters, the West End (*Buddy, Fame*), and repertory companies. Twenty-first century credits in-

clude scenery and lights for *That'll Be the Day* at Swindon's Wyvern Theatre.
Lights: 1990 *Buddy: The Buddy Holly Story*

J. T. McMurray

An electrician, J. T. McMurray resided at 239 East 46th Street in New York.
Lights: 1899 *Papa's Wife* 1900 *Her Majesty, the Girl Queen of Nordenmark*†

Tom McPhillips

Tom McPhillips debuted as a scenic designer on Broadway in 1986. A British designer and art director, he studied at St. Martin's School in London. He began his theater career working for the Young Vic and the National Opera, and as a scenic artist. Since 1977 he has operated his own scenic studio. He is a prolific art director for a wide variety of projects, from commercials and music videos to a time machine exhibition at The Natural History Museum in London. He has designed sets for the concert tours of Ozzy Osbourne, Diana Ross, Michael Jackson, Culture Club, Judas Priest, Luther Vandross, and Jennifer Holiday. He also designed *Sing, Mahalia, Sing, Tony Bennett Unplugged* for MTV, and was art director for the *Chevy Chase Show*.
Sets: 1986 *Uptown...It's Hot*

Robert McQuinn

Robert McQuinn designed costumes and scenery on Broadway between 1907 and 1924. He was an artist and scenic designer who occasionally designed costumes as well. He also illustrated for magazines including *Vogue* and *Vanity Fair*. Robert McQuinn died on June 24, 1975 at the age of 92.
Sets: 1914 *Watch Your Step*† 1915 *Hip-Hip-Hooray; Stop! Look! Listen!* 1916 *The Big Show*† ("Somewhere in Japan") 1917 *Canary Cottage; Love o' Mike* 1918 *Madonna of the Future*†
Costumes: 1907 *Hip! Hip! Hooray!*† (Costumes of the States) 1915 *Hip-Hip-Hooray*†; *Stop! Look! Listen!* 1916 *Betty* (Gown in Act III); *The Big Show*† ("Somewhere in Japan") 1917 *Canary Cottage*† (Gowns); *Cheer-up (Hippodrome)*†; *Eyes of Youth*† 1918 *Everything*† 1922 *Better Times*† ("The Story of

a Fan", other Costumes) 1923 *Stepping Stones*† 1924 *Stepping Stones*†

Roderick McRae

Roderick McRae designed costumes for a 1933 Broadway production. The 1933-1934 edition of Trow's New York and Bronx City Directory lists two men with that name. One resided at 302 West 12th Street, Apartment 2H and the other at 105 West 55th Street in Apartment 2C.
Costumes: 1933 *The First Apple*

Roi Cooper Megrue

Roi Cooper Megrue was a playwright who had several hits on Broadway. His plays, *Potash and Perlmutter*, *Under Cover*, and *It Pays to Advertise* among others were popular light comedies produced in the teens and twenties. He was born on June 12, 1883 in New York City and graduated from Columbia University in 1903. He worked for Elizabeth Marbury brokering plays and while on her staff began to write his own. Roi Megrue died in New York City on February 27, 1927.
Lights: 1917 *Why Marry?*† 1918 *Why Marry?*†

Lang-Fan Mei

Lan-Fang Mei, the famous Chinese actor, lived from 1894 until 1961. He belonged to a family with a long tradition in the Chinese theater, and was trained from the age of nine to appear on the stage. He debuted at age 14, and was known for his characterization of female roles for the Peking Opera. He toured widely, retiring from the stage in 1959, after performing for 50 years. In 1936, while on tour in the U.S., he performed in *Lady Precious Stream* for which he also designed the costumes. His name often appears as Mei Lan-Fang following the Chinese preference to place the surname first.
Costumes: 1936 *Lady Precious Stream*

Meixner

Hans, or Heinz, Meixner was a scenic designer and painter who specialized in creating mechanical effects. He often collaborated with Frank Platzer. Both men often used their last names, as with the 1905 *Pantaloon* play-bill, which simply states: "Scenes by Platzer and Meixner." Meixner died on December 21, 1911 in Milwaukee, Wisconsin at the age of 49.

Sets: 1905 *Fritz in Tammany Hall*† (Scenery and mechanical effects); *Pantaloon*† 1906 *The Clansman*†; *District Leader*†; *The Strength of the Weak*† 1910 *The Winter's Tale*†

Kenneth Mellor

Kenneth Mellor was born in Yorkshire, England and trained as an architect. Productions of *'Tis Pity She's a Whore, The Wood Demon, Phantom of the Opera, You Never Can Tell, Country Life, Eastward Ho, Hobson's Choice* and *The Rules of the Game* are only a small portion of his design activity in Great Britain. He has designed for the Actor's Company, the Lyric Hammersmith and in London's West End. Kenneth Mellor also designs industrial projects, including the lighting on the Thames Bridge. He should not be confused with the Rhode Island education commissioner who has the same name.

Sets: 1984 *Beethoven's Tenth*

Joseph L. Menchen, Jr.

Father and son, Joseph L. Menchen, and Joseph L. Menchen, Jr. became involved with all things electrical at the end of the nineteenth century. The original Joseph Menchen Electrical Company was located at 341 Walworth Road, London, S, E. It was followed with branches in Paris, Berlin, St. Petersburg, and at 360 West 50th Street New York City where the son presided. The company advertised itself as the "Largest Manufacturers of Electrical Appliances and Scenic Effects in the World" at the beginning of the twentieth century. Joseph L. Menchen, Jr. not only designed lights in New York, and London (*Brewster's Millions*, 1913 with T. Digby), he invented and patented mechanical devices. He worked as a consulting engineer from offices at 701 7th Avenue in New York for the United States government, among others, and invented the tracer bullet, liquid fire, and the serial torpedo timer. At the time of his death, as a result of a heart attack on October 7, 1940 in Los Angeles, he was working on additional armament inventions.

Lights: 1899 *A Young Wife* 1900 *Her Majesty, the Girl Queen of Nordenmark*† 1902 *Mrs. Jack*; *Soldiers of Fortune* 1911 *The Lily and the Prince*; *The Triumph of an Empress* 1921 *Nobody's Money*

Pete Menefee

Pete Menefee began professional life as an actor and dancer, appearing in the national companies of *West Side Story, Bye, Bye, Birdie* and other shows. before turning his talents to designing costumes. His costumes, while frequently seen in plays, most often appear for extravaganzas in Las Vegas, at Radio City Music Hall and on television. He has designed specials, series, been nominated for two Emmys for costume design. He won one for *Las Vegas Anniversary Special*, with co-designer Ret Taylor. Television designs include *The Hollywood Palace, Together Again for the First Time: The Third Bill Cosby Special*, and *The 68th AnnualAcademy Awards*. His designs for ice skaters, including Linda Fratianne, and the "Firebird" costumes for *Tom Scallen's Ice Capades* often instigate trends.

Costumes: 1974 *Me and Bessie* 1984 *Shirley MacLaine on Broadway* 1990 *The Christmas Spectacular*† 1991 *Christmas Spectacular*† ("Carol of the Bells, We Need a Little Christmas") 1992 *Radio City Christmas Spectacular*† (We Need a Little Christmas, Santa's Workshop) 1993 *Radio City Christmas Spectacular*† ("Carol of the Bells, We Need a Little Christmas") 1994 *Radio City Christmas Spectacular*† 1995 *Radio City Easter Show*† (Honey Bunny costumes, additional costumes) 1996 *Radio City Christmas Spectacular*†; *Radio City Spring Spectacular*† 1997 *Radio City Christmas Spectacular*†; *Radio City Spring Spectacular*† 1998 *Radio City Christmas Spectacular*† (Christmas in New York)

William H. Mensching

Three generations of men named William Mensching have been involved constructing (and occasionally designing) scenery for opera, theater and television. William H. Mensching operated Mensching & Kilcoyne Studios with Joseph Kilcoyne, constructing opera scenery at 108 W. 15th Street in New York City. He was head carpenter for the original Shubert organization and for Billy Rose. For CBS-TV he worked with his son William G. Mensching, John De Verna and fifty-seven carpenters building scenery for approximately twenty-five shows a week for Jackie Gleason, Arthur Godfrey and Ed Sullivan, among others. William G. Mensching also worked as a carpenter for Studio Alliance, Feller Scenic Studios, Studio 3, and as production manager for Radio City from 1975 until his death on July 28, 1980. Apparently both William H. (who died in 1975) and William G. occasionally designed sets as "William Mensching," as well as through the William H. Mensching Studios during the early 1930s. The third generation, William (Bill) M. Mensching, is president of ShowMotion, a theatrical construction shop in Norwalk, Connecticut which he operates with his brother Peter. They have built sets recently for the Broadway productions of *The Producers*, *Aida*, *42nd Street*, *Jane Eyre*, and *Carnivale* for Radio City Music Hall. among many others as they carry on the family tradition, which actually began with a great-grandfather, Henry Mensching, who hauled scenery for vaudeville by horse and buggy.

Sets: 1932 *Bidding High* **1933** *The Sellout* (as: William H. Mensching Studios) **1934** *Good-Bye Please†*; *Wife Insurance* (as: William H. Mensching Studios)

Chester Menzer

Chester Menzer designed lighting for one production on Broadway in 1947.

Lights: 1947 *Trial Honeymoon*

William Cameron Menzies

In 1928 William Cameron Menzies won the first Oscar for art direction in film for *The Dove* and *The Tempest*. He spent most of his career as a film production designer, occasionally producing and directing. Born William Howe Cameron Menzies on July 29, 1896 in New Haven, Connecticut, he attended Yale University, the University of Edinburgh and the Art Students League, and worked initially an as illustrator. He became Anton Grot's assistant at the Fort Lee, New Jersey Studios of Famous Players-Lasky and collaborated with Grot on his first movie, *The Naulahka*. He worked mostly as an independent art director during his long and prolific career, only occasionally working through a major studio. William Cameron Menzies, who designed *Gone with the Wind* with Lyle Wheeler, was instrumental in developing the fields of art director and production designer for films. He remains widely regarded for his use of realism and carefully controlled details. He died on March 5, 1957 in Hollywood at the age of 60.

Sets: 1923 *The Lullaby*
Costumes: 1923 *The Lullaby*

Mercedes

Mercedes designed settings for two plays on Broadway, one in 1938 and the other in 1941.

Sets: 1938 *Who's Who* **1941** *Tanyard Street*

G. W. Mercier

After completing his M.F.A. at the Yale School of Drama, designer G. W. (Skip) Mercier began amassing an impressive list of credits through collaborations with directors Tom Haas at the Indiana Repertory Theatre, John Russel Brown, Tom Prewitt, and choreographer Margo Sappington, among others. He has designed scenery and costumes for film, television, theater (on and off-Broadway and in regional theaters), opera (in the U.S. and abroad), and dance. He has worked with Julie Taymor and Elliot Goldenthal on *Fool's Fire*, *The Tempest*, *The Taming of the Shrew*, *Liberty's Taken* and *Juan Darién*. Twenty-first century credits include scenery for *Eli's Coming* at the Vineyard Theatre.

Sets: 1996 *Juan Darién: A Carnival Mass†*
Costumes: 1996 *Juan Darién: A Carnival Mass†*

Mary Merrill

Mary Merrill was born in Skowhegan, Maine on November 9, 1907. She started her career as a scenic designer and shifted to costumes. A graduate of Wheaton College, she studied at the Parsons School of Design and at Yale with Donald Oenslager and Frank Poole Bevan. After two years at Yale she succeeded Mr. Bevan as designer for the Hampton Players. She designed for Broadway, the Federal Theatre Project, and U.S.O. wartime shows overseas. She designed and taught costume design and history at the Provincetown Theatre in New York, and was a staff member of the Studio Theatre which Hallie Flanagan transferred to Vassar College for National Theatre Project productions. While at Vassar she designed the costumes for *One Third of a Nation*. Her film designs include *Patterns*, *The Bargain Stick* and *Uncle Vanya*. In 1940 she left theatrical design for display design and was display manager at Bergdorf Goodman from 1942 to 1947. In 1950 she joined the CBS-TV costume department as designer for *You Are There, The Defenders, Man Against Crime* and hundreds of style shows. In 1970 she designed and mounted a large exhibition of theater costumes at the Museum of the City of New York. Mary Merrill died on January 7, 1996.

Sets: 1933 *Double Door*†
Costumes: 1933 *Double Door* 1934 *Post Road*; *Wednesday's Child* (Costume Supervisor) 1935 *Kind Lady* 1936 *Double Dummy*; *The Laughing Woman* 1937 *Cherokee Night*; *Tobias and the Angel* 1938 *The Big Blow*; *Prologue to Glory*; *Sing for Your Supper*

Michael Merritt

Michael Merritt was born in Sioux Falls, South Dakota received a B.A. degree in art history from the University of Chicago and his graduate degree from the University of Illinois. His career was based in the Chicago area, where he designed frequently for the Goodman and Steppenwolf Theatres. As a frequent collaborator of David Mamet, he designed most of the original productions of his plays, including *American Buffalo. Speed-the-Plow*, and *Lakeboat*, and was production designer for three of Mamet's films: *Things Change, Homicide*, and *House of Games*. He also designed for regional theaters including the Milwaukee Repertory Theatre, Woodstock Music Theatre Festival, Arizona Theatre Company and the North Light Repertory, among others, and the television series *Brewster Place*. He had many off-Broadway credits, including the scenery for *Oleanna* which opened shortly after his death on August 3, 1992 at age 47. His ninth Joseph Jefferson award, for *A Summer Remembered* at Steppenwolf Theatre Company, was posthumous. The Michael Merritt Awards for Excellence in Design and Collaboration, initially awarded in 1994, honor his memory. The Michael Merritt Endowment Fund also sponsors an annual scholarship to Columbia College in Chicago where he taught.

Sets: 1984 *Glengarry Glen Ross* 1987 *Speed-the-Plow*

Harley Merry

Born Ebenezer J. Britton (perhaps Brittan) in England circa 1830, Harley Merry was a well-known actor, appearing on stage with his wife Adelaide, James O'Neil, and William Crane. When he retired from the stage, he became an equally well-known scenic artist and designer, creating stage settings for Marlowe and Sothern, and many others. His credits for the last three decades of the nineteenth century are extensive, for productions at the Casino Theatre, the Bijou Opera, and the Brooklyn Opera House, and many more. When the Protective Alliance of Scenic Painters was formed in 1885, Harley Merry was the first president, with Richard Marston as the organizations first chairman. His scenic studio, known as Harley Merry & Sons, although he had one son and one daughter, was located on Franklin Avenue in Brooklyn. He died in 1911, in Flatlands, Long Island, New York.

Sets: 1903 *My Lady Peggy Goes to Town* 1907 *John the Baptist* 1908 *Don*

Quixote† (Act I, II)

Suzanne Mess

Canadian costume designer Suzanne Mess was born in Toronto in 1928 and raised in Ottawa where she studied at the College of Art. After an apprenticeship with Helene Pons in New York she returned to Canada, initially as a costume and wardrobe assistant for the Canadian Opera Company. It was not long before she was promoted to head of wardrobe and then became principal costume designer. Her opera designs have been seen throughout North American and Europe and include many productions for New York City Opera. She has also designed frequently for the Canadian Broadcasting Company television network and the New Play Society.
Costumes: 1990 *The Sound of Music*

Oliver Messel

Oliver Messel was born on January 13, 1904 in London and studied at the Slade School of Art. Well-known for his designs of sets and costumes for the British theater, his first designs in London appeared in 1926. He first designed costumes and scenery in New York in 1928. He designed numerous plays in London's West End, and at the Old Vic, operas in Europe, and for film. A designer of exquisite silhouette and detail, his designs for the stage were admired by his peers and by audiences. In 1955 he won a Tony Award for his set for *House of Flowers*. Mr. Messel died on July 14, 1978. A biography by Charles Castle, *Oliver Messel*, was published by Thames and Hudson in 1987.
Sets: 1928 *This Year of Grace†* **1929** *Wake Up and Dream†* **1936** *The Country Wife* **1948** *The Play's the Thing* **1950** *The Lady's Not for Burning* **1951** *Romeo and Juliet* **1953** *The Little Hut* **1954** *House of Flowers* **1955** *The Dark Is Light Enough* **1959** *Rashomon* **1964** *Traveler without Luggage*
Costumes: 1928 *This Year of Grace†* **1929** *Wake Up and Dream†* **1930** *Symphony in Two Flats†* (Miss Hume's costumes) **1936** *The Country Wife* **1950** *The Lady's Not for Burning* **1951** *Romeo*

and Juliet **1954** *House of Flowers* **1959** *Rashomon* **1964** *Traveler without Luggage* **1973** *Gigi*

Charles Messersmith

An electrician, Charles Messersmith was also known as Charles Messerschmidt. He worked from his home at 318 West 40th Street in the early teens and later from 451 West 44th Street.
Lights: 1913 *A Glimpse of the Great White Way; The Modiste Shop*

M. Messonier

Monsieur Messonier collaborated on the scenery for a 1905 production that played on Broadway.
Sets: 1905 *The Misanthrope†*

Jacob Meth

Jacob Meth collaborated with William Gropper (1897-1977) on the design for several plays in the 1920s. In 1905, he was listed in the Trow Business Directory of Greater New York as a costumer, with a studio at 318 Broome Street. He also designed costumes for productions at the Jewish Art Theatre, and *Samson and Delilah* at the Greenwich Village Theatre in 1920.
Costumes: 1921 *The Idle Inn†* **1923** *Anathema†; The Inspector General†; The Shame Woman†*

Lawrence Metzler

Lawrence Metzler was born in Montclair, New Jersey on February 6, 1937, the son of Pauline Wells and Fred Metzler. His New York debut was *The Bold and the Beautiful* at the off-Broadway Theatre East. He worked at the New York Shakespeare Festival as an electrician during the 1960s, designing *Electra* in 1969 among other productions. He has also worked in theaters throughout the country in various aspects of technical theater, including broadcasting at KCFI in Los Angeles. Active in United Scenic Artists, he served as chair of the Western Region in the early 1990s.
Lights: 1972 *Two Gentlemen of Verona*

William Metzler

William Metzler designed lights on Broadway in 1901. An engineer, he resided at 454 Brook Avenue, New York City in 1907.

Lights: 1901 *Up York State*

Hy Meyer

In 1911, Hy Meyer designed costumes for a Broadway play. At that time he worked as a tailor from 204 East 116th Street in New York. It is possible that the tailor is the same Hyman Meyer, who appeared in the silent movie *The Saturday Night Kid* and the 1922 stage production of *Johannes Kreisher*.

Costumes: 1911 *Everywoman*

Leo B. Meyer

Leo B. Meyer was born in New York City on July 10, 1934 and graduated in 1955 from Carnegie Institute of Technology. The son of a textile designer, he began designing in 1953 at the White Barn Theatre with *The Moon is Blue*, the summer after his sophomore year in college. Since then he has designed scenery and lights for hundreds of productions, taught design at the University of Bridgeport, New York Institute of Technology, Fairfield University and as a guest lecturer at Yale University, painted scenery, and produced plays. As president of Atlas Scenic Studios, Ltd. in Bridgeport, Connecticut he has supervised the painting and construction of productions that have won numerous Tony Awards for designers and producers. Founded in 1968 in Norwalk, Connecticut, the first Broadway production constructed at Atlas was the revival of *Three Men on a Horse*, directed by George Abbott and designed by Boyd Dumrose. Having survived a nearly devastating fire in 1995, Atlas is the oldest, continuously operating scenic supply company in the United States. Recent productions include *The Laramie Project* and *The Heiress* for Broadway, and major national tours.

Sets: 1963 *Pajama Tops* 1967 *The Girl in the Freudian Slip*; *A Minor Adjustment* 1972 *All the Girls Come Out to Play*

Lights: 1963 *Pajama Tops* 1967 *What Did We Do Wrong?* 1972 *All the Girls Come Out to Play*

Stanley A. Meyer

Stanley (Stan) A. Meyer has de-signed many special events for the Disney Company, including a rock 'n roll version of *The Nutcracker* as well as the many national and international versions of *Beauty and the Beast*. His designs for scenery are often seen in regional theaters and off-Broadway. Honors include four Los Angeles Drama-Logue Awards, and nominations for the American Theatre Wing Design and Outer Critics Circle Awards.

Sets: 1994 *Beauty and the Beast*

Keith Michael

Keith Michael received credit for one lighting design in 1970. He has also designed for the New York Ballet Theatre, Balletforte, and Toni Smith and Dancers.

Lights: 1970 *Gloria and Esperanza*

Michi

See Michi Weglyn.

Gordon Micunis

Gordon Jules Micunis was born in Lynn, Massachusetts on June 16, 1933. After receiving his B.A. at Tufts University he studied at Yale University with Donald Oenslager and Frank Poole Bevan, receiving an M.F.A in 1959. He has had a varied career creating contract and residential interior designs, historic renovations and rehabilitations, museum and exhibit installations, logotype and graphic designs, and theatrical and apparel designs. Gordon Micunis' first New York design was *Madame Butterfly* for New York City Opera in 1962, and he has since designed operas for many other companies throughout the United States, including a long time association with the Santa Fe Opera. He has lectured on design at Barnard College, at the Fashion Institute of Technology, Lester Polakov's Studio and Forum of Stage Design and at C. W. Post College. Also a painter, he has exhibited widely on the East Coast and in Santa Fe.

Sets: 1983 *The Ritz*

Jo Mielziner

Jo Mielziner, known primarily as a scenic designer, created numerous costume and lighting designs as well, a common occurrence for designers of his generation. He was born on March 19, 1901 in Paris and attended art schools, including the Art Students League. His father, Leo Mielziner, was a portrait painter and his mother a journalist. He began his career in the theater as an actor, stage manager and scene designer, first in stock and then for the Theatre Guild. His collaborations with Elia Kazan for plays by modern American playwrights are examples of his enormous influence on theater and the quality of design. He received many honors including five Tony Awards for set design, Drama Desk Awards, Critics Awards, Maharam Awards, Donaldson Awards, and a number of honorary degrees, all for his outstanding contributions to the theater. Mr. Mielziner, who died on March 15, 1976, has also received posthumous credit for designs including the revival of *Slaughter on Tenth Avenue* at the New York City Ballet during the 1985-86 season and *Jerome Robbins' Broadway* in 1989. A wonderfully illustrated analysis of his life and work, *Mielziner: Master of Modern Stage Design* was published in 2001 by Mary C. Henderson who also curated an exhibition of Mielziner's designs at the New York Public Library for the Performing Arts at Lincoln Center.

Sets: 1924 *The Awful Mrs. Eaton*; *The Guardsman*; *Nerves* **1925** *The Call of Life*; *Caught*; *The Enemy*; *First Flight*; *Lucky Sam McCarver*; *Mrs. Partridge Presents*; *The Wild Duck* **1926** *Little Eyolf*; *The Masque of Venice*; *Pygmalion*; *Seed of the Brute* **1927** *The Doctor's Dilemma*; *Fallen Angels*; *Mariners*; *The Marquise*; *Right You Are If You Think You Are*; *Saturday's Children*; *The Second Man* **1928** *Cock Robin*; *The Grey Fox*; *The Jealous Moon*; *The Lady Lies*; *A Most Immoral Lady*; *Servant of Two Masters*; *Strange Interlude* **1929** *The Amorous Antic*; *First Mortgage*; *Jenny*; *Judas*; *Karl and Anna*; *The Little Show*; *Meet the Prince*; *Skyrocket*; *Street Scene*; *Young Alexander* **1930** *Café*; *Mr. Gilhooley*; *The Second Little Show*; *Solid South*; *Sweet and Low*; *Uncle Vanya* **1931** *Anatol*; *The Barretts of Wimpole Street*; *Brief Mo-*ment; *The House Beautiful*; *I Love an Actress*; *Of Thee I Sing*; *The Third Little Show* **1932** *Biography*; *Bloodstream*; *Bridal Wise*; *Distant Drums*; *Gay Divorce*; *Hey, Nonny Nonny*†; *Never No More* **1933** *Champagne Sec*; *The Dark Tower*; *A Divine Drudge*; *I Was Waiting for You*; *The Lake*; *Light from St. Agnes, A*; *The Eyes of the Heart, and the R*; *Of Thee I Sing* **1934** *Accent on Youth*; *Biography*; *By Your Leave*; *Dodsworth*; *Merrily We Roll Along*; *The Pure in Heart*; *Romeo and Juliet*; *Spring Song*; *Yellow Jack* **1935** *The Barretts of Wimpole Street*; *De Luxe*; *Flowers of the Forest*; *Hell Freezes Over*; *It's You I Want*; *Jubilee*; *Kind Lady*; *Panic*; *Pride and Prejudice*; *Romeo and Juliet*; *Winterset* **1936** *Co-Respondent Unknown*; *Daughters of Atreus*; *Ethan Frome*; *Hamlet*†; *On Your Toes*; *The Postman Always Rings Twice*; *A Room in Red and White*; *Saint Joan*; *St. Helena*; *The Wingless Victory*; *The Women* **1937** *Barchester Towers*; *Father Malachy's Miracle*; *High Tor*; *The Star Wagon*; *Susan and God*; *Too Many Heroes* **1938** *Abe Lincoln in Illinois*; *The Boys from Syracuse*; *I Married an Angel*; *Knickerbocker Holiday*; *No Time for Comedy*; *On Borrowed Time*; *Save Me the Waltz*; *Sing Out the News*; *Yr. Obedient Husband* **1939** *Christmas Eve*; *Key Largo*; *Morning's at Seven*; *Mrs. O'Brien Entertains*; *Stars in Your Eyes*; *Too Many Girls* **1940** *Flight to the West*; *Higher and Higher*; *Journey to Jerusalem*; *Pal Joey*; *Two on an Island* **1941** *Best Foot Forward*; *Candle in the Wind*; *Cream in the Well*; *The Land Is Bright*; *Mr. and Mrs. North*; *Pal Joey*; *The Seventh Trumpet*; *The Talley Method*; *Watch on the Rhine*; *The Wookey* **1942** *By Jupiter*; *Solitaire* **1943** *Susan and God* **1945** *The Barretts of Wimpole Street*; *Beggars Are Coming to Town*; *Carib Song*; *Carousel*; *Dream Girl*; *The Firebrand of Florence*; *Foolish Notion*; *The Glass Menagerie*; *Hollywood Pinafore*; *The Rugged Path* **1946** *Annie Get Your Gun*; *Another Part of the Forest*; *Happy Birthday*; *Jeb* **1947** *Allegro*; *Barefoot Boy with Cheek*; *The Big Two*; *The Chocolate Soldier*; *Command Decision*; *Finian's Rainbow*; *Street Scene*; *A Streetcar Named Desire* **1948** *Anne of 1000 Days*; *Mr. Roberts*; *Sleepy Hollow*; *Summer and Smoke*†; *Summer and*

Smoke† **1949** *Death of a Salesman; South Pacific* **1950** *Burning Bright; Dance Me a Song; Guys and Dolls; The Innocents; The Man from Mel Dinelli; The Man; The Wisteria Trees* **1951** *The King and I; Point of No Return; Top Banana; A Tree Grows in Brooklyn* **1952** *Flight into Egypt; The Gambler; Wish You Were Here* **1953** *Can-Can; Kind Sir; Me and Juliet; Picnic; Tea and Sympathy* **1954** *All Summer Long; By the Beautiful Sea; Fanny* **1955** *Cat on a Hot Tin Roof; Island of Goats; The Lark; Pipe Dream; Silk Stockings* **1956** *Happy Hunting; Middle of the Night; The Most Happy Fella* **1957** *Look Homeward, Angel; Miss Lonely Hearts; The Square Root of Wonderful* **1958** *The Day the Money Stopped; The Gazebo; Handful of Fire; Oh Captain!; Whoop-Up; The World of Suzie Wong* **1959** *The Gang's All Here; Gypsy; Silent Night, Lonely Night; Sweet Bird of Youth* **1960** *The Best Man; Christine; Little Moon of Alban; Period of Adjustment; There Was a Little Girl* **1961** *All American; The Devil's Advocate; Everybody Loves Opal* **1962** *Mr. President* **1963** *The Milk Train Doesn't Stop Here Anymore* **1964** *After the Fall†; After the Fall†; The Owl and the Pussycat* **1965** *The Playroom* **1966** *Don't Drink the Water; My Sweet Charley* **1967** *Daphne in Cottage D; The Paisley Convertible; That Summer-That Fall* **1968** *I Never Sang for My Father; The Prime of Miss Jean Brodie; The Seven Descents of Myrtle* **1969** *1776* **1970** *Child's Play; Georgy; Look to the Lilies* **1971** *Father's Day* **1972** *Children! Children!; Voices* **1973** *Out Cry* **1974** *In Praise of Love* **1989** *Jerome Robbins' Broadway†*

Costumes: 1924 *The Guardsman* **1926** *Pygmalion* **1927** *Right You Are If You Think You Are* **1929** *Karl and Anna* **1931** *Anatol; The Barretts of Wimpole Street; Brief Moment; The House Beautiful* **1932** *Hey, Nonny Nonny†* (Co-Production Design) **1934** *Romeo and Juliet* **1935** *The Barretts of Wimpole Street; Pride and Prejudice; Romeo and Juliet* **1936** *Ethan Frome; Saint Joan; St. Helena; The Wingless Victory* **1937** *Barchester Towers; Father Malachy's Miracle; High Tor; The Star Wagon* **1938** *The Wild Duck; Yr. Obedient Husband* **1939** *Christmas Eve; Mrs.*

O'Brien Entertains **1945** *The Barretts of Wimpole Street; Dream Girl†*

Lights: 1924 *The Awful Mrs. Eaton; Nerves* **1925** *The Call of Life; Caught; The Enemy; First Flight; Lucky Sam McCarver; Mrs. Partridge Presents; The Wild Duck* **1926** *Little Eyolf; The Masque of Venice; Pygmalion; Seed of the Brute* **1927** *The Doctor's Dilemma; Fallen Angels; Mariners; The Marquise; Right You Are If You Think You Are; Saturday's Children; The Second Man* **1928** *Cock Robin; The Grey Fox; The Jealous Moon; The Lady Lies; A Most Immoral Lady; Strange Interlude* **1929** *The Amorous Antic; First Mortgage; Jenny; Judas; Karl and Anna; The Little Show; Meet the Prince; Skyrocket; Street Scene; Young Alexander* **1930** *Café; Mr. Gilhooley; The Second Little Show; Solid South; Sweet and Low; Uncle Vanya* **1931** *Anatol; The Barretts of Wimpole Street; Brief Moment; The House Beautiful; Of Thee I Sing; The Third Little Show* **1932** *Biography; Bloodstream; Bridal Wise; Distant Drums; Gay Divorce; Hey, Nonny Nonny; Never No More* **1933** *Champagne Sec; The Dark Tower; A Divine Drudge; I Was Waiting for You; The Lake* **1934** *Accent on Youth; By Your Leave; Dodsworth; Merrily We Roll Along; The Pure in Heart; Romeo and Juliet; Spring Song; Yellow Jack* **1935** *De Luxe; Flowers of the Forest; Hell Freezes Over; Jubilee; Kind Lady; Panic; Pride and Prejudice; Winterset* **1936** *Co-Respondent Unknown; Daughters of Atreus; Ethan Frome; Hamlet; On Your Toes; The Postman Always Rings Twice; A Room in Red and White; Saint Joan; St. Helena; The Wingless Victory; The Women†* **1937** *Barchester Towers; Father Malachy's Miracle; High Tor; The Star Wagon; Too Many Heroes* **1938** *Abe Lincoln in Illinois; The Boys from Syracuse; I Married an Angel; Knickerbocker Holiday; No Time for Comedy; On Borrowed Time; Save Me the Waltz; Sing Out the News; Yr. Obedient Husband* **1939** *Christmas Eve; Key Largo; Morning's at Seven; Mrs. O'Brien Entertains; Stars in Your Eyes; Too Many Girls* **1940** *Flight to the West; Higher and Higher; Journey to Jerusalem; Pal Joey; Two on an Island* **1941** *Best Foot Forward; Candle in the Wind; Cream in* the Well; The Land Is Bright; Mr. and Mrs. North; Pal Joey; The Seventh Trumpet; The Talley Method; Watch on the Rhine; The Wookey **1942** By Jupiter; Solitaire **1945** Beggars Are Coming to Town; Carib Song; Carousel; Dream Girl; The Firebrand of Florence; Foolish Notion; The Glass Menagerie; Hollywood Pinafore; The Rugged Path **1946** Annie Get Your Gun; Another Part of the Forest; Happy Birthday; Jeb **1947** Allegro; Barefoot Boy with Cheek; The Big Two; The Chocolate Soldier; Command Decision; Finian's Rainbow; Street Scene; A Streetcar Named Desire **1948** Anne of 1000 Days; Mr. Roberts; Sleepy Hollow **1949** Death of a Salesman; South Pacific **1950** Burning Bright; Dance Me a Song; Guys and Dolls; The Innocents; The Man from Mel Dinelli; The Man; The Wisteria Trees **1951** The King and I; Point of No Return; Top Banana; A Tree Grows in Brooklyn **1952** Flight into Egypt; The Gambler; Wish You Were Here **1953** Can-Can; Kind Sir; Me and Juliet; Picnic; Tea and Sympathy **1954** All Summer Long; By the Beautiful Sea; Fanny **1955** Cat on a Hot Tin Roof; Island of Goats; The Lark; Pipe Dream; Silk Stockings **1956** Happy Hunting; Middle of the Night; The Most Happy Fella **1957** Look Homeward, Angel; Miss Lonely Hearts; The Square Root of Wonderful **1958** The Day the Money Stopped; The Gazebo; Handful of Fire; Oh Captain!; Whoop-Up; The World of Suzie Wong **1959** The Gang's All Here; Gypsy; Rashomon; Silent Night, Lonely Night; Sweet Bird of Youth **1960** The Best Man; Christine; Little Moon of Alban; Period of Adjustment; There Was a Little Girl **1961** All American; The Devil's Advocate; Everybody Loves Opal **1962** Mr. President **1963** The Milk Train Doesn't Stop Here Anymore **1964** The Owl and the Pussycat **1965** The Playroom **1966** Don't Drink the Water; My Sweet Charley **1967** Daphne in Cottage D; The Paisley Convertible; That Summer-That Fall **1968** I Never Sang for My Father; The Prime of Miss Jean Brodie; The Seven Descents of Myrtle **1969** 1776 **1970** Child's Play; Georgy; Look to the Lilies **1971** Father's Day **1972** Children! Children!; Voices **1973** Out Cry **1974** In Praise of Love

Milgrim

Sally Milgrim began her career designing and making garments for private and theatrical customers in the early 1920s from the Lower East Side in New York City. As her business grew, she changed locations, and in 1927 opened the Milgrim Fashion Studio at 57th Street near Fifth Avenue. She was widely regarded for her quality dresses and gowns. At the height of her career there were ten Milgrim stores and her designs were also sold in major department stores. She designed for actresses, among them Ethel Merman, Mae Murray, Pearl White, and Mary Pickford, and the gown Eleanor Roosevelt wore to her husband's first inaugural ball in 1933. She retired in 1960, and died at age 103 on June 11, 1994 in Miami, Florida.

Costumes: 1926 The Donovan Affair; Head or Tail **1927** The Matrimonial Bed (Gowns); Yes, Yes, Yevette

Anne E. Militello

Anne E. Militello began her lighting design career with Josephine the Mouse Singer in 1980 at the Magic Theatre in San Francisco. Since moving to New York City in 1981 she has been working steadily. She was born on April 29, 1957 in Buffalo, New York, the daughter of Emmanuella (Patricia) Pollina and Orazıno (George) Militello. She studied acting at SUNY-Buffalo and design at Lester Polakov's Studio and Forum of Stage Design. Off-Broadway she has designed A Lie of the Mind, productions for Mabou Mines, La Mama E.T.C., and Maria Irene Fornes, among others. Her many designs in regional theaters include productions at American Repertory Theatre, the Mark Taper Forum, South Coast Repertory and in LaJolla. She received the 1984 Obie Award for sustained excellence in lighting design, the 1999 EDDY Award for Amazing Adventures of Spider-Man and the 2000 Lighting Designer of the Year Award for Themed Projects from Lighting Dimensions International.

Lights: 1986 Cuba & His Teddy Bear

Kathleen Millay

Kathleen Millay, author of plays, po-

ems and fairy tales, was born in Union, Maine, sister of Edna St. Vincent Millay. She studied at Vassar and lived most of her life in New York City. Married to playwright Howard I. Young, she died September 21, 1943 at age 46.
Costumes: 1929 *Hawk Island* (Costume Supervisor)

Burton J. Miller

Burton J. Miller, the first costume designer ever elected to the Board of Governors of the Academy of Motion Pictures Arts and Sciences, graduated from Carnegie Institute of Technology and studied at Parsons School of Design. He spent the majority of his career designing costumes for television and films. He shared an Oscar nomination for *Airport '77* with Edith Head and designed *The Sting II, House Calls* and *Sugarland Express*, among many others. Mr. Miller, who died at age 54 on March 5, 1982, also designed fashions for retail stores, including Saks Fifth Avenue and Neiman Marcus.
Costumes: 1952 *I've Got Sixpence* (Costume Supervisor)

Craig Miller

Craig Miller was born on August 7, 1950 in Hugoton, Kansas. He majored in directing at Northwestern University where he received a B.S. in 1972. At the beginning of his career, he worked as an assistant to Thomas Skelton, Jules Fisher, and several other lighting designers. Later, he encouraged his own assistants, and students when he taught at Berra College, to gain experience through that process. He designed theater, opera and dance throughout the United States and was resident lighting designer for the Lar Lubovitch, Elisa Monte and Laura Dean dance companies, and at Santa Fe Opera. When he died in New York city at age 43 on June 7, 1994 after a struggle against cancer, his collaborators in theater, opera and dance all lost a colleague who was an artist with light.
Lights: 1979 *On Golden Pond* **1980** *Barnum* **1981** *The Five O'clock Girl; I Won't Dance* **1983** *Brothers* **1985** *Doubles; Take Me Along; Wind in the Willows* **1987** *Safe Sex* **1988** *Romance/Romance*

1990 *Oh, Kay!* **1992** *The Most Happy Fella* **1993** *White Liars & Black Comedy*

Florence Mason Miller

Florence Mason Miller, mainly known as an abstract painter, was born in 1918 in Washington D.C., and studied at the Phillips Gallery in her home town, at the Corcoran School of Art, and with E. Bisttram in Taos. While living in New York in the late 1930s and early 1940s, she designed costumes for a Broadway production. She resided in Santa Fe, New Mexico beginning in 1945 where she exhibited often, and in the 1960s started creating wall reliefs. In 1938 she married artist Horace Towner Pierce, who also studied with Bisttram,
Costumes: 1938 *Lightnin'*

James M. Miller

Since 1982, James M. Miller, Professor of Theatre at the University of Missouri at Columbia has directed and/or designed more than 80 musicals and plays during the University Theatre's academic season and for its' Summer Repertory Theatre. He has also directed and choreographed for the Arrow Rock Lyceum Theatre, the Stephens College Playhouse, and Tulane University's Summer Lyric Theatre. He studied at the Fashion Institute of Technology, Herbert Berghoff Studios, the School for the Visual Arts, and Parsons School of Design. His M.F.A. is from the University of Southern Mississippi. Among his honors are awards for costume design, directing, and choreography from the Speech and Theatre Association of Missouri and the American College Theatre Festival. His costume designs have been exhibited with the United States Institute of Theatre Technology National and International Exhibit of Design at the New York Public Library for the Performing Arts at Lincoln Center, and at the George Caleb Bingham Gallery in Columbia, Missouri. Also a fine art painter, his works will be exhibited in a one-man show in spring 2002 at the Wilkinson County Historical Museum in Woodville, Mississippi, his hometown. Twenty-first century credits include music and lyrics for *We*

Were Dancing, an adaptation of Horton Foote's *Courtship*.
Costumes: 1982 *Cleavage*†

Joe Miller

Joe Miller had two lighting designs to his credit on Broadway in the early 1930s. An electrician, he resided at 2039 Creston Avenue in 1932. He was associated, also as an electrician, with "Industrial Mexican Drawing Works" at 230 West 29th Street, New York City. Joe Miller appeared in the film *Days of the Buffalo*.
Lights: 1932 *She Loves Me Not* 1934 *The Distaff Side*

Kathryn B. Miller

Kathryn Bache Miller was married to Herbert Miller, the theatrical producer, and often supervised costumes for his productions. The daughter of Jules S. Bache, the investment banker, she was a generous philanthropist, renowned for throwing fabulous parties, often mentioned on the "Best Dressed List" and in 1966 was elected to the Fashion Hall of Fame. The Kathryn Bache Miller Theatre on the Columbia University campus in New York is named in her honor, as is a pavilion at Roosevelt Hospital. She died at age 83 in October 1979.
Costumes: 1948 *The Play's the Thing*† (Costume Supervisor) 1954 *The Living Room*† (Costume Supervisor); *Witness for the Prosecution*† (Costume Supervisor) 1956 *The Reluctant Debutant* (Costume Supervisor) 1957 *Under Milkwood* (Costume Supervisor) 1958 *Patate* (Costume Supervisor)

Lawrence Miller

Lawrence Miller's first New York design was for *Liza Minnelli in Concert* at Carnegie Hall in 1979. He made his New York debut shortly after serving three seasons as resident designer at the Repertory Theatre in Loretto Hilton Center in St. Louis. He was born on August 20, 1944 in Yonkers, New York, and received a B.F.A. at Carnegie Mellon University in graphic arts and an M.F.A. in theater design in 1969, also at Carnegie Mellon. He assisted scenic designers Ming Cho Lee in 1975, Jo Mielziner in 1976 and Tony

Walton from 1976 to 1977. He received a Tony nomination for the set for *Nine* and a Drama Logue Award for the 1985 production of *Teaneck Tanzi: The Venus Flytrap* in Los Angeles. He has designed off-Broadway productions including *Cloud Nine*, and films such as *Equus, Overboard, True Believer, The King of Comedy* and *Aftershock: Earthquake in New York*. He has also designed ballets, operas, and MTV videos. Twenty-first century designs include scenery for *The People vs. Mona* at Pasadena Playhouse, and *Taking Sides* and *Night Sky* at the West Los Angeles Odyssey Theatre.
Sets: 1982 *Nine* 1983 *Teaneck Tanzi: The Venus Flytrap* 1985 *The Loves of Anatol* 1991 *Catskills on Broadway*
Costumes: 1983 *Teaneck Tanzi: The Venus Flytrap*

Michael Miller

Michael Miller was born on June 24, 1953 in Wellington, Kansas. He received a B.F.A. from Southern Oregon State College and an M.F.A. from the University of Washington. He was an intern and assistant designer at the American Conservatory Theatre in San Francisco and began his design career with *Ghosts* at the Intiman Theatre in Seattle, Washington in 1977. Career influences have included John Jensen, Santo Loquasto, Spud Hopkins, William Forrester, Robert Dahlstrom and Margaret Booker. He has also designed in regional and off-Broadway theaters, including scenery for *Hay Fever* and *Kafka's Wick* at the Berkshire Theatre Festival.
Sets: 1982 *Eminent Domain* 1986 *The Boys in Autumn*

Nolan Miller

Nolan Miller, a fashion designer, is best known for his designs for television, including programs such as *Dynasty*. He was born in 1935 in Texas, raised in Louisiana, and graduated from the Chouinard Art Institute in Los Angeles. His interest in fashion and costumes was high even as a young man, and in 1957 he opened his own fashion salon. He caters to glamorous, high fashion television and

movie stars, designing gowns for their personal wardrobes and for their appearances on stage, on television and in the movies. Honors include an Emmy Award in 1983 for the television series *Dynasty*.
Costumes: **1973** *Don Juan in Hell* (Miss Morehead's gown)

Robert Milton

Born Robert Milton Davidor in 1885 in Dinaburg, Russia, Robert Milton came to the United States as a child. He entered theater as an actor with Richard Mansfield, moving on to assisting, stage management, and directing for Mansfield, Mrs. Fiske and William Harris. He directed numerous plays and musicals in New York, beginning in 1911 with *The Return to Jerusalem* and including *Very Good, Eddie, Leave It to Jane, The Charm School, Bride of the Lamb* and *The Dark Angel*. He also designed settings for plays he directed using the acronym "R.M." In the late 1920s he began directing films, mainly for Paramount Studios, beginning with *The Dummy*. Mr. Milton died on January 13, 1956 at age 70.
Sets: **1918** *Oh, My Dear* **1920** *The Unwritten Chapter*

Fania Mindell

Fania (Fanya) Mindell came to the United States from Russia around 1908 and ran a small shop off Washington Square in New York City, where she sold Russian objects and artifacts. When Robert Edmond Jones was designing the set for *Redemption* in 1918 he discovered the shop and its proprietor. He encouraged her interest in the theater and asked Fania Mindell to assist him on the production - - she ultimately designed the costumes and assembled the required properties. This initial collaboration with Robert Edmond Jones led to other design assignments, mainly for costumes and occasionally also for sets. In addition, she was a dancer and choreographer. She married author Ralph Roeder (who also earned Broadway credits as a designer) in 1929. In 1943, they moved to Mexico City where she died in August 1969.

Sets: **1919** *Night Lodging* **1922** *Candida*
Costumes: **1918** *Redemption* **1920** *Medea* **1925** *Morals*; *Rosmersholm* (Women's costumes) **1926** *Easter* (Women's costumes); *Hedda Gabler* (Women's costumes); *Sandalwood* (Costume Supervisor) **1927** *The Brother's Karamazov* (Costume Supervisor); *Mariners*† (All other costumes) **1928** *The Grey Fox*† **1929** *Bond of Interest* (Women principals) **1930** *The Inspector General*; *Uncle Vanya*† (Other women) **1931** *The House of Connelly*; *Wonder Boy*† (Miss Bulgakova's costumes)

Vincente Minnelli

Known primarily as a film director of musicals and large extravaganzas, Vincente (Vincent) Minnelli started his theatrical career as a designer. He began in the Midwest creating sets and costumes for the stage shows which accompanied films. In 1930 he relocated to New York City to design at the Paramount movie theater. He made his Broadway debut as a costume designer for *Earl Carroll's Vanities* in 1931. Appointed art director at Radio City Music Hall for the 1933-34 season, he had responsibility for designing sets, costumes and lights for the weekly stage shows. Gradually he turned his talents to directing and creating revues. His last Broadway designs were costumes for *Very Warm for May* in 1939, which he also staged, although he received posthumous credit in 1998 when his designs for "The Parade of the Wooden Soldiers" were reconstructed at Radio City Music Hall. After moving to Hollywood he directed many award-winning films and won an Oscar for directing *Gigi* in 1958. Minnelli was born in Chicago on February 28, 1903 (some sources say 1910) and died July 25, 1986.
Sets: **1931** *Earl Carroll's Vanities*† **1932** *The Dubarry*; *Earl Carroll's Vanities* **1935** *At Home Abroad* **1936** *The Show Is On*; *Ziegfeld Follies: 1936*; *Ziegfeld Follies: 1936-1937* **1937** *Hooray for What!*; *The Show Is On* **1939** *Very Warm for May*
Costumes: **1930** *Earl Carroll's Vanities*†; *Lew Leslie's Blackbirds* **1931** *Earl Carroll's Vanities*† **1932** *The Dubarry*;

Earl Carroll's Vanities **1935** *At Home Abroad* (Also staged) **1936** *The Show Is On* (Concieved, staged and designed); *Ziegfeld Follies: 1936*†; *Ziegfeld Follies: 1936-1937* **1937** *The Show Is On* (Conceived, staged and designed) **1998** *Radio City Christmas Spectacular*† (The Parade of the Wooden Soldiers)

William Mintzer

William Mintzer, who received a B.F.A. from Carnegie Institute of Technology in 1966 and an M.F.A. from New York University in 1969, was born in 1944.   He designed lights for regional theaters around the United States, including numerous productions for the Milwaukee Repertory Theatre, Arena Stage, Seattle Repertory Theatre, and the Goodman Theatre.   He also amassed numerous credits off-Broadway, and supervised scenery for American tours by the Royal Shakespeare Company, the Abbey Theatre of Dublin and the Comédie Française.   Widely regarded as a pioneer in arena stage lighting, he was a member of the faculty of the State University of New York at Purchase where he began the Professional Conservatory Program, and was also visiting professor at the National Theatre School of Canada.   When he died on July 23, 1997 an endowment fund was created by his former students and collaborators.   In spring 2001, the William Land Mintzer Lighting Laboratory was dedicated.   An award to honor exceptional seniors in the lighting program at SUNY-Purchase was also permanently endowed in his name.
Lights: 1973 *Raisin* **1974** *Yentl* **1977** *Cold Storage* **1978** *Eubie*; *A History of the American Film*

Mr. Minory Mishida

Mr. Minory Mishida supervised costumes for a play in 1928.
Costumes: 1928 *Sakura*† (Japanese costume supervisor)

David Mitchell

David Mitchell has won Tony Awards for the scene design of *Annie* and *Barnum* and received several Tony nominations since his Broadway debut in 1970. He was born on May 12, 1932 in Howesdale, Pennsylvania and studied at Pennsylvania State and Boston Universities. His initial design in New York was *Henry V* for the New York Shakespeare Festival in 1965. He has also designed costumes, notably for the Pennsylvania Ballet, and for *The Steadfast Tin Soldier* for the PBS series *Dance in America*. Films include *One Trick Pony*, *Rich Kids* and *My Dinner with Andre*.   Among his other credits are operas, ballets, and plays. He also received a Maharam Award for *Barnum* (1970), Drama Desk Award for *Short Eyes* (1974), and a Tony Award and an Outer Critics Circle Award for *Annie* (1977). He has been nominated for Tony Awards many times. His numerous credits for the New York City Ballet include *Sleeping Beauty*.

Sets: 1970 *Grin and Bare It!/ Postcards* **1971** *How the Other Half Loves*; *The Incomparable Max* **1976** *Trelawney of the "Wells"* **1977** *Annie*; *The Gin Game*; *I Love My Wife* **1978** *Working* **1979** *I Remember Mama*; *The Price* **1980** *Barnum* **1981** *Bring Back Birdie*; *Can-Can*; *Foxfire* **1983** *Brighton Beach Memoirs*; *Dance a Little Closer*; *La Cage Aux Folles*; *Private Lives* **1985** *Biloxi Blues*; *The Boys of Winter*; *Harrigan 'n Hart*; *The Odd Couple* **1986** *Broadway Bound* **1988** *Legs Diamond* **1989** *Tru* **1991** *The Big Love* **1992** *High Rollers Social and Pleasure Club* **1993** *Ain't Broadway Grand* **1997** *Dream*

Julian Mitchell

Julian Mitchell was an actor, director and producer who began his career staging dance numbers for revues. He was associated with Florenz Ziegfeld among others, and was involved with at least thirteen of the "Follies" productions, beginning with the first one in 1907.   He also directed operettas for Victor Herbert, and at Niblo's Gardens. When necessary, he contributed designs to the productions with which he was involved. He died on June 23, 1926 at age 72 in Long Branch, New Jersey. He should not be confused with the British actor Julien Mitchell (1888-1954).

Sets: 1913 *The Little Café*

Robert Mitchell

Robert Deatrick Mitchell received a
B.A. at Yale University in 1951 after
study with Donald Oenslager. From
1963 to 1968 he assisted Jo Mielziner
and from 1964 assisted Boris Aronson
until Aronson's death. He was born
in New Jersey on April 14, 1929 the
son of Roger Irving and Anna Louise
Mitchell. He was the first American designer invited by the Greek government
to design for the National Theatre of
Greece at Epidaurus, and later represented Greece at the Europalia Festival in Brussels and the 1984 Olympic
Arts Festival in Los Angeles. He has
designed theater and ballet throughout
the United States, Canada and Europe
since his professional debut at the York
Theatre in 1959 with the set design for
The Saintliness of Margery Kempe.
Sets: **1968** *The Sudden and Accidental Reeducation of Horse Johnson* **1973**
Medea **1977** *The Basic Training of Pavlo
Hummel* **1979** *A Meeting in the Air*
1989 *Chu Chem*

Mr. Roy Mitchell

Mr. Roy Mitchell moved to New York
in 1916 to study theater and later
taught folklore at New York University, where he was a member of the
Dramatic Art faculty from 1930 until
his death in 1944. He was born in
St. Clair County, Michigan of Canadian parents in 1884 and studied at the
University of Toronto. After working
in amateur theater and as a reporter,
he began in 1908 to direct plays for the
Arts and Letters Club in Toronto. He
subsequently moved to New York and
worked as a stage manager on Broadway and as technical director of the
Greenwich Village Theatre. Mitchell
then moved to Canada and worked in
the Canadian film industry, becoming
director of the Harthouse Theatre at
the University of Toronto from 1919
until 1930. He designed sets for those
productions that he also directed. Mr.
Mitchell died on July 27, 1944 at age
60.
Sets: **1918** *Karen*; *Pan and the Young
Shepherd*

Danianne Mizzy

Danianne Mizzy was born on November 8, 1960 in New York City into a
family with many theater associations.
Her mother, a Broadway press agent,
worked for producer/director Eddie
Jaffe; her great-grandfather, Charles
Louis LaMarche, ran the Empire Theatre in Cleveland; and her grandmother, Pauline O'Keefe LaMarche,
acted in summer productions of Ohio's
Kenley Players. She received an International Baccalaureate in 1978 from
U.N.I.S.; an A.B. from Brown University in 1982, where she began designing with *Getting Out* in the Production Workshop; and an M.F.A. in design from the Yale University School of
Drama in 1986. Career influences include Jennifer Tipton, Mark Stanley,
Allen Lee Hughes and Mark Reiff.
Lights: **1987** *Fences*

J. Robin Modereger

Jeffery Robin Modereger, a designer
and painter from South Dakota, received an M.F.A. at the University of
Utah. He was a design assistant to Jo
Mielziner and served as artistic director at the Candlewood Playhouse. In
1985 he taught at Long Island University. Additional credits in New York
include *Winslow Boy, Thurber Carnival* and *Jacques Brel is Alive and Well
and Living in Paris.*
Sets: **1980** *Of the Fields, Lately*

Phillip Moeller

Philip Moeller, who founded the Theatre Guild and directed it's first play,
Bonds of Interest in 1916, was also a
playwright. He was born in New York
City on August 26, 1880 and graduated
from Columbia University, after which
he started producing and helped found
the Washington Square players. Occasionally for plays he directed or wrote,
he also provided designs. Between 1925
and 1937 he produced and/or directed
over seventy plays, many of them by
Eugene O'Neil and George Bernard
Shaw. In the mid-1930s he began directing films for RKO-Radio pictures
and in the late 1930s he retired. He
died on April 26, 1958 in New York
City.
Sets: **1915** *Two Blind Beggars and One
Less Blind* (Also directed)

Costumes: 1915 *Two Blind Beggars and One Less Blind* (Also directed)

Mrs. Graham Moffatt

Mrs. Graham Moffatt (Moffat) designed the costumes for a Broadway play in 1912. The play was written and directed by her husband Graham Moffatt (c.1866-1951), a Scottish author and playwright who also wrote *Bunty Pulls the Strings*. Their son, also named Graham Moffatt (1911-1965), was a character actor in British movies. At one time, the entire family performed together in plays. Mrs. Moffatt appeared in movies including *Rolling Home*, made in England in 1935. In 1936, Mr. and Mrs. Moffatt retired to Cape Town, South Africa, where she died in 1943 at age 70.

Costumes: 1912 *The Scrape o' the Pen*

Robert W. Mogel

Robert W. Mogel began designing lights in New York City for the Roundabout Theatre's production of *A Taste of Honey*. He has also designed sets and lights in regional theaters, taught design at Texas Tech University and received extensive credits for outdoor theaters and concerts.

Lights: 1981 *A Taste of Honey*

Leon Mohn

Leo Mohn contributed scenery to two Broadway productions in the first decade of the twentieth century. He collaborated with artist and illustrator Frederick Remington on *On Parole* in 1907.

Sets: 1906 *The Title Mart* 1907 *On Parole†*

Tanya Moiseiwitsch

Tanya Moiseiwitsch, a distinguished British scenic, theater, lighting, and costume designer, was born in London on December 3, 1914. She attended the Central School of Arts and Crafts in London. Her first design assignment was *The Faithful* in London in 1934. A longtime colleague of Tyrone Guthrie, they often collaborated, notably to create the theater for the Stratford (Ontario) Festival, The Guthrie Theatre and the Crucible Theatre in Sheffield, England. Known for her designs for opera and theater in Europe and North America, she served as Principal Designer at The Guthrie Theatre from 1963 to 1969. Other companies for which she has worked include the Royal Shakespeare Company, the Old Vic, the Metropolitan Opera and the Abbey Theatre. Other designs include the 1984 film *King Lear* with Laurence Olivier. In 1975 her costume designs for *The Misanthrope* were nominated for a Tony Award. She was honored with a Commander of the British Empire in 1976 and a Distinguished Service Award in 1987 from the United States Institute of Theatre Technology for fifty years of design.

Sets: 1946 *The Critic*; *Uncle Vanya* 1955 *The Matchmaker* 1968 *The House of Atreus* 1975 *The Misanthrope*

Costumes: 1946 *The Critic*; *Uncle Vanya* 1955 *The Matchmaker* 1968 *The House of Atreus* 1975 *The Misanthrope*

Lights: 1968 *The House of Atreus*

Molyneux

Captain Edward Molyneux was born in Hampstead, England on September 5, 1894 to English-Irish aristocracy. After studying art, he worked for Lucile (Lady Duff Gordon) as a sketch artist. During World War I he served in the British army. He then opened a salon in Paris with branches around France and in London and achieved success dressing his private clientele, which included Gertrude Lawrence and Lynn Fontanne. Known for quality of material, workmanship and elegance of line, he pioneered the use of zippers to create a fluid line in women's gowns. Molyneux occasionally contributed designs to the stage. With only a brief hiatus during World War II, he continued to design until 1950, when he retired. In the mid-1960s he made a brief return, but soon gave the responsibility to a cousin. Molyneux died on March 22, 1974 at the age of 79.

Costumes: 1931 *Private Lives* (Miss Lawrence's gowns) 1934 *And Be My Love†* (Miss Cahill's and Miss Gadd's gowns); *The Shining Hour* (Miss Cooper's gown) 1946 *O Mistress Mine* (Miss Fontanne's dresses)

William Molyneux

William Molyneux designed one set in 1954 on Broadway. In 1953 he designed scenery for the London premiere of Benjamin Britten's opera, *Billy Budd* (also known as *Buddopera*). The production was broadcast by NBC-TV to open its fourth season of opera on television.

Sets: 1954 *Black-Eyed Susan*
Costumes: 1954 *Black-Eyed Susan*

Phil Monat

Lighting designer Phil Monat designs throughout the United States, mainly plays and musicals in regional theaters. He also has extensive off-Broadway credits in theaters including Playwrights Horizons, Manhattan Theatre Club, New York Shakespeare Festival, and Second Stage. His many productions at the Goodspeed Opera House include *Finian's Rainbow*, *Houdini*, *Honky-Tonk Highway* and *Paint Your Wagon*. Honors include a Drama Desk Award nomination for *Goblin Market* at Circle in the Square. Twenty-first century designs include *Hello Muddah, Hello Fadduh!* at the Triad Theatre and *Unwrap Your Candy* at the Vineyard Theatre.

Lights: 1992 *3 from Brooklyn*   1994 *Sally Marr...and Her Escorts*

E. H. Beresford Monck

See Chipmonck.

Monette

Mary M. Monette, a dressmaker, was responsible for the costume designs for a 1910 production on Broadway. Her salon was at 566 Fifth Avenue in New York and she lived at 155 West 48th Street.

Costumes: 1910 *Just A Wife*

Ralph L. Moni

Ralph L. Moni was born on March 6, 1897 and was active on Broadway between 1926 and 1933. He died in Miami, Florida in July 1968.

Costumes: 1926 *Castles in the Air*† (Women's costumes) 1933 *It Pays to Sin* (Miss Starr's costumes)

Robby Monk

Robby Monk designed lights on Broadway beginning in 1979. He was associate lighting designer for *Beatlemania* and assistant set designer for the Broadway and national tours of *Dracula*. His credits for productions in regional theaters include *What I Did Last Summer*, *Cabaret* and *Terra Nova* for Studio Arena Theatre.

Lights: 1979 *Got Tu Go Disco*; *Strider* 1981 *Ned and Jack* 1982 *The World of Shalom Aleichem*

Gladys Monkhouse

Gladys Monkhouse designed costumes on Broadway for revues during the teens and early twenties. Many of her wonderful sketches are in the Billy Rose Theatre Collection at the New York Public Library for the Performing Arts at Lincoln Center. See Figure 9: Gladys Monkhouse: *Better Times*

Costumes: 1917 *Cheer-up (Hippodrome)*†; *Eyes of Youth*† 1918 *Everything*† 1919 *She's a Good Fellow* 1922 *Better Times*† (Other costumes)

Margaret Montague

Margaret Montague, an author, designed costumes for two featured players in a 1934 Broadway show. She was a frequent contributor to *The Atlantic Monthly* and won an O'Henry Award in 1919 for *England to America*. She died in Richmond, Va. at age 76 on September 26, 1955, having lived most of her life in Boston.

Costumes: 1934 *A Ship Comes in* (Miss Bryant's and Miss Stevens' costumes)

Yves Montand

Yves Montand, the popular French actor and singer, was born Yves Livi on October 13, 1921 in Monsummano, Italy and educated in Marseilles. His first film appearance was in 1946 in *Les Portes de la Nuit* after which he appeared in many French and American films, notably *On a Clear Day You Can See Forever*, *Z*, *La Guerre est Finie*, *Is Paris Burning?*, and *Jean De Florette*. He was married to Simone Signoret from 1951 until her death in 1985. He contributed scene and lighting designs to a concert appearance he made

Figure 9: Gladys Monkhouse: *Better Times* Costume rendering, 1922.
By permission, Billy Rose Theatre Collection, The New York Public
Library for the Performing Arts, Astor, Lenox and Tilden Foundations.
Photograph by Jan Juracek.

on Broadway in 1961. He died in Senlis, France on November 9, 1991 at age 70.

Sets: 1961 *An Evening with Yves Montand*

Lights: 1961 *An Evening with Yves Montand*

Elizabeth Montgomery

See Motley.

Patricia Montgomery

Patricia Montgomery designed costumes on Broadway from 1945 to 1950.

Costumes: 1945 *Strange Fruit* 1946 *Jeb* 1947 *This Time Tomorrow* 1950 *A Story for Sunday Evening*

Beni Montresor

Beni Montresor was born in Bussolengo (near Verona), Italy and raised in Venice. He studied at the Academy of Art in Venice after which he designed films for directors Federico Fellini, Roberto Rossellini, and others as well as the autobiographical *Pilgrimage* shown at the Cannes Film Festival in 1972. In 1962 he met Gian Carlo Menotti and subsequently designed Barber's *Vanessa*, his first opera, for the Spoleto Festival. His career was established with *Last Savage* by Menotti at the Metropolitan Opera in 1964 and was soon followed by numerous productions for the major opera companies around the world. His honors were numerous, and included nominations for Tony Awards in 1964 for *Marco Millions* and in 1985 for *The Marriage of Figaro*, a Leonide Massine Award for ballet, and a Caldecott Medal for illustrations for *May I Bring a Friend?*, a children's book written by Beatrice Schenk de Regniers. Among his late twentieth century designs were *Turandot* for New York City Opera and *L'Elisir D'Amore* for the Metropolitan Opera. Montresor died at age 78 on October 11, 2001 in Verona, Italy.

Sets: 1965 *Do I Hear a Waltz?* 1985 *The Marriage of Figaro* 1986 *Rags*

Costumes: 1964 *Marco Millions* 1965 *Do I Hear a Waltz?* 1985 *The Marriage of Figaro*

Lights: 1985 *The Marriage of Figaro*

Madame Mood

Jennie M. Mood designed gowns using Madame Mood as her professional name. Her salon, at 30 West 39th Street in New York City mainly served private clients, but in 1909 she provided gowns for a Broadway show.

Costumes: 1909 *Seven Days* (Miss LaVerne's and Reed's gowns)

Roger Mooney

Roger A. Mooney has designed many sets off-Broadway and in regional theaters. His scenic designs at the Roundabout Theatre include his New York debut *The Blood Knot* and many more, such as *The Master Builder*, *The Winslow Boy*, *Don Juan in Hell*, *Inadmissible Evidence* and *Fallen Angels*. He designed the television versions of *Look Back In Anger* and *The Killing of Sister George*, and the 1987 television special *Puzzle Weekend*. He has designed at the Hudson Theatre Guild, PAF Playhouse, and the Production Company.

Sets: 1981 *A Taste of Honey*

Herbert Moore

Herbert Moore, designed scenery from 1919 to 1935 on Broadway. A painter, he was raised in Claymount, Delaware. *Links With Other Days*, a collection of pen drawings with some notes by Herbert Moore, was published in Melbourne, Australia in 1927 by C.S. Harvey and Company. He shouldn't be confused with lighting pioneer Herbert R. Moore (d. 1991).

Sets: 1919 *Angel Face* 1929 *A Wonderful Night*[†] 1933 *Growing Pains* 1935 *Night of January 16*

John J. Moore

John Jay Moore was born on February 28, 1928 in Sayre, Pennsylvania, and received both a B.S. and an M.A. in drama from Syracuse University where he later taught scenic design for many years. He briefly taught at State University of New York in Albany before starting to designing scenery and lighting on Broadway. He assisted Boris Aronson, Jo Mielziner, Robert Randolph, Tony Walton, Ming Cho Lee, and other designers. In the 1980s he was a scenic consultant for a Disney

Land/Disney World project. He then became Vice-President in Charge of Production for Radio City Music Hall, creating its' production center during his tenure in that position. Film credits include art direction for *Sophie's Choice*, *Wall Street*, *Klute* and *Ghost Busters*. His production designs include *Sea of Love*, *The Wanderers*, *The Cowboy Way*, and *FX2*.

Sets: 1972 *Don Juan* 1976 *Pal Joey*
Lights: 1967 *How to Be a Jewish Mother* 1969 *A Teaspoon Every Four Hours*

Madame Moore

Madame Jennie (Jenny) Moore, of 41 New Bond Street, London, contributed costume designs to productions in England beginning in 1892 with *The Duchess of Malfi* for Opera Comique and remained active until the mid-teens. Among her other credits are *Measure for Measure* in 1893 at the Royalty Theatre, *King Argimenes* in 1911 at the Court Theatre, and *The Pierrot of the Minute* at the Little Theatre in 1913.

Costumes: 1909 *The Love Cure*†

Marion Moore

Marion Moore supervised costumes on Broadway in the mid-1930s.

Costumes: 1934 *Mackerel Skies* (Costume Supervisor) 1935 *Good Men and True* (Costume Supervisor)

Robert Moore

Robert Moore supervised costumes for a play in 1947.

Costumes: 1947 *Tenting Tonight* (Costume Supervisor)

Mark Mooring

Mark Mooring, a fashion and costume designer, designed several shows on Broadway in the 1920s. Between 1933 and 1948 he was a designer in the costume department at Bergdorf Goodman, returning in the early 1960s to create special collections. He also designed for Elizabeth Arden and in Hollywood for Marusia during the 1960s. Mr. Mooring died at age 71 in Hollywood, California on January 5, 1971.

Costumes: 1924 *Be Yourself*† (Dresses) 1925 *Dearest Enemy*† (Act I); *Greenwich Village Follies*†; *Song of the Flame* 1926

The Desert Song†; *Peggy Ann*; *The Wild Rose* 1927 *Golden Dawn* (Costume Research and dresses); *Hit the Deck* 1928 *Good Boy*

Percy Moran

Born in 1862 in Philadelphia, Edward Percy Moran was a painter and illustrator who studied with his father Edward Moran (1829-1901), a landscape painter, at the National Academy of Design, and at the Academy Julian in Paris. His paintings were widely exhibited in Europe and the United States in the late nineteenth century, and won many prizes. He painted landscapes and historical subjects that were reproduced as etchings in magazines and books. Percy Moran, who worked from a studio at 105 East 78th Street, died in New York City on March 25, 1935. The American artist should not be confused with the British actor (1886-1952) with the same name.

Costumes: 1902 *Audrey*

Edward Morange

Edward A. Morange was born in Bronxville, New York. He attended the Chicago Art Institute, the Corcoran School of Fine Arts and the School of Fine Arts at Washington University in St. Louis, where he considered a career in architecture or engineering. While designing exhibitions for the Chicago World's Fair of 1893 and working at the Grand Opera House (Chicago), he began focusing on theatrical design and construction. He began his collaboration with Frank Gates in 1894 and together they founded the scenic studio Gates and Morange in New York. Most of the designs produced by Gates and Morange were credited to the firm, but Edward A. Morange also designed scenery under his own name, both early in the twentieth century and again in 1935. His designs are in the permanent collections of the Brander Matthews Museum at Columbia University and were featured in the 1949 exhibition at the Metropolitan Museum of Art: "Behind American Footlights." He died May 20, 1955 in Torrington, Connecticut at age 90.

Sets: 1899 *Becky Sharp*†; *Children of the Ghetto*† 1900 *Lost River*†; *Monte Cristo*†

1901 *A Gentleman of France*†; *Miranda of the Balcony*†; *Unleavened Bread*†; *The Unwelcome Mrs. Hatch*†; *When Was In Flower* 1902 *The Cavalier*†; *Little Italy*† 1903 *Merely Mary Ann*†; *Nancy Brown*†; *Romeo and Juliet*† 1904 *Becky Sharp*†; *Bird Center*†; *Leah Kleschna*† 1905 *Fantana*†; *The Toast of the Town*† 1906 *Fascinating Mr. Vanderveldt*†; *The Red Mill*† 1907 *Fascinating Flora*†; *The Lady from Lane's*†; *The Ranger*†; *The Rose of Alhambra*†; *Salomy Jane*†; *Sappho and Phaon*† 1908 *The Battle*†; *The Boys and Betty*†; *His Wife's Family*†; *The Man from Home*†; *Marta of the Lowlands*†; *The Soul Kiss*† 1909 *The Conflict*† 1912 *The Daughter of Heaven*† 1935 *For Valor*

James Morcom

James Stewart Morcom was born in Covington, Kentucky on July 28, 1906 and studied at the Grand Central School of Art and the John Murray Anderson-Robert Milton School of the Theatre. He spent the majority of his career in New York City at Radio City Music Hall where he was an assistant to Clarke Robinson in the late 1930s, and then Resident Costume Designer from 1947 to 1950, and Art Director from 1950 until his retirement in 1973. Additional credits include *Five Kings* for Orson Welles' Mercury Theatre Group, and productions for the Federal Theatre Project, the New York Ballet, Ballet Caravan and Jones Beach Theatre. He died in New York on May 28, 1988.
Sets: 1938 *Case History* **1941** *Native Son* **1942** *Native Son*

Dickson Morgan

Dickson Morgan designed sets, directed, and produced plays on Broadway between 1923 and 1926. He moved to Hollywood in the 1930s to head the Mary Pickford Dramatic Academy located at the El Capitan Theatre. He subsequently directed and produced numerous plays on the West Coast, including *Waterloo Bridge* at the Music Box Theatre in Hollywood, and *Mimie Scheller, Loyalties, Lysistrata, Shanghai Gesture, Curtain Call* and *Never Trouble Trouble.* He was also a dialogue coach and associate director for films produced by Universal Studios and Columbia Pictures.
Sets: 1923 *Peter Weston* **1924** *The Road Together*; *Topsy and Eva* **1925** *The Valley of Content* **1926** *Down Stream*

James Morgan [active 1989-]

James Morgan, who designed scenery on Broadway for the first time in 1989 and received a Drama Desk Award nomination for his efforts, was born on March 20, 1952 in Ft. Myers, Florida. He graduated with honors from the University of Florida in 1974 and began designing professionally almost immediately. He is an active designer in regional theaters, off-off and off-Broadway, and has been resident designer for the York Theatre Company in New York City, the American Stage Company in New Jersey and the Caldwell Theatre Company in Florida. He designed the premiere of *The Fan* for the Blackstone Theatre in Chicago, the revival of *Pacific Overtures* in 1985 in the off-Broadway Promenade Theatre, and the national tour of *On the 20th Century*. He also been active with the AIDS benefit *We Need a little Christmas*, as creator, co-director and co-producer. Twenty-first century designs include *Roadside* for the York Theatre Company.
Sets: 1989 *Sweeney Todd* **1990** *The Miser*; *Zoya's Apartment*† **1991** *Getting Married*; *Taking Steps* **1992** *Anna Karenina*

James Morgan [active 1948]

James Morgan supervised costumes for a play in 1948. He should not be confused with the scenic and graphic designer who has the same name.
Costumes: 1948 *Tonight at 8:30*† (Costume Supervisor)

Matt Morgan

Matt (Matthew) Morgan was active in 1907 as a scenic designer. An artist, he had a studio at 630 West 24th Street during the first decade of the twentieth century and lived at 660 West 179th Street.
Sets: 1907 *The Rejuvenation of Aunt Mary*† (Acts I, III)

Robert Morgan

Robert Morgan is a costume designer, set designer, lighting designer and director. He was born in Ocala, Florida on June 15, 1944 and received a B.A. at Dartmouth (1966) and an M.F.A. at Stanford (1969) in costume design and stage direction. His first professional costume designs were for *The House of Blue Leaves* at the American Conservatory Theatre in San Francisco in 1972. He has won numerous awards for costume design, including the Los Angeles Drama Critics Circle, four Drama Logues, several San Diego Critics Association Awards and a Drama Desk nomination for *Loves of Anatol.*
Costumes: 1985 *I'm Not Rappaport*; *The Loves of Anatol* **1987** *Sherlock's Last Case* **2000** *The Full Monty*
Lights: 1981 *Broadway Follies*

Roger Morgan

Roger Morgan was born on December 19, 1938 in New Kensington, Pennsylvania and graduated from the Carnegie Mellon University Department of Drama in 1961. He has designed over two hundred productions on and off-Broadway and in regional theaters and received both Tony and Drama Desk Awards for *The Crucifer of Blood.* He worked for three years as assistant theater designer to Jo Mielziner, assisting with the Vivian Beaumont Theatre at Lincoln Center and the Power Center for the Performing Arts at the University of Michigan. As principal owner of Roger Morgan Studios, Inc. he has had several theater projects honored with regional and national awards, including both the Indiana Repertory Theatre and the Circle Theatre both in Indianapolis, the Playhouse Square in Cleveland, and the Grand Opera House in Wilmington, North Carolina. He is co-author of *Space for Dance* and a founding member of Ensemble Studio Theatre in New York City. Late twentieth century productions include the lighting design for *Peer Gynt* at Trinity Repertory Company.
Sets: 1972 *Dude†*
Lights: 1966 *Under the Weather* **1968** *The Sudden and Accidental Reeducation*

of Horse Johnson **1970** *Wilson in the Promise Land* **1971** *Unlikely Heroes* **1972** *Elizabeth I*; *Ring Round the Bathtub* **1974** *Saturday Sunday Monday* **1977** *Dracula* **1978** *The Crucifer of Blood*; *First Monday in October*; *Gorey Stories* **1979** *Gilda Radner Live from N.Y.*; *I Remember Mama* **1980** *Nuts* **1981** *It Had to Be You* **1982** *Agnes of God*; *Almost an Eagle* **1985** *The Octette Bridge Club* **1987** *Mort Sahl on Broadway!* **1992** *The Visit* **1998** *Colin Quinn - An Irish Wake*

Christopher Morley

Christopher Morley became an associate artist with the Royal Shakespeare Company in 1966 and designed many productions while in residence throughout the following three decades, most recently *Shirley Valentine* at the Barbican in 1992. He has also designed for the Royal Court, the Birmingham Repertory, the Guildhall School, and in London's West End. Opera designs include productions for the English National Opera, the Royal Opera, the English Music Theatre and the Royal Danish Opera. In 1974 he formed Christopher Morley Associates. The British designer should not be confused with the American playwright (1890-1957) or the music critic who writes for the *Birmingham Post.*
Sets: 1971 *Abelard and Heloise*

Ruth Morley

Ruth Morley began designing costumes professionally for plays in 1950 when *Mrs. Warren's Profession* opened at the Bleecker Street Playhouse in New York City. Her credits both on and off-Broadway and at City Center, where she was costume director in the early 1950s, were extensive. She designed for television and many films, including *The Hustler, Kramer vs. Kramer, Taxi Driver, Tootsie, Ghosts, The Prince of Tides* and *The Miracle Worker* for which she received an Oscar nomination. Ruth Morley, who also taught costume design at Brandeis University and other schools died on February 12, 1991 in New York City at age 65.
Costumes: 1951 *Billy Budd*; *The Long Days* **1953** *A Pin to See the Peepshow*; *Take a Giant Step* **1955** *Inherit the Wind* **1957** *The Cave Dwellers*; *A Moon for the*

Misbegotten **1958** *The Shadow of a Gunman; Who Was That Lady I Saw You With?* **1959** *The Miracle Worker; Only in America* **1960** *The Long Dream; Roman Candle; Toys in the Attic* **1962** *In the Counting House; A Thousand Clowns* **1964** *Cafe Crown; Dylan* **1965** *Xmas in Las Vegas* **1966** *Wait until Dark* **1968** *Here's Where I Belong* **1975** *Hughey/ Duet* **1977** *Ladies at the Alamo* **1978** *Death Trap* **1980** *It's So Nice to Be Civilized* **1981** *Twice around the Park* **1984** *Death of a Salesman* **1986** *Shakespeare on Broadway for the Schools* **1988** *Spoils of War*

Carter Morningstar

Carter Morningstar, scenic designer for theater and television, was born in Lanstowne, Pennsylvania and studied at the Philadelphia Academy of Fine Arts and in Europe. He began his professional life as a graphic artist and illustrator, but after service in the Navy during World War II he moved to New York and became a scenic designer. He only rarely designed costumes and lighting. Carter Morningstar died in February 1964 at the age of 53.

Sets: 1960 *Beg, Borrow, or Steal*
Costumes: 1960 *Beg, Borrow, or Steal*
Lights: 1960 *Beg, Borrow, or Steal*

Selma Morosco

Selma Morosco designed scenery on Broadway in 1924.

Sets: 1924 *Artistic Temperament*†

Billy Morris

Billy Morris designed a Broadway set in 1976.

Sets: 1976 *Debbie Reynolds Show*

Madame Morris

Madame Yetta Morris designed costumes for a 1908 Broadway play. She lived and worked from her home at 113 Essex Street.

Costumes: 1908 *The Gentleman from Mississippi*

Charles T. Morrison

Charles T. Morrison designed one set in 1964 on Broadway.

Sets: 1964 *Conversation at Midnight*

Kay Morrison

Kay Morrison designed costumes on Broadway in the 1930s.

Costumes: 1934 *Brittle Heaven* (Miss Gish's and Miss Atwater's costumes); *Mother Lode* 1935 *May Wine; Prisoners of War* (Women's costumes)

Paul Morrison

Paul Morrison, a scenic, lighting and costume designer, was born in Altoona, Pennsylvania on July 9, 1906. He graduated from Lafayette College where he subsequently taught. He began his theater career as an actor and stage manager and first designed costumes in New York in 1939 for *Thunder Rock*. Beginning in 1941 he specialized in scenery and lighting and had numerous shows to his credit on Broadway and in other locations. Mr. Morrison served as Executive Director of the Neighborhood Playhouse beginning in 1963. He died in New York City on December 29, 1980.

Sets: 1941 *Walk into My Parlor* 1942 *Hedda Gabler* 1943 *I'll Take the High Road* 1944 *Love on Leave; Mrs. January and Mr. X; That Old Devil* 1946 *John Gabriel Borkman; What Every Woman Knows* 1948 *The Young and the Fair* 1949 *The Closing Door* 1950 *Affairs of State; Arms and the Man* 1951 *Billy Budd; Faithfully Yours; Twilight Walk* 1952 *Four Saints in Three Acts; Golden Boy* 1953 *On Borrowed Time* 1954 *Abie's Irish Rose; The Confidential Clerk; The Tender Trap* 1955 *Joyce Grenfell Requests the Pleasure*† 1956 *The Loud Red Patrick; Sixth Finger in a Five Finger Glove* 1958 *Make a Million; Maybe Tuesday; The Visit*† 1959 *Masquerade; The Nervous Set* 1960 *Rape of the Belt* 1962 *Cantilevered Terrace* 1963 *Too True to Be Good* 1973 *The Jockey Club Stakes*

Costumes: 1939 *Thunder Rock* 1940 *Night Music* 1941 *Walk into My Parlor* 1943 *Apology* 1946 *John Gabriel Borkman* 1947 *All My Sons* 1950 *Arms and the Man* 1952 *Four Saints in Three Acts; Golden Boy* 1953 *On Borrowed Time* 1954 *Abie's Irish Rose; The Confidential Clerk* 1955 *Bus Stop; Once upon a Tailor* 1956 *The Loud Red Patrick* 1962 *Cantilevered Terrace*

Lights: 1941 *Walk into My Parlor* 1942

Hedda Gabler **1943** *I'll Take the High Road* **1944** *Mrs. January and Mr. X; That Old Devil* **1946** *John Gabriel Borkman; What Every Woman Knows* **1948** *The Young and the Fair* **1949** *The Closing Door* **1950** *Affairs of State; Arms and the Man* **1951** *Billy Budd; Faithfully Yours; Twilight Walk* **1952** *Four Saints in Three Acts; Golden Boy* **1953** *On Borrowed Time* **1954** *Abie's Irish Rose; The Confidential Clerk; The Tender Trap* **1955** *Bus Stop; Joyce Grenfell Requests the Pleasure; Once upon a Tailor; Tiger at the Gate* **1956** *Candide; Cranks; The Loud Red Patrick; Separate Tables; Sixth Finger in a Five Finger Glove; Tamburlaine the Great* **1957** *The Sin of Pat Muldoon; Ziegfeld Follies* **1958** *Make a Million; Maybe Tuesday* **1959** *Flowering Cherry; Happy Town; Kataki; Masquerade; Much Ado About Nothing; The Nervous Set* **1960** *Duel of Angels; Invitation to a March; Rape of the Belt; A Thurber Carnival* **1961** *The Complaisant Lover; A Man for All Seasons* **1962** *Cantilevered Terrace* **1963** *Student Gypsy, or The Prince of Liederkrantz; Too True to Be Good* **1964** *Sponomo* **1968** *The Price* **1973** *The Jockey Club Stakes*

Peggy Morrison

Peggy Elizabeth Morrison was born in New Rochelle, New York on October 5, 1922 and attended Vassar College and the Fashion Academy in New York City. She began designing costumes in 1947 for plays, television, night club revues and industrial shows. Her television designs included *The Jackie Gleason Show, The Honeymooners,* and *The Arthur Murray Show.* In both 1954 and 1955, the Fashion Academy honored her with a Gold Alumni Award for Outstanding Inspirational American Design for her designs at the National Automobile Show in New York City. She should not be confused with Margaret Mackie Morrison (d. 1973), the British author who used the pen-name March Cost.
Costumes: 1948 *Harvest of Years* **1949** *The Mikado; The Pirates of Penzance; Trial by Jury* **1950** *Tickets, Please* **1951** *Four Twelves Are 48* **1952** *Iolanthe; The Mikado; The Pirates of Penzance; Trial by Jury/ H.M.S. Pinafore*

Joan Morse

Joan (Tiger) Morse, daughter of the architect M. Henry Sugarman, was a native New Yorker who studied at the Lincoln School and Syracuse University. She was a fashion designer with a penchant for clever accessories and avant-garde designs. Widely traveled, she searched around the world for unusual fabrics and ideas to sell in her boutiques. She occasionally contributed her designs to plays. Joan Morse, who spent most of her life in London, died April 22, 1972 at age 40 in New York City.
Costumes: 1962 *Rattle of a Simple Man* (Miss Grimes' clothes) **1963** *Rattle of a Simple Man*

Vicki Mortimer

Vicki Mortimer often designs sets and costumes for two of England's best known theaters, the Royal National Theatre and the Royal Shakespeare Company. She also designs for many other major U.K. theaters, including the Abbey Theatre, the Gate Theatre, the Young Vic, Almeida, and Donmar Warehouse. As head of design for Theatre Project Tokyo in Japan, she created sets and costumes for *The Changeling, Electra, Hedda Gabler, Three Sisters* and many more. She has also designed for opera and dance. Twenty-first century designs include *Mountain Language* and *Ashes to Ashes* as part of the Pinter Festival at Lincoln Center 2001, originally produced at the Royal Court Theatre, London.
Sets: 1999 *Closer* **2000** *The Real Thing*
Costumes: 1999 *Closer* **2000** *The Real Thing*

Winn Morton

Winn Morton was born on December 12, 1928 in Lancaster, Texas into a family of artists which included a scenic artist who specialized in opera house drops. He studied at the Parsons School of Design, the Ringling School of Art in Sarasota, Florida, and with Woodman Thompson. He began designing costumes in high school with a production of *The Gondoliers* and professionally for the Ringling Brothers

Circus. He has designed numerous costumes (and occasionally settings) since then on and off-Broadway, for television (*The Ed Sullivan Show* among others), and ice shows. Inspired by the movie musicals of the 1940s and 1950s, Winn Morton has won numerous awards for his creations. Since the mid-1980s he has designed from a ranch outside Dallas, Texas. Late twentieth century designs include a stage show for Six Flags over Georgia and costumes for the Texas Rose Festival,

Sets: 1968 *New Faces of 1968*
Costumes: 1967 *Spofford* **1968** *Avanti!*†; *The Education of H.Y.M.A.N. K.A.P.L.A.N.*; *New Faces of 1968* **1969** *A Teaspoon Every Four Hours* **1971** *How the Other Half Loves* **1980** *Blackstone!*

Jack Moser

Jack Moser designed costumes for a play in 1950.

Costumes: 1950 *Pardon Our French*

Moses and Hamilton

Thomas G. Moses and W. Franklin Hamilton collaborated on Broadway scenic designs during the first decade of the twentieth century, from a studio located at 1358 Broadway in 1902, moving to 1447 Broadway in 1904, in New York City. See their individual names for additional information and credits.

Sets: 1900 *Florodora*† (Designed and painted) **1901** *Under Southern Skies*† **1902** *Robert Emmet* **1904** *Girls Will Be Girls*†; *The Medal and the Maid*; *The Pit*†

Thomas G. Moses

Thomas G. Moses, a landscape painter and scenic artist, was born in Liverpool, England in 1856. He studied painting in Los Angeles and New York and then settled in Chicago, where he worked as a scenic artist for the Sosman & Landis Studio, beginning in 1877. From 1900 to 1904 he designed and painted scenery in New York City, where he was initially associated with the American Theatre, and then worked from a studio on Broadway in collaboration with W. Franklin Hamilton. When he returned to Chicago, he returned as well to Sosman & Landis Studio where he re-

mained until 1929, managing the studio and becoming president in 1915. Among the hundreds of backdrops he designed and painted were many for Masonic initiations and Scottish Rites. He painted landscapes from a studio in Los Angeles in the early 1930s, exhibiting with the Laguna Beach Art Association and the California Art Club. In 1933 he moved to Oak Park, Illinois, where he died in 1934. For additional credits and information, see the entry "Moses and Hamilton."

Sets: 1900 *Marie Antoinette* (Designed and painted); *Mary Stuart*

Jeffrey B. Moss

Jeffrey B. Moss, who designed costumes for two plays in 1974, is known primarily as a scenery and costume designer for network television, and as a producer and director. He was born January 8, 1945 and studied at Pennsylvania State University (B.A., 1966) and Columbia University (M.F.A., 1969). His sets have been seen in many Music Fair productions, including *Fiddler on the Roof* with Zero Mostel and *40 Carats* with Lana Turner, off-Broadway, for Dallas Shakespeare-in-the-Park and for the Carillon Dinner Theatre in Miami. He has directed numerous productions at the Starlight Playhouse since 1969, at Candlewood Playhouse, and *Annie* at the Goodspeed Opera House, among others. He also directed *Some Enchanted Evening* at the Queens Theatre in the Park in 1992 to celebrate the 50th anniversary of the collaboration between Richard Rodgers and Oscar Hammerstein 2d.

Costumes: 1973 *No Sex Please, We're British* **1974** *Fame*

Spencer Mosse

Lighting designer Spencer Mosse was born in New York City on October 17, 1945. He attended the Rudolf Steiner School where he began designing with productions of *The Mikado* and *The Christmas Play*. He has designed lights extensively in regional theaters throughout the United States and off-Broadway since serving an apprenticeship at age fifteen with John

Robertson and Martin Aronstein at the New York Shakespeare Festival. He attended Bard College where he designed over forty-five productions including dance pieces. At the Yale University School of Drama he designed the lighting for six productions and was the first student in the school's history to light a major production (*Coriolanus*) in his first year. He began his career as an assistant working and training with Gilbert V. Hemsley, Jr., Jean Rosenthal, Joan Larkey, H.R. Poindexter, Tharon Musser and John Gleason. Late twentieth century designs include lights for performances by Nina Winthrop and Dancers and productions in the major regional theaters in the U.S.

Lights: 1974 *Lamppost Reunion*; *Mourning Pictures*; *Rainbow Jones* **1976** *Godspell*

Ramsé Mostoller

Ramsé Stevens Mosteller was born February 2, 1924 in Kansas City. She received a B.A. at the University of Kansas, but did not turn her talents to costume design until attending the 57th Street Art School in New York City. She worked as a draper at Brooks Costume Company with Mr. Swan and worked for designers Irene Sharaff, Dorothy Jeakins and Karinska. Her first costume design assignment in New York was *The Thurber Carnival* as Ramsé Stevens. She has designed numerous costumes for plays and lots of television, including shows on all three major commercial networks. She is married to Joseph Frederick Mostoller, who is also a costume designer.

Costumes: 1960 *A Thurber Carnival* (as: Ramsé Stevens) **1962** *The Affair*

Motley

Motley is the trade name of three scenery and costume designers from Britain. The trio consisted of two sisters, Margaret Harris and (Audrey) Sophia Harris Devine, who worked mainly in London, and Elizabeth Montgomery, who represented them in the United States. They first worked together to design a production of *Romeo and Juliet* for the Oxford University Dramatic Society in 1932, and

from then until the early 1970s designed countless plays and operas in England and the United States. The three met in art school and entered a contest at the Old Vic's annual costume ball. They won half the prizes and a job offer from the judge, John Gielgud. Elizabeth Montgomery was born on February 15, 1904 in Kidlington, Oxfordshire, England, and studied at the Westminster School of Art. She died in May 1993. Sophia Harris Devine was born in 1901 and died in 1966. Margaret Frances Harris, known as Percy, had a long term relationship with Riverside Studios and was head of the design course at Almeda Theatre in London, was born May 28, 1904 and died on May 10, 2000. Motley's first Broadway design was *Romeo and Juliet* for Laurence Olivier and Vivian Leigh. Winners of numerous awards, their Tony's include *The First Gentlemen* (1958) and *Becket* (1961) and many additional nominations. Their name is taken from a line of Jacques in *As You Like It*, in which he says "Motley's the only wear." A large collection of their designs are in the permanent collection of the University of Illinois at Urbana-Champaign and in 1996 *Design by Motley*, by Michael Mullin, was published by the University of Delaware Press.

Sets: 1940 *Romeo and Juliet* **1942** *The Three Sisters* **1943** *Lovers and Friends*; *Richard III* **1944** *A Bell for Adano*; *The Cherry Orchard* **1945** *Hope for the Best*; *Skydrift*; *The Tempest*; *You Touched Me* **1946** *The Dancer*; *He Who Gets Slapped*; *Second Best Boy* **1947** *The Importance of Being Earnest* **1950** *Happy As Larry* **1957** *Country Wife* **1959** *Requiem for a Nun†* **1961** *The Complaisant Lover*; *A Man for All Seasons*; *Ross*

Costumes: 1934 *Richard of Bordeaux* **1940** *Romeo and Juliet* **1941** *Doctor's Dilemma* **1942** *The Three Sisters* **1943** *Lovers and Friends* **1944** *A Bell for Adano*; *The Cherry Orchard*; *A Highland Fling*; *Sadie Thompson* **1945** *Carib Song*; *Pygmalion*; *Skydrift*; *The Tempest*; *You Touched Me* **1946** *The Dancer*; *He Who Gets Slapped*; *Second Best Boy* **1947** *The Importance of Being Earnest* (Design by) **1948** *Anne of 1000 Days* **1949**

Miss Liberty; *South Pacific* **1950** *Happy As Larry*; *The Innocents*; *The Liar*; *Peter Pan* **1951** *The Grand Tour*; *Paint Your Wagon* **1952** *Candida*; *To Be Continued* **1953** *Can-Can*; *Mid-summer* **1954** *The Immoralist*; *Mademoiselle Colombe*; *Peter Pan* **1955** *The Honeys*; *Island of Goats*; *The Young and Beautiful* **1956** *Long Day's Journey into Night*; *Middle of the Night*; *The Most Happy Fella* **1957** *Country Wife*; *The First Gentleman*; *Look Homeward, Angel*; *Shinbone Alley* **1958** *The Cold Wind and the Warm*; *Jane Eyre*†; *Love Me Little* **1959** *A Majority of One*; *Requiem for a Nun*; *The Rivalry* **1960** *Becket* **1961** *Kwamina*; *A Man for All Seasons*; *Ross* **1963** *110 Degrees in the Shade*; *Lorenzo*; *Mother Courage and Her Children*; *Tovarich* **1964** *Ben Franklin in Paris* **1965** *Baker Street*; *The Devils* **1966** *Don't Drink the Water*
Lights: **1959** *Requiem for a Nun*

Allen Moyer

Since Allen Moyer completed study at the Tisch School of the Arts at New York University, he has designed scenery for productions throughout the world. He designed *Threepenny Opera* at the Accademia di Santa Cecilia in Rome, *Friend of the People* for the Scottish Opera, as well as productions at the Gate Theatre in Dublin, the Canadian Opera Company, in many regional theaters in the United States and off-Broadway houses. A member of the Drama Dept., he often collaborates with Mark Brokaw. Twenty-first century designs include *Street Scene* and *The Man Who Had all the Luck* at the Williamstown Theatre Festival, *Lobby Hero* at Playwrights Horizons, and *A Thousand Clowns* at the beginning of the 2001-2002 Broadway season.
Sets: **1996** *Tartuffe: Born Again*

Alphonse Mucha

Alphonse Maria Mucha, painter and designer is known mainly for his many poster designs in the Art Nouveau style, particularly those he created for Sarah Bernhardt in the 1890s. He was born in Ivancice, Moravia (Czech Republic) in 1860 and between 1879 and 1884 he worked in Vienna as a scenic artist. He then studied painting at the École des Beaux-Arts in Prague, in Munich and in Paris. In the late 1880s he began creating graphic designs and book illustrations. He taught briefly in New York at the School of Applied Design for Women and returned to America (as he did to other places) when commissioned works required his presence. He also designed jewelry, textiles, wallpaper, furniture, stage settings, and advertisements. Much exhibited and collected, his work was the subject of a retrospective at the Victoria and Albert Museum in London in 1963. Mucha died in 1939.
Sets: **1909** *Kassa*

Mrs. E. J. Muldoon

Mrs. E. J. (Emma J.) Muldoon collaborated on the costumes for one play and designed another in 1917. A dressmaker, she had a small shop at 726 Madison Avenue and made her home at 2688 Broadway during the late teens. In the early 1920s she lived at 300 West 128th Street.
Costumes: **1917** *Lord and Lady Algy*† (Guests Act II dresses, after drawings by Ben Ali Haggin); *The Old Country*

Henry Mulle

Henry Mulle designed costumes on Broadway in 1948.
Costumes: **1948** *Sally*

Joseph Mullen

Joseph Mullen, interior designer and arts philanthropist, designed scenery and costumes on Broadway during the 1920s. His scenic designs also include John Gay's opera *Polly* in 1926, and productions for Gilbert Miller productions, before he devoted his talents to interior design. He was president in the 1940s of the organization which became the American Institute of Interior Designers. Joseph Mullen died at age 73 in 1974.
Sets: **1924** *The Way of the World* **1925** *Wild Birds* **1926** *Bad Habits of 1926*; *The Right to Kill* **1927** *The Garden of Eden* **1930** *Gala Night*; *Petticoat Influence*† **1931** *Paging Danger*
Costumes: **1924** *The Man Who Ate the Popomack* (Chinese Costumes); *The Way of the World* **1926** *Bad Habits of 1926*;

The Right to Kill 1927 *The Garden of Eden*; *A Lady in Love*

Ralph Mulligan

Deborah Shaw received her B.A. from Hampshire College in Amherst, Massachusetts after which she gained experience in the costume shops at Equity Library Theatre and Juilliard, and as an assistant to Jennifer von Mayrhauser. She has designed costumes at many off-Broadway theaters, including Playwrights Horizons, Second Stage, Circle Repertory Company, Double Image, and the Vineyard Theatre. As a member of Ensemble Studio Theatre, she created costumes for many productions, including *To Gillian on Her 37th Birthday*, *Rose Cottages*, *Dream of a Blacklisted Actor* and several evenings of the Marathon (EST's one-act play festival). Among her credits in regional theaters are productions at StageWest, the Berkshire Theatre Festival, Papermill Playhouse, and the Hartmann Theatre. Recent credits include the film *Santa Fe*.

Costumes: 1921 *Music Box Revue*† (Costumes and dresses); *The Rose Girl* 1922 *Music Box Revue* (Costumes for the Diamond Horseshoe, etc.)

Stephen Mullin

Stephen Mullin designed one set in 1964 on Broadway. His review of *The Image of the Architect* by Andrew Saint appeared in the March 1983 issue of *The New Statesman*.

Sets: 1964 *Cambridge Circus*

Marcel Multzer

Marcel Multzer, who designed costumes for a production in the first season of the twentieth century on Broadway, and another in 1911, was known mainly as a costume designer for grand opera. He lived from 1866 to 1937, and designed mostly in Europe, including productions at La Scala. His costume designs have been widely exhibited and examples were included in *Georges Bizet* published by Museo Teatrale alla Scala in 1975, and *Opera Journeys* by Martine Kahane in 1993.

Costumes: 1899 *Robespierre* 1911 *Gypsy Love*† (Other costumes)

Peter Mumford

Peter Mumford, who won the 1995 Laurence Olivier Award for Outstanding Achievement in Dance for designs for *The Glass Blew In* (Siobohn Davies) and *Fearful Symmetries* (Royal Ballet), is also a director for film and television. He studied at the Central School of Art and has designed lights for dance, opera and theater. His designs have been seen at the Royal Shakespeare Company, the Royal National Theatre, Almeida Theatre, and the English National Opera among others. Twenty-first century credits include *Troilus and Cressida* at the Old Vic, *Medea* and *God Only Knows* in London's West End, *Hamlet* in Stratford-upon-Avon, and *Arthur* (Parts 1 and 2) for the Birmingham Royal Ballet.

Lights: 1997 *A Doll's House*; *Stanley*

Leon Munier

Leon Munier, a television art director and production designer, also designed a set in 1967 on Broadway. Off-Broadway productions include of *Torch Song Trilogy* at Actors Playhouse. He served as art director for the made-for-TV movies *Choices*, *King of America* and *Too Far to Go*, among others and was production designer for *Terrible Joe Moran*.

Sets: 1967 *The Ninety-Day Mistress*

Mercedes Muniz

Mercedes Muniz designed costumes for a 1992 flamenco revue.

Costumes: 1992 *Gypsy Passion*

Tom Munn

Thomas J. Munn was born on March 24, 1944 in New Britain, Connecticut. He received a B.F.A. from Boston University School of Fine Arts in 1967, where he studied with Raymond Sovey and Horace Armistead. His professional debut was *The Heiress* at the Theatre-by-the-Sea in Portsmouth, New Hampshire. He credits Dore Schary, producer and playwright, for his first Broadway production, *Brightower*. Since 1976 he has been Lighting Director and Design Consultant for the San Francisco

Opera, where he has amassed numerous credits in lighting, scenic design and special effects. Tom Munn received an Emmy Award in Lighting for the SFO production of *La Gioconda* in 1979 and an Emmy nomination for the world premiere telecast of the opera *A Streetcar Named Desire* in 1998. Lighting designs include *The Ballad of Baby Doe* for New York City Opera, and productions for opera companies in Houston, Dallas, San Diego, Washington, New Orleans, Amsterdam and Sendai, Japan. In addition to designing lights for opera companies, regional theaters, off-Broadway, dance and industrial promotions, he has also served as lighting and theater consultant for projects such as the Muziektheater in Amsterdam and the War Memorial Opera House in San Francisco.

Sets: **1970** *Brightower*

Rob Munnik

Rob Munnik designed lights in 1982 for a Broadway production starring Herman van Veen, a Dutch theater-artist. The production was successful in Europe and the United Kingdom before transferring to New York.

Lights: **1982** *Herman Van Veen: All of Him*

C. Murawski

C. Murawski was 17 years old when he became a stage manager for the Starlight Theatre in Kansas City, Missouri. Television productions include Barbra Streisand specials, Alan King productions and the Kraft Music Hall productions of *Death of a Salesman, The Pueblo,* and *Celebrity Charades.* Productions off-Broadway include *A View from the Bridge, Canterbury Tales* and *Fortune in Men's Eyes.*

Sets: **1975** *Shenandoah*

David Murin

David Murin was born in Pittsburgh, Pennsylvania in 1952. He received a B.F.A. at Yale, where he studied with Oliver Smith, and designed his first costumes for a production of *The Three Sisters.* His M.F.A. was awarded at New York University in 1974. In addition to designing, he worked for Ray

Diffen and in 1978 debuted on Broadway with *Gorey Stories,* collaborating with Edward Gorey on the costumes. David Murin, who is usually considered a period theatrical designer, won an Emmy in 1981 for his costumes on the daytime drama *Ryan's Hope.* He has been resident designer for the Philadelphia Drama Guild and taught at Temple University and Rutgers University. Among his many off-Broadway credits are *Ladyhouse Blues, Fortune's Fools* and *A Quiet End.* Twenty-first century designs include *Funny Girl, Down the Garden Paths* and *The Shadow of Greatness.*

Costumes: **1978** *Gorey Stories* **1979** *Devour the Snow* **1981** *Ned and Jack; The One Act Play Festival; A Talent for Murder* **1982** *Blues in the Night* **1983** *The Caine Mutiny Court Martial* **1990** *Change in the Heir* **1993** *Mixed Emotions*

Rupert Murray

Rupert Murray was born in England and studied at Trinity College, Dublin. His debut as a lighting designer was *Savages* for the Dublin University Players. In addition to credits in the United Kingdom, many for the Gate Theatre, and the Samuel Beckett Centre, he has designed lights in France, Italy, Hong Kong and the United States. He founded Lighting Dimensions in Ireland, a company specializing in theatrical lighting equipment. He has also designed fashion shows, and commercial projects and increasingly works as a theater producer. He coordinated the 1991 Beckett Festival in Dublin, and in 1996 became Director of Dublin's annual St. Patrick's Festival.

Lights: **1988** *Juno and the Paycock* **1996** *Riverdance; Riverdance - The Show* **1997** *Riverdance* **1998** *Riverdance* **2000** *Riverdance on Broadway*

Merrily Murray-Walsh

Merrily Murray-Walsh (Murray) is from Oakland, California. After receiving a B.A. at Mills College in history she worked for four years in the costume shop at the Oregon Shakespeare Festival. She received an M.F.A. from Carnegie Mellon University in Costume Design, and then returned, this time to design costumes for the Oregon Shakespeare Festival beginning with *Tartuffe*. She has also designed for many regional theaters, including *Les Trois Dumas* at the Indiana Repertory Theatre, and on the West Coast. In 1982 she moved to New York and since then has designed costumes both on and off-Broadway, for operas, and for films. Projects for TNT include *In Search of Dr. Seuss, Kingfish: A Story of Huey P. Long*, and *When the Lion Roars*. Late twentieth century credits include the costume design for *Playback* at the Court Theatre.

Costumes: 1983 *Brothers* **1991** *The Speed of Darkness*

Madame Louise Museus

Madame Louise Museus designed costumes on Broadway in 1905.

Costumes: 1905 *Fedora*

Jane Musky

Jane Musky designs primarily for film and has been production designer for *When Harry Met Sally, Young Guns, Raising Arizona, Blood Simple, Company Man, The Object of My Affection* and *Finding Forrester*, among others. She was born Jane Michelle Musky in New Jersey on May 27, 1954 and received a B.F.A. in 1976 at Boston University. Off-Broadway she designed *Marathon 1984* at the Ensemble Studio Theatre and *Hackers* at the Manhattan Punchline Theatre. In 1981 she was production designer of the Second Company of the Williamstown Theatre Festival, and in 1982 was assistant designer on the Mainstage. Her designs have been influenced by travel throughout Europe and work at Harker's Studio, London. She was assistant designer and scenic artist for productions designed by David Hockney, Ralph Koltai and Julia Oman at the English National Opera, Glyndebourne Opera and Pinewood Studios. Honors include an Academy Award nomination for best short film in 1983 for *Split Cherry Tree* and an Emmy Award nomination for production designs in 1984 for an ABC-TV *Afterschool Special*.

Sets: 1985 *The News*

Tharon Musser

Tharon Musser was born on January 8, 1925 in Roanoke, Virginia. She received a B.A. in 1946 from Berea College in Kentucky and an M.F.A. from Yale University in 1950. She worked at the Provincetown Playhouse, the YMHA and for José Limon as a stage manager and lighting designer, gaining background to launch her own prolific career and in the process helping to advance the field of lighting design to its present professional level. Her contributions include being the first lighting designer to use a computer lighting system on Broadway. Her Broadway debut was the premier of *A Long Day's Journey Into The Night* in 1956, the first of over 100 Broadway productions. She has designed plays and many notable musicals and operas throughout the world, and often consults with architects such as Webb & Knapp on lighting for buildings at colleges, universities and theater complexes. One of the dominant lighting designers on Broadway, she has been nominated for numerous Tony Awards and received them for *Follies, A Chorus Line* and *Dreamgirls*. She has lectured widely on lighting design, been the subject of many articles, and influenced scores of assistants and colleagues.

Lights: 1956 *Long Day's Journey into Night* **1957** *The Makropoulos Secret; Monique; Shinbone Alley* **1958** *The Firstborn; J.B.; The Shadow of a Gunman* **1959** *Five Finger Exercise; Only in America; The Rivalry* **1960** *The Long Dream; The Tumbler* **1961** *The Garden of Secrets* **1962** *Calculated Risk; Giants, Sons of Giants; Nowhere to Go But Up* **1963** *Andorra; Here's Love; Marathon '33; Mother Courage and Her Children* **1964** *Alfie; Any Wednesday; The Crucible; Golden Boy; The Seagull* **1965** *All in Good Time; Flora, the Red Menace; Kelly; Minor Miracle* **1966** *A Delicate Balance; The Great Indoors; The Lion in Winter; Malcolm; Mame* **1967** *After the Rain; The Birthday Party; Everything in the Garden; Hallelujah, Baby!; The Imaginary Invalid; The Promise; Tonight at 8:30; A Touch of the Poet* **1968** *Maggie Flynn* **1969** *The Fig Leaves Are Falling; The Gingham Dog* **1970** *Applause; Blood Red Roses; The*

Boy Friend **1971** *Follies; On the Town; The Prisoner of 2nd Avenue; The Trial of the Catonsville Nine* **1972** *The Creation of the World and Other Business; Night Watch; The Sunshine Boys* **1973** *The Good Doctor; A Little Night Music* **1974** *Candide; God's Favorite; Good News; Mack and Mabel; Me and Bessie* **1975** *A Chorus Line; The Wiz* **1976** *1600 Pennsylvania Avenue; California Suite; Pacific Overtures* **1977** *The Act; Chapter Two* **1978** *Ballroom; Tribute* **1979** *Last Licks; Romantic Comedy; They're Playing Our Song; Who's Life Is It Anyway?* **1980** *42nd Street; Children of a Lesser God; I Ought to Be in Pictures; The Roast; Who's Life Is It Anyway?* **1981** *Dreamgirls; Fools; The Moony Shapiro Song Book* **1982** *Special Occasions* **1983** *Brighton Beach Memoirs; Merlin; Private Lives* **1984** *Open Admissions; The Real Thing* **1985** *Biloxi Blues; Jerry's Girls; The Odd Couple* **1986** *Broadway Bound* **1987** *Dreamgirls; A Month of Sundays; Teddy and Alice* **1988** *Rumors* **1989** *Artist Descending a Staircase; Welcome to the Club* **1991** *Lost in Yonkers; The Secret Garden* **1992** *Juno and the Paycock* **1993** *The Goodbye Girl; Laughter on the 23rd Floor* **1995** *Uncle Vanya* **1999** *The Lonesome West*

Pieter Myer

Pieter Myer was active on Broadway between 1919 and 1922 as a scenery and costume designer. He was president in 1922 of Armstrong & Myer, Inc., 200 West 10th Street in New York City, where he worked in collaboration with costume designer Dorothy Armstrong. Also an artist, he had a studio in his home at 50 West 10th Street.

Sets: 1922 *Greenwich Village Follies†*
Costumes: 1919 *Greenwich Village Follies†* (Javanes and batik) **1921** *Tangerine†* ("Tangerian Island")

Helen Myers

Helen Myers designed gowns for a play in 1921. A dressmaker, she resided at 190 East Houston Street in the 1920s.

Costumes: 1921 *The Right Girl* (Act I and II gowns)

John Napier

Born in London on March 1, 1944, John Napier studied at the Hornsey

College of Art before training as a designer of sets and costumes at the Central School of Arts and Crafts. After working at the Leicester Phoenix as Head of Design, he joined the Open Space Theatre as Resident Designer and subsequently became associate designer for the Royal Shakespeare Company. He has designed extensively in London's West End and for the Royal Shakespeare Company, the Royal National Theatre, and the Royal Opera House. His Broadway debut was *Equus* in 1974, and in 1982 he received his first Tony Award for the sets for *The Life and Adventures of Nicholas Nickleby*. He also won Tony Awards for *Cats* (costumes), *Starlight Express* (costumes), *Les Miserables* (sets), and *Sunset Boulevard* (sets). He has designed sets and costumes around the world for television, film and opera, making his Metropolitan Opera debut with *Nabucco* in 2000. He was married at one time to costume and fashion designer Andreane Neofitou, with whom he continues to collaborate. Designs for film include *Hook*, and for video, *Captain Eo* for Disney.

Sets: 1974 *Equus* **1976** *Equus* **1981** *Life and Adventures of Nicholas Nickleby,†* **1982** *Cats* **1987** *Les Miserables; Starlight Express* **1991** *Miss Saigon* **1994** *Sunset Boulevard* **2000** *Jane Eyre*
Costumes: 1974 *Equus* **1976** *Equus* **1981** *Life and Adventures of Nicholas Nickleby,* **1982** *Cats* **1986** *The Life and Adventures of Nicholas Nickleby* **1987** *Starlight Express*

Geoffrey Nares

Geoffrey Nares, actor and designer, was born in London on June 10, 1917. From his debut in 1934 through the end of the 1930s he acted in many plays, mainly in London. He also designed plays such as *Girl Unknown* and *Candida*. One of them, *George and Margaret*, subsequently played on Broadway. He died at age 25 on August 20, 1942.

Sets: 1937 *George and Margaret*

Brian Nason

After receiving an M.F.A. at New York University's Tisch School of the

Arts, Brian Nason assisted Tharon Musser during the 1987-88 season. He has extensive credits off-Broadway including productions at the New York Shakespeare Festival, Manhattan Theatre Club, Jewish Repertory Theatre, Lamb's Theatre, and many more. He also designs for regional theaters including the Long Wharf Theatre, Williamstown Theatre Festival, Seattle Repertory Theatre, Mark Taper Forum, and the Oregon Shakespeare Festival. He is resident designer for both Déja Vu Dance Theatre and the Charles Ragland Dance Company. Brian Nason also designed lights for the feature film, *Sing*, and on television for *O Pioneers* and *Great Performances: Live From Carnegie Hall*. His lighting designs for *Metamorphosis* were nominated for a Tony Award and those for *Birdy* at the Philadelphia Theatre Company won the Barrymore Award.

Lights: 1989 *3Penny Opera†*; *Metamorphosis* 1993 *Cyrano: The Musical†* 1994 *Broken Glass* 1995 *A Month in the Country* 1997 *1776* 2000 *Taller Than a Dwarf*

Mrs. Condé Nast

From 1902 until their divorce in 1923, J. Clairsse Coudert was married to the publishing magnate Condé Nast (1874-1942). They had two children, Natica Nast Warburg and Charles Coudert Nast. Her father was Charles R. Coudert, partner in Coudert Brothers an international law firm with offices in Paris and New York. It is well known that Condé Nast was actively involved in theater, society, and business, so it is not surprising that Mrs. Nast would contribute scenic and costume designs to a Broadway production, as she did in 1914.

Sets: 1914 *The Salamander*
Costumes: 1914 *The Salamander*

L. and H. Nathan

The British costume house L. and H. Nathan's flourished from 1790 until 1972, and was located at 17 Coventry street for most of that time. While the house mainly executed costumes for designers and rented them to a variety of producing organizations, occasionally it was responsible for designs

as well. The designs were created by house designers whose names are not known.

Costumes: 1901 *A Message from Mars†* 1903 *The Proud Prince†* 1908 *The Fool Hath Said: 'There Is No God'†* 1910 *Henry of Navarre†* (Other costumes); *The Scarlet Pimpernel†* (Other costumes) 1911 *Macbeth (Kellerd)†* (Costumes, weapons, and jewelry) 1912 *Milestones†*

Curt Nations

Curt Nations designed one set in 1959 on Broadway.

Sets: 1959 *Happy Town*

Anne Neacy

Anne Neacy designed costumes and masks on Broadway in 1922. At that same time, she resided at 135 West 56th Street in New York City.

Costumes: 1922 *Taboo* (Costumes and masks)

Caspar Neher

Rudolf Ludwig Caspar Neher designed many plays for Bertolt Brecht including *Eduard II, Baal* and *In Dickicht der Stadte*. A German designer, he was born in Augsburg in 1897 and studied at the Munich School of Applied Arts and the Munich Academy of Arts. From 1934 to 1944 he worked at the Deutsches Theatre in Berlin. In 1948 he designed *Antizione* for Brecht in Switzerland and then returned to Germany to design *Herr Puntila* and *Sein Knecht Malti*. He also designed for the Salzburg Festival and the Vienna Opera. Credits at the Metropolitan Opera include *Wozzeck*. Caspar Neher, who died in Vienna on June 30, 1962 has had two major retrospective exhibitions: "Caspar Neher: Brecht's Designer" at Riverside Studios with an accompanying book by the same name by John Willett, published in 1986, and "Bertolt Brecht and Caspar Neher" at the City Museum of Berlin.

Sets: 1933 *The Threepenny Opera†*

Mrs. Seeley Neilson

Mrs. Seeley Neilson designed costumes on Broadway in 1932.

Costumes: 1932 *When Ladies Meet*

Alfred Nelson

Alfred Nelson, a clothing designer, contributed designs to a musical revue in 1921. He specialized in riding apparel and sports clothing and worked for his own company as well as firms in New York, Chicago and Louisville, Kentucky. At the time of his death in 1952, he was head of the custom tailor division of Coffee-Starck Company in Cleveland, Ohio.

Costumes: 1921 *Ziegfeld Follies: 1921*† (Johnny Dress clothes)

Richard Nelson

Richard Nelson was born on December 7, 1938 in Flushing, New York and graduated from the High School of Performing Arts in 1956. His first professional productions were *The Winslow Boy* in 1955 at the Master Institute in New York City (later Equity Library Theatre) and *Hamlet of Stepney Green* in 1958 at the Cricket Theatre off-Broadway. He proceeded to design numerous shows on and off-Broadway, in regional and international theaters. He was principal designer and production manager for the dance companies of Merce Cunningham, José Limon, Louis Falco as well as for other dance and ballet companies. His architectural lighting projects included the Herman Miller Pavilion in Grand Rapids, Michigan, the Palm Court of the Wintergarden at the World Financial Center, and the Con Ed Energy Conservation Center in New York. He received the Tony, Drama Desk and Maharam Awards for *Sunday in the Park with George* and Maharams for *Serenading Louie* and *The Tap Dance Kid*, among other awards. From 1988 to 1991 he was Associate Professor of Theatre at the University of Michigan, and then served on the faculty of the Tisch School of the Arts at New York University. At the time of his death on November 6, 1996 at age 57, he was in the process of designing *Golden Child* for the Joseph Papp Public Theatre.

Lights: 1966 *Caucasian Chalk Circle* 1970 *Water Color/ Criss Crossing* 1971 *All Over* 1972 *The Sign in Sidney Brustein's Window* 1974 *The Magic Show* 1976 *So Long, 174th Street*; *Zal-*

men or the Madness of God 1977 *The Trip Back Down* 1979 *Murder at the Howard Johnson's* 1980 *Censored Scenes from King Kong*; *The Lady from Dubuque*; *Morning's at Seven*; *Onward Victoria* 1981 *Oh, Brother*; *The Supporting Cast* 1982 *A Little Family Business*; *Present Laughter*; *Solomon's Child* 1983 *The Caine Mutiny Court Martial*; *The Corn Is Green*; *Five-Six-Seven-Eight... Dance!*; *The Misanthrope*; *The Tapdance Kid* 1984 *Awake and Sing*; *Sunday in the Park with George* 1985 *Arms and the Man*; *Harrigan 'n Hart* 1986 *The Boys in Autumn*; *Long Day's Journey into Night*; *Loot*; *Precious Sons*; *You Can Never Tell* 1987 *Blithe Spirit*; *Into the Woods*; *Sleight of Hand* 1988 *Mail*; *The Night of the Iguana* 1989 *Cafe Crown*; *The Secret Rapture* 1991 *The Crucible* 1992 *A Little Hotel on the Side*; *The Master Builder*; *Private Lives*; *The Seagull*; *Shimada* 1993 *Saint Joan*; *Three Men on a Horse*; *Timon of Athens* 1994 *Comedy Tonight*; *The Flowering Peach*; *Government Inspector, Then*; *No Man's Land*; *The Shadow Box* 1995 *The Molière Comedies*; *Swinging on a Star*

Andreane Neofitou

Andreane (Andy) Neofitou, a British fashion and costume designer born in 1943, has designed for the Royal Shakespeare Company, often in collaboration with John Napier and Trevor Nunn. She designed *Hedda Gabbler, Once in a Lifetime, Peter Pan, The Changeling,* and others for the Royal Shakespeare Company. She also designed costumes for Gemma Craven and Liz Robertson in *Song & Dance*. Her designs for film include *Rosencrantz and Guildenstern Are Dead*, directed by playwright Tom Stoppard. Among her honors are a Tony Award nomination for *Les Miserables*. Twenty-first century credits include costume designs for *Martin Guerre* by Cameron Mackintosh, and *Nabucco* for the Metropolitan Opera.

Sets: 1986 *The Life and Adventures of Nicholas Nickleby*

Costumes: 1987 *Les Miserables* 1991 *Miss Saigon*† 2000 *Jane Eyre*

Neppel and Brousseau

Neppel and Brousseau collaborated on the scenic design for a Broadway pro-

duction in 1929. Hermann Neppel was a sculptor born in Munich in 1882 who created tombstones, busts and decorative sculpture. His partner, James Brousseau, also operated Brousseau Scenic Construction Company at 428 11th Avenue in New York City in 1927. In 1932, James Brousseau was employed by Cleon Throckmorton, Inc.
Sets: 1929 *White Flame*

Byron Nestor

Byron Nestor was a dressmaker who lived at 25 East 209th street in New York City. His design for "Paco" for *Triana*, one of La Argentina's ballets, was published in a 1929 issue of *Theatre Arts*. He was born January 29, 1898 and died in 1964.
Costumes: 1911 *The Scarcrow*

Mrs. Nettleship

Mrs. Nettleship, of Wigmore Street, London, contributed costume designs to Broadway productions between 1905 and 1912. She often received credit in London playbills in similar circumstances. Credits before 1900 in New York include gowns for Olga Nethersole's appearances with her Repertory Company in *Frou-Frou, Denise, Camille* and *Carmen* in the 1895-1896 season.
Costumes: 1905 *Carmen*† (Miss Nethersole's costumes) **1907** *The Little Michus*† **1908** *Adrienne Lecouvreur*† (Miss Nethersole's costumes); *Carmen*† (Miss Nethersole's costumes) **1910** *Henry of Navarre*† (Miss Nelson's gowns); *The Scarlet Pimpernel*† (Miss Nelson's dresses) **1912** *Lady Patricia* (Dresses)

Siren Nevarro

The credit for costume designs in *The Shoo-Fly Regiment* reads "costume designs and Luneta dances arranged by Miss Siren Nevarro" who also appeared as "Grizelle, a Filipino dancer" in the 1907 production.
Costumes: 1907 *The Shoo-Fly Regiment*† (Also appeared and choreographed)

Newby and Alexander

Newby and Alexander collaborated on scenery for a production on Broadway in 1921. Newby might refer to one of two individuals active at that time:

George Newby was a painter who lived at 641 East 222nd Street and David A. Newby was an engineer who resided at 2436 Marion Avenue.It is possible that Alexander refers to Elizabeth (Mrs. John) Alexander, a costume designer who occasionally designed sets.
Sets: 1921 *Sun-kist*

Gertrude Newell

Gertrude Newell, born and raised in St. Johnsbury, Vermont, studied painting in Italy with Frazatti and in Allegheri's studio. She began professional life as an interior decorator. The design of a door for Grace George's production of *Major Barbara* led her to a theatrical design career. She also produced plays in New York and at the Ambassador Theatre in London. The playbills for *The Earth* and *Major Barbara* refer to her as Gertrude Newell Dudley. She produced *Maya* in 1928 at the Comedy Theatre with sets and costumes by Aline Bernstein. The annotation of "supervisor" for *The Age of Innocence* in 1928 was as a result of a ruling by the scenic artists' union. She also designed as Gertrude Newell Dudley but should not be confused with Professor Gertrude Dudley (d. 1945) for whom Dudley Field at the University of Chicago is named.
Sets: 1915 *The Earth*† (as: Gertrude Newell Dudley); *Major Barbara* (as: Gertrude Newell Dudley) **1916** *Pendennis* **1917** *The Claim*†; *Peter Ibbetson*† **1918** *Forever After* **1921** *The Fair Circassian* (Also produced) **1928** *The Age of Innocence*† (Set supervisor)
Costumes: 1916 *Pendennis* **1917** *The Claim*† (Also accessories); *Hamilton*† (Costume Supervisor); *Peter Ibbetson*† **1920** *Little Old New York* **1921** *The Fair Circassian* (Also produced) **1928** *The Age of Innocence*† (Costume Supervisor)
Lights: 1916 *Pendennis*

Karyl Newman

Costume designer Karyl Newman received her M.F.A. at the Yale University School of Drama. While there, she designed *The Beaux Stratagem*, among productions for the Yale Repertory Theatre. As an active designer

for film and television, she was production designer for the movie *Urban Folk Tales*, and *Leopold and Loeb* and *The Unknown Lincoln*, both for the History Channel. Regional theater designs include productions for Theatre on the Square in San Francisco.
Costumes: 1999 *Not about Nightingales*

Stella Mary Newton
See Stella Mary Pearce.

F. S. Neydhart
F. S. Neydhardt contributed scenic designs to a Broadway production in 1904.
Costumes: 1904 *The Sho-gun*†

Michelle Nezwarsky
Michelle Nezwarsky coordinated costumes for a Broadway show in 1978.
Costumes: 1978 *Neighborhood Playhouse at 50-A Celebration*† (Costume Coordinator)

J. Nievinsky
J. Nievinsky designed scenery for a Broadway production in 1948. He should not be confused with Ignatiy Ignat'evich Nivinsky (1881-1933), the Russian graphic artist whose designs influenced Boris Aronson.
Sets: 1948 *The Golem*

Greta and Agnes Nissen
Greta and Agnes Nissen performed in and contributed costume designs to a musical revue in 1926. Greta was born Grethe Ruzt-Nissen on January 30, 1906 in Oslo, Norway. She danced as a child, and her first stage appearance occurred at age 6. She studied with Michel Fokine, and came to the U.S. in 1923. She was a big star in silent films, discovered on Broadway in *Beggar on Horseback*, and spent 10 years in Hollywood making them. Her movie career faded with the advent of talkies, due to her Scandinavian accent, Producer Howard Hughes replaced her with Jean Harlow in *Hell's Angels*, although she appeared on stage in London in the early 1930s. She retired from stage and film in 1937, married Stuart D. Eckert in 1941, and died in Montecito, California on May 15, 1988. Little is known of Agnes Ruzt-Nissen, who

was born in Oslo on July 23, 1879 and died in Los Angeles on January 6, 1949.
Costumes: 1926 *No Foolin'*†

No Playbill Available
Nearly 10,000 productions occurred on Broadway during the twentieth century. It was impossible to locate playbills for 62 of the plays produced between 1900 and 1914, to see if they contained any information about designers. The index of this book states "NO PLAYBILL" for these productions.

Jacques Noël
Jacques Noël, a French designer, born in Ivry on November 7, 1924, designed scenery and costumes for a play in 1960. He is primarily a scenic designer who has often worked with Jacques Baratier and for the Marcel Marceau Mime Company. His Paris debut, in 1946 at the Théâtre de Babylone for *Le Marchand D'Étoites*, was followed by numerous other productions for a variety of theaters. He has designed often for the Aix-En-Provence Festival, including the 1982 *Il Turco in Italia*, directed by Jean-Louis Thamin. He also designed for the major opera and ballet companies in London. In 1992 he designed *Doublages* in Lille, *Lautrec Sur La Butte* in Paris, *Deux Femmes Pour Un Fantôme* which toured France, and a film version *Le Chapeau Melon* of a mime by Marcel Marceau. A lavishly illustrated book of his designs, *Jacques Noël: Théâtres*, also containing an interview conducted by Christian Guidicelli, was published in Paris in 1993.
Sets: 1960 *The Good Soup*
Costumes: 1960 *The Good Soup*

Madame Najla Nogabgat
Madame Najla Nogabgat (also Najilia Nozobgat) designed costumes for two Broadway plays.
Costumes: 1910 *Mary Magdalene* (Miss Nethersole's costumes) **1915** *The Clever Ones*† (Gowns)

David Noling
David Noling was born on February 6, 1955 in Indianapolis, Indiana. He received a B.A. in 1977 in art and an M.F.A. in 1982 in design at Yale.

He has designed off-Broadway at the New Theatre of Brooklyn, Manhattan Punch Line, Westside Arts Center, SoHo Repertory, Playwrights Horizon and the Manhattan Theatre Club among others. He was nominated for an Audelco Recognition Award for *Sgt. Ola and His Followers* at SoHo Repertory in 1987. He has many credits for regional theaters, dance companies, and as an assistant to lighting designers Frances Aronson, Thomas Skelton and Jennifer Tipton. Through Tapestry Productions he also works with television, film and video.

Lights: 1982 *Master Harold...and the Boys*

"None"

Theater programs published at the end of the twentieth century for Broadway productions almost always acknowledge the contribution made by a scenic, lighting and/ or a costume designer, usually on the title page. When a designers name is missing, it might be for a variety of reasons including artistic disputes, but more often it is simply because no designer contributed to that facet of a production, such as with Patrick Stewart's one-man performance of *A Christmas Carol* in 1991, 1992, 1993 and 2001 on the Broadway stage. At the beginning of the twentieth century, however, designers were rarely mentioned in playbills and when their contribution was cited, it was often in the back of a program, along the acknowledgements for piano tuners, water purifiers, and concession operators. The index of plays in this book lists designers names only when they are known. Acknowledgements of contributions by scenic studios, lighting equipment companies, shoe makers, or any other suppliers are indicated by the citation "ACKS." If a particular design area is not listed, no information about the production's designers could be identified.

James Noone

A native of upstate New York, scene designer James Noone was born on February 17, 1961 in Glens Falls. His exposure and first experiences were close to home, at the Lake George Opera Festival where from the age of twelve he was working as a stage hand. As he gained experience, his responsibility increased. Through exposure to the designers who worked there, including Michael Anania, Pat Collins and Clarke Dunham, he had a custom-made apprenticeship. He studied for a time at Boston University (where he now teaches scene design and history of design) and started his own career as a designer at the Next Move Theatre in Boston, with *Dancing in the Street*. His New York debut was *Paradise* at Playwrights Horizons, where he was also head of the paint and properties departments. His extensive credits in regional theaters, including Goodspeed Opera House, the Williamston Theatre Festival, and Chicago Shakespeare among others, were amassed during the late 1980s and early 1990s, Since the opening of *Inherit the Wind* in 1996 he has designed more productions in New York where his striking originality combined with naturalistic details matches the spirit of twenty-first century theater. Twenty-first century credits include *Krisit* at Primary Stages and *Women in Black* at the Minetta Lane Theatre. See Figure 10: James Noone: *Judgment at Nuremberg*

Sets: 1996 *Inherit the Wind* **1997** *The Gin Game; Jekyll & Hyde†; The Sunshine Boys* **1998** *Getting and Spending* **1999** *Night Must Fall; The Rainmaker* **2001** *A Class Act; Judgment at Nuremberg*

Hilya Nordmark

Hilya Nordmark designed costumes for a featured player in 1932. She was a seamstress in New York City, who often worked for Robert Edmond Jones and Lillian Gish.

Costumes: 1932 *Camille* (Miss Gish's costumes)

Olle Nordmark

Olle (Olof E.) Nordmark designed and executed paintings in the old Nordic "murals" style in churches in New York City and in Sweden, working from his art studio at 30 West 90th Street. An exhibit of his paintings was held at the Delphic Studio in 1934. During the mid-1930s, he was a principal

Figure 10: James Noone: *Judgement at Nuremberg*: Set design, Act I, Scene 7, 2001. Courtesy of James Noone.

in the Louvre Frame Company, at 16 West 22nd Street, together with Earle Waldeman and Karl Folke Emerson. At various times between 1928 to 1944 he worked for the United States Indian Services teaching art. The author of *Fresco Painting* published in 1947, Nordmark was born in Dalecarlia, Sweden on May 21, 1890 and died in France in December 1973.

Sets: 1927 *Rang Tang*
Costumes: 1927 *Rang Tang*

Mr. Norman

Mr. (Karyl) Norman, an actor originally from England, first performed in the United States in 1924 in *Best People*, and in numerous roles following his debut. He had a successful vaudeville career as a female impersonator, in particular with a character called "The Creole Fashion Plate." He played the Orpheum and Keith Circuits in the U.S. and also traveled around the world. He died August 27, 1945 in New York City at the age of 61.

Costumes: 1927 *Lady Do*† ("Costumes by Himself")

Ferris Norris

Ferris Waldo Norris, a British designer, born on December 4, 1894, worked in collaboration with his brother, Herbert Norris for the 1927 design of a play on Broadway. He was the co-author of *An Introductory Study of Electrical Characteristics of Power and Telephone Transmission Lines* with Lloyd Bingham. At the time of publication in 1936, he was Associate Professor of Electrical Engineering at the University of Nebraska. He died in Vermont in 1977.

Costumes: 1927 *The Wandering Jew*†

Herbert Norris

Herbert Norris, author of *Costume and Fashion* published in 1925 in New York and London, studied architecture at the Royal College of Art but specialized in historical and theatrical costumes. He worked as an assistant to costume designer Wilhelm prior to designing costumes for more than 100 productions in England, the United States and Canada. A teacher of design and costume history, he supervised

the historical sections of Madame Tussaud's Exhibition from 1928-1931 and contributed his expertise to many dioramas. His designs are represented in the permanent collection of the Victoria and Albert Museum, and a costume design for Nanki-Poo for a projected 1921 production is reproduced in *Design on Paper*. Herbert Norris, who wrote often on the subjects of costume and architecture died on November 7, 1950.

Costumes: 1927 *The Wandering Jew*†
1930 *Josef Suss*

Christopher Nowak

Christopher A. Nowak was born August 15, 1950 in San Marcos, Texas. In 1972 he received a Bachelor's degree in environmental design at Texas A & M University and in 1975 an M.F.A. from the Yale University School of Drama, where he studied with Ming Cho Lee. He assisted Ben Edwards for a number of years and has designed on and off-Broadway, often at Playwrights Horizons) and in regional theaters. He currently works primarily in movies and television and has been production designer for films including *The Real Blonde, Basketball Diaries, Vampire's Kiss, My Father the Hero*, and *The X-Files* movie. His credits as art director include *Parenthood, Green Card, The Dream Team, Hanky Panky*, and *Fort Apache, the Bronx*. He has also served as production designer for television series including *Trinity, Prince Street* and the current *110 Centre Street*.

Sets: 1977 *Gemini* **1982** *Pump Boys and Dinettes*†

Madame Oaksmith

Two Broadway plays in the first decade of the twentieth century credited Madame Eugenie Oaksmith with costume design. Specializing in gowns, she worked from a small salon at 250 Fifth Avenue in 1903 and from 350 Madison Avenue in 1909. She resided at 8 West 104th Street in New York City.

Costumes: 1902 *The Twin Sister*† (Miss Anglin's gowns) **1909** *The Awakening of Helena Richie*

Chloe Obolensky

Greek designer Chloe Obolensky was born in Athens in 1942, and after studying in England and France began a career in scenic design as assistant to Lila de Nobili. She has designed sets and costumes at La Scala and the Comédie Française, among other producing organizations. She has designed productions for Gian Carlo Menotti, Franco Zeffirelli, and for Peter Brook *The Three Sisters*, *The Mahabharata*, and *Happy Days*, presented in French at the Royal National Theatre in 1997. The author of *The Russian Empire, A Portrait in Photographs*, she lives in Paris. Film designs include *Onegin*. Among her twenty-first century designs are scenery and costumes for *The Tragedy of Hamlet* at the Harvey Theatre in New York City and costume designs for *Le Costume* at the Young Vic in London.

Costumes: **1983** *La Tragedie de Carmen*

Timothy O'Brien

Timothy O'Brien, a designer of sets and sometimes costumes who mainly works in London, was born in Shillong, Assam, India on March 8, 1929, son of soldier Brian Palliser Tiegue and Elinor Laura O'Brien. He studied at Wellington College, Cambridge University (M.A., 1952) and for a year at Yale with Donald Oenslager. His first professional design, sets and costumes for *The Bald Primadonna* and *The New Tenant* occurred in 1956 in London. From 1955 to 1966 he was head of design for BBC-TV, while continuing to design numerous plays, ballets and operas. He has been an associate artist with the Royal Shakespeare Company and from 1961 to 1979 designed in partnership with Tazeena Firth. He has designed exhibitions for Madame Tussaud's in London and Amsterdam, and the film *Night Must Fall*. Honors include the Gold Medal for set design at the Prague Quadriennale (shared with Tazeena Firth, Ralph Koltai and John Bury) 1975, the Golden Triga for best national exhibit in 1991, a Tony nomination for *Evita*, and in 1991 election as Royal Designer for Industry.

Sets: **1964** *Poor Bitos* **1979** *Bedroom*

Farce[†]; *Evita*[†] **1982** *A Doll's Life*[†] **2000** *Macbeth*
Costumes: **1979** *Bedroom Farce*; *Evita*[†] **2000** *Macbeth*

Edward Ocker

Edward Ocker designed lights for two productions in the first season of the twentieth century on Broadway. H.A. Ockershausen was an electrician in New York during the first decade of the twentieth century, working from 103 East Ninth Street, and in 1907 he listed a telephone number in the city directory.

Lights: **1899** *Rogers Brothers in Wall Street* **1900** *The Rogers Brothers in Central Park*

Francis O'Connor

British designer Francis O'Connor, who was named best designer the 1997 at the Irish Theatre Awards for *Tarry Flynn* and *The Leenane Trilogy* designs scenery throughout the United Kingdom. He trained at the Wimbledon School of Art. His designs have been seen at the Royal Shakespeare Company, the Almeida Theatre, the Abbey Theatre, Donmar Warehouse, D'Oyly Carte, the Wexford festival, and in the West End, among others. Twenty-first century credits include *Peer Gynt* for the Royal National Theatre, *La Cava* in the West End, and *Too Late for Logic* directed by Tom Murphy for the Royal Lyceum Theatre Company to open the 2001 Edinburgh Festival.

Sets: **1998** *The Beauty Queen of Leenane* **1999** *The Lonesome West*
Costumes: **1998** *The Beauty Queen of Leenane* **1999** *The Lonesome West*

Carol Oditz

Carol Oditz, a native of New York City, graduated from the University of South Florida. She began as a sculptor before designing costumes for theaters and film. Her earliest New York theater collaborations were with Herbert Berghof and Uta Hagan at their Bank Street Studio and with Jean Erdman at her Theatre for The Open Eye. Among her theater awards is an Obie for *The Last Locomotive* and the San Francisco Critics Award for *The Good Person of Sechuan*. She has also designed at

Lincoln Center, The Kennedy Center, New York Shakespeare Festival, Arena Stage, and many more. Widely regarded for her designs for movies, she was one of five American designers represented in the Biennale della moda di Firenze. Her designs for Jennifer Jason Leigh in *Georgia* were honored by *Vogue* magazine, as were those for *The Ice Storm*. Her design for *Tin Cup* started a world-wide fashion trend with a necklace now referred to as 'The Tin Cup pearls.' Among her other films are *Higher Learning, Ethan Frome, Molly, Staying Together, No Place Like Home, Nobody's Child* and *Autumn in New York*.

Costumes: 1982 *Cleavage*†; *Is There Life after High School?*; *Monday after the Miracle*

Donald Oenslager

Donald Oenslager is known mainly as a scenic designer and a long-time teacher of design at Yale University, where he influenced a generation of designers and they in turn influenced another generation. He was born in Harrisburg, Pennsylvania on May 7, 1902 and graduated from Harvard in 1923. His first designs on Broadway were seen in 1925, the same year he began teaching at Yale, and were followed by over two hundred additional designs for plays and operas. He wrote *Scenery Then and Now* and *Part of a Lifetime* and consulted on the design of many theater spaces. He won a Tony Award for his set design for *A Majority of One* in 1956. He occasionally designed costumes and lighting for productions for which he also created the sets. Donald Oenslager died on June 11, 1975 at the age of 73.

Sets: 1925 *A Bit of Love*; *Morals*; *Sooner or Later* **1927** *Good News*; *Pinwheel* **1928** *Anna*; *The New Moon* **1929** *Follow Through*; *Heads Up*; *Stepping Out* **1930** *Girl Crazy*; *Overture* **1931** *America's Sweetheart*; *East Wind*; *Free for All*; *Rock Me, Juliet*; *You Said It* **1932** *Adam Had Two Sons*; *A Thousand Summers*; *Whistling in the Dark* **1933** *Forsaking All Others*; *Keeper of the Keys*; *Uncle Tom's Cabin* **1934** *Anything Goes*; *Dance with Your Gods*; *Divided by Three*; *Gold Ea-*

gle Guy; *The Lady from the Sea* **1935** *First Lady*; *Something Gay*; *Sweet Mystery of Life*; *Tapestry in Gray* **1936 200** *Were Chosen*; *Johnny Johnson*; *Matrimony RFD*; *Red, Hot and Blue*; *Russet Mantle*; *Stage Door*; *Sweet River*; *Ten Million Ghosts*; *Timber House*; *You Can't Take It with You* **1937** *A Doll's House*; *Edna His Wife*; *I'd Rather Be Right*; *Miss Quis*; *Robin Landing* **1938** *The Circle*; *Fabulous Invalid*; *The Good*; *I Am My Youth*; *Spring Meeting*†; *Spring Thaw*; *A Woman's a Fool to Be Clever* **1939** *The American Way*†; *From Vienna*; *I Know What I Like*; *The Man Who Came to Dinner*; *Margin for Error*; *Off to Buffalo*; *Skylark* **1940** *Beverly Hills*; *My Dear Children*; *My Sister Eileen*; *The Old Foolishness*; *Retreat to Pleasure*; *Young Couple Wanted* **1941** *Claudia*; *Doctor's Dilemma*; *The Lady Who Came to Stay*; *Mr. Bib*; *Pie in the Sky*; *Spring Again*; *Theatre* **1942** *The Flowers of Virtue* **1943** *Hairpin Harmony* **1945** *Pygmalion* **1946** *Born Yesterday*; *Fatal Weakness*; *Land's End*; *Loco*; *On Whitman Avenue*; *Park Avenue*; *Present Laughter*; *Three to Make Ready*; *Years Ago* **1947** *Angel in the Wings*; *The Eagle Has Two Heads*; *Eastward in Eden*; *How I Wonder*; *Lovely Me*; *Message for Margaret*; *Portrait in Black* **1948** *Goodbye, My Fancy*; *The Leading Lady*; *Life with Mother*†; *The Men We Marry*; *Town House* **1949** *At War with the Army*; *The Father*; *The Rat Race*; *The Smile of the World*; *The Velvet Glove* **1950** *The Liar*; *The Live Wire* **1951** *The Constant Wife*; *Second Threshold*; *The Small Hours* **1952** *Candida*; *Paris '90*; *To Be Continued* **1953** *Escapade*; *Horses in Midstream*; *The Prescott Proposals*; *Sabrina Fair* **1954** *Dear Charles* **1955** *Janus*; *A Roomful of Roses*; *The Wooden Dish* **1956** *Major Barbara* **1957** *Four Winds*; *Nature's Way*; *A Shadow of My Enemy* **1958** *The Girls in 509*; *The Man in the Dog Suit*; *The Marriage-Go-Round*; *The Pleasure of His Company* **1959** *The Highest Tree*; *A Majority of One* **1960** *Dear Liar* **1961** *Blood, Sweat and Stanley Poole*; *A Call on Kuprin*; *A Far Country*; *First Love* **1962** *Venus at Large* **1963** *A Case of Libel*; *The Irregular Verb to Love* **1964** *One by One* **1967** *Love in E-Flat*; *Spofford* **1968** *Avanti!* **1969** *The Wrong*

Way Light Bulb **1974** *Good News*
Costumes: 1925 *Sooner or Later* **1927** *Grand Street Follies*† (Finale costumes); *Pinwheel* **1933** *Uncle Tom's Cabin* **1934** *Dance with Your Gods*; *Gold Eagle Guy*; *The Lady from the Sea*† **1935** *Tapestry in Gray* **1936** *Sweet River*† **1937** *A Doll's House* **1938** *The Good*; *I Am My Youth* **1941** *The Lady Who Came to Stay* **1946** *Land's End* **1947** *Eastward in Eden* **1948** *Life with Mother* **1953** *Escapade*; *Horses in Midstream* **1957** *Four Winds*; *A Shadow of My Enemy*
Lights: 1946 *Fatal Weakness*; *On Whitman Avenue*; *Park Avenue* **1947** *Angel in the Wings*; *How I Wonder*; *Lovely Me*; *Portrait in Black* **1948** *Goodbye, My Fancy*; *The Leading Lady*; *The Men We Marry*; *Town House* **1949** *The Father*; *The Rat Race*; *The Smile of the World* **1950** *The Live Wire* **1951** *Second Threshold* **1953** *Escapade*; *Horses in Midstream*; *Sabrina Fair* **1954** *Dear Charles* **1955** *Janus*; *A Roomful of Roses*; *The Wooden Dish* **1956** *Major Barbara* **1957** *Four Winds*; *Nature's Way*; *A Shadow of My Enemy* **1958** *The Girls in 509*; *The Man in the Dog Suit*; *The Marriage-Go-Round*; *The Pleasure of His Company* **1959** *The Highest Tree*; *A Majority of One* **1961** *Blood, Sweat and Stanley Poole*; *A Call on Kuprin*; *A Far Country*; *First Love* **1962** *Venus at Large* **1963** *A Case of Libel*; *The Irregular Verb to Love* **1964** *One by One* **1967** *Love in E-Flat*; *Spofford* **1968** *Avanti!* **1969** *The Wrong Way Light Bulb*

Toshiro Ogawa

Toshiro Ogawa, a native of Tokyo, came to the United States in 1963. He studied at the Hamburg Opera and the Berlin Technical University. He has been lighting designer for the Stuttgart Ballet, the Chautauqua Opera, and American Ballet Theatre and taught at the University of California at Berkeley and the Ohio State University. Off-Broadway credits include productions with the Pan Asian Repertory Theatre. He was production manager/technical director at the Teheran (Iran) Opera House from 1972 until 1975 and at the Performing Arts Center at Manhattan Community College in the mid-1980s.
Lights: 1980 *Goodbye Fidel*

Ogden

H. A. (Harry A.) Ogden, costume designer and authority on U. S. Army uniforms, worked on Broadway during the first two decades of the twentieth century. He also designed costumes for *The Irish Artist* starring Mrs. Chauncey Olcott at the Boston Museum in 1934. An artist, Ogden had a studio in Room 808, 1475 Broadway in the teens and resided in Englewood, New Jersey. He was born in 1856 and died in 1936.
Costumes: 1899 *The Song of the Sword*† (Uniforms) **1900** *Richard Carvel*† **1901** *Garrett O'Magh*; *If I Were King*†; *To Have and to Hold* **1904** *Terence* (Historical costumes); *Twelfth Night* **1905** *Edmund Burke* **1908** *If I Were King* **1913** *If I Were King* **1916** *If I Were King*

Mollie O'Hara

Mollie O'Hara was the proprietor of a firm of dressmakers, at 11 East 8th Street in New York City in 1901. She subsequently worked from 11 East 48th Street.
Costumes: 1905 *Adrea*† (Mrs. Carter's costumes)

Robert O'Hearn

Robert Raymond O'Hearn is a designer of settings, costumes and lights for the opera, ballet and theater. He was born July 19, 1921 in Elkhart, Indiana and studied at Indiana University and the Art Students League. He designed his first play in 1948 for the Brattle Theatre Company in Cambridge, Massachusetts, where he subsequently did sixty productions. Widely regarded as a stage designer for opera, his first opera was *Falstaff* with Sarah Caldwell in 1951. Since that time he has designed for every major opera company in the U.S., and in Austria and Germany. His debut at the Metropolitan Opera was *L'Elisir d'Amore* in 1960 followed by many more to his most recent, *Der Rosenkavalier* in 1993. He credits Robert Messel as an influential figure. His designs have been widely exhibited. In 1987, he was appointed Professor and Chair of Design at Indiana University School of Music.

Sets: 1950 *The Relapse* 1953 *A Date with April* 1955 *Festival* 1956 *The Apple Cart*; *Child of Fortune* 1964 *Abraham Cochrane*
Costumes: 1950 *The Relapse*
Lights: 1955 *Festival* 1956 *The Apple Cart*; *Child of Fortune* 1964 *Abraham Cochrane*

Alexander Okun

Alexander Okun, emigrated to the United States from the Soviet Union where he was Resident Designer for the Moscow Art Theatre. He taught for ten years at the Moscow Art Theatre Academic Institute, and at Boston University after moving the to U.S. He has designed on, off, and off-off-Broadway for productions including *Tales of Tinseltown*. Regional theater credits include *Three Sisters* at the Arena Stage, *La Voie Humane* and *Facade* for the Boston Shakespeare Company, *The Cherry Orchard* at Williams College, and *The Idiot's tale* at Trinity Repertory Theatre. Since 1995, he has been involved with the Eaton Street Theatre in Fort Lauderdale, Florida, which he renovated from a church and where he often designs.
Sets: 1987 *Roza*

Oleksa

Oleksa designed costumes on Broadway in 1981. She was born Jeanette Oleksa in Port Clinton, Ohio on August 23, 1952 and received a B.A. in theater design at the University of Toledo, and an M.F.A. in scene and costume design at Carnegie Mellon. She has designed numerous off- and off-off-Broadway plays, beginning her New York career at The Production Company. She has also done many television shows and Home Box Office specials, including costumes for *Hindenberg, Ship of Doom* and *The Great Plague of 1918*.
Costumes: 1981 *Scenes and Revelations*

Michael Olich

Michael Olich has been designing scenery and costumes throughout the United States for theater, opera and dance since the mid-1980s. Born in 1950, he received an M.F.A. from Carnegie Mellon University in 1975 and studied non-profit management at the University of Washington. He won the 1992 Los Angeles Drama Critics Circle Award for *The Kentucky Cycle* at the Mark Taper Forum. The production which was later performed at The Kennedy Center and on Broadway originated at Seattle's Intiman Theatre where he often designs. His scenic designs have been seen at the Seattle Opera, Pacific Northwest Ballet, The Guthrie Theatre, and the Milwaukee Repertory, among other major theaters. At both American Conservatory Theatre and the Alley Theatre he has served as head of design. From 1996 to 1998 he wasexecutive director of the Seattle Fringe Theatre Festival and in the fall of 2001 joined the faculty of the School of Drama at Carnegie Mellon University as Associate Head. Twenty-first century designs include scenery and costumes for *The Marriage of Figaro* at the Minnesota Opera.
Sets: 1993 *The Kentucky Cycle*

Stephan Olson

Scenic designer Stephan Olson often designs for regional theaters, regional opera companies and off-Broadway. His designs include productions for the WPA Theatre, the Goodspeed Opera House, the INTAR Theatre, and the SoHo Repertory Theatre. He often collaborates with director Gloria Muzio, including *The Truth Teller* at Circle Repertory Company, *Death of a Salesman* at the Manitoba Theatre Center in Toronto, and his 1995 Broadway debut, *The Play's the Thing*. Late twentieth century credits include scenery for *Resident Avow* at the George Street Playhouse.
Sets: 1995 *The Play's the Thing*

Power O'Malley

Power O'Malley was born in County Waterford, Ireland in 1870 and studied at the National Academy of Design, as well as with Henri Shirlaw. His paintings are in the collections of the Fort Worth Museum of Art, the Library of Congress and the Phillips Memorial Gallery among others. He received several prizes for his paintings, etchings and illustrations. Power O'Malley died on July 3, 1946 in New York City.

Sets: 1932 *The Well of the Saints*

Julia Trevelyan Oman

Julia Trevelyan Oman, a British designer of sets and costumes for television, film, and stage, was born in Kensington, England on July 11, 1930. She attended the Royal College of Art and is married to designer Roy Strong. Her first professional design of sets and costumes, *Brief Lives*, played in both London and New York. She has also designed operas and exhibitions, and has created film and television designs, sometimes in collaboration with her husband. Her designs for *La Boheme* for the Royal Opera originally created for a new production in 1974, remain in the repertory, as do her designs for *the Nutcracker* at the Royal Ballet, originally used in 1984. Honors include the Designer of the Year Award in 1967, Royal Designer for Industry in 1977, an ACE Award for art direction in 1983, and Commander of the British Empire in 1986.

Sets: 1967 *Brief Lives* 1974 *Brief Lives*
Costumes: 1967 *Brief Lives* 1974 *Brief Lives*
Lights: 1974 *Brief Lives*

Alice O'Neil

Alice O'Neil (also known as AVON, Av O'Neil, O'Neill) designed numerous costumes and a single setting on Broadway between 1915 and 1924. She appeared as "Ethel Dante" in musical comedies before devoting her talents to design. She was a staff designer for the Schneider-Anderson Costume Company for ten years beginning in 1916. Between 1927 and 1930 she designed films at Fox Studios and for United Artists. In the film industry she collaborated with Stephanie Wachner. Alice O'Neil died in Nottingham, England on March 30, 1954 at age 92.

Sets: 1922 *Greenwich Village Follies†* ("Little Theatre")
Costumes: 1915 *Around the Map†* (as: AVON) 1916 *Miss Springtime†*; *Ziegfeld Follies: 1916†* 1917 *Ziegfeld Follies: 1917†* 1918 *The Rainbow Girl†* 1919 *Aphrodite†*; *The Rose of China†*; *The Royal Vagabond*; *Ziegfeld Midnight Frolic†* ("Little Red Book" costumes) 1920

Sally†; *Ziegfeld Follies: 1920†* (Women's costumes); *Ziegfeld Girls: 1920†* 1921 *George White's Scandals†*; *The Love Letter* (Act II dresses); *Music Box Revue†* (Additional costumes); *The O'Brien Girl* (Ladies gowns, chorus costumes); *Ziegfeld's 9 O'clock Frolic†* 1922 *Greenwich Village Follies†* ("Little Theatre"); *Ziegfeld Follies: 1922†* ("South Seas") 1923 *Kid Boots†*; *Ziegfeld Follies: 1923†* 1924 *The Grab Bag†*; *Sitting Pretty†* (Act II costumes); *Ziegfeld Follies: 1924†*

Horton O'Neil

Horton O'Neil designed one set in 1940 on Broadway.

Sets: 1940 *The Flying Gerardos*

A. Operti

Albert Operti, originally from Turin, Italy where he was born in 1852, was a landscape artist and mural painter who contributed scenery to a 1900 Broadway show. When he was very young, his parents moved to England, and in 1875, he immigrated to America. His studio and home were located at 65 West 36th Street in New York, where he painted, drew newspaper cartoons, and designed theatrical sets. He began designing sets in the 1880s, with *Around the World in Eighty Days* among his early credits. His paintings, which hang in the American Museum of Natural History and the Pittsfield, Massachusetts Museum among other locations, include a record of his travels to the arctic as a member of two expeditions conducted by Admiral Robert Peary. Among the books he illustrated are *Northward Over the Great Ice* and *Snow Land Folk* by Peary. Albert Operti, who was also known as Jasper Ludwig Roccabiglera, died in 1927.

Sets: 1900 *Miss Prinnt*

Hector Orezzoli

A native of Argentina, Hector Orezzoli attended the University of Buenos Aires before studying design at the University of Belgrano. He has designed sets and costumes for many productions in Europe and South America. His collaborations with Claudio Segovia have resulted in the production of several music spectaculars, including a version of *Flamenco Puro* in Seville in 1980, a second version in Paris in 1984, and a Broadway production in 1986. *Tango Argentino* resulted from his continuing collaboration with Mr. Segovia and was honored with a Tony nomination for costume design. Their scenic designs for *Black and Blue* were nominated for a Tony Award in 1989, as were the costumes, which won the Tony Award. He died in New York City on December 5, 1991 at age 38.

Sets: 1985 *Tango Argentino*† 1986 *Flamenco Puro*† 1989 *Black and Blue*† (Also directed)
Costumes: 1985 *Tango Argentino*† (Also producer) 1986 *Flamenco Puro*† 1989 *Black and Blue*†
Lights: 1986 *Flamenco Puro*†

Ben Ormerod

Ben Ormerod, a British lighting designer, has extensive credits in theaters in the United Kingdom, including the Gate Theatre, the Abbey Theatre, the Chichester Festival, the Oxford Stage Company, and the Nottingham Playhouse. In the late 1990s, he began designing more frequently in London, including productions for the Royal National Theatre, the Royal Shakespeare Company, and in the West End. His designs for *The Coronation of Poppea* for the Purcell Quartet were seen both at Royal Festival Hall and in Japan. He also designs for dance, including the Rambert Dance Company and Portugal's Ballet Gulbenkian. Twenty-first century designs include *Remembrance of Things Past*, adapted by Harold Pinter at RNT and *Julius Caesar* for the RSC, directed by Edward Hall.

Lights: 1998 *The Beauty Queen of Leenane*

Robert Ornbo

A British designer of lights, Robert Ornbo was born in Hessle, Yorkshire, England on September 13, 1931 and studied at Hull University. He began designing in London in 1959 with *Urfaust* and has since designed many productions, including operas and plays throughout Europe. He designed lights for the opening production in the Sydney (Australia) Opera House. Together with Richard Pilbrow through

Theatre Projects, Inc., he has been instrumental in the development of the profession of lighting design in the United Kingdom. He designed lights for the 1967 production of *As You Like It* at the Royal National Theatre directed by Clifford Williams.

Lights: 1970 *Company* 1974 *As You Like It*; *London Assurance*; *Travesties*

Orry-Kelly

Orry-Kelly, known primarily as a movie costume designer, began his professional life as an actor on Broadway. He was born Orry George Kelly on December 31, 1897 in Kiama, Australia, and went to New York in 1923. He supported himself painting murals, which led to a job drawing subtitles for silent films. He returned to the theater in the late 1920s as a designer of sets and costumes. When the stock market crash made theater jobs scarce he moved to St. Louis to design for the St. Louis Opera, and then continued west to Hollywood. His name was hyphenated while in California to create a more exotic persona. Making glamour and quality his trademark, he was chief designer for Warner Brothers from 1931 to 1945 and then moved to Fox Studios. He won three Academy Awards for costume design, for *An American in Paris*, *Les Girls* and *Some Like It Hot*. He on died February 26, 1964 at age 67.

Costumes: 1927 *Half a Widow*; *Padlocks of 1927*† ("Summertime") 1928 *The Kingdom of God* 1929 *Boom Boom*†; *George White's Scandals*† (American costumes); *Music in May*†; *Street Singer*; *A Wonderful Night*† 1930 *Nina Rosa*; *Scarlet Sister Mary* 1960 *The World of Carl Sandburg* (Miss Davis' gowns)

Mrs. Robert Osborn

Mrs. Robert Osborn (Osborne) was a dressmaker and milliner who started working in the theater through her association with Daniel Frohman (1851-1940) and his brother Charles (1860-1915) for whom she designed many productions, beginning with Julia Opp's costumes for *The Princess and the Butterfly* in 1897. She would either design and execute gowns specially, or provide them from her stock of imported haute couture. The Mrs. Osborn Company, "Creators of Fashions for Women," was located at 24-26 East 46th Street in New York City, with branches in Paris and Newport. In the early years of the twentieth century, she opened a little theater, Mrs. Osborn's Playhouse, but returned to dressmaking when it wasn't very successful. Sources suggest that Mrs. Osborn died in 1908, although her playbill credits continue through 1911, and Elsie de Wolfe patronized the salon in 1912.

Costumes: 1899 *Wheels within Wheels* **1900** *Brother Officers* (Miss Anglin's gowns); *Hearts Are Trumps* (Misses Bingham and Busley's gowns); *Lady Huntworth's Experiment* (Gowns); *A Man and His Wife* (Gowns) **1901** *The Marriage Game* (Miss Martinot's costumes) **1902** *Aunt Jeannie* (as: Mrs. Osborn Co.: dresses); *Frocks and Frills*; *His Excellency the Governor* (Miss Millard's gowns); *The Joy of Living*† (as: Mrs. Osborn Co.); *The Modern Magdalen* (Miss Bingham's gowns); *The Mummy and the Humming Bird* (as: Mrs. Osborn Co.: dresses); *Tommy Rot* (Gowns) **1903** *Cousin Kate* (as: Mrs. Osborn Co.: gowns); *The Girl from Kay's*; *Miss Elizabeth's Prisoner*†; *The Other Girl* (as: Mrs. Osborn Co.) **1904** *Lady Teazle*† (Miss Russell's costumes); *The Two Roses*† (Miss Scheff's dresses) **1905** *London Assurance*† (Miss Jeffreys' costumes) **1906** *About Town*†; *Clarice*; *The Hypocrites* (Gowns); *The Little Cherub*† (Gowns); *The Love Route* (Miss Tyler's gowns) **1907** *The Dairymaids*; *His Excellency the Governor* (Miss Barrymore's gowns); *The Secret Orchard*; *The Thief* (as: Mrs. Osborn Co.) **1908** *Lady Frederick*; *The World and His Wife* (Gowns) **1909** *Sham*† (Miss Crosman's gowns) **1911** *The Faun*† (Gowns); *The Thief* (as: Mrs. Osborn Co.)

Madame O'Shaughnessy

Madame Mary M. O'Shaughnessy was a dressmaker, working from 150 West 101st in New York City, during the first decade of the twentieth century. She collaborated on the costume designs for a 1904 Broadway show.

Costumes: 1904 *The Pit*†

Mlle. Rachelle Ospovat

Mademoiselle Rachelle Ospovat (Ospo-rat) designed costumes for a featured performer three productions on Broadway and her name was spelled differently each time. Also active in London during the same period, her first name was recorded as Rachelle, Rochelle, and Mrochelle. Among the numerous credits she amassed in London mainly between 1913 and 1933 were *Diplomacy*, *the Doctor's Dilemma*, *Lass o' Laughter* and *On Approval*.

Costumes: 1905 *Beauty and the Barge*† (Miss Maude's gowns) **1913** *Beauty and the Barge*† (Miss Maude's gown); *Grumpy* (Miss Maude's gown)

Curt Ostermann

G. Curtis Ostermann was born on July 20, 1952 in Detroit, the son of G. William and Barbara Ostermann. He received a B.A. with distinction at the University of Michigan and an M.F.A. at New York University Tisch School of the Arts, where he now teaches. From 1978 to 1980 he assisted Tharon Musser, whom he credits as his mentor. He received a nomination for Best Lighting Designer for *A Streetcar Named Desire* from the American Theatre Wing. International credits include productions for the Stuttgart Ballet, the Netherlands Opera, the Theatre Royal de la Monnaie Opera, Toronto's Royal Alexandra Theatre, the Spoleto Festival in Italy and Theatre an der Wein in Vienna. He has also designed at the New York City Opera, in regional theaters throughout the United States, for television and industrial productions. He has received two Emmy Award nominations for his work on *The Maury Povich Show*.

Lights: 1988 *The Devil's Disciple*; *A Streetcar Named Desire*

A. A. Ostrander

Albert A. Ostrander designed sets, lights and costumes for the theater and fashion shows during his career. He initially worked as a technical director for Norman Bel Geddes. He staged several *Fashions of the Times* productions in the late 1940s and also designed for three years for the Ringling Bros. and Barnum & Bailey Circus. A. A. Ostrander died in New York on September 29, 1964 at age 61.

Sets: 1939 *Where There's a Will* 1940
A Case of Youth 1943 *All for All* 1944
Sleep No More 1946 *The Duchess Misbehaves*
Costumes: 1944 *Sleep No More*
Lights: 1944 *Sleep No More*

Samuel Ostrowsky

Samuel Ostrowsky (Ostrovsky) was born on May 5, 1885 (some sources suggest 1886) in Malin, Russia and studied painting in Kiev, Paris and at the Art Institute of Chicago. He exhibited at the Salon d'Automne, Salon des Tuileries, and Sale des Índépendants in Paris, and created illustrations for *Esquire* magazine. Ostrowsky is credited with making the scenic artistry at the Yiddish Art Theatre in New York equivalent to classic levels.
Sets: 1923 *Anathema; The Inspector General*

Kay Otteson

Kay Otteson designed costumes for a Broadway play in 1934.
Costumes: 1934 *Baby Pompadour*

Teo Otto

Teo Otto was born in Remscheid, Germany on February 4, 1904 and studied in Paris and Weimar. He was set designer for the Berlin State Theatre in the early 1930s. In 1933 he moved to Switzerland and designed for the Zurich City Stage until the end of World War II, when he returned to Frankfurt and designed for theater and opera. His designs were seen in operas and plays throughout Europe and in New York. He also painted. Mr. Otto died on June 9, 1968 at age 64.
Sets: 1958 *The Visit*†
Costumes: 1958 *The Visit*†

Paul Ouzounoff

Paul Ouzounoff (Ousonoff), who was also known as Paul Rover, was born in Russia and worked as a seaman, rising to the rank of pilot before devoting his talents to scene painting and design. He spent twelve years on the staff of the Moscow Art Theatre as a scene painter. He moved permanently to the United States in 1923 and worked at Triangle Studios, again as a scene painter. In 1922 he contributed designs for scenery

and costumes to a Broadway show. He died at age 64 on October 24, 1942 in New York City.
Sets: 1922 *Revue Russe*† 1926 *The Scarlet Letter*
Costumes: 1922 *Revue Russe*†

Henry Owen

Henry (or Harry C.) Owen designed scenery on Broadway in 1910. Owen & Carew was a partnership between Henry C. Owen and Vincent P. Carew, both carpenters, in Newark, New Jersey, located at 81 South Boulevard. Owen resided at 106 Pennsylvania Avenue, Newark.
Sets: 1910 *Get-Rich-Quick Wallingford*†

Jean Pace

Jean Pace was born in 1936 in Jackson, Mississippi and was raised in Los Angeles. A dancer and singer, as well as a costume designer, she learned to sew from her grandmother. At the age of six she began creating dances and shows and supplying her own costumes. She has often collaborated on productions with her husband, jazz singer and writer Oscar Brown, Jr. Much of her busy career has been spent in Chicago where highlights include *Summer in the City* in 1967 and *Opportunity Please Knock* which incorporated the street gang Blackstone Rangers as performers into the production. In the mid-1990s Oscar Brown Jr. & Family (the headliner, Jean Pace-Brown, son Bo Brown, and daughter Maggie Brown) appeared at the Jazz Buffet in Chicago.
Costumes: 1969 *Buck White*

Robert Rowe Paddock

Robert Rowe Paddock was born on August 12, 1914 in Mansfield, Ohio. He studied at the Cleveland School of Art and received a B.S. in art and education at Case Western Reserve University. He designed and worked as technical director in summer and stock theaters throughout the United States including the Ivoryton (Connecticut) Playhouse, the Hilltop Lodge, and the Pocono Playhouse during the 1930s and 1940s. From 1951 to 1957 he designed for CBS-TV, creating sets for productions ranging from *Douglas Edwards and the News* and *The Garry Moore Show* to features and series. He also designed special events, including the Inaugural Anniversary Party for John F. Kennedy and New York's "Salute to President Johnson" in Madison Square Garden. Active in professional organizations, he was president of United Scenic Artists for a total of eleven years, and then spent fifteen years as treasurer. He was also on the board of governors of the Television Academy from 1955 to 1958. He retired to Greenwich, Connecticut in the early 1990s and died there on September 3, 2001.

Sets: 1946 *Burlesque* 1947 *Alice in Wonderland and Through the Looking Glass*

Gianfranco Padovani

Ginafranco Padovani, an Italian designer of operas, plays and television, was born on June 20, 1928 in Venice. He studied in Milan at the Accad di Belle Arti Brera and first designed at the Teatro Stabile di Genova in Italy. He has designed for all the major Italian opera companies, and in 1968 designed sets and costumes for a Broadway play.

Sets: 1968 *The Venetian Twins*
Costumes: 1968 *The Venetian Twins*

Martin Pakledinaz

Martin Pakledinaz was born September 1, 1953 in Detroit, Michigan. He received a B.F.A. in directing at Wayne State University and an M.F.A. in costume design at the University of Michigan, where he first designed costumes for a production of *The Trojan Women*. Major influences on his career in costumes in New York have included Barbara Matera, and Theoni V. Aldredge for whom he worked as an assistant designer. Just as he learned much as an assistant designer, so do his own assistants, among them Marion Williams, Eden Miller, Kristin Kraai and Juliet Ouyoung. A designer whose costumes are seen regularly in the regional theaters, off-Broadway, and frequently in opera, he first designed costumes on Broadway in 1981 and made

his debut at the New York City Opera in 1992 with *Xerxes*. Honors include a Tony Award for *Kiss Me, Kate* and the 1998 Irene Sharaff Young Master Award from Theatre Development Fund.

Costumes: 1981 *Inacent Black* 1986 *You Can Never Tell* 1992 *Hamlet (Roundabout)* 1993 *Anna Christie; A Grand Night for Singing* 1994 *Hedda Gabler* 1995 *Holiday* 1996 *The Father*; *Summer and Smoke* 1997 *The Diary of Anne Frank; The Life* 1998 *Golden Child* 1999 *Kiss Me Kate* 2000 *Taller Than a Dwarf*

Reginald Pale

Reginald Pale was primarily a director. In 1923 he contributed costume and scenic designs to Broadway productions which he also directed.

Sets: 1923 *King Lear* (Also directed); *Morphia* (Also directed)
Costumes: 1923 *King Lear* (Costumes and direction)

Elizabeth Palmer

Elizabeth Palmer is from Milford, Connecticut, where she was born February 28, 1946. She studied at the University of Iowa, the Fashion Institute of Technology and the American Academy of Dramatic Art. Her professional debut occurred in 1976 at Center Stage with the costume designs for *Toys in the Attic*. Since that time her designs have been seen in many regional theaters, off-Broadway, and in film, television and commercials. Currently based on the West Coast, her television credits include the television series' *Fortune Dane* and *Wings*, and the NBC-TV movie of the week, *When Your Lover Leaves*. Her designs for *Any Day Now* on Lifetime were nominated for an Emmy Award.

Costumes: 1979 *The Goodbye People* 1984 *Quilters*

John H. Palmer

John H. Palmer was an electrician who resided at 305 West Twelfth Street in New York City in 1898. He worked for the Edison Company, according to the *Fatinitza* and *Girofle-Girofla* programs in 1904. A notice of his death on March 25, 1915 at age 55 was published in the

March 31, 1915 edition of the *New York Dramatic Mirror*. He should not be confused with the British film producer (1916-1991) or the American television reporter also named John Palmer.

Lights: 1904 *Fatinitza*; *Girofle-Girofla*

Gunilla Palmstierna-Weiss

Gunilla Palmstierna-Weiss was born on March 28, 1928 in Lausanne, Switzerland, the daughter of two doctors. Raised and educated in Europe, she studied ceramics, textiles, sculpture and stage design at the Academies of Fine Arts and Crafts in Stockholm, Amsterdam and Paris. She has designed operas, films and plays throughout the world beginning with *The Great Macabre* in 1952 for the Stockholm student theater. She has lectured widely on scenic and costume design during a remarkable career working with many of the major directors and playwrights of the world. Her designs have been honored with many awards, including a Tony Award for *Marat/Sade* in 1966 and a Gold Medal in Prague for *Blood Wedding* in 1969. A son by her first marriage to the graphic artist Mark Sylvan is also a stage designer. She was married to the playwright, author and artist Peter Weiss from 1952 until his death in 1982. They had one daughter, Gern, born in 1972, and collaborated together on many projects. Late twentieth century credits include sets and costumes for the Royal Dramatic Theatre of Sweden, including *A Doll's House* directed by Ingmar Bergman. The production enjoyed a successful run at the Brooklyn Academy of Music in 1991.

Costumes: 1965 *Marat/Sade*

Eric Pape

Eric Pape was born in San Francisco and studied painting in Paris with individual artists and at the École des Beaux Arts. He taught in Boston before opening his own school in New York, the Eric Pape School of Art, where he was director and chief instructor from 1888 to 1918. His studio was located at 200 West 57th Street in New York City in the 1930s. In addition to exhibiting paintings in Europe and the United States, he designed sets and/or costumes for numerous plays, including *Canterbury Pilgrims*, a command performance for President Taft in 1909, and *Trilby* in 1895. Reportedly sponsored for membership at The Players Club by Mark Twain, he died in 1938 at age 68.

Sets: 1924 *Flame of Love*
Costumes: 1914 *Omar, the Tentmaker* 1927 *Julius Caesar* 1930 *Milestones*

Paquin

Paquin was the name of the couture house founded at 3 Rue de la Paix in Paris in 1891 by Jeanne Beckers (1869-1936) and Isadore Jacobs, her husband. Early in the twentieth century "Monsieur and Madame Paquin" had salons in New York, London, Madrid and Buenos Aires. Her elegant gowns were known for their rich fabrics and quality construction, and were popular with private and theatrical customers. She devised garments that were suitable for both day and evening wear, perfectly capturing the spirit of the teens and twenties when the House of Paquin was most successful. Paquin retired in 1920. In 1953 the House of Paquin merged with the House of Worth, becoming Paquin-Worth until closing in 1956.

Costumes: 1902 *The Cross-ways* 1912 *The Perplexed Husband*† (Dresses) 1913 *The Marriage Game*

Yael Pardess

Scenic designer Yael Pardess was born in Israel and majored in theater design at Tel Aviv University. In the late 1980s she began designing in the United States, initially on the West Coast for theaters including the Mark Taper Forum, the San Jose Repertory, and the Sacramento Theatre Company. Since then her designs have been seen throughout the United States for theater, film, industrial promotions, commercials, theme parks and in multimedia special-effects shows. She designed *Movie Magic* for Universal Studios in Japan. Honors include the 1987 Finkel Prize from the Habima Theatre.

Sets: 1990 *Stand Up Tragedy* 2000 *George Gershwin Alone*

Dennis Parichy

Dennis Parichy has been resident lighting designer for the Circle Repertory Company since 1976. He began his professional design career in 1959 with a production of *Richard II* at Eagles Mere Playhouse in Pennsylvania. He was born on November 10, 1938 in Melrose Park, Illinois, the son of Theodore and Eva Parichy. He received a B.S. in 1960 from Northwestern University where he worked with Alvina Krause, and studied at Lester Polakov's Studio and Forum of Stage Design. His mentors include Alvina Krause, Theodore Fuchs and Thomas Skelton. He has received many honors including Maharam Awards for *Talley's Folly* and *The Fifth of July*, a Drama Desk and Obie for *Talley's Folly*, Drama Logue Awards for *Tally's Folly*, *Picnic* and *Burn This*, and Village Awards for *Devour The Snow* and *Angels Fall*. He also received the 1981 Obie Award for sustained excellence and is on the faculty of Brandeis University.

Lights: 1976 *Knock Knock* 1978 *The Best Little Whorehouse in Texas*; *Water Engine, The/ Mr. Happiness* 1979 *Devour the Snow* 1980 *Fifth of July*; *Talley's Folly* 1981 *Crimes of the Heart*; *Duet for One* 1982 *The Best Little Whorehouse in Texas*; *The Curse of an Aching Heart* 1983 *Angels Fall* 1985 *As Is*; *Dancing in the End Zone* 1987 *Burn This*; *Coastal Disturbances*; *The Nerd*; *Penn & Teller* 1989 *Love Letters*; *The Tenth Man* 1991 *Penn & Teller: The Refrigerator Tour* 1992 *Crazy He Calls Me*; *The Price* 1993 *Any Given Day*; *Redwood Curtain* 1996 *Bus Stop*

Carolyn Parker

Carolyn Parker, born June 12, 1935, concentrated her design activity in Minneapolis, Minnesota, amassing many credits for companies including the University of Minnesota, the Walker Art Center Opera Company and the Guthrie Theatre. She designed both sets and costumes, but was mainly known as a costume designer. In 1963 she was design coordinator at the Guthrie Theatre. Other designs include *Romeo and Juliet* at the Stratford (Ontario) Festival in 1968.

She died in Minneapolis in August 1978.

Costumes: 1972 *The Great God Brown* (Costumes and masks) 1973 *Holiday*; *The Visit*

Gerald Parker

Gerald Parker designed the set for a 1961 Broadway play starring George C. Scott. He also worked on the 1981 movie *Growing Up with Sandy Offenheim*.

Sets: 1961 *General Seeger*

Gower Parks

Gower Parks designed sets in 1946 for two Shakespeare plays performed on Broadway.

Sets: 1946 *Henry IV, Part I*; *Henry IV, Part II*

Paul Parnes

Paul Parnes studied at Columbia University and then spent most of his professional life making couture clothes in a Seventh Avenue company named after himself. The Paul Parnes Corporation was founded by his father, Louis Parnes, in 1895 and remained in business until Paul Parnes retired in 1970. He died in July of 1978 at age 80 in Hollywood, Florida. The fashion designer should not be confused with the composer (1925-) who has the same name.

Costumes: 1956 *Sixth Finger in a Five Finger Glove*† (Women's clothes)

Chris Parry

Lighting designer Chris Parry was born in Manchester, England on May 23, 1952. After spending several years as deputy head of stage lighting for the Royal Shakespeare Company, while also designing operas, plays and tours for other companies in the United Kingdom, he began designing in the United States. Since the late 1980s, he has designed more than 100 productions in America's major regional theaters, won numerous awards, and continued to design regularly for the Royal Shakespeare Company. His is also Professor and Head of the lighting design program at the University of California, San Diego. Honors include Tony, Outer Critics Circle, Olivier, and Dora Mavor Moore Awards for *The Who's*

Tommy, and the 1994 Lighting Designer of the Year Award from *Lighting Dimensions International*. Twenty-first century designs include *The Bard of Avon* by Amy Freed at the South Coast Repertory Theatre.
Lights: **1987** *Les Liaisons Dangereuses* **1992** *Search and Destroy* **1993** *The Who's Tommy* **1995** *Translations* **1996** *A Midsummer Night's Dream* **1999** *Not about Nightingales*

Elizabeth Hooker Parsons

Elizabeth Hooker Parsons designed costumes on Broadway in 1934.
Costumes: **1934** *Picnic*; *Roll Sweet Chariot*†

Jeanne Partington

Jeanne Partington designed costumes on Broadway for two shows in the mid-1950s.
Costumes: **1955** *Hear! Hear!* **1956** *Harbour Lights* (Miss Linda Darnell's costumes)

Pascaud

The couture house known as "Maison de Pascaud, Paris" flourished from 1903-1915. In addition to serving private customers, the salon also catered to theatrical clients. Gowns from "Pascaud, Paris" were often used in productions in France, and were also worn in the premiere performance of *The Merry Widow* in London. Those designs were reproduced in the *Souvenir of the First Anniversary Performance of the Merry Widow in London* in 1908 by publisher William Heinemann.
Costumes: **1906** *The Little Cherub*† **1908** *The Soul Kiss*† **1914** *The Passing Show of 1914*† **1920** *Sally*†

Daphne Pascucci

Daphne Pascucci was born in London in 1953. She studied at Barnard College, Juilliard, and in Florence, Italy. She graduated from the Yale School of Drama where she designed costumes for *The Birthday Party* and *The House of York*. While in Italy she designed *Opera Borga*, costumes for television and assisted designer Giovanni Agostinucci. She has worked as an assistant to other costume designers

working on Broadway including Theoni V. Aldredge, and also designed costumes for the film *Overexposed*.
Costumes: **1984** *Ma Rainey's Black Bottom*

Bruce Pask

Bruce Pask designed costumes on Broadway in 2001. In 1995 he was named associate fashion director for *GQ* magazine.
Costumes: **2001** *Design for Living*

Neil Patel

Scenic designer Neil Patel was born on February 27, 1964 in Bangor, Wales, son of Dr. Anoo P. Patel and Dr. Sheila Lang Patel, and raised in Kenosha, Wisconsin. He majored in architecture as an undergraduate at Yale College (B.A. 1986), which he also studied at the Accademia di Belle Arti Brera in Milan, Italy (1986-1988) before pursuing theatrical design at the University of California, San Diego (M.F.A. 1991). Counting Robert Israel and Eiko Ishioka among those who have influenced his career, he spent two years designing sets in Los Angeles before moving to the East Coast. Since the early 1990s, he has been designing steadily in major regional theaters, off-Broadway and abroad. Honors include the 1996 and 2001 Obie Awards for sustained excellence, a 2000 EDDY Award for designs for Anne Bogart, and two Drama Desk nominations for *Quills* (1996) and *Dinner With Friends* (2000). Twenty-first century credits include *Hedda Gabler* at the Steppenwolf Theatre, *Romeo and Juliet* at the McCarter Theater Center, and *Glimmer, Glimmer, Shine* at the Manhattan Theatre Club.
Sets: **1998** *Side Man*

Jean Patou

Jean Patou was born in 1887 and first designed fashion in 1914. After service in World War I as a Captain of Zouaves, he opened a shop in Paris and became one of the great names of French fashion in the 1920s and 1930s, incorporating glamour and business acumen into his fashion house. He was one of the first fashion designers to have fabrics produced especially for him. He often contributed designs to the theater in New York and France. Mr. Patou died in March 1936 at age 49 in Paris, but the couture house remained open under the direction of other designers.

Costumes: 1923 *Little Miss Bluebeard†* (Miss Bordoni's evening gown and cloak in Act I); *Topics of 1923†* (Modern gowns worn by Mlle. Delysia) 1929 *Candle-Light†* (Miss Lawrence's other dresses)

Russell Patterson

Russell Patterson designed scenery and costumes on Broadway in the 1930s. He was known mainly as a cartoonist and illustrator who did much to popularize the "flapper" in the 1920s. He was born in Omaha, Nebraska on December 26, 1894. He studied painting with Monet and at the Art Institute of Chicago, McGill University in Canada and the Academy of Fine Arts. He served as Vice President of the Society of Illustrators and was co-founder of the National Cartoonists Society. During the 1930s he designed scenery and costumes for Broadway and films, later turning his talents solely to illustrations for magazines and advertisements. He also designed Christmas Toy Windows for Macy's, hotel lobbies, restaurants, and the Women's Army Corps (WAC) Uniforms in World War II. Russell Patterson died at age 82 on March 17, 1977.

Sets: 1932 *Ballyhoo of 1932†* 1933 *Hold Your Horses* 1934 *Fools Rush in†* 1935 *George White's Scandals†*
Costumes: 1931 *The Gang's All Here* 1932 *Ballyhoo of 1932†* 1933 *Hold Your Horses* 1934 *Fools Rush in; Ziegfeld Follies: 1934†*

Michael Paul

Michael Paul designed costumes for a Broadway show in 1943.
Costumes: 1943 *The Snark Was a Boojum*

David Paulin

Costume designer David Paulin made his Broadway debut in 1995. He also designed costumes for the national tour of the same production.
Costumes: 1995 *Jesus Christ Superstar*

Herbert Paus

Born in 1880 in Minneapolis, Minnesota, the illustrator Herbert Paus studied at the Art Students League with George Bridgman. He designed covers for many magazines, such as *The Saturday Evening Post, Popular Science, Redbook* and *Collier's* and created book illustrations and posters for Liberty Loan drives and advertisers. He also designed scenery, notably *The Betrothal* by Maurice Maeterlinck in 1913, subsequently performed on Broadway. He died on June 1, 1946.
Sets: 1918 *The Betrothal*

Miss Peacock

Miss Ada (Adaline) Peacock was costume designer on Broadway for a show in 1926 and costume and scenic designer for another in 1929. She was also active in London and designed costumes for *One Dam Thing After Another* in collaboration with Aubrey Hammond, Doris Zinkeisen, and Kitty Shannon, and *The Girl Friend,* both in 1927. In 1928 she designed *This Year of Grace!* with Oliver Messel, G. E. Calthrop and Doris Zinkeisen, and the following year designed costumes for *Wake up and Dream* with Oliver Messel, Louis Curti, Maraud Michael Guiness and Norman Wilkinson. She died in Florida in 1946.
Sets: 1929 *Wake Up and Dream†*
Costumes: 1926 *Happy-Go-Lucky* 1929 *Wake Up and Dream†*

Stella Mary Pearce

Born in London on April 17, 1901, Stella Mary Pearce joined Frank Benson's Shakespeare Company as a performer, after leaving school. Her gift with costumes was soon apparent, and led to a position as assistant to George Sheringham. She also opened a haute couture salon in Bloomsbury, later moving it to Mayfair. In 1934 Martin Browne, director of the Religious Drama Society, asked her to design costumes for T.S. Eliot's first play, *The Rock.* Her designs for the 300 costumes for *The Rock* were a success, and led to additional productions as well as marriage to art historian and critic Eric Newton (who coincidentally designed the set for *The Rock*). She also designed the premiéres of *Murder in the Cathedral* and *The Family Reunion* both by Eliot, as well as numerous other productions in London's West End. When World War II forced the closure of her dress business, she started to write and lecture on the history of dress, becoming a widely recognized expert. In 1965 she founded the first ever postgraduate program in the History of Dress, at the Courtauld Institute of Art. There she taught students to date paintings based on the dress depicted in them, among other courses. Stella Mary Newton was made OBE in 1976, and died at age 100 in London on May 18, 2001.

Costumes: 1938 *Murder in the Cathedral*

Albertine Peck

Mrs. Albertine E. Peck designed costumes for a featured player on Broadway in 1920. Her home was 315 West 79th Street in New York.

Costumes: 1920 *A Hole in the Wall*† (Miss Tindal's and Miss MacDonald's gowns)

Esther Peck

Esther Peck was active on Broadway primarily as a costume designer and occasionally as a scenic designer between 1915 and 1927. She designed numerous sets and costumes for the Neighborhood Playhouse including *Petrouchka*, and also was a fine art painter. One of her costume designs for the Little Theatre Opera company's production of *The Gypsy Baron* was reproduced in the December 1929 issue of *Theatre Arts*. Known in private life as Mrs. David Peck, she resided at 48 East 89th Street in 1915 and at 2095 Creston Avenue, New York City in the early 1930s.

Sets: 1926 *A Burmese Pwe* **1927** *Ritornele*

Costumes: 1915 *Jephthah's Daughter*† **1916** *La Boite a Joujoux*; *Petrouchka* **1926** *A Burmese Pwe* **1927** *Grand Street Follies*† (Finale costumes); *Ritornele* (Production design)

Helene Peck

Helene D. Peck designed costumes for a 1927 production. At the time, she resided at 113 East 14th Street in New York.

Costumes: 1927 *Granite*†

Rose Pederson

Costume designer Rose Pederson first designed costumes on Broadway in 1989. She lives in Seattle, Washington and designs frequently on the West Coast, including *Polish Joke* and *Temporary Help* at A Contemporary Theatre in Seattle.

Costumes: 1989 *Largely New York*

Ernest Peixotto

Ernest Clifford Peixotto was born on October 5, 1869 in San Francisco. He was a painter and author who specialized in travel books about California, the American Southwest and Europe. He studied in California and at the Académie Julien in Paris with Benjamin Constant and Jules Le Febvre. He painted murals, among them "Le Mort d'Arthur" at the Cleveland Public Library in 1911, and public rooms in New York, Paris and California. During World War I he was an official artist with the American Expeditionary Force in France, creating illustrations now in the collections of the National Gallery in Washington, D.C. In 1921 he was made a Chevalier of the Legion of Honor in France, becoming an officer in 1924. He died in New York City on December 6, 1940.

Sets: 1901 *The Brixton Burglary* **1922** *Fools Errand*

Clifford F. Pember

Clifford F. Pember was among a group of designers who were inducted into United Scenic Artists in 1923. Until that time U.S.A. was generally regarded as the union of scenic painters. Clifford Pember, Woodman Thompson, Robert Edmond Jones, Lee Simonson and Joseph Urban were among those who joined the union, thereafter receiving fees on an approved scale, legal contracts, and credit in playbills placed above the cast list. Clifford Pember also worked as an interior decorator. He was active in London during the 1920s, creating scenery and costume designs for plays such as *Lawful, Larceny, Polly Preferred, The Punch*

Bowl, The Odd Spot, Tricks, R.S.V.P., Loose Ends, C.O.D., The Cave Man and *The Last Enemy.*

Sets: 1917 *'Ception Shoals; The Country Cousin; Hamilton; Happiness; The Pipes of Pan; The Wooing of Eve* **1918** *A Doll's House; Getting Together; The Girl Behind the Gun; The Kiss Burglar; Ladies First†; Oh, Lady! Lady!; Sick-a-Bed; Someone in the House; Toot-Toot!* **1919** *Clarence; Five O'clock; The Kiss Burglar; On the Hiring Line* **1920** *Bab; Footloose; His Chinese Wife; Sophie* **1921** *The Circle; Get Together†; Pot-Luck; Sonny Boy; The White Peacock†* **1922** *The Blue Kitten; Daffy Dill; East of Suez; The Faithful Heart; The Fool; Lawful Larceny* **1923** *Anything Might Happen; The Camel's Back; The Guilty One; Hurricane†; The Lady* **1924** *Dancing Mothers; Gypsy Jim* **1947** *Under the Counter*

Margaret Pemberton

Margaret Pemberton, born Margaret McCoy in Orange, New Jersey, studied vocal music in Berlin and Paris, but gave up a singing career to marry the theatrical producer Brock Pemberton (1885-1950) in December 1916. Her love of clothes proved useful in her husband's business and she became the official supervisor of costumes for all the plays he produced. She championed the cause to have an objective source select clothes for stage use in plays requiring contemporary dress. Mrs. Pemberton never claimed to be a designer, nor did she aspire to a career in fashion or theatrical design, but her influence at the time was enormous. She was instrumental in the movement away from allowing a performer to select his or her stage wardrobe. As a result of her active involvement in the selection and purchase of modern clothes for plays, she was appointed to a staff position at Sak's Fifth Avenue as "Director of Modern Costume." Mrs. Pemberton died in 1969.

Costumes: 1926 *The Masque of Venice* (Women's costumes) **1928** *The Lady Lies* (Costume Supervisor); *The Lady of the Orchids* (Costume Supervisor); *Little Accident* (Costume Supervisor); *Mr. Moneypenny†* (Costume Supervisor); *Night Hostess* (Costume Supervisor)

1929 *Maggie the Magnificent* (Costume Supervisor); *A Primer for Lovers* (Costume Supervisor); *Skyrocket; Stepping Out* (Costume Supervisor); *Strictly Dishonorable* (Costume Supervisor) **1930** *An Affair of State†* (Costume Supervisor); *His Majesty's Car†* (Costume Supervisor); *The Song and Dance Man* (Costume Supervisor) **1931** *A Church Mouse* (Costume Supervisor); *The Enemy Within* (Costume Supervisor); *The Great Barrington†* (Modern costumes); *How Money* (Costume Supervisor); *The Joy of Living* (Costume Supervisor); *Lean Harvest* (Costume Supervisor); *The Left Bank* (Costume Supervisor); *Louder, Please†* (Costume Supervisor); *Perfectly Scandalous†* (Costume Supervisor); *She Means Business* (Costume Supervisor); *Three Times the Hour* (Costume Supervisor); *A Woman Denied†* (Miss Nash's costumes) **1934** *By Your Leave* (Costume Supervisor); *Dodsworth* (Costume Supervisor); *Dream Child* (Costume Supervisor); *Order Please* (Costume Supervisor); *Personal Appearance* (Costume Supervisor) **1935** *On to Fortune†* (Costume Supervisor); *Sweet Mystery of Life* (Costume Supervisor) **1937** *Chalked Out* (Costume Supervisor); *Now You've Done It* (Costume Supervisor); *Red Harvest* (Costume Supervisor) **1938** *Kiss the Boys Goodbye* (Costume Supervisor) **1949** *Love Me Long* (Costume Supervisor) **1950** *Mr. Barry's Etchings* (Costume Supervisor)

Harper Pennington

Harper Pennington was an illustrator and painter who was also interested in the theater. He was born in Newport, Rhode Island in 1855 and studied at the Académie Julien in Paris, as well as privately with Gérome and Carolus-Duran. Widely exhibited at the end of the nineteenth century, he died in Baltimore, Maryland in 1920.

Costumes: 1901 *When Knighthood Was in Flower†*

Lights: 1917 *Granny Maumee*

William Pennington

The director of the scenic department of the Washington Square Players, William E. Pennington designed sets for a Broadway play in 1918. He was stage manager of the Bandbox Theatre, 520 E. 77th Street, New York City in 1916. In the early 1930s he was associated with Robert W. Bergman Studios at 142 West 39th Street as secretary of the corporation. His father was the British actor, William H. Pennington (1832-1923), who had appeared as Hamlet at Sadler's Wells in 1872, in productions for the Drury Lane Theatre, and in recitals of Shakespeare for Prime Minister Gladstone at Carlton House Terrace.

Lights: 1918 *Hitchy Koo 1918*

Conrad Penrod

Conrad Penrod studied at Carnegie Institute of Technology and the University of Pittsburgh in his home town of Pittsburgh, Pennsylvania. His first professional designs were for the White Barn Theatre in Pittsburgh. He has worked mainly on the West Coast since designing *Garden District* at the Ivar Theatre in Hollywood - the first of over 400 productions in California. He also owns and operates a construction shop that supplies scenery to theaters in the Los Angeles area.

Lights: 1971 *No Place to be Somebody*

W. Perkins

English scenic artist and designer William Perkins (generally credited as W. or Wm.) was especially prolific in the last three decades of the nineteenth century in London. As early as 1864, he received playbill credit as an assistant to William Beverley and subsequently often collaborated with the other British scene painters of his generation: Robert McCleery, Bruce Smith, Julian Hicks, Harry Emden, and Robert Caney among others. He painted and designed scenery for the major London theaters including the St. James, Vaudeville, Prince of Wales, Princess, and Queen's Theatres, and at Drury Lane. His single Broadway credit was for a production that played in New York after a successful London run.

Sets: 1901 *The Price of Peace*†

Alvin B. Perry

Alvin B. Perry was born in Newport News, Virginia on April 24, 1951 and received a B. S. at Northwestern University, where he studied with Samuel Bell and had his first design assignment, *The Medium*. After two years of study at Yale he worked at the New York Shakespeare Festival with Milo Morrow. He has designed in many regional theaters, and has had a long association with Kent Thompson and the Alabama Shakespeare Festival. Off-Broadway credits include productions at the Manhattan Theatre Club and the Joseph Papp Public Theatre. His costume designs were exhibited in "Onstage: A Century of African American Stage Design" in 1995 at The New York Public Library for the Performing Arts at Lincoln Center. Twenty-first century designs include *Three Mo' Tenors* for Marion Caffey, *A Lesson Before Dying* at the Signature Theatre Company and *St. Lucy's Eyes* at the Cherry Lane Theatre.

Costumes: 1980 *Home*

Joan Personette

Joan Personette, an artist who painted and created collage, was born June 30, 1914 and began her professional life as a costume designer. In the early 1950s she studied with Hans Hofmann in Provincetown, Massachusetts and later with Milton Avery in New York City turning her attention to abstract painting. An exhibition, "Joan Personette, A Retrospective," was held at the National Museum of Women in the Arts in Washington, D.C. in 1990, and her collages were included in the exhibition "Ohio Women Artists" at that same museum in 1991. She died in Nevada on August 29, 1998. The artist should not be confused with the librarian and educator who has the same name.

Costumes: 1951 *Two on the Aisle*

Peters and Kennel

Rollo Peters and Louis Kennel collaborated on the scenic design for a Broadway production in 1918. Rollo Peters, an actor and set designer, worked for the Washington Square Players and the Theatre Guild and also designed under his own name. Louis Kennel has Broadway credits as a costume and lighting designer, but his major activity during fifty years in the theater was scenic design. His primary business was Louis Kennel Scenic Studios, in North Bergen, New Jersey. He also collaborated with Robert C. Entwistle through "Kennel and Entwistle" from 1919 to 1931, and with Rollo Peters through "Peters and Entwistle" in 1918.

Sets: **1918** *The Army with Banners*

Rollo Peters

Rollo Peters, known as an actor and set designer, was born Charles Rollo Peters III in Paris on September 25, 1892. He studied in California and Europe and initially followed his father into the art world as a portrait painter. When he decided to be an actor, he stayed busy designing and building scenery on Broadway for the Washington Square Players and the Theatre Guild while seeking roles. His designs were included in an exhibition of the New American Stagecraft in 1919 at the Bourgeois Galleries, New York City. His first appearance as an actor occurred in 1918 with *Salome* and included several seasons as a leading man for Jane Cowl. Although his acting career was ultimately successful, he continued to design occasionally. He died on January 21, 1967, age 74.

Sets: **1911** *Youth* **1917** *Grasshopper; The Little Man; Madame Sand* **1918** *Josephine* **1919** *The Bonds of Interest; John Ferguson; One Night in Rome; Palmy Days* **1920** *Mixed Marriage; The Prince and the Pauper; Youth* **1922** *Dolly Jordan* **1923** *Pelleas and Melisande; Romeo and Juliet* **1924** *Anthony and Cleopatra* **1925** *The Depths; The Taming of the Shrew* **1927** *Out of the Sea* **1928** *Diversion* **1931** *The Pillars of Society; Streets of New York, or Poverty Is No Crime*

Costumes: **1917** *Grasshopper; The Lady of the Camellias†; Madame Sand* **1918** *Josephine* **1919** *The Bonds of Interest; John Ferguson; Moliere* **1920** *The Prince and the Pauper* **1922** *Dolly Jordan* **1923** *Pelleas and Melisande* **1924** *Anthony and Cleopatra* **1925** *The Taming of the Shrew* **1931** *Streets of New York, or Poverty Is No Crime*

Pamela Peterson

Pamela Peterson debuted on Broadway in 1988.

Costumes: **1988** *Joe Turner's Come and Gone*

Mogens Petri

Mogens Petri designed a set in 1932 on Broadway. A long time resident of Fairfield, Connecticut, he was born May 11, 1903 and died in in June 1980.

Sets: **1932** *Black Souls*

Olga Petrova

Olga Petrova, an actress who wrote and starred in her own plays, was born Muriel Harding in Liverpool, England in 1886 and studied in Paris, London and Brussels. Her stage debut was in London in 1906 and was followed by appearances throughout Great Britain and in New York, initially in vaudeville. She appeared in silent movies under contract with Paramount Pictures beginning in 1914, including *The Vampire, Black Butterfly, The Orchid Lady, Law of the Land, The Soul of Magdalen, Patience Sparhawk, The Silence Sellers,* and *The Panther Woman.* Her autobiography, *Butter with My Bread,* was published in 1942. She died on November 30, 1977 at age 93 in Clearwater, Florida.

Sets: **1921** *The White Peacock†* **1923** *Hurricane†*

Victoria Petrovich

Victoria Petrovich is an active designer of scenery and costumes for productions on the West Coast for theaters including La Jolla Playhouse, Los Angeles Opera, Mark Taper Forum, and Seattle Repertory. Off-Broadway productions include scenery for *Cinderella-Cendrillon, Paradise for the Worried* and *Ladies* at Music Theatre Group and *Of Mice and Men* at GeVa Theatre.

Costumes: **1996** *Scapin*

Victor Petry

Victor J. Petry was born in Philadelphia, son of French parents in 1863, and studied at the Academy of Fine Arts in Philadelphia and the École des Beaux Arts in Paris. He was an interior designer with a studio on Fifth Avenue in

New York City who also designed sets. His specialization in theatrical scenery was with interiors. He began professional life as a newspaper illustrator, later designing jewelry and stationery. After arriving in New York he worked with W. & J. Sloan and Elsie de Wolfe before opening his own business. Victor J. Petry died in July 1924. The scenic and interior designer should not be confused with his son, artist and illustrator Victor Petry (1903-) or with actor Vic Petry (1920-1974).

Sets: 1920 *Call the Doctor*†; *Cornered*†; *One*†

Monroe Pevear

Monroe (Moe, Munroe) Pevear was an early pioneer in the use of color in stage lighting. In his 1924 book, *History of Stage Lighting*, Theodore Fuchs credits him with the first use of primary colors of light in combination with clear tinting to achieve any possible color. Monroe Pevear also developed specialized instruments for direct and indirect light. The Pevear Color Specialty Company, "Theatrical Designers and Lighting Engineers," was located in Boston. An undated brochure advertising the company says "The Pevear Color Specialty Company have been the originators of many unique and successful devices for the lighting of the theater and pageant field, combining the science of light and color with highly efficient and practical light projections of many types."

Lights: 1925 *Edgar Allan Poe*

Michael Philippi

Scenic and lighting designer Michael S. Philippi was born in Appleton, Wisconsin on October 19, 1951 to Ken and Margaret Philippi. He studied at the University of Wisconsin at Madison with two valued teachers, John Ezell and Gilbert V. Hemsley. His professional debut was *Funeral March for a One-Man Band* at the St. Nicholas Theatre Company in Chicago, directed by Amy Saltz. His many designs in Chicago have been rewarded with two Jefferson Awards for lighting, for *In the Belly of the Beast: Letters from Prison* in 1984 and the other for scenery of

Terra Nova in 1985, from sixteen nominations. He has also won two Hollywood Drama-Logue Critic's Awards for lighting design, for *Kabuki Medea* at the Berkeley Repertory Theatre in 1985, and for *Changes of Heart* at the Mark Taper Forum in 1997. Twenty-first century designs include *Breath, Boom* at Playwrights Horizons, *Boy Gets Girl* at the Manhattan Theatre Club and *Blue Surge* at the Goodman Theatre.

Lights: 1991 *The Speed of Darkness* 1999 *Death of a Salesman*

Mardi Philips

Mardi Philips trained for the ballet and appeared professionally for the first time at age 14. She was born on June 30, 1943 in Sacramento, California to Philips and Jean Tedford Jacobs, and graduated from San Francisco State University. She became a member of the San Francisco Ballet, which was founded by Dean and Barbara Crockett, and became interested in costumes through Barbara Crockett, who both danced and designed for the company. Interested in musical theater with the opportunity for both period and fantasy design, she designed *Stardust* and was nominated for an Audelco Award for the costume design for *Blackberries*.

Costumes: 1982 *Torch Song Trilogy* 1986 *Honky Tonk Nights* 1987 *Stardust*

Andy Phillips

The British lighting designer Andy Phillips, who has been designing lights on Broadway since 1974, was resident lighting designer at the Royal Court Theatre for seven seasons from 1965 to 1972, designing nearly eighty shows during his tenure. While there, collaborating often with John Dexter, he pioneered the use of pure white light. He has numerous credits in the West End, at the Royal National Theatre, and for plays and operas in Europe and the United States. In 1960 he formed the theater company Group One in Brighton, England. He is also a playwright, with *The Orange Balloon* and *Cars* among his works. Honors include an American Theatre Wing Award nomination for *M. But-*

terfly. Twenty-first century designs include *Speed-the-Plow* in London. The British lighting designer should not be confused with the Canadian journalist, although they have the same name.
Lights: 1974 *Equus* **1975** *The Misanthrope* **1976** *Equus* **1977** *The Merchant* **1981** *Rose* **1983** *The Glass Menagerie* **1988** *M. Butterfly* **1989** *3Penny Opera*†

George Phillips

George Phillips designed lights on Broadway in 1937 for one show.
Sets: 1937 *Professor Mamlock*

Robin Phillips

British actor and director Robin Phillips was born in Haslemere, Surrey, England on February 28, 1942. He studied with Duncan Ross at the Bristol Old Vic, and began his career as an actor, while also beginning to direct. Associated with some of the world's best theaters, the Royal Shakespeare Company, Stratford (Ontario) Festival Theatre (Artistic Director 1974-1980), the Vivian Beaumont Theatre at Lincoln Center, and Citadel Theatre in Edmonton, Canada (Director General 1990-). Much honored, his directing and acting credits, mainly in the classics, are lengthy. An accomplished painter, he occasionally designs sets for productions he directs.
Sets: 1997 *Jekyll & Hyde*†

Rufus Phillips

Rufus D. Phillips, an engineer, novelist, and stock broker, designed a Broadway set in 1937. Born in 1898 in Newport, Kentucky, his study at Trinity College was interrupted by service in World War I. After returning to graduate (B.S. 1919), he worked as a journalist and then as a stock broker, ultimately forming his own firm. When Colfax Phillips, Inc. failed during the Depression, he worked in the theater and wrote novels including *Sound the Trumpet* published in 1937. After training cadets to fly in World War II, he organized Airways Engineering Corporation, helping construct Philadelphia International Airport among others. A man of varied interests and talents, he died on October 11, 1963 at age 64.

Sets: 1937 *The Lady Has a Heart*†

Tim Phillips

Tim Phillips has designed lights and scenery for many off-Broadway productions and has worked as a scenic painter. He has received two Audelco Awards, one for the scenic design for *Winti Train* in 1978 and a second for the lighting design of *Inacent Black* in 1979.
Lights: 1981 *Inacent Black*

Wendell K. Phillips

Wendell K. Phillips, an actor and director, was born on November 27, 1907 in Blandinsville, Illinois. He graduated from the University of Wisconsin and also attended the Goodman School of Theatre. He studied acting with Lee Strasberg and Michael Chekhov. He began acting in New York City in the early 1930s as a member of the Group Theatre, and began directing in the late 1930s. He received a Tony Award as Best Supporting Actor for *Abe Lincoln in Illinois*, and co-founded the Actors Repertory Theatre Workshop. A member of the Communist Party in the 1930s, his career suffered a five-year lapse in the early 1950s, after which he added television and film to his credits and formed StageGroup in San Francisco in the late 1970s. He occasionally also designed lights and sets, mainly for stock companies. Wendell K. Phillips died at age 83 in Berkeley, California on October 6, 1991. His daughter, actress Wendy Phillips Paulin appeared in the television series' *Homefront, Falcon Crest*, etc., and the film *Bugsy*.
Sets: 1933 *Black Diamond*

Lois Phipps

Lois Phipps designed two sets in 1915 in collaboration with Warren Dahler (1897-1961), a painter and scene designer. Additional information about Warren Dahler can be found under his entry.
Sets: 1915 *The Glittering Gate*†; *Tethered Sheep*†

Ben Phlaum

Ben Phlaum, also cited as Benjamin F. Pflaum, designed lights for one play in 1925. He was associated with the New

York Calcium Company, a supplier of theatrical lighting equipment. In 1925 he resided at 124 Convent Avenue in New York City. He was born on October 11, 1890 and died in February 1974.

Lights: 1925 *The Book of Charm*

Antonios Phocas

Antonio Phocas designed costumes for two Broadway plays in the early 1950s.

Costumes: 1952 *Electra*; *Oedipus Tyrannus*

Joseph Physioc

Joseph Allen Physioc was born in Richmond, Virginia and began designing scenery in small theaters before moving to New York and becoming a scenic painter for the Metropolitan Opera. He was a painter as well as a scenic designer and in the 1930s exhibited widely. Known for a traditional realistic style, he did not readily accept the design trend known as the New American Stagecraft. Some of his designs on Broadway occurred before 1900 and included productions for Richard Mansfield such as *Arms and the Man* (1892), *Richard III* (1896) and *Courted into Court* (1896). He was married to actress and soprano Jessica Eskridge Thomas and together they produced musicals as vehicles for her. He also constructed and painted scenery for other designers through Joseph Physioc Studios and, towards the end of his career, through the Central Park Three Arts Theatre. Also known as Joseph Fisiac and Joseph Physive, he died in Columbia, South Carolina on August 3, 1951 at age 86.

Sets: 1899 *Beau Brummell*; *The Last of the Rohans*; *Rogers Brothers in Wall Street*† (Acts II and III); *The Singing Girl* 1900 *All on Account of Eliza*; *The Belle of Bohemia*†; *Cashel Byron's Profession*; *The Rebel*; *Star and Garter* 1901 *The Bonnie Brier Bush*; *The Climbers*†; *King Washington*; *The Red Kloof*; *Tom Moore* 1902 *The Chaperons*; *Fad and Folly*† (Act I); *Hearts Aflame*†; *The Last Appeal*; *Miss Simplicity*; *The Modern Magdalen*; *Mrs. Jack*; *The Ninety and Nine*; *Soldiers of Fortune*; *The Stubbornness of Geraldine* 1903 *Arrah-Na-Pogue*; *Checkers*; *The Earl of Pawtucket*; *The Frisky*

Mrs. Johnson; *Hearts Courageous*; *Jim Blusdo of the Prairie Belle* (All scenic and mechanical effects designed and painted); *Resurrection*; *Skipper & Co., Wall Street*; *What's the Matter with Susan?* (Designed and painted) 1904 *Sunday*; *That Man and I*†; *Tit For Tat* 1905 *The Lion and the Mouse*; *The Misanthrope*†; *Mrs. Temple's Telegram*; *The Prince Chap*; *Strongheart*; *The System of Dr. Tarr*; *Walls of Jericho* 1906 *Cashel Byron's Profession*; *The Chorus Lady*; *The Daughters of Men* 1907 *Classmates*; *The Struggle Everlasting*† 1908 *The Call of the North*; *Father and the Boys*; *The Offenders*; *The Patriot* (Scene painter); *Pierre of the Plains*; *The Traveling Salesman* 1909 *On the Eve*; *The Third Degree* 1912 *Peg o' My Heart* 1913 *The Love Leash*; *Potash and Perlmutter* 1915 *Abe and Mawruss*; *Fair and Warmer*; *Under Fire* 1916 *The Merry Wives of Windsor*†; *Our Little Wife* 1917 *The Brat*; *Daybreak*; *Doing Our Bit*†; *Losing Eloise*; *The Merry Wives of Windsor* 1918 *The Crowded Hour*; *Lightinin'*; *Madonna of the Future*†; *Roads of Destiny*; *Watch Your Neighbor*; *Where Poppies Bloom* 1920 *Ed Wynn Carnival*; *The Girl with the Carmine Lips*; *Jimmie*; *Tickle Me* 1921 *Wait till We're Married* 1922 *Lady Bug*; *Seventh Heaven* 1923 *Within Four Walls* 1924 *Across the Street*; *Artistic Temperament*†; *The Gift*; *Sweeney Todd* 1925 *Cousin Sonia*; *His Queen*; *Love's Call* 1926 *90 Horse Power*; *Henry's Harem*; *The Man from Toronto*; *The Matinee Girl*; *The Night Duel* 1927 *Dracula* 1929 *Philadelphia* 1931 *Dracula*

Joseph Physioc Studio

Joseph Allen Physioc (c.1865-1951) constructed his own designs and painted scenery for other designers through his scenic studio. Joseph Physioc Studio was located in 1919 at 447 First Avenue, New York City and moved to 416 W. 26th Street in 1927. For additional information and credits, see "Joseph Physioc."

Sets: 1902 *Tommy Rot*† (Act I) 1914 *A Perfect Lady*† (Acts I, IV) 1916 *Rich Man, Poor Man* 1917 *Why Marry?* 1918 *Why Marry?* 1919 *Tumble in* 1920 *The Blue Flame*; *The Bone-*

head; *Scrambled Wives*† **1922** *A Serpent's Tooth*; *The Torch Bearers* **1923** *Not So Fast*† **1925** *The Four Flusher*† **1926** *Autumn Fire*; *A Friend Indeed* **1928** *The Lawyer's Dilemma*

Robin Pidcock

Robin Pidcock, born in 1930 is a British designer of sets and costumes, who has designed numerous shows for the Glasgow Citizens' Theatre since 1965, when he was named head of the design department. *The Critic, The Wild Duck* and *Mrs. Warren's Profession* are only a few of his many credits there. Additional designs include sets and costumes for *Rodelinde* at Sadler's Wells, and productions for the Nottingham Playhouse and the New Shakespeare Company.
Sets: 1968 *A Day in the Death of Joe Egg*
Costumes: 1968 *A Day in the Death of Joe Egg*

Colin Pigott

Colin Pigott, a British scenic designer, debuted on Broadway in 1986. He studied at the Kingston School of Art and received a B.A. in interior design. An active designer of television specials, commercials and feature films, he worked for BBC-TV from 1963 to 1967. He received a Bursary from the Royal Society of Art in 1963 for television and film set design. Twenty-first century credits include production design for *Big Brother*, a United Kingdom reality-based television series.
Sets: 1986 *Jerome Kern Goes to Hollywood*

Richard Pilbrow

Richard Pilbrow has designed over two hundred productions mainly in London. He has also produced plays in New York and Moscow since his professional life began. He founded Theatre Projects in 1957, assembling a team of young lighting designers to encourage the development of the profession and introduce American and German methods and equipment to the United Kingdom. He began his career as a lighting designer and a stage manager. He has also a consulted on developing lighting systems for the Hammer-

smith Lyric Theatre restoration, the Royal National Theatre, the Barbican, A Contemporary Theatre in Seattle, and the Bayfront Center in Toronto among many others. He believes continuing to design is critical to effective theater consulting. Born in Beckenham, Kent, England on April 28, 1933, he studied stage management at the Central School of Speech and Drama and came to the U.S. in 1988. His book *Stage Lighting* was published in 1970.
Lights: 1967 *Rosencrantz and Guildenstern Are Dead* **1968** *Zorba* **1970** *The Rothschilds* **1973** *Shelter* **1992** *Four Baboons Adoring the Sun* **1993** *Tango Pasion*† **1994** *Show Boat* **1997** *The Life*

Lydia Pincus-Gany

Lydia Pincus-Gany (Gani) was born in Bucharest, Rumania on March 24, 1929 and graduated from the Academy of Fine Arts in that city. Between 1953 and 1960 she designed for several state theaters in Bucharest, including the Mic Theatre, Notara Theatre, and the National Theatre Oradea. From 1961 to the present she has worked mainly in Israel where her sets and costumes are often seen at the Habimah Theatre and the Cameri Theatre among many others. She also designs for the modern dance company, Bat Sheva, and the Inbal and Carmon Companies of folk dancers. She has designed over two hundred productions and has often been awarded the equivalent of the Tony Award in Israel. They were featured in "The Curtain Rises in the Museum" exhibition of Beersheba Theatre productions at the Negev Museum in 1991. Mrs. Pincus-Gany has also lectured on set and costume design at Tel-Aviv University. Twenty-first century design credits include the revival of *Romeo and Juliet* for the Israel Classical Ballet Company.
Costumes: 1969 *The New Music Hall of Israel* **1971** *To Live Another Summer*

Scott Pinkney

Scott Pinkney designs lights for the theater and has extensive industrial lighting design credits for clients such as IBM, Estée Lauder, and BMW. He was born on April 7, 1953 in Pittsburgh the son of Marjorie L. Pinkney, an accountant, and Ellwood E. Pinkney, an interior designer and planner from whom he learned drafting and a visual sense. His wife, Debra Smith Pinkney, is a former dancer with BalletWest and a founder of and teacher at the Cape Cod Dance Center. He received a B.F.A. from Boston University in 1976 in lighting design and assisted Richard Winkler for three years. He has also studied and admired designs by Tharon Musser. His first design in the professional world was *The Revels* at the Sanders Theatre in Cambridge, Massachusetts in 1974. His designs have been honored with a Denver Drama Critics Circle Award for lighting design for *Don Juan*, and a Phoebe Award for lighting design for *My Fair Lady* at Theatre Virginia in Richmond.

Lights: 1982 *Torch Song Trilogy*

John Piper

John Egerton Christmas Piper, a British designer and artist, also wrote and illustrated books. He was born in Epsom, Surrey, England on December 13, 1903 and studied at Epsom College, the Royal College of Art (with Sir William Richardson) and at the Slade School of Art. He began exhibiting in 1925 and during World War II recorded bomb damage in paintings for the British government. A retrospective of his art, "50 Years of Work," was held at the Museum of Modern Art, Oxford in 1979. His works are in the permanent collections of the Tate Gallery, the Guggenheim Museum and the Victoria and Albert Museum among others. In addition he has designed many operas and ballets, notably *The Quest* for Sadler's Wells Ballet in 1943 for Frederick Ashton, and the operas of Benjamin Britten. He died in England on June 29, 1992 at age 88. In 2000, an exhibit at London's Imperial War Museum, "John Piper: The Forties," was accompanied by the publication of a lavishly illustrated book with the same title by David Fraser Jenkins.

Sets: 1946 *Oedipus* **1948** *Oedipus Rex*; *The Rape of Lucretia* **1956** *Cranks*

William Pitkin

William Pitkin was born in Omaha, Nebraska on July 15, 1925. A scenic designer, he also occasionally contributed costume and lighting designs to productions. After attending college in the United States and serving in the Army Air Force, he studied in Paris with Christian Bérard at the École Paul Colin. He designed settings in summer stock beginning in 1947 and was a staff designer for Raymond Loewy Associates in 1953. His first New York production was *The Threepenny Opera* starring Lotte Lenya at the Theatre de Lys in 1954. He also designed for opera and extensively for ballet. Mr. Pitkin won an Emmy Award in 1978 for the costumes for *Romeo and Juliet* on PBS. He died on May 10, 1990 in San Antonio, Texas, at age 65.

Sets: 1957 *The Cave Dwellers*; *A Moon for the Misbegotten*; *The Potting Shed* **1960** *Invitation to a March* **1961** *The Conquering Hero†* **1962** *The Beauty Part*; *Seidman and Son*; *Something about a Soldier* **1965** *The Impossible Years* **1968** *The Guide* **1970** *Chinese, The/ Dr. Fish* **1972** *Dear Oscar*

Costumes: 1956 *Child of Fortune* **1962** *Seidman and Son*; *Something about a Soldier* **1968** *The Guide*

Lights: 1962 *The Beauty Part*; *Seidman and Son*

Ben Platt

Benjamin Platt, a tailor, designed costumes for a featured player on Broadway in 1934. He resided with his wife Rebecca at 1772 Vyse Avenue in the early 1930s, according to the Manhattan and Bronx City Directories published in 1931 and 1933.

Costumes: 1934 *Mahogony Hall†* (Miss Baclanova's costumes)

Charles A. Platt

Charles Adams Platt was an architect who worked from offices at 11 East 24th Street in New York City. His designs included buildings at the University of Illinois, the Freer Gallery of Art in Washington, D.C., and apartment houses in New York City. Early in his career, he occasionally designed scenery. He died in New York in 1934.

Sets: 1906 *The Crossing*

Joseph B. Platt

Best remembered as the set designer for *Gone With The Wind*, Joseph Brereton Platt was an industrial and interior designer. He was born on March 26, 1895 in Plainfield, New Jersey and studied at the Parsons School of Design. After service in World War I he worked as a mural painter, magazine illustrator, and interior designer and in 1933 became head of design for Marshall Field and Company in Chicago. In 1936 he formed his own company and designed for various businesses, creating (among other things) the Whitman Sampler Box and cosmetic packages for Elizabeth Arden. He also designed sets for movies and plays and was a member of United Scenic Artists, The Society of Industrial Designers and the Art Directors Club of America. He taught at the Parsons School of Design from 1933 to 1952 and died on February 6, 1968 in Wayne, Pennsylvania.

Sets: 1944 *In Bed We Cry*; *Suds in Your Eye*

Livingston Platt

Livingston Platt was born in Plattsburg, New York in 1874 and went to Europe to develop his skills as a painter. While in Paris he became acquainted with many actors and managers who introduced him to theater and its possibilities. He first designed for a small theater in Bruges, Belgium, which led to designs for several opera productions. He returned to the United States in 1911 and became head of design at the Toy Theatre in Boston, where in 1914 he designed four productions for Margaret Anglin. He preferred to be called a "stage decorator" and designed numerous settings in New York, many of them before 1915, occasionally contributing costume and lighting designs to these same productions. Nothing is known of him after 1933.

Sets: 1915 *Beverly's Balance* 1917 *Billeted* 1918 *East Is West*; *Electra* 1919 *Abraham Lincoln* (Also decorations); *First Is Last*[†]; *Lusmore*; *Shakuntala* 1920 *The Bad Man*; *Thy Name Is*

Woman 1921 *Bluebeard's Eighth Wife*; *The Children's Tragedy*; *Eyvind of the Hills*; *Launcelot and Elaine*; *Mary Stuart*; *Two Blocks Away*; *The White Villa* 1922 *Banco*; *The Ever Green Lady*; *The First 50 Years*; *It Is the Law*; *The Lady Christilinda*; *Madame Pierre* 1923 *Floriani's Wife*; *In Love with Love*; *Robert E. Lee* 1924 *Catskill Dutch*; *Cock O' the Roost*; *The Far Cry*; *The Goose Hangs High*; *No Other Girl*; *The Outsider*; *Outward Bound*; *The Tantrum*[†]; *The Youngest* 1925 *Aloma of the South Seas*; *The Backslapper*; *The Dark Angel*; *Holka Polka*; *It All Depends*; *Oh! Mama*; *Pierrot the Prodigal*; *The School for Scandal*; *She Had to Know*; *Stolen Fruit*; *Stronger than Love*; *Two Married Men* 1926 *The Creaking Chair*; *Daisy Mayme*; *Devils*; *The Great Gatsby*; *Kitty's Kisses*; *Puppy Love*; *Slaves All*; *The Sport of Kings*; *The Witch* 1927 *A La Carte*; *Baby Mine*; *Behold the Bridegroom*; *The Dark*; *Electra*; *House of Shadows*; *L'Aiglon*; *Lally*; *The Legend of Leonora*; *Puppets of Passion*; *The Racket*; *Savage under the Skin*; *Storm Center*; *The Strawberry Blonde*; *Venus* 1928 *Carry On*; *A Distant Drum*; *Elmer Gantry*; *A Free Soul*; *The Great Power*; *In Love with Love*; *Lady Dedlock*[†]; *The Outsider*; *Pleasure Man*; *The Queen's Husband*; *Say When*; *Tomorrow...* 1929 *Abraham Lincoln*; *The First Mrs. Fraser*; *Flight*; *Maggie the Magnificent*; *Merry Andrew*; *Precious*; *A Strong Man's House*; *Thunder in the Air* 1930 *The Greeks Have a Word for It*; *Launcelot and Elaine* 1931 *Berlin*; *A Church Mouse*; *The Guest Room* 1932 *Alice Sit-by-the-Fire/ The Old Lady Shows*; *Dinner at Eight*; *Domino*; *Lilly Turner*; *Mademoiselle*; *The Man Who Reclaimed His Head*; *The Round-Up*; *The Stork Is Dead*; *We Are No Longer Children* 1933 *For Services Rendered*; *Hangman's Whip*; *Her Tin Soldier*; *A Party*; *A Saturday Night*; *Three and One*; *$25.00 an Hour*

Costumes: 1918 *Electra*; *Freedom* 1919 *Abraham Lincoln*; *First Is Last*[†]; *Lusmore*; *Shakuntala* 1921 *Eyvind of the Hills*; *Mary Stuart* 1922 *Banco*[†]; *The First 50 Years* 1925 *Aloma of the South Seas*; *Holka Polka*; *Stronger than Love* 1926 *The Creaking Chair*; *The Sport of Kings* 1927 *Electra*; *L'Aiglon*; *The Racket* 1928 *Elmer Gantry*[†] 1930 *A Lit-*

tle Brother of the Rich **1931** *The Guest Room* **1933** *The Pursuit of Happiness*†
Lights: **1932** *When Ladies Meet*

Frank Platzer

A scenic designer and painter, Frank Platzer was active in New York between 1899 and 1911. He frequently collaborated with Hans Meixner and sometimes they simply used their last names. For example, the 1905 *Pantaloon* playbill says: "Scenes by Platzer and Meixner." He was also responsible for the scenery for *Sportin' Life* at the Acadmey of Music in 1899. Identified as an artist in the 1900 New York City directory, he resided on Prospect Avenue North in Throggs Neck. His design for *As You Like It* was included in "The Art of the Theatre." The exhibition of original designs for the stage was held at 714 Fifth Avenue in November, 1914 by the Stage Society of New York.

Sets: **1900** *Woman and Wine*† **1903** *Way Down East*† (as: Platzer) **1904** *Two Little Sailor Boys* **1905** *The Education of Mr. Pipp*; *Fritz in Tammany Hall*† (as: Platzer: Scenery and mechanical effects); *The Heir to the Hoorah*; *Pantaloon*† **1906** *The Clansman*†; *District Leader*†; *The House of Mirth*; *The Hypocrites*; *The Strength of the Weak*† **1907** *Captain's Brassbound's Conversion*; *Her Sister*; *The Secret Orchard*†; *The Silver Box*; *The Top o' th' World*† (as: Platzer) **1908** *Diana of Dobson's*; *Lady Frederick*; *The Likes o' Me*; *Society and the Bulldog* (as: Platzer) **1909** *Going Some*; *The Sins of Society*† (as: Platzer) **1910** *The Importance of Being Earnest*† (Act I, II); *Love among the Lions*; *Mid-Channel*; *Rebecca of Sunnybrook Farm*† (as: Platzer); *Suzanne*; *We Can't Be As Bad As All That* **1911** *Ben-Hur*; *The Happiest Night of His Life*† (Act II); *Kismet*†; *The Marionettes*†; *The Philosopher in the Apple Orchard*; *The Senator Keeps House*†

Theodore Platzer

Theodore Platzer contributed scenery to a production in Broadway's first season of the twentieth century.
Sets: **1899** *The Ghetto*†

Gertrude Plons

Gertrude Plons, who specialized in gowns from a shop at 963 Madison Avenue in New York City, contributed the designs for gowns to a production on Broadway in 1935. Her husband, Monroe Plonsky, was president of Plonsky & Weiss, Inc. which operated from the same address. A long time resident of Bronx, New York, she was born on September 24, 1898 and died on October 31, 1991.
Costumes: **1936** *In the Bag* (Gowns)

Pluesch

The lighting designs for a 1991 production were created by Pluesch. She is from Germany where she designs frequently.
Lights: **1991** *Andre Heller's Wonderhouse*

Sue Plummer

Susan Jennifer Plummer, a British designer of scenery and costumes, was born on January 20, 1943 in London. She studied at St. Martin's School of Art. Her designs have been seen through the United Kingdom including productions in Sheffield, Glasgow and London, for opera as well as theater. Additional designs in America include scenery and costumes for *Valued Friends* in New Haven. Late twentieth century designs include *The Light Rough* by Brian Thompson and *The Memory of Water* by Shelagh Stephenson at the Hampstead Theatre in London.

Sets: **1985** *Home Front*† (Original design)

Walter Plunkett

Although Walter Plunkett designed numerous movies and received many Academy Award nominations, he is best known for his costume designs for *Gone With the Wind.* He was born in California in 1902 and began designing initially for Ruth St. Denis, instead of pursuing a career as an actor. From 1926 until 1930 and 1932 to 1935, he was head of the wardrobe department for FBO (later RKO) Studios, after which he became a freelance designer. From 1947 until retiring in 1965, he was at M-G-M. He won an Academy Award for *An American in Paris* designed in collaboration with Irene Sharaff and Orry-Kelly. He also received nominations for *The Magnificent Yankee, Kind Lady, That Forsyte Woman, The Actress, Young Bess, Raintree County, Some Came Running, Pocketful of Miracles,* and *How the West Was Won.* Plunkett died in California in 1982.

Costumes: 1951 *Don Juan in Hell* (Miss Moorehead's gown)

Dede Pochos

Dede Pochos is both an actress and a costume designer. In the early 1990s she was a member of the Willow Cabin Theatre Company, and also performed in *As You Like It* at the Anderson Theatre, and *Macbeth* in TriBeCa. She collaborated with Fiona Davis on the costumes for *Wilder, Wilder, Wilder* (in which she also appeared), *S.S. Glencairn - Four Plays of the Sea* at the Clurman Theatre, and *Who Will Carry the Word?* at the Anderson Theatre. She co-designed *A Child's Christmas in Wales* with Tasha Lawrence in 1996 off-Broadway.

Costumes: 1993 *Wilder, Wilder, Wilder*†

Willy Pogany

Willy Pogany was born on August 23, 1882 in Szeged, Hungary and studied in Budapest, Munich and Paris. His career in the visual arts was illustrious and varied. He began as a caricaturist, settled in New York in 1914, created murals (including one for the Ziegfeld Theatre), wrote and illustrated books and magazines, designed buildings, painted portraits and designed sets and costumes. He remains well-recognized as an illustrator by bibliophiles and book collectors. At the height of his theatrical career he was regarded as an authority on the color effects created by lighting. He designed Broadway plays between 1921 and 1930 and also designed costumes and scenery for the Fokine and Adolph Bloom ballets. He founded Willy Pogany Associates, 152 West 46th Street, and collaborated with Joseph Teichner in Pogany-Teichner

Studios. His career also included work in films as an art director. Mr. Pogany died on July 30, 1955 at age 72.

Sets: 1921 *As Ye Mould; Get Together*† (The Thunder Bird); *The Great Broxopp* **1924** *The Little Angel; Madame Pompadour* **1925** *Earl Carroll's Vanities*†; *Florida Girl*†; *The ...* **1926** *2 Girls Wanted*†; *The Jeweled Tree; Queen High* **1928** *Houseboat on the Styx; Kidding Kidders* (as: Willy Pogany Associates) **1929** *Divided Honors; Hawk Island* **1930** *Sari*

Costumes: 1921 *Get Together*† **1924** *The Little Angel* **1925** *The ...* **1930** *Sari*

Lights: 1925 *The ...*

Pogany-Teichner Studios

Scenic designers Willy Pogany (1882-1955) and Joseph Teichner (1888-1966) were associated with Pogany-Teichner Studios where they constructed and painted scenery. In 1925 the studio received credit for the scenic design of a Broadway production. For additional information see the entries under each of their names.

Sets: 1925 *When You Smile*

H. R. Poindexter

H. R. Poindexter was a scenic and lighting designer who worked principally on the West Coast. He was production supervisor and lighting designer for the American Ballet Theatre, the Martha Graham Company, and the Dallas Civic Opera Company. He was technical supervisor at the Mark Taper Forum in Los Angeles from 1969 to 1974, and at the time of his death on September 24, 1977 was technical supervisor for the Ahmanson Theatre. He received a Tony Award for *Paul Sills' Story Theatre* in 1971 and a Los Angeles Drama Critics' Award for *Metamorphoses,* one of many lighting designs created for the Mark Taper Forum. He also created scenery and lighting for many national tours. Two productions he designed, *Paul Robeson* and *Vincent Price in Diversions and Delights,* were on tour prior to their Broadway openings when he died in 1977 at age 41.

Sets: 1974 *Henry Fonda As Clarence*

Darrow **1975** *Henry Fonda As Clarence Darrow* **1976** *The Belle of Amherst; The Night of the Iguana* **1978** *Paul Robeson; Vincent Price in Diversions and Delights*
Lights: **1970** *Ovid's Metamorphoses; Paul Sills' Story Theatre* **1971** *Abelard and Heloise* **1972** *An Evening with Richard Nixon; A Funny Thing Happened on the Way to the Forum* **1974** *Henry Fonda As Clarence Darrow* **1975** *Henry Fonda As Clarence Darrow; Private Lives* **1976** *The Belle of Amherst; Music Is; The Night of the Iguana* **1978** *Vincent Price in Diversions and Delights*

Paul Poiret

Paul Poiret was born on April 20, 1879 in Paris and began his career selling sketches to fashion designers. While working for Doucet in 1896 he discovered his passion for the theater. He reigned between 1904 and 1924 as the fashion designer who banned the corset (although he hobbled legs with narrow skirts). He designed often for the theater in New York and Paris and for the ballet, concentrating on costumes but occasionally contributing scenic designs. Like most of the Parisian art community at that time, he was a great friend of Diaghilev. The same extravagance which brought him fame led to his decline, as he was unable to adjust to the changes created by World War I. He died in poverty in Paris on April 28, 1944.
Sets: **1920** *Afgar* **1925** *Naughty Cinderella*
Costumes: **1911** *Gypsy Love*[†] (Miss Sylvia's first costume) **1912** *Whirl of Society*[†] (Act II headdresses) **1913** *The Great Adventure* (Miss Barton's gowns) **1920** *Afgar* **1922** *The Bunch and Judy*[†] (Costumes in Cabaret Scene in Act II) **1923** *Cinders*[†] (Ladies gowns); *Little Miss Bluebeard*[†] (Miss Bordoni's kimono and P.J.'s, etc.) **1925** *Naughty Cinderella*

Lester Polakov

Lester Polakov (Polikoff) was born in Chicago in 1916 and studied painting in New York with George Grosz, stagecraft with Milton Smith at Columbia University, and drafting with Emeline Roche. He began his career designing sets in summer stock. His New York debut was a 1935 production of *White Trash* at Columbia University, and in 1938 he designed scenery for *The Mother*, making his Broadway debut. He assisted Harry Horner on many productions and credits him as his mentor. After service in the Army Air Corps in World War II he resumed designing and had several exhibitions. In 1958 Polakov established the Lester Polakov Studio of Stage Design, later known as the "Studio and Forum of Stage Design," where he employed some of the best-known designers of sets, lights and costumes to teach. While teaching and overseeing the operation of this school he continued to design sets and costumes for stage and film. His book, *We Live to Fly/Paint Again* was published in 1993.
Sets: **1938** *The Mother* **1946** *Call Me Mister* **1947** *Crime and Punishment*[†] **1950** *The Golden State; The Member of the Wedding* **1952** *Mrs. McThing* **1953** *The Emperor's Clothes* **1954** *The Winner* **1955** *The Skin of Our Teeth* **1961** *Great Day in the Morning* **1980** *Charlotte*
Costumes: **1940** *Reunion in New York* **1941** *Crazy with the Heat*[†] **1947** *Crime and Punishment* **1950** *The Member of the Wedding*
Lights: **1947** *Crime and Punishment* **1950** *The Golden State; The Member of the Wedding* **1953** *The Emperor's Clothes* **1961** *Great Day in the Morning*

Juliet Polcsa

Juliet Polcsa was born in the 1960s and studied at the Fashion Institute of Technology. She worked on Seventh Avenue for four years before a 1985 summer stock experience when she changed her specialization from fashion to costumes. Theater credits include productions off-Broadway and in regional theaters. She collaborated on costumes with Marie Anne Chiment for her 1992 Broadway debut. Best known as the costume designer for the HBO-TV series *The Sopranos*, her first television series, her many film credits include *Big Night, The Imposters, Joe Gould's Secret*, and *Welcome to Collinwood*.
Costumes: **1992** *Metro*[†]

Dominic Poleo

Dominic Poleo graduated from Boston University. He made his professional debut with the Goldovsky Opera Company when he designed costumes for its' performances in Boston and at the Tanglewood Music Festival. Active in regional theaters including the Houston Theatre Center in the 1960s, his Broadway debut in 1970 was also his New York City debut. A resident of Massachusetts for most of his life, he was born on April 26, 1932 and died in March 1974.

Costumes: 1970 *Grin and Bare It!/ Postcards*

Helen Pond

Helen Barbara Pond was born on June 26, 1924 in Cleveland and is the daughter of Ralph Herbert and Charlotte Waters Pond. She studied at Ohio State and Columbia Universities. She began designing at the Chagrin Falls Summer Theatre in Ohio with *Papa is All* and made her New York debut in 1955 with *The House of Connelly*. Since then she has created numerous scenic and lighting designs throughout the United States, including productions for the Paper Mill Playhouse and for thirty-eight seasons at the Cape Playhouse in Dennis, Massachusetts. Opera designs include numerous credits as principal designer for the Opera Company of Boston since 1970 and additional productions for the New York City Opera. She generally works in collaboration with Herbert Senn, and their designs are often exhibited. Honors include the first Robert Edmond Jones Prize, given in 1993, for their contributions to Boston area theater, honoring nearly 50 productions for the Opera Company of Boston and over 300 productions at the Cape Playhouse.

Sets: 1963 *Double Dublin*† 1964 *Roar Like a Dove*†; *What Makes Sammy Run?*† 1968 *Noel Coward's Sweet Potato*† 1973 *No Sex Please, We're British*† 1981 *Macbeth*† 1983 *Show Boat*† 1986 *Oh Coward!*†

Lights: 1963 *Double Dublin*† 1964 *Roar Like a Dove*†; *What Makes Sammy Run?*†

Helene Pons

Helene Pons was born Helene Wermicheff in Tiflis, in the Russian Caucasus, and studied in Switzerland. She took her professional name from her husband, George Pons, who was technical director for Chauve Souris. She designed the costumes for numerous Broadway shows, sometimes the whole show and sometimes for a featured player. As president of Helene Pons Studio, she oversaw the execution of her own designs and those of other costume designers, notably productions at the Metropolitan Opera, American Ballet Theatre, New York City Ballet, and on Broadway, for *My Fair Lady* for Cecil Beaton and *Kiss Me, Kate* for Lemuel Ayers among others. She was nominated for Tony Awards for the three plays she designed on Broadway in 1956. She also designed costumes for many films, including *White Christmas*. In 1963, she closed her studio and moved to California. She never drew "renderings," but started with small rough sketches, made notes and then turned them over to the assistants in her shop to construct. She died on April 19, 1990 in Rome, two weeks before her 92nd birthday.

Costumes: 1926 *The Trumpet Shall Sound* 1927 *The Ivory Door*† 1928 *12,000* (Miss Ellis' costumes); *Macbeth*† 1930 *Marseilles* (Dresses); *The Second Little Show*† 1931 *The Wives of Henry VIII* (After Holbein) 1932 *The Mad Hopes*; *The Wives of Henry VIII* 1933 *The Loves of Charles II*; *Run, Little Chillun*; *Shooting Star* 1934 *The Lady from the Sea*† (Gowns); *Moor Born*; *Theodora, the Queen* 1935 *Mansion on the Hudson* 1936 *The Golden Journey*; *Sweet River*† (Miss Rogers', Miss Philson's, and Miss Hardison's gowns); *Ten Million Ghosts*† (Miss O'Neil's gowns) 1937 *Babes in Arms*; *Brown Sugar*; *Edna His Wife* 1938 *Escape This Night*; *How to Get Tough About It*; *Madame Capet*; *Our Town*; *Shadow and Substance* 1939 *Key Largo*; *The Primrose Path* 1940 *The Flying Gerardos*; *Grey Farm*† (Miss Varden's costumes); *Ladies in Retirement*; *Two on an Island* 1941 *Arsenic and Old Lace* (Miss Hull's and Miss Adair's dresses); *The Distant City*; *Ring around Elizabeth*

(Miss Cowl's Sailing costume); *Theatre†* (Miss Skinner's Act II and Act III costumes); *Watch on the Rhine* **1942** *Lily of the Valley* **1947** *Duet for Two Hands*; *How I Wonder*; *Portrait in Black* (Costume Supervisor) **1948** *Ghosts†* (Miss Le Galliene's costumes); *Hedda Gabler*; *The Men We Marry*; *Where Stars Walk* **1952** *Paris '90*; *The Time of the Cuckoo* **1955** *The Dark Is Light Enough*; *The Diary of Anne Frank*; *The Heavenly Twins*; *The Skin of Our Teeth*; *A View from the Bridge* **1957** *Holiday for Lovers*; *Monique*; *Romanoff and Juliet* **1958** *Epitaph for George Dillon* (Costume Supervisor) **1960** *A Lovely Night* (Miss Stickney's gowns); *Semi-Detached* **1961** *Daughter of Silence†*; *Sail Away†* **1963** *Love and Kisses*

Nananne Porcher

The small number of lighting design credits on the Broadway stage do not reveal the scope of the lighting designs created by Nananne Porcher for ballet, opera, and theater throughout the United States. She was born on December 14, 1922 in LaGrange, Georgia and studied at the University of North Carolina at Chapel Hill and with Jean Rosenthal. Ultimately she focused her talents on theater consulting, including major projects at the Carolina Theatre of the North Carolina School of the Arts, and the George Street Playhouse in New Brunswick, New Jersey among many, many others. She became president of Jean Rosenthal Associates in 1975 and remained in that position when the company became Osprey Designs. Like Jean Rosenthal she was an avid proponent of renovating spacesfor theater. In addition she served as resident designer for American Ballet Theatre and designed lights for major opera companies throughout the United States. World premieres of operas include *Beatrix Cenci* at Opera Society of Washington, D.C. in 1971 and Barber's *Antony and Cleopatra* at the Metropolitan Opera in 1966. She died on June 17, 2001.

Lights: 1971 *Ari* **1974** *Treemonisha*

Ellis E. Porter

Ellis E. Porter was active on Broadway between 1927 and 1937.

Costumes: 1927 *Lady Do†* **1937** *Curtain Call*

Madame Caleb Porter

British actor Caleb Porter (1867-1940) had two wives. The first with Jessie Hannah Neil with whom he had a son, Neil Porter, ended in divorce. The second was the actress Kitty de Legh (1887-?) who was widowed by his death.

Costumes: 1912 *Milestones†*

Mike Porter

Michael (Mike Porter), a painter and designer for stage, film, and television, was born in 1944 (some sources indicate 1948) in Dublin. Prior to designing scenery for *Censored Scenes from King Kong* on Broadway, he designed it in London's West End and for BBC-TV. As a fine art painter, he has had several exhibitions including "Paintings on Wood and Paper" at Keattle's Yard in Cambridge, England. Designs for film include *Krapp's Last Tape.*

Sets: 1980 *Censored Scenes from King Kong*

Kenneth Posner

Kenneth Posner has been involved with the theater since he was five years old, through his mother who designed costumes for the community theater in Westchester, New York where he grew up. He studied at Boston University and then at the State University of New York at Purchase with William Mintzer, widely regarded as a fine teacher and mentor. While assisting Jeff Davis at the Berkshire Theatre Festival, he began designing lights for the Unicorn Theatre, Berkshire's second stage. One of the productions, *Emerald City* was done again the following year at the New York Theatre Workshop, becoming his New York debut. He has designed many productions in major regional theaters, the Guthrie Theatre, Goodman Theatre, and La Jolla Playhouse among them, and in leading theaters off-Broadway. Among his many honors are the 1999 Michael Merritt Award for Excellence in Design and Collaboration, the Lucille Lortel Award for *Side Man*, and

a Joseph Jefferson award for *Richard III* at the Shakespeare Repertory in Chicago. Twenty-first century designs include *The Man Who Had all the Luck* at the Williamstown Theatre Festival and *The Credeaux Canvas* at Playwrights Horizons' Wilder Theatre.
Lights: **1995** *The Rose Tattoo* **1996** *The Father*; *Getting Away with Murder*; *The Rehearsal* **1997** *The Lily and the Prince*; *The Little Foxes*; *View from the Bridge, A* **1998** *Little Me*; *Side Man* **1999** *The Lion in Winter*; *Swing!*; *You're a Good Man, Charlie Brown* **2000** *Uncle Vanya* **2001** *The Adventures of Tom Sawyer*

David Potts

David Potts, son of Edward and Joanne Potts, was born on July 29, 1949 in Cleveland, Ohio. He received a B.A. from Purdue University and an M.F.A. from Brandeis University where he debuted with *Boys in the Band*. He has numerous credits for set designs in regional and off-Broadway theaters and has been resident designer at Circle Repertory Company since 1981. He was Assistant Professor of Design at the State University of New York at Purchase from 1985 to 1988, and design consultant for the Berkshire Theatre Festival from 1978 to 1987. The setting for *Full Hookup* at C.R.C. was nominated for a Drama Desk Award, and his art direction for *Fifth of July* on the PBS-TV series *Theatre in America* was nominated for an ACE Award. David Potts designed the national tours of *I Never Sang For My Father* and *Sleuth*. Twenty-first century designs include *Men* presented by the American Stage Company.
Sets: **1985** *As Is* **1987** *The Musical Comedy Murders* **1989** *Born Yesterday*

George Potts

Costume designer George Potts was born in 1956. He learned about designing and making quality costumes by working with Grace Miceli and Maria Brizzi at Grace Costumes, one of New York's theatrical costume houses, and then assisted Albert Wolsky, Geoffrey Holder, Alvin Colt and other designers on a variety of productions for stage and film. He also designed off-Broadway and in 1983, made his own

debut on Broadway. Shortly before his death, of AIDS, on July 19, 1997 in Fort Lauderdale, Florida, he was associate costume designer for the film *The Age of Innocence*.
Costumes: **1983** *The Ritz*

Nancy Potts

Nancy Potts received a B.F.A. from Washington University in St. Louis, Missouri. After spending some time designing for Seventh Avenue houses, she turned her attention to costume design. Her first New York design assignment was *Right You Are If You Think You Are* for the APA/Phoenix Company in 1964. She worked with that company and its artistic director, Ellis Rabb, for several years, including periods of residency for the company at the University of Michigan in Ann Arbor. She has also designed numerous plays for regional theaters and other off-Broadway companies. She has received many awards, including three Tony Award nominations, the Saturday Review of Literature Best Costume Design Award, the Theatre Yearbook Best Costume Design Award, and a Maharam nomination in 1983 for the revival of *You Can't Take It With You*. For her designs at APA/Phoenix, she received a Maharam Award for three plays which she designed in one season, *The Cherry Orchard, Exit the King,* and *Pantagleize*. Recent credits include a revival of *Porgy and Bess* by the New York City Opera in March 2000.
Costumes: **1965** *You Can't Take It with You* **1966** *Right You Are If You Think You Are*; *The School for Scandal*; *We, Comrades Three* **1967** *Pantagleize*; *The Show-Off*; *War and Peace*; *The Wild Duck*; *You Can't Take It with You* **1968** *The Cherry Orchard*; *The Cocktail Party*; *Exit the King*; *Hair*; *The Misanthrope*; *Pantagleize*; *The Show-Off* **1969** *Cock-a-doodle Dandy*; *Hamlet*; *La Strada* **1970** *Harvey* **1971** *The Grass Harp*; *The School for Wives* **1972** *Don Juan*; *The Selling of the President* **1973** *Chemin De Fer*; *Medea*; *A Streetcar Named Desire*; *Veronica's Room* **1974** *The Rules of the Game*; *Who's Who in Hell* **1976** *Porgy and Bess* **1977** *Hair* **1979** *The Most*

Happy Fella **1980** *Children of a Lesser God*; *I Ought to Be in Pictures*; *The Philadelphia Story* **1981** *Einstein and the Polar Bear*; *Lolita* **1982** *The Curse of an Aching Heart*; *Do Black Patent Leather Shoes Really Reflect Up?* **1983** *Porgy and Bess*; *You Can't Take It with You*

Anthony Powell

Anthony Powell, a designer of sets and costumes, was born in Chorlton-cum-Hardy (near Manchester), Lancashire, England on June 2, 1935 and studied at the Central School of Arts and Crafts in London and at St. Andrew's College in Dublin. His lyrical, creative sets and costumes are seen often in England and Europe for operas, plays and ballets, and occasionally in the United States. A prolific designer of films, his credits include *Indiana Jones and the Temple of Doom, 101 Dalmatians,* and *102 Dalmatians.* Anthony Powell's scenery and costumes for *The School for Scandal* were nominated for Tony Awards in 1963, with the costumes receiving an award. His costume designs for *Sunset Boulevand* were nominated for a Tony in 1995. *travels with My Aunt, Death on the Nile* and *Tess* all won Academy awards, and *102 Dalmatians, Hook* and *Pirates* were nominated. In 2000, the Costume Designers' Guild honored him with a Career Achievement Award.

Sets: 1963 *The School for Scandal* **1975** *Private Lives*
Costumes: 1963 *The School for Scandal* **1990** *Lettice & Lovage†* **1994** *Sunset Boulevard* **2001** *The Adventures of Tom Sawyer*

Michael Warren Powell

Michael Warren Powell, a designer of sets, lights and costumes, is also an actor and director. He has appeared in *Balm in Gilead* as a member of the La Mama E.T.C. acting troupe, and off-Broadway in *Home Free* and *The Owl Answers.* He studied costume design at the Goodman Memorial Art Institute with Theoni V. Aldredge and first designed costumes in Chicago for the Lyric Opera Company and the Drury Lane Theatre. In New York, his costume designs have been seen at Equity Library Theatre, and Circle Repertory Company, his sets at St. Marks Church for Carolyn Lord and her Dance Company, and his lights at the Cubiculo.

Costumes: 1985 *As Is*

John Pratt

John Pratt mainly designed costumes on Broadway, but also created scenery and lights as he did for many of the productions with which he was involved. A naturalized United States citizen, he was born in Saskatchewan, Canada and graduated from the University of Chicago. His credits, in particular designs for dance, were numerous and include costumes for Agnes De Mille, Ruth Page, Miriam Winslow, and his wife, Kathryn Dunham. He worked with the Federal Theatre Project, including costume designs for *Power* at the Blackstone Theatre in Chicago in 1938. Mr. Pratt died at age 74 on March 26, 1986.

Sets: 1955 *Kathryn Dunham and Her Company*
Costumes: 1938 *The Swing Mikado* **1946** *Bal Negre* **1948** *Look Ma, I'm Dancin'* **1950** *Kathryn Dunham and Her Company* **1955** *Kathryn Dunham and Her Company*
Lights: 1946 *Bal Negre*

Shirley Prendergast

Shirley Prendergast received the first Estelle Evans Award presented by Black Women in the Theatre. She has designed lights for many theater companies off-Broadway and in regional theaters, among them the New Federal Theatre, the Negro Ensemble Company, Buffalo's Studio Arena, Washington D.C.'s Arena Stage, Roundabout Theatre Company, George Street Playhouse and the Whole Theatre. Dance designs include lighting for the Alvin Ailey American Dance Theatre and the Dance Theatre of Harlem. She also designed the lights for the 1995 revival of *Paul Robeson.* Late twentieth century designs include lighting design for *Come Down Burning, Last Nite at Ace High* and *The Confessions of Stepin Fetchit.*

Lights: 1968 *Summer of the 17th Doll* **1973** *The River Niger* **1982** *Waltz of the Stork* **1983** *Amen Corner* **1987** *Don't Get God Started* **1988** *Paul Robeson*

Price and O'Brien

The gown for a featured player in a 1908 Broadway production was designed by the "Messers. Price and O'Brien."

Costumes: 1908 *Agnes* (Miss O'Neill's gown)

Margery Price

Margery Price collaborated on a costume design on Broadway in 1920.

Costumes: 1920 *Buzzin' Around*† (Miss Buie's costume)

William E. Price

William E. Price designed lights on Broadway in the 1920s. He was associated with Display Stage Lighting Company, 314 West 11th Street, New York City, in the early 1920s, serving as secretary/treasurer of the company. He lived at 164 Waverly Place in the early 1920s and then moved to White Plains, New York. The president of Display Stage Lighting Company was John Higham, who also designed lights on Broadway.

Lights: 1923 *Fashions of 1924* **1925** *Cape Smoke*

Madame Pulliche

Madame Pulliche collaborated on the costume design for Broadway show in 1920. She ran a dress and costume manufacturing business in New York, designing for and catering to the theatrical trade. She also executed designs created by James Reynolds for a variety of *Follies* productions, and for Alice O'Neill, Ernest De Weerth, Frederick W. Jones III, all of whom were active in the 1920s. She also made costumes for Lee Simonson for *The Road to Rome* in 1928, for Raymond Sovey for *The Jealous Moon* that same year, and for *Four Saints in Three Acts* designed by Kate Drain Lawson in 1934.

Costumes: 1920 *Buzzin' Around*† (Miss Buie's costumes) **1928** *The Jealous Moon*†

Mary Purvis

Mary Purvis designed scenery on Broadway in 1952 for one production.

Sets: 1952 *Women of Twilight*

Robert Pusilio

Robert Pusilio, who designed costumes for a 1975 Broadway show, was born January 30, 1939 in Detroit Michigan, son of John and Jean Pusilio. He received his B.A. from Wayne State University and M.F.A. from the Yale School of Drama. His first experience in New York was as Alex McGowan's assistant for *After the Rain*. Although he has only one Broadway costume design credit, he worked on the costumes for many shows, as an assistant designer to Freddy Wittop, among others. He taught design at Hofstra University, Lester Polakov's Studio and Forum of Stage Design, and as a guest lecturer at Yale University. He owns an antique and gift shop and runs a rental business that supplies antiques and contemporary clothing to commercials and films.

Costumes: 1975 *Hello, Dolly! (Starring Pearl Bailey)*

Marilyn Putnam

Marilyn Putnam supervised the costumes for a Broadway show in 1975.

Costumes: 1976 *George Abbott...a Celebration* (Costume Supervisor)

Paul Pyant

Paul Pyant, a British lighting designer was born July 22, 1953, son of Jean Frampton and Leonard Pyant. He attended the Royal Academy of Dramatic Art, where he studied with Francis Reid and received his diploma, with honors, in 1973. He began his career in the theater as a stage manager for the Kent Opera and then worked with Robert Bryan, head of lighting at Glyndebourne Opera. His professional debut in 1977 was *Die Zauberflote* for the Glyndebourne Touring Opera and his London debut as a lighting designer was *Oberto* for the Bloomsbury Theatre in 1982. He has designed numerous plays and operas throughout the United Kingdom, including productions at the Royal National Theatre and the English National Opera, collaborating often with directors Sir Peter Hall, Jonathan Miller and Nicholas Hytner. He has also designed for the Cameri Theatre in Tel Aviv, the Houston Grand Opera, the Atlanta Ballet, the Dallas Opera, the Los Angeles Opera, and the Metropolitan Opera. Honors include the Critics Circle Award for *Carousel* and Tony Award nominations for *Orpheus Descending* and *Arcadia*. Twenty-first century designs include *Elixir of Love* for the Houston Grand Opera and *Dracula* for the Atlanta Ballet.

Lights: **1989** *Orpheus Descending†* **1994** *Carousel* **1995** *Arcadia* **1998** *Electra*

Howard Pyle

Illustrator and writer Howard Pyle was born in 1853 in Wilmington, Delaware, After completing study at the Art Students League, he did many illustrations for *Harper's Weekly* and gained a reputation for realistic and historically accurate sketches. He was a popular author of books for young people that he also illustrated, including *The Merry Adventures of Robin Hood* in 1883, *The Wonder Clock* in 1888, and *the Story of King Arthur and His Knights* in 1903, among many others. He also illustrated books by other authors. In 1900 he opened an art school adjacent to his studio in Wilmington. In 1909, he designed costumes for a Broadway production, and received credit above the cast list, remarkable for that time, and a tribute to his stature as an artist. His widely respected knowledge of historical artifacts makes it surprising that he was not more active in the theater. His illustrations are in many major collections. He died in 1911, and a biography by Elizabeth Nesbitt, *Howard Pyle*, was published in 1966.

Costumes: **1909** *Springtime* (Costumes and accessories)

Quay Brothers

Twin brothers Stephen and Timothy Quay, generally known as the Brothers Quay, were born in Norristown, Pennsylvania in 1947. They studied at the Philadelphia College of Art and the Royal College of Art in London, where they began filming puppets. In the early 1980s they founded Koninck studios with Keith Griffins, where they make animated short films, music videos, documentaries, and advertisements. They also design scenery

and costumes for theater and opera, often collaborating with director Richard Jones. Honors include the Stockholm Film festival Best Film Award in 1995 for *Institute Benjamenta* and a Drama Desk Award for *The Chairs* in 1998.

Sets: **1998** *The Chairs*

Costumes: **1998** *The Chairs*

Rose le Quesne

Rose le Quesne collaborated on the costumes for a 1902 production performed on Broadway.

Costumes: **1902** *A Cigarette Maker's Romance†* (Ladies costumes)

Erin Quigley

Two of costume designer Erin Quigley's first three Broadway shows were nominated for Tony Awards, *The Grapes of Wrath* in 1990 and *The Song of Jacob Zulu* in 1993. Resident costume designer for the Steppenwolf Theatre, she has designed numerous productions for that company, as well as at the Goodman Theatre, for the Huntington Theatre Company and off-Broadway at the Promenade Theatre and for film. She also designed the television series *Roseanne*. After graduating from California State University at Long Beach, where she majored in acting, she moved to Chicago where some parts led to some costume designs, and a change of career. Twenty-first century designs include *Miss Desmond Behind Bars* which she co-wrote and directed, and for which David Matwijkow designed the costumes.

Costumes: **1990** *The Grapes of Wrath* **1993** *The Song of Jacob Zulu* **1995** *My Thing of Love*

M. J. Quimby

M. J. Quimby designed costumes for a production in the first season of the twentieth century on Broadway. The costumes were constructed by F. H. McCoun, formerly with Lord and Taylor,

Costumes: **1899** *Three Little Lambs*

R. M.

See Robert Milton.

Isaac Rabinovitch

Isaac Rabinovitch was born in Kiev on February 27, 1894 and studied at the School of Fine Art and with Alexander Murashko in Kiev. He began designing sets and costumes in the late teens in Russia for the Moscow Art Theatre and the Musical Studio of the Moscow Art Theatre. Productions include *The Storm* and *Lysistrata* in 1923 and *Hamlet* in 1934. He followed the principles of stage design advocated by the great Russian artist Alexandra Exter. Rabinovitch died in 1961.
Sets: 1925 *Carmencita and the Soldiers*; *Lysistrata*
Costumes: 1925 *Carmencita and the Soldiers*; *Lysistrata*

Peter Radmore

Peter Radmore served on the staff at the Royal National Theatre beginning in the mid-1960s, and was Chief Electrician of the Olivier Theatre in the 1980s. He had numerous credits in fringe theaters in London and regional theaters throughout the U.K. Among his credits were lighting for *Beaux Stratagem, Trelawney of the Wells* and *Hamlet* for Rose Bruford College at Collegiate Theatre. He also designed the British tours of *Heartbreak House, Blithe Spirit, Marriage of Figaro* and others. Radmore died in August 1992 in London.
Lights: 1979 *Bedroom Farce*

Saul Radomsky

Saul Radomsky was born in South Africa and educated in England, where his design activity has been centered. He designed *Small Craft Warnings, Gaslight, The Club, Loot, York Cycle of Mystery Plays*, and many others in the West End. Radomsky also designed productions at the Royal Shakespeare Company, the Hampstead Theatre Club, the Oxford Playhouse Company, Cambridge and Company, and in other regional theaters in the United Kingdom. Honors include a SWET nomination for Designer of the Year for *Tonight at 8:30* in London. Twenty-first century credits include scenic design for *A View from the Bridge* in Edinburgh and *Old World* at the Watermill in Bagnor.

Sets: 1981 *The Moony Shapiro Song Book* 1999 *Kat and the Kings*
Costumes: 1999 *Kat and the Kings*

Frank Rafter

A scenic artist and designer, Frank Rafter worked often in collaboration with D. Frank Dodge and Walter W. Burridge, as well as with Albert Operti, with whom he designed *Around the World in Eighty Days* in 1898. He had additional credits at the end of the nineteenth century, including *The Girl from Paris* at the Herald Square Theatre in 1896 and *The Three Guardsmen* at the Hollis Street Theatre in Boston in 1895.
Sets: 1902 *The Show Girl*

Phil Raiguel

Phil Raiguel designed sets for three plays in the 1940s on Broadway.
Sets: 1943 *The Barber Had Two Sons*; *Slightly Married* 1949 *Mr. Adam*

O. L. Raineri

Orestes L. Raineri designed sets for plays in the 1930s on Broadway. He worked mainly as a scenic artist and lived with his wife Ida at 2551 Cruger Avenue in New York City in 1932. He was associated with the Gates and Morange Scenic Studio.
Sets: 1931 *The Singing Rabbi* 1937 *The Bough Breaks*

Ada Rainey

Ada Rainey is identified as a theatrical manager in a 1907 New York City directory. Her office was located at 1269 Broadway and her home at 114 Madison Avenue. During the teens, she was on the staff of the scenic department for the Washington Square Players, under the direction of William E. Pennington. She also wrote for periodicals, including an article about the interior design in the home of playwright Eleanor Gates, author of *The Poor Little Rich Girl* that appeared in the November 1913 issue of *House Beautiful*.
Sets: 1915 *My Lady's Honor*†; *Saviors*†

Natacha Rambova

Natacha Rambova, was born Winifred Shaughnessy on January 19, 1897 in Salt Lake City, Utah. She changed her name while studying ballet in Europe. After returning to the U.S. she went to California to study with Nazimova, met Rudolf Valentino and became his second wife. She acted in films and on stage, and, in the process of producing a movie, discovered Myrna Loy. After her divorce from Valentino and his subsequent death, she studied voice, designed costumes for plays and had a dress shop in New York. She later abandoned her career in the arts to study languages, after which she edited and translated ancient Egyptian for the Bollinger Foundation, Inc. Miss Rambova returned to California in 1965 and died there June 5, 1966 at the age of 69.

Costumes: 1928 *These Few Ashes*

Karl Ramet

Karl Ramet became a member of the Scenic Artists Association, forerunner of United Scenic Artists, in 1916. The majority of his career, until his retirement in the 1970s, was spent as a scenic painter at the Metropolitan Opera and for the early Ice Capades. He also helped create camouflage effects during the Second World War. Five of his paintings in oils and watercolors were included in an exhibition of painting and designs at the E.B. Dunkel Scenic Studios. He was born in 1891 and died at age 103 on April 29, 1995.

Sets: 1932 *Housewarming*

Dunya Ramicova

Dunya Ramicova was born October 11, 1950 in Bratislava, Czechoslovakia. She received a B.F.A. from the Goodman School of Drama, where she designed costumes for her first play, *Snow Queen*, for the Goodman Children's Theatre in 1971. Prior to attending the Goodman School she studied at Lester Polakov's Studio and Forum of Stage Design with Jane Greenwood, with whom she later taught at the Yale School of Drama. Now on the faculty at the University of California, Los Angeles, her credits for costumes are lengthy for theater, film, and television. She has designed operas around the world, often collaborating with Peter Sellars, Andrei Serban, David Pountney, and

Francesca Zambello, at venues including the Metropolitan Opera, Covent Garden, the Vienna Festival, the Glyndebourne Festival and the Salzburger Festpiele.

Costumes: 1981 *Grown-ups* **1998** *Ah, Wilderness!*

Lewis Rampino

Lewis Rampino was born on November 2, 1942 in Buffalo, New York and attended college in Buffalo, and at Catholic University where he studied with Joe Lewis, and received an M.F.A. in 1968. After graduate school, he was instructor and resident designer at the University of Connecticut, before becoming designer for the Children's Company at Long Wharf. He was resident costume designer for many regional theaters, including the New York Shakespeare Festival, Cincinnati Playhouse in the Park, Seattle Repertory Theatre (for seven years), the Great Lakes Theatre Festival, and principal designer at Actor's Theatre in Louisville, Kentucky. Notable designs include the first American production of *Nicholas Nickleby* for the Walnut Street Theatre in Philadelphia. He died in Louisville, Kentucky on October 29, 1990, shortly before rehearsals began for a revival of *A Christmas Carol*. He had designed the costumes at Actor's Theatre when the production premiered the previous season.

Costumes: 1971 *Solitaire/ Double Solitaire* **1976** *Music Is*

Roger Ramsdell

Roger Ramsdell spent his career as an engineer for Consolidated Edison, but his many avocations included boating, scouring, model railroads, and drawing. He illustrated many of the articles he wrote for *Model Railroader* magazine, among others, and in 1950 used his engineering and artistic talents to create scenery for a Broadway production. He died in March 1999 in Rockville Centre, New York at age 80.

Sets: 1950 *Daphne Laureola*†

C. Alexander Ramsey

Charles Alexander Ramsey designed costumes on Broadway between 1912 and 1914. He was assistant wardrobe manager for Liebler and Company, working with wardrobe mistress Sarah Bolwell. After her death in 1911, he became head of wardrobe for the production company. His interest in historical accuracy was widely regarded, as was the extent of his research. According to Janet Loring in her dissertation, *Costuming on the New York Stage From 1895 to 1915* (State University of Iowa, 1960), he relied heavily on *English Costume* by Fairholdt and consulted with experts from the Metropolitan Museum of Art. Before joining the staff at Liebler and Company he worked for the Russell Uniform Company.

Costumes: 1912 *The Daughter of Heaven*† (Costume Chief); *Racketty-Packetty House* 1914 *The Garden of Paradise*†

Robert Randolph

Robert Randolph was born on March 9, 1926 in Centerville, Iowa, and received both B.F.A. and M.A. degrees at the University of Iowa. Before designing professionally he worked as an architect and industrial designer and taught at Iowa State University. He designed on Broadway for the first time in 1954, creating both sets and costumes for *The Saint of Bleecker Street*. Since that time he has designed numerous shows, concentrating his efforts on scenery but occasionally designing costumes and lights as well. His designs have been nominated for Tony Awards for *Golden Rainbow* and *Applause*, and he has also designed settings for the Tony Award ceremonies. Late twentieth century designs include art direction for the television special *Night of 100 Stars II*.

Sets: 1954 *The Saint of Bleecker Street* 1960 *Bye, Bye, Birdie* 1961 *How to Succeed in Business Without Really Trying* 1962 *Bravo Giovanni*; *Calculated Risk*; *Little Me* 1963 *Sophie* 1964 *Any Wednesday*; *Foxy*; *Funny Girl*; *Something More!* 1965 *Anya*; *Minor Miracle*; *Skyscraper*; *Xmas in Las Vegas* 1966 *It's a Bird...It's a Plane...It's Superman*; *Sweet Charity*; *Walking Happy* 1967 *Henry, Sweet Henry*; *How to Be a Jewish Mother*; *Sherry!* 1968 *Golden Rain-*

bow 1969 *Angela*; *A Teaspoon Every Four Hours* 1970 *Applause* 1971 *70, Girls, 70*; *Ari* 1973 *Good Evening*; *No Hard Feelings* 1974 *Gypsy*; *Words and Music* 1975 *The Norman Conquests*; *We Interrupt this Program* 1976 *Porgy and Bess* 1982 *Seven Brides for Seven Brothers* 1986 *Sweet Charity*

Costumes: 1954 *The Saint of Bleecker Street* 1955 *The Desperate Hours* 1973 *Good Evening* 1974 *Words and Music*

Lights: 1961 *How to Succeed in Business Without Really Trying* 1962 *Bravo Giovanni*; *Little Me* 1963 *Sophie* 1964 *Foxy*; *Funny Girl*; *Something More!* 1965 *Skyscraper*; *Xmas in Las Vegas* 1966 *It's a Bird...It's a Plane...It's Superman*; *Sweet Charity*; *Walking Happy* 1967 *Henry, Sweet Henry*; *Sherry!* 1968 *Golden Rainbow* 1969 *Angela* 1971 *70, Girls, 70* 1973 *Good Evening*; *No Hard Feelings* 1974 *Gypsy* 1975 *The Norman Conquests* 1986 *Sweet Charity*

Germinal Rangel

Germinal Rangel was born in Barcelona, Spain, daughter of French parents, and studied fashion in haute couture houses in Paris. She designed costumes at the Haymarket Theatre in London for *The Duchess of Malfi*, her professional debut in 1945. In 1960, she relocated permanently to London and designed costumes for Maggie Smith, *Private Lives* and several films. She also designed the costumes for *The Protectors* for BBC television. The star of that popular 1970s series about crime-solving, Nyree Dawn Porter, was voted television's best-dressed woman when the series was originally broadcast.

Costumes: 1950 *Captain Brassbound's Conversion* 1975 *Private Lives*

Eva Rapaport

Eva Rapaport designed costumes for a Broadway play in 1935.

Costumes: 1935 *Let Freedom Ring*

Judy Rasmuson

Judy Rasmuson was born in Anchorage, Alaska on August 2, 1945 and studied economics for three years at Smith College prior to beginning her career as a lighting designer. She has also worked in summer stock and off-Broadway as an electrician and assistant lighting designer, and off-off-Broadway as a lighting designer. Her first design was *Brecht on Brecht* at the Austin Riggs Center in Stockbridge, Massachusetts in 1967, and her professional debut was *Heartbreak House* at the Long Wharf Theatre in New Haven, Connecticut in 1970. She has designed in regional theaters from coast to coast and in theearly 1970s also designed rock concerts. Daughter of Elmer (d. 2000) and Mary Louise Rasmuson, prominent Alaskans, she is a member of the Board of Directors of the Rasmuson Foundation, and active with Ronald Wallace in arts and environmental causes.

Lights: 1977 *Annie* **1981** *Twice around the Park* **1994** *A Tuna Christmas*

Mark Ravitz

Mark Ravitz was born on August 18, 1948 in New York City and received a B.F.A. at New York University in 1970. Since he was seven he has been drawing and painting. He attended the Music and Art High School in New York City. Designs for special events include: the Playboy *Bunny of the Year* show in 1970 (which marked his professional debut); Liberty Weekend, the official re-opening of the Statue of Liberty; and industrial promotions. He has designed sets for numerous music tours, clubs, and theater productions such as "The Diamond Dogs Tour," "The Serious Moonlight Tour," and "The Glass Spider Tour," all for David Bowie. He designed the national tour of *Tommy, the Rock Opera*, the "Kiss" world premiere and national tour, the Billy Idol tour, and the Aquacade at the Louisiana World Exposition in New Orleans in 1984. Mark Ravitz is married to Jo Beth Ravitz and they have one son, Miles.

Sets: 1982 *Rock 'n Roll! The First 5,000 Years*

George P. Raymond

George P. Raymond was an actor and a painter. In 1900 he contributed costume designs to a production, in which he did not appear. His residence in 1898 was at 2432 First Avenue and in 1900 was 323 West 59th Street, in New York City.

Costumes: 1900 *Little Nell and the Marchioness*

David Read

David Read designed lighting for a Broadway production in 1965. He was also cinematographer for the movie *Unstable Elements: Atomic Stories 1939-1985*.

Lights: 1965 *Marat/Sade*

Nettie Duff Reade

Nettie Duff Reade designed costumes for two Broadway plays in 1929. She was born on April 5, 1887 and died in San Mateo, California on October 6, 1972.

Costumes: 1929 *Earth Between, The/Before Breakfast*

Ray Recht

Ray Recht was born on August 9, 1947 in Staten Island, New York. He received a B.F.A. in 1969 at Carnegie Mellon University and an M.F.A. in 1972 from the Yale University School of Drama. Ming Cho Lee and Tony Walton have been influential in his career. He began designing in regional theaters with *One Flew Over the Cuckoo's Nest* at Baltimore's Center Stage. He has designed over twenty productions off-Broadway, including *Mrs. Klein* and *Collected Stories*, since his New York debut with *Medal of Honor Rag* at Theatre de Lys. He has also designed for film and television, notably as set designer for *Another World* and *Saturday Night Live*, and in regional theaters, including *The Real Thing* at the Pittsburgh Public Theatre and *Who's Afraid of Virginia Woolf?* at the Stratford (Ontario) Festival. Recht, who has been on the faculty of Marymount College in New York City since 1993 was art director for the films *Amityville II: The Possession, The Search for One Eye Jimmy, Missing Pieces* and *The Babe*.

Sets: 1983 *Slab Boys* **1984** *The Babe* **1994** *The Flowering Peach*

Redfern

In the middle of the nineteenth century, John Redfern had a small custom garment business at 41 High Street in Cowes, on the Isle of Wight. Within twenty years he was selling dry goods as well as providing ladies with mourning wear and tailored garments appropriate for yachting. He relocated to London and opened Redfern & Sons at 26a Conduit Street. Garments for Lillie Langtry, costumes for Sarah Bernhardt, and portions of the 1885 trousseau for Princess Beatrice further enhanced his reputation. He continued to expand, as an advertisement in the 1904 London playbill for *The Cingalee* illustrates: "Paris Models in Dress of All Kinds Produced Simultaneously in London at 26 & 27 Conduit Street." He also opened branches in New York, Chicago and Paris. Upon his death in 1895, his son Ernest Redfern succeeded him, taking responsibility for the London and American salons. Charles Poynter became head of the Paris salon, which belonged to the elite Chambre Syndicale de la Haute Couture. The house of Redfern (fl. 1853-1929) remained successful through the Edwardian era, when the royal appointment granted by Queen Victoria was followed by one granted by Queen Alexandra. The costume and couture designer, and maker of costumes designed by others, should not be confused with William Beales Redfern (c.1840-1923), the British scenic artist and theatrical manager.

Costumes: **1903** *The Marriage of Kitty* **1904** *La Douleureuse* **1907** *All-of-a-Sudden Peggy*† (Miss Woods and Miss Buckley's gowns) **1909** *The Sins of Society* **1912** *Milestones*†; *The Perplexed Husband*†

Henry Redmond

Henry A. (Harry) Redmond designed lights for a 1913 Broadway production. Born in Cincinnati, Ohio in 1881, he worked in the theater in New York during the early teens, but spent the majority of his career in California creating special effects for movies. He died in Canoga Park, California on November 4, 1966.

Lights: **1913** *The Purple Road*

Max Ree

Max Ree spent most of his career as an art director for films. He was born in Copenhagen, Denmark in 1889 and trained as an architect at the Royal Academy of Copenhagen. He met Max Reinhardt and worked with him in Berlin before coming to the United States and contributing designs of sets and costumes to musical revues and Broadway shows. In 1925 he went to work for Metro Goldwyn Mayer designing costumes, serving as costume designer and art director for many films including Max Reinhardt's adaptation of *A Midsummer Night's Dream* in 1935. He also designed for television. Mr. Ree died in California at age 64 on March 7, 1953.

Sets: **1924** *Earl Carroll's Vanities*
Costumes: **1924** *Music Box Revue*† (Act I, Scene 13; Act II, Scene 6)

Doris Reed

Doris Reed designed gowns for a Broadway show in 1923. In 1935 she made her debut as an opera singer in a production of *Carmen* at the New York Hippodrome.

Costumes: **1921** *The Triumph of X*† **1923** *Anything Might Happen* (Gowns)

John Reed

John Reed, who had a furniture business at 369 East 35th Street, New York City in 1900, contributed scenery to a 1902 production.

Sets: **1902** *The Hunchback*†

Pauline Reed

An actress, Pauline Reed resided at 52 West 133rd Street in New York City at the same time she designed the women's costumes for a production on Broadway. Although she did appear in other shows in that era, she was not in the play she designed.

Costumes: **1908** *Bandanna Land*† (Women's costumes)

Allison Reeds

Born in Tulsa, Oklahoma, costume designer Allison Reeds received a B.A. from Oberlin College in 1987 and an M.F.A. at Northwestern University in 1992. She also held an internship at the Costume Institute of the Metropolitan

Museum of art in 1989. She designs for theater throughout the United States and works often for the Steppenwolf and Goodman Theatres, at the Huntington Theatre, and the Seattle and Berkeley Repertory Theatres. Costumes for feature films include *Every Dog Has It's Day* and *Since You've Been Gone* and for short films include *Ladies Room* and *Pam Flam & the Center of the Universe*. Much honored for her costume designs, she has received Drama-Logue Awards for *Arabian Nights* and *The School for Wives* in 1997, Jeff Awards for *Journey to the West* in 1995 and *The Balcony* in 1993, and a Tony nomination for *Buried Child*, among others,

Costumes: 1994 *The Rise and Fall of Little Voice* **1996** *Buried Child*

Larry Reehling

Lawrence Clair Reehling (also known as Lawrence Clair) designed sets for numerous productions in summer stock on Cape Cod and for opera companies in St. Louis, Santa Fe, and Minneapolis. He designed the films *Funny Girl* and *Hello, Dolly* among others and sets for television, including *The Today Show* and *The Tonight Show*. He was born in Hanover, Pennsylvania in 1941 and received degrees from Carnegie Mellon University and the Yale University School of Drama. He died at age 45 on September 5, 1986 in Lancaster, Pennsylvania.

Sets: 1968 *Happiness Is Just a Little Thing Called a Rolls Royce*

Ruth Reeves

Ruth Reeves was a textile designer whose work was widely commissioned and exhibited. She was born in Redlands, California on July 14, 1892 and studied at the Pratt Institute, the California Art School, the Art Students League and in Paris. She contributed designs for costumes and fabric to a Broadway show in 1922. She also designed the fabric which originally covered the walls at Radio City Music Hall. For the WPA she coordinated the "Index of American Design." Widely traveled, she studied native textiles all over the world. She went to India on a Fulbright Scholarship and became a leading authority on their handicrafts. Miss Reeves died on December 23, 1966 in New Delhi, India.

Costumes: 1922 *Bavu* (Batiks and javanes)

Anton Refreigier

Anton Refreiger was born in Moscow on March 2, 1905 and studied sculpture in Paris. After coming to the United States in 1921 he continued his study at the Rhode Island School of Design. He became an American citizen in 1930 and was best known as a mural painter. His paintings are in the permanent collections of museums including the Metropolitan Museum of Art. One of his murals, commissioned for the Rincon Annex Post Office in San Francisco in 1941, was threatened with destruction by the House Un-American Activities Committee in 1953 because it included a Soviet flag. He lived and worked from his home in Woodstock, New York. Anton Refreiger died in Moscow in October 1979 at age 75.

Sets: 1937 *The Pepper Mill*

Adina Reich

Adina Reich was born in 1928. Her costume designs are included in *Scenografia Românească* by Paul Bortnovschi and Liviu Ciulei, published in Bucharest in 1965.

Sets: 1980 *Wish Me Mazel-Tov*
Costumes: 1980 *Wish Me Mazel-Tov*

Alexander Reid

Alexander Reid, a British designer of sets and costumes, who was born in 1929, has designed for many opera companies around the world including the Scottish Opera, Wexford Festival and the English National Opera. In addition he has designed for both the Royal Shakespeare Company (most recently *Poppy)* and the Royal National Theatre in London including *A Little Hotel on the Side*. Both of the productions for which he designed costumes in New York in 1994 were nominated for Tony Awards in the outstanding Costume Design category.

Costumes: 1984 *Cyrano De Bergerac;* *Much Ado About Nothing* **1988** *Carrie*

H. L. Reid

Hugh Logan Reid (Reed), a scene painter and designer who amassed many credits in Boston theaters at the end of the nineteenth century, collaborated on the scenery for a 1904 Broadway production. He often painted with other scenic artists of his generation, such as E. G. Banks, Bruce Smith, William Telbin, St. John Lewis, and John H. Young.

Sets: 1904 *The Virginian*†

Franz Reiner

See Ferry Windberger.

Hilda Reis

Hilda Reis helped coordinate the costumes for a play in 1934. An actress, she appeared in *Peace on Earth*.

Costumes: 1934 *Stevedore* (Costume Committee Chair)

Michele Reisch

Michele Reisch is well known for her designs for television, including *Ryan's Hope* for which she won an Emmy Award, and *As the World Turns*. She also served as head writer for the Canadian Broadcast System's daytime drama *Time of Our Lives*. Designs for the theater include *Carol Leiffer at the Ed Sullivan Theatre*, *Absent Friends* and *Charlotte Sweet*. In addition, she designs decorative accessories for commercial sale and she is a right's advocate for rape victims. She is writing a play about her experience as the victim of an assault.

Costumes: 1999 *Rollin' on the T.O.B.A.*

Theodore Reisig

Theodore Reisig was a designer, scenic artist, and technical director who often worked in collaboration with Julius F. Dowe. He had a scenic studio at 625 East 15th Street, the Theodore Reisig & Co., during the first decade of the twentieth century. By 1912, it was renamed Reisig, Dowe Studios. The *Naughty Marietta* playbill says "Scenery from the Manhattan Opera House under the direction of Theodore Reisig and Julius F. Dowe." A 1921 New York Naturalization Petition lists his address as 627 East 15th Street.

Sets: 1903 *Way Down East*† (Mechanical devices) 1910 *Naughty Marietta*† 1911 *The Red Rose*; *The Red Widow*† 1912 *The Firefly*† (Act I); *The Pearl Maiden* 1913 *The Geisha*; *High Jinks*; *The Honeymoon Express*† 1914 *Experience*

Jane Reisman

Lighting designer Jane Maritza Reisman was born on March 25, 1937 in New York City, the daughter of Lillian and Leo Reisman, an orchestra leader and conductor. She graduated from Vassar College in 1959, studied at Lester Polakov's Studio and Forum of Stage Design, at Bayreuth and with an I.I.E. grant. She has designed off-Broadway, in regional theaters, and for dance companies including the Rome Opera Ballet, American Ballet Theatre, the Banff Festival Ballet and The Pennsylvania Ballet. She has designed more than fifty operas, including productions for the Manhattan School of Music, San Diego Opera, Lake George Opera, Opera Society of Washington, and the Opera Metropolitana de Caracas. She was Visiting Professor of Lighting Design at Emerson College from 1980 to 1982, and since 1991 has been on the Dance and Drama faculty at Bennington College. She founded and chairs the Lighting Internship Program for United Scenic Artists. Honors include a Tony nomination for *Black and Blue*, co-designed with her husband Neil Peter Jampolis. Twenty-first century credits include *St. Lucy's Eyes* for the Cherry Lane Theatre Company and *Forever Plaid* at the Pasadena Playhouse.

Lights: 1973 *Warp* 1974 *The Fifth Dimension* 1976 *Me Jack, You Jill* 1989 *Black and Blue*†

Marvin Reiss

Marvin Reiss was born on August 29, 1923 in St. Louis and received a B.F.A. at the Art Institute of Chicago. He began his career designing for summer stock theaters in Oconomowoc, Wisconsin, Fitchburg, Massachusetts, and Westport, Connecticut. He was art director and original designer for the daytime drama *All My Children*, and art director for the long-running soap opera *The Doctors*. Well known as a scene designer, he created scenic and lighting designs for many Broadway shows and occasionally assisted with the costumes as well. His New York debut was *An Evening with Mike Nichols and Elaine May* off-Broadway. Mr. Reiss, who died on January 18, 2001, worked for many years as a chargeman in New York City shops.

Sets: 1954 *Home Is the Hero* 1958 *Back to Methuselah; Party with Betty Comden and Adolph Green; Third Best Sport* 1959 *Requiem for a Nun†* 1960 *A Thurber Carnival* 1961 *New Faces of '62* 1963 *Love and Kisses* 1968 *Portrait of a Queen*

Costumes: 1954 *Home Is the Hero* 1959 *The Highest Tree*

Lights: 1954 *Home Is the Hero* 1958 *Back to Methuselah; Party with Betty Comden and Adolph Green* 1961 *New Faces of '62* 1963 *Love and Kisses* 1968 *Portrait of a Queen*

Frank Rembach

Frank Rembach has had a varied career in the theater. He has designed in South Africa for Krishna Shah, in London, and in the U.S. In addition, he has been a production stage manager for the national tour of *Mame*, served as literary manager at the Hartman Theatre, and directed. He spent many years in California, mainly writing for television shows including *The Smothers Brothers Comedy Hour, All in the Family* and *Maude*. His plays include *197 ONE!* and *Ataturk*.

Sets: 1966 *Wait a Minim!*
Lights: 1966 *Wait a Minim!*

Frederic Remington

Artist and author Frederic Remington was born in 1861 in Canton, New York and studied at the Yale School of Fine Arts and the Art student League. Well known and widely collected, his paintings, sculpture, books and illustrations were mainly about life in the late nineteenth century American West. He was prolific, creating over 2700 works of art, including illustrations as correspondent during the Spanish-American War for the Hearst papers, illustrations for magazines and books, and even scenic designs. His art is in many museums and private collections, as well as at the Remington Art Memorial Museum in Ogdenburg, New York. He died in 1909.

Sets: 1907 *On Parole†*

Nicholas Remisoff

Nicholas Remisoff (also known as Nikolai Vladimirovich Remisoff, "Re-Mi") contributed designs for scenery and costumes to musical revues in the 1920s. He was born in Petrograd, Russia on May 7, 1887 and studied with Kardovsky at the Imperial Academy of Fine Arts. He worked professionally as an illustrator for the Russian Weekly *Novy Satirikon*, also serving as its editor until its demise. His paintings were exhibited along with those by Alexander Benois and Léon Bakst through the "World of Art." In 1920 he moved to Paris and worked for the impresario Balieff, designing sets and costumes. He also designed in Germany for Max Reinhardt. Balieff brought him to New York with *Chauve Souris* in 1922. He spent many years in Hollywood as a set and production designer for films beginning in 1939 with *Of Mice and Men*, followed by *Ocean's Eleven, Guest in the House, The Strange Woman, Dishonored Lady, The Red Pony*, and *When I Grow Up*, among others. He died in 1979.

Sets: 1922 *Chauve Souris†* 1925 *Chauve Souris†* 1927 *Chauve Souris†* 1929 *Chauve Souris†*
Costumes: 1922 *Chauve Souris†*

Madame Therese Renaud

Madame Therese Renaud contributed costume designs to two Broadway productions in the early 1920s. She was a dressmaker with a salon at 6 East 46th Street in New York City in 1920 and 1921. At that same time, she resided at 529 West 138th Street.

Costumes: 1920 *The Blue Flame†; Crooked Gamblers*

Marilyn Rennagel

Marilyn Rennagel has both a B.A. and M.F.A. in theater arts from the University of California at Los Angeles. Since

1971 she has been an active lighting designer and consultant working throughout the United States on rock concerts, special events, fashion shows, dances, operas. Broadway and off-Broadway productions. Born on June 4, 1943 in Los Angeles, she recognizes electricians Charles Brown and Jim Seagrove, and lighting designer Tharon Musser as major influences. Her New York debut was *Mission* at Playwrights Horizon in 1975. She has been resident designer for the Michigan Opera Company and consultant on lighting systems for the Criterion Center. In 1988 she began taking classes at the New York Botanical Garden in landscape design and at Rutgers University in landscape architecture. She currently designs for theater and television during the winter months and spends spring, summer and fall, designing for landscape clients.

Lights: 1978 *John Curry's Ice Dancing* **1979** *Faith Healer; Peter Allen "Up in One"* **1980** *Clothes for a Summer Hotel* **1981** *Woman of the Year* **1982** *Do Black Patent Leather Shoes Really Reflect Up?* **1986** *Social Security* **1989** *Run for Your Wife*

Eric Renschler

Scenic designer Eric Renschler was born in Evansville, Indiana on July 26, 1961. He received a B.A. degree from the University of Evansville in 1983 and his M.F.A. from the University of Michigan in 1989. A long time associate of John Lee Beatty, he worked on Broadway as an Associate Set Designer on productions including *Proof, The Dinner Party, Footloose, Chicago,* and *The Heiress,* before making his own debut in 1998. He has designed scenery for many productions off-Broadway, including *Riga* and *Trinity* at Circle Repertory Lab where he is a founding member, as well as *The Last Session, Night Blooming Jasmine, I Sing, The Quick Change Room* and *Maybe Baby, It's You.* He has also designed for regional theater and opera companies, commercial projects, films, and videos.

Sets: 1998 *Mamaloshen*

Roy Requa

Roy Requa was active on Broadway in the 1920s as a scenic and costume designer. A long time resident of Brooklyn, New York, he was born on October 9, 1901 and died in November 1964.

Sets: 1925 *Edgar Allan Poe* **1926** *Hush Money*

Costumes: 1924 *Music Box Revue*[†] (Rip Van Winkle) **1925** *Edgar Allan Poe*

John Retsek

John Retsek, who has many credits as an art director and set designer for television, designed scenery in 1971 for a Broadway production. He was born in Michigan City, Indiana and studied at the Goodman Theatre School. Honors include Los Angeles–area Emmy Awards for *Storytime, Life & Times, Dinosaur Hunt: The M.A.D. Scientists* and *Out of the Dumps.* He has designed for KCET-TV in Los Angeles. Among his designs on the West Coast are *Under Milkwood* and *You and Whose Army,* both in the early 1970s.

Sets: 1971 *No Place to be Somebody*

Madame Revare

Madame Lida Revare, also known as Mrs. Emil Revare, was a dressmaker who lived and worked from 535 Eighth Avenue at the beginning of the twentieth century.

Costumes: 1906 *John Hudson's Wife* (Miss Spong's gowns)

W. W. Reville-Terry

W.W. (William Wallace Reville-Terry) was a designer who created gowns for European royalty including Queen Mary and the Princess Royal who became Queen Elizabeth II. He also designed costumes for plays in London and the U.S. Mr. Reville-Terry died in London on October 7, 1948.

Costumes: 1930 *Symphony in Two Flats*[†] (Miss Braithwaite's dresses and hats)

James Reynolds

James Reynolds, an author, artist and illustrator as well as a designer of sets and costumes, was born in Warrenton, Virginia in 1891. Of Irish descent, he wrote *Ghosts in Irish Houses* and later

Ghosts in American Houses, demonstrating a flair for wit and the supernatural. He designed numerous plays on Broadway, contributing both sets and costumes to many before turning his attention to traveling so he might write about his adventures, and paint. He died in Bellagio, Italy, on July 21, 1957 at age 65, from injuries suffered in a traffic accident.

Sets: 1919 *The Tents of the Arabs* 1920 *What's in a Name* 1921 *Greenwich Village Follies†; Ziegfeld Follies: 1921†* 1922 *Greenwich Village Follies†; Ziegfeld Follies: 1922†* 1923 *Sancho Panza* 1924 *Greenwich Village Follies†* 1925 *The Bird Cage; Last Night of Don Juan, The/ The Pilgrimage; The Last of Mrs. Cheyney; Sunny; These Charming People; The Vagabond King* 1926 *Criss Cross; Oh, Please; On Approval* 1927 *Bally Hoo; Lucky; The Royal Family; White Eagle* 1928 *The Furies* 1929 *A Trip to Scarborough* 1934 *Come of Age; The O'Flynn; Thumbs Up†; Within the Gates*
Costumes: 1919 *The Tents of the Arabs* 1920 *What's in a Name†* (All other costumes) 1921 *Ziegfeld Follies: 1921†* (Persian and Dauphin costumes) 1923 *Sancho Panza; Ziegfeld Follies: 1923†* 1924 *Dear Sir†; Greenwich Village Follies†* (Part I, Scene 13, Part II, Scenes 1 and 9, "In Paris"); *Music Box Revue†* (Act II, Scenes 1b and 8); *Ziegfeld Follies: 1924†* 1925 *Dearest Enemy†* (Acts II and III); *Puzzles of 1925†; Sunny; The Vagabond King* 1926 *Criss Cross†; Oh, Please* 1927 *The Command to Love†* (Miss Nash's gowns); *Immortal Isabella?†* (Miss Starr's gowns); *The Royal Family†* (Miss Wright's costumes) 1928 *Chee-Chee†* (Miss Ford's costumes) 1929 *Fifty Million Frenchmen* (Costume Supervisor) 1930 *Sweet and Low* 1931 *A Woman Denied†* 1933 *Hangman's Whip* (Miss Flint's dress) 1934 *Life Begins at 8:40†; The O'Flynn; Within the Gates* 1935 *Jumbo†; On to Fortune†* (Fancy Dress costumes) 1936 *Daughters of Atreus* 1943 *The Vagabond King*

Hill Rheis-Gromes

Hill Rheis-Gromes designed costumes for a play in 1965. He is a native of Austria, where he has designed numerous films, plays and for television. His designs are seen throughout Europe.
Costumes: 1964 *Wiener Blut (Vienna Life)*

Adams T. Rice

Adams T. (Andy) Rice designed lights and scenery, was a technical director, and wrote plays and movies. *Pinocchio, A Fantastic Comedy In Eight Scenes,* was published by Samuel French in 1931. He was appointed technical director of the Children's Theatre in the 1930s after working for the Detroit Civic Theatre, the Washington Square Players, the Theatre Guild, and for his own company, the Detroit Players. Before retiring to Dallas, Texas, he also worked as a screenwriter. Born in 1880, he died on February 17, 1963 in Dallas.
Sets: 1923 *The Enchanted Cottage*
Lights: 1911 *Youth* 1920 *Youth*

Peter Rice

Peter Anthony Morrish Rice, a British designer of sets and costumes, was born on September 13, 1928 in Simla, India and studied at the Royal College of Art. His first design assignment was *Sex and Seraphim* in London in 1951. He designs regularly in England for the theater, ballet and opera, and occasionally in New York. He has numerous credits for productions at the Greenwich Theatre, the Aldeburgh Theatre and at Covent Garden, Glyndebourne Opera, the Royal Opera, the Scottish Opera, the Chichester Festival, and Sadler's Wells. Twenty-first century credits include scenery for the London City Opera's production of *Carmen* that was also performed in the Cerritos Center for the Performing Arts.
Sets: 1972 *Ambassador*
Costumes: 1965 *Pickwick†* 1972 *Ambassador*

William Richardson

William Richardson designed lights for two production on Broadway in the 1940s.
Lights: 1942 *Little Darling* 1944 *A Bell for Adano*

Clive A. Rickabaugh

Clive A. Rickabaugh spent the majority of his career working in the theater in Chicago, Illinois. He was born on October 4, 1906 and died in Chicago in December 1973. Among his many credits with the Federal Theatre Project was scenery for *Power*, part of the "Living Newspaper" series. The production, directed by Edward Vail, originated at the Blackstone Theatre in Chicago. For the Midwest unit of the Federal Theatre Project, he also designed sets for *Frankie and Johnny* and the long-running *O Say Can You Sing*. In the 1930s, his scenic designs were seen on Broadway.

Sets: 1933 *It Pays to Sin* **1938** *The Swing Mikado*

Charles Ricketts

Charles Ricketts, a distinguished designer, artist and author, was born in Geneva, Switzerland on October 2, 1866, and studied in France. After founding and running the Vale Press from 1896 to 1904 he began designing sets and costumes for plays and operas in Europe and occasionally in the United States. He was instrumental in developing modern scene design, using realism creatively to support a production's intent. His sculpture and designs are often displayed in major British museums. Charles Ricketts died on October 31, 1931 at age 65.

Sets: 1908 *Electra* **1947** *The Mikado* **1948** *The Gondoliers* **1951** *The Mikado* **Costumes: 1908** *Electra* **1947** *The Mikado* **1948** *The Gondoliers* **1951** *The Mikado* **1955** *The Mikado*

Richard Riddell

Richard Riddell, who was raised in Missouri, earned a Ph.D. from Stanford University. He has designed productions at theaters including the Guthrie Theatre, the English National Opera, the Royal Shakespeare Company, the American Repertory Theatre, the Oregon Shakespeare Festival and in Berlin as well as for *Akhnaten* and *Satyagraha* by Philip Glass. Since 1992 he has been director of the Program in Drama at Duke University. Prior to that, he was the first director of the Institute for Advanced Theatre Training at Harvard University, associate director of the American Repertory

Theatre in Cambridge, Massachusetts, and Chair of the Drama Department at the University of California at San Diego. Among his honors are Tony, Drama Desk and Maharam Awards for *Big River* in 1985. Recent credits include *Madama Butterfly* for Connecticut Opera, *Otello* for the English National Opera, and *Kudzu* at Ford's Theatre in Washington, D.C.

Lights: 1985 *Big River* **1988** *A Walk in the Woods*

John David Ridge

John David Ridge runs a Hollywood costume shop named for him, where costumes for major motion pictures are produced. He was born on November 6, 1945 in Washington, D.C. and attended Pratt Institute in New York City, where he studied fashion and became interested in costume design. His first assignment as a costume designer was *South Pacific* in 1965 in New Brunswick, Maine. After graduating from New York University, he worked as Costume Supervisor at Juilliard, designed costumes for many productions, managed the costume house then known as Brooks Van Horn, assisted the couture designer Halston and then designed fashion under that label. In addition to executing costumes for designers including Judianna Makovsky, Rita Ryack, and others, he continues to design as time allows, adding to a resume that includes productions for the Acting Company, the Royal National Theatre, and the Joffrey Ballet.

Costumes: 1973 *Measure for Measure*; *Scapin* **1974** *Next Time I'll Sing to You* **1981** *Copperfield*; *My Fair Lady*† (Co-costume Designer) **1999** *Ring 'Round the Moon*

Kevin Rigdon

Kevin Rigdon, a lighting and set designer, was born on February 17, 1956 and raised in Highland Park, Illinois. He studied at Drake University and was an intern at the Guthrie Theatre during the 1975-76 season. He has been resident scenic and lighting designer for the Steppenwolf Company (over 110 productions), the Goodman Theatre, the Alley Theatre, and for Mordine and Company Dance. He has designed for most of the major regional theaters, including the Mark Taper Forum, the Williamstown Theatre Festival and American Repertory Theatre. Honors include several Joseph Jefferson Awards, two American Theatre Design Awards for lighting (*Ghost Stories* in 1986 and *The Grapes of Wrath* in 1990. He was nominated for Tony Awards for both the scenery and the lighting for *The Grapes of Wrath*. He is on the faculty at the University of Houston. Among his twenty-first century credits for set design are *American Buffalo* at Donmar Warehouse, *Unholy Ghost* at the Alley Theatre, and *Ricky Jay Deals a Warm, Winning Show* at the Market Theatre in Boston.

Sets: 1986 *The Caretaker* **1990** *The Grapes of Wrath* **1993** *The Song of Jacob Zulu* **1997** *The Old Neighborhood*

Lights: 1984 *Glengarry Glen Ross* **1986** *The Caretaker* **1987** *Speed-the-Plow* **1988** *Our Town* **1989** *Ghetto* **1990** *The Grapes of Wrath* **1992** *A Streetcar Named Desire* **1994** *The Rise and Fall of Little Voice* **1996** *Buried Child* **2001** *One Flew over the Cuckoo's Nest*

Otis Riggs

Otis M. Riggs, Jr. began his career as a set designer in Hollywood, California in the early 1930s designing for Walter Wanger Productions. After World War II he moved to New York where he designed for television. He was art director for *Another World* and *Lovers and Friends* on NBC-TV and an assistant art director for films. He won three Emmy Awards for art direction, one for the musical version of *Our Town* and two for *Another World* in 1973 and 1976. He died at age 63 on May 4, 1977 in Yonkers, New York.

Sets: 1953 *The Trip to Bountiful*

Albert Rights

Albert Rights, who was born on August 23, 1905, supervised the setting for a Broadway production in 1930. He often worked constructing scenery for theater productions working through a variety of studios. He died in June 1966.

Sets: 1930 *Lysistrata*

James Riley

James Riley designs scenery and lights, as well as working as an electrician. Additional productions include *Dancing in the End Zone* in the 1983-84 season at the Coconut Grove Playhouse in Miami, *Kill Me Again* a Las Vegas stage show in 1989, and the movie *Universal Soldier* in 1992.

Sets: 1976 *So Long, 174th Street*

Constance Ripley

Constance Ripley (also known as Constance Ripley Williams) was active on Broadway during the 1930s. Born and raised in Connecticut, her brother was S. Dillon Ripley, the long-time head of the Smithsonian Museum. She attended the Chapin School in New York City, Miss Porter's School in Farmington, Connecticut and the Windsor School in Boston, after which she was an apprentice to Normal Bel Geddes. For a time in the mid-1930s, she also designed clothing for private customers from her studio at East 55th Street. In 1937, she married Thomas D. Williams and for the next forty years they were in the antique business, based in Litchfield, Connecticut, buying and selling American furniture, decorative arts and paintings. They assisted several museums assemble period rooms and participated in important antique shows. The cover story in the August 19, 1983 *Antiques and the Arts Weekly* profiled her life and career, and included reproductions of costume sketches for some of her Broadway shows. She remains involved with the arts, serving on the Board of Directors of the Artists Collective in Hartford, Connecticut in the mid-1990s.

Costumes: 1931 *The Band Wagon*† (Costumes); *The Cat and the Fiddle*† (Costumes) **1932** *Americana; Flying Colors* **1934** *Revenge with Music* **1935** *Parade*† ("Life Could Be So Beautiful," etc.) **1936** *Red, Hot and Blue*

Madame Ripley

Madame Margaret A. (Alla) Ripley began her career as a dressmaker. She resided at 201 East 39th Street in 1898 and in 1900 at 626 Lexington Avenue, New York City. In 1909, she worked from the Ripley Studio, located at 119

386 Broadway Design Roster

East 19th Street. She contributed designs to productions during the first two decades of the twentieth century, as well as serving private customers. In 1921, as president of the National Fashion Art League, she presided over its annual convention in Chicago.

Costumes: 1899 *The Rounders* **1907** *The Lancers*† (Dancing dresses) **1909** *Old Dutch*† **1910** *The Yankee Girl*† **1912** *Little Women*† (Gowns) **1913** *The Beggar Student*† (Peasant costumes) **1919** *Three's a Crowd*

William Rising

William S. Rising collaborated with H. Robert Law on the scenery for two Broadway productions in the teens. Born in 1851, he graduated from Ohio Wesleyan University and studied voice in Italy. He spent the majority of his career performing on stage, mainly in comic operas, appearing with DeWolf Hopper's Company and opposite Lotta Crabtree. He also appeared in films, directed some silent ones, and performed in radio plays. He died in New York City on October 5, 1930 at age 79.

Sets: 1913 *The Passing Show of 1913*† **1914** *The Passing Show of 1914*†

Mr. Jack Rissman

Mr. Jack Rissman supplied the men's costumes for a play in 1929. Born in Russia on December 19, 1908, he emigrated to America and worked in New York as a tailor before relocating to California. He died in Los Angeles on September 13, 1972.

Costumes: 1929 *Follow Through*† (Men's Costume Supervisor)

Rui Rita

Lighting designer Rui Rita has numerous credits throughout the United States. Designs for major regional theaters including productions at the Alley Theatre, Hartford Stage Company, Long Wharf Theatre, and the American Conservatory Theatre, among others. Designs for dance include *The Nutcracker* for American Ballet Theatre. Off-Broadway he has created lights for the Blue Light Theatre (*Filumena*), at Lincoln Center Theatre (*Far East, Ancestral Voices*), the Variety Arts Theatre (*Dinner With Friends*),

and many more. During a long association with the Williamstown Theatre Festival he has designed dozens of productions, including *Street Scene* and *Philadelphia, Here I Come* in the twenty-first century.

Lights: 1996 *A Thousand Clowns* **1999** *The Price*

William Ritman

William Ritman was well known as a set designer with dozens of Broadway shows to his credit during his twenty-five year theater career, including *Morning's at 7, Who's Afraid of Virginia Woolf?* and *Happy Days*. He sometimes designed lights and occasionally costumes for productions for which he designed the settings. A native of Chicago, he graduated from the Goodman School of Theatre and designed professionally for the first time in 1959, contributing sets and lights to the revival of *On the Town*. Prior to designing for the theater he was active in television. He was producer of the Rebekah Harkness Dance Festival at the New York Shakespeare Festival for eight years, and also taught design at Yale and Buffalo Universities. Born in 1928 in Chicago, Illinois, Mr. Ritman died in New York City on May 6, 1984 at age 56.

Sets: 1962 *Who's Afraid of Virginia Woolf?* **1963** *The Riot Act* **1964** *Absence of a Cello; Tiny Alice* **1965** *Entertaining Mr. Sloane* **1966** *A Delicate Balance; Malcolm* **1967** *The Birthday Party; Come Live with Me; Everything in the Garden; Johnny No-trump; The Promise* **1968** *Loot; Playwrights Repertory–One Acts; We Bombed in New Haven* **1969** *The Gingham Dog; The Mundy Scheme; The Penny Wars; Play It Again, Sam* **1972** *An Evening with Richard Nixon; The Last of Mrs. Lincoln; Moonchildren; The Sign in Sidney Brustein's Window; Six Rms Riv Vu* **1974** *Find Your Way Home; God's Favorite; My Fat Friend; Noel Coward in Two Keys* **1975** *P.S. Your Cat Is Dead* **1976** *California Suite; The Eccentricities of a Nightingale; Who's Afraid of Virginia Woolf?; Zalmen or the Madness of God* **1977** *Chapter Two* **1978** *Death Trap; Tribute* **1979** *Last Licks; Once a Catholic* **1980** *Morning's*

at *Seven*; *Onward Victoria*; *The Roast* **1981** *Lolita*; *The Supporting Cast* **1983** *The Corn Is Green*
Costumes: **1962** *Who's Afraid of Virginia Woolf?* **1964** *Tiny Alice*[†] **1965** *Entertaining Mr. Sloane* **1967** *The Birthday Party*; *Everything in the Garden*; *Johnny No-trump* **1968** *Playwrights Repertory–One Acts*
Lights: **1962** *Who's Afraid of Virginia Woolf?* **1964** *Absence of a Cello* **1965** *Entertaining Mr. Sloane* **1967** *Come Live with Me*; *Johnny No-trump* **1968** *Loot*; *Playwrights Repertory–One Acts* **1969** *The Mundy Scheme* **1970** *Sleuth* **1972** *The Last of Mrs. Lincoln* **1974** *Noel Coward in Two Keys* **1975** *P.S. Your Cat Is Dead* **1976** *Who's Afraid of Virginia Woolf?*

Charles H. Ritter

Charles H. Ritter was a scenic artist and a fine art painter. He was originally from Bloomingburg, New York where he was born on February 13, 1883, and studied at the Art Students League. Between 1872 and 1882 he was on the staff of the Union Square Theatre in New York. He then moved to Chicago where he was a scenic artist at Hooley's Theatre. In 1898 he returned to New York City and worked from a studio at his residence at 634 East 150th Street. His paintings were exhibited in Indianapolis in 1918, 1919, and 1924 after which he settled on the West Coast. Ritter died in Los Angeles on June 28, 1961.
Sets: **1900** *Arizona*[†] **1913** *Arizona*[†] (Acts II, III)

William Riva

William Riva, known primarily as a set designer, was active in theater and television. Occasionally, he would also design costumes and lights, as he did for both his Broadway credits. He not only maintained his own career, but also taught scene design at Fordham University. His wife, Maria Sieber Riva, an actress and author, was the daughter of Marlene Dietrich. Together they helped open the Stamford Playhouse in Stamford, Connecticut in 1955. William Riva died in Bern, Switzerland at age 79 on July 3, 1999.

Sets: **1950** *The Telephone/The Medium* **1951** *Razzle Dazzle*
Costumes: **1950** *The Telephone/The Medium* **1951** *Razzle Dazzle*
Lights: **1950** *The Telephone/The Medium* **1951** *Razzle Dazzle*

Amelie Rives

See Princess Troubetsky.

Carrie F. Robbins

Carrie Fishbein Robbins was born in Baltimore, Maryland on February 7, 1943, and studied at Pennsylvania State University and Yale, where she received an M.F.A., and at art schools. While in college she acted and concentrated on set design, and at Yale University turned her attention to costumes, where it has remained. Her first professional designs were for the Studio Arena Theatre in Buffalo, New York in 1966. Subsequent costume designs have been seen in many regional theaters, on and off-Broadway, and on film and television. She has been nominated for two Tony Awards, for her designs for *Grease* in 1972 and *Over Here* in 1974. She teaches costume design and history at New York University, and has produced theatrical events for venues including the Rockefeller Center Rainbow Room. Twenty-first century designs include *Tallulah Hallelujah!* at the Douglas Fairbanks Theatre, *Toys in the Attic* at the Berkshire Theatre Festival, and *High Infidelity* at the Promenade Theatre.
Costumes: **1970** *Look to the Lilies* **1972** *Grease*; *The Secret Affairs of Mildred Wild* **1973** *The Beggar's Opera*; *The Iceman Cometh*; *Let Me Hear You Smile*; *Molly* **1974** *Over Here*; *Yentl* **1977** *Happy End* **1980** *Fearless Frank* **1981** *The First*; *Frankenstein*; *It Had to Be You*; *Macbeth* **1982** *Agnes of God* **1985** *The Boys of Winter*; *The Octette Bridge Club* **1986** *Raggedy Ann* **1992** *Anna Karenina* **1994** *The Shadow Box* **2001** *A Class Act*

Elinor Robbins

Elinor Robbins designed costumes for a play in 1951.
Costumes: **1951** *Saint Joan*

Jesse J. Robbins

Jesse (Jess) J. Robbins, who designed

lights for one Broadway production in 1917, was born in Dayton, Ohio on April 30, 1886. In 1922 Jess Robbins Productions was located at 220 West 42nd Street in New York City and he resided at 1203 West 42nd Street. He relocated to California and appeared in the film *A Lucky Dog* before becoming a motion picture director which occupied the majority of his career. He died in Los Angeles on March 11, 1973.
Lights: 1917 *Yes or No*

R. N. Robbins

Robert Nelson Robbins was the creative partner and Mitchell Cirker the business manager of Cirker and Robbins Scenic Studio. This studio produced designs for numerous Broadway shows between 1919 and 1944 and also built or painted dozens more for other designers. Robert Robbins also designed sets under his own name in the 1920s and 1930s. Additional information is available under the entry "Cirker and Robbins" in this book.
Sets: 1927 *The Seventh Heart; Synthetic Sin* **1928** *Box Seats; Courage; Gentlemen of the Press; Gods of the Lightning; Night Hostess; Poppa; Ringside* **1929** *Buckaroo* **1932** *Heigh-Ho, Everybody*

Erling Roberts

Erling Roberts designed a set in 1951 on Broadway. He was born on July 22, 1901 and died in Ojai, California in January, 1974.
Sets: 1951 *Jotham Valley*

James Roberts

James Roberts was born in Bath, England in 1835 into a family of distinguished scenic artists that included his father and grandfather. After an apprenticeship at Covent Garden he worked briefly in London before emigrating to America in 1860. At the time of his death on March 21, 1892, he was chief scenic artist for Augustin Daly, with whom he began working in 1869. His designs were used in hundreds of nineteenth century productions in the three theaters Daly operated in succession: the Fifth Avenue Theatre, the 28th Street Theatre, and at 30th Street and Broadway, as well as on tour. Many of his scenic designs were used in productions revived on Broadway, as was the case with his posthumous credit in 1902. Also adept at making scale models, his obituary in the March 22, 1892 edition of *The New York Times* acknowledges that his contribution was more than that of a scenic artist: "Mr. Roberts was one of the best theatrical artists of the day, and most of the elaborate stage pictures that have pleased the eye at Daly's for over twenty years were designed and set under his supervision."
Sets: 1902 *The Hunchback*†

Robin Sanford Roberts

Scenic designer Robin Sanford Roberts received her M.F.A. from the University of California, San Diego. While there she designed *Pericles* and *Love's Labor's Lost*. She has designed for many West Coast theaters including San Diego Repertory (*Avenue X*), The Old Globe Theatre (*The Old Settler, Miracles, The Substance of Fire*, etc.), and the Sacramento Theatre Company (*Three Tall Women*). She has also designed scenery for the Telluride Theatre Festival. Among her honors is a 1997 National Endowment for the Arts/Theatre Communications Group Design Fellowship.
Sets: 1999 *It Ain't Nothing But the Blues*

Ruth Roberts

Ruth Roberts (also known as Ruth Roberts Sabol) designed lights for the world premiere of *The Abduction of Figaro* by Peter Schickele (P.D.Q. Bach) in 1984. She has designed for the theater and opera in the United States and abroad, and has numerous off-Broadway productions to her credit, as well as four Radio City Music Hall extravaganzas. She is the lighting director of *The Late Show with David Letterman*, for which she has been nominated for Emmy Awards.
Lights: 1980 *Fearless Frank* **1985** *The King and I*

Sarah Roberts

Sarah Roberts studied in South Africa and the United Kingdom. She often designs scenery and costumes for the

Market Theatre in Johannesburg including *Born in the R.S.A.*, *Sophiatown*, *Have You Seen Zandile?* and *Strike the Woman, Strike the Rock!*, and for the Junction Avenue Theatre Company of South Africa. Her designs have been seen in the *Woza Africa!* Festival at Lincoln Center, at the Zurich, Berlin and Edinburgh Festivals, and in Basel and Frankfurt.

Sets: 1988 *Sarafina!*
Costumes: 1988 *Sarafina!*

Christine Robinson

Christine Robinson, a British designer, studied at the Lincoln and Hammersmith Schools of Art. She has designed costumes for seasons at Pitlochry, Lincoln Theatre Royal, and Donmar Warehouse. Her credits on television are many, and include specials such as *Cleo Laine and John Dankworth* and the series in England, *Song by Song*. She was also art director for the mid-1970s film *The Waiting Room*.

Costumes: 1986 *Jerome Kern Goes to Hollywood*

Clarke Robinson

Clarke Robinson, who created designs for many productions between 1921 and 1941, was born in Bradford, Pennsylvania on November 26, 1894. He studied voice in Europe and debuted at the age of fifteen singing in opera, light opera and vaudeville. He designed scenery at the Roxy, Rialto and Capitol Theatres, and for Music Box Revues. He replaced Robert Edmund Jones as art director at Radio City Music Hall and was succeeded by his assistant, James Morcom, after six months. He also appeared on radio shows and created television shows. Between World War I and World War II he wrote novels and biographies, designed sets and occasionally lights and costumes, raised horses and became an authority on turf. He died on January 18, 1962 at age 67.

Sets: 1921 *Music Box Revue* 1922 *Music Box Revue* 1923 *Music Box Revue* 1924 *Music Box Revue* 1925 *Dearest Enemy*; *Greenwich Village Follies*; *Gypsy Fires*; *Just Beyond*; *Young Blood* 1926 *No Trespassing*; *Peggy Ann* 1927 *Delmar's Revels*; *Enchantment*; *Patience*; *Revery*; *Rufus LeMaire's Affairs* 1928 *Jarnegan*; *Rain or Shine* 1929 *Fioretta*; *The Ghost Parade*; *Murray Anderson's Almanac*; *Woof, Woof* 1930 *Nine-Fifteen Revue* 1933 *Roberta* 1934 *Keep Moving*; *Say When* 1935 *Earl Carroll's Sketch Book* 1936 *Broadway Sho-Window*; *Granite*; *Mainly for Lovers* 1937 *Call Me Ziggy* 1941 *Viva O'Brien*

Costumes: 1925 *Just Beyond* 1927 *Patience*; *Revery*

Lights: 1927 *Delmar's Revels*; *The New Yorkers* 1931 *Billy Rose's Crazy Quilt*

Emeline Clarke Roche

The daughter of a clergyman, Emeline Clarke Roche was born in Brooklyn, New York. Both a scenic and costume designer, she studied with Norman Bel Geddes before making her Broadway debut in 1940 as costume designer for *The Male Animal*. Emeline Roche worked with Aline Bernstein as an assistant for scenery and costumes, beginning with sets for *The Grand Hotel*, and later assisted Robert Edmond Jones. She worked in summer theater in Newport, Rhode Island from 1935 to 1941 and toured as stage manager with Ruth Draper. Later she designed the backgrounds for the weekly *Kate Smith Show* on NBC-TV, and served as costume director of the New York City Center, designing costumes for over thirty shows. At City Center she designed the costumes for a production of *Anna Christie*, which she considered her greatest personal success. Also active with United Scenic Artist, she died at age 93 on October 20, 1995 in New York City.

Sets: 1938 *Eye on the Sparrow* 1942 *Papa Is All* 1947 *Volpone* 1952 *Anna Christie*

Costumes: 1940 *The Male Animal* 1942 *Mr. Sycamore*; *Papa Is All* 1944 *Jacobowsky and the Colonel*; *Pick-Up Girl* (Costume Supervisor) 1945 *Deep Are the Roots*; *State of the Union†* 1946 *Flamingo Road*; *Loco* 1947 *Love Goes to Press* 1948 *Goodbye, My Fancy*; *Red Gloves* 1949 *Gayden* 1950 *The Devil's Disciple* 1952 *Anna Christie*

Norman Rock

Norman Rock graduated from San Diego Stage College, studied at the Yale University School of Drama, and received an M.A. from Stanford University in 1950. He served in the Naval Reserve during World War II and spent most of his professional career in California. His Broadway debut occurred in 1936 and was followed by an additional production in 1938. He also designed numerous productions for the Hollywood Bowl, Etienne Decroux, the American Mime Theatre, and for television. Norman Rock died at age 77 in Sonoma, California on November 14, 1985.

Sets: 1936 *Reflected Glory* 1938 *Soliloquy*

David Rockwell

Architect David Rockwell, was born in Chicago in 1956, son of Joanne (a vaudeville dancer and choreographer) and Maury Katzenberg. His father was killed in a plane crash when he was four years old. When his mother subsequently remarried, to businessman John Rockwell, he was raised in New Jersey and Guadalajara. After graduating from Syracuse University in 1979 he spent a semester at the Architectural Association in London and then as an assistant to theatrical designer Roger Morgan. In 1984 he founded the Rockwell Group, an architectural firm based in New York City. His projects are wide-ranging and include Grand Central Terminal's dining concourse, sports stadiums, the restaurants Nobu and Next Door Nobu, the Kodak (Academy Awards) Theatre, the Cirque du Soleil Theatre in Orlando, Florida, and the renovation of Radio City Music Hall. He was named the 1998 Designer of the Year by *Interiors* magazine.

Sets: 2000 *The Rocky Horror Show*

Domingo A. Rodriguez

Domingo A. Rodriguez was born September 24, 1929 in Erie, Pennsylvania and has been designing costumes since childhood, initially for puppets and then for a community theater in Harrisburg, Pennsylvania. His costumes first appeared on Broadway in the 1961 production of *Gideon*. He has worked with and learned from Raymond Sovey and Boris Aronson. Mr. Rodriguez teaches at William Woods College as an adjunct professor, and was awarded an honorary doctorate in Fine Arts by that institution. He ran his own costume shop, "Domingo A. Rodriguez, Inc." for a time. He is one in a family of artists: his wife Eva is a dancer, one son is a musician and another an actor.

Costumes: 1961 *Gideon* 1964 *Abraham Cochrane*; *The Passion of Joseph D* 1967 *After the Rain* 1968 *Lovers and Other Strangers*; *The Sudden and Accidental Reeducation of Horse Johnson* 1969 *Trumpets of the Lord* 1977 *The Basic Training of Pavlo Hummel*

Ralph Roeder

Ralph Leclercq Roeder was born in New York City on April 7, 1890 and studied at Columbia University and received his undergraduate degree from Harvard in 1911. During the teens, he was involved with the theater as an actor and director, and occasionally a designer, before turning his attention to writing. On December 3, 1929, he married dancer and costume designer Fania Mindell and in 1930 published his first book, *Savonarola*. They moved to Mexico City in the early 1940s, where he continued to write, including the widely respected *Juarez and His Mexico* (1947) about the Mexican statesman Benito Pablo Juarez won the Aguilla Aztec Award. He died in Mexico City, a suicide, on October 22, 1969, shortly after completing a sequel to Juarez's biography, *Mexico Toward the Future* and the death of his wife in August 1969.

Sets: 1915 *Another Interior* (Also directed)

Costumes: 1915 *Another Interior* (Also directed); *Interior* (Also appeared)

Edward Roelker

Edward Roelker contributed scenic designs to a 1920 Broadway production. He worked as a carpenter in the teens and resided at 368 West 50th Street. In the 1920s he lived at 245 West 50th Street.

Sets: 1920 *Good Times*

Professor Alfred Roller

Alfred Roller, a Viennese scenic designer, was born in Austria in 1864 and died there in 1935. His first sets were for the Viennese Hofoper in 1903. He gained international fame and prominence in 1911 when he designed *Der Rosenkavalier* for Max Reinhardt. That show led to additional collaborations. He designed in the U.S. for the Philadelphia Grand Opera Company and the Metropolitan Opera Company, including *Fidelio* in 1909. He also occasionally designed costumes.

Costumes: 1927 *Jedermann*

Hugo Rombold

Hugo Rombold contributed costume designs to a play on Broadway in 1948.

Costumes: 1948 *Patience†* (Every Day Girls costumes)

Constanza Romero

Costume designer Constanza Romero, originally from Bogotá, Colombia where her father was a commercial artist and photographer and her mother a linguist, moved to Fresno, California with her mother when she was eleven years old. She studied at the California College of Arts and Crafts, in Bogotá, at the University of California at Fresno, and in Florence, Italy. She earned an M.F.A. from the Yale School of Drama. She designs for the Oregon Shakespeare Festival, the Goodman Theatre, the Intiman Theatre, and the Milwaukee Repertory Theatre among others, focusing on costumes, but occasionally designing scenery as well. Productions for The Acting Company include *The Phantom Tollbooth*. Married to playwright August Wilson in 1994, they reside in Seattle with their daughter Azula who was born on August 27, 1997. Twenty-first century designs include costumes for *King Hedley II*.

Costumes: 1990 *The Piano Lesson* **1996** *Seven Guitars*

M. Ronsin

Monsieur Eugene Ronsin (1867-1938) spent most of his career as a scenic artist and designer in Paris, where he did many productions for the Comédie Française, Paris Opera and Théâtre Sarah Bernhardt. His earliest credits were in Belleville. He often collaborated with Emile Bertin and other great French scene painters. His single New York credit does not reflect the prolific career of this artist who successfully made the transition from painted backdrops to the new European stagecraft.

Sets: 1914 *Sari†* (Act II)

John Root

John Root was born in Chicago in 1904 and met his wife, actress Margaret Mullin, during the run of one of his more than fifty Broadway shows, *Red Harvest*. He also designed television, notably *The Armstrong Circle Theatre*, *The Perry Como Show* for several years, and commercials. Prior to working in New York he designed for the Red Barn Theatre, Locust Valley, Long Island. In the early 1960s he changed careers and formed his own company, John Root, Inc. Real Estate, in Lumberville, Pennsylvania. John Root died on March 13, 1990 at age 85 in Doylestown, Pennsylvania.

Sets: 1934 *Piper Paid* **1935** *Ceiling Zero*; *Crime Marches On*; *Cross Ruff*; *If This Be Treason*; *Substitute for Murder*; *There's Wisdom in Women* **1936** *Seen But Not Heard*; *So Proudly We Hail* **1937** *Angel Island*; *Chalked Out*; *Now You've Done It*; *One Thing after Another*; *Red Harvest*; *Sun Kissed* **1938** *All That Glitters*; *Brown Danube*; *The Greatest Show on Earth*; *Kiss the Boys Goodbye*; *Run Sheep Run* **1939** *Pastoral*; *Ring Two*; *Sea Dogs* **1940** *George Washington Slept Here*; *Glamour Preferred*; *Lady in Waiting*; *Out from Under* **1941** *Cuckoos on the Hearth* **1942** *The Cat Screams*; *Janie*; *Jason* **1943** *Counterattack*; *Get Away Old Man*; *Kiss and Tell*; *Nine Girls*; *Pillar to Post* **1944** *Doctors Disagree*; *Harvey*; *A Highland Fling*; *Snafu* **1945** *A Boy Who Lived Twice* **1947** *It Takes Two*; *Tenting Tonight* **1949** *Love Me Long*; *Mrs. Gibbon's Boys* **1950** *Mr. Barry's Etchings* **1951** *Not for Children*

Lights: 1949 *Mrs. Gibbon's Boys* **1951** *Not for Children*

Sonia Rosenberg

Sonia Rosenberg designed costumes for a play on Broadway in 1934. During the 1930s, she and her husband, Abraham Rosenberg, were partners with Gloria Vanderbilt in a dress shop, "Gloria Vanderbilt - Sonia Gowns, Inc." on East 59th Street in New York City. She emigrated to the United States as a young girl, and died in Los Angeles, California on February 28, 1944.

Costumes: 1934 *Piper Paid*[†] (Gowns)

Hilary Rosenfield

Hilary Rosenfield, a native of New York City, was born February 3, 1950 and received a B.F.A. at the New York University School of the Arts, which included a semester at the Royal Academy of Fine Arts in Belgium. Her first costume designs were for a Philadelphia summer stock production of *A Taste of Honey* in 1968 starring Estelle Parsons. Rosenfield designs often for television and was nominated for a Daytime Emmy for *Mom's On Strike*. She specializes in period films, with several to her credit including *Heartland*, *Noon Wine*, and *Desert Bloom*.

Costumes: 1978 *Runaways*

Jean Rosenthal

Jean Rosenthal was one of the pioneers of lighting design. She emerged as a specialist in lighting at a time when the lighting of a production was most often handled by a set designer or an electrician, and in the course of her career made lighting designers crucial members of production teams. Born Eugenia Rosenthal on March 16, 1912 in New York City, she was the daughter of two doctors who were Romanian immigrants. After studying acting and dance at the Neighborhood Playhouse from 1929 to 1930 she became a technical assistant to faculty member Martha Graham, the beginning of a life long association between them. She studied at Yale with Stanley McCandless and joined the Federal Theatre Project in 1935, where she began her professional career. After working with Orson Welles' Mercury Theatre, she formed Theatre Production Service in 1940 and Jean Rosenthal Associates in 1958, for consulting on major theater and architectural projects. During her career she designed over two hundred shows, for Broadway, Martha Graham, the New York City Ballet, and the Metropolitan Opera. Among her major contributions were the elimination of stage shadows by using rich floods of upstage lighting, revising the use of light plots, and controlling angles and mass of illumination to create contrasts without shadows. She died at age 57 on May 1, 1969 after a long battle with cancer, ten days after attending the opening of Martha Graham's *Archaic Hours*. She received the Outer Critics Circle Award for contributions to stage design in 1968-69 and the Henrietta Lord Memorial Award from the Yale School of Drama in 1932. In 1972 *The Magic of Light* was published, the result of a collaboration begun much earlier between Jean Rosenthal and Lael Wertenbaker.

Sets: 1961 *The Conquering Hero*[†] **1963** *The Beast in Me*; *On an Open Roof*

Lights: 1938 *Danton's Death* **1942** *Rosalinda* **1943** *Richard III* **1947** *The Telephone/The Medium* **1948** *Joy to the World*; *Sundown Beach* **1949** *Caesar and Cleopatra* **1952** *The Climate of Eden* **1954** *House of Flowers*; *Ondine*; *Quadrille*; *The Saint of Bleecker Street* **1956** *The Great Sebastian* **1957** *The Dark at the Top of the Stairs*; *A Hole in the Head*; *Jamaica*; *West Side Story* **1958** *The Disenchanted*; *Winesburg, Ohio* **1959** *Destry Rides Again*; *Redhead*; *Saratoga*; *The Sound of Music*; *Take Me Along* **1960** *Becket*; *Caligula*; *Dear Liar*; *A Taste of Honey*; *West Side Story* **1961** *The Conquering Hero*; *Daughter of Silence*; *The Gay Life*; *A Gift of Time*; *The Night of the Iguana* **1962** *A Funny Thing Happened on the Way to the Forum*; *Lord Pengo* **1963** *The Ballad of the Sad Cafe*; *Barefoot in the Park*; *The Beast in Me*; *Jennie*; *On an Open Roof* **1964** *The Chinese Prime Minister*; *Fiddler on the Roof*; *Hamlet*; *Hello, Dolly!*; *Luv*; *Poor Bitos* **1965** *Baker Street*; *The Odd Couple* **1966** *The Apple Tree*; *Cabaret*; *I Do! I Do!*; *Ivanov*; *Show Boat*; *The Star Spangled Girl*; *A*

Time for Singing 1967 *Hello, Dolly!*; *Illya Darling* 1968 *The Exercise*; *The Happy Time*; *Plaza Suite*; *Weekend* 1969 *Dear World* 1980 *West Side Story*

Stephen Ross

Stephen Ross was born on August 18, 1949 in St. Louis, Missouri, the son of David and Ellen Ross. He received a B.A. at Southern Illinois University and an M.F.A. at the University of Wisconsin under Gilbert V. Hemsley, Jr., who influenced his career. His first professional design was *Benvenuto Cellini* with Sarah Caldwell for the Opera Company of Boston. Based in Toronto, he designs primarily opera, productions for regional theater companies, and industrial promotions in Canada and the United States. He has also designed the Annual Mary Kay Canada show for the last fifteen years. Honors include nominations for three Dora Mavor Moore Awards in Toronto. Among his twenty-first century designs are *Madame Butterfly* for Seattle Opera and *Syncopation* by Allan Knee at the Winter Garden Theatre in Toronto.

Lights: 1989 *Shenandoah*

Herman Rosse

Herman Rosse was born in the Hague in 1887, studied at the South Kensington College of Art in London and received a degree in architecture from Stanford University. He created over two hundred sets during his career and taught at both the Art Institute of Chicago and the University of California. He designed relatively few films but received an Oscar for art direction of *King of Jazz*. He also designed many sets for the Chicago Opera Company and the Paper Mill Playhouse. The author of *Masks and Dreams*, written in collaboration with Kenneth Macgowan, he is also remembered as the designer of the medallions for the Antoinette Perry (Tony) Award. Herman Rosse died on April 13, 1965 at age 78.

Sets: 1922 *Ziegfeld Follies: 1922*† 1923 *Little Miss Bluebeard*; *The Swan* 1924 *Greenwich Village Follies*† 1925 *The Stork* 1928 *Americana*†; *Hello, Daddy* 1930 *King Lear* 1931 *The Merchant of Venice* 1932 *Great Magoo*

Costumes: 1925 *Chauve Souris*†

Rossoni

Rossoni designed a set in 1938 on Broadway.

Sets: 1938 *Pasquale Never New*

Karen Roston

Karen Roston is a native of New York City. After receiving a B.A. at Antioch College she studied with Jane Greenwood at Lester Polakov's Studio and Forum of Stage Design. Her professional debut was as costume designer for *The School for Wives* in Dayton, Ohio. The recipient of an Emmy Award for *Saturday Night Live*, she designed her first Broadway show with Franne Lee, who has been influential in her career. She has designed costumes for numerous episodes of NBC-TV's *Saturday Night Live* (notably the Coneheads) and television specials for Steve Martin, David Letterman, Bob and Ray, and Robert Klein among others. Her films include *Muppets Take Manhattan*, *Gilda Live* and *Mondo Video*. Karen Roston is married to Peter Bochan and they have a daughter, Toby.

Sets: 1986 *Into the Light*†
Costumes: 1979 *Gilda Radner Live from N.Y.*† 1989 *Sid Caesar and Company*

Ann Roth

Since designing the costumes for *Maybe Tuesday* on Broadway in 1958, Ann Roth has amassed numerous additional credits. This busy designer has also designed costumes for the American Conservatory Theatre in San Francisco and for the Kennedy Center. Her film credits are numerous and include *Midnight Cowboy, Klute, Working Girl, The Talented Mr. Ripley* (co-designed with her long-time assistant, Gary Jones), and *Places in the Heart*. She shares a loft studio in New York City with Jane Greenwood and David Toser called the Costume Depot. Born in 1931, she graduated from Carnegie Institute of Technology with a major in scene design before turning her considerable talents to costume design. Her first position was assisting Irene Sharaff on the films *The King and I, A Star is Born* and *Brigadoon.* Honors include an Academy Award for *The English Patient* and several additional nominations, the Edith Head Lifetime Achievement Award from the International Fashion Institute, and the 2000 Irene Sharaff Lifetime Achievement Award.

Costumes: 1958 *The Disenchanted; Make a Million; Maybe Tuesday* 1959 *A Desert Incident* 1960 *The Cool World; Face of a Hero* 1961 *A Far Country; Isle of Children; Look: We've Come Through; Purlie Victorious* 1962 *Private Ear, The/ The Public Eye* (Miss McEwan's costumes); *Venus at Large* 1963 *A Case of Libel; Children from Their Games; Natural Affection* 1964 *I Had a Ball; The Last Analysis; Slow Dance on the Killing Ground* 1965 *The Impossible Years; Mrs. Dally; The Odd Couple* 1966 *The Star Spangled Girl; Wayward Stork* 1967 *Something Different* 1968 *Happiness Is Just a Little Thing Called a Rolls Royce* 1969 *My Daughter, Your Son; Play It Again, Sam; The Three Sisters; Tiny Alice*[1] (Miss De Ann Mear's wardrobe) 1970 *The Engagement Baby; Gantry; Purlie* 1971 *Father's Day* 1972 *Children! Children!; Fun City; Purlie; Six Rms Riv Vu* 1973 *Seesaw; The Women* 1975 *The Royal Family* 1976 *The Heiress* 1977 *The Importance of Being Earnest* 1978 *The Best Little Whorehouse in Texas; The Crucifer of Blood; Do You Turn Somersaults?; First Monday in October* 1979 *Strangers; They're Playing Our Song* 1980 *Lunch Hour* 1982 *The Best Little Whorehouse in Texas; Present Laughter* 1983 *The Misanthrope* 1984 *Design for Living; Hurlyburly; Open Admissions*[1] 1985 *Arms and the Man; Biloxi Blues; The Odd Couple; Singin' in the Rain* 1986 *The House of Blue Leaves; Social Security* 1989 *Born Yesterday* 1992 *Death and the Maiden; A Small Family Business* 1993 *Any Given Day* 1994 *What's Wrong with this Picture?* 1996 *Present Laughter* 2000 *The Tale of the Allergist's Wife*

Joseph Roth

Joseph Roth designed lights for a Broadway production in 1925. In the early 1920s he was vice president of Lenox Electric Company, Inc., electricians, located at 396 Lenox Avenue, New York City. He lived at 325 Riverside Drive.

Lights: 1925 *Paid*

Peggy Roth

After the death of her husband Joseph Roth, a garment manufacturer, in 1920, Peggy Roth (also known as Madame Roth) went into the retail business, starting the Peggy Roth Dress Shops with a store on Madison Avenue and one on Broadway at 90th Street. These shops remained open for 38 years, during which time she contributed costume designs to plays. Her shops were also often mentioned in the acknowledgment sections of theater playbills. Mrs. Roth retired in 1960, and died in October 1975 at age 80.

Costumes: 1906 *The Kreutzer Sonata*[1] (as: Madame Roth) 1928 *The Wrecker* (Women's costumes and accessories)

Wolfgang Roth

Wolfgang Roth came to the United States in 1938 from Berlin. Born in the German capital on February 10, 1910, he studied at Berlin's Academy of Art and worked with the Piscator Theatre and Bertolt Brecht. He designed numerous sets for theaters and opera companies around the world, and occasionally designed costumes as well. His credits at the Metropolitan Opera include *A Masked Ball* and at the New York City Opera include *The School for Wives* and *Danton's Death.* He also designed for television and film, painted, illustrated and worked as an architect. Wolfgang Roth died on November 11, 1988 in New York City.

Sets: 1943 *The First Million* 1945 *Too Hot for Maneuvers* 1946 *Pound on Demand* 1947 *Yellow Jack* 1948 *Oh, Mr. Meadowbrook* 1950 *Now I Lay Me Down to Sleep* 1951 *Twentieth Century* 1953 *Porgy and Bess* 1958 *Portofino* 1960 *The Deadly Game* 1979 *Strider*
Costumes: 1946 *Pound on Demand* 1947 *Yellow Jack* 1960 *The Deadly Game*
Lights: 1960 *The Deadly Game*

Albert Rutherston

Albert Daniel Rutherston, also known as Albert Rothenstein, was born December 5, 1881 (sometimes recorded as 1883) in Bradford, England, and studied at the Slade School of Art and with Frederick Brown at University College. He was a painter, and taught as well. His designs for settings and occasionally costumes were seen beginning in 1901. He designed in particular for Granville Barker, including *Le Mariage Forcé* in 1913, and for actress Lillah McCarthy. His address in 1922 was 5 Thurloe Square, SW7 in London. He died in 1953.

Costumes: 1915 *Androcles and the Lion*

Lucille Rothschild

Lucille Rothschild, who designed costumes for a Broadway play in 1930, was president of the Carroll Dress and Coat Company, 455 Seventh Avenue, New York City. She resided at 325 Riverside Drive with her husband, William L. Rothschild, who was resident buyer for the salon.

Costumes: 1930 *Let and Sub-Let*

Paul Rover

See Paul Ouzounoff.

Hazel Roy

Hazel Roy (1902-1964) was active on Broadway in the early 1950s. She was primarily a dancer and concert soloist, and created costumes initially for her own performances. In 1952, she was elected chairman of the Costume Designers division of United Scenic Artists. In private life she was known as Hazel Roy Timberg, after her marriage to scriptwriter and vaudeville headliner Herman Timberg. When he died on April 16, 1952, they were living at the Hotel Greystone at the corner of Broadway and Ninety-first Street in New York City.

Costumes: 1951 *Lace on Her Petticoat*; *To Dorothy, a Son* (Clothes by) **1952** *Gertie*

Steven Rubin

Steven Rubin was born in Portland, Oregon in 1942 and studied at the University of Utah and at Yale, where he also taught design for two years. When possible, he prefers to do both sets and costumes for productions, but has designed numerous sets working with other designers who contribute costumes. He has designed for the Indiana Repertory Theatre, the San Diego Shakespeare Festival, and the Old Globe. An especially gifted designer for dance, he has designed scenery and/or costumes for many productions for Pennsylvania Ballet, Fort Worth Ballet Company, Milwaukee Ballet, and the New York City Ballet. He has also held the position of resident designer with several companies. Late twentieth century credits include costumes for *Square Dance* co-designed with Barbara Matera for New York City Ballet and *The Snow Ball*, a co-production by Hartford Stage and San Diego Shakespeare Festival.

Sets: 1975 *Ah, Wilderness!* **1979** *Devour the Snow*; *On Golden Pond* **1980** *Horowitz and Mrs. Washington* **1981** *The Survivor* **1988** *Romance/Romance*
Costumes: 1979 *On Golden Pond*

Bernard Rudofsky

Bernard Rudofsky, architect and social critic, was born April 13, 1905 in Vienna, Austria and studied architecture at the Polytechnic University in Vienna. Long interested in the human body and its coverings, he wrote many books, including *Are Clothes Modern?* (1947), *The Unfashionable Human Body* (1971),and *Now I Lay Me Down to Eat* (1980). He designed exhibits at museums, such as "Architecture without Architects" for the Museum of Modern Art in 1964, held positions at Yale University, the Royal Academy of Fine Art in Copenhagen, and at Waseda University in Tokyo, among others. A retrospective of his work, "Sparta/Sybaris " was held in Vienna in 1987, accompanied by a book of the same title. He mainly lived and worked from New York City, where he died in March 1988.

Costumes: 1951 *Barefoot in Athens*

Kevin Rupnik

Scenic designer Kevin Rupnik was born on February 28, 1956 in Warren, Ohio and received a B.F.A. at Carnegie Mellon University in 1978 and an M.F.A. at the Yale University School of Drama in 1981. His initial professional productions were for the

Pittsburgh Civic Light Opera. He designs mainly for television and theater, and has credits as companies including the Williamstown Theatre Festival, the Alaska Repertory Theatre, GeVa Theatre, the Santa Fe Opera, the New York City Opera, and the Coconut Grove Playhouse. Designs for television include the daytime dramas *One Life to Live*, *All My Children*, and currently *As the World Turns*. He also designed the prime-time series *The Arthel and Fred Show* when based in California. Awards include the Los Angeles Drama Logue Award for the scenic design of *Greater Tuna*.

Sets: 1982 *Ghosts*

Charles E. Rush

Charles E. Rush designed lights for a Broadway show in 1924. He also designed in London, creating lights for *Lilac Time* in 1928 at Daly's Theatre.

Lights: 1924 *Hassard Short's Ritz Revue*

James Russell

James Spencer Russell was born on April 7, 1915 in Monticello, Indiana. He studied at the University of New Mexico with Raymond Johnson. He also studied with Donald Oenslager at Yale University and has both B.F.A. and M.F.A. degrees. A painter, he exhibited at the American Federation of Arts, the Rhode Island School of Design and Small Environments.

Sets: 1949 *The Happiest Years*

Steven Rust

Steven J. Rust, a lighting designer and theater consultant, was born in Burlington, Vermont on May 3, 1959, son of Helen Ann and Charles B. Rust. He majored in Economics at Connecticut College, graduating in 1981. A year as a lighting design intern through United Scenic Artists led to work as an assistant lighting designer with Neil Peter Jampolis, Mary Jo Dondlinger and Anne Militello, while he designed productions for the Willow Cabin Theatre Company and Theatre Row Theatre, and other New York theaters. Through Columbia Artists Management, Inc., Charles Cosler Theatre Design, Inc., Associated Press Studio, and currently Sachs Morgan Studio he has

provided a variety of theater consulting services and project management. Late twentieth century designs include *The Manchurian Candidate* at Theatre Row Theatre and *The Director* at New Voices Theatre Company.

Lights: 1993 *Wilder, Wilder, Wilder*

Rita Ryack

Rita Ryack received an M.F.A. in costume design at Yale University and is principally as a costume designer for major motion pictures. She was born in Boston, Massachusetts and started professional life as illustrator and film animator, but decided to pursue a career in theatrical design. Her first costume designs in New York were for *Sister Susie Cinema* for Mabou Mines at the New York Shakespeare Festival. She was also Principal Designer at the American Repertory Theatre at Harvard for a time and has designed at the Goodman Theatre, Indiana Repertory Theatre, the New York Shakespeare Festival and the Manhattan Theatre Club. Movies include *Les Compreres*, *The Fan*, *Apollo 13*, *Casino*, *Dr. Seuss' How the Grinch Stole Christmas*, and *Ransom*. Her costume designs for *My One and Only* were nominated for Tony and Drama Desk Awards. In 1986, she won the Obie Award for three plays, *Anteroom*, *A Lie of the Mind* and *It's Only a Play*. Recent films include *After Hours* directed by Martin Scorsese and *House on Sullivan Street* directed by Peter Yates. Twenty-first century designs include costumes for the movies *Rush Hour 2* and *A Beautiful Mind*.

Costumes: 1983 *My One and Only* **1984** *The Human Comedy*

D. D. Ryan

Mrs. D. D. Ryan designed costumes for a Broadway play in 1970. Her wide-ranging experience with clothes and costumes includes being fashion editor for *Harper's Bazaar* and design coordinator for Elaine May's film *A New Leaf*. As one of fashion designer Halston's inner circle during the 1970s and 1980s, she was often mentioned in fashion columns for her highly individual style.

Costumes: 1970 *Company*

E. H. Ryan

E. H. Ryan contributed scenic designs to a Broadway production in 1905. The show was originally staged in London and subsequently imported by the Shubert Brothers with the original scenery. E. H. Ryan often collaborated with the other active scenic painters of his time including Robert McCleary, Stafford Hall and Robert Caney. Additional credits include *Sardanapalus* (Booth Theatre, New York, 1876) and *The Derby Winner* (Shakespeare Theatre, Liverpool, England, 1895)

Sets: **1905** *The Babes and the Baron*†

Oscar Ryan

Oscar Ryan was born June 27, 1904 in Montreal, Quebec, Canada. Active in Canadian theater, he helped found the Canadian Workers Theatre Movement, and is also known as a theater critic, playwright, and author. Among other plays, he co-wrote *Eight Men Speak, A Political Play in Six Acts* presented by the Progressive Arts Club of Canada. The play dramatized the attempted murder of Tim Buck in his cell at Kingston Penitentiary in 1933 and the reluctance of authorities to investigate.

Lights: **1938** *The Swing Mikado*

T. E. Ryan

T. E. Ryan was a scenic artist and designer who amassed credits in London and in the United States, mainly in Boston, Philadelphia, and New York. Productions in London in the 1880s include *Fourteen Days, Boccaccio, Beauty and the Beast* and *Dick Whittington and His Cat*. He collaborated with many of the leading British scene painters of his era, such as Robert Caney, Walter Spong, William Telbin, and Walter Hann, and others. *Love in Harness* in 1886 and *Rose d'Amour* in 1888 were among his nineteenth century New York credits. He died on October 21, 1920.

Sets: **1901** *The Messenger Boy*† **1902** *The Hunchback*† **1906** *Caesar and Cleopatra*† **1911** *Betsy* **1913** *The Man with Three Wives*

Albert Rybeck

Albert Rybeck (also known as Albert

J. Ribicki) designed lights in 1925 for a Broadway show. Albert J. Rybicki was a photo-engraver active in New York from the teens through the thirties.

Lights: **1925** *George White's Scandals*

Richard Rychtarik

Richard Rychtarik was born in Czechoslovakia on July 20, 1894 and studied architecture in Prague prior to coming to the United States in 1923. He designed scenery and costumes for the Cleveland Playhouse in the late 1920s and in 1935 designed the set for the United States premiere of *Lady Macbeth of Mtensk* by Shostakovitch which the Cleveland Orchestra performed at the Metropolitan Opera House. He subsequently relocated to New York City and designed for the City Center Opera and Metropolitan Opera, becoming technical director of the Metropolitan Opera in 1947. From 1949 until 1964 he was Chief Scenic Designer for CBS-TV. He died in New York City at age 87 on July 10, 1982.

Sets: **1942** *Once over Lightly*

Sylvia Saal

Sylvia Saal designed costumes for a Broadway play in 1946.

Costumes: **1946** *Present Laughter*†
(Other costumes supervised)

Anthony Sabatino

Anthony Sabatino, born in Galveston, Texas on October 30, 1944, received a B.A. degree from the University of Houston, and an M.F.A. from Brandeis University, where he studied with Howard Bay. An art director, production designer, and producer, he spent his career primarily designing for television. During his seven year association with Don Cornelius and *Soul Train* he designed the dance show, the Annual Soul Train Music Awards, and television specials. He was art director for several series, including *Let's Make a Deal, Doctor Dean* and *Fun House*, for which he won the 1989 Emmy Award for excellence in design. He designed many award shows (*Golden Globes*, etc.) and television specials. Anthony Sabatino died at age 48 in Los Angeles on April 10, 1993, of AIDS.

Sets: **1977** *Toller Cranston's Ice Show*

Florence Sachnoff

Florence Sachnoff designed costumes for a play in 1937 on Broadway.

Costumes: 1937 *Native Ground*

Sackman

The credit for "Sackman" probably refers to one of two men active in New York during the first two decades of the twentieth century with that surname. William Sackman (1893-1984) was a fine art painter who resided at 625 Jeff Place in Queens, New York during the teens before moving to Connecticut. John G. Sackman was a carpenter who lived at 70 East 115th Street in New York in 1909.

Sets: 1912 *Milestones*

Sada Sacks

Sada Sacks, who was born on March 30, 1900, designed gowns for a play on Broadway in 1935. She was the proprietor of a dress-making shop at 671 Madison Avenue in the 1920s and 1930s. She lived for most of her life with her husband Samuel Sacks at 49 East 96th Street in New York City, although she was a resident of Beachwood, Ohio at the time of her death in November 1978.

Costumes: 1935 *Blind Alley* (Gowns)

Ruth St. Denis

Ruth St. Denis was a pioneer of the modern dance movement in the U.S. She was born Ruth Dennis in Newark, New Jersey and began to study dance at age ten. After some years of dancing in plays and with dance companies, and creating her own pieces, she engaged Ted Shawn as a dancing partner. They were married in 1914, started the Denishawn School in Los Angeles, and then formed the Denishawn Company. Her pupils included the major American choreographers to-be: Martha Graham, Doris Humphrey and Charles Weidman. Miss St. Denis often created costumes for herself and their company, and in 1932 contributed costume designs to a show on Broadway. This legendary dancer, choreographer and teacher, who published an autobiography, *An Unfinished Life*, died in Los Angeles on July 21, 1968.

Costumes: 1932 *Singapore* (Miss Caubaye's and native dancer's costumes)

Yves Saint Laurent

Yves Saint Laurent was born in 1936 in Oran, Algeria. He studied languages at school and in 1954 attended the Chambre Syndicale in Paris. At a young age he won two prizes in the International Wool Secretariat design contest. Dior offered him a position in his salon on the basis of a fifteen minute interview, and in 1957 when Dior died, Saint Laurent became head of the Dior house. After service in the Algerian War, he opened his own couture house in Paris, quickly becoming one of the foremost fashion designers of the twentieth century. His collections are invariably original, much copied, and often honored with awards. In 1983, he became the first living designer to have a retrospective of his designs on exhibition at the Metropolitan Museum of Art. In addition to his fashion designs, he occasionally contributes costume designs (his first love) to ballets, plays and films.

Costumes: 1964 *Zizi*

Ruth St. Moritz

Ruth St. Moritz designed costumes for a Broadway show in the mid-1960s.

Costumes: 1964 *Sponomo*

Loudon Sainthill

Loudon Sainthill, a painter and designer, was born in Hobart, Tasmania, Australia in 1919 and in early 1950 moved to London where he did most of his design work, both sets and costumes. In London his paintings were widely exhibited. His first major success in the theater was *The Tempest* for the Royal Shakespeare Company in Stratford-upon-Avon in 1951, and was followed by many designs in London's West End and for ballet companies. In the United States he won a Tony for *Canterbury Tales* and a nomination for *The Right Honorable Gentleman*. He died on June 9, 1969 in London at age 50.

Sets: 1955 *Tiger at the Gate* **1956** *Romeo and Juliet* **1965** *Half a Sixpence*; *The Right Honorable Gentleman*

Costumes: 1955 *Tiger at the Gate* 1956 *Romeo and Juliet* 1965 *Half a Sixpence*†; *The Right Honorable Gentleman* 1969 *Canterbury Tales*

Serge de Salomko

The playbill for *The Echo* states that the costumes were made in Paris from designs by Serge de Salomko of St. Petersburg.

Costumes: 1910 *The Echo*

Lucielle Samuels

Lucielle (Lucille) Samuels designed costumes for a Broadway play in 1938.

Costumes: 1938 *Bright Rebel*

James D. Sandefur

James D. Sandefur was born on February 26, 1958 in St. Louis. He received a B.F.A. in 1981 from Southern Methodist University and an M.F.A. from the Yale School of Drama in 1985, where he was a Donald Oenslager Scholar. His early experience in theater was as an actor. As a designer, he believes that having performed aids his understanding of actors' and dancers' needs. Sandefur also uses his background in various skilled areas such as scenic painting, properties, and construction in regional theaters to realize designs. He includes Ming Cho Lee and William and Jean Eckart as mentors. In 1987 he received the American Theatre Wing Design Award for *Fences*.

Sets: 1987 *Fences*

Annie Sanse

Annie E. Sanse, known in private life as Mrs. David Sanse designed costumes for plays at the beginning of the twentieth century. She worked from her home at 281 West 11th Street in New York City.

Costumes: 1905 *King Lear*†; *Macbeth*† 1906 *His Honor, the Barber* 1907 *King Lear*†; *Macbeth*

Bruno Santini

Bruno Santini, a native of Switzerland, studied at the Wimbledon School of Theatre Design with Richard Negri and assisted several designers, including Barry Kaye early in his career. He has designed sets for the Royal National Theatre (including *Single Spies*), for the Lyric Studio (Hammersmith), the Scottish Opera, English Music Theatre, D'Oyly Carte, Welsh National Opera and many others. He has collaborated with director Simon Callow in the United Kingdom on productions including *Shirley Valentine*, which subsequently moved to Broadway and his 1991 film version of Carson McCullers' novel *Ballad of the Sad Cafe*. Additional credits include production design for the movie *The Proprietor* directed by Ismail Merchant and starring Jeanne Moreau, Sam Waterston and Jean-Pierre Aumont, and scenery for *Pericles* at the 2000 Theatre Ludlow Festival.

Sets: 1989 *Shirley Valentine*
Costumes: 1989 *Shirley Valentine*

Susan Santoian

Costume designer Susan Santoian made her Broadway debut in 1997 with a production that originated in Boston, where she is located. She has also designed *Old, Wicked Songs* for the Jewish Theatre of New England and *Who's Afraid of Virginia Woolf?* performed by the Cambridge Theatre Company at the Hasty Pudding Theatre in Boston.

Costumes: 1997 *Jackie*

Allessandro Sapelli

See Caramba.

Madame Sara

Madame Sara collaborated on the designs for a play in 1930.

Costumes: 1930 *The Challenge of Youth*†

Tony Sarg

An artist and puppeteer, Tony Sarg originated the large balloons now universally associated with Macy's Thanksgiving Day Parade. Born on April 24, 1882 in Guatemala and educated in Europe, he began professional life as an illustrator in London where he became fascinated with Holden, the great English puppet master. He subsequently established his own puppet theater at the Old Curiosity Shop. He came to the United States in 1915 and became a citizen

in 1921, working mainly as an illustrator for magazines and newspapers such as *The New York Times, Saturday Evening Post* and *Colliers.* In the late 1920s he formed the Tony Sarg Company (later the Tony Sarg Marionette Workshop), which produced marionette shows, window displays, and animated cartoons. He also illustrated children's books and designed furnishings. Tony Sarg died on March 7, 1942 in New York City.
Sets: 1917 *The Morris Dance*

Alexander Saron

Alexander Saron designed costumes for a Broadway play in 1937.
Costumes: 1937 *A Hero Is Born*

William Noel Saulter

William Noel Saulter designed two sets in the mid-1940s on Broadway.
Sets: 1945 *Make Yourself at Home* **1946** *The Haven*

Steele Savage

Artist Steele Savage, who occasionally designed scenery, costumes, and furniture, was born in Detroit, Michigan in 1900 and studied at the Detroit School of Fine Arts, the Chicago Art Institute and the Slade School in London. He traveled in Europe, worked for magazines in France, and lived and painted in the West Indies for some years. He was primarily a magazine and book illustrator who illustrated a number of books for children including M. Komroff's *Bible Dictionary for Boys and Girls.* He also drew for science fiction, covers for paperbacks, and advertisements. Savage died in 1970.
Sets: 1934 *Caviar*†
Costumes: 1934 *Caviar* (All Costumes except Miss Guilford's)

Pierre Saveron

Pierre Saveron designed lighting for a Broadway production in 1958.
Lights: 1958 *Théâtre National Populaire*

Carol Sax

Mr. Carol Sax established several theaters including the Vagabond Theatre in Baltimore in 1918 and the Romany Theatre in Lexington, Kentucky. He produced plays in Paris with a company of American actors for the 1929-30 season and was managing producer of the Manchester Repertory Company in England. He was also on the faculty at the Universities of Kentucky and Iowa as a professor of art. Mr. Sax died at age 76 on September 28, 1961.
Sets: 1928 *Lady Dedlock*†

Scaasi

Born in Montreal, Canada in 1931, Arnold Isaacs designs under his name spelled backwards, Scaasi. After studying in Montreal and Paris, he worked on 7th Avenue, first in retail, then wholesale and finally couture. He began his own costume business with a salon on East 56th Street in 1963. He specializes in evening wear made of sumptuous fabrics and has many actresses as private customers. His clients also include first ladies Nancy Reagan, Barbara Bush, and Laura Bush.
Costumes: 1958 *Once More, with Feeling*† (Miss Francis' costumes); *Present Laughter*† (Miss Eva Gabor's gowns) **1960** *From A to Z*† (Miss Hermione Gingold's gowns)

George Schaaf

George Schaaf, a master electrician, worked closely with Robert Edmond Jones on numerous productions in the Plymouth Theatre that were directed and produced by Arthur Hopkins. The close association between Schaaf and Jones was responsible for developments in instrumentation as well as ways to gently move and shift light. Schaaf was probably responsible for more designs than his few credits reveal. His training with lights did not begin in the theater. He was hired to work at the Empire Theatre by producer Charles Frohman after making and installing an electric sign in his theater building.
Lights: 1923 *Hamlet* **1924** *Madame Pompadour*

George Schaefer

George Schaefer, a director and producer with many Broadway and television shows to his credit, was born on December 16, 1920 in Wallingford, Connecticut. He received a B.A. in

1941 from Lafayette College and attended the Yale University School of Drama until drafted into service in World War II. His directorial debut in New York was *Hamlet* with Maurice Evans in 1945, followed by an illustrious career directing for stage and television. His television credits began in 1953 with *Hallmark Hall of Fame* and continued for four decades. His many honors include Emmy, Sylvania, Radio Television Daily, and Directors' Guild of America Awards, and a Tony Award shared with Maurice Evans for producing *Teahouse of the August Moon*. Shortly before he died on September 10, 1997 in Los Angeles, California at age 76, he directed the television remake of *Harvey* starring Harry Anderson.

Lights: 1947 *Man and Superman*

Schaffner and Sweet Studio

Walter Schaffner and Chandos Sweet ran a scenic studio at 449 First Avenue in New York City in the 1920s. They produced their own designs, and constructed and painted scenery for other designers. Chandos Sweet moved to New York from his native Kansas City, Missouri in 1910. He was a stage manager and theatrical manager for producers including Charles Frohman, Arthur Hopkins and Henry W. Savage. Chandos Sweet died at age 77 in Queens, New York on February 29, 1960. Walter Schaffner was a scenic painter and landscape artist who worked for the Shuberts in addition to his association with Sweet. Walter Schaffner also designed under his own name and additional information is available under that heading.

Sets: 1925 *Easy Terms* **1926** *New York Exchange* **1927** *We All Do* **1928** *This Thing Called Love* **1929** *Kibitzer*

Walter Schaffner

Walter Schaffner studied at the National Academy of Design and was a landscape painter in addition to being a scenic painter and designer. He was associated with Chandos Sweet in the scenic studio Schaffner and Sweet in the 1920s. His designs were no doubt more extensive than those credited to him because he also worked for the Shuberts and other producers. He died on September 30, 1934 in Montrose, New York.

Sets: 1924 *Bye, Bye, Barbara* **1925** *China Rose*; *Oh! Oh! Nurse*

Anna Scheer

An actress, Anna Scheer designed costumes on Broadway in the 1920s, during the time she was president of Newport Costume Company, 105 Madison Avenue in New York City. In 1985, a British documentary about hostels, *Enter the Adventure*, featured students from the Anna Scheer Theatre School.

Costumes: 1923 *The Wasp* (Gowns) **1924** *Garden of Weeds*† (Costumes and principal role)

Mary Percy Schenck

Mary Percy Schenck was born in Jersey City, New Jersey on June 16, 1917, and studied at Yale University in both the fine arts and drama schools. In addition to her Broadway credits, she designed costumes for the Metropolitan Opera Company including *The Flying Dutchman* and *Il Trovatore*. She won a Tony Award in 1948 for *The Heiress* costume designs. Mrs. Eugene J. Cosgrove in private life, she married in 1952 and had three children.

Costumes: 1942 *The Skin of Our Teeth* **1944** *Catherine Was Great*† **1945** *Hollywood Pinafore*† (Period costumes); *Kiss Them for Me* (Costume Supervisor); *The Next Half Hour* **1947** *Dear Judas* (Also masks); *The Heiress*

Nancy Schertler

Nancy Schertler has had a long association with the Arena Stage where she spent eight years as an electrician and assistant lighting designer. Her association with mentors Garland Wright and Allen Lee Hughes stems from Arena Stage as does her professional debut as lighting designer, for *Quartermaines Terms*. She was born in Washington, D.C. on December 16, 1954, the daughter of Jean and Leon Schertler, and received a B.A. in speech and theater at the College of St. Catherine in St. Paul, Minnesota. She has received many nominations for Helen Hayes Awards and a Tony Award nomination for *Largely New York*. Recent credits include *Sisters Matsumoto, Mrs. Warren's Profession, The Glass Menagerie* and *Gross Indecency* for the Huntington Theatre Company, and *Texts for Nothing*, a prose work by Samuel Beckett for the Classic Stage Company.

Lights: **1989** *Largely New York* **1993** *Fool Moon* **1995** *Fool Moon* **1996** *Scapin* **1998** *Fool Moon*

Douglas W. Schmidt

Douglas Wocher Schmidt has designed sets for numerous shows both on and off-Broadway and in regional theaters around the United States. Born on October 4, 1942 in Cincinnati, Ohio, he studied at Boston University with Horace Armistead and Raymond Sovey and with Lester Polakov at the Studio and Forum of Stage Design. His theater experience includes directing and stage management and occasionally costume design. He began designing with *The Thirteen Clocks* by James Thurber at High Mowing School in Wilton, New Hampshire in 1960 and in summer stock. Design activity in regional theaters includes Cincinnati Playhouse in the Park, Center Stage in Baltimore, the Old Globe, the Ahmanson Theatre, the Mark Taper Forum and The Guthrie Theatre. He has designed many sets for operas at the Tanglewood Festival and the Juilliard School. Often honored for outstanding scenic design, Mr. Schmidt received a Maharam Award for *Enemies* in 1973, and Drama Desk Awards for *Veronica's Room* and *Over Here!*. He has also designed sets for television, film, opera and ballet. Twenty-first century credits include scenery for the 2002 revival of *Into the Woods*.

Sets: **1970** *Paris Is Out* **1972** *The Country Girl*; *Grease*; *The Love Suicide at Schofield Barracks* **1973** *Measure for Measure*; *A Streetcar Named Desire*; *Veronica's Room* **1974** *An American Millionaire*; *Fame*; *Over Here*; *Who's Who in Hell* **1975** *Angel Street* **1976** *Herzl*; *Let My People Come*†; *The Robber Bridegroom* **1977** *The Threepenny*

Opera **1978** *Runaways*†; *Stages* **1979** *The Most Happy Fella*; *Peter Allen "Up in One"*; *Romantic Comedy*; *They're Playing Our Song* **1981** *Frankenstein* **1983** *Porgy and Bess* **1985** *Dancing in the End Zone* **1986** *Smile* **1991** *Nick & Nora* **1994** *Damn Yankees* **1995** *The School for Scandal* **1996** *Getting Away with Murder* **1999** *Band in Berlin*; *The Civil War* **2001** *42nd Street*

Costumes: **1972** *The Love Suicide at Schofield Barracks* **1976** *Let My People Come*

Lights: **1972** *The Country Girl*

Jacques Schmidt

Costume designer Jacques Schmidt who spent most of his professional life working with Patrice Chereau and other producers in France, made his Broadway debut in 1989. After studying at the Sorbonne he designed haute couture, and stage costumes for the theater, opera and film during a career that lasted over thirty-five years. His designs were seen throughout Europe in theaters in Poland, Marseille, Milan, Lyon, and Lenz. Born on March 16, 1933 in Briancon (Hautes-Alpes), he was completing designs for a new production of *Rigoletto* when he died on September 8, 1996 in Paris.

Costumes: **1989** *Metamorphosis*

M. Schmidt

Mrs. Minna Moscherosch Schmidt was born March 18, 1866 in Sindelfingen, Germany moved to Chicago, Illinois in 1886 where she created and exhibited historic figurines, ran a dance school, owned a wig and costume shop, promoted women's issues, and was a philanthropist. She traveled extensively and was an advocate of authentic costumes and stage settings, which she also designed. Author of *400 Outstanding Women of the World* and *Costumeology of Their Time* published in 1933, she died at age 95 in 1961.

Sets: **1948** *David's Crown*

F. C. Schmitz

F. C. Schmitz, a scenic artist and designer collaborated on two Broadway sets. According to the 1912 *Tantalizing Tommy* playbill, he was from London.

Sets: 1906 *Mauricette* 1912 *Tantalizing Tommy*† (Painted)

Susanne Schmoegner

Susanne Schmoegner designed costumes for a 1991 Broadway production.
Costumes: 1991 *Andre Heller's Wonderhouse*

Fritz Schoultz

Fritz Schoultz collaborated on costumes for a Broadway play in 1900.
Costumes: 1900 *Prince Otto*†

Tom Schraeder

Tom Schraeder is Lighting Director for the Hilberry Repertory Theatre and Professor of Lighting Design at Wayne State University in Detroit, Michigan. Born on January 29, 1959 in Chicago, he received a B.A. in 1974 from Loyola University and an M.F.A. in 1978 from the Yale University School of Drama. Career influences include Thomas Skelton, Ming Cho Lee and Bill Warfel. He has designed sets and lights for numerous off-Broadway and regional theater productions. From 1984 to 1999 he was set and lighting designer for the *Stephen Foster Story*, an outdoor historical drama in Bardstown, Kentucky. The production toured Japan in 1985 and was broadcast on Japanese television. Since 1998, he has been the resident lighting designer for the Detroit Repertory Theatre.
Lights: 1979 *Wings*

Ernest Schraps

Ernest Schraps designed costumes for numerous shows on Broadway between 1917 and 1948. In addition he worked for the Paramount Astoria Studios on Long Island and then in Hollywood at Hal Roach Studios. He designed movie costumes for featured players Patsy Kelly, Lyda Roberti, Rosina Lawrence, and Grace Moore, among others but never received credit for designing an entire feature film. He spent the fifteen years before his death on June 6, 1956 at the age of 65 as head costume designer at Brooks Costume Company.
Costumes: 1917 *A Night in Spain* 1922 *The Passing Show of 1922* (Raduin number) 1923 *Artists and Models* 1924 *Artists and Models*† 1925 *The Love Song*

(Act I and Act III costumes); *Princess Flavia* 1926 *Gay Paree*† (Some designs); *Hans, the Flute Player* (Some costumes); *Hello, Lola*†; *A Night in Paris*†; *The Pearl of Great Price*†; *The Two Orphans* 1927 *Artists and Models*†; *Cherry Blossoms*; *The Circus Princess*; *Immortal Isabella?*† (Other costumes); *The Love Call*† (Act I and II); *A Night in Spain* 1928 *Angela*†; *Greenwich Village Follies*; *Luckee Girl*; *The Red Robe*†; *White Lilacs*† 1929 *Broadway Nights*†; *The Lady from the Sea*; *Music in May*†; *Pleasure Bound*†; *A Wonderful Night*† 1930 *Artists and Models*; *Joseph*; *Three Little Girls*; *Three's a Crowd*† 1931 *Everybody's Welcome*†; *Experience Unnecessary*† (Gowns); *The School for Scandal* 1932 *If Booth Had Missed*; *A Little Rocketeer*† (Wardrobe Design); *Marching By*; *The Perfect Marriage*; *Smiling Faces* 1934 *Music Hath Charms*; *The Only Girl*; *So Many Paths* 1939 *Foreigners* (Costume Supervisor) 1940 *The Corn Is Green*; *Romantic Mr. Dickens* 1941 *Golden Wings*; *Night of Love*; *The Wookey* 1942 *Hedda Gabler*; *I Killed the Count* (Costume Supervisor); *Laugh, Town, Laugh*† (Gowns for Miss Schramm, Miss Grabow, and Miss Kirk); *Under this Roof* 1943 *The Corn Is Green* 1944 *Catherine Was Great*†; *No Way Out* (Costume Supervisor) 1945 *Up in Central Park*† 1948 *Set My People Free*; *The Silver Whistle*

William Schroder

William Schroder, designer of sets and costumes, was born May 11, 1947 in Bronxville, New York and received his B.A. degree in 1969 from Wesleyan University. Since an apprenticeship at Stratford (Ontario) Festival where he worked with Leslie Hurry and Ralph Pendleton, he has designed extensively in regional theaters and in Europe. Off-Broadway credits include productions at The American Jewish Theatre. Author of the children's book *Pea Soup and Sea Serpents*, his designs for the Minnesota Children's Theatre include *The Wind in the Willows* and *A Wrinkle in Time*.
Sets: 1976 *Your Arms Too Short to Box with God* 1979 *But Never Jam Today* 1980 *Your Arms Too Short to Box with God* 1982 *Your Arms Too Short to Box*

with God

Costumes: 1976 *Your Arms Too Short to Box with God* **1979** *But Never Jam Today* **1980** *Horowitz and Mrs. Washington*; *Your Arms Too Short to Box with God* **1982** *Your Arms Too Short to Box with God*

Edwin J. Schruers

Edwin Judson Schruers, born on July 2, 1903 in Oil City, Pennsylvania (some sources state 1913), spent the majority of his career as an architect. He graduated from Harvard in 1935 and in 1938 contributed scenic designs to a Broadway production. He worked on the East Coast until 1952 when he formed his own architectural firm in Berkeley, California. Among the buildings he designed are hospitals in San Francisco and Berkeley. He died on March 8, 1994 in Contra Costa, California.

Sets: 1938 *On the Rocks*

Duane Schuler

Duane Schuler was planning to major in engineering at the University of Wisconsin-Madison when he took a course in lighting design from Gilbert V. Hemsley, Jr., which led to a three year stint as his assistant and a career in lighting design. He was born in Wisconsin on June 20, 1950 and received his B.S. in 1972. He has designed lights for major regional theaters and opera companies throughout the United States. After serving as resident lighting designer at the Guthrie Theatre from 1974 to 1978 he became Resident Lighting Designer at the Lyric Opera of Chicago. One of the most widely known and respected lighting designers for opera, he is also a theater consultant and an architectural lighting designer. Duane Schuler received a Drama Desk Award nomination for *Teibele and her Demon* and a Hollywood Drama Critic Award for *Uncle Vanya* at A.C.T. Twenty-first century designs include *The Great Gatsby* and *Fidelio* for the Metropolitan Opera, *Rigoletto* at the San Diego Opera and *Cold Sassy Tree* for the Houston Grand Opera.

Lights: 1979 *Teibele and Her Demon* **1987** *South Pacific* **1991** *Brigadoon* **1996** *Brigadoon*

Karen Schulz

Karen Schultz was born in Wisconsin in 1951. She received a B.A. at the University of Wisconsin at Madison in 1974 under John Ezell and an M.F.A. at Yale in 1977 under Ming Cho Lee. She began designing for the Madison Civic Theatre with *Scenes from American Life* and since then has designed dance, music videos, television commercials and scenery for films including *The Last Day of Frank and Jesse James, Mr. And Mrs. Bridge, Slaves of New York* and an NBC-TV Movie of the Week. Late twentieth century off-Broadway designs include *Only Kidding* for West Side Arts. She is married to designer and art director David Gropman.

Sets: 1978 *The Inspector General*

Clara Schuman

Clara Schuman designed costumes for a play on Broadway in 1926.

Costumes: 1926 *Broadway*

Richard Schurkamp

Costume designer Richard Schurkamp made his Broadway debut when he collaborated with Alison Chitty in 1989, although his experience on Broadway began as an assistant to Will Kim for *Song & Dance* in 1985. Additional New York credits include costume designs for *Exactly Like You* for the York Theatre Company in 1999. Among his honors is an Emmy Award nomination for his designs for *All My Children*, a daytime drama on ABC-TV.

Costumes: 1989 *Orpheus Descending†*

Ernest Schütte

Ernest Heinrich Conrad Schütte designed one set on Broadway in 1928. A painter and an architect, he was born on April 5, 1890 in Hanover, Germany and spent his career in Berlin.

Sets: 1928 *Redemption*

Tom Schwinn

Tom Schwinn was born on November 20, 1947 in Sendai, Japan and received a B.A. at Wichita State University, where he began designing in the experimental theater. His M.F.A. is from the

University of Iowa. He has been a visiting artist at the University of Delaware and has designed sets for industrial promotions, for regional theaters including the Long Wharf, and for off-Broadway theaters including the Manhattan Theatre Club. Herman Sichter and William Ritman have been instrumental in his career. Designs for television include *New Music Awards* and *A Tribute to Roy Orbison* (on the Showtime Network) which was nominated for an ACE Award. His wife, Helene Beba Shamash, is a costume designer.
Sets: 1980 *Nuts*

Mr. Scotson-Clark

Mr. George Frederick Scotson-Clark, a British artist and author, was born February 9, 1872 in Brighton, Sussex, England. He studied painting at the Slade School in London and came to the United States in 1891, where he worked as a commercial artist specializing in posters. He then moved back to England and after several years in London illustrating magazines returned to the United States to paint portraits and landscapes, while continuing to create advertising illustrations. Between 1918 and 1921 he was art director for *Century Magazine*. After service in World War I with the New York National Guard he became a U.S. citizen. Mr. Scotson-Clark died on December 20, 1927 in Connecticut.
Sets: 1916 *Beau Brummell*
Costumes: 1916 *Beau Brummell* (Costume Supervisor)

Ashmead Eldridge Scott

Ashmead Eldridge Scott, who designed one Broadway set in 1922, was born November 27, 1893. He spent the majority of career associated with Stagecraft Studios, "Stage Decorators," 17 East 39th Street, New York City in the 1920s, together with Elmer Johnson and Cecil Owen. Mr. Scott, who resided at 44 East 79th Street, also appeared in *The Mask of Hamlet* in 1921. He was living in Texas at the time of his death in February 1965.
Sets: 1922 *The Cat and the Canary*

Mrs. Bessie Scott

Mrs. Bessie Scott designed costumes in 1904. She is identified as an actress, residing at 175 West 94th Street in the 1903-1904 New York City Directory. The costume designer and actress should not be confused with the Massachusetts dentist (d. 1947) with the same name.
Costumes: 1904 *Judith of Bethulia*†

J. Hutchinson Scott

J. Hutchinson Scott designed sets and costumes for two plays in the late 1960s. A British designer of sets and costumes, he was born in Northumberland, England in 1924. He studied at the Edward VII Art School, Durham University and the People's Theatre in Newcastle-Upon-Tyne. His first London production was *The Circle of Chalk* in 1945. At various times he served as resident set designer for the Oxford Playhouse and the Bristol Old Vic. He was a founding member of the Crest Theatre in Toronto. Mr. Scott died in September 1977 at age 53.
Sets: 1965 *Boeing-Boeing* **1966** *Help Stamp Out Marriage* **1967** *There's a Girl in My Soup* **1968** *The Flip Side*
Costumes: 1965 *Boeing-Boeing* **1968** *The Flip Side*†

Harry Sears

Harry (Harold) Sears designed lights for one play in 1920. The 1920 playbill for *What's in a Name* has this acknowledgement: "All of the mechanical effects invented by Harry Sears and the entire scenic construction was under his direction." An engineer, he resided at 15 Van Nest Place in 1917 and at 1642 Madison Avenue, New York City in 1920.
Lights: 1920 *Pitter Patter*

L. W. Seavey

Lafayette W. Seavey had his own scenic studio at Walton Avenue and 138th Street in New York City, where he designed, constructed and painted scenery for many Augustin Daly productions, a Daly's Fifth Avenue Theatre and tours. The majority of his designs were during the nineteenth century, beginning in 1869 with *Twelfth Night* and *Patrie*. Although he died in New York City on June 18, 190, his scenery continued to be used, as it was

for a 1911 Broadway production that
had been on tour before playing the
Garden Theatre.
Sets: 1901 *The Merchant of Venice*†
1911 *The Lily and the Prince*† (Acts I,
III)

Arthur P. Segal

Arthur P. Segal, who designed sets
on Broadway between 1926 and 1934,
spent the majority of career as president and manager of Studio Alliance,
a scenery shop that constructed and
painted scenery for many designers. He
also worked as a manager for scenery at
ABC-TV for many years, prior to retiring in 1968. He died on January 17,
1993. He should not be confused with
the abstract painter (1875-1944) with
the same name.
Sets: 1926 *Broadway* 1933 *Both Your
Houses*; *The First Apple*; *Her Man Max*;
Three-Cornered Moon 1934 *But Not for
Love*; *The Sky's the Limit*

David F. Segal

David F. Segal was born in New York
City on June 2, 1943, the son of Rabbi
Samuel M. Segal and Cynthia Shapiro
Segal. He attended the University of
Pennsylvania and received a B.A. from
New York University, in 1964. He
also attended Lester Polakov's Studio
and Forum of Stage Design before becoming a member of its' faculty. He
became Tharon Musser's first United
Scenic Artist assistant and was greatly
inspired by the person he considers the
world's greatest lighting designer. His
New York debut was *Say Nothing* at
the Jan Hus Theatre in 1965. He is
an associate artist at the Old Globe
Theatre and has designed throughout
the United States including *The History of Sex* and *The Folies Bergère* in
Las Vegas. Partial New York credits include *Full Gallop*, *Boesman and Lena*,
Translations and *A...My Name is Alice*. Credits in the twenty-first century
include *The Boswell Sisters* at the Old
Globe Theatre.
Sets: 1972 *That's Entertainment*
Lights: 1969 *The World's a Stage* 1970
Happy Birthday, Wanda June 1971
Oh! Calcutta!; *Twigs* 1972 *Dear Os-
car*; *That's Entertainment* 1973 *Irene*

1974 *Summer Brave* 1976 *The Heiress*;
The Robber Bridegroom 1977 *The Basic
Training of Pavlo Hummel* 1979 *Loose
Ends*; *Sarava* 1980 *Manhattan Showboat*
1981 *Hey, Look Me Over!*; *Lolita* 1994
Damn Yankees

Louise Segal

Louise Segal designed costumes for two
Broadway shows in 1937. At that time,
she was the bookkeeper for Strauss
Textiles, Inc. in New York City and
resided at 1975 Walton Avenue, Apartment #1E. Two years later, in 1939,
she appeared in *The American Way*
and subsequently in other shows. Her
sister was Vivienne Segal, a musical
comedy and vaudeville performer.
Costumes: 1937 *In Clover* (Costume
Supervisor); *The Lady Has a Heart*† (Miss
Landis' gowns, hats and accessories)

George Segare

George Segare designed a set on Broadway in 1932.
Sets: 1932 *The Laughing Past*

Richard Seger

Richard Seger studied at the Art Institute of Chicago and the Royal Poinciana Playhouse in Palm Beach, California where he had a scholarship to
work and study theater. He was born
in Hinsdale, Illinois on May 3, 1937 and
began designing for community theaters in Chicago, where he made his
debut as a set designer with *The Importance of Being Earnest*. His New York
productions include *Day of Absence
and Happy Ending* and *The World of
Günter Grass* as well as his shows on
Broadway. His many awards include
Drama Logues for *Little Foxes*, *Hotel Paradiso*, *End of the World With
Symposium to Follow* and *5th of July*
at A.C.T., and *The Country Wife*,
Rashomon, *Pygmalion*, *Tartuffe*, *Anthony and Cleopatra*, and *The Night of
the Iguana* at the Old Globe. During
the 1990s, he concentrated on painting
large figurative works in oil. He died
on December 25, 2000.
Sets: 1969 *Butterflies Are Free* 1976
Something's Afoot

Claudio Segovia

Claudio Segovia was born in Buenos

Aires where he studied scenery and painting at the Academia Naçional de Artes Visuales. He has designed sets and costumes for plays and operas around the world since 1965. In addition he creates productions using popular music and folk traditions such as *Flamenco Puro*, performed for the first time in Seville, Spain, and in a second edition in 1984 in Paris. Mr. Segovia collaborated as a director, creator, and set and costume designer with the late Hector Orezzoli for nearly twenty years. *Tango Argentino* was honored with a Tony nomination for costume design. Their costume designs for *Black and Blue* won the Tony Award in 1989, while the scenic designs were also nominated.

Sets: 1985 *Tango Argentino*† 1986 *Flamenco Puro*† 1989 *Black and Blue*†

Costumes: 1985 *Tango Argentino*† 1986 *Flamenco Puro*† 1989 *Black and Blue*†

Lights: 1986 *Flamenco Puro*†

Roderick Seidenberg

Roderick Seidenberg graduated from Columbia University with a degree in architecture. He was a member of the New York architectural firm Sugarman & Berger and designed the New Yorker Hotel and the Garment Center Building. In 1927 he also designed scenery for a Broadway play. In the late 1930s he left New York and moved to Bucks County, Pennsylvania where he wrote, painted and continued to work as an architect, specializing in restoring and rebuilding old houses. His books include *Post-Historic Man* and *Anatomy of the Future*. He died in Doylestown, Pennsylvania at age 83 on August 27, 1973.

Sets: 1927 *The Prisoner*

Richard Harrison Senie

Richard Harrison Senie, who was born on May 22, 1916, designed scenery in New York for the Theatre Guild and the Balinese Dancers among other companies. He also designed a Broadway production in 1951 and was an active designer for television. He died in New York City in May 1986.

Sets: 1951 *Saint Joan*

Herbert Senn

(Charles) Herbert Senn was born on October 9, 1924 in Ilion, New York and studied at Columbia University with his mentor Woodman Thompson. He began designing while in high school and made his debut in London's West End with *The Boys From Syracuse* at the Drury Lane Theatre in November 1963. He often designs in collaboration with Helen Pond, concentrating on sets but occasionally designing lights. The team has designed extensive productions off-Broadway, for 38 summer seasons at the Cape Play House, Dennis, Massachusetts, over 50 productions for Sarah Caldwell at the Boston Opera Company, and for operas and ballets throughout the United States. An exhibit of their designs was held at the New York Theatre Company in winter 2000-2001.

Sets: 1963 *Double Dublin*† 1964 *Roar Like a Dove*†; *What Makes Sammy Run?*† 1968 *Noel Coward's Sweet Potato*† 1973 *No Sex Please, We're British*† 1975 *A Musical Jubilee* 1981 *Macbeth*† 1983 *Show Boat*† 1986 *Oh Coward!*†

Lights: 1963 *Double Dublin*† 1964 *Roar Like a Dove*†; *What Makes Sammy Run?*†

Seyfried

Seyfried was the scenic artist and designer for a 1907 Broadway production.

Sets: 1907 *The Builders*† (Also painted)

Victoria Shaffer

Victoria Shaffer made her theater debut with costumes for *Don't Get God Started* on Broadway in 1987, although her designs for television and featured performers were seen before that time. She has designed fashions for private customers as well as stage appearances by Cher, Madonna, and Donna Summer. Television credits include the wardrobe for Kim Fields on *Facts of Life*, and for video both *Let My People Go* and *Live in Concert* for The Winans.

Costumes: 1987 *Don't Get God Started*

Beba Shamash

Costume designer Beba Shamash received an M.F.A. from the Tisch School of the Arts at New York University.

She has designed extensively for regional theater as well as for film and television, and many productions for the York Theatre in New York City, notably *Merrily We Roll Along.* Her credits include industrial promotions (International Barbie, Microsoft, MCI, etc.), national tours (*The Rocky Horror Show*), and for regional opera (Kentucky Opera, Tulsa Opera, etc.) Among other productions, she designed costumes for *Arthur: The Musical* at Goodspeed Opera House, *Most Happy Fella* at New York City Opera, and the 1989 revival of *Sweeney Todd* at Circle in the Square. Twenty-first century credits include *Spunk* and *Threepenny Opera* at the Berrie Center at Ramapo College where she teaches theater to undergraduate students. Her husband, Tom Schwinn, is a scenic designer.
Costumes: 1989 *Sweeney Todd* **1991** *The Most Happy Fella*

James Shannon

James Shannon designed one set in 1932 on Broadway. A painter, he resided at 240 West 17th Street, New York City in 1918.
Sets: 1932 *The Marriage of Cana*

Irene Sharaff

During an illustrious career Irene Sharaff designed costumes for twenty-two ballets in New York, London, Tokyo, Milan, Copenhagen and San Francisco; thirty movies, seventeen of which were musicals, two television specials, and sixty-one productions on Broadway, thirty-three of which were musicals. For her efforts she was rewarded with a Donaldson Award, the Antoinette Perry Award for *The King And I* in 1951and five Academy Awards (out of sixteen nominations). Originally from Boston where she was born on January 23, 1910, she studied at the Art Students League, the New York School of Fine and Applied Arts and in Paris at the Grande Chaumière. Miss Sharaff was introduced to Aline Bernstein in 1928 and became her assistant for costumes, sets and properties at the Civic Repertory Theatre. It was her designs for the scenery and costumes of *Alice In Wonderland* at the

Civic in 1932 which launched her own career. Shortly afterward she debuted on Broadway with the costume designs for *As Thousands Cheer.* The revivals of *The King and I* in 1981 using her original designs and *Jerome Robbins' Broadway* in 1988 were the culmination of a Broadway career which spanned five decades for one of the premier costume designers of the twentieth century. In June 1993, Theatre Development Fund honored her with its first lifetime achievement award and the following year named the award in her honor. She died on August 16, 1993 in New York City. See Figure 11: Irene Sharaff: *On Your Toes*
Sets: 1932 *Alice in Wonderland* **1935** *Crime and Punishment*; *Rosmersholm* **1939** *The American Way*†
Costumes: 1929 *On the High Road*† (Assistant to Miss Bernstein); *The Seagull*† (Assistant to Miss Bernstein) **1930** *The Green Cockatoo*† (Assistant to Miss Bernstein); *The Lady from Alfaqueque*† (Assistant to Miss Bernstein); *Siegfried*† (Assistant to Miss Bernstein) **1932** *Alice in Wonderland* (After Tenniel) **1933** *As Thousands Cheer*† ("The Funnies, Easter Parade") **1934** *The Great Waltz*† (Bridesmaids and Ballet); *Life Begins at 8:40*†; *Union Pacific* **1935** *The Great Waltz* (Bridesmaids and Ballet); *Jubilee*†; *Parade*† ("I'm Telling You Louie," etc.); *Rosmersholm* **1936** *Idiot's Delight*† (Chorus costumes); *On Your Toes*; *White Horse Inn* **1937** *I'd Rather Be Right*†; *Virginia* **1938** *The Boys from Syracuse* **1939** *The American Way*; *From Vienna*; *Streets of Paris* **1940** *All in Fun*; *Boys and Girls Together* **1941** *Banjo Eyes*; *Lady in the Dark*† (Costumes); *The Land Is Bright*; *Mr. Bib* (Costume Supervisor); *Sunny River* **1942** *By Jupiter*; *Count Me in*; *Star and Garter* **1943** *Lady in the Dark*† **1945** *Billion Dollar Baby*; *Hamlet* **1946** *The Would-Be Gentleman* **1948** *Magdalena* **1949** *Montserrat* **1950** *Dance Me a Song*; *Michael Todd's Peep Show* **1951** *The King and I*; *The Lady of the Slipper*; *A Tree Grows in Brooklyn* **1952** *Of Thee I Sing* **1953** *Me and Juliet* **1954** *By the Beautiful Sea*; *On Your Toes* **1956** *Candide*; *Happy Hunting*; *Shangri-La* **1957** *Small War on Murray Hill*; *West Side Story* **1958** *Flower Drum Song* **1959**

Figure 11: Irene Sharaff: On Your Toes: "Slaughter on Tenth Avenue,"
Ballet Sequence: "Tough Boy," 1954. From the collection of Arthur
and Barbara Matera. Courtesy of Arthur Matera. Photograph by Jan
Juracek.

Juno **1960** *Do Re Mi; West Side Story* **1963** *The Girl Who Came to Supper;* *Jennie* **1964** *Funny Girl* **1966** *Sweet Charity* **1967** *Hallelujah, Baby!* **1973** *Irene*† (Miss Debbie Reynold's costumes) **1977** *The Lady of the Slipper* (Original designs) **1980** *West Side Story* **1985** *The King and I*† (Original designs) **1989** *Jerome Robbins' Broadway*†

Redington Sharpe

Redington Sharpe, a set designer born Robert Redington Sharpe, studied at the Art Institute in Cleveland before moving to New York at the age of seventeen to study with and assist Norman Bel Geddes. His mother was an actress who had performed with Maude Adams. In 1924, when he was nineteen, he became Art Director of the Pasadena Community Playhouse in California, where he designed sets and occasionally costumes. He also designed in Los Angeles and Europe. A story about his success at a relatively young age appeared in the *The New York Times* on November 25, 1928, just after the opening of *Major Barbara*, his Broadway debut. His essay, "Where Symbolism Matters, A Stage Designer Discusses the Essentials of His Art," was published in the April 1931 issue of *Theatre Magazine*. He died in New York City on May 14, 1934 at the age of 29.

Sets: **1928** *Major Barbara* **1929** *Claire Adams* **1930** *Joseph* **1933** *Saint Wench; Tobacco Road* **1937** *Tobacco Road* (Original design) **1942** *Tobacco Road* (Original design) **1943** *Tobacco Road* (Original design)

Costumes: **1928** *Major Barbara*

Bob Shaw

Bob Shaw designed scenery on Broadway throughout the 1980s and has extensive credits at the Public Theatre, including *Tacky Stuff* in 1988. He was born in Philadelphia on January 1, 1957 and received a B.F.A. at the Pratt Institute in 1978. He collaborated with his mentor Wilford Leach, principal director of the New York Shakespeare Festival, on twelve productions including his New York debut, *The Mandrake*. Awards include Drama Desk

nominations for *The Pirates of Penzance, The Mystery of Edwin Drood* and *Hamlet*, and an Outer Critics Circle Award for *The Mystery of Edwin Drood*. Since 1990 he has worked mainly in television and is production designer for the HBO series *The Sopranos*.

Sets: **1981** *The Pirates of Penzance*† **1984** *The Human Comedy* **1985** *The Mystery of Edwin Drood* **1987** *Coastal Disturbances*

Deborah Shaw

Deborah Shaw received her B.A. from Hampshire College in Amherst, Massachusetts after which she gained experience in the costume shops at Equity Library Theatre and Juilliard, and as an assistant to Jennifer von Mayrhauser. She has designed costumes at many off-Broadway theaters, including Playwrights Horizons, Second Stage, Circle Repertory Theatre, Double Image, and the Vineyard Theatre. As a member of Ensemble Studio Theatre, she created costumes for many productions, including *To Gillian on Her 37th Birthday, Rose Cottages, Dream of a Blacklisted Actor* and several evenings of the Marathon (EST's one-act play festival). Among her credits in regional theaters are productions at StageWest, the Berkshire Theatre Festival, Papermill Playhouse, and the Hartmann Theatre.

Costumes: **1987** *The Nerd*

Edith Shayne

Edith Shayne, an actress, was born in Brooklyn and studied at the Sargent School of Acting. She first appeared on stage at age 16 in *The Count of Monte Cristo* with Edmund Breese. For many years she was the leading lady for John Drew, performing on both the British and American stages. In 1935 she appeared on Broadway in *Crime Marches On*, for which she also designed the costumes. She also appeared in early films, including *Poor Little Pepina*.

Costumes: **1935** *Crime Marches On* (Costume Supervisor)

William Sheafe

William Sheafe, Jr. designed both scenery and lighting on Broadway during the teens. In collaboration with George H. Shelton he ran a design business, Sheafe & Shelton at 1547 Broadway in New York City in 1917. He resided at 359 West 46th Street in 1917, at 64 West 9th Street in 1922, and at 307 Broadway in 1927.

Sets: 1916 *Six Who Passed while the Lentils Boiled*
Lights: 1919 *The Phantom Legion*

Paul Shelving

Paul Shelving, a British designer and artist, was born in Rowley Regis, Staffordshire, England in 1889 and studied art in London. He designed sets and costumes for the first time at the Court Theatre in 1914 for *The Cockyolly Bird*. After World War I he became resident designer for the Birmingham Repertory Theatre Company, designing numerous shows there over the next several years. He also created many sets and costumes at the Malvern Festival during the 1930s, in addition to numerous credits in London. He usually designed sets and costumes for the same production. Mr. Shelving, who was also known as F. W. Severne North, died at age 79 in June 1968.

Sets: 1927 *Yellow Sands*
Costumes: 1927 *Yellow Sands*

Theresa Shepherd

Theresa Shepherd designed costumes for a featured player in 1929 on Broadway.

Costumes: 1929 *Broken Dishes* (Miss Davis's dresses)

Helen Sheppard

Helen Sheppard designed gowns on Broadway between 1914 and 1918. She was born July 31, 1878 in St. Louis and studied at Washington (St. Louis) University, Chase School of Art, the Art Students League and the Julian Academy in Paris. As president and treasurer of Sheppard and Co., located at 102 East 75 Street in New York, she designed and imported gowns for private and theatrical customers and also did interior design. In private life, as Helen Louise Sheppard Plimpton, after marrying Albert Plimpton on November 27, 1909, she was active in the suffrage movement. She died in March 1937 in Paris, at age 58.

Costumes: 1914 *The Lie* (Gowns) **1918** *The Unknown Purple*† (Miss Frost's gowns)

Paul Sheriff

Paul Sheriff, an art director, was born Paul Shouvalov in Moscow on November 13, 1903. When he became a British citizen in 1930 he took his professional name. His grandfather was the Czar's Ambassador to London in the 1880s. He studied at Oxford and worked as an architect and mining engineer before studying film design with Lazare Meerson and working in the British film industry in the late 1930s. He was highly regarded in England for his set designs for films which included *Henry V, The Millionairess, The Grass is Greener, Dark Journey* and *Moulin Rouge*, for which he received an Academy Award for Art Direction in 1952. He occasionally also designed costumes and in 1948 designed a Broadway show. Paul Sheriff died at age 57 on September 28, 1965.

Sets: 1947 *Crime and Punishment*† **1948** *Macbeth*
Costumes: 1948 *Macbeth*

Mimi Jordan Sherin

Lighting designer Mimi Jordan Sherin works frequently in regional theaters around the United States, for opera companies throughout the world, off-Broadway, and with choreographers. Her designs are regularly seen at Pittsburgh Public Theatre, Center Stage, McCarter Theater Center, Hartford Stage Company, American Repertory Theatre, Long Wharf Theatre, Actors Theatre of Louisville, and Trinity Repertory Company, among others. New York credits include productions at the New York Theatre Workshop, the Roundabout Theatre, and at the Joseph Papp Public Theatre and in London she has designed for the Royal National Theatre and the Royal Shakespeare Company. Among her honors are an American Theatre Wing Award, two Obie Awards, and five Drama Desk nominations. She is lighting designer for SITI, a New York based company; SITI's design team won the 2000

EDDY Award for design collaboration. Her designs for opera include productions in Vienna, Glyndebourne, Wales, Denmark, Chicago, Houston, Washington, Seattle, Santa Fe, Glimmerglass, and in Australia where she won the 1999 Greenroom Award.

Lights: 1991 *Our Country's Good* (as: Mimi Jordan Sherin) 1994 *The Glass Menagerie* (as: Mimi Jordan)

George Sheringham

George Sheringham, a British painter and designer, was born in London on November 13, 1885 and studied art at the Slade School and in Paris. He began designing sets and costumes in 1924 in London with *Midsummer Madness* and often worked in collaboration with Sir Nigel Playfair. He first designed in New York in 1931. His paintings were exhibited throughout Europe and are in the collections of the South Kensington Museum, the Musée de Luxembourg, the Manchester Whitworth Gallery and the Ottawa Gallery. Honors include the Paris Grand Prix for theater design and architectural decoration in 1925 and an award from the Royal Society of Arts in 1936. He died on November 11, 1937 at age 53.

Sets: 1948 *Patience; The Pirates of Penzance*

Costumes: 1931 *The Unknown Warrier* (Miss Fuller's costumes); *The Venetian* 1948 *H.M.S. Pinafore; Patience†* (Aesthetic Maidens); *The Pirates of Penzance* 1951 *Trial by Jury/ H.M.S. Pinafore* 1955 *H.M.S. Pinafore; The Pirates of Penzance; Trial by Jury* (Ladies costumes)

Loren Sherman

Loren Sherman was born on January 21, 1955 in Chicago. He has designed numerous off-Broadway productions including the Playwright Horizons' premieres of *Romance Language, The Dining Room, Baby with the Bathwater* and *The Nice and the Nasty.* He designed *Coriolanus, Coming of Age in Soho, The Marriage of Bette and Boo, Richard III* and *Wenceslaus Square* among others for the New York Shakespeare Festival. He has also designed for the Roundabout, Cir-

cle Repertory Company, INTAR, Juilliard, and the Young Playwrights Festival, and in regional theaters throughout the United States. In 1985 he won an Obie Award for sustained excellence in set design. He acknowledges Robert Keil at the University of Chicago High School, Henry May at the University of California at Berkeley, and Ming Cho Lee at the Yale University School of Drama as mentors.

Sets: 1986 *Shakespeare on Broadway for the Schools* 1987 *Sleight of Hand* 1990 *Shogun: The Musical* 1992 *Crazy He Calls Me; Private Lives* 1994 *A Tuna Christmas* 1995 *Uncle Vanya*

André Sherri

André Sherri owned a theatrical business at 108 West 45th Street in New York City prior to his death October 21, 1924. He operated the shop with his wife, Antoinette. He began professional life as a dancer and went on to producing cabarets and vaudeville sketches before entering the costume business. Madame Sherri hired Charles LeMaire, when he was a young man, to assist customers in their costume business, where he learned much about costumes and also met many people involved in New York theater.

Costumes: 1918 *Atta Boy; Listen Lester*

Walter Sherwood

Walter Sherwood designed sets for three plays in the mid-1920s on Broadway. A painter, he resided at 1344 St. Nicholas Avenue in New York City in 1918. It is possible that he was the writer and painter Walter J. Sherwood, born in 1865 in Wauscon, Ohio, who contributed to many magazines, including *Magazine of Art.* He could also be Walter Scott Sherwood, a portrait painter who died at age 75 in Providence, Rhode Island in 1950.

Sets: 1925 *Night Hawk* 1926 *The Blonde Sinner; Night Hawk*

Everett Shinn

Everett Shinn, born on November 6, 1873 in Woodstown, New Jersey, was best known as a mural painter, illustrator and set designer. He studied at the Pennsylvania Academy of Fine Arts before moving to New York, where he worked as an illustrator for various newspapers and magazines. A member of "The Eight" (also known as the "Ashcan School"), he painted many street scenes in addition to clowns, dancers and actors. He also painted the murals in the Belasco Theatre in New York. Mr. Shinn, who died at age 79 on May 1, 1953, was elected to the National Institute of Arts and Letters in 1951 in recognition of his artistic contributions during a career spanning fifty years.

Sets: 1913 *The Poor Little Rich Girl†* (Color scheme) 1917 *In for the Night*
Costumes: 1930 *Roadside*

John Shipley

John Shipley, who is designer and art director, designed sets in 1980 for a Broadway play. His varied credits include serving as attraction lighting designer for Disney's Animal Kingdom in Florida and as art director for a 30-second television advertisement for the BackCare mattress manufactured by the Simmons Company.

Sets: 1980 *Quick Change†*

Hassard Short

(Hubert) Hassard Short was born in Edlington, Lincolnshire, England on October 15, 1877 and made his acting debut at the Drury Lane Theatre in 1895. He came to the United States in 1901 and continued acting but became interested in directing and producing. In 1920 he directed *Honeydew*, the first of more than fifty hit musicals. He installed his own lighting system at the Music Box Theatre for *Honeydew* and often designed lights and occasionally scenery for plays he also directed. He produced many popular musicals such as *Roberta, Show Boat, Music Box Revues, The Great Waltz* and *As Thousands Cheer*. An innovative director, he used colored lights and other effects and is considered by many to be the first to replace footlights with lights hung from the ceiling over the audience and directed toward the stage. Hassard Short died in Nice, France on October 9, 1956.

Sets: 1924 *Hassard Short's Ritz Revue*
Costumes: 1920 *Honey Girl*

Lights: 1920 *Honey Girl* 1933 *Roberta* 1934 *The Great Waltz* 1937 *Frederika* 1939 *The American Way; From Vienna* 1941 *Banjo Eyes; Lady in the Dark* 1943 *Carmen Jones; Lady in the Dark* 1944 *Mexican Hayride; Seven Lively Arts†* 1947 *Music in My Heart* 1948 *Make Mine Manhattan* 1950 *Michael Todd's Peep Show*

Vassily Shoukhoeff

Vassily Shoukhoeff (also known as Vasilii Ivanovich Shukhaev, Zhoukoff, and Jhoukoff) collaborated on the scenery and costume designs for a musical revue in 1925 which had originated in London. He was born on January 12, 1887 in Moscow and died May 14, 1973 in Tbilisi, U.S.S.R. He studied at the Academy of Arts in St. Petersburg and became a member of the World of Art Society in 1917. He exhibited frequently and emigrated to western Europe in 1922 living mainly in Paris. He also painted portraits, illustrated books, created murals, and designed the interior of La Maisonnette Russe in Paris. He moved to Leningrad in 1935 and was Professor of Drawing at the Academy of Arts in Tbilisi beginning in 1947.

Sets: 1925 *Chauve Souris†*
Costumes: 1925 *Chauve Souris†*

Howard Shoup

Howard Shoup worked in the salon of New York designer Hattie Carnegie and for major department stores before moving to California to design films for Metro-Goldwyn-Meyer in 1935. He left M-G-M to serve in World War II, and as Sgt. Howard Shoup, designed a play on Broadway in 1943. He returned to Hollywood after the war. In all, he designed costumes for approximately 130 films during his career for M-G-M, Warner Brothers and other studios. His designs for the films *The Young Philadelphians, The Rise and Fall of Legs Diamond, Claudelle Inglish, Kisses for My President* and *A Rage to Live* were all nominated for Academy Awards. In addition, he had a dress shop in Beverly Hills from 1950 to 1970. He died in Woodland Hills, California at age 83 on May 29, 1987.

Costumes: 1932 *Nona* 1943 *Winged Victory*

Mrs. J. J. Shubert

Mrs. J. J. Shubert designed costumes for three Broadway shows in 1915. Born Catherine Dealey in Kansas on February 9, 1894, she was Jacob J. Shubert's (d. 1963) first wife and the mother of John Shubert who succeeded his father as manager, until killed in a train accident in 1962. Catherine Dealey Shubert died in Los Angeles on December 23, 1981. The costume designer should not be confused with the second Mrs. J. J. Shubert, Muriel Knowles (d. 1970) who moved to New York City from Ohio in 1919, and quickly found employment as a show girl in musicals for the Shubert's and other producers.

Costumes: 1915 *The Passing Show of 1915*; *The Passing Show*; *A World of Pleasure*

James Shute

James Lovell Shute designed sets for two shows in the mid-1920s. A playwright, he wrote *Trapped* in 1928 with F.G. Johnson and *Fools for Scandal* with Nancy Hamilton and Rosemary Casey in 1938. He was born in Illinois on May 7, 1864 and died in San Bernardino, California on July 2, 1953.

Sets: 1926 *The Trumpet Shall Sound* 1927 *Granite*

Muriel Sibell

Muriel Vincent Sibell Wolle was born in Brooklyn, New York in 1898 and studied at the New York School of Fine and Applied Art, and at New York University. Her early career aspirations were in theater, but after relocating to Boulder, Colorado where she received an M.A. and taught at the University of Colorado from 1926 to 1966, she devoted her talents to western subjects. She wrote and illustrated *Stampede to Timberline, Cloud Cities of Colorado* and *Montana Pay Dirt*, among other books about Colorado and Montana ghost towns. Her watercolors and lithographs have been widely exhibited and collected. She died in 1977.

Costumes: 1920 *The Light of the World*† ("Passion Play")

Eduardo Sicangco

Designer Eduardo V. Sicangco was born on February 1, 1954 in Bacolod City, Philippines, son of Jose Sicangco and Gloria Varela. His B.A. in communication arts is from Ateneo University in the Philippines, and his M.F.A. from the Tisch School of the Arts at New York University. While he has successfully designed scenery and costumes for many of the classics, he is best known for his designs for musicals and revues, which have been seen throughout the country since his professional debut with *Gotta Getaway*, the 1984 Summer Spectacular at Radio City Music Hall. Credits in major regional theaters include productions at the Goodspeed Opera House, the Seattle Repertory Theatre, Center Stage, and Hartford Stage. Late twentieth century credits include *Queen Amarantha* at the WPA Theatre and *Romeo and Juliet* for Ballet Philippines.

Sets: 1993 *Radio City Easter Show*† 1994 *Radio City Easter Show*† 1995 *Gentlemen Prefer Blondes*; *Radio City Easter Show*† (Additional scenery) 1996 *Radio City Spring Spectacular*† 1997 *Radio City Spring Spectacular*†

Costumes: 1994 *Radio City Easter Show*† 1995 *Gentlemen Prefer Blondes*; *Radio City Easter Show*†; *Radio City Easter Show*† 1996 *Radio City Spring Spectacular*† 1997 *Radio City Spring Spectacular*†

Carl Sidney

Carl Sidney, a women's clothing designer, was active on Broadway in 1936. He died in New York City on February 1, 1958 at the age of 47.

Costumes: 1936 *The Illustrator's Show*

Mrs. Caroline Siedle

Caroline F. Siedle was born in London, daughter of an artist, and started to design costumes when young. She came to the United States after marrying Edward Siedle, property master at the Metropolitan Opera House, and launched her American career with *The Princess Nicotine* in 1892. Among other productions prior to 1900, she designed costumes for *The Belle of New York* in 1897 for the Casino Theatre. That musical comedy is generally considered the first production to originate in New York and then transfer to London, complete with original cast, costumes and scenery. She also designed *El Capitan* in 1896. There were many variations of her name, including Mrs. or Madame at the front and as many spellings of Siedle as possible, including Seidel, Siedel, and Seidle. Even the obituaries printed at the time of her death on February 26, 1907 in Ludlow Park, Yonkers, New York spelled her name in different ways. Her posthumous credits were for productions in rehearsal or on tour while she was still alive. They were completed at her studio where her designs, and those for other designers, were executed.

Costumes: 1900 *The Belle of Bohemia*; *The Greatest Thing in the World*; *In the Palace of the King*; *The Princess Chic*; *Quo Vadis* **1901** *The Forest Lovers*; *The Helmet of Navarre*; *The King's Carnival*; *The Little Duchess†*; *A Romance of Athlone*; *The Strollers†* **1902** *A Chinese Honeymoon*; *Dolly Varden*; *The Emerald Isle†*; *Joan o' the Shoals*; *Miss Simplicity†*; *Sally in Our Alley*; *When Johnny Comes Marching Home* **1903** *Babes in Toyland*; *Babette†* (Miss Scheff's costumes); *The Jewel of Asia*; *Red Feather*; *The Runaways*; *Whoop-Dee-Doo*; *The Wizard of Oz†* (Fancy costumes) **1904** *Babette†* (Miss Scheff's costumes); *Higgledy-Piggledy*; *It Happened in Nordland*; *Lady Teazle†*; *Sergeant Kitty†*; *The Two Roses†*; *A Venetian Romance* **1905** *The Earl and the Girl*; *Miss Dolly Dollars* (All character costumes and Miss Glaser's dresses) **1906** *About Town†*; *The Parisian Model†*; *The Red Mill†*; *The Rich Mr. Hoggenheimer*; *The Social Whirl†*; *The Tourists* **1907** *Fascinating Flora*; *The Tattooed Man* **1912** *The Merry Countess* (as: Siedle Studios) **1913** *Somewhere Else†* (as: Siedle Studios)

Harry Silverglat

Harry Silverglat has designed lights for rock concerts and musical events, as well as the national tours of *Equus* and *Bubbling Brown Sugar*. As assistant to

James Tilton, he worked on the television special *Uncommon Women and Others* in 1978, and in 1980 designed scenery for *Fourtune* off-Broadway.
Lights: 1976 *Oh! Calcutta!*

B. J. Simmons

Playbills from the first decade of the twentieth century cite the contributions of costume designer B. J. Simmons, of 7 King Street, Covent Garden, London. The costumes he designed in New York were for productions imported to Broadway after successful London runs.
Costumes: 1904 *My Lady Molly* **1907** *The Little Michus†* **1908** *Adrienne Lecouvreur†* (as: Simmonds: Men's costumes) **1910** *Pomander Walk*

Pat Simmons

Lighting designer Pat Simmons made her Broadway debut in 1970. Born in 1936, she amassed credits throughout the United States in stock and regional theaters, including lights for the 1983-84 season production of *When Hell Freezes Over, I'll Skate* at the Coconut Grove Playhouse. A long-time member of United Scenic Artists, she died in 1999.
Lights: 1970 *The Cherry Orchard*

Rowayne Simmons

Rowayne Simmons supervised costumes for a Broadway show in 1919.
Costumes: 1919 *Shubert Gaieties of 1919* (Costume Supervisor)

Stanley Simmons

Stanley Simmons was born in New Orleans in 1927 and took drawing classes there as a child. After moving to New York he studied for a time at the Art Students League, but gave up drawing to devote himself to dancing. As a dancer he performed in several Broadway shows, including *Out of this World* in 1950 and with various dance companies. He studied with Louis Chalif, Anatole Vilzak and Madame Alexander among others. His first major assignment as a designer was *On Your Toes* in summer stock, but it was Agnes De Mille who pushed him into design. She choreographed a piece for him and gave him a ballet to design as incentive. Karinska constructed the costumes and encouraged him further. He subsequently designed costumes regularly for dance companies in the United States, Europe and Canada, including the Joffrey Ballet, American Ballet Theatre, the New York City Ballet, and the Eliot Feld Ballet, and Baryshnikov's *The Specter of the Rose*. Additional designs include television specials, productions for the Vienna State Opera, the Spoleto Festival, industrial promotions, and *Lena: The Lady and Her Music*, the concert series featuring Lena Horne in a Broadway theater. He died on September 4, 1999 at age 71 in Los Angeles.

Sets: 1956 *Waiting for Godot*
Costumes: 1955 *Almost Crazy* **1956** *Waiting for Godot* **1957** *Waiting for Godot* **1961** *Come Blow Your Horn* **1966** *Show Boat* **1967** *There's a Girl in My Soup* **1969** *Come Summer* **1975** *Rogers and Hart* **1976** *So Long, 174th Street* **1977** *The King and I* (With Irene Sharaff: Original Designs) **1980** *Brigadoon*; *The Music Man* **1985** *The King and I*†

Victor Simoff

Victor Simoff, also known as Victor Andreyevich Simov, lived from 1858 until 1935. An artist, he designed scenery for the Moscow Art Theatre when it opened in 1898. As a painter of the Russian realistic school, he was instrumental in the transition from using stock scenery for productions to creating realistic settings for each play performed. *My Life in the Russian Theatre* recounts a story of a child at a performance of *The Seagull* asking his mother if they might walk through the garden on stage. Both of his Broadway credits were for productions that toured to America.

Sets: 1923 *The Lower Depths*†; *Tsar Fyodor Ivanovitch*

Elizabeth Simon

A costumer, according to the 1905 Trow Business Directory of Greater New York and the Polk's 1909-1910 New York and Bronx City Directory, Elizabeth Simon had a studio at 462 Third Avenue.

Costumes: 1911 *The Faun*† (Costumes)

Louis M. Simon

Louis Mortimer Simon worked in the theater in many capacities, including actor, stage manager, director, administrator, and once as a costume designer. He was born in Salt Lake City, Utah on October 25, 1906 and studied at the University of Pennsylvania, Harvard University, at Yale with George Pierce Baker, and in Europe with Max Reinhardt, before working for Doris Keane at the Theatre Guild as stage manager. Active with many professional organizations, Mr. Simon served in the Special Services branch of the Army during World War II, as managing director of Veterans Hospital Camp Shows after the war, as Executive Secretary of Actors Equity Association from 1949 to 1952, and as director of the Professional Training Program of the American Theatre Wing from 1952 to 1959. He was also public relations director for the Actors Fund of America, and in 1972 wrote *A History of the Actors Fund of America*. He died in Manchester, New Hampshire on October 28, 1996.

Costumes: 1930 *Garrick Gaieties*†

Lee Simonson

Lee Simonson, a designer of sets, costumes and occasionally lights, was born on June 26, 1888 in New York City and graduated from Harvard in 1909. He designed scenery for the Washington Square Players from 1917 until drafted into the service a year later. After World War I he helped found the Theatre Guild and served as one of its directors from 1919 to 1940. He debuted on Broadway with the Theatre Guild's production of *The Faithful*. He designed sets and costumes for numerous plays and operas and also taught design. In 1947 he designed Wagner's *Ring Cycle* for the Metropolitan Opera, one of his many designs there. He wrote several books about scene design, including *The Art of Scenic Design*, *The Stage is Set* and an autobiography, *Part of a Lifetime* published in 1943. This talented, prolific designer died at age 78 on January 23, 1967. His second wife was the costume designer Carolyn Hancock.

Sets: 1915 *Love of One's Neighbor*; *A Miracle of St. Anthony* 1919 *The Faithful*; *Moliere* 1920 *The Cat Bird*; *Heartbreak House*; *Jane Clegg*; *Martinique*; *The Mirage†*; *The Power of Darkness*; *The Treasure* 1921 *Don Juan*; *Liliom*; *Mr. Pim Passes By*; *Tangerine* 1922 *Back to Methuselah*; *From Morn Till Midnight*; *He Who Gets Slapped*; *The Lucky One*; *R.U.R.*; *The Tidings Brought to Mary†*; *The World We Live In* 1923 *The Adding Machine*; *As You Like It*; *The Failures*; *Peer Gynt*; *Spring Cleaning* 1924 *Carnival*; *Fata Morgana*; *Man and the Masses*; *The Mongrel*; *Sweet Little Devil* 1925 *Arms and the Man*; *The Glass Slipper* 1926 *Goat Song*; *Juarez and Maximillian* 1927 *Mr. Pim Passes By†*; *The Road to Rome* 1928 *Marco Millions*; *The Road to Rome*; *Volpone* 1929 *Camel Through the Needle's Eye*; *Carnival*; *Damn Your Honor*; *Dynamo* 1930 *The Apple Cart*; *Elizabeth the Queen*; *Hotel Universe*; *Marco Millions*; *Roar China*; *Volpone* 1931 *Lean Harvest*; *Miracle at Verdun* 1932 *Collision*; *The Good Earth*; *Red Planet* 1933 *American Dream*; *The Mask and the Face*; *Masks and Faces*; *School for Husbands* 1934 *Days without End*; *Jigsaw*; *Rain from Heaven*; *A Sleeping Clergyman*; *They Shall Not Die* 1935 *Parade*; *Simpleton of the Unexpected Isles* 1936 *Call It a Day*; *End of Summer*; *Idiot's Delight*; *Prelude to Exile* 1937 *Amphitryon 38*; *Madame Bovary*; *The Masque of Kings*; *Virginia* 1938 *Lorelei*; *Wine of Choice* 1944 *The Streets Are Guarded* 1945 *Foxhole in the Parlor* 1946 *Joan of Lorraine*

Costumes: 1915 *A Miracle of St. Anthony* 1919 *The Faithful* 1920 *Jane Clegg*; *Martinique*; *The Power of Darkness*; *The Treasure* 1921 *Don Juan* (Women, Mr. Tellegen's costumes); *Liliom* 1922 *Back to Methuselah*; *He Who Gets Slapped*; *R.U.R.*; *The Tidings Brought to Mary* 1923 *The Adding Machine*; *As You Like It*; *The Failures*; *Peer Gynt* 1924 *Fata Morgana*; *Man and the Masses* 1925 *Arms and the Man*; *The Glass Slipper* 1926 *Goat Song*; *Juarez and Maximillian* 1927 *The Road to Rome* 1928 *Marco Millions*; *The Road to Rome*; *Volpone* 1929 *Camel Through the Needle's Eye*;

Damn Your Honor; *Dynamo* 1930 *The Apple Cart*; *Elizabeth the Queen*; *Marco Millions*; *Roar China*; *Volpone* 1932 *Collision†* 1933 *School for Husbands* 1934 *A Sleeping Clergyman* 1935 *Parade†* (Bourgeois Processional); *Simpleton of the Unexpected Isles* 1936 *Prelude to Exile* 1937 *Madame Bovary*; *The Masque of Kings* 1945 *Foxhole in the Parlor* 1946 *Joan of Lorraine*

Lights: 1920 *Martinique* 1924 *Carnival* 1929 *Camel Through the Needle's Eye*; *Dynamo* 1932 *Collision* 1933 *American Dream* 1945 *Foxhole in the Parlor* 1946 *Joan of Lorraine*

Rosaria Sinisi

Scenic designer Rosaria Sinisi studied at New York University with Oliver Smith and subsequently became one of his assistants. After his death in 1994, she supervised the use of his original designs for the revival of *Hello, Dolly!* on Broadway. Additional theater credits in New York include scenery for *To Heaven in a Swing* at the American Place Theatre and *The Day, The Night* at St. Clement's. She was art director for the 1992 television broadcast of the Tony Awards.

Sets: 1995 *Hello, Dolly!†* (Scenic supervision)

Jerome Sirlin

Jerome Sirlin was born in San Diego and received his undergraduate degree at the University of California, Berkley after which he spent a year studying architecture and urban design at the University of California, Los Angeles. He worked as an architect for a while, including two years in South America before joining the faculty at Antioch College, and then Cornell University. In 1981, he designed scenery for a ballet based on *Legend of the Invisible City of Kitezh* which led to a career change. His first major design was *The Ring Cycle* for Artpark, the Buffalo, New York summer festival, followed by national tours for Madonna and Paul Simon, and other operas, including *Magic Flute* for the Baltimore Opera and *Esther* and *Marilyn* (which he also directed) at the New York City Opera. He has collaborated with Philip Glass on *Hydrogen Jukebox* and *1,000*

Airplanes on the Roof. His designs often incorporate holographic projections. Honors include a Tony Award nomination for the scenery for *The Kiss of the Spider Woman.*

Sets: 1993 *Kiss of the Spider Woman* (Also projections)

Noble Sissle

Noble Sissle, a composer and lyricist, teamed with Eubie Blake to perform in vaudeville and create songs for hit musicals. In 1921 he helped create the first black musical to play at a Broadway theater in the regular season, *Shuffle Along.* The partnership with Eubie Blake ultimately ended but each continued successful careers. Sissle was born on July 10, 1889 in Indianapolis, Indiana and after the death of his father sang with the Jubilee Singers on the Chautauqua Circuit. He served in World War I in the 369th Regiment and was in their orchestra along with Blake. Sissle was founder and first President of the Negro Actors Guild and a member of the American Society of Composers, Authors and Publishers. In 1972 he received an Ellington Medal at Yale University along with thirty black instrumentalists and singers. He died at age 86 on December 17, 1975 in Tampa, Florida. In 1948 he directed and designed *Harlem Cavalcade* on Broadway in collaboration with Ed Sullivan.

Lights: 1942 *Harlem Cavalcade*†

Narelle Sissons

Born in Great Britain on September 17, 1965, Narelle Sissons received her B.A. with honors from Central St. Martins College in theater design and her M.F.A. in production design from the Royal College of Art. She designed in London's fringe theaters before coming to the United States where she has designed extensively in regional theaters and off-Broadway, including the original production of *How I Learned to Drive.* She collaborates regularly with director Barry Edelstein, with whom she has done *As You Like It* at the Williamstown Theatre Festival, *Julius Caesar* for the New York Shakespeare Festival (Delacorte Theatre), *The Misanthrope* at the Classic Stage

Company, and her Broadway debut at the Roundabout Theatre, among others. Honors include a Backstage West Award for *Sideman,* an American Theatre Wing nomination for *The Misanthrope,* and a Drama Desk nomination for *Entertaining Mr. Sloane.* Known for her bold use of materials and space, twenty-first century designs include *Jesus Hopped the A Train* at Donmar Warehouse in London.

Sets: 1997 *All My Sons*

Thomas Skelton

Thomas R. Skelton, who was initially a stage manager, entered the field of lighting design as an apprentice electrician under Jean Rosenthal while on a scholarship at the American Dance Festival. Interestingly he later influenced the career of lighting designer Jennifer Tipton under similar circumstances. He was born in Bridgton, Maine on September 24, 1927 and received a B.F.A. at Middlebury College. His New York debut was *The Enchanted* in 1958, soon followed by an extensive list on and off-Broadway and throughout the United States. He was associated with major dance companies such as the Joffrey Ballet, New York City Ballet, Paul Taylor, and José Limon and was co-founder and associate artistic director of the Ohio Ballet. Primarily a lighting designer, he occasionally designed sets. Honors included Tony Award nominations for *The Iceman Cometh, Indians* and *All God's Chillun Got Wings,* a Carbonelle Award for *Peter Pan* and a Los Angeles Drama Critics Award for *The Iceman Cometh.* During the course of his career Thomas Skelton, who died on August 9, 1994 in Akron, Ohio at age 66, was instrumental in making lighting designers indispensable members of production teams and fostering the talents of new generations of lighting designers.

Sets: 1962 *Tiao Ch'in, or The Beautiful Bait*

Lights: 1963 *Oh Dad, Poor Dad, Mamma's Hung You...* 1964 *Wiener Blut (Vienna Life); Zizi* 1968 *Jimmy Shine; Mike Downstairs* 1969 *Coco; Come Summer; Does a Tiger Wear a*

Necktie?; *Indians*; *A Patriot for Me* **1970** *Henry V*; *Lovely Ladies, Kind Gentlemen*; *Purlie* **1972** *The Lincoln Mask*; *Purlie*; *The Secret Affairs of Mildred Wild*; *The Selling of the President* **1973** *Gigi*; *Status Quo Vadis*; *The Waltz of the Toreadors* **1974** *Absurd Person Singular*; *Where's Charley?* **1975** *All God's Chillun Got Wings*; *Death of a Salesman*; *The First Breeze of Summer*; *The Glass Menagerie*; *A Musical Jubilee*; *Shenandoah* **1976** *Days in the Trees*; *Guys and Dolls*; *Kings*; *The Lady from the Sea*; *Legend*; *A Matter of Gravity* **1977** *Caesar and Cleopatra*; *The King and I*; *Romeo and Juliet* **1978** *The Kingfisher*; *The November People* **1979** *Oklahoma!*; *Peter Pan*; *Richard III* **1980** *Brigadoon*; *Camelot*; *Filumena* **1981** *Camelot*; *Can-Can*; *The West Side Waltz* **1982** *Seven Brides for Seven Brothers* **1983** *Dance a Little Closer*; *Mame*; *Peg*; *Show Boat* **1984** *Death of a Salesman* **1985** *The Iceman Cometh* **1986** *Lillian* **1989** *A Few Good Men* **1991** *Park Your Car in Harvard Yard* **1993** *Shakespeare for My Father*

Marjorie Slaiman

Costume designer Marjorie Slaiman attended the School of Industrial Art at the University of Buffalo, and American University in Washington, D.C. Resident designer at Arena Stage between 1965 and 1993, among her first designs there were the costumes for *The Great White Hope*. At Arena Stage, she supervised the costume shop as well as designed more than 130 productions, for which she was much honored with Helen Hayes Awards and nominations. She also designed costumes for the Payne Theatre in Austin, Texas and the Boston University Theatre. Born Marjorie Lawler in 1925 in Bronx, New York, she died in Fairfax, Virginia on September 13, 2002.
Costumes: 1969 *Indians* **1972** *Moonchildren* **1976** *Zalmen or the Madness of God* **1978** *A History of the American Film*; *Working*

Chris Slingsby

Chris Slingsby was production designer for a 1996 Broadway production. He also created photomontage backdrops for *The Risen People* at the Dublin Theatre Festival in 1994.
Sets: 1996 *Riverdance*† (Production design)

Aino Sllmola

Aino Sllmola designed costumes for a play on Broadway in 1942.
Costumes: 1942 *A Ball in Old Vienna*

J. Blanding Sloan

James Blanding Sloan, a painter, illustrator, woodcarver, and scenic designer, was active on Broadway between 1918 and 1923. Earlier he had designed sets for the Little Theatre in Chicago for fellow scenic designers Ellen Von Volkenburg and Maurice Browne. His designs were included in an exhibition of the New American Stagecraft at the Bourgeois Galleries in New York City in 1919. A member of the Wits and Fingers Scenic Studio in the 1920s, he worked with marionette units of the Federal Theatre Project, and then had a puppet theater in San Francisco. He was born in Corsicana, Texas on September 19, 1886 and studied at the Chicago Academy of Fine Arts with B.J.O. Nordfeldt and George Senseney. Widely exhibited, his art is in the permanent collections of the Brooklyn Museum, the Museum of New Mexico, and the de Young Museum. He died in Hayward, California in 1975.
Sets: 1918 *Jonathan Makes a Wish*† **1922** *Greenwich Village Follies*† **1923** *Uptown West*†

Enid Smiley

Enid Smiley designed costumes for a Broadway play in 1949.
Costumes: 1949 *How Long Till Summer*

Bruce Smith

W. (Wally) Bruce Smith, a leading British scenic artist designed and painted dozens of productions and also created numerous mechanical effects in London beginning in 1876, when he assisted Julian Hicks with the scenery for a group of plays including *Jo, Hunted Down, A Will with a Vengeance, The Invisible Prince, Miss Guilt,* and *The Way of the Wind* at the Theatre Royal

Globe. He was born in London on January 23, 1855, son of Thomas Smith, an upholsterer and died at age 87 on November 8, 1942. He appeared on stage when young, and then studied at South Kensington's Science and Art Departments before working as an apprentice at the Alhambra Theatre under Joseph Harker. His scenic art appeared on most of the London theaters, but was mainly used at Drury Lane, the Adlephi Theatre and Covent Garden. In 1985 a biography, *"Sensation" Smith of Drury Lane* by Dennis Castle, his grandson, was published by Charles Skilton Ltd., London.

Sets: 1901 *The Price of Peace*†; *The Sleeping Beauty and the Beast*† 1903 *Mother Goose*† 1905 *The White Cat*† 1910 *Get-Rich-Quick Wallingford*† 1913 *Hop o' My Thumb*† 1915 *Stolen Orders*†

Carolyn Smith

Canadian costume designer Carolyn Smith collaborated on the costumes for a 1990 Broadway production. She also designed the costumes for *Our Country's Good* at the Martha Cohen Theatre in Alberta, Canada and both scenery and costumes for *Scary Stories* at Buddies in Bad Times Theatre in Toronto. The costume designer should not be confused with the academic and author Carolyn J. Smith.

Costumes: 1990 *Buddy: The Buddy Holly Story*†

Ernest Allen Smith

Ernest Allen Smith, born in Erie, Pennsylvania on May 9, 1943, earned a B.A. at Pennsylvania State University where he performed regularly as the lead dancer in many musicals. After moving to New York City for graduate studies in marketing/economics at New York University, he defined his interest in theater design. In 1968 his graduate design studies began at Columbia University under Patton Campbell, David Hays and James Gohl. His studies continued under Charles Elson at Hunter College, where he earned an M.A. in theater directing, history and design. From 1968 to 1986 he designed over 250 shows on and off-Broadway, for opera, film, industrial promotions and in regional theaters. From 1972 until 1976,

while continuing to design, he taught at State University of New York at Purchase, establishing the theater design program with Norris Houghton. In 1986, with Andrew B. Marlay, he co-founded Penn & Fletcher, Inc., a fine embroidery and design services company, where his creative energies remain focused.

Sets: 1980 *Musical Chairs*
Costumes: 1977 *Gemini*

Kiki Smith

Kiki Smith graduated from Smith College in 1971, and then completed graduate degrees at the University of Virginia (M.A.) and the University of Texas (M.F.A.) She was born in Charlottesville, Virginia on December 4, 1949. She is a costume designer for the theater and ballet, and professor of theater at Smith College where she supervises Smith's collection of vintage clothing has taught costume design since 1974. A founding member of Shakespeare & Company in Lenox, Massachusetts, she has designed costumes for that theater for over 25 years, many in collaboration with Tina Packer. Additional designs include productions for the Talking Band Theatre with its' founder Paul Zimet, including *Star Messengers* performed at La MaMa E.T.C. in late 2001. The costume designer should not be confused with the contemporary artist known for prints and sculptures containing human symbols who has the same name.

Costumes: 1981 *Heartland*

Oliver Smith

Oliver Lemuel Smith was born in Waupun (Wawpawn), Wisconsin on February 13, 1918 and graduated from the Pennsylvania State University in 1939. Known primarily as a scenic designer, he first designed professionally for the Ballet Russe de Monte Carlo's performance of *Saratoga* at the Metropolitan Opera in 1941, making his debut on Broadway the following year with the scenic design for *Rosalinda*. Since that time he has designed sets for over four hundred productions for ballet, opera, theater and film, and occasionally contributed costume and lighting designs to those productions. The recipient of Tony Awards for scenic design for *My Fair Lady*, *West Side Story*, *The Sound of Music*, *Becket*, *Camelot*, *Hello, Dolly* and *Baker Street*, he received many other nominations. He was also nominated for an Academy Award for *Guys and Dolls* and produced many of the shows he designed. From 1945 to 1981 he was co-director of the Ballet Theatre with Lucia Chase, with whom he transformed it into the American Ballet Theatre. He returned as Artistic Co-Director in 1989 following the departure of Mikhail Baryshnikov until 1992 when he became emeritus. During his long and illustrious career as a designer, he also took the time to teach and mentor young designers, both as a member of the faculty at New York University School of the Arts for 22 years and as his assistants. Oliver Smith died at age 75 on January 23, 1994 in Brooklyn Heights, New York.

Sets: 1942 *Rosalinda* 1944 *On the Town*; *The Perfect Marriage*; *Rhapsody* 1945 *Billion Dollar Baby* 1946 *Beggar's Holliday* 1947 *Brigadoon*; *High Button Shoes*; *Topaz* 1948 *Look Ma, I'm Dancin'* 1949 *Along Fifth Avenue*; *Gentlemen Prefer Blondes*; *Miss Liberty*†; *Miss Liberty*† 1950 *Bless You All* 1951 *Paint Your Wagon* 1952 *Pal Joey* 1953 *Carnival in Flanders*; *In the Summer House* 1954 *The Burning Glass*; *On Your Toes* 1955 *Will Success Spoil Rock Hunter?* 1956 *Auntie Mame*; *Candide*; *Mr. Wonderful*; *My Fair Lady* 1957 *A Clearing in the Woods*; *Eugenia*; *Juno and the Paycock*; *Nude with Violin*; *Time Remembered*; *A Visit to a Small Planet*; *West Side Story* 1958 *Flower Drum Song*; *Present Laughter*; *Say, Darling*; *Winesburg, Ohio* 1959 *Cheri*; *Destry Rides Again*; *Five Finger Exercise*; *Goodbye Charlie*; *Juno*; *The Sound of Music*; *Take Me Along* 1960 *Becket*; *Camelot*; *A Taste of Honey*; *Under the Yum-Yum Tree*; *The Unsinkable Molly Brown*; *West Side Story* 1961 *Daughter of Silence*; *The Gay Life*; *Mary, Mary*; *The Night of the Iguana*; *Sail Away*; *Show Girl* 1962 *Come on Strong*; *Lord Pengo*; *Romulus*; *Tiger Tiger Burning Bright* 1963

110 Degrees in the Shade; *Barefoot in the Park*; *Children from Their Games*; *The Girl Who Came to Supper*; *Natural Affection* 1964 *Bajour*; *Beeckman Place*; *Ben Franklin in Paris*; *The Chinese Prime Minister*; *Dylan*; *Hello, Dolly!*; *I Was Dancing*; *Luv*; *Poor Richard*; *Slow Dance on the Killing Ground* 1965 *Baker Street*; *Cactus Flower*; *Kelly*; *The Odd Couple*; *On a Clear Day You Can See Forever*; *A Very Rich Woman* 1966 *The Best Laid Plans*; *I Do! I Do!*; *Show Boat*; *The Star Spangled Girl* 1967 *Hello, Dolly!*; *How Now Dow Jones*; *Illya Darling*; *Song of the Grasshopper* 1968 *Darling of the Day*; *The Exercise*; *Plaza Suite*; *Weekend* 1969 *But, Seriously*; *Come Summer*; *Dear World*; *Indians*; *Jimmy*; *Last of the Red Hot Lovers*; *A Patriot for Me* 1970 *Lovely Ladies, Kind Gentlemen* 1971 *Four in a Garden* 1972 *The Little Black Book*; *Lost in the Stars* 1973 *Gigi*; *Tricks*; *The Women* 1974 *All over Town* 1975 *Don't Call Back*; *Hello, Dolly! (Starring Pearl Bailey)*; *The Royal Family* 1976 *The Heiress*; *My Fair Lady* 1978 *Do You Turn Somersaults?*; *First Monday in October*; *Hello, Dolly!* 1979 *Carmelina* 1980 *Clothes for a Summer Hotel*; *Lunch Hour*; *Mixed Couples*; *West Side Story* 1981 *My Fair Lady*; *A Talent for Murder* 1982 *84 Charing Cross Road* 1989 *Jerome Robbins' Broadway*† 1995 *Hello, Dolly!*†

Costumes: 1955 *Will Success Spoil Rock Hunter?* (Design by) 1959 *Five Finger Exercise*† 1961 *Daughter of Silence*†; *Sail Away*†

Lights: 1963 *Children from Their Games*

Rae Smith

A British designer of sets and costumes, Rae Smith has designed often for the Royal Shakespeare Company, the Welsh National Opera, and the Royal National Theatre and is a frequent collaborator with composer Sarah Collins. Additional designs in the United States include *The Street of Crocodiles* at Lincoln Center and *The Visit* and *Dinner* at the Spoleto Festival in Charleston, South Carolina. As a director, her productions include *Lucky* for the David Glass Ensemble, *Mysteria* for RSC, and *The Terminatrix* for the Studio at RNT. Twenty-first cen-

tury credits include *Pinocchio* at the Lyric Hammersmith, and *Juno and the Paycock* at the Roundabout Theatre.
Sets: 1999 *The Weir*
Costumes: 1999 *The Weir*

Rusty Smith

Russell (Rusty) Smith is from Winder, Georgia and is married to the actress Anne Allgood. He has designed productions at the Yale University School of Drama, in regional theaters, for films and summer stock. Productions include the national tour of *One Mo' Time* and *Guys and Dolls* at the StageWest Theatre. He was assistant production designer for the film *Sticky Fingers* and production designer for *Camp Nowhere.*
Sets: 1985 *Blood Knot*

Charles Smithline

Charles Smithline, who created the lights for a Broadway production in the first season of the twentieth century, resided at 2580 8th Avenue in 1905.
Lights: 1900 *In the Palace of the King*

Edna Sobol

Edna Sobol was born in Haifa, Israel and graduated from the Sorbonne with a major in art history. She designs scenery and costumes for theaters throughout Israel, often in collaboration with scenic designer Adrian Vaux. Her designs for the Haifa Municipal Theatre include sets and costumes for *Shell Shock* and costumes for *Amadeus, The Physicists,* and *The Tenants.* Her designs for the Beersheba Municipal Theatre include costumes for *Remembrance, Breaking Legs, Don Juan* and *The Three Sisters.* She has also designed costumes at the Cameri and Beit Liessen theaters.
Costumes: 1989 *Ghetto*

Susan L. Soetaert

Susan L. Soetaert has been resident designer for the Jean Cocteau Repertory Theatre since the early 1990s, and has designed costumes for numerous productions for that company and others. Among her designs at the Bouwerie Lane Theatre are costumes for *The First Lulu, Much Ado About Nothing, The Brothers Karamazov,* and *The*

Keepers. Additional design-related activities include *The Ripper,* an interactive computer game. On the faculty at the City University of New York where she teaches costume design, she has also worked for Barbara Matera, Ltd., Eaves-Brooks Costume Company, Ringling Bros. and Barnum & Bailey Circus, and the Ice Theatre of New York.

Costumes: 2001 *The Gathering*

M. Solotaroff

M. (Moi) Solotaroff, who designed for Diaghilev in Russia, also designed a set on Broadway. He taught workshops at the 92nd street Y, and in the 1930s helped establish a puppet theater with a group of former students using the puppets for social commentary.

Sets: 1935 *Recruits*

Pearl Somner

Pearl Somner was born on May 5, 1923 in Chicago, Illinois and studied at the University of Illinois and the Art Institute of Chicago. She grew up surrounded by the arts in her native city, which remains a major influence on her career. She served as an assistant to Lee Simonson, and spent two years at the Berliner Ensemble. Her first professional costumes were for a production of *The Summer of the 17th Doll* at the Provincetown Playhouse, and most recent ones, for a production of *the Music Man* in Beijing in the late 1980s. Her extensive designs for film and television include the movies *The Cross and the Switchblade* and *Love Story* as well as commercials, industrial promotions, and specials. Interested in the conservation of costumes, she has been active in the Association of Professional Women.

Costumes: 1967 *The Ninety-Day Mistress* **1969** *But, Seriously*† **1974** *Ulysses in Nighttown* **1975** *Shenandoah; We Interrupt this Program* **1976** *Herzl* **1977** *The Trip Back Down* **1978** *Angel* **1979** *Last Licks; Who's Life Is It Anyway?* **1980** *Who's Life Is It Anyway?* **1982** *84 Charing Cross Road; The World of Shalom Aleichem*

George C. Somnes

George C. Somnes was born in Boston, Massachusetts and studied in Europe. He performed on the Broadway stage during the early teens and in 1915 became the first American actor to attain success with the Old Vic Company in London, performing Claudius in *Hamlet* among other roles. After service in World War I he began directing and in 1929 moved to California to work in the film industry. He returned to New York in the early 1930s to direct additional productions and from 1936 to 1954 was director of the Elitch Garden Theatre in Denver, Colorado. Married to Helen Bonfils, daughter of the founder of the Denver Post, they were active in the theater in Denver where she performed, as well as in New York where Bonfils & Somnes, produced plays that he directed. He served on the Board of Directors of the American National Theatre Academy (ANTA). At the time of his death on February 8, 1956, he was supervising the design and construction of the Bonfils Memorial Theatre in Denver.
Costumes: 1914 *The Marriage of Columbine†*

Hans Sondheimer

Hans Sondheimer was born in Gelnhausen, Germany on December 6, 1901 and worked as an engineer and in the technical departments of theaters in Germany. He moved to the United States in 1939 and joined Erwin Piscator's New School Dramatic Workshop. He spent most of his professional life with the New York City Opera beginning in the inaugural season of 1944, and serving as technical director, lighting designer and production coordinator until he retired in 1980. During that time, he designed lights for the majority of the company's productions. A founding member of the United States Institute of Theatre Technology (USITT), he was an active theater consultant and designer and was technical consultant, designer and manager for other companies. After his retirement, until the time of his death on September 1, 1984, he remained active with New York City Opera as a technical consultant.
Lights: 1942 *Winter Soldiers*

Terence Tam Soon

Terence Tam Soon studied with costume design with Dorothy Jeakins, Theodora Van Runkle and Rudi Gernrich. He works mainly on the West Coast and in 1966 and 1967 received the Best Costume Design Award from the Los Angeles Fashion Guild. A founding member of the Asian Fashion Designers of Los Angeles, his costume designs have been seen at the Mark Taper Forum's New Theatre for Now, the Hollywood Bowl, the Inner City Dance Company and the East-West Players. He also designs costumes for television.
Costumes: 1976 *I Have a Dream*

Janusz Sosnowski

Janusz Sosnowski first designed on Broadway in 1992. An active designer for movies, his credits include art direction for *Miss Nobody*, a Polish film and *Zero Degrees Kelvin*, a Norwegian film. He was production designer for the Norway/U.K. film *Eddie Cockrell.*
Sets: 1992 *Metro*

Sergi Soudeikine

Sergi Soudeikine (also known as Sergei Yurievich Soudeikine, Serge Urevitch Sudeikine) was born in Tiflis, Russia on March 19, 1882 and studied at the Moscow Fine Arts School, the Imperial Academy in St. Petersburg and the Grande Chaumière in Paris. He began his career designing stage sets in Moscow in 1905 for Maeterlinck's *The Death of Tintagiles* and soon became one of Russia's foremost designers. At the onset of the Russian Revolution he settled in Paris. His designs were first seen in New York in 1922 when the impresario Balieff brought *Chauve Souris* to New York. His success led him to many more opportunities in the theater and opera designing sets and occasionally costumes. He became a member of the stage production staff at Radio City Music Hall in New York in 1934 and worked there for many years. In addition he ran a decorative arts studio in Stony Point, New York. Married to the operatic soprano Jeanne Palmer,

Mr. Soudeikine died on August 12, 1946 in Nyack, New York.

Sets: 1922 *Chauve Souris†*; *Revue Russe†* 1925 *Chauve Souris†* 1926 *The Chief Thing†* 1927 *Chauve Souris†* 1929 *Chauve Souris†* 1934 *The Chinese Nightingale*; *New Faces* 1935 *Porgy and Bess* 1936 *Forbidden Melody* 1943 *Chauve Souris: 1943*

Costumes: 1922 *Chauve Souris†*; *Revue Russe†* 1926 *The Chief Thing* 1927 *Chauve Souris* 1929 *Chauve Souris* 1934 *The Chinese Nightingale*; *New Faces* 1943 *Chauve Souris: 1943*

Raymond Sovey

Raymond Sovey was a prolific scenic designer who followed the common practice of his time of creating costumes for productions he was engaged to design. He occasionally also designed lights. Born in 1897 in Torrington, Connecticut, he studied at Columbia University and taught art in Baltimore before beginning his association with the theater. He began as an actor, appearing on Broadway in 1919 before designing his first production in 1920. The following forty years were busy ones for him, filled with designs for numerous plays. He received Tony Award nominations for his scenic designs for *The Great Sebastians* and for his costume designs for *All the Way Home*. Mr. Sovey died at age 72 on June 25, 1966.

Sets: 1920 *George Washington†*; *The Mirage†* 1921 *Iphigenia in Aulis* 1923 *Icebound*; *The Jolly Roger†*; *Saint Joan*; *White Desert*; *You and I* 1924 *Cheaper to Marry*; *Dear Sir*; *The Mask and the Face*; *Nancy Ann*; *New Toys* 1925 *The Butter and Egg Man*; *Harvest*; *Puppets*; *Something to Brag About* 1926 *The Adorable Liar*; *Gentlemen Prefer Blondes*; *Glory Hallelujah*; *The Ladder*; *A Proud Woman*; *The Ramblers* 1927 *The Brother's Karamazov*; *Coquette*; *The Letter*; *The Mikado*; *The Wild Man of Borneo* 1928 *Animal Crackers*; *The Command Performance*; *The Front Page*; *Goin' Home*; *Hotbed*; *Little Accident*; *She's My Baby*; *Three Cheers†*; *Tonight at 12*; *Wings over Europe* 1929 *Meteor*; *Other Men's Wives*; *Scarlet Pages*; *Strictly Dishonorable*; *Top Speed* 1930

Art and Mrs. Bottle; *As Good As New*; *The Inspector General*; *Strike Up the Band*; *That's the Woman*; *Twelfth Night*; *The Vinegar Tree*; *Waterloo Bridge* 1931 *After All*; *Cloudy with Showers*; *Counselor-at-Law*; *Fast Service*; *Green Grow the Lilacs*; *The Left Bank*; *The Way of the World*; *The Wiser They Are*; *Wonder Boy* 1932 *Black Sheep*; *Counselor-at-Law*; *Here Today*; *Hey, Nonny Nonny†*; *Honeymoon*; *I Loved You Wednesday*; *Men Must Fight*; *She Loves Me Not*; *Wild Waves* 1933 *The Blue Widow*; *Conquest*; *Doctor Monica*; *Her Master's Voice*; *Lone Valley*; *She Loves Me*; *Shooting Star* 1934 *The Distaff Side*; *Oliver! Oliver!*; *Portrait of Gilbert*; *Post Road*; *Ragged Army*; *The Wooden Slipper* 1935 *Bright Star*; *The Distant Shore*; *The Dominant Sex*; *The Eldest*; *Fly Away Home*; *Libel*; *Life's Too Short*; *May Wine*; *Most of the Game*; *The Petrified Forest* 1936 *Alice Takat*; *The Promise*; *Star Spangled*; *Sweet Aloes*; *Tovarich* 1937 *Amazing Dr. Clitterhouse*; *And Now Good-Bye*; *Babes in Arms*; *French Without Tears*; *Loves of Women*; *Yes, My Darling Daughter* 1938 *Dance Night*; *If I Were You*; *Knights of Song*; *Once Is Enough*; *Oscar Wilde*; *Our Town* 1939 *Miss Swan Expects*; *The Woman Brown* 1940 *Delicate Story*; *Grey Farm*; *Jupiter Laughs*; *Ladies in Retirement* 1941 *Arsenic and Old Lace*; *Boudoir*; *The Happy Days*; *Letters to Lucerne*; *Ring around Elizabeth*; *Village Green*; *The Walrus and the Carpenter*; *Your Loving Son* 1942 *Broken Journey*; *Counselor-at-Law*; *The Damask Cheek*; *Flare Path*; *Guest in the House*; *Strip for Action* 1943 *Another Love Story*; *Murder without Crime*; *Outrageous Fortune*; *Tomorrow the World*; *The Vagabond King* 1944 *Feathers in a Gale*; *For Keeps*; *Jackpot†*; *Lower North*; *Over Twenty-One*; *Sleep, My Pretty One*; *Soldier's Wife* 1945 *And Be My Love*; *The Hasty Heart*; *Mermaids Singing*; *A Place of Our Own*; *The Rich Full Life*; *The Ryan Girl*; *State of the Union*; *Therese* 1946 *Antigone*; *Apple of His Eye*; *Temper the Wind*; *This, Too, Shall Pass*; *Wonderful Journey* 1947 *For Love or Money*; *The Heiress*; *I Gotta Get Out*; *Love Goes to Press*; *Parlor Story* 1948 *Edward, My Son*; *Grandma's Diary*; *The Hallams*; *Harvest of Years* 1949 *The Traitor* 1950 *Cocktail*

Party; Ring 'Round the Moon **1951** Four Twelves Are 48; Gigi; Gramercy Ghost; Remains to Be Seen **1952** One Bright Day **1954** The Living Room; Witness for the Prosecution **1956** The Great Sebastian; The Reluctant Debutant **1957** Under Milkwood **1958** Patate
Costumes: 1920 George Washington† **1921** Macbeth† **1923** Saint Joan **1924** Flame of Love **1927** Coquette; The Mikado **1928** The Command Performance; The Jealous Moon†; La Gringa† (Miss Colbert's costumes); She's My Baby† **1930** As Good As New; The Second Little Show†; Twelfth Night **1931** The Third Little Show; The Way of the World **1932** Gay Divorce; Here Today; Hey, Nonny Nonny† (Co-Production Design); Wild Waves **1933** Her Master's Voice† **1934** Portrait of Gilbert; Ragged Army (Period costumes) **1935** The Distant Shore† (Ladies costumes) **1936** Tovarich **1938** Oscar Wilde **1939** The Woman Brown **1940** Grey Farm†; Jupiter Laughs **1942** The Damask Cheek **1944** Lower North **1945** The Hasty Heart; Therese **1951** Gramercy Ghost **1954** The Living Room†; Witness for the Prosecution† **1960** All the Way Home
Lights: 1930 As Good As New **1931** The Way of the World **1932** Here Today; Wild Waves **1933** Her Master's Voice **1934** Portrait of Gilbert **1936** Tovarich **1939** The Woman Brown **1940** Jupiter Laughs **1944** Lower North **1945** The Hasty Heart **1948** Edward, My Son; Grandma's Diary **1950** Cocktail Party; Ring 'Round the Moon **1951** Gramercy Ghost **1954** The Living Room; Witness for the Prosecution **1955** The Chalk Garden **1959** Look after Lulu

Anna Spencer

Anna (Ann) Spencer designed costumes and executed them for other designers. She worked with the Klaw and Erlanger Costume Company before starting her own business where she helped created costumes for the "Follies" productions to which she undoubtedly contributed designs as well, being particularly adept at musical revues. Married to William H. Riordan, her daughter was four years old when Anna Spencer Riordan died on May 4, 1922 in New York City, at age 30.

Costumes: 1915 Moloch **1919** Clarence (Miss Hays' gowns) **1920** Poor Little Ritz Girl† (Flower costumes) **1922** The Blue Kitten† (Costume Supervisor); Make It Snappy† (Additional costumes); The Rose of Stamboul; Up the Ladder (Gowns)

Frank Spencer

Frank Spencer was born on January 7, 1911 in Portland, Maine. He studied both design and directing at Yale, where he directed Orphee and studied with Donald Oenslager and Frank Poole Bevan. He assisted many other costume designers, including Robert Edmond Jones, Irene Sharaff, Miles White when he designed for the circus, and Raoul Pène Du Bois. For five decades, he designed costumes at Radio City Music Hall, where his original designs continue to be used. In a interview in the late 1970s, he commented that he watched the prices for a Rockette costume increase from $10 in 1932 to between $300 and $350 in 1978. In 1981, Frank Spencer retired to San Francisco, California, where he died April 29, 1996.
Costumes: 1941 Little Dark Horse **1955** Tonight on Samarkind **1956** The Ponder Heart **1958** Jane Eyre† **1979** The Magnificent Christmas Spectacular; New York Summer; Snow White and the Seven Dwarfs **1980** It's Spring; The Magnificent Christmas Spectacular; Manhattan Showboat; A Rockette Spectacular with Ginger Rogers **1988** Christmas Spectacular (Original costume designer) **1990** The Christmas Spectacular† (Original costume designer) **1991** Christmas Spectacular† (Original costume designer) **1992** Radio City Christmas Spectacular† (Original costume designer) **1993** Radio City Christmas Spectacular† (Original costume designer) **1994** Radio City Christmas Spectacular† (Original costume designer) **1996** Radio City Christmas Spectacular† (Original costume designer) **1997** Radio City Christmas Spectacular† (Original costume designer) **1998** Radio City Christmas Spectacular† (The Living Nativity)

David Spero

David Spero collaborated on the costume designs for a Broadway show in 1931. He was the president of D. Spero,

Inc. and resided at 1070 Park Avenue, New York City in the mid-1930s.

Costumes: 1931 *The Singing Rabbit*†

Neil Spisak

Neil Spisak is best known for his designs for major motion pictures, beginning with *Driving Miss Daisy* in 1985. He was born in 1942 and graduated from Carnegie Mellon University where he began designing both sets and costumes. After completing graduate school, he assisted William Ivey Long and Ann Roth and then took responsibility from Roth for the touring productions of *The Best Little Whorehouse in Texas*. He subsequently designed the London production. In addition to working with Roth on Broadway shows he assisted her on the films *Silkwood* and *Morning After*. Since then his design activity has been mainly in film, as costume designer, art director and production designer. Among his films are *Pacific Heights, Benny and Joon* and *Disclosures*. He was production designer for *Trip to Bountiful, Tiger Town, For Love of the Game,* and *End of the Line*. His honors include a nomination for an Emmy Award for the Elizabethan costumes he designed for the PBS television series *Roanoak*. Twenty-first century credits include the film *Spider-Man*.

Costumes: 1987 *Stepping Out*

Walter B. Spong

British scenic artist Walter Brookes (W.B.) Spong was well known for his designs for exterior scenes in England and Australia where he worked for eleven years with Dion Boucicault and Robert Brough. His designs in London were often seen at Drury Lane, Sadler's Wells, and the Royal Court Theatre, beginning as early as 1864. He often worked in collaboration with scene painter E.G. Banks (who also has credits on Broadway) for shows including *A Very Little Hamlet* in 1894. Spong died in Nice, Alpes-Maritimes, France on March 2, 1929 at age 80, three months after the death of his wife. Their daughter, Hilda Spong (1875-1955) was a very popular actress in London prior to emigrating to New York in 1915 where she was equally successful.

Sets: 1905 *The Man on the Box; Zira* **1906** *Lady Jim*

John Spradbery

British lighting designer John Spradbery (Spradbury) frequently collaborates with director Lindsay Kemp, as with his Broadway credit in 1974. He designs frequently in Europe for theater and dance. Late twentieth century credits include *Cinderella* at Covent Garden and for the Lyon Opera Ballet, *The Master and Margarita* in London's West End, and lighting designs for Ballet Victor Ullate de la Zarzuela in Madrid.

Lights: 1974 *Flowers*†

Franca Squarciapino

Franca Squarciapino, an Italian costume designer, designed costumes for a Broadway play in 1981 and received a Tony Award nomination for her designs. She has designed many productions at La Scala, the Netherlands Opera, the Paris Opera, the Metropolitan Opera, and the Royal Opera House in Covent Garden. Major motion picture designs include costumes for *The Horseman on the Roof* (Le Hussard Surletoit), *Volaverunt*, Honors include BAFTA and Academy Awards for the costumes for the film *Cyrano de Bergerac* in 1990.

Costumes: 1981 *Can-Can*

Bill Stabile

Bill Stabile began his career in theater in Ohio with the Kenley Players. He moved to the East Coast in the early 1970s to paint floats for Macy's Thanksgiving Day Parade but quickly became involved with experimental theaters. He has designed sets for numerous productions at La MaMa E.T.C., Circle Repertory Company, New York Shakespeare Festival, North Shore Music Theatre, and Spookhouse. He has also collaborated often with Tom O'Horgan, including *Lily* at the New York State Opera and *The Architect and the Emperor of Assyria*. Additional credits include Leonard Bernstein's *Mass* broadcast by PBS-TV to celebrate the Kennedy Center's tenth anniversary, the Umbria Jazz Festival, concerts for Max Roach, and the 1998 film *Went to Coney Island on a Mission from God...Be Back by Five*. He also designed the scenery for *Senator Joe*, a production that previewed but never opened on Broadway in 1989.

Sets: 1981 *I Won't Dance* 1982 *Torch Song Trilogy* 1995 *Jesus Christ Superstar*

Paul Staheli

Paul Staheli is known as a production designer and art director for television and film. He specializes in mysteries, and has served in either capacity for all the "Perry Mason" made-for-television movies of the 1980s and 1990s. He was the production designer for the CBS-TV series *Diagnosis Murder* and art director for the *Father Dowling Mysteries* series. He has been production designer for numerous major motion pictures, including *Destroyer, Revenge of the Ninja, The Boogens, Earthbound, Hangar 18* and *In Search of the Historic Jesus*, among others.

Sets: 1969 *The Three Sisters*

Mark W. Stanley

Mark W. Stanley designed lights for two Broadway productions during the last decade of the twentieth century. Among his many designs for the New York City Opera are *La Traviata, The Desert Song,* and *Norma.* Off-Broadway productions include *Curse of the Starving Class* and *Mireille.* He designed the lighting for *United States* at the Brooklyn Academy of Music.

Lights: 1991 *The Most Happy Fella* 1995 *The Merry Widow*

Everett Staples

Everett Staples designed costumes for a Broadway play in 1946.

Costumes: 1946 *Hidden Horizon*

Stavropoulos

George Peter Stavropoulos, a fashion designer born in Tripolis, Greece in 1920, designed in his own couture house, Nikis B, in Athens from 1949 to 1960. In 1961, he opened a salon on West 57th Street in New York, featuring his specialty: softly draped evening clothes, often made from multiple layers of silk chiffon. He designed expensive and luxurious clothing for fine shops and private customers, and was a favorite designer of Maria Callas, Lady Bird Johnson when her husband was president, and Elizabeth Taylor. As a young man in Greece, he designed costumes for plays and ballet, and in 1969 he contributed designs to a Broadway play. He died in New York city in 1990 at age 70.

Costumes: 1969 *But, Seriously†* (Act II dresses)

James Hart Stearns

James Hart Stearns, who was born in New Jersey on January 3, 1896, received an M.A. in Drama from Stanford University, where he also spent a year as artist-in-residence. He worked as display director for Gump's Department Store in San Francisco for seven years, beginning as a display assistant, and spent thirteen years as resident designer for the San Francisco Actor's Workshop. He also designed for the Stratford (Ontario) Festival, the first season of the Repertory Theatre of Lincoln Center and on Broadway. Mr. Stearns, who made his professional debut with *The Plough and the Stars* in 1956 for the San Francisco Actor's Workshop, died in California on December 26, 1971.

Sets: 1966 *Caucasian Chalk Circle*
Costumes: 1966 *Caucasian Chalk Circle* (Also masks) 1967 *Halfway Up the Tree*

George S. Steele

George S. Steele designed one set on Broadway in 1936. An architect, he worked at 420 Madison Avenue in New York City and resided in Shrewsbury, New Jersey.

Sets: 1936 *Fresh Fields*

Douglas Stein

Douglas Stein graduated from the Yale University School of Drama in 1982 and has since been an active scenic designer for theater, opera and dance. A native of Harrisburg, Pennsylvania, where he was born on November 5, 1948, he has designed for the major regional theaters including the Goodman and La Jolla Theatres, Arena Stage, and enjoyed a long association at the Guthrie Theatre. Off-Broadway credits include productions at the Manhattan Theatre Club, Classic Stage Company, and Lincoln Center Theatre. He has taught at New York and Princeton Universities, and the School of Visual Arts, and served on the boards of Theatre Communications Group and Theatre for a New Audience. Honors include an Obie Award for *Through the Leaves*. Twenty-first century designs include *Saved* and *Troilus and Cressida* produced by the Theatre for a New Audience.

Sets: **1988** *Our Town* **1989** *Largely New York* **1992** *Falsettos* **1993** *Fool Moon*; *Timon of Athens* **1994** *Government Inspector, Then* **1995** *Fool Moon*; *The Molière Comedies* **1996** *Scapin* **1998** *Fool Moon*; *Freak* **2000** *Dirty Blonde*

Miss E. M. A. Steinmetz

Miss E.M.A. Steinmetz was a fashion designer and illustrator who worked for Stein & Blaine during the teens and twenties. Stein & Blaine "Furriers and Ladies' Tailors" was located originally at 8-10 West 36th Street, and then became Stein & Blaine "A Creative House" located at 13 and 15 West 57th Street. The store used twice-a-day fashion shows to entice customers for whom each garment was then custommade. Many of her charming designs for gowns are in the permanent collection of the Fashion Institute of Technology in New York City.

Costumes: **1922** *The Endless Chain* (Gowns)

Charles Stepanek

Karel (Charles) Stepanek, an actor, was born in Brno, Czechoslovakia on October 29, 1899 and debuted on stage in his hometown in 1920. Occasionally he contributed ideas for designs of productions in which he also performed, and for a short time westernized his first name, although he returned to the original spelling for his major stage and film roles. He appeared for several seasons in Berlin with major companies, one of which toured the United States in the early 1930s. In 1940 he moved

to London, initially working as a political commentator for the BBC before resuming his acting career in 1941, after which he appeared on stage and in many movies. He appeared on stage in New York in 1951 as Baron Prus in *The Makropoulos Secret*, and starred in the 1960s movies *Licensed to Kill* and *Sink the Bismarck* among many more. He died in 1980.

Sets: **1931** *If Love Were All*

Alfred Stern, Jr.

Alfred Stern Jr. designed costumes on Broadway in 1939. An American nephew of the German designer Ernest Stern, he was resident costume designer at Radio City Music Hall from 1933 to 1937. A specialist in planning celebrations, he designed the Crystal Palace at the New York World's Fair. He has also planned numerous celebrations for cities around the U.S., including Detroit's 250th Birthday Festival and the West Virginia Centennial. During the late 1940s he wrote a column, "Costume Design Review," in *Dance Magazine* with Morton Haack, answering questions on costume design and giving technical advice on production. Mr. Stern also served as a director of the American National Theatre and Academy's Department of Community and Industrial Showmanship.

Costumes: **1939** *I Must Love Someone*

Ernest Stern

Ernest (Ernst) Stern was born in 1876 in Bucharest, Romania and trained in Munich at the Academy of Arts. In 1906 he joined Max Reinhardt's theater as art director and created designs of sets and costumes for numerous plays during the following years. In 1911 his designs were first seen in London and in 1912 a production of *Sumurum*, with sets and costumes by Ernest Stern, came to New York from Berlin. His designs in London, included *Kismet* and *Bitter-Sweet* in 1925. Between 1943 and 1945 he designed for Sir Donald Wolfit. He also designed films both in London and Hollywood, mainly for Ernst Lubitsch. His book of reminiscences, *My Life, My Stage*, was published in London in 1951. Ernest Stern died in 1954.

Sets: 1912 *Sumurun*† 1927 *Danton's Tod* 1929 *Bitter Sweet*† 1936 *White Horse Inn* 1937 *Young Madame Conti* 1947 *As You Like It*; *King Lear*

Costumes: 1912 *Sumurun* 1927 *Danton's Tod* 1929 *Bitter Sweet*† 1947 *As You Like It*; *King Lear*

Dale Stetson

Dale Stetson debuted on Broadway with the set for *The New Yorkers*, designed from sketches by Peter Arno, who wrote the musical extravaganza in 1927. While he specialized in scenic design he occasionally designed costumes. Also a mural painter, he created a large painting of the East River for the opening of the East River Savings Bank on Cortlandt Street in New York City in 1935. Born on August 23, 1904, he died in Washington, Vermont on July 29, 1989.

Sets: 1927 *The New Yorkers* 1930 *The New Yorkers*† 1931 *Here Goes the Bride*†; *Three Times the Hour* 1932 *Christopher Comes Across*; *The Fatal Alibi*

Costumes: 1932 *Christopher Comes Across*

Florine Stettheimer

Florine Stettheimer was a portrait painter and set designer who lived and worked at the Beaux Arts Studio, the legendary arts salon run by Florine with her sisters Carrie and Ettie, at 80 West 40th Street in New York City. She was born on August 19, 1871 and studied at the Art Students League. She began painting portraits by doing studies of members of her family. Her designs for *Four Saints in Three Acts* were remarkable since few established artists of the time also designed for the theater. Although the practice is now more common, Florine Stettheimer was one of the first established mainstream artists to design for the Broadway theater. She died on May 12, 1944 in New York City. Her paintings are in the collections of the Museum of Modern Art and at Columbia University because her sisters ignored her wish that her creative work be destroyed when she died. A retrospective exhibition at the Museum of Modern Art was held in 1946, and the very successful "Florine Stettheimer: Manhattan Fantastica" at the Whitney Museum of American Art in 1995 resurrected the stature of this remarkable artist.

Sets: 1934 *Four Saints in Three Acts*†

Frank W. Stevens

Frank W. Stevens designed sets for two Broadway productions in the early 1940s. He was associated with Joseph Teichner Studios, Inc. at 152 West 46th Street in New York City in 1931 and was a company director.

Sets: 1942 *Keep 'Em Laughing*; *Laugh, Town, Laugh*

John Wright Stevens

John Wright Stevens has designed sets for film, television, operas, industrial promotions and theater. He has designed for the New York Shakespeare Festival at Lincoln Center and for Early Music Dramas presented by the Waverly Consort. He also designed the set for *Without Willie* off-Broadway in 1983. His film work includes *The Lathe of Heaven*, *La Voix Humaine*, and art direction for *Rooftops* and *The Last Action Hero*. He received a B.A. at Catholic University and an M.F.A. from the Yale University School of Drama.

Sets: 1981 *Animals*; *The One Act Play Festival*

Ramsé Stevens

See Ramsé Mostoller.

Robert Ten Eyck Stevenson

Robert Ten Eyck Stevenson was active on Broadway between 1925 and 1936, returning in 1949 to design an additional production. He was vice president of Ten Eyck Couturier, Inc., located at 1 West 47th Street, in New York City during the mid-1930s.

Costumes: 1925 *The Crooked Friday* 1927 *Kiss Me*; *Padlocks of 1927*†; *Sidewalks of New York*† 1930 *The Vanderbilt Revue* 1932 *Shuffle Along of 1933*† 1933 *Pardon My English* 1934 *Keep Moving*† 1936 *Forbidden Melody* (as: Ten Eyck) 1949 *The Closing Door*

Victor Stiebel

Victor Stiebel, a fashion designer who worked mainly in London, was born in Durban, South Africa in 1907. He studied architecture at Cambridge University before entering the fashion business. Known for his designs for Princess Margaret, he wrote an autobiography, *South African Childhood*, which was published in 1968. He died in London in 1976.

Costumes: 1955 *Joyce Grenfell Requests the Pleasure* (Miss Grenfell's gowns)

Allan Stitchbury

Allan Stitchbury has designed lights for theater companies throughout his native Canada. He graduated from the University of Alberta, where he began designing, and spent two years as resident lighting designer for Victoria's Bastion Theatre. As resident designer for Edmonton's Northern Light Theatre he created lights for *Wings, Side by Side by Sondheim, Overruled, Take Me Where the Water's Warm* and *Piaf* among others. Among his many productions at the Banff Centre are *Baal, A Doll House, Ghosts* and *The Importance of Being Earnest*. He also produced daily highlights of the Commonwealth Games for the Canadian Broadcasting Company.

Lights: 1980 *Mister Lincoln*

John E. Stone

John E. Stone, who was born in New York City on September 12, 1888, designed costumes for two plays on Broadway in 1925. He spent the majority of his life on the West Coast working in a variety of capacities in the film industry, including directing, acting, producing, and writing screen plays. He died in Los Angeles, California on June 3, 1961.

Costumes: 1925 *Florida Girl*; *Louie the 14th* (Ladies costumes)

Mary Stonehill

Mary McAndrew Stonehill, a mural painter, was born in Brooklyn on October 23, 1900. She studied at Parsons School of Design and the École des Beaux Arts and the Academie Moderne in France, and often painted pictures of carousels. Her costume designs were always done in collaboration, with other designers, often William Henry

Matthews. Married to George Stonehill, also a mural painter, she died in February, 1951.

Costumes: 1931 *Hamlet*†; *Julius Caesar*†; *The Merchant of Venice*†

Emily Stoner

Emily Stoner designed costumes for a Broadway play in 1936.

Costumes: 1936 *The Lights o' London*

Frank Stout

Frank Stout, who designed a set on Broadway in 1915, spent the majority of his professional career as director of scenic art at the Carnegie Institute of Technology. While he was teaching at Carnegie Tech, scenic design changed. He was an important factor as a generation of scenic painters departed from nineteenth century methods to embrace the "New American Stagecraft." Stout also painted still lifes and landscapes. He died on April 10, 1955 at age 79 in Sharon, Connecticut.

Sets: 1915 *The Maker of Dreams*

Frederick Stover

Although primarily a designer for film and television, Frederick Stover designed sets and lights on Broadway during the 1940s. He was one of the first students in the graduate program at Yale University where he studied with Donald Oenslager. He was an active designer on the West Coast and was chief designer of the Los Angeles unit of the Federal Theatre Project. In the late 1940s, he designed scenery and lighting at the McCarter Theatre. He died at age 74 in February 1979 in East Hampton, New York. His ghost is said to inhabit the pre-Revolutionary War "Brown House" now occupied by the Ladies Village Improvement Society of East Hampton.

Sets: 1940 *Meet the People* **1945** *Hamlet* **1947** *Man and Superman* **1949** *Browning Version, The and A Harlequinade*
Lights: 1949 *A Harlequinade/The Browning Version*

C. Strahlendorff

Carl Strahlendorff was listed in the Manhattan and Bronx directories during the first two decades of the twentieth century as an artistic decorator.

His studio was located at 122 East 23rd Street.

Sets: 1918 *The Passing Show of 1918†*

Tony Straiges

Tony (Anthony) Straiges was born in Minersville, Pennsylvania on October 31, 1942. While living in Washington, D.C. he became involved with theater through the American Light Opera Company and the American Puppet Theatre. After serving in the army he studied briefly at Carnegie Mellon University and worked as a design assistant in San Francisco. He subsequently studied with Eldon Elder at Brooklyn College and with Ming Cho Lee at the Yale School of Drama and credits both men as mentors along with technical director Pete Feller. Tony Straiges has designed in major regional theaters in the United States and off-Broadway. He is the recipient of a Maharam and a Tony Award for *Sunday in the Park with George*, a Phoebe Award, a Boston Critics Award, a Drama Desk Award and an Outer Critics Circle Award in New York City.

Sets: 1978 *A History of the American Film*; *Timbuktu* 1979 *Richard III* 1980 *Harold and Maude* 1981 *Copperfield* 1984 *Sunday in the Park with George* 1986 *Long Day's Journey into Night* 1987 *Into the Woods* 1988 *Rumors* 1989 *Artist Descending a Staircase*; *Dangerous Games* 1991 *I Hate Hamlet* 1992 *Shimada* 1998 *Golden Child*

Stephen Strawbridge

Stephen Strawbridge was born on October 24, 1954 in Baltimore. He graduated from Towson State University where he became involved with theater, and received a Master of Fine Arts degree from the Yale University School of Drama. While establishing his career, he assisted Jennifer Tipton, whom he considers his mentor. He is an especially active designer in regional theaters, off-Broadway, and for dance (Pilobolus, Nina Weaver, Spencer Colton, etc.) and opera companies (New York City Opera, San Francisco Opera, Dallas Opera, etc.). On the faculty of the Yale University School of Drama, he is co-chair of the Design Department and resident designer for the Yale

Repertory Theatre. Honors include a Helen Hayes Award nomination for *Maspeth* at the Folger Theatre, and for an American Theatre Wing Award for *Ice Cream with Hot Fudge* at the New York Shakespeare Festival.

Lights: 1989 *Mastergate*

Hazel Strayer

Hazel Strayer was born October 29, 1891 in Lawn Hill, Iowa. She received a B.A. from Iowa State Teachers College (now University of Northern Iowa) in 1914 and a M.A. at Columbia University in 1923. She spent the majority of her career as professor of oral interpretation and drama at Iowa State Teachers College, from 1916 to 1956, serving as director of theater from 1929 to 1956. She took occasional sabbaticals to pursue post-graduate work, including study at Yale with George Pearce Baker. During these periods, she also worked in summer stock and on Broadway. Her contribution to theater and design has been through the generations of talented students she taught and directed. This includes those who currently perform in a theater named for her and a colleague, Stan Wood, at the University of Northern Iowa: Strayer-Wood Theatre. Miss Strayer, who retired in 1956, died in 1959.

Costumes: 1936 *Russet Mantle* (Costume Supervisor)

Anthony W. Street

Anthony W. Street (also known as A. W. Street) designed scenery on Broadway during the 1930s.

Sets: 1908 *The Great Question* 1930 *The International Review* 1932 *Zombie* 1934 *Furnished Rooms* 1935 *Satellite*

Walter Street

Walter Street designed a Broadway show in 1934. He resided with his wife Annie at 1851 7th Avenue in New York City in 1932.

Sets: 1934 *Late Wisdom†*

Oscar Strnad

Oscar (Oska) Strnad, an Austrian architect and designer was associated with Max Reinhardt at the Kunstgewerbe Schule in Vienna. He built the

Schloss Theatre in the park at Rein-
hardt's Castle in Leopoldskron near
Salzburg. He also rebuilt the Salzburg
Festspielhaus and "Faust-town" in the
Salzburg Felsenreitschule. He designed
Don Juan at Théâtre des Champs-
Élysées in Paris in 1928. Both Robert
Edmond Jones and Jo Mielziner stud-
ied his theories of architecture and de-
sign. Professor Strnad, who was born
in Vienna in 1879, died at age 56 on
September 3, 1935 in Vienna.
Sets: **1927** *A Midsummer Night's Dream*
1928 *Peripherie*

Austin Strong

Austin Strong, the playwright who
wrote the popular comedy *Seventh
Heaven*, was born in San Francisco in
1881 and raised in New Zealand and
Samoa. He attended Wellington College in Australia and studied in France
and Italy as a landscape architect. The
grand-stepson of Robert Louis Stevenson, he began writing soon after settling in London and his first play, *The
Exile*, was produced in 1903. He wrote
several hit plays, among them *A Good
Little Devil*, *Three Wise Fools* and
A Play Without A Name, for which
he also designed the set. He contributed to the *New York Times*, *Saturday Review of Literature*, *The Atlantic Monthly* and other publications
and served for several years on the
Pulitzer Prize Drama jury, resigning in
1934 due to restrictions placed on the
jury. He died on September 17, 1952 in
Nantucket, Massachusetts.
Sets: **1928** *A Play without Name*

Bianca Stroock

Bianca Stroock was born Bianca Hirsh-
field on November 11, 1892 (occasionally 1896) in New York City and studied at Hunter College. She was married
in 1915 to James Stroock, the president of Brooks Costume Company, and
had two actress daughters, Geraldine
Brooks and Gloria Stroock Stern. She
made her Broadway debut as costume
designer in 1916, and was especially active during the 1930 and 1940s, mainly
as a costume supervisor or coordinator. She died in Los Angeles on May
17, 1984.

Costumes: **1916** *The Big Show*† **1931**
Papavert† (Women's gowns) **1932** *Collision*† (Costume Supervisor); *The In-
side Story* (Costume Supervisor); *New
York to Cherbourg* (Costume Supervisor); *She Loves Me Not*; *The Stork Is
Dead* (Costume Supervisor) **1934** *The
Red Cat* (Costume Supervisor); *The
Wooden Slipper* (Costume Supervisor)
1935 *Abide with Me* (Costume Supervisor); *Field of Ermine*; *It's You I Want*
(Costume Supervisor); *Night of January
16* (Costume Supervisor); *The Ragged
Edge* (Costume Supervisor); *To See Ourselves* (Costume Supervisor) **1936** *And
Stars Remain* (Costume Supervisor); *Arrest That Woman* (Miss Emerson's gown)
1937 *Loves of Women* (Costume Supervisor); *Miss Quis* (Costume Supervisor) **1938** *Lorelei* (Costume Supervisor);
Spring Thaw (Costume Supervisor) **1939**
The Philadelphia Story† (Costume Supervisor); *Ring Two*† (Costume Supervisor)
1940 *My Dear Children* (Costume Supervisor) **1941** *Claudia*†; *Pie in the Sky*
(Costume Supervisor) **1942** *The Doughgirls*† **1943** *Lady, Behave* (Costume Supervisor); *The Voice of the Turtle* (Costume Supervisor) **1944** *Dear Ruth* (Costume Supervisor); *Decision* (Costume
Supervisor); *The Odds on Mrs. Oakley* (Costume Supervisor); *Soldier's Wife*;
Wallflower (Costume Supervisor) **1945**
Round Trip (Clothes) **1946** *Christopher
Blake* (Costume Supervisor); *Fatal Weakness* (Costume Supervisor); *Wonderful
Journey* (Costume Supervisor) **1947** *The
Big Two*; *Parlor Story* **1948** *The Hallams*
1949 *Metropole* **1953** *Sabrina Fair*

Stroppa

Stroppa, who created scenery for a
Broadway production in 1923, is also
credited with scenery for the London
productions of *Thais* at the Drury Lane
Theatre in 1920, and for *Ghosts* and
Cosi Sia at the New Oxford Theatre in
1923. The New York playbill identifies
the designer as being "of Milan."
Sets: **1923** *Laugh, Clown, Laugh*

Zenobius Strzelecki

Zenobius Strzelecki, a Polish theatrical
designer, created scenery for a production on Broadway in 1967. The production originated at the Jewish State

Theatre of Poland with Ida Kaminska as Artistic Director. He was born in Burgstadt, Germany on October 23, 1915 and studied at the Warsaw Academy of Fine Arts and the State Theatrical Institute with L. Schiller. An active scenic designer in Poland, he wrote *Polska plastyka teatralna (Polish Theatrical Plastic Art)*, a history of stage design in Poland, published in 1966, *Kierunki scenografii wsyólczesnez (Trends in Modern Polish Scenery)* in 1979 and *Konwencje scenograficzne (Contemporary Scenography)* in 1973.
Sets: 1967 *Mother Courage*

Michel Stuart

Michel Stuart began professional life as a dancer, appearing in *West Side Story* in London at the age of 13. He created the role of George in *A Chorus Line*, but left the show to pursue other interests. He designed costumes and a line of clothes for Giorgio Sant'Angelo on 7th Avenue, and directed plays. Mr. Stuart also became an important theatrical producer with many successful productions to his credit, including *Nine, The Tap Dance Kid* and *Cloud Nine*. Born in Manhattan, he died September 7, 1997 at age 54, in an automobile accident in Malibu, California.
Costumes: 1980 *A Day in Hollywood/A Night in the Ukraine*

Patricia Quinn Stuart

Costume designer Patricia Quinn Stuart was born on November 16, 1938 and received a B.A. at Antioch College, where she designed costumes for the first time for *The Waltz of the Toreadors* in 1960. Additional study in design and media has occurred in various schools since that time, including the Fashion Institute of Technology, where she has been Adjunct Instructor of Fashion Design in the Art Department since 1981. She assisted both her mentors, Patricia Zipprodt and Domingo Rodriguez as her own career developed. Her debut was *The Waltz of Toreadors* at Antioch College, when she was an undergraduate student. Her costume design activities range from theater and opera to television and film.

Costumes: 1968 *A Cry of Players; The Cuban Thing* 1970 *The Me Nobody Knows* 1972 *The Lincoln Mask; Lost in the Stars*

Bruce Stuios

Bruce Stuios designed costumes for a 1929 Broadway show.
Costumes: 1929 *Carnival*

Tom Sturge

Lighting designer Tom Sturge has designed over 250 productions since receiving his B.F.A. from Boston University. His designs range from theater to dance, opera, national tours, international shows, industrial promotions, television and movies. Credits in regional theaters include productions at the Goodspeed Opera House, Theatre-by-the-Sea, the Pittsburgh Public Theatre, George Street Playhouse, Alliance Theatre and the Paper Mill Playhouse. Off-Broadway he has designed at Theatre Four, Circle Repertory Company, La MaMa E.T.C. and the Jewish Repertory Theatre creating lights for premieres of *Amazing Grace, Sheba, Theda Bara and the Frontier Rabbi, All that Glitters* and *The Size of the World* among others. On the faculty at Boston University, he is an Assistant Professor, teaching lighting design in the School of Theatre Arts. Twenty-first century designs include *Sweet Charity, Peter Pan* and *Joseph and the Amazing Technicolor Dreamcoat* all at the North Shore Music Theatre, and *King o' the Moon* at Merrimack Repertory Theatre.
Lights: 1990 *Those Were the Days* 1992 *Gypsy Passion*

Jason Sturm

Jason Sturm, who has designed lighting extensively in the West, made his East Coast and Broadway debut with *Chu Chem* in 1989. He was born in Miami Beach, Florida on August 12, 1951 and received a B.A. in liberal arts from the University of New Mexico. He credits a college professor in New Mexico, John Malolepsy, and designer Robert Mitchell as influences on his career. Although his brother tried to involve him in backstage activity at a local college theater when he was growing up, he received little formal training in the theater and spent a number of years in other professions before being drawn into the theater. His professional debut was *The Fantasticks* for the Albuquerque Civic Light Opera Association. He has designed for many different theater companies including the New Mexico Repertory Theatre, Opera Southwest, Milwaukee Repertory Theatre, and the Vortex Theatre, where he has also served on the Board of Directors. Twenty-first century designs include *How Happy Barbies Are! (Qué Felices Son las Barbies!)* written by and starring Wanda Arriaga and presented internationally by Teatro Circulo; he won an ACE Award for the design. He also created the Intrepid Sea Air Space Museum Event Hall, frequently used by this nation's President, and the Wintergarden Performance Stage in the World Financial Center in New York City.

Lights: 1989 *Chu Chem*; *Miss Margarida's Way*

Dennis Sullivan

Dennis Sullivan was an interior decorator, who resided at 141 East 50th Street, New York City. In 1916, he used his talents to create lighting for a Broadway production. He died on January 31, 1940 at age 46.

Lights: 1916 *The Queen's Enemies*

Ed Sullivan

Edward Vincent Sullivan, known to television audiences for the *Ed Sullivan Show* which ran Sunday nights on CBS-TV for twenty-three years, was involved in many aspects of show business. He was born on September 28, 1902 in New York City. He worked for a series of newspapers, settling at *The Evening Graphic* in 1927 where he became Broadway columnist in 1929. He produced vaudeville shows and emceed radio shows, organized benefits during World War II and wrote film scripts. In 1947 he was hired to emcee *Toast of the Town* which became the *Ed Sullivan Show*. An early advocate for hiring black performers on television, he practiced his own philosophy, providing

audiences with an extraordinary performance by Marian Anderson in 1952 among others. As a young sportswriter he had helped publicize a basketball game between the original Celtics and Bob Douglas' Renaissance team at the Armory. He later produced vaudeville and legitimate productions and in 1948 with Noble Sissle directed and designed *Harlem Cavalcade*, the first Broadway production with a black cast. Ed Sullivan died on October 13, 1974 at age 72.

Sets: 1942 *Harlem Cavalcade*

Elizabeth Higgins Sullivan

Elizabeth Higgins Sullivan was born December 14, 1875 (or according to some sources, 1874) in Columbus, Nebraska. She began professional life as a newspaper writer and became interested in social settlement work and the suffragist movement, which led her to costume design for a Broadway show in 1932. She later became interested in horticulture and wrote articles on that subject and on agriculture in the South. Her plays include *The Beacon* with Joy Higgins and *The Strongest Man*.

Costumes: 1932 *Carrie Nation*

John Sullivan

John Sullivan designed lights in 1946 and 1948 for several productions on Broadway. At least two lighting designers share this name, but the Broadway designer is not the same John Sullivan who was lighting director for WGBH-TV (1933-1995).

Lights: 1946 *The Critic*; *Henry IV, Part I*; *Henry IV, Part II*; *Oedipus*; *Uncle Vanya* **1948** *Oedipus Rex*

John Carver Sullivan

John Carver Sullivan, a graduate of Carnegie Mellon University made his New York debut with *The Guardsman* at The Production Company. He has taught at Webster College, Dartmouth College, and the Pacific Conservatory of the Performing Arts. His designs have been seen in many regional theaters, including the Alley Theatre, Missouri Repertory Theatre, StageWest, the Opera Theatre of St. Louis, Goodspeed Opera House, and for the Hartford Ballet. Mr. Sullivan designs sets as well as costumes.

Costumes: 1983 *Moose Murders*

Paul Sullivan

Paul Sullivan has designed lights for theaters in Canada, Mexico, France and Germany as well as for the Pennsylvania Ballet Company, Brooklyn Academy of Music, The Kennedy Center in Washington, D.C. and Carnegie Hall. Additional productions in New York City include *Broadway Soul*. Late twentieth century credits include many designs for the Dance Theatre of Harlem.

Lights: 1968 *New Faces of 1968* **1972** *Heathen!*; *Lost in the Stars*; *Mother Earth* **1984** *The Wiz*

Josef Sumbatsivily

Josef Sumbatsivily has been designing scenery in the former Soviet Union since 1950. His scenery has been used extensively at the BolshoiBallet, the Moscow Satire Theatre, the Pushkin Theatre, and the Theatre of the Soviet Army. These productions and additional designs at the Mayakovsky Theatre and Leningrad's Komissarjevsky Theatre have garnered him many awards, among them a Gold Medal in set design for *Ivan the Terrible* in Czechoslovakia.

Sets: 1990 *Zoya's Apartment*† (Original designs)

David Sumner

Scenic designer David Sumner was born in Cambridge, England in 1954. He earned his B.S. at the University of Louisville where he studied with Michael Hottois, and attended graduate school at Brandeis University, studying with Howard Bay. Since the early 1980s, he has been an active designer, illustrator and scenic artist with numerous credits for industrial promotions, corporate meetings, exhibits, and theatrical productions. His wide-ranging designs include the world premiere of the ballet *Shim Chung*, in Seoul, Korea, a European tour of *Funny Girl*, a series of interiors for nightclubs at the 1980 Winter Olympic

Games in Lake Placid, New York, and the New York City-sponsored outdoor concert *Broadway on Broadway*. He designs often for the Pittsburgh Public Theatre.

Sets: 1992 *Gypsy Passion*

Ed Sundquist

Ed Sundquist was an easel painter, scenic artist and designer. He designed and painted sets in New York, San Francisco, and Pittsburgh. As proprietor of the Ed Sundquist Studio during the teens, he designed additional productions and painted sets for other designers. Known for his marine paintings, he died on October 11, 1961 at age 80 in Taconic, Connecticut.

Sets: 1915 *The Ware Case*† **1916** *Her Soldier Boy*† **1917** *De Luxe Annie*†; *The Fugitive* (as: Ed Sundquist Studio); *The Imaginary Invalid* (as: Ed Sundquist Studio) **1918** *A Cure for Curables* **1930** *Brown Buddies*† **1935** *Weather Permitting* **1938** *The Wild Duck*†

Charles Suppon

Charles Suppon, fashion designer, was born in Collinsville, Illinois on January 12, 1949. He received a B.F.A. from the School of the Art Institute, University of Chicago and worked as an assistant to Calvin Klein from 1971 to 1976. His designs for Intre Sport won a Coty American Fashion Critics Award in 1978, only two years after the sportswear line for women was launched. In addition, he designed costumes for Peter Allen's stage and cabaret appearances beginning in 1979. With Harvey Fierstein, he co-authored *Legs Diamond*. The musical, starring Peter Allen had a short Broadway run in 1988, the year before Charles Suppon died at age 40 on March 21, 1989.

Costumes: 1979 *Peter Allen "Up in One"*

James Surridge

James Surridge was known as a "propertyman" and in that capacity was active in the theater, often assisting scene designers. He maintained a studio at 2100 Tiebout Avenue in the Bronx at the beginning of the twentieth century where he crafted properties and constructed scenery. Born on June 22,

1893, he was 18 years old when his name first appeared in a Broadway playbill. Surridge died in Rochester, New York in February 1972.

Sets: 1911 *The Wedding Trip†* (Designed and built) **1913** *Oh, I Say†*

Jean Sutherland

Jean Sutherland designed costumes for a Broadway play in 1937.

Costumes: 1937 *Robin Landing*

Millie Sutherland

Millie Sutherland was active on Broadway from 1942 to 1950.

Costumes: 1942 *The First Crocus* (Costume Supervisor) **1948** *A Story for Strangers* **1949** *Detective Story* (Costume Supervisor) **1950** *Pride's Crossing*

Josef Svoboda

Josef Svoboda was an internationally renowned Czechoslovakian architect and scenographer. He was born on May 10, 1920 in Caslav, Czechoslovakia and trained as an architect in Prague. His career began in 1948, when he became the head designer at the National Theatre, Prague after which he designed sets and costumes throughout the world for operas, ballets, plays and films. An advocate of a blend of contemporary technology and traditional scenic design techniques effectively using projections and mirror effects, he designed over five hundred productions and influenced the design of others. His British debut was *The Storm* in 1966 at the Royal National Theatre. His designs were seen only rarely in the United States, but included *Otello* and *Carmen* at the Metropolitan Opera in the 1970s. Svoboda, who died on April 8, 2002 in Prague, was honored with numerous prizes and honorary degrees.

Sets: 1974 *Jumpers*

Miss Gloria Swanson

Miss Gloria Swanson, the actress, was born March 27, 1899 in Chicago, Illinois. She had a successful career on stage, beginning as a child in Key West, Florida, and in both silent and sound films. She also had a flair for clothes and a reputation as a dress designer and in 1951 designed her own gown for a Broadway show. Miss Swanson died on April 4, 1983 at the age of 84.

Costumes: 1951 *Nina†* (Her own gowns and hats)

E. Lyall Swete

Lyall Swete, a British actor, playwright and producer, was born in Wrington, Somerset, England on July 25, 1865 and studied at Trinity College at Stratford-upon-Avon. He debuted as an actor in 1887 in Margate, England in *The Road to Ruin*, and made his first appearance in London in 1900 in *Henry V*. He produced *Chu-Chin-Chow* in New York in 1917, subsequently appearing and producing other plays including *Clair de Lune*, for which he also designed the settings. He died on February 19, 1930.

Sets: 1921 *Clair De Lune†*

Anthea Sylbert

Anthea Sylbert, who was born October 6, 1939 in New York City, has been designing costumes for films since 1967. Her movies include *Chinatown* and *Julia* for which she received Oscar nominations, as well as *Carnal Knowledge, Rosemary's Baby, Shampoo*, and *The Heartbreak Kid*. The majority of her career has been spent in Hollywood (and on location), but she has two Broadway plays to her credit. She received a B.A. from Barnard College and an M.A. from Parsons School of Design but she left New York in the late 1970s to join Warner Brothers and subsequently United Artists as a vice president for production. In 1982 she formed Hawn-Sylbert Movie Company in association with Goldie Hawn. She returned to New York in 1984 to work once again with Mike Nichols on *The Real Thing*.

Costumes: 1971 *The Prisoner of 2nd Avenue* **1984** *The Real Thing*

Paul Sylbert

Paul Sylbert was born April 16, 1928 in New York City and spent the early part of his career painting scenery for television productions. Since the early 1950s, he has worked mainly in the film industry, occasionally designing scenery for theater and opera. His credits as art director for movies are extensive, beginning with *Baby Doll* and *A Face in the Crowd*, designed in collaboration with his twin brother, Richard Sylbert. He has also worked with his former wife, Anthea Sylbert. Paul Sylbert was production designer for *Kramer vs. Kramer, One Flew Over the Cuckoo's Nest, Gorky Park, Biloxi Blues, Rosewood*, and many others, Honors include an Academy Award for Best Art Direction for *Heaven Can Wait*, shared with Edwin O'Donovan. He received a nomination in that same category for *Prince of Tides* (with Caryl Heller).

Sets: 1990 *Street Scene*

Richard Sylbert

Richard Sylbert, known primarily as a production designer for movies, was born in Brooklyn, New York in April 1928, twin brother to Paul He attended the Tyler School of Fine Arts and Temple University, hoping to be a painter, and began his design career with NBC-TV in 1952. His mentor was William Cameron Menzies, one of the great American film designers, with whom he was associated for two months just prior to Menzies' death. His list of film credits reads like a list of great films: *Carnal Knowledge, Tequilla Sunrise, Fat City, Baby Doll, Face in the Crowd, The Graduate, The Manchurian Candidate, Splendor in the Grass, Rosemary's Baby*, and *Bonfire of the Vanities*. He was nominated for Academy Awards for *Shampoo, Chinatown, The Cotton Club*, and *Reds* and received Oscars for art direction for *Who's Afraid of Virginia Woolf?* and *Dick Tracy*. He also designed the set for the long running television series, *Cheers. Setting the Scene* by Robert S. Sennett, published in 1994, includes a profile of the life and career of this creative designer, who died at age 73 on March 23, 2002 in Woodland Hills, California.

Sets: 1957 *The Egghead* **1971** *The Prisoner of 2nd Avenue*

Vic Symonds

Vic Symonds, a British designer, has often worked in collaboration with Alan Pickford during the past thirty-five years. He was art director and production designer with Pickford for *The Jewel in the Crown* shown on *Mobil Masterpiece Theatre* on PBS in 1984. The production won the Royal Television Society Design Award for 1983-1984 and was nominated for six Emmy Awards when shown in the United States, including one for art direction. Vic Symonds has designed other television films including *Bedroom Farce, Occupations* and the feature film *The Long Good Friday*.

Sets: 1962 *Rattle of a Simple Man* **1963** *Rattle of a Simple Man*

S. Syrjala

Sointu Syrjala, born in Toronto on December 30, 1904, grew up in Fitchburg, Massachusetts. He attended the Worcester Museum School, the National Academy of Design and the Boston Museum School of Fine Arts. He designed scenery for the theater and television beginning with *Precedent* in the early 1930s. Earlier he had performed in the chorus in several musicals before becoming an assistant to Jo Mielziner and Willy Pogany. With Ben Hecht he organized pageants to aid Israel, including *We Will Never Die* in 1943 and *Salute to Israel* in 1970. During 1968 he designed the restoration of Ford's Theatre in Washington, D.C. Mr. Syrjala also designed regularly for television beginning in 1951. For CBS-TV his credits included *The Guiding Light* and *Secret Storm*. He retired in 1972 due to failing eyesight and died at age 74 in April 1979.

Sets: 1928 *Heavy Traffic* **1931** *Devil in the Mind*; *Precedent* **1933** *Armourette*; *Far-Away Horses* **1934** *The Milky Way*; *Stevedore* **1935** *Blind Alley*; *Remember the Day* **1936** *Double Dummy*; *Stark Mad*; *Swing Your Lady* **1937** *Pins and Needles* **1938** *Pins and Needles* **1951** *The Fourposter*

Costumes: 1936 *Swing Your Lady* (Production design) **1937** *Pins and Needles*†

Julia Sze

Julia Sze, the daughter of a former Chinese ambassador to the U.S. and England, was born in Tientsin, China and came to the U.S. at the age of nine. She was educated in Europe and graduated from Cornell in 1938, never studying costume design. She began designing costumes on Broadway in 1947. In the early 1950s she joined CBS-TV where she progressed through the ranks to became head costume designer, coordinating six other designers and costumes for 30 shows per week.

Costumes: 1947 *Angel in the Wings*; *Command Decision* (Costume Supervisor) 1948 *Hold It* 1949 *Death of a Salesman* 1950 *The Man from Mel Dinelli*; *The Man* 1958 *Drink to Me Only* 1966 *Help Stamp Out Marriage* 1967 *The Girl in the Freudian Slip*; *Love in E-Flat*

Samuel L. Tabor

Samuel L. Tabor designed a set in 1934 on Broadway. On January 18, 1916, he filed a naturalization petition in New York City, while residing at 202 Broome Street. In 1918 he worked as a cap maker and lived at 632 East 11th Street, New York City. He should not be confused with the physics educator who has the same name.

Sets: 1934 *Late Wisdom†*

Elmer Taflinger

Elmer Taflinger, a painter who began to draw when he was six years old, was born in Indianapolis, Indiana on March 3, 1891, and studied at the Art Students League and with George Bridgman. He designed costumes for two plays in the teens, and because he worked as art director for David Belasco, was surely responsible for additional designs. He taught at the Minneapolis School of Art, and then for nearly forty years from his studio in Indianapolis, where he died August 6, 1981 at age 90.

Costumes: 1916 *Little Lady in Blue* 1917 *Tiger Rose†*

Alan Tagg

Alan Tagg trained for a career in theater at the Mansfield College of Art and the Old Vic Theatre School. He was born in Sutton-in-Ashfield, England on April 13, 1928 and began his career as assistant to Oliver Messel and Cecil Beaton. He has been designing in London since 1952, when *The River Line* opened, and was a founding member of the English Stage Company in 1956. He has designed numerous productions

in the West End, for the Royal Court Theatre, the Royal Shakespeare Company, the Royal National Theatre, and in Chichester as well as in New York, Europe and Australia. Alan Tagg has also designed exhibitions at the Victoria and Albert Museum and other locations.

Sets: 1957 *Look Back in Anger* 1958 *The Entertainer* 1965 *All in Good Time* 1967 *Black Comedy* 1974 *London Assurance* 1978 *The Kingfisher* 1979 *Who's Life Is It Anyway?* 1980 *Who's Life Is It Anyway?* 1986 *Corpse!* 1990 *Lettice & Lovage*

Costumes: 1967 *Black Comedy*

Ron Talsky

Ron Talsky, a costume designer based on the West Coast, worked for Western Costume Company and designed several films featuring Raquel Welch, including *The Three Musketeers* and *The Four Musketeers*. After service in the Navy in Korea, Mr. Talsky, a Los Angeles native, worked in craft services, then as an electrician at 20th Century Fox before serving his apprenticeship to join the Costumer's Union. Other film credits include *The Man Who Shot Liberty Valance, The Manchurian Candidate* and *How the West Was Won*. He was also well known for the elegant gowns he designed with Carole Little through Carole Little for Saint-Tropez West, that were worn by many Hollywood stars to fashionable events, such as the Academy Awards. Born November 7, 1934, he died in California in September 1995.

Costumes: 1977 *I Love My Wife*

Victor En Yu Tan

Victor En Yu Tan, who attended Columbia University, has designed lights in regional theaters around the country, from Syracuse Stage and GEVA on the East Coast to the Cincinnati Playhouse and Milwaukee Repertory Theatre in the Midwest and the Alaska Repertory Theatre in Anchorage. His New York debut was *The Year of the Dragon* at the American Place Theatre in 1974, before which he had assisted other lighting designers. He received an Obie Award for sustained excellence for his designs at the New York Shakespeare Festival, the Opera at 92nd Street, the Pan Asian Repertory (where he has been resident lighting designer since 1980) and the New Federal Theatre. En Yu Tan, who taught lighting design at the University of Michigan, is currently associate professor and head of the lighting design program at the University of Missouri at Kansas City.

Lights: 1986 *Shakespeare on Broadway for the Schools*

Herman Patrick Tappé

Herman Patrick Tappé had a varied career in New York. He was a successful women's dress designer and proprietor of shops on East 50th and West 57th streets in New York City, and also headed the millinery manufacturers Chez Tappé LaMode,Inc. He designed scenery and costumes for productions on Broadway spanning four decades, specializing in costumes. In addition John and Herman Tappé operated a saloon, "Tappé Brothers," in 1919 at 383 West 125th Street. Herman Tappé died at age 78 on September 20, 1954.

Sets: 1917 *Polly with a Past*†
Costumes: 1921 *Good Morning, Dearie*† **1927** *The Ivory Door*† (Miss Watkin's clothes) **1930** *Uncle Vanya*† (Miss Gish's costumes) **1940** *Joan o' the Shoals* (Modern clothes)

Tarazona Brothers

Tarazona Brothers received credit for one set in 1917. Enrique Tarazona and Luis Crispo were proprietors of Acme Scenery & Decorating Company, supplying "High Grade European Art on Guaranteed Fire Proof Material" at 1547 Broadway, New York City in 1916. Enrique was also an artist and maintained a studio at 336 Mott Avenue in that same year.

Sets: 1917 *The Land of Joy*

Miss Tashman

Miss (Lilyan) Tashman, an actress, was born in Brooklyn, New York on October 23, 1899. She began her career as an artist's model and appeared for the first time on stage in *The Lilac Domino*

in October 1914. She subsequently appeared in many plays, including *The Garden of Weeds,* for which she also designed her own costumes. Miss Tashman also appeared in many films prior to her death at age 34 on March 21, 1934.

Costumes: 1924 *Garden of Weeds*† (Her own Act I costume)

Jean Tate

Jean Tate supervised costumes for two plays in the mid-1930s.

Costumes: 1935 *Porgy and Bess* (Costume Supervisor) **1937** *And Now Good-Bye* (Costume Direction and Assistant to Mr. Sovey)

Yan Tax

Yan Tax, who is known mainly as a costume designer for European movies and television, designed costumes on Broadway in 1993, his New York debut. Additional credits include costumes for the films *Left Luggage, Between the Devil and the Deep Blue Sea* and *Le Huitieme Jour (The Eighth Day).* Among his other designs for theater is *Mozart!,* a musical staged in Vienna, Austria. Honors include a nomination for a Tony Award for *Cyrano: The Musical.*

Costumes: 1993 *Cyrano: The Musical*

James A. Taylor

James A. Taylor, who designed scenery on Broadway in 1965, had extensive credits for ABC-TV and CBS-TV, including the daytime dramas *The Nurses* and *As the World Turns,* special news events, and the series *Kojak.* He was art director for countless commercials, and designed scenery off-Broadway, for stock companies, the St. Paul Civic Opera, Theatre Under The Stars in Atlanta, Georgia and for the Papermill Playhouse, among others. He was born in 1932 and died in Pioneer, California at age 68 on February 10, 2001.

Sets: 1965 *The Glass Menagerie*†

Marochka Taylor

Marochka Taylor designed costumes for a Broadway play in 1940.

Costumes: 1940 *Fledgling* (Clothes)

Morris Taylor

Morris Taylor is the pseudonym that
Buddy Sheffield used for his design
and technical work with the Sheffield
Ensemble Theatre in Biloxi, Mississippi. SET, founded by Buddy, David
and Rita Sheffield in 1972, received
many honors including the Jennie Hei-
den Award for Excellence in Children's
Theatre. Sheffield's designs, as Morris Taylor, included the scenery for
Bananas, Beans, Feats and *Videosyn-
crasies.* When David Sheffield moved
to New York to write for *Saturday
Night Live,* Buddy and Rita Sheffield
went to California, to write for television and movies. They created, produced and wrote *Roundhouse* for four
seasons on Nickelodeon. He was also
the head writer for the first two seasons of *In Living Color* and then became executive consultant for the Fox
Television series.
Sets: 1982 *Cleavage*

Noel Taylor

Noel Taylor, originally from Youngs-
town, Ohio, was born on January 17,
1917, and studied in France. He first
worked in the theater as an actor and
playwright, appearing in stock productions, and in *Reunion in Vienna* on
Broadway in 1931. His first Broadway costume activity was for featured
players in 1946 and as a costume supervisor. Since that time he has designed costumes for numerous shows
on Broadway and the West Coast, including the Mark Taper Forum. He
also designed for several television series, variety shows and approximately
60 productions on the Hallmark Hall
of Fame. Taylor won a Maharam
Award in 1966 for his costume designs for *Gnadige Fraulein* and *Slapstick Tragedy.* Twenty-first century
credits include *Women in Black* at the
Minetta Lane Theatre.
Costumes: 1946 *A Family Affair* (Costume Supervisor, Miss Curtis' suit); *The
Haven* (Costume Supervisor) **1947** *Alice
in Wonderland and Through the Looking
Glass* **1951** *Stalag 17*; *Twentieth Century* **1952** *Bernadine*; *Dial "M" for Murder*; *The Grey Eyed People*; *The Male
Animal*; *One Bright Day* **1953** *In the*
Summer House; *The Ladies of the Cor-
ridor*; *The Teahouse of the August Moon*
1954 *The Burning Glass*† **1955** *Festival*;
No Time for Sergeants **1956** *The Apple
Cart*; *Auntie Mame*†; *Time Limit* **1957**
Good As Gold; *The Square Root of Won-
derful* **1958** *The Body Beautiful*; *Maria
Golovin* **1959** *Tall Story* **1960** *Little
Moon of Alban*; *The Wall* **1961** *Every-
body Loves Opal*; *General Seeger*; *Great
Day in the Morning*; *The Night of the
Iguana*; *A Shot in the Dark*; *Write Me a
Murder* **1963** *Marathon '33*; *One Flew
over the Cuckoo's Nest*; *The Riot Act*;
Strange Interlude† **1964** *Hughie*; *What
Makes Sammy Run?* **1965** *And Things
That Go Bump in the Night* **1966** *The
Great Indoors*; *The Loves of Cass Mc
Guire*; *Slapstick Tragedy*; *We Have Al-
ways Lived in the Castle* **1967** *Dr. Cook's
Garden*; *Song of the Grasshopper* **1968**
We Bombed in New Haven **1969** *The
Mundy Scheme* **1970** *Brightower*; *Ovid's
Metamorphoses* **1972** *A Funny Thing
Happened on the Way to the Forum*; *The
Last of Mrs. Lincoln*; *Mourning Be-
comes Electra* **1975** *The Norman Con-
quests* **1976** *The Night of the Iguana*
1977 *Chapter Two* **1978** *Paul Robeson*;
Vincent Price in Diversions and Delights
1980 *Mixed Couples* **1991** *Lucifer's Child*
1994 *The Glass Menagerie* **1997** *The
Gin Game*; *The Sunshine Boys*

Robert U. Taylor

Robert U. Taylor was born in 1941
in Lexington, Pennsylvania. He studied at the University of Pennsylvania, the Pennsylvania Academy of Fine
Arts and the Yale University School of
Drama. He has taught at Hunter College and Princeton. Since his Broadway debut he has designed for many of
the foremost regional theaters, including the Goodman, McCarter Theater
Center and Guthrie Theatres, among
others. He received a Drama Desk and
Maharam Award for *Beggars' Opera* in
1972. As design coordinator he designed many productions for the Colon-
nades Theatre Lab in the 1970s including *A Month in the Country.* He
has also worked with the Chelsea Theatre Group and the off-off-Broadway
Greek Theatre. He has devoted increasing attention to art direction of

television commercials, including advertisements for Anacin, Canada Dry, Charmin, Nyquil and Scott Paper.
Sets: 1971 *Unlikely Heroes* 1973 *The Beggar's Opera*†; *Raisin* 1974 *Lamppost Reunion* 1975 *Boccaccio* 1977 *Happy End*

Suzanne Taylor

Suzanne Taylor servedas costume consultant for a Broadway play in 1964. In 1958, she worked as a wardrobe consultant to Edith Head on the Broadway production of *The Pleasure of His Company*.
Costumes: 1964 *Beeckman Place* (Clothes Consultant)

Julie Taymor

Born in 1952 in Newton, Massachusetts, Julie Taymor's interest in puppets and mythology began when she was very young, staging shows in the backyard and performing with the Boston Children's Theatre and the Theatre Workshop of Boston. She graduated from Oberlin College where she studied with Herbert Blau and then traveled. Staying in Indonesia for nearly five years, she formed a company, Teatr Loh, and with them created her first major work: *Way of Snow*, using Balinese and Javanese mask and puppet forms. When she returned to the United States she began designing and in the mid-1980s started directing, often incorporating puppet forms into her productions. Much honored for her creativity, she received a MacArthur Foundation Grant and a Tony Award for the costumes for *The Lion King*. Her designs and creations have been widely exhibited, and are the subject of two books, *Julie Taymor, Playing with Fire* and *The Lion King: Pride Rock on Broadway*. Twenty-first century credits include *The King Stag*.
Sets: 1996 *Juan Darién: A Carnival Mass*† 2000 *The Green Bird*† (Also masks and puppets)
Costumes: 1996 *Juan Darién: A Carnival Mass*† 1997 *The Lion King*

Paul Tazewell

Paul Tazewell, originally from Baltimore, Maryland, completed his B.F.A. at the North Carolina School of the Arts in 1986, and his M.F.A. from New York University in 1989. His costume designs are often seen at the Goodman Theatre, the Joseph Papp Public Theatre, the Guthrie Theatre, Center Stage and Hartford Stage. Honors include a Tony Award nomination for *Bring in 'da Noise, Bring in 'da Funk*, a Michael Merritt Award for Excellence in Design and Collaboration, a Helen Hayes Award for Arena Stage's *The African Company Presents 'Richard III'*, and the 1997 Young Master Award from Theatre Development Fund. Twenty-first century designs include the ballet *Resurrection* and *Once Around the City* for Second Stage Theatre.
Costumes: 1996 *Bring in 'da Noise, Bring in 'da Funk* 1998 *On the Town* 1999 *The Gershwins' Fascinating Rhythm*

John Tedesco

John Tedesco was born in New York City on October 13, 1948, the son of Pasquale and Marie Tedesco. He studied at New York University, receiving a B.F.A. in theater in 1970, and acknowledges Jules Fisher as his mentor. He has designed productions in New York City since his 1971 debut, *The House of Blue Leaves*. He was responsible for the 1986 lighting design of the Statue of Liberty, designed and supplied special effects for the Han River Festival opening ceremonies of the 1988 Olympics in Seoul, South Korea, and did the Anaheim arena lighting for the movie *The Mighty Ducks*. He is the owner of Phoebus Lighting in San Francisco.
Lights: 1972 *Grease* 1973 *Bette Midler*

Edith Teets

Edith Teets supervised costumes for a 1936 Broadway play.
Costumes: 1936 *The Fields Beyond* (Women's Costume Supervisor)

Charles Teichner

Charles Teichner designed scenery for Broadway plays between 1928 and 1930 under his own name and through his scenic studio. Born on December 14, 1899, he worked primarily as a scenic artist and resided with his wife Martha at 735 Mace Avenue, New York City in 1933. He died in Miami, Florida in September 1974.

Sets: **1928** *Parisiana* (as: Charles Teichner Studios) **1930** *Dora Mobridge*

Joseph Teichner

Joseph Teichner was active on Broadway during the 1920s under his own name and through his studio, Joseph Teichner Scenic Studios. He was born in Gyoma, Hungary on February 18, 1888 and studied painting with J. Carlson and at the National Academy of Design. Joseph Teichner received credit for productions under various spellings of his name, including Josef Tichenor and Joseph Tickner. He died in Fresno, California on June 14, 1966.

Sets: **1925** *Earl Carroll's Vanities*[†]; *Florida Girl*[†] **1927** *Babbling Brooks*; *The Bottom of the Cup*; *Junk*; *What Do We Know?*

Joseph Teichner Studio

Joseph Teichner (1888-1966) operated a scenic studio at 314 Eleventh Avenue in the 1920s. In the early 1930s, in association with Armin and Bertha Teichner, and Frank W. Stevens, Joseph Teichner Studios was located at 152 West 46th Street. In addition to theatrical work the firm also provided services as interior decorators. For additional information, see "Joseph Teichner" and "Pogany-Teichner Studios."

Sets: **1927** *Africana*[†] **1929** *Earl Carroll's Sketch Book*[†] **1932** *Girls in Uniform*; *Tell Her the Truth* **1933** *Man Bites Dog* **1934** *Caviar*[†]

M. Teitelman

M. Teitelman collaborated on the costume designs for a Broadway musical in 1931. The production featured music by Harry Lubin and Joseph Rumshinsky with a book by Boris and Harry Thomashefsky.

Costumes: **1931** *The Singing Rabbi*[†]

W. L. Telbin

British scenic artist and painter William Lewis Telbin was born into a family of scenic artists in 1846 and had a long and successful career in the major London theaters, including Drury Lane, the Alhambra Palace Theatre, and the Lyceum Theatre from 1878-1898, among others. He was widely regarded for his ability to paint intricate drapery and was one of Henry Irving's favorite designers. Both W. L. and his elder brother Henry (d. 1866) learned to paint from their father, William T. Telbin (1813-1873), one of the best known mid-nineteenth century scenic artists. All three family members were also fine art painters. W. L. Telbin's nineteenth century credits in America include *Henry VIII* in 1878 on Broadway and *Claudian* in Brooklyn's Park Theatre, among many others for Henry Irving and Herbert Beerbohm Tree's tours. He died at Twyford Abbey, Park Royal, London on December 3, 1931 at age 85.

Sets: **1899** *The Merchant of Venice*[†] **1900** *The Man of Forty*[†] **1906** *Paolo and Francesca* **1907** *The Merchant of Venice*[†]

Lou Tellegen

Lou Tellegen (Lou-Tellegen) was born Isidor Louis Bernard van Dammeler in St. Oedenrode, Netherlands on November 26, 1883. He made his stage debut in 1903 and soon after moved to Paris where he appeared often with Sarah Bernhardt. He toured with her to America in 1910 and made his London debut with her in 1912. Between the opening of *Mama Rosa* in 1914 at the Longacre Theatre and 1931, he appeared steadily on the New York stage. He also acted in and directed movies. His autobiography, *Women Have Been Kind* was published in 1931. Tellegen died in Los Angeles, California on October 29, 1934.

Costumes: **1914** *Maria Rosa* (Also starred)

Rouben Ter-Arutunian

Rouben Ter-Arutunian, a scenic and costume designer, was born on July 24, 1920 in Tiflis, Georgia, Russia. He studied concert piano in Berlin and art in both Berlin and Paris. His first design was for *The Bartered Bride* in Dresden in 1941, followed by costumes for the Berlin State Opera Ballet. In 1951 he moved to the United States, becoming a citizen in 1957. His extensive designs included scenery, costumes, and occasionally lights for ballets, operas and theaters in the United

States and around the world. He was staff designer for all three major television networks and also designed variety shows and specials. Mr. Ter-Arutunian received an Emmy Award for art direction in 1957 for *Twelfth Night*, an Outer Critics Circle Award for *Who Was that Lady I Saw You With?* in 1958, as well as a Tony Award for costume design for *Redhead* in 1959. A large collection of his theatrical designs are in the Jerome Robbins Dance Division of the New York Public Library for the Performing Arts at Lincoln Center. He died on October 17, 1992 at age 72.

Sets: 1957 *New Girl in Town* 1958 *Maria Golovin*; *Who Was That Lady I Saw You With?* 1959 *Redhead* 1960 *Advise and Consent* 1961 *Donnybrook!* 1962 *A Passage to India* 1963 *Arturo Ui*; *Hot Spot* 1964 *The Deputy*; *The Milk Train Doesn't Stop Here Anymore* 1965 *The Devils* 1966 *Ivanov* 1968 *Exit the King*; *I'm Solomon* 1969 *The Dozens* 1971 *All Over* 1975 *Goodtime Charley* 1976 *Days in the Trees*; *The Lady from the Sea* 1980 *Goodbye Fidel*; *The Lady from Dubuque*

Costumes: 1957 *New Girl in Town* (Design by) 1959 *Redhead* 1961 *Donnybrook!* (Design by) 1962 *A Passage to India* (Design by) 1963 *Arturo Ui*; *Hot Spot* 1964 *The Milk Train Doesn't Stop Here Anymore* (Design by) 1966 *Ivanov* 1969 *The Dozens* 1971 *All Over* 1976 *Days in the Trees*; *The Lady from the Sea*

Lights: 1957 *New Girl in Town* 1963 *Arturo Ui*

Max Teuber

Max Teuber designed lights in 1929 and scenery in 1933 on Broadway. He was born in Germany on June 6, 1879. Upon emigrating to America, he worked mainly as a theatrical producer in New York City. He both lived and worked from 203 West 103rd Street. Teuber died in Los Angeles, California on January 8, 1960.

Sets: 1933 *Murder at the Vanities*
Lights: 1929 *Earl Carroll's Sketch Book*

Cheryl Thacker

Cheryl Thacker is from Birmingham, Alabama, where she was born on August 18, 1948. She received a B.A.

at Birmingham Southern College in 1970 (cum laude, Phi Beta Kappa) and an M.F.A. from New York University Tisch School of the Arts in theater design in 1973. Her New York debut was the lighting design for the Laura Foreman Dance Company in 1973 at the American Laboratory Theatre. She designed lighting for more than fifty off- and off-off-Broadway productions including *Fugue in a Nursery* (Orpheum), *Say Goodnight, Gracie* (Actors' Playhouse, *The Club* (Circle in the Square), *The Shortchanged Review* (Mitzi Newhouse), and *When You Comin' Back, Red Ryder?* at the Eastside Playhouse. In recent years most of her work has been in television. She was staff lighting director at NBC-TV for fourteen years where she lit the first one thousand episodes of *Late Night with David Letterman*. Now incorporated as The Lighting Unit, Inc., her twenty-first century credits include *The Irish Tenors* at Ellis Island (PBS-TV), *Four Seasons/American Seasons*, *Newsmakers of the Year Awards 2000*, and *Inside the Law* for NYU School of Law which airs on over 150 PBS stations.

Lights: 1976 *The Runner Stumbles* 1977 *Unexpected Guests*

Forrest Thayer

Forrest Thayer, Jr. attended Parsons School of Design and worked as an assistant to costume designer Ellen Goldsborough. He first designed costumes on Broadway in the late 1940s. He died at age 32 on October 1, 1951.

Costumes: 1949 *The Smile of the World*† 1950 *The Live Wire*

Peggy Thayer

Peggy Thayer designed costumes for a 1944 Broadway show. She also performed in plays including *The Marriage Tax* and *Girls from Quakertown*. Her father, John Borland Taylor, vice president of the Pennsylvania Railroad, died on the Titanic. Peggy Thayer, an active sportswoman, was married to Harold E. Talbott. Born on March 16, 1916, she died in July 1992.

Costumes: 1944 *The Man Who Had All the Luck*† (Miss Eugenia Rawl's costumes)

Clara Fargo Thomas

Muralist Mrs. Clara Fargo Thomas was born in Bedford, New York, and studied in Paris. Her father, James M. Fargo was a member of the Wells Fargo family and developed the American Express Traveler's Check. She painted her first mural was when her son, Joseph Thomas, Jr. was born and she redecorated his room. She subsequently painted murals for many public buildings in the twenties and thirties and also for private residences, as well as designed scenery and furniture. Commissions included projects for the Grosvenor House Hotel in London, the Chicago Tribune Building, and Elizabeth Arden's country home. Widely exhibited, her studio was located on East 19th Street, New York City. She died in Mount Desert Island, Maine on April 26, 1970.

Sets: 1924 *The Second Mrs. Tanqueray* **1928** *The High Road*

Frank D. Thomas

Frank D. Thomas designed lights for a 1917 Broadway production. A specialist in stage effects and novelties, his business was located in Room 506 at 1547 Broadway, New York City during the teens and twenties. He lived in East Orange, New Jersey.

Sets: 1911 *The Revue of Revues*† (Battleship effect)
Lights: 1917 *Going Up*

Hugh S. Thomas

Hugh S. Thomas designed lights for two Broadway productions during the first decade of the twentieth century.

Lights: 1905 *The Raiders* **1909** *Springtime*

Susan Thomas

Susan Thomas, Inc. produced designs for exclusive women's clothing. Founded in 1947 by William B. Thomas and his father, Victor Tomshinsky, the business started as a small custom salon catering to private customers and theatrical performers. It flourished until 1968 when Susan Thomas, Inc. became part of Genesco. Thomas then formed Vivanti Sportswear with his sons. A long time resident of Englewood, New Jersey, he

died in Durham, North Carolina at age 66 on November 9, 1985.

Costumes: 1956 *Sixth Finger in a Five Finger Glove*† (Women's clothes)

William Thomas

William Thomas designed lights in the 1920s and 1940s on Broadway. It is possible that the lighting designer active in 1924 is different than the one active in 1945. The lighting designer(s) shouldnot be confused with Bill Thomas, originally William Thomas Peterson (1920-2000) who designed costumes for movies.

Lights: 1924 *Marjorie* **1945** *A Lady Says Yes; Many Happy Returns*

Frank Thompson

Frank Thompson, part Cherokee Indian, was born in Shawnee, Oklahoma and studied at the University of California. He designed costumes for theater, film, ballet and opera starting in 1947 with *Louisiana Lady* on Broadway. He created costumes for television specials and spent five years as Miles White's assistant on costumes for Ringling Bros. and Barnum & Bailey Circus. Shortly before his death on June 4, 1977, Mr. Thompson designed the costumes for *The Nutcracker* choreographed by Mikhail Baryshnikov for the American Ballet Theatre.

Costumes: 1947 *Louisiana Lady* (Costume Supervisor) **1948** *The Linden Tree*; *The Rape of Lucretia* (Costume Supervisor) **1953** *Late Love*; *The Little Hut* (Costume Supervisor) **1954** *His and Hers* **1957** *Nature's Way*; *Nude with Violin* **1958** *Present Laughter*† **1959** *Moonbirds*; *The Tenth Man* **1960** *Viva Madison Avenue* **1961** *How to Make a Man* **1962** *Harold*; *The Perfect Setup* **1963** *The Irregular Verb to Love*; *Photo Finish* **1964** *Never Live over a Pretzel Factory* **1965** *The Zulu and the Zayda* **1966** *Annie Get Your Gun* **1970** *The Gingerbread Lady*; *A Place for Polly* **1971** *Frank Merriwell (or Honor Changed)*; *Unlikely Heroes* **1972** *The Country Girl*; *Wild and Wonderful*

Frederick W. Thompson

Frederick W. Thompson was born in Nashville, Tennessee (one source suggests Ironton, Ohio) in 1872, studied to be an architect, and spent the majority of career in management. He created Luna Park, making Coney Island a major attraction, and then produced spectacles at the New York Hippodrome. He also wrote, produced and directed plays, and for some of them, designed scenery. His Broadway shows included *Brewster's Millions, Polly of the Circus* and *A Fool There Was*. The *My Man* playbill refers to the scenery as built and painted in "Frederick Thompson's Luna Park Studios." A flamboyant businessman, he madeand lost several fortunes during his lifetime. He died on June 6, 1919 at age 47.

Sets: 1905 *The Raiders*† (Also wrote); *A Yankee Circus on Mars*† (Also wrote) 1906 *Brewster's Millions*† 1908 *Via Wireless* (Also wrote)

Mark Thompson

British designer (Owen) Mark Thompson was born April 12, 1957. His B. A., with honors in drama and theater arts was awarded at Radley College, Birmingham University. His early professional designs were for regional theater and opera companies throughout the United Kingdom. Since the late 1980s, he has designed principally in London's West End, for the Royal Shakespeare Company, the Royal National Theatre and in major European and American theaters. His honors are numerous, and include Olivier Awards for both sets and costumes for *The Comedy of Errors* and for *Joseph and the Amazing Technicolor Dreamcoat*, and set design for *Hysteria* and *The Wind in the Willows*. Twenty-first century designs includes *Life x 3*, and sets and costumes for *Mamma Mia!* in the 2001-2002 Broadway season.

Sets: 1990 *Shadowlands* 1993 *Joseph and the Amazing Technicolor Dreamcoat* 1995 *Arcadia* 1998 *Art*; *The Blue Room* 2001 *Blast!*; *Follies*
Costumes: 1990 *Shadowlands* 1993 *Joseph and the Amazing Technicolor Dreamcoat* 1995 *Arcadia* 1998 *Art*; *The Blue Room* 2001 *Blast!*

Woodman Thompson

Woodman Thompson was a scenic designer who also created costumes and occasionally lights. Born in 1889, he began his theatrical career in 1918 and worked steadily in the theater until his death on August 30, 1955 at the age of 66. He was a member of the faculty at the Carnegie Institute of Technology when the undergraduate theater program was established, but left for New York City in 1921, a move that would prove permanent. He was resident designer for the Theatre Guild, the Actor's Theatre, and the Equity Theatre and taught design both privately and at Columbia University. A member of United Scenic Artists from 1923, he served his fellow designers as President, Vice President and Treasurer at various times.

Sets: 1922 *Malvaloca*; *The Rivals*; *Why Not?* 1923 *The Business Widow*; *The Chastening*; *Neighbors*; *Queen Victoria*; *Roger Bloomer*; *Sweet Nell of Old Drury* 1924 *The Admiral*; *Beggar on Horseback*; *Candida*; *Close Harmony*; *Expressing Willie*; *The Firebrand*; *The Habitual Husband*; *Hedda Gabler*; *Macbeth*; *Marjorie*; *Minick*; *The New Englander*; *What Price Glory?* 1925 *Beggar on Horseback*; *Candida*; *The Cocoanuts* 1926 *The Desert Song*; *God Loves Us*; *Hedda Gabler*; *The Importance of Being Earnest*; *Iolanthe*; *The Pirates of Penzance*; *The Shelf*; *White Wings* 1927 *Iolanthe*; *The Pirates of Penzance* 1928 *The Merchant of Venice*; *These Few Ashes* 1929 *A Primer for Lovers* 1930 *The Merchant of Venice*; *Midnight*; *This One Man* 1932 *Dangerous Corner*; *The Warrior's Husband* 1933 *Dangerous Corner* 1934 *Lady Jane* 1935 *The Bishop Misbehaves*; *Tomorrow's a Holiday* 1936 *Plumes in the Dust* 1937 *Candida*; *The Ghost of Yankee Doodle* 1942 *Candida* 1946 *Candida*; *Hear the Trumpet*; *Magnificent Yankee*
Costumes: 1922 *Malvaloca* 1923 *Neighbors*; *Queen Victoria*; *Sweet Nell of Old Drury* 1924 *Beggar on Horseback*; *The Firebrand*; *Hedda Gabler* 1925 *Beggar on Horseback*; *Candida* 1926 *Iolanthe*; *The Pirates of Penzance*; *The Shelf* 1928 *The Merchant of Venice* 1930 *The Merchant of Venice* 1932 *The Warrior's Husband* 1936 *Plumes in the Dust* 1937 *Candida* 1942 *Candida* 1946 *Hear the Trumpet*; *Magnificent Yankee*
Lights: 1926 *The Shelf* 1936 *Plumes in the Dust* 1946 *Hear the Trumpet*

Brian Thomson

Australian scenic designer Brian Thomson was born in Sydney on January 5,1946. He studied architecture before starting to work in the theater, beginning with *Tommy* in 1970. His credits in Australia and the United Kingdom are numerous, especially since the early 1970s when he began collaborating with director Jim Sharman, initially with *Hair* and *Jesus Christ Superstar*. Since then he has designed plays, operas, musicals, films and special events. Among his many credits for opera are *Death in Venice* in 1980 and *Tristan und Isolde* in 1990 for the State Opera of South Australia. He served as production designer for the closing ceremonies of the Sydney 2000 Olympic Games and also designed the medal podiums. Honors include a Tony Award for *The King and I*.
Sets: 1975 *The Rocky Horror Show* 1995 *The King and I* 1996 *The King and I*

Clarke W. Thornton

Clarke W. Thornton is active in regional theaters and has designed the national tours of *Man of La Mancha, Fiddler on the Roof*, and *Anything Goes*. He designed *Gotta Getaway* and other productions at Radio City Music Hall as well as productions off-Broadway. For three years he was resident designer for the Dance Theatre of Harlem. He is also a consultant for new and renovated theaters.
Lights: 1979 *A Meeting in the Air*

Mary C. Thornton

Mary C. Thornton was born in Hamilton, Ontario, Canada in 1916. Her parents emigrated to Canada from Ascoli Piceno, Italy and she studied in both Ontario and Italy. She apprenticed with ceramics and fabrics artisans. After considering a career as an opera singer, she became wardrobe mistress for the Hamilton Opera Company. Since 1974, she has been associated, as scenic and costume designer with Famous People Players, whose artistic director is her daughter, Diana Dupuy.

Sets: 1986 *A Little Like Magic* 1994 *A Little More Magic* (Visual arts effects)
Costumes: 1986 *A Little Like Magic* 1994 *A Little More Magic* (Visual arts effects)

Cleon Throckmorton

Cleon Throckmorton was supposed to play a part in the premiere of Eugene O'Neill's play *The Emperor Jones* at the Provincetown Players, but ended up designing the setting. "Throck" was born October 18, 1896 in Atlantic City, New Jersey. After earning a degree in engineering he studied design at the Carnegie Institute of Technology and George Washington University. He designed hundreds of plays during his career, and although his name is not as well known as his contemporary Robert Edmond Jones, he was instrumental in advancing the art and profession of scenic design. During the Depression he produced melodramas in Hoboken, New Jersey, as well as plays at the Old Rialto and The Lyric Theatre in New York City, and the Millpond Playhouse in Roslyn, Long Island. He was associated with many theater groups including the Provincetown Players, the Theatre Guild, the Neighborhood Playhouse and the Civic Repertory Theatre. Cleon Throckmorton died on October 23, 1965 at age 68 in Atlantic City, New Jersey. See Figure 12: Cleon Throckmorton: *Porgy*
Sets: 1921 *The Hand of the Potter*; *The Verge* 1922 *The God of Vengeance*; *Greenwich Village Follies*†; *The Hairy Ape*†; *Mr. Faust*; *The Old Soak*; *The Pigeon*; *The Red Geranium*; *Six Characters in Search of an Author* 1923 *Children of the Moon*; *The Potters*; *We've Got to Have Money* 1924 *All God's Chillun Got Wings*; *The Crime in the Whistler Room*; *The Emperor Jones*; *Fashion*†; *George Dandin, or the Husband Confounded*†; *S.S. Glencairn*; *Six Characters in Search of an Author*; *The Spook Sonata*†; *The Tantrum*† 1925 *Adam Solitaire*; *The Blue Peter*; *The Devil to Pay*; *The Emperor Jones / The Dreamy Kid*; *Houses of Sand*; *Lovely Lady*; *The Man Who Never Did*; *A Man's Man*; *O, Nightingale*; *Odd Man Out*; *Outside Looking in*; *Rosmersholm*; *Ruint*; *The Triumph of the Egg*; *Weak*

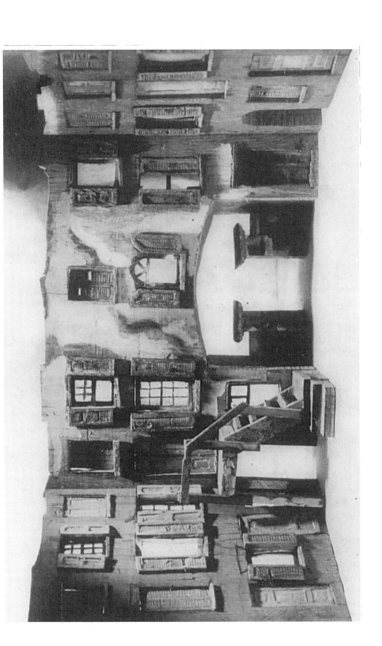

Figure 12: Cleon Throckmorton: *Porgy*: Set model design, 1927. By permission, Billy Rose Theatre Collection, The New York Public Library for the Performing Arts, Astor, Lenox and Tilden Foundations. Photograph by Jan Juracek.

Sisters; The Wise-crackers **1926** *Beyond Evil; Beyond the Horizon; Bride of the Lamb; The Dream Play; East Lynne; The Emperor Jones; In Abraham's Bosom; The Makropoulos Secret; Sandalwood; Saturday Night; The Silver Cord* (as: Cleon Throckmorton Studios) **1927** *Burlesque; Earth; The Good Hope†; In Abraham's Bosom; Inheritors; The Ivory Door; Jacob Slovak; The King Can Do No Wrong; Lovely Lady; Menace; Paradise; Porgy†; Rapid Transit; The Stairs; Triple Crossed; The Triumphant Bachelor; Wall Street* **1928** *Congai; Hot Pan; Killers; Napoleon; On Call; Patience; Rope; The Scarlet Fox; These Modern Women* **1929** *Fiesta; Getting Even; Inspector Kennedy; Man's Estate; Porgy; The Unsophisticates* **1930** *The Old Rascal; Penny Arcade; Stepping Sisters; Torch Song* **1931** *Brass Ankle; The Bride the Sun Shines On; Did I Say No?; Doctor X; Gray Shadow; Hobo; The House of Connelly; How Money; Just to Remind You; A Regular Guy; Sentinels; She Means Business; Six Characters in Search of an Author; Springtime for Henry; Two Seconds; A Widow in Green* **1932** *Another Language; Back Fire; Bulls, Bears, and Asses; Chyrasalis; Criminal at Large; The Dark Hours; Hired Husband; Monkey; The Moon in the Yellow River; The Other One; Page Pygmalion; Rendezvous; Take a Chance; The Truth about Blayds* **1933** *Alien Corn; Another Language; Birthright* (as: Cleon Throckmorton Studios); *The Comic Artist; Eight Bells; Give Us This Day; Is Life Worth Living?; Peace on Earth; Run, Little Chillun; Springtime for Henry; The Threepenny Opera†* **1934** *The Gods We Make; The Lord Bless the Bishop; Ode to Liberty; Sing and Whistle* **1935** *Bitter Oleander; Creeping Fire; Noah; Prisoners of War* **1936** *Bitter Stream; I Want a Policeman; In Heaven and Earth†; Jefferson Davis; The Lights o' London†; Searching for the Sun; A Woman of Destiny* **1937** *Curtain Call; Love in My Fashion; Without Warning* **1941** *Ghost for Sale* **1942** *Nathan the Wise*

Costumes: 1930 *Torch Song*

Nancy Thun

Daughter of Herman Thun, Jr. and Clara Ann Haberkorn, scenic designer Nancy Thun was born in Watseka, Illinois on September 27, 1952. She received a B.F.A. at the University of Illinois and an M.F.A. at the Yale University School of Drama, as well as studying at the Brighton Polytechnic Art College and Art Students League. In addition to amassing numerous credits on television, in major regional theaters and off-Broadway, she has assisted and been an associate designer for Ming Cho Lee and Mark Thompson, both of whom she considers mentors, and others. Her professional debut was *Orpheus in the Underworld* for the Santa Fe Opera. She has served as set designer for the daytime dramas *Another World, As the World Turns* and *Guiding Light.* Honors include the Cleveland Critics Award for the set of *Sweeney Todd.*

Sets: 1995 *Buttons on Broadway*

Jane Thurn

Jane Thurn has designed numerous off-Broadway productions at the Manhattan Theatre Club, the Vineyard Theatre, and others. She designed the set for *Silent Dancing,* the PBS documentary on the Joffrey Ballet, and was art director for the New York unit of the film *Honky Tonk Freeway.* She has an M.F.A. in scenic design from Carnegie Mellon University and has also designed television commercials.

Sets: 1981 *Scenes and Revelations*

Howard Thurston

Howard Thurston was a magician who performed in vaudeville shows and on tours. In 1913, he collaborated on a special effect with Langdon McCormick for *The Honeymoon Express.* They recorded a patent for the device that looked like an automobile racing a train. Theodore Reisig also collaborated on the scenic designs for that production. In 1935 Thurston married Pauline Martin, who danced in an act with her twin sister Irene Martin when they were young. When Mrs. Pauline Thurston died in North Adams, Massachusetts on February 10, 1943, she was a widow.

Sets: 1913 *The Honeymoon Express†*

Jan Tichacek

Jan Tichacek designed one set in 1938. An artist named Stephen Tichacek resided at 541 East 83rd Street, New York City in 1932.

Sets: 1938 *Danton's Death*

Martin Tilley

British designer Martin Tilley who received his training at the Leicester Phoenix Theatre, specializes in scenery, working in theaters around the United Kingdom. Theatrical designs include the tour of *Suez* starring Roy Dotrice and the opera *Cosi Fan Tutti* at the 1978 Oxford Festival. He has designed several productions for the King's Head in London, including *Kingdom Come* and *Catchpenny Twist*. He also creates graphic designs through McIlroy Coates in Edinburgh, where he is senior designer

Sets: 1980 *Fearless Frank* 1983 *Edmund Kean*

Costumes: 1983 *Edmund Kean*

James Tilton

James Floyd Tilton began designing while in the United States Army Special Services Division (1959-1962) becoming Resident Designer at the Frankfurt, Germany Playhouse. After his discharge in 1963 he became principal designer for the A.P.A.-Phoenix Repertory Theatre. From 1963 to 1971 he designed numerous plays for A.P.A., including the first production at the Phoenix Theatre, *Scapin*. He designed for many regional theaters, industrial promotions, and for other New York theaters. In 1970 he designed his first film, *Dear Dead Delilah*. Honors include a Tony Award nomination for *Seascape* and several Carbonelle Awards. James Tilton was born in Rochelle, Illinois on July 30, 1937 and received a B.A. at the University of Iowa in 1959. He died in East Hampton, New York in April 1998 at age 60.

Sets: 1965 *You Can't Take It with You* 1966 *Right You Are If You Think You Are*; *The School for Scandal*; *We, Comrades Three* 1967 *Pantagleize*; *The Show-Off*; *War and Peace*; *The Wild Duck*; *You Can't Take It with You* 1968 *The Cherry Orchard*; *The Cocktail Party*; *The Misanthrope*; *Pantagleize*; *The Show-Off* 1969 *Cock-a-doodle Dandy*; *Hamlet*; *Private Lives* 1970 *Harvey* 1971 *The Grass Harp*; *Oh! Calcutta!*; *The School for Wives* 1975 *Seascape* 1976 *Comedians†*; *Oh! Calcutta!* 1977 *Vieux Carre* 1981 *Twice around the Park* 1983 *You Can't Take It with You*

Lights: 1965 *You Can't Take It with You* 1967 *Pantagleize*; *The Show-Off* 1968 *The Cherry Orchard*; *The Cocktail Party*; *Exit the King*; *The Misanthrope*; *Pantagleize*; *The Show-Off* 1969 *Cock-a-doodle Dandy*; *Hamlet*; *Private Lives* 1970 *Harvey* 1971 *The Grass Harp*; *The School for Wives* 1975 *Seascape* 1977 *Vieux Carre* 1983 *You Can't Take It with You*

Hal Tiné

Hal Tiné has designed scenery for over one hundred forty productions New York, regional theater, opera and Broadway productions. He was born in Cambridge, Massachusetts on July 24, 1943 and studied stage design under Oren Parker at Carnegie Mellon University, graduating in 1968 after spending a season as design intern at the Guthrie Theatre. Career influences include Tyrone Guthrie, Tanya Moiseiwitsch, Peter Wexler and Ming Cho Lee. Mr. Tiné began his professional career off-Broadway in 1972 and worked at among others, Alice Tully Hall, Carnegie Hall, Circle-in-the-Square, Actors Playhouse, the Guthrie Theatre, Long Wharf Theatre, Actors Theatre of Louisville, Studio Arena, and Syracuse Stage. With Peter Wexler he worked on the Metropolitan Opera's 1973 production of *LesTroyens* and was associate designer for the Met's *Le Prophete* and *Un Ballo in Maschera*, as well as the Carlos Mosley Pavilion. Additional credits include New York Grand Opera, *Saturday Night Live*, *Good Morning, America*, *ABC World News* and *20/20*. With his company, Pinxit, and Peter Wexler, he has also designed several museum and media-based exhibits. Since 1986 he has been head of the set design program at the Conservatory of Theatre Arts and Film, Purchase College, State University of New York.

Sets: 1977 *The Trip Back Down* 1985 *Jerry's Girls*

Ben Tipton

Ben Tipton designed scenery for a 1949 Broadway production.
Sets: 1949 *Ken Murray's Blackout of 1949*

Jennifer Tipton

Few contemporary lighting designers have the versatility of Jennifer Tipton, who designs not only for theater but for dance and opera as well. She was born in Columbus, Ohio on September 11, 1937 and received a B.A. at Cornell University in 1958. Though initially a dance student at Connecticut College, she studied lighting design under Thomas Skelton. Her first design was a dance piece by Pauline De Groot at the Connecticut College School of Dance. She began her professional career with Paul Taylor and Twyla Tharp and has designed for most major modern and ballet companies and choreographers. Her theater design includes productions in the major regional theaters, and in London's West End, the Spoleto Festival in Italy and the Netherlands Dans Theatre. She maintains an ongoing collaboration with Robert Wilson for whom she has designed *CIVIL warS*, *Alcestes*, and *Hamletmachine* at the Lyric Opera of Chicago and *Parsifal* at the Hamburg Opera. Her designs have been much honored: Tony Awards for *Jerome Robbins' Broadway* and *The Cherry Orchard*, two Drama Desks, Obie Awards, Bessie Awards, the 1989 American Theatre Wing Design Award, a Brandeis Arts Award, Medal in Dance, Joseph Jefferson Awards, a Kudo Award, a Commonwealth Award, a 1991 *Dance Magazine* Award, an Olivier Award, a Guggenheim, and the National Endowment of the Arts Distinguished Theatre Artist Award in 1991. In 2001, she received the Dorothy and Lillian Gish Prize. Twenty-first century designs include *The Seagull* at the Delacorte Theatre and the 2001 premiere of Twyla Tharp's *Westerly Round* at Jacob's Pillow.
Lights: 1969 *Our Town* 1975 *Habeas Corpus*; *Murder among Friends* 1976 *For Colored Girls Who Have Considered Suicide*; *Rex* 1977 *The Cherry Orchard*; *Happy End* 1978 *Runaways* 1979 *Bosoms and Neglect*; *The Goodbye People* 1980 *Lunch Hour* 1981 *The Pirates of Penzance*; *Sophisticated Ladies* 1982 *Alice in Wonderland*; *The Wake of Jamie Foster* 1984 *Hurlyburly*; *Whoopi Goldberg* 1985 *Singin' in the Rain* 1988 *Ah, Wilderness!*; *Long Day's Journey into Night* 1989 *Jerome Robbins' Broadway* 1991 *La Bête* 1993 *In the Summer House* 2000 *James Joyce's The Dead*; *Wrong Mountain*

Raymond Tomlinson

Raymond Tomlinson designed costumes for a 1927 Broadway play. The costume designer should not be confused with the biochemist who has the same name.
Costumes: 1927 *Lace Petticoat*

Carl Toms

Carl Toms, a British designer of sets and costumes, was born on May 29, 1927 (1929 is sometimes cited) in Kirkby-in-Ashfield, England and studied at the Mansfield College of Art, the Royal College of Art and the Old Vic Theatre School. His mentors were Margaret Harris (Motley) and Oliver Messel, whom he assisted for six years. His stage creations were seen extensively in theater, opera and films after his debut, *The Apollo de Bellac*, at the Royal Court in 1957. When the Young Vic Company was established he was appointed Head of Design and Associate Director. He worked often in London's West End and at the Royal National Theatre. In 1967 he received the Order of the British Empire (O.B.E.) and won both a Tony Award and Drama Desk Award in 1975 for his set for *Sherlock Holmes*, originally produced by the Royal Shakespeare Company. He also received the Laurence Olivier Award in 1981 for *The Provoked Wife* at the Royal National Theatre and a 1984 Drama Logue Award in Hollywood. In 1987 he became a Fellow of the Royal Society of Arts. He died at age 72 on August 4, 1999 in Hertfordshire, England.
Sets: 1970 *Sleuth* 1972 *Vivat! Vivat Regina!* 1974 *Scapino*; *Sherlock Holmes*;

Travesties 1975 *Habeas Corpus* 1979
Night and Day 1996 *An Ideal Husband*
Costumes: 1970 *Sleuth* 1972 *Vivat!*
Vivat Regina! 1974 *Scapino*; *Sherlock*
Holmes; *Travesties* 1975 *Habeas Corpus*
1979 *Night and Day* 1996 *An Ideal Husband*

David Toser

David Toser was born in Milwaukee, Wisconsin and received a B.A. at Brown and an M.F.A. at Yale Drama School. He received related training at Parsons School of Design, the Art Students League, and at the Rhode Island School of Design. Further training came from assisting Raoul Pène Du Bois, Miles White, Willa Kim and Florence Klotz. He made his debut on Broadway in 1968 with two productions opening at the same time. An active regional theater designer, he has done fifty-two shows for the Goodspeed Opera House, seventeen for the Pittsburgh Public Theatre, six for A.C.T., plus many more. He designed costumes for the last fourteen *Tony Award Shows*, for two *Comic Relief* shows, and three PBS-TV specials. His credits also include more than 300 industrial shows. "In Costume Inc." in New York City is Mr. Toser's costume rental business.

Costumes: 1968 *The Great White Hope*; *Noel Coward's Sweet Potato* 1969 *Does a Tiger Wear a Necktie?*; *Our Town* 1973 *Status Quo Vadis* 1975 *Very Good, Eddie* 1976 *Going Up* 1979 *Whoopee* 1985 *Take Me Along* 1986 *Oh Coward!*

Johanna Town

Johanna Town designs lights throughout the United Kingdom, and in London's fringe and West End theaters. She designed lights for the British tour of *Top Girls*. Among her credits in the United States are *Out Lady of Sligo* for the Irish Repertory Theatre, *The Steward of Christendom* at the Brooklyn Academy of Music and *Some Explicit Polaroids* at Smith College. Late twentieth century credits include *Sliding with Suzanne*, *Feelgood*, *Spinning into Butter* and *Rita, Sue and Bob, Too* in London.

Lights: 2000 *Rose*

Ethel Traphagen

Ethel Traphagen established the first school of fashion in the U.S., the Traphagen School of Fashion, in 1923. She was a central force in making the United States a fashion center, utilizing designs and fabrics produced in the U.S. She was born in New York City on October 10, 1882, and studied at the National Academy of Design and at Cooper Union, where she won design prizes. She started teaching in 1910 and during her career as an educator, fashion designer and author exerted a major influence on costume and fashion designers. She died on April 29, 1963 in New York City.

Costumes: 1919 *39 East*

Michael Travis

Michael Travis made his debut as a costume designer on Broadway in 1958 after beginning in stock productions in the mid-1950s. He was born Louis Torakis on April 13, 1928 in Detroit, Michigan, and studied in Paris. He has designed many productions in the theater on- and off-Broadway, and in regional theaters. Television productions include *Rowan & Martin's Laugh-In*. He also designed for Liberace for thirteen years, and did concert costumes for Eartha Kitt, Judy Garland, and Dionne Warwick, among others. He should not be confused with the character actor (d. 1994) nor the environmental scientist who share the same name.

Costumes: 1958 *Once More, with Feeling*† (Men's clothes); *Portofino*; *Third Best Sport*† 1959 *Happy Town* 1960 *Rape of the Belt*† 1961 *Blood, Sweat and Stanley Poole*; *A Cook for Mr. General*; *Rhinoceros* 1962 *Come on Strong*† 1963 *The Advocate* 1964 *I Was Dancing*; *Roar Like a Dove* 1967 *How to Be a Jewish Mother* 1974 *The Fifth Dimension*

Mildred Trebor

Mildred Morse Trebor designed costumes for productions at the Theatre Guild, and then on Broadway in the early 1950s. She spent the majority of her professional career designing daytime dramas for CBS-TV and NBC-TV. Born in 1911, she died on June 28, 1993.

Costumes: 1951 *Legend of Lovers* 1952
Seagulls over Sorrento; *Venus Observed*[†]
1953 *Picnic*

Dolly Tree

Dolly Tree (born Dorothy Tree) spent
the majority of her career as a costume
designer in England designing musical
revues and then in the film industry in
California. Her numerous movies between 1930 and 1942 include *Babes in
Arms*, *Hullabaloo*, and *Two Girls on
Broadway*. Between these two associations, she lived in New York City,
primarily working for Brooks Costume
Company with Charles Le Maire. She
was born in Westbury-upon-Tryme,
England in 1899 and died in 1962.
Costumes: 1928 *Diamond Lil*; *Pleasure
Man* 1929 *How's Your Health* (Act II
costumes) 1930 *The International Review*[†]

James Trittipo

James Trittipo was known mainly as a
set designer and art director for television. He was born in Ohio and graduated from the Carnegie Institute of
Technology. He began designing for
television in its' early days, for both
live variety shows and dramatic productions. The recipient of three Emmy
Awards for his designs for *Hollywood
Palace*, which he designed for eight
years, he also worked in theater on the
West Coast. As a set designer his work
on Broadway included *On the Town*
and *A Funny Thing Happened on the
Way to the Forum* which he designed
just prior to his death in 1971 at the
age of 43.
Sets: 1962 *The Captains and the Kings*
1970 *Ovid's Metamorphoses* 1971 *On the
Town* 1972 *A Funny Thing Happened on
the Way to the Forum*
Costumes: 1962 *The Captains and the
Kings*
Lights: 1962 *The Captains and the
Kings*

Princess Troubetsky

Princess Troubetsky (also known as
Amelie Rives) was born in Richmond,
Virginia on August 23, 1863, the
daughter of Sadie McMurdo Rives and
Colonel Alfred Landon Rives. Raised
in Alabama, she studied art in Paris.

When her first marriage ended in divorce in 1895, Oscar Wilde introduced
her to Prince Pierre Troubetsky (Trou-
betzkoy), a Russian artist who became her second husband. She was a
successful romantic fiction writer and
playwright. Several of her plays were
produced including four on Broadway:
Prince and the Pauper (1920), *Love-in-
a-Mist* (1926), *Allegiance* (1918) and
The Fear Market (1916), for which she
also designed the set. She died at age
81 on June 15, 1945 in Charlottesville,
Virginia.
Sets: 1916 *The Fear Market*[†]

Hannah Troy

Hannah Troy was born in Brooklyn,
New York on February 10, 1900 (some
sources state 1905), daughter of Lewis
and Rachel Swisgold. An important American fashion designer, she
founded Hannah Troy, Inc. in 1937.
Among her innovations were importing Italian designs as early as 1951
and the Troyfigure which was her name
for petite sizing that she invented after studying measurements of women-
volunteers in the Second World War.
Her designs were carried by the leading
New York stores, including Saks Fifth
Avenue, Bergdorf Goodman, and Henri
Bendel, and worn by First Lady Pat
Nixon and Mamie van Doren, among
many others. An active member of
civic and charitable organizations, she
retired in 1968 and died on June 22,
1993 in Miami Beach, Florida at age
93.
Costumes: 1964 *One by One*[†] (Women's
clothes)

William Troy

William Troy spent 25 years as art director for the Colgate-Palmolive Company. He also worked as a consultant to
other manufacturers for product packaging. Prior to designing in industry,
he created costumes for a Broadway
show. Mr. Troy died at age 66 in June,
1965.
Costumes: 1922 *Raymond Hitchcock's
Pinwheel*[†] (Gypsy, Brigand, Faun, and
Nymph)

Tryon

Tryon collaborated on the costumes for a 1911 Broadway production. The costume designer should not be confused with Henry C. Tryon (d. 1892) who was a Boston-based scenic artist.

Costumes: **1911** *Ziegfeld Follies of 1911*†

Dean Tschetter

Dean Tschetter, who designed a production on Broadway in 1983, has also been Art Director for *Another World* on NBC-TV. He began designing in regional theaters and for opera and ballet after serving an apprenticeship at the National Opera in Munich, Germany. His designs have been honored with nominations for a Bay Area Critics Award in San Francisco for *The Passion of Dracula* and a nomination for a Maharam Award for *Goose and Tom-Tom* by David Rabe at the Public Theatre. He was art director for the 1989 film *Fright Night, Part 2*.

Sets: **1983** *Breakfast with Les and Bess*

Susan Tsu

Susan Tsu, who received both a B.F.A. and M.F.A. from Carnegie Mellon University, was born in State College, Pennsylvania. in November 1950. She has designed costumes in many major regional theaters, as well as *The Balcony* for the Bolshoi Theatre as part of a U.S./Soviet Arts Exchange and *The Joy Luck Club*, a collaboration between The Shanghai People's Art Theatre and the Long Wharf Theatre in Connecticut. Her costume designs have won many honors, including the New York Drama Desk, Drama Critics Circle and Los Angeles Distinguished Designer Awards. Susan Tsu has been David Bruton, Jr. Regents Professor of Fine Arts at the University of Texas at Austin since 1991, after heading the costume design department of the School of Theatre Arts at Boston University for eight years. Also active in professional organizations, her twenty-first century designs include *Two Sisters and a Piano* at the Oregon Shakespeare Festival, *King Lear* at the Cincinnati Playhouse, *Macbeth* at Hartford Stage, and

The Greeks, Part I at the Alley Theatre.

Costumes: **1972** *Elizabeth I* **1976** *Godspell*

George Tsypin

George Tsypin was born on January 1, 1954 in Kazakhstan, Russia and studied architecture at the Moscow Architectural Institute, earning an M.F.A. in 1977. He emigrated to the United States in 1979 and in 1984 received his second M.F.A. degree, from New York University in theater design. His sculptural scenery, seen in major regional theaters in the U.S. and opera houses throughout the world is well matched to the productions directed by his many frequent collaborators, JoAnne Akalatis, Julie Taymor, Peter Sellars, and Robert Falls, among others. His varied credits include the opera *The Death of Klinghoffer* in Brussels, the film *The Cabinet of Dr. Ramirez* and an exhibit of sculpture at the Twining gallery in New York City. The recipient of an Obie Award for sustained excellence, his twenty-first century designs include scenery for *The Gambler* at the Metropolitan Opera.

Sets: **1993** *In the Summer House*

Bert Tuchman

Identified as a carpenter in the 1904-05 New York City directory, Bert Tuchman resided at 253 West 39th Street in New York City. His last name in playbills was reproduced with these variations: Tuchman, Tucman, and Tuckman. Albert Tuchman was listed without trade in the 1917 directory, residing 850 West 179 Street.

Sets: **1904** *Girls Will Be Girls*† **1905** *King Lear*† (Production and mechanical effects); *The Marriage of William Ashe*† (Mechanical effects) **1907** *King Lear*† (Production and mechanical effects) **1909** *The Dollar Mark*† (Designed and built) **1911** *Bunty Pulls the Strings*† (Designed and built); *The Lights o' London*†; *Miss Jack*† (Design and construction); *An Old New Yorker*†; *The Rack*† (Designed and built) **1912** *Little Women*† (Designed and constructed); *Making Good*†; *The Point of View*† (Designed and built) **1913** *Divorcons*† (Set and properties); *The Things That Count*† (Designed and built) **1914** *The Charm of Isabel*[†] (Designed and built); *Don't Weaken*[†] (Designed and built)

Martin Tudor

Martin Tudor, who spent two years as an assistant to Jennifer Tipton, has designed many off-Broadway productions including *I'm Getting My Act Together and Taking It On The Road* and *Marie and Bruce.* He was born on December 17, 1954 in Jersey City, New Jersey and graduated from the Bergen School. He attended Rutgers University and studied at Lester Polakov's Studio and Forum of Stage Design. He designed Barry Manilow's European Tour and produced and designed the Meat Loaf World Tour. He is also president and executive producer of B&D Communications, a film and television production company, and served as executive producer for the made-for-television movie *Heads.*
Lights: 1977 *Miss Margarida's Way*

Richard Walton Tully

Playwright Richard Walton Tully was born in Nevada City, California on May 7, 1877. He studied at the University of California, winning the Junior Farce Contest in 1899 with his first play and graduating with a Bachelor of Law degree. He produced many of his own plays and also designed some of them. His plays, including *The Bird of Paradise, Omar the Tentmaker, The Poor Little Rich Girl* and others, were especially popular in the teens but his later works were less successful. Richard Walton Tully died on January 31, 1945 at age 67 in New York City.
Sets: 1914 *Omar, the Tentmaker*[†] (Also author, director, producer) **1916** *The Flame* **1917** *The Masquerader* **1918** *Keep Her Smiling*

Barney Turner

In 1937 Barney Turner designed for scenery for one play on Broadway.
Sets: 1937 *The Cat and the Canary*

Kay Turner

Kay Turner designed costumes for a 1920 Broadway show
Costumes: 1920 *What's in a Name*[†] ("Georgian" dresses)

Ret Turner

Ret Turner is an especially active costume designer for television specials, movies, awards shows, and series. He works primarily on the West Coast and occasionally designs costumes for the theater. Honors include five Emmy Awards, for the *Mitzi Gaynor Special* (with Bob Mackie), *Mama's Family* (with Bob Mackie), *Carol & Co.* (with Bob Mackie), *Las Vegas Anniversary Special* (with Pete Menefee), and *Diana Ross Special* (with Ray Aghayan).
Costumes: 1960 *Vintage '60*[†] (Men's clothes)

David M. Twachtman

David M. Twachtman designed one set in 1938 on Broadway.
Sets: 1938 *Shadow and Substance*

Reiner Tweebeeke

Reiner Tweebeeke designs lights in his native Holland as well as throughout Europe. He has also designed in Canada. His first designs were for a musical theater group and since 1987 has designed professionally for Toneelgroep Amsterdam, the Nationale Toneel, The Holland Festival, and in Tomoso, Norway, for the Halogaland Theatre. Among his honors is a Dutch Proscenium Award nomination for *Moortje* at Nationale Toneel and *Cyrano: The Musical*
Lights: 1993 *Cyrano: The Musical*[†]

Mr. George C. Tyler

George C. Tyler was a successful Broadway producer for forty years, beginning as a manager for James O'Neill, and then forming Liebler and Company in 1897 with Theodore Liebler (1852-1941). He introduced the Irish Players from the Abbey Theatre to the United States, promoted Booth Tarkington as a playwright and with Arnold Daly first presented George Bernard Shaw's plays in America. Although he amassed many credits as a director and produced more than 350 plays, he never claimed to be nor aspired to be a designer. He is included in this volume because the Broadway playbill for *Love's Comedy* includes this reference: "Scenery Loaned by Mr.

George C. Tyler." In an era when references to design elements were often omitted, it is significant that he was cited. He was born in Chillicothe, Ohio on April 12, 1967 and died in Yonkers, New York at age 78 on March 13, 1946.
Sets: 1908 *Love's Comedy* ("Scenery loaned")

Efim Udler

Efim Udler made his Broadway debut as a lighting designer in 1997, with a play produced by the Sovremennik Theatre. Usually plays are brought into New York after successful runs in other locations, but this particular version of *The Cherry Orchard* had an American debut in 1997 before it was performed in Moscow. His other credits include the lighting design for the *A Teacher of Russian* performed by the Oleg Tabakov Moscow Theatre-Studio at the Triplex Theatre on Chamber Street in New York City. The production was part of an exchange with the Acting Company.
Lights: 1997 *The Cherry Orchard*

Ultz

David Ultz, a British designer of scenery and costumes, has many credits in London's West End and designs regularly for the Royal Shakespeare Company. Born in 1951, he attended the Central School of Speech and Drama in London, where he studied with Ralph Kolta) and Sadler's Wells Design School. He also studied with Margaret Harris (Motley) and Hayden Griffen. After college he assisted Griffen at the Exeter Repertory for two years, followed by design for the Citizen's Theatre of Glasgow. He subsequently returned to London where his innovative designs soon attracted attention. He has designed many productions, including *The Twin Rivals* and *Our Friends of the North* at Cambridge Arts Theatre, *Our Friends of the North* at The Pit/Barbican Centre, and scenery and costumes for *A Comedy of Errors* at Stratford-upon-Avon. He has also designed for the National Arts Center in Ottawa, Canada among many other theaters and locations, and increasingly directs or co-directs productions with which he is involved.

Sets: 1982 *Good*

Edith Unger

Edith Unger designed costumes in 1919 on Broadway.
Costumes: 1919 *Hobohemia* (Smocks)

Unitt and Wickes

The scenic studio Unitt and Wickes was operated at 152 West 46th Street, New York City during the teens and twenties by Edward G. Unitt and Joseph Wickes. The studio location is the same as that of Emens and Unitt. Edward G. Unitt and Joseph Wickes were active designers who received individual credit for many productions. Additional information is available under their entries.

Sets: 1900 *The Master Builder* **1903** *The Other Girl* **1904** *Letty*; *Little Mary*; *Ransom's Folly*[†] (as: Unitt and Co.: Designed and painted); *Richelieu* **1905** *Richelieu* **1906** *Eileen Asthore*[†] **1907** *Jeanne d'Arc*[†]; *The Lancers*; *O'Neill of Derry*[†] (Acts II, III); *Richelieu* **1908** *The American Idea*[†]; *The Fool Hath Said: 'There Is No God'*; *Golden Butterfly*[†] (Act III); *Hamlet*; *If I Were King*; *The Master Builder*; *Our American Cousin*; *The Queen of the Moulin Rouge*[†] (Designed and painted); *Sister Beatrice*[†]; *What Every Woman Knows*; *The Winterfeast* **1909** *The Awakening of Helena Richie*; *The Bachelor's Baby*; *The Builder of Bridges*; *The Chocolate Soldier*[†] (Acts II, III); *Cottage in the Air*[†]; *An Englishman's Home*; *The Fires of Fate*[†]; *The Harvest Moon*; *Inconstant George*; *The Man Who Owns Broadway*[†] (Act II); *Penelope* **1910** *The Brass Bottle*; *Girlies*[†]; *The Importance of Being Earnest*[†] (Act III); *The Impostor*; *Little Eyolf*; *Merry Wives of Windsor*[†]; *Mrs. Dot*; *Sister Beatrice*[†]; *The Spitfire*; *The Upstart*[†] (Interior set) **1911** *The Blue Bird*[†]; *Green Stockings*[†] (Act III); *Kismet*[†]; *The Little Millionaire*[†]; *Macbeth (Kellerd)*; *Nobody's Daughter*[†]; *The Runaway*[†] (Acts I and II); *Ziegfeld Follies of 1911*[†] **1912** *The Affairs of Anatol*; *The Argyle Case*[†]; *Broadway Jones*; *Eva*; *The Flower of the Palace of Han*[†] (Painted); *June Madness*; *Oh! Oh! Delphine*[†]; *The Pigeon*; *Rutherford and Son*; *The Terrible Meek*[†] (Painted) **1913** *Good Little Devil*; *The Great Adventure*;

Her Own Money; *The New Henrietta*† (Design and painting); *The Philanderer*†; *Prunella*; *The Tyranny of Tears*; *The Will* **1914** *The Beauty Shop*; *The Dummy*; *Lady Windermere's Fan*; *Omar, the Tentmaker*†; *A Pair of Silk Stockings*†; *Papa's Darling*†; *The Rule of Three*; *The Truth*†; *The Truth*†; *Ziegfeld Follies of 1914*† **1915** *The Girl Who Smiles* **1916** *Hush!*; *The Passing Show of 1916*†; *The Pride of the Race* **1917** *His Little Widows*†; *The Lassoo*; *Misalliance*; *Romance and Arabella* **1919** *The Little Whopper*; *Too Many Husbands* **1920** *The Americans in France*; *The Cave Girl*; *Crooked Gamblers*; *Genius and the Crowd*†; *Honey Girl*; *Just Suppose*; *The Tavern* **1921** *The Green Goddess*; *The Intimate Strangers*†; *The O'Brien Girl*; *The Tavern*; *Toto*

Edward G. Unitt

Edward G. Unitt, a scenic painter, maintained a studio at the Lyceum Theatre of Daniel and Charles Frohman, for whom he designed and painted many shows, often being acknowledged as E. G. Unitt, or simply as Unitt. He designed many productions prior to 1900: *Aristocracy* (1892), *Under the Red Robe* (1896) scenery and costumes, *The Little Minister* scenery and costumes (1897), *The Conquerors* and *The Liars* (1898), *Barbara Frietchie* (1899), and *Trelawney of the "Wells."* He later maintained a studio at Daly's Fifth Avenue Theatre, collaborated with Homer Emens through "Emens and Unitt," and was involved in 1915, in Morosco-Wagner, Co. Inc., amusements, with Oliver Morosco and Charles Wagner.

Sets: 1899 *The Cowboy and the Lady*; *The Girl from Maxim's*; *The Manoeuvres of Jane*; *Miss Hobbs*; *The Song of the Sword*; *Tyranny of Tears*; *Wheels within Wheels* **1900** *The Ambassador*; *Borderside*; *Coralie and Company, Dressmakers*; *David Harum*; *Hamlet*; *L'Aiglon*† (Act I, III); *Lady Huntworth's Experiment*; *Mrs. Dane's Defense*; *The Pride of Jennico*; *Richard Carvel*; *The Rose of Persia*; *A Royal Family*; *The Sunken Bell*; *The Surprises of Love* **1901** *Are You A Mason?*; *Captain Jinks of the Horse Marines*; *Colorado*; *Diplomacy*; *The Forest Lovers*; *The Girl and the Judge*; *If I Were King*;

The Lash of a Whip; *The Love Match*; *On and Off*; *Quality Street*; *A Royal Rival*; *The Second in Command*; *The Wilderness* **1902** *Carrots*; *A Country Girl*†; *A Country Mouse*; *The Eternal City*†; *Frocks and Frills*; *The Girl with the Green Eyes*; *Hearts Aflame*†; *Iris*; *The New Clown*; *Notre Dame*; *A Rose o' Plymouth-Town*; *Sally in Our Alley*†; *Sky Farm* **1903** *The Bird in the Cage*; *Captain Dieppe*†; *Lady Rose's Daughter*; *Mice and Men*; *The Proud Prince*† **1904** *Granny*†; *Hamlet*; *The Light That Lies in Woman's Eyes*; *A Madcap Princess*†; *Piff! Paff! Pouf!*†; *That Man and I*†; *The Winter's Tale*† **1905** *Beauty and the Barge*†; *Cousin Billy*†; *Just Out of College*†; *The School for Husbands*†; *Wonderland*† **1906** *About Town*†; *The Blue Moon*†; *Cymbeline*†; *The Great Divide*†; *His House in Order*†; *The Mountain Climber*†; *Pippa Passes*†; *The Red Mill*† **1907** *A Grand Army Man*†; *His Excellency the Governor*†; *Miss Hook of Holland*†; *My Wife*†; *The Rose of Alhambra*†; *The Spoilers*†; *The Straight Road*†; *The Sunken Bell*†; *The Talk of New York*†; *Twelfth Night*† **1908** *Don Quixote*† (Act III, IV); *Fluffy Ruffles*†; *Funabashi*†; *Jack Straw*†; *The Mollusc*†; *Nearly a Hero*† **1909** *The Beauty Spot*†; *The Commanding Officer*; *A Fool There Was*† **1910** *Diplomacy* **1913** *The Amazons* **1915** *The Adventure of Lady Ursula*†; *Rosemary* **1923** *Cymbeline*†

Gretl Urban

Gretl Urban (sometimes Gretl Thurlow), was born Margarete Urban, daughter of Joseph Urban. She worked with her father beginning in 1920 for productions at the Metropolitan Opera including *Lohengrin* in 1921. Many scholars consider her to be an important partner in her father's extensive design activity. She designed costumes for many productions at the Metropolitan Opera, often collaborating with her father who designed the scenery. She designed costumes for films, some with her father, and some on her own, including *When Knighthood Was in Flower* (1922), *Enemies of Women* (1923), and *Zander the Great* and *Never the Twain Shall Meet* (1925). Gretl Urban died in 1998.

Sets: 1925 *Louie the 14th* **1935** *The Sea-*

son Changes

Joseph Urban

Joseph Urban was born in Vienna in 1872 and studied both architecture and stage design. He is credited with introducing many Continental stagecraft techniques to the United States. After working in Vienna for several years, he came to Boston in 1910 to design an opera. The success of the production led to an opportunity to design at the Metropolitan Opera. He designed scenery and costumes for many revues presented by Florenz Ziegfeld and also designed the Ziegfeld Theatre, unfortunately demolished in 1966. He was art director for numerous films between 1920 and 1931. Productions in London included scenery for *Snow Flakes*, *Giselle* and *Macbeth* in 1920, and revivals of *Snow Flakes* in 1924 and 1927. Urban died in 1933 in New York City, and his archive is located in the permanent collections at Columbia University. His designs for architecture and stage have been much published and exhibited including the book *Joseph Urban: Architecture, Theatre, Opera, Film*, published in 1994 and the exhibit *Architect of Dreams: The Theatrical Vision of Joseph Urban* at Columbia University in 2000.

Sets: 1914 *The Garden of Paradise*; *Twelfth Night* 1915 *Around the Map†*; *Ziegfeld Follies: 1915*; *Ziegfeld Midnight Frolic* 1916 *The Century Girl*; *FloraBella*; *Macbeth†*; *Miss Springtime*; *Pom-Pom*; *Ziegfeld Follies: 1916* 1917 *Jack O'Lantern†*; *Miss 1917*; *Nju*; *The Riviera Girl*; *Ziegfeld Follies: 1917* 1918 *By Pigeon Post*; *The Canary*; *Glorianna*; *Head over Heels†*; *The Invisible Foe*; *Nothing But Lies*; *The Rainbow Girl*; *Ziegfeld Follies: 1918* 1919 *Apple Blossoms*; *Hitchy Koo 1919†*; *The Rose of China*; *Smilin' Through*; *A Young Man's Fancy*; *Ziegfeld Midnight Frolic* 1920 *Sally*; *Ziegfeld Follies: 1920* 1921 *The Love Letter*; *The Merry Widow*; *Ziegfeld Follies: 1921†*; *Ziegfeld Midnight Follies*; *Ziegfeld's 9 O'clock Frolic* 1922 *Sally, Irene and Mary*; *The Yankee Princess*; *Ziegfeld Follies: 1922†* 1923 *Ziegfeld Follies: 1923* 1924 *Moonlight*; *Ziegfeld Follies: 1924†* 1925 *Antonia*; *Human Nature*; *Song of the Flame*; *A Tale of the Wolf* 1926 *Betsy†*; *No Foolin'†*; *The Wild Rose* 1927 *Golden Dawn*; *Rio Rita*; *Show Boat*; *Yours Truly*; *Ziegfeld Follies: 1927* 1928 *Rosalie*; *The Three Musketeers*; *Treasure Girl*; *Whoopee*; *Yours Truly* 1929 *Midnite Frolics*; *Show Girl*; *Sons o' Guns* 1930 *Flying High*; *Princess Charming*; *Ripples*; *Simple Simon*; *Smiles* 1931 *George White's Scandals*; *The Good Fairy*; *Simple Simon*; *Ziegfeld Follies: 1931* 1932 *A Good Fairy*; *Hot-Cha!*; *Music in the Air*; *Show Boat* 1933 *Melody* 1948 *Sally*
Costumes: 1925 *A Tale of the Wolf*
Lights: 1914 *The Garden of Paradise*; *Yosemite*

Stasy Uskinsky

Stasy Uskinsky, also known as Stasys Uinskas and Stacy Ušinskas was a Lithuanian stage designer who lived from 1905 to 1975. In addition to designing a 1938 Broadway play, a 1937 issue of *Theatre Arts* reproduced designs for a ballet performed in New York. References to his credits as a book illustrator and glass etcher are also contained in *Allgemeines Lexikon der Bildenden Künstler des XX* and *Encyclopedia Lituanica*.
Costumes: 1938 *Bridal Crown* (Costumes and marionettes)

Brian Vahey

Brian Vahey was born on May 31, 1956 in Dublin, Ireland and earned a diploma at the Dunlaoghaire School of Arts where he studied animation and sculpture. He has served as resident designer, assistant and tutor at Riverside Studios, assisting Miss Margaret Harris (Motley) with whom he studied in 1982. He has held a Cincellin Fellowship at Bristol University and served as assistant designer at the Abbey Theatre, where he has contributed designs for scenery and costumes to many productions. He made his debut in 1982 at the Abbey Theatre with *Mr. Joyce is Leaving Paris*. He has been production designer at R.T.E. Television in Ireland and designed the film *The Walk of Life*. Major influences include Margaret Harris and John Dexter. He worked with Dexter at the

Buxton Opera Festival in 1985 and designed *The Cocktail Party* for him in London in 1986.
Sets: 1984 *A Moon for the Misbegotten*
Costumes: 1984 *A Moon for the Misbegotten*

Vail Studios

Vail Studios was established in 1892 by George M. Vail and operated through the Grand Opera House, becoming Vail Scenic Construction Company in 1910 when it was located at 318-322 West 24th Street in New York. In 1950, the business was absorbed into Chester Rakeman Scenic Studios. Vail Scenic Construction Company built sets for *Ziegfeld Follies, George White's Scandals, Kiss Me, Kate, Bloomer Girl, Mr. Pickwick*, and many, many more. They also supplied settings to CBS-TV. George Vail died at age 81 on November 14, 1952.
Sets: 1934 *House of Ramsen*

Valentina

Valentina was born Valentina Nicholaevna Sanina on May 1, 1899 (some sources cite 1904) in Kiev. Her dramatic art studies were cut short by the Russian Revolution, and she was forced to flee for safety. At age 17 she met and married George Schlee in Sevastopol, and lived afterwards in various cities in Europe. Her talent for designing clothes to fit personality rather than conform to contemporary style was encouraged in Paris by Léon Bakst. In 1923, she moved to New York with her husband and his family, and in 1928, opened her own establishment, Valentina Gowns, Inc. where all the garments were made to order. She was an instant success and was immediately in demand by private customers and performers. Her reputation for glamorous and intricate gowns contributed to her popularity in the theater and for films. She closed her shop in 1957. Noted film designs include Katherine Hepburn's gowns in *Philadelphia Story*. She died in New York at age 90 on September 14, 1989.
Costumes: 1934 *Come of Age* (Gowns and hats) **1935** *Bright Star* (Gowns) **1936** *Idiot's Delight†* (Miss Fontanne's costumes) **1937** *Amphitryon 38* **1938** *No Time for Comedy†* **1939** *The Philadelphia Story†* (Miss Hepburn's gowns) **1940** *Goodbye in the Night* (Miss Mason's and Miss Schafer's dresses); *There Shall Be No Night* **1941** *Candle in the Wind* (Miss Hayes clothes); *Hope for a Harvest* (Miss Eldridge's costumes); *Theatre†* (Miss Skinner's Act I, Miss Flint's gowns) **1942** *Laugh, Town, Laugh†* (Miss Froman gown) **1943** *This Rock* (Gowns for Miss Burke and Miss Sterling) **1944** *Seven Lively Arts†* (Modern gowns) **1945** *One Man Show†* (Miss Constance Cummings' gowns); *The Rugged Path†* (Gowns) **1946** *Antigone*; *Lute Song†* (Miss Mary Martin's costumes) **1947** *Anthony and Cleopatra†* (Women's costumes); *Message for Margaret†* (Miss Hopkins' gowns) **1950** *Bell, Book and Candle†* (Miss Lilli Palmer's costumes) **1951** *The Constant Wife* (Miss Cornell's clothes) **1952** *Venus Observed†* **1954** *The Burning Glass†* (Miss Maria Riva's dresses) **1964** *The Chinese Prime Minister*

C. W. Valentine

C. W. Valentine, also known as Washington and W.C. was a scenic artist and designer active in New York in the last decade of the nineteenth and the first one of the twentieth century. He was associated, as a staff scenic artist, with the Gaiety Theatre in Brooklyn, and the Olympic Theatre and Hyde and Behman's Theatre, both in New York City.
Sets: 1903 *Running for Office*

E. Van Ackerman

In 1927 Earl Van Ackerman created sets for a Broadway play. In the early 1920s he operated Beaux Arts Scenic Studios with George W. Korb in Newark, New Jersey, where he also resided. He also painted the sets for *Made for Each Other* in 1939, which were constructed by Nolan Brothers.
Sets: 1924 *The Green Beetle* **1927** *Tia Juana*

Ellen Van der Horst

Ellen Van der Horst designed costumes for a 1982 Broadway play, starring Herman van Veen, a Dutch performer. The production played throughout Europe and the United Kingdom before transferring to New York. She also designed *El Paseo* at the Theatre Cosmic in Amsterdam in 1993.

Costumes: 1982 *Herman Van Veen: All of Him*

Gerda Vanderneers

Gerda Vanderneers collaborated on the costume design for a 1940 Broadway show.

Costumes: 1940 *Meet the People*†

Edwin H. Vandernoot

Edwin H. Vandernoot designed scenery for an evening of one-act plays in 1940 on Broadway.

Sets: 1940 *What D' You Call It/ According to Law/ etc.*

Joe Vaněk

Joe Vaněk is a scenic and costume designer who has had long term collaborations with two of Dublin's major theaters. He has been an associate of the Gate Theatre since 1984 and been Director of Design at the National Theatre since 1994. He was also head of design at Watford Palace Theatre when Michael Attenborough was artistic director. His designs have also been often seen in London's West End and in major European opera houses. Much honored for his realistic stage settings, both the scenery and costumes for *Dancing at Lughnasa* were nominated for Tony Awards and were part of the British entry that won the Gold Medal at the 1991 Prague Quadriennale. He has also received three Harvey's Theatre Awards in Ireland, and two West Coast Critic's Awards for *The Phantom of the Opera* in San Francisco.

Sets: 1991 *Dancing at Lughnasa* 1993 *Wonderful Tennessee*
Costumes: 1991 *Dancing at Lughnasa* 1993 *Wonderful Tennessee*

Franklin Van Horn

Franklin M. Van Horn was responsible for costume designs on Broadway during the last decade of the nineteenth and first decade of the twentieth century. He was proprietor of the New York branch of Van Horn & Son, theatrical costumers, located at 34 East 20th Street in New York City. The business mainly executed costumes for other designers, but during the early years of the twentieth century also contributed original designs to productions. Although Franklin Van Horn died on April 20, 1909 in Atlantic City, New Jersey, the company he founded in Philadelphia in 1852 and expanded to New York City in the early 1890s thrived throughout most of the twentieth century, forming alliances with many similar firms, before becoming part of Dodger Costumes in 1998.

Costumes: 1900 *Mistress Nell* (as: Van Horn & Son) 1902 *As You Like It*† (Other costumes); *The Cavalier* (as: Van Horn & Son); *Mistress Nell* 1904 *Judith of Bethulia*†; *The Two Orphans*† 1905 *At the Threshold*; *A Blot in the 'Scutcheon* (Miss Gerson's costumes); *King Lear*†; *London Assurance*† (Other costumes); *Macbeth*†; *The System of Dr. Tarr* 1906 *Clothes*†; *Hamlet (Mantell)*; *Pippa Passes* 1907 *King Lear*†; *O'Neill of Derry*

Vannio Vanni

Vannio Vanni designed lights for a Broadway production in 1964.

Lights: 1964 *Rugantino*

Robert Van Rosen

Robert Van Rosen, a surrealist painter, often lectured on art and theater in major museums in the greater New York area. He occasionally contributed designs to plays. He worked as an industrial designer in the 1940s and 1950s designing packaging and consulting on packaging. The author of *Comeback* (1949), a book about his recovery from a stroke, he died at age 62 on November 16, 1966.

Sets: 1926 *Princess Turandot* 1931 *Bloody Laughter* 1932 *Wolves* 1938 *Empress of Destiny*
Costumes: 1926 *Princess Turandot* 1938 *Empress of Destiny*

Hugh Vanstone

British lighting designer Hugh Vanstone, born on August 8, 1965 in Exeter, England, trained at the Northcott Theatre in Exeter from 1980 to 1986, and as an assistant to Andrew Bridge. His professional debut was *The Deep Blue Sea* in 1982 at the Northcott. He designs frequently in London's

West End, for the Royal Shakespeare Company, the Royal National Theatre, and Royal Opera House. A proponent of clean, fluid light, his honors include nominations for Olivier Awards in 1996 for *Art* in the West End, in 1997 for *Hamlet* for the RSC, and in 2001 for *The Cherry Orchard* and *The Graduate*. He won the Olivier Award in 1999 and again in 2001 for Best Lighting Designer. Twenty-first century designs include *Life x 3* for the Royal National Theatre, *The Caretaker* in London's West End, and *The Unexpected Man* at the Promenade Theatre in New York City.

Lights: 1998 *Art*; *The Blue Room* **1999** *Closer* **2001** *Blast!*; *Follies*

Ellen Van Volkenburg

Ellen Van Volkenburg founded the Little Theatre of Chicago in 1912 with her husbandMaurice Browne (1881-1955). With its' opening the little theater movement in the United States began. The Little Theatre of Chicago operated at the Fine Arts Building on Michigan Avenue and was active for three years. Van Volkenburg was born in Battle Creek, Michigan in 1882 and attended the University of Michigan. An actress, puppeteer, and producer, she toured the United States as a performer. Browne produced plays in New York, including a production of *Medea* in 1920, after which they moved to London. In 1931 Van Volkenburg directed, designed and acted in a Broadway production, after which she returned to London where she appeared in plays until the late 1930s. She died in 1978.

Sets: 1931 *The Venetian*†

Dorothy Van Winkle

Dorothy F. Van Winkle, an artist, designed costumes for a Broadway play in 1935. Her studio and home was located at 305 West 72nd Street In New York City.

Costumes: 1935 *Smile at Me*

Leo Van Witsen

Leo Van Witsen was born July 12, 1912 in the Hague, Netherlands where he studied at the Royal Academy of Art. He also studied in Paris at the Grande Chaumière, and in and Berlin.

He began designing costumes in the Hague for a cabaret which parodied Dutch folk songs. After that time his designs, with an emphasis in opera, graced many stages. For many years he was resident designer at Brooks-Van Horn Costume Company, heading the Opera department and from 1945 to 1985, was the staff costume designer for the Goldovsky Opera Institute in New York City. He received an Obie nomination for *Seven at Dawn* and is the author of *Costuming for Opera: Who Wears What and Why*. Volume I was published in 1981 and Volume II in 1994. His third book about opera costumes is scheduled for publication in Spring 2002.

Costumes: 1938 *Danton's Death* (Costume Supervisor) **1963** *The Beast in Me*

Varady

Frederick Varady, born in 1908 in Budapest, was an illustrator who studied at the Royal Hungarian Academy of Art. After leaving Hungary in 1927, he worked throughout Europe, and designed and illustrated fashion in Paris and Berlin. He opened a studio at 20 West 46th Street in New York City after emigrating to the United States where he also painted murals, created fine art and continued to design fashion, and occasionally theatrical costumes. In the early 1930s he was associated with George S. Tarkay in the Twain Art Studios at 350 West 57th Street. By the late 1930s, he was drawing for major magazines, including *Cosmopolitan*, *McCall's*, *The Saturday Evening Post* and *Good Housekeeping*.

Costumes: 1933 *As Thousands Cheer*† (Modern gowns)

Adrian Vaux

Adrian Vaux designs extensively in England and Israel. He was resident designer for the Mermaid Theatre from 1964 to 1970 and created sets for *Treasure Island*, *Fanny's First Play*, *The Imaginary Invalid* and *The Philanderer* among others. From 1971 to 1980 he was resident designer at the Leicester Haymarket. He has also been resident designer at the Old Vic and has extensive credits in the West End. At the Haifa Municipal Theatre in Israel he designed *Soul of a Jew, Magda, Ghetto* and *The Jerusalem Syndrome.* His designs for *The Comedy of Errors* were included in a 1991 exhibit in Jerusalem, "The Curtain Rises in the Museum," featuring designs for the Beersheba Theatre.

Sets: 1989 *Ghetto*

Kaj Velden

Kaj (Karl) Velden, a scenic and interior designer, was the proprietor of Karl Velden Studios. His wife, Mrs. Inge Jesperson Velden (d. 1971) was a fashion designer who worked for Christian Dior in Paris. Velden was born on May 25, 1901 and died in New York in December 1975.

Sets: 1944 *Take a Bow*

Mariann Verheyen

Mariann Verheyen was born on March 9, 1950 and received her B.A. from St. Norbert College (1972), where she first designed costumes, and her M.F.A. from the University of Wisconsin at Madison (1978). While working at a design assistant at Brooks Van Horn from 1978 to 1980 and with costume designer Jane Greenwood from 1980 to 1981, she began establishing her own career. Her many designs in regional theaters include productions at the North Shore Music Theatre, Colorado Shakespeare Festival, the Hartmann Theatre, the Missouri Repertory Theatre, the Alley Theatre and for the Huntington Theatre Company, among others. She has off-Broadway credits at the Joseph Papp Public Theatre (*Everybody's Ruby*), the New York Theatre (*Philemon*), and Second Stage (*Something Different*). Honors include the Villager Downtown Theatre Award for Outstanding Costumes in 1983 for her designs for *Wednesday, Accounts* and *Blood Relations* at the Hudson Guild and the 1984 Boston Theatre Critics Award for *On the Razzle* at the Huntington Theatre Company. Since 1991, she has been on the faculty of the School of Theatre Arts at Boston University.

Costumes: 1990 *Peter Pan* **1991** *Peter Pan*

James Vermeulen

James Vermeulen, who graduated from the State University of New York at Purchase, has designed lights in many off-Broadway theaters. He frequently designs for directors Loretta Greko, Joe Mantello, Andy Goldberg and Michael Sexton. Among the regional theaters where he has worked are the Oregon Shakespeare Festival, the Milwaukee Repertory Theatre, PlayMakers Repertory Company and the Walnut Street Theatre. His designs for *Stop Kiss* at the Joseph Papp Public Theatre were nominated for a Hewes Design Award. Off-Broadway credits include productions at the Promenade Theatre, St. Clement's, the New York Theatre Workshop, Intar Theatre, Theatre Four, and the Greenwich House Theatre. Twenty-first century designs include *Bomb-itty of Errors* at 45 Bleeker, *The Square* at the Joseph Papp Public Theatre, *Early on in the Shape of Things* at the Promenade Theatre and *Good Thing* at the Theatre at St. Clement's Church.

Lights: 2001 *Design for Living*

Levino Verna

Levino Verna designed costumes for a play on Broadway in 1974. The credit line for *Absurd Person Singular* reads "Costumes designed by LEVINO VERNA for Laurence Gross." In Spring 1980, his fall-and-winter collection of evening wear, silk dresses appropriate for late-day wear, and furs were all favorably reviewed. The dressy blouses in the collection were manufactured in South Norwalk, Connecticut by the Mayehoff Company. His fall-and-winter collection in 1983 was also well-received.

Costumes: 1974 *Absurd Person Singular*

Veronica

Veronica (Veronica Blythe) worked primarily executing costume designs for the Shubert Organization and doing wardrobe work. She was active from 1920 until the mid-1940s, in a variety of incarnations, including Eaves,

Schneider & Blythe, Veronica Costume Company, Veronica Stage Costumes, Inc., and was often acknowledged in playbills for her contributions to productions. Ernest Schrapps, Kirah Markham, Lee Simonson, and Irene Sharaff were among the designers who valued her execution of their designs. Born on October 9, 1881, she died in March 1965, in Queens, New York.

Costumes: **1938** *Hellzapoppin*† **1939** *Yokel Boy*† **1942** *Harlem Cavalcade* **1944** *Robin Hood*

Marcel Vertès

Marcel Vertès was born in Budapest, Hungary in 1895 and spent most of his life in France as a painter and illustrator, gaining an international reputation. He participated in a 1920 exhibition of paintings and began theatrical design with the support of Ferenc Molnar. His first designs were seen in Paris in 1933 and for many years he designed sets and costumes for plays, operas and ballets in Paris and New York. He also designed eight hundred circus costumes for Ringling Bros. and Barnum & Bailey Circus. Marcel Vertès, the recipient of Academy Awards for both sets and costumes for *Moulin Rouge*, died at age 66 on October 31, 1961 in Paris.

Sets: **1955** *Seventh Heaven*
Costumes: **1955** *Seventh Heaven*

Sheldon K. Viele

Sheldon Knickerbocker Viele designed sets and occasionally costumes for many plays in the 1920s on Broadway. He was originally from Buffalo, New York and in 1927 was instrumental in founding the Studio Theatre in that city. A graduate of Yale, he served in World War I in France in the Camouflage Corps. For two years Mr. Viele, who also was a painter, was technical director of the Theatre Guild. He died on September 23, 1934 at the age of 42.

Sets: **1920** *Enter Madame*; *Miss Lulu Bett* at **1921** *Ambush*; *The Cloister*; *John Hawthorne*; *We Girls* **1922** *Fashions for Men*; *The Plot Thickens*†; *The Shadow* **1923** *Helen of Troy, New York*†; *Meet the Wife*†; *Rita Coventry*; *The Shadow* **1924** *The Easy Mail*; *The Fake*†; *Lollipops*†; *The Rising Sun*; *The Show-Off* **1925**

Craig's Wife; *The Enchanted April*; *Jane, Our Stranger*; *One of the Family*; *The Servant in the House* **1927** *Sidewalks of New York*; *The Wasp's Nest* **1928** *Three Cheers*†
Costumes: **1921** *The Cloister*; *John Hawthorne*

Miss Vila

Miss Vila was costume supervisor for a Broadway play in 1926.
Costumes: **1926** *Queen High* (Costume Supervisor)

Villi

Villi collaborated on the costume design for a Broadway play in 1930. The 1925 Manhattan City Directory identifies Antonio Villi as a ladies tailor, living and working from 63 West 48th Street. It is unlikely that this is actress Olga Villi (d. 1989) who appeared on stage and in films in Italy.
Costumes: **1930** *The Challenge of Youth*†

August Vimnera

August (Auguste) Vimnera, who designed sets for several plays on Broadway in the 1920s, was born on July 17, 1891. The playbill for *Earl Carroll Vanities* (1926) referred to him as "A. Vimnera of Paris." He also designed through the August Vimnera Studio. He retired to Broward, Florida, and died there in December 1967.
Sets: **1925** *The Small Timer*; *Tell Me More*† **1926** *Earl Carroll's Vanities* **1927** *Footlights*; *Hearts and Trumps*; *Kiss Me*; *The Mulberry Bush*; *Tales of Rigo* **1928** *The Breaks*; *Diamond Lil* (as: August Vimnera Studio); *Forbidden Roads*; *Girl Trouble*; *The Intruder*; *Red Dust*; *The Silver Box* **1929** *Red Dust*

H. A. Vincent

Harold Aiken Vincent collaborated on the scenery for a Broadway play in 1915. He was born in Boston on February 14, 1864 and died on September 27, 1931. During the teens, he was employed at Emil Lakner and Co., which sold dry goods, including garments. A self-taught painter, he exhibited widely and won several prizes for his marine paintings.
Sets: **1915** *You Never Can Tell*†

Madame Viola

Otto Viola was the proprietor of the Maison Viola, located at 27, Albemarle Street/Bond Street in London. As "Court Dressmaker and Creator of Fashions" the salon was allowed to use the Royal Seal in advertisements, and often did so in theatrical playbills in London. He often contributed original designs, that he also executed, for featured players in productions in London. Examples of Viola's designs are included in *Theatre and Fashion: Oscar Wilde to the Suffragettes* published in 1994.

Costumes: **1902** *The Joy of Living*† **1904** *The Rich Mrs. Repton* **1906** *Mauricette; Mr. Hopkinson*† **1907** *All-of-a-Sudden Peggy*† (Miss Sergeantson's gowns) **1914** *Jerry*

Miss Violet

Miss Violet supervised costumes for a 1932 Broadway play.

Costumes: **1932** *Page Pygmalion* (Costume Supervisor)

Madame Virion

Madame Virion contributed designs to three productions on Broadway during the first decade of the twentieth century. Widow of August Virion, she was a dressmaker who resided at 360 West 121st Street in New York City.

Costumes: **1901** *Miranda of the Balcony*† (Gowns) **1902** *Divorcons; Hon. John Grigsby*†

Ruth Vivian

Ruth Vivian, an actress, was born in England and performed with her brothers and sisters in an act called "Les Petites Viviennes." She came to the U.S. on a tour of Shakespearean plays with Sir Philip Ben Greet, staying to perform in many Broadway plays including *The Man Who Came to Dinner* and *Sweet Aloes*. She was also interested in teaching the blind and was largely responsible for establishing a school to train drama teachers to work with blind students. In addition, she helped create a library of plays for the American Foundation for the Blind. Miss Vivian died on October 24, 1949 at age 66.

Costumes: **1915** *Treasure Island* (Costume Supervisor)

Arthur Voegtlin

Arthur Voegtlin, who was born in Chicago in 1858, studied painting with his father, William T. Voegtlin, a scenic artist who emigrated to America from Switzerland in 1850. The family relocated to New York in the 1880s and Arthur Voegtlin was a scenic artist for Hoyt & McKee at the Madison Square Theatre. He also designed and painted scenery, including *A Runaway Colt* in 1899. The early part of his career was spent creating, designing, and directing productions at the New York Hippodrome, beginning with it's opening in 1904 with *A Yankee Circus on Mars* and continuing until 1918. He also designed and directed productions at Coney Island's Luna Park. Following World War I, he was instrumental in importing shows from London, and sending American productions abroad. His studio was located at 33 West 24th Street. In 1937 he moved to California, initially to supervise a movie about the New York Hippodrome. Although the movie was not made, he remained in Los Angeles, where he died on January 18, 1948 at age 90.

Sets: **1899** *My Innocent Boy* **1900** *Hodge, Podge, & Co.; Janice Meredith*† **1901** *Don Caesar's Return; On the Quiet* **1902** *The Crisis*†; *The Diplomat* **1903** *The Bishop's Move; John Ermine of the Yellowstone* **1904** *Harriet's Honeymoon* **1905** *The Raiders*†; *A Society Circus; A Yankee Circus on Mars*† **1906** *About Town*†; *The House of Silence; Neptune's Daughter*†; *Pioneer Days* **1907** *Auto Race, The; The Four Seasons; Circus Events; The Gay White Way; The Girl Behind the Counter; The White Hen*† (Act II) **1908** *The Battle in the Skies; The Land of the Birds; Marcelle; The Mimic World*† (Last act); *Nearly a Hero*†; *Sporting Days* **1909** *Havanna; The Midnight Sons*†; *A Trip to Japan*† **1910** *Inside the Earth; The International Cup/The Battle of Niagara and The Ear; The Jolly Bachelors*† (Scenic equipment by); *The King of Cadonia; The Summer Widowers* **1911** *Around the World; The Hen-Pecks; The Never Homes; Winter Garden*† (Also wrote) **1912** *The Ne'er-Do-Well*; *Sumu-run*[†]; *Under Many Flags* **1913** *America*; *Joseph and His Brethren* **1914** *H.M.S. Pinafore*; *Wars of the World*

Fred Voelpel

Fred Voelpel was born in Peoria, Illinois and attended the University of Illinois and Yale, where he studied with Donald Oenslager and Frank Poole Bevan. He has been designing costumes, lights and sets since 1943 when he debuted at both Peoria Players Little Theatre and Peoria Central High School, and professionally since 1956 for television and the theater. Among his television credits are *Robert Montgomery Presents* for NBC-TV and the musical variety series' *Patti Page Show*, *Andy Williams Show* and the *Pat Boone Show* for ABC-TV. He has won two New York Critics Circle Awards for set design, an Obie Award for *The Effect of Gamma Rays on Man-in-the-Moon Marigolds*, a Variety Poll Award, an Esquire Dubious Achievement Award for *Oh, Calcutta*, and a Miami (Florida) L.O.R.T. Award for *Seascape*. He was master teacher of design at New York University's Tisch School of the Arts from 1966 to 1992, winning a "Great Teacher Award" in his final year. During that same period he designed for the National Theatre for the Deaf, for which he received an Honorary Tony Award. He was also Resident Designer for the National Playwrights' Conference beginning in 1965, and on the faculty of the National Theatre Institute from its founding in 1970. From 1964 to 1987 he designed sets and costumes for Paul Green's *The Lost Colony*, the nation's longest running outdoor drama, located in Manteo, North Carolina.

Sets: 1960 *From A to Z*; *Vintage '60* **1961** *Young Abe Lincoln* **1969** *Home Fires/ Cop Out* **1970** *Sganarelle* **1971** *And Miss Reardon Drinks a Little* **1972** *Hurry, Harry* **1975** *Very Good, Eddie* **1981** *Einstein and the Polar Bear*
Costumes: 1960 *From A to Z*[†] **1961** *Young Abe Lincoln* **1963** *The Milk Train Doesn't Stop Here Anymore*; *Sophie* **1964** *Absence of a Cello*; *A Murderer among Us*; *The Sign in Sidney Brustein's Win-*dow **1965** *Drat! the Cat!*; *Peterpat* **1969** *Home Fires/ Cop Out* **1970** *Sganarelle*; *Songs from Milkwood*; *Two by Two* **1971** *Oh! Calcutta!* **1975** *Seascape* **1981** *Bring Back Birdie*
Lights: 1960 *From A to Z* **1961** *Young Abe Lincoln*

Virginia Volland

Virginia Volland was born in Chicago, Illinois on August 2, 1909 and studied at Stanford University. She began her career as a dress designer and actress before turning to costume design. She debuted off-Broadway in 1937 with the costume design for *The Infernal Machine*. The author of *Designing Woman*, about life as a designer, Miss Volland's own career as a costume designer was cut short when she lost her sight. She died in New York City in March 1968

Costumes: 1934 *But Not for Love* **1952** *Time Out for Ginger*[†] (Miss Rowles' clothes, Miss Malone's cape) **1953** *Gently Does It* **1954** *The Integration Show Case*; *One Eye Closed* **1955** *The Grand Prize* **1956** *The Hot Corner* **1957** *The Genius and the Goddess*; *Hide and Seek*; *The Tunnel of Love* **1958** *The Gazebo*; *Sunrise at Campobello*; *Two for the Seesaw* **1959** *A Raisin in the Sun* **1960** *A Mighty Man Is He*

Egon Von Furstenberg

Prince Egon Von Furstenburg, also known as Egon Furstenburg, a fashion designer, was born in Lausanne, Switzerland on June 29, 1946. After working in the financial industry he became a buyer in department stores including Macy's, and studied at the Fashion Institute of Technology before creating his business, Egon Von Furstenburg, Ltd. A successful designer of men's wear during the 1970s and 1980s, he wrote *The Power Book*. In summer 2001, he introduced a new line of men's fashion in Milan, Italy: "EA 92."

Costumes: 1975 *Don't Call Back*[†]

Elfi Von Kantzow

Elfi Von Kantzow designed scenery and costumes for Broadway shows in the early 1950s.

Sets: 1952 *The Brass Ring*; *Jane*

Costumes: 1950 *Edwina Black* 1952 *The Brass Ring*; *Jane*

Jennifer von Mayrhauser

Jennifer von Mayrhauser was born in Ithaca, New York on January 26, 1948, the daughter of Thomas and Florence Bergen. She received a B.S. in Theatre from Northwestern University in 1970 and studied at Lester Polakov's Studio and Forum of Stage Design. Her designs for costumes have been seen in New York since 1972 when *Press Cuttings* opened at the Cubiculo Theatre. She has designed numerous productions in regional theaters, and off-Broadway including the New York Shakespeare Festival, Circle Repertory Theatre, Second Stage Theatre, Playwrights Horizons, and as resident designer for many years at Circle Repertory Company. Movies include *Mystic Pizza, The Real Blonde, Lean On Me,* and others. Among her designs for television are *The Days and Nights of Molly Dodd* (HBO), numerous American Playhouse specials, and the long-running series *Law and Order*, for which she received an Emmy Award nomination in 1999. Among her other honors is the 1995 Obie Award for Sustained Excellence in Costume Design. On the faculty at Brandeis University as adjunct professor, she is married to Richard Cottrell and the mother of two children, Julia and Lucy Cottrell.

Costumes: 1976 *Knock Knock* 1978 *Da* 1980 *Censored Scenes from King Kong*; *Hide and Seek*; *John Gabriel Borkman*; *Talley's Folly* 1981 *The Father* 1982 *Beyond Therapy*; *Eminent Domain*; *Solomon's Child*; *Special Occasions*; *Steaming*; *The Wake of Jamie Foster* 1983 *Angels Fall*; *Baby*; *Passion* 1984 *Awake and Sing* 1985 *Hay Fever* 1986 *The Boys in Autumn*; *Execution of Justice,* 1987 *The Musical Comedy Murders* 1988 *The Night of the Iguana* 1989 *The Heidi Chronicles* 1992 *Crazy He Calls Me* 1996 *A Thousand Clowns*

Patrizia von Brandenstein

Patrizia von Brandenstein is well known as a costume and production designer for movies, including *Working Girl, A Chorus Line, The Untouchables, Silkwood, Six Degrees of Separation, Just Cause, The People vs. Larry Flynt,* and *Amadeus* for which she won an Academy Award. She has also designed for dance, theater, and often collaborates on projects with her husband, scenic designer Stuart Wurtzel. Off-Broadway productions include costumes for *Narnia*, presented by the New York State Theatre Institute. Twenty-first century credits include production design for the films *Shaft* and *Rodgers and Hammerstein's South Pacific.*

Costumes: 1989 *Hizzoner*

Carl H. Vose

Carl Vose designed sets and costumes for two shows on Broadway in the late 1920s. In 1928 he wrote *Radio Fundamentals, Volume 1: Sources of Electromotive Force* with A.G. Zimmerman. He received a B.S. in Electrical Engineering. He was a member of the Radio Engineering Department, General Electric Company and also worked at one time as an electrician for Western Electric Company.

Sets: 1927 *The Arabian* (Also properties) 1928 *Sakura*

Costumes: 1927 *The Arabian* 1928 *Sakura*†

Harriet Voyt

Harriet Voyt made her debut in 1992 as a costume designer with *Oleanna* at the Orpheum Theatre in New York City, after working for two years as an assistant to playwright David Mamet. She attended the University of Maryland, and then spent twelve years as a model, working through the Eileen Ford Agency. Beginning in the 1970s she often appeared in major fashion magazines and on runways in New York, Paris, Milan, and Tokyo. Designs at the American Repertory Theatre include *Boston Marriage* and *The Cryptogram*. Twenty-first century designs include costumes for *The Square Root of Minus One, Amazons* and *The Imperialist's* at the Club Cave Canem for the Market Theatre in Boston.

Costumes: 1997 *The Old Neighborhood*

Voytek

Voytek Roman, a Polish designer, has designed extensively in the United Kingdom. His set designs for *Strange Interlude* in London were nominated for the Sir Laurence Oliver Award for design of the year. He has also directed plays for television and designed the film *Man in a Glass Booth*. Late twentieth century credits include production design for *Dandelion Dead* on Great Performances and the film *Stealing Heaven*.

Sets: 1985 *Strange Interlude*†

James Wade [British]

British designer James Wade designed sets and costumes for a Gilbert and Sullivan operetta on Broadway in 1955. That same production was also performed by the D'Oyly Opera Company at London's Savoy Theatre in 1962. Representative designs are reproduced in *Gilbert and Sullivan: The Official D'Oyly Carte Picture History* by Robin Wilson and Lloyd Frederic, published by Knopf in 1984. He should not be confused with either the American engineer (d. 1950) or the assistant movie director (1895-1949) all of whom share the same name.

Sets: 1955 *Princess Ida* (Scenic supervisor)

Costumes: 1955 *Princess Ida*

James Wade

James Wade, an engineer, was born in Ireland and graduated from the Darlington (England) Technical College. He emigrated to New York in 1909 and served in the United States Army during World War I. Active with the Yonkers Amateur Opera Company where he directed and designed, he also contributed scenery to a Broadway production. He then worked for the Otis Elevator Company, until 1938 and at the Control Instrument Company during World War II. He died on November 10, 1950 in Yonkers, New York at age 69.

Sets: 1921 *Dear Me*

Robin Wagner

"Robin" (Samuel Anton) Wagner was born on August 31, 1933 in San Francisco. After attending the California School of Fine Arts he began designing in San Francisco for the Golden Gate Opera Workshop in 1953. His first New York production was *And the Wind Blows* at St. Mark's Playhouse in 1959. Since then he has designed many productions, including some of Broadway's most popular musicals of the last twenty years: *A Chorus Line, Dreamgirls, Hair, Kiss Me, Kate*, and *The Producers*. Many of these productions incorporated his trademarks: movable (often automated) scenery containing large-scale structures. He has also designed in Europe, off-Broadway and for opera, ballet, and film. He received the Tony Award, a Drama Desk and Outer Critic's Circle Award for *On the Twentieth Century*, a second Tony Award for *City of Angels*, a third Tony Award for *The Producers*, a Drama Desk Award for *Lenny*, Maharam Awards for *Seesaw, Dreamgirls* and *Chorus Line*, and a Lumen Award for a Rolling Stones tour of the United States. In 1999, he was inducted into the Theatre Hall of Fame.

Sets: 1967 *The Trial of Lee Harvey Oswald* 1968 *The Cuban Thing*; *The Great White Hope*; *Hair*; *Lovers and Other Strangers*; *Promises, Promises* 1969 *My Daughter, Your Son*; *The Watering Place* 1970 *The Engagement Baby*; *Gantry* 1971 *Jesus Christ Superstar*; *Lenny* 1972 *Inner City*; *Lysistrata*; *Sugar* 1973 *Full Circle*; *Seesaw* 1974 *The Fifth Dimension*; *Mack and Mabel* 1975 *A Chorus Line* 1977 *Hair* 1978 *Ballroom*; *On the Twentieth Century* 1979 *Comin' Uptown* 1980 *42nd Street* 1981 *Dreamgirls* 1983 *Merlin* 1985 *Song & Dance* 1987 *Dreamgirls*; *Teddy and Alice* 1988 *Chess* 1989 *City of Angels*; *Jerome Robbins' Broadway*†; *Jerome Robbins' Broadway*† (Supervising set designer) 1992 *Crazy for You*; *Jelly's Last Jam* 1993 *Angels in America, Part II: Perestroika*; *Angels in America: Millennium Approaches* 1995 *Victor/Victoria* 1996 *Big* 1997 *The Life*; *Side Show* 1999 *Kiss Me Kate*; *Saturday Night Fever* 2000 *The Wild Party* 2001 *The Producers*

John Wain

John Wain collaborated on the designs for a 1977 Broadway production. In

1978, he was assistant director of the movie *Licensed to Love and Kill.* He should not be confused with his father, British novelist (1925-1994) and author of *Hurry On Down* among many others.

Sets: 1977 *Ipi Tombi*†

Susan Wain

Susan Wain designed lights and costumes for a 1977 Broadway play, collaborating with her husband, John Wain who designed the scenery. She has served as director of costumes and make-up for Roy Cooney Productions, Ltd. in England, the organization that produced the show. Additional credits include wardrobe for the 1986 movie *Shanghai Surprise.*

Costumes: 1977 *Ipi Tombi* (Costume Supervisor)
Lights: 1977 *Ipi Tombi*†

Frances Waite

Frances Resor Waite was the daughter of the general attorney for the Baltimore & Ohio Railroad's Western lines, Morrison R. Waite and was born and raised in Cincinnati, Ohio. She graduated from Bryn Mawr in 1927 and while taking a class in theatrical design met her future husband, the designer Norman Bel Geddes, becoming his second wife in 1933. Working with the various theater-based activities of her husband, she designed costumes for many productions, two of them on Broadway during the 1930s. Known socially as Mrs. Frances Resor Waite Geddes and professionally as Frances Waite, she died on January 20, 1943.

Costumes: 1930 *Lysistrata* (Costume Supervisor) 1937 *Seige*

Walter Walden

Walter Walden conceived costume, lighting and particularly scenic designs for Broadway productions in the 1920s and 1930s. Additional designs include *The Jayhawker* by Sinclair Lewis, directed by Joe Losey which was performed briefly at the Garrick Theatre in Philadelphia. In February 1937, he appeared at the Studio Club of the Y.W.C.A. and spoke on "Scenic Designing as a Profession" for the members. It is unlikely that the theatrical designer is the same person as the Walter Walden who wrote romantic adventure stories using the pen name Miles Irving.

Sets: 1928 *The Dark Mirror* 1929 *The Subway*; *The Vegetable* 1930 *At the Bottom*; *The Life Line*; *The Seagull* 1932 *Lost Boy* 1934 *Jayhawker* 1937 *Swing It*†† 1938 *Prologue to Glory*
Costumes: 1930 *At the Bottom*; *Troyka* (Costumes conceived)
Lights: 1928 *The Dark Mirror*

Bill Walker

Bill Walker has had a long affiliation with the Long Wharf Theatre, where he served as resident costume designer from 1970 to 1976 and then designed on a regular basis. He has designed costumes for many other regional theaters, including the Indiana Repertory Theatre, Actor's Theatre of Louisville, and at the Kennedy Center, as well as on and off-Broadway. Additional designs include the national tours of *The Lion in Winter* and *Private Lives.* Twenty-first century credits include production design for *George M!* and *Art* for the Le Petit Theatre du Vieux Carre in New Orleans.

Costumes: 1974 *Sizwe Banzi is Dead* 1975 *Ah, Wilderness!*; *The Island* 1977 *The Gin Game*; *The Shadow Box* 1979 *Spokesong* 1980 *Watch on the Rhine* 1981 *The Survivor* 1983 *American Buffalo*; *A View from the Bridge* 1985 *Joe Egg*; *Requiem for a Heavyweight* 1986 *Loot* 1987 *All My Sons*

Billy B. Walker

Billy B. Walker is head electrician and resident lighting designer at Radio City Music Hall where he has designed lights for approximately three hundred productions. He graduated from the University of Illinois. His professional career began with sound design and he created the first sound system for the Indianapolis 500 auto race. After serving as technical director for *Skating Vanities,* he moved to New York City in the mid-1950s and has spent most of the last forty years at Radio City. His responsibilities at Radio City include not only the stage lighting system but the entire electrical operations.

Lights: 1979 *New York Summer* 1995 *Radio City Easter Show*† (The Glory of Easter)

David Walker

David Walker, a British designer of sets and costumes, was born in Calcutta, India on July 18, 1934. He studied at the Central School of Arts and Crafts and with designer Jeannetta Cochrane. He first designed costumes for the Theatre Workshop in England in 1960, working prior to that time in costume and property shops. His designs for opera have been seen at the Metropolitan Opera, the San Francisco Opera, Royal Opera at Covent Garden, at Glyndebourne, in Italy, and in Sweden. In addition, he designs for television and film and does illustrations.

Costumes: 1974 *London Assurance*

Natalie Barth Walker

Natalie Barth Walker first designed costumes on Broadway in 1943, receiving playbill credit both as Natalie Barth and as Natalie Barth Walker. She designed costumes for the theater, ballet, opera, film and television, and worked an assistant to Paul DuPont, Emeline Roche and Millie Sutherland while starting in the costume field. In addition she served as staff designer at both Dazian's and at Stage Costumes, Inc. Films include *Good Bye, New York* and *Hey, Let's Twist*. In the late 1980s she designed costumes for *Peggy and Jackson* for Festival Latino, *An American Solution*, *Faust*, a Bel Canto Opera production, and *Maternity Miasma* at American Folk Theatre among other productions. Born May 24, 1922, she died on January 16, 2000, in Evanston, Illinois.

Costumes: 1943 *Manhattan Nocturne* 1945 *The Wind is Ninety* 1947 *The First Mrs. Fraser* (Costuming); *I Gotta Get Out* (Costume Supervisor) 1948 *Cup of Trembling* 1949 *Two Blind Mice* 1950 *Black Chiffon*; *Season in the Sun* (Costume supervisor) 1951 *Borscht Capades* 1956 *Double in Hearts* 1981 *Marlowe*

Bernhardt Wall

Bernhardt Wall, an artist, worked in a studio at 1869 Bathgate Avenue in New York City during the teens. He was born in Buffalo, New York on December 29, 1872 and studied at the Art Students League in Buffalo, as well as privately. After serving with the 202nd Volunteers in the Spanish-American War, he worked in New York as a commercial artist, occasionally designing costumes until 1913. He then traveled aroundf the United States and produced a series of etchings "Under Western Skies." His works, mainly etchings and lithographies of the American West, are in the permanent collections of the British Museum, the New York Historical Society, the Huntington Library, and the National Library in Madrid. Also a commercial artist and illustrator of historical biographies, he died in Los Angeles, California on February 9, 1956.

Costumes: 1911 *The Lily and the Prince*; *The Triumph of an Empress*

Ben Wallace

Ben Wallace designed costumes for a 1944 Broadway show.

Costumes: 1944 *Take a Bow*

Eugene Wallace

Eugene Wallace designed lights for a 1911 Broadway production.

Lights: 1911 *The Faun*

Janice Wallace

Janice Wallace designed costumes in 1945 on Broadway.

Costumes: 1945 *Make Yourself at Home*

Jean Wallace

Jean Wallace designed costumes on Broadway in 1976. It is not likely that the costume designer is the actress (d. 1990) married to Franchot Tone from 1941-1949 and Cornel Wilde from 1951-1989 with the same name.

Costumes: 1976 *Wheelbarrow Closers*

Ronald Wallace

Ronald Wallace began a long association with the Long Wharf Theatre when it was formed in 1965, amassing extensive credits. He also designed many productions off-Broadway (especially for the New York Shakespeare Festival), at the Edinburgh International Festival of the Arts and in London's West End. In addition, his designs have been seen at the Kennedy Center and in regional theaters including the Cleveland Playhouse, the Actors Theatre of Louisville, and StageWest, and on television. Together with lighting designer Judy Rasmuson, he is active in arts and environmental causes. He should not be confused with the poet and academic who has the same name.

Lights: 1971 *Solitaire/ Double Solitaire* 1973 *The Changing Room* 1974 *The National Health; Sizwe Banzi is Dead* 1975 *Ah, Wilderness!; The Island* 1976 *Comedians; Pal Joey* 1977 *The Gin Game; The Shadow Box* 1979 *Strangers* 1980 *Watch on the Rhine* 1983 *American Buffalo; Passion; A View from the Bridge* 1985 *Joe Egg; Requiem for a Heavyweight* 1987 *All My Sons* 1988 *Checkmates*

Jane Wallack

Jane Wallack designed sets for a 1919 Broadway production.

Sets: 1919 *An Exchange of Wives*†

William Oden Waller

William Oden Waller, known as W. Odenwaller, William Oldenwald and by other variations on his name, was active on Broadway between 1921 and 1940. In 1924 the W. Oden Waller Scenic Studio was located at 530 West 47th Street and he resided in Woodcliff, New Jersey. In 1932 he resided at 1813 2nd Avenue, New York City with Charles Odenwald, a decorator, Karl Odenwald, a painter, and Max Odenwald, an electrician. It is possible that the designer is the same U.S. Army Private William Odenwald, recipient of the Purple Heart and a Silver Star, who died in Luxembourg on February 16, 1945.

Sets: 1921 *Dover Road* 1922 *Lights Out* 1923 *The Nervous Wreck; Red Light Annie; A Square Peg* 1924 *In His Arms* 1925 *Paid; The Sea Woman* 1926 *Chicago; George White's Scandals*†; *Loose Ends* 1927 *Manhattan Mary; The Spider; Take the Air* 1928 *George White's Scandals*†; *He Understood Women; The Song Writer; The Spider* 1929 *George White's Scandals*†; *June Moon* 1930 *Suspense* 1931 *The Social Register*† 1933 *June*

Moon 1935 *Rain; Seven Keys to Baldpate* 1936 *Bright Honor; The County Chairman; Dear Old Darling* 1937 *Fulton of Oak Falls* 1940 *Boys and Girls Together; Return of the Vagabond*

Betty Walls

Betty Walls designed gowns for a featured player in a 1921 Broadway play.

Costumes: 1921 *Golden Days* (Miss Helen Hayes' gowns)

Mary Walls

Mary Walls was active on Broadway between 1920 and 1936. She worked for many years as a buyer for a New York department store before opening her own shop, featuring women's fashions, in the early 1920s.

Costumes: 1920 *Merchants of Venus* (Miss McComa's gowns) 1921 *The Survival of the Fittest* (Miss Hall's gowns) 1930 *Room of Dreams* (Women's costumes) 1936 *A Private Affair* (Miss Linley's costumes)

Andy Walmsley

Andy Walmsley was born into a 'showbiz' family on September 23, 1966 in Blackpool, England and studied interior design at the Leeds Polytechnic. With both parents appearing on stage, he was familiar with backstage areas, and by the time he was 15 had enough experience to begin designing. His wide experience for television game shows for ITV and BBC includes his first design, *The Paul Daniels Magic Show*, and the extraordinarily-popular and often-duplicated set for *Who Wants to be a Millionaire*. Inspired by the artistry and work ethic of John Napier, Walmsley was the youngest designer, at age 22, to work in London's West End. He designed such successful shows in the early 1990s, that much of his time in the middle of the decade was occupied with creating sets for subsequent versions throughout the world. Recent designs include *Oliver!* in the West End and *Greed*, hosted by Jerry Springer on London's Channel 5.

Sets: 1990 *Buddy: The Buddy Holly Story* 1993 *Blood Brothers*

Costumes: 1993 *Blood Brothers*

Thomas A. Walsh

Thomas A. Walsh was born on September 20, 1955 in Burbank, California and attended Hollywood High School and the California Institute of the Arts. His father, Arthur Walsh, was a Metro-Goldwyn-Meyer contract actor and a night-club comedian. He has worked as a scenic artist, union stagehand, assistant designer (to Sally Jacobs at the Mark Taper Forum), and carpenter as well as a designer. His credits include television, interior design, theaters and the film *The Handmaid's Tale.* He credits Sally Jacobs, Tony Walton and Edward Burbridge as major influences. Late twentieth century credits include the set design for *Playback* at the Court Theatre.

Sets: 1979 *Zoot Suit* 1980 *Children of a Lesser God* 1983 *Brothers*

Tony Walton

Tony (Anthony John) Walton, a scenic and costume designer, was born in Walton-on-Thames, Surrey, England on October 24, 1934, and studied at Radley College, the City of Oxford School of Technology, Art and Commerce and at the Slade School of Fine Arts. Prior to designing for the theater he worked as a commercial artist and illustrator. His theatrical designs have often been seen in both England and the United States, beginning with the 1955-56 season for Peter Haddon's Company at the Wimbledon Theatre. His designs for film include *Mary Poppins* and *Murder on the Orient Express, All That Jazz, The Wiz* and *The Boy Friend.* A prolific and creative designer, Mr. Walton has won many awards and nominations for set design in both theater and film, including Tony Awards for *Pippin, The House of Blue Leaves,* and *Guys and Dolls,* an Emmy Award for *Death of a Salesman,* an Academy Award for *All That Jazz,* membership in the Theater Hall of Fame in 1991, and membership in the Interior Design Hall of Fame in 1993. A 1989 exhibit at the American Museum of the Moving Image, "Tony Walton: Designing for Stage and Screen," featured his designs, as have most books written about major scenic designers in the last fifty years.

Sets: 1961 *Once There Was a Russian* 1962 *A Funny Thing Happened on the Way to the Forum* 1964 *Golden Boy* 1966 *The Apple Tree* 1972 *Pippin* 1973 *The Good Doctor; Shelter; Uncle Vanya* 1975 *Bette Midler's Clams on the Half Shell Revue; Chicago* 1976 *1600 Pennsylvania Avenue*† 1977 *The Act* 1980 *A Day in Hollywood/A Night in the Ukraine* 1981 *Sophisticated Ladies; Woman of the Year* 1982 *Little Me* 1984 *Hurlyburly; The Real Thing; Whoopi Goldberg* 1985 *I'm Not Rappaport; Leader of the Pack* 1986 *The House of Blue Leaves; Social Security* 1987 *The Front Page* 1989 *Anything Goes; Grand Hotel, The Musical; Lend Me a Tenor* 1990 *Six Degrees of Separation* 1991 *Will Rogers Follies* 1992 *Conversations with My Father; Death and the Maiden; Four Baboons Adoring the Sun; Guys and Dolls; Tommy Tune Tonite! A Song and Dance Act* 1993 *A Grand Night for Singing; Laughter on the 23rd Floor; She Loves Me* 1994 *A Christmas Carol; Picnic* 1995 *A Christmas Carol; Company* 1996 *A Christmas Carol; A Funny Thing Happened on the Way to the Forum* 1997 *1776; A Christmas Carol; King David; Steel Pier* 1998 *A Christmas Carol* 1999 *Annie Get Your Gun* 2000 *The Man Who Came to Dinner; Taller Than a Dwarf; Uncle Vanya*

Costumes: 1961 *Once There Was a Russian* 1962 *A Funny Thing Happened on the Way to the Forum* 1963 *The Rehearsal* 1964 *Golden Boy* (Also projections) 1966 *The Apple Tree* 1973 *The Good Doctor; Shelter* (Also projections); *Uncle Vanya* 1975 *Bette Midler's Clams on the Half Shell Revue* 1976 *1600 Pennsylvania Avenue* 1982 *Little Me* 1984 *Whoopi Goldberg* (Visual Consultant) 1989 *Anything Goes* 1996 *A Funny Thing Happened on the Way to the Forum* 2000 *Uncle Vanya*

Ward

The gowns for a 1905 Broadway production were designed by "Ward." The credit most likely belongs to Agnes Ward, a dressmaker, who maintained a small salon at 777 East 174th Street in New York City at that time. She resided at 1740 Bathgate Avenue.

Costumes: 1905 *De Lancy* (Gowns)

Ward and Harvey Studios

Ward and Harvey Studios, comprised of designers Herbert Ward and Walter M. Harvey (d. 1945), received credit for the scenic design of Broadway productions from 1921 to 1932. Ward & Harvey Studios, Inc. was located at 502 West 38th Street, New York City. Both men designed productions individually as well, and additional information and credits can be found under their names.

Sets: 1927 *Oh, Ernest*; *Talk about Girls*; *White Lights* 1928 *Atlas and Eva*; *Divorce a La Carte*; *Present Arms* 1929 *The Booster*; *The Crooks Convention*; *Lady Fingers*; *The Silver Swan* 1930 *Bad Girl*; *Lew Leslie's Blackbirds*; *So Was Napoleon* 1931 *Old Man Murphy* 1932 *The Surgeon*

Lights: 1930 *The Vanderbilt Revue*†

Anthony Ward

British designer Anthony Robert Ward was born on January 6, 1957 and received his B.A. degree from the Wimbledon School of Art. He started his career designing in small regional and London theaters, but soon began designing for the major ones, including the Royal Shakespeare Company, the Royal National Theatre, the Royal Ballet, Donmar Warehouse and the English National Opera. He lives and works from a studio in London, and often travels to the European continent where his designs have been commissioned by the Paris and Bastille Opera Companies and De Vlaamse Opera in Antwerp, among others. Additional productions in the United States include sets and costumes for *The Winter's Tale* for RSC, which also ran at the Brooklyn Academy of Music, directed by Adrian Noble, *The Makropulos Case* for the Metropolitan Opera, and *Oklahoma!* in the 2001-2002 Broadway season. Honors include several Olivier Award nominations, and the Olivier Award for costume design in 1996 for *A Midsummer Night's Dream* and for scenic design in 1999 for *Oklahoma!*. He was also nominated for a Tony Award for the scenery for *A Midsummer Night's Dream*.

Sets: 1996 *A Midsummer Night's Dream*
Costumes: 1996 *A Midsummer Night's Dream*

Herbert Ward

Herbert Ward designed scenery for Broadway plays from 1921 to 1934 and through Ward & Harvey Studios, Inc. Herbert Ward was president and Walter Harvey was secretary and treasurer of the scenic studio where they painted scenery for their own designs as well as for other designers. The scenic artist and designer who resided at 502 West 38th Street, should not be confused with the fiction writer (1861-1932) with the same name.

Sets: 1921 *George White's Scandals* 1922 *George White's Scandals*† 1923 *Adrienne*; *Nifties of 1923*† 1927 *Bye, Bye, Bonnie*; *Caste* 1930 *First Night*† 1931 *Papavert*†; *Unexpected Husband*† 1932 *Through the Years*†; *Trick for Trick*† 1933 *It Happened Tomorrow*† 1934 *All the King's Horses*; *A Ship Comes in*†

Toni Ward

Toni Ward designed costumes for two plays in the 1942-43 Broadway season. She spent most of her career as an interior designer, but worked as well in the theater department of the William Morris Agency. Addition credits for costume design include *Sand Hog*. Known in private life as Mrs. Toni W. Holzager, she died on December 5, 1973 at age 66 in Great Neck, Long Island, New York.

Costumes: 1937 *One Third of a Nation* 1942 *The Eve of Saint Mark* 1943 *The Patriots*†

William B. Warfel

William B. Warfel was born in Amherst, Massachusetts on February 12, 1933. He received both a B.A. (1955) and an M.F.A. (1957) at Yale University studying lighting design with Stanley McCandless. In 1967 he was appointed Lighting Director at Yale Repertory, where he amassed many credits at the same time he taught and mentored numerous students. After a distinguished career, he became Emeritus Professor of Theatre

Design at Yale University. Respected for his expertise as a theater consultant, he is president of Systems Design Associates, a consulting company for performance spaces, comprised of Ming Cho Lee, John R. Hood and Eugene C. Leitermann.

Lights: 1985 *Blood Knot*

Leon R. Warren

Leon R. Warren designed a set in 1932 for a Broadway show. At that same time, he was secretary and treasurer of Warren Brothers., Inc., dress manufacturers, located at 463 Seventh Avenue New York City. He resided at 3521 168th street in Flushing, Long Island, New York in the mid-1930s.

Sets: 1932 *Incubator*

Mary Mease Warren

Mary Meese Warren designed costumes on Broadway in 1975. She has also designed costumes for *Generations of the Dead in the Abyss of Coney Island Madness* at Long Wharf and both *Candida, Ma Rainey's Black Bottom* at Center Stage in Baltimore and *Slow Dance on the Killing Ground* at the Crossroads Theatre in New Brunswick, New Jersey. Recent credits include costumes for *Ceremonies in Dark Old Men* at Long Wharf Theatre.

Costumes: 1975 *The First Breeze of Summer*

William Warren

William Warren, an actor and company manager, died at age 73 on February 28, 1941. He spent sixteen years as head carpenter at the Metropolitan Opera House, beginning in 1925. He toured with the production of *Uncle Tom's Cabin* at the beginning of the twentieth century, performed often in Boston, and played a role in *Dr. Clyde*. His father, the actor William Warren, Sr., was a long time member of the company at the Walnut Street Theatre in Philadelphia in the latter half of the nineteenth century.

Sets: 1933 *Thoroughbred*

Will Washcoe

Will (Wilfred) Washcoe designed lights in 1941 on Broadway. Born on August 30, 1917, he spent the majority of his life in New York City. After he died in March 1966, his wife, Emma Washcoe (1914-1985), moved to Houston, Texas where she died in 1985.

Lights: 1941 *They Walk Alone*

Perry Watkins

Perry Watkins worked as a flower seller, journalist and insurance salesman before taking a trip to New York City and discovering scene design. He broke the color barrier by becoming the first black member of United Scenic Artists in the late 1930s when *Mamba's Daughter's* opened on Broadway. The productions he designed between 1935 and 1938 were all part of the Harlem unit of the Federal Theatre project, performed in what were considered at the time to be Broadway houses, if not necessarily Broadway productions. He worked as a producer, beginning with *Beggars' Holiday* in 1946 and *Moon of Mah'no'men* in 1947, working through Production Associates with Thomas Ward Lanyan and Dale Wasserman. He was also a director and art director for films and was preparing to go to Africa to make a film at the time of his death. Mr. Watkins died in Newburgh, New York at age 67 on August 14, 1974.

Sets: 1937 *Moon of the Caribees, Etc.* (Federal Theater Project production) **1938** *Haiti* (Federal Theater Project production); *Pinocchio* (Federal Theater Project production) **1939** *Mamba's Daughter's* **1940** *Big White Fog*; *Mamba's Daughter's* **1942** *Heart of a City*; *Three Men on a Horse*; *You'll See the Stars* **1943** *Bright Lights of 1943*; *Manhattan Nocturne*; *Run, Little Chillun* **1944** *Take It As It Comes* **1945** *Blue Holiday* **1949** *Forward the Heart* **1954** *The Integration Show Case* **1956** *Harbour Lights*

Costumes: 1935 *Three Men on a Horse* (Federal Theater Project production) **1938** *Androcles and the Lion* (Federal Theater Project production) **1939** *Mamba's Daughter's* **1940** *Mamba's Daughter's* **1942** *Three Men on a Horse* **1943** *Bright Lights of 1943*; *Run, Little Chillun* **1945** *Blue Holiday* (Designed and supervised)

Lights: 1940 *Big White Fog* **1945** *Blue Holiday* **1949** *Forward the Heart*

David Watson

David Watson was born on March 13, 1941 in London and was orphaned by the death of his parents in the 1941 London blitz. He was adopted by Leonard and Vera Watson and studied music on scholarship at Westminster Abbey School and the Royal Academy of Music. Known as an actor and singer, he appeared in the London productions of *West Side Story* and *The Fantasticks* prior to moving to the United States and appearing on television and in the theater. He also began directing. In the mid-1980s he was Producing Director for the Sharon Playhouse, and in 1994 was executive director of the Emelin Theatre in Mamaroneck, New York.

Lights: 1974 *Scapino*

Edna Watson

Edna Watson, who created costumes in 1973 on Broadway, began designing off-Broadway in 1966. Originally from Chicago, she began her career in theater as a costume maker. Her New York debut, *The Black Terror* in the early 1970s, occurred when the performers at the Public Theatre successfully lobbied for a black designer. Additional credits include *The Connection, Don't Bother Me, I Can't Cope* and *Step Lively, Boy*. Her career was among those profiled in "Scenes in New York Drama" in the April 1973 issue of *Ebony*.

Costumes: 1973 *The River Niger*

Kristina Watson

Kristina Watson has designed costumes in many regional theaters in the U.S. Credits include *Moby Dick – Rehearsed* and *The Learned Ladies* at the Denver Theatre Center and the national tour of *Oklahoma!* She has designed at Juilliard, Williamstown Theatre Festival, Wolf Trap Farm Park, the Philadelphia Drama Guild and for PBS-TV.

Costumes: 1979 *Loose Ends* **1980** *Past Tense*

Lee Watson

Leland Hale Watson worked steadily in the theater after his professional debut at the Provincetown Playhouse in 1950. He was principally a lighting designer who worked in theater, ballet, opera and television. Born on February 18, 1926 in Charleston, Illinois, he received an M.F.A. at Yale in 1951 after service in World War II and work as a radio engineer. His interest in the theater began in high school. Occasionally Mr. Watson also designed scenery for plays and more rarely costumes. He served as lighting director for CBS-TV from 1951 to 1955, and taught design in many universities and at Lester Polakov's Studio and Forum of Stage Design. He also wrote articles about lighting design and two books, beginning with *Theatrical Lighting Practice* in 1955. *Lighting Design Handbook*, one of the few comprehensive books about lighting design, was published posthumously in 1990. His awards included an Obie for *Machinal* in 1957. Lee Watson died on December 10, 1989 at age 63.

Sets: 1958 *Next President, The-A Musical Salamagundi* **1960** *A Lovely Night* **1961** *The Importance of Being Oscar*
Costumes: 1958 *Next President, The-A Musical Salamagundi* **1961** *The Importance of Being Oscar* (Design by)
Lights: 1955 *The Diary of Anne Frank*; *A View from the Bridge* **1956** *Girls of Summer*; *Harbour Lights*; *Protective Custody* **1957** *The Cave Dwellers*; *Mask and Gown*; *Miss Isobel*; *A Moon for the Misbegotten* **1958** *Next President, The-A Musical Salamagundi*; *The Night Circus*; *Portofino* **1959** *Legend of Lizzie* **1960** *A Lovely Night* **1961** *Do You Know the Milky Way?*; *The Importance of Being Oscar* **1962** *Moby Dick*

Walter Watson

Walter Watson was born December 21, 1928 in Seattle, Washington and learned his craft through workshops, practical classes and under the tutelage of Helene Pons and Ray Diffen. He has designed costumes mainly on the West Coast beginning with designs for the Bon Marche department store and an opera company in Seattle. He also taught pattern drafting at Louise Salinger Academy of Fashion. His costume designs have been recognized with nominations for awards for *The Couch* at the Magic Theatre

and *Too Good to be True* at the Berkeley Repertory Theatre by the Bay Area Critics in California.
Costumes: 1969 *Tiny Alice*† (Men's costumes) **1976** *Something's Afoot*†

John Watt

John Watt, a mechanical engineer by training, designs primarily for television and occasionally for theater. His career in television began in 1958.
Lights: 1983 *Edmund Kean*

Miss Gwyneth Waugh

Miss Gwyneth Waugh designed costumes for featured players in a 1922 Broadway production.
Costumes: 1922 *Billeted*† (Costumes for the Ushers)

Ned Wayburn

The director and producer Ned Wayburn was born in Pittsburgh and began his career in vaudeville playing ragtime piano and singing. He created over 600 productions, including revues, dances, musical comedies, plays and pantomimes, through the Klaw and Erlanger, Shubert, and Florenz Ziegfeld organizations for which he worked at various times. He was especially well known for his incarnations of *The Ziegfeld Follies*. Occasionally he also contributed designs to productions he stages. Wayburn died at age 68 in New York City on September 6, 1942.
Sets: 1913 *The Passing Show of 1913*† (Scene 6 in Acts I, II, also directed and wrote)
Lights: 1912 *The Sun Dodgers* (Also directed and devised)

Rollo Wayne

Rollo Wayne, the designer of the first revolving stage set used in the United States, was born in Louisville, Kentucky on March 5, 1899. He studied at Harvard University and with George Pierce Baker at Workshop 47. The first revolving stage set was used for a production of *H.M.S. Pinafore* produced by the Shuberts in 1926. He worked for the Shuberts for twelve years and also for Florenz Ziegfeld, Lew Leslie and Max Gordon. He died at age 55 on March 18, 1954 in Louisville.

Sets: 1916 *Such Is Life* **1921** *The Chocolate Soldier* **1922** *Springtime of Youth*† **1924** *Parasites*; *Top-Hole* **1925** *The Crooked Friday*; *Man or Devil*; *The Man with a Load of Mischief*; *The Offence*; *Taps* **1926** *H.M.S. Pinafore* **1927** *Murray Will*; *Ruddigore*; *Such Is Life* **1928** *The Common Sin*; *Exceeding Small*; *Gang Way*; *The Great Necker*; *A Lady for a Night*; *Sign of the Leopard*; *So Am I*; *White Lilacs*; *Within the Law* **1929** *Babes in Toyland*; *Cape Cod Follies*; *Congratulations*; *Death Takes a Holiday*; *The First Law*; *Jonesy*; *Nigger Rich*; *Rope's End*; *Security*; *Stripped*; *Young Sinners* **1930** *Babes in Toyland*; *Bird in Hand*; *The Chocolate Soldier*; *The Count of Luxembourg*; *His Majesty's Car*; *The Infinite Shoeblack*†; *Insult*; *Ladies All*; *Lady Clara*; *The Last Enemy*; *The Man in Possession*; *Nine Till Six*; *On the Spot*; *The Prince of Pilsen*; *Purity*; *The Serenade*; *Topaz*; *The Truth Game*; *Up Pops the Devil* **1931** *The Constant Sinner*; *Death Takes a Holiday*; *Everybody's Welcome*; *The Good Companions*; *Marriage for Three*; *Melo*; *A Modern Virgin*; *The Silent Witness*; *Topaz*; *Young Sinners* **1932** *Autumn Crocus*; *Best Years*; *Blessed Event*; *The Boy Friend*; *Happy Landing*; *If Booth Had Missed*; *Peacock*; *The Perfect Marriage*; *The Silent House* **1933** *Best Sellers*; *Double Door*†; *Going Gay*; *Young Sinners* **1934** *First Episode*; *Spring Freshet* **1935** *If a Body*; *A Journey by Night* **1936** *In Heaven and Earth*†; *The Kick Back* **1937** *The Trial of Dr. Beck*

William Weaver

William Weaver received an award for outstanding period design from *Stage Magazine* in the mid-1930s. He was active as a costume and scenic designer for twenty years, designing on Broadway, for the Metropolitan Opera Company, and for the 1933 *Showboat Revue*, which was performed aboard the steamers of the Hudson River Day Line. Mr. Weaver, originally from Asheville, North Carolina, died on August 14, 1937.
Sets: 1920 *The Passing Show of 1921* **1921** *The Rose Girl* **1924** *Princess April* **1925** *Bringing Up Father*
Costumes: 1923 *Music Box Revue*

(Eighth Note Dresses in "Scale" Number) **1924** *Bye, Bye, Barbara*; *Princess April* **1926** *George White's Scandals*† (Additional designs) **1927** *Much Ado About Nothing* **1930** *The Rivals* **1936** *Broadway Sho-Window* **1937** *Frederika*

Bryon Webb

Byron Webb worked as technical director for the Federal Theatre Project in New York and designed lights for the FTP production of *Androcles and the Lion*.
Lights: 1938 *Haiti* (Federal Theater Project production)

Clifton Webb

Clifton Webb, an actor and singer, was born Webb Parmalee Hottenbeck in Indianapolis, Indiana and appeared on stage at the age of seven at Carnegie Hall. He appeared continuously in roles in plays and operas until 1946 when he moved to Hollywood to do films. In 1923 he performed a leading role in a play for which he also designed the men's costumes. He died in Beverly Hills, California on October 13, 1966, with his age reported between 69 and 76.
Costumes: 1923 *Jack and Jill*† (Men's costumes and leading role)

Virginia Dancy Webb

Virginia Dancy Webb was born in New York City on April 8, 1940. She has a B.A. from Vassar College and an M.F.A. from Yale University. She often works in collaboration with her husband, Elmon Webb. Their designs include *Prince Igor*, a joint production of the Cincinnati Conservatory and the New York City Opera, many productions during several seasons at Long Wharf Theatre, and the film *Cold Sweat*. Virginia Dancy Webb has designed for the Mark Taper Forum, Syracuse Stage, Pittsburgh Public Theatre, and off-Broadway. She was staff artist for CBS-TV from 1975 to 1978 and has taught at Vassar and Marymount Colleges.
Sets: 1974 *The National Health*

Florence Weber

Florence Weber designed costumes for a musical revue in 1929 on Broadway.

Costumes: 1929 *Earl Carroll's Sketch Book*

Ben Webster

Ben Webster designed scenery and costumes for a Broadway play in 1925. The designer should not be confused with the British actor (1864-1947) who was appearing in *Gloriana* in London at the time, nor the American jazz tenor saxophonist (d. 1973).
Sets: 1925 *Merchants of Glory*
Costumes: 1925 *Merchants of Glory*

Gil Wechsler

Gilbert Wechsler is from Brooklyn, New York where he was born on February 5, 1942, the son of Arnold and Miriam Wechsler. In 1964 he received a B.S. from New York University and in 1967 an M.F.A. from the Yale University School of Drama. He assisted Jo Mielziner on *Mata Hari* in 1967 and toured with the Harkness Ballet prior to working for various ballet companies, the Guthrie Theatre, and the Shaw and Stratford (Ontario) Festivals in Canada. As principal lighting designer for the Metropolitan Opera he designed nearly one hundred operas in the repertory, reworked earlier designs, and supervised lighting for many televised productions of operas from the Met. Between 1972 and 1976 he was resident lighting designer for the Lyric Opera of Chicago. He credits Charles Elson as a major influence on his career. Recent designs include *Equus* at Stratford, Ontario and both *Die Fledermaus* and *Il Barbiere di Siviglia* at the Metropolitan Opera.
Lights: 1968 *Staircase* **1972** *There's One in Every Marriage*

Michi Weglyn

Michi Nishiura Weglyn was born in Stockton, California on November 29, 1926. Beginning in 1952, simply as "Michi" she designed costumes for the theater, television, night clubs and ice shows, and between 1964 and 1967 she headed a costume construction and design studio, Michi Associates, Ltd. During the civil rights movement in the 1960s she began to tell the story of the internment of Japanese-Americans during World War II, based in part on her own experience. This resulted in eight years of research culminating in the critically acclaimed *Years of Infamy: The Untold Story of America's Concentration Camps* published in 1976 and then adapted for on television. Between the publication of the book and her death in New York City on April 26, 1999, she worked on behalf of former internees.

Costumes: 1952 *Collector's Item* (as: Michi: Costume Supervisor) **1954** *Hit the Trail* (as: Michi)

Gustav Weidhaas

Gustav A. Weidhaas designed sets and special effects for *George White's Scandals* throughout the 1920s. He also worked for other producers of plays, musicals and variety shows such as Billy Rose, Florenz Ziegfeld, David Belasco and Charles Frohman, specializing in "illusions." Gustav Weidhaas was the head of Weidhaas Studios, 536 West 29th Street. His wife was the costume designer Frances Feist and they had one son, Ted Weidhaas, also a theatrical designer. He died at age 62 in Bronxville, New York on August 21, 1938.

Sets: 1923 *George White's Scandals†* **1924** *George White's Scandals†* **1925** *George White's Scandals†* **1926** *George White's Scandals†* **1928** *George White's Scandals†* **1929** *George White's Scandals†*

Ted Weidhaas

Francis "Ted" Weidhaas was born into a family of theatrical designers. His mother, Frances Feist, for whom he was named, was a costume designer active on Broadway in the 1930s who also designed for the Cotton Club. His father, Gustav Weidhaas, created scenic designs and effects on Broadway and for other theaters during the teens and twenties. Ted Weidhaas, who designed the contour curtain for Radio City Music Hall also created masks and murals as well as scenic designs. He died on December 19, 1986.

Sets: 1929 *George White's Scandals†*; *Ned Wayburn's Gambols* **1934** *Thumbs Up†*

Michael Weight

Michael Weight was born in Somerset West, Cape Colony, South Africa on May 31, 1906. He studied at the University of Cape Town and the Slade School of Art after moving to England. His debut as a set designer was *Dandy Dick* at the Hammersmith Lyric Theatre in 1930, followed by many productions throughout the United Kingdom and in London from the 1930s to the 1950s. He designed the *Sherlock Holmes Exhibition* for the Festival of Britain in 1951, and also designed films and television plays. He died in Rome, Italy on January 14, 1973 at age 66.

Sets: 1956 *Separate Tables*

David Weiner

Lighting designer David Weiner has many credits in off-Broadway theaters including the Music-Theatre Group, the American Place Theatre, the Vineyard Theatre, and the Joseph Papp Public Theatre. He began his professional activity working with Paul Gallo as an intern in 1992 and subsequently became his assistant on productions including *Titanic*. He occasionally designs scenery, notably *Oxygen* and *Sweeney Todd*, for the San Diego Repertory Company. Twenty-first century designs include lights for *Saved* produced by the Theatre for a New Audience and *References to Salvador Dali Make Me Hot* at the Joseph Papp Public Theatre.

Lights: 1999 *Amy's View†* **2000** *Betrayal; The Real Thing†*

Jules Weiss

Jules C. Weiss was a tailor who founded a small, exclusive firm, Jules C. Weiss & Co., at 321 Fifth Avenue in 1870, remaining in business until he retired in 1928. Among his private and theatrical customers was James Buchanon Brady, more commonly known as Diamond Jim Brady. He died at age 88 in Coney Island, New York on January 18, 1940. The tailor should not be confused with the La MaMa E.T.C. patron (d. 1985) although their names are the same.

Costumes: 1913 *The Amazons†* (Miss Burke's clothes)

Julie Weiss

Julie Weiss, who first designed costumes on Broadway in 1979, graduated from the University of California and received an M.F.A. from Brandeis University. She has designed costumes for many shows at the Mark Taper Forum, including *Gethsemane*, *Ashes* and *Says I, Says He*. Her designs for television include *For Richer, For Poorer*. Best known for her designs for film, her designs include *Searching for Bobby Fischer*, *Tequila Sunrise*, *Independence Day*, *Steel Magnolias*, *Twelve Monkeys*, and *The Freshman*. Honors include Emmy Awards for *Woman of Independent Means* and the ABC television special *The Dollmaker*, a Tony Award nomination for *The Elephant Man* and the 2000 Costume Designers Guild Award for *American Beauty*.

Costumes: 1979 *The Elephant Man* **1981** *Piaf* **1982** *Macbeth* **1983** *Total Abandon* **1991** *Liza Minnelli: Stepping Out at Radio City*

Marc B. Weiss

Marc B. Weiss studied biology in college but soon discovered theater, first as an avocation and subsequently as a career. He began his professional career designing for the Washington Ballet and Arena Stage in Washington, D.C. He has designed for television, regional theaters, nightclub acts, and productions for the American Shakespeare Festival. Additional credits are lights for *The March on Russia*, presented by the Chelsea Stage in association with the Cleveland Playhouse, the international tours of *The Music of Andrew Lloyd Webber* and *My One and Only*, and sets and lights for *Scaramouche*. His combined credits number over two hundred-fifty productions. Weiss is also an international theater consultant. Honors include a Tony Award nomination for *A Moon for the Misbegotten*.

Lights: 1972 *Six Rms Riv Vu* **1973** *Medea* **1974** *Cat on a Hot Tin Roof*; *Find Your Way Home*; *Words and Music* **1975** *Hughey/ Duet*; *We Interrupt this Program* **1976** *The Eccentricities of a Nightingale* **1977** *Ladies at the Alamo* **1978** *Death Trap* **1979** *Break a Leg*; *Once a Catholic*

1980 *Horowitz and Mrs. Washington*; *A Life* **1981** *Animals*; *The First*; *The One Act Play Festival*; *Shakespeare's Cabaret*; *To Grandmother's House We Go* **1982** *84 Charing Cross Road*; *Othello* **1983** *Zorba* **1984** *Design for Living*; *A Moon for the Misbegotten*; *The Rink* **1986** *Raggedy Ann*; *Uptown...It's Hot* **1987** *Cabaret* **1988** *Macbeth* **1993** *Anna Christie* **1994** *Hedda Gabler* **1995** *Garden District*

Polaire Weissman

Polaire Weissman and Alice Beer ran the costume workshop of the Neighborhood Playhouse during its' height of activity in the 1920s. She then was instrumental in forming The Costume Institute' along with Aline Bernstein, Lee Simonson, and Irene Lewisohn, working initially as aide to Irene Lewisohn. Founded in 1937 as the Museum of Costume Art, Costume Institute, Inc., Polaire Weissman was the first executive director, supervising a collection of about 500 items, mainly theatrical and regional costumes, located in a loft on West 46th Street. In 1946 the collection, then about 10,000 items, was given space at the Metropolitan Museum of Art and granted curatorial status in 1959. By the time she retired in 1968 (succeeded by Adolph Cavallo for two years, and then Stella Blum), the Institute was firmly established, supported by annual fund raising events, and focused on fashion. Born on April 22, 1897, she died in New York City in November 1986.

Costumes: 1935 *Bitter Oleander*

Ena Welch

Ena Welch, who designed costumes for two productions in the first decade of the twentieth century, was associated with the Klaw and Erlanger costume company. Playbills of that era also refer to her on the staff at Daly's Theatre as "Mistress of Wardrobe."

Costumes: 1905 *The Mayor of Tokio*[†] **1908** *Mary's Lamb*[†] (Fancy costumes)

Max Weldy

Max Weldy first designed costumes for the Folies Bergère. He had his own business in Paris in the 1920s and early 1930s (Weldy, Paris) where he executed costume designs for use in Paris and

New York. In the late 1930s he moved to London where John Ringling saw his designs and invited him to work for Ringling Brothers Circus. He remained with the circus until the 1960s, spending time in the United States designing and executing costumes for the circus, movies and the theater. His credits on Broadway include costume designs and a single scenic design in 1931. Born in France on June 18, 1895, Weldy died in November 1983.

Sets: 1931 *The Laugh Parade*
Costumes: **1926** *Gay Paree*[†]; *Katja* **1927** *Artists and Models*[†] (Additional costumes) **1931** *The Laugh Parade*; *Of Thee I Sing*[†] **1932** *Face the Music*[†] **1933** *Of Thee I Sing*[†] **1942** *Heart of a City*[†] (Revue costumes)

Orson Welles

Orson Welles is remembered as the "boy wonder" who took Hollywood by storm with the film classic *Citizen Kane*, and who scared thousands of Americans with a radio broadcast about a Martian invasion of Earth, *War of the Worlds*. He was born George Orson Welles on May 6, 1915 in Kenosha, Wisconsin and began performing at the age of two. He spent most of his life at the center of various controversies. In 1937, while working with the Federal Theatre Project, he designed and directed a production of *Dr. Faustus* notable for its austerity. Mr. Welles died at the age of 70 on October 10, 1985.

Sets: 1937 *Dr. Faustus* **1938** *The Cradle Will Rock*
Costumes: 1937 *Dr. Faustus* (Designed and directed)

Alice Wellman

Alice Wellman was born May 11, 1900 in Salt Lake City, Utah. She was an actress and singer in films and on stage from 1926 to 1949, working in New York and Europe. In 1937 she supervised costumes for a play on Broadway. She also worked as a theater manager, director and as a casting director for films. In the 1960s she turned her attention to writing books, particularly for children. She grew up in Angola, Portuguese West Africa, the daughter

of missionaries, and many of her stories recorded her memories and adventures in Africa. Alice Wellman died in 1984.
Costumes: **1937** *Straw Hat* (Costume Supervisor)

Milnor Wells

Milnor H. Wells, often acknowledged in playbills as M. H. Wells, designed lights for productions during the first decade of the twentieth century. He was an electrical engineer with offices at 22 East 24th Street in Manhattan during that time, while residing at 403 McDonough Street in Brooklyn. He also served as staff electrician at various Broadway theaters and in that capacity probably contributed designs to many more productions than those for which he is credited.

Lights: 1900 *Borderside* **1901** *The Forest Lovers* **1904** *The Serio-Comic Governess* **1907** *The Boys of Company "B"* (as: M. H. Wells) **1908** *The Prisoner of Zenda* **1909** *Penelope* **1910** *Mrs. Dot*

Pauline Wells

Pauline Wells designed costumes for a 1922 Broadway production.
Costumes: 1922 *A Fantastic Fricassee*

Mark Wendland

Mark Wendland received a B.A. from Carnegie Mellon University and has designed scenery and costumes throughout the United States and off-Broadway since the mid-1980s. Known for his strikingly original abstract designs he often collaborates with director Brian Kulick, Among his many designs on the West Coast are scenery for *Billy the Kid, Cosmonaut, School for Wives*, and *Sheridan* at the La Jolla Playhouse while in residence on a Pew Artist's Grant, and *Much Ado about Nothing* at the Berkeley Repertory Theatre. He has designed at Trinity Repertory Theatre, the St. Louis Repertory, the Denver Theatre Center, the Mark Taper Forum, the Huntington Theatre, the Alley Theatre, the Guthrie Theatre, and the Goodman Theatre, among others. Off-Broadway credits include *A Dybbuk* at the Joseph Papp Public Theatre, both *Timon of Athens* and *Cymbeline* at the Delacorte

Theatre and productions at the Atlantic Theatre, Playwrights Horizons, the Classic Stage Company and the New York Theatre Workshop. Twenty-first century credits include *A Fair Country* for the Hungtinton Theatre Company and *Almost Holy Picture* in the 2001-2002 Broadway season.

Sets: **1999** *Death of a Salesman*

Angela Wendt

Angela Wendt, who is from Germany, studied in Berlin at Hochschule der Kunste before emigrating to New York in 1981 pursuing a career in acting and dance. She claims that stage fright caused her to change focus, initially to scene painting and then to fashion and theatrical design. She has designed numerous music videos, the feature film *Montreal Childhood's End*, and for dance. Her many off-Broadway credits include productions at the New York Theatre Workshop, the Classic Stage Company, the Samuel Beckett Theatre, the Joseph Papp Public Theatre. Honors include a Drama Desk Award nomination for the costumes for *Rent*.

Costumes: **1996** *Rent* **1997** *All My Sons*

John Wenger

John Wenger was born in Elizabeth, Odessa, Russia on June 16, 1891. He studied at the Imperial Art School in Odessa and the National Academy of Design. After moving to the United States in 1903 he found work as a jewelry designer and scenic artist. He designed settings for the Boston Opera Company, the Metropolitan Opera, and the Greenwich Village Theatre and was art director for the Rivoli, Capital and Roxy movie theaters. His film designs included *Paramount on Parade* in 1929. He was the first designer to use gauze backdrops and lateral moving scenery, for *Good Boy* in 1928. This innovative designer and watercolorist died on August 24, 1976 in Manhattan at age 89. His designs and paintings are in the permanent collections of the Museum of the City of New York, the Metropolitan Museum of Art, and the Museum of Modern Art.

Sets: **1921** *The Poppy God* **1922** *George White's Scandals*† **1924** *Great Music*; *Round the Town*†; *Ziegfeld Follies: 1924*† **1925** *Bridge of Distances*; *The Master of the Inn*; *The Monkey Talks*; *Tip Toes* **1926** *No Foolin'*†; *Oh, Kay* **1927** *Funny Face*; *Hit the Deck*; *Piggy*; *Spring Song* **1928** *Good Boy*; *Here's Howe*; *Oh, Kay*; *Ups-a-Daisy* **1929** *Spring Is Here* **1933** *Pardon My English* **1946** *Walk Hard*

Lights: **1946** *Walk Hard*

L. Wenzelberg

L. Wenzelberg collaborated on the designs for a 1917 Broadway show.

Costumes: **1917** *Furs and Frills*†

Christina Weppner

Christina Weppner, the daughter of architect, Robert Arthur Weppner, Jr., was born on June 29, 1948 in Washington, D.C. She studied at Connecticut College, where she designed her first play, *Tiger at the Gates*, and received a B.F.A. at the New York University School of the Arts. A designer of both sets and costumes, she has been influenced by designers including Ming Cho Lee, Oliver Smith, Ben Edwards and Douglas Schmidt. Additional designs include scenery for the plays *The Breaks* and *Estrella!: Who Can You Trust in a City of Lies?* and for *Water on the Moon* a solo dance piece by Maureen Fleming.

Costumes: **1980** *Nuts*

Lou Wertheim

Lou Wertheim, who designed sets on Broadway in 1929 and 1930, was credited in the *Messin' Around* playbill as the former manager of Willy Pogany Studios. Louis and Hyman Wertheim produced ladies hats at 49 West 37th Street in New York City in the 1920s and 1930s.

Sets: **1929** *Messin' 'Round* **1930** *With Privileges*

Roland West

Roland West was a film director who began acting in plays and vaudeville in his native Cleveland, Ohio, where he was born on February 20, 1885. He began writing some of his own sketches prior to joining the Lowe Circuit as a producer of short acts and skits. His first film was the silent *Lost Souls*, which he directed and co-produced. Later films included several starring Norma Talmadge. The first talkie he directed was *Alibi* with Chester Morris in 1928. He died on March 31, 1952 in Santa Monica, California at age 65.

Sets: 1918 *The Unknown Purple*
Lights: 1918 *The Unknown Purple*

Peter Wexler

Peter Wexler received a B.S. in design in 1958 from the University of Michigan, where he majored in photography and painting. He attended graduate school at Yale University. Born on October 31, 1936 in New York City, he began designing with sets, costumes and lights for the New York Shakespeare Festival's production of *Anthony and Cleopatra* in 1959. Since then he has amassed extensive credits for plays, operas, television and films throughout the United States. In the early 1970s he began producing musical events based on his work with the Promenades and Rug Concerts at the New York Philharmonic. His company has produced, programmed, designed, and directed museum exhibitions, concerts, public spaces, and media events for major symphony orchestras, opera companies, museums, government agencies and the private sector. His models and drawings have been widely collected and exhibited. Peter Wexler has been married to Emmy Award winning costume designer Constance Ross Wexler since 1962. Among his many awards are Maharam and Drama Desk Awards for *The Happy Time*, a Los Angeles Drama Critics Circle Award in 1971, and the 1996 Bard Award for Excellence in Architecture and Urban Design.

Sets: 1966 *A Joyful Noise* **1968** *The Happy Time* **1970** *Minnie's Boys* **1971** *The Trial of the Catonsville Nine* **1978** *A Broadway Musical*
Lights: 1966 *A Joyful Noise*

James Whale

James Whale was born on July 22, 1896 in Dudley, Staffordshire, England and spent his career as an actor, designer and film director. He started work as a cartoonist for *The Bystander* but began acting while a prisoner of war in Germany in 1917 and 1918. After the war he performed and designed for the Birmingham Repertory Company, followed by ten years of theater performances and designs throughout England. He moved to New York City in 1929 where he directed and produced plays before going to Hollywood. His films include *Frankenstein, The Invisible Man, The Road Back*, and *Show Boat*. He died on May 29, 1957 in Hollywood, California.

Sets: 1929 *A Hundred Years Old*; *Journey's End*

George Whalen

George Whalen, an electrician, lived and worked from 268 West 17th Street in New York in 1908.

Lights: 1908 *Marcelle*

John Whalen

John J. Whalen was an electrician who worked for Shubert Enterprises, particularly on productions at the Lyric Theatre. He also created special effects. He was active on Broadway in the teens and probably was responsible for more productions than those for which he received credit. He resided at 563 West 170th Street, New York City in 1915.

Lights: 1908 *Mlle. Mischief*; *Mr. Hamlet of Broadway*† (as: J. J. Whalen) **1909** *The Girl and the Wizard*; *Old Dutch* **1910** *The Prince of Bohemia* **1912** *The Passing Show of 1912*† **1915** *Alone at Last*; *Hands-Up*; *Taking Chances* **1916** *Fixing Sister*

Albertine Randall Wheelan

Albertine Randall Wheelan, an illustrator and costume designer, was born on May 27, 1863 in San Francisco, California. She studied at the San Francisco School of Design and with Virgil Williams before marrying Farifax H. Wheelan in 1887. An active illustrator of books, magazines and stained glass windows, she designed costumes for many productions directed by David Belasco, with whom she was associated for eighteen years. She also created illustrations for *St. Nicholas Magazine* for twenty-five years. Mrs. Wheelan died at age 90 on January 9, 1954 in Litchfield, Connecticut.

Costumes: 1906 *The Rose of the Rancho* 1907 *A Grand Army Man* 1914 *Sari†* 1917 *Tiger Rose†* 1919 *The Son-Daughter* 1921 *George White's Scandals†*; *The Perfect Fool†* 1922 *George White's Scandals†*

Gary James Wheeler

Gary James Wheeler designed a set in 1973 on Broadway.

Sets: 1973 *The River Niger*

Melissa Whiffen

Melissa Whiffen designed gowns for a Broadway show in 1934.

Costumes: 1934 *Good-Bye Please* (Gowns Designed By)

Rex Whistler

Rex Whistler, a theatrical designer, etcher and painter, was born in Eltham, Kent, England on June 24, 1905. He studied at the Architectural Association, the Slade School of Art and in Rome. His first designs were seen at Covent Garden in 1934, and he was widely regarded for his designs for ballet. He was also known for his murals, notably the one at the Tate Gallery Restaurant, and book illustrations. He fought with the British forces during World War II and died at Normandy, France on July 27, 1944.

Sets: 1929 *Wake Up and Dream†* 1935 *Victoria Regina* 1936 *Victoria Regina* 1938 *Victoria Regina* 1947 *Love for Love* Costumes: 1929 *Wake Up and Dream†* 1935 *Victoria Regina* 1936 *Victoria Regina* 1938 *Victoria Regina* Lights: 1935 *Victoria Regina* 1936 *Victoria Regina†* 1938 *Victoria Regina*

D. T. White

D. T. White designed scenery for a production in the first Broadway season of the twentieth century.

Sets: 1900 *The Man of Forty†*

Miles White

Miles White made his debut on Broadway in 1938 with the costume designs for *Right This Way*. Unlike many designers of his era, he is unique in his early specialization in costume – resisting the then common practice to design

both sets and costumes. The son of a lawyer, he was born in Oakland, California on July 27, 1914 (some sources suggest 1920) and studied at the University of California and the California School of Fine Arts before moving to New York and completing his education at the Art Student's League. Mr. White received nominations for four Tony Awards and received two. These were for *Bless You All* in 1951 and *Hazel Flagg* in 1953. He also received Donaldson awards for *Gentlemen Prefer Blondes, Pal Joey, Bloomer Girl* and *High Button Shoes*. In addition to designing many popular musicals, including *Oklahoma!* and *Carousel,* he created costumes for several movies (receiving three Oscar nominations), ten productions for Ringling Bros. and Barnum & Bailey Circus, television shows, ballets and night club revues during his distinguished career. In 1997, he received the Irene Sharaff Lifetime Achievement Award from Theatre Development Fund. Miles White died on February 17, 2000 at age 85.

Costumes: 1938 *Right This Way* 1939 *George White's Scandals* 1941 *Best Foot Forward* 1942 *The Pirate* 1943 *Early to Bed*; *Get Away Old Man* (Designer and Supervisor); *Oklahoma!*; *Ziegfeld Follies: 1943* 1944 *Allah Be Praised; Bloomer Girl; Dream with Music* 1945 *Carousel; The Day before Spring* 1946 *Duchess of Malfi; Gypsy Lady* 1947 *High Button Shoes* 1949 *Gentlemen Prefer Blondes* 1950 *Bless You All* 1951 *Oklahoma!* 1952 *Pal Joey; Three Wishes for Jamie; Two's Company* 1953 *Hazel Flagg* 1954 *The Girl in Pink Tights* 1955 *Ankles Aweigh* 1957 *Eugenia; Jamaica; Time Remembered* 1958 *Oh Captain!* 1959 *Cheri; Take Me Along* 1960 *Bye, Bye, Birdie; The Unsinkable Molly Brown* 1961 *Milk and Honey; Show Girl* 1970 *Candida* 1973 *Tricks* 1976 *Best Friend* 1977 *Toller Cranston's Ice Show* 1989 *Jerome Robbins' Broadway†*

John Biddle Whitelaw

John Biddle Whitelaw was active on Broadway in the mid-1930s. He was born in Chicago and served in the army during and after World War II. Also known as an artist, he died on August

6, 1948 in New York City.
Sets: **1934** *Bridal Quilt* **1935** *Reprise*

Michael J. Whitfield

Michael J. Whitfield was born on April 11, 1944. He received a B.A. from the University of Victoria, British Columbia in 1967, an M.A. from Villanova University in 1970, and attended the University of Illinois at Champaign-Urbana from 1971-1974. From 1974 to 1976, he was assistant to his mentor, Gil Wechsler, at the Stratford (Ontario) Festival, making his professional design debut with the Third Stage Season for the Stratford (Ontario) Festival in 1974. He has remained with that company ever since, and is currently resident lighting designer. He is also regularly designs for the Canadian Opera Company in Toronto and received the Dora Mavor Moore Award in 1988 for the lighting design of *Observe the Sons of Ulster Marching Towards the Somme*. He often collaborates on productions with his wife, scenic and costume designer Susan Benson.
Lights: **1987** *The Mikado*

Vantile Whitfield

Vantile E. Whitfield was born on September 8, 1930 in Washington, D.C. and received a B.A. at Howard University and an M.A. at the University of California. In his varied career as an administrator and designer he has held positions such as art director for Ad Graphics in Hollywood, general manager of the American Theatre of Being, and set designer for Universal Studios. He has also served as program director, Expansion Arts, at the National Endowment for the Arts in Washington, D.C. Honors include Los Angeles Critics Circle Award in 1970 for design.
Sets: **1965** *The Amen Corner*
Costumes: **1965** *The Amen Corner*
Lights: **1965** *The Amen Corner*

Miss Gertrude Whitty

Miss Gertrude Whitty, a British actress, appeared in numerous plays in London, and *An Old New Yorker* on Broadway in 1911, among other roles. She designed costumes for a Shakespeare play on Broadway in which she appeared in 1917. The role of Falstaff was played by her husband, Thomas A. Wise, a noted actor. They were married from 1895 until his death on March 21, 1928 in New York City.
Costumes: **1917** *The Merry Wives of Windsor*

Richard Whorf

Richard Whorf, who was born in Winthrop, Massachusetts on June 4, 1906, worked in the theater as an actor, director and designer. He first appeared on stage in 1921 in Boston. He had an active career as an actor and director for theater and film and occasionally also designed costumes and lights. He began designing in the early 1940s and in 1949 played the title role in *Richard III*, while also designing the costumes and scenery. He also directed numerous television programs, including episodes of *Gunsmoke*, *Alfred Hitchcock* and *The Beverly Hillbillies*. In 1954 he received both a Donaldson Award and a Tony Award for his costume design for *Ondine*. Richard Whorf died in 1966 in Santa Monica, California.
Sets: **1940** *Fledgling*; *Old Acquaintance*; *There Shall Be No Night* **1944** *But Not Goodbye* **1949** *Richard III* **1957** *The Genius and the Goddess*
Costumes: **1949** *Richard III* **1954** *Ondine*
Lights: **1957** *The Genius and the Goddess*

Joseph Wickes

Joseph Wickes was active on Broadway between 1906 and 1931. He designed productions both under his own name and through Joseph Wickes Studio which was located at 241 West 62nd Street In New York City. He often worked in collaboration with Edward G. Unitt through Unitt and Wickes, and also collaborated with Homer Emens, through Emens, Unitt and Wickes. Joseph Wickes died on January 20, 1950.
Sets: **1906** *The Blue Moon*†; *The Great Divide*†; *Pippa Passes*†; *The Red Mill*† **1907** *His Excellency the Governor*†; *Miss Hook of Holland*†; *My Wife*†; *The Spoilers*†; *The Straight Road*†; *The Sunken*

Bell†; *The Talk of New York†*; *Twelfth Night†* **1908** *Don Quixote†* (Act III, IV); *Fluffy Ruffles†*; *Jack Straw†*; *The Mollusc†* **1909** *The Beauty Spot†*; *A Fool There Was†* **1914** *On Trial* **1922** *Marjolaine*; *Secrets* (as: Joseph Wickes Studio); *The Texas Nightingale†* (as: Joseph Wickes Studio) **1923** *The Rise of Rosie O'Reilly* **1924** *The Harem*; *Ladies of the Evening*; *Tiger Cats* **1925** *Accused* (as: Joseph Wickes Studio); *American Born* (as: Joseph Wickes Studio); *Canary Dutch* (as: Joseph Wickes Studio); *The Dove*; *Tangletoes* (as: Joseph Wickes Studio) **1926** *Fanny*; *The Home Towners*; *Lilly Sue*; *Lulu Belle*; *What Never Dies*; *Yellow* **1927** *Baby Cyclone* (as: Joseph Wickes Studio); *Hidden*; *Merry Malones* **1928** *The Bachelor Father*; *The Big Fight*; *Billie*; *Minna* **1929** *The Judge and the Jury* **1930** *Dancing Partner*; *The Rhapsody* (as: Joseph Wickes Studio); *Tonight or Never* **1931** *Friendship* (as: Joseph Wickes Studio)

Robert Wierzel

Lighting designer Robert Wierzel designs for dance and theater companies throughout the United States in addition to serving on the faculty at New York University. Principal designer for choreographer Bill T. Jones and Bill T. Jones/Arne Zane and Co., he has also designed for composer Philip Glass. Industrial lighting projects include *Baule: African Art/Western Eyes* at the Yale University Art Gallery and the Art Institute of Chicago. Among his honors is the 1991 American Theatre Wing Design Award for *Hydrogen Jukebox*. Twenty-first century designs include *The Tender Land* for Virginia Opera, *Love's Fire* and *Romeo and Juliet* for the Acting Company, *Paul Bunyan* for New York City Opera, and *Othello* at the Joseph Papp Public Theatre.
Lights: **1996** *Dreams & Nightmares†* (Additional lighting) **1998** *The Deep Blue Sea*

Bolton Wilder

Bolton Wilder designed lights for a Broadway production in 1939. He was born on January 14, 1915 and died in New Haven, Connecticut in June 1982.
Lights: **1939** *Once upon a Time*

Clement Wilenchick

Clement Wilenchick was born in New York City on October 28, 1900. He studied art in Cardiff, Wales and in Paris at the École des Beaux Arts, after which he returned to the United States to paint. His first involvement in the theater was as an actor at the Neighborhood Playhouse and the Provincetown Playhouse. He also performed in Europe while continuing to paint and exhibit. He returned to New York City in 1931 and performed with the Group Theatre as an artist-actor and in several plays on Broadway, supplying sets and costume designs for one play. As "Crane Whiley" and "Clem Wilenchick" he appeared in a few films in 1938 and 1939, among them *The Lazy Warning* and *Charlie McCarthy, Detective*. He died on February 28, 1957 in Los Angeles.
Sets: **1928** *Dr. Knock*
Costumes: **1928** *Dr. Knock*

Thomas Wilfred

Thomas Wilfred invented the Clavilus, an organ with keys connected to projectors behind a translucent screen. He became known for his "lumina" compositions which he performed throughout the United States, first demonstrated at the Neighborhood Playhouse in 1922. In 1930 he founded the Art Institute of Light. He also made a variety of light machines for theatrical productions and designed and installed lighting systems at the University of Washington Playhouse and the Center Theatre at the University of Georgia. In 1930 he contributed designs for sets and costumes to a Broadway production. His work is in the collections of the Cleveland Museum of Art, the Museum of Modern Art and the Metropolitan Museum of Art. He was born on June 18, 1889 in West Nyack, New York and died there at age 79 on August 15, 1968
Sets: **1930** *The Vikings*
Costumes: **1930** *The Vikings*

Wilhelm

C. Wilhelm (also known as William John Charles Pitcher) was born in

Northfleet, Kent, England on March 21, 1858. After apprenticing with two of England's best known nineteenth century scenic artists, William Roxby Beverley and James Robinson Planche, he began a prolific career. During the last quarter of the nineteenth century he designed sets and costumes for pantomimes in Drury Lane in London, later working at the Empire Theatre designing sets, costumes and creating ballets. He designed the original productions of *Iolanthe* in 1882 and *Ruddigore* in 1887, and worked as a production designer for directors and producers. A watercolor painter, he also contributed designs to revues on Broadway. Wilhelm died at age 67 in 1925.

Sets: 1923 *Stepping Stones*[†] **1924** *Stepping Stones*[†]

Costumes: 1902 *The Toreador*[†] **1905** *The Babes and the Baron* **1906** *The Red Mill*[†] **1908** *The Soul Kiss*[†] (Divertissements and Mlle Genne's costume) **1910** *The Arcadians*; *The Bachelor Belles*[†]; *The Girl in the Train*[†]; *The Old Town*[†] **1912** *The Lady of the Slipper* **1922** *Better Times*[†] **1923** *Stepping Stones*[†] **1924** *Stepping Stones*[†]

Norman Wilkerson

Norman Wilkerson was active on Broadway between 1948 and 1951.

Costumes: 1948 *Iolanthe* **1951** *Iolanthe* (Fairy costumes)

Norman Wilkinson

The distinguished British designer Norman Wilkinson, of Four Oaks, was born in Abbotsholme, Derbyshire, in 1882 and studied at the Birmingham School of Art and in Paris. He worked with Charles Frohman, D'Oyly Carte and Harley Granville-Barker. While a governor of the Shakespeare Memorial Theatre, he designed a *A Midsummer Night's Dream* in 1932 for that theater, among many others. He was known in the United States primarily as the designer of *Androcles and the Lion* in 1915, which included *The Man Who Married a Dumb Wife* as a curtain raiser. The designs for the curtain raiser by Robert Edmond Jones are generally regarded as the beginning of both the "New American Stage-

craft" and the modern era on Broadway. Norman Wilkinson, who used "of Four Oaks" (his former address) to distinguish himself from his namesake, a marine painter, died in London in 1934.

Sets: 1915 *Androcles and the Lion*; *The Doctor's Dilemma*[†]; *The Doctor's Dilemma*[†]; *A Midsummer Night's Dream*[†]; *A Midsummer Night's Dream*[†] **1929** *Wake Up and Dream*[†]

Costumes: 1915 *A Midsummer Night's Dream*[†] **1929** *Wake Up and Dream*[†]

Frances Willard

Frances Willard, costume designer, lived in Greenwich, Connecticut, but maintained a firm of dressmakers at 9 East 42st Street in New York City, where she provided gowns and accessories to private and theatrical customers.

Costumes: 1915 *Children of Earth*[†] (Designs by); *Taking Chances* (Miss Troutman's gowns)

Anna Wille

Anna Wille designed costumes for a 1926 Broadway play. Her home at that time was 18 Christopher Street in New York City.

Costumes: 1926 *The Scarlet Letter*

Maria Willenz

Maria Willenz designed costumes in 1927 on Broadway.

Costumes: 1927 *A La Carte*

Clement M. Williams

Clement M. Williams designed settings for two plays in the mid-1930s. An architect, he resided at 405 East 54th Street, New York City in 1932.

Sets: 1934 *Come What May* **1936** *The Puritan*

George Williams

George Williams, who designed scenery for five productions in the first decade of the twentieth century, was a character actor who appeared on stage in the teens and in movies in the twenties. Films include *The Silent Stranger*, *Geared to Go*, and *Little Miss Smiles*. He was born in 1854 and died in Los Angeles, California on February 21, 1936.

Sets: 1908 *Mlle. Mischief*; *Mr. Hamlet of Broadway* **1909** *The Midnight Sons*[†]; *A*

Trip to Japan† (Mechanical devises) **1910**
The Prince of Bohemia† (Designed and built)

Robert T. Williams

Robert T. Williams designed sets for Broadway in the 1960s and early 1970s. For one production he also designed lights. As production supervisor of Artpark-at-the-Church in Lewiston, New York, his designs for that company include lights for *Into the Woods* and *Brighton Beach Memoirs* and scenery for *Damn Yankees, Oliver,* and *The Medium*. Additional designs include a touring production of *Annie* in the early 1990s.

Sets: 1964 *A Girl Could Get Lucky* **1965** *The Glass Menagerie*† **1967** *A Warm Body* **1970** *Charley's Aunt*
Lights: 1967 *A Warm Body*

Hugh Willoughby

Hugh Willoughby was born in Croyden, England on October 15, 1891 and first designed costumes for a musical revue in The Hague, Netherlands. He went on to design costumes for many shows throughout Europe and occasionally contributed sets as well. He designed costumes and scenery on Broadway in the 1920s and 1930s. He also collaborated with John Newton Booth and Frederick Jones III; additional information and credits can be found under each name and in "Booth-Willoughby." Some of his designs are in the permanent collection of the Austrian National Library, and examples were reproduced in *Wake up and Dream! Costume Designs for Broadway Musicals 1900-1925* published in 1986. Hugh Willoughby died at age 82 on April 4, 1973.

Sets: 1926 *Castles in the Air*† **1928** *Earl Carroll's Vanities* **1929** *Earl Carroll's Sketch Book*† **1930** *Earl Carroll's Vanities* **1931** *Earl Carroll's Vanities*† **1934** *Saluta* **1937** *Tide Rising* **1938** *Where Do We Go from Here?*
Costumes: 1925 *Mercenary Mary* **1927** *Judy; Piggy*

Mary Wills

Mary Wills, a prolific costume designer for the movies, designed costumes on Broadway in 1980 for the first time. She received Academy Award Nominations for *Hans Christian Anderson* in 1952, *The Virgin Queen* in 1954, *Teenage Rebel* in 1956, *A Certain Smile* in 1958, *The Diary of Anne Frank* in 1959, *The Wonderful World of the Brothers Grimm* in 1962 and *The Passover Plot* in 1976. She often collaborated with Charles Le Maire, and worked mainly for Samuel Goldwyn Productions and for Twentieth Century-Fox. An active member of the Costume Designers Guild, she was born in 1914 and died on February 7, 1997 in Sedona, Arizona.

Costumes: 1980 *Quick Change*

Wilma

Wilma designed gowns for a 1942 Broadway play.

Costumes: 1942 *They Should Have Stood in Bed* (Gowns)

Andrea Wilson

In 1977, Andrea Wilson designed lights for a show on Broadway and also served as assistant to Mitch Miller, the production's technical director. Additional designs include lights for *Big Maggie* and *Jose Feliciano at the Palace* as well as for Cleo Laine in concert and productions for Antonio Gades Ballet Company in the mid-1980s.

Lights: 1977 *Party with Betty Comden and Adolph Green*

Claggett Wilson

Claggett Wilson, a painter and scene designer, was born in Washington, D.C. and studied art in New York and Paris. He painted many pictures of natives in the Basque region of Spain, World War II paintings and a collection of twenty paintings interpreting the "Song of Solomon." His theater and designs activity was mainly designing sets for productions starring Alfred Lunt and Lynn Fontanne. Mr. Wilson, who taught art at Columbia University from 1913 to 1917, died on May 19, 1952 at the age of 64.

Sets: 1940 *The Taming of the Shrew*†
Costumes: 1940 *The Taming of the Shrew*

Joseph Wilson

Joseph G. Wilson designed lights for many Broadway productions between 1900 and 1925, long before the profession was formally developed, receiving playbill credit mainly as an electrical engineer. The lighting designer should not be confused with the British scene painter active in the middle of the nineteenth century, the Irish actor and manager (1858-1940) who appeared throughout Great Britain, or the New Jersey Psychiatrist, although they all have the same name.
Lights: 1900 *The Devil's Disciple* **1904** *The College Widow* (as: Joseph G. Wilson); *Woodland* **1907** *The Merry Widow* (as: Joseph G. Wilson); *A Yankee Tourist* (as: Joseph G. Wilson) **1908** *Mary Jane's Pa* **1909** *The Florist Shop*; *The Gay Hussars* (as: Joseph G. Wilson) **1910** *Miss Patsy* **1911** *Everywoman* (as: Joseph G. Wilson); *Excuse Me* (as: Joseph G. Wilson); *Little Boy Blue* **1912** *What Ails You?* **1913** *Somewhere Else* **1914** *A Mix-Up* **1917** *Have a Heart* **1918** *Toot-Toot!* **1920** *Lady Billy* **1922** *The Clinging Vine* **1923** *The Magic Ring*; *White Desert* **1925** *Lass o' Laughter*; *A Lucky Break*

Kathryn Wilson

Kathryn Wilson designed lights for a play in 1936. A decorator, she worked for A. M. Kemper at 1441 Broadway, New York City in 1932.
Lights: 1936 *The Living Newspaper*[†]

Scott Wilson

Scott Wilson spent most of his professional career as an industrial designer. Active in professional organizations, he served as National Director of the Inter-Society Color Council and President of the National Society for Decoration Design in the mid-1950s. A 1926 graduate of Harvard College, he died on May 2, 1951.
Costumes: 1937 *As You Like It*[†]

E. Carlton Winckler

The lighting designer E. Carlton Winckler was born on January 20, 1908 in Jersey City, New Jersey. For twenty years he worked with John Murray Anderson, who encouraged his interest in lighting design while they created "units" for Paramount Movie Theatres. He worked for producer Billy Rose for nearly thirty years while also designing lights throughout the United States for theater and films. He designed numerous shows for which he did not receive program credit, working at a time when the profession of lighting design was only beginning to emerge. He was also an active designer during the period when United Scenic Artists and IATSE Local One struggled over jurisdiction of theatrical lighting design. He designed the lights for Walt Disney's *Fantasia*, pioneering new techniques in film lighting. In 1943 he became involved in television, working in New York and on the West Coast, and in 1951 became General Manager of the Program Department for CBS-TV, where he remained until retirement in 1973. He then joined Imero Fiorentino Associates as senior production consultant and director of the Education Division. In 1977 the Society of Motion Picture and Television Engineers honored him with their Progress Award Gold Medal for contributions to television's development.
Sets: 1927 *Lace Petticoat*
Lights: 1929 *Murray Anderson's Almanac* **1940** *Earl Carroll's Vanities*; *Louisiana Purchase* **1941** *Ah, Wilderness!*; *Clash by Night*; *Hope for a Harvest*; *Liz the Mother*; *Sunny River* **1942** *New Faces of 1943*; *R.U.R.* **1943** *Counterattack* **1944** *Seven Lively Arts*[†] **1945** *The Assassin*; *Concert Varieties*; *Hamlet* **1946** *The Duchess Misbehaves*; *If the Shoe Fits* **1948** *Light Up the Sky*

Ferry Windberger

Ferry Windberger, also known as Franz V. Reiner, is a stage designer from Austria. Among his credits is the new "ghost train" that he designed in the mid-1980s for Vienna's Prater Fairground. Built along the Danube River, the section of Prater Park containing the fairgrounds is a popular public attraction. It was destroyed twice, at the end of World War II and by vandals in 1983, but rebuilt both times. Windberger's design contains 45 ghosts, skeletons, and ghouls as well as special effects configured to frighten those who take the three-minute ride on a train through a dark tunnel.

Sets: 1964 *Wiener Blut (Vienna Life)*

Helen Windsor

Helen Windsor designed gowns for four Broadway productions in the early seasons of the twentieth century. Her credits begin as early as 1893, when she designed and executed costumes for *Aristocracy* at Palmer's Theatre, starring Viola Allen and Wilton Lackaye. Additional productions before 1900 include *Rosemary* in 1896, gowns for Miss Allen in *Under the Red Robe* in 1896, gowns for Jessie Millward in *Phroso* in 1898 and gowns for Margaret Anglin in *Romeo and Juliet* in the 1898-1899 season.

Costumes: 1899 *My Lady's Lord†* (Gowns) **1900** *L'Aiglon†* (Gowns); *Richard Carvel†* (Miss Conquest's gowns) **1903** *The Pretty Sister of José†* (Miss Adams' costumes)

Rose Windsor

Rose Windsor was the president of Rose Windsor, Inc., a company of dressmakers located at 7 West 30th Street. Her husband, J. Craven Windsor, was the company secretary. They resided at 320 Manhattan Avenue. In both 1914 and 1915 she contributed gowns to Broadway productions.

Costumes: 1914 *Twin Beds†* (Gowns) **1915** *Rosemary†* (Gowns)

Richard Winkler

Lighting designer Richard Winkler was born on June 20, 1948 in Detroit, Michigan, the son of Edith and Leslie Winkler. He received a B.S. at the University of Michigan and continued his study at Lester Polakov's Studio and Forum of Stage Design and with Tharon Musser, who has had a major influence on his career. His first design was for *Once Upon A Mattress* at the University of Michigan. With extensive credits for opera and regional theaters in the United States, he has also designed concert appearances, world tours, and for theaters throughout Europe. He has received a Helen Hayes Award nomination for *A Midsummer Night's Dream* at the Folger Theatre in Washington, D.C., and a Hollywood

Dramalogue Award for Best Lighting for *Once in a Lifetime* at the La Jolla Playhouse. Twenty-first century designs include *Jerusalem* at the Cleveland Playhouse and *Fame: The Musical* in Pasadena.

Lights: 1973 *The Play's the Thing* **1976** *Best Friend; George Abbott...a Celebration; Something's Afoot* **1978** *Neighborhood Playhouse at 50-A Celebration* **1980** *Your Arms Too Short to Box with God* **1982** *Your Arms Too Short to Box with God* **1985** *The Loves of Anatol* **1986** *Corpse!* **1987** *Barbara Cook: A Concert for the Theatre* **1994** *Ian McKellen: A Knight Out at the Lyceum*

Nancy Winters

Nancy Winters designed a Broadway set in 1984. In 1986 she designed the set for *Africanis Instructus*, directed by Richard Foreman, with whom she often works. She has also designed *The Golem* and *Don Juan* at the Delacorte Theatre and *Egyptology* for the New York Shakespeare Festival. Nancy Winters, who is also a landscape painter, created a ceiling mosaic for *Samuel's Major Problems* in 1993.

Sets: 1984 *The Three Musketeers*

Birgit Rattenborg Wise

Birgit Rattenborg Wise is a costume designer based in Chicago. She was born in Copenhagen, Denmark on May 2, 1953, daughter of Dr. and Mrs. Chrsten C. Rattenborg. The family immigrated to Chicago in 1959. Her B.A. is from Coe College (1974) and her M.A. from the University of Kansas (1976). She has designed extensively for the Goodman Theatre (where she is head draper), and the Chicago Opera Theatre, as well as productions for Steppenwolf Theatre Company, the Milwaukee Ballet Company, Hubbard Street Dance, and others. Honors include nominations for Joseph Jefferson Award Awards for *Blues for an Alabama Sky*, Goodman Theatre 1998, and *Voice of the Turtle*, Goodman Theatre 1992, and a Black Theatre Alliance Award for *Knock Me a Kiss*. Among her twenty-first century designs is *Blue Surge* at the Goodman Theatre.

Costumes: 1999 *Death of a Salesman*

Figure 13: Freddy Wittop: *Dear World*: Aurelia, 1969. Courtesy of Hargrett Rare Book & Manuscript Library / University of Georgia Libraries. Photograph by Jan Juracek.

Freddy Wittop

Freddy Wittop, born Fred Wittop Koning in Bossum, Holland on July 26, 1911 (some sources state 1921), began his theatrical career as a dancer using the name Frederico Rey. He both performed and designed beginning in the late 1930s. He served in the U.S. Army during World War II and then returned to performing. From 1951 to 1958 he toured throughout Europe and the U.S. with his own dance company. He designed for operas, ballet and the theater in the U.S. and Europe, including costumes for Josephine Baker, the Folies Bergère, Latin Quarter revues, Holiday on Ice tours, and many more or equal variety. Mr. Wittop was nominated six times for the Tony Award for Outstanding Costume Design, winning in 1964 for *Hello, Dolly*, for which he created one of theater's best known garments. He died on February 2, 2001 in Florida at age 89, shortly before the Irene Sharaff Lifetime Achievement Award was bestowed on this charming, creative man. Some of his designs are in the Museum of the City of New York. The main archive is in the permanent collection of the Hargrett Rare Book and Manuscript Library at The University of Georgia.   See Figure 13: Freddy Wittop: *Dear World*

Costumes: 1939 *Folies Bergère* 1942 *Beat the Band* 1959 *Heartbreak House* 1961 *Carnival*; *Subways Are for Sleeping* 1964 *Bajour*; *Hello, Dolly!* 1965 *Kelly*; *On a Clear Day You Can See Forever*; *Roar of the Greasepaint – The Smell of the Crowd* 1966 *I Do! I Do!*; *Three Bags Full* 1967 *Hello, Dolly!* 1968 *George M!*; *The Happy Time* 1969 *Dear World*; *A Patriot for Me* 1970 *Lovely Ladies, Kind Gentlemen* 1978 *Hello, Dolly!* 1984 *The Three Musketeers* 1985 *Wind in the Willows*

Ed Wittstein

Ed Wittstein was born in Mt. Vernon, New York on April 7, 1929 and received a B.S. at New York University. He also studied at the Parsons School of Design, Cooper Union, and Erwin Piscator's Dramatic Workshop in New York City, beginning in 1947. He has designed sets for numerous plays

and in addition often designs costumes and/or lights. He has also designed sets and costumes for operas, ballets and television.   Credits include the long-running off-Broadway play *The Fantasticks*, *The Adams Chronicles*, *Echoes in the Darkness* and *Sarah, Plain and Tall* on television, and the films *Endless Love*, *Bananas*, *Fame* and *Play it Again, Sam*.   He received an Obie Award in 1966 for *Sergeant Musgrave's Dance* and a Maharam Award in 1974 for *Ulysses in Nighttown*. His paintings and drawings have been widely exhibited.

Sets: 1961 *Kean* 1963 *Enter Laughing*; *A Rainy Day in Newark* 1964 *The White House* 1965 *And Things That Go Bump in the Night*; *The Yearling* 1967 *The Natural Look*; *You Know I Can't Hear You When the Water's Running* 1968 *Before You Go*; *The Man in the Glass Booth* 1969 *Celebration* 1970 *Blood Red Roses*; *Happy Birthday, Wanda June* 1972 *Ring Round the Bathtub*; *Tough to Get Help* 1974 *Ulysses in Nighttown*

Costumes: 1961 *Kean* 1962 *Bravo Giovanni* 1963 *Enter Laughing*; *A Rainy Day in Newark* 1964 *The White House* 1965 *The Yearling* 1969 *Celebration*

Lights: 1963 *Enter Laughing*; *A Rainy Day in Newark* 1969 *Celebration*

Robert Wojewodski

Robert Wojewodski first designed costumes in New York for *House Beautiful*. He graduated from the University of Scranton with a major in English Literature and a minor in Studio Art.   He has designed costumes for many plays off-Broadway including *Table Settings* and *Key Exchange*. For the New York Shakespeare Festival his designs include *Fathers and Sons*, *A Prayer for My Daughter* and *Taken in Marriage*. Costume designs by Mr. Wojewodski have also been seen at Long Wharf, Center Stage and Seattle Repertory Theatres, among others.

Costumes: 1979 *Bent*; *The Price* 1980 *The American Clock* 1983 *Slab Boys* 1992 *Conversations with My Father* 1996 *Getting Away with Murder*

Peter Wolf

Peter Wolf debuted on Broadway as a set designer in 1947 and as a lighting designer in 1950. During that same time he also designed many productions for Maurice Evans' New York City Theatre company. After rejecting acting as a career, he studied at the Grand Central School of Art and the Yale School of Drama. He then worked as an assistant for several New York-based scenic designers and at the New York City Center with Maurice Evans. A position supplying scenery for summer musicals in Dallas led to considerable travel and eventual relocation to Texas. His firm, Peter Wolf Concepts (formerly Peter Wolf Associates), began as a major scenic studio and has become a firm which designs and builds commercial buildings, industrial promotions, restaurants, exhibits, etc. He has credits for settings for hundreds of plays, musicals and operas throughout the United States.

Sets: 1947 *Sweethearts* 1948 *The Linden Tree* 1950 *The Devil's Disciple* 1977 *The King and I* 1979 *Peter Pan* 1980 *Blackstone!*; *The Music Man* 1983 *Mame* 1984 *The Wiz* 1985 *The King and I*
Lights: 1950 *The Devil's Disciple*

Donald Wolfit

Sir Donald Wolfit, a British actor, was born in Newark-on-Trent, Nottinghamshire, England on April 20, 1902. He was one of the last of the actor-managers and earned his reputation as a Shakespearean actor at the Old Vic and Stratford-upon-Avon. In 1937 he formed his own company and toured around the world. During World War II he entertained the troops, resuming the presentation of plays in a repertory format at the end of the war. In 1955 he published his autobiography, *First Interval.* Knighted in 1957, Sir Donald Wolfit died in February 1968 at the age of 65. His papers and designs are in the permanent collection of the Harry Ransom Humanities Research Center at The University of Texas at Austin.

Sets: 1947 *Hamlet*†; *The Merchant of Venice*
Costumes: 1947 *Hamlet*†

Albert Wolsky

Albert Wolsky was born in Paris, France on November 24, 1930 and received a B.A. at City University of New York. His training for costume design came through positions as an apprentice and assistant to designers including Patricia Zipprodt, Irene Sharaff, Stanley Simmons, A. Domingo Rodriguez, Robert Fletcher and Ann Roth. He has designed costumes for numerous plays off-Broadway, for theaters including the Phoenix and the New York Shakespeare Festival. His major costume design work has been in the films *The Heart is a Lonely Hunter, Striptease, Up Close and Personal, Grease, Manhattan* and *The Turning Point,* among others He was nominated for Academy Awards for *Sophie's Choice, Toys* and *The Journey of Natty Gann* and won them for *All That Jazz* in 1980 and *Bugsy* in 1991.

Costumes: 1965 *Generation* 1971 *The Trial of the Catonsville Nine* 1972 *The Sunshine Boys* 1973 *The Jockey Club Stakes* 1974 *All over Town* 1976 *Sly Fox* 1980 *Tricks of the Trade* 1981 *Wally's Cafe*

Beatrice Wood

Beatrice Wood not only designed costumes for a 1926 Broadway play, she designed scarves for Isadora Duncan, was the inspiration for Henri-Pierre Roche's novel, *Jules et Jim* that in turn inspired Francois Truffault, was the subject of a 1993 documentary, *Beatrice Wood, the Mama of Dada* and was the basis for the character of Rose in James Cameron's movie *Titanic.* Born in 1893 in San Francisco, she studied art and acting in Paris and then formed the Society of Independent Artists with Henri-Pierre Roche and Marcel Duchamp. In the 1930s she became a ceramic artist, so successful that her first exhibition in 1949 in New York was followed many others, including a retrospective being held in New York at the time of her death on March 12, 1998 in Ojai, California. She died a few days after her 105th birthday.

Costumes: 1926 *The Great Adventure*

Mr. Chester Woodard

Mr. Chester Woodard designed sets for a 1915 play on Broadway.

Sets: 1915 *Three of Hearts*†

Patricia Woodbridge

Patricia Woodbridge was born on August 9, 1946 in Philadelphia and received a B.A. from Bennington College and an M.F.A. at New York University's Tisch School of the Arts. She counts Ben Edwards, Tony Walton and Ming Cho Lee, (all of whom she has assisted) as influential in her career. Her first design as a professional was *The Wonderful Ice Cream Suit* for the Puerto Rico Traveling Theatre. She has designed for many regional theaters including Arena Stage, the Goodman Theatre, the Philadelphia Drama Guild and the Cincinnati Playhouse. Productions off-Broadway include the premieres of *The Runner Stumbles, Nightclub Cantata, Fishing, The Other Half, How I Got that Story, Dispatches,* and Faith, Hope and Charity. Currently, she works entirely in film, with credits including production design for *Johnny Suede* and art direction for *City by the Sea, Down, Company Man, The Hurricane, The Object of My Affection, Cadillac Man,* and *My Father, the Hero.*
Sets: **1976** *The Runner Stumbles*

Beverly Woodner

Beverly Woodner designed costumes on Broadway in 1948. Her brother, Ian Woodner (1903-1990), was an architect and developer who amassed an important collection of Old Master drawings
Costumes: **1948** *Joy to the World*

F. W. Woods

Frank W. Woods, an architect with offices at 10 East 43rd Street, Room 905 in New York City, collaborated on the design for a 1921 Broadway play. He resided at 8 East 8th Avenue at that time.
Costumes: **1921** *Sun-kist*† (Miss Clark's gowns)

Jack Woodson

Born in Richmond, Virginia on January 23, 1913, John Waddie, Jr., has used his mother's maiden name throughout his career as an artist and illustrator. He is known professionally as Jack Woodson and as John Waddie Woodson, Jr. Early in his career he collaborated on scenery for a Broadway production, but since then has created illustrations for numerous textbooks, children's stories, and publications of the National Park Service.
Sets: **1954** *The Honor of the Family*

David C. Woolard

David C. Woolard, born in Houston, Texas, earned his B.F.A. at Southern Methodist University. He has designed costumes for opera, dance and theater throughout the United States at theaters including La Jolla Playhouse, The Old Globe, Hartford Stage, The Guthrie Theatre, the Alley Theatre, and Santa Fe Opera among others. He has designed numerous off-Broadway shows including *Jeffrey, Mrs. Klein,* and *The Donkey Show.* He has been nominated for two Tony Awards, for *The Who's Tommy* and *The Rocky Horror Show,* and received many other honors in his career to date. Twenty-first century productions include *Barry Manilow's Copacabana,* and *Wonder of the World* in the 2001-2002 Broadway season.
Costumes: **1989** *A Few Good Men* **1993** *The Who's Tommy* **1994** *Damn Yankees; Sally Marr...and Her Escorts*† (Production costumes) **1997** *The Young Man from Atlanta* **1998** *Wait until Dark* **1999** *Marlene; Voices in the Dark* **2000** *The Rocky Horror Show* **2001** *Bells Are Ringing*

Reginald Woolley

Reginald Harry Angus Woolley was born in Hong Kong in 1912 and spent his career as a set designer, illustrator, director and theater manager. He was resident designer for Players Theatre Club, a 250-seat house in Villiers Street, London for fifty years, where among numerous shows, he designed the original production of Sandy Wilson's *The Boyfriend* which he commissioned. A member of Williams and Woolley, Theatrical Managers, he also designed in the West End, for the Old Vic, many operas at Sadler's Wells, and for the Wexford Festival. *Playing With Punch* by Frank Baker, published in 1944, was illustrated by Reginald Woolley and Douglas Campbell. He died on March 14, 1993 at age 80.

Sets: 1954 *The Boyfriend*
Costumes: 1954 *The Boyfriend*

John Workman

John Workman designed costumes for a 1954 Broadway production.
Costumes: 1954 *Hayride*

Beryl Wormser

Beryl Wormser supervised the costumes for two plays in 1936.
Costumes: 1936 *So Proudly We Hail*† (Women's Costume Supervisor); *Stark Mad* (Costume Supervisor)

Worth

Charles Frederick Worth founded haute couture. Born in Bourne, Lincolnshire, England in 1825, he started working at age twelve in the garment trade. He spent seven years as an apprentice in a haberdashery and in 1845 moved to Paris where within five years he opened a dressmaking department at Maison Gagelin. By 1858 he had his own couture house and was making gowns for Empress Eugenie. A gown from the House of Worth, especially an evening gown, was highly valued by members of society around the world and by European royalty, as well as by actresses Sarah Bernhardt, Eleanora Duse and others. Worth died in 1895, but his sons Gaston (1853-1924) and Jean-Philippe (1856-1926) continued the business. The House of Worth remained a family concern until 1953 when the House of Paquin merged with the House of Worth, becoming Paquin-Worth until closing in 1956. Gowns and accessories carrying a Worth label are in the collections of major museums around the world, including the Museum of the City of New York and the Metropolitan Museum of Art.
Costumes: 1900 *David Garrick* (Miss More's gowns) 1901 *Du Barry*† (Mrs. Carter's gowns); *Miranda of the Balcony*† (Gowns) 1902 *The Silver Slipper*† (Evening gowns) 1903 *Resurrection* 1904 *Mrs. Gorringe's Necklace* (Gowns); *The Pit*†

Michael Wright

Michael Wright designed a Broadway set in 1947. The set designer active in

the 1940s should not be confused with the actor who appeared in *Streamers* among other films, or the television designer who designed for KCBS in Los Angeles, WBBM in Chicago and Newsnight Minnesota in the mid-1990s.
Sets: 1947 *The Winslow Boy*

Russel Wright

Russel Wright, an industrial designer, was born on April 3, 1905 in Lebanon, Ohio. Exhibiting an artistic talent as a young boy, he took classes at the Cincinnati Art Academy before going to New York to study at the Art Students League. While in college at Princeton he directed plays and designed sets, which led to an offer from Norman Bel Geddes to travel to Paris. He left school and began work as a theatrical designer assisting designers and creating sets for the Theatre Guild, the Neighborhood Playhouse and the Group Theatre. A workshop where he produced theatrical properties grew into a small factory as his talent and originality with custom-made furniture and decorative accessories became known. He gradually gave up a career in theater to concentrate on designing functional, modernist home furnishings, at which he was very successful. Exhibitions include *Russel Wright, American Designer* at the Hudson River Museum in 1983, *Design Since 1945* at the Philadelphia Museum in 1983, and *High Style: 20th Century American Design* at the Whitney Museum in 1985. His designs are in major museums, including the Museum of Modern Art, the Cooper-Hewitt Museum, and the Metropolitan Museum of Art, among others. He died at age 72 on December 22, 1976 in New York City.
Sets: 1925 *Exiles*; *Grand Street Follies*
Costumes: 1925 *Exiles*; *Grand Street Follies*†

John Wulp

John E. Wulp began working as a paint boy in his teens and then designed for the Boston Summer Theatre. He attended Yale University prior to military service. He is a Broadway producer *(Dracula* Tony Award, 1978 among others), a playwright *(The*

Saintliness of Marjery Kempe among others) and a designer. He is also a painter and editor (the magazine *Readers' Digest*), teacher (set design at Carnegie Mellon University) and a director. He has served on the Board of Directors of Playwrights Horizons and the Eglevsky Ballet. Honors include an Obie Award for directing *Red Eye of Love* and a Tony nomination for the set design of *Crucifer of Blood*, which was also honored with Drama Desk, Outer Critics' Circle and Los Angeles Critics Awards. A resident of Vinalhaven, Maine, an island in Penobscot Bay, his twenty-first century productions include *Islands* by singer-songwriter Carol Bullens. The show, based on interviews with islanders tells the story of Maine-island life and was performed in Portland, and in October 2001 at the New Victory Theater off-Broadway.

Sets: 1978 *The Crucifer of Blood* **1979** *Bosoms and Neglect*

Stuart Wurtzel

Stuart Wurtzel was bornAugust 2, 1940 in Hillside, New Jersey. After receiving a B.F.A. in 1962 and an M.F.A. in 1964 from Carnegie Mellon University he joined Bill Ball at the Pittsburgh Playhouse and traveled with him to the American Conservatory Theatre as an assistant designer. He designed forty productions for A.C.T., as well as productions for the Alliance Theatre, Cincinnati's Playhouse in the Park, and off-Broadway. His first feature film was *Hester Street* in 1975, followed by many more as production designer, such as *Hair, Simon, The Purple Rose of Cairo, Brighton Beach Memoirs, An Innocent Man, The Old Gringo, Staying Together, I.Q., When a Man Loves a Woman,* and *Three Men and a Little Lady.* Honors include an Academy Award nomination for *Hannah and Her Sisters* and an Emmy Award nomination for *Little Gloria...Happy at Last.* He is married to production designer Patrizia Von Brandenstein, with whom he began working at A.C.T. and frequently collaborates.

Sets: 1969 *A Flea in Her Ear; Tiny Alice* **1974** *Sizwe Banzi is Dead†; Summer*

Brave **1975** *The Island* **1977** *Unexpected Guests* **1981** *Wally's Cafe*

John Wyckham

John Wyckham Suckling was born on May 18, 1926 in Solihull, Warwickshire, England. He first worked in theater as a stage manager in the early 1950s and began his career as a lighting designer in 1955. He has extensive credits for lighting in the West End, for the Royal Shakespeare Company, and Sadler's Wells among others. He is senior partner in John Wyckham Associates, theater consultants, and was a founding member of the Society of Theatre Consultants. He has also consulted on the design and renovation of many theaters in the United Kingdom.

Sets: 1965 *Beyond the Fringe*
Lights: 1963 *Oliver!* **1965** *Beyond the Fringe†; Oliver!*

Alexander Wyckoff

Alexander Wyckoff, who was active on Broadway in the 1920s and 1930s was born in Leonia, New Jersey on August 17, 1898 and studied at Columbia College and Carnegie Institute of Technology where he later taught scene design and scene painting with Woodman Thompson. One of his many students was the lighting designer Abe Feder. He also founded a school in Edgewater, New Jersey associated with the summer season at the Ogunquit (Maine) Playhouse to train stagecraft instructors. He wrote *Early American Dress* with Edward Warwick and Henry C. Pitz, *Aboriginal Dress, Western Hemisphere, Post-Glacial to 1866 A.D.,* and other books. Active with the Leonia Players from 1920 to 1953, he also was involved with theater in and around Tustin, California from 1971 to 1988. He died on October 29, 1995.

Sets: 1925 *Cain†; White Gold* **1932** *The Anatomist; When the Bough Breaks*
Costumes: 1925 *Cain†*

Wynn

Wynn was a pseudonym for Irwin Cooper, also known as Wynn Cooper. The son of vaudeville comedian Harry Cooper, he studied construction and engineering at New York University. He was active working backstage on

theater productions, before becoming a sports announcer. Wynn, who collaborated with designer Charles LeMaire and others, died on October 28, 1936.
Costumes: 1929 *Murray Anderson's Almanac*† **1934** *Life Begins at 8:40*†

Shigeru Yaji

Shigeru Yaji was born in Tokyo, Japan on May 7, 1949. He earned his B.A. degree at Tamagawa University in Tokyo and his M.A. at California State University, Long Beach. Since 1994 he has been on the faculty at the University of California, Irvine, teaching part-time while actively designing on the West Coast. He has been the principal designer at South Coast Repertory since 1983, when he made his professional debut with the costume designs for *As You Like It*, directed by Lee Shallat. His designs have also been featured at Berkeley Repertory Theatre, Intiman Theatre, The Globe Theatres, the Oregon Shakespeare Festival, San Jose Repertory Theatre, and American Conservatory Theatre, as well as Disneyland International. Among his many honors are five Los Angeles Drama Critics Circle Awards, twenty-nine Drama-Logue Awards, a Bay Area Theatre Critics Circle Award, and an Emmy Award nomination.
Costumes: 1998 *Peter Pan*

Michael H. Yeargan

Michael H. Yeargan was born in Dallas, Texas on February 13, 1946. He studied at Stetson University, the University of Madrid and Yale University, where he received an M.F.A. in 1972, and now serves as Associate Professor of stage design. An elementary school teacher, Miss Frances Parr, first interested him in set design, which remains his primary interest. His first professional designs were seen in the Yale Repertory Theatre production of *Happy End* and his New York debut came in 1974. He has frequently collaborated on productions with the director Andrei Serban, an association that began at Yale and continues around the world with productions of plays and operas (another of his interests). Mr. Yeargan occasionally designs both

sets and costumes for productions to achieve an integration of style and effect. His designs for *Otello* and *Così Fan Tutte* for the Metropolitan Opera were subsequently seen on television in the series *Life from the Met.* Among his honors is a Connecticut Critics Award for the scenic designs for *Misalliance* at Long Wharf. Twenty-first century designs include *Dead Man Walking* for the San Francisco Opera.
Sets: 1974 *Bad Habits* **1975** *The Ritz*† **1980** *A Lesson from Aloes* **1981** *It Had to Be You*† **1985** *Hay Fever* **1988** *Ah, Wilderness!* **1999** *The Gershwins' Fascinating Rhythm*
Costumes: 1974 *Bad Habits* **1976** *Me Jack, You Jill*† **1977** *Something Old, Something New*†

Nicholas Yellenti

Nicholas Yellenti, who was born in Pittsburgh, Pennsylvania in on July 7, 1894, studied painting at the Swain School of Design with C. Riddell, I. Caliga, and P. Little. He exhibited paintings at the Corcoran Gallery Biennial in 1937, and won prizes at art exhibitions in Toledo, Ohio in 1920 and 1921. His activity on Broadway between 1923 to 1963, was mainly scenic design but he designed lights for one production. In addition, he constructed and painted sets for other designers. Yellenti died on July 18, 1991.
Sets: 1923 *The Breaking Point* **1924** *Bluffing Bluffers*; *Flossie* **1925** *Easy Come, Easy Go*; *The Family Upstairs*; *The Mud Turtle*; *Solid Ivory*; *Twelve Miles Out* **1926** *Ashes of Love*; *The Bells*; *Black Boy*; *The Donovan Affair*; *Gertie*; *If I Was Rich*; *Just Life*; *Kongo*; *She Couldn't Say No*; *They All Want Something*; *This Woman Business*; *We Americans* **1927** *Bless You, Sister*; *Fog*; *Fog Bound*; *Her First Affairs*; *The Jazz Singer*; *A Lady in Love*; *The Mystery Shop*; *Nightstick*; *Restless Women*; *Set a Thief*; *The Shannons of Broadway*; *Skin Deep*; *Take My Advice*; *Tenth Avenue* **1928** *Adventure*; *The Behavior of Mrs. Crane*; *Brothers*; *Get Me in the Movies*; *The Golden Age*; *The Happy Husband*; *A Man with Red Hair*; *Mirrors*; *The Mystery Man*; *Quicksand*; *Tin Pan Alley*; *The War Song* **1929** *House Un-*

guarded; *Ladies Don't Lie*; *Scotland Yard*; *Veneer* **1930** *Love, Honor and Betray*; *Made in France*; *Schoolgirl*; *Sweet Chariot* **1931** *Her Supporting Cast*; *In Times Square*; *In the Best of Families* **1932** *Absent Feather*; *The Web* **1933** *The Curtain Rises*; *The Family Upstairs* **1934** *American–Very Early*; *Baby Pompadour*; *Theodora, the Queen*; *When in Rome* **1935** *Good Men and True*; *The Ragged Edge*; *A Woman of the Soil* **1936** *Around the Corner*; *Arrest That Woman*; *Love on the Dole* **1937** *Behind Red Lights*; *Places Please*; *Something for Nothing* **1938** *Bright Rebel*; *Censored* **1939** *Aries Is Rising* **1948** *The Vigil* **1963** *The Golden Age*
Lights: **1948** *The Vigil*

Alison Yerxa

Alison Yerxa was born on February 2, 1952 in Woodland, California the daughter of Charles and Virginia Yerxa, a fourth generation northern California farming family. She received a B.A. in art from the University of California at Santa Cruz and made her design debut with *Prelude to a Death in Venice*. She works extensively in motion pictures, as art director for *Fantasia/2000* an animated IMAX film, and with visual special effects for movies including *Star Trek, The Motion Picture*, *Star Trek: Insurrection* and *Brainstorm*. As art director for Blue Sky/VIFX, she worked on *The X-Files* film. Yerxa won an American Theatre Wing Design Award (formerly the Maharam Award) for special theatrical effects in 1989 for *The Warrior Ant*. In addition to creating the original production design for *The Gospel at Colonus* at the Brooklyn Academy of Music with playwright and director Lee Breuer, she collaborated with him on *The Shaggy Dog*, *Animation*, and *Lear*.
Sets: **1988** *The Gospel at Colonus*

Genjiro Yeto

Genjiro Yeto, also known as Genjiro Katoaka, was born in 1867 in Arita, Japan. He studied painting in New York City and exhibited widely in the United States between 1889 and 1912. He also illustrated books including *A Japanese Nightingale* by Onoto Watanna, published in 1904. A 1906 New York City directory lists Genjiro Yeto as a landscape artist with studios located at both 114th West 12th Street and 6 East 17th Street. His paintings are popular with private collectors and some of his illustrations are in the collection of Victorian and Edwardian Collection of Popular Fiction in the State Library of Tasmania.
Costumes: **1902** *The Darling of the Gods*† **1903** *Darling of the Gallery Gods, The* and *The Dress Parade*†

Robert Yodice

Robert Yodice (Iodice) was resident designer at Juilliard from 1973 to 1977. He is a painter as well as a set designer and received an Obie Award in 1978 for Joseph Papp's *Museum*. He also designed *Alice at the Palace* for the New York Shakespeare Festival. Related experience includes positions as technical director for various theaters and service on the staffs of Ride and Show Engineering, Stage Engineering International and The Great American Market. Born in New York City, he studied painting with Robert Rabinowitz in addition to earning B.F.A. and M.F.A. degrees. He began his career as an assistant to Ming Cho Lee and Wolfgang Roth and has also been an assistant professor and resident designer at the University of California (now UCLA).
Sets: **1973** *The Beggar's Opera*†

Akira Yoshimura

Akira "Leo" Yoshimura has an M.F.A. from the Yale University School of Drama. He also studied painting at the Art Institute of Chicago and the American Academy of Art in Chicago. Additional credits include designs for television (with two Emmy nominations for *Saturday Night Live*) and regional theaters, such as the Dallas Theatre Center, the Joseph Papp Public Theatre and the Hartman Theatre. His career began with Paul Sills at the Second City Repertory. He should not be confused with the Japanese novelist (1927-) with the same name, nor Lee Yoshimura (1940-), a construction company executive.
Sets: **1979** *Gilda Radner Live from N.Y.*†

James Youmans

James Youmans designs scenery on both coasts of the United States. He has credits at the South Coast Repertory, the Mark Taper Forum, La Jolla Playhouse, Pasadena Playhouse, and the Seattle Repertory Theatre in the west, and the Goodspeed Opera House, the Huntington Theatre Company, and the Long Wharf Theatre in the east, among many others. Off-Broadway credits include *The Petrified Prince* at the New York Shakespeare Festival for which he was nominated for a Drama Desk Award, and productions at Westbeth Theatre Center, the Manhattan Theatre Club, Playwrights Horizons, the Vineyard Theatre, and the WPA Theatre. He received his B.F.A. at State University of New York, at Purchase in 1986. Twenty-first century designs include the national tour of *Cinderella* starring Eartha Kitt as the Fairy Godmother, *The Boswell Sisters* at the Old Globe Theatre, and *Summer of '42* at the Variety Arts Theatre.

Sets: 1995 *Swinging on a Star*

Young Brothers

John H. Young (1858-1944) and Louis C. Young (1864-1915) were partners in Young Brothers and worked primarily as scene painters. The business was located at 536 West 29th Street, New York City and was active between 1900 and 1920. John and Louis Young resided in Pelham, New York.

Sets: 1909 *The Bridge†* (Act II) **1910** *The Jolly Bachelors†* (as: J.H. and L.C. Young) **1912** *Broadway to Paris* (as: John and Louie Young); *The Passing Show of 1912* (as: John H. and Louis) **1913** *All Aboard†*; *The Ghost Breaker†*; *The Passing Show of 1913†*; *The Tongues of Men* **1914** *Life†* (Acts I, III, IV, V); *The Passing Show of 1914†* **1915** *Two is Company*

Young Brothers and Boss

John H. Young (1858-1944) and Louis C. Young (1864-1915) were partners in Young Brothers and also collaborated with Charles E. Boss (c.1875-1940) through Young Brothers and Boss between 1906 and 1909. All three men designed productions under their own names, as well as in collaboration with other scene painters. Additional information can be found under each heading.

Sets: 1906 *The Love Letter†* (Act I, II); *The Two Mr. Wetherbys* **1907** *The Coming of Mrs. Patrick*; *The Rejuvenation of Aunt Mary†* (Act II) **1908** *Fifty Miles from Boston†*; *Funabashi†*; *Little Nemo†*; *The Worth of a Woman* **1909** *A Fool There Was†*; *Springtime*; *Strife†*

Clive Young

Clive Young designed gowns for a 1921 Broadway play.

Costumes: 1921 *Ambush* (Miss Eldridge's gowns in Acts I and III)

John H. Young

John H. Young was born in Grand Rapids, Michigan in 1858 and worked as a scenic designer and painter in Chicago and New York City. He moved to Chicago after attending school in Michigan to be a scenic painter. He then moved to New York at the turn of the twentieth century and designed shows for major producers such as Florenz Ziegfeld, Earl Carroll and George White. His brother Louis C. Young (1864-1915) was also a scenic painter and the often worked together. A specialist in mechanical displays, he amassed a large library of photographs for use in creating authentic scenes. He died in North Pelham, New York on January 5, 1944 at age 86.

Sets: 1899 *The Ghetto†* **1900** *Caleb West†*; *Fiddle-Dee-Dee*; *Her Majesty, the Girl Queen of Nordenmark†*; *Monte Cristo†*; *Woman and Wine†* **1901** *The Auctioneer†*; *The Governor's Son*; *Hoity Toity*; *Lovers' Lane†*; *Under Southern Skies†* **1902** *Twirly Whirly* **1903** *Babes in Toyland†*; *Captain Barrington*; *Whoop-Dee-Doo*; *The Wizard of Oz†* (Act I, Scenes 2, 4, 5; Act III) **1904** *Bird Center†*; *The Cingalee*; *An English Daisy*; *It Happened in Nordland*; *Much Ado About Nothing*; *Olympe†*; *The Pit†* **1905** *Wonderland†* **1906** *Forty-five Minutes from Broadway†*; *George Washington, Jr.†* **1907** *Lola from Berlin*; *The Round Up*; *The Talk of New York†*; *Ziegfeld Follies of 1907†* **1908** *The American Idea†*; *The Gay Musician†*; *The Girl Question*; *Little Nemo†*; *The Merry Widow Burlesque*; *The*

Soul Kiss†; *The Yankee Prince*; *Ziegfeld Follies of 1908*† (Designed and painted) **1909** *The Candy Shop*† (Act II); *Old Dutch* **1910** *Mary Magdalene*† (Act II); *The Merry Whirl*† (Act I); *The Prince of Bohemia*† (Designed and painted) **1911** *The Wife Hunters* **1912** *Hokey-Pokey and Bunty, Bulls and Strings*; *The Master of the House*† (as: Young); *The Merry Countess*; *Roly Poly and Without the Law*; *The Sun Dodgers* **1913** *Ziegfeld Follies of 1913*† (and Co.) **1914** *Ziegfeld Follies of 1914*† **1916** *Robinson Crusoe, Jr.*† **1917** *Doing Our Bit*† **1921** *In the Night Watch*†

Leonard Young

Leonard Young, a native of Canada, designed sets and costumes and served as assistant director for a Broadway show in 1921. He managed the Community Players of Montreal, Canada from 1920 to 1923, when it closed, unable to compete with larger, commercial theaters. He then worked as a newspaper illustrator in Montreal until the Second World War when he served with the Ninth Field Ambulance Unit of the Third Canadian Division. During the war, he designed for *Dumbbells*, a concert troupe from that same military unit.
Sets: 1921 *Biff! Biff! Bang!*
Costumes: 1921 *Biff! Biff! Bang!*
(Also Assistant Director)

Louis C. Young

Louis C. Young was born in Grand Rapids, Michigan in 1864, and like his brother, John H. Young (1858-1944), he worked initially as a scenic designer and painter in Chicago before moving to New York City at the end of the nineteenth century where he first worked as an assistant to Phillip Goatcher at Niblo's Gardens as a scene painter. Credits before 1900 include *An Errant Knave* in 1890 and *The Christian* in 1898. He died in North Pelham, New York in 1915.
Sets: 1900 *Mistress Nell* **1901** *Garrett O'Magh*; *A Romance of Athlone* **1902** *Hon. John Grigsby*; *Joan o' the Shoals*†; *Mistress Nell*; *The Sword of the King*† **1904** *Terence* **1905** *Edmund Burke*; *Mary, Mary, Quite Contrary*† **1906** *Fasci-*

nating Mr. Vanderveldt† **1910** *Mary Magdalene*† (Act II)

Roland Young

Roland Young's career as an actor began in the United States with the Washington Square Players. He was born in London on November 11, 1887 and performed in the West End before coming to America. He was a star of stage and screen and was nominated for an Academy Award for Best Supporting Actor in 1937 for *Topper*, one of numerous films including *Ruggles of Red Gap* and *The Man Who Could Work Miracles* in which he appeared. He also was a successful actor in New York City in plays such as *Beggar on Horseback*, *The Queen's Husband*, *Good Gracious Annabelle*, *A Touch of Brimstone* and *Rollo's Wild Oats*, for which he also designed the settings. He was a caricaturist and author of the verse collection *Not for Children*. Married to the actress Dorothy Patience May, Roland Young died on June 7, 1953 at age 65.
Sets: 1920 *Rollo's Wild Oat*

Ross B. Young

Ross B. Young designed costumes on Broadway in 1970. He first designed *The Cherry Orchard* for the John Fernald Company at the Meadow Brook Theatre at Oakland University in Rochester, Michigan.
Costumes: 1970 *The Cherry Orchard*

Sylvia Younin

Sylvia Younin, a native New Yorker, designed a set on Broadway in 1967. She received a B.A. from Brooklyn College and an M.A. from Columbia University. In addition to writing Yiddish short stories she translates books from Yiddish into English.
Sets: 1967 *Sing, Israel, Sing*

Kenneth M. Yount

Kenneth M. Yount was born in Washington, D.C. on August 10, 1949 and attended Hastings College, St. Paul's School of Theology, and the University of Missouri, where he studied with Vincent Scassotti and received a Master of Arts degree. His costumes were seen in many regional theaters and off-Broadway in *Scrambled Feet* and

Sea Marks, among other shows. As an in-house designer at Eaves-Brooks he amassed many credits and also supervised all facets of costume production for other designers. In 1993 he was named director of the TDF's Costume Collection where he supervised rentals to not-for-profit theaters and helped begin the Irene Sharaff Awards for Excellence in Costume. Dance credits include productions for the Nutmet Ballet Company and between 1983 and 1993, productions for Jacques d'Amboise's National Dance Institute. He died on February 24, 1996 in New York City, a victim of AIDS.
Costumes: 1976 *Oh! Calcutta!* **1989** *Chu Chem*

Vyacheslav Zaitsev

Vyacheslav Mikhailovich Zaitsev was born in Ivanovo, Russia on March 2, 1938 and studied at the Moscow Textile Institute, where he now teaches. Primarily a fashion designer, he was chief designer at the All Union Fashion House from 1965 to 1978. In 1982 he formed "Slava Zaitsev" the Moscow fashion house that exported Soviet fashions designs to the United States through Intertorg, Inc. in the late 1980s. A member of the Artists' Union since 1976, he has participated in Paris fashion shows since 1988, and in 1989 won a Japanese award for his couture designs. Author of *The Changing Fashion* and *This Many-Faced World of Fashion* he designed a Russian fashion doll, Marusya, initially available in 1996.
Costumes: 1997 *The Cherry Orchard*

S. Zalud

Sam Zalud mainly designed sets and occasionally costumes for plays and musical revues. He was employed by the Shuberts and also was involved with several of the *Ziegfeld Follies*. He was born in 1886 and died on March 27, 1963 at the age of 77.
Costumes: 1914 *Madam Moselle*† (Costumes) **1918** *Little Simplicity*; *The Passing Show of 1918*†; *Sinbad*† **1919** *Good Morning, Judge*; *Hello, Alexander*; *Monte Cristo, Jr.*; *Take It from Me*† **1920** *Cinderella on Broadway*†

Victor Zanoff

Victor Zanoff designed one Broadway set in 1937.
Sets: 1937 *Swing It*†

Franco Zeffirelli

Franco Zeffirelli originally planned to become an actor or join the family textile import business. Born on February 12, 1923 in Florence, Italy, he attended the University of Architecture in Florence. He began acting in 1945 but soon turned to design and gradually began directing. He designed films for Luchino Visconti, Vittorio de Sica and Michelangelo Antonioni. He has designed operas at La Scala and the Metropolitan Opera, most recently *Turandot* and *La Boheme*. Notable film work as director and designer include *Romeo and Juliet*, *Brother Sun, Sister Moon*, *The Taming of The Shrew*, *Otello* and *Hamlet*. Among his many honors are Academy Award nominations for direction for *Romeo and Juliet* in 1968 and a Special Prize for Outstanding Contribution to World Cinema at the Karlovy Vary International Film Festival in 1999. Additional New York credits include directing *Filumena* in 1980 and many productions at the Metropolitan Opera. He is author of *Zeffirelli by Zeffirelli* (1986).
Sets: 1963 *The Lady of the Camellias* **1974** *Saturday Sunday Monday*

Madame Frances Ziebarth

Madame Frances M. Ziebarth was best known as the costumer at the New York Hippodrome. She supervised the execution of designs for John Murray Anderson, Alfredo Edel, Mark Lawson, and Arthur Voegtlin among other, and was also responsible for wardrobe maintenance. Occasionally she also collaborated on costume designs.
Costumes: 1908 *The Battle in the Skies*; *Sporting Days* **1914** *Wars of the World*† (Costumer)

Klara Zieglerova

Scenic designer Klara Zieglerova, daughter of a graphic designer and an architect, is from Prague. She studied graphic design at the Academy of Applied Arts and spent a year at Miami University of Ohio studying scenic design before working in graphics in Czechoslovakia. After returning to America and receiving an M.F.A. from the Yale University School of Drama in 1996, she assisted Ming Cho Lee and then Tony Walton. While at Yale, she designed *The Good Person of Zechwan* and *Mrs. Warren's Profession* for the Yale Repertory Theatre. Her many credits in regional theaters include productions at the Williamstown Theatre Festival, the McCarter Theater Center, the Old Globe Theatre, and the Intar Theatre. Off-Broadway she has designed *What You Get and What You Expect* at the New York Theatre Workshop, *Eclipsed* for the Irish Repertory Theatre, and *Mirandolina* for the Pearl Theatre Company. Twenty-first century designs include *First Love* at the New York Theatre Workshop and *Light Up the Sky* for the Williamstown Theatre Festival.

Sets: 2000 *The Search for Signs of Intelligent Life in the Universe*

Frank J. Zimmerer

Frank J. Zimmerer was born in Nebraska City, Nebraska in 1882 and studied at the Art Institute of Chicago, the Glasgow School of Art, and in Paris. During the teens he was active in New York, creating sets for Broadway plays, and painting. He served in administrative positions at the Kansas City Art Institute and Northwest Missouri Normal before relocating to California in the mid-1920s to work as a commercial artist and exhibit his paintings. Zimmerer died in Los Angeles, California on October 17, 1965.

Sets: 1916 *The Birthday of the Infanta*; *The Golden Doom*; *King Arimenes and the Unknown Warrior*; *Petrouchka*; *The Trimplet* 1918 *Jonathan Makes a Wish†*; *Seventeen* 1919 *A Night in Avignon*

Costumes: 1916 *The Golden Doom*; *King Arimenes and the Unknown Warrior†* 1919 *A Night in Avignon*

Frank Zimmerman

Frank Zimmerman was the son of one of New York's most influential theatrical managers, J. Fred Zimmerman. He

graduated from the University of Pennsylvania in 1903 and spent six years as business manager of the Garrick Theatre. In 1913 he began working in management for Zimmerman Vaudeville enterprises. Mr. Zimmerman died, a suicide, on July 12, 1927.

Sets: 1916 *The Gods of the Mountain* 1919 *Book of Job*; *The Golden Doom*; *Laughter of the Gods*; *Stingy*

Costumes: 1916 *The Gods of the Mountain* 1919 *Book of Job*; *The Golden Doom*; *Laughter of the Gods*; *Stingy*

Madame Zimmerman

The 1906 London playbill for *The Merry Widow* credits the costume designs to "Madame Zimmerman, Paris." Her designs were seen in subsequent versions in London as well as in New York. She also contributed costumes to other plays in both cities.

Costumes: 1907 *The Merry Widow†* 1909 *The Love Cure†* 1913 *Somewhere Else†* (Children's costumes)

Doris Zinkeisen

Doris Claire Zinkeisen was born July 31, 1898 in Kilcreggan, Scotland. She studied at the Royal Academy School, where an early painting was exhibited in 1917. She also won medals at the Paris salon when young. She designed mainly in England for the theater and the ballet, beginning in 1923 with sets and costumes for *The Insect Play* and often collaborated with Nigel Playfair, Charles B. Cochran and Noel Coward. She designed regularly at the Old Vic and for opera. She served in St. John's Ambulance Brigade during the Second World War and in 1945 traveled to the Belsen Concentration Camp after which she painted scenes that are in the permanent collection of the Imperial War Museum. After the war she painted murals on the Queen Mary as part of the effort to restore it from troop ship to passenger liner. Author of *Designing for the Stage*, and an avid horsewoman, she died on January 3, 1991 at age 92 in Badingham, England.

Sets: 1929 *Wake Up and Dream†*

Costumes: 1928 *This Year of Grace†* 1929 *Wake Up and Dream†* 1934 *The Great Waltz†*

Patricia Zipprodt

Patricia Zipprodt designed costumes for plays, ballets, operas, film and television during a remarkable career. She was born in Evanston, Illinois on February 24, 1925 and graduated from Wellesley College. She trained for a career in costume design at the Chicago Art Institute, the Fashion Institute of Technology and as an assistant costume designer. Her New York debut occurred in 1957 after which she became especially active as a designer, and well known as a mentor to young designers for were her devoted assistants. Notable films include *The Graduate*. Her talent was rewarded with eight Tony nominations and three Tony Awards, for *Fiddler on the Roof* in 1965, *Cabaret* in 1967 and *Sweet Charity* in 1986 and the 1997 Irene Sharaff Lifetime Achievement Award, and in 1992 was inducted into the Theater Hall of Fame. She died on July 17, 1999 at age 73.

Costumes: 1957 *Miss Lonely Hearts*; *The Potting Shed* (Costume Supervisor); *The Rope Dancers*; *A Visit to a Small Planet* (Costume Supervisor) **1958** *Back to Methuselah*; *The Night Circus* **1959** *The Gang's All Here* **1960** *Period of Adjustment* **1961** *The Garden of Secrets*; *Sunday in New York* **1962** *Step on a Crack* **1963** *Oh Dad, Poor Dad, Mamma's Hung You...*; *She Loves Me* **1964** *Fiddler on the Roof* **1965** *Anya* **1966** *Cabaret*; *Pousse-Cafe* **1968** *Plaza Suite*; *Zorba* **1969** *1776*; *The National Theatre of the Deaf* **1970** *Georgy* **1971** *Scratch* **1972** *Pippin* **1974** *Mack and Mabel* **1975** *All God's Chillun Got Wings*; *Chicago* **1976** *Fiddler on the Roof*; *Poor Murderer* **1978** *King of Hearts*; *Stages* **1980** *Charlotte* **1981** *Fiddler on the Roof*; *Fools*; *Kingdoms* **1982** *Alice in Wonderland*; *Whodunnit* **1983** *Brighton Beach Memoirs*; *The Glass Menagerie* **1984** *Accidental Death of an Anarchist*; *Sunday in the Park with George*† **1986** *Big Deal*; *Sweet Charity*

1987 *Cabaret* **1988** *Macbeth* **1989** *Dangerous Games*; *Jerome Robbins' Broadway*† **1990** *Cat on a Hot Tin Roof*; *Fiddler on the Roof*; *Shogun: The Musical* **1991** *The Crucible* **1992** *A Little Hotel on the Side*; *The Master Builder*; *My Favorite Year* **1993** *My Fair Lady*

Elizabeth Zook

Elizabeth Zook designed costumes on Broadway in 1933.

Costumes: 1933 *Tattle Tales*

Catherine Zuber

Catherine Zuber received the Obie Award in for Sustained Excellence in Costume Design in 1997, a tribute to her many successful designs for productions off-Broadway in theaters such as the Manhattan Theatre Club, the Laura Pels Theatre, Playwrights Horizons, La MaMa E.T.C., Minetta Lane Theatre, and the Joseph Papp Public Theatre. Her credits in regional theaters are equally prolific, including shows at Hartford Stage, Goodman Theatre, Center Stage, La Jolla Playhouse, Dallas Theatre Center, Guthrie Theatre, McCarter Theatre, the Berkeley Repertory, and the American Repertory Theatre where she is resident costume designer. Zuber was born in England and moved to Queens, New York with her family when she was a child. She attended the Museum School of Fine Arts in Boston, where she studied photography and then Yale University School of Drama, where she studied with Ming Cho Lee and Jane Greenwood, and earned an M.F.A. Twenty-first century designs include *Saved* produced by the Theatre for a New Audience and *Othello* at the Joseph Papp Public Theatre.

Costumes: 1993 *The Red Shoes* **1994** *Philadelphia, Here I Come!* **1995** *The Rose Tattoo* **1997** *Ivanov*; *London Assurance*; *Triumph of Love* **1998** *The Sound of Music*; *Twelfth Night*

Appendix 1: The Tony Awards

The Tony Award is given at the end of each Broadway season for an outstanding contribution in several categories, including scenic, costume and lighting design. The award honors Antoinette Perry (1888-1946), an actress and director who was Chairman of the Board of the American Theatre Wing during World War II. Under the auspices of the American Theatre Wing, nominees and winners are selected by members of the governing boards of professional organizations, opening night press lists, the board of directors of the American Theatre Wing, and members of the League of New York Theatres and Producers. Since 1947 when the awards were first given, there have been many changes in the number of categories (Stage Technicians were eliminated after 1962), the title of categories (from Costumes to Costume Design), and the format. Currently there is a maximum of four nominations in each category and it is possible for a designer to be nominated for more than one production in a season. Winners are in bold.

1947
SETS: **David Ffolkes** for *Henry VIII*.
COSTUMES: **Lucinda Ballard** for *Another Part of the Forest; Happy Birthday; Street Scene, John Loves Mary; The Chocolate Soldier.*

1948
SETS: **Horace Armistead** for *The Medium*.
COSTUMES: **Mary Percy Schenck** for *The Heiress*.

1949
SETS: **Jo Mielziner** for *Sleepy Hollow; Summer and Smoke; Anne of the Thousand Days; Death of a Salesman; South Pacific.*
COSTUMES: **Lemuel Ayers** for *Kiss Me, Kate.*

1950
SETS: **Jo Mielziner** for *The Innocents*.
COSTUMES: **Aline Bernstein** for *Regina*.

1951
SETS: **Boris Aronson** for *The Rose Tattoo; The Country Girl; Season in the Sun.*
COSTUMES: **Miles White** for *Bless You All.*

1952
SETS: **Jo Mielziner** for *The King and I.*

COSTUMES: **Irene Sharaff** for *The King and I.*
1953
SETS: **Raoul Pène du Bois** for *Wonderful Town.*
COSTUMES: **Miles White** for *Hazel Flagg.*
1954
SETS: **Peter Larkin** for *Ondine; The Teahouse of the August Moon.*
COSTUMES: **Richard Whorf and Edith Lutyens Bel Geddes** for *Ondine.*
1955
SETS: **Oliver Messel** for *House of Flowers.*
COSTUMES: **Cecil Beaton** for *Quadrille.*
1956
SETS: **Peter Larkin** for *Inherit the Wind; No Time for Sergeants.* Boris Aronson for *The Diary of Anne Frank; Bus Stop; Once Upon A Tailor; A View from the Bridge.* Ben Edwards for *The Ponder Heart; Someone Waiting; The Honeys.* Jo Mielziner for *Cat on a Hot Tin Roof; The Lark; Middle of the Night; Pipe Dream.* Raymond Sovey for *The Great Sebastians.*
COSTUMES: **Alvin Colt** for *Pipe Dream.* Alvin Colt for *The Lark; Phoenix '55.* Mainbocher for *The Great Sebastians.* Helene Pons for *The Diary of Anne Frank; Heavenly Twins; A View from the Bridge.*
1957
SETS: **Oliver Smith** for *My Fair Lady.* Boris Aronson for *A Hole In The Head; Small War On Murray Hill.* Ben Edwards for *The Waltz Of The Toreadors.* George Jenkins for *The Happiest Millionaire; Too Late The Phalarope.* Donald Oenslager for *Major Barbara.* Oliver Smith for *A Clearing in the Woods; Candide; Auntie Mame; Eugenia; A Visit to a Small Planet.*
COSTUMES: **Cecil Beaton** for *My Fair Lady.* Cecil Beaton for *Little Glass Clock.* Alvin Colt for *Li'l Abner; The Sleeping Prince.* Dorothy Jeakins for *Major Barbara; Too Late the Phalarope.* Irene Sharaff for *Candide; Happy Hunting; Shangri La; Small War on Murray Hill.*
1958
SETS: **Oliver Smith** for *West Side Story.* Boris Aronson for *Orpheus Descending; A Hole in the Head; The Rope Dancers.* Ben Edwards for *The Dark at the Top of the Stairs.* Peter Larkin for *Look Homeward, Angel; Miss Lonelyhearts; The Square Root of Wonderful; Oh, Captain!; The Day the Money Stopped.* Oliver Smith for *Brigadoon; Carousel; Jamaica; Nude with Violin; Time Remembered.*
COSTUMES: **Motley** for *The First Gentleman.* Lucinda Ballard for *Orpheus Descending.* Motley for *Look Back in Anger; Look Homeward, Angel; Shinbone Alley; The Country Wife.* Irene Sharaff for *West Side Story.* Miles White for *Jamaica; Time Remembered; Oh, Captain!*
1959
SETS: **Donald Oenslager** for *A Majority of One.* Boris Aronson for *J.B.* Ballou for *The Legend of Lizzie.* Ben Edwards for *Jane Eyre.* Oliver Messel for *Rashomon.* Teo Otto for *The Visit.*
COSTUMES: **Rouben Ter-Arutunian** for *Redhead.* Castillo for *Goldilocks.* Dorothy Jeakins for *The World of Suzie Wong.* Oliver Messel for *Rashomon.* Irene Sharaff for *Flower Drum Song.*
1960
SETS MUSICAL: **Oliver Smith** for *The Sound of Music.* Cecil Beaton for *Saratoga.* William and Jean Eckart for *Fiorello!* Peter Larkin for *Greenwillow.* Jo Mielziner for *Gypsy.*
SETS DRAMATIC: **Howard Bay** for *Toys in the Attic.* Will Steven Armstrong for *Caligula.* David Hays for *The Tenth Man.* George Jenkins for *The Miracle Worker.* Jo Mielziner for *The Best Man.*
COSTUMES: **Cecil Beaton** for *Saratoga.* Raoul Pène du Bois for *Gypsy.* Alvin Colt for *Greenwillow.* Miles White for *Take Me Along.*

1961

SETS MUSICAL: **Oliver Smith** for *Camelot*.   George Jenkins for *13 Daughters*.   Robert Randolph for *Bye, Bye Birdie*.

SETS DRAMATIC: **Oliver Smith** for *Becket*.   Roger Furse for *Duel of the Angels*. David Hays for *All the Way Home*.   Jo Mielziner for *The Devil's Advocate*.   Rouben Ter-Arutunian for *Advise and Consent*.

COSTUMES MUSICAL: **Adrian and Tony Duquette** for *Camelot*.   Cecil Beaton for *Tenderloin*.   Rolf Gerard for *Irma la Douce*.

COSTUMES DRAMATIC: **Motley** for *Becket*.   Theoni V. Aldredge for *The Devil's Advocate*.   Raymond Sovey for *All the Way Home*.

1962

SETS: **Will Steven Armstrong** for *Carnival*.   David Hays for *No Strings*.   Oliver Smith for *The Gay Life*.   Rouben Ter-Arutunian for *A Passage to India*.

COSTUMES: **Lucinda Ballard** for *The Gay Life*.   Donald Brooks for *No Strings*. Motley for *Kwamina*.   Miles White for *Milk and Honey*.

1963

SETS: **Sean Kenny** for *Oliver!*   Will Steven Armstrong for *Tchin-Tchin*.   Anthony Powell for *The School for Scandal*.   Franco Zeffirelli for *The Lady of the Camellias*.

COSTUMES: **Anthony Powell** for *The School for Scandal*.   Marcel Escoffier for *The Lady of the Camellias*.   Robert Fletcher for *Little Me*.   Motley for *Mother Courage and Her Children*.

1964

SETS: **Oliver Smith** for *Hello, Dolly!*   Raoul Pène Du Bois for *The Student Gypsy*. Ben Edwards for *The Ballad of the Sad Cafe*.   David Hays for *Marco Millions*.

COSTUMES: **Freddy Wittop** for *Hello, Dolly!*   Beni Montresor for *Marco Millions*. Irene Sharaff for *The Girl Who Came to Supper*.   Rouben Ter-Arutunian for *Arturo Ui*.

1965

SETS: **Oliver Smith** for *Baker Street; Luv; The Odd Couple*.   Boris Aronson for *Fiddler on the Roof; Incident at Vichy*.   Sean Kenny for *The Roar of the Greasepaint - The Smell of the Crowd*.   Beni Montresor for *Do I Hear A Waltz?*

COSTUMES: **Patricia Zipprodt** for *Fiddler on the Roof*.   Jane Greenwood for *Tartuffe*. Motley for *Baker Street*.   Freddy Wittop for *The Roar of the Greasepaint-The Smell of the Crowd*.

1966

SETS: **Howard Bay** for *Man of La Mancha*.   William and Jean Eckart for *Mame*. David Hays for *Drat! The Cat!*   Robert Randolph for *Anya; Skyscraper; Sweet Charity*.

COSTUMES: **Gunilla Palmstierna-Weiss** for *Marat/Sade*.   Howard Bay and Patton Campbell for *Man of La Mancha*.   Loudon Sainthill for *The Right Honorable Gentleman*.   Irene Sharaff for *Sweet Charity*.

1967

SETS: **Boris Aronson** for *Cabaret*.   John Bury for *The Homecoming*.   Oliver Smith for *I Do! I Do!*   Alan Tagg for *Black Comedy*.

COSTUMES: **Patricia Zipprodt** for *Cabaret*.   Nancy Potts for *The Wild Duck; The School for Scandal*.   Tony Walton for *The Apple Three*.   Freddy Wittop for *I Do! I Do!*

1968

SETS: **Desmond Heeley** for *Rosencrantz and Guildenstern are Dead*.   Boris Aronson for *The Price*.   Robert Randolph for *Golden Rainbow*.   Peter Wexler for *The Happy Time*.

COSTUMES: **Desmond Heeley** for *Rosencrantz and Guildenstern are Dead*.   Jane Greenwood for *More Stately Mansions*.   Irene Sharaff for *Hallelujah, Baby!*   Freddy Wittop for *The Happy Time*.

1969

SETS: **Boris Aronson** for *Zorba.* Derek Cousins for *Canterbury Tales.* Jo Mielziner for *1776.* Oliver Smith for *Dear World.*

COSTUMES: **Loudon Sainthill** for *Canterbury Tales.* Michael Annals for *Morning, Noon and Night.* Robert Fletcher for *Hadrian VII.* Particia Zipprodt for *Zorba.*

1970

SETS: **Jo Mielziner** for *Child's Play.* Howard Bay for *Cry for Us All.* Ming Cho Lee for *Billy.* Robert Randolph for *Applause.*

COSTUMES: **Cecil Beaton** for *Coco.* Ray Aghayan for *Applause.* W. Robert LaVine for *Jimmy.* Freddy Wittop for *A Patriot for Me.*

LIGHTS: **Jo Mielziner** for *Child's Play.* Tharon Musser for *Applause.* Thomas Skelton for *Indians.*

1971

SETS: **Boris Aronson** for *Company.* John Bury for *The Rothschilds.* Sally Jacobs for *A Midsummer Night's Dream.* Jo Mielziner for *Father's Day.*

COSTUMES: **Raoul Pène du Bois** for *No, No, Nanette.* Jane Greenwood for *Les Blancs.* Jane Greenwood for *Hay Fever.* Freddy Wittop for *Lovely Ladies, Kind Gentlemen.*

LIGHTS: **H.R. Poindexter** for *Story Theatre.* Robert Ornbo for *Company.* William Ritman for *Sleuth.*

1972

SETS: **Boris Aronson** for *Follies.* John Bury for *Old Times.* Kert Lundell for *Ain't Supposed to Die a Natural Death.* Robin Wagner for *Jesus Christ Superstar.*

COSTUMES: **Florence Klotz** for *Follies.* Theoni V. Aldredge for *Two Gentlemen of Verona.* Randy Barcelo for *Jesus Christ Superstar.* Carrie F. Robbins for *Grease.*

LIGHTS: **Tharon Musser** for *Follies.* Martin Aronstein for *Ain't Supposed to Die a Natural Death.* John Bury for *Old Times.* Jules Fisher for *Jesus Christ Superstar.*

1973

SETS: **Tony Walton** for *Pippin.* Boris Aronson for *A Little Night Music.* David Jenkins for *The Changing Room.* Santo Loquasto for *That Championship Season.*

COSTUMES: **Florence Klotz** for *A Little Night Music.* Theoni V. Aldredge for *Much Ado About Nothing.* Miles White for *Tricks.* Patricia Zipprodt for *Pippin.*

LIGHTS: **Jules Fisher** for *Pippin.* Martin Aronstein for *Much Ado About Nothing.* Ian Calderon for *That Championship Season.*   Tharon Musser for *A Little Night Music.*

1974

SETS: **Franne and Eugene Lee** for *Candide.* John Conklin for *The Au Pair Man.* Santo Loquasto for *What the Wine Sellers Buy.* Oliver Smith for *Gigi.* Ed Wittstein for *Ulysses in Nighttown.*

COSTUMES: **Franne Lee** for *Candide.* Theoni V. Aldredge for *The Au Pair Man.* Finlay James for *Crown Matrimonial.* Oliver Messel for *Gigi.* Carrie F. Robbins for *Over Here!*

LIGHTS: **Jules Fisher** for *Ulysses in Nighttown.* Marton Aronstein for *Boom Boom Room.* Ken Billlington for *The Visit.* Ben Edwards for *A Moon for the Misbegotten.* Tharon Musser for *The Good Doctor.*

1975

SETS: **Carl Toms** for *Sherlock Holmes.* Scott Johnson for *Dance With Me.* Tanya Moiseiwitsch for *The Misanthrope.* William Ritman for *God's Favorite.* Rouben Ter-Arutunian for *Goodtime Charley.* Robert Wagner for *Mack and Mabel.*

COSTUMES: **Geoffrey Holder** for *The Wiz.* Arthur Boccia for *Where's Charley?* Raoul Pène du Bois for *Doctor Jazz.* Willa Kim for *Goodtime Charley.* Tanya Moiseiwitsch for *The Misanthrope.* Patricia Zipprodt for *Mack and Mabel.*

LIGHTS: **Neil Peter Jampolis** for *Sherlock Holmes.* Chipmonck for *The Rocky Horror Show.* Abe Feder for *Goodtime Charley.* Andy Phillips for *Equus.* Thomas Skelton for *All God's Chillun.* James Tilton for *Seascape.*

1976

SETS: **Boris Aronson** for *Pacific Overtures*.   Ben Edwards for *A Matter of Gravity*.
David Mitchell for *Trelawny of the "Wells"*.   Tony Walton for *Chicago*.
COSTUMES: **Florence Klotz** for *Pacific Overtures*.   Theoni V. Aldredge for *A Chorus
Line*.   Ann Roth for *The Royal Family*.   Patricia Zipprodt for *Chicago*.
LIGHTS: **Tharon Musser** for *A Chorus Line*.   Ian Calderon for *Trelawny of the
"Wells"*.   Jules Fisher for *Chicago*.   Tharon Musser for *Pacific Overtures*.

1977

SETS: **David Mitchell** for *Annie*.   Santo Loquasto for *The Cherry Orchard*.   Santo
Loquasto for *American Buffalo*.   Robert Randolph for *Porgy and Bess*.
COSTUMES: **Theoni V. Aldredge** (tie) for *Annie*.   **Santo Loquasto** (tie) for *The
Cherry Orchard*.   Theoni V. Aldredge for *Threepenny Opera*.   Nancy Potts for *Porgy
and Bess*.
LIGHTS: **Jennifer Tipton** for *The Cherry Orchard*.   John Bury for *No Man's Land*.
Pat Collins for *Threepenny Opera*.   Neil Peter Jampolis for *The Innocents*.

1978

SETS: **Robin Wagner** for *On The Twentieth Century*.   Zack Brown for *The Impor-
tance of Being Earnest*.   Edward Gorey for *Dracula*.   David Mitchell for *Working*.
COSTUMES: **Edward Gorey** for *Dracula*.   Halston for *The Act*.   Geoffrey Holder for
Timbucktu!   Willa Kim for *Dancin'*.
LIGHTS: **Jules Fisher** for *Dancin'*.   Ken Billington for *Working*.   Jules Fisher for
Beatlemania.   Tharon Musser for *The Act*.

1979

SETS: **Eugene Lee** for *Sweeney Todd*.   Karl Eigsti for *Knockout*.   David Jenkins for
The Elephant Man.   John Wulp for *The Crucifer of Blood*.
COSTUMES: **Franne Lee** for *Sweeney Todd*.   Theoni V. Aldredge for *Ballroom*.   Ann
Roth for *The Crucifer of Blood*.   Julie Weiss for *The Elephant Man*.
LIGHTS: **Roger Morgan** for *The Crucifer of Blood*.   Ken Billington for *Sweeney
Todd*.   Beverly Emmons for *The Elephant Man*.   Tharon Musser for *Ballroom*.

1980

SETS: **John Lee Beatty** (tie) for *Tally's Folly*.   **David Mitchell** (tie) for *Barnum*.
Timothy O'Brien and Tazeena Firth for *Evita*.   Tony Walton for *A Day in Hollywood/A
Night in Ukraine*.
COSTUMES: **Theoni V. Aldredge** for *Barnum*.   Pierre Balmain for *Happy New Year*.
Raoul Pène du Bois for *Sugar Babies*.   Timothy O'Brien and Tazeena Firth for *Evita*.
LIGHTS: **David Hersey** for *Evita*.   Beverly Emmons for *A Day in Hollywood/A Night
in the Ukraine*.   Craig Miller for *Barnum*.   Dennis Parichy for *Talley's Folly*.

1981

SETS: **John Bury** for *Amadeus*.   John Lee Beatty for *Fifth of July*.   Santo Loquasto
for *The Suicide*.   David Mitchell for *Can-Can*.
COSTUMES: **Willa Kim** for *Sophisticated Ladies*.   Theoni V. Aldredge for *42nd Street*.
John Bury for *Amadeus*.   Franca Squarciapino for *Can-Can*.
LIGHTS: **John Bury** for *Amadeus*.   Tharon Musser for *42nd Street*.   Dennis Parichy
for *Fifth of July*.   Jennifer Tipton for *Sophisticated Ladies*.

1982

SETS: **John Napier and Dermot Hayes** for *The Life and Adventures of Nicholas
Nickleby*.   Ben Edwards for *Medea*.   Lawrence Miller for *Nine*.   Robin Wagner for
Dreamgirls.
COSTUMES: **William Ivey Long** for *Nine*.   Theoni V. Aldredge for *Dreamgirls*.   Jane
Greenwood for *Medea*.   John Napier for *The Life and Adventures of Nicholas Nickleby*.
LIGHTS: **Tharon Musser** for *Dreamgirls*.   Martin Aronstein for *Medea*.   David
Hersey for *The Life and Adventures of Nicholas Nickleby*.   Marcia Madeira for *Nine*.

1983

SETS: **Ming Cho Lee** for *K-2*.   John Gunter for *All's Well That Ends Well*.   David
Mitchell for *Foxfire*.   John Napier for *Cats*.

COSTUMES: **John Napier** for *Cats*. Lindy Hemming for *All's Well That Ends Well*. Rita Ryack for *My One and Only*. Patricia Zipprodt for *Alice in Wonderland*.
LIGHTS: **David Hersey** for *Cats*. Ken Billington for *Foxfire*. Robert Bryan for *All's Well That Ends Well*. Allen Lee Hughes for *K2*.

1984
SETS: **Tony Straiges** for *Sunday in the Park with George*. Clarke Dunham for *End of the World*. Peter Larkin for *The Rink*. Tony Walton for *The Real Thing*.
COSTUMES: **Theoni V. Aldredge** for *La Cage Aux Folles*. Jane Greenwood for *Heartbreak House*. Patricia Zipprodt and Ann Hould-Ward for *Sunday in the Park with George*. Anthea Sylbert for *The Real Thing*.
LIGHTS: **Richard Nelson** for *Sunday in The Park With George*. Ken Billington for *End of the World*. Jules Fisher for *La Cage aux Folles*. Marc B. Weiss for *A Moon for the Misbegotten*.

1985
SETS: **Heidi Landesman** for *Big River*. Clarke Dunham for *Grind*. Ralph Koltai for *Much Ado About Nothing*. Voytek and Michael Levine for *Strange Interlude*.
COSTUMES: **Florence Klotz** for *Grind*. Patricia McGourty for *Big River*. Alexander Reid for *Cyrano de Bergerac*. Alexander Reid for *Much Ado About Nothing*.
LIGHTS: **Richard Riddell** for *Big River*. Terry Hands and Jeffrey Beecroft for *Cyrano de Bergerac*. Terry Hands and Jeffrey Beecroft for *Much Ado About Nothing*. Allen Lee Hughes for *Strange Interlude*.

1986
SETS: **Tony Walton** for *The House of Blue Leaves*. Ben Edwards for *The Iceman Cometh*. David Mitchell for *The Boys in Winter*. Beni Montresor for *The Marriage of Figaro*.
COSTUMES: **Patricia Zipprodt** for *Sweet Charity*. Willa Kim for *Song & Dance*. Beni Montresor for *The Marriage of Figaro*. Ann Roth for *The House of Blue Leaves*.
LIGHTS: **Pat Collins** for *I'm Not Rappaport*. Jules Fisher for *Song & Dance*. Paul Gallo for *The House of Blue Leaves*. Thomas R. Skelton for *The Iceman Cometh*.

1987
SETS: **John Napier** for *Les Miserables*. Bob Crowley for *Les Liaisons Dangereuses*. Martin Johns for *Me and My Girl*. Tony Walton for *The Front Page*.
COSTUMES: **John Napier** for *Starlight Express*. Bob Crowley for *Les Liaisons Dangereuses*. Ann Curtis for *Me and My Girl*. Andreane Neofitou for *Les Miserables*.
LIGHTS: **David Hersey** for *Les Miserables*. Martin Aronstein for *Wild Honey*. David Hersey for *Starlight Express*. Beverly Emmons and Chris Parry for *Les Liaisons Dangereuses*.

1988
SETS: **Maria Björnson** for *The Phantom of the Opera*. Eiko Ishioka for *M. Butterfly*. Tony Straiges for *Into the Woods*. Tony Walton for *Anything Goes*.
COSTUMES: **Maria Björnson** for *The Phantom of the Opera*. Ann Hould-Ward for *Into the Woods*. Eiko Ishioka for *M. Butterfly*. Tony Walton for *Anything Goes*.
LIGHTS: **Andrew Bridge** for *The Phantom of the Opera*. Paul Gallo for *Anything Goes*. Richard Nelson for *Into the Woods*. Andy Phillips for *M. Butterfly*.

1989
SETS: **Santo Loquasto** for *Cafe Crown*. Thomas Lynch for *The Heidi Chronicles*. Claudio Segovia and Hector Orezzoli for *Black and Blue*. Tony Walton for *Lend Me a Tenor*.
COSTUMES: **Claudio Segovia and Hector Orezzoli** for *Black and Blue*. Jane Greenwood for *Our Town*. Willa Kim for *Legs Diamond*. William Ivey Long for *Lend Me a Tenor*.
LIGHTS: **Jennifer Tipton** for *Jerome Robbins' Broadway*. Brian Nason for *Metamorphosis*. Neil Peter Jampolis and Jane Reisman for *Black and Blue*. Nancy Schertler for *Largely New York*.

1990

SETS: **Robin Wagner** for *City of Angels*.   Alexandra Byrne for *Some Americans Abroad*. Kevin Rigdon for *The Grapes of Wrath*. Tony Walton for *The Grand Hotel, The Musical*.

COSTUMES: **Santo Loquasto** for *Grand Hotel, The Musical*. Theoni V. Aldredge for *Gypsy*. Florence Klotz for *City of Angels*. Erin Quigley for *The Grapes of Wrath*.

LIGHTS: **Jules Fisher** for *Grand Hotel, The Musical*. Paul Gallo for *City of Angels*. Paul Pyant and Neil Peter Jampolis for *Orpheus Descending*. Kevin Rigdon for *The Grapes of Wrath*.

1991

SETS: **Heidi Landesman** for *The Secret Garden*. Richard Hudson for *La Bête*. John Napier for *Miss Saigon*. Tony Walton for *The Will Rogers Follies*.

COSTUMES: **Willa Kim** for *The Will Rogers Follies*. Theoni V. Aldredge for *The Secret Garden*. Judy Dearing for *Once on This Island*. Patricia Zipprodt for *Shogun: The Musical*.

LIGHTS: **Jules Fisher** for *The Will Rogers Follies*. David Hersey for *Miss Saigon*. Allen Lee Hughes for *Once on This Island*. Jennifer Tipton for *La Bête*.

1992

SETS: **Tony Walton** for *Guys and Dolls*.   John Lee Beatty for *A Small Family Business*. Robin Wagner for *Jelly's Last Jam*. Joe Vaněk for *Dancing at Lughnasa*.

COSTUMES: **William Ivey Long** for *Crazy for You*. Jane Greenwood for *Two Shakespearean Actors*. Toni-Leslie James for *Jelly's Last Jam*. Joe Vaněk for *Dancing at Lughnasa*.

LIGHTS: **Jules Fisher** for *Jelly's Last Jam*. Paul Gallo for *Guys and Dolls*. Paul Gallo for *Crazy for You*. Richard Pilbrow for *Four Baboons Adoring the Sun*.

1993

SETS: **John Arnone** for *The Who's Tommy*. John Lee Beatty for *Redwood Curtain*. Jerome Sirlin for *Kiss of the Spider Woman*. Robin Wagner for *Angels in America: Millennium Approaches*.

COSTUMES: **Florence Klotz** for *Kiss of the Spider Woman*. Jane Greenwood for *The Sisters Rosensweig*. Erin Quigley for *The Song of Jacob Zulu*. David C. Woolard for *The Who's Tommy*.

LIGHTS: **Chris Parry** for *The Who's Tommy*. Howell Binkley for *Kiss of the Spider Woman*.   Jules Fisher for *Angels in America: Millennium Approaches*.   Dennis Parichy for *Redwood Curtain*.

1994

SETS: **Bob Crowley** for *Carousel*. Peter J. Davison for *Medea*. Ian MacNeil for *An Inspector Calls*. Tony Walton for *She Loves Me*.

COSTUMES: **Ann Hould-Ward** for *Beauty and the Beast*.   Jane Greenwood for *Passion*. David Charles and Jane Greenwood for *She Loves Me*. Yan Tax for *Cyrano: The Musical*.

LIGHTS: **Rick Fisher** for *An Inspector Calls*. Beverly Emmons for *Passion*. Jules Fisher for *Angels in America: Perestroika*. Natasha Katz for *Beauty and the Beast*.

1995

SETS: **John Napier** for *Sunset Boulevard*. John Lee Beatty for *The Heiress*. Stephen Brimson Lewis for *Indiscretions*. Mark Thompson for *Arcadia*.

COSTUMES: **Florence Klotz** for *Show Boat*.   Jane Greenwood for *The Heiress*. Stephen Brimson Lewis for *Indiscretions*. Anthony Powell for *Sunset Boulevard*.

LIGHTS: **Andrew Bridge** for *Sunset Boulevard*.   Beverly Emmons for *The Heiress*. Mark Henderson for *Indiscretions*. Paul Pyant for *Arcadia*.

1996

SETS: **Brian Thomson** for *The King and I*. John Lee Beatty for *A Delicate Balance*. Scott Bradley for *Seven Guitars*. Anthony Ward for *A Midsummer Night's Dream*.

COSTUMES: **Roger Kirk** for *The King and I*. Jane Greenwood for *A Delicate Balance*. Alison Reeds for *Buried Child*. Paul Tazewell for *Bring in 'da Noise, Bring in 'da Funk*.

LIGHTS: **Jules Fisher and Peggy Eisenhauer** for *Bring in 'da Noise, Bring in 'da Funk.* Christopher Akerlind for *Seven Guitars.* Blake Burba for *Rent.* Nigel Levings for *The King and I.*

1997

SETS: **Steward Laing** for *Titanic.* John Lee Beatty for *The Little Foxes.* G.W. Mercier and Julie Taymor for *Juan Darién.* Tony Walton for *Steel Pier.*

COSTUMES: **Judith Dolan** for *Candide.* Ann Curtis for *Jekyll & Hyde.* William Ivey Long for *Chicago.* Martin Pakledinaz for *The Life.*

LIGHTS: **Ken Billington** for *Chicago.* Beverly Emmons for *Jekyll & Hyde.* Donald Holder for *Juan Darién.* Richard Pilbrow for *The Life.*

1998

SETS: **Richard Hudson** for *The Lion King.* Quay Brothers for *The Chairs.* Bob Crowley for *The Capeman.* Eugene Lee for *Ragtime.*

COSTUMES: **Julie Taymor** for *The Lion King.* William Ivey Long for *Cabaret.* Santo Loquasto for *Ragtime.* Martin Pakledinaz for *Golden Child.*

LIGHTS: **Donald Holder** for *The Lion King.* Paul Anderson for *The Chairs.* Peggy Eisenhauer and Mike Baldassari for *Cabaret.* Jules Fisher and Peggy Eisenhauer for *Ragtime.*

1999

SETS: **Richard Hoover** for *Not About Nightingales.* Bob Crowley for *The Iceman Cometh.* Bob Crowley for *Twelfth Night.* Riccardo Hernandez for *Parade.*

COSTUMES: **Lez Brotherston** for *Swan Lake.* Santo Loquasto for *Fosse.* John David Ridge for *Ring Round the Moon.* Catherine Zuber for *Twelfth Night.*

LIGHTS: **Andrew Bridge** for *Fosse.* Mark Henderson for *The Iceman Cometh.* Natasha Katz for *Twelfth Night.* Chris Parry for *Not About Nightingales.*

2000

SETS: **Bob Crowley** for *Aida.* Thomas Lynch for *The Music Man.* Robin Wagner for *Kiss Me, Kate.* Tony Walton for *Uncle Vanya.*

COSTUMES: **Martin Pakledinaz** for *Kiss Me, Kate.* Bob Crowley for *Aida.* Constance Hoffman for *The Green Bird.* William Ivey Long for *The Music Man.*

LIGHTS: **Natasha Katz** for *Aida.* Jules Fisher and Peggy Eisenhauer for *Marie Christine.* Jules Fisher and Peggy Eisenhauer for *The Wild Party.* Peter Kaczorowski for *Kiss Me, Kate.*

2001

SETS: **Robin Wagner** for *The Producers.* Bob Crowley for *The Invention of Love.* Heidi Ettinger for *The Adventures of Tom Sawyer.* Douglas W. Schmidt for *42nd Street.*

COSTUMES: **William Ivey Long** for *The Producers.* Theoni V. Aldredge for *Follies.* Roger Kirk for *42nd Street.* David C. Woolard for *The Rocky Horror Show.*

LIGHTS: **Peter Kaczorowski** for *The Producers.* Jules Fisher and Peggy Eisenhauer for *Jane Eyre.* Paul Gallo for *42nd Street.* Kenneth Posner for *The Adventures of Tom Sawyer.*

Appendix 2: The Donaldson Awards

The Donaldson Awards for outstanding Broadway design were given annually in July, beginning with the 1943-1944 season and ending with the 1954-1955 season. They honored W.H. Donaldson, founder of *The Bill Board*. The winners were selected by a poll of theater people. Two awards were given in the scenic and costume design categories, one for a musical and the other for a play.

1944
SETS PLAY: **Stewart Chaney** for *The Voice of the Turtle*.
SETS MUSICAL: **Howard Bay** for *Carmen Jones*.
COSTUMES PLAY: **Motley** for *Lovers and Friends*.
COSTUMES MUSICAL: **Raoul Pène Du Bois** for *Carmen Jones*.

1945
SETS PLAY: **George Jenkins** for *I Remember Mama*.
SETS MUSICAL: **Howard Bay** for *Up in Central Park*.
COSTUMES PLAY: **Lucinda Ballard** for *I Remember Mama*.
COSTUMES MUSICAL: **Miles White** for *Bloomer Girl*.

1946
SETS PLAY: **Jo Mielziner** for *Dream Girl*.
SETS MUSICAL: **Robert Edmond Jones** for *Lute Song*.
COSTUMES PLAY: **Motley** for *Pygmalion*.
COSTUMES MUSICAL: **Robert Edmond Jones** for *Lute Song*.

1947
SETS PLAY: **Cecil Beaton** for *Lady Windermere's Fan*.
SETS MUSICAL: **Oliver Smith** for *Brigadoon*.
COSTUMES PLAY: **Cecil Beaton** for *Lady Windermere's Fan*.
COSTUMES MUSICAL: **David Ffolkes** for *Brigadoon*.

1948
SETS PLAY: **Jo Mielziner** for *A Streetcar Named Desire*.
SETS MUSICAL: **Oliver Smith** for *High Button Shoes*.
COSTUMES PLAY: **David Ffolkes** for *Man and Superman*.
COSTUMES MUSICAL: **Miles White** for *High Button Shoes*.

1949
SETS PLAY: **Jo Mielziner** for *Death of a Salesman*.
SETS MUSICAL: **Lemuel Ayers** for *Kiss Me, Kate*.

COSTUMES PLAY: **Christian Béard** for *Madwoman of Chaillot.*
COSTUMES MUSICAL: **Lemuel Ayers** for *Kiss Me, Kate.*

1950

SETS PLAY: **Jo Mielziner** for *The Innocents.*
SETS MUSICAL: **Oliver Smith** for *Gentlemen Prefer Blondes.*
COSTUMES PLAY: **James Bailey** for *As You Like It.*
COSTUMES MUSICAL: **Miles White** for *Gentlemen Prefer Blondes.*

1951

SETS PLAY: **Frederick Fox** for *Darkness at Noon.*
SETS MUSICAL: **Jo Mielziner** for *The King and I.*
COSTUMES PLAY: **Castillo** (tie) for *Ring 'Round the Moon.* **Oliver Messel** (tie) for *Romeo and Juliet.*
COSTUMES MUSICAL: **Irene Sharaff** for *The King and I.*

1952

SETS PLAY: **Cecil Beaton** for *The Grass Harp.*
SETS MUSICAL: **Oliver Smith** for *Pal Joey.*
COSTUMES PLAY: **Audrey Cruddas** for *Caesar and Cleopatra.*
COSTUMES MUSICAL: **Miles White** for *Pal Joey.*

1953

SETS PLAY: **Lemuel Ayers** for *Camino Real.*
SETS MUSICAL: **Raoul Pène du Bois** for *Wonderful Town.*
COSTUMES PLAY: **Lemuel Ayers** for *Camino Real.*
COSTUMES MUSICAL: **Lemuel Ayers** for *My Darlin' Aida.*

1954

SETS PLAY: **Peter Larkin** for *Teahouse of the August Moon.*
SETS MUSICAL: **William and Jean Eckart** for *The Golden Apple.*
COSTUMES PLAY: **Edith Lutyens Bel Geddes and Richard Whorf** for *Ondine.*
COSTUMES MUSICAL: **Lemuel Ayers** for *Kismet.*

1955

SETS PLAY: **Peter Larkin** for *Inherit the Wind.*
SETS MUSICAL: **Oliver Messel** for *House of Flowers.*
COSTUMES PLAY: **Cecil Beaton** for *Quadrille.*
COSTUMES MUSICAL: **Oliver Messel** for *House of Flowers.*

Appendix 3: The Maharam, American Theater Wing, and Henry Hewes Awards

The Maharam Awards were presented each fall to recognize distinguished design on, off and off-off Broadway. The awards were named for Joseph Maharam, a theatrical fabric manufacturer, and sponsored through the Joseph Maharam Foundation. In 1986, they were renamed the American Theatre Wing Design Awards, after that organization took responsibility for administering them. In 1998 they were renamed once again to honor Henry Hewes, long-time theater critic of the *Saturday Review*.

As The Maharam Award

1965
SETS: **Boris Aronson** (tie) for *Fiddler on the Roof.* **Ming Cho Lee** (tie) for *Electra.*
COSTUMES: **Jane Greenwood** for *Tartuffe.*

1966
SETS: **Howard Bay** for *Man of La Mancha.*
COSTUMES: **Noel Taylor** for *Gnadige Fraulein; Slapstick Tragedy.*

1967
SETS: **Boris Aronson** for *Cabaret.*
COSTUMES: **Jeanne Button** for *Macbird.*

1968
SETS: **Ming Cho Lee** (tie) for *Ergo.* **Nancy Potts** for *Pantagleize; Hair.* **Peter Wexler** (tie) for *The Happy Time.*

1969
SETS: **Julian Beck** (tie) for *Frankenstein.* **Jo Melziner** (tie) for *1776.*
COSTUMES: **Patricia Zipprodt** for *1776.*

1970
SETS: **Boris Aronson** (tie) for *Company.* **Jo Mielziner** (tie) for *Child's Play.*
COSTUMES: **Theoni V. Aldredge** for *Peer Gynt.*

1971
SETS: **Boris Aronson** (tie) for *Follies.* **Peter Larkin** (tie) for *Les Blancs.*
COSTUMES: **Raoul P''ene Du Bois** for *No, No, Nanette.*

1972
SETS: **Kurt Lundell** (tie) for *Ain't Supposed To Die a Natural Death.* **Robert U. Taylor** (tie) for *Begger's Opera.*
COSTUMES: **Willa Kim** for *Screens.*

1973

SETS: **Douglas Schmidt** (tie) for *Enemies*. **Robin Wagner** (tie) for *Seesaw*.
COSTUMES: **Theoni V. Aldredge** for *Much Ado About Nothing*.

1974

SETS: **Franne and Eugene Lee** (tie) for *Candide*. **Ed Wittstein** (tie) for *Ulysses in Nighttown*.
COSTUMES: **Franne Lee** for *Candide*.

1975

SETS: **Robin Wagner** (tie) for *A Chorus Line*. **Robert Wilson** (tie) for *Letter for Queen Victoria*.
COSTUMES: **Carrie Robbins** for *Polly*.

1976

SETS: **Boris Aronson** (tie) for *Pacific Overtures*. **John Lee Beatty** (tie) for *Knock Knock*.
COSTUMES: **Florence Klotz** for *Pacific Overtures*.

1977

SETS: **Santo Loquasto** (tie) for *American Buffalo*. **Douglas W. Schmidt** (tie) for *Agamemnon*.
COSTUMES: **Santo Loquasto** for *Agamemnon*.

1978

SETS: **John Lee Beatty** (tie) for *A Life in The Theatre*. **Edward Gorey and Lynn Pecktal** (tie) for *Dracula*.
COSTUMES: **Theoni V. Aldredge** for *On the 20th Century*.
LIGHTS: **Jules Fisher** for *Dancin'*.

1979

SETS: **Karl Eigsti** (tie) for *Knockout*. **David Jenkins** (tie) for *The Elephant Man*. **Michael H. Yeardon** (tie) for *The Umbrellas of Cherbourg*.
COSTUMES: **Peter Schumann** for *Wolkenstein; Joan of Arc*.
LIGHTS: **Beverly Emmons** for *The Elephant Man*.

1980

SETS: **David Mitchell** (tie) for *Barnum*. **Stuart Wurtzel** (tie) for *The Sorrows of Stephen*.
SETS, COSTUMES AND PUPPETS: **Julie Taymor** for *The Haggadah (also puppet design)*.
LIGHTS: **Dennis Parichy** for *Talley's Folly*.

1981

SETS: **Douglas E. Ball** (tie) for *Request Concert*. **John Lee Beatty** (tie) for *Fifth of July*. **Manuel Lutgenhorst** (tie) for *Request Concert*.
COSTUMES: **Patricia McGourty** for *The Pirates of Penzance*.
SPECIAL CITATION: **Clarke Dunham** for *The Me Nobody Knows*.
LIGHTS: **Dennis Parichy** for *Fifth of July*.

1982

SETS: **David Chapman** (tie) for *The First*. **Edward T. Gianfrancesco** (tie) for *Big Apple Messenger; The Little Shop of Horrors*.
COSTUMES: **William Ivey Long** for *Nine*.
LIGHTS: **Tharon Musser and Robin Wagner** for *Dreamgirls*.
COLLABORATION: **Beverly Emmons, Dermot Hayes, David Hersey, Neil Peter Jampolis, and John Napier** for *The Life and Adventures of Nicholas Nickleby*.

1983

SETS: **Julie Archer, Linda Hartinian, Greg Mehrten, Bryan St. John Schofield, L. B. Dallas, Craig Miller, Stephanie Rudolph, Craig Jones, and David Hardy** (tie) for *Cold Harbor / Company / Haff*. **Ming Cho Lee and Leslie Taylor** (tie) for *K2*.
COSTUMES: **Patricia Zipprodt** (tie) for *Alice in Wonderland; Don Juan*.
LIGHTS: **Allen Lee Hughes** for *K2*.

1984

SETS: **Tony Straiges and Bran Ferren** (tie) for *Sunday in the Park with George.* **Bill Stable** (tie) for *Spookhouse.*

COSTUMES: **Theoni V. Aldredge** for *La Cage aux Folles.* **Patricia Zipprodt and Ann Hould-Ward** for *Sunday in the Park with George.*

LIGHTS: **Paul Gallo** (tie) for *The Garden of Earthly Delights.* **Richard Nelson** (tie) for *Sunday in the Park with George.*

EFFECTS: **Tony Straiges and Bran Ferren** for *Sunday in the Park with George.*

1985

SETS: **Heidi Landesman** (tie) for *Big River.* **Charles Ludlam** (tie) for *The Mystery of Irma Vep.* **Angus Moss** (tie) for *Nosferatu.*

COSTUMES: **Mel Carpenter** for *Nosferatu.* **Patricia McGourty** for *Big River.* **Everett Quinton** for *The Mystery of Irma Vep.*

LIGHTS: **Blu** (tie) for *Nosferatu.* **Lawrence Eichler** (tie) for *The Mystery of Irma Vep.* **Richard Riddell** (tie) for *Big River.*

> As The American Theater Wing Award

1986

SETS: **Tony Walton** (tie) for *The House of Blue Leaves.*

COSTUMES: **Everett Quinton** for *Salammbo.*

LIGHTS: **Kevin Rigdon** for *Ghost Stories.*

EFFECTS: **Eva Buchmuller, Theo Cremona and Rudi Stern** for *Dreamland Burns.*

COLLABORATION: **Robert Israel and Paul Gallo** for *Vienna Lusthaus.*

1987

SETS: **Robert Israel** (tie) for *The Hunger Artist.* **James D. Sandefur** (tie) for *Fences.*

COSTUMES: **John Napier** for *Starlight Express.*

LIGHTS: **Paul Gallo** (tie) for *The Hunger Artist.* **Jennifer Tipton** (tie) for *Worstward Ho.*

EFFECTS: **Tomm Kamm and Robert Wilson** for *CIVIL warS.*

1988

SETS: **John Lee Beatty** for *Burn This.*

EFFECTS: **Eva Buchmuller** for *L-Train to Eldorado.*

COSTUME AND SCENIC DESIGN: **Eiko Ishioka** for *M. Butterfly.*

CONCEPT, PUPPETRY AND MASKS: **Julie Taymor** for *Juan Darién.*

1989

SETS: **Jerome Sirlin** for *1000 Airplanes on the Roof.*

COSTUMES: **Susan Young** for *A Tale of Two Cities.*

LIGHTS: **Jennifer Tipton** for *Long Day's Journey Into Night / Jerome Robbin's Broadway / Waiting for Godot / The Rimers of Eldrich.*

EFFECTS: **Alison Yerxa** for *Warrior Ant.*

1990

SETS: **Kevin Rigdon** for *The Grapes of Wrath.*

COSTUMES: **Santo Loquasto** for *Grand Hotel, Tthe Musical.*

LIGHTS: **Jules Fisher** for *Grand Hotel, The Musical.*

EFFECTS: **Fred Curchack** for *Stuff as Dreams Are Made Of.*

1991

COSTUMES: **Patricia Zipprodt** for *Shogun.*

SETS AND COSTUMES: **Richard Hudson** for *La Bête.*

LIGHTS: **Robert Wierzel** for *Hydrogen Jukebox.*

EFFECTS: **Paul Zaloom** for *My Civilization.*

1992

SETS: **John Arnone** for *Pericles.*

COSTUMES: **Toni Leslie-James** for *Jelly's Last Jam.*

MASKS, PUPPETS AND COSTUMES: **Ralph Lee and Casey Compton** for *Wichikapache Goes Walking.*
LIGHTS: **Jules Fisher** for *Jelly's Last Jam.*

1993

SETS: **John Arnone** for *The Who's Tommy.*
COSTUMES: **Elizabeth Fried** for *Brother Truckers.*
LIGHTS: **Mimi Jordan Sherin** for *Woyzeck.*
EFFECTS: **Wendall K. Harrington** for *The Who's Tommy.*

1994

SETS: **Tony Walton** for *She Loves Me.*
COSTUMES: **Ann Hould-Ward** for *Beauty and the Beast.*
LIGHTS: **Beverly Emmons** for *Passion.*
EFFECTS: **David Schulder** for *MovieLand.*

1995

SETS: **John Lee Beatty** for *The Heiress.* **Jane Greenwood** for *The Heiress.*
PUPPETS AND MASKS: **Ralph Lee** for *Heart of the Earth: A Popul Vuh Sotry.*
LIGHTS: **Beverly Emmons** for *The Heiress.*

1996

SETS: **Christopher Barreca** for *Chronicle of a Death Fortold.*
COSTUMES: **Angela Wendt** for *Rent.*
PUPPETS: **Julie Archer** for *Rose the Dog; Sri Moo.*
PROJECTIONS: **Karen Ten Eyck** for *An Epidog.*
LIGHTS: **Jules Fisher and Peggy Eisenhauer** for *Bring in 'da Noise, Bring in 'da Funk.*

1997

SETS: **Robin Phillips, James Noone and Christina Poddubiuk** for *Jekyll & Hyde.*
COSTUMES: **Howard Crabtree** for *When Pigs Fly.*
LIGHTS: **Beverly Emmons** for *Jekyll & Hyde; When the World Was Green.*
EFFECTS: **Julie Archer** for *Peter & Wendy.*

1998

SETS: **Eugene Lee** for *Ragtime.*
COSTUMES: **Julie Taymor** for *The Lion King.*
LIGHTS: **Jules Fisher and Peggy Eisenhauer** for *Ragtime.*
EFFECTS: **Julie Taymor and Michael Curry** for *The Lion King.*

> As The Henry Hewes Award

1999

SETS: **Robert Brill with Scott Pask** for *The Mineola Twins.*
COSTUMES: **Jess Goldstein** for *The Mineola Twins.*
LIGHTS: **Michael Chybowski** for *Cymbeline; Wit.*
EFFECTS: **Theodora Skipitares** for *A Harlot's Progress.*

2000

SETS: **David Gallo** for *Jitney; The Wild Party.*
COSTUMES: **William Ivey Long** for *Contact, The Music Man; Swing!*
LIGHTS: **Peter Kaczorowski** for *Contact, The Music Man; Kiss Me, Kate.*
EFFECTS: **Steve O'Hearn** for *Squonk.*

2001

SETS: **John Moran** for *Book of the Dead.*
COSTUMES: **Roger Kirk** (tie) for *42nd Street.* **David C. Woolard** (tie) for *The Rocky Horror Show.*
LIGHTS: **Brian MacDevitt** for *The Invention of Love.*
EFFECTS: **Rudi Stem** for *Theater of Light.*

Appendix 4: The Irene Sharaff Awards

Costume designer Irene Sharaff was honored by the Theatre Development Fund in 1993 with a lifetime achievement award. When she died later that year, Theatre Development Fund established two awards to honor her memory and accomplishments: a Lifetime Acheivement Award and a Young Master Award. In 1999, two additional awards were created, a Posthumous Honor and an Artisan Award. Now presented annually, a committee comprised of professional costume designers and artisans selects the winners. As part of their missions to honor excellence in theater and develop a wider audience for the arts, Theatre Development Fund also sponsors annual Astaire Awards for "excellence in dance on Broadway" to choreographers and dancers.

1993
LIFETIME ACHIEVEMENT: **Irene Sharaff**
1994
YOUNG MASTER: **Gregg Barnes**
LIFETIME ACHIEVEMENT: **Desmond Heeley**
1996
YOUNG MASTER: **Toni-Leslie James**
LIFETIME ACHIEVEMENT: **Alvin Colt and Miles White**
1997
YOUNG MASTER: **Paul Tazewell**
LIFETIME ACHIEVEMENT: **Patricia Zipprodt**
1998
YOUNG MASTER: **Martin Pakledinaz**
LIFETIME ACHIEVEMENT: **Jane Greenwood**
1999
YOUNG MASTER: **Suzy Benzinger**
POSTHUMOUS: **Raoul Pène du Bois**
LIFETIME ACHIEVEMENT: **Willa Kim**
ARTISAN: **Ray Diffen**

2000
YOUNG MASTER: **Robert Perdziola**
POSTHUMOUS: **Lucinda Ballard**
LIFETIME ACHIEVEMENT: **Ann Roth**

ARTISAN: **Woody Shelp**

2001

YOUNG MASTER: **Constance Hoffman**
POSTHUMOUS: **Aline Bernstein.**
LIFETIME ACHIEVEMENT: **Freddy Wittop**
ARTISAN: **Barbara Matera**

Selected Bibliography

Anderson, Barbara and Cletus. *Costume Design.* Fort Worth: Harcourt Brace, 2nd ed., 1999.

Anderson, Kristen and Imogen Ross. *Performance Design in Australia.* Sydney, NSW: Craftsman House, 2001.

Appia, Adolphe. *Music and the Art of the Theatre.* Coral Gables: University of Miami Press, 1962.

Aronson, Arnold. *American Set Design.* New York: Theatre Communications Group, 1985.

Asakura, Setsu. *The Scenic Art of Setsu Asakura.* Tokyo: Parco Shupan, 1981.

Atkinson, W. Patrick, comp. *Theatrical Design in the Twentieth Century: An Index to Photographic Reproductions of Scenic Designs.* Westport: Greenwood Press, 1996.

Bay, Howard. *Stage Design.* New York: Drama Book Specialists, 1974.

Beaumont, Cyril W. and Browse, Lillian, eds. *Leslie Hurry, Settings and Costumes for Sadler's Wells Ballets.* London: For the Shenval Press by Faber and Faber, 1946.

Bel Geddes, Norman. *Miracle in the Evening.* Garden City, NY: Doubleday & Co., Inc., 1960.

Bellman, Willard F. *Scene Design, Stage Lghting, Sound, Costume & Make-up: A Scenographic Approach.* New York: Harper, 1983.

————. *Lighting the Stage: Art and Practice.* New York: Thomas Y. Crowell Co., 1974.

Bentham, Frederick P. *The Art of Stage Lighting.* London: Pitman & Sons, 1980.

Bentley, Toni. *Costumes by Karinska.* New York: Harry N. Abrams, 1995.

Bergman, Gösta M. *Lighting in the Theatre.* Stockholm: Almqvist & Wiksell International, 1977.

Binnie, Eric. *The Theatrical Designs of Charles Ricketts.* Ann Arbor: University of Michigan Research Press, 1985.

Blumenthal, Arthur R. *Theater Designs in the Collection of the Cooper-Hewitt Museum.* New York: Smithsonian Institution, 1986.

Boll, André. *Du Decor de Theatre.* Paris: E. Chiron, 1926

Bowlt, John E. *Russian Stage Design: Scenic Innovation, 1900-1930.* Jackson: Mississippi Museum of Art, 1982.

Bowman, Wayne. *Modern Theatre Lighting.* New York: Harper & Brothers, 1957.

Breitman, Ellen. *Art and the Stage.* Cleveland: Cleveland Art Museum in cooperation with Indiana University Press, 1981

Burdick, Elizabeth B., Peggy C. Hansen, and Brenda Zanger, eds. *Contemporary Stage Design, U.S.A.* Middletown, CT: Wesleyan UP, 1974.

Carter, Randolph. *Joseph Urban: Architecture, Theatre, Opera, Film.* New York: Abberville Press, 1992.

Castle, Charles. *Oliver Messel.* New York: Thames and Hudson, 1986.

Castle, Dennis. *"Sensation" Smith of Drury Lane.* London: Charles Skilton, Ltd., 1985.

Cheney, Sheldon. *The New Movement in the Theatre.* Westport: Greenwood Press, 1971.

———. *Stage Decoration.* New York: The John Day Company, 1928.

Cheshire, David F. *Bibliography of Theatre and Stage Design: A Select List of books and Articles Published 1960-1970.* London: Commission for a British Theatre Institute, 1974.

Cogniat, Raymond. *Les Décorateurs de Théâtre.* Paris: Librairie Théâtrale, 1955.

Columbia University Dramatic Museum. *A Catalog of Models and of Stage-sets in the Dramatic Museum of Columbia University.* New York: Printed for the Dramatic Museum of Columbia University, 1916.

Courtney, Cathy, ed. *Jocelyn Herbert: A Theatre Workbook.* London: Art Books International, 1993.

Craig, Edward Gordon. *The Art of the Theatre.* Edinburgh: T.N. Foulis, 1905.

———. *Craig on Theatre.* London: Methuen, 1983.

———. *On the Art of the Theatre.* New York: Dodd, Mead, & Co., 1925.

———. *Towards a New Theatre.* New York: Benjamin Blom, 1969.

De Marly, Diana. *Costume on the Stage 1600-1940.* New York: Barnes & Noble Books, 1982.

Diaghilev and Russian Stage Designers. Washington: The Foundation, 1972.

Cunningham, Rebecca. *The Magic Garment.* Prospect Heights: Waveland Press, Inc., 1989.

Docherty, Peter. ed. *Design for Performance: From Diaghilev to the Pet Shop Boys.* London: Lund Humphries, in association with Lethaby Press, 1996.

Elder, Eldon. *Designs for the Theatre.* New York: Drama Book Specialists, 1978.

Finkel, Alicia. *Romantic Stages: Set and Costume Design in Victorian England.* Jefferson, NC: McFarland & Company, Inc..

Fuchs, Theodore. *Stage Lighting.* Boston: Little Brown and Co., 1929.

Fuerst, Walter Rene and Samuel J. Hume. *Twentieth Century Stage Decoration.* Vol. 1, text. Vol. 2 ill. New York: Dover Publications, 1929.

Goodwin, John, ed. *British Theatre Design*. London: George Weidenfeld & Nicholson, Ltd., 1989.

Gorelik, Mordecai. *New Theatres for Old*. New York: Samuel French, 1940.

Hainaux, Rene and Yves-Bonnat. *Stage Design Throughout the World Since 1935*. New York: Theatre Arts Books, 1964.

———. *Stage Design Throughout the World Since 1950*. New York: Theatre Arts Books, 1964.

———. *Stage Design Throughout the World Since 1960*. New York: Theatre Arts Books, 1972.

———. *Stage Design Throughout the World: 1970-1975*. New York: Theatre Arts Books, 1976.

Hardberger, Linda. *Setting the Stage American Style: A Gift of Scene Designs from Robert L.B. Tobin*. San Antonio: Marion Koogler McNay Art Museum.

Harris, Andrew B. *Broadway Theatre*. London; New York: Routledge, 1994.

Hartmann, Louis. *Theatre Lighting*. New York: D. Appleton, 1930.

Hay, Richard L. *A Space for Magic*. Ashland: Oregon Shakespearean Fesival, 1979.

Hays, David. *Light on the Subject*. New York: Limelight Editions, 1990.

Heffner, Hubert, Samuel Selden and Hunton Sellman. *Modern Theatre Practice*. New York: Appledon-Century-Crofts, 1959.

Henderson, Mary. *Jo Mielziner: Master of Modern Stage Design*. New York: Watson Guptil Publications, 2001.

Hodgman, Ann. *A Day in the Life of a Theater Set Designer*. Mahwah, NJ: Troll Associates, 1988.

Holt, Michael. *Stage Design and Properties*. New York: Schirmer Books, 1989.

Hoover, Marjorie L. *Meyerhold and His Set Designers*. New York: P. Lang, 1988.

Howard, Pamela. *What is Scenography?* London; New York: Routledge, 2001.

International Federation for Theatre Research. *Innovations in Stage and Theatre Design*. New York: American Society for Theatre Research, 1972.

International Theatre Institute of the United States, Inc. *Contemporary Stage Design U.S.A.* Middletown, CT: Wesleyan UP, 1974.

International Theatre Institute. *Stage Design Throughout the World Since 1935*. London: G.G. Harrap, 1956.

———. *Stage Design Throughout the World Since 1950*. Middletown, Conn.: Wesleyan University Press, 1964

Ishioka, Eiko. *Eiko on Stage*. New York: Callaway, 2000.

Jenkins, David Fraser, et al. *John Piper*. London: Tate Gallery of Art, 1983. (Catalogue of Exhibition at the Tate Gallery).

Jones, Robert Edmond. *The Dramatic Imagination*. New York: Theatre Arts Books, 1941.

———. *Drawings for the Theatre*. New York: Theatre Art Books, 1978.

Jowers, Sidney and John Cavanagh. *Theatrical Costume, Masks, Make-up and Wigs: A Bibliography and Iconography*. London: Routledge, 2000.

Keller, Max. *Light Fantastic: The Art and Design of Stage Lighting*. Munich; New York: Prestel, 1999.

Kessler, Jackson. *Theatrical Costume: A Guide to Information Sources*. Detroit: Gale Research Co., 1979.

Komisarjevsky, Theodore. *The Costume of the Theatre*. London: Geoffrey Bles, 1931.

Komisarjevsky, Theodore, and Lee Simonson. *Settings and Costumes for the Modern Stage*. New York: Benjamin Blom, 1966.

Lacy, Robin Thurlow. *A Biographical Dictionary of Scenographers, 500 B.C. to 1900 A.D.* New York, Westport: Greenwood Press, 1990.

Larson, Orville K. *Scene Design for Stage and Screen*. East Lansing, MI: Michigan State UP, 1961.

———. *Scene Design in the American Theatre from 1915 to 1960*. Fayetteville: Arkansas UP, 1989.

Laver, James. *Drama, Its Costume and Décor*. London, Studio Publications, 1951.

———. *Costume in the Theatre*. London: Harrap, 1964.

Macgowan, Kenneth, and Robert Edmond Jones. *Continental Stagecraft*. New York: Bemjamin Blom, 1964.

Marion Koogler McNay Art Museum. *Robert Edmond Jones and the American Theatre*. San Antonio: Marion Koogler McNay Art Museum, 1986.

Mason, Rupert. George Sheringham and B. Morrison, eds. *Robes of Thespis, Costume Design by Modern Artists*. London: E. Benn, Ltd., 1928.

McCandless, Stanley. *A Method of Lighting the Stage*. New York: Theatre Arts Books, 1958.

———. *A Syllabus of Stage Lighting*. 11th ed. New Haven: Drama Book Specialists, 1964.

Melvill, Harald. *Designing and Painting Scenery for the Theatre*. London: Art Trade Press, 1963.

Mielziner, Jo. *Designing for the Theatre*. New York: Atheneum, 1965.

Mikotowicz, Thomas J, ed. *Theatrical Designers: An International Biographical Dictionary*. Westport: Greenwood Press, 1992.

Minnelli, Vincente. *Vincente Minnelli from Stage to Screen*. Palm Springs: The Museum, 1983.

Motley. *Designing and Making Stage Costumes, rev. ed.* New York: Theatre Arts Books/Routledge, 1992.

Mullin, Michael. *Design by Motley*. Newark: University of Delaward Press, 1996.

Niedermoser, Otto. *Oskar Strnad, 1879-1935*. Vienna: Bergland, 1965.

Noël, Jacques. *Jacques Noël: Théâtres*. Paris: Bibliothèque Historique de la Ville de Paris, 1993.

Oenslager, Donald. *Stage Design: Four Centuries of Scenic Invention*. New York: Viking Press, 1975.

———. *Scenery Then and Now*. New York: Russell and Russell, 1966.

———. *The Theatre of Donald Oenslager*. Middletown, Conn.: Wesleyan University Press, 1978.

Ost, Geoffrey. *Stage Lighting*. London: Herbert Jenkins, Ltd., 1957.

Owen, Bobbi. *Costume Design on Broadway: Designers and Their Credits, 1915-1985*. Westport: Greenwood Press, Inc., 1987.

———. *Lighting Design on Broadway: Designers and Their Credits, 1915-1990*. Westport: Greenwood Press, Inc., 1991.

———. *Scenic Design on Broadway: Designers and Their Credits, 1915-1990*. Westport: Greenwood Press, Inc., 1991.

Palmer, Richard H. *The Lighting Art: The Aesthetics of Stage Lighting Design.* Englewood Cliffs: Prentice-Hall, 1985.

Parker, W. Oren and Harvey K. Smith. *Scene Design and Stage Lighting.* New York: Holt, Rinehart and Winston, 1979.

Payne, Darwin Reed. *The Scenographic Imagination.* Carbondale and Edwardsvile, IL: Southern Illinois UP, 1981.

Pecktal, Lynn. *Costume Design: Techniques of Modern Masters.* New York: Back Stage Books, 1993.

———. *Designing and Drawing for the Theatre.* New York: McGraw-Hill, 1995.

———. *Designing and Painting for the Theatre.* New York: Holt, Reinhart, and Winston, 1975.

Pendleton, Ralph (ed). *The Theatre of Robert Edmond Jones.* Middletown: Wesleyan UP, 1958.

Pilbrow, Richard. *Stage Lighting Design: The Art, the Craft, the Life.* London: Nick Hern Books, 1997.

Polakov, Lester. *We Live to Fly/Paint Again.* New York: Longbooks Press, 1993.

Ptackova, Vera. *Josef Svoboda.* Praha: Divadelni Ustav, 1984.

Rees, Terence. *Theatre Lighting in the Age of Gas.* London: Society for Theatre Research, 1978.

Reid, Francis. *Lighting the Stage: A Lighting Designer's Experiences.* Oxford, Boston: Focal Press, 1995.

———. *Stage Lighting Handbook.* New York: Theatre Arts Books/Methuen, 1982

Rich, Frank, with Lisa Aronson. *The Theatre Art of Boris Aronson.* New York: Knopf, 1987.

Rischbieter, Henning. *Art and the Stage in the 20th Century: Painters and Sculptors Work for the Theater.* Greenwich: New York Graphic Society, 1968.

Robinson, Alice M., Vera Mowry Roberts, and Milly S. Barranger. *Notable Women in the American Theatre: A Biographical Dictionary.* Westport: Greenwood Press, Inc., 1989.

Rose, Enid. *Gordon Craig and the Theatre.* London: Sampson Row, Marston, 1931.

Rosenthal, Jean and Lael Wertenbacker. *The Magic of Light.* Boston: Little Brown and Co., 1972.

Rowell, Kenneth. *Stage Design.* London: Studio Vista, 1968.

Rubin, Joel E. and Leland H. Watson. *Theatrical Lighting Practice.* New York: Theatre Arts Books, 1954.

Sainthill, Loudon. *Loudon Sainthill.* London: Hutchinson, 1973.

Sayler, Oliver Martin. *Max Reinhardt and His Theatre.* New York: Benjamin Blom, 1968.

Sheringham, George and Laver, James (eds.) *Design in the Theatre.* London: The Studio, Ltd., 1927.

Schouvaloff, Alexander. *Set and Costume Designs for Ballet and Theatre.* (Catalogue of the Thyssen-Bornemisza Collection). New York: Vendome Press, 1987

————. *Theatre on Paper*. London: Sotheby's, 1990.

Selden, Samuel and Hunton D. Sellman. *Stage Scenery and Lighting*. Rev. ed. New York: Appleton-Century-Crofts, 1959.

Sharaff, Irene. *Broadway and Hollywood: Costumes Designed by Irene Sharaff*. Cincinnati: Van Nostrand Reinhold Co., 1976.

Shubert, Hannelore. *The Modern Theatre: Architecture, Stage Design, Lighting*. New York: Praeger, 1971.

Simonson, Lee. *The Art of Scenic Design*. New York: Reinhold, 1950.

————. *The Designer in the Theatre*. New York, 1934

————. *Part of a Lifetime*. New York: Duell, Sloan, and Pearce, 1943.

————. *The Stage is Set*. New York: Theatre Arts Books, 1932.

Smith, Ronn. *American Set Design 2*. New York: Theatre Communications Group, 1991.

Society of British Theatre Designers. *British Theatre Design 1983-1987*. Faringdon, Oxfordshire: Twynam, c1987.

Spencer, Charles. *Cecil Beaton: Stage and Film Designs*. London: Academy Editions, 1994.

The Stage Is All the World: The Theatrical Designs of Tanya Moiseiwitsch. Chicago: The David and Alfred Smart Museum of Art, The University of Chicago, in association with the University of Washington Press, 1994.

Strzelecki, Zenobiusz. *Wspo Czesna Scenografia Polska*. Warszawa: Arkady. 1983-1984.

Svoboda, Josef. *The Secret of Theatrical Space*. New York: Applause Theatre Books, 1993.

University Art Museum. *The Twin City Scenic Collection: Popular Entertainment 1895-1929*. Minneapolis: University of Minnesota Press, 1987.

Warfel, William B. *Handbook of Stage Lighting Graphics*. New York: Drama Book Specialists, 1974.

Watson, Lee. *Lighting Design Handbook*. New York: McGraw-Hill, Inc., 1990

Wengrow, Arnold. *Robert Redington Sharpe: The Life of a Theatre Designer*. Cambridge: Harvard Theatre Collection, Harvard College Library, 1990.

Welker, David Harold. *Theatrical Set Design, The Basic Techniques*. Boston: Allyn and Bacon, 1969.

Willett, John. *Caspar Neher, Brecht's Designer*. London, New York: Methuen, 1986.

Winkelbauer, Stefanie M. *Wake up and Dream! Costume Design for Broadway Musicals 1900-1025 from the Theatre Collection of the Austrian National Library*. Vienna: H. Böhlhaus, 1986.

Index of Plays

This index lists the twentieth century Broadway productions in alphabetical order. The designers for each production are also listed in *alphabetical* order. Each designer's name has superscripts to indicate what they designed. So R.E. Jones $^{(S)(L)}$ indicates he did sets and lights; the reader is referred to the list of credits following his brief biography to obtain additional details. When a program had no design credits, the single entry NONE appears. When a program gave general acknowledgements for design work rather than identifying a specific designer, ACK$^{(C)}$(with appropriate superscript) appears. In about sixty cases no playbill could be located and NO PLAYBILL appears.

Robert Randolph[S][L]

84 Charing Cross Road (1982) Oliver Smith[S]; Pearl Somner[C]; Marc B. Weiss[L]

90 Horse Power (1926) Joseph Physioc[S]; ACK[C][L]

90 in the Shade (1915) Dodge and Castle[S]; ACK[C][L]

A La Broadway (1911) NONE

A La Carte (1927) Livingston Platt[S]; Maria Willenz[C]

Abbey Theatre Irish Players (1932) ACK[L]

Abbey Theatre Players (1937) ACK[L]

Abbey Theatre Players in Repertory (1934) ACK[L]

Abe and Mawruss (1915) Joseph Physioc[S]; ACK[C][L]

Abe Lincoln in Illinois (1938) Rose Bogdanoff[C]; Jo Mielziner[S][L]

Abe Lincoln in Illinois (1993) John Lee Beatty[S]; Beverly Emmons[L]; Jane Greenwood[C]

Abelard and Heloise (1971) Daphne Dare[C]; Christopher Morley[S]; H. R. Poindexter[L]

Abide with Me (1935) P. Dodd Ackerman[S]; Bianca Stroock[C]

Abie's Irish Rose (1922) ACK[C]

Abie's Irish Rose (1937) Cirker and Robbins[S]; Mildred Manning[C]

Abie's Irish Rose (1954) Paul Morrison[S][C][L]

Abigail (1905) NONE

About Town (1906) Homer Emens[S]; Mrs. Robert Osborn[C]; Mrs. Caroline Siedle[C]; Edward G. Unitt[S]; Arthur Voegtlin[S]

Above the Clouds (1922) NONE

Abraham Cochrane (1964) Robert O'Hearn[S][L]; Domingo A. Rodriguez[C]

Abraham Lincoln (1919) Livingston Platt[S][C]; ACK[L]

Abraham Lincoln (1929) Livingston Platt[S]

Absence of a Cello (1964) William Ritman[S][L]; Fred Voelpel[C]

Absent Feather (1932) Nicholas Yellenti[S]; ACK[C]

Absurd Person Singular (1974) Edward Burbridge[S]; Thomas Skelton[L]; Levino Verna[C]

Abyssinia (1906) NONE

Accent on Youth (1934) Jo Mielziner[S][L]; ACK[C]

Accidental Death of an Anarchist (1984) Karl Eigsti[S]; Allen Lee Hughes[L]; Patricia Zipprodt[C]

Accomplice (1990) Martin Aronstein[L]; Alvin Colt[C]; David Jenkins[S]

According to Law (1944) Harry Gordon Bennett[S]; Leo Kerz[L]

Accused (1925) Henri Bendel[C]; Louis Hartmann[L]; Joseph Wickes[S]

Achilles had a Heel (1935) Claude Bragdon[S][C]; ACK[L]

Acquittal, The (1920) Hickson[C]; ACK[L]

Across the Street (1924) Joseph Physioc[S]; ACK[C]

Act, The (1977) Halston[C]; Tharon Musser[L]; Tony Walton[S]

Ada Beats the Drum (1930) Cirker and Robbins[S]; ACK[C][L]

Adam and Eva (1919) Henri Bendel[C]; Harry Collins[C]; ACK[L]

Adam Had Two Sons (1932) Donald Oenslager[S]; ACK[C]

Adam Solitaire (1925) Blanche Hays[C]; Cleon Throckmorton[S]

Adam's Apple (1929) ACK[L]

Adam's Wife (1931) ACK[S][L]

Adding Machine, The (1923) Lee Simonson[S][C]

Adele (1913) NONE

Admirable Crichton, The (1903) Ernest Gros[S]

Admirable Crichton, The (1931) De Guary[C]; Gates and Morange[S]; Anthony Greshoff[L]

Admiral, The (1924) Grace O. Clarke[C]; Woodman Thompson[S]

Adorable Liar, The (1926) Raymond Sovey[S]; ACK[C]

Adrea (1905) Percy Anderson[C]; Wilfred Buckland[S]; Ernest Gros[S]; Mollie O'Hara[C]

Adrienne (1923) Anthony Greshoff[L]; Herbert Ward[S]; ACK[C]

Adrienne Lecouvreur (1908) Mrs. Nettleship[C]; B. J. Simmons[C]

Adventure (1928) Nicholas Yellenti[S]; ACK[C]

Adventure of Lady Ursula, The (1915) Edward G. Unitt[S]; ACK[S][C][L]

Adventures of Tom Sawyer, The (2001) Heidi Ettinger[S]; Kenneth Posner[L]; Anthony Powell[C]

Adventurous Age, The (1927) Anthony Greshoff[L]; ACK[S][C]

Advertising of Kate, The (1922) P.

Dodd Ackerman[S]; Edward Crowe[C]

Advise and Consent (1960) John
Boxer[C]; Klaus Holm[L]; Rouben
Ter-Arutunian[S]

Advocate, The (1963) Ralph
Alswang[S][L]; Michael Travis[C]

Aero Club, The (1907) ACK[C]

Affair of Honor (1956) Ralph
Alswang[S][L]; Gene Coffin[C]

Affair of State, An (1930) Henry
Dreyfuss[S][C]; Margaret Pemberton[C]

Affair, The (1962) Eldon Elder[S][L];
Ramsé Mostoller[C]

Affairs of Anatol, The (1912) Madame
Allouise[C]; Henri Bendel[C]; Lucile[C];
Unitt and Wickes[S]

Affairs of State (1950) Dorothy
Jeakins[C]; Paul Morrison[S][L]

Affinity, The (1910) NONE

Afgar (1920) Paul Poiret[S][C]

African Millionaire, An (1904) NONE

Africana (1927) Charles LeMaire[C];
Walter Lewis[S]; Joseph Teichner
Studio[S]; ACK[L]

Africana (1934) Anthony Continer[S]

After All (1931) Elsie and Camille[C];
Raymond Sovey[S]

After Five (1913) NONE

After Office Hours (1900) NONE

After Such Pleasures (1934) ACK[S][L]

After the Fall (1964) Anna Hill
Johnstone[C]; Jo Mielziner[S]

After the Opera (1907) NONE

After the Rain (1967) Brian Currah[S];
Tharon Musser[L]; Domingo A.
Rodriguez[C]

After Tomorrow (1931) ACK[L]

Agatha Dene (1904) NONE

Agatha Sue, I Love You (1966)
Patton Campbell[C]; William and Jean
Eckart[S][L]

Age of Innocence, The (1928) Georges
Barbier[C]; J. F. Gallagher[S]; Gertrude
Newell[S][C]

Aged 26 (1936) Stewart Chaney[S][C]

Ages of Man (1958) Ben Edwards[L]

Agnes (1908) C. Lovat Fraser[S]; Price
and O'Brien[C]

Agnes of God (1982) Eugene Lee[S];
Roger Morgan[L]; Carrie F. Robbins[C]

Ah, Wilderness! (1933) Robert
Edmond Jones[S]; ACK[C]

Ah, Wilderness! (1941) Watson
Barratt[S]; E. Carlton Winckler[L]

Ah, Wilderness! (1975) Steven
Rubin[S]; Bill Walker[C]; Ronald

Wallace[L]

Ah, Wilderness! (1988) Jane
Greenwood[C]; Jennifer Tipton[L];
Michael H. Yeargan[S]

Ah, Wilderness! (1998) Peter
Kaczorowski[L]; Thomas Lynch[S];
Dunya Ramicova[C]

Aida (2000) Bob Crowley[S][C]; Natasha
Katz[L]

Ain't Broadway Grand (1993) Suzy
Benzinger[C]; Ken Billington[L]; David
Mitchell[S]

Ain't Misbehavin' (1978) Randy
Barcelo[C]; John Lee Beatty[S]; Pat
Collins[L]

Ain't Misbehavin' (1988) Randy
Barcelo[C]; John Lee Beatty[S]; Pat
Collins[L]

**Ain't Supposed to Die a Natural
Death** (1971) Martin Aronstein[L];
Bernard Johnson[C]; Kert Lundell[S]

Air Minded (1932) Charles J. Auburn[S]

Airways, Inc. (1929) John Dos
Passos[S]; ACK[C]

Alarm Clock, The (1923) Paul Allen[S]

Alaskan, The (1907) NONE

Alfie (1964) Lloyd Burlingame[S][C];
Tharon Musser[L]

Algeria (1908) Ernest Albert[S]; Alfredo
Edel[C]; Kliegl Brothers[L]

Alias Jimmy Valentine (1910) NONE

Alias Jimmy Valentine (1921) Gates
and Morange[S]; Anthony Greshoff[L];
ACK[C]

Alias the Deacon (1925) P. Dodd
Ackerman[S]

Alibi Bill (1912) NONE

Alice in Arms (1945) Frederick
Fox[S][C][L]

Alice in Wonderland (1915) William
Penhallow Henderson[S][C]

Alice in Wonderland (1932) Irene
Sharaff[S][C]

Alice in Wonderland (1982) John Lee
Beatty[S]; Jennifer Tipton[L]; Patricia
Zipprodt[C]

**Alice in Wonderland and Through
the Looking Glass** (1947) Robert
Rowe Paddock[S]; Noel Taylor[C]

Alice of Old Vincennes (1901) Henry
Dazian[C]; Ernest Gros[S]

Alice Sit-by-The-Fire (1905) Madame
Dubosc[C]; Walter Hann[S]; Madame
Hayward[C]; Lucile[C]

Alice Sit-by-The-Fire (1911) NONE

Alice Sit-by-the-Fire/ The Old Lady

Shows (1932) Livingston Platt[S]; ACK[C][L]

Alice Takat (1936) Hattie Carnegie[C]; Raymond Sovey[S]; ACK[C]

Alien Corn (1933) Cleon Throckmorton[S]; ACK[C][L]

Alison's House (1930) Aline Bernstein[S][C]

Alive and Kicking (1950) Mason Arvold[L]; Raoul Pène Du Bois[S][C]

All Aboard (1913) David Atchison[L]; Melville Ellis[C]; H. Robert Law[S]; Young Brothers[S]

All American (1961) Patton Campbell[C]; Jo Mielziner[S][L]

All Comforts of Home (1942) Harry Gordon Bennett[S]; Paul du Pont[C]

All Dressed Up (1925) P. Dodd Ackerman[S]; Frances Clyne[C]; ACK[L]

All Editions (1936) Cirker and Robbins[S]; DuWico[L]; ACK[C]

All for a Girl (1908) NONE

All for All (1943) A. A. Ostrander[S]; ACK[C]

All for Love (1949) Larry Gebhardt[L]; Edward Gilbert[S]; Billy Livingston[C]

All for the Ladies (1912) Melville Ellis[C]

All God's Chillun Got Wings (1924) Cleon Throckmorton[S]

All God's Chillun Got Wings (1975) Ming Cho Lee[S]; Thomas Skelton[L]; Patricia Zipprodt[C]

All Good Americans (1933) Virginia Estes Cates[C]; Mordecai Gorelik[S]

All in Favor (1942) Samuel Leve[S]; ACK[C]

All in Fun (1940) Edward Gilbert[S]; Irene Sharaff[C]

All in Good Time (1965) Peter Harvey[C]; Tharon Musser[L]; Alan Tagg[S]

All in One, Trouble in Tahiti (1955) Patton Campbell[C]; Eldon Elder[S][L]

All Men Are True (1941) Frederick Fox[S]

All My Sons (1947) Mordecai Gorelik[S][L]; Paul Morrison[C]

All My Sons (1987) Hugh Landwehr[S]; Bill Walker[C]; Ronald Wallace[L]

All My Sons (1997) Donald Holder[L]; Narelle Sissons[S]; Angela Wendt[C]

All on Account of Eliza (1900) Joseph Physioc[S]

All Over (1971) Richard Nelson[L]; Rouben Ter-Arutunian[S][C]

All over Town (1974) John Gleason[L]; Oliver Smith[S]; Albert Wolsky[C]

All Rights Reserved (1934) Tom Adrian Cracraft[S]; ACK[C]

All Soul's Eve (1920) Arthur T. Hewlett[S]; J. Monroe Hewlett[S]

All Star Gambol (1913) Henri Bendel[C]; Marie Dressler[S][C]

All Star Variety Jubilee (1913) No PLAYBILL

All Summer Long (1954) Anna Hill Johnstone[C]; Jo Mielziner[S][L]

All That Glitters (1938) Hattie Carnegie[C]; John Root[S]

All the Girls Come Out to Play (1972) Joseph G. Aulisi[C]; Leo B. Meyer[S][L]

All the King's Horses (1934) John N. Booth, Jr.[C]; Herbert Ward[S]; ACK[C]

All the King's Men (1929) Cirker and Robbins[S]; ACK[C]

All the Living (1938) Harry Horner[S]; ACK[C]

All the Way Home (1960) David Hays[S][L]; Raymond Sovey[C]

All Wet (1925) ACK[C][L]

All You Need Is One Good Break (1950) Peggy Clark[L]; Paul du Pont[C]; Samuel Leve[S]

All's Well That Ends Well (1983) Robert Bryan[L]; Beverly Emmons[L]; John Gunter[S]; Lindy Hemming[C]; John Kasarda[S]

All-of-a-Sudden Peggy (1907) Callot Soeurs[C]; Madame Hayward[C]; Redfern[C]; Madame Viola[C]

Allah Be Praised (1944) George Jenkins[S][L]; Miles White[C]

Allah, The (1911) Ben Beerwald[L]; Madame Sara Bolwell[C]

Allegiance (1918) ACK[S][L]

Allegro (1947) Lucinda Ballard[C]; Jo Mielziner[S][L]

Alleluia (1907) NONE

Allez-Oop (1927) Mabel E. Johnston[C]; Bernard Lohmuller[S]

Alloy (1924) P. Dodd Ackerman[S]; ACK[L]

Alma, Where Do You Live (1910) ACK[S][C][L]

Almost an Eagle (1982) Karl Eigsti[S][C]; Roger Morgan[L]

Almost Crazy (1955) John Robert Lloyd[S][L]; Stanley Simmons[C]

Almost Perfect Person, An (1977) Ben Edwards[S][L]; Jane Greenwood[C]

Aloma of the South Seas (1925) Livingston Platt[(S)(C)]; Ack[(L)]

Alone at Last (1915) John Whalen[(L)]; Ack[(S)(C)]

Alone Together (1984) Karl Eigsti[(S)]; Arden Fingerhut[(L)]; Jane Greenwood[(C)]

Along Came Ruth (1914) NONE

Along Fifth Avenue (1949) Peggy Clark[(L)]; David Ffolkes[(C)]; Oliver Smith[(S)]

Altar of Friendship, The (1902) NONE

Always You (1920) Ack[(L)]

Amadeus (1980) John Bury[(S)(C)(L)]

Amadeus (1999) Paule Constable[(L)]; William Dudley[(S)(C)]

Amazing Dr. Clitterhouse (1937) Raymond Sovey[(S)]

Amazons, The (1913) Henri Bendel[(C)]; Edward G. Unitt[(S)]; Jules Weiss[(C)]

Ambassador (1972) Martin Aronstein[(L)]; Peter Rice[(S)(C)]

Ambassador, The (1900) Edward G. Unitt[(S)]

Amber Heart, The (1899) NONE

Ambitious Mrs. Alcott, The (1907) Alexander Corbett[(S)]

Ambush (1921) Sheldon K. Viele[(S)]; Clive Young[(C)]; Ack[(L)]

Ameer, The (1899) Gates and Morange[(S)]; Ernest Gros[(S)]; Archie Gunn[(C)]; Richard Marston[(S)]

Amen Corner (1983) Felix E. Cochren[(C)]; Karl Eigsti[(S)]; Shirley Prendergast[(L)]

Amen Corner, The (1965) Vantile Whitfield[(S)(C)(L)]

America (1913) Arthur Voegtlin[(S)]

America (1981) Ken Billington[(L)]; Michael Casey[(C)]; Robert Guerra[(S)]

America's Sweetheart (1931) Yetta Kiviette[(C)]; Charles LeMaire[(C)]; Donald Oenslager[(S)]

American (1926) John Held, Jr.[(S)(C)]

American Ace, An (1918) Lincoln J. Carter[(S)]; Ack[(C)]

American Born (1925) Madame Frances[(C)]; Joseph Wickes[(S)]

American Buffalo (1977) Jules Fisher[(L)]; Santo Loquasto[(S)(C)]

American Buffalo (1983) Marjorie Bradley Kellogg[(S)]; Bill Walker[(C)]; Ronald Wallace[(L)]

American Clock, The (1980) Karl Eigsti[(S)]; Neil Peter Jampolis[(L)]; Robert Wojewodski[(C)]

American Daughter, An (1997) John Lee Beatty[(S)]; Pat Collins[(L)]; Jane Greenwood[(C)]

American Dream (1933) Lee Simonson[(S)(L)]; Ack[(C)]

American Holiday (1936) Tom Adrian Cracraft[(S)]; Ack[(C)]

American Idea, The (1908) Unitt and Wickes[(S)]; John H. Young[(S)]

American Invasion, An (1902) Ernest Albert[(S)]

American Landscape (1938) Aline Bernstein[(S)(C)]

American Lord, The (1906) Ernest Gros[(S)]

American Maid, The (1913) Frederica DeWolfe[(C)]; Homer Emens[(S)]

American Millionaire, An (1974) Theoni V. Aldredge[(C)]; Martin Aronstein[(L)]; Douglas W. Schmidt[(S)]

American Tragedy, An (1926) Carolyn Hancock[(S)]; Ack[(C)(L)]

American Tragedy, An (1931) Ack[(C)(L)]

American Way, The (1939) Donald Oenslager[(S)]; Irene Sharaff[(S)(C)]; Hassard Short[(L)]

American Widow, An (1909) H. Robert Law[(S)]

American–Very Early (1934) Nicholas Yellenti[(S)]

Americana (1928) John Held, Jr.[(S)(C)]; Herman Rosse[(S)]

Americana (1932) Albert R. Johnson[(S)(L)]; Constance Ripley[(C)]

Americans in France, The (1920) Unitt and Wickes[(S)]; Ack[(L)]

Among the Married (1929) Gates and Morange[(S)]; Ack[(C)]

Among Those Present (1902) NONE

Among Those Sailing (1936) P. Dodd Ackerman[(S)]; Ack[(C)]

Amorous Antic, The (1929) Jo Mielziner[(S)(L)]; Ack[(C)]

Amoureuse (1904) NONE

Amphitryon (1952) Christian Bérard[(S)(C)]

Amphitryon 38 (1937) Lee Simonson[(S)]; Valentina[(C)]

Amy's View (1999) Bob Crowley[(S)(C)]; Mark Henderson[(L)]; David Weiner[(L)]

Anastasia (1954) Ben Edwards[(S)(C)(L)]

Anathema (1923) William Gropper[(C)]; Jacob Meth[(C)]; Samuel Ostrowsky[(S)]

Anatol (1931) Jo Mielziner[(S)(C)(L)]

Anatomist, The (1932) Alexander

Wyckoff[S]; ACK[C]

Ancient Mariner, The (1924) ACK[L]

And Be My Love (1934) David Homan[S]; Anna Hill Johnstone[C]; Molyneux[C]

And Be My Love (1945) Anna Hill Johnstone[C]; Raymond Sovey[S]

And Miss Reardon Drinks a Little (1971) Martin Aronstein[L]; Sara Brook[C]; Fred Voelpel[S]

And Now Good-Bye (1937) Raymond Sovey[S]; Jean Tate[C]

And So to Bed (1927) James B. Fagan[S]; ACK[L]

And Stars Remain (1936) Aline Bernstein[S]; Bianca Stroock[C]

And Things That Go Bump in the Night (1965) Jules Fisher[L]; Noel Taylor[C]; Ed Wittstein[S]

Andersonville Trial, The (1959) Will Steven Armstrong[S][C][L]

Andorra (1963) Boris Aronson[S]; Ray Diffen[C]; Tharon Musser[L]

Andre Charlot's Revue of 1924 (1924) G. K. Benda[C]; Guy DeGerald[C]; Marc Henri[S]; Laverdet[S]

Andre Heller's Wonderhouse (1991) Andre Heller[S]; Pluesch[L]; Susanne Schmoegner[C]

Androcles and the Lion (1915) Albert Rutherston[C]; Norman Wilkinson[S]; ACK[L]

Androcles and the Lion (1925) Miguel Covarrubias[S][C]; ACK[L]

Androcles and the Lion (1938) Manuel Essman[S]; A. H. Feder[L]; Perry Watkins[C]

Angel (1978) John Gleason[L]; Ming Cho Lee[S]; Pearl Somner[C]

Angel Face (1919) O'Kane Conwell[C]; Anthony Greshoff[L]; Herbert Moore[S]

Angel in the House, The (1915) ACK[L]

Angel in the Pawnshop (1951) John E. Blankenchip[S][C][L]

Angel in the Wings (1947) Donald Oenslager[S][L]; Julia Sze[C]

Angel Island (1937) John Root[S]; ACK[C][L]

Angel Street (1941) Lemuel Ayers[S][C]; A. H. Feder[L]

Angel Street (1975) Patricia Adshead[C]; Leon Di Leone[L]; Douglas W. Schmidt[S]

Angela (1928) Georges Barbier[C]; Watson Barratt[S]; Ernest Schraps[C]

Angela (1969) Jane Greenwood[C]; Robert Randolph[S][L]

Angeline Moves in (1932) Karle O. Amend[S]

Angels Don't Kiss (1932) ACK[S][C]

Angels Fall (1983) John Lee Beatty[S]; Dennis Parichy[L]; Jennifer von Mayrhauser[C]

Angels in America, Part II: Perestroika (1993) Peggy Eisenhauer[L]; Jules Fisher[L]; Toni-Leslie James[C]; Robin Wagner[S]

Angels in America: Millennium Approaches (1993) Peggy Eisenhauer[L]; Jules Fisher[L]; Toni-Leslie James[C]; Robin Wagner[S]

Angels Kiss Me (1951) Kenn Barr[C]; Frederick Fox[S][L]

Animal Crackers (1928) Mabel E. Johnston[C]; Raymond Sovey[S]

Animal Kingdom, The (1932) Aline Bernstein[S]; ACK[C]

Animals (1981) Marilyn Bligh-White[C]; John Wright Stevens[S]; Marc B. Weiss[L]

Ankles Aweigh (1955) George Jenkins[S][L]; Miles White[C]

Ann Boyd (1913) ACK[C]

Anna (1928) Yetta Kiviette[C]; Donald Oenslager[S]

Anna Ascends (1920) Harry Collins[C]; ACK[S][L]

Anna Christie (1921) Robert Edmond Jones[S]

Anna Christie (1952) Emeline Clarke Roche[S][C]

Anna Christie (1977) Ben Edwards[S][L]; Jane Greenwood[C]

Anna Christie (1993) John Lee Beatty[S]; Martin Pakledinaz[C]; Marc B. Weiss[L]

Anna Karenina (1907) H. Robert Law[S]

Anna Karenina (1992) Mary Jo Dondlinger[L]; James Morgan [active 1989-][S]; Carrie F. Robbins[C]

Anna Lucasta (1944) Paul du Pont[C]; Frederick Fox[S]

Anna Russell and Her Little Show (1953) Ralph Alswang[L]

Anne of 1000 Days (1948) Jo Mielziner[S][L]; Motley[C]

Anne of England (1941) M. Dobuzhinsky[S][C][L]

Annie (1977) Theoni V. Aldredge[C]; David Mitchell[S]; Judy Rasmuson[L]

Annie (1997) Theoni V. Aldredge[C]; Ken Billington[L]; Kenneth Foy[S]

Annie Dear (1924) ACK[S][C][L]

Annie Get Your Gun (1946) Lucinda Ballard[C]; Jo Mielziner[S][L]

Annie Get Your Gun (1966) Peter Hunt[L]; Paul McGuire[S]; Frank Thompson[C]

Annie Get Your Gun (1999) Beverly Emmons[L]; William Ivey Long[C]; Tony Walton[S]

Anniversary Waltz (1954) Frederick Fox[S][L]; Robert Mackintosh[C]

Another Interior (1915) Ralph Roeder[S][C]

Another Language (1932) Cleon Throckmorton[S]; ACK[C]

Another Language (1933) Cleon Throckmorton[S]; ACK[C]

Another Love (1934) Robert Brunton[S]; ACK[C]

Another Love Story (1943) Hattie Carnegie[C]; Raymond Sovey[S]

Another Man's Shoes (1918) Dodge and Castle[S]; ACK[L]

Another Part of the Forest (1946) Lucinda Ballard[C]; Jo Mielziner[S][L]

Another Sun (1940) Paul du Pont[C]; Ben Edwards[S]

Anthony and Cleopatra (1924) Rollo Peters[S][C]

Anthony and Cleopatra (1947) John Boyt[C]; Leo Kerz[S]; Valentina[C]; ACK[L]

Anthony in Wonderland (1917) ACK[S][C][L]

Anti-Matrimony (1910) NONE

Antigone (1946) Raymond Sovey[S]; Valentina[C]

Antonia (1925) Joseph Urban[S]; ACK[C]

Antony and Cleopatra (1909) Ernest Albert[S]; E. Hamilton Bell[C]; Jules Guérin[S]

Antony and Cleopatra (1951) Audrey Cruddas[C]; Roger Furse[S]; ACK[L]

Any Given Day (1993) Marjorie Bradley Kellogg[S]; Dennis Parichy[L]; Ann Roth[C]

Any House (1916) P. Dodd Ackerman[S]; ACK[L]

Any Wednesday (1964) Theoni V. Aldredge[C]; Tharon Musser[L]; Robert Randolph[S]

Anya (1965) Richard Casler[L]; Robert Randolph[S]; Patricia Zipprodt[C]

Anybody Home (1949) Louis Kennel[S][C][L]

Anybody's Game (1932) Philip Gelb[S]; ACK[C]

Anyone Can Whistle (1964) Theoni V. Aldredge[C]; William and Jean Eckart[S]; Jules Fisher[L]

Anything Goes (1934) George Jenkins[C]; Donald Oenslager[S]

Anything Goes (1989) Paul Gallo[L]; Tony Walton[S][C]

Anything Might Happen (1923) Clifford F. Pember[S]; Doris Reed[C]; ACK[L]

Apache, The (1923) ACK[L]

Apartment 12-K (1914) Joseph[C]

Aphrodite (1919) Percy Anderson[C]; Léon Bakst[C]; Paul Bismarck[L]; Joseph and Phil Harker[S]; Henry Kliegl[L]; Alice O'Neil[C]

Apology (1943) Samuel Leve[S][L]; Paul Morrison[C]

Apothecary, The (1926) Aline Bernstein[S][C]; ACK[L]

Appearances (1925) ACK[L]

Appearances (1929) ACK[L]

Applause (1970) Raymond Aghayan[C]; Tharon Musser[L]; Robert Randolph[S]

Apple Blossoms (1919) Joseph Urban[S]; ACK[C][L]

Apple Cart, The (1930) Lee Simonson[S][C]

Apple Cart, The (1956) Robert O'Hearn[S][L]; Noel Taylor[C]

Apple Doesn't Fall, The (1996) Ken Billington[L]; Gail Cooper-Hecht[C]; Kenneth Foy[S]

Apple of His Eye (1946) Edward DeForrest[C]; Raymond Sovey[S]

Apple Tree, The (1966) Jean Rosenthal[L]; Tony Walton[S][C]

Applesauce (1925) ACK[L]

April (1918) Gates and Morange[S]; ACK[C][L]

Apron Strings (1930) Louis Kennel[S]; ACK[C]

Arab, The (1911) NONE

Arabesque (1925) Norman Bel Geddes[S][C]

Arabian Nightmare (1927) ACK[S][C][L]

Arabian, The (1927) Carl H. Vose[S][C]

Arcadia (1995) Paul Pyant[L]; Mark Thompson[S][C]

Arcadians, The (1910) Homer Emens[S]; Wilhelm[C]

Are You A Crook? (1913) NONE

Are You A Mason? (1901) Edward G.

Unitt(S)

Are You Decent? (1934) Joan Adrian(C); ACK(S)(L)

Are You My Father? (1903) NONE

Are You with It? (1945) Raoul Pène Du Bois(C); George Jenkins(S)(L)

Aren't We All? (1923) P. Dodd Ackerman Studio(S); Evelyn McHorter(C); ACK(L)

Aren't We All? (1925) P. Dodd Ackerman Studio(S); ACK(L)

Aren't We All? (1985) Judith Bland(C); Finlay James(S); Natasha Katz(L)

Argyle Case, The (1912) H. Robert Law(S); Unitt and Wickes(S); ACK(C)

Ari (1971) Sara Brook(C); Nananne Porcher(L); Robert Randolph(S)

Ariadne (1925) Carolyn Hancock(S)(C)

Aries Is Rising (1939) Nicholas Yellenti(S); ACK(C)

Arizona (1900) Will R. Barnes(C); Walter W. Burridge(S); Charles H. Ritter(S)

Arizona (1913) Walter W. Burridge(S); Charles H. Ritter(S)

Arlequin Poli Par 'Amour (1955) Emile Bertin(S)

Armourette (1933) S. Syrjala(S); ACK(C)

Arms and the Girl (1950) Horace Armistead(S); Audré(C); ACK(L)

Arms and the Man (1899) NONE

Arms and the Man (1906) NONE

Arms and the Man (1915) Charles E. Boss(S); William Henry Matthews(C); ACK(L)

Arms and the Man (1925) Lee Simonson(S)(C)

Arms and the Man (1950) Paul Morrison(S)(C)(L)

Arms and the Man (1985) Thomas Lynch(S); Richard Nelson(L); Ann Roth(C)

Arms for Venus (1937) Herbert Callister(C); Nat Karson(S)

Army Play by Play, The (1943) Cirker and Robbins(S)

Army with Banners, The (1918) Grace O. Clarke(C); Peters and Kennel(S); ACK(L)

Around the Corner (1936) Nicholas Yellenti(S)

Around the Map (1915) F. Richards Anderson(C); Robert Brunton(S); O'Kane Conwell(C); Cora MacGeachy(C); Alice O'Neil(C); Joseph Urban(S)

Around the World (1911) Alfredo Edel(C); Arthur Voegtlin(S)

Around the World in Eighty Days (1946) Alvin Colt(C); Robert Davison(S)

Arrah-Na-Pogue (1903) Joseph Physioc(S)

Arrest That Woman (1936) Bianca Stroock(C); Nicholas Yellenti(S)

Arrow Maker, The (1911) E. Hamilton Bell(S)(C)

Arsene Lupin (1909) Ernest Gros(S)

Arsenic and Old Lace (1941) Helene Pons(C); Raymond Sovey(S); ACK(L)

Arsenic and Old Lace (1986) Jeanne Button(C); Pat Collins(L); Marjorie Bradley Kellogg(S)

Art (1998) Mark Thompson(S)(C); Hugh Vanstone(L)

Art and Mrs. Bottle (1930) Raymond Sovey(S)

Art and Opportunity (1917) Mary Blackburn(C); ACK(S)(L)

Artie (1907) Homer Emens(S)

Artist Descending a Staircase (1989) Joseph G. Aulisi(C); Tharon Musser(L); Tony Straiges(S)

Artistic Temperament (1924) Selma Morosco(S); Joseph Physioc(S); ACK(C)(L)

Artists and Models (1923) Watson Barratt(S); Ernest Schraps(C)

Artists and Models (1924) Watson Barratt(S); Charles LeMaire(C); Ernest Schraps(C)

Artists and Models (1925) Watson Barratt(S); Erté(C)

Artists and Models (1927) Watson Barratt(S); Ernest Schraps(C); Max Weldy(C); ACK(L)

Artists and Models (1930) Watson Barratt(S); Ernest Schraps(C)

Artists and Models (1943) Watson Barratt(S); Kathryn Kuhn(C)

Arturo Ui (1963) Rouben Ter-Arutunian(S)(C)(L)

As a Man Thinks (1911) H. Robert Law(S)

As Good As New (1930) Raymond Sovey(S)(C)(L)

As Husbands Go (1931) Cirker and Robbins(S); ACK(C)(L)

As Husbands Go (1933) ACK(S)(C)

As Is (1985) Dennis Parichy(L); David Potts(S); Michael Warren Powell(C)

As the Girls Go (1948) Howard Bay(S); Oleg Cassini(C); ACK(L)

(1909) Madame Oaksmith[C]; Unitt and Wickes[S]

Awakening, The (1908) NONE

Awakening, The (1918) Millard France[S]; H. P. Scenic Studio Knight[S]; ACK[L]

Awful Mrs. Eaton, The (1924) Jo Mielziner[S][L]; ACK[C]

Awful Truth, The (1922) Lanvin[C]; ACK[C]

Aztec Romance, An (1912) NONE

Bab (1920) Anthony Greshoff[L]; Clifford F. Pember[S]

Babbling Brooks (1927) Joseph Teichner[S]; ACK[C]

Babe, The (1984) F. Mitchell Dana[L]; Judy Dearing[C]; Ray Recht[S]

Babes and the Baron, The (1905) Stafford Hall[S]; T. Holmes[S]; Phillip Howden[S]; R. McCleery[S]; E. H. Ryan[S]; Wilhelm[C]

Babes in Arms (1937) Helene Pons[C]; Raymond Sovey[S]

Babes in Toyland (1903) Homer Emens[S]; Kliegl Brothers[L]; P. J. McDonald[S]; Mrs. Caroline Siedle[C]; John H. Young[S]

Babes in Toyland (1929) Rollo Wayne[S]; ACK[C][L]

Babes in Toyland (1930) Rollo Wayne[S]; ACK[C]

Babette (1903) F. Richards Anderson[C]; Emens and Unitt[S]; Mrs. Caroline Siedle[C]

Babette (1904) F. Richards Anderson[C]; Emens and Unitt[S]; Mrs. Caroline Siedle[C]

Babies a la Carte (1927) ACK[S][L]

Baby (1983) John Lee Beatty[S]; Pat Collins[L]; Jennifer von Mayrhauser[C]

Baby Cyclone (1927) Joseph Wickes[S]; ACK[C]

Baby Mine (1910) Lucile[C]

Baby Mine (1927) Livingston Platt[S]; ACK[C][L]

Baby Pompadour (1934) Kay Otteson[C]; Nicholas Yellenti[S]

Baby Wants a Kiss (1964) Peter Harvey[S][C]; David Hays[L]

Bacchae, The (1980) Pat Collins[L]; John Conklin[S][C]

Bachelor Belles, The (1910) F. Richards Anderson[C]; T. Bernard McDonald[S]; Wilhelm[C]

Bachelor Born (1938) Watson Barratt[S]; ACK[C]

Bachelor Father, The (1928) Louis Hartmann[L]; Joseph Wickes[S]; ACK[C]

Bachelor's Baby, The (1909) Unitt and Wickes[S]

Bachelor's Night, A (1921) ACK[S][C][L]

Bachelor, The (1909) Arthur Law[S]

Bachelors and Benedicts (1912) Dodge and Castle[S]; Madame Julie[C]

Bachelors' Brides (1925) ACK[L]

Back Fire (1932) Cleon Throckmorton[S]

Back Here (1928) ACK[S][C][L]

Back Home (1915) ACK[L]

Back Pay (1921) ACK[C][L]

Back Seat Drivers (1928) ACK[C][L]

Back to Earth (1918) ACK[C][L]

Back to Methuselah (1922) Lee Simonson[S][C]

Back to Methuselah (1958) Marvin Reiss[S][L]; Patricia Zipprodt[C]

Backfire (1916) ACK[S][L]

Backslapper, The (1925) Lester M. Livingston[C]; Livingston Platt[S]; ACK[L]

Bad Girl (1930) Ward and Harvey Studios[S]; ACK[C]

Bad Habits (1974) Ken Billington[L]; Michael H. Yeargan[S][C]

Bad Habits of 1926 (1926) Joseph Mullen[S][C]; ACK[L]

Bad Man, The (1920) Livingston Platt[S]; ACK[C][L]

Bad Manners (1933) ACK[S][L]

Bad Samaritan, The (1905) NONE

Bad Seed, The (1954) Sal Anthony[C]; George Jenkins[S][L]

Badges (1924) William F. Ash[L]

Bagels and Yox (1951) Bruno Maine[L]; ACK[S][C]

Bajour (1964) Peggy Clark[L]; Oliver Smith[S]; Freddy Wittop[C]

Baker Street (1965) Motley[C]; Jean Rosenthal[L]; Oliver Smith[S]

Bal Negre (1946) John Pratt[C][L]

Balkan Princess, The (1911) Melville Ellis[C]; Joseph[C]; H. Robert Law[S]

Ball in Old Vienna, A (1942) Aino Sllmola[C]; ACK[L]

Ballad of the Sad Cafe, The (1963) Ben Edwards[S]; Jane Greenwood[C]; Jean Rosenthal[L]

Ballet Ballads (1948) Nat Karson[S][C][L]

Ballroom (1978) Theoni V. Aldredge[C]; Tharon Musser[L]; Robin Wagner[S]

Bally Hoo (1927) James Reynolds[S]

Ballyhoo (1930) Cirker and Robbins[S]; Charles LeMaire[C]

Ballyhoo of 1932 (1932) Yetta Kiviette[S][C]; Charles LeMaire[S][C]; Russell Patterson[S][C]

Bamboula (1929) Ack[S][L]

Banco (1922) Livingston Platt[S][C]; Ack[C]

Band in Berlin (1999) Jonathan Bixby[C]; Kirk Bookman[L]; Gregory Gale[C]; Douglas W. Schmidt[S]

Band Wagon, The (1931) Albert R. Johnson[S]; Yetta Kiviette[C]; Constance Ripley[C]

Bandanna Land (1908) Pauline Reed[C]; Ack[S][C]

Banjo Eyes (1941) Harry Horner[S]; Irene Sharaff[C]; Hassard Short[L]

Banshee, The (1927) Frank Garrison[S]; Benjamin Leffler[L]

Baptiste (1952) Mayo[S]

Barbara (1917) P. Dodd Ackerman Studio[S]; Homer Conant[C]

Barbara Cook: A Concert for the Theatre (1987) Joseph G. Aulisi[C]; John Falabella[S]; Richard Winkler[L]

Barbara's Millions (1906) None

Barber Had Two Sons, The (1943) Phil Raiguel[S]

Barber of New Orleans, The (1909) Eleanor Plaisted Abbott[C]; Ernest Albert[S]

Barchester Towers (1937) Jo Mielziner[S][C][L]

Bare Facts of 1926 (1926) Ack[S][L]

Barefoot (1925) Ack[L]

Barefoot Boy with Cheek (1947) Alvin Colt[C]; Jo Mielziner[S][L]

Barefoot in Athens (1951) Boris Aronson[S]; Bernard Rudofsky[C]; Ack[L]

Barefoot in the Park (1963) Donald Brooks[C]; Jean Rosenthal[L]; Oliver Smith[S]

Bargain, The (1915) Ack[L]

Barker, The (1927) P. Dodd Ackerman[S]; Ack[C]

Barnum (1980) Theoni V. Aldredge[C]; Craig Miller[L]; David Mitchell[S]

Barnum Was Right (1923) Ack[S][C][L]

Baron Trenck (1912) Hugo Baruch[S][C]

Baroness Fiddlesticks, The (1904) None

Barretts of Wimpole Street, The (1931) Jo Mielziner[S][C][L]

Barretts of Wimpole Street, The (1935) Jo Mielziner[S][C]

Barretts of Wimpole Street, The (1945) Jo Mielziner[S][C]

Barrier, The (1910) Gates and Morange[S]

Barrier, The (1950) H. A. Condell[S]; Ack[L]

Barrister, The (1932) Theodore Kahn[S]; Ack[C]

Barrymore (1997) Natasha Katz[L]; Santo Loquasto[S][C]

Barton Mystery, The (1917) Ack[L]

Basic Training of Pavlo Hummel, The (1977) Robert Mitchell[S]; Domingo A. Rodriguez[C]; David F. Segal[L]

Bat, The (1920) Gates and Morange[S]; Ack[L]

Bat, The (1937) Frederick Fox[S]; Ack[L]

Bat, The (1953) Ralph Alswang[S][L]; Alice Gibson[C]

Bathsheba (1947) Stewart Chaney[S][C][L]

Battle Cry, The (1914) None

Battle Hymn (1936) Herbert Andrews[C]; Howard Bay[S]; Emanuel Berian[L]

Battle in the Skies, The (1908) Joseph Elsner[L]; Arthur Voegtlin[S]; Madame Frances Ziebarth[C]

Battle of the Butterflies, The (1908) None

Battle, The (1908) Frank E. Gates[S]; Edward Morange[S]

Battleship Gertie (1935) Boris Aronson[S]; Virginia Estes Cates[C]

Battling Buckler (1923) William E. Castle[S]; Yetta Kiviette[C]

Bavu (1922) Henry Herbert[S]; Ruth Reeves[C]

Baxter's Partner (1911) None

Be Calm, Camilla (1918) Robert Edmond Jones[S]

Be So Kindly (1937) Ack[S][C][L]

Be Your Age (1929) P. Dodd Ackerman Studio[S]; Ack[C][L]

Be Your Age (1953) Ralph Alswang[S]; Jocelyn[C]

Be Yourself (1924) H. Robert Studio Law[S]; Charles LeMaire[C]; Mark Mooring[C]; Ack[L]

Bear, A (1915) P. T. Frankl[S]

Beast in Me, The (1963) Jean Rosenthal[S][L]; Leo Van Witsen[C]

Beat the Band (1942) Samuel Leve[S]; Freddy Wittop[C]

Beau Brummell (1899) Joseph Physioc[S]

Beau Brummell (1905) NONE
Beau Brummell (1906) NONE
Beau Brummell (1907) NONE
Beau Brummell (1916) Mr. Scotson-Clark[S][C]
Beau Gallant (1926) Henry Dreyfuss[S]; ACK[C][L]
Beau-Strings (1926) Henry Dreyfuss[S]
Beaucaire (1901) Richard Marston[S]
Beautiful Adventure, The (1914) Lucile[C]; ACK[C]
Beautiful People, The (1941) Samuel Leve[S]
Beauty and the Barge (1905) Homer Emens[S]; Lucile[C]; Mlle. Rachelle Ospovat[C]; Edward G. Unitt[S]
Beauty and the Barge (1913) Emens and Unitt[S]; Lucile[C]; Mlle. Rachelle Ospovat[C]
Beauty and the Beast (1994) Ann Hould-Ward[C]; Natasha Katz[L]; Stanley A. Meyer[S]
Beauty and the Jacobin (1912) NONE
Beauty Part, The (1962) Alvin Colt[C]; William Pitkin[S][L]
Beauty Queen of Leenane, The (1998) Francis O'Connor[S][C]; Ben Ormerod[L]
Beauty Shop, The (1914) Unitt and Wickes[S]; ACK[C]
Beauty Spot, The (1909) H. Robert Law[S]; Edward G. Unitt[S]; Joseph Wickes[S]
Beaux Stratagem, The (1928) Jules Guérin[S][C]
Becket (1960) Motley[C]; Jean Rosenthal[L]; Oliver Smith[S]
Becky Sharp (1899) Percy Anderson[C]; Madame Freisinger[C]; Frank E. Gates[S]; William Grogan[L]; Edward Morange[S]
Becky Sharp (1904) Percy Anderson[C]; Frank E. Gates[S]; William Grogan[L]; Edward Morange[S]
Becky Sharp (1911) Gates and Morange[S]
Becky Sharpe (1929) Robert Edmond Jones[S][C]
Bedfellows (1929) ACK[L]
Bedford's Hope (1906) Henry Buhler[S]; Lincoln J. Carter[S]
Bedroom Farce (1979) Tazeena Firth[S]; Timothy O'Brien[S][C]; Peter Radmore[L]
Beeckman Place (1964) Jack Brown[L]; Oliver Smith[S]; Suzanne Taylor[C]

Bees and the Flowers, The (1946) Enid Gilbert[S][C][L]
Beethoven (1910) E. Hamilton Bell[S][C]
Beethoven's Tenth (1984) Martin Aronstein[L]; Madeline Ann Graneto[C]; Kenneth Mellor[S]
Before and After (1905) NONE
Before Morning (1933) Karle O. Amend[S]; ACK[C]
Before You Go (1968) Theoni V. Aldredge[C]; Jules Fisher[L]; Ed Wittstein[S]
Before You're 25 (1929) ACK[S][C][L]
Beg, Borrow, or Steal (1960) Carter Morningstar[S][C][L]
Beggar on Horseback (1924) Woodman Thompson[S][C]
Beggar on Horseback (1925) Woodman Thompson[S][C]
Beggar Student, The (1913) Melville Ellis[C]; H. Robert Law[S]; Madame Ripley[C]
Beggar's Holiday (1946) Peggy Clark[L]
Beggar's Holliday (1946) Walter Florell[C]; Oliver Smith[S]
Beggar's Opera, The (1920) C. Lovat Fraser[S][C]
Beggar's Opera, The (1928) C. Lovat Fraser[S][C]
Beggar's Opera, The (1973) Martin Aronstein[L]; Carrie F. Robbins[C]; Robert U. Taylor[S]; Robert Yodice[S]
Beggars Are Coming to Town (1945) Ralph Alswang[C]; Charles James[C]; Jo Mielziner[S][L]
Behavior of Mrs. Crane, The (1928) Nicholas Yellenti[S]; ACK[C]
Behind Red Lights (1937) Nicholas Yellenti[S]
Behold the Bridegroom (1927) Livingston Platt[S]; ACK[C]
Behold This Dreamer (1927) Gates and Morange[S]; Anthony Greshoff[L]
Believe Me Xantippe (1913) NONE
Belinda (1918) Homer Emens[S]; ACK[C][L]
Belinda/New Word/ Old Friends/Old Lady, The (1917) Homer Emens[S]; ACK[C][L]
Bell for Adano, A (1944) Motley[S][C]; William Richardson[L]
Bell, Book and Candle (1950) George Jenkins[S][L]; Anna Hill Johnstone[C]; Valentina[C]
Bella Donna (1912) Jean[C]
Bellamy Trial, The (1931) ACK[C][L]

Belle Marseillaise, La (1905) Henry
Dazian(C); Ernest Gros(S)
Belle of Amherst, The (1976) Theoni
V. Aldredge(C); H. R. Poindexter(S)(L)
Belle of Bohemia, The (1900) Ernest
Albert(S); D. Frank Dodge(S); Joseph
Physioc(S); Mrs. Caroline Siedle(C)
Belle of Bond Street, The (1914)
NONE
Belle of Bridgeport, The (1900) Fox
and Vincent(S); St. John Lewis(S);
MacCoughtry(S)
Belle of Brittany (1909) Melville
Ellis(C)
Belle of Broadway, The (1902) No
PLAYBILL
Belle of London Town, The (1907)
NONE
Belle of Mayfair, The (1906) NONE
Bells Are Ringing (1956) Peggy
Clark(L); Raoul Pène Du Bois(S)(C)
Bells Are Ringing (2001) Riccardo
Hernández(S); Donald Holder(L); David
C. Woolard(C)
Bells, The (1899) NONE
Bells, The (1926) Nicholas Yellenti(S);
ACK(L)
Belmont Varieties (1932) Annette
Brod(C); ACK(L)
Belt, The (1927) Evelyn T. Clifton(C);
John Dos Passos(S)
Ben Franklin in Paris (1964) Jack
Brown(L); Motley(C); Oliver Smith(S)
Ben Greet Rep (1910) NONE
Ben Hur (1899) Ernest Albert(S); F.
Richards Anderson(C); Alexander
Grinager(S); Ernest Gros(S); H.
Harndin(L)
Ben Hur (1902) Ernest Albert(S); F.
Richards Anderson(C); George
Enright(L); Ernest Gros(S); H.
Harndin(L)
Ben-Hur (1911) Frank Platzer(S)
Ben-Hur (1916) F. Richards
Anderson(C); ACK(S)(L)
Benefactors (1985) Michael Annals(S);
Martin Aronstein(L); John Dunn(C)
Bent (1979) Arden Fingerhut(L); Santo
Loquasto(S); Robert Wojewodski(C)
Berenice (1963) Diane Esmond(S)(C)
Berkeley Square (1929) Sir Edwin
Lutyens(S); ACK(C)
Berlin (1931) Livingston Platt(S)
Bernadine (1952) John Robert
Lloyd(S)(L); Noel Taylor(C)
Bertha, the Sewing Machine Girl

(1935) Ilmar and Tames(S)(C)
Best Foot Forward (1941) Jo
Mielziner(S)(L); Miles White(C)
Best Friend (1976) Andrew Greenhut(S);
Miles White(C); Richard Winkler(L)
Best House in Naples, The (1956)
Ralph Alswang(S)(L); Jerry Boxhorn(C)
Best Laid Plans, The (1966) Peggy
Clark(L); Florence Klotz(C); Oliver
Smith(S)
Best Little Whorehouse Goes
Public, The (1994) John Arnone(S);
Peggy Eisenhauer(L); Jules Fisher(L);
Bob Mackie(C)
Best Little Whorehouse in Texas,
The (1978) Marjorie Bradley
Kellogg(S); Dennis Parichy(L); Ann
Roth(C)
Best Little Whorehouse in Texas,
The (1982) Marjorie Bradley
Kellogg(S); Dennis Parichy(L); Ann
Roth(C)
Best Man, The (1960) Theoni V.
Aldredge(C); Jo Mielziner(S)(L)
Best Man, The (2000) Theoni V.
Aldredge(C); John Arnone(S); Howell
Binkley(L)
Best of Friends, The (1903) No
PLAYBILL
Best People, The (1924) ACK(C)(L)
Best People, The (1933) ACK(S)
Best Sellers (1933) Rollo Wayne(S);
ACK(C)
Best Years (1932) Rollo Wayne(S)
Bet Your Life (1937) ACK(S)
Betrayal (1980) John Bury(S)(C)(L)
Betrayal (2000) Rob Howell(S)(C); David
Weiner(L)
Betrothal, The (1918) O'Kane
Conwell(C); Herbert Paus(S)
Betsy (1911) T. E. Ryan(S)
Betsy (1926) Gates and Morange(S);
Charles LeMaire(C); Joseph Urban(S);
ACK(L)
Bette Midler (1973) Robert DeMora(C);
Richard Mason(S); John Tedesco(L)
Bette Midler's Clams on the Half
Shell Revue (1975) Beverly
Emmons(L); Tony Walton(S)(C)
Better 'Ole, The (1918) Ernest
Albert(S); ACK(C)(L)
Better Times (1922) Will R. Barnes(C);
Edward Demmler(L); Mark Lawson(S);
Cora MacGeachy(C); William Henry
Matthews(C); Robert McQuinn(C);
Gladys Monkhouse(C); Wilhelm(C);

ACK[S]

Betty (1916) Homer Emens[S]; Robert McQuinn[C]; ACK[L]

Betty at Bay (1918) NONE

Betty Be Good (1920) P. Dodd Ackerman Studio[S]; Yetta Kiviette[C]; ACK[L]

Betty Lee (1924) P. Dodd Ackerman[S]; Charles LeMaire[C]; ACK[L]

Betty, Be Careful (1931) ACK[S][L]

Between the Devil (1937) Albert R. Johnson[S]; Yetta Kiviette[C]

Between Two Worlds (1934) Aline Bernstein[S]; ACK[C]

Beverly Hills (1940) Donald Oenslager[S]; ACK[C]

Beverly's Balance (1915) Livingston Platt[S]; ACK[C][L]

Beware of Dogs (1921) ACK[L]

Beware of Widows (1925) Gladys E. Calthrop[S]; ACK[L]

Beyond (1925) Robert Edmond Jones[S][C][L]

Beyond Evil (1926) Cleon Throckmorton[S]

Beyond Human Power (1902) NONE

Beyond the Fringe (1965) Ralph Alswang[L]; John Wyckham[S][L]; ACK[C]

Beyond the Horizon (1920) Hewlett & Basing[S]; ACK[L]

Beyond the Horizon (1926) Cleon Throckmorton[S]

Beyond Therapy (1982) Paul Gallo[L]; Andrew Jackness[S]; Jennifer von Mayrhauser[C]

Bicycle Ride to Nevada (1963) Howard Bay[S][L]; Edith Lutyens Bel Geddes[C]

Bidding High (1932) William H. Mensching[S]

Biff! Bang! (1918) ACK[S][L]

Biff! Biff! Bang! (1921) Leonard Young[S][C]

Big (1996) Paul Gallo[L]; William Ivey Long[C]; Robin Wagner[S]

Big Blow, The (1938) A. H. Feder[L]; Samuel Leve[S]; Mary Merrill[C]

Big Boy (1925) Watson Barratt[S]

Big Chance, The (1918) ACK[L]

Big City, The (1942) H. Heckroth[S][C]; ACK[L]

Big Deal (1986) Jules Fisher[L]; Peter Larkin[S]; Patricia Zipprodt[C]

Big Fight, The (1928) Joseph Wickes[S]; ACK[C][L]

Big Fish, Little Fish (1961) Ben Edwards[S][L]; Mary Grant[C]

Big Game (1920) ACK[L]

Big Hearted Herbert (1934) Marie Crisp[C]; ACK[S][L]

Big Idea, The (1914) NONE

Big Jim Garrity (1914) NONE

Big Knife, The (1949) Howard Bay[S]; Lucille Little[C]; ACK[L]

Big Lake (1927) Lewis Barrington[S]; Gertrude Brown[C]; ACK[L]

Big Love, The (1991) Ken Billington[L]; Jane Greenwood[C]; David Mitchell[S]

Big Mogul, The (1925) ACK[S][C][L]

Big Night (1933) Mordecai Gorelik[S]; ACK[C]

Big Pond, The (1928) A. J. Lundborg[S]; ACK[C]

Big River (1985) Heidi Ettinger[S]; Patricia McGourty[C]; Richard Riddell[L]

Big Show, The (1916) Léon Bakst[S][C]; Robert McQuinn[S][C]; Bianca Stroock[C]; ACK[L]

Big Two, The (1947) Jo Mielziner[S][L]; Bianca Stroock[C]

Big White Fog (1940) Anne De Paur[C]; Perry Watkins[S][L]

Biggest Thief in Town, The (1949) Eleanor Goldsmith[C]; Leo Kerz[S][L]

Bill of Divorcement, A (1921) Henri Bendel[C]; Gates and Morange[S]

Billeted (1917) Livingston Platt[S]; ACK[C]

Billeted (1922) John Dwyer[S]; Thyza Head[C]; Miss Gwyneth Waugh[C]; ACK[L]

Billie (1928) Joseph Wickes[S]; ACK[C][L]

Billion Dollar Baby (1945) Irene Sharaff[C]; Oliver Smith[S]

Billionaire, The (1902) Ernest Albert[S]; F. Richards Anderson[C]

Billy (1909) NONE

Billy (1969) Theoni V. Aldredge[C]; Martin Aronstein[L]; Ming Cho Lee[S]

Billy Barnes People, The (1961) Spencer Davies[S]; Grady Hunt[C]

Billy Barnes Revue (1959) Peggy Clark[L]; Glen Holse[S]; ACK[C]

Billy Budd (1951) Ruth Morley[C]; Paul Morrison[S][L]

Billy Draws a Horse (1939) Watson Barratt[S]; ACK[C]

Billy Rose's Crazy Quilt (1931) Fanny Brice[C]; Clarke Robinson[L]; ACK[S]

Billy the Kid (1938) Jared French[C];

Blood Money (1927) P. Dodd Ackerman Studio[S]; Ack[C][L]

Blood Red Roses (1970) Deirdre Cartier[C]; Tharon Musser[L]; Ed Wittstein[S]

Blood, Sweat and Stanley Poole (1961) Donald Oenslager[S][L]; Michael Travis[C]

Bloodstream (1932) Jo Mielziner[S][L]; Ack[C]

Bloody Laughter (1931) Robert Van Rosen[S]

Bloomer Girl (1944) Lemuel Ayers[S][L]; Miles White[C]

Blossom Time (1921) Watson Barratt[S]; Ack[C][L]

Blossom Time (1924) Watson Barratt[S]

Blossom Time (1926) Watson Barratt[S]

Blossom Time (1931) Watson Barratt[S]; Ack[C]

Blossom Time (1938) Watson Barratt[S]; Ack[C]

Blossom Time (1943) Watson Barratt[S]; Ack[C]

Blot in the 'Scutcheon, A (1905) Franklin Van Horn[C]; Ack[S]

Blow Ye Winds (1937) Cirker and Robbins[S]; Maxine Leigh[C]

Bludgeon, The (1914) None

Blue Bandana, The (1924) Ack[L]

Blue Bird, The (1911) E. Hamilton Bell[S][C]; Unitt and Wickes[S]

Blue Bird, The (1923) Ack[C][L]

Blue Bird, The (1932) Ack[L]

Blue Denim (1958) Alvin Colt[C]; Charles Elson[L]; Peter Larkin[S]

Blue Envelope, The (1916) Henri Bendel[C]; Ack[S][L]

Blue Eyes (1921) Ack[S][C][L]

Blue Flame, The (1920) Hickson[C]; Joseph Physioc Studio[S]; Madame Therese Renaud[C]

Blue Ghost, The (1930) Cirker and Robbins[S]; Ack[C][L]

Blue Grass (1908) None

Blue Holiday (1945) Perry Watkins[S][C][L]

Blue Kitten, The (1922) Shirley Barker[C]; Clifford F. Pember[S]; Anna Spencer[C]

Blue Lagoon, The (1921) Ack[S][C][L]

Blue Monday (1932) Louis Bromberg[S]

Blue Moon, The (1906) Ernest Albert[S]; Homer Emens[S]; Edward G. Unitt[S]; Joseph Wickes[S]

Blue Mouse, The (1908) H. Robert Law[S]

Blue Paradise, The (1915) Ack[C][L]

Blue Pearl, The (1918) Ack[L]

Blue Peter, The (1925) Cleon Throckmorton[S]

Blue Room, The (1998) Mark Thompson[S][C]; Hugh Vanstone[L]

Blue Widow, The (1933) Selma Alexander[C]; Raymond Sovey[S]

Bluebeard's Eighth Wife (1921) Livingston Platt[S]; Ack[C]

Bluebird, The (1910) E. Hamilton Bell[S][C]

Blues for Mr. Charley (1964) A. H. Feder[S][C][L]

Blues in the Night (1982) Ken Billington[L]; John Falabella[S]; David Murin[C]

Bluffing Bluffers (1924) Nicholas Yellenti[S]; Ack[C][L]

Bluffs (1908) None

Blushing Bride, The (1922) Ack[C]

Blythe Spirit (1943) Stewart Chaney[S]; Ack[C]

Bobby Burnit (1910) H. Robert Law[S]

Boccaccio (1904) None

Boccaccio (1975) Patrika Brown[L]; Linda Fisher[C]; Robert U. Taylor[S]

Body Beautiful, The (1935) Boris Aronson[S]; Ack[C]

Body Beautiful, The (1958) William and Jean Eckart[S][L]; Noel Taylor[C]

Boeing-Boeing (1965) Lloyd Burlingame[L]; J. Hutchinson Scott[S][C]

Bohemian Girl, The (1933) Ack[L]

Bold Sojer Boy, The (1903) None

Bombo (1921) Watson Barratt[S]; Ack[C]

Bond of Interest (1929) Claude Bragdon[S]; Fania Mindell[C]

Bonds of Interest, The (1919) Rollo Peters[S][C]

Bonehead, The (1920) Joseph Physioc Studio[S]; Ack[C][L]

Bonnie Brier Bush, The (1901) Joseph Physioc[S]

Book of Charm, The (1925) Lewis Barrington[S]; Mrs. Marcus Harrison[C]; Ben Phlaum[L]

Book of Job (1919) Frank Zimmerman[S][C]

Boom Boom (1929) Georges Barbier[C]; Watson Barratt[S]; Orry-Kelly[C]; Ack[C]

Boom Boom Room (1973) Theoni V. Aldredge[C]; Martin Aronstein[L];

Santo Loquasto[S]

Boomerang, The (1915) Henri Bendel[C]; Ernest Gros[S]

Booster, The (1929) Ward and Harvey Studios[S]

Bootleggers, The (1922) Ack[C][L]

Border Land (1932) Karle O. Amend[S]; Ack[C]

Borderside (1900) Edward G. Unitt[S]; Milnor Wells[L]

Born Yesterday (1946) Charles Elson[L]; Ruth Kanin[C]; Donald Oenslager[S]

Born Yesterday (1989) Jeff Davis[L]; David Potts[S]; Ann Roth[C]

Borrowed Love (1929) Cirker and Robbins[S]; Ack[C]

Borscht Capades (1951) Charles Elson[S][L]; Natalie Barth Walker[C]

Borstal Boy (1970) Neil Peter Jampolis[S][L]; Tomas MacAnna[C]

Bosom Friends (1917) Ack[S][L]

Bosoms and Neglect (1979) Willa Kim[C]; Jennifer Tipton[L]; John Wulp[S]

Boss, The (1911) Wilfred Buckland[S]; H. Robert Law[S]

Bostonians, The (1900) Ernest Albert[S]; Walter W. Burridge[S]

Both Your Houses (1933) Charles LeMaire[C]; Arthur P. Segal[S]; Ack[C]

Bottled (1928) Wiard Ihnen[S]; Ack[C]

Bottom of the Cup, The (1927) Joseph Teichner[S]; Ack[L]

Bottomland (1927) Ack[L]

Boudoir (1941) Raymond Sovey[S]; Ack[C]

Bough Breaks, The (1937) O. L. Raineri[S]; Ack[C]

Bought and Paid For (1911) H. Robert Law[S]

Bought and Paid for (1921) None

Boundary Line, The (1930) Henry Dreyfuss[S]; Ack[C]

Box Seats (1928) Evelyn T. Clifton[C]; Mabel E. Johnston[C]; R. N. Robbins[S]

Boy and the Girl, The (1909) None

Boy Friend, The (1932) Rollo Wayne[S]

Boy Friend, The (1970) Andrew and Margaret Brownfoot[S][C]; Tharon Musser[L]

Boy Growing Up, A (1957) Ack[L]

Boy Meets Girl (1935) A. J. Lundborg[S]; Ack[C]

Boy Meets Girl (1943) Cirker and Robbins[S]; Ack[C]

Boy Who Lived Twice, A (1945) John Root[S]; Ack[C]

Boyd's Daughter (1940) Johannes Larsen[S][L]

Boyfriend, The (1954) A. H. Feder[L]; Reginald Woolley[S][C]

Boys and Betty, The (1908) Frank E. Gates[S]; Edward Morange[S]

Boys and Girls Together (1940) Irene Sharaff[C]; William Oden Waller[S]

Boys from Syracuse, The (1938) Jo Mielziner[S][L]; Irene Sharaff[C]

Boys in Autumn, The (1986) Michael Miller[S]; Richard Nelson[L]; Jennifer von Mayrhauser[C]

Boys of Company "B", The (1907) Emens and Unitt[S]; Milnor Wells[L]

Boys of Winter, The (1985) Pat Collins[L]; David Mitchell[S]; Carrie F. Robbins[C]

Boys Will Be Boys (1919) Ack[L]

Brain Sweat (1934) Ack[S]

Braisley Diamond, The (1906) None

Brand (1910) E. Hamilton Bell[S][C]

Branded (1917) Ack[C][L]

Brass Ankle (1931) Cleon Throckmorton[S]

Brass Bottle, The (1910) Henry Dazian[C]; Unitt and Wickes[S]

Brass Buttons (1927) Ack[S][L]

Brass Ring, The (1952) Elfi Von Kantzow[S][C]

Brat, The (1917) Joseph Physioc[S]; Ack[C][L]

Bravo (1948) Rose Bogdanoff[C]; Leo Kerz[S]; Ack[L]

Bravo Giovanni (1962) Robert Randolph[S][L]; Ed Wittstein[C]

Breadwinner, The (1931) Ack[S][C][L]

Break a Leg (1979) Theoni V. Aldredge[C]; Peter Larkin[S]; Marc B. Weiss[L]

Breakfast in Bed (1920) Ack[L]

Breakfast with Les and Bess (1983) Ian Calderon[L]; Timothy Dunleavy[C]; Dean Tschetter[S]

Breaking Point, The (1923) Nicholas Yellenti[S]; Ack[L]

Breaking the Code (1987) Natasha Katz[L]; Liz da Costa[S][C]

Breaks, The (1928) August Vimnera[S]; Ack[L]

Brewster's Millions (1906) Ernest Albert[S]; Frederick W. Thompson[S]

Bridal Crown (1938) Eugene Dunkel[S]; Stasy Uskinsky[C]

Bridal Path, The (1913) NONE
Bridal Quilt (1934) John Biddle
Whitelaw⁽ˢ⁾; ACK⁽ᶜ⁾
Bridal Wise (1932) Jo Mielziner⁽ˢ⁾⁽ᴸ⁾;
ACK⁽ᶜ⁾
Bride of the Lamb (1926) Cleon
Throckmorton⁽ˢ⁾
Bride of Torozko, The (1934) Stewart
Chaney⁽ˢ⁾
Bride Retires, The (1925) ACK⁽ᴸ⁾
Bride the Sun Shines On, The (1931)
Cleon Throckmorton⁽ˢ⁾; ACK⁽ᶜ⁾
Bride, The (1924) ACK⁽ᶜ⁾⁽ᴸ⁾
Bridge of Distances (1925) John
Wenger⁽ˢ⁾
Bridge, The (1909) Gates and
Morange⁽ˢ⁾; Young Brothers⁽ˢ⁾
Brief Lives (1967) Lloyd Burlingame⁽ᴸ⁾;
Julia Trevelyan Oman⁽ˢ⁾⁽ᶜ⁾
Brief Lives (1974) Julia Trevelyan
Oman⁽ˢ⁾⁽ᶜ⁾⁽ᴸ⁾
Brief Moment (1931) Jo
Mielziner⁽ˢ⁾⁽ᶜ⁾⁽ᴸ⁾
Brigadier Gerard (1906) Henry
Dazian⁽ᶜ⁾; Ernest Gros⁽ˢ⁾
Brigadoon (1947) Peggy Clark⁽ᴸ⁾; David
Ffolkes⁽ᶜ⁾; Oliver Smith⁽ˢ⁾
Brigadoon (1980) Paul de Pass⁽ˢ⁾;
Michael J. Hotopp⁽ˢ⁾; Stanley
Simmons⁽ᶜ⁾; Thomas Skelton⁽ᴸ⁾
Brigadoon (1991) Desmond Heeley⁽ˢ⁾⁽ᶜ⁾;
Duane Schuler⁽ᴸ⁾
Brigadoon (1996) Desmond Heeley⁽ˢ⁾⁽ᶜ⁾;
Duane Schuler⁽ᴸ⁾
Bright Boy (1944) Watson Barratt⁽ˢ⁾
Bright Eyes (1910) P. Dodd Ackerman
Studio⁽ˢ⁾; Frank Callaghan⁽ᴸ⁾;
Corrigan and DeSoria⁽ᴸ⁾; Kliegl
Brothers⁽ᴸ⁾; Cora MacGeachy⁽ᶜ⁾
Bright Honor (1936) William Oden
Waller⁽ˢ⁾; ACK⁽ᶜ⁾
Bright Lights of 1943 (1943) Al
Alloy⁽ᴸ⁾; Perry Watkins⁽ˢ⁾⁽ᶜ⁾
Bright Rebel (1938) Lucielle
Samuels⁽ᶜ⁾; Nicholas Yellenti⁽ˢ⁾
Bright Star (1935) Raymond Sovey⁽ˢ⁾;
Valentina⁽ᶜ⁾
Brighten the Corner (1945) Willis
Knighton⁽ˢ⁾
Brighton Beach Memoirs (1983)
David Mitchell⁽ˢ⁾; Tharon Musser⁽ᴸ⁾;
Patricia Zipprodt⁽ᶜ⁾
Brightower (1970) John Gleason⁽ᴸ⁾;
Tom Munn⁽ˢ⁾; Noel Taylor⁽ᶜ⁾
Bring Back Birdie (1981) David
Hays⁽ᴸ⁾; David Mitchell⁽ˢ⁾; Fred

Voelpel⁽ᶜ⁾
Bring in 'da Noise, Bring in 'da
Funk (1996) Peggy Eisenhauer⁽ᴸ⁾;
Jules Fisher⁽ᴸ⁾; Riccardo Hernández⁽ˢ⁾;
Paul Tazewell⁽ᶜ⁾
Bringing Up Father (1925) Benjamin
C. Davis⁽ᶜ⁾; William Weaver⁽ˢ⁾; ACK⁽ᴸ⁾
Brittle Heaven (1934) P. Dodd
Ackerman⁽ˢ⁾; Kay Morrison⁽ᶜ⁾; ACK⁽ᴸ⁾
Brixton Burglary, The (1901)
Joseph⁽ᶜ⁾; Ernest Peixotto⁽ˢ⁾
Broadway (1926) Clara Schuman⁽ᶜ⁾;
Arthur P. Segal⁽ˢ⁾; ACK⁽ᴸ⁾
Broadway and Buttermilk (1916)
ACK⁽ᴸ⁾
Broadway Bound (1986) Joseph G.
Aulisi⁽ᶜ⁾; David Mitchell⁽ˢ⁾; Tharon
Musser⁽ᴸ⁾
Broadway Boy (1932) Karle O.
Amend⁽ˢ⁾
Broadway Brevities of 1920 (1920)
Charles LeMaire⁽ᶜ⁾; ACK⁽ˢ⁾⁽ᴸ⁾
Broadway Follies (1981) Alvin Colt⁽ᶜ⁾;
Peter Larkin⁽ˢ⁾; Robert Morgan⁽ᴸ⁾
Broadway Interlude (1934) Karle O.
Amend⁽ˢ⁾; Jacques⁽ᶜ⁾
Broadway Jones (1912) Cassidy and
Sons⁽ᴸ⁾; Unitt and Wickes⁽ˢ⁾
Broadway Musical, A (1978) Randy
Barcelo⁽ᶜ⁾; John De Santis⁽ᴸ⁾; Peter
Wexler⁽ˢ⁾
Broadway Nights (1929) Georges
Barbier⁽ᶜ⁾; Watson Barratt⁽ˢ⁾; Ernest
Schraps⁽ᶜ⁾
Broadway Shadows (1930) ACK⁽ᴸ⁾
Broadway Sho-Window (1936) Clarke
Robinson⁽ˢ⁾; William Weaver⁽ᶜ⁾
Broadway to Paris (1912) Melville
Ellis⁽ᶜ⁾; Max & Mahieu⁽ᶜ⁾; Young
Brothers⁽ˢ⁾
Broadway to Tokio (1900) Ernest
Albert⁽ˢ⁾; D. Frank Dodge⁽ˢ⁾; Henry E.
Hoyt⁽ˢ⁾
Broadway Whirl, The (1921)
Hickson⁽ᶜ⁾; ACK⁽ˢ⁾
Broken Branches (1922) ACK⁽ˢ⁾⁽ᶜ⁾⁽ᴸ⁾
Broken Chair, The (1929) Louis
Bromberg⁽ˢ⁾
Broken Dishes (1929) Eddie Eddy⁽ˢ⁾;
Theresa Shepherd⁽ᶜ⁾
Broken Glass (1994) Santo
Loquasto⁽ˢ⁾⁽ᶜ⁾; Brian Nason⁽ᴸ⁾
Broken Idol, A (1909) D. Frank
Dodge⁽ˢ⁾; ACK⁽ᶜ⁾
Broken Journey (1942) Raymond
Sovey⁽ˢ⁾; ACK⁽ᶜ⁾

Broken Threads (1917) Henri
Bendel[C]; Dodge and Castle[S];
Hickson[C]; Ack[L]

Broken Wing, The (1920) P. Dodd
Ackerman[S]; Lucile[C]

Bronx Express, The (1922) Mabel A.
Buell[S]; Ack[C]

Brook, The (1923) Ack[L]

Brooklyn Biarritz (1941) Frederick
Fox[S]; Ack[C]

Brooklyn, U.S.A. (1941) Howard
Bay[S]; Moe Hack[L]

Broomsticks, Amen! (1934) Tom
Adrian Cracraft[S]

Brother Cain (1941) Louis Kennel[S];
Ack[C]

Brother Elks (1925) Daniel J. Carey[L];
Ack[S][C]

Brother Jacques (1904) Ernest Gros[S];
Hitchins & Balcom[C]

Brother Officers (1900) Mrs. Robert
Osborn[C]

Brother Rat (1936) Cirker and
Robbins[S]; Ack[C]

Brother's Karamazov, The (1923)
Ack[L]

Brother's Karamazov, The (1927)
Fania Mindell[C]; Raymond Sovey[S]

Brothers (1928) Nicholas Yellenti[S];
Ack[C]

Brothers (1983) Craig Miller[L]; Merrily
Murray-Walsh[C]; Thomas A. Walsh[S]

Brown Buddies (1930) Theodore
Kahn[S]; Ed Sundquist[S]

Brown Danube (1938) John Root[S];
Ack[C]

Brown of Harvard (1906) Ack[C]

Brown Sugar (1937) Cirker and
Robbins[S]; Helene Pons[C]

Browning Version, The and A
Harlequinade (1949) David
Ffolkes[C]; Frederick Stover[S]

Brute, The (1912) None

Bubble, The (1915) None

Bubbling Brown Sugar (1976) Barry
Arnold[L]; Clarke Dunham[S]; Bernard
Johnson[C]

Buccaneer, The (1925) Robert Edmond
Jones[S][C][L]

Buck White (1969) Martin Aronstein[L];
Edward Burbridge[S]; Jean Pace[C]

Buckaroo (1929) R. N. Robbins[S];
Ack[C]

Buddies (1919) Ack[C][L]

Buddy: The Buddy Holly Story
(1990) Bill Butler[C]; Graham

McLusky[L]; Carolyn Smith[C]; Andy
Walmsley[S]

Budget, The (1932) P. Dodd
Ackerman[S]; Mildred Manning[C]

Bugle Call, The (1900) Walter Hann[S];
Madame Hayward[C]; Ack[C]

Builder of Bridges, The (1909) Unitt
and Wickes[S]

Builders, The (1907) Benjamin Craig[S];
Seyfried[S]

Bulldog Drummond (1921) Ack[C]

Bulls, Bears, and Asses (1932) Selma
Alexander[C]; Cleon Throckmorton[S]

Bully (1977) John Conklin[S][C]; Peter
Hunt[L]

Bully, The (1924) Ack[L]

Bunch and Judy, The (1922) Georges
Barbier[C]; Gates and Morange[S]; Paul
Poiret[C]; Ack[L]

Bunny (1916) Lucile[C]; Ack[L]

Bunty Pulls the Strings (1911)
Angel[C]; Mary Fisher[C]; H. Robert
Law[S]; Bert Tuchman[S]

Burgomaster of Belgium, A (1919)
John Brunton[S]; Ack[L]

Burgomaster, The (1900) None

Buried Child (1996) Robert Brill[S];
Allison Reeds[C]; Kevin Rigdon[L]

Burlesque (1927) Cleon
Throckmorton[S]; Ack[C]

Burlesque (1946) Grace Houston[C];
Robert Rowe Paddock[S]

Burmese Pwe, A (1926) Esther
Peck[S][C]; Ack[L]

Burn This (1987) John Lee Beatty[S];
Laura Crow[C]; Dennis Parichy[L]

Burning Bright (1950) Aline
Bernstein[C]; Jo Mielziner[S][L]

Burning Deck, The (1940) Harry
Horner[S]; Ack[C]

Burning Glass, The (1954) John
Davis[L]; Oliver Smith[S]; Noel
Taylor[C]; Valentina[C]

Bury the Dead (1936) Ack[S][C]

Bus Stop (1955) Boris Aronson[S]; Paul
Morrison[C][L]

Bus Stop (1996) Linda Fisher[C]; Hugh
Landwehr[S]; Dennis Parichy[L]

Business before Pleasure (1917)
Hickson[C]; Ack[L]

Business Is Business (1904) Ernest
Gros[S]

Business Widow, The (1923)
Woodman Thompson[S]; Ack[C]

Buster Brown (1905) None

Busybody, The (1924) Ack[L]

But for the Grace of God (1937) Stewart Chaney[S]

But Never Jam Today (1979) William Schroder[S][C]

But Not for Love (1934) Arthur P. Segal[S]; Virginia Volland[C]

But Not Goodbye (1944) Richard Whorf[S]

But, Seriously (1969) Jules Fisher[L]; Oliver Smith[S]; Pearl Somner[C]; Stavropoulos[C]

Butley (1972) Eileen Diss[S]; Neil Peter Jampolis[C][L]

Butter and Egg Man, The (1925) Raymond Sovey[S]; ACK[C]

Butterflies Are Free (1969) Jules Fisher[L]; Robert Mackintosh[C]; Richard Seger[S]

Butterfly on the Wheel, A (1912) Lucile[C]; ACK[S]

Button, Button (1929) ACK[S][C][L]

Buttons on Broadway (1995) Ken Billington[L]; Nancy Thun[S]

Buttrio Square (1952) Sal Anthony[C]; Samuel Leve[S][L]

Buy Me Blue Ribbons (1951) Jack Landau[S][C]; ACK[L]

Buy, Buy, Baby (1926) ACK[C][L]

Buzzard, The (1928) ACK[L]

Buzzin' Around (1920) Margery Price[C]; Madame Pulliche[C]; ACK[L]

By Jupiter (1942) Jo Mielziner[S][L]; Irene Sharaff[C]

By Pigeon Post (1918) Joseph Urban[S]

By Request (1928) ACK[L]

By the Beautiful Sea (1954) Jo Mielziner[S][L]; Irene Sharaff[C]

By the Way (1925) Guy DeGerald[C]; ACK[S][L]

By Your Leave (1934) Jo Mielziner[S][L]; Margaret Pemberton[C]

Bye, Bye, Barbara (1924) Walter Schaffner[S]; William Weaver[C]; ACK[L]

Bye, Bye, Birdie (1960) Peggy Clark[L]; Robert Randolph[S]; Miles White[C]

Bye, Bye, Bonnie (1927) Helen Mahieu[C]; Herbert Ward[S]; ACK[L]

C.O.D. (1912) ACK[S]

Cabalagata (a.k.a. A Night in Spain) (1949) Daniel Cordoba[C]; Luis Márquez[S]; ACK[L]

Cabaret (1966) Boris Aronson[S]; Jean Rosenthal[L]; Patricia Zipprodt[S]

Cabaret (1987) David Chapman[S]; Marc B. Weiss[L]; Patricia Zipprodt[C]

Cabaret (1998) Mike Baldassari[L];

Robert Brill[S]; Peggy Eisenhauer[L]; William Ivey Long[C]

Cabin in the Sky (1940) Boris Aronson[S][C]

Cactus Flower (1965) Theoni V. Aldredge[C]; Martin Aronstein[L]; Oliver Smith[S]

Cadet Girl, The (1900) D. Frank Dodge[S]; Archie Gunn[C]; Edward La Moss[S]

Caesar and Cleopatra (1906) Joseph Harker[S]; J. McCreery[S]; T. E. Ryan[S]

Caesar and Cleopatra (1913) NONE

Caesar and Cleopatra (1925) Aline Bernstein[C]; Frederick W. Jones III[S]

Caesar and Cleopatra (1949) Rolf Gérard[S][C]; Jean Rosenthal[L]

Caesar and Cleopatra (1951) Audrey Cruddas[C]; Roger Furse[S]; ACK[L]

Caesar and Cleopatra (1977) Jane Greenwood[C]; Ming Cho Lee[S]; Thomas Skelton[L]

Café (1930) Jo Mielziner[S][L]

Café De Danse (1929) ACK[L]

Cafe Crown (1942) Boris Aronson[S]; ACK[C]

Cafe Crown (1963) Samuel Leve[L]

Cafe Crown (1964) Samuel Leve[S]; Ruth Morley[C]

Cafe Crown (1989) Santo Loquasto[S][C]; Richard Nelson[L]

Cain (1925) Elizabeth Stuart Close[C]; Bassett Jones[S][C][L]; Alexander Wyckoff[S][C]

Caine Mutiny Court Martial, The (1954) ACK[L]

Caine Mutiny Court Martial, The (1983) John Falabella[S]; David Murin[C]; Richard Nelson[L]

Calculated Risk (1962) Mary McKinley[C]; Tharon Musser[L]; Robert Randolph[S]

Caleb West (1900) Frisbie & Mayerhofer[L]; William Kellam[S]; John H. Young[S]

Caliban by the Yellow Sands (1916) Robert Edmond Jones[S][C]

Calico Wedding (1945) Frederick Fox[S]

California Suite (1976) Jane Greenwood[C]; Tharon Musser[L]; William Ritman[S]

Caligula (1960) Will Steven Armstrong[S][C]; Jean Rosenthal[L]

Call It a Day (1936) Lee Simonson[S]; ACK[C]

Call Me Madam (1950) Raoul Pène Du Bois[(S)(C)]; Mainbocher[(C)]; ACK[(L)]
Call Me Mister (1946) Grace Houston[(C)]; Lester Polakov[(S)]
Call Me Ziggy (1937) Clarke Robinson[(S)]; ACK[(C)]
Call of Life, The (1925) Jo Mielziner[(S)(L)]
Call of the Cricket, The (1910) NONE
Call of the North, The (1908) Joseph Physioc[(S)]
Call on Kuprin, A (1961) Florence Klotz[(C)]; Donald Oenslager[(S)(L)]
Call the Doctor (1920) Henri Bendel[(C)]; Alexander Grinager[(S)]; Victor Petry[(S)]; ACK[(L)]
Calling All Stars (1934) A. H. Feder[(L)]; Nat Karson[(S)]; Billy Livingston[(C)]
Cambridge Circus (1964) Judy Birdwood[(C)]; Robert Darling[(L)]; Stephen Mullin[(S)]
Camel Through the Needle's Eye (1929) Lee Simonson[(S)(C)(L)]
Camel's Back, The (1923) Clifford F. Pember[(S)]; ACK[(C)]
Camelot (1960) Gilbert Adrian[(C)]; Tony Duquette[(C)]; A. H. Feder[(L)]; Oliver Smith[(S)]
Camelot (1980) Desmond Heeley[(S)(C)]; Thomas Skelton[(L)]
Camelot (1981) Desmond Heeley[(S)(C)]; Thomas Skelton[(L)]
Camelot (1993) Neil Peter Jampolis[(S)(L)]; Franne Lee[(C)]
Camels Are Coming, The (1931) ACK[(L)]
Cameo Kirby (1909) Maurice Hermann[(C)]
Camille (1904) Robert T. McKee[(S)]
Camille (1908) ACK[(S)(C)]
Camille (1911) NONE
Camille (1931) Robert Edmond Jones[(S)(C)(L)]
Camille (1932) Robert Edmond Jones[(S)]; Hilya Nordmark[(C)]
Camille (1935) Aline Bernstein[(S)(C)]; ACK[(L)]
Camino Real (1953) Lemuel Ayers[(S)(C)(L)]
Can-Can (1953) Jo Mielziner[(S)(L)]; Motley[(C)]
Can-Can (1981) David Mitchell[(S)]; Thomas Skelton[(L)]; Franca Squarciapino[(C)]
Canaries Sometimes Sing (1930) ACK[(C)(L)]

Canary Cottage (1917) Madame Keeler[(C)]; Robert McQuinn[(S)(C)]; ACK[(L)]
Canary Dutch (1925) Louis Hartmann[(L)]; Joseph Wickes[(S)]; ACK[(C)]
Canary, The (1918) Joseph Urban[(S)]; ACK[(C)(L)]
Candida (1903) NONE
Candida (1905) NONE
Candida (1907) NONE
Candida (1915) ACK[(L)]
Candida (1922) Fania Mindell[(S)]; ACK[(L)]
Candida (1924) Woodman Thompson[(S)]; ACK[(C)(L)]
Candida (1925) Daniel J. Carey[(L)]; Woodman Thompson[(S)(C)]
Candida (1937) Woodman Thompson[(S)(C)]
Candida (1942) Woodman Thompson[(S)(C)]
Candida (1946) Woodman Thompson[(S)]
Candida (1952) Motley[(C)]; Donald Oenslager[(S)]
Candida (1970) John Braden[(S)]; John Gleason[(L)]; Miles White[(C)]
Candida (1981) Kenneth Foy[(S)]; Paul Gallo[(L)]; Richard Hornung[(C)]
Candida (1993) Jess Goldstein[(C)]; David Jenkins[(S)]; Peter Kaczorowski[(L)]
Candide (1933) Pauline Lawrence[(C)]
Candide (1956) Paul Morrison[(L)]; Irene Sharaff[(C)]; Oliver Smith[(S)]
Candide (1974) Eugene Lee[(S)]; Franne Lee[(C)]; Tharon Musser[(L)]
Candide (1997) Ken Billington[(L)]; Judith Dolan[(C)]; Clarke Dunham[(S)]
Candle in the Wind (1941) Jo Mielziner[(S)(L)]; Valentina[(C)]
Candle-Light (1929) Chanel[(C)]; Jean Patou[(C)]; ACK[(L)]
Candy Shop, The (1909) Homer Emens[(S)]; John H. Young[(S)]; ACK[(C)]
Canterbury Tales (1969) Derek Cousins[(S)]; Jules Fisher[(L)]; Loudon Sainthill[(C)]
Canterbury Tales (1980) Michael Anania[(S)]; Sigrid Insull[(C)]; Gregg Marriner[(L)]
Cantilevered Terrace (1962) Paul Morrison[(S)(C)(L)]
Cap't Jinks of the Horse Marines (1938) Ben Edwards[(S)(C)]; A. H. Feder[(L)]
Cape Cod Folks (1906) Gates and Morange[(S)]; ACK[(L)]
Cape Cod Follies (1929) Rollo

Wayne[S]; ACK[C]

Cape Smoke (1925) William E. Price[L]; ACK[S][C]

Capeman, The (1998) Bob Crowley[S][C]; Natasha Katz[L]

Caponsacchi (1926) Claude Bragdon[S][C]

Caponsacchi (1928) Claude Bragdon[S][C]

Caponsacchi (1929) Claude Bragdon[S][C]

Cappy Ricks (1919) Hickson[C]; ACK[L]

Caprice (1928) Aline Bernstein[S]; ACK[C]

Captain Applejack (1921) Henri Bendel[C]; Helen Dryden[C]; Samuel Lorber[C]

Captain Barrington (1903) John H. Young[S]

Captain Brassbound's Conversion (1915) Elizabeth Axtman[C]; ACK[S][L]

Captain Brassbound's Conversion (1950) Ben Edwards[S][L]; Germinal Rangel[C]

Captain Brassbound's Conversion (1972) Michael Annals[S]; William H. Batchelder[L]; Sara Brook[C]

Captain Dieppe (1903) Homer Emens[S]; Edward G. Unitt[S]

Captain Jinks (1925) Frederick W. Jones III[S]; Yetta Kiviette[C]

Captain Jinks of the Horse Marines (1901) Percy Anderson[C]; Edward G. Unitt[S]

Captain Kidd, Jr. (1916) ACK[L]

Captain Molly (1902) Gates and Morange[S]; Maurice Hermann[C]; ACK[C]

Captain's Brassbound's Conversion (1907) Frank Platzer[S]

Captains and the Kings, The (1962) James Trittipo[S][C][L]

Captive, The (1926) William E. Castle[S]; Evelyn McHorter[C]; ACK[C]

Caravan (1928) P. Dodd Ackerman[S]

Cardinal's Edict, The (1905) NONE

Career Angel (1944) Frederick Fox[L]; Carl Kent[S]; ACK[C]

Caretaker, The (1964) Brian Currah[S]; Marvin March[L]; ACK[C]

Caretaker, The (1986) John Malkovich[C]; Kevin Rigdon[S][L]

Carib Song (1945) Jo Mielziner[S][L]; Motley[C]

Caribbean Carnival (1947) Herbert Brodkin[S]; Lou Eisele[C]; ACK[L]

Carmelina (1979) Donald Brooks[C]; A.

H. Feder[L]; Oliver Smith[S]

Carmen (1905) W. T. Hemsley[S][C]; Mrs. Nettleship[C]

Carmen (1908) W. T. Hemsley[S][C]; Mrs. Nettleship[C]

Carmen Amaya and Her Company (1955) ACK[L]

Carmen Jones (1943) Howard Bay[S]; Raoul Pène Du Bois[C]; Hassard Short[L]

Carmencita and the Soldiers (1925) Isaac Rabinovitch[S][C]

Carnival (1919) P. Dodd Ackerman[S]; Henri Bendel[C]; ACK[L]

Carnival (1924) Lee Simonson[S][L]; ACK[C]

Carnival (1929) Lee Simonson[S]; Bruce Stuios[C]

Carnival (1961) Will Steven Armstrong[S][L]; Freddy Wittop[C]

Carnival in Flanders (1953) Lucinda Ballard[C]; Oliver Smith[S]

Caroline (1923) Watson Barratt[S]; ACK[C]

Carousel (1945) Jo Mielziner[S][L]; Miles White[C]

Carousel (1994) Bob Crowley[S][C]; Paul Pyant[L]

Carpetbagger, The (1900) NONE

Carrie (1988) Terry Hands[L]; Ralph Koltai[S]; Alexander Reid[C]

Carrie Nation (1932) Charles E. Boss[S]; Elizabeth Higgins Sullivan[C]

Carrots (1902) Edward G. Unitt[S]

Carry Me Back to Morningside Heights (1968) Kert Lundell[S][C][L]

Carry On (1928) Livingston Platt[S]; ACK[C]

Casanova (1923) Georges Barbier[S][C]

Case History (1938) James Morcom[S]; ACK[C]

Case of Arson, A (1906) NONE

Case of Becky, The (1912) Ernest Gros[S]; Louis Hartmann[L]

Case of Clyde Griffiths, The (1936) Watson Barratt[S]; Pierre Du Bois[C]

Case of Frenzied Finance, A (1905) NONE

Case of Lady Camber, The (1917) Henri Bendel[C]; Homer Emens[S]; ACK[L]

Case of Libel, A (1963) Donald Oenslager[S][L]; Ann Roth[C]

Case of Phillip Lawrence, The (1937) ACK[S]

Case of Rebellious Susan, The (1905)

Ack[C]

Case of Youth, A (1940) A. A. Ostrander[S]; Ack[C]

Casey Jones (1938) Michael Gordon[L]; Mordecai Gorelik[S]; Mildred Manning[C]

Cashel Byron's Profession (1900) Peter W. King[L]; Joseph Physioc[S]

Cashel Byron's Profession (1906) Joseph Physioc[S]

Casino Girl, The (1900) Ernest Albert[S]; D. Frank Dodge[S]

Caste (1910) No PLAYBILL

Caste (1927) Henri Bendel[C]; Herbert Ward[S]

Castles in the Air (1926) P. Dodd Ackerman[S]; John N. Booth, Jr.[C]; DuWico[L]; Ralph L. Moni[C]; Hugh Willoughby[S]

Cat and the Canary, The (1922) Ashmead Eldridge Scott[S]; Ack[C][L]

Cat and the Canary, The (1937) Barney Turner[S]; Ack[C]

Cat and the Fiddle, The (1931) Henry Dreyfuss[S]; Yetta Kiviette[C]; Constance Ripley[C]; Ack[L]

Cat Bird, The (1920) Lee Simonson[S]; Ack[L]

Cat on a Hot Tin Roof (1955) Lucinda Ballard[C]; Jo Mielziner[S][L]

Cat on a Hot Tin Roof (1974) John Conklin[S]; Jane Greenwood[C]; Marc B. Weiss[L]

Cat on a Hot Tin Roof (1990) William Dudley[S]; Mark Henderson[L]; Patricia Zipprodt[C]

Cat Screams, The (1942) Mary Grant[C]; John Root[S]

Catch a Star (1955) Ralph Alswang[S]; Thomas Becher[C]

Catch Me If You Can (1965) George Jenkins[S][L]; Peter Joseph[C]

Catch of the Season, The (1905) Ernest Gros[S]

Catherine Was Great (1944) Howard Bay[S]; Mary Percy Schenck[C]; Ernest Schraps[C]

Cats (1982) David Hersey[L]; John Napier[S][C]

Catskill Dutch (1924) Livingston Platt[S]

Catskills on Broadway (1991) Peggy Eisenhauer[L]; Lawrence Miller[S]; Ack[C]

Caucasian Chalk Circle (1966) Richard Nelson[L]; James Hart

Stearns[S][C]

Caught (1925) Jo Mielziner[S][L]

Caught in the Rain (1906) NONE

Caught Wet (1931) Cirker and Robbins[S]; Ack[C]

Cavalier, The (1902) Frank E. Gates[S]; Edward Morange[S]; Franklin Van Horn[C]

Cave Dwellers, The (1957) Ruth Morley[C]; William Pitkin[S]; Lee Watson[L]

Cave Girl, The (1920) Charles Howard[C]; Unitt and Wickes[S]

Cave Man, The (1911) NONE

Caviar (1934) Steele Savage[S][C]; Joseph Teichner Studio[S]

Ceiling Zero (1935) John Root[S]

Celebrated Case, A (1915) Henri Bendel[C]; Homer Emens[S]; Ack[C][L]

Celebration (1969) Ed Wittstein[S][C][L]

Celebrity (1927) William E. Castle[S]; Rose Keane[C]; Ack[L]

Cemetery Club, The (1990) John Lee Beatty[S]; Lindsay W. Davis[C]; Natasha Katz[L]

Censor and the Dramatists, The (1913) No PLAYBILL

Censored (1938) Nicholas Yellenti[S]

Censored Scenes from King Kong (1980) Richard Nelson[L]; Mike Porter[S]; Jennifer von Mayrhauser[C]

Centuries (1927) John Dos Passos[S]

Century Girl, The (1916) Marie Cooke[C]; Raphael Kirchner[C]; Cora MacGeachy[C]; William Henry Matthews[C]; Joseph Urban[S]; Ack[L]

Century Revue, The (1920) Homer Conant[S][C]

'Ception Shoals (1917) Clifford F. Pember[S]; Ack[L]

Certain Party, A (1911) Owen Hitchins[C]; Lucile[C]; Max & Mahieu[C]

Chains (1912) Ack[S]

Chairs, The (1998) Paul Anderson[L]; Quay Brothers[S][C]

Chalk Dust (1936) Howard Bay[S]; Ack[C]

Chalk Garden, The (1955) Cecil Beaton[S][C]; Raymond Sovey[L]

Chalked Out (1937) Margaret Pemberton[C]; John Root[S]

Challenge of Youth, The (1930) P. Dodd Ackerman[S]; Madame Sara[C]; Villi[C]

Challenge, The (1919) Henri Bendel[C];

ACK[L]

Chamberlain Brown's Scrapbook
(1932) ACK[L]

Chameleon, The (1932) ACK[L]

Champagne Complex (1955) Charles
Elson[S][C][L]

Champagne Sec (1933) Jo
Mielziner[S][L]; ACK[C]

Champion, The (1921) NONE

Change (1914) NONE

Change in the Heir (1990) Michael
Anania[S]; Jeff Davis[L]; David
Murin[C]

Change Your Luck (1930) Norman Bel
Geddes[S][C]; Hilda Farnham[C]

Changelings, The (1923) ACK[C][L]

Changing Room, The (1973) Whitney
Blausen[C]; David Jenkins[S]; Ronald
Wallace[L]

Channel Road, The (1929) Robert
Edmond Jones[S][C]; ACK[L]

Chantecler (1911) John Alexander[S];
Alexander Grinager[S]; J. Monroe
Hewlett[S]; ACK[C]

Chaperons, The (1902) Archie Gunn[C];
Joseph Physioc[S]

Chaperons, The (1908) Ernest Albert[S]

Chapter Two (1977) Tharon Musser[L];
William Ritman[S]; Noel Taylor[C]

Charity Girl, The (1912) NONE

Charlatan, The (1922) Henri Bendel[C];
Robert W. Bergman Studio[S]; ACK[L]

Charles I (1906) NONE

Charley's Aunt (1906) ACK[S][C][L]

Charley's Aunt (1925) ACK[L]

Charley's Aunt (1940) John
Koenig[S][C]; ACK[L]

Charley's Aunt (1970) Richard
Anderson[C]; F. Mitchell Dana[L];
Robert T. Williams[S]

Charlie and Algernon (1980) Kate
Edmunds[S]; Jess Goldstein[C]; Hugh
Lester[L]

Charlot Revue (1925) Marc Henri[S];
Laverdet[S]; ACK[C][L]

Charlotte (1980) Pat Collins[L]; Lester
Polakov[S]; Patricia Zipprodt[C]

Charm (1929) ACK[L]

Charm of Isabel, The (1914) H.
Robert Law[S]; Bert Tuchman[S]

Charm School, The (1920) Gordon
Conway[C]; ACK[L]

Chase, The (1952) George Bockman[C];
Albert R. Johnson[S]

Chastening, The (1923) Grace O.
Clarke[C]; Woodman Thompson[S];

ACK[L]

Chauve Souris (1922) Nicholas
Remisoff[S][C]; Sergi Soudeikine[S][C];
ACK[L]

Chauve Souris (1925) Alexander
Benois[C]; Nicholas Benois[C]; Nicholas
Remisoff[S]; Herman Rosse[C]; Vassily
Shoukhoeff[S][C]; Sergi Soudeikine[S]

Chauve Souris (1927) M.
Dobuzhinsky[S]; Nicholas Remisoff[S];
Sergi Soudeikine[S][C]; ACK[L]

Chauve Souris (1929) Nicholas
Remisoff[S]; Sergi Soudeikine[S][C];
ACK[L]

Chauve Souris: 1943 (1943) Sergi
Soudeikine[S][C]

Cheaper to Marry (1924) Raymond
Sovey[S]

Cheater, The (1910) NONE

Cheaters (1978) Ian Calderon[L]; Jane
Greenwood[C]; Lawrence King[S]

Cheating Cheaters (1916) ACK[C][L]

Checkerboard, The (1920) ACK[L]

Checkers (1903) Joseph Physioc[S]

Checking Out (1976) Ken Billington[L];
David Jenkins[S]; Carol Luiken[C]

Checkmates (1988) Edward
Burbridge[S]; Judy Dearing[C]; Ronald
Wallace[L]

Chee-Chee (1928) John N. Booth, Jr.[C];
John Hawkins[S]; James Reynolds[C];
ACK[L]

Cheer Up (1913) NONE

Cheer-up (Hippodrome) (1917) Will
R. Barnes[C]; Joseph Elsner[L]; H.
Robert Law[S]; Mark Lawson[S];
Katherine H. Lovell[C]; William Henry
Matthews[C]; Robert McQuinn[C];
Gladys Monkhouse[C]

Chemin De Fer (1973) Ken
Billington[L]; Edward Burbridge[S];
Nancy Potts[C]

Cheri (1959) Peggy Clark[L]; Oliver
Smith[S]; Miles White[C]

Cherokee Night (1937) Samuel Leve[S];
Mary Merrill[C]; ACK[L]

Cherry Blossoms (1927) Watson
Barratt[S]; Ernest Schraps[C]

Cherry Orchard, The (1923) ACK[L]

Cherry Orchard, The (1928) Aline
Bernstein[S][C]; James B. Fagan[S]

Cherry Orchard, The (1929) Aline
Bernstein[S]; ACK[L]

Cherry Orchard, The (1933) Aline
Bernstein[S][C]

Cherry Orchard, The (1944)

Motley[(S)(C)]

Cherry Orchard, The (1968) Nancy Potts[(C)]; James Tilton[(S)(L)]

Cherry Orchard, The (1970) Richard Davis[(S)]; Pat Simmons[(L)]; Ross B. Young[(C)]

Cherry Orchard, The (1977) Santo Loquasto[(S)(C)]; Jennifer Tipton[(L)]

Cherry Orchard, The (1997) Pavel Kaplevich[(S)]; Peter Kirillov[(S)]; Efim Udler[(L)]; Vyacheslav Zaitsev[(C)]

Chess (1988) Theoni V. Aldredge[(C)]; David Hersey[(L)]; Robin Wagner[(S)]

Chicago (1926) DuWico[(L)]; William Oden Waller[(S)]; Ack[(C)]

Chicago (1975) Jules Fisher[(L)]; Tony Walton[(S)]; Patricia Zipprodt[(C)]

Chicago (1996) John Lee Beatty[(S)]; Ken Billington[(L)]; William Ivey Long[(C)]

Chicken Every Sunday (1944) Howard Bay[(S)(L)]; Rose Bogdanoff[(C)]

Chicken Feed (1923) P. Dodd Ackerman[(S)]; Ack[(C)]

Chief Thing, The (1926) Kate Drain Lawson[(S)]; Sergi Soudeikine[(S)(C)]

Chief, The (1915) Homer Emens[(S)]; Ack[(L)]

Chiffon Girl, The (1924) Ack[(S)(C)(L)]

Child of Fortune (1956) Robert O'Hearn[(S)(L)]; William Pitkin[(C)]

Child of Manhattan (1932) Jonel Jorgulesco[(S)]; Ack[(C)]

Child of Nature, A (1908) None

Child's Play (1970) Sara Brook[(C)]; Jo Mielziner[(S)(L)]

Children from Their Games (1963) Ann Roth[(C)]; Oliver Smith[(S)(L)]

Children of a Lesser God (1980) Tharon Musser[(L)]; Nancy Potts[(C)]; Thomas A. Walsh[(S)]

Children of Darkness (1930) Robert Edmond Jones[(S)(C)]; Ack[(L)]

Children of Destiny (1910) H. Robert Law[(S)]

Children of Earth (1915) Franklin Booth[(S)]; John A. Higham[(L)]; Frances Willard[(C)]; Ack[(S)(C)(L)]

Children of Kings, The (1902) Ack[(S)(C)]

Children of the Ghetto (1899) Charles Bingham[(L)]; Frank E. Gates[(S)]; Edward Morange[(S)]

Children of the Moon (1923) Cleon Throckmorton[(S)]; Ack[(L)]

Children of the Wind (1973) Sara Brook[(C)]; Leo Kerz[(S)(L)]

Children of Today (1913) No Playbill

Children! Children! (1972) Jo Mielziner[(S)(L)]; Ann Roth[(C)]

Children's Hour (1934) Aline Bernstein[(S)]; Ack[(C)]

Children's Hour, The (1953) Howard Bay[(S)]; Anna Hill Johnstone[(C)]

Children's Tragedy, The (1921) Livingston Platt[(S)]

Chimes of Normandy, The (1931) Ack[(C)(L)]

Chin-Chin (1914) Ack[(C)]

China Doll, A (1904) None

China Rose (1925) Walter Schaffner[(S)]; Ack[(C)(L)]

Chinese Coffee (1992) Zack Brown[(S)(C)]; Arden Fingerhut[(L)]

Chinese Honeymoon, A (1902) D. Frank Dodge[(S)]; Mrs. Caroline Siedle[(C)]

Chinese Nightingale, The (1934) Sergi Soudeikine[(S)(C)]

Chinese O'Neill (1929) Captain Cushing Donnell[(S)(C)]

Chinese Prime Minister, The (1964) Jean Rosenthal[(L)]; Oliver Smith[(S)]; Valentina[(C)]

Chinese, The/ Dr. Fish (1970) Martin Aronstein[(L)]; Sara Brook[(C)]; William Pitkin[(S)]

Chippies (1929) Ack[(L)]

Chips with Everything (1963) Jocelyn Herbert[(S)(C)(L)]

Chivalry (1925) R. Forester[(S)]; Ack[(L)]

Chocolate Dandies, The (1924) John N. Booth, Jr.[(S)]; Booth-Willoughby[(S)]; Anthony Greshoff[(L)]; Yetta Kiviette[(C)]

Chocolate Soldier, The (1909) Hugo Baruch[(S)]; Unitt and Wickes[(S)]

Chocolate Soldier, The (1921) Rollo Wayne[(S)]; Ack[(C)]

Chocolate Soldier, The (1930) Rollo Wayne[(S)]; Ack[(C)]

Chocolate Soldier, The (1931) Ack[(C)(L)]

Chocolate Soldier, The (1934) Ack[(C)(L)]

Chocolate Soldier, The (1942) Paul du Pont[(C)]; Eugene Dunkel[(S)]

Chocolate Soldier, The (1947) Lucinda Ballard[(C)]; Jo Mielziner[(S)(L)]

Chorus Lady, The (1906) Joseph Physioc[(S)]

Chorus Line, A (1975) Theoni V. Aldredge[(C)]; Tharon Musser[(L)]; Robin Wagner[(S)]

Chosen People, The (1912) NONE
Chris and the Wonderful Lamp
(1900) F. Richards Anderson[C];
Homer Emens[S]; Gates and
Morange[S]; Ernest Gros[S]; H.
Harndin[L]
Christian Pilgrim, The (1907)
Hermann Burghart[S]; Homer
Emens[S]; Gates and Morange[S];
Ernest Gros[S]; Kliegl Brothers[L];
Benjamin Leffler[C]
Christine (1960) Alvin Colt[C]; Jo
Mielziner[S][L]
Christmas Carol, A (1990) Ben
Edwards[S]; Jane Greenwood[C]
Christmas Carol, A (1994) Peggy
Eisenhauer[L]; Jules Fisher[L]; William
Ivey Long[C]; Tony Walton[S]
Christmas Carol, A (1995) Jules
Fisher[L]; William Ivey Long[C]; Tony
Walton[S]
Christmas Carol, A (1996) Peggy
Eisenhauer[L]; Jules Fisher[L]; William
Ivey Long[C]; Tony Walton[S]
Christmas Carol, A (1997) Peggy
Eisenhauer[L]; Jules Fisher[L]; William
Ivey Long[C]; Tony Walton[S]
Christmas Carol, A (1998) Peggy
Eisenhauer[L]; Jules Fisher[L]; William
Ivey Long[C]; Tony Walton[S]
Christmas Carol, A (Stewart) (1991)
Fred Allen[L]
Christmas Carol, A (Stewart) (1992)
Fred Allen[L]
Christmas Carol, A (Stewart) (1994)
Fred Allen[L]
Christmas Eve (1939) Jo
Mielziner[S][C][L]
Christmas Spectacular (1988) Charles
Lisanby[S]; Frank Spencer[C]
Christmas Spectacular (1991) Ken
Billington[L]; Jose Lengson[C]; Charles
Lisanby[S]; Pete Menefee[C]; Frank
Spencer[C]
Christmas Spectacular, The (1988)
Ken Billington[L]
Christmas Spectacular, The (1990)
Ken Billington[L]; Jose Lengson[C];
Charles Lisanby[S]; Pete Menefee[C];
Frank Spencer[C]
Christopher Blake (1946) Harry
Horner[S][L]; Leo Kerz[L]; Bianca
Stroock[C]
Christopher Comes Across (1932)
Dale Stetson[S][C]
Chronicle of a Death Foretold (1995)

Christopher Barreca[S]; Beverly
Emmons[L]; Jules Fisher[L]; Toni-Leslie
James[C]
Chu Chem (1989) Robert Mitchell[S];
Jason Sturm[L]; Kenneth M. Yount[C]
Chu Chin Chow (1917) Percy
Anderson[C]; Paul Bismarck[L]; Joseph
and Phil Harker[S]
Church Mouse, A (1931) Margaret
Pemberton[C]; Livingston Platt[S];
ACK[L]
Church Mouse, A (1933) George
Allgier[S]; ACK[C]
Chyrasalis (1932) Cleon
Throckmorton[S]; ACK[C]
Cigarette Maker's Romance, A
(1902) Angel[C]; Rose le Quesne[C];
ACK[S]
Cinderelative (1930) ACK[L]
Cinderella (1993) Henry Bardon[S];
Gregg Barnes[C]; Jeff Davis[L]
Cinderella (1995) Henry Bardon[S];
Gregg Barnes[C]; Jeff Davis[L]
Cinderella Man, The (1916) ACK[L]
Cinderella on Broadway (1920)
Watson Barratt[S]; Homer Conant[S][C];
Madame Haverstick[C]; Cora
MacGeachy[C]; S. Zalud[C]; ACK[L]
Cinders (1923) Evelyn McHorter[C];
Paul Poiret[C]; ACK[S][L]
Cingalee, The (1904) Percy
Anderson[C]; John H. Young[S]
Cipher Code, The (1901) NONE
Circle, The (1921) Lucile[C]; Clifford F.
Pember[S]
Circle, The (1938) Hattie Carnegie[C];
Donald Oenslager[S]
Circle, The (1989) J. Michael Deegan[L];
Jane Greenwood[C]; Desmond Heeley[S]
Circus Princess, The (1927) Watson
Barratt[S]; Ernest Schraps[C]
Citizen's Home, A (1909) P. Dodd
Ackerman[S]
Citta Morta, La (1902) NONE
City Haul (1929) Murray Mayer[C];
ACK[S][L]
City of Angels (1989) Paul Gallo[L];
Florence Klotz[C]; Robin Wagner[S]
City, The (1909) H. Robert Law[S]
Civic Light Opera Company Season
(1935) ACK[L]
Civil War, The (1999) Paul Gallo[L];
William Ivey Long[C]; Douglas W.
Schmidt[S]
Civilian Clothes (1919) ACK[C][L]
Claim, The (1917) Elizabeth

Axtman(S)(C); Caroline Dudley(S)(C); Gertrude Newell(S)(C)

Clair De Lune (1921) John Barrymore(S); E. Lyall Swete(S); ACK(C)

Claire Adams (1929) Redington Sharpe(S); ACK(C)

Clansman, The (1906) Meixner(S); Frank Platzer(S)

Clarence (1919) Anthony Greshoff(L); Clifford F. Pember(S); Anna Spencer(C)

Clarice (1906) Ernest Gros(S); Mrs. Robert Osborn(C)

Clash by Night (1941) Boris Aronson(S); E. Carlton Winckler(L); ACK(C)

Class Act, A (2001) Kevin Adams(L); James Noone(S); Carrie F. Robbins(C)

Class of '29 (1936) Tom Adrian Cracraft(S)

Classmates (1907) Joseph Physioc(S)

Claudia (1941) Donald Oenslager(S); Bianca Stroock(C); ACK(C)

Claw, The (1921) Robert Edmond Jones(S); ACK(C)

Claw, The (1927) Robert Edmond Jones(S); ACK(C)

Clean Beds (1939) Watson Barratt(S)

Clean Slate, A (1903) ACK(S)(C)

Clear All Wires (1932) Aline Bernstein(S)(C)

Clearing in the Woods, A (1957) Lucinda Ballard(C); A. H. Feder(L); Oliver Smith(S)

Cleavage (1982) Paul de Pass(L); Michael J. Hotopp(L); James M. Miller(C); Carol Oditz(C); Morris Taylor(S)

Clever Ones, The (1915) C. Tomlinson Dare(C); Madame Najla Nogabgat(C); ACK(S)(L)

Climate of Eden, The (1952) Kenn Barr(C); Frederick Fox(S); Jean Rosenthal(L)

Climax, The (1909) NONE

Climax, The (1910) NONE

Climax, The (1919) ACK(L)

Climax, The (1926) P. Dodd Ackerman(S); Benjamin Leffler(L)

Climax, The (1933) ACK(C)(L)

Climbers, The (1901) Ernest Albert(S); Joseph Physioc(S)

Clinging Vine, The (1922) William E. Castle(S); Peggy Hoyt(C); Joseph Wilson(L)

Cloister, The (1921) Sheldon K. Viele(S)(C)

Close Harmony (1924) Woodman Thompson(S)

Close Quarters (1939) Watson Barratt(S)

Closer (1999) Vicki Mortimer(S)(C); Hugh Vanstone(L)

Closing Door, The (1949) Paul Morrison(S)(L); Robert Ten Eyck Stevenson(C)

Clothes (1906) H. Robert Law(S); Robert T. McKee(S); Franklin Van Horn(C); ACK(C)

Clothes for a Summer Hotel (1980) Theoni V. Aldredge(C); Marilyn Rennagel(L); Oliver Smith(S)

Cloud 7 (1958) Alice Gibson(C); Albert R. Johnson(S)(L)

Clouds (1925) ACK(L)

Clouds, The (1911) NONE

Cloudy with Showers (1931) Raymond Sovey(S); ACK(C)

Clubs Are Trumps (1924) ACK(S)(C)(L)

Clutching Claw, The (1928) DuWico(L); ACK(S)

Clutterbuck (1949) Alvin Colt(C); Samuel Leve(S); ACK(L)

Co-Respondent Unknown (1936) Jo Mielziner(S)(L); ACK(C)

Co-Respondent, The (1916) Harry Collins(C); Dodge and Castle(S); ACK(L)

Coastal Disturbances (1987) Susan Hilferty(C); Dennis Parichy(L); Bob Shaw(S)

Coastwise (1931) Karle O. Amend(S); ACK(L)

Coat-Tales (1916) ACK(C)(L)

Cobra (1924) Peggy Hoyt(C); ACK(S)(C)(L)

Cock O' the Roost (1924) Livingston Platt(S); ACK(C)

Cock O' the Walk (1915) Homer Emens(S); Hickson(C)

Cock Robin (1928) A. S. Fishback(C); Jo Mielziner(S)(L)

Cock-a-doodle Dandy (1969) Nancy Potts(C); James Tilton(S)(L)

Cocktail Party (1950) Raymond Sovey(S)(L); ACK(C)

Cocktail Party, The (1968) Nancy Potts(C); James Tilton(S)(L)

Coco (1969) Cecil Beaton(S)(C); Thomas Skelton(L)

Cocoanuts, The (1925) Charles LeMaire(C); Woodman Thompson(S)

Coggerers, The/Mr. Banks of Birmin/The Red Velvet Coat (1939) Manuel Essman(S)

Coggerers, The/The Red Velvet Coat/Mr. Banks of Birmin (1939)

NONE
Cohan and Harris Minstrels (1908)
NONE
Cohan and Harris Minstrels (1909)
NONE
Cohan Revue of 1918, The (1917)
ACK(S)(C)(L)
Cohan Revue, The (1916) Lucile(C);
Cora MacGeachy(C); ACK(S)(L)
Cold Feet (1923) ACK(S)(C)(L)
Cold in Sables (1931) P. Dodd
Ackerman(S); ACK(C)
Cold Storage (1977) Karl Eigsti(S)(C);
William Mintzer(L)
Cold Wind and the Warm, The
(1958) Boris Aronson(S); A. H.
Feder(L); Motley(C)
Colin Quinn - An Irish Wake (1998)
Eugene Lee(S)(C); Roger Morgan(L)
Collector's Item (1952) Charles
Elson(S)(L); Michi Weglyn(C)
College Widow, The (1904) Will R.
Barnes(C); Walter W. Burridge(S);
Joseph Wilson(L)
Collision (1932) Lee Simonson(S)(C)(L);
Bianca Stroock(C)
Colonel Newcome (1917) Gates and
Morange(S); Joseph Harker(S); Percy
Macquoid(C); ACK(L)
Colonel Satan (1931) De Guary(C);
Gates and Morange(S); ACK(C)
Colorado (1901) Edward G. Unitt(S)
Come Across (1938) Watson Barratt(S);
ACK(C)
Come Along (1919) Homer Emens(S);
Gates and Morange(S); ACK(C)(L)
Come Angel Band (1936) Watson
Barratt(S)
Come Back to the 5 & Dime,
Jimmy Dean, Jimmy Dean (1982)
Scott Bushnell(C); Paul Gallo(L); David
Gropman(S)
Come Back, Little Sheba (1950)
Howard Bay(S); Lucille Little(C); ACK(L)
Come Blow Your Horn (1961) Ralph
Alswang(S)(L); Stanley Simmons(C)
Come Easy (1933) Philip Gelb(S); ACK(C)
Come Live with Me (1967) Patton
Campbell(C); William Ritman(S)(L)
Come of Age (1934) James Reynolds(S);
Valentina(C)
Come on Charlie (1919) ACK(S)(L)
Come on Strong (1962) Oleg Cassini(C);
John Harvey(L); Oliver Smith(S);
Michael Travis(C)
Come Seven (1920) ACK(S)(L)

Come Summer (1969) Stanley
Simmons(C); Thomas Skelton(L); Oliver
Smith(S)
Come to Bohemia (1916) NONE
Come What May (1934) Mildred
Manning(C); Clement M. Williams(S);
ACK(C)
Come-on Man, The (1929) Eddie
Eddy(S)
Comedian, The (1923) Ernest Gros(S);
ACK(C)(L)
Comedians (1976) John Gunter(S)(C);
James Tilton(S); Ronald Wallace(L)
Comedienne, The (1924) ACK(L)
Comedy in Music Opus 2 (1964)
Ralph Alswang(S)(C)(L)
Comedy of Women, A (1929) Eddie
Eddy(S); ACK(C)
Comedy Tonight (1994) Alvin Colt(C);
Ray Klausen(S); Richard Nelson(L)
Comes the Revelation (1942) Ralph
Alswang(S); ACK(C)
Comet, The (1907) H. Robert Law(S)
Comforts of Ignorance, The (1918)
ACK(L)
Comic Artist, The (1933) Cleon
Throckmorton(S); ACK(C)
Comic, The (1927) M. Paul Dodge(S);
ACK(C)(L)
Comin' Thro' the Rye (1906) NONE
Comin' Uptown (1979) Ann Emonts(C);
Gilbert V. Hemsley, Jr.(L); Robin
Wagner(S)
Coming of Mrs. Patrick, The (1907)
Madame Laurent(C); Young Brothers
and Boss(S)
Command Decision (1947) Jo
Mielziner(S)(L); Julia Sze(C)
Command Performance, The (1928)
Raymond Sovey(S)(C)
Command to Love, The (1927) Miss
Ouida Bergere(S); Hattie Carnegie(C);
James Reynolds(C)
Commanding Officer, The (1909)
Edward G. Unitt(S)
Commedia del'Arte (1927) Aline
Bernstein(S)(C); ACK(L)
Committee, The (1966) Ralph
Alswang(S)(L)
Commodore Marries, The (1929)
Robert Edmond Jones(S); ACK(C)
Common Clay (1915) Elsie de Wolfe(S);
Madame Julie(C); ACK(L)
Common Ground (1945) George
Jenkins(S)(C)(L)
Common Sense Bracket (1904) Walter

W. Burridge[S]

Common Sin, The (1928) Rollo Wayne[S]; ACK[C]

Commuters, The (1910) H. Robert Law[S]; ACK[C]

Company (1970) Boris Aronson[S]; Robert Ornbo[L]; D. D. Ryan[C]

Company (1995) Peter Kaczorowski[L]; William Ivey Long[C]; Tony Walton[S]

Company's Coming (1931) Stanley Bell[S]; ACK[C]

Complaisant Lover, The (1961) Paul Morrison[L]; Motley[S]

Complex, The (1925) ACK[C][L]

Compulsion (1957) John Boxer[C]; Charles Elson[L]; Peter Larkin[S]

Comtesse Coquette (1907) Frederica DeWolfe[C]; Ernest Gros[S]

Con and Co. (1910) NONE

Concert Varieties (1945) Carl Kent[S][C]; E. Carlton Winckler[L]

Concert, The (1910) Ernest Gros[S]; Louis Hartmann[L]; ACK[C]

Conduct Unbecoming (1970) Finlay James[S][C][L]

Confession, The (1911) NONE

Confidential Clerk, The (1954) Paul Morrison[S][C][L]

Conflict (1929) P. Dodd Ackerman[S]

Conflict, The (1909) Frank E. Gates[S]; Edward Morange[S]

Congai (1928) Yetta Kiviette[C]; Cleon Throckmorton[S]; ACK[C]

Congratulations (1929) Rollo Wayne[S]; ACK[C]

Conjur Man Dies, The (1936) Manuel Essman[S]; A. H. Feder[L]

Connecticut Yankee, A (1927) John Hawkins[S][C]; ACK[L]

Connecticut Yankee, A (1943) Nat Karson[S][L]; ACK[C]

Connie Goes Home (1923) ACK[C][L]

Conquering Hero, The (1961) Patton Campbell[C]; William Pitkin[S]; Jean Rosenthal[S][L]

Conquest (1933) Raymond Sovey[S]; ACK[C]

Conscience (1924) P. Dodd Ackerman[S]; ACK[L]

Conscience (1952) Ralph Alswang[S]

Consequences (1914) ACK[C]

Conspiracy, The (1912) NONE

Constant Nymph, The (1926) George W. Harris[S]; ACK[C]

Constant Sinner, The (1931) Rollo Wayne[S]; ACK[C][L]

Constant Wife, The (1926) ACK[C][L]

Constant Wife, The (1951) Donald Oenslager[S]; Valentina[C]

Consul, The (1903) NONE

Consul, The (1950) Horace Armistead[S]; Grace Houston[C]; ACK[L]

Contact (2000) Peter Kaczorowski[L]; William Ivey Long[C]; Thomas Lynch[S]

Continental Varieties (1934) Lydia Chaliapine[C]; Henry Dreyfuss[S]

Continental Varieties (1935) Henry Dreyfuss[S]

Conversation at Midnight (1964) Barry Garlinger[L]; Charles T. Morrison[S]; ACK[C]

Conversation Piece (1934) Gladys E. Calthrop[S][C]

Conversations with My Father (1992) Pat Collins[L]; Tony Walton[S]; Robert Wojewodski[C]

Cook for Mr. General, A (1961) Will Steven Armstrong[S][L]; Michael Travis[C]

Cool World, The (1960) Howard Bay[S][L]; Ann Roth[C]

Copenhagen (2000) Peter J. Davison[S][C]; Mark Henderson[L]; Michael Lincoln[L]

Copper and Brass (1957) Alvin Colt[C]; William and Jean Eckart[S][L]

Copperfield (1981) Ken Billington[L]; John David Ridge[C]; Tony Straiges[S]

Copperhead, The (1918) ACK[S][L]

Coquette (1927) Raymond Sovey[S][C]; ACK[L]

Coralie and Company, Dressmakers (1900) Edward G. Unitt[S]

Cordelia Blossom (1914) ACK[C]

Coriolanus (1938) Ben Edwards[S][C]; A. H. Feder[L]

Corn Is Green, The (1940) Howard Bay[S]; Ernest Schraps[C]; ACK[L]

Corn Is Green, The (1943) Howard Bay[S]; Ernest Schraps[C]

Corn Is Green, The (1983) Theoni V. Aldredge[C]; Richard Nelson[L]; William Ritman[S]

Cornered (1920) Victor Petry[S]; ACK[S][C][L]

Coronet of the Duchess, The (1904) NONE

Corpse! (1986) Lowell Detweiler[C]; Alan Tagg[S]; Richard Winkler[L]

Cortez (1929) Louis Bromberg[S]; ACK[C][L]

Cottage in the Air (1909) E. Hamilton Bell[S]; Unitt and Wickes[S]

Counselor-at-Law (1931) Raymond Sovey[S]; ACK[C]

Counselor-at-Law (1932) Raymond Sovey[S]; ACK[C]

Counselor-at-Law (1942) Raymond Sovey[S]; ACK[C]

Count Me in (1942) Howard Bay[S]; Irene Sharaff[C]

Count of Luxembourg, The (1912) Ernest Albert[S]; Comelli[C]

Count of Luxembourg, The (1930) Rollo Wayne[S]

Counterattack (1943) John Root[S]; E. Carlton Winckler[L]; ACK[C]

Countess Cathleen, The (1905) NONE

Countess Julia (1913) NONE

Countess Maritza (1926) Watson Barratt[S]; ACK[C]

Countess Maritza (1928) Watson Barratt[S]; ACK[C]

Country Boy, The (1910) H. Robert Law[S]

Country Cousin, The (1917) Clifford F. Pember[S]; ACK[C]

Country Girl, A (1902) Percy Anderson[C]; Walter W. Burridge[S]; Henry E. Hoyt[S]; George McCurdy[L]; Edward G. Unitt[S]

Country Girl, The (1911) NONE

Country Girl, The (1950) Boris Aronson[S][L]; Anna Hill Johnstone[C]

Country Girl, The (1972) Douglas W. Schmidt[S][L]; Frank Thompson[C]

Country Mouse, A (1902) Edward G. Unitt[S]

Country Wife (1957) Motley[S][C]

Country Wife, The (1936) Oliver Messel[S][C]

Country, Girl, The and Lilli Tse (1906) Henry E. Hoyt[S]

County Chairman, The (1903) Sam'l B. Budd[L]; Walter W. Burridge[S]; ACK[C]

County Chairman, The (1936) William Oden Waller[S]

Courage (1928) R. N. Robbins[S]; ACK[C]

Courtesan (1930) P. Dodd Ackerman[S]; ACK[C]

Courtin' Time (1951) Ralph Alswang[S]; Saul Bolasni[C]

Courting (1925) ACK[L]

Courtship of Then, Now and Tomorrow, The (1915) NONE

Cousin Billy (1905) Homer Emens[S];

Ernest Gros[S]; Edward G. Unitt[S]

Cousin Kate (1903) Mrs. Robert Osborn[C]

Cousin Kate (1912) NONE

Cousin Louisa (1906) Emens and Unitt[S]; Kliegl Brothers[L]

Cousin Lucy (1915) Melville Ellis[C]; ACK[S][L]

Cousin Sonia (1925) Joseph Physioc[S]; ACK[C]

Cowboy and the Lady, The (1899) Edward G. Unitt[S]

Cradle Snatchers (1925) Evelyn McHorter[C]; ACK[S][L]

Cradle Snatchers (1932) Mabel A. Buell[S]

Cradle Song, The (1927) Gladys E. Calthrop[S][C]

Cradle Song, The (1930) Gladys E. Calthrop[S][C]; ACK[L]

Cradle Will Rock, The (1938) A. H. Feder[L]; Orson Welles[S]

Cradle Will Rock, The (1947) ACK[C][L]

Craig's Wife (1925) Sheldon K. Viele[S]; ACK[C]

Craig's Wife (1947) Stewart Chaney[S]; ACK[C]

Cranks (1956) Paul Morrison[L]; John Piper[S]

Crashing Through (1928) P. Dodd Ackerman[S]; ACK[C]

Crazy for You (1992) Paul Gallo[L]; William Ivey Long[C]; Robin Wagner[S]

Crazy He Calls Me (1992) Dennis Parichy[L]; Loren Sherman[S]; Jennifer von Mayrhauser[C]

Crazy with the Heat (1941) Marie Humans[C]; Albert R. Johnson[S][L]; Lester Polakov[C]

Creaking Chair, The (1926) Livingston Platt[S][C]

Cream in the Well (1941) Rose Bogdanoff[C]; Jo Mielziner[S][L]

Creation of the World and Other Business, The (1972) Boris Aronson[S]; Hal George[C]; Tharon Musser[L]

Creeping Fire (1935) Marguerite Gidden[C]; Cleon Throckmorton[S]

Creoles (1927) Norman Bel Geddes[S]; ACK[C]

Crier at Night, The (1916) NONE

Crime (1927) P. Dodd Ackerman[S]; ACK[C]

Crime and Punishment (1908) No

PLAYBILL

Crime and Punishment (1935) Irene Sharaff[S]

Crime and Punishment (1947) Lester Polakov[S][C][L]; Paul Sheriff[S]

Crime in the Whistler Room, The (1924) Cleon Throckmorton[S]

Crime Marches On (1935) John Root[S]; Edith Shayne[C]

Crimes of the Heart (1981) John Lee Beatty[S]; Patricia McGourty[C]; Dennis Parichy[L]

Criminal at Large (1932) Cleon Throckmorton[S]; ACK[C]

Criminal Code, The (1929) Albert R. Johnson[S]

Crimson Alibi, The (1919) Henri Bendel[C]; Mrs. Lillian Trimble Bradley[S]

Crinoline Girl, The (1914) Dodge and Castle[S]; Julian Eltinge[C]

Crisis, The (1902) William Camph[S]; Arthur Voegtlin[S]

Criss Cross (1926) Mabel E. Johnston[C]; James Reynolds[S][C]; ACK[L]

Critic, The (1915) Millard France[S]; ACK[C][L]

Critic, The (1925) Aline Bernstein[S]

Critic, The (1946) Tanya Moiseiwitsch[S][C]; John Sullivan[L]

Critics' Choice (1960) Oleg Cassini[C]; George Jenkins[S]

Critics'Choice (1960) George Jenkins[L]

Crooked Friday, The (1925) Robert Ten Eyck Stevenson[C]; Rollo Wayne[S]

Crooked Gamblers (1920) Madame Therese Renaud[C]; Unitt and Wickes[S]

Crooked Square, The (1923) ACK[S][C][L]

Crooks Convention, The (1929) Ward and Harvey Studios[S]

Crops and Croppers (1918) Harriet Klamroth[S]

Cross My Heart (1928) P. Dodd Ackerman[S]; Mabel E. Johnston[C]

Cross Roads (1929) Robert Edmond Jones[S]; Yetta Kiviette[C]

Cross Ruff (1935) Sybyl Nash Hogan[C]; John Root[S]

Cross-Town (1937) Karle O. Amend[S]

Cross-ways, The (1902) E. G. Banks[S]; H. K. Browne[S]; Paquin[C]

Crossing, The (1906) Madame Castle-Bert[C]; Charles A. Platt[S]

Crowded Hour, The (1918) Hickson[C]; Joseph Physioc[S]; ACK[L]

Crown Matrimonial (1973) Finlay James[S][C]; Neil Peter Jampolis[L]

Crown Prince, The (1904) NONE

Crown Prince, The (1927) Watson Barratt[S]; ACK[C]

Crucible (1933) Karle O. Amend Studio[S]; ACK[C]

Crucible, The (1953) Boris Aronson[S]; Edith Lutyens Bel Geddes[C]

Crucible, The (1964) Alvin Colt[C]; Peter Larkin[S]; Tharon Musser[L]

Crucible, The (1991) David Jenkins[S]; Richard Nelson[L]; Patricia Zipprodt[C]

Crucifer of Blood, The (1978) Roger Morgan[L]; Ann Roth[C]; John Wulp[S]

Cry for Us All (1970) Howard Bay[S][L]; Robert Fletcher[C]

Cry of Players, A (1968) John Gleason[L]; David Hays[S]; Patricia Quinn Stuart[C]

Cry of the Peacock (1950) Cecil Beaton[S][C]; ACK[L]

Cub, The (1910) NONE

Cuba & His Teddy Bear (1986) Gabriel Berry[C]; Anne E. Militello[L]

Cuban Thing, The (1968) Jules Fisher[L]; Patricia Quinn Stuart[C]; Robin Wagner[S]

Cuckoos on the Hearth (1941) John Root[S]

Cue for Passion (1940) Herbert Andrews[S]

Cue for Passion (1958) Dorothy Jeakins[C]; George Jenkins[S][L]

Cup of Trembling (1948) Charles Elson[S][L]; Natalie Barth Walker[C]

Cup, The (1923) ACK[L]

Cupid Outwits Adam (1900) NONE

Cure for Curables, A (1918) Ed Sundquist[S]

Cure for Matrimony (1939) Dolaro Belasco[C]; Melville Bernstein[S]

Curiosity (1919) Lucile[C]; ACK[S][L]

Curioso Accidente, Un (1907) NONE

Curious Savage, The (1950) George Jenkins[S][C][L]; Anna Hill Johnstone[C]; ACK[L]

Curse of an Aching Heart, The (1982) John Lee Beatty[S]; Dennis Parichy[L]; Nancy Potts[C]

Curtain Call (1937) Ellis E. Porter[C]; Cleon Throckmorton[S]

Curtain Rises, The (1933) Nicholas Yellenti[S]; ACK[C]

Cut of the Axe (1960) Audré[C]; Howard Bay[S][L]
Cyclone Lover, The (1928) Ack[S][C][L]
Cymbeline (1906) Homer Emens[S]; Edward G. Unitt[S]
Cymbeline (1923) Gates and Morange[S]; Edward G. Unitt[S]
Cynara (1931) Watson Barratt[S]; Ack[C][L]
Cynthia (1903) D. Frank Dodge[S]
Cyrano (1973) Desmond Heeley[C]; Gilbert V. Hemsley, Jr.[L]; John Jensen[S]
Cyrano De Bergerac (1899) Richard Marston[S]
Cyrano De Bergerac (1900) None
Cyrano De Bergerac (1923) Claude Bragdon[S][C]
Cyrano De Bergerac (1926) Claude Bragdon[S]
Cyrano De Bergerac (1928) Claude Bragdon[S][C]
Cyrano De Bergerac (1932) Claude Bragdon[S]
Cyrano De Bergerac (1936) Claude Bragdon[S][C]
Cyrano De Bergerac (1946) Lemuel Ayers[S][C]
Cyrano De Bergerac (1984) Jeffrey Beecroft[L]; Terry Hands[L]; John Kasarda[S]; Ralph Koltai[S]; Alexander Reid[C]
Cyrano: The Musical (1993) Paul Gallis[S]; Brian Nason[L]; Yan Tax[C]; Reiner Tweebeeke[L]
Czar Paul (1912) None
Czarina, The (1922) Henri Bendel[C]; Warren Dahler[S]; Ack[L]
D'Arcy of the Guards (1901) Percy Macquoid[S][C]
D'Oyly Carte Opera Company (1934) Ack[L]
D'Oyly Carte Opera Company (1936) Ack[L]
D'Oyly Carte Opera Company (1939) Ack[L]
Déclasé (1919) Ack[L]
Déclassé (1919) Henri Bendel[C]; Homer Emens[S]
Da (1978) Arden Fingerhut[L]; Marjorie Bradley Kellogg[S]; Jennifer von Mayrhauser[C]
Daddies (1918) Elsie de Wolfe[S]; Hickson[C]; Ack[L]
Daddy Dufard (1910) None
Daddy Dumplins (1920) Gates and Morange[S]; Ack[C][L]
Daddy Long Legs (1918) Dodge and Castle[S]; Ack[L]
Daddy Long-Legs (1914) None
Daddy's Gone A-Hunting (1921) Robert Edmond Jones[S]; Ack[C]
Daffy Dill (1922) Charles LeMaire[C]; Clifford F. Pember[S]; Ack[L]
Dagger and the Cross, The (1905) Mathias Armbruster[S]; Mrs. Louise Haggeman[C]
Dagger, The (1925) Karle O. Amend[S]; Ack[C][L]
Dagmar (1923) Frederick W. Jones III[S]; Ack[C]
Dairy Farm, The (1899) Ack[S]
Dairymaids, The (1907) Ernest Gros[S]; Mrs. Robert Osborn[C]
Daisy Mayme (1926) Maybelle Manning[C]; Livingston Platt[S]; Ack[L]
Damaged Goods (1913) None
Damaged Goods (1937) Ack[L]
Damask Cheek, The (1942) Raymond Sovey[S][C]
Dame Aux Camelias, La (1900) Ack[S][C]
Dame aux Camelias, La (1904) Ack[S][C]
Dame Edna (1999) Stephen Adnitt[C]; Kenneth Foy[S]; Jason Kantrowitz[L]
Dame Nature (1938) Norris Houghton[S]; Ack[C]
Damn the Tears (1927) Norman Bel Geddes[S]; Kay Francis[C]; Julia Hoyt[C]
Damn Yankees (1955) William and Jean Eckart[S][C]; Peter Larkin[L]
Damn Yankees (1994) Douglas W. Schmidt[S]; David F. Segal[L]; David C. Woolard[C]
Damn Your Honor (1929) Lee Simonson[S][C]
Dance a Little Closer (1983) Donald Brooks[C]; David Mitchell[S]; Thomas Skelton[L]
Dance Me a Song (1950) Jo Mielziner[S][L]; Irene Sharaff[C]
Dance Night (1938) Raymond Sovey[S]
Dance with Your Gods (1934) Donald Oenslager[S][C]
Dancer, The (1919) Watson Barratt[S]; Ack[L]
Dancer, The (1946) Motley[S][C]
Dancers of God (1955) Noël Ballif[S][C]
Dancers, The (1923) Ack[C][L]
Dancin' (1978) Jules Fisher[L]; Willa

Kim[C]; Peter Larkin[S]

Dancing Around (1914) P. Dodd Ackerman[S]; Melville Ellis[C]; Nick Kronyack[L]; H. Robert Law[S]

Dancing at Lughnasa (1991) Trevor Dawson[L]; Joe Vaněk[S][C]

Dancing Duchess, The (1914) Will R. Barnes[C]; Arthur D. Brooks[C]

Dancing Girl, The (1923) Watson Barratt[S]; ACK[C]

Dancing in the End Zone (1985) Patricia McGourty[C]; Dennis Parichy[L]; Douglas W. Schmidt[S]

Dancing Mothers (1924) Clifford F. Pember[S]; ACK[C]

Dancing Partner (1930) Henri Bendel[C]; Louis Hartmann[L]; Joseph Wickes[S]

Danger (1921) P. Dodd Ackerman[S]; Peggy Hoyt[C]; ACK[L]

Dangerous Corner (1932) Brownie[C]; Woodman Thompson[S]

Dangerous Corner (1933) Woodman Thompson[S]

Dangerous Games (1989) Peggy Eisenhauer[L]; Tony Straiges[S]; Patricia Zipprodt[C]

Dante (1903) C. Karl[C]

Danton's Death (1938) Jean Rosenthal[L]; Jan Tichacek[S]; Leo Van Witsen[C]

Danton's Tod (1927) Ernest Stern[S][C]; ACK[L]

Daphne in Cottage D (1967) Theoni V. Aldredge[C]; Jo Mielziner[S][L]

Daphne Laureola (1950) Ralph Alswang[L]; Roger Furse[S]; Roger Ramsdell[S]

Dark Angel, The (1925) Livingston Platt[S]

Dark at the Top of the Stairs, The (1957) Lucinda Ballard[C]; Ben Edwards[S]; Jean Rosenthal[L]

Dark Eyes (1943) Stewart Chaney[S]

Dark Hammock (1944) Jack Daniels[L]; Samuel Leve[S]; Kermit Love[C]

Dark Hours, The (1932) Cleon Throckmorton[S]; ACK[C]

Dark Is Light Enough, The (1955) Oliver Messel[S]; Helene Pons[C]

Dark Mirror, The (1928) Walter Walden[S][L]

Dark of the Moon (1945) Peggy Clark[C]; George Jenkins[S][L]

Dark Rosaleen (1919) John P. Campbell[S][C]; ACK[L]

Dark Tower, The (1933) Jo Mielziner[S][L]; ACK[C]

Dark Victory (1934) Robert Edmond Jones[S]; ACK[C]

Dark, The (1927) Livingston Platt[S]

Darkness at Noon (1951) Kenn Barr[C]; Frederick Fox[S][L]

Darling of the Day (1968) Peggy Clark[L]; Raoul Pène Du Bois[C]; Oliver Smith[S]

Darling of the Gallery Gods, The and The Dress Parade (1903) Wilfred Buckland[S]; Madame Freisinger[C]; Ernest Gros[S]; Louis Hartmann[L]; Kliegl Brothers[L]; Genjiro Yeto[C]

Darling of the Gods, The (1902) Wilfred Buckland[S]; Madame Freisinger[C]; Ernest Gros[S]; Louis Hartmann[L]; Kliegl Brothers[L]; Genjiro Yeto[C]

Date with April, A (1953) Robert O'Hearn[S]; ACK[L]

Daughter of Heaven, The (1912) Ben Beerwald[L]; Caramba[C]; Gates and Morange[S]; Edward Morange[S]; C. Alexander Ramsey[C]

Daughter of Madame Angot, The (1925) Maria Gortinskaya[S][C]

Daughter of Silence (1961) Helene Pons[C]; Jean Rosenthal[L]; Oliver Smith[S][C]

Daughter of the Tumbrils, The (1906) NONE

Daughters of Atreus (1936) Jo Mielziner[S][L]; James Reynolds[C]

Daughters of Men, The (1906) Joseph Physioc[S]

David Garrick (1900) Worth[C]

David Garrick (1905) NONE

David Garrick (1916) Maurice Hermann[C]; H. Robert Law[S]; ACK[L]

David Garrick on the Art of Acting (1904) No PLAYBILL

David Harum (1900) Edward G. Unitt[S]

David's Crown (1948) Madame Chilek[C]; M. Schmidt[S]; ACK[L]

Dawn (1924) H. Robert Studio Law[S]; ACK[C][L]

Dawn of a Tomorrow, The (1909) Gates and Morange[S]

Day after Tomorrow, The (1950) Edward Gilbert[S]

Day before Spring, The (1945) Robert Davison[S]; Miles White[C]

Day Before, The (1906) No Playbill

Day by the Sea, A (1955) Jay
Krause(S)(C)(L)

Day in Hollywood/A Night in the
Ukraine, A (1980) Beverly
Emmons(L); Michel Stuart(C); Tony
Walton(S)

Day in the Death of Joe Egg, A
(1968) Lloyd Burlingame(L); Robin
Pidcock(S)(C)

Day in the Sun (1938) Louis Kennel(S);
Ack(C)

Day the Money Stopped, The (1958)
Betty Coe Armstrong(C); Jo
Mielziner(S)(L)

Day Will Come, The (1944) Frederick
Fox(S)

Daybreak (1917) Joseph Physioc(S);
Ack(C)(L)

Days in the Trees (1976) Thomas
Skelton(L); Rouben Ter-Arutunian(S)(C)

Days to Come (1936) Aline
Bernstein(S); Ack(C)

Days without End (1934) Lee
Simonson(S); Ack(C)

De Lancy (1905) Ernest Gros(S); Ward(C)

De Luxe (1935) Jo Mielziner(S)(L); Ack(C)

De Luxe Annie (1917) P. Dodd
Ackerman(S); Harry Collins(C); Ed
Sundquist(S); Ack(L)

Deacon and the Lady, The (1910) D.
Frank Dodge(S); Joseph C. Fischer(C);
William Henry Matthews(C)

Dead End (1935) Norman Bel
Geddes(S)(C)

Dead Pigeon (1953) William and Jean
Eckart(S); Ack(C)

Deadfall (1955) Ralph Alswang(S)(C)(L)

Deadlock, The (1914) None

Deadly Game, The (1960) Wolfgang
Roth(S)(C)(L)

Dear Barbarians (1952) A. H. Feder(L);
Jack Landau(S)(C)

Dear Brutus (1918) Homer Emens(S);
Ack(C)(L)

Dear Charles (1954) Gene Coffin(C);
Donald Oenslager(S)(L)

Dear Fool, The (1914) No Playbill

Dear Judas (1947) Albert R.
Johnson(S)(L); Mary Percy Schenck(C)

Dear Liar (1960) Cecil Beaton(C);
Donald Oenslager(S); Jean Rosenthal(L)

Dear Me (1921) Harry Collins(C); James
Wade(S)

Dear Me, the Sky Is Falling (1963)
Will Steven Armstrong(S)(L); Edith

Lutyens Bel Geddes(C)

Dear Octopus (1939) Gladys E.
Calthrop(S); Ack(C)

Dear Old Charlie (1912) Ack(C)

Dear Old Darling (1936) William Oden
Waller(S); Ack(C)

Dear Old England (1930) P. Dodd
Ackerman(S); Ack(C)

Dear Oscar (1972) Mary McKinley(C);
William Pitkin(S); David F. Segal(L)

Dear Ruth (1944) Frederick Fox(S);
Bianca Stroock(C)

Dear Sir (1924) Yetta Kiviette(C); James
Reynolds(C); Raymond Sovey(S)

Dear Unfair Sex, The (1906) Ack(S)

Dear World (1969) Jean Rosenthal(L);
Oliver Smith(S); Freddy Wittop(C)

Dearest Enemy (1925) Hubert Davis(C);
Mark Mooring(C); James Reynolds(C);
Clarke Robinson(S)

Death and the King's Horseman
(1987) Pat Collins(L); Judy Dearing(C);
David Gropman(S)

Death and the Maiden (1992) Jules
Fisher(L); Ann Roth(C); Tony Walton(S)

Death of a Salesman (1949) Jo
Mielziner(S)(L); Julia Sze(C)

Death of a Salesman (1975) Arthur
Boccia(C); Marjorie Bradley Kellogg(S);
Thomas Skelton(L)

Death of a Salesman (1984) Ben
Edwards(S); Ruth Morley(C); Thomas
Skelton(L)

Death of a Salesman (1999) Michael
Philippi(L); Mark Wendland(S); Birgit
Rattenborg Wise(C)

Death Takes a Holiday (1929) Rollo
Wayne(S); Ack(C)(L)

Death Takes a Holiday (1931) Rollo
Wayne(S)

Death Trap (1978) Ruth Morley(C);
William Ritman(S); Marc B. Weiss(L)

Debbie Reynolds Show (1976) Jerry
Grollnek(L); Bob Mackie(C); Billy
Morris(S)

Debtors, The (1909) Frederica
DeWolfe(C); D. Frank Dodge(S); Ack(C)

Deburau (1920) Ernest Gros(S); Louis
Hartmann(L); Ack(C)

Debut (1956) John Boyt(S)(C)(L)

Debutante, The (1914) Cora
MacGeachy(C); William Henry
Matthews(C)

Decision (1929) Anthony Continer(S);
Ack(L)

Decision (1944) Frederick Fox(S); Bianca

Stroock(C)

Decorating Clementine (1910) Ernest Gros(S)

Decoy, The (1932) ACK(L)

Deep Are the Roots (1945) Howard Bay(S); Emeline Clarke Roche(C)

Deep Blue Sea, The (1952) Charles Elson(S)(L)

Deep Blue Sea, The (1998) John Arnone(S); Jane Greenwood(C); Robert Wierzel(L)

Deep Channels (1929) Anne Cone(C); ACK(L)

Deep Harlem (1929) ACK(L)

Deep Mrs. Sykes, The (1945) Eleanor Farrington(S)(C)(L)

Deep Purple, The (1911) NONE

Deep Tangled Wildwood, The (1923) William Henry Matthews(S)(C)

Defender, The (1902) D. Frank Dodge(S); Archie Gunn(C); ACK(L)

Degenerates, The (1900) W. T. Hemsley(S)

Delicate Balance, A (1966) Theoni V. Aldredge(C); Tharon Musser(L); William Ritman(S)

Delicate Balance, A (1995) John Lee Beatty(S); Pat Collins(L); Jane Greenwood(C)

Delicate Balance, A (1996) John Lee Beatty(S); Pat Collins(L); Jane Greenwood(C)

Delicate Story (1940) Raymond Sovey(S); ACK(C)

Delmar's Revels (1927) Jeanette Hackett(C); Clarke Robinson(S)(L)

Deluge, The (1917) Robert Edmond Jones(S); ACK(L)

Deluge, The (1922) Robert Edmond Jones(S); ACK(L)

Demi-Virgin, The (1921) H. George Brandt(S)(C)

Democracy's King/ Master, The (1918) NONE

Depths, The (1925) Rollo Peters(S); ACK(L)

Deputy, The (1964) Edith Lutyens Bel Geddes(C); John Harvey(L); Rouben Ter-Arutunian(S)

Desert Flower, The (1924) NONE

Desert Incident, A (1959) Howard Bay(S)(L); Ann Roth(C)

Desert Sands (1922) ACK(S)(C)(L)

Desert Song, The (1926) Vyvian Donner(C); Mark Mooring(C); Woodman Thompson(S)

Deserters, The (1910) H. Robert Law(S)

Design for a Stained Glass Window (1950) Stewart Chaney(S)(C)(L)

Design for Living (1933) Gladys E. Calthrop(S); Yetta Kiviette(C); ACK(C)

Design for Living (1984) Thomas Lynch(S); Ann Roth(C); Marc B. Weiss(L)

Design for Living (2001) Robert Brill(S); Bruce Pask(C); James Vermeulen(L)

Desire under the Elms (1924) Millia Davenport(C); Robert Edmond Jones(S)

Desire under the Elms (1952) Ben Edwards(C); Mordecai Gorelik(S)

Desk Set, The (1955) George Jenkins(S)(C)(L)

Desperate Hours, The (1955) Howard Bay(S)(L); Robert Randolph(C)

Destruction (1932) NONE

Destry Rides Again (1959) Alvin Colt(C); Jean Rosenthal(L); Oliver Smith(S)

Detective Sparks (1909) NONE

Detective Story (1949) Boris Aronson(S); Millie Sutherland(C); ACK(L)

Detour, The (1921) NONE

Devil and Daniel Webster, The (1938) Robert Edmond Jones(S)(C)(L)

Devil in the Cheese (1926) Norman Bel Geddes(S)(C)

Devil in the Mind (1931) S. Syrjala(S)

Devil of Pei-Ling, The (1936) Karle O. Amend(S)

Devil Passes, The (1932) P. Dodd Ackerman(S); ACK(C)

Devil Takes a Bride, The (1938) Lawrence L. Goldwasser(S); ACK(C)

Devil to Pay, The (1925) Cleon Throckmorton(S); ACK(C)

Devil's Advocate, The (1961) Theoni V. Aldredge(C); Jo Mielziner(S)(L)

Devil's c, The (1988) Zack Brown(C)

Devil's Disciple (1899) NONE

Devil's Disciple, The (1900) Walter W. Burridge(S); Joseph Wilson(L)

Devil's Disciple, The (1923) Carolyn Hancock(S)(C)

Devil's Disciple, The (1950) Emeline Clarke Roche(C); Peter Wolf(S)(L)

Devil's Disciple, The (1988) Zack Brown(S); Curt Ostermann(L)

Devil's Galore (1945) Howard Bay(S); Peggy Clark(C)

Devil's Garden, The (1915) Robert

Edmond Jones[S][C]; ACK[L]

Devil's Host, The (1931) Karle O. Amend[S]; ACK[C]

Devil's Little Game, The (1932) Hiram Hoover[S]

Devil, The (Adapted by Herford) (1908) Walter W. Burridge[S]

Devil, The (Adapted by Konta and Trowbridge) (1908) Gates and Morange[S]

Devils (1926) Livingston Platt[S]

Devils, The (1965) Jules Fisher[L]; Motley[C]; Rouben Ter-Arutunian[S]

Devour the Snow (1979) David Murin[C]; Dennis Parichy[L]; Steven Rubin[S]

Dew Drop Inn (1923) Watson Barratt[S]; ACK[C][L]

Dial "M" for Murder (1952) Peter Larkin[S][L]; Noel Taylor[C]

Diamond Lil (1928) Dolly Tree[C]; August Vimnera[S]; ACK[L]

Diamond Lil (1949) William De Forest[S]; Paul du Pont[C]; DuWico[L]; Ben Edwards[S]

Diamond Lil (1951) Paul du Pont[S][C][L]

Diamond Orchid (1965) Donald Brooks[C]; David Hays[S][L]

Diana (1929) Cirker and Robbins[S]; Mildred Manning[C]

Diana of Dobson's (1908) Frank Platzer[S]

Diary of Anne Frank, The (1955) Boris Aronson[S]; Helene Pons[C]; Lee Watson[L]

Diary of Anne Frank, The (1997) Adrianne Lobel[S]; Brian MacDevitt[L]; Martin Pakledinaz[C]

Dice of the Gods, The (1923) Gates and Morange[S]; ACK[C]

Dickey Bird, The (1914) Gates and Morange[S]

Dictator, The (1904) NONE

Dictator, The (1911) NONE

Did I Say No? (1931) Cleon Throckmorton[S]; ACK[L]

Diff'rent (1938) Ben Edwards[S][C]; A. H. Feder[L]

Difference in Gods, A (1917) ACK[L]

Difference in Gods, A (1918) ACK[L]

Different Times (1972) Martin Aronstein[L]; David Guthrie[S][C]

Dinner at Eight (1932) Omar Kiam[C]; Livingston Platt[S]

Dinner at Eight (1966) Ray Diffen[C]; David Hays[S][L]

Dinner Is Served (1929) DuWico[L]; ACK[S][C]

Dinner Party, The (2001) John Lee Beatty[S]; Jane Greenwood[C]; Brian MacDevitt[L]

Dinosaur Wharf (1951) Samuel Leve[S][C][L]

Diplomacy (1901) Edward G. Unitt[S]

Diplomacy (1910) Edward G. Unitt[S]

Diplomacy (1914) NONE

Diplomacy (1928) Gates and Morange[S]; Anthony Greshoff[L]

Diplomat, The (1902) Arthur Voegtlin[S]

Dirty Blonde (2000) Susan Hilferty[C]; David J. Lander[L]; Douglas Stein[S]

Dirty Linen/ New Found Land (1977) Martin Aronstein[L]; Gabriella Falk[S][C]

Discovering America (1912) No PLAYBILL

Disenchanted, The (1958) Ben Edwards[S]; Jean Rosenthal[L]; Ann Roth[C]

Disengaged (1909) NONE

Dishonored Lady (1930) Stanley Bell[S]; Omar Kiam[C]; ACK[L]

Disraeli (1911) Joseph F. Driscoll[L]

Disraeli (1912) Joseph F. Driscoll[L]

Disraeli (1917) Gates and Morange[S]; ACK[C][L]

Distaff Side, The (1934) Joe Miller[L]; Raymond Sovey[S]

Distant Bell, A (1960) Theoni V. Aldredge[C]; Peggy Clark[L]; Mordecai Gorelik[S]

Distant City, The (1941) Samuel Leve[S]; Helene Pons[C]

Distant Drum, A (1928) Livingston Platt[S]; ACK[C]

Distant Drums (1932) Bernice Ladd[C]; Jo Mielziner[S][L]

Distant Shore, The (1935) Raymond Sovey[S][C]; ACK[C]

District Leader (1906) Meixner[S]; Frank Platzer[S]

Diversion (1928) Rollo Peters[S]; ACK[C]

Divided by Three (1934) Donald Oenslager[S]; ACK[C]

Divided Honors (1929) Willy Pogany[S]; ACK[C]

Divine Drudge, A (1933) Jo Mielziner[S][L]

Divine Moment, A (1934) P. Dodd Ackerman[S]; ACK[C]

Division Street (1980) Martin

Aronstein(L); Robert Blackman(C); Ralph Funicello(S)

Divorce (1909) NONE

Divorce a La Carte (1928) DuWico(L); Ward and Harvey Studios(S); ACK(C)

Divorce Me, Dear (1931) P. Dodd Ackerman Studio(S); ACK(L)

Divorcons (1902) Gates and Morange(S); Madame Virion(C)

Divorcons (1907) H. Robert Law(S)

Divorcons (1913) H. Robert Law(S); Bert Tuchman(S)

Dixie to Broadway (1924) ACK(C)(L)

Do Black Patent Leather Shoes Really Reflect Up? (1982) James Maronek(S); Nancy Potts(C); Marilyn Rennagel(L)

Do I Hear a Waltz? (1965) Jules Fisher(L); Beni Montresor(S)(C)

Do Re Mi (1960) Boris Aronson(S); Irene Sharaff(C)

Do You Know the Milky Way? (1961) Edith Lutyens Bel Geddes(C); Colin Low(S); Lee Watson(L)

Do You Turn Somersaults? (1978) Ken Billington(L); Ann Roth(C); Oliver Smith(S)

Doctor Jazz (1975) Raoul Pène Du Bois(S)(C); A. H. Feder(L)

Doctor Monica (1933) Raymond Sovey(S); ACK(C)

Doctor Social (1948) Stewart Chaney(S)(C)(L)

Doctor X (1931) Cleon Throckmorton(S); ACK(C)

Doctor's Dilemma (1941) Motley(C); Donald Oenslager(S)

Doctor's Dilemma, The (1915) Lucile(C); Norman Wilkinson(S); ACK(C)(L)

Doctor's Dilemma, The (1927) Aline Bernstein(C); Jo Mielziner(S)(L); ACK(C)

Doctors Disagree (1944) John Root(S)

Dodsworth (1934) Jo Mielziner(S)(L); Margaret Pemberton(C)

Does a Tiger Wear a Necktie? (1969) Edward Burbridge(S); Thomas Skelton(L); David Toser(C)

Dogg's Hamlet, Cahoot's Macbeth (1979) Norman Coates [British](S)(C); Howard Eaton(L)

Doing Our Bit (1917) Homer Conant(C); Joseph Physioc(S); John H. Young(S); ACK(L)

Dolce (1906) NONE

Doll Girl, The (1913) NONE

Doll's House, A (1902) Mrs. Julia Bacon(C); Emens, Unitt and Wickes(S)

Doll's House, A (1908) Mrs. Julia Bacon(C); Emens, Unitt and Wickes(S)

Doll's House, A (1918) Clifford F. Pember(S); ACK(C)(L)

Doll's House, A (1937) Donald Oenslager(S)(C)

Doll's House, A (1997) Deirdre Clancy(S)(C); Peter Mumford(L)

Doll's Life, A (1982) Ken Billington(L); Tazeena Firth(S); Florence Klotz(C); Timothy O'Brien(S)

Dollar Mark, The (1909) H. Robert Law(S); Bert Tuchman(S)

Dollar Princess, The (1909) Ernest Gros(S); ACK(C)

Dolly Jordan (1922) Rollo Peters(S)(C)

Dolly Varden (1902) Homer Emens(S); Claude Hagen(S); Mrs. Caroline Siedle(C)

Dominant Sex, The (1935) Lydia Furbush(C); Raymond Sovey(S)

Domino (1932) Livingston Platt(S); ACK(C)

Don (1909) NONE

Don Caesar's Return (1901) Arthur Voegtlin(S)

Don Carlos (1906) NONE

Don Juan (1921) Lee Simonson(S)(C)

Don Juan (1972) John J. Moore(S); Nancy Potts(C)

Don Juan in Hell (1951) Walter Plunkett(C); ACK(L)

Don Juan in Hell (1973) Nolan Miller(C); ACK(L)

Don Q., Jr. (1926) ACK(L)

Don Quixote (1908) Mrs. Lulu Fralik(C); Madame Freisinger(C); Kliegl Brothers(L); Harley Merry(S); Edward G. Unitt(S); Joseph Wickes(S); ACK(L)

Don't Bother Mother (1925) DuWico(L); Miss Mary Fox(S)

Don't Call Back (1975) Whitney Blausen(C); John Gleason(L); Oliver Smith(S); Egon Von Furstenberg(C)

Don't Drink the Water (1966) Jo Mielziner(S)(L); Motley(C)

Don't Get God Started (1987) Llewellyn Harrison(S); Shirley Prendergast(L); Victoria Shaffer(C)

Don't Listen Ladies (1948) Leon Davey(S); DuWico(L)

Don't Look Now (1936) Lou Bromley(S); ACK(C)

Don't Play Us Cheap (1972) Martin

Aronstein[L]; Bernard Johnson[C]; Kert Lundell[S]
Don't Tell (1920) Thomas F. Dunn[S]; Ack[L]
Don't Throw Glass Houses (1938) Louis Kennel[S]; Ack[C]
Don't Weaken (1914) H. Robert Law[S]; Bert Tuchman[S]; Ack[C]
Donnybrook! (1961) Klaus Holm[L]; Rouben Ter-Arutunian[S][C]
Donovan Affair, The (1926) Milgrim[C]; Nicholas Yellenti[S]
Doonesbury (1983) Beverly Emmons[L]; Peter Larkin[S]; Patricia McGourty[C]
Doormat, The (1922) Ack[L]
Dora Mobridge (1930) Charles Teichner[S]; Ack[C]
Dorian Gray (1928) Ack[S][L]
Dorothy Vernon of Haddon Hall (1903) None
Double Door (1933) Mary Merrill[S][C]; Rollo Wayne[S]
Double Dublin (1963) Helen Pond[S][L]; Herbert Senn[S][L]; Ack[C]
Double Dummy (1936) Mary Merrill[C]; S. Syrjala[S]
Double Exposure (1918) Ack[L]
Double in Hearts (1956) Samuel Leve[S]; Natalie Barth Walker[C]
Double Life, The (1906) None
Doubles (1985) Robert Fletcher[S][C]; Craig Miller[L]
Doug Henning and His World of Magic (1984) Jef Billings[C]; Bill Bohnert[S]; Michael McGiveney[L]
Doughgirls, The (1942) Frederick Fox[S]; Bianca Stroock[C]; Ack[C]
Douleureuse, La (1904) Redfern[C]; Ack[S]
Dove of Peace, The (1912) None
Dove, The (1925) Louis Hartmann[L]; Joseph Wickes[S]; Ack[C]
Dover Road (1921) William Oden Waller[S]; Ack[C]
Dowerless Bride, The (1908) No Playbill
Down Stream (1926) Dickson Morgan[S]; Ack[C]
Down to Miami (1944) Stewart Chaney[S][L]
Dozens, The (1969) Martin Aronstein[L]; Rouben Ter-Arutunian[S][C]
Dr. Cook's Garden (1967) David Hays[S][L]; Noel Taylor[C]
Dr. De Luxe (1911) P. Dodd Ackerman[S]; Castle and Harvey[S];

Ack[C]
Dr. Faustus (1937) Orson Welles[S][C]
Dr. Jekyll and Mr. Hyde (1899) None
Dr. Jekyll and Mr. Hyde (1905) None
Dr. Jekyll and Mr. Hyde (1906) None
Dr. Knock (1928) Clement Wilenchick[S][C]
Dr. Wake's Patient (1907) W. H. Bull[S]; Ack[C]
Dracula (1927) Joseph Physioc[S]; Ack[C]
Dracula (1931) Joseph Physioc[S]; Ack[L]
Dracula (1977) Edward Gorey[S][C]; Roger Morgan[L]
Dragon's Claw, The (1914) F. Richards Anderson[C]; Grinager and Beardsley[S]
Dragon, The (1929) Frances Keating[S]
Drat! the Cat! (1965) David Hays[S][L]; Fred Voelpel[C]
Dream (1997) Ken Billington[L]; Ann Hould-Ward[C]; David Mitchell[S]
Dream Child (1934) Stewart Chaney[S]; Margaret Pemberton[C]
Dream City (1906) Will R. Barnes[C]
Dream Girl (1945) Mainbocher[C]; Jo Mielziner[S][C][L]
Dream Girl, The (1924) Watson Barratt[S]; Ack[C]
Dream Play, The (1926) Cleon Throckmorton[S]; Ack[C]
Dream with Music (1944) Stewart Chaney[S]; Miles White[C]
Dreamgirls (1981) Theoni V. Aldredge[C]; Tharon Musser[L]; Robin Wagner[S]
Dreamgirls (1987) Theoni V. Aldredge[C]; Tharon Musser[L]; Robin Wagner[S]
Dreams & Nightmares (1996) Eiko Ishioka[S][C][L]; Robert Wierzel[L]
Dreams for Sale (1922) Ack[S][C][L]
Dresser, The (1981) Laurie Dennett[S]; Stephen Doncaster[C]; Beverly Emmons[L]
Drifting (1910) Kliegl Brothers[L]; Ack[S][C]
Drink (1903) None
Drink to Me Only (1958) John Robert Lloyd[S][L]; Julia Sze[C]
Driven (1914) None
Drone, The (1912) None
Druid Circle, The (1947) Stewart Chaney[S][L]; Gladys Cobb[C]

Drums Begin, The (1933) Cirker and
Robbins(S); Frances Clyne(C)
Drums of Jeopardy, The (1922)
Anthony Greshoff(L); ACK(S)(C)
Drunkard, The (1934) Franklyn
Ambrose(S); ACK(C)
Du Barry (1901) Adolphe Bellotte(C);
Henry Dazian(C); Ernest Gros(S);
Archie Gunn(C); Worth(C)
Du Barry Was a Lady (1939) Raoul
Pène Du Bois(S)(C)
Dubarry, The (1932) Vincente
Minnelli(S)(C)
Duchess Misbehaves, The (1946)
Willa Kim(C); A. A. Ostrander(S); E.
Carlton Winckler(L)
Duchess of Dantzic, The (1905)
Thomas Mangan(S)
Duchess of Malfi (1946) Harry Gordon
Bennett(S); Miles White(C)
Duchess, The (1911) Melville Ellis(C)
Dude (1972) Randy Barcelo(C); Eugene
Lee(S); Franne Lee(S); Roger Morgan(S)
Duel of Angels (1960) Roger Furse(S);
Paul Morrison(L); ACK(C)
Duel, The (1906) Ernest Gros(S)
Duet for One (1981) John Lee Beatty(S);
Jane Greenwood(C); Dennis Parichy(L)
Duet for Two Hands (1947) Charles
Elson(S)(L); Helene Pons(C)
Duke in Darkness, The (1944) Stewart
Chaney(S)(C); ACK(L)
Duke of Duluth, The (1905) Will R.
Barnes(C); D. Frank Dodge(S); Gates
and Morange(S); Joseph George(L)
Duke of Killicrankie (1904) Ernest
Gros(S)
Duke of Killicrankie, The (1915)
Henri Bendel(C); Homer Emens(S);
ACK(L)
Dulcy (1921) Anthony Greshoff(L); H.
Robert Studio Law(S); ACK(C)
Dumb and the Blind, The (1914)
ACK(C)
Dumb Bell (1923) NONE
Dummy, The (1914) Unitt and
Wickes(S)
Dunce Boy, The (1925) ACK(L)
Dunnigan's Daughter (1945) Stewart
Chaney(S)(C)
Dust Heap, The (1924) ACK(L)
Dybbuck, The (1925) Aline
Bernstein(S)(C); ACK(L)
Dybbuck, The (1926) Nathan
Altman(S); Aline Bernstein(S)(C)
Dybbuck, The (1948) Nathan

Altman(S); ACK(L)
Dybbuck, The (1982) Samuel Leve(S)(L)
Dylan (1964) Jack Brown(L); Ruth
Morley(C); Oliver Smith(S)
Dynamo (1929) Lee Simonson(S)(C)(L)
Eagle Has Two Heads, The (1947)
Aline Bernstein(C); Donald
Oenslager(S)
Earl and the Girl, The (1905) Ernest
Albert(S); Thomas J. Cleland(L); D.
Frank Dodge(S); Mrs. Caroline
Siedle(C)
Earl Carroll's Sketch Book (1929)
Joseph Teichner Studio(S); Max
Teuber(L); Florence Weber(C); Hugh
Willoughby(S)
Earl Carroll's Sketch Book (1935)
Clarke Robinson(S)
Earl Carroll's Vanities (1924) Max
Ree(S); ACK(C)
Earl Carroll's Vanities (1925) Karle O.
Amend(S); Charles LeMaire(C); Willy
Pogany(S); Joseph Teichner(S); ACK(L)
Earl Carroll's Vanities (1926)
Madame Arlington(C);
Booth-Willoughby(C); Charles
LeMaire(C); August Vimnera(S); ACK(L)
Earl Carroll's Vanities (1928) Mabel
E. Johnston(C); William Henry
Matthews(C); Hugh Willoughby(S)
Earl Carroll's Vanities (1930) Charles
LeMaire(C); Vincente Minnelli(C); Hugh
Willoughby(S)
Earl Carroll's Vanities (1931) Charles
LeMaire(C); Vincente Minnelli(S)(C);
Hugh Willoughby(S)
Earl Carroll's Vanities (1932)
Vincente Minnelli(S)(C)
Earl Carroll's Vanities (1940) Jean le
Seyeux(S)(C); E. Carlton Winckler(L)
Earl of Pawtucket, The (1903) Joseph
Physioc(S)
Earl of Ruston (1971) Neil Peter
Jampolis(S)(C)(L)
Early to Bed (1943) George
Jenkins(S)(L); Miles White(C)
Earth (1927) Evelyn T. Clifton(C); Cleon
Throckmorton(S)
Earth Between, The/ Before
Breakfast (1929) James Light(S);
Nettie Duff Reade(C); ACK(L)
Earth Journey (1944) Hildegart
Heitland(C); W. Emerton Heitland(S);
Leo Herbert(L)
Earth, The (1915) Elizabeth Axtman(C);
H. Robert Law(S); Gertrude Newell(S);

ACK[L]

Easiest Way, The (1909) Ernest Gros[S]

Easiest Way, The (1921) Ernest Gros[S]; Louis Hartmann[L]

East Is West (1918) Mary Blackburn[C]; Livingston Platt[S]; ACK[L]

East Lynne (1926) Millia Davenport[C]; Cleon Throckmorton[S]

East of Broadway (1932) P. Dodd Ackerman[S]; ACK[C]

East of Suez (1922) Clifford F. Pember[S]; ACK[C][L]

East Wind (1931) Charles LeMaire[C]; Donald Oenslager[S]; ACK[L]

Easter (1926) Albert Bliss[S]; Fania Mindell[C]

Eastern Standard (1989) Donald Holder[L]; Philipp Jung[S]; William Ivey Long[C]

Easterner, The (1908) NONE

Eastward in Eden (1947) Donald Oenslager[S][C][L]

Easy Come, Easy Go (1925) Nicholas Yellenti[S]; ACK[L]

Easy Dawson (1905) NONE

Easy Mail, The (1924) Sheldon K. Viele[S]

Easy Street (1924) Eugene Cox[S]; ACK[C][L]

Easy Terms (1925) DuWico[L]; Schaffner and Sweet Studio[S]; ACK[C]

Easy Virtue (1925) George W. Harris[S]; ACK[C]

Ebb Tide (1931) Karle O. Amend Studio[S]; ACK[L]

Eben Holden (1901) Ernest Gros[S]

Eccentricities of a Nightingale, The (1976) Theoni V. Aldredge[C]; William Ritman[S]; Marc B. Weiss[L]

Echo, The (1910) Serge de Salomko[C]; ACK[S]

Ed Wynn Carnival (1920) Joseph Physioc[S]; ACK[C][L]

Eden End (1935) Kate Drain Lawson[S]

Edgar Allan Poe (1925) Monroe Pevear[L]; Roy Requa[S][C]

Editha's Burglar (1916) ACK[L]

Edmund Burke (1905) Ogden[C]; Louis C. Young[S]

Edmund Kean (1983) Martin Tilley[S][C]; John Watt[L]

Edna His Wife (1937) Donald Oenslager[S]; Helene Pons[C]

Education of H.Y.M.A.N. K.A.P.L.A.N., The (1968) Martin Aronstein[L]; William and Jean

Eckart[S]; Winn Morton[C]

Education of Mr. Pipp, The (1905) Frank Platzer[S]

Edward, My Son (1948) Raymond Sovey[S][L]

Edwin Booth (1958) Zvi Geyra[S][L]; Edith Head[C]

Edwina Black (1950) Leo Kerz[S][L]; Elfi Von Kantzow[C]

Effect of Gamma Rays on Man-in-the-Moon Marigolds, The (1978) Ian Calderon[L]; Peter Harvey[S][C]

Egg, The (1962) Raymond Aghayan[C]; Bob Brannigan[L]; Robert Kelly[S]

Egghead, The (1957) Anna Hill Johnstone[C]; Richard Sylbert[S]

Egotist, The (1922) ACK[L]

Eight Bells (1933) Cleon Throckmorton[S]; ACK[C]

Eight O'clock Tuesday (1941) Lemuel Ayers[S]; ACK[C]

Eileen (1917) Raymond Newton Hyde[C]; Kliegl Brothers[L]; H. Robert Studio Law[S]

Eileen Asthore (1906) Homer Emens[S]; Unitt and Wickes[S]

Einstein and the Polar Bear (1981) Arden Fingerhut[L]; Nancy Potts[C]; Fred Voelpel[S]

El Gran Galeoto (1899) NONE

Elder Miss Blossom, The (1899) NONE

Elder Son, The (1914) NONE

Eldest, The (1935) Raymond Sovey[S]

Electra (1908) Kliegl Brothers[L]; Charles Ricketts[S][C]

Electra (1918) Livingston Platt[S][C]

Electra (1927) Livingston Platt[S][C]; ACK[L]

Electra (1932) ACK[L]

Electra (1952) C. Clonis[S]; Antonios Phocas[C]

Electra (1998) Johan Engels[S][C]; Paul Pyant[L]

Electricity (1910) Homer Emens[S]

Elektra (1930) ACK[L]

Elephant Man, The (1979) Beverly Emmons[L]; David Jenkins[S]; Julie Weiss[C]

Elevating A Husband (1912) Dodge and Castle[S]

Eliza Comes to Stay (1914) NONE

Elizabeth I (1972) Robert Anton[S]; Roger Morgan[L]; Susan Tsu[C]

Elizabeth Sleeps Out (1936) ACK[S]

Elizabeth the Queen (1930) Lee

Simonson[(S)(C)]
Elmer Gantry (1928) William Henry
Matthews[(C)]; Livingston Platt[(S)(C)];
ACK[(L)]
Elmer the Great (1928) ACK[(C)(L)]
Elsie (1923) ACK[(S)(C)(L)]
Elsie Janis and Her Gang (1919) Will
R. Barnes[(C)]; Charles LeMaire[(C)];
ACK[(S)(L)]
Elsie Janis and Her Gang (1922) Will
R. Barnes[(C)]; Charles LeMaire[(C)];
ACK[(S)(L)]
Elton Case, The (1921) Henri
Bendel[(C)]; ACK[(S)]
Embarrassment of Riches, The
(1906) NONE
Embassy Ball, The (1906) NONE
Embers (1926) ACK[(L)]
Embezzled Heaven (1944) Stewart
Chaney[(S)(C)]
Emerald Isle, The (1902) Percy
Anderson[(C)]; Mrs. Caroline Siedle[(C)]
Eminent Domain (1982) Lowell ·
Achziger[(L)]; Michael Miller[(S)]; Jennifer
von Mayrhauser[(C)]
Emlyn Williams As Charles Dickens
(1952) ACK[(L)]
Emlyn Williams As Charles Dickens
(1953) ACK[(L)]
Emperor Henry IV (1973) Abd'el
Farrah[(S)(C)]; Neil Peter Jampolis[(L)]
**Emperor Jones / The Dreamy Kid,
The** (1925) Cleon Throckmorton[(S)]
Emperor Jones, The (1924) Cleon
Throckmorton[(S)]
Emperor Jones, The (1926) Cleon
Throckmorton[(S)]
Emperor's Clothes, The (1953) Ben
Edwards[(C)]; Lester Polakov[(S)(L)]
Empress Eugenie, The (1932)
ACK[(C)(L)]
Empress of Destiny (1938) Robert Van
Rosen[(S)(C)]
Enchanted April, The (1925) Sheldon
K. Viele[(S)]
Enchanted Cottage, The (1923)
Adams T. Rice[(S)]
Enchanted Isle (1927) Ida Hoyt
Chamberlain[(S)]; ACK[(C)(L)]
Enchanted, The (1950) Robert
Edmond Jones[(S)(C)]; ACK[(L)]
Enchantment (1927) Clarke Robinson[(S)]
Enchantress, The (1911) William
Camph[(S)]; Joseph[(C)]; Lucile[(C)]; William
Henry Matthews[(C)]
End As a Man (1953) Mel Bourne[(S)(C)]

End of Summer (1936) Lee
Simonson[(S)]; ACK[(C)]
End of the World (1984) Ken
Billington[(L)]; Clarke Dunham[(S)];
William Ivey Long[(C)]
Endless Chain, The (1922) H. Robert
Studio Law[(S)]; Miss E. M. A.
Steinmetz[(C)]; ACK[(L)]
Enemy of the People, An (1927)
Claude Bragdon[(S)(C)]
Enemy of the People, An (1928)
Claude Bragdon[(S)(C)]
Enemy of the People, An (1937)
Claude Bragdon[(S)(C)]
Enemy of the People, An (1950) Aline
Bernstein[(C)]; Charles Elson[(S)(L)]
Enemy Within, The (1931) Margaret
Pemberton[(C)]; ACK[(S)(L)]
Enemy, The (1925) Jo Mielziner[(S)(L)]
Engagement Baby, The (1970) Jules
Fisher[(L)]; Ann Roth[(C)]; Robin
Wagner[(S)]
English Daisy, An (1904) John H.
Young[(S)]
Englishman's Home, An (1909) Unitt
and Wickes[(S)]
Enigma, The (1908) NONE
Enter Laughing (1963) Ed
Wittstein[(S)(C)(L)]
Enter Madame (1920) Sheldon K.
Viele[(S)]; ACK[(C)(L)]
Entertainer, The (1958) Clare
Jeffrey[(C)]; Alan Tagg[(S)]
Entertaining Mr. Sloane (1965)
William Ritman[(S)(C)(L)]
Epic Proportions (1999) David Gallo[(S)];
Paul Gallo[(L)]; William Ivey Long[(C)]
Episode (1925) David S. Gaither[(S)];
ACK[(C)]
Epitaph for George Dillon (1958)
Ralph Alswang[(L)]; Stephen
Doncaster[(S)]; Helene Pons[(C)]
Equus (1974) John Napier[(S)(C)]; Andy
Phillips[(L)]
Equus (1976) John Napier[(S)(C)]; Andy
Phillips[(L)]
Ermine (1921) Norman Bel Geddes[(S)(C)]
Erminie (1903) Frank Lentz[(S)]; ACK[(C)]
Errant Lady (1934) Victor Graziano[(S)]
Erstwhile Susan (1916) ACK[(L)]
Escapade (1953) Donald
Oenslager[(S)(C)(L)]
Escape (1927) ACK[(S)(C)(L)]
Escape Me Never (1935) Theodore
Komisarjevsky[(S)]; ACK[(C)]
Escape This Night (1938) Harry

Horner[S]; Helene Pons[C]
Escape, The (1913) No PLAYBILL
Eternal City, The (1902) Ernest
Gros[S]; Edward G. Unitt[S]; ACK[C]
Eternal Magdalene, The (1915)
ACK[C][L]
Eternal Road, The (1937) Norman Bel
Geddes[S][C][L]
Ethan Frome (1936) Jo Mielziner[S][C][L]
Eubie (1978) Karl Eigsti[S]; Bernard
Johnson[C]; William Mintzer[L]
Eugenia (1957) Peggy Clark[L]; Oliver
Smith[S]; Miles White[C]
Eugenically Speaking (1915) Englebert
Gminska[S]; B. Russell Herts[S]
Eva (1912) F. Richards Anderson[C];
Unitt and Wickes[S]
Eva the Fifth (1928) Cirker and
Robbins[S]; ACK[C][L]
Evangeline (1913) Arthur Hopkins[S]
Evangelist, The (1907) NONE
Eve of Saint Mark, The (1942)
Howard Bay[S]; Moe Hack[L]; Toni
Ward[C]
Eve's Leaves (1925) ACK[S][C][L]
Evening with Beatrice Lillie, An
(1952) Rolf Gérard[S]
**Evening with Harry Connick, Jr.
and His Orchestra, An** (1990)
John Falabella[S]; Alexander Julian[C];
Marilyn Lowey[L]
Evening with Jerry Herman, An
(1998) Ken Billington[L]; Kenneth
Foy[S]; ACK[C]
Evening with Richard Nixon, An
(1972) Joseph G. Aulisi[C]; H. R.
Poindexter[L]; William Ritman[S]
Evening with Yves Montand, An
(1961) Yves Montand[S][L]
Evensong (1933) Laurence Irving[S];
ACK[C]
Ever Green Lady, The (1922)
Livingston Platt[S]; ACK[C][L]
Every Man for Himself (1940) Ernest
Glover[S]
Every Thursday (1934) P. Dodd
Ackerman Studio[S]
Everybody Loves Opal (1961) Jo
Mielziner[S][L]; Noel Taylor[C]
Everybody's Welcome (1931) Allison
McLellan Hunter[C]; Ernest Schraps[C];
Rollo Wayne[S]; ACK[L]
Everyday (1921) ACK[S][C]
Everyman (1902) NONE
Everyman (1907) NONE
Everyman (1913) NONE

Everyman (1918) ACK[L]
Everything (1918) Will R. Barnes[C];
Joseph Elsner[L]; William Henry
Matthews[C]; Robert McQuinn[C];
Gladys Monkhouse[C]; ACK[S]
Everything in the Garden (1967)
Tharon Musser[L]; William
Ritman[S][C]
Everything's Joke (1930) Edgar
Bohlman[S]
Everywhere I Roam (1938) Robert
Edmond Jones[S][C]
Everywoman (1911) Walter W.
Burridge[S]; Hy Meyer[C]; Joseph
Wilson[L]
Evidence (1914) NONE
Evita (1979) Tazeena Firth[S][C];
Timothy O'Brien[S][C]
Exceeding Small (1928) Rollo Wayne[S]
Excess Baggage (1927) P. Dodd
Ackerman[S]; DuWico[L]; ACK[C]
Exchange of Wives, An (1919) Harry
Collins[C]; Dodge and Castle[S]; Jane
Wallack[S]; ACK[L]
Exciters, The (1922) ACK[S][C][L]
Excursion (1937) Gladys E. Calthrop[S];
ACK[C]
Excuse Me (1911) Walter W.
Burridge[S]; Joseph Wilson[L]
Execution of Justice, (1986) Pat
Collins[L]; Ming Cho Lee[S]; Jennifer
von Mayrhauser[C]
Exercise, The (1968) Jean Rosenthal[L];
Oliver Smith[S]; ACK[C]
Exile, The (1923) Gates and Morange[S];
Kliegl Brothers[L]; ACK[C]
Exiles (1925) Russel Wright[S][C]
Exit the King (1968) Nancy Potts[C];
Rouben Ter-Arutunian[S]; James
Tilton[L]
Experience (1914) Melville Ellis[C];
Joseph[C]; Theodore Reisig[S]
Experience (1918) Henri Bendel[C];
ACK[L]
Experience Unnecessary (1931)
Watson Barratt[S]; Allison McLellan
Hunter[C]; Ernest Schraps[C]
Explorer, The (1912) Henri Bendel[C];
Lucile[C]
Expressing Willie (1924) Woodman
Thompson[S]; ACK[C]
Extra (1923) ACK[L]
Eye on the Sparrow (1938) Emeline
Clarke Roche[S]; ACK[C]
Eyes of the Heart, The (1906) NONE
Eyes of Youth (1917) Will R. Barnes[C];

Katherine H. Lovell[C]; William Henry Matthews[C]; Robert McQuinn[C]; Gladys Monkhouse[C]; ACK[S][L]

Eyvind of the Hills (1921) Livingston Platt[S][C]

Fabulous Invalid (1938) John Hambleton[C]; Donald Oenslager[S]

Face of a Hero (1960) Ben Edwards[S][L]; Ann Roth[C]

Face the Music (1932) Albert R. Johnson[S]; Yetta Kiviette[C]; Max Weldy[C]

Face the Music (1933) Albert R. Johnson[S]

Facing the Music (1903) Madame Francis[C]; ACK[S][C]

Fad and Folly (1902) D. Frank Dodge[S]; Joseph Physioc[S]; ACK[C]

Fade Out-Fade In (1964) Donald Brooks[C]; William and Jean Eckart[S][L]

Fade Out-Fade In (1965) Donald Brooks[C]; William and Jean Eckart[S][L]

Fads and Fancies (1915) F. Richards Anderson[C]; Anthony Greshoff[L]; Cora MacGeachy[C]; ACK[S]

Failures, The (1923) Lee Simonson[S][C]

Fair and Warmer (1915) Joseph Physioc[S]; ACK[C][L]

Fair Circassian, The (1921) Gertrude Newell[S][C]

Fair Co-Ed, The (1909) William Camph[S]; Homer Emens[S]; T. Bernard McDonald[S]

Fair Exchange, A (1905) NONE

Fair Game (1957) Frederick Fox[S]; Robert Mackintosh[C]

Fair Games for Lovers (1964) Ralph Alswang[S][C][L]

Faith Healer (1979) John Lee Beatty[S]; Jane Greenwood[C]; Marilyn Rennagel[L]

Faith Healer, The (1910) No PLAYBILL

Faithful Heart, The (1922) Clifford F. Pember[S]

Faithful, The (1919) Lee Simonson[S][C]

Faithfully Yours (1951) Paul Morrison[S][L]

Fake, The (1924) Henri Bendel[C]; Wilson Hungate[S]; Sheldon K. Viele[S]; ACK[L]

Fall and Rise of Susan Lennox (1920) ACK[L]

Fall Guy, The (1925) ACK[L]

Fall of Eve, The (1925) John W.

Baxter[S]; C. B. DuMoulin[S]; ACK[L]

Fallen Angels (1927) Frances Clyne[C]; Jo Mielziner[S][L]

Fallen Angels (1956) Patton Campbell[C]; Eldon Elder[S][L]

Fallen Idol, The (1915) ACK[L]

False Dreams, Farewell (1934) Selma Alexander[C]; A. J. Lundborg[S]

Falsettos (1992) Frances Aronson[L]; Ann Hould-Ward[C]; Douglas Stein[S]

Falstaff (1928) Millia Davenport[C]; Louis Kennel[S]; ACK[L]

Fame (1974) Martin Aronstein[L]; Jeffrey B. Moss[C]; Douglas W. Schmidt[S]

Family Affair, A (1946) Samuel Leve[S]; Noel Taylor[C]

Family Affair, A (1962) Robert Fletcher[C]; David Hays[S][L]

Family Affairs (1929) Cirker and Robbins[S]; Madame Frances[C]; Mildred Manning[C]

Family Cupboard, The (1913) Joseph[C]; Richard T. Lingley[S]

Family Exit/ Counsel's Opinion/ etc. (1932) ACK[L]

Family Failing, The (1925) ACK[L]

Family Portrait (1939) Harry Horner[S][C]

Family Upstairs, The (1925) Nicholas Yellenti[S]; ACK[L]

Family Upstairs, The (1933) Nicholas Yellenti[S]; ACK[L]

Family Way, The (1965) Thomas Becher[C]; Ben Edwards[S][L]

Family, The (1910) No PLAYBILL

Family, The (1943) Boris Aronson[S]; Moe Hack[L]; Carolyn Hancock[C]

Famous Mrs. Fair, The (1919) ACK[L]

Fan, The (1921) Cora Bulger[C]; Rose Hagan[C]; Agnes Lenners[C]

Fanatics, The (1927) ACK[L]

Fancy Meeting You Again (1952) Kathleen Ankers[C]; Albert R. Johnson[S]

Fanny (1926) Joseph Wickes[S]; ACK[C]

Fanny (1954) Alvin Colt[C]; Jo Mielziner[S][L]

Fanny Hawthorn (1922) ACK[L]

Fanny's First Play (1912) NONE

Fantana (1905) D. Frank Dodge[S]; Frank E. Gates[S]; Edward Morange[S]

Fantasia/ A Temporary Husband/ Crescendo (1933) Bernard Brooks[S]

Fantasia/ Crescendo/ A Temporary Husband (1933) ACK[C]

Fantastic Fricassee, A (1922) André

Chotin(S); Pauline Wells(C)
Far Country, A (1961) Donald
Oenslager(S)(L); Ann Roth(C)
Far Cry, The (1924) Livingston Platt(S);
Ack(C)
Far-Away Horses (1933) Selma
Alexander(C); S. Syrjala(S)
Farewell Summer (1937) Frederick
Fox(S); Linda Lee Hill(C)
Farewell to Arms, A (1930) P. Dodd
Ackerman(S)
Farewell, Farewell, Eugene (1960)
Robert Fletcher(S)(C)
Farm of Three Echoes (1939) Cirker
and Robbins(S); Ack(C)
Farmer's Wife, The (1924) Watson
Barratt(S); Henri Bendel(C)
Fascinating Flora (1907) Frank E.
Gates(S); Edward Morange(S); Mrs.
Caroline Siedle(C)
Fascinating Mr. Vanderveldt (1906)
Madame Gabbetio(C); Frank E.
Gates(S); Madame Hayward(C);
Edward Morange(S); Louis C. Young(S)
Fascinating Widow, The (1911)
Madame Frances(C); Ack(C)
Fashion (1924) Robert Edmond
Jones(S)(C); Kirah Markham(C);
Reginald Marsh(S); Cleon
Throckmorton(S)
Fashions for Men (1922) Aline
Bernstein(C); Sheldon K. Viele(S);
Ack(L)
Fashions of 1924 (1923) Gilbert
Adrian(C); William E. Price(L); Ack(S)
Fast and Furious (1931) Cirker and
Robbins(S); Ack(C)(L)
Fast and Grow Fat (1916) Dodge and
Castle(S); Ack(C)(L)
Fast Life (1928) Ack(S)(L)
Fast Service (1931) Lucinda(C);
Raymond Sovey(S)
Fata Morgana (1924) Lee Simonson(S)(C)
Fata Morgana (1931) Dave Caddy(C);
Ack(C)
Fatal Alibi, The (1932) Dale Stetson(S);
Ack(C)
Fatal Weakness (1946) Donald
Oenslager(S)(L); Bianca Stroock(C)
Fatal Wedding, The (1901) NONE
Fatal Wedding, The (1924) Millard
France(S); Ack(C)(L)
Father and Son (1908) NONE
Father and the Boys (1908) Joseph
Physioc(S)
Father Malachy's Miracle (1937) Jo

Mielziner(S)(C)(L)
Father's Day (1971) Jo Mielziner(S)(L);
Ann Roth(C)
Father, The (1912) NONE
Father, The (1928) P. Dodd
Ackerman(S); Ack(L)
Father, The (1949) Eleanor
Goldsmith(C); Donald Oenslager(S)(L)
Father, The (1962) Sven Fahlstedt(S);
Gunnar Gelbort(C); Ack(C)
Father, The (1981) Arden Fingerhut(L);
Marjorie Bradley Kellogg(S); Jennifer
von Mayrhauser(C)
Father, The (1996) John Lee Beatty(S);
Martin Pakledinaz(C); Kenneth
Posner(L)
Father, The/ Barbara's Wedding
(1931) Ack(L)
Fatinitza (1904) Percy Anderson(C);
Joseph Clare(S); Henry E. Hoyt(S);
Richard Marston(S); John H. Palmer(L)
Fatted Calf, The (1912) NONE
Faun, The (1911) Ernest Albert(S); Mrs.
Robert Osborn(C); Elizabeth Simon(C);
Eugene Wallace(L)
Fear Market, The (1916) Lucile(C);
Princess Troubetsky(S); Ack(S)(L)
Fearless Frank (1980) Carrie F.
Robbins(C); Ruth Roberts(L); Martin
Tilley(S)
Feathers in a Gale (1944) Aline
Bernstein(C); Raymond Sovey(S)
Fedora (1905) James Fox(S); F. G.
Gaus(L); Madame Louise Museus(C)
Fedora (1922) Ack(S)(L)
Fences (1987) Candice Donnelly(C);
Danianne Mizzy(L); James D.
Sandefur(S)
Festival (1955) Robert O'Hearn(S)(L);
Noel Taylor(C)
Few Are Chosen (1935) Alfred
Bauer(S); Greta Baum(C)
Few Good Men, A (1989) Ben
Edwards(S); Thomas Skelton(L); David
C. Woolard(C)
Few Wild Oats, A (1932) Karle O.
Amend(S); Ack(C)(L)
Fickle Women (1937) Ack(L)
Fiddle-Dee-Dee (1900) Will R.
Barnes(C); John H. Young(S)
Fiddler on the Roof (1964) Boris
Aronson(S); Jean Rosenthal(L); Patricia
Zipprodt(C)
Fiddler on the Roof (1976) Boris
Aronson(S); Ken Billington(L); Patricia
Zipprodt(C)

Fiddler on the Roof (1981) Boris Aronson(S); Ken Billington(L); Patricia Zipprodt(C)

Fiddler on the Roof (1990) Boris Aronson(S); Ken Billington(L); Patricia Zipprodt(C)

Fiddler's Three (1918) Mary Blackburn(C); ACK(S)(L)

Field God, The (1927) Louis Bromberg(S)

Field of Ermine (1935) Bianca Stroock(C); ACK(L)

Fields Beyond, The (1936) Horace Armistead(S); Edith Teets(C)

Fiesta (1929) Mordecai Gorelik(C); Evelyn McHorter(C); Cleon Throckmorton(S)

Fifteen Minute Hamlet, The (1992) John Lee Beatty(S); Pat Collins(L); Jess Goldstein(C)

Fifth Column, The (1940) Howard Bay(S); Paul du Pont(C)

Fifth Dimension, The (1974) Jane Reisman(L); Michael Travis(C); Robin Wagner(S)

Fifth of July (1980) John Lee Beatty(S); Laura Crow(C); Dennis Parichy(L)

Fifth Season, The (1953) Edythe Gilfond(C); Samuel Leve(S)

Fifty Miles from Boston (1908) Ernest Albert(S); Young Brothers and Boss(S)

Fifty Million Frenchmen (1929) Norman Bel Geddes(S); James Reynolds(C)

Fifty-Fifty (1919) ACK(C)(L)

Fig Leaves Are Falling, The (1969) William and Jean Eckart(S); Robert Mackintosh(C); Tharon Musser(L)

Fight, The (1913) Hickson(C); H. Robert Law(S)

Fighting Cock, The (1959) Howard Bay(L); Rolf Gérard(S)(C)

Fighting Hope, The (1908) Ernest Gros(S)

Filumena (1980) Raimonda Gaetani(S)(C); Thomas Skelton(L)

Final Balance, The (1928) Mordecai Gorelik(S)

Find the Fox (1930) ACK(S)(C)(L)

Find Your Way Home (1974) Theoni V. Aldredge(C); William Ritman(S); Marc B. Weiss(L)

Fine and Dandy (1930) Henry Dreyfuss(S); Charles LeMaire(C)

Fine Feathers (1913) NONE

Finian's Rainbow (1947) Eleanor

Goldsmith(C); Jo Mielziner(S)(L)

Finishing Touches (1973) Ben Edwards(S)(L); Jane Greenwood(C)

Fiorello (1959) William and Jean Eckart(S)(C)(L)

Fioretta (1929) Charles LeMaire(C); William Henry Matthews(C); Clarke Robinson(S)

Fire! (1969) Howard Bay(S)(L); Lewis Brown(C)

Firebird (1932) Aline Bernstein(S); ACK(C)

Firebrand of Florence, The (1945) Raoul Pène Du Bois(C); Jo Mielziner(S)(L)

Firebrand, The (1924) Woodman Thompson(S)(C)

Firefly, The (1912) P. Dodd Ackerman(S); William Henry Matthews(C); Theodore Reisig(S)

Firefly, The (1931) ACK(C)(L)

Fireman's Flame, The (1937) Eugene Dunkel(S); Kermit Love(C)

Fires of Fate, The (1909) Ernest Gros(S); Unitt and Wickes(S)

Fires of St. John, The (1904) NONE

Fires of St. John, The (1908) NONE

Firm of Cunningham, The (1905) Gates and Morange(S); ACK(C)

First 50 Years, The (1922) Livingston Platt(S)(C); ACK(L)

First American Dictator (1939) ACK(L)

First Apple, The (1933) Roderick McRae(C); Arthur P. Segal(S)

First Breeze of Summer, The (1975) Edward Burbridge(S); Thomas Skelton(L); Mary Mease Warren(C)

First Crocus, The (1942) Johannes Larsen(S); Millie Sutherland(C)

First Episode (1934) Rollo Wayne(S); ACK(C)

First Flight (1925) Jo Mielziner(S)(L)

First Gentleman, The (1957) Ralph Alswang(S)(L); Motley(C)

First Impressions (1959) Alvin Colt(C); Charles Elson(L); Peter Larkin(S)

First Is Last (1919) Henri Bendel(C); Harry Collins(S)(C); Lucile(C); Livingston Platt(S)(C); ACK(L)

First Lady (1935) John Hambleton(C); Donald Oenslager(S)

First Lady in the Land, The (1911) H. Robert Law(S)

First Law, The (1929) Rollo Wayne(S)

First Legion, The (1934) Eddie Eddy(S); John F. McEvoy(C)

First Love (1926) Watson Barratt[S]; ACK[C]

First Love (1961) Theoni V. Aldredge[C]; Donald Oenslager[S][L]

First Million, The (1943) Paul du Pont[C]; Wolfgang Roth[S]

First Monday in October (1978) Roger Morgan[L]; Ann Roth[C]; Oliver Smith[S]

First Mortgage (1929) Jo Mielziner[S][L]; ACK[C]

First Mrs. Fraser, The (1929) Livingston Platt[S]; ACK[C]

First Mrs. Fraser, The (1947) Charles Elson[S][L]; Natalie Barth Walker[C]

First Night (1930) Walter Harvey[S]; Herbert Ward[S]; ACK[C]

First One Asleep, Whistle (1966) Theoni V. Aldredge[C]; Lloyd Burlingame[S][L]

First Stone, The (1928) Aline Bernstein[S][C]

First Stop to Heaven (1941) Louis Kennel[S]; ACK[C]

First Violin, The (1899) NONE

First Year, The (1920) Gates and Morange[S]; ACK[C][L]

First, The (1981) David Chapman[S]; Carrie F. Robbins[C]; Marc B. Weiss[L]

Firstborn, The (1958) Boris Aronson[S]; Robert Fletcher[C]; Tharon Musser[L]

Fisher Maiden, The (1903) Ernest Albert[S]; Henry Dazian[C]; ACK[C]

Five Alarm Waltz (1941) Harry Horner[S]

Five Finger Exercise (1959) Ray Diffen[C]; Tharon Musser[L]; Oliver Smith[S][C]

Five Frankforters, The (1913) Hugo Baruch[S]

Five Guys Named Moe (1992) Andrew Bridge[L]; Tim Goodchild[S]; Noel Howard[C]

Five Million, The (1919) ACK[C][L]

Five O'clock (1919) Mary Blackburn[C]; Clifford F. Pember[S]; ACK[L]

Five O'clock Girl (1927) Norman Bel Geddes[S]; Charles LeMaire[C]

Five O'clock Girl, The (1981) Nanzi Adzima[C]; John Lee Beatty[S]; Craig Miller[L]

Five Star Final (1930) P. Dodd Ackerman Studio[S]

Five-Six-Seven-Eight... Dance! (1983) Lindsay W. Davis[S][C]; Tom John[S]; Richard Nelson[L]

Fixing Sister (1916) H. Robert Law[S]; John Whalen[L]; ACK[C]

Flag Is Born, A (1946) John Boyt[C]; Robert Davison[S]

Flag Lieutenant (1909) Henry Dazian[C]; Ernest Gros[S]

Flag Station, The (1907) NONE

Flahooey (1951) Howard Bay[S][L]; David Ffolkes[C]

Flame of Love (1924) Eric Pape[S]; Raymond Sovey[C]

Flame, The (1916) Richard Walton Tully[S]; ACK[L]

Flamenco Puro (1986) Hector Orezzoli[S][C][L]; Claudio Segovia[S][C][L]

Flamingo Road (1946) Watson Barratt[S]; Leo Kerz[L]; Emeline Clarke Roche[C]

Flare Path (1942) Raymond Sovey[S]; ACK[C]

Flashing Stream, The (1938) Joseph and Phil Harker[S]; ACK[C]

Flea in Her Ear, A (1969) Lewis Brown[C]; John McLain[L]; Stuart Wurtzel[S]

Fledgling (1940) Marochka Taylor[C]; Richard Whorf[S]

Flesh (1925) Louis Bromberg[S]; ACK[C][L]

Flight (1929) Livingston Platt[S]; ACK[C]

Flight into Egypt (1952) Anna Hill Johnstone[C]; Jo Mielziner[S][L]

Flight to the West (1940) Jo Mielziner[S][L]

Flight, The (1912) NO PLAYBILL

Flip Side, The (1968) Lloyd Burlingame[L]; Galanos[C]; J. Hutchinson Scott[S][C]

Flo-Flo (1917) Mrs. R. Kerner[C]; ACK[S][L]

Floating Light Bulb, The (1981) Pat Collins[L]; Santo Loquasto[S][C]

Flora, the Red Menace (1965) Donald Brooks[C]; William and Jean Eckart[S]; Tharon Musser[L]

FloraBella (1916) Mrs. R. Kerner[C]; Joseph Urban[S]; ACK[L]

Floradora (1920) Watson Barratt[S]; Cora MacGeachy[C]

Floriani's Wife (1923) Livingston Platt[S]; ACK[C]

Florida Girl (1925) Karle O. Amend[S]; Willy Pogany[S]; John E. Stone[C]; Joseph Teichner[S]; ACK[L]

Florist Shop, The (1909) Charles E. Brown[S]; Walter W. Burridge[S]; Joseph Wilson[L]

Florodora (1900) Joseph[C]; T. Bernard McDonald[S]; Moses and Hamilton[S]

Flossie (1924) Benjamin Leffler[L]; Nicholas Yellenti[S]; Ack[C]

Flower Drum Song (1958) Peggy Clark[L]; Irene Sharaff[C]; Oliver Smith[S]

Flower of the Palace of Han, The (1912) E. Hamilton Bell[S][C]; Unitt and Wickes[S]

Flower of the Ranch, The (1908) NONE

Flower of Yamato, The (1908) Gates and Morange[S]; Kliegl Brothers[L]; Ack[C]

Flowering Cherry (1959) Theoni V. Aldredge[C]; Boris Aronson[S]; Paul Morrison[L]

Flowering Peach, The (1954) Ballou[C]; A. H. Feder[L]; Mordecai Gorelik[S]

Flowering Peach, The (1994) Theoni V. Aldredge[C]; Richard Nelson[L]; Ray Recht[S]

Flowers (1974) John Gleason[L]; Lindsay Kemp[S][C]; John Spradbery[L]

Flowers of the Forest (1935) Jo Mielziner[S][L]; Ack[C]

Flowers of Virtue, The (1942) Joseph Fretwell III[C]; Donald Oenslager[S]

Fluffy Ruffles (1908) Hugo Baruch[S]; Edward G. Unitt[S]; Joseph Wickes[S]

Fly Away Home (1935) Raymond Sovey[S]; Ack[C]

Fly by Night (1933) Joseph Hansen[S]; Ack[C]

Flying Colors (1932) Norman Bel Geddes[S][L]; Constance Ripley[C]

Flying Gerardos, The (1940) Horton O'Neil[S]; Helene Pons[C]

Flying High (1930) Charles LeMaire[C]; Joseph Urban[S]

Fog (1927) Nicholas Yellenti[S]; Ack[C]

Fog Bound (1927) Nicholas Yellenti[S]

Folies Bergère (1939) Emile Bertin[S]; Raymond Deshays[S]; Grosvois and Lambert[S]; Lavignac & Pellegry[S]; Freddy Wittop[C]; Ack[L]

Folies Bergère (1964) Michel Gyarmathy[S][C]

Folies Bergère (1965) Ack[L]

Follies (1971) Boris Aronson[S]; Florence Klotz[C]; Tharon Musser[L]

Follies (2001) Theoni V. Aldredge[C]; Mark Thompson[S]; Hugh Vanstone[L]

Follow Me (1916) Homer Conant[C]; Ack[L]

Follow the Girl (1918) Ack[L]

Follow the Girls (1944) Howard Bay[S][L]; Lou Eisele[C]

Follow Through (1929) Yetta Kiviette[C]; Donald Oenslager[S]; Mr. Jack Rissman[C]; Ack[L]

Fool and His Money, A (1903) NONE

Fool Hath Said: 'There Is No God', The (1908) Madame Freisinger[C]; L. and H. Nathan[C]; Unitt and Wickes[S]

Fool Moon (1993) Bill Kellard[C]; Nancy Schertler[L]; Douglas Stein[S]

Fool Moon (1995) Bill Kellard[C]; Nancy Schertler[L]; Douglas Stein[S]

Fool Moon (1998) Bill Kellard[C]; Nancy Schertler[L]; Douglas Stein[S]

Fool of Fortune, A (1912) Walter W. Burridge[S]

Fool There Was, A (1909) T. Bernard McDonald[S]; Edward G. Unitt[S]; Joseph Wickes[S]; Young Brothers and Boss[S]

Fool's Bells (1925) DuWico[L]; Ack[S][C]

Fool, The (1922) Travis Banton[C]; Clifford F. Pember[S]; Ack[L]

Foolish Notion (1945) Mainbocher[C]; Jo Mielziner[S][L]

Foolish Virgin, The (1910) Ernest Gros[S]

Fools (1981) John Lee Beatty[S]; Tharon Musser[L]; Patricia Zipprodt[C]

Fools Errand (1922) Ernest Peixotto[S]; Ack[C]

Fools Rush in (1934) Eugene Dunkel[S]; Russell Patterson[S][C]

Foolscap (1933) David S. Gaither[S]; Kirah Markham[C]

Footlights (1927) Helen Mahieu[C]; August Vimnera[S]

Footloose (1920) Clifford F. Pember[S]; Ack[C][L]

Footloose (1998) John Lee Beatty[S]; Ken Billington[L]; Toni-Leslie James[C]

For All of Us (1923) Watson Barratt[S]; Ack[C]

For Better or Worse (1927) Ack[L]

For Colored Girls Who Have Considered Suicide (1976) Judy Dearing[C]; Ming Cho Lee[S]; Jennifer Tipton[L]

For Goodness Sake (1922) P. Dodd Ackerman[S]; Ack[C][L]

For Heaven's Sake, Mother (1948) Leo Kerz[S][L]

For Keeps (1944) Raymond Sovey[S]

For Love or Money (1947) DuWico[L];

Anna Hill Johnstone(C); Raymond Sovey(S)

For Love's Sweet Sake (1903) NONE

For Services Rendered (1933) Omar Kiam(C); Livingston Platt(S)

For the Defense (1919) Hewlett & Basing(S); ACK(C)

For Valor (1935) Edward Morange(S)

For Value Received (1923) Charles J. Auburn(S); ACK(C)(L)

For Your Pleasure (1943) Kathryn Kuhn(C); ACK(L)

Forbidden (1919) Henri Bendel(C); Gates and Morange(S)

Forbidden Fruit (1915) Robert E. Locher(S)(C)

Forbidden Melody (1936) Sergi Soudeikine(S); Robert Ten Eyck Stevenson(C)

Forbidden Roads (1928) August Vimnera(S); ACK(C)(L)

Foreign Affairs (1932) Albert R. Johnson(S); ACK(C)

Foreigners (1939) Watson Barratt(S); Ernest Schraps(C)

Forest Lovers, The (1901) Mrs. Caroline Siedle(C); Edward G. Unitt(S); Milnor Wells(L)

Forever After (1918) Henri Bendel(C); Gertrude Newell(S); ACK(L)

Forever Tango (1997) Argemira Affonso(C); Luis Bravo(L)

Forsaking All Others (1933) Hattie Carnegie(C); Emmett Joyce(C); Donald Oenslager(S)

Fortune Hunter, The (1909) Gates and Morange(S)

Fortune Teller, The (1919) ACK(C)(L)

Fortune Teller, The (1929) ACK(L)

Fortunes of the King, The (1904) Charles E. Boss(S); Maurice Hermann(C)

Forty Carats (1968) Will Steven Armstrong(S); Martin Aronstein(L); William McHone(C)

Forty-five Minutes from Broadway (1906) Ernest Albert(S); F. Richards Anderson(C); William Hoover(S); Frank Marsden(S); John H. Young(S)

Forty-ninth Cousin, The (1960) Stewart Chaney(S)(L); Gene Coffin(C)

Forward the Heart (1949) Perry Watkins(S)(L)

Fosse (1999) Andrew Bridge(L); Santo Loquasto(S)(C)

Fountain of Youth, The (1918) ACK(S)(C)(L)

Fountain, The (1925) Robert Edmond Jones(S)(C)

Four Baboons Adoring the Sun (1992) Willa Kim(C); Richard Pilbrow(L); Tony Walton(S)

Four Flusher, The (1925) Charles J. Auburn(S); Hickson(C); Joseph Physioc Studio(S); ACK(L)

Four in a Garden (1971) Martin Aronstein(L); William McHone(C); Oliver Smith(S)

Four O'clock (1933) Cirker and Robbins(S); ACK(C)

Four Saints in Three Acts (1934) A. H. Feder(L); Kate Drain Lawson(S)(C); Florine Stettheimer(S)

Four Saints in Three Acts (1952) Paul Morrison(S)(C)(L)

Four Twelves Are 48 (1951) Peggy Morrison(C); Raymond Sovey(S)

Four Walls (1927) Cirker and Robbins(S)

Four Winds (1957) Donald Oenslager(S)(C)(L)

Fourposter, The (1951) Lucinda Ballard(C); S. Syrjala(S); ACK(L)

Fourth Estate, The (1909) Gates and Morange(S)

Foxfire (1981) Ken Billington(L); Linda Fisher(C); David Mitchell(S)

Foxhole in the Parlor (1945) Lee Simonson(S)(C)(L)

Foxy (1964) Robert Fletcher(C); Robert Randolph(S)(L)

Foxy Grandpa (1902) NONE

Foxy Quiller (1900) F. Richards Anderson(C); Ernest Gros(S)

Fragile Fox (1954) Ralph Alswang(S)(L)

Francesca Da Rimini (1901) NONE

Francesca Da Rimini (1902) NONE

Frank Fay's Fables (1922) P. Dodd Ackerman(S); Ann Burrows(C); Helen A. Haas(C); William Henry Matthews(C); ACK(L)

Frank Merriwell (or Honor Changed) (1971) John Gleason(L); Tom John(S); Frank Thompson(C)

Frankenstein (1981) Jules Fisher(L); Carrie F. Robbins(C); Douglas W. Schmidt(S)

Frankie and Johnnie (1930) P. Dodd Ackerman(S); ACK(C)

Freak (1998) Jan Kroeze(L); Douglas Stein(S)

Freckles (1912) Dodge and Castle(S)

Freddy (1929) P. Dodd Ackerman(S);

ACK(C)

Frederika (1937) Watson Barratt(S); Hassard Short(L); William Weaver(C)

Free for All (1931) Yetta Kiviette(C); Donald Oenslager(S)

Free Lance, The (1906) F. Richards Anderson(C); Ernest Gros(S)

Free Soul, A (1928) Livingston Platt(S); ACK(C)(L)

Freedom (1918) J. Monroe Hewlett(S); Livingston Platt(C)

Freedom of Suzanne, The (1905) Walter Hann(S)

Freedom of the City, The (1974) F. Mitchell Dana(L); Alicia Finkel(C); David Jenkins(S)

Freiburg Passion Play, The (1929) Kurd Albrecht(S); ACK(C)

French Doll, The (1922) H. Robert Studio Law(S); ACK(C)(L)

French Leave (1920) Irma Campbell(C); Dodge and Castle(S); Paul Iribe(C); ACK(L)

French Touch, The (1945) George Jenkins(S)(C)(L)

French Without Tears (1937) Raymond Sovey(S)

Fresh Fields (1936) George S. Steele(S); ACK(C)

Friend Indeed, A (1926) Joseph Physioc Studio(S); ACK(L)

Friend Martha (1917) Dodge and Castle(S); ACK(L)

Friendly Enemies (1918) ACK(C)(L)

Friendship (1931) Joseph Wickes(S); ACK(C)(L)

Friquet (1905) Ernest Gros(S)

Frisky Mrs. Johnson, The (1903) Joseph Physioc(S)

Fritz in Tammany Hall (1905) F. Richards Anderson(C); Henry Bissing(L); Meixner(S); Frank Platzer(S)

Frivolities of 1920 (1920) Dodge and Castle(S); ACK(C)(L)

Frocks and Frills (1902) Mrs. Robert Osborn(C); Edward G. Unitt(S)

Frogs of Spring, The (1953) Boris Aronson(S)(L); Alvin Colt(C)

From A to Z (1960) Scaasi(C); Fred Voelpel(S)(C)(L)

From Morn Till Midnight (1922) Lee Simonson(S); ACK(C)

From the Second City (1961) Frederick Fox(S)(L); ACK(C)

From Vienna (1939) Donald Oenslager(S); Irene Sharaff(C); Hassard

Short(L)

Front Page, The (1928) Raymond Sovey(S); ACK(L)

Front Page, The (1946) Irene Aronson(C); Nat Karson(S)

Front Page, The (1969) Will Steven Armstrong(S)(L); Sara Brook(C)

Front Page, The (1987) Paul Gallo(L); Willa Kim(C); Tony Walton(S)

Frou Frou (1902) NONE

Frou-Frou (1912) Gates and Morange(S)

Fugitive, The (1917) O'Kane Conwell(C); Ed Sundquist(S)

Full Circle (1973) Hope Bryce(C); Jules Fisher(L); Robin Wagner(S)

Full House, A (1915) Dodge and Castle(S); ACK(L)

Full Monty, The (2000) John Arnone(S); Howell Binkley(L); Robert Morgan(C)

Fulton of Oak Falls (1937) John Hambleton(C); William Oden Waller(S)

Fun City (1972) Ralph Alswang(S); Jules Fisher(L); Ann Roth(C)

Fun Couple, The (1962) Ray Diffen(C); Eldon Elder(S)(L)

Funabashi (1908) Homer Emens(S); Edward G. Unitt(S); Young Brothers and Boss(S)

Funny Face (1927) Yetta Kiviette(C); John Wenger(S); ACK(L)

Funny Girl (1964) Robert Randolph(S)(L); Irene Sharaff(C)

Funny Thing Happened on the Way to the Forum, A (1962) Jean Rosenthal(L); Tony Walton(S)(C)

Funny Thing Happened on the Way to the Forum, A (1972) H. R. Poindexter(L); Noel Taylor(C); James Trittipo(S)

Funny Thing Happened on the Way to the Forum, A (1996) Paul Gallo(L); Tony Walton(S)(C)

Furies, The (1928) James Reynolds(S); ACK(C)

Furnished Rooms (1934) Anthony W. Street(S); ACK(C)

Furs and Frills (1917) P. Dodd Ackerman(S); Harry Collins(C); Lucile(C); L. Wenzelberg(C); ACK(L)

Gabrielle (1941) Kenn Barr(C); Peggy Clark(S)(L)

Gaby (1911) Ernest Albert(S); Joseph(C)

Gadfly, The (1899) Colin Campbell(L); Gates and Morange(S); ACK(C)

Gala Night (1930) Joseph Mullen(S); ACK(C)

Galileo (1947) Robert Davison(S); ACK(C)
Galloper, The (1906) Walter W. Burridge(S); ACK(C)
Gallops (1906) Ernest Albert(S); Arthur Corbault(S); ACK(C)
Gambler, The (1952) Robert Mackintosh(C); Jo Mielziner(S)(L)
Gamblers All (1917) ACK(C)(L)
Gamblers, The (1910) NONE
Gambling (1929) George Jenkins(C); ACK(L)
Game of Love and Death, The (1929) Aline Bernstein(S)(C)
Game of Love, The (1909) NONE
Gammer Gurton's Needle (1916) ACK(L)
Gang Way (1928) Rollo Wayne(S); ACK(C)
Gang's All Here, The (1931) Henry Dreyfuss(S); Russell Patterson(C)
Gang's All Here, The (1959) Jo Mielziner(S)(L); Patricia Zipprodt(C)
Gantry (1970) Jules Fisher(L); Ann Roth(C); Robin Wagner(S)
Garden District (1995) Zack Brown(S)(C); Marc B. Weiss(L)
Garden of Allah, The (1911) Madame Sara Bolwell(C); Gates and Morange(S); Kliegl Brothers(L); D. Lellouch(C); ACK(C)
Garden of Allah, The (1918) Gates and Morange(S); Henry L. Gebhardt(L); ACK(C)
Garden of Eden, The (1927) Joseph Mullen(S)(C)
Garden of Paradise, The (1914) Caramba(C); C. Alexander Ramsey(C); Joseph Urban(S)(L)
Garden of Secrets, The (1961) Boris Aronson(S); Tharon Musser(L); Patricia Zipprodt(C)
Garden of Weeds (1924) George W. Howe(S); Anna Scheer(C); Miss Tashman(C)
Garrett O'Magh (1901) Ogden(C); Louis C. Young(S)
Garrick Gaieties (1925) Miguel Covarrubias(S); Carolyn Hancock(S)(C); ACK(L)
Garrick Gaieties (1926) Miguel Covarrubias(S)(C); Carolyn Hancock(S)(C)
Garrick Gaieties (1930) Raoul Pène Du Bois(C); Kate Drain Lawson(S)(C); Louis M. Simon(C)
Gasoline Gypsies (1931) ACK(S)(C)(L)

Gathering, The (2001) Michael Anania(S); Scott Clyve(L); Susan L. Soetaert(C)
Gay Divorce (1932) Jo Mielziner(S)(L); Raymond Sovey(C)
Gay Hussars, The (1909) Walter W. Burridge(S); Landolff of Paris(C); Joseph Wilson(L)
Gay Life, The (1909) Gates and Morange(S)
Gay Life, The (1961) Lucinda Ballard(C); Jean Rosenthal(L); Oliver Smith(S)
Gay Lord Quex, The (1900) William Harford(S)
Gay Lord Quex, The (1917) Gates and Morange(S); ACK(C)(L)
Gay Musician, The (1908) Ernest Albert(S); James Fox(S); John H. Young(S)
Gay Paree (1925) Watson Barratt(S); ACK(C)
Gay Paree (1926) Watson Barratt(S); Ernest Schraps(C); Max Weldy(C)
Gay White Way, The (1907) Arthur Voegtlin(S)
Gayden (1949) DuWico(L); Willis Knighton(S); Emeline Clarke Roche(C)
Gazebo, The (1958) Jo Mielziner(S)(L); Virginia Volland(C)
Geisha, The (1913) Melville Ellis(C); Theodore Reisig(S)
Geisha, The (1931) ACK(C)(L)
Gemini (1977) Larry Crimmins(L); Christopher Nowak(S); Ernest Allen Smith(C)
General John Regan (1913) Angel(C); Gates and Morange(S)
General John Regan (1930) Jennie Covan(C); William Gaskin(S)
General Post (1917) ACK(C)(L)
General Seeger (1961) Ralph Holmes(L); Gerald Parker(S); Noel Taylor(C)
Generation (1965) George Jenkins(S)(L); Albert Wolsky(C)
Genesee of the Hills (1907) D. Frank Dodge(S)
Geneva (1940) ACK(S)(C)(L)
Genius and the Crowd (1920) Shirley Barker(C); Gates and Morange(S); Unitt and Wickes(S); ACK(L)
Genius and the Goddess, The (1957) Virginia Volland(C); Richard Whorf(S)(L)
Genius, The (1906) NONE
Gentile Wife, The (1918) Robert

Edmond Jones[S]

Gentle Grafters (1926) ACK[C][L]

Gentle People, The (1939) Boris Aronson[S]; Michael Gordon[L]; ACK[C]

Gentleman from Mississippi, The (1908) H. Robert Law[S]; Madame Morris[C]

Gentleman of France, A (1901) Frank E. Gates[S]; Edward Morange[S]

Gentleman of Leisure, A (1911) ACK[S][C]

Gentlemen from Athens, The (1947) Ralph Alswang[S][L]; ACK[C]

Gentlemen from Number 19, The (1913) NONE

Gentlemen of the Press (1928) R. N. Robbins[S]; ACK[C]

Gentlemen Prefer Blondes (1926) Peggy Clark[L]; Raymond Sovey[S]; ACK[C]

Gentlemen Prefer Blondes (1949) Peggy Clark[L]; Oliver Smith[S]; Miles White[C]

Gentlemen Prefer Blondes (1995) Kirk Bookman[L]; Eduardo Sicangco[S][C]

Gentlewoman (1934) Lydia Furbush[C]; Mordecai Gorelik[S]

Gently Does It (1953) George Jenkins[S][L]; Virginia Volland[C]

George Abbott...a Celebration (1976) Marilyn Putnam[C]; Richard Winkler[L]

George and Margaret (1937) Geoffrey Nares[S]

George Dandin, or the Husband Confounded (1924) Millia Davenport[C]; Robert Edmond Jones[S][C]; Cleon Throckmorton[S]

George Gershwin Alone (2000) James F. Ingalls[L]; Yael Pardess[S]

George M! (1968) Martin Aronstein[L]; Tom John[S]; Freddy Wittop[C]

George Washington (1920) Robert Edmond Jones[S][C]; Raymond Sovey[S][C]; ACK[L]

George Washington Slept Here (1940) John Root[S]; ACK[C]

George Washington, Jr. (1906) Ernest Albert[S]; John H. Young[S]

George White's Music Hall Varieties (1932) Yetta Kiviette[C]; Charles LeMaire[C]; ACK[S]

George White's Scandals (1919) ACK[S][C][L]

George White's Scandals (1921)

Gilbert Adrian[C]; Ada B. Fields[C]; Alice O'Neil[C]; Herbert Ward[S]; Albertine Randall Wheelan[C]

George White's Scandals (1922) Erté[C]; Herbert Ward[S]; John Wenger[S]; Albertine Randall Wheelan[C]

George White's Scandals (1923) Erté[C]; Cora MacGeachy[C]; Gustav Weidhaas[S]; ACK[S][L]

George White's Scandals (1924) Erté[C]; Gustav Weidhaas[S]; ACK[S][L]

George White's Scandals (1925) Erté[C]; Juliet[C]; Albert Rybeck[L]; Gustav Weidhaas[S]; ACK[S]

George White's Scandals (1926) Erté[C]; William Oden Waller[S]; William Weaver[C]; Gustav Weidhaas[S]; ACK[L]

George White's Scandals (1928) Erté[C]; Charles LeMaire[C]; William Oden Waller[S]; Gustav Weidhaas[S]

George White's Scandals (1929) Erté[C]; Charles LeMaire[C]; Cora MacGeachy[C]; Orry-Kelly[C]; William Oden Waller[S]; Gustav Weidhaas[S]; Ted Weidhaas[S]

George White's Scandals (1931) Yetta Kiviette[C]; Charles LeMaire[C]; Joseph Urban[S]; ACK[L]

George White's Scandals (1935) Walter Jagemann[S]; Charles LeMaire[C]; Russell Patterson[S]

George White's Scandals (1939) DuWico[L]; Albert R. Johnson[S]; Miles White[C]

Georgy (1970) Jo Mielziner[S][L]; Patricia Zipprodt[C]

Geraniums in My Window (1934) Philip Gelb[S]

Gershwins' Fascinating Rhythm, The (1999) Peggy Eisenhauer[L]; Paul Tazewell[C]; Michael H. Yeargan[S]

Gertie (1926) Nicholas Yellenti[S]

Gertie (1952) William and Jean Eckart[S]; Hazel Roy[C]

Get Away Old Man (1943) John Root[S]; Miles White[C]

Get Me in the Movies (1928) Charles LeMaire[C]; Nicholas Yellenti[S]; ACK[C]

Get Rich Quick, Wallingford (1917) ACK[S][L]

Get Together (1921) Will R. Barnes[C]; Clifford F. Pember[S]; Willy Pogany[S][C]; ACK[L]

Get-Rich-Quick Wallingford (1910)

Angel[C]; W. T. Hemsley[S]; Henry Owen[S]; Bruce Smith[S]; ACK[C]

Getting a Polish (1910) Joseph F. Driscoll[L]; Gates and Morange[S]

Getting and Spending (1998) Kevin Adams[L]; Michael Krass[C]; James Noone[S]

Getting Away with Murder (1996) Kenneth Posner[L]; Douglas W. Schmidt[S]; Robert Wojewodski[C]

Getting Even (1929) Cleon Throckmorton[S]; ACK[C]

Getting Gertie's Garter (1921) H. George Brandt[S]; ACK[C]

Getting Married (1916) Dodge and Castle[S]; ACK[C][L]

Getting Married (1931) Aline Bernstein[S]; ACK[C]

Getting Married (1991) Mary Jo Dondlinger[L]; Holly Hynes[C]; James Morgan [active 1989-][S]

Getting Together (1918) Clifford F. Pember[S]; ACK[C]

Ghetto (1989) Kevin Rigdon[L]; Edna Sobol[C]; Adrian Vaux[S]

Ghetto, The (1899) Theodore Platzer[S]; John H. Young[S]

Ghost Between, The (1921) P. Dodd Ackerman[S]; ACK[C]

Ghost Breaker, The (1913) Madame Julie[C]; T. Bernard McDonald[S]; Young Brothers[S]

Ghost for Sale (1941) Cleon Throckmorton[S]; ACK[C]

Ghost of Jerry Bundler, The (1913) NONE

Ghost of Yankee Doodle, The (1937) John Hambleton[C]; Woodman Thompson[S]

Ghost Parade, The (1929) Clarke Robinson[S]

Ghost Train, The (1926) P. Dodd Ackerman[S]; Langdon McCormick[L]; ACK[C]

Ghost Writer (1933) Cirker and Robbins[S]; ACK[C]

Ghosts (1903) NONE

Ghosts (1912) NONE

Ghosts (1915) ACK[L]

Ghosts (1919) ACK[L]

Ghosts (1926) David S. Gaither[S]; ACK[L]

Ghosts (1927) David S. Gaither[S][C][L]

Ghosts (1933) ACK[L]

Ghosts (1935) Stewart Chaney[S][C]; A. H. Feder[L]

Ghosts (1948) Watson Barratt[S]; Edith Lutyens Bel Geddes[C]; Helene Pons[C]; ACK[C][L]

Ghosts (1982) Theoni V. Aldredge[C]; Martin Aronstein[L]; Kevin Rupnik[S]

Giants, Sons of Giants (1962) Edith Lutyens Bel Geddes[C]; Peter Larkin[S]; Tharon Musser[L]

Giddy Thing, The (1900) St. John Lewis[S]; MacCoughtry[S]

Gideon (1961) David Hays[S][L]; Domingo A. Rodriguez[C]

Gift of Time, A (1961) Boris Aronson[S]; Edith Lutyens Bel Geddes[C]; Jean Rosenthal[L]

Gift, The (1924) Joseph Physioc[S]; ACK[C]

Gigi (1951) Raymond Sovey[S]; ACK[C][L]

Gigi (1973) Oliver Messel[C]; Thomas Skelton[L]; Oliver Smith[S]

Gilbert and Sullivan Opera (1915) NONE

Gilbert's Engaged (1925) NONE

Gilda Radner Live from N.Y. (1979) Eugene Lee[S]; Franne Lee[C]; Roger Morgan[L]; Karen Roston[C]; Akira Yoshimura[S]

Gin Game, The (1977) David Mitchell[S]; Bill Walker[C]; Ronald Wallace[L]

Gin Game, The (1997) Kirk Bookman[L]; James Noone[S]; Noel Taylor[C]

Ginger (1923) P. Dodd Ackerman[S]; Max Cohen[C]

Gingerbread Lady, The (1970) Martin Aronstein[L]; David Hays[S]; Frank Thompson[C]

Gingerbread Man, The (1905) Will R. Barnes[C]; Archie Gunn[C]; J Hegeman[C]; Lee Lash Studios[S]

Gingham Dog, The (1969) Theoni V. Aldredge[C]; Tharon Musser[L]; William Ritman[S]

Gingham Girl, The (1922) ACK[S][C][L]

Gioconda Smile, The (1950) A. H. Feder[S][L]

Gioconda, La (1902) NONE

Girl and the Governor, The (1907) NONE

Girl and the Judge, The (1901) Edward G. Unitt[S]

Girl and the Kaiser, The (1910) Melville Ellis[C]; Joseph[C]

Girl and the Pennant, The (1913) Madame Julie[C]; ACK[S]

Girl and the Wizard, The (1909)
Melville Ellis(C); H. Robert Law(S);
John Whalen(L)

Girl Behind the Counter, The (1907)
Arthur Voegtlin(S)

Girl Behind the Gun, The (1918)
Clifford F. Pember(S); ACK(C)(L)

Girl Can Tell, A (1953) Edith Lutyens
Bel Geddes(C); Stewart Chaney(S)

Girl Could Get Lucky, A (1964) Will
Steven Armstrong(C); Jules Fisher(L);
Robert T. Williams(S)

Girl Crazy (1930) Yetta Kiviette(C);
Donald Oenslager(S)

Girl Friend, The (1926) P. Dodd
Ackerman(S)

Girl from Brazil, The (1916) Homer
Conant(S)(C); ACK(L)

Girl from Brighton, The (1912) Paul
Arlington(C)

Girl from Dixie, The (1903) NONE

Girl from Home, The (1920) O'Kane
Conwell(C); ACK(L)

Girl from Kay's, The (1903) Mrs.
Robert Osborn(C)

Girl from Maxim's, The (1899)
Edward G. Unitt(S)

Girl from Montmartre, The (1912)
Homer Emens(S); ACK(C)

Girl from Nantucket, The (1945) Lou
Eisele(C); Albert R. Johnson(S)(L)

Girl from Rector's, The (1909) NONE

Girl from Up There, The (1901)
Ernest Albert(S); Ernest Gros(S)

Girl from Utah, The (1914) Henri
Bendel(C); ACK(C)

Girl from Wyoming, The (1938)
Eugene Dunkel(S); ACK(C)

Girl He Couldn't Leave Behind,
The (1910) NONE

Girl in Pink Tights, The (1954) Eldon
Elder(S)(L); Miles White(C)

Girl in the Barracks (1899) ACK(C)

Girl in the Freudian Slip, The (1967)
Clarke Dunham(L); Leo B. Meyer(S);
Julia Sze(C)

Girl in the Limousine, The (1919)
ACK(L)

Girl in the Spotlight, The (1920)
Anthony Greshoff(L); William Henry
Matthews(C); ACK(S)

Girl in the Taxi, The (1910) Hugo
Baruch(S)(C); T. J. Digby(L)

Girl in the Train, The (1910) Anna
Conkwright(C); Wilhelm(C)

Girl o' Mine (1918) Watson Barratt(S);

Henri Bendel(C); ACK(L)

Girl of My Dreams, The (1911) P.
Dodd Ackerman Studio(S); ACK(C)(L)

Girl of the Golden West, The (1905)
Ernest Gros(S)

Girl on the Film, The (1913)
Comelli(C); Lucile(C); ACK(S)

Girl on the Via Flamina, The (1954)
Keith Cuerden(S)(C); Klaus Holm(L)

Girl Outside, The (1932) P. Dodd
Ackerman(S); ACK(C)

Girl Patsy, The (1906) Carns and
Williams(S)

Girl Question, The (1908) John H.
Young(S)

Girl Trouble (1928) August Vimnera(S);
ACK(C)(L)

Girl Who Came to Supper, The
(1963) Peggy Clark(L); Irene Sharaff(C);
Oliver Smith(S)

Girl Who Has Everything, The
(1906) NONE

Girl Who Smiles, The (1915) Unitt
and Wickes(S); ACK(C)(L)

Girl with the Carmine Lips, The
(1920) Joseph Physioc(S); ACK(L)

Girl with the Green Eyes, The
(1902) Edward G. Unitt(S)

Girl with the Whooping Cough,
The (1910) Callot Soeurs(C)

Girlies (1910) Unitt and Wickes(S);
ACK(S)

Girls (1908) H. Robert Law(S)

Girls Against the Boys, The (1959)
Ralph Alswang(S)(L); Sal Anthony(C)

Girls in 509, The (1958) Lucinda
Ballard(C); Donald Oenslager(S)(L)

Girls in Uniform (1932) Joseph
Teichner Studio(S); ACK(C)

Girls of Gottenburg, The (1908)
Percy Anderson(C); ACK(S)

Girls of Holland, The (1907) NONE

Girls of Summer (1956) Boris
Aronson(S); Kenn Barr(C); Lee
Watson(L)

Girls Will Be Girls (1904) Moses and
Hamilton(S); Bert Tuchman(S)

Girofle-Girofla (1904) Percy
Anderson(C); Joseph Clare(S); William
Hoover(S); Henry E. Hoyt(S); Richard
Marston(S); John H. Palmer(L)

Give and Take (1923) ACK(S)(L)

Give Me Yesterday (1931) Thomas
Farrar(S); Ellen Goldsborough(C)

Give Us This Day (1933) Cleon
Throckmorton(S)

Glad of It (1903) NONE
Glad Tidings (1951) John Derro[C];
William and Jean Eckart[S]
Glamour Preferred (1940) John
Root[S]; ACK[C]
Glass Clock, The (1956) Cecil
Beaton[S]; Charles Lisanby[L]
Glass Menagerie, The (1945) Jo
Mielziner[S][L]; ACK[C]
Glass Menagerie, The (1965) Patton
Campbell[C]; V. C. Fuqua[L]; James A.
Taylor[S]; Robert T. Williams[S]
Glass Menagerie, The (1975) Sydney
Brooks[C]; Ming Cho Lee[S]; Thomas
Skelton[L]
Glass Menagerie, The (1983) Ming
Cho Lee[S]; Andy Phillips[L]; Patricia
Zipprodt[C]
Glass Menagerie, The (1994) Loy
Arcenas[S]; Mimi Jordan Sherin[L];
Noel Taylor[C]
Glass of Water, A (1930) Jean
Bilibine[S][C]
Glass Slipper, The (1925) Lee
Simonson[S][C]
Glengarry Glen Ross (1984) Nan
Cibula-Jenkins[C]; Michael Merritt[S];
Kevin Rigdon[L]
Glimpse of the Great White Way, A
(1913) Charles Messersmith[L]; ACK[S]
Glittering Gate, The (1915) Warren
Dahler[S]; Lois Phipps[S]; ACK[L]
Glittering Gloria (1904) NONE
Gloria and Esperanza (1970) The
Birdie Sisters[C]; Daffi[S]; Peter
Harvey[C]; Ella Luxembourg[C]; Keith
Michael[L]
Gloriana (1938) John Koenig[S]
Glorianna (1918) Mary Blackburn[C];
Joseph Urban[S]; ACK[L]
Glorious Betsy (1908) H. Robert Law[S]
Glorious Morning (1938) John
Koenig[S]; ACK[L]
Glory (1922) ACK[S][C][L]
Glory Hallelujah (1926) Raymond
Sovey[S]; ACK[L]
Go Easy, Mabel (1922) P. Dodd
Ackerman[S]; ACK[C][L]
Go West, Young Man (1923) Charles
J. Auburn[S]
Go-Go (1923) Shirley Barker[C]; ACK[S][L]
Goat Alley (1921) NONE
Goat Alley (1927) ACK[S][L]
Goat Song (1926) Lee Simonson[S][C]
God and Kate Murphy (1959) Betty
Coe Armstrong[C]; Ben Edwards[S][L]

God Loves Us (1926) Woodman
Thompson[S]; ACK[C]
God of Vengeance, The (1922) Cleon
Throckmorton[S]; ACK[L]
God Said Ha! (1996) Russell H.
Champa[L]; Connie Martin[C]; Michael
McGarty[S]
God's Favorite (1974) Joseph G.
Aulisi[C]; Tharon Musser[L]; William
Ritman[S]
God's Heart (1997) Robert Brill[S];
Toni-Leslie James[C]; Brian
MacDevitt[L]
Goddess of Liberty, The (1909) Lee
Lash Studios[S]; ACK[C]
Goddess of Reason, The (1909)
Florence Froelich[C]; H. Robert Law[S]
Gods of the Lightning (1928)
Benjamin Leffler[L]; R. N. Robbins[S];
ACK[C]
Gods of the Mountain, The (1916)
Frank Zimmerman[S][C]; ACK[L]
Gods We Make, The (1934) Cleon
Throckmorton[S]; ACK[C]
Godspell (1976) Spencer Mosse[L]; Susan
Tsu[C]; ACK[S]
Goin' Home (1928) Raymond Sovey[S];
ACK[C]
Going Gay (1933) Rollo Wayne[S];
ACK[C]
Going Some (1909) Frank Platzer[S]
Going Up (1917) Harry Collins[C]; Frank
D. Thomas[L]; ACK[S]
Going Up (1976) Peter M. Ehrhardt[L];
Edward Haynes[S]; David Toser[C]
Gold (1921) NONE
Gold Braid (1930) David S. Gaither[S][C]
Gold Diggers, The (1919) Henri
Bendel[C]; Ernest Gros[S]; ACK[L]
Gold Eagle Guy (1934) Donald
Oenslager[S][C]
Golda (1977) Jules Fisher[L]; Santo
Loquasto[S][C]
Golden Age, The (1928) Charles
Christie[C]; Nicholas Yellenti[S]
Golden Age, The (1963) Nicholas
Yellenti[S]; ACK[C][L]
Golden Apple, The (1954) Alvin
Colt[C]; William and Jean Eckart[S];
Klaus Holm[L]
Golden Boy (1952) Paul Morrison[S][C][L]
Golden Boy (1964) Tharon Musser[L];
Tony Walton[S][C]
Golden Butterfly (1908) Ernest
Albert[S]; Gates and Morange[S];
William Henry Matthews[C]; Unitt

and Wickes[S]; Ack[L]

Golden Child (1998) David J. Lander[L]; Martin Pakledinaz[C]; Tony Straiges[S]

Golden Dawn (1927) Mark Mooring[C]; Joseph Urban[S]; Ack[L]

Golden Days (1921) Anthony Greshoff[L]; H. Robert Studio Law[S]; Betty Walls[C]

Golden Doom, The (1916) Frank J. Zimmerer[S][C]

Golden Doom, The (1919) Frank Zimmerman[S][C]

Golden Fleecing (1959) Frederick Fox[S][C][L]

Golden Journey, The (1936) Watson Barratt[S]; Helene Pons[C]

Golden Rainbow (1968) Alvin Colt[C]; Robert Randolph[S][L]

Golden State, The (1950) Grace Houston[C]; Lester Polakov[S][L]

Golden Wings (1941) Watson Barratt[S]; Ernest Schraps[C]

Goldfish, The (1922) Watson Barratt[S]; Ack[L]

Goldilocks (1958) Castillo[C]; A. H. Feder[L]; Peter Larkin[S]

Golem, The (1948) J. Nievinsky[S]; Ack[L]

Gondoliers, The (1931) Ack[L]

Gondoliers, The (1932) Ack[L]

Gondoliers, The (1948) Charles Ricketts[S][C]; Ack[L]

Gondoliers, The (1951) Ack[L]

Gone Tomorrow/ Home Life of a Buffalo/Hope is the Thing (1948) Mordecai Gassner[S]; Moe Hack[L]

Good (1982) Beverly Emmons[L]; Linda Fisher[C]; Ultz[S]

Good As Gold (1957) Al Alloy[L]; Peter Larkin[S]; Noel Taylor[C]

Good Bad Woman, A (1919) Ack[L]

Good Bad Woman, A (1925) Ack[L]

Good Boy (1928) Mark Mooring[C]; John Wenger[S]

Good Companions, The (1931) Rollo Wayne[S]; Ack[C][L]

Good Doctor, The (1973) Tharon Musser[L]; Tony Walton[S][C]

Good Earth, The (1932) Lee Simonson[S]; Ack[C]

Good Evening (1973) Robert Randolph[S][C][L]

Good Fairy, A (1932) Joseph Urban[S]; Ack[C]

Good Fairy, The (1931) Joseph Urban[S]; Ack[C]

Good Fellow, The (1926) Ack[C][L]

Good Gracious, Annabelle (1916) Robert Edmond Jones[S]; Ack[C]

Good Hope, The (1907) None

Good Hope, The (1927) Millia Davenport[C]; William Kline[S]; Cleon Throckmorton[S]

Good Hunting (1938) Frances Feist[C]; Norris Houghton[S]

Good Little Devil (1913) Percy Anderson[C]; Louis Hartmann[L]; Unitt and Wickes[S]

Good Men and True (1935) Marion Moore[C]; Nicholas Yellenti[S]

Good Men Do, The/ Her Honor, the Mayor (1918) Ack[L]

Good Morning Corporal (1944) Robert Barnhart[S]; Ack[C]

Good Morning, Dearie (1921) Earl Benham[C]; Gates and Morange[S]; Herman Patrick Tappé[C]

Good Morning, Judge (1919) Dodge and Castle[S]; S. Zalud[C]; Ack[L]

Good Morning Rosamond (1917) Mabel A. Buell[S]; Ack[C][L]

Good Neighbor (1941) Frederick Fox[S]

Good News (1927) Yetta Kiviette[C]; Donald Oenslager[S]; Ack[L]

Good News (1974) Donald Brooks[C]; Tharon Musser[L]; Donald Oenslager[S]

Good Night Ladies (1945) Frederick Fox[S][L]; Billy Livingston[C]

Good Night, Paul (1917) Ack[C][L]

Good Old Days, The (1923) Ack[L]

Good Soup, The (1960) Al Alloy[L]; Jacques Noël[S][C]

Good Times (1920) Will R. Barnes[C]; Joseph Elsner[L]; Edward Roelker[S]

Good Woman, Poor Thing, A (1933) Aline Bernstein[S]; Hattie Carnegie[C]; Emmett Joyce[C]

Good, The (1938) Donald Oenslager[S][C]

Good-Bye Please (1934) Theodore Kahn[S]; William H. Mensching[S]; Melissa Whiffen[C]

Goodbye Again (1932) Tom Adrian Cracraft[S]; Ack[C]

Goodbye Again (1943) Tom Adrian Cracraft[S]

Goodbye Again (1956) Samuel Leve[S]

Goodbye Charlie (1959) Peggy Clark[L]; Oliver Smith[S]

Goodbye Fidel (1980) Florence Klotz[C]; Toshiro Ogawa[L]; Rouben Ter-Arutunian[S]

Goodbye Girl, The (1993) Santo

Loquasto$^{(S)(C)}$; Tharon Musser$^{(L)}$
Goodbye in the Night (1940) Cirker and Robbins$^{(S)}$; Valentina$^{(C)}$
Goodbye People, The (1968) Alvin Colt$^{(C)}$; David Hays$^{(S)(L)}$
Goodbye People, The (1979) Santo Loquasto$^{(S)}$; Elizabeth Palmer$^{(C)}$; Jennifer Tipton$^{(L)}$
Goodbye, My Fancy (1948) Donald Oenslager$^{(S)(L)}$; Emeline Clarke Roche$^{(C)}$
Goodtime Charley (1975) A. H. Feder$^{(L)}$; Willa Kim$^{(C)}$; Rouben Ter-Arutunian$^{(S)}$
Goose for the Gander, A (1945) Frederick Fox$^{(S)}$; Ack$^{(C)}$
Goose Hangs High, The (1924) Livingston Platt$^{(S)}$; Ack$^{(C)(L)}$
Gorey Stories (1978) Edward Gorey$^{(S)}$; Roger Morgan$^{(L)}$; David Murin$^{(C)}$
Gorilla, The (1925) Charles J. Auburn$^{(S)}$; Ack$^{(C)(L)}$
Gospel at Colonus, The (1988) Julie Archer$^{(L)}$; Ghretta Hynd$^{(C)}$; Alison Yerxa$^{(S)}$
Gossipy Sex, The (1927) Cirker and Robbins$^{(S)}$; Ack$^{(C)(L)}$
Got Tu Go Disco (1979) Joe Eula$^{(C)}$; James Hamilton$^{(S)}$; Robby Monk$^{(L)}$
Government Inspector, The (1994) Lewis Brown$^{(C)}$
Government Inspector, Then (1994) Richard Nelson$^{(L)}$; Douglas Stein$^{(S)}$
Governor's Boss, The (1914) Dodge and Castle$^{(S)}$; Ack$^{(C)}$
Governor's Lady, The (1912) Ernest Gros$^{(S)}$
Governor's Son, The (1901) Klaw & Erlanger$^{(C)}$; John H. Young$^{(S)}$
Grab Bag, The (1924) Mabel E. Johnston$^{(C)}$; Charles LeMaire$^{(C)}$; Alice O'Neil$^{(C)}$; Ack$^{(S)(L)}$
Grain of Dust, The (1912) NONE
Gramercy Ghost (1951) Raymond Sovey$^{(S)(C)(L)}$
Grand Army Man, A (1907) Wilfred Buckland$^{(S)}$; Ernest Gros$^{(S)}$; Edward G. Unitt$^{(S)}$; Albertine Randall Wheelan$^{(C)}$
Grand Duchess/ The Waiter, The (1925) Ernest Gros$^{(S)}$; Ack$^{(C)(L)}$
Grand Duke, The (1921) Henri Bendel$^{(C)}$; Ernest Gros$^{(S)}$
Grand Hotel (1930) Aline Bernstein$^{(S)(C)}$
Grand Hotel, The Musical (1989) Jules Fisher$^{(L)}$; Santo Loquasto$^{(C)}$;

Tony Walton$^{(S)}$
Grand Mogul, The (1907) Ernest Albert$^{(S)}$; F. Richards Anderson$^{(C)}$
Grand Music Hall of Israel, The (1968) Jules Fisher$^{(L)}$; Hovav Kruvi$^{(C)}$; Ack$^{(S)}$
Grand Night for Singing, A (1993) Natasha Katz$^{(L)}$; Martin Pakledinaz$^{(C)}$; Tony Walton$^{(S)}$
Grand Prize, The (1955) Patton Campbell$^{(S)(L)}$; Virginia Volland$^{(C)}$
Grand Street Follies (1925) Aline Bernstein$^{(C)}$; Russel Wright$^{(S)(C)}$; Ack$^{(L)}$
Grand Street Follies (1926) Aline Bernstein$^{(S)(C)}$; Ack$^{(L)}$
Grand Street Follies (1927) Aline Bernstein$^{(S)(C)}$; Donald Oenslager$^{(C)}$; Esther Peck$^{(C)}$; Ernest de Weerth$^{(C)}$; Ack$^{(L)}$
Grand Street Follies (1928) Aline Bernstein$^{(S)(C)}$; Ack$^{(L)}$
Grand Street Follies (1929) Aline Bernstein$^{(S)(C)}$; Ack$^{(L)}$
Grand Tour, The (1951) Howard Bay$^{(S)}$; Motley$^{(C)}$
Grand Tour, The (1979) Theoni V. Aldredge$^{(C)}$; Martin Aronstein$^{(L)}$; Ming Cho Lee$^{(S)}$
Grandma's Diary (1948) Raymond Sovey$^{(S)(L)}$; Ack$^{(C)}$
Granite (1927) Helene Peck$^{(C)}$; James Shute$^{(S)}$; Ack$^{(C)}$
Granite (1936) Georges Marix$^{(C)}$; Clarke Robinson$^{(S)}$
Granny (1904) Homer Emens$^{(S)}$; Edward G. Unitt$^{(S)}$
Granny Maumee (1914) NONE
Granny Maumee (1917) Robert Edmond Jones$^{(S)(C)}$; Harper Pennington$^{(L)}$
Grapes of Wrath, The (1990) Erin Quigley$^{(C)}$; Kevin Rigdon$^{(S)(L)}$
Grass Harp, The (1952) Cecil Beaton$^{(S)(C)}$
Grass Harp, The (1971) Nancy Potts$^{(C)}$; James Tilton$^{(S)(L)}$
Grass Widow, The (1917) P. Dodd Ackerman$^{(S)}$; Ack$^{(C)(L)}$
Grasshopper (1917) Rollo Peters$^{(S)(C)}$
Gray Shadow (1931) Cleon Throckmorton$^{(S)}$
Grease (1972) Carrie F. Robbins$^{(C)}$; Douglas W. Schmidt$^{(S)}$; John Tedesco$^{(L)}$
Grease (1994) John Arnone$^{(S)}$; Howell

Binkley[L]; Willa Kim[C]

Great Adventure, The (1913) Paul Poiret[C]; Unitt and Wickes[S]; ACK[L]

Great Adventure, The (1926) Frederick Bentley[S]; Beatrice Wood[C]

Great Barrington, The (1931) Cirker and Robbins[S]; De Guary[C]; Margaret Pemberton[C]; ACK[C][L]

Great Big Doorstop, The (1942) Howard Bay[S]; Peggy Clark[C]

Great Broxopp, The (1921) Aline Bernstein[C]; Willy Pogany[S]

Great Day (1929) Gates and Morange[S]; Mabel E. Johnston[C]

Great Day in the Morning (1961) Lester Polakov[S][L]; Noel Taylor[C]

Great Divide, The (1906) Homer Emens[S]; Edward G. Unitt[S]; Joseph Wickes[S]

Great Divide, The (1917) ACK[S][L]

Great Gatsby, The (1926) Livingston Platt[S]; ACK[C][L]

Great God Brown, The (1926) Robert Edmond Jones[S][C]; ACK[L]

Great God Brown, The (1972) Boris Aronson[S]; Carolyn Parker[C]

Great Indoors, The (1966) Peter Larkin[S]; Tharon Musser[L]; Noel Taylor[C]

Great John Ganton, The (1909) H. Robert Law[S]

Great Katherine (1916) Warren Dahler[S][C]

Great Lady (1938) Lucinda Ballard[C]; Albert R. Johnson[S]

Great Lover, The (1915) Lucile[C]; ACK[L]

Great Lover, The (1932) ACK[S]

Great Magoo (1932) Allison McLellan Hunter[C]; Herman Rosse[S]

Great Man, The (1931) John N. Booth, Jr.[C]; Leopold De Sola[C]; ACK[L]

Great Music (1924) John Wenger[S]; ACK[C]

Great Name, The (1911) NONE

Great Necker, The (1928) Yetta Kiviette[C]; Rollo Wayne[S]

Great Power, The (1928) Livingston Platt[S]; ACK[C]

Great Pursuit, The (1916) Henri Bendel[C]; ACK[S][L]

Great Question, The (1908) Anthony W. Street[S]

Great Scott (1929) Anthony Continer[S]; ACK[C]

Great Sebastian, The (1956) Mainbocher[C]; Jean Rosenthal[L]; Raymond Sovey[S]

Great Temptations (1926) Watson Barratt[S]

Great to Be Alive (1950) Stewart Chaney[S][C]; ACK[L]

Great Waltz, The (1934) Albert R. Johnson[S]; Irene Sharaff[C]; Hassard Short[L]; Doris Zinkeisen[C]

Great Waltz, The (1935) Albert R. Johnson[S]; Irene Sharaff[C]

Great Way, The (1921) Ernest de Weerth[S][C]

Great White Hope, The (1968) John Gleason[L]; David Toser[C]; Robin Wagner[S]

Greater Love (1931) ACK[S][L]

Greater Love, The (1906) P. Dodd Ackerman[S]; Charles E. Boss[S]; Castle and Harvey[S]; ACK[C]

Greatest Man Alive, The (1957) Frederick Fox[S][C][L]

Greatest Show on Earth, The (1938) Frank Bevan[C]; John Root[S]

Greatest Thing in the World, The (1900) Gates and Morange[S]; Mrs. Caroline Siedle[C]

Greek Slave, A (1899) Ernest Albert[S]; F. Richards Anderson[C]; Ernest Gros[S]

Greeks Have a Word for It, The (1930) Livingston Platt[S]; ACK[C]

Green Bay Tree, The (1933) Robert Edmond Jones[S]; ACK[C]

Green Beetle, The (1924) E. Van Ackerman[S]; ACK[L]

Green Bird, The (2000) Constance Hoffman[C]; Donald Holder[L]; Christine Jones[S]; Julie Taymor[S]

Green Cockatoo, The (1910) Madame Freisinger[C]

Green Cockatoo, The (1930) Aline Bernstein[S][C]; Irene Sharaff[C]

Green Goddess, The (1921) Unitt and Wickes[S]; ACK[C]

Green Grow the Lilacs (1931) Miss Bessie B. Cunningham[C]; Raymond Sovey[S]

Green Hat, The (1925) P. Dodd Ackerman[S]; ACK[C]

Green Pastures (1935) Robert Edmond Jones[S][C][L]

Green Pastures (1951) Robert Edmond Jones[S][C]

Green Pastures, The (1930) Robert Edmond Jones[S]; ACK[C]

Green Stick (1934) Jay Doten[S]; Vincent Mallory[S]

Green Stockings (1911) Gates and Morange[S]; Unitt and Wickes[S]; ACK[C]

Green Table, The (1942) H. Heckroth[S][C]; ACK[L]

Green Waters (1936) Watson Barratt[S]; ACK[C]

Greenwich Village Follies (1919) Shirley Barker[C]; Charles Ellis[C]; Charles B. Falls[S]; Pieter Myer[C]; ACK[L]

Greenwich Village Follies (1920) Robert E. Locher[S]; ACK[C][L]

Greenwich Village Follies (1921) Robert E. Locher[S][C]; James Reynolds[S]

Greenwich Village Follies (1922) E. Amies[C]; Dorothy Armstrong[S]; Georgianna Brown[S][C]; Erté[S]; Erle Payne Franke[S][C]; Howard Greer[S][C]; Mrs. Ingeborg Hansell[S][C]; Reginald Marsh[S]; Pieter Myer[S]; Alice O'Neil[S][C]; James Reynolds[S]; J. Blanding Sloan[S]; Cleon Throckmorton[S]

Greenwich Village Follies (1923) John Murray Anderson[S]; Norman Levinson[C]; Robert E. Locher[S][C]; ACK[L]

Greenwich Village Follies (1924) John Murray Anderson[C]; Mrs. Ingeborg Hansell[S][C]; Yetta Kiviette[C]; James Reynolds[S][C]; Herman Rosse[S]

Greenwich Village Follies (1925) Charles LeMaire[C]; Mark Mooring[C]; Clarke Robinson[S]

Greenwich Village Follies (1928) Watson Barratt[S]; Ernest Schraps[C]; ACK[L]

Greenwillow (1960) Alvin Colt[C]; A. H. Feder[L]; Peter Larkin[S]

Gretna Green (1903) NONE

Grey Eyed People, The (1952) Eldon Elder[S][L]; Noel Taylor[C]

Grey Farm (1940) Helene Pons[C]; Raymond Sovey[S][C]

Grey Fox, The (1928) Jo Mielziner[S][L]; Fania Mindell[C]; ACK[C]

Greyhound, The (1912) NONE

Grierson's Way (1906) Robert T. McKee[S]

Grin and Bare It!/ Postcards (1970) Martin Aronstein[L]; David Mitchell[S]; Dominic Poleo[C]

Grind (1985) Ken Billington[L]; Clarke Dunham[S]; Florence Klotz[C]

Growing Pains (1933) Sol Cornberg[L]; Herbert Moore[S]; ACK[C]

Grown-ups (1981) Paul Gallo[L]; Andrew Jackness[S]; Dunya Ramicova[C]

Grumpy (1913) Mlle. Rachelle Ospovat[C]

Guardsman, The (1924) Jo Mielziner[S][C]

Guest in the House (1942) Raymond Sovey[S]; ACK[C]

Guest of Honor, The (1920) P. Dodd Ackerman[S]; ACK[L]

Guest Room, The (1931) Livingston Platt[S][C]; ACK[L]

Guide, The (1968) Martin Aronstein[L]; William Pitkin[S][C]

Guilty Conscience, The (1913) NONE

Guilty Man, The (1916) O'Kane Conwell[C]; ACK[L]

Guilty One, The (1923) Clifford F. Pember[S]; ACK[C][L]

Guinea Pig, The (1929) William Bradley Studio[S]; ACK[C]

Guns (1928) ACK[L]

Guys and Dolls (1950) Alvin Colt[C]; Jo Mielziner[S][L]

Guys and Dolls (1976) Tom John[S]; Bernard Johnson[C]; Thomas Skelton[L]

Guys and Dolls (1992) Paul Gallo[L]; William Ivey Long[C]; Tony Walton[S]

Guys in the Truck, The (1983) John Falabella[S][C]; John Gleason[L]

Gypsy (1903) NONE

Gypsy (1929) ACK[C][L]

Gypsy (1959) Raoul Pène Du Bois[C]; Jo Mielziner[S][L]

Gypsy (1974) Raoul Pène Du Bois[C]; Robert Randolph[S][L]

Gypsy (1989) Theoni V. Aldredge[C]; Kenneth Foy[S]; Natasha Katz[L]

Gypsy (1991) Theoni V. Aldredge[C]; Kenneth Foy[S]; Natasha Katz[L]

Gypsy Blonde (1934) Karle O. Amend[S]; ACK[C]

Gypsy Fires (1925) Florence Froelich[C]; Clarke Robinson[S]

Gypsy Jim (1924) Clifford F. Pember[S]

Gypsy Lady (1946) Boris Aronson[S]; Adrian Awan[L]; Miles White[C]

Gypsy Love (1911) Ernest Albert[S]; Madame Frances[C]; Marcel Multzer[C]; Paul Poiret[C]; ACK[L]

Gypsy Passion (1992) Mercedes Muniz(C); Tom Sturge(L); David Sumner(S)

Gypsy Trail, The (1917) Lucile(C); ACK(L)

Gypsy, The (1912) No PLAYBILL

H.M.S. Pinafore (1911) H. Robert Law(S)

H.M.S. Pinafore (1912) H. Robert Law(S)

H.M.S. Pinafore (1913) H. Robert Law(S)

H.M.S. Pinafore (1914) Arthur Voegtlin(S)

H.M.S. Pinafore (1926) Rollo Wayne(S)

H.M.S. Pinafore (1931) ACK(L)

H.M.S. Pinafore (1948) Joseph and Phil Harker(S); George Sheringham(C); ACK(L)

H.M.S. Pinafore (1955) Joseph and Phil Harker(S); George Sheringham(C)

Habeas Corpus (1975) Jennifer Tipton(L); Carl Toms(S)(C)

Habitual Husband, The (1924) Woodman Thompson(S); ACK(C)

Hadrian VII (1969) Lloyd Burlingame(L); Robert Fletcher(S)(C)

Hail and Farewell (1923) ACK(S)(C)(L)

Hail Scrawdyke! (1966) Jules Fisher(L); Willa Kim(C); Peter Larkin(S)

Hair (1968) Jules Fisher(L); Nancy Potts(C); Robin Wagner(S)

Hair (1977) Jules Fisher(L); Nancy Potts(C); Robin Wagner(S)

Hairpin Harmony (1943) Jeanette Hackett(L); Helen Mahieu(C); Donald Oenslager(S)

Hairy Ape, The (1922) Robert Edmond Jones(S); Cleon Throckmorton(S); ACK(L)

Haiti (1938) James Cochran(C); Perry Watkins(S); Bryon Webb(L)

Hal Holbrook in Mark Twain Tonight (1977) ACK(C)(L)

Half a Sixpence (1965) Jules Fisher(L); Jane Greenwood(C); Loudon Sainthill(S)(C)

Half a Widow (1927) P. Dodd Ackerman(S); Orry-Kelly(C)

Half an Hour (1913) Ernest Albert(S); Elizabeth Axtman(C)

Half Gods (1929) Albert R. Johnson(S); ACK(C)

Half Moon, The (1920) ACK(S)(C)(L)

Half Naked Truth, The (1926) ACK(C)(L)

Half-Caste, The (1926) Connors and Bennett(S); DuWico(L); Kliegl Brothers(L); ACK(C)

Halfway to Hell (1934) Philip Gelb(S); ACK(C)

Halfway Up the Tree (1967) Ralph Alswang(S)(L); James Hart Stearns(C)

Hall of Fame, The (1902) St. John Lewis(S)

Hallams, The (1948) DuWico(L); Raymond Sovey(S); Bianca Stroock(C)

Hallelujah, Baby! (1967) William and Jean Eckart(S); Tharon Musser(L); Irene Sharaff(C)

Halloween (1936) Louis Kennel(S); ACK(C)

Ham Tree, The (1905) F. Richards Anderson(C); Ernest Gros(S); William Hoover(S)

Hamilton (1917) Caroline Dudley(C); Gertrude Newell(C); Clifford F. Pember(S); ACK(L)

Hamlet (1900) C. Karl(C); Edward G. Unitt(S)

Hamlet (1904) C. Karl(C); Edward G. Unitt(S)

Hamlet (1905) NONE

Hamlet (1907) NONE

Hamlet (1908) Maurice Hermann(C); Unitt and Wickes(S); ACK(C)

Hamlet (1912) Joseph Harker(S)

Hamlet (1913) Hawes Craven(S); Joseph Harker(S)

Hamlet (1918) Claude Bragdon(S); Maurice Hermann(C); ACK(L)

Hamlet (1922) Robert Edmond Jones(S)(C)

Hamlet (1923) Robert Edmond Jones(S)(C); George Schaaf(L)

Hamlet (1925) Henri Bendel(C); Aline Bernstein(C); Frederick W. Jones III(S); ACK(L)

Hamlet (1931) Norman Bel Geddes(S)(C)(L); William Henry Matthews(C); Mary Stonehill(C)

Hamlet (1934) Claude Bragdon(S)

Hamlet (1936) Stewart Chaney(S)(C); Jo Mielziner(S)(L)

Hamlet (1938) David Ffolkes(S)(C)

Hamlet (1939) David Ffolkes(S)(C)

Hamlet (1945) Irene Sharaff(C); Frederick Stover(S); E. Carlton Winckler(L)

Hamlet (1947) Eric Adeney(S)(C); Donald Wolfit(S)(C)

Hamlet (1952) André Masson(S)(C)

Hamlet (1958) Audrey Cruddas(S)(C)(L)

Hamlet (1964) Ben Edwards(S); Jane Greenwood(C); Jean Rosenthal(L)

Hamlet (1969) Nancy Potts(C); James Tilton(S)(L)

Hamlet (1992) Christopher Barreca(S)

Hamlet (Kellerd) (1911) NONE

Hamlet (Mantell) (1906) H. Robert Law(S); Franklin Van Horn(C)

Hamlet (Roundabout) (1992) Christopher Barreca(S); Natasha Katz(L); Martin Pakledinaz(C)

Hamlet (starring Nichol Williamson) (1969) John Gleason(L); Jocelyn Herbert(S)(C)

Hammerstein's Nine O'clock Revue (1923) Charles LeMaire(S)(C)

Hand in Glove (1944) Robert Davison(C); Samuel Leve(S)(L)

Hand of the Potter, The (1921) Cleon Throckmorton(S)

Handful of Fire (1958) Lucinda Ballard(C); Jo Mielziner(S)(L)

Hands-Up (1915) John Whalen(L); ACK(S)(C)

Handy Man, The (1925) Clara Butler(S); ACK(C)(L)

Hangman's House (1926) Louis Kennel(S)

Hangman's Whip (1933) Livingston Platt(S); James Reynolds(C)

Hanky Panky (1912) Cora MacGeachy(C)

Hannele (1910) Madame Freisinger(C); Ernest Gros(S)

Hans, the Flute Player (1910) NONE

Hans, the Flute Player (1926) Ernest Schraps(C)

Happiest Days, The (1938) P. Dodd Ackerman(S)

Happiest Girl in the World, The (1961) William and Jean Eckart(S)(L); Robert Fletcher(C)

Happiest Millionaire, The (1956) Audré(C); George Jenkins(S)(L)

Happiest Night of His Life, The (1911) Ernest Albert(S); Frank Platzer(S); ACK(C)

Happiest Years, The (1949) James Russell(S); ACK(C)(L)

Happily Ever After (1945) Watson Barratt(S)

Happiness (1917) Clifford F. Pember(S); ACK(C)(L)

Happiness Is Just a Little Thing Called a Rolls Royce (1968) John Harvey(L); Larry Reehling(S); Ann Roth(C)

Happy (1927) ACK(C)(L)

Happy As Larry (1950) Motley(S)(C); ACK(L)

Happy Birthday (1946) Lucinda Ballard(C); Jo Mielziner(S)(L)

Happy Birthday, Wanda June (1970) Joseph G. Aulisi(C); David F. Segal(L); Ed Wittstein(S)

Happy Days (1919) Will R. Barnes(C); Marie Cooke(C); ACK(L)

Happy Days, The (1941) Raymond Sovey(S)

Happy End (1977) Carrie F. Robbins(C); Robert U. Taylor(S); Jennifer Tipton(L)

Happy Ending, The (1916) Robert Edmond Jones(S)

Happy Hunting (1956) Jo Mielziner(S)(L); Irene Sharaff(C)

Happy Husband, The (1928) Nicholas Yellenti(S); ACK(C)

Happy Hypocrite, The (1902) E. G. Banks(S); Walter Hann(S)

Happy Journey/ The Respectful Prostitute, The (1948) Ralph Alswang(C); Robert Gundlach(S); ACK(L)

Happy Landing (1932) Rollo Wayne(S); ACK(C)

Happy Marriage, The (1909) NONE

Happy New Year (1980) Pierre Balmain(C); Ken Billington(L); Michael Eagan(S)

Happy Time, The (1950) Aline Bernstein(S)(C); ACK(L)

Happy Time, The (1968) Jean Rosenthal(L); Peter Wexler(S); Freddy Wittop(C)

Happy Town (1959) Paul Morrison(L); Curt Nations(S); Michael Travis(C)

Happy-Go-Lucky (1920) ACK(S)(L)

Happy-Go-Lucky (1926) Miss Peacock(C); ACK(S)(L)

Happyland (1905) Ernest Albert(S); ACK(C)

Harbour Lights (1956) Jeanne Partington(C); Perry Watkins(S); Lee Watson(L)

Harem, The (1924) Joseph Wickes(S); ACK(C)

Harlem (1929) ACK(S)(L)

Harlem Cavalcade (1942) Noble Sissle(L); Ed Sullivan(S); Veronica(C); ACK(L)

Harlequinade/The Browning Version, A (1949) Frederick Stover(L)

Harold (1962) Ben Edwards(S)(L); Frank Thompson(C)

Harold and Maude (1980) Neil Peter Jampolis(L); Florence Klotz(C); Tony Straiges(S)

Harp of Life, The (1916) ACK(C)

Harriet (1943) Lemuel Ayers(S); Aline Bernstein(C)

Harriet's Honeymoon (1904) Arthur Voegtlin(S)

Harrigan 'n Hart (1985) Ann Hould-Ward(C); David Mitchell(S); Richard Nelson(L)

Harvest (1925) Raymond Sovey(S); ACK(L)

Harvest Moon, The (1909) Unitt and Wickes(S)

Harvest of Years (1948) Peggy Morrison(C); Raymond Sovey(S); ACK(L)

Harvester, The (1904) Walter W. Burridge(S)

Harvey (1944) John Root(S); ACK(C)

Harvey (1970) Nancy Potts(C); James Tilton(S)(L)

Hassan (1924) George W. Harris(S)(C)

Hassard Short's Ritz Revue (1924) Charles LeMaire(C); Charles E. Rush(L); Hassard Short(S)

Hasty Heart, The (1945) Raymond Sovey(S)(C)(L)

Hatful of Rain, A (1955) Mordecai Gorelik(S)(C)(L)

Hats Off to Ice (1944) Eugene Braun(L); Grace Houston(C); Billy Livingston(C); Bruno Maine(S)

Haunted House, The (1924) ACK(S)(L)

Havanna (1909) Arthur Voegtlin(S)

Have a Heart (1917) Henry Ives Cobb, Jr.(S); Joseph Wilson(L); ACK(C)

Have I Got a Girl for You (1963) Willa Kim(C); Samuel Leve(S)(L)

Haven, The (1946) William Noel Saulter(S); Noel Taylor(C)

Having Our Say (1995) Judy Dearing(C); Allen Lee Hughes(L); Thomas Lynch(S)

Having Wonderful Time (1937) Stewart Chaney(S); ACK(C)

Havoc (1924) ACK(C)(L)

Havoc, The (1911) NONE

Hawk Island (1929) Kathleen Millay(C); Willy Pogany(S)

Hawk, The (1914) ACK(C)

Hawthorne of the U.S.A. (1912) NONE

Hay Fever (1925) Gladys E. Calthrop(S)(C)

Hay Fever (1931) ACK(S)(C)(L)

Hay Fever (1970) Ben Edwards(S)(L); Jane Greenwood(C)

Hay Fever (1985) Arden Fingerhut(L); Michael H. Yeargan(S); Jennifer von Mayrhauser(C)

Hayride (1954) Jack Derrenberger(S); John Workman(C)

Hazel Flagg (1953) Harry Horner(S)(L); Miles White(C)

He (1931) ACK(S)(C)(L)

He and She (1920) ACK(L)

He Came from Milwaukee (1910) H. Robert Law(S); Lucile(C)

He Comes Up Smiling (1914) ACK(C)

He Didn't Want to Do It (1918) Henri Bendel(C); ACK(S)(L)

He Loved the Ladies (1927) ACK(L)

He Understood Women (1928) William Oden Waller(S); ACK(C)

He Walked in Her Sleep (1929) ACK(L)

He Who Gets Slapped (1922) Lee Simonson(S)(C)

He Who Gets Slapped (1946) Motley(S)(C)

Head First (1926) ACK(L)

Head or Tail (1926) P. Dodd Ackerman Studio(S); DuWico(L); Milgrim(C)

Head over Heels (1918) Gates and Morange(S); Joseph Urban(S); ACK(C)(L)

Headquarters (1929) P. Dodd Ackerman(S); ACK(C)

Heads or Tails (1947) Watson Barratt(S); Alice Gibson(C); Leo Kerz(L)

Heads Up (1929) Yetta Kiviette(C); Donald Oenslager(S)

Hear the Trumpet (1946) Woodman Thompson(S)(C)(L)

Hear! Hear! (1955) Samuel Leve(S); Jeanne Partington(C)

Heart of a City (1942) Perry Watkins(S); Max Weldy(C); ACK(C)

Heart of a Thief, The (1914) NONE

Heart of Wetona, The (1916) Ernest Gros(S); ACK(L)

Heartaches of a Pussycat (1980) Emilio Carcano(S); Beverly Emmons(L); Claudie Gastine(C)

Heartbreak House (1920) Lee Simonson(S)

Heartbreak House (1938) Millia Davenport(C); John Koenig(S)

Heartbreak House (1959) Ben Edwards(S)(L); Freddy Wittop(C)

Heartbreak House (1983) Paul Gallo(L); Jane Greenwood(C); Marjorie

Cracraft[S]; Alexander Saron[C]

Hero, The (1921) NONE

Herod (1909) Ernest Albert[S]; Percy Anderson[C]

Heroine, The (1963) Charles Brandon[S]; Klaus Holm[L]; Mary McKinley[C]

Herzl (1976) John Gleason[L]; Douglas W. Schmidt[S]; Pearl Somner[C]

Hey, Look Me Over! (1981) Karen Eifert[C]; David F. Segal[L]

Hey, Nonny Nonny (1932) Jo Mielziner[S][C][L]; Raymond Sovey[S][C]

Hickory Stick (1944) Frederick Fox[S]

Hidden (1927) Joseph Wickes[S]; ACK[C]

Hidden Horizon (1946) Charles Elson[S][L]; Everett Staples[C]

Hidden River, The (1957) Stewart Chaney[S][L]; Anna Hill Johnstone[C]

Hidden Stranger (1963) Audré[C]; Peter Cotes[S][L]

Hide and Seek (1957) Ralph Alswang[S][L]; Virginia Volland[C]

Hide and Seek (1980) John Lee Beatty[S]; Arden Fingerhut[L]; Jennifer von Mayrhauser[C]

Higgledy-Piggledy (1904) Mrs. Caroline Siedle[C]

High Button Shoes (1947) Peggy Clark[L]; Oliver Smith[S]; Miles White[C]

High Cost of Loving, The (1914) NONE

High Gear (1927) ACK[S][C][L]

High Ground, The (1951) Peggy Clark[S][C][L]

High Hatters, The (1928) Anne Caldwell[C]; ACK[S][L]

High Jinks (1913) Callot Soeurs[C]; Theodore Reisig[S]

High Kickers (1941) Nat Karson[S]; ACK[C]

High Road, The (1912) Homer Emens[S]; Gates and Morange[S]; Alice Kauser[S]

High Road, The (1928) Clara Fargo Thomas[S]; ACK[C]

High Rollers Social and Pleasure Club (1992) Theoni V. Aldredge[C]; Beverly Emmons[L]; David Mitchell[S]

High Society (1998) Loy Arcenas[S]; Howell Binkley[L]; Jane Greenwood[C]

High Spirits (1964) Jules Fisher[L]; Robert Fletcher[S][C]

High Stakes (1924) ACK[S][C][L]

High Tor (1937) Jo Mielziner[S][C][L]

Higher and Higher (1940) Lucinda Ballard[C]; Jo Mielziner[S][L]

Highest Tree, The (1959) Donald Oenslager[S][L]; Marvin Reiss[C]

Highland Fling, A (1944) Motley[C]; John Root[S]

Highway of Life, The (1914) NONE

Highwayman, The (1917) ACK[S][C][L]

Hilda Cassidy (1933) Selma Alexander[C]; Tom Adrian Cracraft[S]; ACK[C]

Hilda Crane (1950) Harriet Ames[C]; Howard Bay[S][C]; ACK[L]

Hill Between, The (1938) Tom Adrian Cracraft[S]; ACK[C]

Him (1928) Eugene Fitsch[S][C]; ACK[L]

Hindle Wakes (1912) NONE

Hindu, The (1922) ACK[S][C][L]

Hip! Hip! Hooray! (1907) Joseph Elsner[L]; Homer Emens[S]; Gates and Morange[S]; Mark Lawson[S]; Cora MacGeachy[C]; William Henry Matthews[C]; Robert McQuinn[C]

Hip-Hip-Hooray (1915) Joseph Elsner[L]; Cora MacGeachy[C]; William Henry Matthews[C]; Robert McQuinn[S][C]

Hipper's Holiday (1934) Louis Bromberg[S]; Olga Hunt[C]

Hired Husband (1932) Cleon Throckmorton[S]

His and Hers (1954) Charles Elson[S][L]; Frank Thompson[C]

His Bridal Night (1916) Lucile[C]; ACK[S][L]

His Chinese Wife (1920) Clifford F. Pember[S]; ACK[C][L]

His Excellency the Governor (1902) Mrs. Robert Osborn[C]

His Excellency the Governor (1907) Homer Emens[S]; Mrs. Robert Osborn[C]; Edward G. Unitt[S]; Joseph Wickes[S]

His Excellency the Governor (1912) Hawes Craven[S]

His Excellency the Governor (1995) James Acheson[C]; Peter J. Davison[S]; Mark Henderson[L]

His Honor the Mayor (1906) Joseph C. Fischer[C]

His Honor the Mayor (1922) Robert Edmond Jones[L]

His Honor, Abe Potash (1919) Henri Bendel[C]; ACK[S][L]

His Honor, the Barber (1906) Annie Sanse[C]

His Honor, the Barber (1911) NONE
His House in Order (1906) Homer Emens[S]; Edward G. Unitt[S]
His Little Widows (1917) Dodge and Castle[S]; Unitt and Wickes[S]; ACK[L]
His Majesty (1906) NONE
His Majesty Bunker Bean (1916) H. Robert Studio Law[S]; ACK[L]
His Majesty's Car (1930) Omar Kiam[C]; Margaret Pemberton[C]; Rollo Wayne[S]
His Name on the Door (1909) Gates and Morange[S]; ACK[C]
His Queen (1925) Joseph Physioc[S]; ACK[L]
His Wife by His Side (1912) William Birns[S]
His Wife's Family (1908) Frank E. Gates[S]; Edward Morange[S]
History of the American Film, A (1978) William Mintzer[L]; Marjorie Slaiman[C]; Tony Straiges[S]
Hit the Deck (1927) Mark Mooring[C]; John Wenger[S]
Hit the Trail (1954) Leo Kerz[S][L]; Michi Weglyn[C]
Hit the Trail Holiday (1915) ACK[L]
Hitch Your Wagon (1937) Watson Barratt[S]; Nat Lewis[C]; Mildred Manning[C]
Hitchy Koo (1917) Harry Collins[C]; ACK[L]
Hitchy Koo 1918 (1918) Madame Arlington[C]; Mary Blackburn[C]; H. Robert Law[S]; William Pennington[L]
Hitchy Koo 1919 (1919) H. Robert Studio Law[S]; Joseph Urban[S]; ACK[C][L]
Hitchy Koo 1920 (1920) O'Kane Conwell[C]; H. Robert Studio Law[S]; ACK[L]
Hizzoner (1989) Eldon Elder[S]; John McLain[L]; Patrizia von Brandenstein[C]
Hobo (1931) Cleon Throckmorton[S]
Hobohemia (1919) Edith Unger[C]; ACK[S][L]
Hoboken Blues (1928) Evelyn T. Clifton[C]; William Gaskin[S]
Hobson's Choice (1915) ACK[L]
Hodge, Podge, & Co. (1900) Will R. Barnes[C]; Arthur Voegtlin[S]
Hoity Toity (1901) Will R. Barnes[C]; John H. Young[S]; ACK[L]
Hokey-Pokey and Bunty, Bulls and Strings (1912) David Atchison[L];

Cora MacGeachy[C]; John H. Young[S]
Hold Everything (1928) Henry Dreyfuss[S]; Yetta Kiviette[C]
Hold It (1948) Edward Gilbert[S]; Julia Sze[C]; ACK[L]
Hold onto Your Hats (1940) Raoul Pène Du Bois[S][C]; A. H. Feder[L]
Hold Your Horses (1933) Russell Patterson[S][C]
Hole in the Head, A (1957) Boris Aronson[S]; Patton Campbell[C]; Jean Rosenthal[L]
Hole in the Wall, A (1920) Henri Bendel[C]; Anton Grot[S]; Albertine Peck[C]; ACK[L]
Holiday (1916) NONE
Holiday (1928) Hattie Carnegie[C]; Robert Edmond Jones[S]; Charles Kondazian[C]
Holiday (1973) Ken Billington[L]; Edward Burbridge[S]; Carolyn Parker[C]
Holiday (1995) Donald Holder[L]; Derek McLane[S]; Martin Pakledinaz[C]
Holiday for Lovers (1957) John Robert Lloyd[S][L]; Helene Pons[C]
Holka Polka (1925) Livingston Platt[S][C]
Hollow Crown, The (1962) ACK[C][L]
Hollywood Pinafore (1945) Kathryn Kuhn[C]; Jo Mielziner[S][L]; Mary Percy Schenck[C]
Holmses of Baker Street, The (1936) Kate Drain Lawson[S]
Holy Terror, A (1925) ACK[L]
Home (1970) Jules Fisher[L]; Jocelyn Herbert[S][C]
Home (1980) Martin Aronstein[L]; Felix E. Cochren[S]; Alvin B. Perry[C]
Home Again (1918) ACK[L]
Home Fires (1923) ACK[C][L]
Home Fires/ Cop Out (1969) John Gleason[L]; Fred Voelpel[S][C]
Home Folks (1904) William Hoover[S]; Thomas Mangan[S]; Richard Marston[S]; ACK[C]
Home Front (1985) Ken Billington[L]; Frank J. Boros[S]; John Falabella[C]; Sue Plummer[S]
Home Is the Hero (1954) Marvin Reiss[S][C][L]
Home of the Brave (1945) Ralph Alswang[S][C][L]
Home Sweet Homer (1976) Howard Bay[S][C][L]; Ray Diffen[C]
Home Towners, The (1926) Joseph Wickes[S]; ACK[C]

Homecoming, The (1967) John Bury[(S)(C)(L)]
Homecoming, The (1991) John Arnone[(S)]; Peter Kaczorowski[(L)]; William Ivey Long[(C)]
Hon. John Grigsby (1902) Henry Dazian[(C)]; Madame Virion[(C)]; Louis C. Young[(S)]; Ack[(C)]
Honest Jim Blunt (1912) NONE
Honest Liars (1926) William E. Castle[(S)]; Ack[(L)]
Honey Girl (1920) Hassard Short[(C)(L)]; Unitt and Wickes[(S)]
Honeydew (1920) Ack[(L)]
Honeymoon (1932) Raymond Sovey[(S)]; Ack[(C)]
Honeymoon Express, The (1913) Callot Soeurs[(C)]; Nick Kronyack[(L)]; Lucile[(C)]; Langdon McCormick[(S)]; Theodore Reisig[(S)]; Howard Thurston[(S)]
Honeymoon Lane (1926) Ack[(S)(C)(L)]
Honeymoon, The (1913) NONE
Honeys, The (1955) Ben Edwards[(S)]; Motley[(C)]
Honky Tonk Nights (1986) Robert Cothran[(S)]; Natasha Katz[(L)]; Mardi Philips[(C)]
Honor Be Damned (1927) P. Dodd Ackerman[(S)(L)]
Honor Bright (1937) William Kline[(S)]
Honor Code, The (1931) Ack[(L)]
Honor of the Family, The (1908) Ernest Gros[(S)]
Honor of the Family, The (1919) Ack[(L)]
Honor of the Family, The (1926) Ack[(S)(L)]
Honor of the Family, The (1954) Jack Woodson[(S)]
Honors Are Even (1921) Ack[(S)(C)]
Honour (1998) Jane Greenwood[(C)]; Peter Kaczorowski[(L)]; Derek McLane[(S)]
Hook 'n Ladder (1952) Jerry Boxhorn[(C)]; Eldon Elder[(S)]
Hook-Up, The (1935) A. H. Feder[(L)]; Sydne Hoffman[(C)]; Nat Karson[(S)]
Hooray for What! (1937) Raoul Pène Du Bois[(C)]; Vincente Minnelli[(S)]
Hop o' My Thumb (1913) Henry Emden[(S)]; C. Formilli[(S)]; Joseph Harker[(S)]; R. McCleery[(S)]; Bruce Smith[(S)]; Ack[(C)]
Hope for a Harvest (1941) Watson Barratt[(S)]; Valentina[(C)]; E. Carlton Winckler[(L)]

Hope for the Best (1945) Motley[(S)]; Ack[(C)]
Horowitz and Mrs. Washington (1980) Steven Rubin[(S)]; William Schroder[(C)]; Marc B. Weiss[(L)]
Horse Fever (1940) Louis Kennel[(S)]; Ack[(C)]
Horses in Midstream (1953) Donald Oenslager[(S)(C)(L)]
Hostage, The (1960) Margaret Bury[(C)]; Frederick Fox[(S)(L)]
Hostile Witness (1905) Ack[(C)]
Hostile Witness (1959) Ralph Alswang[(S)(L)]; Ack[(C)]
Hot Chocolates (1929) P. Dodd Ackerman[(L)]; Ack[(S)(L)]
Hot Corner, The (1956) Ralph Alswang[(S)(L)]; Virginia Volland[(C)]
Hot Mikado, The (1939) Nat Karson[(S)(C)]
Hot Pan (1928) Hubert Davis[(C)]; Cleon Throckmorton[(S)]
Hot Rhythm (1930) Ack[(S)(C)]
Hot Spot (1963) Rouben Ter-Arutunian[(S)(C)]
Hot Water (1929) Ack[(C)(L)]
Hot-Cha! (1932) John W. Harkrider[(C)]; Charles LeMaire[(C)]; Joseph Urban[(S)]
Hotbed (1928) Raymond Sovey[(S)]
Hotel Alimony (1934) P. Dodd Ackerman[(S)]; Phil MacDonald[(C)]
Hotel Mouse, The (1922) Watson Barratt[(S)]; Ack[(L)]
Hotel Paradiso (1957) Osbert Lancaster[(S)(C)]; Charles Lisanby[(S)]; Ack[(L)]
Hotel Universe (1930) Lee Simonson[(S)]; Ack[(C)(L)]
Hothouse, The (1982) William T. Lane[(C)]; Eugene Lee[(S)(L)]
Hottentot, The (1920) Ack[(C)(L)]
Hour Glass, The (1904) NONE
Hour Glass, The (1907) NONE
House Beautiful, The (1931) Jo Mielziner[(S)(C)(L)]
House in Paris, The (1944) Stewart Chaney[(S)]; Ack[(C)]
House in the Country, A (1937) P. Dodd Ackerman[(S)]; Ack[(C)]
House Next Door, The (1909) Ernest Albert[(S)]; John Brunton[(S)]; T. Bernard McDonald[(S)]
House of a Thousand Candles, The (1908) NONE
House of Atreus, The (1968) Tanya Moiseiwitsch[(S)(C)(L)]

House of Blue Leaves, The (1986) Paul Gallo⁽ᴸ⁾; Ann Roth⁽ᶜ⁾; Tony Walton⁽ˢ⁾
House of Bondage, The (1914) ACK⁽ˢ⁾⁽ᶜ⁾
House of Burnside, The (1904) ACK⁽ˢ⁾
House of Connelly, The (1931) Fania Mindell⁽ᶜ⁾; Cleon Throckmorton⁽ˢ⁾; ACK⁽ᴸ⁾
House of Doom, The (1932) Henry Landish⁽ˢ⁾; ACK⁽ᴸ⁾
House of Fear, The (1929) ACK⁽ᴸ⁾
House of Flowers (1954) Oliver Messel⁽ˢ⁾⁽ᶜ⁾; Jean Rosenthal⁽ᴸ⁾
House of Glass, The (1915) ACK⁽ᶜ⁾⁽ᴸ⁾
House of Mirth, The (1906) Frank Platzer⁽ˢ⁾
House of Ramsen (1934) Vail Studios⁽ˢ⁾; ACK⁽ᶜ⁾
House of Shadows (1927) Livingston Platt⁽ˢ⁾; ACK⁽ᶜ⁾
House of Silence, The (1906) Arthur Voegtlin⁽ˢ⁾
House of Women, The (1927) Robert Edmond Jones⁽ˢ⁾⁽ᶜ⁾
House That Jack Built, The (1900) NONE
House Unguarded (1929) Nicholas Yellenti⁽ˢ⁾; ACK⁽ᶜ⁾
Houseboat on the Styx (1928) John N. Booth, Jr.⁽ᶜ⁾; Willy Pogany⁽ˢ⁾; ACK⁽ᴸ⁾
Houseparty (1929) Gates and Morange⁽ˢ⁾; Anthony Greshoff⁽ᴸ⁾; Evelyn McHorter⁽ᶜ⁾
Houses of Sand (1925) Cleon Throckmorton⁽ˢ⁾; ACK⁽ᶜ⁾⁽ᴸ⁾
Housewarming (1932) Karl Ramet⁽ˢ⁾; ACK⁽ᶜ⁾
How Beautiful with Shoes (1935) P. Dodd Ackerman⁽ˢ⁾; ACK⁽ᶜ⁾
How Come, Lawd? (1937) ACK⁽ˢ⁾
How He Lied to Her Husband (1904) NONE
How He Lied to Her Husband (1905) NONE
How He Lied to Her Husband (1906) NONE
How He Lied to Her Husband (1907) NONE
How I Wonder (1947) Donald Oenslager⁽ˢ⁾⁽ᴸ⁾; Helene Pons⁽ᶜ⁾
How Long Till Summer (1949) Ralph Alswang⁽ˢ⁾⁽ᴸ⁾; Enid Smiley⁽ᶜ⁾
How Money (1931) Margaret Pemberton⁽ᶜ⁾; Cleon Throckmorton⁽ˢ⁾
How Now Dow Jones (1967) Martin

Aronstein⁽ᴸ⁾; Robert Mackintosh⁽ᶜ⁾; Oliver Smith⁽ˢ⁾
How the Other Half Loves (1971) Peggy Clark⁽ᴸ⁾; David Mitchell⁽ˢ⁾; Winn Morton⁽ᶜ⁾
How to Be a Jewish Mother (1967) John J. Moore⁽ᴸ⁾; Robert Randolph⁽ˢ⁾; Michael Travis⁽ᶜ⁾
How to Get Tough About It (1938) Norris Houghton⁽ˢ⁾; Helene Pons⁽ᶜ⁾
How to Make a Man (1961) Harry Horner⁽ˢ⁾⁽ᴸ⁾; Frank Thompson⁽ᶜ⁾
How to Succeed in Business Without Really Trying (1961) Robert Fletcher⁽ᶜ⁾; Robert Randolph⁽ˢ⁾⁽ᴸ⁾
How to Succeed in Business Without Really Trying (1995) John Arnone⁽ˢ⁾; Howell Binkley⁽ᴸ⁾; Susan Hilferty⁽ᶜ⁾
How's the World Treating You? (1966) Ben Edwards⁽ˢ⁾⁽ᴸ⁾; Jane Greenwood⁽ᶜ⁾
How's Your Health (1929) Cirker and Robbins⁽ˢ⁾; Dolly Tree⁽ᶜ⁾
Howdy Mr. Ice of 1950 (1949) Eugene Braun⁽ᴸ⁾; Grace Houston⁽ᶜ⁾; Kathryn Kuhn⁽ᶜ⁾; Billy Livingston⁽ᶜ⁾; Bruno Maine⁽ˢ⁾
Howdy Stranger (1937) Karle O. Amend⁽ˢ⁾; ACK⁽ᶜ⁾
Howdy, Mr Ice (1948) Eugene Braun⁽ᴸ⁾
Howdy, Mr. Ice (1948) Kathryn Kuhn⁽ᶜ⁾; Billy Livingston⁽ᶜ⁾; Bruno Maine⁽ˢ⁾
Howie (1958) Patton Campbell⁽ᶜ⁾; Frederick Fox⁽ˢ⁾⁽ᴸ⁾
Hoyden, The (1907) Homer Emens⁽ˢ⁾
Hughey/ Duet (1975) Kert Lundell⁽ˢ⁾; Ruth Morley⁽ᶜ⁾; Marc B. Weiss⁽ᴸ⁾
Hughie (1964) David Hays⁽ˢ⁾⁽ᴸ⁾; Noel Taylor⁽ᶜ⁾
Hughie (1996) Candice Donnelly⁽ᶜ⁾; David Gallo⁽ˢ⁾; Donald Holder⁽ᴸ⁾
Human Comedy, The (1984) James F. Ingalls⁽ᴸ⁾; Rita Ryack⁽ᶜ⁾; Bob Shaw⁽ˢ⁾
Human Nature (1925) Joseph Urban⁽ˢ⁾
Humbug, The (1929) P. Dodd Ackerman⁽ˢ⁾; ACK⁽ᶜ⁾
Humming Bird, The (1923) ACK⁽ᶜ⁾⁽ᴸ⁾
Humming Sam (1933) DuWico⁽ᴸ⁾; ACK⁽ˢ⁾⁽ᶜ⁾
Humoresque (1923) ACK⁽ˢ⁾⁽ᴸ⁾
Humpty Dumpty (1904) NONE
Humpty Dumpty (1918) Henri Bendel⁽ᶜ⁾; Homer Emens⁽ˢ⁾

Hunchback, The (1902) John Reed[S]; James Roberts[S]; T. E. Ryan[S]

Hundred Years Old, A (1929) James Whale[S]; ACK[C][L]

Hundreth Man, The (1913) NONE

Hunky Dory (1922) ACK[L]

Hurdy-Gurdy Girl, The (1907) Oliver P. Bernard[S]

Hurlyburly (1984) Ann Roth[C]; Jennifer Tipton[L]; Tony Walton[S]

Hurricane (1923) Clifford F. Pember[S]; Olga Petrova[S]

Hurry, Harry (1972) Martin Aronstein[L]; Sara Brook[C]; Fred Voelpel[S]

Husband and Wife (1915) B. Russell Herts[S]

Husbands of Leontine, The (1900) Ernest Gros[S]

Hush Money (1926) Roy Requa[S]; ACK[L]

Hush! (1916) O'Kane Conwell[C]; Unitt and Wickes[S]; ACK[L]

Hyphen, The (1915) ACK[L]

Hypocrites, The (1906) Mrs. Robert Osborn[C]; Frank Platzer[S]

I Am a Camera (1951) Boris Aronson[S]; Ellen Goldsborough[C]

I Am My Youth (1938) Donald Oenslager[S][C]

I Can Get It for You Wholesale (1961) Theoni V. Aldredge[C]; Will Steven Armstrong[S][L]

I Do! I Do! (1966) Jean Rosenthal[L]; Oliver Smith[S]; Freddy Wittop[C]

I Gotta Get Out (1947) DuWico[L]; Raymond Sovey[S]; Natalie Barth Walker[C]

I Had a Ball (1964) Will Steven Armstrong[S]; Ann Roth[C]

I Hate Hamlet (1991) Paul Gallo[L]; Tony Straiges[S]

I Have a Dream (1976) Martin Aronstein[L]; Donald Harris[S]; Terence Tam Soon[C]

I Have Been Here Before (1938) Laurence Irving[S]

I Killed the Count (1942) Emil Holak[S]; Ernest Schraps[C]

I Know My Love (1949) Stewart Chaney[S][C][L]

I Know What I Like (1939) Donald Oenslager[S]; ACK[C]

I Like It Here (1946) Ralph Alswang[S]; ACK[C]

I Love an Actress (1931) Jo Mielziner[S]; ACK[C][L]

I Love My Wife (1977) Gilbert V. Hemsley, Jr.[L]; David Mitchell[S]; Ron Talsky[C]

I Love You (1919) ACK[C][L]

I Loved You Wednesday (1932) Raymond Sovey[S]; ACK[C]

I Married an Angel (1938) John Hambleton[C]; Jo Mielziner[S][L]

I Must Love Someone (1939) Karle O. Amend[S]; Alfred Stern, Jr.[C]

I Never Sang for My Father (1968) Theoni V. Aldredge[C]; Jo Mielziner[S][L]

I Ought to Be in Pictures (1980) David Jenkins[S]; Tharon Musser[L]; Nancy Potts[C]

I Pagliacci (1908) NONE

I Remember Mama (1944) Lucinda Ballard[C]; George Jenkins[S][L]

I Remember Mama (1979) Theoni V. Aldredge[C]; David Mitchell[S]; Roger Morgan[L]

I Want a Policeman (1936) Cleon Throckmorton[S]; ACK[C]

I Want My Wife (1930) P. Dodd Ackerman Studio[S]; ACK[C]

I Was Dancing (1964) Martin Aronstein[L]; Oliver Smith[S]; Michael Travis[C]

I Was Waiting for You (1933) Jo Mielziner[S][L]; ACK[C]

I Won't Dance (1981) Craig Miller[L]; Bill Stabile[S]

I'd Rather Be Right (1937) A. H. Feder[L]; John Hambleton[C]; Donald Oenslager[S]; Irene Sharaff[C]

I'll Be Hanged If I Do (1910) NONE

I'll Say She Is (1924) H. Robert Studio Law[S]; ACK[C][L]

I'll Take the High Road (1943) Rose Bogdanoff[C]; Paul Morrison[S][L]

I'm Not Rappaport (1985) Pat Collins[L]; Robert Morgan[C]; Tony Walton[S]

I'm Solomon (1968) Martin Aronstein[L]; Jane Greenwood[C]; Rouben Ter-Arutunian[S]

I've Got Sixpence (1952) Boris Aronson[S][L]; Burton J. Miller[C]

I, Myself (1934) Tom Adrian Cracraft[S]; ACK[C]

I.O.U. (1917) Norman Bel Geddes[S][L]

I.O.U. (1918) Norman Bel Geddes[S][L]

Ian McKellen: A Knight Out at the Lyceum (1994) Norbert U. Kolb[S];

Jones(S); ACK(C)

In Abraham's Bosom (1926) Cleon Throckmorton(S)

In Abraham's Bosom (1927) Evelyn T. Clifton(C); Cleon Throckmorton(S); ACK(L)

In Any Language (1952) Raoul Pène Du Bois(S)(C)

In April (1915) Robert E. Locher(S)(C)

In Bed We Cry (1944) Gilbert Adrian(C); Joseph B. Platt(S)

In Clover (1937) Norris Houghton(S); Louise Segal(C)

In Dahomey (1903) NONE

In for the Night (1917) Hickson(C); Everett Shinn(S); ACK(L)

In Hayti (1909) NONE

In Heaven and Earth (1936) Cleon Throckmorton(S); Rollo Wayne(S); ACK(C)

In His Arms (1924) Julia Carroll(C); O'Kane Conwell(C); William Oden Waller(S); ACK(L)

In Love with Love (1923) Gilbert Clark(C); Livingston Platt(S)

In Love with Love (1928) Livingston Platt(S)

In Newport (1904) Ernest Albert(S); D. Frank Dodge(S); Richard Marston(S)

In Paradise (1899) NONE

In Praise of Love (1974) Theoni V. Aldredge(C); Jo Mielziner(S)(L)

In the Bag (1936) P. Dodd Ackerman(S); Gertrude Plons(C)

In the Best of Families (1931) Beatrice Maude(C); Nicholas Yellenti(S)

In the Bishop's Carriage (1907) Gates and Morange(S)

In the Counting House (1962) David Hays(S)(L); Ruth Morley(C)

In the Long Run (1909) NONE

In the Near Future (1925) ACK(S)(L)

In the Next Room (1923) ACK(L)

In the Night Watch (1921) Watson Barratt(S); Charles Davis(L); John H. Young(S)

In the Palace of the King (1900) Ernest Albert(S); Mrs. Caroline Siedle(C); Charles Smithline(L)

In the Palace of the King (1923) DuWico(L); ACK(S)(C)

In the Summer House (1953) Peggy Clark(L); Oliver Smith(S); Noel Taylor(C)

In the Summer House (1993) Ann Hould-Ward(C); Jennifer Tipton(L);

George Tsypin(S)

In Time to Come (1941) Harry Horner(S); John Koenig(C)

In Times Square (1931) Nicholas Yellenti(S)

Inacent Black (1981) Felix E. Cochren(S); Martin Pakledinaz(C); Tim Phillips(L)

Inadmissable Evidence (1965) Lloyd Burlingame(L); Jocelyn Herbert(S)(C)

Inca of Jerusalem, The (1916) Aline Bernstein(C)

Inca of Perusalem, The (1916) Warren Dahler(S); Ruth Deike(C); ACK(L)

Incognito (1904) NO PLAYBILL

Incomparable Max, The (1971) Theoni V. Aldredge(C); Martin Aronstein(L); David Mitchell(S)

Inconstant George (1909) Unitt and Wickes(S)

Incubator (1932) Leon R. Warren(S); ACK(C)

Incubus, The (1909) NONE

Indestructible Wife, The (1918) Hickson(C); Robert T. McKee(S)

Indian Summer (1913) NONE

Indians (1969) Thomas Skelton(L); Marjorie Slaiman(C); Oliver Smith(S)

Indiscretion (1929) Eddie Eddy(S)

Indiscretion of Truth, The (1912) Ernest Albert(S); H. Robert Law(S)

Indiscretions (Les Parents Terribles) (1995) Mark Henderson(L); Stephen Brimson Lewis(S)(C)

Inferior Sex, The (1910) Ernest Albert(S)

Infinite Shoeblack, The (1930) Leslie Banks(S); Rollo Wayne(S); ACK(C)

Ingomar (1904) ACK(S)(C)

Inherit the Wind (1955) A. H. Feder(L); Peter Larkin(S); Ruth Morley(C)

Inherit the Wind (1996) Ken Billington(L); Jess Goldstein(C); James Noone(S)

Inheritors (1927) Gladys E. Calthrop(C); Cleon Throckmorton(S)

Ink (1927) Albert Bliss(S); ACK(C)

Inner City (1972) Joseph G. Aulisi(C); John Dodd(L); Robin Wagner(S)

Inner Man, The (1917) ACK(L)

Innkeeper, The (1956) David Hays(S)(L); Guy Kent(C)

Innocent (1914) ACK(C)

Innocent Eyes (1924) Watson Barratt(S); Charles German(C); Larry J. Margulies(C)

Innocent Idea, An (1920) Cirker and Robbins⁽ˢ⁾; Harry Collins⁽ᶜ⁾; Aᴄᴋ⁽ᴸ⁾
Innocent Voyage, The (1943) Aline Bernstein⁽ᶜ⁾; Stewart Chaney⁽ˢ⁾
Innocents, The (1950) Jo Mielziner⁽ˢ⁾⁽ᴸ⁾; Motley⁽ᶜ⁾
Innocents, The (1976) John Lee Beatty⁽ˢ⁾; Deirdre Clancy⁽ᶜ⁾; Neil Peter Jampolis⁽ᴸ⁾; Mary McKinley⁽ᶜ⁾
Inquest (1970) Sara Brook⁽ᶜ⁾; Karl Eigsti⁽ˢ⁾; Jules Fisher⁽ᴸ⁾
Inside Story, The (1932) P. Dodd Ackerman⁽ˢ⁾; Bianca Stroock⁽ᶜ⁾; Aᴄᴋ⁽ᴸ⁾
Inside the Earth (1910) Arthur Voegtlin⁽ˢ⁾
Inside the Lines (1915) Gates and Morange⁽ˢ⁾; Aᴄᴋ⁽ˢ⁾⁽ᶜ⁾⁽ᴸ⁾
Inside U.S.A. (1948) Lemuel Ayers⁽ˢ⁾; Castillo⁽ᶜ⁾; Eleanor Goldsmith⁽ᶜ⁾
Inspector Calls, An (1947) Stewart Chaney⁽ˢ⁾⁽ᶜ⁾⁽ᴸ⁾
Inspector Calls, An (1994) Rick Fisher⁽ᴸ⁾; Ian MacNeil⁽ˢ⁾⁽ᶜ⁾
Inspector General, The (1923) William Gropper⁽ᶜ⁾; Jacob Meth⁽ᶜ⁾; Samuel Ostrowsky⁽ˢ⁾; Aᴄᴋ⁽ᴸ⁾
Inspector General, The (1930) Fania Mindell⁽ᶜ⁾; Raymond Sovey⁽ˢ⁾
Inspector General, The (1978) F. Mitchell Dana⁽ᴸ⁾; William Ivey Long⁽ᶜ⁾; Karen Schulz⁽ˢ⁾
Inspector Kennedy (1929) Cleon Throckmorton⁽ˢ⁾
Insult (1930) Rollo Wayne⁽ˢ⁾; Aᴄᴋ⁽ᶜ⁾
Integration Show Case, The (1954) Virginia Volland⁽ᶜ⁾; Perry Watkins⁽ˢ⁾; Aᴄᴋ⁽ᴸ⁾
Interference (1927) William E. Castle⁽ˢ⁾; Aᴄᴋ⁽ᶜ⁾⁽ᴸ⁾
Interior (1915) Robert Edmond Jones⁽ˢ⁾; Ralph Roeder⁽ᶜ⁾
Interlock (1958) Howard Bay⁽ˢ⁾⁽ᴸ⁾; Robert Mackintosh⁽ᶜ⁾
International Cup/The Battle of Niagara and The Ear, The (1910) Arthur Voegtlin⁽ˢ⁾
International Cup/The Battle of Niagara and the Ear, The (1964) Will Steven Armstrong⁽ᴸ⁾
International Incident, An (1940) Aᴄᴋ⁽ᶜ⁾
International Marriage, An (1991) Jane Greenwood⁽ᶜ⁾
International Review, The (1930) Yetta Kiviette⁽ᶜ⁾; Anthony W. Street⁽ˢ⁾; Dolly Tree⁽ᶜ⁾

International, The (1928) John Dos Passos⁽ˢ⁾; Helen Johnson⁽ᶜ⁾
Intimate Relations (1932) Louis Bromberg⁽ˢ⁾
Intimate Strangers, The (1921) Anthony Greshoff⁽ᴸ⁾; H. Robert Law⁽ˢ⁾; Unitt and Wickes⁽ˢ⁾; Aᴄᴋ⁽ᶜ⁾
Into the Light (1986) Neil Peter Jampolis⁽ᶜ⁾⁽ᴸ⁾; Hervig Libowitzky⁽ˢ⁾; Karen Roston⁽ˢ⁾
Into the Whirlwind (1996) Michael Frenkel⁽ˢ⁾⁽ᶜ⁾⁽ᴸ⁾
Into the Woods (1987) Ann Hould-Ward⁽ᶜ⁾; Richard Nelson⁽ᴸ⁾; Tony Straiges⁽ˢ⁾
Intruder, The (1909) No Pʟᴀʏʙɪʟʟ
Intruder, The (1928) August Vimnera⁽ˢ⁾; Aᴄᴋ⁽ᶜ⁾
Invention of Love, The (2001) Bob Crowley⁽ˢ⁾⁽ᶜ⁾; Brian MacDevitt⁽ᴸ⁾
Investigation, The (1966) Martin Aronstein⁽ᴸ⁾; Anna Hill Johnstone⁽ᶜ⁾; Kert Lundell⁽ˢ⁾
Invisible Foe, The (1918) Henri Bendel⁽ᶜ⁾; Joseph Urban⁽ˢ⁾
Invitation to a March (1960) Lucinda Ballard⁽ᶜ⁾; Paul Morrison⁽ᴸ⁾; William Pitkin⁽ˢ⁾
Invitation to Murder (1934) Robert Barnhart⁽ˢ⁾
Iolanthe (1913) Melville Ellis⁽ᶜ⁾
Iolanthe (1926) Woodman Thompson⁽ˢ⁾⁽ᶜ⁾; Aᴄᴋ⁽ᴸ⁾
Iolanthe (1927) Woodman Thompson⁽ˢ⁾
Iolanthe (1948) Norman Wilkerson⁽ᶜ⁾; Aᴄᴋ⁽ᴸ⁾
Iolanthe (1951) Norman Wilkerson⁽ᶜ⁾; Aᴄᴋ⁽ᴸ⁾
Iolanthe (1952) Ralph Alswang⁽ˢ⁾; Peggy Morrison⁽ᶜ⁾
Iolanthe (1955) Pat Freeborn⁽ᶜ⁾; Aᴄᴋ⁽ᴸ⁾
Iole (1913) Ernest Albert⁽ˢ⁾; Henry Dazian⁽ᶜ⁾; Frederica DeWolfe⁽ᶜ⁾; Lucile⁽ᶜ⁾
Iphigenia in Aulis (1921) Raymond Sovey⁽ˢ⁾
Ipi Tombi (1977) Timothy Heale⁽ᴸ⁾; Elizabeth MacLeish⁽ˢ⁾; John Wain⁽ˢ⁾; Susan Wain⁽ᶜ⁾⁽ᴸ⁾
Irene (1973) Raoul Pène Du Bois⁽ˢ⁾⁽ᶜ⁾; David F. Segal⁽ᴸ⁾; Irene Sharaff⁽ᶜ⁾
Irene Wycherley (1908) Joseph Harker⁽ˢ⁾; Aᴄᴋ⁽ᶜ⁾
Iris (1902) Edward G. Unitt⁽ˢ⁾
Irish Players (1911) Nᴏɴᴇ
Irish Players, The (1913) Nᴏɴᴇ

Irma La Douce (1960) Joe Davis[L]; Rolf Gérard[S)(C)

Iron Cross, The (1917) ACK[S)(C)(L]

Iron Men (1936) Norman Bel Geddes[S)(C]

Irregular Verb to Love, The (1963) Donald Oenslager[S)(L]; Frank Thompson[C]

Is Life Worth Living? (1933) Cleon Throckmorton[S]

Is Matrimony A Failure? (1909) Ernest Gros[S]

Is There Life after High School (1982) John Lee Beatty[S]

Is There Life after High School? (1982) Beverly Emmons[L]; Carol Oditz[C]

Isabel (1925) ACK[C)(L]

Island of Goats (1955) Jo Mielziner[S)(L]; Motley[C]

Island, The (1975) Bill Walker[C]; Ronald Wallace[L]; Stuart Wurtzel[S]

Isle o' Dreams, The (1913) NONE

Isle of Children (1961) Howard Bay[S)(L]; Ann Roth[C]

Isle of Spice, The (1904) W. Franklin Hamilton[S]

Israel (1909) Ernest Gros[S]

It Ain't Nothing But the Blues (1999) Don Darnutzer[L]; Robin Sanford Roberts[S]

It All Depends (1925) Livingston Platt[S]; ACK[C]

It Can't Happen Here (1936) Tom Adrian Cracraft[S]; Charles Hawkins[C]

It Had to Be You (1981) Lawrence King[S]; Roger Morgan[L]; Carrie F. Robbins[C]; Michael H. Yeargan[S]

It Happened in Nordland (1904) Mrs. Caroline Siedle[C]; John H. Young[S]

It Happened Tomorrow (1933) Walter Harvey[S]; Phil MacDonald[C]; Herbert Ward[S]

It Happens on Ice (1940) Norman Bel Geddes[S)(C)(L]

It Happens on Ice (1941) Norman Bel Geddes[S)(C]

It Happens to Everybody (1919) ACK[L]

It Is the Law (1922) Livingston Platt[S]; ACK[C)(L]

It Is to Laugh (1927) P. Dodd Ackerman[S]; ACK[C]

It Never Rains (1931) P. Dodd Ackerman[S]; ACK[L]

It Pays to Advertise (1914) ACK[S]

It Pays to Sin (1933) Ralph L. Moni[C]; Clive A. Rickabaugh[S]

It Takes Two (1947) John Root[S]; ACK[C]

It's a Bird...It's a Plane...It's Superman (1966) Florence Klotz[C]; Robert Randolph[S)(L]

It's a Boy (1922) ACK[S)(C)(L]

It's a Gift (1945) Rose Bogdanoff[C]; Samuel Leve[S]

It's a Grand Life (1930) Anthony Greshoff[L]; Evelyn McHorter[C]; ACK[S]

It's a Wise Child (1929) Louis Hartmann[L]; ACK[C]

It's a Wise Child (1933) ACK[S)(C]

It's All Your Fault (1906) NONE

It's So Nice to Be Civilized (1980) Charles E. Hoefler[S)(L]; Ruth Morley[C]

It's Spring (1980) Ken Billington[L]; John William Keck[S]; Frank Spencer[C]

It's Up to You (1921) ACK[C]

It's You I Want (1935) Jo Mielziner[S]; Bianca Stroock[C]

Ivan the Terrible (1904) NONE

Ivan the Terrible (1905) NONE

Ivan the Terrible (1906) NONE

Ivan the Terrible (1920) ACK[L]

Ivanov (1966) Jean Rosenthal[L]; Rouben Ter-Arutunian[S)(C]

Ivanov (1997) John Lee Beatty[S]; James F. Ingalls[L]; Catherine Zuber[C]

Ivory Door, The (1927) Helene Pons[C]; Herman Patrick Tappé[C]; Cleon Throckmorton[S]; ACK[L]

Ivy Green, The (1949) Stewart Chaney[S)(C]; DuWico[L]

Izzy (1924) ACK[S)(C)(L]

J.B. (1958) Boris Aronson[S]; Lucinda Ballard[C]; Tharon Musser[L]

Jack and Jill (1923) Gilbert Clark[C]; Howard Greer[C]; Frederick W. Jones III[S)(C]; Robert E. Locher[C]; Clifton Webb[C]

Jack and the Beanstalk (1931) Margaret Linley[S]; ACK[L]

Jack O'Lantern (1917) Ernest Albert[S]; Helen Dryden[C]; Homer Emens[S]; Joseph Urban[S]; ACK[C)(L]

Jack Straw (1908) Edward G. Unitt[S]; Joseph Wickes[S]

Jack's Little Surprise (1904) NONE

Jackie (1997) David Gallo[S]; Peter Kaczorowski[L]; Susan Santoian[C]

Jackie Mason: Politically Incorrect (1994) Neil Peter Jampolis[(S)(C)(L)]
Jackie Mason: Brand New (1990) Neil Peter Jampolis[(S)(L)]
Jackpot (1944) Stewart Chaney[(C)]; Robert Edmond Jones[(S)]; Raymond Sovey[(S)]
Jackson White (1935) ACK[(L)]
Jacob Slovak (1927) Cleon Throckmorton[(S)]
Jacobowsky and theColonel (1944) Stewart Chaney[(S)]; Emeline Clarke Roche[(C)]
Jacques Brel Is Alive and Living in Paris (1972) Les Lawrence[(S)]; ACK[(C)(L)]
Jade God, The (1929) ACK[(C)(L)]
Jake's Women (1992) Santo Loquasto[(S)]
Jamaica (1957) Jean Rosenthal[(L)]; Miles White[(C)]
Jamboree (1932) Philip Gelb[(S)]; ACK[(C)]
James Joyce's The Dead (2000) Jane Greenwood[(C)]; David Jenkins[(S)]; Jennifer Tipton[(L)]
James Whitmore in Will Rogers' U.S.A. (1974) Eldon Elder[(S)(C)(L)]
Jane (1952) Elfi Von Kantzow[(S)(C)]
Jane Clegg (1920) Lee Simonson[(S)(C)]
Jane Eyre (1958) Ben Edwards[(S)]; Motley[(C)]; Frank Spencer[(C)]
Jane Eyre (2000) Peggy Eisenhauer[(L)]; Jules Fisher[(L)]; John Napier[(S)]; Andreane Neofitou[(C)]
Jane, Our Stranger (1925) Frances Clyne[(C)]; Sheldon K. Viele[(S)]
Janice Meredith (1900) Ernest Gros[(S)]; Arthur Voegtlin[(S)]
Janie (1942) DuWico[(L)]; Yetta Kiviette[(C)]; John Root[(S)]
January Thaw (1946) Watson Barratt[(S)]; ACK[(C)]
Janus (1955) Jane Derby[(C)]; Donald Oenslager[(S)(L)]
Japanese Doll, A (1907) NONE
Japanese Lady, A (1907) NO PLAYBILL
Japanese Nightingale, A (1903) Ernest Albert[(S)]; F. Richards Anderson[(C)]; Henry Bissing[(L)]; Ernest Gros[(S)]
Japanese Ophelia, A (1907) No PLAYBILL
Jarnegan (1928) E.J. Herrett[(C)]; Clarke Robinson[(S)]
Jason (1942) John Root[(S)]; ACK[(C)]
Jay Walker, The (1926) Cirker and Robbins[(S)]; ACK[(C)(L)]

Jayhawker (1934) Helen Grayson[(C)]; Walter Walden[(S)]
Jazz Singer, The (1925) ACK[(S)(C)(L)]
Jazz Singer, The (1927) Nicholas Yellenti[(S)]; ACK[(C)(L)]
Jealous Moon, The (1928) Jo Mielziner[(S)(L)]; Madame Pulliche[(C)]; Raymond Sovey[(C)]
Jealousy (1928) P. Dodd Ackerman[(S)]; ACK[(C)(L)]
Jeanne d'Arc (1907) Homer Emens[(S)]; Unitt and Wickes[(S)]
Jeb (1946) Jo Mielziner[(S)(L)]; Patricia Montgomery[(C)]
Jedermann (1927) Professor Alfred Roller[(C)]; ACK[(S)(L)]
Jefferson Davis (1936) Ivan Glidden[(C)]; Cleon Throckmorton[(S)]
Jekyll & Hyde (1997) Ann Curtis[(C)]; Beverly Emmons[(L)]; James Noone[(S)]; Robin Phillips[(S)]
Jelly's Last Jam (1992) Jules Fisher[(L)]; Toni-Leslie James[(C)]; Robin Wagner[(S)]
Jennie (1963) George Jenkins[(S)]; Jean Rosenthal[(L)]; Irene Sharaff[(C)]
Jenny (1929) Jo Mielziner[(S)(L)]; ACK[(C)]
Jenny Kissed Me (1948) Ralph Alswang[(S)]; Eleanor Goldsmith[(C)]; ACK[(L)]
Jephthah's Daughter (1915) Alice and Irene Lewisohn[(S)(C)]; Esther Peck[(C)]; ACK[(L)]
Jeremiah (1939) Harry Horner[(S)(C)]
Jerome Kern Goes to Hollywood (1986) Ken Billington[(L)]; Colin Pigott[(S)]; Christine Robinson[(C)]
Jerome Robbins' Broadway (1989) Boris Aronson[(S)]; Joseph G. Aulisi[(C)]; Alvin Colt[(C)]; Raoul Pène Du Bois[(C)]; Jo Mielziner[(S)]; Irene Sharaff[(C)]; Oliver Smith[(S)]; Jennifer Tipton[(L)]; Robin Wagner[(S)]; Miles White[(C)]; Patricia Zipprodt[(C)]
Jerry (1914) Madame Viola[(C)]; ACK[(S)]
Jerry's Girls (1985) Florence Klotz[(C)]; Tharon Musser[(L)]; Hal Tiné[(S)]
Jersey Lily, The (1903) Joseph George[(L)]; Archie Gunn[(C)]; Claude Hagen[(S)]; William Kellam[(S)]
Jest, The (1919) Maurice Hermann[(C)]; Robert Edmond Jones[(S)]; ACK[(L)]
Jest, The (1926) Robert Edmond Jones[(S)(C)(L)]
Jesters, The (1908) Henry Dazian[(C)]; Ernest Gros[(S)]
Jesus Christ Superstar (1971) Randy

Barcelo[C]; Jules Fisher[L]; Robin Wagner[S]

Jesus Christ Superstar (1995) Rick Belzer[L]; David Paulin[C]; Bill Stabile[S]

Jesus Christ Superstar (2000) Peter J. Davison[S]; Roger Kirk[C]; Mark McCullough[L]

Jewel of Asia, The (1903) Ernest Albert[S]; Joseph George[L]; Mrs. Caroline Siedle[C]

Jewel Robbery (1932) Aline Bernstein[S]; ACK[C]

Jeweled Tree, The (1926) Willy Pogany[S]; ACK[C]

Jigsaw (1934) Lee Simonson[S]; ACK[C]

Jim Blusdo of the Prairie Belle (1903) Joseph Physioc[S]

Jim Jam Jems (1920) ACK[S][C][L]

Jim the Penman (1910) NONE

Jimmie (1920) Joseph Physioc[S]; ACK[C][L]

Jimmie's Women (1927) Gates and Morange[S]; ACK[C]

Jimmy (1969) Peggy Clark[L]; W. Robert La Vine[C]; Oliver Smith[S]

Jimmy Shine (1968) Lewis Brown[C]; Edward Burbridge[S]; Thomas Skelton[L]

Jinny, the Carrier (1905) Emens and Unitt[S]

Jitta's Atonement (1923) ACK[C][L]

Joan o' the Shoals (1902) P. J. McDonald[S]; Mrs. Caroline Siedle[C]; Louis C. Young[S]

Joan o' the Shoals (1909) NONE

Joan o' the Shoals (1940) Stewart Chaney[S]; Herman Patrick Tappé[C]

Joan of Lorraine (1946) Lee Simonson[S][C][L]

Jockey Club Stakes, The (1973) Paul Morrison[S][L]; Albert Wolsky[C]

Joe Egg (1985) Marjorie Bradley Kellogg[S]; Bill Walker[C]; Ronald Wallace[L]

Joe Turner's Come and Gone (1988) Scott Bradley[S]; Michael Giannitti[L]; Pamela Peterson[C]

John (1927) Norman Bel Geddes[S]

John Brown (1934) Cirker and Robbins[S]; ACK[C]

John Brown's Body (1953) ACK[L]

John Bull's Other Island (1905) NONE

John Bull's Other Island (1948) Molly MacEwan[S]; ACK[L]

John Curry's Ice Dancing (1978)

Marilyn Rennagel[L]

John Ermine of the Yellowstone (1903) Arthur Voegtlin[S]

John Ferguson (1919) Rollo Peters[S][C]

John Ferguson (1933) ACK[S]

John Gabriel Borkman (1915) H. P. Scenic Studio Knight[S]; ACK[L]

John Gabriel Borkman (1926) Gladys E. Calthrop[S][C]

John Gabriel Borkman (1946) Paul Morrison[S][C][L]

John Gabriel Borkman (1980) Paul Gallo[L]; Andrew Jackness[S]; Jennifer von Mayrhauser[C]

John Gladye's Honor (1907) ACK[C]

John Hawthorne (1921) Sheldon K. Viele[S][C]

John Henry (1903) NONE

John Henry (1940) John Hambleton[C]; Albert R. Johnson[S]

John Hudson's Wife (1906) Madame Revare[C]

John Loves Mary (1947) Lucinda Ballard[C]; Frederick Fox[S][L]

John Murray Anderson's Almanac (1953) Thomas Becher[C]; Raoul Pène Du Bois[S]

John the Baptist (1907) Harley Merry[S]

John the Baptist (1913) H. Robert Law[S]

Johnny 2x4 (1942) Howard Bay[S]

Johnny Belinda (1940) A. H. Feder[L]; Frederick Fox[S]; ACK[C]

Johnny Johnson (1936) Paul du Pont[C]; Donald Oenslager[S]

Johnny No-trump (1967) William Ritman[S][C][L]

Johnny on a Spot (1942) Frederick Fox[S][C]

Johnny, Get Your Gun (1917) ACK[C][L]

Joker, The (1925) NONE

Jolly Bachelors, The (1910) Melville Ellis[C]; Gates and Morange[S]; Arthur Voegtlin[S]; Young Brothers[S]

Jolly Roger, The (1923) John Wolcott Adams[S]; Raymond Sovey[S]; ACK[C]

Jolly's Progress (1959) Gene Coffin[C]; George Jenkins[S]

Jonathan Makes a Wish (1918) J. Blanding Sloan[S]; Frank J. Zimmerer[S]

Jonesy (1929) Rollo Wayne[S]

Jonica (1930) William Hawley[S]; ACK[C][L]

Josef Suss (1930) Boris Aronson(S); Herbert Norris(C)

Joseph (1930) Ernest Schraps(C); Redington Sharpe(S)

Joseph and His Bretheren (1912) Ben Beerwald(L)

Joseph and His Brethren (1913) Melville Ellis(C); Arthur Voegtlin(S)

Joseph and the Amazing Technicolor Dreamcoat (1982) Barry Arnold(L); Judith Dolan(C); Karl Eigsti(S)

Joseph and the Amazing Technicolor Dreamcoat (1993) Andrew Bridge(L); Mark Thompson(S)(C)

Joseph Entangled (1904) Robert T. McKee(S)

Josephine (1918) Rollo Peters(S)(C)

Jotham Valley (1951) Erling Roberts(S)

Journey by Night, A (1935) Rollo Wayne(S); Ack(C)

Journey to Jerusalem (1940) Millia Davenport(C); Jo Mielziner(S)(L)

Journey's End (1929) James Whale(S); Ack(C)

Journey's End (1939) Lemuel Ayers(S)

Journeyman (1938) Nat Karson(S)

Joy Forever, A (1946) Stewart Chaney(S)(C)

Joy of Living, The (1902) Ernest Gros(S); Mrs. Robert Osborn(C); Madame Viola(C)

Joy of Living, The (1931) Margaret Pemberton(C); Ack(S)(L)

Joy to the World (1948) Harry Horner(S); Jean Rosenthal(L); Beverly Woodner(C)

Joyce Grenfell in Monologues and Songs (1958) Ack(L)

Joyce Grenfell Requests the Pleasure (1955) Paul Morrison(S)(L); Victor Stiebel(C); Joan and David deBethel(S)

Joyful Noise, A (1966) Peter Joseph(C); Peter Wexler(S)(L)

Joyous Season (1934) Robert Edmond Jones(S); Muriel King(C)

Juan Darién: A Carnival Mass (1996) Donald Holder(L); G. W. Mercier(S)(C); Julie Taymor(S)(C)

Juarez and Maximillian (1926) Lee Simonson(S)(C)

Jubilee (1935) Connie DePinna(C); Jo Mielziner(S)(L); Irene Sharaff(C)

Judas (1929) Richard Boleslavski(C); Jo Mielziner(S)(L)

Judas Kiss, The (1998) Bob Crowley(S)(C); Mark Henderson(L)

Judge and the Jury, The (1906) Ernest Gros(S)

Judge and the Jury, The (1929) Joseph Wickes(S)

Judge's Husband, The (1926) Mabel A. Buell(S); Ack(C)(L)

Judgement Day (1934) Aline Bernstein(S)

Judgment at Nuremberg (2001) Jess Goldstein(C); Brian MacDevitt(L); James Noone(S)

Judith of Bethulia (1904) Gates and Morange(S); J. G. Hammond(S); Mrs. Bessie Scott(C); Franklin Van Horn(C)

Judith Zaraine (1911) None

Judy (1927) DuWico(L); Hugh Willoughby(C); Ack(S)

Judy Drops In (1924) Ack(S)(C)(L)

Judy Forgot (1910) Ack(C)

Julie (1927) Ack(S)(L)

Julie Bonbon (1906) None

Julius Caesar (1907) None

Julius Caesar (1912) Sir Laurence Alma-Tadema(S); Joseph Harker(S)

Julius Caesar (1918) Ack(C)

Julius Caesar (1922) Ack(L)

Julius Caesar (1927) Norman Bel Geddes(S); Eric Pape(C)

Julius Caesar (1931) William Henry Matthews(C); Mary Stonehill(C); Ack(S)(L)

Julius Caesar (1937) Samuel Leve(S)(L); Ack(C)

Julius Caesar (1950) Ralph Alswang(S)(L); Beulah Frankel(C)

Julius Caesar (Richard Mansfield) (1902) Sir Laurence Alma-Tadema(S)

Jumbo (1935) Raoul Pène Du Bois(C); Albert R. Johnson(S); James Reynolds(C)

Jumpers (1974) Gilbert V. Hemsley, Jr.(L); Willa Kim(C); Josef Svoboda(S)

Jumping Jupiter (1911) D. Frank Dodge(S); Lee Lash Studios(S); Lucile(C); Ack(C)

June Days (1925) Watson Barratt(S); Ack(L)

June Love (1921) Ada B. Fields(C)

June Madness (1912) Unitt and Wickes(S)

June Moon (1929) William Oden Waller(S); Ack(C)

June Moon (1933) William Oden

Waller[S]; ACK[C][L]
Junior Miss (1941) Rose Bogdanoff[C]; Frederick Fox[S]; ACK[L]
Junk (1927) Joseph Teichner[S]
Juno (1959) Peggy Clark[L]; Irene Sharaff[C]; Oliver Smith[S]
Juno and the Paycock (1926) ACK[S][L]
Juno and the Paycock (1927) ACK[S][L]
Juno and the Paycock (1940) Robert Edmond Jones[S]; ACK[C]
Juno and the Paycock (1957) Oliver Smith[S]
Juno and the Paycock (1988) Consolata Boyle[C]; Frank Hallinan Flood[S]; Rupert Murray[L]
Juno and the Paycock (1992) Santo Loquasto[S][C]; Tharon Musser[L]
Jupiter Laughs (1940) Raymond Sovey[S][C][L]
Just a Minute (1919) ACK[C][L]
Just a Minute (1928) P. Dodd Ackerman[S]; Helen Mahieu[C]
Just A Wife (1910) Ernest Gros[S]; Louis Hartmann[L]; Monette[C]
Just a Woman (1916) ACK[L]
Just around the Corner (1919) ACK[C][L]
Just Because (1922) H. Robert Studio Law[S]; ACK[C][L]
Just Beyond (1925) Clarke Robinson[S][C]
Just Boys (1915) ACK[L]
Just Fancy (1927) P. Dodd Ackerman[S]; E.J. Herrett[C]; ACK[L]
Just Herself (1914) ACK[C]
Just Life (1926) Nicholas Yellenti[S]; ACK[C]
Just Like John (1912) NONE
Just Married (1921) ACK[C]
Just Out of College (1905) Homer Emens[S]; Edward G. Unitt[S]
Just Outside the Door (1915) Grinager and Beardsley[S]
Just Suppose (1920) Unitt and Wickes[S]; ACK[L]
Just to Get Married (1912) NONE
Just to Remind You (1931) Cleon Throckmorton[S]
Justice (1916) ACK[S][L]
K Guy, The (1928) Theodore Kahn[S]
K-2 (1983) Allen Lee Hughes[L]
K2 (1983) Noël Borden[C]; Ming Cho Lee[S]
Kairn of Koridwen, The (1916) Herbert Crowley[C]; ACK[L]
Karen (1918) Mina Loy[C]; Mr. Roy

Mitchell[S]; ACK[L]
Karl and Anna (1929) Jo Mielziner[S][C][L]
Kassa (1909) Alphonse Mucha[S]
Kat and the Kings (1999) Howard Harrison[L]; Saul Radomsky[S][C]
Kataki (1959) Peter Dohanos[S]; Anne Graham[C]; Paul Morrison[L]
Katerina (1929) Aline Bernstein[S]
Kathleen (1948) Rose Bogdanoff[C]; Charles Elson[S][L]
Kathleen Ni Houlihan (1900) NONE
Kathleen Ni Houlihan (1907) NONE
Kathryn Dunham and Her Company (1950) Ralph Alswang[S]; John Pratt[C]; ACK[L]
Kathryn Dunham and Her Company (1955) John Pratt[S][C]; ACK[L]
Katinka (1915) ACK[S][C][L]
Katja (1926) Watson Barratt[S]; Max Weldy[C]; ACK[L]
Katy Did (1927) ACK[L]
Katy's Kisses (1919) ACK[L]
Kean (1961) John Harvey[L]; Ed Wittstein[S][C]
Kean, On Desordre Et Genie (1907) NONE
Keep 'Em Laughing (1942) Frank W. Stevens[S]
Keep Her Smiling (1918) Richard Walton Tully[S]; ACK[L]
Keep It Clean (1929) ACK[L]
Keep It in the Family (1967) Lloyd Burlingame[S]; Mary McKinley[C]; ACK[L]
Keep It to Yourself (1918) Mrs. Lillian Trimble Bradley[S]; ACK[C][L]
Keep Kool (1924) H. Robert Law[S]
Keep Moving (1934) Raoul Pène Du Bois[C]; Clarke Robinson[S]; Robert Ten Eyck Stevenson[C]
Keep Off the Grass (1940) Nat Karson[S][C]
Keep Shufflin' (1928) Karle O. Amend[S]; Helen Mahieu[C]; ACK[L]
Keeper of the Keys (1933) Donald Oenslager[S]; ACK[C]
Keeping Expenses Down (1932) ACK[L]
Keeping Up Appearances (1910) Joseph[C]
Keeping Up Appearances (1916) ACK[C][L]
Keeping Up Appearances (1918) ACK[C][L]

Kelly (1965) Tharon Musser(L); Oliver Smith(S); Freddy Wittop(C)

Kempy (1922) P. Dodd Ackerman(S); Ack(C)

Kempy (1927) P. Dodd Ackerman(S); Ack(L)

Ken Murray's Blackout of 1949 (1949) Ben Tipton(S); Ack(L)

Ken Murray's Hollywood (1965) Ralph Alswang(S)(C)(L)

Kennedy's Children (1975) Martin Aronstein(L); Santo Loquasto(S)(C)

Kentucky Cycle, The (1993) Frances Kenny(C); Peter Maradudin(L); Michael Olich(S)

Kept (1926) Albert Bliss(S); Ack(C)

Key Largo (1939) Jo Mielziner(S)(L); Helene Pons(C)

Kibitzer (1929) Schaffner and Sweet Studio(S); Ack(L)

Kick Back, The (1936) Rollo Wayne(S)

Kick In (1914) Madame Julie(C)

Kid Boots (1923) Henri Bendel(C); Evelyn McHorter(C); Alice O'Neil(C); Ack(S)(L)

Kidding Kidders (1928) Willy Pogany(S); Ack(C)(L)

Kill That Story (1934) Stewart Chaney(S); Ack(C)

Killers (1928) Cleon Throckmorton(S); Ack(C)(L)

Killing of Sister George, The (1966) Catherine Browne(S)(C)(L); Jane Greenwood(C)

Kind Lady (1935) Mary Merrill(C); Jo Mielziner(S)(L)

Kind Lady (1940) Watson Barratt(S); Ack(C)

Kind Sir (1953) Mainbocher(C); Jo Mielziner(S)(L)

Kindling (1911) H. Robert Law(S)

Kindred (1939) Robert Edmond Jones(S)

King and I, The (1951) Jo Mielziner(S)(L); Irene Sharaff(C)

King and I, The (1977) Stanley Simmons(C); Thomas Skelton(L); Peter Wolf(S)

King and I, The (1985) Ruth Roberts(L); Irene Sharaff(C); Stanley Simmons(C); Peter Wolf(S)

King and I, The (1995) Roger Kirk(C); Nigel Levings(L); Brian Thomson(S)

King and I, The (1996) Roger Kirk(C); Nigel Levings(L); Brian Thomson(S)

King Arimenes and the Unknown Warrior (1916) Frank J.

Zimmerer(S)(C)

King Can Do No Wrong, The (1927) Cleon Throckmorton(S); Ack(C)(L)

King David (1997) David Agress(L); William Ivey Long(C); Tony Walton(S)

King Dodo (1902) Walter W. Burridge(S)

King Hedley II (2001) David Gallo(S); Donald Holder(L); Toni-Leslie James(C)

King Henry V (1928) Claude Bragdon(S)(C)

King Henry VIII (1916) Percy Macquoid(C); Ack(S)

King Highball (1902) No Playbill

King Lear (1905) H. Robert Law(S); Annie Sanse(C); Bert Tuchman(S); Franklin Van Horn(C)

King Lear (1907) H. Robert Law(S); Annie Sanse(C); Bert Tuchman(S); Franklin Van Horn(C)

King Lear (1923) Reginald Pale(S)(C); Ack(L)

King Lear (1930) William Henry Matthews(C); Herman Rosse(S); Ack(L)

King Lear (1947) Ernest Stern(S)(C)

King Lear (1950) Ralph Alswang(S)(L); Dorothy Jeakins(C)

King of Cadonia, The (1910) Arthur Voegtlin(S)

King of Friday's Men, The (1951) Stewart Chaney(S)(C)(L)

King of Hearts (1954) Frederick Fox(S)(C)(L)

King of Hearts (1978) Pat Collins(L); Santo Loquasto(S); Patricia Zipprodt(C)

King of Nowhere, A (1916) Ack(C)(L)

King Rene's Daughter (1906) None

King Richard II (1937) David Ffolkes(S)(C)

King Richard II (1940) David Ffolkes(S)(C)

King Richard III (1907) None

King Washington (1901) Joseph Physioc(S)

King's Carnival, The (1901) St. John Lewis(S); Mrs. Caroline Siedle(C)

King, The (1917) Ack(C)(L)

Kingdom of God, The (1928) Watson Barratt(S); Orry-Kelly(C)

Kingdoms (1981) Paul Gallo(L); David Hays(S); Patricia Zipprodt(C)

Kingfisher, The (1978) Jane Greenwood(C); Thomas Skelton(L); Alan Tagg(S)

Kings (1976) Ben Benson(C); John Falabella(S); Thomas Skelton(L)

Kipling (1984) Pamela Howard[S][C]; Neil Peter Jampolis[L]

Kismet (1911) Percy Anderson[C]; Walter W. Burridge[S]; Homer Emens[S]; Gates and Morange[S]; Frank Platzer[S]; Unitt and Wickes[S]

Kismet (1953) Lemuel Ayers[S][C]; Peggy Clark[L]

Kiss and Tell (1943) John Root[S]; ACK[C]

Kiss Burglar, The (1918) William Henry Matthews[C]; Clifford F. Pember[S]; ACK[L]

Kiss Burglar, The (1919) Clifford F. Pember[S]; ACK[L]

Kiss for Cinderella, A (1916) Mrs. John Alexander[S][C]; ACK[L]

Kiss for Cinderella, A (1942) Paul du Pont[C]; DuWico[L]; Harry Horner[S]

Kiss in a Taxi, A (1925) P. Dodd Ackerman[S]; ACK[C][L]

Kiss Me (1927) Robert Ten Eyck Stevenson[C]; August Vimnera[S]

Kiss Me Kate (1948) Lemuel Ayers[S][C]; ACK[L]

Kiss Me Kate (1952) Lemuel Ayers[S][C]; Peggy Clark[L]

Kiss Me Kate (1999) Peter Kaczorowski[L]; Martin Pakledinaz[C]; Robin Wagner[S]

Kiss Me Quick (1913) ACK[S]

Kiss of Importance, A (1930) Henry Dreyfuss[S]; ACK[C]

Kiss of the Spider Woman (1993) Howell Binkley[L]; Florence Klotz[C]; Jerome Sirlin[S]

Kiss the Boys Goodbye (1938) Margaret Pemberton[C]; John Root[S]

Kiss Them for Me (1945) Frederick Fox[S]; Mary Percy Schenck[C]

Kiss Waltz, The (1911) Melville Ellis[C]; H. Robert Law[S]

Kissing Time (1920) Dodge and Castle[S]; ACK[C][L]

Kitty Darlin' (1917) ACK[L]

Kitty Grey (1909) NONE

Kitty Mackay (1914) Adrienne Brugard[C]

Kitty's Kisses (1926) Livingston Platt[S]; ACK[C][L]

Knickerbocker Holiday (1938) Frank Bevan[C]; Jo Mielziner[S][L]

Knickerbocker Holiday (1977) Ken Billington[L]; Donald Brooks[C]

Knife, The (1917) Hickson[C]; ACK[L]

Knight For A Day, A (1907) D. Frank

Dodge[S]; ACK[C]

Knights of Song (1938) Kate Drain Lawson[C]; Raymond Sovey[S]

Knock Knock (1976) John Lee Beatty[S]; Dennis Parichy[L]; Jennifer von Mayrhauser[C]

Knock on Wood (1935) Watson Barratt[S]; ACK[C]

Knockout (1979) Karl Eigsti[S]; Jane Greenwood[C]; Neil Peter Jampolis[L]

Know Thyself (1909) NONE

Kongo (1926) Nicholas Yellenti[S]

Kosher Kitty Kelly (1925) DuWico[L]; H. Robert Studio Law[S]; ACK[C]

Kreutzer Sonata, The (1906) Madame Freisinger[C]; Gates and Morange[S]; John A. Higham[L]; Peggy Roth[C]

Kreutzer Sonata, The (1924) ACK[S][C][L]

Kultur (1933) Tom Adrian Cracraft[S]; ACK[C]

Kwamina (1961) Will Steven Armstrong[S][L]; Motley[C]

Kwan Yin (1926) Ernest de Weerth[S][C]; ACK[L]

Kykunkor (1934) Asadata Dafora[S][C]

L'Aiglon (1900) Henry Dazian[C]; Ernest Gros[S]; Edward G. Unitt[S]; Helen Windsor[C]

L'Aiglon (1924) ACK[L]

L'Aiglon (1927) Livingston Platt[S][C]; ACK[L]

L'Aiglon (1934) Aline Bernstein[S][C]

L'Elevation (1917) Elizabeth Axtman[C]; Robert T. McKee[S]; ACK[L]

L'Hirondelle (1904) NONE

L'Invitation Au Voyage (1928) Aline Bernstein[S]

La Bête (1991) Richard Hudson[S][C]; Jennifer Tipton[L]

La Belle Paree (1911) Cora MacGeachy[C]; William Henry Matthews[C]

La Boite a Joujoux (1916) Esther Peck[C]; ACK[L]

La Cage Aux Folles (1983) Theoni V. Aldredge[C]; Jules Fisher[L]; David Mitchell[S]

La Grasse Valise (1965) Jacques Dupont[S][C]; Frederick Fox[C]; John Gleason[L]

La Gringa (1928) P. Dodd Ackerman[S]; Raymond Sovey[C]; ACK[C]

La Nativite (1933) Natalie Hays Hammond[C]; Alice Laughlin[S]

La Perichale (1925) Pierre

Kontchalovsky(S)(C)

La Repetition Ou l'Amour Puni
(1952) Jean-Denis Malclès(S)(C); Ack(L)

La Strada (1969) Ming Cho Lee(S);
Nancy Potts(C)

La Tendresse (1922) Ack(C)(L)

La Tragedie de Carmen (1983)
Jean-Guy Lecat(S); Chloe
Obolensky(C); Ack(L)

La, La, Lucille (1919) Mary
Blackburn(C); Ack(L)

Laburnum Grove (1935) Watson
Barratt(S); Ack(C)

Labyrinth, The (1905) None

Lace on Her Petticoat (1951) Samuel
Leve(S); Hazel Roy(C)

Lace Petticoat (1927) Raymond
Tomlinson(C); E. Carlton Winckler(S);
Ack(L)

Ladder, The (1926) Madame
Freisinger(C); Raymond Sovey(S)

Ladies All (1930) Rollo Wayne(S)

Ladies and Gentlemen (1939) Boris
Aronson(S); Ack(C)

Ladies at the Alamo (1977) Peter
Larkin(S); Ruth Morley(C); Marc B.
Weiss(L)

Ladies Don't Lie (1929) Nicholas
Yellenti(S); Ack(C)

Ladies First (1918) Dodge and Castle(S);
Clifford F. Pember(S); Ack(L)

Ladies in Retirement (1940) Helene
Pons(C); Raymond Sovey(S)

Ladies Leave (1929) Robert Edmond
Jones(S); Ack(C)

Ladies Night (1920) H. George
Brandt(S); Ack(S)(C)(L)

Ladies of Creation (1931) Eugene
Fitsch(S); Ack(C)

Ladies of the Corridor, The (1953)
Ralph Alswang(S)(L); Noel Taylor(C)

Ladies of the Evening (1924) Louis
Hartmann(L); Joseph Wickes(S); Ack(C)

Ladies of the Jury (1929) Gates and
Morange(S); Evelyn McHorter(C)

Ladies Paradise, The (1901) None

Ladies' Battle, The (1900) None

Ladies' Money (1934) Boris Aronson(S);
Virginia Estes Cates(C)

Lady Across the Hall, The (1905)
None

Lady Alone (1927) P. Dodd
Ackerman(S); Ack(C)(L)

Lady Beyond the Moon (1931) Cleon
Throckmorton(S); Ack(C)

Lady Billy (1920) Arnold A.

Kraushaar(S); Joseph Wilson(L); Ack(C)

Lady Bookie, The (1905) None

Lady Bug (1922) Joseph Physioc(S);
Ack(C)(L)

Lady Butterfly (1923) Shirley
Barker(C); Ack(S)(L)

Lady Christilinda, The (1922)
Livingston Platt(S)

Lady Clara (1930) Rollo Wayne(S)

Lady Comes Across, The (1942)
Stewart Chaney(S)(C)

Lady Dedlock (1928) Lucien
Labaudt(C); Livingston Platt(S); Carol
Sax(S)

Lady Detained, A (1935) P. Dodd
Ackerman Studio(S); Ack(C)

Lady Do (1927) Kennel and
Entwistle(S)(L); Mr. Norman(C); Ellis E.
Porter(C)

Lady Fingers (1929) Yetta Kiviette(C);
Ward and Harvey Studios(S)

Lady for a Night, A (1928) Yetta
Kiviette(C); Rollo Wayne(S); Ack(L)

Lady Frederick (1908) Mrs. Robert
Osborn(C); Frank Platzer(S)

Lady from Alfaqueque, The (1929)
Aline Bernstein(S)(C); Ack(L)

Lady from Alfaqueque, The (1930)
Aline Bernstein(S)(C); Irene Sharaff(C);
Ack(L)

Lady from Dubuque, The (1980) John
Falabella(C); Richard Nelson(L);
Rouben Ter-Arutunian(S)

Lady from Lane's, The (1907)
Frederica DeWolfe(C); D. Frank
Dodge(S); Frank E. Gates(S); Edward
Morange(S)

Lady from Lobster Square, The
(1910) None

Lady from Oklahoma, The (1913)
None

Lady from the Provinces, The (1923)
Ack(L)

Lady from the Sea, The (1911) No
Playbill

Lady from the Sea, The (1923) Ack(L)

Lady from the Sea, The (1929)
Watson Barratt(S); Ernest Schraps(C);
Ack(L)

Lady from the Sea, The (1934)
Donald Oenslager(S)(C); Helene Pons(C)

Lady from the Sea, The (1976)
Thomas Skelton(L); Rouben
Ter-Arutunian(S)(C)

Lady Has a Heart, The (1937) Watson
Barratt(S); Edna Hume(C); Stanley R.

McCandless[L]; Rufus Phillips[S]; Louise Segal[C]
Lady Huntworth's Experiment (1900) Mrs. Robert Osborn[C]; Edward G. Unitt[S]
Lady in Danger (1945) Harry Gordon Bennett[S]; ACK[C]
Lady in Ermine, The (1922) Watson Barratt[S]; ACK[C][L]
Lady in Love, A (1927) Joseph Mullen[C]; Nicholas Yellenti[S]; ACK[L]
Lady in Red, The (1919) Hickson[C]; Lucile[C]; ACK[S][L]
Lady in the Dark (1941) Hattie Carnegie[C]; Harry Horner[S]; Irene Sharaff[C]; Hassard Short[L]
Lady in the Dark (1943) Hattie Carnegie[C]; Harry Horner[S]; Irene Sharaff[C]; Hassard Short[L]
Lady in Waiting (1940) John Root[S]
Lady Jane (1934) Woodman Thompson[S]; ACK[C]
Lady Jim (1906) Walter B. Spong[S]
Lady Killer, The (1924) P. Dodd Ackerman[S]; ACK[C]
Lady Lies, The (1928) Jo Mielziner[S][L]; Margaret Pemberton[C]
Lady Luck (1936) ACK[S]
Lady Luxury (1914) ACK[C]
Lady Margaret (1902) NONE
Lady of Coventry, The (1911) NONE
Lady of Dreams, The (1912) Gates and Morange[S]
Lady of Letters (1935) Mildred Manning[C]; ACK[S]
Lady of Lyons, The (1902) NONE
Lady of the Camellias, The (1917) O'Kane Conwell[C]; Homer Emens[S]; Rollo Peters[C]; ACK[L]
Lady of the Camellias, The (1963) Lloyd Burlingame[L]; Marcel Escoffier[C]; Franco Zeffirelli[S]
Lady of the Lamp, The (1920) Earl Carroll[S]; William Henry Matthews[C]
Lady of the Orchids, The (1928) P. Dodd Ackerman[S]; Margaret Pemberton[C]; ACK[L]
Lady of the Rose, The (1925) ACK[L]
Lady of the Slipper, The (1912) Homer Emens[S]; Wilhelm[C]
Lady of the Slipper, The (1951) Irene Sharaff[C]
Lady of the Slipper, The (1977) Irene Sharaff[C]
Lady of the Weeping Willow Tree, The (1916) ACK[L]

Lady Patricia (1912) Mrs. Nettleship[C]; ACK[S]
Lady Precious Stream (1936) Watson Barratt[S]; Lang-Fan Mei[C]; ACK[L]
Lady Refuses, The (1933) DuWico[L]; ACK[C]
Lady Remembers, The (1932) ACK[L]
Lady Rose's Daughter (1903) Edward G. Unitt[S]
Lady Says Yes, A (1945) Watson Barratt[S]; Lou Eisele[C]; William Thomas[L]
Lady Screams, The (1927) Benjamin Leffler[L]; ACK[S][C]
Lady Shore, The (1905) Emens and Unitt[S]
Lady Teazle (1904) D. Frank Dodge[S]; Gates and Morange[S]; Mrs. Robert Osborn[C]; Mrs. Caroline Siedle[C]
Lady Who Came to Stay, The (1941) Donald Oenslager[S][C]
Lady Windermere's Fan (1914) Unitt and Wickes[S]
Lady Windermere's Fan (1932) ACK[C][L]
Lady Windermere's Fan (1946) Cecil Beaton[S][C][L]
Lady with a Lamp, The (1931) Robert Edmond Jones[S]; ACK[C]
Lady's Name, A (1916) Earl Carroll[S]; ACK[C]
Lady's Not for Burning, The (1950) Charles Elson[L]; Oliver Messel[S][C]
Lady's Virtue, A (1925) Watson Barratt[S]; ACK[C]
Lady, Be Good (1924) Norman Bel Geddes[S]; ACK[C]
Lady, Behave (1943) Frederick Fox[S]; Bianca Stroock[C]
Lady, The (1923) Clifford F. Pember[S]; ACK[C]
Laff That Off (1925) ACK[C][L]
Laffing Room Only (1944) Stewart Chaney[S]; Billy Livingston[C]
Lake, The (1933) Howard Greer[C]; Jo Mielziner[S][L]
Lally (1927) Livingston Platt[S]
Lamppost Reunion (1974) Judy Dearing[C]; Spencer Mosse[L]; Robert U. Taylor[S]
Lancashire Lass, The (1931) ACK[L]
Lancers, The (1907) Henri Bendel[C]; Miss Finch[C]; Madame Ripley[C]; Unitt and Wickes[S]
Land Is Bright, The (1941) Jo Mielziner[S][L]; Irene Sharaff[C]

Land of Fame (1943) Frederick Fox[S];
Grace Houston[C]
Land of Heart's Desire, The (1900)
Homer Emens[S]; Virginia Gerson[C]
Land of Joy, The (1917) Tarazona
Brothers[S]; ACK[C]
Land of Nod, The (1907) NONE
Land of Promise, The (1913) Homer
Emens[S]
Land of the Birds, The (1908) Alfredo
Edel[C]; Arthur Voegtlin[S]
Land of the Free (1917) ACK[L]
Land's End (1946) Charles Elson[L];
Donald Oenslager[S][C]
Largely New York (1989) Rose
Pederson[C]; Nancy Schertler[L];
Douglas Stein[S]
Lark, The (1955) Alvin Colt[C]; Jo
Mielziner[S][L]
Lash of a Whip, The (1901) Edward
G. Unitt[S]
Lass o' Laughter (1925) Joseph
Wilson[L]; ACK[S][C]
Lassie (1920) ACK[S][C][L]
Lassoo, The (1917) Unitt and Wickes[S];
ACK[C][L]
Last Analysis, The (1964) David
Hays[S][L]; Ann Roth[C]
Last Appeal, The (1902) Joseph
Physioc[S]
Last Dance, The (1948) Ralph
Alswang[S][C]; ACK[L]
Last Enemy, The (1930) Rollo Wayne[S]
Last Laugh, The (1915) ACK[C][L]
Last Licks (1979) Tharon Musser[L];
William Ritman[S]; Pearl Somner[C]
Last Night of Don Juan, The/ The
Pilgrimage (1925) Millia
Davenport[C]; James Reynolds[S]
Last of Mrs. Cheyney, The (1925)
Chanel[C]; James Reynolds[S]; ACK[L]
Last of Mrs. Lincoln, The (1972)
William Ritman[S][L]; Noel Taylor[C]
Last of the Red Hot Lovers (1969)
Donald Brooks[C]; Peggy Clark[L];
Oliver Smith[S]
Last of the Rohans, The (1899)
Joseph Physioc[S]
Last of the Rohans, The (1900) NONE
Last Resort, The (1914) NONE
Last Stop (1944) Rose Bogdanoff[C];
Samuel Leve[S]
Last Waltz, The (1921) Watson
Barratt[S]; ACK[C]
Last Warning, The (1922) ACK[S][C]
Late Christopher Bean, The (1932)

NONE
Late George Apley, The (1944) Al
Alloy[L]; Stewart Chaney[S][C]
Late Love (1953) Stewart Chaney[S][L];
Frank Thompson[C]
Late Nite Comic (1987) Ken
Billington[L]; Gail Cooper-Hecht[C];
Clarke Dunham[S]
Late One Evening (1933) Eddie
Eddy[S]; ACK[C]
Late Wisdom (1934) Walter Street[S];
Samuel L. Tabor[S]; ACK[C]
Laugh Parade, The (1931) Frank
Detering[L]; Max Weldy[S][C]
Laugh Time (1943) ACK[S][L]
Laugh, Clown, Laugh (1923) Henri
Bendel[C]; George Haddon[C];
Stroppa[S]
Laugh, Town, Laugh (1942) Ernest
Schraps[C]; Frank W. Stevens[S];
Valentina[C]; ACK[L]
Laughing Husband, The (1914) Henri
Bendel[C]; ACK[C]
Laughing Lady, The (1923) Henri
Bendel[C]; Robert Edmond Jones[S]
Laughing Past, The (1932) George
Segare[S]
Laughing Woman, The (1936) Watson
Barratt[S]; Mary Merrill[C]
Laughs and Other Events (1960) John
Robert Lloyd[S][C][L]
Laughter of the Gods (1919) Frank
Zimmerman[S][C]
Laughter on the 23rd Floor (1993)
William Ivey Long[C]; Tharon
Musser[L]; Tony Walton[S]
Launcelot and Elaine (1921)
Livingston Platt[S]; ACK[C]
Launcelot and Elaine (1930)
Livingston Platt[S]
Launzi (1923) Robert Edmond Jones[S][C]
Laura (1947) Stewart Chaney[S]; Robert
Lanza[C]; ACK[L]
Law and the Man, The (1906) H.
Robert Law[S]
Law and the Man, The (1925) Pierre
Kontchalovsky[S]
Law Breaker, The (1922) ACK[C][L]
Law of the Land, The (1914) ACK[C]
Law of the Land, The (1969) Martin
Aronstein[L]
Lawful Larceny (1922) Clifford F.
Pember[S]; ACK[C][L]
Lawyer's Dilemma, The (1928) Joseph
Physioc Studio[S]; ACK[L]
Le Barbier de Seville (1955) Emile

Bertin[S]

Le Bourgeois Gentilhomme (1955) Suzanne Lalique[S][C]

Le Jeu De l'Amour et Du Hasard (1955) Suzanne Lalique[C]; Ack[L]

Le Process (1952) Félix Labisse[S][L]

Leader of the Pack (1985) Pamela Cooper[L]; Robert DeMora[C]; Tony Walton[S]

Leading Lady, The (1948) Mainbocher[C]; Donald Oenslager[S][L]

Leaf and Bough (1949) Rouben Mamoulian[L]

Leaf People (1974) Randy Barcelo[C]; John Conklin[S]; John McLain[L]

Leah Kleschna (1904) Madame Freisinger[C]; Frank E. Gates[S]; Edward Morange[S]

Leah Kleschna (1924) Entwistle[S]; Louis Kennel[S]; Ack[C]

Lean Harvest (1931) Margaret Pemberton[C]; Lee Simonson[S]; Ack[L]

Learned Ladies, The (1911) NONE

Leave Her to Heaven (1940) Watson Barratt[S]; Ack[C]

Leave It to Me! (1938) Raoul Pène Du Bois[C]; Albert R. Johnson[S]

Leave It to Me! (1939) Raoul Pène Du Bois[C]; Albert R. Johnson[S]

Ledge, A (1929) Jean Blackburne[C]; Edgar Bohlman[S]

Left Bank, The (1931) Margaret Pemberton[C]; Raymond Sovey[S]; Ack[L]

Legal Murder (1934) Thomas Fowler[S]; Ack[L]

Legend (1976) Florence Klotz[C]; Santo Loquasto[S]; Thomas Skelton[L]

Legend of Leonora, The (1914) John Alexander[S]

Legend of Leonora, The (1927) Livingston Platt[S]; Ack[C]

Legend of Lizzie (1959) Ballou[S][C]; Lee Watson[L]

Legend of Lovers (1951) Eldon Elder[S]; Mildred Trebor[C]

Legend of Sarah (1950) Ralph Alswang[S]; Ben Edwards[C]; Ack[L]

Legend of the Dance, The (1925) Aline Bernstein[S][C]

Legs Diamond (1988) Jules Fisher[L]; Willa Kim[C]; David Mitchell[S]

Lemonade Boy, The (1907) NONE

Lend an Ear (1948) Raoul Pène Du Bois[S][C][L]

Lend Me a Tenor (1989) Paul Gallo[L];

William Ivey Long[C]; Tony Walton[S]

Lend Me Your Ears (1936) Cirker and Robbins[S]; Ack[C]

Lenin's Dowry (1932) Aline Bernstein[S]

Lenny (1971) Randy Barcelo[C]; Jules Fisher[L]; Robin Wagner[S]

Les Blancs (1970) Jane Greenwood[C]; Neil Peter Jampolis[L]; Peter Larkin[S]

Les Fausses Confidences (1952) Maurice Brianchon[S][C]; Ack[L]

Les Fourberies de Scapin (1952) Christian Bérard[S][C]; Maurice Brianchon[S]; Ack[L]

Les Liaisons Dangereuses (1987) Bob Crowley[S][C]; Chris Parry[L]

Les Miserables (1987) David Hersey[L]; John Napier[S]; Andreane Neofitou[C]

Lesson from Aloes, A (1980) William Armstrong[L]; Susan Hilferty[C]; Michael H. Yeargan[S]

Lesson in Love, A (1923) Ack[C][L]

Let 'em Eat Cake (1933) Albert R. Johnson[S]; Yetta Kiviette[C]

Let and Sub-Let (1930) Lucille Rothschild[C]; Ack[L]

Let Freedom Ring (1935) Mordecai Gorelik[S]; Eva Rapaport[C]

Let Freedom Sing (1942) Herbert Andrews[S]; Paul du Pont[C]

Let It Ride! (1961) William and Jean Eckart[S][L]; Guy Kent[C]

Let Me Hear You Smile (1973) Neil Peter Jampolis[L]; Peter Larkin[S]; Carrie F Robbins[C]

Let My People Come (1976) Duane F. Mazey[S][L]; Douglas W. Schmidt[S][C]

Let Us Be Gay (1929) Cirker and Robbins[S]; Ack[C][L]

Let's Face It (1941) John W. Harkrider[C]; Harry Horner[S]

Let's Face It (1942) John W. Harkrider[C]; Harry Horner[S]

Let's Go (1918) Ack[C][L]

Let's Make an Opera (1950) Ralph Alswang[S][L]; Aline Bernstein[C]

Letter for Queen Victoria, A (1975) Beverly Emmons[L]; Peter Harvey[S][C]

Letter of the Law, The (1920) Ack[L]

Letter, The (1927) Raymond Sovey[S]; Ack[C][L]

Letters to Lucerne (1941) Raymond Sovey[S]; Ack[C]

Lettice & Lovage (1990) Ken Billington[L]; Frank Krenz[C]; Anthony Powell[C]; Alan Tagg[S]

Letty (1904) Unitt and Wickes[S]

Letty Pepper (1922) ACK[(C)(L)]
Lew Dockstader's Minstrels (1904)
 NONE
Lew Dockstader's Minstrels (1906)
 NONE
Lew Leslie's Blackbirds (1930)
 Vincente Minnelli[(C)]; Ward and
 Harvey Studios[(S)]
Lew Leslies' Blackbirds of 1939
 (1939) Mabel A. Buell[(S)]; Frances
 Feist[(C)]
Li'l Abner (1956) Alvin Colt[(C)]; William
 and Jean Eckart[(S)(L)]
Liar, The (1950) Motley[(C)]; Donald
 Oenslager[(S)]; ACK[(L)]
Liars, The (1915) Elizabeth Axtman[(C)];
 B. Russell Herts[(S)]
**Libby Holman's Blues, Ballads and
 Sin Song** (1954) ACK[(C)(L)]
Libel (1935) Raymond Sovey[(S)]; ACK[(C)]
Liberty Belles, The (1901) Ernest
 Albert[(S)]
Liberty Hall (1913) ACK[(S)(C)]
Liberty Jones (1941) Raoul Pène Du
 Bois[(C)]
Licensed (1915) NONE
Lido Girl, The (1928) ACK[(C)(L)]
Lie, The (1914) Helen Sheppard[(C)]
Lieber Augustin (1913) Melville
 Ellis[(C)]; Lee Lash Studios[(S)]; H. Robert
 Law[(S)]
Lieutenant, The (1975) Frank J.
 Boros[(S)(C)]; Ian Calderon[(L)]
Life (1902) NONE
Life (1914) H. Robert Law[(S)]; Young
 Brothers[(S)]; ACK[(C)]
**Life and Adventures of Nicholas
 Nickleby,** (1981) Beverly Emmons[(L)];
 Dermot Hayes[(S)]; David Hersey[(L)]; Neil
 Peter Jampolis[(L)]; John Napier[(S)(C)]
**Life and Adventures of Nicholas
 Nickleby, The** (1981) David
 Hersey[(L)]
**Life and Adventures of Nicholas
 Nickleby, The** (1986) David
 Hersey[(L)]; John Napier[(C)]; Andreane
 Neofitou[(S)]
Life and Death of an American
 (1938) Howard Bay[(S)]; Moe Hack[(L)];
 Alexander Jones[(C)]
Life and Loves of Dorian Gray, The
 (1936) Joel[(S)]; Lucile[(S)]; ACK[(C)(L)]
Life Begins (1932) P. Dodd
 Ackerman[(S)]; ACK[(C)(L)]
Life Begins at 8:40 (1934) Raoul Pène
 Du Bois[(C)]; Albert R. Johnson[(S)];

Yetta Kiviette[(C)]; Pauline Lawrence[(C)];
 Billy Livingston[(C)]; James Reynolds[(C)];
 Irene Sharaff[(C)]; Wynn[(C)]
Life Is Like That (1930) Philip Gelb[(S)]
Life Line, The (1930) Walter Walden[(S)];
 ACK[(C)]
Life of Reilly, The (1942) Samuel
 Leve[(S)]
Life with Father (1939) Stewart
 Chaney[(S)(C)]; ACK[(L)]
Life with Mother (1948) Stewart
 Chaney[(S)]; Donald Oenslager[(S)(C)];
 ACK[(L)]
Life's Too Short (1935) Raymond
 Sovey[(S)]; ACK[(C)]
Life, A (1980) Robert Fletcher[(S)(C)];
 Marc B. Weiss[(L)]
Life, The (1997) Martin Pakledinaz[(C)];
 Richard Pilbrow[(L)]; Robin Wagner[(S)]
Lifting the Lid (1905) F. Richards
 Anderson[(C)]; Castle and Harvey[(S)];
 Richard Marston[(S)]
Light Eternal, The (1906) Percy
 Anderson[(S)]; Emens, Unitt and
 Wickes[(S)]; Ernest Gros[(S)]; Kliegl
 Brothers[(L)]; ACK[(C)]
**Light from St. Agnes, A; The Eyes
 of the Heart, and The R** (1905)
 NONE
**Light from St. Agnes, A; The Eyes
 of the Heart, and the R** (1933) Jo
 Mielziner[(S)]
Light from St. Agnes, The (1906)
 NONE
Light of Asia, The (1928) Claude
 Bragdon[(S)(C)]
Light of the World, The (1920) Miss
 Sarah Hecht[(C)]; Muriel Sibell[(C)]; ACK[(L)]
Light That Failed, The (1903) Walter
 Hann[(S)]; Joseph Harker[(S)]; W. T.
 Hemsley[(S)]
Light That Failed, The (1913) Walter
 Hann[(S)]; Joseph Harker[(S)]; W. T.
 Hemsley[(S)]
**Light That Lies in Woman's Eyes,
 The** (1904) Edward G. Unitt[(S)]
Light Up the Sky (1948) Frederick
 Fox[(S)]; Yetta Kiviette[(C)]; E. Carlton
 Winckler[(L)]
Light Wines and Beer (1930)
 DuWico[(L)]; ACK[(S)]
Light, Lively, and Yiddish (1970)
 Sylvia Friedlander[(C)]; Joseph Ijaky[(S)];
 ACK[(L)]
Lightinin' (1918) Henri Bendel[(C)];
 Joseph Physioc[(S)]; ACK[(L)]

Lightnin' (1938) Cirker and Robbins(S); Florence Mason Miller(C)

Lights o' London, The (1911) H. Robert Law(S); Bert Tuchman(S)

Lights o' London, The (1936) Nils Asther(S); Emily Stoner(C); Cleon Throckmorton(S)

Lights Out (1922) William Oden Waller(S); ACK(C)(L)

Like a King (1921) NONE

Likes o' Me, The (1908) Frank Platzer(S)

Lilac Domino, The (1914) ACK(C)

Lilac Room, The (1907) NONE

Lilac Time (1917) ACK(L)

Lilies of the Field (1921) ACK(S)(C)

Liliom (1921) Lee Simonson(S)(C)

Liliom (1932) Aline Bernstein(S)(C)

Liliom (1940) Nat Karson(S)(C)

Lillian (1986) Jane Greenwood(C); Thomas Skelton(L); ACK(S)

Lilly Sue (1926) Joseph Wickes(S)

Lilly Turner (1932) Livingston Platt(S)

Lily and the Prince, The (1911) P. Dodd Ackerman(S); Howard Church(S); Homer Emens(S); Joseph L. Menchen, Jr.(L); L. W. Seavey(S); Bernhardt Wall(C)

Lily and the Prince, The (1925) ACK(L)

Lily and the Prince, The (1930) Henry Dreyfuss(S)

Lily and the Prince, The (1997) John Lee Beatty(S); Jane Greenwood(C); Kenneth Posner(L)

Lily of the Valley (1942) Harry Horner(S)(L); Helene Pons(C)

Lily Tomlin in "Appearing Nightly" (1977) Daniel Adams(L); J. Allen Highfill(C)

Lily, The (1909) Wilfred Buckland(S); Ernest Gros(S); Louis Hartmann(L); ACK(C)

Lincoln (1906) Ernest Albert(S); ACK(C)

LincolnMask, The (1972) Kert Lundell(S); Thomas Skelton(L); Patricia Quinn Stuart(C)

Linden Tree, The (1948) Frank Thompson(C); Peter Wolf(S)

Lion and the Mouse, The (1905) Peter W. King(L); Joseph Physioc(S)

Lion and the Mouse, The (1922) Benjamin Leffler(L)

Lion and the Mouse, The (1932) Aline Bernstein(S)

Lion in Winter, The (1966) Will Steven Armstrong(S)(C); Tharon Musser(L)

Lion in Winter, The (1999) David Gallo(S); Michael Krass(C); Kenneth Posner(L)

Lion King, The (1997) Donald Holder(L); Richard Hudson(S); Julie Taymor(C)

Lion Tamer, The (1926) Aline Bernstein(S)(C)

Listen Lester (1918) H. Robert Studio Law(S); André Sherri(C); ACK(L)

Listen Professor (1944) Lucinda Ballard(C); Howard Bay(S)

Listening In (1922) Anthony Greshoff(L); ACK(S)(C)

Literary Sense, The (1907) NONE

Little A (1947) Watson Barratt(S); Leo Kerz(L); ACK(C)

Little Accident (1928) Margaret Pemberton(C); Raymond Sovey(S)

Little Angel, The (1924) Willy Pogany(S)(C)

Little Bit of Everything, A (1904) Richard Marston(S)

Little Bit of Fluff, A (1916) ACK(C)(L)

Little Black Book, The (1932) Louis Kennel(S)

Little Black Book, The (1972) Martin Aronstein(L); Sara Brook(C); Oliver Smith(S)

Little Blue Devil, The (1919) Henri Bendel(C); Mary Blackburn(C); ACK(L)

Little Boy Blue (1911) Charles E. Brown(S); Frederica DeWolfe(C); Ernest Gros(S); Joseph Wilson(L)

Little Brother of the Rich, A (1909) NONE

Little Brother of the Rich, A (1930) Livingston Platt(C)

Little Brother, The (1918) ACK(L)

Little Brown Jug (1946) Frederick Fox(S)(L); ACK(C)

Little Café, The (1913) F. Richards Anderson(C); Julian Mitchell(S)

Little Cherub, The (1906) Ernest Gros(S); Mrs. Robert Osborn(C); Pascaud(C)

Little Clay Cart, The (1924) Aline Bernstein(S)(C)(L)

Little Clay Cart, The (1926) Aline Bernstein(S)(C)

Little Damozel, The (1910) Walter W. Burridge(S)

Little Dark Horse (1941) John Koenig(S); Frank Spencer(C)

Little Darling (1942) Watson Barratt[S]; William Richardson[L]; ACK[C]

Little Duchess, The (1901) Ernest Albert[S]; Will R. Barnes[C]; Archie Gunn[C]; Mrs. Caroline Siedle[C]

Little Eyolf (1910) Mrs. Julia Bacon[C]; Unitt and Wickes[S]

Little Eyolf (1926) Robert Edmond Jones[C]; Jo Mielziner[S][L]

Little Family Business, A (1982) Theoni V. Aldredge[C]; David Gropman[S]; Richard Nelson[L]

Little Father of the Wilderness, The (1906) NONE

Little Father of the Wilderness, The (1949) Carl Kent[S]

Little Foxes, The (1939) Howard Bay[S]; Aline Bernstein[C]; ACK[L]

Little Foxes, The (1981) Paul Gallo[L]; Andrew Jackness[S]; Florence Klotz[C]

Little Foxes, The (1997) John Lee Beatty[S]; Jane Greenwood[C]; Kenneth Posner[L]

Little Glass Clock, The (1955) Cecil Beaton[S][C]; Charles Lisanby[L]

Little Gray Lady, The (1906) NONE

Little Hotel on the Side, A (1992) David Jenkins[S]; Richard Nelson[L]; Patricia Zipprodt[C]

Little Hut, The (1953) Charles Elson[L]; Oliver Messel[S]; Frank Thompson[C]

Little Italy (1902) Frank E. Gates[S]; Hollander[C]; Edward Morange[S]

Little Jessie James (1923) P. Dodd Ackerman[S]; Mabel E. Johnston[C]

Little Johnny Jones (1904) W. Franklin Hamilton[S]

Little Journey, A (1918) Watson Barratt[S]; ACK[C][L]

Little Lady in Blue (1916) Ernest Gros[S]; Elmer Taflinger[C]; ACK[L]

Little Like Magic, A (1986) Ken Billington[L]; Mary C. Thornton[S][C]

Little Lord Fauntleroy (1903) ACK[S][C]

Little Man, The (1917) Rollo Peters[S]; ACK[C][L]

Little Mary (1904) Unitt and Wickes[S]

Little Me (1962) Robert Fletcher[C]; Robert Randolph[S][L]

Little Me (1982) Beverly Emmons[L]; Tony Walton[S][C]

Little Me (1998) David Gallo[S]; Ann Hould-Ward[C]; Kenneth Posner[L]

Little Michus, The (1907) Mary Fisher[C]; Mrs. Nettleship[C]; B. J. Simmons[C]

Little Millionaire, The (1911) H. Robert Law[S]; Unitt and Wickes[S]; ACK[C][L]

Little Minister, The (1904) NONE

Little Minister, The (1925) ACK[L]

Little Miss Bluebeard (1923) Boué Soeurs[C]; Jean Patou[C]; Paul Poiret[C]; Herman Rosse[S]

Little Miss Brown (1912) H. Robert Law[S]

Little Miss Charity (1920) P. Dodd Ackerman[S]; ACK[C][L]

Little Miss Fix-It (1911) D. Frank Dodge[S]; Gates and Morange[S]

Little Moon of Alban (1960) Jo Mielziner[S][L]; Noel Taylor[C]

Little More Magic, A (1994) Ken Billington[L]; Mary C. Thornton[S]; Mary C. Thornton[C]

Little Murders (1967) Theoni V. Aldredge[C]; Jules Fisher[L]; Ming Cho Lee[S]

Little Nell and the Marchioness (1900) William Gill[S]; George P. Raymond[C]

Little Nemo (1908) Ernest Albert[S]; F. Richards Anderson[C]; Young Brothers and Boss[S]; John H. Young[S]

Little Night Music, A (1973) Boris Aronson[S]; Florence Klotz[C]; Tharon Musser[L]

Little Night Music, A (1990) Michael Anania[S]; Dawn Chiang[L]; Lindsay W. Davis[C]

Little Ol' Boy (1933) Mordecai Gorelik[S]; Helen Grayson[C]

Little Old New York (1920) Gertrude Newell[C]; ACK[S][L]

Little Orchid Annie (1930) ACK[C][L]

Little Poor Man, The (1925) Albert Bliss[S]; Howard Claney[S]; Marion De Peu[C]

Little Princess, The (1903) NONE

Little Ray of Sunshine, A (1899) E. G. Banks[S]

Little Red Riding Hood (1900) NONE

Little Rocketeer, A (1932) Watson Barratt[S]; Allison McLellan Hunter[C]; Ernest Schraps[C]

Little Shop (1935) P. Dodd Ackerman[S]; ACK[C]

Little Show, The (1929) Ruth Brenner[C]; Jo Mielziner[S][L]

Little Simplicity (1918) Watson Barratt[S]; S. Zalud[C]; ACK[L]

Little Spitfire, The (1926) Cirker and

Robbins(S); ACK(L)
Little Stranger, The (1905) ACK(S)(C)
Little Teacher, The (1918) ACK(L)
Little Water on the Side, A (1914) ACK(C)
Little Water on the Side, A (1920) Hewlett & Basing(S)
Little Whopper, The (1919) Harry Collins(C); Unitt and Wickes(S); ACK(L)
Little Women (1912) H. Robert Law(S); Madame Ripley(C); Bert Tuchman(S); ACK(C)
Little Women (1916) ACK(S)(C)(L)
Little Women (1931) Charles Chrisdie(C); H. Robert Studio Law(S); ACK(L)
Littlest Rebel, The (1911) Dodge and Castle(S)
Live and Learn (1930) ACK(C)(L)
Live Life Again (1945) Grace Houston(C); Albert R. Johnson(S)(L)
Live Wire, The (1950) Donald Oenslager(S)(L); Forrest Thayer(C)
Living Corpse, The (1929) Aline Bernstein(S)(C)
Living Dangerously (1935) Watson Barratt(S)(C)
Living Mask, The (1924) Robert Edmond Jones(S)(C)
Living Newspaper, The (1936) Hjalmar Hermanson(S); Kathryn Wilson(L); ACK(L)
Living Room, The (1954) Kathryn B. Miller(C); Raymond Sovey(S)(C)(L)
Liz the Mother (1910) E. Hamilton Bell(S)(C)
Liz the Mother (1941) Raoul Pène Du Bois(S); E. Carlton Winckler(L)
Liza (1922) Nina Gilman(C); ACK(S)(L)
Liza Minnelli: Stepping Out at Radio City (1991) David Agress(L); Michael J. Hotopp(S); Julie Weiss(C)
Lo and Behold! (1951) Stewart Chaney(S)(C)(L)
Locked Door, The (1924) Carolyn Hancock(S); ACK(C)(L)
Locked Room, The (1933) Karle O. Amend(S); Hattie Carnegie(C); ACK(L)
Loco (1946) Charles Elson(L); Donald Oenslager(S); Emeline Clarke Roche(C)
Lodger, The (1917) Dodge and Castle(S); ACK(L)
Loggerheads (1925) ACK(L)
Lola from Berlin (1907) F. Richards Anderson(C); John H. Young(S)
Lolita (1981) Nancy Potts(C); William

Ritman(S); David F. Segal(L)
Lollipops (1924) William E. Castle(S); Sheldon K. Viele(S); ACK(C)
Lolly (1929) Edgar Bohlman(S)(C)
Lolotte (1904) NONE
Lombardi, Ltd. (1917) John Collette(S); ACK(C)(L)
Lombardi, Ltd. (1927) ACK(C)(L)
London Assurance (1905) Mrs. Robert Osborn(C); Franklin Van Horn(C)
London Assurance (1937) Robert Byrne(C); Louis Kennel(S)
London Assurance (1974) Robert Ornbo(L); Alan Tagg(S); David Walker(C)
London Assurance (1997) Blake Burba(L); Derek McLane(S); Catherine Zuber(C)
London Calling (1930) Cirker and Robbins(S)
London Follies (1911) NONE
Lone Valley (1933) Raymond Sovey(S)
Lonely Romeo, A (1919) P. Dodd Ackerman(S); Cora MacGeachy(C); ACK(L)
Lonesome Town (1908) Homer Emens(S); ACK(C)
Lonesome West, The (1999) Tharon Musser(L); Francis O'Connor(S)(C)
Long Dash, The (1918) ACK(L)
Long Day's Journey into Night (1956) David Hays(S); Motley(C); Tharon Musser(L)
Long Day's Journey into Night (1962) Gunnar Gelbort(C); Georg Magnusson(S)
Long Day's Journey into Night (1986) Willa Kim(C); Richard Nelson(L); Tony Straiges(S)
Long Day's Journey into Night (1988) Ben Edwards(S); Jane Greenwood(C); Jennifer Tipton(L)
Long Days, The (1951) Eldon Elder(S)(L); Ruth Morley(C)
Long Dream, The (1960) Zvi Geyra(S); Ruth Morley(C); Tharon Musser(L)
Long Road, The (1930) P. Dodd Ackerman(S)
Long Watch, The (1952) John E. Blankenchip(S)(C)
Look after Lulu (1959) Cecil Beaton(S)(C); Raymond Sovey(L)
Look Back in Anger (1957) Howard Bay(C)(L); Alan Tagg(S)
Look Homeward, Angel (1957) Jo Mielziner(S)(L); Motley(C)

Look Ma, I'm Dancin' (1948) John Pratt(C); Oliver Smith(S); Ack(L)
Look to the Lilies (1970) Jo Mielziner(S)(L); Carrie F. Robbins(C)
Look Who's Here (1920) H. Robert Studio Law(S); Ack(C)(L)
Look: We've Come Through (1961) David Hays(S)(L); Ann Roth(C)
Loose Ankles (1926) Ack(S)(C)(L)
Loose Ends (1926) William Oden Waller(S); Ack(C)(L)
Loose Ends (1979) Zack Brown(S); David F. Segal(L); Kristina Watson(C)
Loose Moments (1935) Cirker and Robbins(S); Mildred Manning(C); Ack(L)
Loot (1968) Patton Campbell(C); William Ritman(S)(L)
Loot (1986) John Lee Beatty(S); Richard Nelson(L); Bill Walker(C)
Lord and Lady Algy (1899) None
Lord and Lady Algy (1917) Marie Decker(C); Howard Greenley(S); Ben Ali Haggin(C); Lucile(C); Mrs. E. J. Muldoon(C); Ack(L)
Lord Bless the Bishop, The (1934) Cleon Throckmorton(S); Ack(C)
Lord Pengo (1962) Lucinda Ballard(C); Jean Rosenthal(L); Oliver Smith(S)
Lorelei (1938) Lee Simonson(S); Bianca Stroock(C)
Lorelei (1974) Raymond Aghayan(C); Alvin Colt(C); John Conklin(S); John Gleason(L); Bob Mackie(C)
Lorenzo (1963) David Hays(S)(L); Motley(C)
Los Angeles (1927) Ack(L)
Losing Eloise (1917) Julia Carroll(C); Joseph Physioc(S); Ack(L)
Loss of Roses, A (1959) Boris Aronson(S); Lucinda Ballard(C); A. H. Feder(L)
Lost (1927) P. Dodd Ackerman(S); Ack(C)
Lost Boy (1932) Walter Walden(S); Ack(C)
Lost Co-Respondent, The (1915) Ack(L)
Lost Horizons (1934) G. Bradford Ashworth(S); Ack(C)
Lost in the Stars (1949) George Jenkins(S); Anna Hill Johnstone(C); Ack(L)
Lost in the Stars (1972) Oliver Smith(S); Patricia Quinn Stuart(C); Paul Sullivan(L)
Lost in Yonkers (1991) Santo

Loquasto(S)(C); Tharon Musser(L)
Lost River (1900) Homer Emens(S); Frank E. Gates(S); Edward Morange(S)
Lost Sheep (1930) Watson Barratt(S); Yetta Kiviette(C); Ack(C)
Lottery Man, The (1909) H. Robert Law(S)
Loud Red Patrick, The (1956) Paul Morrison(S)(C)(L)
Loud Speaker (1927) Mordecai Gorelik(S); Ack(C)
Louder, Please (1931) Margaret Pemberton(C); Cleon Throckmorton(S); Ack(C)
Louie the 14th (1925) John E. Stone(C); Gretl Urban(S); Ack(L)
Louis XI (1907) None
Louisiana (1933) Ack(L)
Louisiana Lady (1947) Watson Barratt(S); Leo Kerz(L); Frank Thompson(C)
Louisiana Purchase (1940) Tom Lee(S)(C); E. Carlton Winckler(L)
Love 'em and Leave 'em (1926) Robert Edmond Jones(S); Ack(C)(L)
Love among the Lions (1910) Frank Platzer(S)
Love among the Lions (1911) Madame Freisinger(C)
Love and Babies (1933) Tom Adrian Cracraft(S)
Love and Death/ Aleko/ Fountain of Bakkchi Sarai/ etc. (1925) Ivan Gremislavsky(S)(C); Nikolai Iznar(S)(C)
Love and Kisses (1963) Helene Pons(C); Marvin Reiss(S)(L)
Love and Let Love (1951) Ralph Alswang(S); Jean Louis(C)
Love and Libel (1960) Marie Day(C); David Hays(S)(L)
Love and the Man (1905) Joseph Harker(S)
Love Call, The (1927) Watson Barratt(S); Charles LeMaire(C); Ernest Schraps(C); Ack(L)
Love City, The (1926) Karle O. Amend Studio(S); Ack(C)(L)
Love Cure, The (1909) Walter W. Burridge(S); Madame Moore(C); Madame Zimmerman(C)
Love Dreams (1921) Yetta Kiviette(C)
Love Drive, The (1917) Ack(L)
Love Duel, The (1929) Watson Barratt(S)
Love Expert, The (1929) Ack(S)(C)(L)
Love for Love (1925) Millia

Davenport^(C); Robert Edmond
Jones^{(S)(C)}
Love for Love (1940) Millia
Davenport^(C); Robert Edmond Jones^(S)
Love for Love (1947) Jeanetta
Cochrane^(C); William Conway^(L); Rex
Whistler^(S)
Love for Love (1974) Ken Billington^(L);
Douglas Higgins^(S); Franne Lee^(C)
Love from a Stranger (1936) Kate
Drain Lawson^(S); ACK^(S)
Love Goes to Press (1947) Emeline
Clarke Roche^(C); Raymond Sovey^(S)
Love Habit, The (1923) ACK^{(S)(C)(L)}
Love in a Mist (1926) ACK^{(S)(C)(L)}
Love in E-Flat (1967) Donald
Oenslager^{(S)(L)}; Julia Sze^(C)
Love in Idleness (1904) NONE
Love in My Fashion (1937) Cleon
Throckmorton^(S); ACK^(C)
Love in the Tropics (1927) Eddie
Eddy^(S); Edward Jacobi^(L); ACK^(C)
Love Is a Time of Day (1969) Lloyd
Burlingame^{(S)(C)(L)}
Love Is Like That (1927) William E.
Castle^(S); ACK^{(C)(L)}
Love Kills (1934) ACK^{(C)(L)}
Love Laughs (1919) Mabel A. Buell^(S);
ACK^{(C)(L)}
Love Leash, The (1913) Kliegl
Brothers^(L); Joseph Physioc^(S); ACK^(C)
Love Letter, The (1906) Gates and
Morange^(S); Young Brothers and
Boss^(S)
Love Letter, The (1921) Alice
O'Neil^(C); Joseph Urban^(S)
Love Letters (1989) Dennis Parichy^(L)
Love Life (1948) Boris Aronson^(S);
Lucinda Ballard^(C); Peggy Clark^(L)
Love Match, The (1901) Edward G.
Unitt^(S)
Love Me Little (1958) Ralph
Alswang^(S); Motley^(C)
Love Me Long (1949) DuWico^(L);
Margaret Pemberton^(C); John Root^(S)
Love Mill, The (1918) Hickson^(C);
ACK^{(S)(L)}
Love Nest, The (1927) Aline
Bernstein^{(S)(C)}
Love o' Mike (1917) Robert
McQuinn^(S); ACK^{(C)(L)}
Love of Four Colonels, The (1953)
Rolf Gérard^{(S)(C)}
Love of One's Neighbor (1915) Lee
Simonson^(S); ACK^(C)
Love on Leave (1944) Paul Morrison^(S)

Love on the Dole (1936) Frances
Hooper^(C); Nicholas Yellenti^(S)
Love Route, The (1906) Thomas J.
Cleland^(L); H. Robert Law^(S); Mrs.
Robert Osborn^(C)
Love Scandal, A (1923) William E.
Castle^(S); ACK^(C)
Love Set, The (1923) Charles J.
Auburn^(S)
Love Song, The (1925) Watson
Barratt^(S); Ernest Schraps^(C)
**Love Suicide at Schofield Barracks,
The** (1972) John Gleason^(L); Douglas
W. Schmidt^{(S)(C)}
Love They Neighbor (1996) Neil Peter
Jampolis^{(S)(C)(L)}
Love Thief, The (1927) Benjamin
Leffler^(L); ACK^{(S)(C)}
Love Watches (1908) Ernest Gros^(S)
Love! Valour! Compassion! (1995)
Loy Arcenas^(S); Jess Goldstein^(C);
Brian MacDevitt^(L)
Love's Call (1925) Edward Hartford^(L);
Joseph Physioc^(S); ACK^(C)
Love's Comedy (1908) Mr. George C.
Tyler^(S)
Love's Lightning (1918) ACK^{(C)(L)}
Love's Lottery (1904) NONE
Love's Old Sweet Song (1940) Watson
Barratt^(S); ACK^(C)
Love's Pilgrimage (1904) NONE
Love, Honor and Betray (1930)
Nicholas Yellenti^(S); ACK^(C)
Lovely Ladies, Kind Gentlemen
(1970) Thomas Skelton^(L); Oliver
Smith^(S); Freddy Wittop^(C)
Lovely Lady (1925) Cleon
Throckmorton^(S)
Lovely Lady (1927) Cleon
Throckmorton^(S)
Lovely Me (1947) Eleanor Goldsmith^(C);
Donald Oenslager^{(S)(L)}
Lovely Night, A (1960) Helene Pons^(C);
Lee Watson^{(S)(L)}
Lovers and Enemies (1927) Aline
Bernstein^{(S)(C)}; ACK^(L)
Lovers and Friends (1943) Motley^{(S)(C)}
Lovers and Other Strangers (1968)
John Gleason^(L); Domingo A.
Rodriguez^(C); Robin Wagner^(S)
Lovers' Lane (1901) D. Frank Dodge^(S);
John H. Young^(S)
Lovers, The (1956) John Boyt^(C);
Charles Elson^{(S)(L)}
Loves of Anatol, The (1985) Lawrence
Miller^(S); Robert Morgan^(C); Richard

Winkler[L]

Loves of Cass Mc Guire, The (1966) Lloyd Burlingame[S][L]; Noel Taylor[C]

Loves of Charles II, The (1933) Helene Pons[C]; Ack[L]

Loves of Lulu, The (1925) Ack[C][L]

Loves of Women (1937) Raymond Sovey[S]; Bianca Stroock[C]

Low Bridge (1933) Ack[L]

Lower Depths, The (1923) Ivan Gremislavsky[S]; Victor Simoff[S]; Ack[L]

Lower North (1944) Raymond Sovey[S][C][L]

Loyalties (1922) Ack[S][C][L]

Luana (1930) Cirker and Robbins[S]; Charles LeMaire[C]

Lucifer's Child (1991) Pat Collins[L]; Marjorie Bradley Kellogg[S]; Noel Taylor[C]

Luck in Pawn (1919) H. Robert Studio Law[S]; Ack[L]

Luck of MacGregor, The (1908) NONE

Luck of the Navy, The (1919) Ack[L]

Luckee Girl (1928) Watson Barratt[S]; Ernest Schraps[C]

Lucky (1927) Mabel E. Johnston[C]; James Reynolds[S]

Lucky Break, A (1925) Joseph Wilson[L]; Ack[S]

Lucky Miss Dean (1906) Ack[S][C]

Lucky O'Shea (1917) Ack[S][L]

Lucky One, The (1922) Lee Simonson[S]; Ack[C]

Lucky Sam McCarver (1925) Jo Mielziner[S][L]; Ack[C]

Lucky Sambo (1925) Mrs. A. E. Mathieson[C]; Ack[S][L]

Lucky Star, The (1910) Percy Anderson[C]

Lucrece (1932) Robert Edmond Jones[S][C]

Lullaby (1954) Ben Edwards[S][L]

Lullaby, The (1923) Don Casey[L]; William Cameron Menzies[S][C]

Lulu Belle (1926) George Haddon[C]; Joseph Wickes[S]

Lulu's Husbands (1910) NONE

Lunatics and Lovers (1954) Frederick Fox[S][C][L]

Lunch Hour (1980) Ann Roth[C]; Oliver Smith[S]; Jennifer Tipton[L]

Lure, The (1913) H. Robert Law[S]

Lusmore (1919) Livingston Platt[S][C]

Lute Song (1946) Robert Edmond Jones[S][C][L]; Valentina[C]

Luther (1963) Jocelyn Herbert[S][C][L]

Luv (1964) Theoni V. Aldredge[C]; Jean Rosenthal[L]; Oliver Smith[S]

Lydia Gilmore (1912) NONE

Lyons Mail, The (1906) Hawes Craven[S]

Lysistrata (1925) Isaac Rabinovitch[S][C]

Lysistrata (1930) Albert Rights[S]; Frances Waite[C]; Ack[L]

Lysistrata (1946) Ralph Alswang[S][L]; Rose Bogdanoff[C]

Lysistrata (1972) Jules Fisher[L]; Willa Kim[C]; Robin Wagner[S]

M. Butterfly (1988) Eiko Ishioka[S][C]; Andy Phillips[L]

Ma Cousine (1904) Ack[S]

Ma Rainey's Black Bottom (1984) Peter Maradudin[L]; Charles Henry McClennahan[S]; Daphne Pascucci[C]

Macbeth (1899) Alexander Corbett[S]; Maurice Hermann[C]

Macbeth (1900) Alexander Corbett[S]; Maurice Hermann[C]

Macbeth (1905) H. Robert Law[S]; Annie Sanse[C]; Franklin Van Horn[C]

Macbeth (1907) H. Robert Law[S]; Annie Sanse[C]

Macbeth (1916) Percy Anderson[S][C]; Joseph Urban[S]; Ack[L]

Macbeth (1918) Ack[L]

Macbeth (1921) Ami Mali Hicks[C]; Robert Edmond Jones[S][C]; Raymond Sovey[C]

Macbeth (1924) Percy Anderson[C]; Woodman Thompson[S]

Macbeth (1928) Gordon Craig[S][C]; Helene Pons[C]; Ack[L]

Macbeth (1935) P. Dodd Ackerman[S]; Charles B. Falls[C]

Macbeth (1936) A. H. Feder[L]; Nat Karson[S][C]

Macbeth (1941) Lemuel Ayers[C]; Samuel Leve[S]

Macbeth (1948) Paul Sheriff[S][C]; Ack[L]

Macbeth (1956) Audrey Cruddas[S][C]

Macbeth (1981) John Gleason[L]; Helen Pond[S]; Carrie F. Robbins[C]; Herbert Senn[S]

Macbeth (1982) William Armstrong[L]; Kenneth Foy[S]; Julie Weiss[C]

Macbeth (1988) Daphne Dare[S]; Marc B. Weiss[L]; Patricia Zipprodt[C]

Macbeth (2000) Terry Hands[L]; Timothy O'Brien[S][C]

Macbeth (Kellerd) (1911) Callot Soeurs[C]; Mrs. Lulu Fralik[C]; Maurice

Thomas Farrar[S]; Ben Platt[C]

Maid and the Millionaire, The (1907) No PLAYBILL

Maid and the Mummy, The (1904) D. Frank Dodge[S]; Archie Gunn[C]

Maid in America (1915) Melville Ellis[C]; Nick Kronyack[L]; H. Robert Law[S]

Maid Marian (1902) F. Richards Anderson[C]; Ernest Gros[S]

Maid of Athens (1914) NONE

Maid of the Mountains, The (1918) ACK[S][C][L]

Maid of the Ozarks (1946) ACK[L]

Mail (1988) Vicki Baral[S]; Gerry Hariton[S]; William Ivey Long[C]; Richard Nelson[L]

Main Line, The (1924) Arthur Ebbetts[S]

Main Street (1921) NONE

Mainly for Lovers (1936) Charles LeMaire[C]; Clarke Robinson[S]

Major Andre (1903) NONE

Major Barbara (1915) Elizabeth Axtman[C]; Gertrude Newell[S]; ACK[L]

Major Barbara (1928) Redington Sharpe[S][C]; ACK[L]

Major Barbara (1956) Dorothy Jeakins[C]; Donald Oenslager[S][L]

Major Barbara (1980) Zack Brown[S][C]; John McLain[L]

Majority of One, A (1959) Motley[C]; Donald Oenslager[S][L]

Make a Million (1958) Paul Morrison[S][L]; Ann Roth[C]

Make a Wish (1951) Raoul Pène Du Bois[S][C]

Make It Snappy (1922) Watson Barratt[S]; Cleveland Bronner[S][C]; Cora MacGeachy[C]; Anna Spencer[C]

Make Me Know It (1929) ACK[S][C][L]

Make Mine Manhattan (1948) Frederick Fox[S]; Morton Haack[C]; Hassard Short[L]

Make Way for Lucia (1948) Lucinda Ballard[S][C]; ACK[L]

Make Way for the Ladies (1899) Ernest Gros[S]

Make Yourself at Home (1945) William Noel Saulter[S]; Janice Wallace[C]

Maker of Dreams, The (1915) Frank Stout[S]

Maker of Men, A (1905) ACK[S][C]

Making Good (1912) H. Robert Law[S]; Bert Tuchman[S]

Makropoulos Secret, The (1926) Cleon Throckmorton[S]; ACK[C][L]

Makropoulos Secret, The (1957) Patton Campbell[C]; Norris Houghton[S]; Tharon Musser[L]

Malcolm (1966) Willa Kim[C]; Tharon Musser[L]; William Ritman[S]

Male Animal, The (1940) Aline Bernstein[S]; Emeline Clarke Roche[C]

Male Animal, The (1952) Mel Bourne[S]; Noel Taylor[C]

Malvaloca (1922) Woodman Thompson[S][C]

Mam'selle 'Awkins (1900) NONE

Mam'selle Napoleon (1903) Ernest Albert[S]

Mama Loves Papa (1926) ACK[C][L]

Mama's Baby Boy (1912) No PLAYBILL

Mamaloshen (1998) Eric Cornwell[L]; Eric Renschler[S]

Mamba's Daughter's (1939) Perry Watkins[S][C]

Mamba's Daughter's (1940) Perry Watkins[S][C]

Mame (1966) William and Jean Eckart[S]; Robert Mackintosh[C]; Tharon Musser[L]

Mame (1983) Robert Mackintosh[C]; Thomas Skelton[L]; Peter Wolf[S]

Mamma's Affair (1920) Hickson[C]; ACK[L]

Mamselle Sallie (1906) ACK[S]

Mamzelle Champagne (1906) NONE

Man and His Angel (1906) NONE

Man and His Wife, A (1900) Mrs. Robert Osborn[C]

Man and Superman (1905) NONE

Man and Superman (1912) NONE

Man and Superman (1947) David Ffolkes[C]; George Schaefer[L]; Frederick Stover[S]

Man and Superman (1978) Zack Brown[S][C]; F. Mitchell Dana[L]

Man and the Masses (1924) Lee Simonson[S][C]

Man Bites Dog (1933) Joseph Teichner Studio[S]; ACK[C]

Man Crazy (1932) ACK[L]

Man for All Seasons, A (1961) Paul Morrison[L]; Motley[S][C]

Man from Blankley's, The (1903) NONE

Man from Cairo, The (1938) Frederick Fox[S]; ACK[C]

Man from China, The (1904) Ernest Albert[S]

Man from Cook's, The (1912) F.
Richards Anderson[C]; Walter W.
Burridge[S]; Ernest Gros[S]
Man from Home, The (1908) Frank E.
Gates[S]; Edward Morange[S]
Man from Mel Dinelli, The (1950) Jo
Mielziner[S][L]; Julia Sze[C]
Man from Mexico, The (1909) NONE
Man from Now, The (1906) Walter W.
Burridge[S]; Archie Gunn[C]
Man from Toronto, The (1926)
Benjamin Leffler[L]; Joseph Physioc[S];
ACK[C]
Man in Evening Clothes, The (1924)
William E. Castle[S]; ACK[C][L]
Man in Possession, The (1930) Rollo
Wayne[S]
Man in the Dog Suit, The (1958)
Anna Hill Johnstone[C]; Donald
Oenslager[S][L]
Man in the Glass Booth, The (1968)
Joseph G. Aulisi[C]; Jules Fisher[L]; Ed
Wittstein[S]
Man Inside, The (1913) Ernest Gros[S]
Man of Destiny (1925) Miguel
Covarrubias[S]; Carolyn Hancock[S][C];
ACK[L]
Man of Destiny, The (1903) NONE
Man of Destiny, The (1904) NONE
Man of Destiny, The (1905) NONE
Man of Forty, The (1900) W. L.
Telbin[S]; D. T. White[S]
Man of Honor, A (1911) John
Collette[S]
Man of La Mancha (1977) Howard
Bay[S][C][L]; Patton Campbell[C]
Man of La Mancha (1992) Howard
Bay[S][C]; Patton Campbell[C]; Gregory
Allen Hirsch[L]
Man of the Hour, The (1906) H.
Robert Law[S]
Man of the People, A (1920) ACK[C][L]
Man on Stilts, The (1931) Henry
Dreyfuss[S]; ACK[C]
Man on the Box, The (1905) Walter
B. Spong[S]
Man on the Case, The (1907) Castle
and Harvey[S]
Man or Devil (1925) Rollo Wayne[S]
Man Proposes (1904) Robert T.
McKee[S]
Man Who Ate the Popomack, The
(1924) Frederick W. Jones III[S];
Joseph Mullen[C]
Man Who Came Back, The (1916) H.
Robert Law[S]; ACK[C][L]

Man Who Came to Dinner, The
(1939) Omar Kiam[C]; Donald
Oenslager[S]; ACK[L]
Man Who Came to Dinner, The
(1980) Zack Brown[S][C]; Jeff Davis[L]
Man Who Came to Dinner, The
(2000) Paul Gallo[L]; William Ivey
Long[C]; Tony Walton[S]
Man Who Changed His Name, The
(1932) Karle O. Amend Studio[S];
ACK[C]
Man Who Had All the Luck, The
(1944) Frederick Fox[S]; Peggy
Thayer[C]; ACK[C]
Man Who Had Three Arms, The
(1983) Jeff Davis[L]; John Falabella[C];
John Jensen[S]
Man Who Killed Lincoln, The (1940)
Rose Bogdanoff[C]; Eugene Dunkel[S]
Man Who Married a Dumb Wife,
The (1915) Robert Edmond
Jones[S][C]; ACK[L]
Man Who Never Did, The (1925)
Cleon Throckmorton[S]
Man Who Owns Broadway, The
(1909) Ernest Albert[S]; Unitt and
Wickes[S]; ACK[C][L]
Man Who Reclaimed His Head, The
(1932) Livingston Platt[S]; ACK[C]
Man Who Stayed at Home, The
(1918) Hickson[C]; ACK[L]
Man Who Stole the Castle (1903)
Edith Craig[S]; ACK[L]
Man Who Stood Still, The (1908) H.
Robert Law[S]
Man with a Load of Mischief, The
(1925) Rollo Wayne[S]; ACK[C]
Man with Blond Hair, The (1941)
Howard Bay[S]
Man with Red Hair, A (1928)
Nicholas Yellenti[S]; ACK[C][L]
Man with Three Wives, The (1913)
Melville Ellis[C]; T. E. Ryan[S]
Man's Estate (1929) Cleon
Throckmorton[S]; ACK[C]
Man's Friends, A (1913) Gates and
Morange[S]
Man's Man, A (1925) Cleon
Throckmorton[S]; ACK[L]
Man's Name, The (1921) ACK[C]
Man's World, A (1910) H. Robert
Law[S]
Man, The (1950) Jo Mielziner[S][L]; Julia
Sze[C]
Mandarin, The (1920) ACK[L]
Mandingo (1961) Frederick Fox[S][C][L]

Manhattan (1922) Marjorie Dalmain(S);
Jesse Fremont(C); Ack(L)
Manhattan Mary (1927) Erté(C);
William Oden Waller(S); Ack(L)
Manhattan Nocturne (1943) Natalie
Barth Walker(C); Perry Watkins(S)
Manhattan Showboat (1980) Robert
Guerra(S); David F. Segal(L); Frank
Spencer(C)
Manhatters, The (1927) Henry
Dreyfuss(S)(C)
Manoeuvres of Jane, The (1899)
Edward G. Unitt(S)
Manon Lescaut (1901) None
Mansion on the Hudson (1935)
Helene Pons(C); Ack(L)
Many a Slip (1930) Cirker and
Robbins(S); Ack(C)
Many Happy Returns (1945) Stewart
Chaney(S); William Thomas(L)
Many Mansions (1937) Mary
Binning(C); Julia Cerrell(C); John
Koenig(S); Stanley R. McCandless(L)
Many Waters (1929) Ack(L)
Marat/Sade (1965) Sally Jacobs(S);
Gunilla Palmstierna-Weiss(C); David
Read(L)
Marat/Sade (1967) Martin Aronstein(L);
Lewis Brown(C); Edward Burbridge(S)
Marathon (1933) P. Dodd Ackerman(S)
Marathon '33 (1963) Peter Larkin(S);
Tharon Musser(L); Noel Taylor(C)
Marcelle (1900) F. Richards
Anderson(C); Henry Bissing(L); Ernest
Gros(S)
Marcelle (1908) Melville Ellis(C); Arthur
Voegtlin(S); George Whalen(L)
March Hares (1921) Joseph(C)
March Hares (1928) Ack(L)
Marching By (1932) Watson Barratt(S);
Ernest Schraps(C)
Marching Song (1937) Howard Bay(S)
Marco Millions (1928) Lee
Simonson(S)(C)
Marco Millions (1930) Lee
Simonson(S)(C)
Marco Millions (1964) David Hays(S)(L);
Beni Montresor(C)
Margaret Schiller (1916) Homer
Emens(S); Ack(L)
Margery Daw (1916) Ack(L)
Margin for Error (1939) Donald
Oenslager(S); Ack(C)
Maria Golovin (1958) Charles Elson(L);
Noel Taylor(C); Rouben
Ter-Arutunian(S)

Maria Rosa (1914) Dodge and Castle(S);
Kliegl Brothers(L); Lou Tellegen(C)
Marie Antoinette (1900) Thomas G.
Moses(S)
Marie Christine (1999) Christopher
Barreca(S); Peggy Eisenhauer(L); Jules
Fisher(L); Toni-Leslie James(C)
Marie Odile (1915) Ernest Gros(S);
Ack(L)
Marie-Odile (1915) Ernest Gros(S)
Marigold (1930) Edith Barber(C);
Captain H. Oaks Jones(C); Ian Lloyd
MacKenzie(S)
Marilyn (1983) Joseph G. Aulisi(C); Tom
John(S); Marcia Madeira(L)
Marilyn's Affairs (1933) Ack(S)(L)
Mariners (1927) Henri Bendel(C);
Frances Clyne(C); Jo Mielziner(S)(L);
Fania Mindell(C)
Marinka (1945) Howard Bay(S); Mary
Grant(C)
Marionettes, The (1911) Homer
Emens(S); Frank Platzer(S); Ack(C)(L)
Marjolaine (1922) William Henry
Matthews(C); Joseph Wickes(S); Ack(L)
Marjorie (1924) William Thomas(L);
Woodman Thompson(S); Ack(C)
Mark of the Beast, The (1915) Ack(L)
Markheim (1906) Hawes Craven(S);
Joseph Harker(S)
Marlene (1999) John Arnone(S); Mark
Jonathan(L); David C. Woolard(C)
Marlowe (1981) Mitch Acker(L); Cary
Chalmers(S); Natalie Barth Walker(C)
Marquis De Priola, The (1919)
Ack(C)(L)
Marquise, The (1927) Ben Ali
Haggin(C); Jo Mielziner(S)(L)
Marriage a La Carte (1911) Joseph(S)
Marriage Bed, The (1929) Hans
Dreier(S); Ack(C)(L)
Marriage for Three (1931) Rollo
Wayne(S); Ack(C)
Marriage Game, The (1901) Richard
Marston(S); Mrs. Robert Osborn(C)
Marriage Game, The (1913) Richard
Marston(S); Paquin(C)
Marriage is for Single People (1945)
Frederick Fox(S)
Marriage Market, The (1913)
Comelli(C); Homer Emens(S)
Marriage of a Star, The (1910) None
Marriage of Cana, The (1932) James
Shannon(S)
Marriage of Columbine, The (1914)
Rufus Clarke(C); Gates and

Morange(S); George C. Somnes(C)

Marriage of Convenience, A (1918) ACK(C)(L)

Marriage of Figaro, The (1985) Beni Montresor(S)(C)(L)

Marriage of Kitty, The (1903) William Harford(S); Redfern(C)

Marriage of Kitty, The (1914) ACK(C)

Marriage of Reason, The (1907) Ernest Gros(S); Richard Marston(S)

Marriage of William Ashe, The (1905) H. Robert Law(S); Bert Tuchman(S); ACK(C)

Marriage on Approval (1928) P. Dodd Ackerman(S)

Marriage-Go-Round, The (1958) Castillo(C); Donald Oenslager(S)(L); ACK(C)

Marriage-Not, The (1912) Boss and Ormston(S); ACK(C)

Married Woman, The (1916) ACK(L)

Married Woman, The (1921) Madame Julie Levick(C); ACK(S)

Married—and How! (1928) ACK(L)

Marry the Man (1929) ACK(S)(L)

Marry the Poor Girl (1920) ACK(C)(L)

Marrying Mary (1906) Gates and Morange(S); ACK(C)

Marrying Money (1914) Lucile(C)

Marseilles (1930) Stanley Bell(S); Helene Pons(C)

Marta of the Lowlands (1903) Gates and Morange(S)

Marta of the Lowlands (1908) Frank E. Gates(S); Edward Morange(S)

Martine (1928) Robert Edmond Jones(S)(C)

Martinique (1920) Lee Simonson(S)(C)(L)

Mary (1920) ACK(S)(C)(L)

Mary and John (1905) NO PLAYBILL

Mary Goes First (1914) ACK(C)

Mary Jane McKane (1923) Gates and Morange(S); Charles LeMaire(C)

Mary Jane's Pa (1908) Charles E. Brown(S); Walter W. Burridge(S); Joseph Wilson(L)

Mary Magdalene (1910) Gates and Morange(S); Madame Najla Nogabgat(C); John H. Young(S); Louis C. Young(S)

Mary of Magdala (1902) Percy Anderson(C); Homer Emens(S); Gates and Morange(S)

Mary of Scotland (1933) Robert Edmond Jones(S)(C)(L)

Mary Rose (1920) Homer Emens(S)

Mary Stuart (1900) Thomas G. Moses(S)

Mary Stuart (1921) Livingston Platt(S)(C)

Mary the 3rd (1923) ACK(S)(C)(L)

Mary's Ankle (1917) ACK(L)

Mary's Lamb (1908) Ena Welch(C); ACK(C)

Mary's Maneuvers (1913) NONE

Mary, Mary (1961) Theoni V. Aldredge(C); Peggy Clark(L); Oliver Smith(S)

Mary, Mary, Quite Contrary (1905) T. Bernard McDonald(S); Louis C. Young(S)

Mary, Mary, Quite Contrary (1923) Henri Bendel(C); Ernest Gros(S); Louis Hartmann(L)

Mascot, The (1909) NONE

Mask and Gown (1957) Lee Watson(L)

Mask and the Face, The (1924) Raymond Sovey(S)

Mask and the Face, The (1933) Frances Clyne(C); Lee Simonson(S)

Mask of Hamlet, The (1921) NONE

Masked Woman, The (1922) ACK(C)(L)

Masks and Faces (1907) NONE

Masks and Faces (1933) Lee Simonson(S); ACK(C)

Masque of Kings, The (1937) Lee Simonson(S)(C)

Masque of Venice, The (1926) Jo Mielziner(S)(L); Margaret Pemberton(C)

Masquerade (1959) Robert Mackintosh(C); Paul Morrison(S)(L)

Masquerader, The (1917) Richard Walton Tully(S); ACK(C)(L)

Mass Appeal (1981) F. Mitchell Dana(C); David Gropman(S); William Ivey Long(C)

Master Builder (1925) Gladys E. Calthrop(S)(C)

Master Builder, The (1900) Unitt and Wickes(S)

Master Builder, The (1908) Unitt and Wickes(S)

Master Builder, The (1926) Gladys E. Calthrop(S)(C)

Master Builder, The (1992) David Jenkins(S); Richard Nelson(L); Patricia Zipprodt(C)

Master Class (1995) Jane Greenwood(C); Brian MacDevitt(L); Michael McGarty(S)

Master Harold...and the Boys (1982) Jane Clark(S); Sheila McLamb(C); David Noling(L)

Master Key, The (1909) NONE
Master Mind, The (1913) Dodge and
Castle(S); H. Robert Law(S); Lucile(C);
Max & Mahieu(C); ACK(L)
Master of the House, The (1912)
Dodge and Castle(S); John H. Young(S)
Master of the Inn, The (1925) John
Wenger(S); ACK(C)
Master, The (1916) H. Robert Studio
Law(S); ACK(L)
Mastergate (1989) Candice Donnelly(C);
Philipp Jung(S); Stephen
Strawbridge(L)
Matchmaker, The (1955) Tanya
Moiseiwitsch(S)(C); ACK(L)
Mater (1908) NONE
Maternity (1915) O'Kane Conwell(C);
Robert Larkin(S); Lucile(C)
Matilda (1906) ACK(L)
Matinee Girl, The (1926) DuWico(L);
Joseph Physioc(S); ACK(C)
Matinee Hero, The (1918) ACK(C)(L)
Matinee Idol, The (1910) NONE
Mating Dance (1965) Eldon Elder(S);
John Harvey(L); Florence Klotz(C)
Mating Season, The (1927) ACK(C)(L)
Matriarch, The (1930) ACK(S)(C)(L)
Matrimonial Bed, The (1927)
Milgrim(C); ACK(S)(L)
Matrimony RFD (1936) Donald
Oenslager(S); ACK(C)
Matter of Gravity, A (1976) Ben
Edwards(S); Jane Greenwood(C);
Thomas Skelton(L)
Mauricette (1906) T. J. Digby(L); F. C.
Schmitz(S); Madame Viola(C)
May Wine (1935) Kay Morrison(C);
Raymond Sovey(S)
Maya (1928) Aline Bernstein(S)(C)
Maybe Tuesday (1958) Paul
Morrison(S)(L); Ann Roth(C)
Mayfair (1930) ACK(L)
Mayflowers (1925) Watson Barratt(S)
Mayor of Tokio, The (1905) Henry
Bissing(L); Thomas Bradley(S); D.
Frank Dodge(S); Eugene Dupuis(L);
Madame Freisinger(C); Gates and
Morange(S); Ena Welch(C)
Maytime (1917) Homer Conant(S)(C);
Robert Larkin(L)
Me (1925) ACK(L)
Me and Bessie (1974) Donald Harris(S);
Pete Menefee(C); Tharon Musser(L)
Me and Juliet (1953) Jo Mielziner(S)(L);
Irene Sharaff(C)
Me and Molly (1948) Rose

Bogdanoff(C); Harry Horner(S); Leo
Kerz(L)
Me and My Girl (1986) Ann Curtis(C);
Chris Ellis(L); Martin Johns(S)
Me and Thee (1965) Charles
Evans(S)(C); V. C. Fuqua(L); A.
Christina Giannini(C)
Me Jack, You Jill (1976) Lawrence
King(S)(C); Jane Reisman(L); Michael H.
Yeargan(C)
Me Nobody Knows, The (1970)
Clarke Dunham(S)(L); Patricia Quinn
Stuart(C)
Meanest Man in the World, The
(1920) ACK(C)(L)
Measure for Measure (1973) Martin
Aronstein(L); John David Ridge(C);
Douglas W. Schmidt(S)
Measure of a Man, The (1906) ACK(C)
Mecca (1920) Percy Anderson(C); Léon
Bakst(C); Joseph and Phil Harker(S)
Medal and the Maid, The (1904)
Comelli(C); Moses and Hamilton(S)
Medea (1920) Fania Mindell(C)
Medea (1947) Castillo(C); Peggy Clark(L);
Ben Edwards(S)
Medea (1973) Robert Mitchell(S); Nancy
Potts(C); Marc B. Weiss(L)
Medea (1982) Martin Aronstein(L); Ben
Edwards(S); Jane Greenwood(C)
Medea (1994) Paul Brown(C); Peter J.
Davison(S); Wayne Dowdeswell(L)
Medicine Show (1940) Samuel Leve(S)(L)
Meek Mouse (1928) Albert Bliss(S)
Meet a Body (1944) Willis
Knighton(S)(C)
Meet Me in Saint Louis (1989) Keith
Anderson(S)(C); Ken Billington(L)
Meet My Sister (1930) Watson
Barratt(S); ACK(C)
Meet the People (1940) Roy Holmes(L);
Kate Drain Lawson(C); Frederick
Stover(S); Gerda Vanderneers(C)
Meet the Prince (1929) Jo
Mielziner(S)(L)
Meet the Wife (1923) Gertrude
Lennox(S); Sheldon K. Viele(S); ACK(C)
Meeting in the Air, A (1979)
Marianne Custer(C); Robert
Mitchell(S); Clarke W. Thornton(L)
Melo (1931) Rollo Wayne(S); ACK(C)
Melody (1933) Charles LeMaire(C);
Joseph Urban(S)
Melody Man, The (1924) ACK(L)
Melody of Youth, The (1916) ACK(S)(L)
Melting of Molly, The (1918) Watson

Barratt[S]; ACK[C][L]

Melting Pot, The (1909) Gates and Morange[S]

Member of the Wedding, The (1950) Lester Polakov[S][C][L]

Member of the Wedding, The (1975) Ken Billington[L]; Donald Brooks[C]; Douglas Higgins[S]

Memphis Bound (1945) Lucinda Ballard[C]; George Jenkins[S][L]

Men in Shadow (1943) Frederick Fox[S][L]; ACK[C]

Men in White (1933) Lydia Furbush[C]; Mordecai Gorelik[S]; ACK[L]

Men Must Fight (1932) Raymond Sovey[S]; ACK[C]

Men of Distinction (1953) David Ffolkes[S][C]

Men to the Sea (1944) Howard Bay[S][L]; Grace Houston[C]

Men We Marry, The (1948) Donald Oenslager[S][L]; Helene Pons[C]

Menace (1927) Cleon Throckmorton[S]; ACK[C]

Mendel, Inc (1929) Cirker and Robbins[S]; ACK[C][L]

Mercenary Mary (1925) Karle O. Amend[S]; Hugh Willoughby[C]; ACK[L]

Merchant of Venice (1907) NONE

Merchant of Venice, The (1899) Hawes Craven[S]; Edwin William Godwin[C]; Walter Hann[S]; W. L. Telbin[S]

Merchant of Venice, The (1901) Walter Hann[S]; Maurice Hermann[C]; Henry E. Hoyt[S]; L. W. Seavey[S]

Merchant of Venice, The (1904) NONE

Merchant of Venice, The (1905) C. Karl[C]

Merchant of Venice, The (1906) NONE

Merchant of Venice, The (1907) Hawes Craven[S]; Walter Hann[S]; C. Karl[C]; W. L. Telbin[S]

Merchant of Venice, The (1908) NONE

Merchant of Venice, The (1913) Joseph Harker[S]; W. T. Hemsley[S]

Merchant of Venice, The (1916) Homer Emens[S]; Percy Macquoid[C]; ACK[L]

Merchant of Venice, The (1918) ACK[S][L]

Merchant of Venice, The (1922) Ernest Gros[S]; ACK[C][L]

Merchant of Venice, The (1925) Claude Bragdon[S][C]

Merchant of Venice, The (1928)

Woodman Thompson[S][C]

Merchant of Venice, The (1930) Woodman Thompson[S][C]; ACK[L]

Merchant of Venice, The (1931) William Henry Matthews[C]; Herman Rosse[S]; Mary Stonehill[C]

Merchant of Venice, The (1947) Sheila Jackson[C]; Donald Wolfit[S]

Merchant of Venice, The (1989) Chris Dyer[S][C]; Barbara Forbes[C]; Neil Peter Jampolis[L]

Merchant of Venice, The (Kellerd) (1911) NONE

Merchant of Yonkers, The (1938) Boris Aronson[S][C]

Merchant, The (1977) Jocelyn Herbert[S][C]; Andy Phillips[L]

Merchants of Glory (1925) Ben Webster[S][C]

Merchants of Venus (1920) Mary Walls[C]; ACK[S][L]

Mere Man (1912) H. Robert Law[S]; ACK[C]

Merely Mary Ann (1903) Frank E. Gates[S]; Edward Morange[S]

Merely Murder (1937) Watson Barratt[S]; ACK[C]

Merlin (1983) Theoni V. Aldredge[C]; Tharon Musser[L]; Robin Wagner[S]

Mermaids Singing (1945) Raymond Sovey[S]

Merrily We Roll Along (1934) John Hambleton[C]; Jo Mielziner[S][L]

Merrily We Roll Along (1981) Judith Dolan[C]; David Hersey[L]; Eugene Lee[S]

Merry Andrew (1929) Livingston Platt[S]; ACK[C][L]

Merry Christmas, Daddy (1916) B. Russell Herts[S][C]; ACK[L]

Merry Countess, The (1912) Mrs. Caroline Siedle[C]; John H. Young[S]

Merry Malones (1927) E.J. Herrett[C]; Mabel E. Johnston[C]; Cora MacGeachy[C]; Joseph Wickes[S]; ACK[L]

Merry Whirl, The (1910) Homer Emens[S]; Kliegl Brothers[L]; John H. Young[S]; ACK[C]

Merry Widow Burlesque, The (1908) John H. Young[S]

Merry Widow, The (1907) Percy Anderson[C]; Walter W. Burridge[S]; Landolff of Paris[C]; Joseph Wilson[L]; Madame Zimmerman[C]

Merry Widow, The (1921) Peggy

Hoyt(C); Joseph Urban(S)

Merry Widow, The (1929) Ack(C)(L)

Merry Widow, The (1931) Ack(C)(L)

Merry Widow, The (1942) Ack(S)(C)(L)

Merry Widow, The (1943) Howard Bay(S); Walter Florell(C)

Merry Widow, The (1995) Michael Anania(S); Gregg Barnes(C); Mark W. Stanley(L)

Merry Wives of Gotham (1924) John N. Booth, Jr.(C); William E. Castle(S); Yetta Kiviette(C); William Henry Matthews(C); Ack(L)

Merry Wives of Windsor (1910) E. Hamilton Bell(S)(C); Gates and Morange(S); Unitt and Wickes(S)

Merry Wives of Windsor, The (1916) Percy Anderson(S)(C); Joseph Physioc(S); Ack(L)

Merry Wives of Windsor, The (1917) Joseph Physioc(S); Miss Gertrude Whitty(C); Ack(L)

Merry Wives of Windsor, The (1928) Henry Dreyfuss(C); Gates and Morange(S); Ack(L)

Merry Wives of Windsor, The (1938) Howard Bay(S)(C)

Merry World, The (1926) Watson Barratt(S); Ack(L)

Merry, Merry (1925) P. Dodd Ackerman(S); Charles LeMaire(C)

Merry-Go-Round (1927) P. Dodd Ackerman Studio(S); Daisy Garson(C); Walt Kuhn(C); Ack(L)

Merry-Go-Round (1932) Isaac Benesch(S)

Merry-Go-Round, The (1908) No Playbill

Message for Margaret (1947) Charles Elson(L); Donald Oenslager(S); Valentina(C); Ack(C)

Message from Mars, A (1901) Angel(C); Madame Francis(C); Walter Hann(S); L. and H. Nathan(C)

Messenger Boy, The (1901) Joseph Harker(S); T. E. Ryan(S)

Messin' 'Round (1929) DuWico(L); Lou Wertheim(S); Ack(C)

Metamorphosis (1989) Duke Durfee(S); Brian Nason(L); Jacques Schmidt(C)

Meteor (1929) Elizabeth Hawes(C); Raymond Sovey(S); Ack(C)

Metro (1992) Ken Billington(L); Marie Anne Chiment(C); Juliet Polcsa(C); Janusz Sosnowski(S)

Metropole (1949) DuWico(L); Edward

Gilbert(S); Bianca Stroock(C)

Mexican Hayride (1944) Mary Grant(C); George Jenkins(S); Hassard Short(L)

Mexicana (1906) None

Mexicana (1938) Julio Castellanos(S); Augustín Lazo(C)

Meyer & Son (1909) H. P. Scenic Studio Knight(S); Ack(L)

Mia Moglie Non Ha Chic (1907) None

Mice and Men (1903) Edward G. Unitt(S)

Mice and Men (1913) Walter Hann(S); W. T. Hemsley(S)

Michael and Mary (1929) Thomas Farrar(S); Ack(C)

Michael Drops In (1938) Eleanor Farrington(S); Ack(C)

Michael Feinstein in Concert (1988) Beverly Emmons(L); Andrew Jackness(S)

Michael Feinstein in Concert (1990) David Agress(L)

Michael Todd's Peep Show (1950) Howard Bay(S); Irene Sharaff(C); Hassard Short(L)

Michel Auclair (1925) Robert Edmond Jones(S)

Mid-Channel (1910) Frank Platzer(S)

Mid-summer (1953) Howard Bay(S)(L); Motley(C)

Mid-West (1936) Watson Barratt(S)

Middle of the Night (1956) Jo Mielziner(S)(L); Motley(C)

Middle Watch, The (1929) Ack(L)

Middleman, The (1900) Richard Marston(S)

Midgie Purvis (1961) Ben Edwards(S)(L); Guy Kent(C)

Midnight (1930) Woodman Thompson(S); Ack(C)

Midnight Girl, The (1914) Melville Ellis(C); H. Robert Studio Law(S)

Midnight Rounders of 1921, The (1921) None

Midnight Rounders, The (1920) Ack(L)

Midnight Sons, The (1909) Arthur Voegtlin(S); George Williams(S)

Midnite Frolics (1929) John W. Harkrider(C); Charles LeMaire(C); Joseph Urban(S); Ack(L)

Midsummer Night's Dream, A (1903) Ernest Albert(S); F. Richards Anderson(C)

Midsummer Night's Dream, A
(1915) Norman Wilkinson[S][C]

Midsummer Night's Dream, A
(1927) Oscar Strnad[S]; Ernest de
Weerth[C]; Ack[L]

Midsummer Night's Dream, A
(1932) Ack[S][C][L]

Midsummer Night's Dream, A
(1954) Christopher Ironside[S][C];
Robin Ironside[S][C]

Midsummer Night's Dream, A
(1971) Lloyd Burlingame[L]; Sally
Jacobs[S][C]

Midsummer Night's Dream, A
(1996) Chris Parry[L]; Anthony
Ward[S][C]

Mighty Gents, The (1978) Judy
Dearing[C]; Gilbert V. Hemsley, Jr.[L];
Santo Loquasto[S]

Mighty Man Is He, A (1960) Frederick
Fox[S][L]; Virginia Volland[C]

Mikado, The (1902) None
Mikado, The (1910) None
Mikado, The (1912) None
Mikado, The (1913) None
Mikado, The (1925) None

Mikado, The (1927) Raymond
Sovey[S][C]; Ack[L]

Mikado, The (1931) Ack[L]

Mikado, The (1933) Watson Barratt[S];
Ack[C][L]

Mikado, The (1947) Charles
Ricketts[S][C]; Ack[L]

Mikado, The (1949) Ralph
Alswang[S][L]; Peggy Morrison[C]

Mikado, The (1951) Charles
Ricketts[S][C]

Mikado, The (1952) Ralph Alswang[S];
Peggy Morrison[C]

Mikado, The (1955) Peter Goffin[S];
Charles Ricketts[C]; Ack[L]

Mikado, The (1987) Susan Benson[S][C];
Michael J. Whitfield[L]

Mikado, The (1993) Thierry
Bosquet[S][C]; John Gleason[L]

Mike Angelo (1923) Ack[L]

Mike Downstairs (1968) Edward
Burbridge[S]; Hal George[C]; Thomas
Skelton[L]

Milady's Boudoir (1914) Ack[C]

Mile-a-Minute Kendall (1916) Ack[L]

Milestones (1912) L. and H. Nathan[C];
Madame Caleb Porter[C]; Redfern[C];
Sackman[S]

Milestones (1930) Eric Pape[C]; Ack[L]

Military Mad (1904) None

Military Maid, The (1900) None

Milk and Honey (1961) Howard
Bay[S][L]; Miles White[C]

Milk Train Doesn't Stop Here
Anymore, The (1963) Jo
Mielziner[S][L]; Fred Voelpel[C]

Milk Train Doesn't Stop Here
Anymore, The (1964) Martin
Aronstein[L]; Rouben
Ter-Arutunian[S][C]

Milky Way, The (1934) Brymer[C]; S.
Syrjala[S]

Milky Way, The (1943) Cirker and
Robbins[S]; Ack[C]

Million Dollars, A (1900) D. Frank
Dodge[S]; James Fox[S]; St. John
Lewis[S]; MacCoughtry[S]

Million, The (1911) None

Millionairess, The (1952) James
Bailey[S]; Pierre Balmain[C]

Mills of the Gods, The (1907) None

Mimic and the Maid, The (1907)
None

Mimic World, The (1908) H. Robert
Law[S]; Arthur Voegtlin[S]

Mimic World, The (1921) Watson
Barratt[S]

Mimie Scheller (1936) Cirker and
Robbins[S]; Mildred Manning[C]

"Mind-the-Paint" Girl, The (1912)
None

Minick (1924) Woodman Thompson[S]

Minna (1928) George Haddon[C]; Joseph
Wickes[S]; Ack[L]

Minnie and Mr. Williams (1948)
Mordecai Gassner[S][C]; Ack[L]

Minnie's Boys (1970) Donald Brooks[C];
Jules Fisher[L]; Peter Wexler[S]

Minor Adjustment, A (1967) Saul
Bolasni[C]; Jules Fisher[L]; Leo B.
Meyer[S]

Minor Miracle (1965) Theoni V.
Aldredge[C]; Tharon Musser[L]; Robert
Randolph[S]

Miracle at Verdun (1931) Charles
Chrisdie[C]; Lee Simonson[S]; Ack[C]

Miracle in the Mountains (1947)
Robert Davison[S][C]

Miracle Man, The (1914) John
Collette[S]

Miracle of St. Anthony, A (1915)
Kliegl Brothers[L]; Lee Simonson[S][C]

Miracle of St. Anthony, The (1908)
No Playbill

Miracle Worker, The (1959) George
Jenkins[S][L]; Ruth Morley[C]

Miracle, The (1924) Norman Bel Geddes[(S)(C)(L)]

Mirage, The (1920) Madame Frances[(C)]; Lee Simonson[(S)]; Raymond Sovey[(S)]; ACK[(L)]

Miranda of the Balcony (1901) Frank E. Gates[(S)]; Maurice Hermann[(C)]; Edward Morange[(S)]; Madame Virion[(C)]; Worth[(C)]

Mirrors (1928) Nicholas Yellenti[(S)]; ACK[(L)]

Mis' Nelly of N'Orleans (1919) Homer Emens[(S)]; ACK[(C)(L)]

Misalliance (1917) Unitt and Wickes[(S)]; ACK[(C)(L)]

Misanthrope, The (1905) M. Messonier[(S)]; Joseph Physioc[(S)]

Misanthrope, The (1968) Nancy Potts[(C)]; James Tilton[(S)(L)]

Misanthrope, The (1975) Tanya Moiseiwitsch[(S)(C)]; Andy Phillips[(L)]

Misanthrope, The (1983) Marjorie Bradley Kellogg[(S)]; Richard Nelson[(L)]; Ann Roth[(C)]

Miser, The (1990) Gail Brassard[(C)]; Mary Jo Dondlinger[(L)]; James Morgan [active 1989-][(S)]

Miser, The/Snickering Horses/The Great Cat (1936) NONE

Miser/ The Great Cat/ Snickering Horses, The (1937) Samuel Leve[(S)]

Misleading Lady, The (1913) Jean[(C)]; H. Robert Law[(S)]

Mismates (1925) ACK[(L)]

Miss 1917 (1917) Lucile[(C)]; Joseph Urban[(S)]; ACK[(L)]

Miss Daisy (1914) ACK[(C)]

Miss Dolly Dollars (1905) Emens and Unitt[(S)]; Mrs. Caroline Siedle[(C)]

Miss Elizabeth's Prisoner (1903) Henry Dazian[(C)]; Mrs. Robert Osborn[(C)]

Miss Gulliver's Travels (1931) Cirker and Robbins[(S)]; ACK[(C)]

Miss Hobbs (1899) Edward G. Unitt[(S)]

Miss Hook of Holland (1907) Percy Anderson[(C)]; Edward G. Unitt[(S)]; Joseph Wickes[(S)]

Miss Information (1915) Melville Ellis[(C)]; ACK[(L)]

Miss Innocence (1908) T. Bernard McDonald[(S)]

Miss Isobel (1957) Audré[(C)]; Peter Larkin[(S)]; Lee Watson[(L)]

Miss Jack (1911) Charles E. Brown[(S)]; Mr. Bothwell Browne[(C)]; Kliegl

Brothers[(L)]; H. Robert Studio Law[(S)]; Bert Tuchman[(S)]

Miss Julie (1962) Gunnar Gelbort[(C)]; Yngve Larson[(S)]

Miss Liberty (1949) Motley[(C)]; Oliver Smith[(S)]

Miss Lonely Hearts (1957) Jo Mielziner[(S)(L)]; Patricia Zipprodt[(C)]

Miss Lulu Betat (1920) Sheldon K. Viele[(S)]

Miss Margarida's Way (1972) Santo Loquasto[(S)]

Miss Margarida's Way (1977) Santo Loquasto[(S)(C)]; Martin Tudor[(L)]

Miss Margarida's Way (1989) Santo Loquasto[(C)]; Jason Sturm[(L)]

Miss Millions (1919) Henri Bendel[(C)]; Mark Lawson[(S)]; ACK[(L)]

Miss Patsy (1910) Walter W. Burridge[(S)]; Joseph Wilson[(L)]

Miss Phoenix (1913) NONE

Miss Pocahontas (1907) J. G. Hammond[(S)]; ACK[(C)(L)]

Miss Princess (1912) NONE

Miss Prinnt (1900) A. Operti[(S)]

Miss Quis (1937) Donald Oenslager[(S)]; Bianca Stroock[(C)]

Miss Saigon (1991) Suzy Benzinger[(C)]; David Hersey[(L)]; John Napier[(S)]; Andreane Neofitou[(C)]

Miss Simplicity (1902) Madame Castle-Bert[(C)]; Joseph Physioc[(S)]; Mrs. Caroline Siedle[(C)]; ACK[(L)]

Miss Springtime (1916) F. Richards Anderson[(C)]; Ben Beerwald[(L)]; Alice O'Neil[(C)]; Joseph Urban[(S)]

Miss Swan Expects (1939) Raymond Sovey[(S)]; ACK[(C)]

Missouri Legend (1938) John Koenig[(S)(C)]

Mistakes Will Happen (1906) NONE

Mister Johnson (1956) William and Jean Eckart[(S)(C)]

Mister Lincoln (1980) David L. Lovett[(S)(C)]; Allan Stitchbury[(L)]

Mister Malatesta (1923) ACK[(L)]

Mister Romeo (1927) ACK[(S)(C)(L)]

Mistress Nell (1900) Franklin Van Horn[(C)]; Louis C. Young[(S)]

Mistress Nell (1902) Franklin Van Horn[(C)]; Louis C. Young[(S)]

Mix-Up, A (1914) Dodge and Castle[(S)]; Marie Dressler[(S)]; Robert Kalloch[(C)]; Joseph Wilson[(L)]

Mixed Couples (1980) Martin Aronstein[(L)]; Oliver Smith[(S)]; Noel

Taylor[C]

Mixed Doubles (1927) Watson Barratt[S]

Mixed Emotions (1993) Neil Peter Jampolis[S][L]; David Murin[C]

Mixed Marriage (1920) Rollo Peters[S]

Mizpah (1906) Henry Dazian[C]; Ernest Gros[S]

Mlle. Mischief (1908) Melville Ellis[C]; John Whalen[L]; George Williams[S]

Mlle. Modiste (1905) Homer Emens[S]

Mlle. Modiste (1913) Henry Dazian[C]; Homer Emens[S]; Joseph[C]; ACK[C]

Moby Dick (1962) David Craven[C]; Klaus Holm[S]; Lee Watson[L]

Mocking Bird, The (1902) Will R. Barnes[C]; John Cunningham[S]

Model, The (1912) ACK[S]

Modern Eve, A (1915) William Henry Matthews[C]; ACK[L]

Modern Eve, The (1915) William Henry Matthews[C]

Modern Girl, A (1914) ACK[C]

Modern Magdalen, The (1902) Anthony Greshoff[L]; Mrs. Robert Osborn[C]; Joseph Physioc[S]

Modern Marriage (1911) Lee Lash Studios[S]

Modern Virgin, A (1931) Rollo Wayne[S]; ACK[C]

Modest Suzanne (1912) Dodge and Castle[S]; Madame Frances[C]

Modiste Shop, The (1913) Charles Messersmith[L]; ACK[S][C]

Molière Comedies, The (1995) Ann Hould-Ward[C]; Richard Nelson[L]; Douglas Stein[S]

Moliere (1919) Rollo Peters[C]; Lee Simonson[S]; ACK[L]

Mollusc, The (1908) Edward G. Unitt[S]; Joseph Wickes[S]

Molly (1973) Marsha L. Eck[S]; Jules Fisher[L]; Carrie F. Robbins[C]

Molly Darling (1922) H. Robert Studio Law[S]; ACK[C][L]

Molly May (1910) NO PLAYBILL

Molly O' (1916) ACK[C][L]

Moloch (1915) Anna Spencer[C]; ACK[L]

Moment of Death, The (1900) Ernest Albert[S]

Monday after the Miracle (1982) John Lee Beatty[S]; F. Mitchell Dana[L]; Carol Oditz[C]

Money Business (1926) NONE

Money from Home (1927) Gates and Morange[S]; ACK[L]

Money Lender, The (1928) Robert Edmond Jones[S]; ACK[C]

Money Mad (1937) ACK[S]

Money Makers, The (1905) Ernest Albert[S]; ACK[C]

Money Makers, The (1914) ACK[S][C]

Mongrel, The (1924) Lee Simonson[S]

Monique (1957) John Robert Lloyd[S]; Tharon Musser[L]; Helene Pons[C]

Monkey (1932) Cleon Throckmorton[S]; ACK[C]

Monkey Talks, The (1925) John Wenger[S]; ACK[C][L]

Monkey's Paw, The (1907) NONE

Monks of Malabar, The (1900) Henry E. Hoyt[S]

Monna Vanna (1905) Gates and Morange[S]; Maurice Hermann[C]; John A. Higham[L]

Monsieur Beaucaire (1912) NONE

Monsieur Beaucaire (1919) Percy Anderson[C]; ACK[L]

Monster, The (1922) John H. M. Dudley[S]

Monster, The (1933) ACK[S]

Monte Cristo (1900) Homer Emens[S]; Frank E. Gates[S]; Edward Morange[S]; John H. Young[S]

Monte Cristo, Jr. (1919) Watson Barratt[S]; S. Zalud[C]; ACK[L]

Monteith and Rand (1979) Donald Brooks[C]; Gilbert V. Hemsley, Jr.[L]

Month in the Country, A (1930) M. Dobuzhinsky[S][C]

Month in the Country, A (1995) Jane Greenwood[C]; Santo Loquasto[S]; Brian Nason[L]

Month of Sundays, A (1987) Joseph G. Aulisi[C]; Marjorie Bradley Kellogg[S]; Tharon Musser[L]

Montmartre (1922) John Brunton[S]; ACK[L]

Montserrat (1949) Howard Bay[S]; Irene Sharaff[C]; ACK[L]

Moon Besieged, The (1962) Robert Fletcher[C]; Ming Cho Lee[S][L]

Moon Flower, The (1924) Henri Bendel[C]; ACK[S][L]

Moon for the Misbegotten, A (1957) Ruth Morley[C]; William Pitkin[S]; Lee Watson[L]

Moon for the Misbegotten, A (1973) Ben Edwards[S][L]; Jane Greenwood[C]

Moon for the Misbegotten, A (1984) Brian Vahey[S][C]; Marc B. Weiss[L]

Moon for the Misbegotten, A (2000)

Pat Collins[L]; Jane Greenwood[C]; Eugene Lee[S]

Moon in the Yellow River, The (1932) Cleon Throckmorton[S]

Moon Is a Gong, The (1926) Rose T. Briggs[C]; John Dos Passos[S]; Mordecai Gorelik[S]

Moon Is Blue, The (1951) Stewart Chaney[S][L]; Ack[C]

Moon Is Down, The (1942) Howard Bay[S]; Rose Bogdanoff[C]

Moon of the Caribees, Etc. (1937) Perry Watkins[S]

Moon over Buffalo (1995) Ken Billington[L]; Heidi Ettinger[S]; Bob Mackie[C]

Moon over Mulberry Street (1935) Selma Alexander[C]; Louis Kennel[S]

Moon Vine, The (1943) Lucinda Ballard[S][C]

Moonbirds (1959) Leo Kerz[S][L]; Frank Thompson[C]

Moonchildren (1972) Martin Aronstein[L]; William Ritman[S]; Marjorie Slaiman[C]

Moondown (1915) NONE

Moonlight (1924) Mabel E. Johnston[C]; Joseph Urban[S]

Moonlight Mary (1916) Ack[L]

Moonshine (1905) NO PLAYBILL

Moony Shapiro Song Book, The (1981) Franne Lee[C]; Tharon Musser[L]; Saul Radomsky[S]

Moor Born (1934) Louis Kennel[S]; Helene Pons[C]

Moose Murders (1983) Pat Collins[L]; Marjorie Bradley Kellogg[S]; John Carver Sullivan[C]

Moral Fabric (1932) Bernard Brooks[S]

Morals (1925) Fania Mindell[C]; Donald Oenslager[S]

Morals of Marcus, The (1907) Ernest Gros[S]

More Stately Mansions (1967) Ben Edwards[S]; Jane Greenwood[C]; John Harvey[L]

More Than Queen (1899) Homer Emens[S]

More the Merrier, The (1941) Stewart Chaney[S]; Ack[C]

More to Love (1998) David Gallo[S]; Ann Hould-Ward[C]; Michael Lincoln[L]

Morey Amsterdam's Hilarities (1948) Crayon[S]; Ack[L]

Mormon Wife, The (1901) NONE

Morning After, The (1925) NONE

Morning Noon and Night (1968) Michael Annals[S][C]; Martin Aronstein[L]

Morning Star (1940) Howard Bay[S]; Alexander Jones[C]

Morning Star (1942) Hattie Carnegie[C]; Stewart Chaney[S]; Ack[C]

Morning's at Seven (1939) Lucinda Ballard[C]; Jo Mielziner[S][L]

Morning's at Seven (1980) Linda Fisher[C]; Richard Nelson[L]; William Ritman[S]

Morphia (1923) Reginald Pale[S]

Morris Dance, The (1917) Tony Sarg[S]; Ack[C]

Mort Sahl on Broadway! (1987) Roger Morgan[L]

Morte Civile, La (1907) NONE

Moscow Circus (1991) Stephen Bickford[S][L]; Audrey Carter[C]

Most Happy Fella, The (1956) Jo Mielziner[S][L]; Motley[C]

Most Happy Fella, The (1979) Gilbert V. Hemsley, Jr.[L]; Nancy Potts[C]; Douglas W. Schmidt[S]

Most Happy Fella, The (1991) Michael Anania[S]; Beba Shamash[C]; Mark W. Stanley[L]

Most Happy Fella, The (1992) John Lee Beatty[S]; Jess Goldstein[C]; Craig Miller[L]

Most Immoral Lady, A (1928) Jo Mielziner[S][L]; Ack[C]

Most of the Game (1935) Raymond Sovey[S]; Ack[C]

Mother (1910) NO PLAYBILL

Mother (1935) Charles Friedman[L]; Mordecai Gorelik[S]; Ack[C]

Mother Carey's Chickens (1917) Ack[L]

Mother Courage (1967) Charles Elson[L]; Zenobius Strzelecki[S]

Mother Courage and Her Children (1963) Ming Cho Lee[S]; Motley[C]; Tharon Musser[L]

Mother Earth (1972) Alan Kimmel[S]; Mary McKinley[C]; Paul Sullivan[L]

Mother Goose (1903) Robert Caney[S]; Henry Emden[S]; C. Formilli[S]; R. McCleery[S]; Bruce Smith[S]

Mother Lode (1934) Leigh Allen[S]; Kay Morrison[C]

Mother Lover, The (1969) Ben Edwards[S][L]; Jane Greenwood[C]

Mother Sings (1935) Harry Gordon

Bennett[S]; ACK[C]

Mother's Liberty Bond (1918) ACK[S][C][L]

Mother, The (1938) Lester Polakov[S]

Motor Girl, The (1909) Lee Lash Studios[S]; ACK[C]

Mountain Climber, The (1906) Homer Emens[S]; Edward G. Unitt[S]

Mountain Fury (1929) P. Dodd Ackerman[S]

Mountain Man, The (1921) Robert Edmond Jones[S]; ACK[C]

Mountain, The (1933) Stanley Fort[S]; Roy LaPaugh[S]

Mountebank, The (1923) René Hubert[C]; ACK[S][L]

Mourning Becomes Electra (1931) Robert Edmond Jones[S][C]; ACK[L]

Mourning Becomes Electra (1932) Robert Edmond Jones[S][C]; ACK[L]

Mourning Becomes Electra (1972) Marsha L. Eck[S]; Jules Fisher[L]; Noel Taylor[C]

Mourning Pictures (1974) Whitney Blausen[C]; John Jacobsen[S]; Spencer Mosse[L]

Move On, Sister (1933) P. Dodd Ackerman[S]

Move-On (1926) ACK[L]

Movers, The (1907) Ernest Gros[S]; ACK[C]

Mozart (1926) Edouard Jonas[S]; ACK[C][L]

Mr. Adam (1949) Phil Raiguel[S]; ACK[L]

Mr. and Mrs. Daventry (1910) E. G. Banks[S]; Walter Hann[S]

Mr. and Mrs. North (1941) Mildred Manning[C]; Jo Mielziner[S][L]

Mr. Barnum (1918) ACK[S][L]

Mr. Barry's Etchings (1950) Margaret Pemberton[C]; John Root[S]; ACK[L]

Mr. Bib (1941) Donald Oenslager[S]; Irene Sharaff[C]

Mr. Bluebeard (1903) Ernest Albert[S]; Arthur D. Brooks[S]; Henry Emden[S]; Bruce Gresham[S]; Julian Hicks[S]; R. McCleery[S]

Mr. Buttles (1910) NONE

Mr. Faust (1922) Lucy L'Engle[C]; Cleon Throckmorton[S]

Mr. Gilhooley (1930) Jo Mielziner[S][L]; ACK[C]

Mr. Hamlet of Broadway (1908) Melville Ellis[C]; John Whalen[L]; George Williams[S]; ACK[L]

Mr. Hopkinson (1906) Julian Hicks[S]; Madame Marte[C]; Madame Viola[C]

Mr. Lode of Koal (1909) NONE

Mr. Moneypenny (1928) Robert Edmond Jones[S][C]; Margaret Pemberton[C]

Mr. Myd's Mystery (1915) H. Robert Studio Law[S]; ACK[L]

Mr. Peebles and Mr. Hooker (1946) Frederick Fox[S]; Eleanor Goldsmith[C]

Mr. Pickwick (1903) NONE

Mr. Pickwick (1952) Kathleen Ankers[S][C][L]

Mr. Pim Passes By (1915) Henri Bendel[C]

Mr. Pim Passes By (1921) Lee Simonson[S]

Mr. Pim Passes By (1927) Kate Drain Lawson[S]; Lee Simonson[S]; ACK[C]

Mr. Preedy and the Countess (1910) ACK[C]

Mr. President (1962) Theoni V. Aldredge[C]; Jo Mielziner[S][L]

Mr. Roberts (1948) Jo Mielziner[S][L]; ACK[C]

Mr. Samuel (1930) Gates and Morange[S]; Anthony Greshoff[L]; Evelyn McHorter[C]

Mr. Smooth (1899) NONE

Mr. Strauss Goes to Boston (1945) Stewart Chaney[S]; Walter Florell[C]

Mr. Sycamore (1942) Samuel Leve[S]; Emeline Clarke Roche[C]

Mr. Wix of Wickham (1904) NONE

Mr. Wonderful (1956) Peggy Clark[L]; Robert Mackintosh[C]; Oliver Smith[S]

Mr. Wu (1914) ACK[C]

Mrs. Avery (1911) Walter W. Burridge[S]

Mrs. Battle's Bath (1905) No PLAYBILL

Mrs. Black Is Back (1904) NONE

Mrs. Boltay's Daughters (1915) NONE

Mrs. Bumpstead-Leigh (1911) D. Frank Dodge[S]

Mrs. Bumpstead-Leigh (1929) Gates and Morange[S]

Mrs. Dakon (1909) NONE

Mrs. Dally (1965) David Hays[S][L]; Ann Roth[C]

Mrs. Dane's Defense (1900) Robert Caney[C]; Edward G. Unitt[S]

Mrs. Dane's Defense (1928) Yetta Kiviette[C]; ACK[L]

Mrs. Deering's Divorce (1903) NONE

Mrs. Dot (1910) Unitt and Wickes[S];

Milnor Wells[L]

Mrs. Gibbon's Boys (1949) John Robert Lloyd[C]; John Root[S][L]

Mrs. Gorringe's Necklace (1904) Worth[C]

Mrs. Jack (1902) Julia Carroll[C]; Joseph L. Menchen, Jr.[L]; Joseph Physioc[S]

Mrs. January and Mr. X (1944) Gilbert Adrian[C]; Paul Morrison[S][L]

Mrs. Kimball Presents (1944) Cirker and Robbins[S]

Mrs. Leffingwell's Boots (1905) NONE

Mrs. McThing (1952) Lucinda Ballard[C]; Lester Polakov[S]

Mrs. Moonlight (1930) Thomas Farrar[S]; Ellen Goldsborough[C]

Mrs. O'Brien Entertains (1939) Jo Mielziner[S][C][L]

Mrs. Partridge Presents (1925) Jo Mielziner[S][L]

Mrs. Patterson (1954) Raoul Pène Du Bois[S][C]

Mrs. Peckham's Carouse (1913) Gates and Morange[S]

Mrs. Temple's Telegram (1905) Joseph Physioc[S]; ACK[L]

Mrs. Warren's Profession (1905) NONE

Mrs. Warren's Profession (1907) NONE

Mrs. Warren's Profession (1922) ACK[L]

Mrs. Wiggs of the Cabbage Patch (1904) NONE

Mrs. Wilson, That's All (1906) NONE

Mrs. Xmas Angel (1912) NONE

Much Ado About Nothing (1900) ACK[C]

Much Ado About Nothing (1904) C. Karl[C]; John H. Young[S]

Much Ado About Nothing (1907) Emens and Unitt[S]

Much Ado About Nothing (1912) Grace O. Clarke[S]; Mr. Albert Herter[C]

Much Ado About Nothing (1913) E. Hamilton Bell[C]; Callot Soeurs[C]; Madame Freisinger[C]; Maurice Hermann[C]

Much Ado About Nothing (1927) Gates and Morange[S]; William Weaver[C]; ACK[L]

Much Ado About Nothing (1952) Stewart Chaney[S][C]

Much Ado About Nothing (1959)

Mariano Andreu[S][C]; Paul Morrison[L]

Much Ado About Nothing (1972) Theoni V. Aldredge[C]; Martin Aronstein[L]; Ming Cho Lee[S]

Much Ado About Nothing (1984) Jeffrey Beecroft[L]; Terry Hands[L]; John Kasarda[S]; Ralph Koltai[S]; Alexander Reid[C]

Mud Turtle, The (1925) Nicholas Yellenti[S]; ACK[L]

Mulatto (1935) Franklyn Ambrose[S]; Stephen Golding[S]

Mulberry Bush, The (1927) Edward Knoblock[C]; August Vimnera[S]

Mule Bone (1991) Lewis Brown[C]; Edward Burbridge[S]; Allen Lee Hughes[L]

Mum's the Word (1940) ACK[L]

Mummenschanz (1986) Beverly Emmons[L]

Mummy and the Humming Bird, The (1902) Mrs. Robert Osborn[C]

Mundy Scheme, The (1969) William Ritman[S][L]; Noel Taylor[C]

Murder among Friends (1975) Joseph G. Aulisi[C]; Santo Loquasto[S]; Jennifer Tipton[L]

Murder at the Howard Johnson's (1979) Sara Brook[C]; Karl Eigsti[S]; Richard Nelson[L]

Murder at the Vanities (1933) John N. Booth, Jr.[C]; Brymer[C]; Mabel E. Johnston[C]; Max Teuber[S]

Murder in the Cathedral (1936) Tom Adrian Cracraft[S][C]

Murder in the Cathedral (1938) Andre Bicat[S]; Stella Mary Pearce[C]

Murder on the Second Floor (1929) P. Dodd Ackerman[S]

Murder without Crime (1943) Raymond Sovey[S]

Murderer among Us, A (1964) David Hays[S][L]; Fred Voelpel[C]

Murray Anderson's Almanac (1929) Peter Arno[C]; Jacques Darcy[C]; Charles LeMaire[C]; Robert E. Locher[C]; Clarke Robinson[S]; E. Carlton Winckler[L]; Wynn[C]

Murray Will (1927) Rollo Wayne[S]; ACK[C]

Music Box Revue (1921) Henri Bendel[C]; Cora MacGeachy[C]; Ralph Mulligan[C]; Alice O'Neil[C]; Clarke Robinson[S]

Music Box Revue (1922) Ralph Mulligan[C]; Clarke Robinson[S];

Ack(L)

Music Box Revue (1923) Clarke Robinson(S); William Weaver(C)

Music Box Revue (1924) Mabel E. Johnston(C); Max Ree(C); Roy Requa(C); James Reynolds(C); Clarke Robinson(S)

Music Hath Charms (1934) Watson Barratt(S); Ernest Schraps(C)

Music in May (1929) Watson Barratt(S); Orry-Kelly(C); Ernest Schraps(C)

Music in My Heart (1947) Alvin Colt(S)(C); Hassard Short(L)

Music in the Air (1932) John W. Harkrider(C); Joseph Urban(S)

Music in the Air (1951) Lemuel Ayers(S)(C); Charles Elson(L)

Music Is (1976) Eldon Elder(S); H. R. Poindexter(L); Lewis Rampino(C)

Music Man, The (1957) Howard Bay(S)(L); Raoul Pène Du Bois(C)

Music Man, The (1980) Marcia Madeira(L); Stanley Simmons(C); Peter Wolf(S)

Music Man, The (2000) Peter Kaczorowski(L); William Ivey Long(C); Thomas Lynch(S)

Music Master, The (1904) Wilfred Buckland(S); Ernest Gros(S); Louis Hartmann(L)

Music Master, The (1916) Ernest Gros(S); Ack(C)(L)

Musical Chairs (1980) Michael J. Cesario(C); Peggy Clark(L); Ernest Allen Smith(S)

Musical Comedy Murders, The (1987) Jeff Davis(L); David Potts(S); Jennifer von Mayrhauser(C)

Musical Jubilee, A (1975) Donald Brooks(C); Herbert Senn(S); Thomas Skelton(L)

Musk (1920) Ack(S)(C)(L)

My Aunt from Yplilanti (1923) Ack(C)

My Aunt from Ypsilanti (1923) Charles J. Auburn(S); Ack(L)

My Best Girl (1912) H. Robert Law(S); Ack(S)

My Country (1926) Ack(L)

My Darlin' Aida (1952) Lemuel Ayers(S)(C)(L)

My Daughter, Your Son (1969) John Harvey(L); Ann Roth(C); Robin Wagner(S)

My Dear Children (1940) Donald Oenslager(S); Bianca Stroock(C)

My Dear Public (1943) Lucinda Ballard(C); Albert R. Johnson(S)

My Fair Ladies (1941) Watson Barratt(S); Mabel E. Johnston(C)

My Fair Lady (1956) Cecil Beaton(C); A. H. Feder(L); Oliver Smith(S)

My Fair Lady (1976) Cecil Beaton(C); John Gleason(L); Oliver Smith(S)

My Fair Lady (1981) Cecil Beaton(C); Ken Billington(L); John David Ridge(C); Oliver Smith(S)

My Fair Lady (1993) Natasha Katz(L); Ralph Koltai(S); Patricia Zipprodt(C)

My Fat Friend (1974) Martin Aronstein(L); Sara Brook(C); William Ritman(S)

My Favorite Year (1992) Jules Fisher(L); Thomas Lynch(S); Patricia Zipprodt(C)

My Girl (1924) P. Dodd Ackerman(S); Travis Banton(C); Ack(L)

My Girl Friday (1929) Ack(S)(L)

My Golden Girl (1920) Ack(L)

My Heart's in the Highlands (1938) Herbert Andrews(S)(C); Michael Gordon(L)

My Innocent Boy (1899) Arthur Voegtlin(S)

My Lady (1901) William Gill(S)

My Lady Dainty (1901) None

My Lady Friends (1919) Ack(C)(L)

My Lady Molly (1904) B. J. Simmons(C); Ack(S)(L)

My Lady Peggy Goes to Town (1903) Marie Cummings(C); Harley Merry(S); Ack(C)

My Lady's Dress (1914) Lucile(C); Ack(C)

My Lady's Garter (1915) Ack(L)

My Lady's Glove (1917) Ack(C)(L)

My Lady's Honor (1915) B. Russell Herts(S); Ada Rainey(C)

My Lady's Lord (1899) Henry Dazian(C); Ernest Gros(S); Henry E. Hoyt(S); Helen Windsor(C)

My Lady's Maid (1906) No Playbill

My Little Friend (1913) None

My Magnolia (1926) Ack(L)

My Man (1910) Ack(S)

My Maryland (1927) Watson Barratt(S)

My Milliner's Bill and Marietta (1904) No Playbill

My Mother, My Father and Me (1963) Howard Bay(S)(L); Dorothy Jeakins(C)

My Name Is Aquilon (1949) Stewart Chaney(S); Ack(L)

My One and Only (1983) Adrianne Lobel[S]; Marcia Madeira[L]; Rita Ryack[C]

My Princess (1927) P. Dodd Ackerman[S]; Charles LeMaire[C]

My Romance (1948) Watson Barratt[S]; Lou Eisele[C]; ACK[L]

My Sister Eileen (1940) Mildred Manning[C]; Donald Oenslager[S]

My Sister, My Sister (1974) Kathleen Ankers[C]; Larry Crimmins[L]; Lawrence King[S]

My Sweet Charley (1966) Jack Martin Lindsay[C]; Jo Mielziner[S][L]

My Thing of Love (1995) John Lee Beatty[S]; Howell Binkley[L]; Erin Quigley[C]

My Three Angels (1953) Boris Aronson[S]; Lucinda Ballard[C]

My Wife (1907) Edward G. Unitt[S]; Joseph Wickes[S]

My Wife Won't Let Me (1906) No PLAYBILL

My Wife's Husbands (1903) NONE

Myself - Bettina (1908) NONE

Mystery Man, The (1928) Nicholas Yellenti[S]

Mystery Moon (1930) ACK[S][C]

Mystery of Edwin Drood, The (1985) Lindsay W. Davis[C]; Paul Gallo[L]; Bob Shaw[S]

Mystery Shop, The (1927) Nicholas Yellenti[S]; ACK[C]

Naked (1926) ACK[L]

Naked Genius, The (1943) Frederick Fox[S]; Billy Livingston[C]

Nan (1913) NONE

Nance Oldfield (1899) NONE

Nance Oldfield (1907) NONE

Nancy Ann (1924) Raymond Sovey[S]; ACK[C]

Nancy Brown (1903) Frank E. Gates[S]; Edward Morange[S]

Nancy Lee (1918) Henri Bendel[C]; ACK[S][L]

Nancy Stair (1905) Emens and Unitt[S]

Nancy's Private Affair (1930) Eddie Eddy[S]; ACK[C]

Napi (1931) ACK[S][C][L]

Napoleon (1928) Cleon Throckmorton[S]; ACK[C]

Narrow Path, The (1909) NONE

Nash at Nine (1973) Theoni V. Aldredge[C]; Martin Aronstein[L]; David Chapman[S]

Nathan the Wise (1942) Rose

Bogdanoff[C]; Cleon Throckmorton[S]

Nathan Weinstein, Mystic, Connecticut (1966) Ben Edwards[S][L]; Jane Greenwood[C]

National Anthem, The (1922) ACK[S][C][L]

National Health, The (1974) Whitney Blausen[C]; Ronald Wallace[L]; Virginia Dancy Webb[S]

National Theatre of the Deaf, The (1969) John Gleason[L]; David Hays[S]; Patricia Zipprodt[C]

Native Ground (1937) Howard Bay[S]; A. H. Feder[L]; Florence Sachnoff[C]

Native Son (1941) Nat Lewis[C]; James Morcom[S]; ACK[L]

Native Son (1942) James Morcom[S]

Natja (1925) ACK[S][C][L]

Natural Affection (1963) Jack Brown[L]; Ann Roth[C]; Oliver Smith[S]

Natural Law, The (1915) Henri Bendel[C]; Homer Emens[S]

Natural Look, The (1967) Patton Campbell[C]; Jules Fisher[L]; Ed Wittstein[S]

Nature's Nobleman (1921) ACK[C]

Nature's Way (1957) Donald Oenslager[S][L]; Frank Thompson[C]

Naughty Anthony (1900) Ernest Gros[S]

Naughty Cinderella (1925) Paul Poiret[S][C]

Naughty Marietta (1910) Will R. Barnes[C]; Julius F. Dowe[S]; Theodore Reisig[S]

Naughty Marietta (1929) ACK[C][L]

Naughty Marietta (1931) ACK[C][L]

Naughty Naught '00 (1937) Eugene Dunkel[S]; Kermit Love[C]

Naughty Riquette (1926) ACK[C][L]

Ne'er-Do-Well, The (1912) Arthur Voegtlin[S]; ACK[C]

Near Santa Barbara (1921) NONE

Nearly a Hero (1908) Edward G. Unitt[S]; Arthur Voegtlin[S]

Nearly Married (1913) Madame Julie[C]

Necken, The (1913) ACK[C]

Ned and Jack (1981) James Leonard Joy[S]; Robby Monk[L]; David Murin[C]

Ned Mc Cobb's Daughter (1926) Aline Bernstein[S][C]

Ned Wayburn's Gambols (1929) Charles LeMaire[C]; Ted Weidhaas[S]; ACK[L]

Ned Wayburn's Town Topics (1915) Vyvian Donner[C]; Lucile[C]; Cora

MacGeachy[C]; Ack[S][L]

Neighborhood Playhouse at 50–A Celebration (1978) Pat Britten[C]; Michelle Nezwarsky[C]; Richard Winkler[L]

Neighbors (1923) Woodman Thompson[S][C]

Nell Go In (Nell Gwynne) (1900) NONE

Nellie Bly (1946) Nat Karson[S][C][L]

Nemesis (1921) Ack[C]

Neptune's Daughter (1906) H. M. Bowdoin[S]; Arthur Voegtlin[S]

Nerd, The (1987) John Lee Beatty[S]; Dennis Parichy[L]; Deborah Shaw[C]

Nerves (1924) Jo Mielziner[S][L]; Ack[C]

Nervous Set, The (1959) Theoni V. Aldredge[C]; Paul Morrison[S][L]

Nervous Wreck, The (1923) William Oden Waller[S]

Nest Egg, The (1910) NONE

Nest, The (1922) Kennel and Entwistle[S][L]; Ack[C]

Net, The (1919) Ack[C][L]

Never Homes, The (1911) David Atchison[L]; Cora MacGeachy[C]; Arthur Voegtlin[S]

Never Live over a Pretzel Factory (1964) Howard Bay[S][L]; Frank Thompson[C]

Never No More (1932) Julia Carlisle[C]; Jo Mielziner[S][L]

Never Say Die (1912) NONE

Never Say Never (1951) Frederick Fox[S]; Alice Gibson[C]

Never Too Late (1962) William and Jean Eckart[S][L]; Florence Klotz[C]

Nevertheless (1916) Ack[S][L]

New Brooms (1924) Gates and Morange[S]; Mrs. Raymond Hitchcock[C]; Ack[L]

New Chauve-Souris (1931) Yury Annyenkov[S][C]; Natalia Gontcharova[S][C]

New Clown, The (1902) Edward G. Unitt[S]

New Dominion, The (1906) NONE

New England Folks (1901) Homer Emens[S]

New Englander, The (1924) Woodman Thompson[S]

New Faces (1934) Sergi Soudeikine[S][C]

New Faces of '56 (1956) Thomas Becher[C]; Peggy Clark[L]; Peter Larkin[S]

New Faces of '62 (1961) Thomas

Becher[C]; Marvin Reiss[S][L]

New Faces of 1936 (1936) Stewart Chaney[S][C]; A. H. Feder[L]

New Faces of 1943 (1942) Edward Gilbert[S][C]; E. Carlton Winckler[L]

New Faces of 1952 (1952) Thomas Becher[C]; Raoul Pène Du Bois[S]

New Faces of 1968 (1968) Winn Morton[S][C]; Paul Sullivan[L]

New Gallantry, The (1925) Ack[S][C][L]

New Girl in Town (1957) Rouben Ter-Arutunian[S][C][L]

New Henrietta, The (1913) Frank Detering[L]; T. Bernard McDonald[S]; Unitt and Wickes[S]

New Lady Bantock, The (1909) Ack[C]

New Life, A (1943) Howard Bay[S]

New Moon, The (1928) Charles LeMaire[C]; Donald Oenslager[S]

New Moon, The (1942) Ack[L]

New Morality, The (1921) NONE

New Music Hall of Israel, The (1969) James Hamilton[S][L]; Lydia Pincus-Gany[C]

New Poor, The (1924) H. Robert Studio Law[S]; Ack[C]

New Priorities of 1943 (1942) Helen Mahieu[C]; Ack[L]

New Secretary, The (1913) Ernest Gros[S]

New Sin, The (1912) NONE

New Toys (1924) Raymond Sovey[S]; Ack[C]

New York (1910) NO PLAYBILL

New York (1927) Ack[C][L]

New York Exchange (1926) Schaffner and Sweet Studio[S]; Ack[C][L]

New York Idea, The (1906) Gates and Morange[S]; Ack[C]

New York Idea, The (1915) Elizabeth Axtman[C]; B. Russell Herts[S]

New York Idea, The (1933) Ack[S][C][L]

New York Summer (1979) Frank Spencer[C]; Billy B. Walker[L]; Ack[S]

New York to Cherbourg (1932) Stephen Gordon[S]; Bianca Stroock[C]; Ack[L]

New Yorkers, The (1901) Ernest Albert[S]; D. Frank Dodge[S]

New Yorkers, The (1927) Peter Arno[C]; Charles LeMaire[C]; Clarke Robinson[L]; Dale Stetson[S]

New Yorkers, The (1930) Peter Arno[S][C]; Charles LeMaire[C]; Dale Stetson[S]

Newcomers, The (1923) Karle O. Amend Studio[S]; ACK[C][L]

Newlyweds and Their Baby, The (1909) P. Dodd Ackerman[S]

News, The (1985) Norman Coates [American][L]; Richard Hornung[C]; Jane Musky[S]

Next Half Hour, The (1945) Edward Gilbert[S]; Mary Percy Schenck[C]

Next of Kin, The (1909) NONE

Next President, The-A Musical Salamagundi (1958) Lee Watson[S][C][L]

Next Time I'll Sing to You (1974) Martin Aronstein[L]; John David Ridge[C]

Next! (1911) NONE

Nic Nax of 1926 (1926) John Dwyer[S]

Nica (1926) Miss Dora Malet[C]; ACK[L]

Nice People (1921) Henri Bendel[C]; Peggy Hoyt[C]; Lucile[C]; ACK[S]

Nice Wanton (1911) E. Hamilton Bell[S]

Nice Women (1929) Karle O. Amend Studio[S]; Cirker and Robbins[S]; ACK[C][L]

Nick & Nora (1991) Theoni V. Aldredge[C]; Jules Fisher[L]; Douglas W. Schmidt[S]

Nifties of 1923 (1923) Gilbert Adrian[C]; Ernest Gros[S]; Yetta Kiviette[C]; Herbert Ward[S]

Nigger Rich (1929) Rollo Wayne[S]; ACK[C]

Nigger, The (1909) Homer Emens[S]

Night and Day (1979) Neil Peter Jampolis[L]; Carl Toms[S][C]

Night before Christmas, The (1941) Boris Aronson[S]; ACK[C]

Night Boat, The (1920) O'Kane Conwell[C]; Dodge and Castle[S]; ACK[L]

Night Call, The (1922) John Brunton[S]; ACK[C][L]

Night Circus, The (1958) David Hays[S]; Lee Watson[L]; Patricia Zipprodt[C]

Night Duel, The (1926) Joseph Physioc[S]; ACK[C][L]

Night Hawk (1925) Walter Sherwood[S]; ACK[L]

Night Hawk (1926) Walter Sherwood[S]; ACK[C][L]

Night Hostess (1928) Margaret Pemberton[C]; R. N. Robbins[S]; ACK[L]

Night in Avignon, A (1919) Frank J. Zimmerer[S][C]

Night in Paris, A (1926) Watson Barratt[S]; Erté[C]; Ernest Schraps[C]; ACK[C]

Night in Spain, A (1917) Watson Barratt[S]; Ernest Schraps[C]; ACK[L]

Night in Spain, A (1927) Watson Barratt[S]; Ernest Schraps[C]

Night in the House (1935) Aline Bernstein[S][C]

Night in Venice, A (1929) Watson Barratt[S]

Night Life (1962) Alice Gibson[C]; Albert R. Johnson[S][L]

Night Lodging (1919) Fania Mindell[S]; ACK[L]

'night Mother (1983) Heidi Ettinger[S][C]; James F. Ingalls[L]

Night Music (1940) Michael Gordon[L]; Mordecai Gorelik[S]; Paul Morrison[C]

Night Must Fall (1936) Edward Carrick[S]; ACK[C][L]

Night Must Fall (1999) Jess Goldstein[C]; Brian MacDevitt[L]; James Noone[S]

Night of 100 Stars III (1990) Alvin Colt[C]; Jeff Engel[L]; Ray Klausen[S]

Night of January 16 (1935) Herbert Moore[S]; Bianca Stroock[C]

Night of Love (1941) Watson Barratt[S]; Ernest Schraps[C]

Night of the 4th, The (1901) Gates and Morange[S]; Al. Lawrence[S]; P. J. McDonald[S]; ACK[C]

Night of the Auk (1956) Howard Bay[S][L]; ACK[C]

Night of the Iguana, The (1961) Jean Rosenthal[L]; Oliver Smith[S]; Noel Taylor[C]

Night of the Iguana, The (1976) H. R. Poindexter[S][L]; Noel Taylor[C]

Night of the Iguana, The (1988) Zack Brown[S]; Richard Nelson[L]; Jennifer von Mayrhauser[C]

Night of the Iguana, The (1996) Loy Arcenas[S]; Susan Hilferty[C]; James F. Ingalls[L]

Night of the Party, The (1902) ACK[C]

Night of the Tribades, The (1977) Jane Greenwood[C]; Lawrence King[S]; John McLain[L]

Night over Taos (1932) Robert Edmond Jones[S][C]

Night Remembers, The (1934) ACK[L]

Night That Made America Famous, The (1975) Randy Barcelo[C]; Imero Fiorentino[L]; Kert Lundell[S]

Night Watch (1972) Donald Brooks[C]; George Jenkins[S]; Tharon Musser[L]

Nightcap, The (1921) P. Dodd Ackerman[S]; ACK[C]

Nightie Night (1919) ACK[S][L]

Nightingale, The (1927) Watson Barratt[S]; ACK[C]

Nightstick (1927) Nicholas Yellenti[S]; ACK[C]

Nikki (1931) P. Dodd Ackerman[S]; Karle O. Amend[S]; ACK[C][L]

Nina (1951) Charles Elson[S][C][L]; Miss Gloria Swanson[C]

Nina Rosa (1930) Watson Barratt[S]; Orry-Kelly[C]; ACK[L]

Nine (1982) William Ivey Long[C]; Marcia Madeira[L]; Lawrence Miller[S]

Nine Girls (1943) John Root[S]; ACK[C]

Nine Pine Street (1933) Robert Edmond Jones[S][C]

Nine Till Six (1930) Mercie McHardy[C]; Rollo Wayne[S]

Nine-Fifteen Revue (1930) Yetta Kiviette[C]; Clarke Robinson[S]

Nineteenth Hole, The (1927) ACK[C][L]

Ninety and Nine, The (1902) Kliegl Brothers[L]; Joseph Physioc[S]

Ninety-Day Mistress, The (1967) Clarke Dunham[L]; Leon Munier[S]; Pearl Somner[C]

Ninth Guest, The (1930) P. Dodd Ackerman[S]; ACK[C]

Nirvana (1926) ACK[L]

Nju (1917) Joseph Urban[S]; ACK[L]

No Exit (1946) Frederick Kiesler[S][L]; ACK[C]

No Foolin' (1926) John W. Harkrider[C]; Greta and Agnes Nissen[C]; Joseph Urban[S]; John Wenger[S]

No Hard Feelings (1973) Theoni V. Aldredge[C]; Robert Randolph[S][L]

No Man's Land (1976) John Bury[S][C][L]

No Man's Land (1994) Jane Greenwood[C]; David Jenkins[S]; Richard Nelson[L]

No More Blondes (1920) ACK[L]

No More Frontier (1931) John Marshall Coombs[S][L]; ACK[C]

No More Ladies (1934) Watson Barratt[S]; Yetta Kiviette[C]; ACK[C]

No More Peace (1938) Ben Edwards[S][C]; A. H. Feder[L]

No More Women (1926) ACK[C][L]

No Other Girl (1924) Erle Payne Franke[C]; Livingston Platt[S]; ACK[L]

No Place to Be Somebody (1969) Theoni V. Aldredge[C]; Michael Davidson[S][L]

No Place to be Somebody (1971) Conrad Penrod[L]; John Retsek[S]; ACK[C]

No Questions Asked (1934) P. Dodd Ackerman[S]; Brymer[C]

No Sex Please, We're British (1973) John Harvey[L]; Jeffrey B. Moss[C]; Helen Pond[S]; Herbert Senn[S]

No Strings (1961) Donald Brooks[C]; David Hays[S][L]

No Time for Comedy (1938) Lucile[C]; Jo Mielziner[S][L]; Valentina[C]

No Time for Sergeants (1955) Peggy Clark[L]; Peter Larkin[S]; Noel Taylor[C]

No Trespassing (1926) Clarke Robinson[S]; ACK[C]

No Way Out (1944) Edward Gilbert[S]; Ernest Schraps[C]

No, No Nanette (1925) P. Dodd Ackerman[S]; Corinne Barker[C]

No, No, Nanette (1971) Raoul Pène Du Bois[S][C]; Jules Fisher[L]

Noah (1935) Ludwig Bemelmans[C]; Cleon Throckmorton[S]

Noah's Flood (1911) NO PLAYBILL

Noble Experiment, The (1930) Louis Bromberg[S]

Noble Rogue, A (1929) ACK[L]

Noble Spaniard, The (1909) Mr. Tom Heslewood[C]; ACK[S]

Nobody Home (1915) Elsie de Wolfe[S]; ACK[C][L]

Nobody Loves an Albatross (1963) Will Steven Armstrong[S][L]; Florence Klotz[C]

Nobody's Business (1923) ACK[C][L]

Nobody's Daughter (1911) E. Hamilton Bell[S][C]; Homer Emens[S]; Unitt and Wickes[S]

Nobody's Money (1921) P. Dodd Ackerman[S]; Joseph L. Menchen, Jr.[L]; ACK[C]

Nobody's Widow (1910) Ernest Gros[S]

Nocturne (1925) David S. Gaither[S]

Noel Coward in Two Keys (1974) Ray Diffen[C]; William Ritman[S][L]

Noel Coward's Sweet Potato (1968) Peter Hunt[L]; Helen Pond[S]; Herbert Senn[S]; David Toser[C]

Noises Off (1983) Michael Annals[S][C]; Martin Aronstein[L]

Nona (1932) P. Dodd Ackerman[S];

Howard Shoup[C]

None So Blind (1910) Gates and Morange[S]

Noose, The (1926) P. Dodd Ackerman Studio[S]; ACK[C][L]

Norman Conquests, The (1975) Robert Randolph[S][L]; Noel Taylor[C]

Norman, Is That You? (1970) Fred Allison[L]; William and Jean Eckart[S]; Florence Klotz[C]

Not about Nightingales (1999) Richard Hoover[S]; Karyl Newman[C]; Chris Parry[L]

Not for Children (1951) Edith Lutyens Bel Geddes[C]; Mainbocher[C]; John Root[S][L]

Not Herbert (1926) Hartmann and Fantana[S]; ACK[C]

Not Now, Darling (1970) Lloyd Burlingame[S][C][L]

Not So Fast (1923) P. Dodd Ackerman Studio[S]; Joseph Physioc Studio[S]; ACK[C][L]

Not So Long Ago (1920) ACK[L]

Not with My Money (1918) ACK[L]

Nothing But Lies (1918) Henri Bendel[C]; Joseph Urban[S]; ACK[L]

Nothing But Love (1919) Vincent Collins[S]; Homer Conant[C]; John H. M. Dudley[S]; Hickson[C]; ACK[L]

Notorious Mrs. Ebbsmith, The (1902) NONE

Notre Dame (1902) Edward G. Unitt[S]

November People, The (1978) Joseph G. Aulisi[C]; Kert Lundell[S]; Thomas Skelton[L]

Novice and the Duke, The (1929) Edgar Bohlman[S]

Now I Lay Me Down to Sleep (1950) John Derro[C]; Wolfgang Roth[S]; ACK[L]

Now You've Done It (1937) Margaret Pemberton[C]; John Root[S]

Now-a-Days (1929) ACK[S][L]

Nowhere Bound (1935) Karle O. Amend[S]

Nowhere to Go But Up (1962) Robert Fletcher[C]; Peter Larkin[S]; Tharon Musser[L]

Nude with Violin (1957) Peggy Clark[L]; Oliver Smith[S]; Frank Thompson[C]

Number 7 (1926) ACK[L]

Number, The (1951) Ralph Alswang[S]; Jocelyn[C]

Nurse Marjorie (1906) NONE

Nut Farm, The (1929) A. J. Lundborg[S]; ACK[C]

Nuts (1980) Roger Morgan[L]; Tom Schwinn[S]; Christina Weppner[C]

O Evening Star (1936) Stewart Chaney[S]; ACK[C]

O Mistress Mine (1946) Robert Davison[S]; Molyneux[C]

O'Brien Girl, The (1921) Alice O'Neil[C]; Unitt and Wickes[S]

O'Flynn, The (1934) James Reynolds[S][C]

O'Neill of Derry (1907) Homer Emens[S]; T. Bernard McDonald[S]; Unitt and Wickes[S]; Franklin Van Horn[C]

O, Nightingale (1925) Cleon Throckmorton[S]; ACK[C]

Oba Oba (1987) Steve Cochrane[L]; ACK[S]

Obsession (1946) Gilbert Adrian[C]; Stewart Chaney[S][L]

Occupe Toi d'Amelie (1952) Félix Labisse[S]; Jean-Denis Malclès[C]; ACK[L]

Octette Bridge Club, The (1985) John Lee Beatty[S]; Roger Morgan[L]; Carrie F. Robbins[C]

Octoroon, The (1929) Charles Chrisdie[C]; Benjamin Leffler[L]; ACK[S]

Odd Couple, The (1965) Jean Rosenthal[L]; Ann Roth[C]; Oliver Smith[S]

Odd Couple, The (1985) David Mitchell[S]; Tharon Musser[L]; Ann Roth[C]

Odd Man Out (1925) Cleon Throckmorton[S]; ACK[C][L]

Odds and Ends of 1917 (1917) Henri Bendel[C]; Yetta Kiviette[C]; ACK[S][L]

Odds on Mrs. Oakley, The (1944) Frederick Fox[S]; Bianca Stroock[C]

Ode to Liberty (1934) Cleon Throckmorton[S]; ACK[C]

Oedipus (1913) NONE

Oedipus (1946) Marie-Hèléne Dasté[C]; John Piper[S]; John Sullivan[L]

Oedipus Rex (1907) NONE

Oedipus Rex (1911) NONE

Oedipus Rex (1923) ACK[L]

Oedipus Rex (1948) Marie-Hèléne Dasté[C]; John Piper[S]; John Sullivan[L]

Oedipus Tyrannus (1952) C. Clonis[S]; Antonios Phocas[C]

Of Love Remembered (1967) Saul

Bolasni[C]; Eldon Elder[S][L]

Of Mice and Men (1974) William and Jean Eckart[S][C][L]

Of the Fields, Lately (1980) Richard Dorfman[L]; Dolores Gamba[C]; J. Robin Modereger[S]

Of Thee I Sing (1931) Charles LeMaire[C]; Jo Mielziner[S][L]; Max Weldy[C]

Of Thee I Sing (1933) Charles LeMaire[C]; Jo Mielziner[S]; Max Weldy[C]

Of Thee I Sing (1952) Peggy Clark[L]; Albert R. Johnson[S]; Irene Sharaff[C]

Of V We Sing (1942) ACK[S][C][L]

Off Chance, The (1918) Henri Bendel[C]; Homer Emens[S]; ACK[L]

Off to Buffalo (1939) Donald Oenslager[S]

Off-Key (1927) DuWico[L]; ACK[S][C]

Offence, The (1925) Rollo Wayne[S]

Offenders, The (1908) Joseph Physioc[S]

Office Boy, The (1903) NONE

Officer 666 (1912) NONE

Oh Boy! (1917) D. M. Akin[S]; ACK[C][L]

Oh Captain! (1958) Jo Mielziner[S][L]; Miles White[C]

Oh Coward! (1986) F. Mitchell Dana[L]; Helen Pond[S]; Herbert Senn[S]; David Toser[C]

Oh Dad, Poor Dad, Mamma's Hung You... (1963) William and Jean Eckart[S]; Thomas Skelton[L]; Patricia Zipprodt[C]

Oh What a Lovely War (1964) John Bury[S][L]; Una Collins[C]

Oh! Calcutta! (1971) David F. Segal[L]; James Tilton[S]; Fred Voelpel[C]

Oh! Calcutta! (1976) Harry Silverglat[L]; James Tilton[S]; Kenneth M. Yount[C]

Oh! Mama (1925) Henri Bendel[C]; Livingston Platt[S]; ACK[C][L]

Oh! Oh! Delphine (1912) F. Richards Anderson[C]; Frank Detering[L]; Homer Emens[S]; Unitt and Wickes[S]

Oh! Oh! Nurse (1925) Walter Schaffner[S]; ACK[C][L]

Oh, Brother (1945) Samuel Leve[S]; ACK[C]

Oh, Brother (1981) Paul de Pass[S]; Ann Emonts[C]; Michael J. Hotopp[S]; Richard Nelson[L]

Oh, Ernest (1927) Ward and Harvey Studios[S]; ACK[C][L]

Oh, Henry (1920) Dodge and Castle[S]; ACK[L]

Oh, I Say (1913) Lee Lash Studios[S]; James Surridge[S]; ACK[C]

Oh, Kay (1926) John Wenger[S]; ACK[C]

Oh, Kay (1928) John Wenger[S]; ACK[C]

Oh, Kay! (1990) Theoni V. Aldredge[C]; Kenneth Foy[S]; Craig Miller[L]

Oh, Lady! Lady! (1918) Eugene Braun[L]; Harry Collins[C]; Clifford F. Pember[S]

Oh, Look! (1918) H. Robert Law[S]; ACK[C][L]

Oh, Men! Oh, Women! (1953) Paul du Pont[C]; William and Jean Eckart[S]

Oh, Mr. Meadowbrook (1948) Lucille Little[C]; Wolfgang Roth[S]; ACK[L]

Oh, My Dear (1918) Eugene Braun[L]; Harry Collins[C]; Robert Milton[S]

Oh, Please (1926) James Reynolds[S][C]

Oh, Professor (1930) ACK[C][L]

Oh, Promise Me (1930) Cirker and Robbins[S]; ACK[C]

Oh, What a Girl (1919) Watson Barratt[S]; ACK[C][L]

Oklahoma! (1943) Lemuel Ayers[S]; Miles White[C]

Oklahoma! (1951) Lemuel Ayers[S]; Miles White[C]

Oklahoma! (1979) Paul de Pass[S]; Bill Hargate[C]; Michael J. Hotopp[S]; Thomas Skelton[L]

'Ol Man Satan (1932) Continer and Golding[S]

Old Acquaintance (1940) Richard Whorf[S]; ACK[C]

Old Bill, M.P. (1926) DuWico[L]; David S. Gaither[S]; ACK[C]

Old Country, The (1917) Mrs. E. J. Muldoon[C]; ACK[L]

Old Dutch (1909) Madame Castle-Bert[C]; Frederica DeWolfe[C]; Madame Ripley[C]; John Whalen[L]; John H. Young[S]

Old English (1924) Robert W. Bergman Studio[S]; ACK[C]

Old Firm, The (1913) NONE

Old Foolishness, The (1940) Mildred Manning[C]; Donald Oenslager[S]

Old Heidelberg (1903) NONE

Old Heidelberg (1910) E. Hamilton Bell[S][C]

Old Homestead, The (1904) Homer Emens[S]

Old Lady Says "No", The (1948) Hilton Edwards[L]; Micheal MacLiammoir[S][C]

Old Limerick Town (1902) NONE

Old Maid, The (1935) Stewart Chaney(S)(C)

Old Man Murphy (1931) Ward and Harvey Studios(S); ACK(C)

Old Neighborhood, The (1997) John Ambrosone(L); Kevin Rigdon(S); Harriet Voyt(C)

Old New Yorker, An (1911) H. Robert Law(S); Bert Tuchman(S)

Old Rascal, The (1930) Cleon Throckmorton(S)

Old Soak, The (1922) Cleon Throckmorton(S)

Old Times (1971) John Bury(S)(L); Beatrice Dawson(C)

Old Town, The (1910) Will R. Barnes(C); Homer Emens(S); Wilhelm(C)

Olive Latimer's Husband (1910) Ernest Gros(S); Lee Lash Studios(S); ACK(C)

Oliver Goldsmith (1900) NONE

Oliver Twist (1912) Gates and Morange(S)

Oliver! (1963) Sean Kenny(S)(C); John Wyckham(L)

Oliver! (1965) Sean Kenny(S)(C); John Wyckham(L)

Oliver! (1984) Andrew Bridge(L); Sean Kenny(S)(C)

Oliver! Oliver! (1934) Omar Kiam(C); Raymond Sovey(S)

Olympe (1904) D. Frank Dodge(S); John H. Young(S)

Olympia (1928) ACK(S)(C)(L)

Omar, the Tentmaker (1914) Wilfred Buckland(S); Kliegl Brothers(L); Eric Pape(C); Richard Walton Tully(S); Unitt and Wickes(S)

On a Clear Day You Can See Forever (1965) A. H. Feder(L); Oliver Smith(S); Freddy Wittop(C)

On an Open Roof (1963) Florence Klotz(C); Jean Rosenthal(S)(L)

On and Off (1901) Edward G. Unitt(S)

On Approval (1926) James Reynolds(S); ACK(C)

On Borrowed Time (1991) Mary Jo Dondlinger(L); Holly Hynes(C); Marjorie Bradley Kellogg(S)

On Borrowed Time (1938) Jo Mielziner(S)(L); ACK(C)

On Borrowed Time (1953) Paul Morrison(S)(C)(L)

On Call (1928) Cleon Throckmorton(S)

On Golden Pond (1979) Craig Miller(L);

Steven Rubin(S)(C)

On Location (1937) ACK(S)(C)

On Parole (1907) William Camph(S); Leon Mohn(S); Frederic Remington(S)

On Stage (1935) G. Bradford Ashworth(S); ACK(C)

On the Eve (1909) Hugo Baruch(C); Peter W. King(L); Joseph Physioc(S); ACK(C)

On the High Road (1929) Aline Bernstein(S)(C); Irene Sharaff(C)

On the Hiring Line (1919) Anthony Greshoff(L); Clifford F. Pember(S)

On the Make (1932) Cirker and Robbins(S); ACK(C)

On the Quiet (1901) Arthur Voegtlin(S)

On the Rocks (1938) Alexander Jones(C); Edwin J. Schruers(S)

On the Spot (1930) Rollo Wayne(S); ACK(C)

On the Stairs (1922) ACK(L)

On the Town (1944) Alvin Colt(C); Oliver Smith(S)

On the Town (1971) Raymond Aghayan(C); Bob Mackie(C); Tharon Musser(L); James Trittipo(S)

On the Town (1998) Paul Gallo(L); Adrianne Lobel(S); Paul Tazewell(C)

On the Twentieth Century (1978) Ken Billington(L); Florence Klotz(C); Robin Wagner(S)

On the Waterfront (1995) Ann Hould-Ward(C); Peter Kaczorowski(L); Eugene Lee(S)

On to Fortune (1935) Stewart Chaney(S); Margaret Pemberton(C); James Reynolds(C)

On Trial (1914) Joseph Wickes(S)

On Whitman Avenue (1946) Ricki Grisman(C); Donald Oenslager(S)(L)

On with the Dance (1917) Henri Bendel(C); Harry Collins(C); Hickson(C); ACK(L)

On Your Toes (1936) Jo Mielziner(S)(L); Irene Sharaff(C)

On Your Toes (1954) Peggy Clark(L); Irene Sharaff(C); Oliver Smith(S)

On Your Toes (1983) Zack Brown(S)(C); John McLain(L)

Once a Catholic (1979) Patricia Adshead(C); William Ritman(S); Marc B. Weiss(L)

Once for the Asking (1963) Audré(C); A. H. Feder(S)(L)

Once in a Lifetime (1930) Cirker and Robbins(S); ACK(C)

Once in a Lifetime (1978) F. Mitchell Dana[L]; Karl Eigsti[S]; Carol Luiken[C]

Once Is Enough (1938) Raymond Sovey[S]; ACK[C]

Once More, with Feeling (1958) George Jenkins[S][L]; Scaasi[C]; Michael Travis[C]

Once on This Island (1990) Loy Arcenas[S]; Judy Dearing[C]; Allen Lee Hughes[L]

Once over Lightly (1942) Richard Rychtarik[S]; ACK[C]

Once There Was a Russian (1961) Klaus Holm[L]; Tony Walton[S][C]

Once upon a Mattress (1996) John Lee Beatty[S]; Pat Collins[L]; Jane Greenwood[C]

Once upon a Tailor (1955) Boris Aronson[S]; Paul Morrison[C][L]

Once upon a Time (1905) Ernest Albert[S]

Once upon a Time (1918) ACK[L]

Once upon a Time (1939) Cirker and Robbins[S]; Bolton Wilder[L]

Ondine (1954) Peter Larkin[S]; Jean Rosenthal[L]; Richard Whorf[C]

One (1920) Henri Bendel[C]; Alexander Grinager[S]; Ernest Gros[S]; Victor Petry[S]; ACK[L]

One Act Play Festival, The (1981) David Murin[C]; John Wright Stevens[S]; Marc B. Weiss[L]

One Bright Day (1952) Raymond Sovey[S]; Noel Taylor[C]

One by One (1964) Florence Klotz[C]; Donald Oenslager[S][L]; Hannah Troy[C]

One Eye Closed (1954) Eldon Elder[S][L]; Virginia Volland[C]

One Flew over the Cuckoo's Nest (1963) Will Steven Armstrong[S][L]; Noel Taylor[C]

One Flew over the Cuckoo's Nest (2001) Laura Bauer[C]; Robert Brill[S]; Kevin Rigdon[L]

One for All (1927) Millard France[S]; ACK[L]

One for the Money (1939) John Murray Anderson[L]; Raoul Pène Du Bois[S][C]; Edward Clarke Lilley[L]

One Glorious Hour (1927) William Birns[S]; ACK[C][L]

One Good Year (1935) Karle O. Amend[S]; ACK[C]

One Heluva Night (1924) ACK[L]

One Kiss (1923) Ernest Gros[S]; Cora MacGeachy[C]; ACK[L]

One Man Show (1945) Stewart Chaney[S]; Valentina[C]; ACK[C]

One Man's Woman (1926) Louis Kennel[S]; ACK[L]

One More Honeymoon (1934) Karle O. Amend Studio[S]; ACK[C]

One More River (1960) George Jenkins[S][L]; Anna Hill Johnstone[C]

One Night in Rome (1919) Rollo Peters[S]; ACK[C][L]

One of the Family (1925) Sheldon K. Viele[S]; ACK[C][L]

One of Us (1918) ACK[S][L]

One Sunday Afternoon (1933) Eugene Dunkel[S]; A. H. Feder[L]; ACK[C]

One Thing after Another (1937) Phil MacDonald[C]; John Root[S]

One Third of a Nation (1937) Howard Bay[S]; Moe Hack[L]; Toni Ward[C]

One Touch of Venus (1943) Howard Bay[S]; Paul du Pont[C]

One Way Street (1928) ACK[L]

One Wife or Another (1933) Bernard Brooks[S]; ACK[L]

One, Two, Three/ The Violet (1930) Stanley Bell[S]; ACK[C][L]

Only 38 (1921) Edward B. Corey[S]

Only Game in Town, The (1968) Theoni V. Aldredge[C]; Jules Fisher[L]; George Jenkins[S]

Only Girl, The (1914) ACK[C]

Only Girl, The (1934) Dodge and Castle[S]; Ernest Schraps[C]; ACK[L]

Only in America (1959) Peter Larkin[S]; Ruth Morley[C]; Tharon Musser[L]

Only Law, The (1909) P. Dodd Ackerman[S]; ACK[C]

Only Son, The (1911) ACK[S][L]

Only the Heart (1944) Frederick Fox[S][L]

Only the Young (1932) ACK[S]

Only Way, The (1899) Henry Dazian[C]; Ernest Gros[S]

Onward Victoria (1980) Theoni V. Aldredge[C]; Richard Nelson[L]; William Ritman[S]

Op o' Me Thumb (1904) NONE

Open Admissions (1984) David Gropman[S]; Gary Jones[C]; Tharon Musser[L]; Ann Roth[C]

Open House (1947) Leo Kerz[S][C][L]

Opera Ball, The (1912) Dodge and Castle[S]; ACK[C]

Opportunity (1920) ACK[L]

Optimist, The (1906) NONE

Optimists, The (1928) ACK[L]

Orange Blossoms (1922) Norman Bel Geddes[S]; Ack[C]

Orchid, The (1907) None

Orchids Preferred (1937) Frederick Fox[S]; Ack[C]

Order Please (1934) Louis Kennel[S]; Margaret Pemberton[C]

Orpheus Descending (1957) Boris Aronson[S]; Lucinda Ballard[C]; A. H. Feder[L]

Orpheus Descending (1989) Alison Chitty[S][C]; Neil Peter Jampolis[L]; Paul Pyant[L]; Richard Schurkamp[C]

Oscar Wilde (1938) Raymond Sovey[S][C]; Ack[L]

Ostriches (1925) Ack[L]

Othello (1905) Mathias Armbruster[S]; Maurice Hermann[C]

Othello (1907) None

Othello (1913) None

Othello (1914) None

Othello (1925) Claude Bragdon[S][C]

Othello (1935) P. Dodd Ackerman[S]; Charles B. Falls[C]

Othello (1937) Robert Edmond Jones[S][C]

Othello (1943) Robert Edmond Jones[S][C][L]

Othello (1970) Karl Eigsti[S]; John Gleason[L]; Jane Greenwood[C]

Othello (1982) David Chapman[S]; Robert Fletcher[C]; Marc B. Weiss[L]

OtherFellow, The (1910) D. Frank Dodge[S]

Other Girl, The (1903) Mrs. Robert Osborn[C]; Unitt and Wickes[S]

Other House, The (1907) None

Other Men's Wives (1929) Raymond Sovey[S]; Ack[C]

Other One, The (1932) Cleon Throckmorton[S]; Ack[C]

Other Rose, The (1923) George Haddon[S]; Ack[C]

Otherwise Engaged (1977) Eileen Diss[S]; Jane Greenwood[C]; Neil Peter Jampolis[L]

Ouija Board, The (1920) Ack[L]

Our American Cousin (1908) Madame Freisinger[C]; Unitt and Wickes[S]

Our American Cousin (1915) Ack[L]

Our Betters (1917) Gates and Morange[S]; Hickson[C]; Ack[L]

Our Betters (1928) William E. Castle[S]; Ack[C][L]

Our Children (1915) Ack[L]

Our Country's Good (1991)

Christopher Barreca[S]; Candice Donnelly[C]; Mimi Jordan Sherin[L]

Our Lan' (1947) Ralph Alswang[S][L]

Our Little Wife (1916) Henri Bendel[C]; Ruth Carnegie[C]; Joseph Physioc[S]

Our Miss Gibbs (1910) Henry Dazian[C]; Ack[C]

Our Mrs. McChesney (1915) Homer Emens[S]

Our Nell (1922) H. Robert Studio Law[S]; Ack[C][L]

Our Pleasant Sins (1919) P. Dodd Ackerman Studio[S]; Ack[L]

Our Town (1938) Helene Pons[C]; Raymond Sovey[S]

Our Town (1944) Ack[S][L]

Our Town (1969) Edward Burbridge[S]; Jennifer Tipton[L]; David Toser[C]

Our Town (1988) Jane Greenwood[C]; Kevin Rigdon[L]; Douglas Stein[S]

Our Wives (1912) Eugene V. Adams[S]; Walter Harvey[S]; Ack[L]

Our World (1911) None

Ourselves (1913) None

Out Cry (1973) Sandy Cole[C]; Jo Mielziner[S][L]

Out from Under (1940) John Root[S]; Ack[C]

Out of a Blue Sky (1930) Honor Leeming[S]; Ack[C][L]

Out of Step (1925) Ack[S][C][L]

Out of the Frying Pan (1941) Cirker and Robbins[S]

Out of the Night (1927) Cirker and Robbins[S]; Ack[C][L]

Out of the Sea (1927) Rollo Peters[S]; Ack[C]

Out of the Seven Seas (1923) Ack[L]

Out of This World (1950) Lemuel Ayers[S][C]; Charles Elson[L]

Out There (1917) H. Robert Law[S]

Out There (1918) Ack[L]

Out West of Eighth (1951) Ralph Alswang[S]; Jocelyn[C]

Outcast (1914) None

Outrageous Fortune (1943) Raymond Sovey[S]

Outrageous Mrs. Palmer, The (1920) Watson Barratt[S]; Hickson[C]; Peggy Hoyt[C]; Lucile[C]; Ack[L]

Outside Looking in (1925) Cleon Throckmorton[S]

Outsider, The (1924) Livingston Platt[S]; Ack[C]

Outsider, The (1928) Livingston Platt[S]; Ack[L]

Outward Bound (1924) Livingston Platt[S]; Ack[C][L]

Outward Bound (1938) Watson Barratt[S]; Ack[C]

Over a Welsh Rarebit (1903) None

Over a Welsh Rarebit (1904) None

Over Here (1918) Ack[S][L]

Over Here (1974) John Gleason[L]; Carrie F. Robbins[C]; Douglas W. Schmidt[S]

Over Night (1911) Joseph[C]; H. Robert Law[S]

Over the 'Phone (1917) Harry Collins[C]; Dodge and Castle[S]; Ack[L]

Over the River (1912) Frederica DeWolfe[S]

Over the Top (1917) Homer Conant[C]; Ack[S][L]

Over Twenty-One (1944) Raymond Sovey[S]; Ack[C]

Overtons, The (1945) Hattie Carnegie[C]; Edward Gilbert[S]

Overture (1930) Donald Oenslager[S]; Ack[C]

Ovid's Metamorphoses (1970) H. R. Poindexter[L]; Noel Taylor[C]; James Trittipo[S]

Owl and the Pussycat, The (1964) Florence Klotz[C]; Jo Mielziner[S][L]

Oy Is Dus a Leben! (1942) Harry Gordon Bennett[S]

P.S. I Love You (1964) Raoul Pène Du Bois[S][C]; Jules Fisher[L]

P.S. Your Cat Is Dead (1975) Frank J. Boros[C]; William Ritman[S][L]

Pacific Overtures (1976) Boris Aronson[S]; Florence Klotz[C]; Tharon Musser[L]

Pacific Paradise (1972) Ack[S][C][L]

Pack of Lies (1985) Natasha Katz[L]; Ralph Koltai[S][C]

Paddy the Best Thing (1920) Ack[L]

Padlocks of 1927 (1927) Orry-Kelly[C]; Robert Ten Eyck Stevenson[C]; Ack[L]

Padre, The (1926) Watson Barratt[S]

Pagan Lady (1930) Henry Dreyfuss[S]; Emmett Joyce[C]

Pagans (1921) None

Page Miss Glory (1934) A. J. Lundborg[S]; Ack[C]

Page Pygmalion (1932) Cleon Throckmorton[S]; Miss Violet[C]

Paging Danger (1931) Joseph Mullen[S]; Ack[C]

Paid (1925) Joseph Roth[L]; William Oden Waller[S]; Ack[C]

Paid Companions (1931) Ack[L]

Paid in Full (1908) Ack[S][C][L]

Paint Your Wagon (1951) Peggy Clark[L]; Motley[C]; Oliver Smith[S]

Painted Woman, The (1913) No Playbill

Pair of Petticoats, A (1918) Ack[L]

Pair of Queens, A (1916) Ack[L]

Pair of Silk Stockings, A (1914) O'Kane Conwell[S][C]; Cyril Harcourt[S]; Lucile[C]; Unitt and Wickes[S]

Pair of Sixes, A (1914) Dodge and Castle[S]; Lucile[C]

Paisley Convertible, The (1967) Alvin Colt[C]; Jo Mielziner[S][L]

Pajama Game, The (1954) Lemuel Ayers[S][C]

Pajama Game, The (1973) John Gleason[L]; David Guthrie[S][C]

Pajama Tops (1963) Vilma Auld[C]; Leo B. Meyer[S][L]

Pal Joey (1940) John Koenig[C]; Jo Mielziner[S][L]

Pal Joey (1941) John Koenig[C]; Jo Mielziner[S][L]

Pal Joey (1952) Peggy Clark[L]; Oliver Smith[S]; Miles White[C]

Pal Joey (1976) Arthur Boccia[C]; John J. Moore[S]; Ronald Wallace[L]

Palmy Days (1919) Rollo Peters[S]; Ack[L]

Pals First (1917) Ack[S][L]

Pan and the Young Shepherd (1918) Mr. Roy Mitchell[S]; Ack[C]

Panama Hattie (1940) Raoul Pène Du Bois[S][C]; Billy Livingston[C]; Ack[L]

Panic (1935) Jo Mielziner[S][L]

Pansy (1929) Benjamin Leffler[L]; Ack[S][C]

Pantagleize (1967) Nancy Potts[C]; James Tilton[S][L]

Pantagleize (1968) Nancy Potts[C]; James Tilton[S][L]

Pantaloon (1905) Meixner[S]; Frank Platzer[S]

Panthea (1914) None

Paolo and Francesca (1906) Percy Macquoid[C]; W. L. Telbin[S]

Paolo and Francesca (1924) Frederick W. Jones III[S]

Paolo and Francesca (1929) Eleanor Eustis[S]

Papa (1919) Ack[S][L]

Papa Is All (1942) Emeline Clarke Roche[S][C]

Papa Lebonnard (1907) NONE
Papa Lebonnard (1908) NONE
Papa's Darling (1914) Ernest Albert(S);
Unitt and Wickes(S); ACK(C)
Papa's Wife (1899) D. Frank Dodge(S);
Landolff of Paris(C); Richard
Marston(S); J. T. McMurray(L)
Papavert (1931) Walter Harvey(S);
Bianca Stroock(C); Herbert Ward(S);
ACK(C)
Paper Chase, The (1912) NONE
Parade (1935) Billy Livingston(C);
Constance Ripley(C); Irene Sharaff(C);
Lee Simonson(S)(C)
Parade (1998) Howell Binkley(L); Judith
Dolan(C); Riccardo Hernández(S)
Paradise (1927) Cleon Throckmorton(S);
ACK(C)
Paradise Alley (1924) Gates and
Morange(S); ACK(L)
Paradise Lost (1935) Boris Aronson(S);
ACK(C)
Paradise of Mahoumet, The (1911)
NONE
Parasites (1924) Rollo Wayne(S);
ACK(C)(L)
Pardon My English (1933) Robert Ten
Eyck Stevenson(C); John Wenger(S)
Pardon Our French (1950) Albert R.
Johnson(S); Jack Moser(C); ACK(L)
Pariah (1913) NONE
Paris (1928) William E. Castle(S);
Elizabeth Hawes(C); ACK(L)
Paris '90 (1952) Donald Oenslager(S);
Helene Pons(C)
Paris Bound (1927) Robert Edmond
Jones(S); ACK(C)
Paris by Night (1904) P. Dodd
Ackerman(S); Madame Dowling(C)
Paris Is Out (1970) Martin Aronstein(L);
Florence Klotz(C); Douglas W.
Schmidt(S)
Parish Priest, The (1900) NONE
Parisian Model, The (1906) Ernest
Albert(S); Landolff of Paris(C); Mrs.
Caroline Siedle(C)
Parisian Romance, A (1899) NONE
Parisian Romance, A (1905) NONE
Parisian Romance, A (1906) NONE
Parisian Romance, A (1907) NONE
Parisiana (1928) Gwendolyn Cumnor(C);
Charles Teichner(S); ACK(L)
Parisienne (1950) Howard Bay(S); Paul
du Pont(C); ACK(L)
Parisienne, La (1904) NONE
Park (1970) Martin Aronstein(L); Peter

Harvey(S)(C)
Park Avenue (1946) Tina Leser(C);
Mainbocher(C); Donald Oenslager(S)(L)
Park Avenue, Ltd. (1932) ACK(L)
Park Your Car in Harvard Yard
(1991) Ben Edwards(S); Jane
Greenwood(C); Thomas Skelton(L)
Parlor Story (1947) Raymond Sovey(S);
Bianca Stroock(C)
Parlor, Bedroom, and Bath (1917)
ACK(L)
Parnell (1935) Stewart Chaney(S)(C)
Parnell (1936) Stewart Chaney(S)(C)
Parson's Bride, The (1929) ACK(L)
Partners Again (1922) ACK(C)(L)
Party with Betty Comden and
Adolph Green (1958) Marvin
Reiss(S)(L); ACK(C)
Party with Betty Comden and
Adolph Green (1977) Donald
Brooks(C); Andrea Wilson(L)
Party's Over, The (1933) Cirker and
Robbins(S); ACK(C)
Party, A (1933) Livingston Platt(S);
ACK(C)
Pasquale Never New (1938) Rossoni(S)
Passage to India, A (1962) John
Harvey(L); Rouben Ter-Arutunian(S)(C)
Passenger to Bali, A (1940) A. H.
Feder(L); Lawrence L. Goldwasser(S);
ACK(C)
Passers-By (1911) C. Haddon
Chambers(S); Gates and Morange(S)
Passing of the Idle Rich, The (1913)
NONE
Passing of the Third Floor Back,
The (1909) NONE
Passing of the Third Floor Back,
The (1913) NONE
Passing Present, The (1931) Robert
Edmond Jones(S)(C)(L)
Passing Show of 1912, The (1912)
Melville Ellis(C); Nick Kronyack(L);
John Whalen(L); Young Brothers(S)
Passing Show of 1913, The (1913)
Melville Ellis(C); Nick Kronyack(L); H.
Robert Law(S); William Rising(S); Ned
Wayburn(S); Young Brothers(S)
Passing Show of 1914, The (1914)
Melville Ellis(C); Joseph(C); Nick
Kronyack(L); H. Robert Law(S); Max &
Mahieu(C); Pascaud(C); William
Rising(S); Young Brothers(S)
Passing Show of 1915, The (1915)
Mrs. J. J. Shubert(C)
Passing Show of 1916, The (1916) P.

Newell[(S)(C)(L)]

Penelope (1909) Madame Hayward[(C)]; Unitt and Wickes[(S)]; Milnor Wells[(L)]

Penn & Teller (1987) John Lee Beatty[(S)]; Dennis Parichy[(L)]

Penn & Teller: The Refrigerator Tour (1991) John Lee Beatty[(S)]; Dennis Parichy[(L)]

Penny Arcade (1930) Cleon Throckmorton[(S)]

Penny Wars, The (1969) Martin Aronstein[(L)]; Jane Greenwood[(C)]; William Ritman[(S)]

Penny Wise (1919) Cirker and Robbins[(S)]; DuWico[(L)]

Penny Wise (1937) Cirker and Robbins[(S)]; Ack[(C)]

Penrod (1918) Ack[(L)]

People Don't Do Such Things (1927) Ack[(C)(L)]

People on the Hill (1931) Isaac Benesch[(S)]; Maxine Levy[(C)]; Ack[(L)]

People, The (1916) Ack[(L)]

Pepper Mill, The (1937) Anton Refreigier[(S)]

Perfect Alibi, The (1928) Thomas Farrar[(S)]

Perfect Fool, The (1921) Ada B. Fields[(C)]; Anthony Greshoff[(L)]; Cora MacGeachy[(C)]; Albertine Randall Wheelan[(C)]; Ack[(S)]

Perfect Lady, A (1914) H. Robert Studio Law[(S)]; Joseph Physioc Studio[(S)]

Perfect Marriage, The (1932) Ernest Schraps[(C)]; Rollo Wayne[(S)]

Perfect Marriage, The (1944) Oliver Smith[(S)]

Perfect Setup, The (1962) Charles Elson[(L)]; Jack McCullagh[(S)]; Frank Thompson[(C)]

Perfectly Frank (1980) Ken Billington[(L)]; John Falabella[(S)(C)]

Perfectly Scandalous (1931) Hattie Carnegie[(C)]; Margaret Pemberton[(C)]; Ack[(L)]

Perfumed Lady, The (1934) Watson Barratt[(S)]; Elizabeth Hawes[(C)]

Period of Adjustment (1960) Jo Mielziner[(S)(L)]; Patricia Zipprodt[(C)]

Peripherie (1928) Oscar Strnad[(S)]; Ernest de Weerth[(C)]; Ack[(L)]

Perkins (1918) Ack[(L)]

Perplexed Husband, The (1912) Paquin[(C)]; Redfern[(C)]

Personal (1907) None

Personal Appearance (1934) Margaret Pemberton[(C)]; Ack[(S)(L)]

Personality (1921) Ack[(C)]

Persons Unknown (1922) H. Robert Studio Law[(S)]; Ack[(L)]

Peter Allen "Up in One" (1979) Marilyn Rennagel[(L)]; Douglas W. Schmidt[(S)]; Charles Suppon[(C)]

Peter Flies High (1931) Ack[(S)(L)]

Peter Ibbetson (1917) Caroline Dudley[(S)(C)]; Gertrude Newell[(S)(C)]

Peter Ibbetson (1931) Watson Barratt[(S)]

Peter Pan (1912) Mrs. John Alexander[(C)]; Charles Basing[(S)]; Ernest Gros[(S)]; Arthur T. Hewlett[(S)]; J. Monroe Hewlett[(S)]; Bassett Jones[(L)]

Peter Pan (1915) Ernest Gros[(S)]; Ack[(L)]

Peter Pan (1924) George W. Harris[(S)(C)]

Peter Pan (1928) Aline Bernstein[(S)(C)]

Peter Pan (1950) Ralph Alswang[(S)(L)]; Motley[(C)]

Peter Pan (1954) Peggy Clark[(L)]; Peter Larkin[(S)]; Motley[(C)]

Peter Pan (1979) Bill Hargate[(C)]; Thomas Skelton[(L)]; Peter Wolf[(S)]

Peter Pan (1990) James Leonard Joy[(S)]; Natasha Katz[(L)]; Mariann Verheyen[(C)]

Peter Pan (1991) Paul de Pass[(S)]; Michael J. Hotopp[(S)]; James Leonard Joy[(S)]; Natasha Katz[(L)]; Mariann Verheyen[(C)]

Peter Pan (1998) Martin Aronstein[(L)]; John Iacovelli[(S)]; Shigeru Yaji[(C)]

Peter Pan (Maude Adams) (1905) John Alexander[(C)]; Ernest Gros[(S)]

Peter Stuyvesant (1899) Homer Emens[(S)]

Peter Weston (1923) Dickson Morgan[(S)]; Ack[(C)]

Peter's Mother (1918) Ack[(L)]

Peterpat (1965) David Hays[(S)(L)]; Fred Voelpel[(C)]

Petite Marquise, La (1904) None

Petition, The (1986) John Bury[(S)(C)(L)]

Petrified Forest, The (1935) Raymond Sovey[(S)]

Petrified Forest, The (1943) Tom Adrian Cracraft[(S)]

Petrouchka (1916) Esther Peck[(C)]; Frank J. Zimmerer[(S)]; Ack[(L)]

Petticoat Fever (1935) Selma Alexander[(C)]; Robert Barnhart[(S)]

Petticoat Influence (1930) Stanley Bell[(S)]; Robert Heller[(S)]; Joseph Mullen[(S)]; Ack[(C)(L)]

Phaedre (1963) Jacques Dupont[S][C]

Phantom Legion, The (1919) Kennel and Entwistle[S]; William Sheafe[L]

Phantom Lover, The (1928) Jones and Erwin[S]; ACK[C][L]

Phantom of the Opera, The (1988) Maria Bjørnson[S][C]; Andrew Bridge[L]

Phantom Rival, The (1914) Ernest Gros[S]

Phantoms (1930) P. Dodd Ackerman[S]

Philadelphia (1929) Joseph Physioc[S]

Philadelphia Story, The (1939) Hattie Carnegie[C]; Robert Edmond Jones[S]; Bianca Stroock[C]; Valentina[C]

Philadelphia Story, The (1980) John Conklin[S]; John Gleason[L]; Nancy Potts[C]

Philadelphia, Here I Come (1966) Lloyd Burlingame[S][C][L]

Philadelphia, Here I Come! (1994) Christopher Akerlind[L]; John Lee Beatty[S]; Catherine Zuber[C]

Philanderer, The (1913) J. P. Allen[C]; Madame Mary Grey[C]; Mr. Owen Little[S]; Unitt and Wickes[S]

Philanthropist, The (1971) Sara Brook[C]; Lloyd Burlingame[L]; John Gunter[S]

Philip Goes Forth (1931) Henry Dreyfuss[S]

Philosopher in the Apple Orchard, The (1911) Frank Platzer[S]

Phoebe of Quality Street (1921) ACK[C]

Phoenix '55 (1955) Alvin Colt[C]; Eldon Elder[S]; Klaus Holm[L]

Phoenix Too Frequent, A (1950) Jack Landau[S][C]; ACK[L]

Photo Finish (1963) Don Ashton[S]; Charles Elson[L]; Frank Thompson[C]

Physicists, The (1964) John Bury[S][C][L]

Piaf (1981) Beverly Emmons[L]; David Jenkins[S]; Julie Weiss[C]

Piano Lesson, The (1990) Christopher Akerlind[L]; E. David Cosier, Jr.[S]; Constanza Romero[C]

Pick-Up Girl (1944) Watson Barratt[S]; Roy Hargrave[L]; Emeline Clarke Roche[C]

Pickwick (1927) William E. Castle[S]; ACK[C]

Pickwick (1965) Jules Fisher[L]; Roger Furse[C]; Sean Kenny[S]; Peter Rice[C]

Picnic (1934) P. Dodd Ackerman[S]; Elizabeth Hooker Parsons[C]

Picnic (1953) Jo Mielziner[S][L]; Mildred Trebor[C]

Picnic (1994) Peter Kaczorowski[L]; William Ivey Long[C]; Tony Walton[S]

Pie in the Sky (1941) Donald Oenslager[S]; Bianca Stroock[C]

Pied Piper, The (1908) No PLAYBILL

Pierre of the Plains (1908) Peter W. King[L]; Joseph Physioc[S]

Pierrot the Prodigal (1925) Livingston Platt[S]; ACK[C]

Pietro (1920) Homer Emens[S]; ACK[L]

Piff! Paff! Pouf! (1904) Homer Emens[S]; Edward G. Unitt[S]

Pigeon, The (1912) Unitt and Wickes[S]

Pigeon, The (1922) Cleon Throckmorton[S]; ACK[L]

Pigeons and People (1933) ACK[L]

Piggy (1927) John Wenger[S]; Hugh Willoughby[C]

Pigs (1924) P. Dodd Ackerman[S]; ACK[C][L]

Piker, The (1925) P. Dodd Ackerman[S]; ACK[C][L]

Pilate's Daughter (1914) NONE

Pilgrim's Progress (1924) ACK[L]

Pillar to Post (1943) John Root[S]

Pillars of Society (1904) Wilfred Buckland[S]; Ernest Gros[S]

Pillars of Society (1910) Wilfred Buckland[S]; John A. Higham[L]

Pillars of Society, The (1931) Rollo Peters[S]; ACK[C][L]

Pin to See the Peepshow, A (1953) Ariel Ballif[S]; A. H. Feder[L]; Ruth Morley[C]

Pinch Hitter, A (1922) Gates and Morange[S]; ACK[L]

Pink Elephant, The (1953) Ralph Alswang[S][L]; Guy Kent[C]

Pink Lady, The (1911) Ernest Albert[S]; F. Richards Anderson[C]; Frank Detering[L]

Pinocchio (1938) James Cochran[C]; Moe Hack[L]; Perry Watkins[S]

Pins and Needles (1922) ACK[S][C][L]

Pins and Needles (1937) Norma Fuller[C]; S. Syrjala[S][C]

Pins and Needles (1938) S. Syrjala[S]; ACK[C][L]

Pinwheel (1927) Donald Oenslager[S][C]

Pioneer Days (1906) Arthur Voegtlin[S]

Pipe Dream (1955) Alvin Colt[C]; Jo Mielziner[S][L]

Piper Paid (1934) Ruth Edell[C]; John Root[S]; Sonia Rosenberg[C]

Piper, The (1911) E. Hamilton Bell[S][C]

Piper, The (1920) Ack⁽ᴸ⁾
Pipes of Pan, The (1917) Clifford F.
Pember⁽ˢ⁾
Pippa Passes (1906) Homer Emens⁽ˢ⁾;
Edward G. Unitt⁽ˢ⁾; Franklin Van
Horn⁽ᶜ⁾; Joseph Wickes⁽ˢ⁾
Pippin (1972) Jules Fisher⁽ᴸ⁾; Tony
Walton⁽ˢ⁾; Patricia Zipprodt⁽ᶜ⁾
Pirate, The (1942) Lemuel Ayers⁽ˢ⁾;
Miles White⁽ᶜ⁾
Pirates of Penzance, The (1912) NONE
Pirates of Penzance, The (1926)
Woodman Thompson⁽ˢ⁾⁽ᶜ⁾; Ack⁽ᴸ⁾
Pirates of Penzance, The (1927)
Woodman Thompson⁽ˢ⁾
Pirates of Penzance, The (1931)
Ack⁽ᴸ⁾
Pirates of Penzance, The (1936)
Franklyn Ambrose⁽ˢ⁾; Billy
Livingston⁽ᶜ⁾
Pirates of Penzance, The (1948)
George Sheringham⁽ˢ⁾⁽ᶜ⁾; Ack⁽ᴸ⁾
Pirates of Penzance, The (1949)
Ralph Alswang⁽ˢ⁾⁽ᴸ⁾; Peggy Morrison⁽ᶜ⁾
Pirates of Penzance, The (1952)
Ralph Alswang⁽ˢ⁾; Peggy Morrison⁽ᶜ⁾
Pirates of Penzance, The (1955)
George Sheringham⁽ᶜ⁾; Ack⁽ᴸ⁾
Pirates of Penzance, The (1981)
Wilford Leach⁽ˢ⁾; Patricia
McGourty⁽ᶜ⁾; Bob Shaw⁽ˢ⁾; Jennifer
Tipton⁽ᴸ⁾
Pit, The (1904) Félix⁽ᶜ⁾; Gates and
Morange⁽ˢ⁾; Hitchins & Balcom⁽ᶜ⁾;
Moses and Hamilton⁽ˢ⁾; Madame
O'Shaughnessy⁽ᶜ⁾; Worth⁽ᶜ⁾; John H.
Young⁽ˢ⁾
Pitter Patter (1920) Harry Sears⁽ᴸ⁾;
Ack⁽ˢ⁾⁽ᶜ⁾
Place for Polly, A (1970) Clarke
Dunham⁽ˢ⁾⁽ᴸ⁾; Frank Thompson⁽ᶜ⁾
Place in the Sun, A (1918) Ack⁽ᴸ⁾
Place of Our Own, A (1945) Lucinda
Ballard⁽ᶜ⁾; Raymond Sovey⁽ˢ⁾
Places Please (1937) Nicholas
Yellenti⁽ˢ⁾; Ack⁽ᶜ⁾
Plain and Fancy (1955) Peggy Clark⁽ᴸ⁾;
Raoul Pène Du Bois⁽ˢ⁾⁽ᶜ⁾
Plain Jane (1924) Mabel A. Buell⁽ˢ⁾;
Evelyn McHorter⁽ᶜ⁾; Ack⁽ᴸ⁾
Plan M (1942) Lemuel Ayers⁽ˢ⁾; Ack⁽ᶜ⁾
Plantation Revue (1922) Gertrude
Johnson⁽ᶜ⁾; Lew Leslie⁽ˢ⁾; Ack⁽ᴸ⁾
Platinum (1978) John Gleason⁽ᴸ⁾; David
Hays⁽ˢ⁾; Bob Mackie⁽ᶜ⁾
Play It Again, Sam (1969) Martin

Aronstein⁽ᴸ⁾; William Ritman⁽ˢ⁾; Ann
Roth⁽ᶜ⁾
Play Memory (1984) Ken Billington⁽ᴸ⁾;
Clarke Dunham⁽ˢ⁾; William Ivey
Long⁽ᶜ⁾
Play On! (1997) Jeff Davis⁽ᴸ⁾; Marianna
Elliott⁽ᶜ⁾; James Leonard Joy⁽ˢ⁾
Play without Name, A (1928) Omar
Kiam⁽ᶜ⁾; Austin Strong⁽ˢ⁾
Play's the Thing, The (1926) Jean
Dary⁽ˢ⁾; Ack⁽ᶜ⁾
Play's the Thing, The (1928) Ack⁽ᴸ⁾
Play's the Thing, The (1948) Ralph
Alswang⁽ᴸ⁾; Castillo⁽ᶜ⁾; Oliver
Messel⁽ˢ⁾; Kathryn B. Miller⁽ᶜ⁾
Play's the Thing, The (1973) Holmes
Easley⁽ˢ⁾; Mimi Maxmen⁽ᶜ⁾; Richard
Winkler⁽ᴸ⁾
Play's the Thing, The (1995) Jess
Goldstein⁽ᶜ⁾; Peter Kaczorowski⁽ᴸ⁾;
Stephan Olson⁽ˢ⁾
Play, Genius, Play (1935) Cirker and
Robbins⁽ˢ⁾; Ack⁽ᶜ⁾
Playboy of the Western World, The
(1921) Harriet Klamroth⁽ˢ⁾
Playboy of the Western World, The
(1930) William Gaskin⁽ˢ⁾⁽ᶜ⁾
Playboy of the Western World, The
(1946) John Boyt⁽ˢ⁾⁽ᶜ⁾
Player Maid, The (1905) NONE
Players (1978) Martin Aronstein⁽ᴸ⁾;
Hayden Griffin⁽ˢ⁾⁽ᶜ⁾
Players from Japan, The (1930)
Ack⁽ᴸ⁾
Playing the Game (1927) Ack⁽ᴸ⁾
Playroom, The (1965) Theoni V.
Aldredge⁽ᶜ⁾; Jo Mielziner⁽ˢ⁾⁽ᴸ⁾
Playwrights Repertory–One Acts
(1968) William Ritman⁽ˢ⁾⁽ᶜ⁾⁽ᴸ⁾
Plaza Suite (1968) Jean Rosenthal⁽ᴸ⁾;
Oliver Smith⁽ˢ⁾; Patricia Zipprodt⁽ᶜ⁾
Please Get Married (1919) Ack⁽ˢ⁾⁽ᶜ⁾⁽ᴸ⁾
Please Help Emily (1916) Ack⁽ᶜ⁾⁽ᴸ⁾
Please Mrs. Garibaldi (1939) Ack⁽ᶜ⁾⁽ᴸ⁾
Pleasure Bound (1929) Georges
Barbier⁽ᶜ⁾; Watson Barratt⁽ˢ⁾; Ernest
Schraps⁽ᶜ⁾
Pleasure Man (1928) Livingston
Platt⁽ˢ⁾; Dolly Tree⁽ᶜ⁾
Pleasure of His Company, The (1958)
Edith Head⁽ᶜ⁾; Donald Oenslager⁽ˢ⁾⁽ᴸ⁾
Pleasure Seekers, The (1913) Cora
MacGeachy⁽ᶜ⁾; William Henry
Matthews⁽ᶜ⁾
Plenty (1983) Arden Fingerhut⁽ᴸ⁾; Jane
Greenwood⁽ᶜ⁾; John Gunter⁽ˢ⁾

Plot Thickens, The (1922) Ruby Ross
Goodnow(S); Sheldon K. Viele(S);
ACK(C)(L)
Plough and the Stars, The (1927)
ACK(C)(L)
Plumes in the Dust (1936) Woodman
Thompson(S)(C)(L)
Plutocrat, The (1930) Louis Kennel(S);
ACK(L)
Pocahontas (1938) Karl R. Free(C)
Poetasters of Ispahan, The (1912)
NONE
Point of Honor, A (1937) Kate Drain
Lawson(S)(C)
Point of No Return (1951)
Mainbocher(C); Jo Mielziner(S)(L)
Point of View, The (1912) H. Robert
Studio Law(S); Bert Tuchman(S)
Point Valaine (1935) Gladys E.
Calthrop(S); Mrs. Robert L. Holt(C)
Poison Tree, The (1976) Martin
Aronstein(L); Judy Dearing(C);
Marjorie Bradley Kellogg(S)
Poldekin (1920) Anthony Greshoff(L); H.
Robert Studio Law(S); ACK(S)
Polish Jew, The (1899) NONE
Polly of Hollywood (1927) Paul
Aimes(C); ACK(S)(L)
Polly of the Circus (1907) Frank
Marsden(S)
Polly Preferred (1923) P. Dodd
Ackerman(S); ACK(C)
Polly with a Past (1917) Elsie de
Wolfe(S); Ernest Gros(S); Herman
Patrick Tappé(S); ACK(C)(L)
Polonaise (1945) Howard Bay(S); Mary
Grant(C)
Polygamy (1914) Gates and Morange(S);
ACK(S)(C)
Pom-Pom (1916) Joseph Urban(S);
ACK(C)(L)
Pomander Walk (1910) Gates and
Morange(S); B. J. Simmons(C)
Pomeroy's Past (1926) ACK(C)(L)
Ponder Heart, The (1956) Ben
Edwards(S)(L); Frank Spencer(C)
Poor Bitos (1964) Donald Brooks(C);
Timothy O'Brien(S); Jean Rosenthal(L)
Poor Little Rich Girl, The (1913)
Madame Freisinger(C); Ernest Gros(S);
Kliegl Brothers(L); Everett Shinn(S)
Poor Little Ritz Girl (1920) Cora
MacGeachy(C); Anna Spencer(C);
ACK(S)(L)
Poor Little Thing (1914) ACK(C)
Poor Murderer (1976) Howard

Bay(S)(L); Patricia Zipprodt(C)
Poor Nut, The (1925) ACK(C)(L)
Poor Richard (1964) Theoni V.
Aldredge(C); Peggy Clark(L); Oliver
Smith(S)
Poppa (1928) R. N. Robbins(S)
Poppy (1923) Ralph Barton(S); Charles
LeMaire(C); ACK(L)
Poppy God, The (1921) John Wenger(S)
Popsy (1941) Tom Adrian Cracraft(S);
ACK(C)
Popularity (1906) NONE
Porgy (1927) Rouben Mamoulian(S)(C);
Cleon Throckmorton(S); ACK(L)
Porgy (1929) Cleon Throckmorton(S);
ACK(L)
Porgy and Bess (1935) Sergi
Soudeikine(S); Jean Tate(C)
Porgy and Bess (1942) Herbert
Andrews(S); Paul du Pont(C)
Porgy and Bess (1943) Herbert
Andrews(S); Paul du Pont(C)
Porgy and Bess (1944) Herbert
Andrews(S); Paul du Pont(C)
Porgy and Bess (1953) Jed Mace(C);
Wolfgang Roth(S)
Porgy and Bess (1976) Gilbert V.
Hemsley, Jr.(L); Nancy Potts(C);
Robert Randolph(S)
Porgy and Bess (1983) Gilbert V.
Hemsley, Jr.(L); Nancy Potts(C);
Douglas W. Schmidt(S)
Port o' London (1926) ACK(L)
Portofino (1958) Wolfgang Roth(S);
Michael Travis(C); Lee Watson(L)
Portrait in Black (1947) Donald
Oenslager(S)(L); Helene Pons(C)
Portrait of a Lady (1954) Cecil
Beaton(C); William and Jean
Eckart(S)(L)
Portrait of a Queen (1968) Theoni V.
Aldredge(C); Marvin Reiss(S)(L)
Portrait of Gilbert (1934) Raymond
Sovey(S)(C)(L)
Possessed, The (1939) M.
Dobuzhinsky(S)
Post Road (1934) Mary Merrill(C);
Raymond Sovey(S)
Postman Always Rings Twice, The
(1936) Jo Mielziner(S)(L); ACK(C)
Postmark Zero (1965) Jack
Blackman(S)(C)(L)
Pot of Broth, A (1900) NONE
Pot of Broth, A (1908) NONE
Pot-Luck (1921) Clifford F. Pember(S);
ACK(C)

Potash and Perlmutter (1913) Joseph Physioc[S]

Potash and Perlmutter (1935) Karle O. Amend[S]

Potash and Perlmutter, Detectives (1926) Karle O. Amend[S]; ACK[L]

Potiphar's Wife (1928) Eddie Eddy[S]; ACK[C][L]

Potters, The (1923) Cleon Throckmorton[S]; ACK[C][L]

Potting Shed, The (1957) Peggy Clark[L]; William Pitkin[S]; Patricia Zipprodt[C]

Pound on Demand (1946) Wolfgang Roth[S][C]

Pousse-Cafe (1966) Will Steven Armstrong[S]; V. C. Fuqua[L]; Patricia Zipprodt[C]

Power (1937) Howard Bay[S]

Power of Darkness, The (1920) Lee Simonson[S][C]

Power without Glory (1948) Charles Elson[S][L]

Pre-Honeymoon (1936) Cirker and Robbins[S]; ACK[C]

Precedent (1931) S. Syrjala[S]

Precious (1929) Livingston Platt[S]; ACK[C]

Precious Sons (1986) Joseph G. Aulisi[C]; Andrew Jackness[S]; Richard Nelson[L]

Prelude (1936) ACK[C][L]

Prelude to a Kiss (1990) Loy Arcenas[S]; Walker Hicklin[C]; Debra J. Kletter[L]

Prelude to Exile (1936) Lee Simonson[S][C]

Prescott Proposals, The (1953) Mainbocher[C]; Donald Oenslager[S]

Present Arms (1928) DuWico[L]; Ward and Harvey Studios[S]; ACK[C]

Present Laughter (1946) Castillo[C]; Charles Elson[L]; Donald Oenslager[S]; Sylvia Saal[C]

Present Laughter (1958) Peggy Clark[L]; Scaasi[C]; Oliver Smith[S]; Frank Thompson[C]

Present Laughter (1982) Marjorie Bradley Kellogg[S]; Richard Nelson[L]; Ann Roth[C]

Present Laughter (1996) Brian MacDevitt[L]; Derek McLane[S]; Ann Roth[C]

Preserving Mr. Panmure (1912) NONE

President's Daughter, The (1970) Barry Arnold[S][C][L]

Press Agent, The (1905) NONE

Pressing Business (1930) Cirker and Robbins[S]; ACK[L]

Pretty Little Parlor (1944) Stewart Chaney[S]; Paul du Pont[C]

Pretty Mrs. Smith (1914) Clarise[C]; Melville Ellis[C]; Lucile[C]

Pretty Peggy (1903) NONE

Pretty Sister of José, The (1903) Henry Dazian[C]; Helen Windsor[C]

Pretty Soft (1919) ACK[C][L]

Price of Money, The (1906) NONE

Price of Peace, The (1901) Robert Caney[S]; Henry Emden[S]; Julian Hicks[S]; R. McCleery[S]; W. Perkins[S]; Bruce Smith[S]; ACK[C]

Price, The (1911) Harry Gordon Bennett[S]

Price, The (1968) Boris Aronson[S][C]; Paul Morrison[L]

Price, The (1979) Todd Elmer[L]; David Mitchell[S]; Robert Wojewodski[C]

Price, The (1992) John Lee Beatty[S]; Jane Greenwood[C]; Dennis Parichy[L]

Price, The (1999) Michael Brown[S]; Laurie A. Churba[C]; Rui Rita[L]

Pride (1923) ACK[S][L]

Pride and Prejudice (1935) Jo Mielziner[S][C][L]

Pride of Jennico, The (1900) Maurice Hermann[C]; Edward G. Unitt[S]

Pride of the Race, The (1916) Unitt and Wickes[S]

Pride's Crossing (1950) Ralph Alswang[S][L]; Millie Sutherland[C]

Prima Donna, The (1901) NONE

Prima Donna, The (1908) Frederica DeWolfe[C]; Homer Emens[S]

Prime of Miss Jean Brodie, The (1968) Jane Greenwood[C]; Jo Mielziner[S][L]

Primer for Lovers, A (1929) Margaret Pemberton[C]; Woodman Thompson[S]

Primrose Path, The (1907) NONE

Primrose Path, The (1939) Cirker and Robbins[S]; Helene Pons[C]

Prince and the Pauper, The (1920) Rollo Peters[S][C]; ACK[L]

Prince Chap, The (1905) Joseph Physioc[S]

Prince Consort, The (1905) NONE

Prince Karl (1899) NONE

Prince of Bohemia, The (1910) Melville Ellis[C]; John Whalen[L]; George Williams[S]; John H. Young[S]

Prince of Central Park (1989) Michael Bottari[(S)(C)]; Ronald Case[(S)(C)]; Norman Coates [American][(L)]

Prince of India, The (1906) F. Richards Anderson[(C)]; ACK[(L)]

Prince of Pilsen, The (1903) Will R. Barnes[(C)]; Walter W. Burridge[(S)]; Archie Gunn[(C)]

Prince of Pilsen, The (1930) Rollo Wayne[(S)]

Prince Otto (1900) Henry Buhler[(S)]; Walter W. Burridge[(S)]; Edith Craig[(C)]; Frederick Gibson[(S)]; Henry Martin[(S)]; Fritz Schoultz[(C)]

Prince There Was, A (1918) ACK[(L)]

Princess April (1924) William Weaver[(S)(C)]

Princess Beggar (1907) NO PLAYBILL

Princess Charming (1930) Charles LeMaire[(C)]; Joseph Urban[(S)]

Princess Chic, The (1900) E. Castle-Bert[(S)]; Mrs. Caroline Siedle[(C)]

Princess Flavia (1925) Watson Barratt[(S)]; Ernest Schraps[(C)]

Princess Ida (1925) Lloyd Kelly[(L)]; ACK[(S)(C)]

Princess Ida (1936) Percy Anderson[(C)]; ACK[(L)]

Princess Ida (1955) James Wade [British][(S)(C)]; ACK[(L)]

Princess of Kensington, A (1903) Charles Alias[(C)]; Madame Freisinger[(C)]

Princess Pat, The (1915) ACK[(S)(C)(L)]

Princess Players, The (1913) H. Robert Law[(S)]; ACK[(L)]

Princess Players, The (1914) NONE

Princess Turandot (1926) Robert Van Rosen[(S)(C)]

Princess Virtue (1921) ACK[(S)(C)]

Priorities of 1942 (1942) Kathryn Kuhn[(C)]; ACK[(L)]

Prisoner of 2nd Avenue, The (1971) Tharon Musser[(L)]; Anthea Sylbert[(C)]; Richard Sylbert[(S)]

Prisoner of Zenda, The (1908) William Camph[(S)]; William Hawley[(S)]; Milnor Wells[(L)]

Prisoner, The (1927) Roderick Seidenberg[(S)]

Prisoners of War (1935) Kay Morrison[(C)]; Cleon Throckmorton[(S)]

Private Affair, A (1936) Mary Walls[(C)]; ACK[(S)]

Private Ear, The/ The Public Eye (1962) Klaus Holm[(S)(L)]; Ann Roth[(C)]

Private Lives (1931) Gladys E. Calthrop[(S)]; Molyneux[(C)]

Private Lives (1948) Charles Elson[(S)(L)]; ACK[(C)]

Private Lives (1969) Joe Eula[(C)]; Barbara Matera[(C)]; James Tilton[(S)(L)]

Private Lives (1975) H. R. Poindexter[(L)]; Anthony Powell[(S)]; Germinal Rangel[(C)]

Private Lives (1983) Theoni V. Aldredge[(C)]; David Mitchell[(S)]; Tharon Musser[(L)]

Private Lives (1992) William Ivey Long[(C)]; Richard Nelson[(L)]; Loren Sherman[(S)]

Private Secretary, The (1910) William H. Day[(S)]

Privilege Car (1931) Eddie Eddy[(S)]

Processional (1925) Mordecai Gorelik[(S)(C)]

Processional (1937) Manuel Essman[(S)]

Prodigal Husband, The (1914) Homer Emens[(S)]

Prodigal Son, The (1905) Ernest Albert[(S)]; Comelli[(C)]; Richard Marston[(S)]

Prodigal Son, The (1942) Dimitri Bouchène[(S)(C)]

Producers, The (2001) Peter Kaczorowski[(L)]; William Ivey Long[(C)]; Robin Wagner[(S)]

Professor Mamlock (1937) George Phillips[(S)]

Professor's Love Story, The (1900) NONE

Professor's Love Story, The (1917) ACK[(L)]

Prologue to Glory (1938) A. H. Feder[(L)]; Mary Merrill[(C)]; Walter Walden[(S)]

Promenade, All! (1972) Martin Aronstein[(L)]; David Chapman[(S)]; James Berton Harris[(C)]

Promise, The (1936) Hattie Carnegie[(C)]; Raymond Sovey[(S)]

Promise, The (1967) Tharon Musser[(L)]; William Ritman[(S)]; ACK[(C)]

Promises, Promises (1968) Martin Aronstein[(L)]; Donald Brooks[(C)]; Robin Wagner[(S)]

Proof (2000) John Lee Beatty[(S)]; Pat Collins[(L)]; Jess Goldstein[(C)]

Proof through the Night (1942) Moe Hack[(L)]; Albert R. Johnson[(S)]

Proposals (1997) John Lee Beatty[(S)]; Jane Greenwood[(C)]; Brian MacDevitt[(L)]

Protective Custody (1956) Peter Larkin[S][C]; Lee Watson[L]

Proud Laird, The (1905) NONE

Proud Prince, The (1903) Homer Emens[S]; Maurice Hermann[C]; Kliegl Brothers[L]; L. and H. Nathan[C]; Edward G. Unitt[S]

Proud Woman, A (1926) Raymond Sovey[S]; ACK[C]

Provincetown Follies (1935) John Plummer Ludlum[S]

Provincetown Players: One Acts (1917) ACK[L]

Prunella (1913) O'Kane Conwell[C]; Unitt and Wickes[S]

Public Relations (1944) Stewart Chaney[S]

Pump Boys and Dinettes (1982) Fred Buchholz[L]; Doug Johnson[S]; Patricia McGourty[C]; Christopher Nowak[S]

Punch, Judy & Co. (1903) NONE

Puppet Show (1930) ACK[L]

Puppets (1925) Raymond Sovey[S]

Puppets of Passion (1927) Livingston Platt[S]; ACK[C]

Puppy Love (1926) Livingston Platt[S]; ACK[C]

Pure in Heart, The (1934) Jo Mielziner[S][L]; ACK[C]

Puritan, The (1936) Clement M. Williams[S]; ACK[C]

Purity (1930) Rollo Wayne[S]

Purlie (1970) Ben Edwards[S]; Ann Roth[C]; Thomas Skelton[L]

Purlie (1972) Ben Edwards[S]; Ann Roth[C]; Thomas Skelton[L]

Purlie Victorious (1961) Ben Edwards[S][L]; Ann Roth[C]

Purple Mask, The (1920) ACK[S][L]

Purple Road, The (1913) P. Dodd Ackerman[S]; Walter Harvey[S]; Henry Redmond[L]; ACK[C]

Pursuit of Happiness, The (1933) Livingston Platt[C]; ACK[C][L]

Putting It Together (1999) Bob Crowley[S][C]; Howard Harrison[L]

Puzzles of 1925 (1925) Mabel E. Johnston[C]; James Reynolds[C]; ACK[S][L]

Pygmalion (1914) Gates and Morange[S]

Pygmalion (1926) Jo Mielziner[S][C][L]

Pygmalion (1938) Ben Edwards[S][C]; A. H. Feder[L]

Pygmalion (1945) Charles Elson[L]; Motley[C]; Donald Oenslager[S]

Pygmalion (1987) Martin Aronstein[L];

Terence Emery[C]; Douglas Heap[S]

Pyramids (1926) ACK[C][L]

Quadrille (1954) Cecil Beaton[S][C]; Jean Rosenthal[L]

Quaker Girl, The (1911) NONE

Quality Street (1901) Percy Anderson[C]; Edward G. Unitt[S]

Quarantine (1924) Norman Bel Geddes[S]; ACK[C]

Queen and the Rebels, The (1982) Jane Greenwood[C]; David Jenkins[S]; John McLain[L]

Queen at Home (1930) ACK[C]

Queen Bee (1929) David S. Gaither[S]; ACK[C]

Queen High (1926) Willy Pogany[S]; Miss Vila[C]

Queen o' Hearts (1922) H. Robert Studio Law[S]; ACK[C][L]

Queen of the Moulin Rouge, The (1908) Will R. Barnes[C]; T. Bernard McDonald[S]; Unitt and Wickes[S]

Queen of the Movies, The (1914) Hugo Baruch[S][C]

Queen Victoria (1923) Woodman Thompson[S][C]

Queen's Enemies, The (1916) Aline Bernstein[C]; Warren Dahler[S]; Howard Kretz[S]; Dennis Sullivan[L]

Queen's Husband, The (1928) Livingston Platt[S]; ACK[C][L]

Queer People (1934) P. Dodd Ackerman[S]; ACK[C]

Question, The (1912) NONE

Quick Change (1980) Chris Flower[S]; John Shipley[S]; Mary Wills[C]

Quicksand (1928) Nicholas Yellenti[S]; ACK[C]

Quiet Please (1940) Everett Burgess[S]; Howard Greer[C]

Quilters (1984) Ursula Belden[S]; Allen Lee Hughes[L]; Elizabeth Palmer[C]

Quincy Adams Sawyer (1902) ACK[S]

Quinneys (1915) Joseph and Phil Harker[S]; ACK[C]

Quo Vadis (1900) D. Frank Dodge[S]; Mrs. Caroline Siedle[C]; ACK[L]

R.U.R. (1922) Lee Simonson[S][C]

R.U.R. (1942) Boris Aronson[S]; E. Carlton Winckler[L]

Race of Hairy Men, A (1965) Ben Edwards[S][L]; Jane Greenwood[C]

Race with the Shadow, The (1923) Carolyn Hancock[S][C]

Rachel (1913) Will R. Barnes[C]; Dodge and Castle[S]; Samuel J. Friedman[S];

Kliegl Brothers[L]
Racing Demon (1995) Bob
    Crowley[S)(C)]; Mark Henderson[L]
Rack, The (1911) H. Robert Law[S];
    Bert Tuchman[S]
Racket, The (1927) Livingston
    Platt[S)(C)]
Racketty-Packetty House (1912) Ben
    Beerwald[L]; Gates and Morange[S]; C.
    Alexander Ramsey[C]
Radio City Christmas Spectacular
    (1992) Ken Billington[L]; Michael J.
    Hotopp[S]; Jose Lengson[C]; Charles
    Lisanby[S]; Pete Menefee[C]; Frank
    Spencer[C]
Radio City Christmas Spectacular
    (1993) Ken Billington[L]; Michael J.
    Hotopp[S]; Charles Lisanby[S]; Pete
    Menefee[C]; Frank Spencer[C]
Radio City Christmas Spectacular
    (1994) Gregg Barnes[C]; Ken
    Billington[L]; Michael J. Hotopp[S];
    Charles Lisanby[S]; Pete Menefee[C];
    Frank Spencer[C]
Radio City Christmas Spectacular
    (1995) Gregg Barnes[C]; Ken
    Billington[L]; Michael J. Hotopp[S];
    Jason Kantrowitz[L]
Radio City Christmas Spectacular
    (1996) Gregg Barnes[C]; Ken
    Billington[L]; Michael J. Hotopp[S];
    Jason Kantrowitz[L]; Charles
    Lisanby[S]; Pete Menefee[C]; Frank
    Spencer[C]
Radio City Christmas Spectacular
    (1997) Gregg Barnes[C]; Ken
    Billington[L]; Michael J. Hotopp[S];
    Jason Kantrowitz[L]; Charles
    Lisanby[S]; Pete Menefee[C]; Frank
    Spencer[C]
Radio City Christmas Spectacular
    (1998) Gregg Barnes[C]; Ken
    Billington[L]; Michael J. Hotopp[S];
    Jason Kantrowitz[L]; Charles
    Lisanby[S]; Pete Menefee[C]; Vincente
    Minnelli[C]; Frank Spencer[C]
Radio City Easter Show (1993) Ken
    Billington[L]; Erté[S)(C)]; Jason
    Kantrowitz[L]; Jose Lengson[C];
    Eduardo Sicangco[S]
Radio City Easter Show (1994) Ken
    Billington[L]; Erté[S)(C)]; Jason
    Kantrowitz[L]; Jose Lengson[C];
    Eduardo Sicangco[S)(C)]
Radio City Easter Show (1995) Ken
    Billington[L]; Erté[S]; Jason

Kantrowitz[L]; Jose Lengson[C]; Bob
    Mackie[C]; Pete Menefee[C]; Eduardo
    Sicangco[S)(C)]; Billy B. Walker[L]
Radio City Spring Spectacular
    (1996) Ken Billington[L]; Erté[S)(C)];
    Michael J. Hotopp[S]; Jason
    Kantrowitz[L]; Frank Krenz[C]; Jose
    Lengson[C]; Bob Mackie[C]; Pete
    Menefee[C]; Eduardo Sicangco[S)(C)]
Radio City Spring Spectacular
    (1997) Ken Billington[L]; Erté[S)(C)];
    Michael J. Hotopp[S]; Jason
    Kantrowitz[L]; Frank Krenz[C]; Jose
    Lengson[C]; Bob Mackie[C]; Pete
    Menefee[C]; Eduardo Sicangco[S)(C)]
Raffles (1910) NONE
Raffles, the Amateur Cracksman
    (1903) Gates and Morange[S]
Ragged Army (1934) Raymond
    Sovey[S)(C)]
Ragged Edge, The (1935) Bianca
    Stroock[C]; Nicholas Yellenti[S]
Raggedy Ann (1986) Vicki Baral[S];
    Gerry Hariton[S]; Carrie F. Robbins[C];
    Marc B. Weiss[L]
Rags (1986) Jules Fisher[L]; Florence
    Klotz[C]; Beni Montresor[S]
Ragtime (1998) Peggy Eisenhauer[L];
    Jules Fisher[L]; Eugene Lee[S]; Santo
    Loquasto[C]
Raiders, The (1905) Hugh S.
    Thomas[L]; Frederick W. Thompson[S];
    Arthur Voegtlin[S]; ACK[C]
Rain (1922) ACK[L]
Rain (1935) William Oden Waller[S];
    ACK[C]
Rain from Heaven (1934) Lee
    Simonson[S]; ACK[C]
Rain or Shine (1928) Charles
    LeMaire[C]; Clarke Robinson[S]
Rainbow (1928) Gates and Morange[S];
    Charles LeMaire[C]; ACK[L]
Rainbow Girl, The (1918) Alice
    O'Neil[C]; Joseph Urban[S]; ACK[C)(L)]
Rainbow Jones (1974) Richard
    Ferrer[S]; James Berton Harris[C];
    Spencer Mosse[L]
Rainbow Rose (1926) ACK[S)(C)(L)]
Rainbow, The (1912) NONE
Rainmaker, The (1954) Ralph
    Alswang[S)(L)]; Saul Bolasni[C]
Rainmaker, The (1999) Jess
    Goldstein[C]; Peter Kaczorowski[L];
    James Noone[S]
Rainy Day in Newark, A (1963) Ed
    Wittstein[S)(C)(L)]

Raisin (1973) Bernard Johnson[C]; William Mintzer[L]; Robert U. Taylor[S]

Raisin in the Sun, A (1959) Ralph Alswang[S][L]; Virginia Volland[C]

Rambler Rose (1917) Henri Bendel[C]; Homer Emens[S]; ACK[L]

Ramblers, The (1926) Charles LeMaire[C]; Raymond Sovey[S]; ACK[L]

Ramshackle Inn (1944) Peggy Clark[C]; Frederick Fox[S]

Rang Tang (1927) Olle Nordmark[S][C]

Ranger, The (1907) Walter W. Burridge[S]; Frank E. Gates[S]; Kliegl Brothers[L]; Edward Morange[S]; ACK[C]

Ransom's Folly (1904) Peter W. King[L]; P. J. McDonald[S]; Unitt and Wickes[S]

Rap, The (1931) ACK[L]

Rape of Lucretia, The (1948) Peggy Clark[L]; John Piper[S]; Frank Thompson[C]

Rape of the Belt (1960) Pierre Balmain[C]; Paul Morrison[S][L]; Michael Travis[C]

Rapid Transit (1927) Evelyn T. Clifton[C]; Cleon Throckmorton[S]

Rashomon (1959) Oliver Messel[S][C]; Jo Mielziner[L]

Rat Race, The (1949) Lucinda Ballard[C]; Joseph Fretwell III[C]; Donald Oenslager[S][L]

Rat, The (1925) ACK[L]

Rats of Norway, The (1948) William De Forest[S][C][L]

Rattle of a Simple Man (1962) Joan Morse[C]; Vic Symonds[S]; ACK[L]

Rattle of a Simple Man (1963) Joan Morse[C]; Vic Symonds[S]; ACK[L]

Ratto Sabine, Il (1907) NONE

Raw Meat (1933) Hugh Mason[S]

Raymond Hitchcock's Pinwheel (1922) Lillian Greenfield[C]; William Troy[C]

Razzle Dazzle (1951) William Riva[S][C][L]

Re-Echo (1934) Louis Kennel[S][C]

Ready Money (1912) Cassidy and Sons[L]; Dodge and Castle[S]

Ready When You Are (1964) Theoni V. Aldredge[C]; Will Steven Armstrong[S][L]

Real Inspector Hound, The (1992) John Lee Beatty[S]; Pat Collins[L]; Jess Goldstein[C]

Real Thing, The (1984) Tharon Musser[L]; Anthea Sylbert[C]; Tony Walton[S]

Real Thing, The (2000) Mark Henderson[L]; Vicki Mortimer[S][C]; David Weiner[L]

Real Thing, The (C. Cushing) (1911) NONE

Rebecca (1945) Watson Barratt[S]

Rebecca of Sunnybrook Farm (1910) John Brunton[S]; T. Bernard McDonald[S]; Frank Platzer[S]; ACK[L]

Rebel, The (1900) Charles Chrisdie[C]; Maurice Hermann[C]; Joseph Physioc[S]

Rebellion (1911) NONE

Rebound (1930) Hattie Carnegie[C]; Robert Edmond Jones[S]; Charles Kondazian[C]

Recapture (1930) P. Dodd Ackerman[S]; ACK[C]

Reckoning, The (1907) NONE

Reclining Figure (1954) Frederick Fox[S][C][L]

Recruits (1935) S. Anisfield[C]; M. Solotaroff[S]

Rector's Garden, The (1908) NONE

Red Blinds (1926) Gladys E. Calthrop[S]; ACK[L]

Red Canary, The (1914) NONE

Red Cat, The (1934) P. Dodd Ackerman[S]; Bianca Stroock[C]

Red Dawn, The (1919) ACK[C][L]

Red Dust (1928) August Vimnera[S]; ACK[C]

Red Dust (1929) August Vimnera[S]; ACK[C]

Red Falcon, The (1924) Constance Bellamy[S]; ACK[L]

Red Feather (1903) Ernest Albert[S]; Mrs. Caroline Siedle[C]

Red Geranium, The (1922) Cleon Throckmorton[S]

Red Gloves (1948) Stewart Chaney[S]; Emeline Clarke Roche[C]; ACK[L]

Red Harvest (1937) Margaret Pemberton[C]; John Root[S]

Red Kloof, The (1901) Charles Chrisdie[C]; Joseph Physioc[S]

Red Light Annie (1923) William Oden Waller[S]; ACK[C]

Red Mill, The (1906) Homer Emens[S]; Frank E. Gates[S]; Edward Morange[S]; Mrs. Caroline Siedle[C]; Edward G. Unitt[S]; Joseph Wickes[S]; Wilhelm[C]

Red Mill, The (1945) Adrian

Awan[S][L]; Walter J. Israel[C]

Red Moon, The (1909) NONE

Red Pepper (1922) ACK[L]

Red Petticoat, The (1912) NONE

Red Planet (1932) Lee Simonson[S]; ACK[C]

Red Poppy, The (1922) ACK[C][L]

Red Robe, The (1928) Georges Barbier[C]; Watson Barratt[S]; Ernest Schraps[C]

Red Rose, The (1911) Callot Soeurs[C]; Madame Frances[C]; Madame Freisinger[C]; Theodore Reisig[S]; ACK[L]

Red Roses for Me (1955) Ballou[C]; Howard Bay[S][L]

Red Shoes, The (1993) Ken Billington[L]; Heidi Ettinger[S]; Catherine Zuber[C]

Red White and Maddox (1969) Richard Casler[L]; David Chapman[S][C]

Red Widow, The (1911) Theodore Reisig[S]

Red, Hot and Blue (1936) Donald Oenslager[S]; Constance Ripley[C]

Redemption (1918) Robert Edmond Jones[S]; Fania Mindell[C]; ACK[L]

Redemption (1928) Ernest Schütte[S]; ACK[C][L]

Redemption of David Corson, The (1906) NO PLAYBILL

Redhead (1959) Jean Rosenthal[L]; Rouben Ter-Arutunian[S][C]

Redskin, The (1906) H. Robert Law[S]

Redwood Curtain (1993) John Lee Beatty[S]; Laura Crow[C]; Dennis Parichy[L]

Reflected Glory (1936) Howard Greer[C]; Norman Rock[S]

Regeneration, The (1908) NONE

Reggae (1980) Edward Burbridge[S]; Raoul Pène Du Bois[C]; Beverly Emmons[L]

Regina (1949) Horace Armistead[S]; Aline Bernstein[C]; Charles Elson[L]

Regina (1992) Joseph A. Citarella[C]; Jeff Davis[L]; James Leonard Joy[S]

Regular Feller, A (1919) ACK[L]

Regular Guy, A (1931) Cleon Throckmorton[S]

Rehearsal, The (1963) Will Steven Armstrong[L]; Jane Graham[S]; Tony Walton[C]

Rehearsal, The (1996) Robert Brill[S]; Michael Krass[C]; Kenneth Posner[L]

Rejuvenation of Aunt Mary, The (1907) Matt Morgan[S]; Young Brothers and Boss[S]; ACK[L]

Relapse, The (1950) Robert O'Hearn[S][C]; ACK[L]

Relations (1928) P. Dodd Ackerman[S]; ACK[C][L]

Reluctant Debutant, The (1956) Kathryn B. Miller[C]; Raymond Sovey[S]

Remains to Be Seen (1951) Raymond Sovey[S]; ACK[C]

Remarkable Mr. Pennypacker, The (1953) Ben Edwards[S][C]

Remember the Day (1935) S. Syrjala[S]; ACK[C][L]

Remnant (1918) Henri Bendel[C]; Ernest Gros[S]; Edna Hartman[C]; ACK[L]

Remote Control (1929) Henry Dreyfuss[S]; ACK[C]

Rendezvous (1932) Cleon Throckmorton[S]

Rent (1996) Blake Burba[L]; Paul Clay[S]; Angela Wendt[C]

Rented Earl, The (1915) ACK[S][L]

Reprise (1935) John Biddle Whitelaw[S]

Requiem for a Heavyweight (1985) Marjorie Bradley Kellogg[S]; Bill Walker[C]; Ronald Wallace[L]

Requiem for a Nun (1959) Motley[S][C][L]; Marvin Reiss[S]

Rescuing Angel, The (1917) Robert Edmond Jones[S]; ACK[L]

Resistible Rise of Arturo Ui, The (1968) Richard L. Hay[S][C]

Respect for Riches (1920) William Henry Matthews[C]; ACK[L]

Restless Women (1927) Nicholas Yellenti[S]

Resurrection (1903) Joseph Physioc[S]; Worth[C]

Retreat to Pleasure (1940) Paul du Pont[C]; Donald Oenslager[S]

Return Engagement (1940) Johannes Larsen[S]

Return from Jerusalem, The (1912) Lucile[C]

Return of Eve, The (1909) H. Robert Law[S]

Return of Peter Grimm, The (1911) Ernest Gros[S]

Return of Peter Grimm, The (1921) Ernest Gros[S]; Louis Hartmann[L]

Return of the Vagabond (1940) William Oden Waller[S]; ACK[C]

Reunion (1938) ACK[L]

Reunion in New York (1940) Harry Horner[S]; Lester Polakov[C]
Reunion in Vienna (1931) Aline Bernstein[S]; Ack[C]
Reveil, Le (1908) None
Revellers, The (1909) None
Revenge or The Pride of Lillian Le Mar (1913) No Playbill
Revenge with Music (1934) Albert R. Johnson[S]; Constance Ripley[C]
Revery (1927) Clarke Robinson[S][C]
Revisor (1935) Yury Annyenkov[S]
Revolt (1928) Ack[S][C][L]
Revolt, The (1915) Ack[L]
Revue of Revues, The (1911) H. Robert Law[S]; Max & Mahieu[C]; Frank D. Thomas[S]
Revue Russe (1922) Léon Bakst[S][C]; Paul Ouzounoff[S][C]; Sergi Soudeikine[S][C]
Rex (1976) John Conklin[S][C]; Jennifer Tipton[L]
Rhapsody (1944) Frank Bevan[C]; Stanley R. McCandless[L]; Oliver Smith[S]
Rhapsody in Black (1931) Ack[L]
Rhapsody, The (1930) Joseph Wickes[S]; Ack[C]
Rhinoceros (1961) Leo Kerz[S][L]; Michael Travis[C]
Rich Full Life, The (1945) Raymond Sovey[S]
Rich Man's Son, A (1899) None
Rich Man's Son, A (1912) None
Rich Man, Poor Man (1916) Joseph Physioc Studio[S]; Ack[L]
Rich Mr. Hoggenheimer, The (1906) Ernest Gros[S]; Mrs. Caroline Siedle[C]
Rich Mrs. Repton, The (1904) Madame Viola[C]; Ack[S]
Richard B. Mantell Repertory (1909) None
Richard Carvel (1900) Ogden[C]; Edward G. Unitt[S]; Helen Windsor[C]
Richard III (1904) None
Richard III (1905) None
Richard III (1906) None
Richard III (1908) None
Richard III (1943) David Ffolkes[C]; Motley[S]; Jean Rosenthal[L]
Richard III (1949) Richard Whorf[S][C]; Ack[L]
Richard III (1956) Leslie Hurry[S][C]
Richard III (1979) Jeanne Button[C]; Thomas Skelton[L]; Tony Straiges[S]
Richard Lovelace (1901) None

Richard of Bordeaux (1934) P. Dodd Ackerman[S]; Motley[C]
Richard Savage (1901) Alexander Corbett[S]; Maurice Hermann[C]
Richelieu (1904) Mrs. Lulu Fralik[C]; Madame Freisinger[C]; Unitt and Wickes[S]
Richelieu (1905) Mrs. Lulu Fralik[C]; Madame Freisinger[C]; Unitt and Wickes[S]
Richelieu (1907) Mrs. Lulu Fralik[C]; Madame Freisinger[C]; Unitt and Wickes[S]
Richelieu (1909) Mrs. Lulu Fralik[C]; Madame Freisinger[C]
Richelieu (1929) Claude Bragdon[S][C]
Richest Girl, The (1909) Ernest Gros[S]
Richter's Wife (1905) No Playbill
Riddle Me This (1932) David S. Gaither[S]; Ack[C]
Riddle Me This (1933) David S. Gaither[S]
Riddle: Woman, The (1918) P. Dodd Ackerman Studio[S]; Lucile[C]; Ack[L]
Ride Down Mt. Morgan (2000) John Arnone[S]; Elizabeth Hope Clancy[C]; Brian MacDevitt[L]
Rider of Dreams, The/ Granny Maumee/ Simon (1917) Robert Edmond Jones[S][C]; Ack[L]
Right Age to Marry, The (1926) Ack[L]
Right Girl, The (1921) Helen Myers[C]; Ack[S]
Right Honorable Gentleman, The (1965) Lloyd Burlingame[L]; Loudon Sainthill[S][C]
Right Next to Broadway (1944) Karle O. Amend[S]; Ack[C]
Right of Happiness (1931) Madame Frances[C]; Maritza[C]; Ack[S][L]
Right of Way, The (1907) Homer Emens[S]; Richard Marston[S]
Right This Way (1938) Nat Karson[S]; Miles White[C]
Right to Be Happy, The (1912) H. Robert Law[S]
Right to Dream, The (1924) Ack[L]
Right to Happiness, The (1912) None
Right to Kill, The (1926) Joseph Mullen[S][C]
Right to Love, The (1925) Ack[L]
Right to Strike, The (1921) None
Right You Are If You Think You Are (1927) Jo Mielziner[S][C][L]
Right You Are If You Think You

Are (1966) Gilbert V. Hemsley, Jr.[L];
Nancy Potts[C]; James Tilton[S]
Righteous Are Bold, The (1955)
Audré[C]; Watson Barratt[S]; Peggy
Clark[L]
Ring 'Round the Moon (1950)
Castillo[C]; Raymond Sovey[S][L]
Ring 'Round the Moon (1999) John
Lee Beatty[S]; Natasha Katz[L]; John
David Ridge[C]
Ring around Elizabeth (1941) Helene
Pons[C]; Raymond Sovey[S]
Ring Round the Bathtub (1972)
Joseph G. Aulisi[C]; Roger Morgan[L];
Ed Wittstein[S]
Ring Two (1939) Hattie Carnegie[C];
John Root[S]; Bianca Stroock[C]
Ringmaster, The (1909) NONE
Ringside (1928) R. N. Robbins[S]
Ringside Seat (1938) Lawrence L.
Goldwasser[S]; ACK[C]
Rink, The (1984) Theoni V. Aldredge[C];
Peter Larkin[S]; Marc B. Weiss[L]
Rio Grande (1914) Gates and
Morange[S]
Rio Grande (1916) Gates and
Morange[S]
Rio Rita (1927) John W. Harkrider[C];
Joseph Urban[S]
Riot Act, The (1963) William
Ritman[S]; Noel Taylor[C]
Rip Van Winkle (1905) NONE
Ripples (1930) Charles LeMaire[C];
Joseph Urban[S]
Rise and Fall of Little Voice, The
(1994) Thomas Lynch[S]; Allison
Reeds[C]; Kevin Rigdon[L]
Rise of Rosie O'Reilly, The (1923)
Ada B. Fields[C]; Cora MacGeachy[C];
Joseph Wickes[S]
Rising of the Moon, The (1908) NONE
Rising Sun, The (1924) Sheldon K.
Viele[S]
Rita Coventry (1923) Sheldon K.
Viele[S]; ACK[C][L]
Ritornele (1927) Esther Peck[S][C];
ACK[L]
Ritz, The (1975) Martin Aronstein[L];
Lawrence King[S][C]; Michael H.
Yeargan[S]
Ritz, The (1983) Todd Lichtenstein[L];
Gordon Micunis[S]; George Potts[C]
Ritzy (1930) Cirker and Robbins[S];
ACK[L]
Rivalry, The (1959) David Hays[S];
Motley[C]; Tharon Musser[L]

Rivals, The (1899) NONE
Rivals, The (1912) Grace O. Clarke[S]
Rivals, The (1922) Woodman
Thompson[S]; ACK[C][L]
Rivals, The (1923) David S. Gaither[S];
Anthony Greshoff[L]; ACK[C]
Rivals, The (1930) Gates and
Morange[S]; Anthony Greshoff[L];
William Weaver[C]
Rivals, The (1942) Watson Barratt[S][C]
River Niger, The (1973) Shirley
Prendergast[L]; Edna Watson[C]; Gary
James Wheeler[S]
Riverdance (1996) Robert Ballagh[S];
Jen Kelly[C]; Rupert Murray[L]; Chris
Slingsby[S]
Riverdance (1997) Robert Ballagh[S];
Jen Kelly[C]; Rupert Murray[L]
Riverdance (1998) Robert Ballagh[S];
Margaret Crosse[C]; Jen Kelly[C];
Rupert Murray[L]
Riverdance - The Show (1996) Robert
Ballagh[S]; Jen Kelly[C]; Rupert
Murray[L]
Riverdance on Broadway (2000)
Robert Ballagh[S]; Joan Bergin[C]; Jen
Kelly[C]; Rupert Murray[L]
Riviera Girl, The (1917) Joseph
Urban[S]; ACK[C][L]
Road to Arcady, The (1912) NONE
Road to Happiness, The (1915) ACK[L]
Road to Happiness, The (1927) ACK[L]
Road to Mandalay, The (1916) ACK[L]
Road to Rome, The (1927) Lee
Simonson[S][C]; ACK[L]
Road to Rome, The (1928) Lee
Simonson[S][C]
Road to Yesterday, The (1906) NONE
Road Together, The (1924) Dickson
Morgan[S]; ACK[L]
Roads of Destiny (1918) Hickson[C];
Joseph Physioc[S]; ACK[L]
Roadside (1930) Robert Edmond
Jones[S]; Everett Shinn[C]
Roar China (1930) Lee Simonson[S][C]
Roar Like a Dove (1964) Helen
Pond[S][L]; Herbert Senn[S][L]; Michael
Travis[C]
**Roar of the Greasepaint – The
Smell of the Crowd** (1965) Sean
Kenny[S][L]; Freddy Wittop[C]
Roast, The (1980) Alvin Colt[C]; Tharon
Musser[L]; William Ritman[S]
Rob Roy (1913) Will R. Barnes[C];
Gates and Morange[S]
Robber Bridegroom, The (1976)

Jeanne Button[C]; Douglas W. Schmidt[S]; David F. Segal[L]

Robe Rouge, La (1904) ACK[S]

Robert B. Mantell Repertory (1911) NONE

Robert B. Mantell Repertory (1915) NONE

Robert Burns (1905) NONE

Robert E. Lee (1923) Livingston Platt[S]; ACK[C]

Robert Emmet (1902) Moses and Hamilton[S]

Roberta (1933) Yetta Kiviette[C]; Clarke Robinson[S]; Hassard Short[L]

Robespierre (1899) Hawes Craven[S]; Joseph Harker[S]; Marcel Multzer[C]

Robin Hood (1902) Madame Freisinger[C]; Ernest Gros[S]

Robin Hood (1912) Will R. Barnes[C]; Homer Emens[S]; Gates and Morange[S]

Robin Hood (1929) ACK[C][L]

Robin Hood (1932) ACK[C][L]

Robin Hood (1944) Veronica[C]; ACK[S]

Robin Landing (1937) Donald Oenslager[S]; Jean Sutherland[C]

Robinson Crusoe, Jr. (1916) P. Dodd Ackerman[S]; Aloys Bohnen[C]; H. Robert Law[S]; John H. Young[S]; ACK[L]

Rock 'n Roll! The First 5,000 Years (1982) Jules Fisher[L]; Franne Lee[C]; Mark Ravitz[S]

Rock Me, Juliet (1931) Donald Oenslager[S]

Rock-a-Bye Baby (1918) ACK[S][C][L]

Rockabye Hamlet (1976) Joseph G. Aulisi[C]; Jules Fisher[L]; Kert Lundell[S]

Rockbound (1929) ACK[S][C][L]

Rockefeller and the Red Indians (1968) Lloyd Burlingame[L]; Hayden Griffin[S][C]

Rocket to the Moon (1938) Michael Gordon[L]; Mordecai Gorelik[S]; ACK[C]

Rockette Spectacular with Ginger Rogers, A (1980) Ken Billington[L]; John William Keck[S]; Frank Spencer[C]

Rocky Horror Show, The (1975) Sue Blane[C]; Chipmonck[L]; Peter Harvey[C]; Brian Thomson[S]

Rocky Horror Show, The (2000) Paul Gallo[L]; David Rockwell[S]; David C. Woolard[C]

Roger Bloomer (1923) Kate Drain Lawson[C]; Woodman Thompson[S]

Rogers and Hart (1975) Ken Billington[L]; David Jenkins[S]; Stanley Simmons[C]

Rogers Brothers in Central Park, The (1900) F. Richards Anderson[C]; Ernest Gros[S]; Edward Ocker[L]

Rogers Brothers in Harvard, The (1902) F. Richards Anderson[C]; Ernest Gros[S]

Rogers Brothers in Ireland, The (1905) F. Richards Anderson[C]; Henry Bissing[L]; Ernest Gros[S]

Rogers Brothers in London, The (1903) Ernest Albert[S]; F. Richards Anderson[C]; Henry Bissing[L]; Ernest Gros[S]

Rogers Brothers in Panama, The (1907) Ernest Albert[S]; Will R. Barnes[C]; Walter W. Burridge[S]; Homer Emens[S]; Gates and Morange[S]; Kliegl Brothers[L]; P. J. McDonald[S]; ACK[C]

Rogers Brothers in Paris, The (1904) F. Richards Anderson[C]; Ernest Gros[S]

Rogers Brothers in Wall Street (1899) F. Richards Anderson[C]; Gates and Morange[S]; Edward Ocker[L]; Joseph Physioc[S]

Rogers Brothers in Washington, The (1901) Ernest Gros[S]

Roll Sweet Chariot (1934) Tom Adrian Cracraft[S]; Alice McFadden[C]; Elizabeth Hooker Parsons[C]

Rollicking Girl, The (1905) Ernest Gros[S]

Rollin' on the T.O.B.A. (1999) Larry W. Brown[S]; Jon Kusner[L]; Michele Reisch[C]

Rolling Stones (1915) ACK[C][L]

Rollo's Wild Oat (1920) Maurice Hermann[C]; Roland Young[S]; ACK[L]

Roly Poly and Without the Law (1912) David Atchison[L]; Cora MacGeachy[C]; John H. Young[S]

Roman Candle (1960) David Hays[S][L]; Ruth Morley[C]

Roman Servant, A (1934) Watson Barratt[S]; Melanie Kahane[C]; Murray Mayer[C]

Romance (1921) O'Kane Conwell[C]

Romance and Arabella (1917) Unitt and Wickes[S]; ACK[L]

Romance of Athlone, A (1901) Mrs. Caroline Siedle[C]; Louis C. Young[S]

Romance/Romance (1988) Steven Jones[C]; Craig Miller[L]; Steven Rubin[S]

Romancing 'Round (1927) Frank Detering[L]; ACK[S][C]

Romanoff and Juliet (1957) Howard Bay[L]; Jean-Denis Malclès[S]; Helene Pons[C]

Romantic Comedy (1979) Jane Greenwood[C]; Tharon Musser[L]; Douglas W. Schmidt[S]

Romantic Mr. Dickens (1940) Watson Barratt[S]; Ernest Schraps[C]

Romantic Young Lady, The (1926) Aline Bernstein[S][C]

Romeo and Juliet (1903) Frank E. Gates[S]; Edward Morange[S]

Romeo and Juliet (1904) C. Karl[C]

Romeo and Juliet (1905) C. Karl[C]

Romeo and Juliet (1907) C. Karl[C]

Romeo and Juliet (1915) ACK[L]

Romeo and Juliet (1922) Robert Edmond Jones[S][C]

Romeo and Juliet (1923) Henri Bendel[C]; Madame Freisinger[C]; Rollo Peters[S]; ACK[L]

Romeo and Juliet (1930) Aline Bernstein[S][C]

Romeo and Juliet (1934) Jo Mielziner[S][C][L]

Romeo and Juliet (1935) Jo Mielziner[S][C]

Romeo and Juliet (1940) Robert Edmond Jones[L]; Motley[S][C]

Romeo and Juliet (1951) Oliver Messel[S][C]

Romeo and Juliet (1956) Loudon Sainthill[S][C]

Romeo and Juliet (1977) John Conklin[C]; Ming Cho Lee[S]; Thomas Skelton[L]

Romulus (1962) Lucinda Ballard[C]; Peggy Clark[L]; Oliver Smith[S]

Roof, The (1931) Thomas Farrar[S]; Ellen Goldsborough[C]; ACK[L]

Room 349 (1930) Eddie Eddy[S]; ACK[C]

Room in Red and White, A (1936) Elizabeth Hawes[C]; Jo Mielziner[S][L]

Room of Dreams (1930) Eddie Eddy[S]; Mary Walls[C]

Room Service (1937) Cirker and Robbins[S]; ACK[C]

Room Service (1953) Frederick Fox[S][L]

Roomful of Roses, A (1955) Audré[C]; Donald Oenslager[S][L]

Roosty (1938) Nat Karson[S]; ACK[C]

Rope (1928) Cleon Throckmorton[S]

Rope Dancers, The (1957) Boris Aronson[S][L]; Patricia Zipprodt[C]

Rope's End (1929) Rollo Wayne[S]; ACK[L]

Rosa Machree (1922) ACK[S][L]

Rosalie (1928) John W. Harkrider[C]; Joseph Urban[S]

Rosalinda (1942) Ladislas Czettel[C]; Jean Rosenthal[L]; Oliver Smith[S]

Rosary, The (1910) NONE

Rose (1981) Linda Fisher[C]; John Gunter[S]; Andy Phillips[L]

Rose (2000) Stephen Brimson Lewis[S][C]; Johanna Town[L]

Rose Bernd (1922) Robert Edmond Jones[S]; ACK[C]

Rose Briar (1922) Ben Ali Haggin[C]; ACK[L]

Rose Girl, The (1921) Ralph Mulligan[C]; William Weaver[S]; ACK[L]

Rose Maid, The (1912) Will R. Barnes[C]; Dodge and Castle[S]

Rose o' Plymouth-Town, A (1902) Edward G. Unitt[S]; ACK[C]

Rose of Algeria, The (1909) Ernest Albert[S]; T. Bernard McDonald[S]; ACK[C][L]

Rose of Alhambra, The (1907) Homer Emens[S]; Frank E. Gates[S]; Edward Morange[S]; Edward G. Unitt[S]

Rose of China, The (1919) Helen Dryden[C]; Alice O'Neil[C]; Joseph Urban[S]; ACK[L]

Rose of Panama, The (1912) No PLAYBILL

Rose of Persia, The (1900) Percy Anderson[C]; Edward G. Unitt[S]

Rose of Stamboul, The (1922) Watson Barratt[S]; Anna Spencer[C]

Rose of the Rancho, The (1906) Wilfred Buckland[S]; Ernest Gros[S]; Louis Hartmann[L]; Albertine Randall Wheelan[C]

Rose Tattoo, The (1951) Boris Aronson[S]; Rose Bogdanoff[C]; Charles Elson[L]

Rose Tattoo, The (1995) Santo Loquasto[S]; Kenneth Posner[L]; Catherine Zuber[C]

Rose-Marie (1924) Gates and Morange[S]; Charles LeMaire[C]; ACK[L]

Roseanne (1923) Robert Peter Davis[S]; Daisy Martin[C]

Rosedale (1913) ACK[S][C][L]

Rosemary (1915) Henry Dazian[C];

Edward G. Unitt[S]; Rose Windsor[C];
ACK[L]

**Rosencrantz and Guildenstern Are
Dead** (1967) Desmond Heeley[S][C];
Richard Pilbrow[L]

Rosmersholm (1904) NONE

Rosmersholm (1925) Fania Mindell[C];
Cleon Throckmorton[S]

Rosmersholm (1935) Irene Sharaff[S][C];
ACK[L]

Ross (1961) Al Alloy[L]; Motley[S][C]

Rothschilds, The (1970) John
Bury[S][C]; Ann Curtis[C]; Richard
Pilbrow[L]

Rotters, The (1922) P. Dodd
Ackerman[S]; ACK[L]

Rouget De L'Isle (1902) ACK[S][C][L]

Round the Town (1924) John
Wenger[S]; ACK[S][L]

Round Trip (1945) Samuel Leve[S];
Bianca Stroock[C]

Round Up, The (1907) Klaw &
Erlanger[C]; John H. Young[S]

Round-Up, The (1932) Livingston
Platt[S]; ACK[C]

Rounders, The (1899) Madame
Ripley[C]; ACK[S][L]

Rowan Atkinson at the Atkinson
(1986) Will Bowen[S][C]; Mark
Henderson[L]

Royal Box, The (1928) Madame
Freisinger[C]; ACK[S][L]

Royal Chef, The (1904) NONE

Royal Family, A (1900) Edward G.
Unitt[S]

Royal Family, The (1927) Peggy
Hoyt[C]; James Reynolds[S][C]; ACK[L]

Royal Family, The (1975) John
Gleason[L]; Ann Roth[C]; Oliver
Smith[S]

Royal Fandango, A (1923) Robert
Edmond Jones[S]; ACK[C]

Royal Hunt of the Sun (1965) Michael
Annals[S][C]; Martin Aronstein[L]

Royal Mounted, The (1908) NONE

Royal Rival, A (1901) Henry Dazian[C];
Edward G. Unitt[S]

Royal Rogue, A (1900) NONE

Royal Vagabond, The (1919) Alice
O'Neil[C]; ACK[L]

Royal Virgin, The (1930) Watson
Barratt[S]; ACK[C]

Roza (1987) Ken Billington[L]; Florence
Klotz[C]; Alexander Okun[S]

Rubicon, The (1922) ACK[C][L]

Ruddigore (1927) Rollo Wayne[S]

Ruddigore (1955) Peter Goffin[S][C]

Rufus LeMaire's Affairs (1927)
Charles LeMaire[C]; Clarke Robinson[S]

Rugantino (1964) Giulio Coltellacci[S][C];
Vannio Vanni[L]

Rugged Path, The (1945) Rose
Bogdanoff[C]; Jo Mielziner[S][L];
Valentina[C]

Ruggles of Red Gap (1915) ACK[L]

"Ruined" Lady, The (1920) Robert T.
McKee[S]; ACK[L]

Ruint (1925) Cleon Throckmorton[S]

Rule of Three, The (1914) Henri
Bendel[C]; Kliegl Brothers[L]; Unitt
and Wickes[S]

Rules of the Game, The (1974) Ken
Billington[L]; Douglas Higgins[S];
Nancy Potts[C]

Ruling Power, The (1904) Ernest
Gros[S]; St. John Lewis[S]

Rumors (1988) Joseph G. Aulisi[C];
Tharon Musser[L]; Tony Straiges[S]

Rumple (1957) Alvin Colt[C]; George
Jenkins[S][L]

Run for Your Wife (1989) Michael
Anania[S]; Joseph G. Aulisi[C]; Marilyn
Rennagel[L]

Run Sheep Run (1938) John Root[S];
ACK[C]

Run, Little Chillun (1933) Helene
Pons[C]; Cleon Throckmorton[S]

Run, Little Chillun (1943) Perry
Watkins[S][C]

Runaway, The (1911) Ernest Gros[S];
Unitt and Wickes[S]

Runaways (1978) Woods Mackintosh[S];
Hilary Rosenfield[C]; Douglas W.
Schmidt[S]; Jennifer Tipton[L]

Runaways, The (1903) D. Frank
Dodge[S]; Mrs. Caroline Siedle[C]

Runner Stumbles, The (1976) James
Berton Harris[C]; Cheryl Thacker[L];
Patricia Woodbridge[S]

Runnin' Wild (1923) H. Robert Studio
Law[S]; ACK[C]

Running for Office (1903) C. W.
Valentine[S]

Russet Mantle (1936) Donald
Oenslager[S]; Hazel Strayer[C]

Russian Bank (1940) Louis Bromberg[S]

Russian People, The (1942) Boris
Aronson[S]; ACK[C]

Rust (1924) ACK[L]

Ruth Draper (1934) ACK[L]

Ruth Draper (1936) ACK[L]

Ruth Draper (1957) ACK[L]

Ruth Draper and Paul Draper (1954) ACK[L]

Rutherford and Son (1912) Unitt and Wickes[S]

Rutherford and Son (1927) Charles Friedman[S]; ACK[L]

Ryan Girl, The (1945) Hattie Carnegie[C]; Raymond Sovey[S]

S.S. Glencairn (1924) Cleon Throckmorton[S]

S.S. Glencairn (1929) Martha Andrews[C]; ACK[S][L]

S.S. Tenacity, The (1922) Robert Edmond Jones[S]; ACK[L]

Sabrina Fair (1953) Donald Oenslager[S][L]; Bianca Stroock[C]

Sacrament of Judas, The (1903) NONE

Sacrament of Judas, The (1913) NONE

Sacred and Profane Love (1920) Homer Emens[S]

Sacred Flame, The (1928) ACK[S][C][L]

Sacred Flame, The (1952) Leo Kerz[S][L]

Sacrifice, The (1921) NONE

Sacrilege (1995) John Arnone[S]; Howell Binkley[L]; Alvin Colt[C]

Sadie Love (1915) ACK[C][L]

Sadie Thompson (1944) Boris Aronson[S]; Motley[C]

Safe Sex (1987) Nanzi Adzima[C]; John Falabella[S]; Craig Miller[L]

Sag Harbor (1900) Ernest Albert[S]; Gates and Morange[S]

Sail Away (1961) Peggy Clark[L]; Helene Pons[C]; Oliver Smith[S][C]

Sailor, Beware (1933) P. Dodd Ackerman[S]; Virginia Estes Cates[C]

Sailor, Beware (1935) P. Dodd Ackerman[S]; Virginia Estes Cates[C]; ACK[L]

Sailors of Cattaro (1934) Mordecai Gorelik[S]; ACK[C]

Saint Joan (1923) Raymond Sovey[S][C]

Saint Joan (1936) Jo Mielziner[S][C][L]

Saint Joan (1951) Elinor Robbins[C]; Richard Harrison Senie[S]

Saint Joan (1977) Zack Brown[C]; David Jenkins[S]; John McLain[L]

Saint Joan (1993) Ann Hould-Ward[C]; Marjorie Bradley Kellogg[S]; Richard Nelson[L]

Saint of Bleecker Street, The (1954) Robert Randolph[S][C]; Jean Rosenthal[L]

Saint Wench (1933) Madame Valentina Kachouba[C]; Redington Sharpe[S]

Saint, The (1924) Robert Edmond Jones[S]

Sakura (1928) Mr. Minory Mishida[C]; Carl H. Vose[S][C]

Salamander, The (1914) Mrs. Condé Nast[S][C]

Sally (1920) Lucile[C]; Alice O'Neil[C]; Pascaud[C]; Joseph Urban[S]; ACK[L]

Sally (1948) Henry Mulle[C]; Joseph Urban[S]; ACK[L]

Sally (1987) Peter M. Ehrhardt[L]; Roger LaVoie[S]

Sally in Our Alley (1902) D. Frank Dodge[S]; Mrs. Caroline Siedle[C]; Edward G. Unitt[S]

Sally Marr...and Her Escorts (1994) William Barclay[S]; David Dangle[C]; Phil Monat[L]; David C. Woolard[C]

Sally, Irene and Mary (1922) Joseph Urban[S]; ACK[C][L]

Sally, Irene and Mary (1925) ACK[S][C][L]

Salome (1922) ACK[S][C][L]

Salome (1923) George Clisbee[S][C]

Salome (1992) Zack Brown[S][C]; Arden Fingerhut[L]

Salomy Jane (1907) Frank E. Gates[S]; Kliegl Brothers[L]; Edward Morange[S]

Salt Water (1929) Mildred Manning[C]; ACK[L]

Saluta (1934) John N. Booth, Jr.[C]; Hugh Willoughby[S]

Salvation (1928) Robert Edmond Jones[S]; ACK[C]

Salvation Nell (1908) D. Frank Dodge[S]; Madame Freisinger[C]; Ernest Gros[S]

Sam Abramovitch (1927) NONE

Sam Houston (1906) NONE

Samson (1908) NONE

Samson and Delilah (1920) Robert Edmond Jones[S]; ACK[L]

San Toy (1900) Percy Anderson[C]

Sancho Panza (1923) James Reynolds[S][C]

Sandalwood (1926) Fania Mindell[C]; Cleon Throckmorton[S]

Sandro Botticelli (1923) Ernest de Weerth[S][C]; ACK[L]

Sap Runs High, The (1936) Karle O. Amend[S]; ACK[C]

Sap, The (1924) ACK[L]

Sapho (1900) Ernest Albert[S]

Sapho (1904) NONE

Sapho (1908) NONE

Sapphire Ring, The (1925) NONE

Sappho and Phaon (1907) Percy Anderson[C]; Frank E. Gates[S]; Edward Morange[S]

Sarafina! (1988) Mannie Manim[L]; Sarah Roberts[S][C]

Sarah Bernhardt in Rep (1910) Mathias Armbruster[S]

Saratoga (1959) Cecil Beaton[S][C]; Jean Rosenthal[L]

Sarava (1979) Santo Loquasto[S][C]; David F. Segal[L]

Sari (1914) Ernest Gros[S]; M. Ronsin[S]; Albertine Randall Wheelan[C]; ACK[C]

Sari (1930) Willy Pogany[S][C]

Satellite (1935) Anthony W. Street[S]; ACK[C]

Saturday Night (1926) Gladys E. Calthrop[C]; Cleon Throckmorton[S]

Saturday Night Fever (1999) Suzy Benzinger[C]; Andrew Bridge[L]; Andy Edwards[C]; Robin Wagner[S]

Saturday Night, A (1933) Livingston Platt[S]; ACK[C]

Saturday Sunday Monday (1974) Raimonda Gaetani[C]; Roger Morgan[L]; Franco Zeffirelli[S]

Saturday to Monday (1917) ACK[C][L]

Saturday's Children (1927) Jo Mielziner[S][L]

Sauce for the Goose (1911) No PLAYBILL

Saucy Sally (1904) NONE

Savage Rhythm (1931) Kennel and Entwistle[S]

Savage under the Skin (1927) Livingston Platt[S]

Save Me the Waltz (1938) John Hambleton[C]; Jo Mielziner[S][L]

Saving Grace, The (1918) Henri Bendel[C]; Homer Emens[S]; ACK[L]

Saviors (1915) Robert E. Locher[S][C]; Ada Rainey[S]

Say It with Flowers (1926) ACK[S][L]

Say When (1928) Livingston Platt[S]; ACK[C]

Say When (1934) Charles LeMaire[C]; Clarke Robinson[S]

Say, Darling (1958) Peggy Clark[L]; Alvin Colt[C]; Oliver Smith[S]

Scalawag (1927) ACK[L]

Scandal (1919) Lucile[C]; ACK[S][L]

Scandal, The (1910) ACK[S][C]

Scandals of 1920 (1920) H. Robert Studio Law[S]; ACK[C][L]

Scapin (1973) Martin Aronstein[L]; John David Ridge[C]; ACK[S]

Scapin (1996) Victoria Petrovich[C]; Nancy Schertler[L]; Douglas Stein[S]

Scapino (1974) Carl Toms[S][C]; David Watson[L]

Scaramouche (1923) T. M. Cleland[S][C]

Scarcrow, The (1911) H. Robert Law[S]; Byron Nestor[C]

Scarlet Fox, The (1928) Cleon Throckmorton[S]

Scarlet Letter, The (1906) NONE

Scarlet Letter, The (1907) NONE

Scarlet Letter, The (1926) Paul Ouzounoff[S]; Anna Wille[C]

Scarlet Lily, The (1927) Watson Barratt[S]

Scarlet Man, The (1921) Boué Soeurs[C]

Scarlet Pages (1929) Raymond Sovey[S]; ACK[C]

Scarlet Pimpernel, The (1910) R. McCleery[S]; L. and H. Nathan[C]; Mrs. Nettleship[C]

Scarlet Pimpernel, The (1997) Jane Greenwood[C]; Andrew Jackness[S]; Natasha Katz[L]

Scarlet Pimpernel, The (1998) Jane Greenwood[C]; Andrew Jackness[S]; Natasha Katz[L]

Scarlet Sister Mary (1930) Watson Barratt[S]; Orry-Kelly[C]

Scene of the Crime (1940) Cirker and Robbins[S]

Scenes and Revelations (1981) William Armstrong[L]; Oleksa[C]; Jane Thurn[S]

Schemers (1924) NONE

School (1913) NONE

School Days (1908) Madame Castle-Bert[C]; D. Frank Dodge[S]

School for Brides (1944) Ernest Glover[S]; ACK[C]

School for Husbands (1933) Lee Simonson[S][C]

School for Husbands, The (1905) Homer Emens[S]; Edward G. Unitt[S]

School for Scandal, The (1899) Mathias Armbruster[S]

School for Scandal, The (1902) Mathias Armbruster[S]

School for Scandal, The (1904) Mathias Armbruster[S]

School for Scandal, The (1909) E. Hamilton Bell[S][C]

School for Scandal, The (1925) Livingston Platt[S]; ACK[C]

School for Scandal, The (1931)

Watson Barratt[S]; Ernest Schraps[C]

School for Scandal, The (1963) Ralph Alswang[L]; Anthony Powell[S][C]

School for Scandal, The (1966) Gilbert V. Hemsley, Jr.[L]; Nancy Potts[C]; James Tilton[S]

School for Scandal, The (1995) Theoni V. Aldredge[C]; Mary Jo Dondlinger[L]; Douglas W. Schmidt[S]

School for Virtue (1931) Karle O. Amend[S]; ACK[C][L]

School for Wives, The (1971) Nancy Potts[C]; James Tilton[S][L]

School Girl, The (1904) Ernest Gros[S]

School Houses onthe Lot (1938) A. J. Lundborg[S]

Schoolgirl (1930) Alice Armstrong[C]; Nicholas Yellenti[S]

Schweiger (1926) Boris Anisfield[S][C]

Scorpion, The (1933) Eugene Dunkel[S]; ACK[C]

Scotch Mist (1926) ACK[S][C][L]

Scotland Yard (1929) Nicholas Yellenti[S]; ACK[C]

Scoundrel (1935) Allison McLellan Hunter[C]; ACK[L]

Scrambled Wives (1920) Henri Bendel[C]; Alexander King, Jr.[S]; Joseph Physioc Studio[S]; ACK[L]

Scrap of Paper, A (1914) ACK[C]

Scrap of Paper, The (1917) ACK[S][C][L]

Scrape o' the Pen, The (1912) Mrs. Graham Moffatt[C]

Scratch (1971) John Conklin[S]; A. H. Feder[L]; Patricia Zipprodt[C]

Sea Dogs (1939) John Root[S]

Sea Legs (1937) Mabel A. Buell[S]; Alfred Cheney Johnston[L]; ACK[C]

Sea Woman, The (1925) William Oden Waller[S]; ACK[L]

Seagull, The (1929) Aline Bernstein[S][C]; Irene Sharaff[C]

Seagull, The (1930) Walter Walden[S]; ACK[L]

Seagull, The (1938) Robert Edmond Jones[S][C]

Seagull, The (1964) Alvin Colt[C]; Peter Larkin[S]; Tharon Musser[L]

Seagull, The (1992) Laura Crow[C]; Marjorie Bradley Kellogg[S]; Richard Nelson[L]

Seagulls over Sorrento (1952) Mel Bourne[S][L]; Mildred Trebor[C]

Search and Destroy (1992) Christopher Barreca[S]; Candice Donnelly[C]; Chris Parry[L]

Search for Signs of Intelligent Life in the Universe, The (1985) Neil Peter Jampolis[S][L]; ACK[C]

Search for Signs of Intelligent Life in the Universe, The (2000) Ken Billington[L]; Klara Zieglerova[S]

Search Me (1915) ACK[S][L]

Searching for the Sun (1936) Cleon Throckmorton[S]

Searching Wind, The (1944) Howard Bay[S]; Aline Bernstein[C]

Seascape (1975) James Tilton[S][L]; Fred Voelpel[C]

Season Changes, The (1935) Gretl Urban[S]; ACK[C]

Season in the Sun (1950) Boris Aronson[S][L]; Natalie Barth Walker[C]

Second Best Boy (1946) Motley[S][C]

Second Comin', The (1931) ACK[L]

Second Fiddle, The (1904) NONE

Second in Command, The (1901) Henry Dazian[C]; Edward G. Unitt[S]

Second in Command, The (1913) NONE

Second Little Show, The (1930) Jo Mielziner[S][L]; Helene Pons[C]; Raymond Sovey[C]

Second Man, The (1927) Hattie Carnegie[C]; Jo Mielziner[S][L]

Second Mrs. Tanqueray, The (1902) NONE

Second Mrs. Tanqueray, The (1908) H. P. Hall[S]; Walter Hann[S]

Second Mrs. Tanqueray, The (1913) Madame Frances[C]

Second Mrs. Tanqueray, The (1924) Clara Fargo Thomas[S]

Second String, A (1960) Ben Edwards[S][L]; Robert Mackintosh[C]

Second Threshold (1951) Donald Oenslager[S][L]

Secret Afairs of Mildred Wild, The (1972) Carrie F. Robbins[C]; Thomas Skelton[L]

Secret Garden, The (1991) Theoni V. Aldredge[C]; Heidi Ettinger[S]; Tharon Musser[L]

Secret of Polichinelle, The (1904) NONE

Secret Orchard, The (1907) Homer Emens[S]; Mrs. Robert Osborn[C]; Frank Platzer[S]

Secret Rapture, The (1989) Jane Greenwood[C]; Santo Loquasto[S]; Richard Nelson[L]

Secret Room, The (1945) Frederick

Fox[L]; Carolyn Hancock[S]

Secret Service (1910) Henry E. Hoyt[S]

Secret Strings (1914) Maurice Hermann[C]; ACK[S][C][L]

Secret, The (1913) NONE

Secrets (1922) Miss Margaret Lawrence[C]; Joseph Wickes[S]; ACK[L]

Security (1929) Rollo Wayne[S]

See America First (1916) Gates and Morange[S]; ACK[L]

See My Lawyer (1915) ACK[L]

See My Lawyer (1939) Cirker and Robbins[S]; ACK[C][L]

See Naples and Die (1929) Robert Edmond Jones[S][C]; Yetta Kiviette[C]

See the Jaguar (1952) Lemuel Ayers[S][C]

Seed of the Brute (1926) Jo Mielziner[S][L]

Seeds in the Wind (1948) Ralph Alswang[S]

Seeing New York (1906) William Adler[C]

Seeing Things (1920) Henri Bendel[C]; ACK[L]

Seen But Not Heard (1936) John Root[S]; ACK[C]

Seesaw (1973) Jules Fisher[L]; Ann Roth[C]; Robin Wagner[S]

Seidman and Son (1962) William Pitkin[S][C][L]

Seige (1937) Norman Bel Geddes[S]; Frances Waite[C]

Self and Lady (1900) Ernest Gros[S]

Selling of the President, The (1972) Tom John[S]; Nancy Potts[C]; Thomas Skelton[L]

Sellout, The (1933) William H. Mensching[S]

Semi-Detached (1960) Boris Aronson[S]; Klaus Holm[L]; Helene Pons[C]

Semi-Detached (1963) Will Steven Armstrong[L]; Kenneth Bridgeman[S][C]

Senator Keeps House, The (1911) John Brunton[S]; T. Bernard McDonald[S]; Frank Platzer[S]

Send Me No Flowers (1960) Frederick Fox[S][C][L]

Sentinels (1931) Cleon Throckmorton[S]; ACK[C]

Separate Rooms (1940) DuWico[L]; ACK[C]

Separate Tables (1956) Paul Morrison[L]; Michael Weight[S]; ACK[C]

Septimus (1909) Ernest Gros[S]

Seremonda (1917) Homer Emens[S];

Kliegl Brothers[L]; ACK[C]

Serena Blandish (1929) Robert Edmond Jones[S]; ACK[C]

Serenade, The (1930) Rollo Wayne[S]

Sergeant Brue (1905) Richard Marston[S]

Sergeant Kitty (1904) D. Frank Dodge[S]; Madame Freisinger[C]; Archie Gunn[C]; Mrs. Caroline Siedle[C]

Serio-Comic Governess, The (1904) Emens and Unitt[S]; Milnor Wells[L]

Serious Money (1988) Rick Fisher[L]; Peter Hartwell[S][C]

Serpent's Tooth, A (1922) Joseph Physioc Studio[S]; ACK[C][L]

Servant in the House, The (1908) H. Robert Law[S]

Servant in the House, The (1918) ACK[L]

Servant in the House, The (1921) NONE

Servant in the House, The (1925) Sheldon K. Viele[S]; ACK[C]

Servant in the House, The (1926) Claude Bragdon[S]; ACK[C]

Servant of Two Masters (1928) Oscar Laske[C]; Jo Mielziner[S]; ACK[L]

Service (1918) Gates and Morange[S]; ACK[L]

Sesostra (1912) NONE

Set a Thief (1927) Nicholas Yellenti[S]; ACK[L]

Set My People Free (1948) Ralph Alswang[S]; Ernest Schraps[C]; ACK[L]

Set to Music (1939) Gladys E. Calthrop[S][C]

Seussical the Musical (2000) Natasha Katz[L]; Eugene Lee[S]; William Ivey Long[C]

Seven (1929) Cirker and Robbins[S]; Yetta Kiviette[C]; ACK[C][L]

Seven Brides for Seven Brothers (1982) Robert Fletcher[C]; Robert Randolph[S]; Thomas Skelton[L]

Seven Chances (1916) Ernest Gros[S]; ACK[C][L]

Seven Days (1909) Madame Mood[C]

Seven Days' Leave (1918) ACK[C][L]

Seven Descents of Myrtle, The (1968) Jane Greenwood[C]; Jo Mielziner[S][L]

Seven Guitars (1996) Christopher Akerlind[L]; Scott Bradley[S]; Constanza Romero[C]

Seven Keys to Baldpate (1913) NONE

Seven Keys to Baldpate (1935) William Oden Waller[S]

Seven Lively Arts (1944) Norman Bel Geddes[S]; Mary Grant[C]; Hassard Short[L]; Valentina[C]; E. Carlton Winckler[L]

Seven Sisters (1911) NONE

Seven Year Itch, The (1952) Frederick Fox[S][C][L]

Seventeen (1918) Frank J. Zimmerer[S]; ACK[L]

Seventeen (1951) Stewart Chaney[S]; David Ffolkes[C]

Seventh Heart, The (1927) R. N. Robbins[S]; ACK[L]

Seventh Heaven (1922) Joseph Physioc[S]; ACK[L]

Seventh Heaven (1955) A. H. Feder[L]; Marcel Vertès[S][C]

Seventh Trumpet, The (1941) Jo Mielziner[S][L]; ACK[C]

Severed Head, A (1964) Martin Aronstein[L]; Stewart Chaney[S][C]

Sex (1926) ACK[L]

Sex and Longing (1996) John Arnone[S]; Susan Hilferty[C]; Brian MacDevitt[L]

Sex Fable, The (1931) ACK[C][L]

Sganarelle (1970) John Gleason[L]; Fred Voelpel[S][C]

Sh! the Octopus (1928) Karle O. Amend[S]; ACK[L]

Shades of Night, The (1901) Mrs. Charles Hone[S]

Shadow and Substance (1938) Helene Pons[C]; David M. Twachtman[S]

Shadow Box, The (1977) Ming Cho Lee[S]; Bill Walker[C]; Ronald Wallace[L]

Shadow Box, The (1994) David Jenkins[S]; Richard Nelson[L]; Carrie F. Robbins[C]

Shadow of a Gunman, The (1958) Peter Larkin[S]; Ruth Morley[C]; Tharon Musser[L]

Shadow of My Enemy, A (1957) Donald Oenslager[S][C][L]

Shadow, The (1915) Lucile[C]; ACK[L]

Shadow, The (1922) Sheldon K. Viele[S]; ACK[L]

Shadow, The (1923) Sheldon K. Viele[S]; ACK[L]

Shadowed (1913) Hickson[C]; H. Robert Law[S]

Shadowlands (1990) J. Michael Deegan[L]; Mark Thompson[S][C]

Shady Lady (1933) Tom Adrian Cracraft[S]; ACK[C]

Shakespeare for My Father (1993) Thomas Skelton[L]; ACK[S]

Shakespeare on Broadway for the Schools (1986) Ruth Morley[C]; Loren Sherman[S]; Victor En Yu Tan[L]

Shakespeare's Cabaret (1981) Frank J. Boros[S][C]; Marc B. Weiss[L]

Shakuntala (1919) Livingston Platt[S][C]

Sham (1909) Mrs. Robert Osborn[C]; ACK[C]

Shame Woman, The (1923) William Gropper[C]; Jacob Meth[C]; ACK[L]

Shameen Dhu (1914) NONE

Shanghai (1926) Frederick W. Jones III[S]; ACK[C]

Shanghai Gesture (1928) Frederick W. Jones III[S]; ACK[C]

Shangri-La (1956) Peter Larkin[S][L]; Irene Sharaff[C]

Shannons of Broadway, The (1927) Nicholas Yellenti[S]; ACK[C]

Sharlee (1923) Reid McGuire[S]

Shatter'd Lamp, The (1934) Watson Barratt[S]; ACK[C]

Shavings (1920) ACK[L]

She Couldn't Say No (1926) Nicholas Yellenti[S]; ACK[C]

She Got What She Wanted (1929) ACK[L]

She Had to Know (1925) Livingston Platt[S]; ACK[C]

She Lived Next to the Firehouse (1931) Cirker and Robbins[S]; Mildred Manning[C]

She Loves Me (1933) Raymond Sovey[S]

She Loves Me (1963) William and Jean Eckart[S][L]; Patricia Zipprodt[C]

She Loves Me (1977) Ken Billington[L]; Donald Brooks[C]; ACK[S]

She Loves Me (1993) David Charles[C]; Jane Greenwood[C]; Peter Kaczorowski[L]; Tony Walton[S]

She Loves Me Not (1932) Joe Miller[L]; Raymond Sovey[S]; Bianca Stroock[C]

She Means Business (1931) Margaret Pemberton[C]; Cleon Throckmorton[S]

She Stoops to Conquer (1905) NONE

She Stoops to Conquer (1912) F. Richards Anderson[C]; Henri Bendel[C]; Richard Marston[S]

She Stoops to Conquer (1924) Norman Bel Geddes[S]; Aline Bernstein[C]

She Stoops to Conquer (1928)

Norman Bel Geddes[S]; Ack[C]

She Walked in Her Sleep (1918) Henri Bendel[C]; Ack[L]

She Would and She Did (1919) Ack[L]

She's a Good Fellow (1919) Dodge and Castle[S]; Gladys Monkhouse[C]; Ack[L]

She's in Again (1915) Ack[S][L]

She's My Baby (1928) Raymond Sovey[S][C]; Ack[C][L]

Sheep of the Runway (1970) Jules Fisher[L]; Jane Greenwood[C]; Peter Larkin[S]

Sheik of Avenue B, The (1992) Robert Bessoir[L]; Deidre Burke[C]; Bruce Goodrich[S]

Shelf, The (1926) Woodman Thompson[S][C][L]

Shelter (1973) Richard Pilbrow[L]; Tony Walton[S][C]

Shenandoah (1975) C. Murawski[S]; Thomas Skelton[L]; Pearl Somner[C]

Shenandoah (1989) Guy Geoly[C]; Kert Lundell[S]; Stephen Ross[L]

Shepherd in the Distance, The (1915) Robert E. Locher[S][C]

Shepherd King, The (1904) Castle and Harvey[S]

Sheppy (1944) Watson Barratt[S]

Sherlock Holmes (1899) Ernest Gros[S]

Sherlock Holmes (1910) Ernest Gros[S]

Sherlock Holmes (1928) Gates and Morange[S]; Anthony Greshoff[L]; Yetta Kiviette[C]; Ack[C]

Sherlock Holmes (1929) Gates and Morange[S]; Anthony Greshoff[L]; Ack[C]

Sherlock Holmes (1953) Stewart Chaney[S][C][L]

Sherlock Holmes (1974) Neil Peter Jampolis[L]; Carl Toms[S][C]

Sherlock Holmes/Secret Service (1915) None

Sherlock's Last Case (1987) Pat Collins[L]; David Jenkins[S]; Robert Morgan[C]

Sherman Was Right (1915) Ack[L]

Sherry! (1967) Robert Mackintosh[C]; Robert Randolph[S][L]

Shimada (1992) Judy Dearing[C]; Richard Nelson[L]; Tony Straiges[S]

Shinbone Alley (1957) Eldon Elder[S]; Motley[C]; Tharon Musser[L]

Shining Hour, The (1934) Aubrey Hammond[S]; Molyneux[C]; Ack[L]

Ship Comes in, A (1934) Walter Harvey[S]; Margaret Montague[C];

Herbert Ward[S]

Shipwrecked (1924) P. Dodd Ackerman Studio[S]; Ack[L]

Shirkers, The (1907) None

Shirley Kaye (1916) Ack[C][L]

Shirley Maclaine on Broadway (1984) Ken Billington[L]; Pete Menefee[C]

Shirley Valentine (1989) Nick Chelton[L]; Bruno Santini[S][C]

Sho-gun, The (1904) Will R. Barnes[C]; Walter W. Burridge[S]; F. S. Neydhart[C]

Shoemaker's Holiday, The (1938) Millia Davenport[C]; Samuel Leve[S][L]

Shogun: The Musical (1990) Natasha Katz[L]; Loren Sherman[S]; Patricia Zipprodt[C]

Shoo-Fly Regiment, The (1907) Ernest Albert[S]; Siren Nevarro[C]; Ack[C]

Shoot the Works (1931) Henry Dreyfuss[S][L]; Yetta Kiviette[C]; Charles LeMaire[C]

Shooting Shadows (1924) Charles J. Auburn[S]

Shooting Star (1933) Helene Pons[C]; Raymond Sovey[S]

Shop at Sly Corner, The (1949) Willis Knighton[S][C]; Ack[L]

Shore Leave (1922) Henri Bendel[C]; Ernest Gros[S]; Ack[L]

Shot in the Dark, A (1961) Ben Edwards[S][L]; Noel Taylor[C]

Show Boat (1927) Frank Detering[L]; John W. Harkrider[C]; Joseph Urban[S]

Show Boat (1932) John W. Harkrider[C]; Joseph Urban[S]

Show Boat (1946) Lucinda Ballard[C]; Howard Bay[S]

Show Boat (1966) Jean Rosenthal[L]; Stanley Simmons[C]; Oliver Smith[S]

Show Boat (1983) Molly Maginnis[C]; Helen Pond[S]; Herbert Senn[S]; Thomas Skelton[L]

Show Boat (1994) Florence Klotz[C]; Eugene Lee[S]; Richard Pilbrow[L]

Show Girl (1929) John W. Harkrider[C]; Joseph Urban[S]

Show Girl (1961) Peggy Clark[L]; Oliver Smith[S]; Miles White[C]

Show Girl, The (1902) Frank Rafter[S]

Show Is On, The (1936) Vincente Minnelli[S][C]

Show Is On, The (1937) Vincente Minnelli[S][C]

Show Shop, The (1914) Ack[(C)(L)]
Show-Off, The (1924) Sheldon K. Viele[(S)]; Ack[(C)]
Show-Off, The (1932) Philip Maltese[(S)]; Ack[(C)]
Show-Off, The (1950) Beulah Frankel[(C)(L)]
Show-Off, The (1967) Nancy Potts[(C)]; James Tilton[(S)(L)]
Show-Off, The (1968) Nancy Potts[(C)]; James Tilton[(S)(L)]
Show-Off, The (1992) David Charles[(C)]; Ben Edwards[(S)]; Peter Kaczorowski[(L)]
Shrike, The (1952) Howard Bay[(S)]; Edith Lutyens Bel Geddes[(C)]
Shubert Gaieties of 1919 (1919) Watson Barratt[(S)]; Rowayne Simmons[(C)]; Ack[(L)]
Shuffle Along (1921) None
Shuffle Along (1952) Waldo Angelo[(C)]; Albert R. Johnson[(S)]
Shuffle Along of 1933 (1932) Karle O. Amend[(S)]; Helen Mahieu[(C)]; Robert Ten Eyck Stevenson[(C)]
Shulamite, The (1906) None
Siberia (1905) None
Sick-a-Bed (1918) Clifford F. Pember[(S)]; Ack[(L)]
Sid Caesar and Company (1989) Neil Peter Jampolis[(S)(L)]; Karen Roston[(C)]
Side by Side by Sondheim (1977) Ken Billington[(L)]; Peter Docherty[(S)]; Florence Klotz[(C)]
Side Man (1998) Tom Broecker[(C)]; Neil Patel[(S)]; Kenneth Posner[(L)]
Side Show (1997) Gregg Barnes[(C)]; Brian MacDevitt[(L)]; Robin Wagner[(S)]
Sidewalks of New York (1927) Maybelle Manning[(C)]; Robert Ten Eyck Stevenson[(C)]; Sheldon K. Viele[(S)]; Ack[(C)(L)]
Siegfried (1930) Aline Bernstein[(S)(C)]; Irene Sharaff[(C)]
Sign in Sidney Brustein's Window, The (1964) Jack Blackman[(S)]; Jules Fisher[(L)]; Fred Voelpel[(C)]
Sign in Sidney Brustein's Window, The (1972) Theoni V. Aldredge[(C)]; Richard Nelson[(L)]; William Ritman[(S)]
Sign of the Leopard (1928) Rollo Wayne[(S)]
Sign of the Rose, The (1911) Gates and Morange[(S)]
Sign on the Door, The (1919) Ack[(S)(C)(L)]
Signature (1945) Stewart Chaney[(S)]

Silence (1924) Ack[(S)(L)]
Silent Assertion, The (1917) Ack[(L)]
Silent Call, The (1911) Gates and Morange[(S)]
Silent House, The (1928) Watson Barratt[(S)]
Silent House, The (1932) Rollo Wayne[(S)]; Ack[(C)(L)]
Silent Night, Lonely Night (1959) Theoni V. Aldredge[(C)]; Jo Mielziner[(S)(L)]
Silent Voice, The (1914) Mr. Beardsley[(L)]; Grinager and Beardsley[(S)]; Mr. Maxwell[(L)]
Silent Witness, The (1916) Ack[(L)]
Silent Witness, The (1931) Rollo Wayne[(S)]
Silk Stockings (1955) Lucinda Ballard[(C)]; Robert Mackintosh[(C)]; Jo Mielziner[(S)(L)]
Silks and Satins (1920) Yetta Kiviette[(C)]; Ack[(S)(L)]
Silver Box, The (1907) Frank Platzer[(S)]
Silver Box, The (1928) August Vimnera[(S)]
Silver Cord, The (1926) Cleon Throckmorton[(S)]; Ack[(C)(L)]
Silver Fox, The (1921) Watson Barratt[(S)]; Ack[(C)]
Silver Girl, The (1907) None
Silver Slipper, The (1902) Charles Alias[(C)]; Joseph[(C)]; Worth[(C)]; Ack[(S)(L)]
Silver Star, The (1909) Ernest Albert[(S)]; F. Richards Anderson[(C)]
Silver Swan, The (1929) John N. Booth, Jr.[(C)]; DuWico[(L)]; William Henry Matthews[(C)]; Ward and Harvey Studios[(S)]
Silver Tassie, The (1929) Charles Friedman[(S)]; Ena Hourwich[(C)]; Ack[(L)]
Silver Wedding, The (1913) None
Silver Whistle, The (1948) Herbert Brodkin[(S)(L)]; Ernest Schraps[(C)]
Sim Sala Bim (1940) Ack[(L)]
Simon Called Peter (1924) Ack[(L)]
Simple Simon (1930) John W. Harkrider[(C)]; Joseph Urban[(S)]
Simple Simon (1931) Joseph Urban[(S)]; Ack[(C)]
Simpleton of the Unexpected Isles (1935) Lee Simonson[(S)(C)]
Simply Heavenly (1957) Norman Blumenfield[(L)]; Charles Brandon[(S)]
Sin of Pat Muldoon, The (1957) Mordecai Gorelik[(S)]; Anna Hill Johnstone[(C)]; Paul Morrison[(L)]

Sinbad (1918) Watson Barratt[S]; Homer Conant[C]; Cora MacGeachy[C]; S. Zalud[C]; Ack[L]

Sing and Whistle (1934) Cleon Throckmorton[S]; Ack[C]

Sing for Your Supper (1938) Herbert Andrews[S]; A. H. Feder[L]; Mary Merrill[C]

Sing Out the News (1938) John Hambleton[C]; Jo Mielziner[S][L]

Sing Out, Sweet Land (1944) Lucinda Ballard[C]; Albert R. Johnson[S]

Sing Till Tomorrow (1953) Ralph Alswang[S][L]; Ack[C]

Sing, Israel, Sing (1967) Judith[C]; Sylvia Younin[S]; Ack[L]

Singapore (1932) Eddie Eddy[S]; Ruth St. Denis[C]

Singin' in the Rain (1931) Yetta Kiviette[C]; Ack[L]

Singin' in the Rain (1985) Santo Loquasto[S]; Ann Roth[C]; Jennifer Tipton[L]

Singing Girl, The (1899) Joseph Physioc[S]

Singing Jailbirds (1928) Manuel Essman[S]

Singing Rabbi, The (1931) O. L. Raineri[S]; David Spero[C]; M. Teitelman[C]

Single Man, A (1911) Lucile[C]

Sinner (1927) P. Dodd Ackerman[S]; Ack[C]

Sinners (1915) Ack[C][L]

Sins of Society, The (1909) Oliver P. Bernard[S]; Frank Platzer[S]; Redfern[C]; Ack[L]

Sir Anthony (1906) Ack[S][C]

Sire (1911) Ernest Gros[S]

Siren, The (1911) Henry Dazian[C]; Homer Emens[S]; Ack[C]

Sister Beatrice (1908) E. Hamilton Bell[S][C]; Unitt and Wickes[S]

Sister Beatrice (1910) E. Hamilton Bell[S][C]; Unitt and Wickes[S]

Sister Mary (1899) Henry E. Hoyt[S]

Sisters (1927) Ack[C][L]

Sisters of the Chorus (1930) Ack[C][L]

Sisters Rosensweig, The (1993) John Lee Beatty[S]; Pat Collins[L]; Jane Greenwood[C]

Sitting Pretty (1924) P. Dodd Ackerman[S]; Charles LeMaire[C]; Alice O'Neil[C]

Six Characters in Search of an Author (1922) Cleon Throckmorton[S]; Ack[C][L]

Six Characters in Search of an Author (1924) Cleon Throckmorton[S]

Six Characters in Search of an Author (1931) Cleon Throckmorton[S]; Ack[C]

Six Degrees of Separation (1990) Paul Gallo[L]; William Ivey Long[C]; Tony Walton[S]

Six Month's Option (1917) Ack[C][L]

Six Rms Riv Vu (1972) William Ritman[S]; Ann Roth[C]; Marc B. Weiss[L]

Six Who Passed while the Lentils Boiled (1916) S. J. Dawkins[L]; W. Emerton Heitland[C]; William Sheafe[S]

Six-Fifty, The (1921) P. Dodd Ackerman Studio[S]; Ack[C]

Sixth Finger in a Five Finger Glove (1956) Paul Morrison[S][L]; Paul Parnes[C]; Susan Thomas[C]

Sizwe Banzi is Dead (1974) Douglas Heap[S]; Bill Walker[C]; Ronald Wallace[L]; Stuart Wurtzel[S]

Ski-Hi (1908) No PLAYBILL

Skidding (1928) DuWico[L]; Ack[S][C]

Skin Deep (1927) Nicholas Yellenti[S]; Ack[C]

Skin Game, The (1920) Kennel and Entwistle[S][L]; Ack[C]

Skin of Our Teeth, The (1942) Albert R. Johnson[S]; Mary Percy Schenck[C]

Skin of Our Teeth, The (1955) A. H. Feder[L]; Lester Polakov[S]; Helene Pons[C]

Skin of Our Teeth, The (1975) Ken Billington[L]; Eugene Lee[S]; Franne Lee[C]

Skipper & Co., Wall Street (1903) Joseph Physioc[S]

Skipper Next to God (1948) Boris Aronson[S]; Ack[L]

Skirt, The (1921) P. Dodd Ackerman[S]; Peggy Hoyt[C]

Skull, The (1928) Cirker and Robbins[S]; Ack[C][L]

Sky Farm (1902) Edward G. Unitt[S]

Sky's the Limit, The (1934) Arthur P. Segal[S]

Skydrift (1945) Motley[S][C]

Skylark (1939) Hattie Carnegie[C]; Donald Oenslager[S]

Skylark, A (1910) Frederica DeWolfe[C]; Peter W. King[L]; H. Robert Law[S]; William Henry Matthews[C]

Skylark, The (1921) NONE

Skylight (1996) Paul Gallo[L]; John Gunter[S][C]; Michael Lincoln[L]

Skyrocket (1929) Jo Mielziner[S][L]; Margaret Pemberton[C]

Skyscraper (1965) Theoni V. Aldredge[C]; Robert Randolph[S][L]

Slab Boys (1983) Arden Fingerhut[L]; Ray Recht[S]; Robert Wojewodski[C]

Slapstick Tragedy (1966) Martin Aronstein[L]; Ming Cho Lee[S]; Noel Taylor[C]

Slaves All (1926) William Henry Matthews[C]; Livingston Platt[S]; ACK[L]

Sleep No More (1944) A. A. Ostrander[S][C][L]

Sleep of Prisoners, A (1951) A. H. Feder[L]

Sleep, My Pretty One (1944) Raymond Sovey[S]

Sleeping Beauty and the Beast, The (1901) Robert Caney[S]; Henry Emden[S]; Julian Hicks[S]; R. McCleery[S]; Bruce Smith[S]

Sleeping Clergyman, A (1934) Lee Simonson[S][C]

Sleeping Partners (1918) Watson Barratt[S]; ACK[C][L]

Sleeping Prince, The (1956) Alvin Colt[C]; Norris Houghton[S]

Sleepless Night, A (1919) Watson Barratt[S]; ACK[C][L]

Sleepy Hollow (1948) David Ffolkes[C]; Jo Mielziner[S][L]

Sleight of Hand (1987) William Ivey Long[C]; Richard Nelson[L]; Loren Sherman[S]

Sleuth (1970) William Ritman[L]; Carl Toms[S][C]

Slice of Life, A (1912) NONE

Slight Case of Murder, A (1935) Kate Drain Lawson[S][C]

Slightly Delirious (1934) Karle O. Amend[S]; Hattie Carnegie[C]

Slightly Married (1943) Phil Raiguel[S]

Slightly Scandalous (1944) Gilbert Adrian[C]; Harry Dworkin[S]

Slim Princess, The (1911) Percy Anderson[C]; Frederica DeWolfe[C]; ACK[S]

Slow Dance on the Killing Ground (1964) Jack Brown[L]; Ann Roth[C]; Oliver Smith[S]

Sly Fox (1976) George Jenkins[S][L]; Albert Wolsky[C]

Small Family Business, A (1992) John Lee Beatty[S]; Peter Kaczorowski[L]; Ann Roth[C]

Small Hours, The (1951) Alice Gibson[C]; Donald Oenslager[S]

Small Miracle (1934) Boris Aronson[S]; Virginia Estes Cates[C]

Small Timer, The (1925) August Vimnera[S]; ACK[L]

Small War on Murray Hill (1957) Boris Aronson[S][L]; Irene Sharaff[C]

Small Wonder (1948) Ralph Alswang[S][L]; John Derro[C]

Smile (1986) Paul Gallo[L]; William Ivey Long[C]; Douglas W. Schmidt[S]

Smile at Me (1935) Karle O. Amend[S]; Dorothy Van Winkle[C]

Smile of the World, The (1949) Mainbocher[C]; Donald Oenslager[S][L]; Forrest Thayer[C]

Smiles (1930) John W. Harkrider[C]; Joseph Urban[S]

Smilin' Through (1919) Henri Bendel[C]; Joseph Urban[S]; ACK[L]

Smiling Faces (1932) Watson Barratt[S]; Ernest Schraps[C]

Smith (1910) Walter Hann[S]; Madame Hayward[C]; ACK[C]

Smokey Joe's Cafe (1995) Heidi Ettinger[S]; Timothy Hunter[L]; William Ivey Long[C]

Smoldering Flame, The (1913) NONE

Smooth as Silk (1921) NONE

Snafu (1944) John Root[S]; ACK[C]

Snapshots of 1921 (1921) ACK[C]

Snark Was a Boojum, The (1943) Frederick Fox[S]; Michael Paul[C]

Snobs (1911) NONE

Snookie (1941) Frederick Fox[S]; ACK[L]

Snow White and the Seven Dwarfs (1912) NO PLAYBILL

Snow White and the Seven Dwarfs (1979) Ken Billington[L]; John William Keck[S]; Frank Spencer[C]

So Am I (1928) Rollo Wayne[S]; ACK[L]

So Long, 174th Street (1976) Richard Nelson[L]; James Riley[S]; Stanley Simmons[C]

So Long, Letty (1916) ACK[S][L]

So Many Paths (1934) Watson Barratt[S]; Ernest Schraps[C]

So Much for So Much (1914) John Collette[S]

So Proudly We Hail (1936) John Root[S]; Beryl Wormser[C]; ACK[C]

So This Is London (1922) Hickson[C];

ACK[L]

So This Is Politics (1924) ACK[S][L]

So Was Napoleon (1930) DuWico[L]; George Jenkins[C]; Ward and Harvey Studios[S]

Social Register, The (1931) Natalie Hays Hammond[S]; William Oden Waller[S]; ACK[C]

Social Security (1986) Marilyn Rennagel[L]; Ann Roth[C]; Tony Walton[S]

Social Whirl, The (1906) Joseph[C]; Mrs. Caroline Siedle[C]

Society and the Bulldog (1908) Frank Platzer[S]

Society Circus, A (1905) Alfredo Edel[C]; Archie Gunn[C]; Arthur Voegtlin[S]

Society Girl (1931) Cirker and Robbins[S]; ACK[C]

Sold and Paid For (1900) No PLAYBILL

Soldier's Wife (1944) Raymond Sovey[S]; Bianca Stroock[C]

Soldiers (1968) Ralph Koltai[S][C][L]

Soldiers and Women (1929) ACK[S][L]

Soldiers of Fortune (1902) Joseph L. Menchen, Jr.[L]; Joseph Physioc[S]

Solid Gold Cadillac, The (1953) Edward Gilbert[S]; ACK[C]

Solid Ivory (1925) Nicholas Yellenti[S]; ACK[L]

Solid South (1930) Jo Mielziner[S][L]; ACK[C]

Soliloquy (1938) Norman Rock[S]

Solitaire (1942) Lucinda Ballard[C]; Jo Mielziner[S][L]

Solitaire/ Double Solitaire (1971) Kert Lundell[S]; Lewis Rampino[C]; Ronald Wallace[L]

Solitary Confinement (1992) William Barclay[S]; Kathleen Detoro[C]; Donald Holder[L]

Solomon's Child (1982) Marjorie Bradley Kellogg[S]; Richard Nelson[L]; Jennifer von Mayrhauser[C]

Some Americans Abroad (1990) Alexandra Byrne[S][C]; Rick Fisher[L]

Some Baby (1915) ACK[L]

Some Night (1918) ACK[S][L]

Some of My Best Friends (1977) Ken Billington[L]; Eugene Lee[S]; Franne Lee[C]

Some Party (1922) ACK[L]

Somebody's Luggage (1916) ACK[L]

Somebody's Sweetheart (1918) Homer Conant[C]; ACK[L]

Someone in the House (1918) Emmett Joyce[C]; Clifford F. Pember[S]; ACK[C][L]

Someone Waiting (1956) Gene Coffin[C]; Ben Edwards[S][L]

Someone Who'll Watch over Me (1992) Robin Don[S][C]; Natasha Katz[L]

Something about a Soldier (1962) Klaus Holm[L]; William Pitkin[S][C]

Something Different (1967) Will Steven Armstrong[S][L]; Ann Roth[C]

Something for Nothing (1937) Nicholas Yellenti[S]

Something for the Boys (1943) Howard Bay[S]; Billy Livingston[C]

Something Gay (1935) Donald Oenslager[S]; ACK[C]

Something More Important/The Old Woman/etc. (1935) Jack Maclennan[S][L]; ACK[C]

Something More! (1964) Alvin Colt[C]; Robert Randolph[S][L]

Something Old, Something New (1977) Clarke Dunham[L]; Lawrence King[S][C]; Michael H. Yeargan[C]

Something to Brag About (1925) Raymond Sovey[S]; ACK[L]

Something's Afoot (1976) Clifford Capone[C]; Richard Seger[S]; Walter Watson[C]; Richard Winkler[L]

Sometime (1918) ACK[C][L]

Somewhere Else (1913) William Adler[C]; Madame Freisinger[C]; Ernest Gros[S]; Mrs. Caroline Siedle[C]; Joseph Wilson[L]; Madame Zimmerman[C]; ACK[C]

Son of the People, A (1910) E. Hamilton Bell[S][C]

Son-Daughter, The (1919) Ernest Gros[S]; Louis Hartmann[L]; Albertine Randall Wheelan[C]

Song & Dance (1985) Jules Fisher[L]; Willa Kim[C]; Robin Wagner[S]

Song and Dance Man, The (1923) ACK[S][C][L]

Song and Dance Man, The (1930) Margaret Pemberton[C]; ACK[L]

Song of Bernadette (1946) Ralph Brown[S]; Willis Knighton[S]; ACK[L]

Song of Jacob Zulu, The (1993) Robert Christen[L]; Erin Quigley[C]; Kevin Rigdon[S]

Song of Norway (1944) Lemuel Ayers[S]; Robert Davison[C]; Walter J. Israel[C]

Song of Songs, The (1914) NONE
Song of the Flame (1925) Mark
Mooring[C]; Joseph Urban[S]
Song of the Grasshopper (1967)
Martin Aronstein[L]; Oliver Smith[S];
Noel Taylor[C]
Song of the Sword, The (1899)
Maurice Hermann[C]; Ogden[C];
Edward G. Unitt[S]
Song Writer, The (1928) William Oden
Waller[S]; ACK[C][L]
Songs from Milkwood (1970) John
Gleason[L]; David Hays[S]; Fred
Voelpel[C]
Sonny Boy (1921) Clifford F. Pember[S];
ACK[C]
Sons and Soldiers (1943) Norman Bel
Geddes[S][C]
Sons o' Fun (1941) Edward Duryea
Dowling[L]; Raoul Pène Du Bois[S][C]
Sons o' Guns (1929) Charles
LeMaire[C]; Joseph Urban[S]
Sonya (1921) P. T. Frankl[S]; ACK[C]
Sooner or Later (1925) Donald
Oenslager[S][C]; ACK[L]
Sophie (1920) Helen Dryden[C]; Clifford
F. Pember[S]
Sophie (1944) Rose Bogdanoff[C]; Samuel
Leve[S]
Sophie (1963) Robert Randolph[S][L];
Fred Voelpel[C]
Sophisticated Ladies (1981) Willa
Kim[C]; Jennifer Tipton[L]; Tony
Walton[S]
Sophisticrats, The (1933) Selma
Alexander[C]; Isaac Benesch[S]
Sorceress, The (1904) Ernest Gros[S]
Sothern and Marlowe Repertory
(1910) NONE
Sothern and Marlowe Repertory
(1911) NONE
Sothern and Marlowe Repertory
(1912) NONE
Sothern and Marlowe Repertory
(1913) NONE
Soul Kiss, The (1908) Ernest Albert[S];
F. Richards Anderson[C]; Frank E.
Gates[S]; Edward Morange[S];
Pascaud[C]; Wilhelm[C]; John H.
Young[S]
Sound of Hunting, A (1945) Samuel
Leve[S]
Sound of Music, The (1959) Lucinda
Ballard[C]; Mainbocher[C]; Jean
Rosenthal[L]; Oliver Smith[S]
Sound of Music, The (1990) Neil Peter

Jampolis[S][L]; Suzanne Mess[C]
Sound of Music, The (1998) Heidi
Ettinger[S]; Paul Gallo[L]; Catherine
Zuber[C]
Sour Grapes (1926) ACK[C][L]
South Pacific (1949) Jo Mielziner[S][L];
Motley[C]
South Pacific (1987) Desmond
Heeley[S][C]; Duane Schuler[L]
South Pacific by Rigsby (1903) NONE
South Pacific by Rigsby (1943) Boris
Aronson[S]; ACK[L]
Southern Exposure (1950) Kenn
Barr[C]; Frederick Fox[S][L]
Southerners, The (1904) NO PLAYBILL
Southwest Corner, The (1955) Ralph
Alswang[S][L]; Paul McGuire[C]
Spanish Love (1920) Robert W.
Bergman Studio[S]; ACK[C][L]
Speakeasy (1927) ACK[C][L]
Speaking of Murder (1956) Frederick
Fox[S][L]; Alice Gibson[C]
Special Occasions (1982) David
Jenkins[S]; Tharon Musser[L]; Jennifer
von Mayrhauser[C]
Speckled Band, The (1910) Homer
Emens[S]
Speed (1911) Boss and Ormston[S]
Speed of Darkness, The (1991)
Thomas Lynch[S]; Merrily
Murray-Walsh[C]; Michael Philippi[L]
Speed-the-Plow (1987) Nan
Cibula-Jenkins[C]; Michael Merritt[S];
Kevin Rigdon[L]
Spell, The (1907) NONE
Spellbinder, The (1904) NONE
Spellbound (1927) Robert W. Bergman
Studio[S]; Anthony Greshoff[L]
Spenders, The (1903) NONE
Spendthrift, The (1910) NONE
Spice of 1922 (1922) Joseph Law[S];
ACK[C]
Spider, The (1927) DuWico[L]; William
Oden Waller[S]; ACK[C]
Spider, The (1928) DuWico[L]; William
Oden Waller[S]; ACK[C]
Spiritualist, The (1913) Emens and
Unitt[S]; William Kellam[S]
Spite Corner (1922) Ernest Gros[S]
Spitfire, The (1910) Unitt and Wickes[S]
Spofford (1967) Winn Morton[C]; Donald
Oenslager[S][L]
Spoilers, The (1907) Homer Emens[S];
Edward G. Unitt[S]; Joseph Wickes[S]
Spoils of War (1988) Paul Gallo[L];
Andrew Jackness[S]; Ruth Morley[C]

Spokesong (1979) Marjorie Bradley Kellogg(S); John McLain(L); Bill Walker(C)

Sponomo (1964) Pamela Lewis(S); Paul Morrison(L); Ruth St. Moritz(C)

Spook House (1930) Karle O. Amend Studio(S)

Spook Sonata, The (1924) Robert Edmond Jones(S)(C)(L); Cleon Throckmorton(S)

Spooks (1925) ACK(L)

Sport of Kings, The (1926) Livingston Platt(S)(C)

Sporting Days (1908) Arthur Voegtlin(S); Madame Frances Ziebarth(C)

Sporting Thing to Do, The (1923) ACK(L)

Spread Eagle (1927) Norman Bel Geddes(S); ACK(C)

Sprightly Romance of Marsac, The (1900) NONE

Spring 3100 (1928) DuWico(L); ACK(S)

Spring Again (1941) Donald Oenslager(S); ACK(C)

Spring Board, The (1927) P. Dodd Ackerman(S); ACK(C)

Spring Chicken, The (1906) NONE

Spring Cleaning (1923) Lee Simonson(S); ACK(C)

Spring Dance (1936) Evan Bennett(C); Stewart Chaney(S)

Spring Fever (1925) ACK(L)

Spring Freshet (1934) Rollo Wayne(S); ACK(C)

Spring in Autumn (1933) ACK(S)

Spring Is Here (1929) Yetta Kiviette(C); John Wenger(S)

Spring Maid, The (1910) Will R. Barnes(C); M. J. Caldwell(L); D. Frank Dodge(S); Owen Hitchins(C); ACK(L)

Spring Meeting (1938) Roger Furse(S); Donald Oenslager(S); ACK(C)

Spring Song (1927) John Wenger(S); ACK(C)

Spring Song (1934) Jo Mielziner(S)(L); ACK(C)

Spring Thaw (1938) DuWico(L); Donald Oenslager(S); Bianca Stroock(C)

Springtime (1909) Howard Pyle(C); Hugh S. Thomas(L); Young Brothers and Boss(S)

Springtime Folly (1951) Louis Kennel(S); ACK(L)

Springtime for Henry (1931) Cleon Throckmorton(S); ACK(C)

Springtime for Henry (1933) Cleon Throckmorton(S); ACK(C)(L)

Springtime for Henry (1951) H. A. Condell(S); David Ffolkes(C); Louis Kennel(S); Lawrence Mansfield(S)

Springtime of Youth (1922) Watson Barratt(S); Rollo Wayne(S); ACK(C)

Spunk (1990) Loy Arcenas(S); Donald Holder(L); Toni-Leslie James(C)

Spy, The (1913) NONE

Squab Farm, The (1918) ACK(L)

Square Crooks (1926) ACK(L)

Square Peg, A (1923) William Oden Waller(S)

Square Root of Wonderful, The (1957) Jo Mielziner(S)(L); Noel Taylor(C)

Square, The (1926) William E. Castle(S); Millia Davenport(C)

Squaring the Circle (1935) Cirker and Robbins(S); ACK(C)

Squaw Man, The (1905) Gates and Morange(S)

Squaw Man, The (1911) Gates and Morange(S)

Squaw Man, The (1921) Henri Bendel(C); Mabel A. Buell Scenic Studio(S); Madame Haverstick(C)

Squealer, The (1928) ACK(L)

St. Helena (1936) Jo Mielziner(S)(C)(L)

St. Louis Woman (1946) Lemuel Ayers(S)(C)

Stage Door (1936) John Hambleton(C); Donald Oenslager(S)

Stages (1978) Pat Collins(L); Douglas W. Schmidt(S); Patricia Zipprodt(C)

Staircase (1968) Michael Annals(S)(C); Gil Wechsler(L)

Stairs, The (1927) Barbara Allen(C); Cleon Throckmorton(S)

Stalag 17 (1951) John Robert Lloyd(S)(L); Noel Taylor(C)

Stand Up Tragedy (1990) Carol Brolaski(C); Michael Gilliam(L); Yael Pardess(S)

Stand-Up Tragedy (1990) Carol Brolaski(C)

Stanley (1997) Tim Hatley(S)(C); Peter Mumford(L)

Star and Garter (1900) F. Richards Anderson(C); Peter W. King(L); Joseph Physioc(S)

Star and Garter (1942) Harry Horner(S); Irene Sharaff(C)

Star Gazer, The (1917) ACK(L)

Star Spangled (1936) Raymond Sovey(S)

Star Spangled Family (1945) Lou

Eisele(C); Edward Gilbert(S)

Star Spangled Girl, The (1966) Jean Rosenthal(L); Ann Roth(C); Oliver Smith(S)

Star Wagon, The (1937) Jo Mielziner(S)(C)(L)

Starbucks, The (1903) NONE

Starcross Story, The (1954) Audré(C); Watson Barratt(S)

Stardust (1987) Ken Billington(L); David Jenkins(S); Mardi Philips(C)

Stark Mad (1936) S. Syrjala(S); Beryl Wormser(C)

Starlight (1925) Ruth Brenner(S)(C); Frederick W. Jones III(S)

Starlight Express (1987) David Hersey(L); John Napier(S)(C)

Starmites (1989) Lowell Detweiler(S); Susan Hirschfield(C); Jason Kantrowitz(L)

Stars in Your Eyes (1939) John Hambleton(C); Jo Mielziner(S)(L)

Stars on Ice (1942) Lucinda Ballard(C); Eugene Braun(L); Bruno Maine(S)

State Fair (1996) Michael Bottari(C); Ronald Case(C); James Leonard Joy(S); Natasha Katz(L)

State of the Union (1945) Hattie Carnegie(C); Emeline Clarke Roche(C); Raymond Sovey(S)

Status Quo Vadis (1973) Edward Burbridge(S); Thomas Skelton(L); David Toser(C)

Steadfast (1923) NONE

Steam Roller, The (1924) ACK(L)

Steaming (1982) Pat Collins(L); Marjorie Bradley Kellogg(S); Jennifer von Mayrhauser(C)

Steel (1931) P. Dodd Ackerman(S)

Steel (1939) Melville Bernstein(S); Edward Fitzpatrick(L); Margaret Karns(C)

Steel Pier (1997) Peter Kaczorowski(L); William Ivey Long(C); Tony Walton(S)

Step on a Crack (1962) George Jenkins(S)(L); Patricia Zipprodt(C)

Step This Way (1916) ACK(L)

Step-Sister, The (1907) Homer Emens(S)

Stepdaughters of War (1930) Stanley Bell(S); ACK(C)

Stepping Out (1929) Donald Oenslager(S); Margaret Pemberton(C)

Stepping Out (1987) Beverly Emmons(L); David Jenkins(S); Neil Spisak(C)

Stepping Sisters (1930) Cleon Throckmorton(S); ACK(C)

Stepping Stones (1923) P. Dodd Ackerman(S); Will R. Barnes(C); Cora MacGeachy(C); Robert McQuinn(C); Wilhelm(S)(C); ACK(L)

Stepping Stones (1924) P. Dodd Ackerman(S); Will R. Barnes(C); Cora MacGeachy(C); Robert McQuinn(C); Wilhelm(S)(C); ACK(L)

Steve (1912) NONE

Stevedore (1934) Hilda Reis(C); S. Syrjala(S)

Stick-in-the-Mud (1935) P. Dodd Ackerman(S); Kate Drain Lawson(C)

Sticks and Bones (1972) Theoni V. Aldredge(C); Ian Calderon(L); Santo Loquasto(S)

Still Waters (1926) ACK(L)

Stingy (1919) Frank Zimmerman(S)(C)

Stitch in Time, A (1918) H. Robert Studio Law(S); ACK(C)(L)

Stolen Fruit (1925) Livingston Platt(S)

Stolen Orders (1915) R. McCleery(S); Bruce Smith(S); ACK(C)(L)

Stolen Story, The (1906) Walter W. Burridge(S)

Stones in His Pockets (2001) Jack Kirwan(S)(C); James McFetridge(L)

Stop Press (1939) ACK(L)

Stop the World, I Want to Get Off (1962) Sean Kenny(S)(L)

Stop Thief (1912) NONE

Stop! Look! Listen! (1915) Robert McQuinn(S)(C); ACK(L)

Stop-Over (1938) Norris Houghton(S)

Stork Is Dead, The (1932) Livingston Platt(S); Bianca Stroock(C)

Stork, The (1925) Herman Rosse(S); ACK(C)

Storm Center (1927) Livingston Platt(S)

Storm Operation (1944) Howard Bay(S); Moe Hack(L); ACK(C)

Storm over Patsy (1937) Aline Bernstein(S)

Storm, The (1900) NONE

Storm, The (1919) Langdon McCormick(S)(L); ACK(C)

Story for Strangers, A (1948) Ralph Alswang(S)(L); Millie Sutherland(C)

Story for Sunday Evening, A (1950) Theodore Cooper(S)(L); Patricia Montgomery(C)

Story of Mary Surratt, The (1947) Girvan Higginson(L); Samuel Leve(S)

Story of the Rosary, The (1914)

ACK(C)

StraightRoad, The (1907) Alexander Corbett(S); Homer Emens(S); Edward G. Unitt(S); Joseph Wickes(S)

Straight through the Door (1928) Mabel A. Buell Scenic Studio(S); Saul F. Burger(C); ACK(L)

Strange Bedfellows (1948) Ralph Alswang(S)(L); Morton Haack(C)

Strange Fruit (1945) George Jenkins(S)(L); Patricia Montgomery(C)

Strange Gods (1933) P. Dodd Ackerman(S); ACK(C)

Strange Interlude (1928) Jo Mielziner(S)(L); ACK(C)

Strange Interlude (1963) Theoni V. Aldredge(C); David Hays(S)(L); Noel Taylor(C)

Strange Interlude (1985) Deirdre Clancy(C); Allen Lee Hughes(L); Michael Levine(S); Voytek(S)

Strange Play, A (1944) Harry Gordon Bennett(S); Leo Kerz(L)

Strange Woman, The (1913) Gates and Morange(S); T. Bernard McDonald(S); ACK(C)

Stranger In a Strange Land, A (1899) NONE

Stranger Than Fiction (1917) ACK(L)

Stranger, The (1911) NO PLAYBILL

Stranger, The (1945) Boris Aronson(S)(L); Rose Bogdanoff(C)

Strangers (1979) David Jenkins(S); Ann Roth(C); Ronald Wallace(L)

Strangers at Home (1934) P. Dodd Ackerman(S); Miriam Frone(C)

Strangler Fig, The (1940) Frederick Fox(S); ACK(C)

Straw Hat (1937) Mabel A. Buell Scenic Studio(S); Alice Wellman(C)

Straw Hat Revue (1939) Zoe de Salle(C); Edward Gilbert(S)

Straw Hat, The (1926) Lillian Gaertner(S)(C)

Straw, The (1921) Gates and Morange(S)

Strawberry Blonde, The (1927) Livingston Platt(S)

Stray Leaves (1933) ACK(C)(L)

Street Corner Symphony (1997) Jonathan Bixby(C); Peggy Eisenhauer(L); Jules Fisher(L); Neil Peter Jampolis(S)

Street Scene (1929) Jo Mielziner(S)(L)

Street Scene (1947) Lucinda Ballard(C); Jo Mielziner(S)(L)

Street Scene (1990) Gilbert V. Hemsley, Jr.(L); Marjorie McCown(C); Paul Sylbert(S)

Street Singer (1929) Watson Barratt(S); Orry-Kelly(C)

Street Wolf, The (1928) DuWico(L); ACK(S)(C)

Streetcar Named Desire, A (1947) Lucinda Ballard(C); Jo Mielziner(S)(L)

Streetcar Named Desire, A (1973) John Gleason(L); Nancy Potts(C); Douglas W. Schmidt(S)

Streetcar Named Desire, A (1988) John Conklin(S); Jess Goldstein(C); Curt Ostermann(L)

Streetcar Named Desire, A (1992) Ben Edwards(S); Jane Greenwood(C); Kevin Rigdon(L)

Streets Are Guarded, The (1944) Lee Simonson(S)

Streets of New York, or Poverty Is No Crime (1931) Rollo Peters(S)(C); ACK(L)

Streets of Paris (1939) Edward Duryea Dowling(L); Lawrence L. Goldwasser(S); Irene Sharaff(C)

Strength of the Weak, The (1906) Meixner(S); Frank Platzer(S)

Strictly Dishonorable (1929) Margaret Pemberton(C); Raymond Sovey(S); ACK(L)

Strider (1979) Andrew B. Marlay(C); Robby Monk(L); Wolfgang Roth(S)

Strife (1909) E. Hamilton Bell(S)(C); Young Brothers and Boss(S)

Strike Me Pink (1933) Henry Dreyfuss(S); Yetta Kiviette(C)

Strike Up the Band (1930) Charles LeMaire(C); Raymond Sovey(S)

Strings, My Lord, Are False, The (1942) Howard Bay(S); Paul du Pont(C)

Strip for Action (1942) Raymond Sovey(S)

Strip Girl (1935) Dave Caddy(C); Cirker and Robbins(S)

Stripped (1929) Rollo Wayne(S); ACK(C)

Strollers, The (1901) D. Frank Dodge(S); Mrs. Caroline Siedle(C); ACK(L)

Strolling Players (1905) NONE

Strong Are Lonely, The (1953) Rolf Gérard(S)(C)

Strong Man's House, A (1929) Livingston Platt(S); ACK(C)

Strong, The (1924) Charles J. Auburn(S)

Stronger Sex, The (1908) ACK(C)

Stronger than Love (1925) Livingston Platt(S)(C)

Stronger, The (1913) NONE
Strongheart (1905) Joseph Physioc[S]
Struggle Everlasting, The (1907)
Peter W. King[L]; P. J. McDonald[S];
Joseph Physioc[S]; ACK[C]
Strugglers, The (1911) NONE
Strut, Miss Lizzie (1922) ACK[S][L]
Stubborn Cinderella, A (1909) NONE
Stubbornness of Geraldine, The
(1902) Joseph Physioc[S]
Student Gypsy, or The Prince of
Liederkrantz (1963) Raoul Pène Du
Bois[S][C]; Paul Morrison[L]
Student King, The (1906) Will R.
Barnes[C]; Walter W. Burridge[S]
Student Prince, The (1924) Watson
Barratt[S]; ACK[C]
Student Prince, The (1931) Watson
Barratt[S]; ACK[C][L]
Student Prince, The (1943) Watson
Barratt[S]
Student Prince, The (1993) Patton
Campbell[C]; Gilbert V. Hemsley,
Jr.[L]; Jack Hofsiss[S][C][L]; David
Jenkins[S]
Subject Was Roses, The (1964) Jules
Fisher[L]; Donald Foote[C]; Edgar
Lansbury[S]
Substitute for Murder (1935) John
Root[S]; ACK[C]
Subway Express (1929) Cirker and
Robbins[S]; ACK[L]
Subway, The (1929) Walter Walden[S]
Subways Are for Sleeping (1961) Will
Steven Armstrong[S][L]; Freddy
Wittop[C]
Success (1918) Gates and Morange[S];
ACK[C][L]
Success Story (1932) Mordecai
Gorelik[S]; ACK[C]
Successful Calamity, A (1917) Robert
Edmond Jones[S]; ACK[C]
Successful Calamity, A (1934) Aubrey
Hammond[S]
Such a Little Queen (1909) H. Robert
Law[S]
Such Is Life (1916) Rollo Wayne[S];
ACK[C][L]
Such Is Life (1927) Rollo Wayne[S];
ACK[L]
Sudden and Accidental Reeducation
of Horse Johnson, The (1968)
Robert Mitchell[S]; Roger Morgan[L];
Domingo A. Rodriguez[C]
Suds in Your Eye (1944) Kermit
Love[C]; Joseph B. Platt[S]

Sue, Dear (1922) ACK[S][C][L]
Sugar (1972) Martin Aronstein[L]; Alvin
Colt[C]; Robin Wagner[S]
Sugar Babies (1979) Raoul Pène Du
Bois[S][C]; Gilbert V. Hemsley, Jr.[L]
Sugar Hill (1931) Theodore Kahn[S];
Helen Mahieu[C]
Suicide, The (1980) F. Mitchell Dana[L];
Santo Loquasto[S][C]
Sultan of Sulu, The (1902) Walter W.
Burridge[S]; John T. McCutcheon[C]
Summer and Smoke (1948) Rose
Bogdanoff[C]; Jo Mielziner[S]
Summer and Smoke (1996) Brian
MacDevitt[L]; Derek McLane[S];
Martin Pakledinaz[C]
Summer Brave (1974) Donald
Brooks[C]; David F. Segal[L]; Stuart
Wurtzel[S]
Summer Night (1939) Robert Edmond
Jones[S][C][L]
Summer of the 17th Doll (1968)
Gertha Brock[C]; Edward Burbridge[S];
Shirley Prendergast[L]
Summer Widowers, The (1910)
Arthur Voegtlin[S]
Summer Wives (1936) Mabel A. Buell
Scenic Studio[S]; ACK[C]
Sumurun (1912) Ernest Stern[S][C];
Arthur Voegtlin[S]
Sun Dodgers, The (1912) Cora
MacGeachy[C]; Ned Wayburn[L]; John
H. Young[S]
Sun Field, The (1942) Kenn Barr[C];
Ernest Glover[S]
Sun Kissed (1937) John Root[S]; ACK[C]
Sun Showers (1923) Mabel E.
Johnston[C]; H. Robert Law[S];
ACK[S][L]
Sun-kist (1921) Miss Fanchon[C]; Newby
and Alexander[S]; F. W. Woods[C]
Sun-Up (1923) Oscar Liebetrau[S];
ACK[L]
Sun-Up (1928) Oscar Liebetrau[S];
ACK[L]
Sunday (1904) Joseph Physioc[S]
Sunday Breakfast (1952) Ben
Edwards[S][C]
Sunday in New York (1961) David
Hays[S][L]; Patricia Zipprodt[C]
Sunday in the Park with George
(1984) Ann Hould-Ward[C]; Richard
Nelson[L]; Tony Straiges[S]; Patricia
Zipprodt[C]
Sunday Man, The (1964) Donald F.
Jensen[S][C][L]

Sweet Nell of Old Drury (1900) Ernest Gros[S]

Sweet Nell of Old Drury (1923) Woodman Thompson[S][C]

Sweet River (1936) Donald Oenslager[S][C]; Helene Pons[C]; ACK[C]

Sweet Seventeen (1924) P. Dodd Ackerman Studio[S]; Lester M. Livingston[C]; ACK[L]

Sweet Stranger (1930) Henry Dreyfuss[S]

Sweet Sue (1987) Ken Billington[L]; Jess Goldstein[C]; Santo Loquasto[S]

Sweetheart Shop, The (1920) ACK[S][C][L]

Sweetheart Time (1926) ACK[L]

Sweethearts (1913) Dodge and Castle[S]

Sweethearts (1929) ACK[C][L]

Sweethearts (1947) Michael Lucyk[C]; Peter Wolf[S]; ACK[L]

Swifty (1922) Kennel and Entwistle[S]; ACK[C][L]

Swing It (1937) Alexander Jones[C]; Maxine Jones[C]; Walter Walden[S]; Victor Zanoff[S]

Swing Mikado, The (1938) John Pratt[C]; Clive A. Rickabaugh[S]; Oscar Ryan[L]

Swing Your Lady (1936) S. Syrjala[S][C]

Swing! (1999) William Ivey Long[C]; Thomas Lynch[S]; Kenneth Posner[L]

Swingin' the Dream (1939) Herbert Andrews[S][C]; Walter Jagemann[S]

Swinging on a Star (1995) Judy Dearing[C]; Richard Nelson[L]; James Youmans[S]

Sword of the King, The (1902) P. J. McDonald[S]; Louis C. Young[S]

Swords (1921) Robert Edmond Jones[S][C]

Sybil (1916) Henri Bendel[C]; Homer Emens[S]; ACK[L]

Sylvia (1923) Oscar Liebetrau[S]; ACK[L]

Sylvia Runs Away (1914) NONE

Symphony (1935) Tom Adrian Cracraft[S]; ACK[C]

Symphony in Two Flats (1930) Oliver Messel[C]; W. W. Reville-Terry[C]; ACK[L]

Synthetic Sin (1927) R. N. Robbins[S]; ACK[L]

System of Dr. Tarr, The (1905) Kliegl Brothers[L]; Joseph Physioc[S]; Franklin Van Horn[C]

'T Is to Blame for Everything (1928) Ernest de Weerth[S][C]; ACK[L]

Taboo (1922) Anne Neacy[C]; ACK[S][L]

Tailor-Made Man, A (1917) Harry Collins[C]; Hickson[C]; ACK[C][L]

Tailor-Made Man, A (1929) ACK[S][C][L]

Tainted Philanthropy (1912) NONE

Take a Bow (1944) Kaj Velden[S]; Ben Wallace[C]

Take a Chance (1932) Yetta Kiviette[C]; Charles LeMaire[C]; Cleon Throckmorton[S]

Take a Giant Step (1953) Eldon Elder[S][L]; Ruth Morley[C]

Take Her, She's Mine (1961) William and Jean Eckart[S][L]; Florence Klotz[C]

Take It As It Comes (1944) Perry Watkins[S]; ACK[C]

Take It from Me (1919) P. Dodd Ackerman[S]; Arline Gardiner[C]; S. Zalud[C]; ACK[L]

Take Me Along (1959) Jean Rosenthal[L]; Oliver Smith[S]; Miles White[C]

Take Me Along (1985) James Leonard Joy[S]; Craig Miller[L]; David Toser[C]

Take My Advice (1911) ACK[S]

Take My Advice (1927) Nicholas Yellenti[S]; ACK[L]

Take My Tip (1932) Cirker and Robbins[S]; Yetta Kiviette[C]

Take the Air (1927) Charles LeMaire[C]; Cora MacGeachy[C]; Evelyn McHorter[C]; William Oden Waller[S]

Taking Chances (1915) William Birns[S]; John Whalen[L]; Frances Willard[C]

Taking Sides (1996) Theoni V. Aldredge[C]; Howell Binkley[L]; David Jenkins[S]

Taking Steps (1991) Gail Brassard[C]; Mary Jo Dondlinger[L]; James Morgan [active 1989-][S]

Tale of the Allergist's Wife, The (2000) Christopher Akerlind[L]; Santo Loquasto[S]; Ann Roth[C]

Tale of the Wolf, A (1925) Joseph Urban[S][C]

Talent for Murder, A (1981) Ken Billington[L]; David Murin[C]; Oliver Smith[S]

Tales of Rigo (1927) August Vimnera[S]; ACK[L]

Talk about Girls (1927) DuWico[L]; Ward and Harvey Studios[S]; ACK[C]

Talk of New York, The (1907) F. Richards Anderson[C]; Edward G. Unitt[S]; Joseph Wickes[S]; John H.

Young[S]

Talker, The (1912) Henry Dreyfuss[S][C]

Talking Parrot, The (1923) Ack[S][C][L]

Tall Story (1959) George Jenkins[S][L]; Noel Taylor[C]

Taller Than a Dwarf (2000) Brian Nason[L]; Martin Pakledinaz[C]; Tony Walton[S]

Talley Method, The (1941) Jo Mielziner[S][L]; Ack[C]

Talley's Folly (1980) John Lee Beatty[S]; Dennis Parichy[L]; Jennifer von Mayrhauser[C]

Tambourines to Glory (1963) John Conklin[S][C]; Peter Hunt[L]

Tamburlaine the Great (1956) Leslie Hurry[S][C]; Paul Morrison[L]

Taming of Helen, The (1903) Alexander Corbett[S]

Taming of the Shrew, The (1904) Mrs. Lulu Fralik[C]; Maurice Hermann[C]

Taming of the Shrew, The (1905) C. Karl[C]

Taming of the Shrew, The (1907) None

Taming of the Shrew, The (1925) Rollo Peters[S][C]

Taming of the Shrew, The (1935) Carolyn Hancock[S]; Ack[C]

Taming of the Shrew, The (1940) Carolyn Hancock[S]; Claggett Wilson[S][C]

Tangerine (1921) Dorothy Armstrong[C]; Henri Bendel[C]; Pieter Myer[C]; Lee Simonson[S]; Ack[L]

Tangletoes (1925) Joseph Wickes[S]; Ack[C][L]

Tango Argentino (1985) Hector Orezzoli[S][C]; Claudio Segovia[S][C]; Ack[L]

Tango Pasion (1993) Dawn Chiang[L]; John Falabella[S][C]; Richard Pilbrow[L]

Tantalizing Tommy (1912) Percy Anderson[S]; Madame Frances[C]; F. C. Schmitz[S]

Tante (1913) Grace E. Brady[C]; C. Haddon Chambers[S]; Ack[C]

Tantrum, The (1924) Livingston Platt[S]; Cleon Throckmorton[S]; Ack[C][L]

Tanyard Street (1941) Mercedes[S]; Ack[C]

Tapdance Kid, The (1983) Paul de Pass[S]; Ann Emonts[C]; Michael J. Hotopp[S]; Richard Nelson[L]

Tapestry in Gray (1935) Donald Oenslager[S][C]

Taps (1904) D. Frank Dodge[S]; Ack[C]

Taps (1925) Rollo Wayne[S]; Ack[C][L]

Tarnish (1923) Ack[C][L]

Tartuffe (1977) Zack Brown[S][C]; John McLain[L]

Tartuffe: Born Again (1996) Jeff Davis[L]; Jess Goldstein[C]; Allen Moyer[S]

Tarzan of the Apes (1921) Henri Bendel[C]; Ack[S]

Taste of Honey, A (1960) Dorothy Jeakins[C]; Jean Rosenthal[L]; Oliver Smith[S]

Taste of Honey, A (1981) A. Christina Giannini[C]; Robert W. Mogel[L]; Roger Mooney[S]

Tattle Tales (1933) Martin[S]; Elizabeth Zook[C]

Tattooed Man, The (1907) Emens, Unitt and Wickes[S]; Mrs. Caroline Siedle[C]; Ack[L]

Tavern, The (1920) Unitt and Wickes[S]; Ack[L]

Tavern, The (1921) Unitt and Wickes[S]; Ack[C]

Tavern, The (1930) Ack[L]

Tchin-Tchin (1962) Theoni V. Aldredge[C]; Will Steven Armstrong[S][L]

Tea and Sympathy (1953) Anna Hill Johnstone[C]; Jo Mielziner[S][L]

Tea for Three (1918) Ack[C][L]

Teahouse of the August Moon, The (1953) Peter Larkin[S][L]; Noel Taylor[C]

Teaneck Tanzi: The Venus Flytrap (1983) Arden Fingerhut[L]; Lawrence Miller[S][C]

Teaser, The (1921) Ack[C]

Teaspoon Every Four Hours, A (1969) John J. Moore[L]; Winn Morton[C]; Robert Randolph[S]

Teddy and Alice (1987) Theoni V. Aldredge[C]; Tharon Musser[L]; Robin Wagner[S]

Teibele and Her Demon (1979) Desmond Heeley[S][C]; Duane Schuler[L]

Telephone/The Medium, The (1947) Horace Armistead[S][C]; Jean Rosenthal[L]

Telephone/The Medium, The (1950) William Riva[S][C][L]

Tell Her the Truth (1932) Joseph Teichner Studio[S]; Ack[C]

Tell Me More (1925) H. Robert Studio Law[S]; Charles LeMaire[C]; August Vimnera[S]; Ack[L]

Tell Me, Pretty Maiden (1937) Watson Barratt[S]

Tell My Story (1939) Ack[C][L]

Temper the Wind (1946) Anna Hill Johnstone[C]; Raymond Sovey[S]; Ack[L]

Temperamental Journey, The (1913) Ernest Gros[S]; Louis Hartmann[L]

Tempest, The (1916) Thomas D. Benrimo[S][C]; Ack[L]

Tempest, The (1945) Moe Hack[L]; Motley[S][C]

Tempest, The (1995) Paul Gallo[L]; Riccardo Hernández[S]; Toni-Leslie James[C]

Temptations (1911) Ernest Albert[S]; Joseph[C]

Ten Little Indians (1944) Howard Bay[S]; Ack[C]

Ten Million Ghosts (1936) Donald Oenslager[S]; Helene Pons[C]; Ack[C]

Ten Minute Alibi (1933) Watson Barratt[S]; Ack[C]

Ten Nights in a Barroom (1932) Ack[L]

Tender Trap, The (1954) Anna Hill Johnstone[C]; Paul Morrison[S][L]

Tenderfoot, The (1904) Ack[S][C]

Tenderloin (1960) Cecil Beaton[S][C]

Tenement Tragedy, The (1906) None

Tenth Avenue (1927) Nicholas Yellenti[S]

Tenth Man, The (1959) David Hays[S][L]; Frank Thompson[C]

Tenth Man, The (1989) Jane Greenwood[C]; Santo Loquasto[S]; Dennis Parichy[L]

Tenting Tonight (1947) Robert Moore[C]; John Root[S]

Tents of the Arabs, The (1919) James Reynolds[S][C]

Terence (1904) Ogden[C]; Louis C. Young[S]; Ack[L]

Terrible Meek, The (1912) E. Hamilton Bell[S][C]; Unitt and Wickes[S]

Tess of the D'Urbervilles (1902) No Playbill

Tethered Sheep (1915) Warren Dahler[S]; Lois Phipps[S]; Ack[L]

Texas Nightingale, The (1922) Joseph Wickes[S]; Ack[S][C][L]

Texas Trilogy, A (1976) Ben Edwards[S][L]; Jane Greenwood[C]

Texas, Li'l Darlin' (1949) Theodore Cooper[S][L]; Eleanor Goldsmith[C]

Théâtre National Populaire (1958) Léon Gischia[C]; Jacques Le Marquet[S]; Pierre Saveron[L]

Thais (1911) P. Dodd Ackerman[S]; Castle and Harvey[S]; Kliegl Brothers[L]; William Henry Matthews[C]

Thais (1931) Ernest de Weerth[C]; Ack[L]

Thank You (1921) Wade Douglas[S]; Ack[C]

Thank You, Svoboda (1944) Moe Hack[L]; Samuel Leve[S]

Thanksgiving (1916) Alice and Irene Lewisohn[S][C]; Ack[L]

That Championship Season (1972) Theoni V. Aldredge[C]; Ian Calderon[L]; Santo Loquasto[S]

That Day (1922) Ack[C][L]

That Ferguson Family (1928) William Birns[S]; Ack[C][L]

That French Lady (1927) William E. Castle[S]; Ack[C][L]

That Lady (1949) Rolf Gérard[S][C]; Ack[L]

That Man and I (1904) Homer Emens[S]; Ernest Gros[S]; Joseph Physioc[S]; Edward G. Unitt[S]

That Old Devil (1944) Anna Hill Johnstone[C]; Paul Morrison[S][L]

That Sort (1914) Jean[C]

That Summer-That Fall (1967) Theoni V. Aldredge[C]; Jo Mielziner[S][L]

That's Entertainment (1972) Jane Greenwood[C]; David F. Segal[S][L]

That's Gratitude (1930) Louis Kennel[S]; Ack[C]

That's Gratitude (1932) Cirker and Robbins[S]; Ack[C]

That's the Woman (1930) Raymond Sovey[S]; Ack[C]

The ... (1925) Willy Pogany[S][C][L]

Theatre (1941) Donald Oenslager[S]; Helene Pons[C]; Valentina[C]

Them's the Reporters (1935) Karle O. Amend[S]

Theodora, the Queen (1934) Helene Pons[C]; Nicholas Yellenti[S]

There and Back (1903) D. Frank Dodge[S]

There Shall Be No Night (1940) Valentina[C]; Richard Whorf[S]

There Was a Little Girl (1960) Patton

Campbell[C]; Jo Mielziner[S][L]

There You Are (1932) Bertha Beres[C]; ACK[S][C]

There's a Girl in My Soup (1967) Lloyd Burlingame[L]; J. Hutchinson Scott[S]; Stanley Simmons[C]

There's Always a Breeze (1938) Frederick Fox[S]; ACK[C]

There's Always Juliet (1932) Gordon Conway[C]; Laurence Irving[S]; ACK[C]

There's Many a Slip (1902) Ernest Gros[S]

There's One in Every Marriage (1972) Alan Barlow[S][C]; Gil Wechsler[L]

There's Wisdom in Women (1935) Muriel King[C]; John Root[S]

Therese (1945) Raymond Sovey[S][C]

These Charming People (1925) James Reynolds[S]; ACK[C][L]

These Days (1928) Robert Edmond Jones[S]; ACK[C]

These Few Ashes (1928) Natacha Rambova[C]; Woodman Thompson[S]

These Modern Women (1928) Cleon Throckmorton[S]; ACK[C]

These Two (1934) ACK[C][L]

They All Come to Moscow (1933) Tom Adrian Cracraft[S]; Fannie Gallent[C]

They All Want Something (1926) Nicholas Yellenti[S]

They Don't Mean Any Harm (1932) ACK[S][C][L]

They Knew What They Wanted (1924) Carolyn Hancock[S][C]

They Knew What They Wanted (1939) Lemuel Ayers[S]; ACK[C]

They Knew What They Wanted (1949) Frederick Fox[S][C]; ACK[L]

They Never Grow Up (1930) Edgar Bohlman[S][C]

They Shall Not Die (1934) Lee Simonson[S]; ACK[C]

They Should Have Stood in Bed (1942) Samuel Leve[S]; Wilma[C]

They Walk Alone (1941) Lemuel Ayers[S]; Will Washcoe[L]; ACK[C]

They're Playing Our Song (1979) Tharon Musser[L]; Ann Roth[C]; Douglas W. Schmidt[S]

Thief, The (1907) Ernest Gros[S]; Mrs. Robert Osborn[C]

Thief, The (1911) Ernest Gros[S]; Mrs. Robert Osborn[C]

Thief, The (1927) ACK[S][C][L]

Thieves (1974) Joseph G. Aulisi[C]; Jules Fisher[L]; Peter Larkin[S]

Thin Ice (1922) Watson Barratt[S]; ACK[C][L]

Things That Count, The (1913) Warren Dahler[S]; H. Robert Law[S]; Bert Tuchman[S]

Third Best Sport (1958) Robert Mackintosh[C]; Marvin Reiss[S]; Michael Travis[C]; ACK[L]

Third Degree, The (1909) Joseph Physioc[S]

Third Little Show, The (1931) Jo Mielziner[S][L]; Raymond Sovey[C]

Third Party, The (1914) ACK[S][L]

Thirsty Soil (1937) Louis Bromberg[S]; ACK[C]

Thirteen Daughters (1961) Alvin Colt[C]; George Jenkins[S][L]

This Is New York (1930) Henry Dreyfuss[S]; ACK[C]

This Is the Army (1942) John Koenig[S][C]

This Man's Town (1930) Cirker and Robbins[S]

This One Man (1930) Woodman Thompson[S]

This Our House (1935) Eddie Eddy[S]; ACK[C]

This Rock (1943) Watson Barratt[S]; Valentina[C]

This Thing Called Love (1928) Schaffner and Sweet Studio[S]; ACK[C]

This Time Tomorrow (1947) Herbert Brodkin[S]; Patricia Montgomery[C]; ACK[L]

This Was a Man (1926) Gladys E. Calthrop[S]; George W. Harris[S]; ACK[L]

This Was Burlesque (1964) ACK[L]

This Was Burlesque (1965) Rex Huntington[C]; ACK[C]

This Was Burlesque (1981) Rex Huntington[C]; ACK[L]

This Way Out (1917) ACK[L]

This Woman and This Man (1909) NONE

This Woman Business (1926) Nicholas Yellenti[S]

This Year of Grace (1928) Gladys E. Calthrop[S][C]; Marc Henri[S]; Laverdet[S]; Oliver Messel[S][C]; Doris Zinkeisen[C]

This, Too, Shall Pass (1946) Raymond Sovey[S]; ACK[C]

Thoroughbred (1933) William

Warren[S]; ACK[C]

Thoroughbreds (1924) ACK[L]

Those Endearing Young Charms (1943) Frederick Fox[S]

Those That Play the Clowns (1966) Michael Annals[S][C]; Martin Aronstein[L]

Those We Love (1930) Louis Kennel[S]; ACK[C]

Those Were the Days (1990) Gail Cooper-Hecht[C]; Tom Sturge[L]

Those Who Walk in Darkness (1919) ACK[L]

Thousand Clowns, A (1962) George Jenkins[S][L]; Ruth Morley[C]

Thousand Clowns, A (1996) Ben Edwards[S]; Rui Rita[L]; Jennifer von Mayrhauser[C]

Thousand Summers, A (1932) Donald Oenslager[S]; ACK[C]

Thousand Years Ago, A (1914) H. Robert Law[S]

Three and One (1933) Livingston Platt[S]; ACK[C]

Three Bags Full (1966) Will Steven Armstrong[S][L]; Freddy Wittop[C]

Three Bears, The (1917) Homer Emens[S]

Three Cheers (1928) Charles LeMaire[C]; Raymond Sovey[S]; Sheldon K. Viele[S]

Three Daughters of Monsieur Dupont, The (1910) NONE

Three Doors (1925) ACK[S][C][L]

Three Faces East (1918) Lucile[C]; ACK[L]

Three for Diana (1919) NONE

Three Lights, The (1911) George Kanlan[S]; ACK[L]

Three Little Girls (1930) Watson Barratt[S]; Ernest Schraps[C]

Three Little Lambs (1899) Ernest Gros[S]; Henry E. Hoyt[S]; M. J. Quimby[C]

Three Little Maids (1903) NONE

Three Live Ghosts (1920) P. Dodd Ackerman[S]; ACK[L]

Three Men and a Woman (1932) ACK[L]

Three Men on a Horse (1935) Boris Aronson[S]; Perry Watkins[C]

Three Men on a Horse (1942) Perry Watkins[S][C]

Three Men on a Horse (1969) Fred Allison[L]; Boyd Dumrose[S]; A. Christina Giannini[C]

Three Men on a Horse (1993) Ann Hould-Ward[C]; Marjorie Bradley Kellogg[S]; Richard Nelson[L]

Three Musketeers, The (1921) ACK[S][C]

Three Musketeers, The (1928) John W. Harkrider[C]; Joseph Urban[S]; ACK[L]

Three Musketeers, The (1984) Ken Billington[L]; Nancy Winters[S]; Freddy Wittop[C]

Three of Hearts (1915) H. Robert Law[S]; Mr. Chester Woodard[S]; ACK[L]

Three of Us, The (1906) P. Dodd Ackerman[S]

Three Romeos, The (1911) Lucile[C]

Three Showers (1920) Irma Campbell[C]; Gates and Morange[S]; ACK[L]

Three Sisters (1997) Theoni V. Aldredge[C]; Peter Kaczorowski[L]; Derek McLane[S]

Three Sisters, The (1923) ACK[L]

Three Sisters, The (1926) Gladys E. Calthrop[S][C]; ACK[L]

Three Sisters, The (1939) Lucinda Ballard[C]; Johannes Larsen[S]

Three Sisters, The (1942) Motley[S][C]

Three Sisters, The (1964) Theoni V. Aldredge[C]; Will Steven Armstrong[S]; Ray Diffen[C]; A. H. Feder[L]

Three Sisters, The (1969) John McLain[L]; Ann Roth[C]; Paul Staheli[S]

Three Times the Hour (1931) Margaret Pemberton[C]; Dale Stetson[S]

Three to Make Ready (1946) Audré[C]; Charles Elson[L]; Donald Oenslager[S]

Three Twins (1908) D. M. Akin[S]; Corrigan and DeSoria[S]; William Kellam[S]; ACK[C][L]

Three Waltzes (1937) Watson Barratt[S]; Connie DePinna[C]

Three Wise Fools (1918) ACK[C][L]

Three Wise Fools (1936) Hattie Carnegie[C]; ACK[L]

Three Wishes for Jamie (1952) A. H. Feder[L]; George Jenkins[S]; Miles White[C]

Three's a Crowd (1919) Madame Ripley[C]; ACK[S][L]

Three's a Crowd (1930) Albert R. Johnson[S]; Yetta Kiviette[C]; Ernest Schraps[C]

Three's a Family (1943) Stewart

Chaney(S); ACK(C)

Three-Cornered Moon (1933) Arthur P. Segal(S); ACK(C)

Threepenny Opera, The (1933) Caspar Neher(S); Cleon Throckmorton(S); ACK(C)

Threepenny Opera, The (1977) Theoni V. Aldredge(C); Pat Collins(L); Douglas W. Schmidt(S)

Thrills (1925) ACK(S)(L)

Through the Night (1930) ACK(L)

Through the Years (1932) John N. Booth, Jr.(C); Walter Harvey(S); Herbert Ward(S)

Thumbs Down (1923) P. Dodd Ackerman(S); ACK(C)

Thumbs Up (1934) Raoul Pène Du Bois(S); James Reynolds(S); Ted Weidhaas(S)

Thunder (1919) Wade Douglas(S); ACK(L)

Thunder in the Air (1929) Livingston Platt(S); ACK(C)

Thunder on the Left (1933) Aline Bernstein(S)

Thunder Rock (1939) Michael Gordon(L); Mordecai Gorelik(S); Paul Morrison(C)

Thunderbolt, The (1910) E. Hamilton Bell(S)(C)

Thunderbolt, The (1911) Gates and Morange(S)

Thurber Carnival, A (1960) Paul Morrison(L); Ramsé Mostoller(C); Marvin Reiss(S)

Thy Name Is Woman (1920) Edna Hartman(C); Livingston Platt(S)

Thy Neighbor's Wife (1911) NONE

Ti-Coq (1951) Leo Kerz(L); Jean Fournier deBelleval(S)(C)

Tia Juana (1927) E. Van Ackerman(S)

Tiao Ch'in, or The Beautiful Bait (1962) Thomas Skelton(S); ACK(L)

Tick-Tack-Toe (1920) Watson Barratt(S); Homer Conant(C); ACK(L)

Tickets, Please (1950) Ralph Alswang(S); Peggy Morrison(C); ACK(L)

Tickle Me (1920) Joseph Physioc(S); ACK(C)(L)

Tidbits of 1946 (1946) ACK(L)

Tide Rising (1937) Elizabeth Beard(C); Hugh Willoughby(S)

Tidings Brought to Mary, The (1922) Theodore Komisarjevsky(S); Lee Simonson(S)(C)

Tiger at the Gate (1955) Paul Morrison(L); Loudon Sainthill(S)(C)

Tiger Cats (1924) Louis Hartmann(L); Joseph Wickes(S); ACK(C)

Tiger Rose (1917) Ernest Gros(S); Edna Hartman(C); Louis Hartmann(L); Elmer Taflinger(C); Albertine Randall Wheelan(C)

Tiger Tiger Burning Bright (1962) Lucinda Ballard(C); A. H. Feder(L); Oliver Smith(S)

Tiger! Tiger! (1918) ACK(L)

Tight Britches (1934) G. Bradford Ashworth(S)

Tightwad (1927) ACK(L)

Till the Day I Die (1935) NONE

Tillie (1919) ACK(L)

Tillie's Nightmare (1910) John H. M. Dudley(S); Melville Ellis(C)

Timber House (1936) Donald Oenslager(S); ACK(C)

Timbuktu (1978) Ian Calderon(L); Geoffrey Holder(C); Tony Straiges(S)

Time (1923) Frederick Ford(S); ACK(L)

Time and the Conways (1938) P. Dodd Ackerman(S)

Time for Elizabeth (1948) George Jenkins(S); ACK(L)

Time for Singing, A (1966) Theoni V. Aldredge(C); Ming Cho Lee(S); Jean Rosenthal(L)

Time Limit (1956) Ralph Alswang(S)(L); Noel Taylor(C)

Time of the Cuckoo, The (1952) Ben Edwards(S)(L); Helene Pons(C)

Time of Your Life, The (1939) Watson Barratt(S); Paul du Pont(C)

Time of Your Life, The (1940) Watson Barratt(S); Paul du Pont(C)

Time Out for Ginger (1952) Eldon Elder(S)(L); Virginia Volland(C); ACK(C)

Time Remembered (1957) A. H. Feder(L); Oliver Smith(S); Miles White(C)

Time, the Place and the Girl, The (1907) Will R. Barnes(C)

Time, the Place, and the Girl, The (1942) Karle O. Amend(S); Paul du Pont(C)

Times Have Changed (1935) Stewart Chaney(S); Madame Georgette(C)

Timon of Athens (1993) Ann Hould-Ward(C); Richard Nelson(L); Douglas Stein(S)

Tin Pan Alley (1928) Nicholas Yellenti(S); ACK(C)

Tintypes (1980) Paul Gallo(L); Jess Goldstein(C); Thomas Lynch(S)

Tiny Alice (1964) Martin Aronstein[L]; Mainbocher[C]; William Ritman[S][C]

Tiny Alice (1969) John McLain[L]; Ann Roth[C]; Walter Watson[C]; Stuart Wurtzel[S]

Tip Toes (1925) Yetta Kiviette[C]; John Wenger[S]

Tip Top (1920) Dodge and Castle[S]; ACK[S][L]

Tipping the Winner (1914) NONE

Tired Business Man (1929) ACK[L]

'Tis of Thee (1940) Carl Kent[S]; ACK[C]

Tit For Tat (1904) Joseph Physioc[S]

Titanic (1997) Paul Gallo[L]; Stewart Laing[S][C]

Title Mart, The (1906) Leon Mohn[S]

Title, The (1921) P. Dodd Ackerman[S]; ACK[C]

To Be Continued (1952) Motley[C]; Donald Oenslager[S]

To Dorothy, a Son (1951) William and Jean Eckart[S]; Hazel Roy[C]

To Grandmother's House We Go (1981) Ben Edwards[S]; Jane Greenwood[C]; Marc B. Weiss[L]

To Have and to Hold (1901) Ernest Gros[S]; Ogden[C]

To Live Another Summer (1971) Neil Peter Jampolis[S][L]; Lydia Pincus-Gany[C]

To Love (1922) ACK[S][C][L]

To My Husband (1936) Jules Laurentz[S]; ACK[C]

To Quito and Back (1937) Aline Bernstein[S][C]

To See Ourselves (1935) Kate Drain Lawson[S]; Bianca Stroock[C]

To the Ladies (1922) Gates and Morange[S]; ACK[C]

Toast of the Town, The (1905) Percy Anderson[C]; Frank E. Gates[S]; Edward Morange[S]

Tobacco Road (1933) Redington Sharpe[S]

Tobacco Road (1937) Redington Sharpe[S]; ACK[L]

Tobacco Road (1942) Redington Sharpe[S]

Tobacco Road (1943) Redington Sharpe[S]

Tobacco Road (1950) ACK[L]

Tobias and the Angel (1937) Samuel Leve[S]; Mary Merrill[C]

Toby's Bow (1919) Mrs. Sidney Harris[S]; ACK[L]

Today (1913) NONE

Toddles (1908) Adrienne King[C]

Toller Cranston's Ice Show (1977) D. Scott Linder[L]; Anthony Sabatino[S]; Miles White[C]

Tom Jones (1907) Walter W. Burridge[S]

Tom Moore (1901) Maurice Hermann[C]; Joseph Physioc[S]

Tom Pinch (1900) NONE

Tom Sawyer/ Treasure Island (1931) M. L. Keen[C]; ACK[S]

Tommy (1927) Karle O. Amend[S]; Marcus Harrison[C]; ACK[C][L]

Tommy (1933) Karle O. Amend Studio[S]

Tommy Rot (1902) D. Frank Dodge[S]; Mrs. Robert Osborn[C]; Joseph Physioc Studio[S]

Tommy Tune Tonite! A Song and Dance Act (1992) Peggy Eisenhauer[L]; Jules Fisher[L]; Willa Kim[C]; Tony Walton[S]

Tomorrow and Tomorrow (1931) Aline Bernstein[S]; ACK[C]

Tomorrow the World (1943) Raymond Sovey[S]

Tomorrow's a Holiday (1935) John Hambleton[C]; Woodman Thompson[S]

Tomorrow's Harvest (1934) Lee Lash Studios[S]; ACK[C]

Tomorrow... (1928) Livingston Platt[S]; ACK[C]

Tone Pictures/The White Peacock (1927) Aline Bernstein[S][C]

Tongues of Men, The (1913) Young Brothers[S]; ACK[C]

Tonight at 12 (1928) Rose Clark[C]; Raymond Sovey[S]

Tonight at 8:30 (1936) Gladys E. Calthrop[S]; ACK[C]

Tonight at 8:30 (1948) Hattie Carnegie[C]; George Jenkins[S]; James Morgan [active 1948][C]

Tonight at 8:30 (1967) Will Steven Armstrong[S]; Alvin Colt[C]; Tharon Musser[L]

Tonight on Samarkind (1955) Ben Edwards[S][L]; Frank Spencer[C]

Tonight or Never (1930) George Haddon[C]; Joseph Wickes[S]

Tonight's the Night (1914) ACK[C]

Too Hot for Maneuvers (1945) Lou Eisele[C]; Wolfgang Roth[S]

Too Late the Phalarope (1956) Dorothy Jeakins[C]; George Jenkins[S][L]

Too Many Boats (1934) Robert Barnhart[S]; Mildred Manning[C];

ACK(C)

Too Many Cooks (1914) NONE

Too Many Girls (1939) Raoul Pène Du Bois(C); Jo Mielziner(S)(L)

Too Many Heroes (1937) Jo Mielziner(S)(L)

Too Many Husbands (1919) Harry Collins(C); Unitt and Wickes(S)

Too Much Johnson (1910) NONE

Too Much Party (1934) Karle O. Amend(S); Viola Cohn(C)

Too True to Be Good (1932) Jonel Jorgulesco(S)(C)

Too True to Be Good (1963) Edith Lutyens Bel Geddes(C); Paul Morrison(S)(L)

Toot Sweet (1919) ACK(L)

Toot-Toot! (1918) Clifford F. Pember(S); Joseph Wilson(L); ACK(C)

Top Banana (1951) Alvin Colt(C); Jo Mielziner(S)(L)

Top o' th' World, The (1907) D. Frank Dodge(S); Archie Gunn(C); Frank Platzer(S)

Top o' the Hill (1929) John Decker(S); ACK(C)(L)

Top Speed (1929) Yetta Kiviette(C); Raymond Sovey(S)

Top-Hole (1924) Rollo Wayne(S); ACK(C)(L)

Top-Notchers (1942) ACK(C)(L)

Topaz (1930) Rollo Wayne(S); ACK(C)

Topaz (1931) Rollo Wayne(S); ACK(C)

Topaz (1947) Audré(C); Peggy Clark(L); Oliver Smith(S)

Topics of 1923 (1923) Watson Barratt(S); Erté(C); Jean Patou(C); ACK(L)

Toplitzky of Notre Dame (1946) Kenn Barr(C); Edward Gilbert(S)

Topsy and Eva (1924) Madame Keeler(C); Dickson Morgan(S); ACK(L)

Torch Bearers, The (1922) Joseph Physioc Studio(S); ACK(C)

Torch Song (1930) Cleon Throckmorton(S)(C)

Torch Song Trilogy (1982) Mardi Philips(C); Scott Pinkney(L); Bill Stabile(S)

Torches, The (1917) ACK(L)

Toreador, The (1902) F. Richards Anderson(C); Ernest Gros(S); Wilhelm(C)

Tortilla Flat (1938) Mordecai Gorelik(S); Barbara Guerdon(C)

Tosca, La (1900) NONE

Total Abandon (1983) Beverly Emmons(L); David Jenkins(S); Julie Weiss(C)

Toto (1921) Unitt and Wickes(S); ACK(C)(L)

Touch and Go (1949) Peggy Clark(L); John Robert Lloyd(S)(C)

Touch of Brimstone, A (1935) P. Dodd Ackerman(S); Elizabeth Hawes(C); Mildred Manning(C)

Touch of the Poet, A (1958) Ben Edwards(S)(C)(L)

Touch of the Poet, A (1967) Will Steven Armstrong(S); Alvin Colt(C); Tharon Musser(L)

Touch of the Poet, A (1977) Ben Edwards(S)(L); Jane Greenwood(C)

Touchstone (1953) George Jenkins(S)(L)

Tough to Get Help (1972) Joseph G. Aulisi(C); John Gleason(L); Ed Wittstein(S)

Tourists, The (1906) Ernest Albert(S); Mrs. Caroline Siedle(C)

Tovarich (1936) Raymond Sovey(S)(C)(L)

Tovarich (1963) Rolf Gérard(S); John Harvey(L); Motley(C)

Town Boy (1929) Karle O. Amend(S)

Town House (1948) John Derro(C); Donald Oenslager(S)(L)

Town's Woman, The (1929) Eddie Eddy(S); ACK(C)

Toymaker of Nuremberg, The (1907) Ernest Gros(S)

Toys in the Attic (1960) Howard Bay(S)(L); Ruth Morley(C)

Traffic, The (1914) NONE

Tragedy of Nan, The (1920) ACK(L)

Tragedy of Richard III, The (1920) Robert Edmond Jones(S)(C); ACK(L)

Tragic 18 (1926) ACK(L)

Trail of the Lonesome Pine, The (1912) Walter W. Burridge(S); Lee Lash Studios(S)

Traitor, The (1930) Charles J. Auburn(S); Charles Chrisdie(C); ACK(L)

Traitor, The (1949) Joseph Fretwell III(C); Raymond Sovey(S); ACK(L)

Translations (1995) Joan Bergin(C); Ashley Martin-Davis(S); Chris Parry(L)

Transplanting Jean (1921) Dodge and Castle(S); ACK(C)

Trap, The (1915) ACK(L)

Trapped (1928) ACK(C)(L)

Traveler without Luggage (1964) Gerald Feil(L); Oliver Messel(S)(C)

Traveling Lady, The (1954) Ben

Edwards[S][C][L]
Traveling Man, The (1916) Ack[L]
Traveling Salesman, The (1908)
Joseph Physioc[S]
Travesties (1974) Robert Ornbo[L]; Carl
Toms[S][C]
Treasure Girl (1928) Yetta Kiviette[C];
Joseph Urban[S]
Treasure Island (1915) Gates and
Morange[S]; Ruth Vivian[C]
Treasure, The (1920) Lee
Simonson[S][C]; Ack[L]
Treat 'Em Rough (1926) P. Dodd
Ackerman Studio[S]; Ack[L]
Tree Grows in Brooklyn, A (1951) Jo
Mielziner[S][L]; Irene Sharaff[C]
Tree, The (1932) Serge Edgerly[S];
Ack[C]
Treemonisha (1974) Franco
Colavecchia[S][C]; Nananne Porcher[L]
Trelawney of the "Wells" (1911)
None
Trelawney of the "Wells" (1925)
Robert Edmond Jones[S][C][L]
Trelawney of the "Wells" (1927)
Robert Edmond Jones[S]; Ack[C]
Trelawney of the "Wells" (1976) Ian
Calderon[L]; David Mitchell[S]
Trial by Jury (1948) Ralph Alswang[S][L]
Trial by Jury (1949) Ralph
Alswang[S][L]; Peggy Morrison[C]
Trial by Jury (1955) Joseph and Phil
Harker[S]; George Sheringham[C]
Trial by Jury/ H.M.S. Pinafore
(1951) Joseph and Phil Harker[S];
George Sheringham[C]
Trial by Jury/ H.M.S. Pinafore
(1952) Ralph Alswang[S]; Peggy
Morrison[C]
Trial Honeymoon (1947) Philip
Kessler[S][C]; Chester Menzer[L]
Trial Marriage, The (1912) Madame
Julie[C]; H. Robert Law[S]
Trial of Dr. Beck, The (1937) Rollo
Wayne[S]
Trial of Joan of Arc, The (1921)
Ernest de Weerth[S]; Ack[C]
Trial of Lee Harvey Oswald, The
(1967) Theoni V. Aldredge[C]; Jules
Fisher[L]; Robin Wagner[S]
Trial of Mary Dugan (1927) P. Dodd
Ackerman[S]; Ack[C][L]
Trial of the Catonsville Nine, The
(1971) Tharon Musser[L]; Peter
Wexler[S]; Albert Wolsky[C]
Triangle, The (1906) No Playbill

Tribute (1978) Lowell Detweiler[C];
Tharon Musser[L]; William Ritman[S]
Trick for Trick (1932) Walter Harvey[S];
Herbert Ward[S]; Ack[C]
Tricks (1973) Martin Aronstein[L]; Oliver
Smith[S]; Miles White[C]
Tricks of the Trade (1980) Peter
Dohanos[S][L]; Albert Wolsky[C]
Trifler, The (1905) None
Trigger (1927) Ack[S][L]
Trilby (1900) Madame Freisinger[C]; H.
Robert Studio Law[S]
Trilby (1915) Madame Freisinger[C];
Robert Edmond Jones[S]; Ack[C][L]
Trilby (1921) Ack[C]
Trimmed in Scarlet (1920) Ack[L]
Trimplet, The (1916) S. J. Dawkins[L];
Frank J. Zimmerer[S]
Trio (1944) Stewart Chaney[S]
Trip Back Down, The (1977) Richard
Nelson[L]; Pearl Somner[C]; Hal Tiné[S]
Trip to Bountiful, The (1953) Rose
Bogdanoff[C]; Peggy Clark[L]; Otis
Riggs[S]
Trip to Japan, A (1909) H. M.
Bowdoin[S]; Joseph Elsner[L]; Landolff
of Paris[C]; Arthur Voegtlin[S]; George
Williams[S]; Ack[C]
Trip to Scarborough, A (1929) James
Reynolds[S]
Triple Crossed (1927) Cleon
Throckmorton[S]
Triple Play (1959) David Hays[S][L];
Anna Hill Johnstone[C]
Triplets (1932) Ned Crane[S]
Triumph (1935) Hattie Carnegie[C];
Philip Gelb[S]
Triumph of an Empress, The (1911)
Ernest Albert[S]; Joseph L. Menchen,
Jr.[L]; Bernhardt Wall[C]
Triumph of Love (1997) Heidi
Ettinger[S]; Paul Gallo[L]; Catherine
Zuber[C]
Triumph of Love, The (1904) Ernest
Albert[S]; Ack[C]
Triumph of the Egg, The (1925)
Cleon Throckmorton[S]; Ack[L]
Triumph of X, The (1921) Mabel A.
Buell[S]; Charles Howard[C]; Doris
Reed[C]
Triumphant Bachelor, The (1927)
Cleon Throckmorton[S]; Ack[C]
Troilus and Cressida (1932) P. Dodd
Ackerman Studio[S]; Charles
Chrisdie[C]
Troilus and Cressida (1956) Frederick

Crooke[(S)(C)]; Аск[(L)]

Trois Jeunes Filles Nues (1929) Аск[(S)(C)(L)]

Trojan Incident (1938) Howard Bay[(S)(C)]

Troubadour, A (1900) NONE

Trouser, The (1926) Аск[(L)]

Troyka (1930) Eddie Eddy[(S)]; Walter Walden[(C)]

Tru (1989) Ken Billington[(L)]; Sarah Edwards[(C)]; Jason Kantrowitz[(L)]; David Mitchell[(S)]

Truckline Cafe (1946) Boris Aronson[(S)]; Millia Davenport[(C)]

True West (2000) Rob Howell[(S)(C)]; Brian MacDevitt[(L)]

Truly Blessed (1990) Fred Kolo[(S)(L)]; Andrew B. Marlay[(C)]

Truly Valiant (1936) Louis Bromberg[(S)]; Аск[(C)]

Trumpet Shall Sound, The (1926) Helene Pons[(C)]; James Shute[(S)]

Trumpets of the Lord (1969) Marsha L. Eck[(S)]; Jules Fisher[(L)]; Domingo A. Rodriguez[(C)]

Truth about Blayds, The (1922) Norman Bel Geddes[(S)]; Аск[(C)(L)]

Truth about Blayds, The (1932) Cleon Throckmorton[(S)]; Аск[(C)]

Truth Game, The (1930) Rollo Wayne[(S)]; Аск[(C)]

Truth Wagon, The (1912) Homer Emens[(S)]; Madame Frances[(C)]

Truth, The (1907) Clyde Fitch[(S)]

Truth, The (1914) Elizabeth Axtman[(C)]; Unitt and Wickes[(S)]; Аск[(C)]

Try and Get It (1943) DuWico[(L)]; Norman Edwards[(C)]; Аск[(S)]

Try It with Alice (1924) Margaret Lathem[(S)]; Аск[(C)(L)]

Tsar Fyodor Ivanovitch (1923) Victor Simoff[(S)]

Tumble in (1919) Henri Bendel[(C)]; Joseph Physioc Studio[(S)]; Аск[(L)]

Tumbler, The (1960) Roger Furse[(S)]; Tharon Musser[(L)]; Аск[(C)]

Tuna Christmas, A (1994) Linda Fisher[(C)]; Judy Rasmuson[(L)]; Loren Sherman[(S)]

Tunnel of Love, The (1957) Ralph Alswang[(S)(L)]; Virginia Volland[(C)]

Turn to the Right (1916) Gates and Morange[(S)]; William Hanna[(S)]

Turning Point (1910) E. Hamilton Bell[(S)]; Madame Freisinger[(C)]

Tweedles (1923) Аск[(L)]

Twelfth Night (1900) NONE

Twelfth Night (1904) Homer Emens[(S)]; Ogden[(C)]

Twelfth Night (1905) C. Karl[(C)]

Twelfth Night (1907) Homer Emens[(S)]; Maurice Hermann[(C)]; Edward G. Unitt[(S)]; Joseph Wickes[(S)]

Twelfth Night (1910) Ernest Albert[(S)]; E. Hamilton Bell[(S)(C)]; Homer Emens[(S)]; Gates and Morange[(S)]

Twelfth Night (1914) Caramba[(C)]; Joseph Urban[(S)]

Twelfth Night (1926) Gladys E. Calthrop[(S)]

Twelfth Night (1930) Raymond Sovey[(S)(C)]; Аск[(L)]

Twelfth Night (1940) Stewart Chaney[(S)(C)]; Аск[(L)]

Twelfth Night (1941) Michael Chekhov[(S)(C)]

Twelfth Night (1949) Louis Kennel[(S)(C)]; Аск[(L)]

Twelfth Night (1958) Desmond Heeley[(S)(C)]

Twelfth Night (1998) Bob Crowley[(S)]; Natasha Katz[(L)]; Catherine Zuber[(C)]

Twelve Miles Out (1925) Nicholas Yellenti[(S)]

Twelve Months Later (1900) NONE

Twelve Pound Look, The (1911) Homer Emens[(S)]

Twentieth Century (1951) Wolfgang Roth[(S)]; Noel Taylor[(C)]

Twenty Days in the Shade (1908) Ernest Gros[(S)]

Twenty Seven Wagons Full of Cotton (1955) Patton Campbell[(C)]; Eldon Elder[(S)(L)]

Twice around the Park (1981) Ruth Morley[(C)]; Judy Rasmuson[(L)]; James Tilton[(S)]

Twiddle-Twaddle (1906) Ernest Albert[(S)]

Twigs (1971) Sara Brook[(C)]; Peter Larkin[(S)]; David F. Segal[(L)]

Twilight of the Golds, The (1993) Martin Aronstein[(L)]; Jeanne Button[(C)]; John Iacovelli[(S)]

Twilight Walk (1951) Paul Morrison[(S)(L)]

Twilight: Los Angeles, 1992 (1994) John Arnone[(S)]; Jules Fisher[(L)]; Toni-Leslie James[(C)]

Twin Beds (1914) Bob Davis[(C)]; Madame Julie[(C)]; Lucile[(C)]; Rose Windsor[(C)]

Twin Sister, The (1902) Henry Dazian[C]; Madame Oaksmith[C]

Twinkle, Twinkle (1926) P. Dodd Ackerman[S]; Charles LeMaire[C]

Twirly Whirly (1902) Will R. Barnes[C]; John H. Young[S]

Two Blind Beggars and One Less Blind (1915) Phillip Moeller[S][C]

Two Blind Mice (1949) Albert R. Johnson[S]; Natalie Barth Walker[C]; ACK[L]

Two Blocks Away (1921) Peggy Hoyt[C]; Livingston Platt[S]

Two by Two (1925) Charles J. Auburn[S]; ACK[C]

Two by Two (1970) John Gleason[L]; David Hays[S]; Fred Voelpel[C]

Two Fellows and a Girl (1923) ACK[S][C][L]

Two for the Seesaw (1958) George Jenkins[S][L]; Virginia Volland[C]

Two for the Show (1940) John Murray Anderson[L]; Raoul Pène Du Bois[S][C]

Two Gentlemen of Verona (1972) Theoni V. Aldredge[C]; Ming Cho Lee[S]; Lawrence Metzler[L]

Two is Company (1915) Young Brothers[S]; ACK[L]

Two Little Brides (1912) No PLAYBILL

Two Little Girls (1921) Shirley Barker[C]; Anthony Greshoff[L]; H. Robert Studio Law[S]

Two Little Sailor Boys (1904) Frank Platzer[S]

Two Married Men (1925) Livingston Platt[S]

Two Mr. Wetherbys, The (1906) Young Brothers and Boss[S]

Two Mrs. Carrolls, The (1943) Frederick Fox[S]; Grace Houston[C]; ACK[L]

Two on an Island (1940) Jo Mielziner[S][L]; Helene Pons[C]

Two on the Aisle (1951) Howard Bay[S]; Joan Personette[C]

Two Orphans, The (1904) Richard Marston[S]; Franklin Van Horn[C]; ACK[C]

Two Orphans, The (1926) Ernest Schraps[C]; ACK[L]

Two Roses, The (1904) Emens and Unitt[S]; Mrs. Robert Osborn[C]; Mrs. Caroline Siedle[C]

Two Schools, The (1902) Ernest Gros[S]

Two Seconds (1931) Cleon Throckmorton[S]; ACK[C][L]

Two Shakespearean Actors (1992) Jules Fisher[L]; Jane Greenwood[C]; David Jenkins[S]

Two Strange Women (1933) David S. Gaither[S]; ACK[C]

Two Strangers from Nowhere (1924) Henry Dreyfuss[S]

Two Trains Running (1992) Tony Fanning[S]; Chrisi Karvonides[C]; Geoff Korff[L]

Two Virtues, The (1915) ACK[S][L]

Two Women (1910) Homer Emens[S]; Kliegl Brothers[L]

Two Women and That Man (1909) A. R. Barker[C]; ACK[S]

Two's Company (1952) Ralph Alswang[S]; Miles White[C]

Typhoon, The (1912) Madame Frances[C]; Gates and Morange[S]; Peter W. King[L]; Kliegl Brothers[L]

Tyranny of Love, The (1921) ACK[C]

Tyranny of Tears (1899) Edward G. Unitt[S]

Tyranny of Tears, The (1913) Unitt and Wickes[S]

Tyrant, The (1930) P. Dodd Ackerman[S]; De Guary[C]

Ulysses (1903) Percy Anderson[C]; Hawes Craven[S]

Ulysses in Nighttown (1974) Jules Fisher[L]; Pearl Somner[C]; Ed Wittstein[S]

Un Caprice (1955) ACK[L]

Unborn, The (1915) ACK[L]

Unchastened Woman, The (1915) Henri Bendel[C]; George Hopkins[C]; ACK[S][L]

Unchastened Woman, The (1926) ACK[S][L]

Uncle Harry (1942) Howard Bay[S]; Peggy Clark[C]

Uncle Sam (1911) NONE

Uncle Tom's Cabin (1901) NONE

Uncle Tom's Cabin (1933) Donald Oenslager[S][C]

Uncle Vanya (1929) Anthony Continer[S]

Uncle Vanya (1930) Jo Mielziner[S][L]; Fania Mindell[C]; Herman Patrick Tappé[C]; ACK[C]

Uncle Vanya (1946) Tanya Moiseiwitsch[S][C]; John Sullivan[L]

Uncle Vanya (1973) Jules Fisher[L]; Tony Walton[S][C]

Uncle Vanya (1995) Mimi Maxmen[C]; Tharon Musser[L]; Loren Sherman[S]

Uncle Vanya (2000) Kenneth Posner(L); Tony Walton(S)(C)

Uncle Willie (1956) Ralph Alswang(S)(L); Guy Kent(C)

Unconquered, The (1940) Boris Aronson(S); Ack(C)

Under Cover (1903) Gates and Morange(S)

Under Cover (1914) Gates and Morange(S); Madame Julie(C)

Under Fire (1915) Joseph Physioc(S)

Under Glass (1933) Karle O. Amend(S); Hattie Carnegie(C)

Under Many Flags (1912) Arthur Voegtlin(S)

Under Milkwood (1957) Kathryn B. Miller(C); Raymond Sovey(S)

Under Pressure (1918) Ack(L)

Under Sentence (1916) Ack(L)

Under Southern Skies (1901) Moses and Hamilton(S); John H. Young(S)

Under the Counter (1947) Clifford F. Pember(S); Ack(L)

Under the Gaslight (1929) Ack(L)

Under the Greenwood Tree (1907) None

Under the Weather (1966) Kert Lundell(S)(C); Roger Morgan(L)

Under the Yum-Yum Tree (1960) Peggy Clark(L); Ray Diffen(C); Oliver Smith(S)

Under this Roof (1942) Harry Horner(S); Ernest Schraps(C)

Under Two Flags (1901) Ernest Gros(S)

Undercurrent, The (1925) None

Undesirable Lady, An (1933) P. Dodd Ackerman(S); Ack(C)

Unexpected Guests (1977) Joseph G. Aulisi(C); Cheryl Thacker(L); Stuart Wurtzel(S)

Unexpected Husband (1931) Walter Harvey(S); Herbert Ward(S); Ack(C)

Unforeseen, The (1903) Ernest Gros(S)

Uninvited Guest, The (1927) Ack(L)

Union Pacific (1934) Albert R. Johnson(S); Irene Sharaff(C)

Unknown Purple, The (1918) Hickson(C); Helen Sheppard(C); Roland West(S)(L)

Unknown Warrier, The (1931) George Sheringham(C); Ack(S)

Unknown Warrior, The (1928) Henri Bendel(C); Frederick W. Jones III(S)

Unknown Woman, The (1919) Henri Bendel(C); Ack(S)(L)

Unleavened Bread (1901) Frank E. Gates(S); Edward Morange(S)

Unlikely Heroes (1971) Roger Morgan(L); Robert U. Taylor(S); Frank Thompson(C)

Unsinkable Molly Brown, The (1960) Peggy Clark(L); Oliver Smith(S); Miles White(C)

Unsophisticates, The (1929) Cleon Throckmorton(S)

Unto the Third (1933) Ack(C)(L)

Unwelcome Mrs. Hatch, The (1901) Frank E. Gates(S); Edward Morange(S)

Unwritten Chapter, The (1920) Robert Milton(S); Ack(L)

Unwritten Law, The (1913) None

Up and Down Broadway (1910) Melville Ellis(C); Lee Lash Studios(S)

Up and Up, The (1930) Ack(S)

Up from Nowhere (1919) Mrs. Sidney Harris(S); Ack(L)

Up in Central Park (1945) Howard Bay(S)(L); Grace Houston(C); Ernest Schraps(C)

Up in Mabel's Room (1919) Hickson(C); Ack(L)

Up Pops the Devil (1930) Rollo Wayne(S)

Up the Ladder (1922) Marjorie Dalmain(S); Anna Spencer(C); Ack(L)

Up the Line (1926) P. Dodd Ackerman(S); Ack(L)

Up York State (1901) Walter W. Burridge(S); William Metzler(L)

Ups-a-Daisy (1928) John Wenger(S)

Upstart, The (1910) Henri Bendel(C); Unitt and Wickes(S); Ack(S)(C)

Uptown West (1923) Michael Carr(S); J. Blanding Sloan(S); Ack(L)

Uptown...It's Hot (1986) Ellen Lee(C); Tom McPhillips(S); Marc B. Weiss(L)

Usurper, The (1904) Ernest Albert(S)

Utter Glory of Morrissey Hale, The (1979) Howard Bay(S)(L); David Graden(C)

Vagabond King, The (1925) James Reynolds(S)(C)

Vagabond King, The (1943) James Reynolds(C); Raymond Sovey(S)

Valley Forge (1934) Carroll French(C); Kate Drain Lawson(S)

Valley of Content, The (1925) Dickson Morgan(S); Ack(L)

Vamp, The (1955) Raoul Pène Du Bois(S)(C)

Vampire, The (1909) None

Van Dyck, The (1907) None

Vanderbilt Cup, The (1906) NONE

Vanderbilt Revue, The (1930) Robert Ten Eyck Stevenson(C); Ward and Harvey Studios(L); ACK(L)

Vanities of 1923 (1923) Brymer(C); Mabel E. Johnston(C); Reid McGuire(S); ACK(L)

Vanity Fair (1911) E. Hamilton Bell(S)(C)

Vegetable, The (1929) Walter Walden(S)

Veils (1928) DuWico(L); Mabel E. Johnston(C)

Velvet Glove, The (1949) Joseph Fretwell III(C); Donald Oenslager(S); ACK(L)

Velvet Lady, The (1919) Mary Blackburn(C); H. Robert Studio Law(S); ACK(L)

Veneer (1929) Nicholas Yellenti(S); ACK(C)

Venetian Glass Nephew, The (1931) Edgar Bohlman(S)(C)

Venetian Romance, A (1904) Henry Bissing(L); Mrs. Caroline Siedle(C); ACK(S)

Venetian Twins, The (1968) Gianfranco Padovani(S)(C)

Venetian, The (1931) Peter Bax(S); George Sheringham(C); Ellen Van Volkenburg(S); ACK(L)

Venus (1927) Evelyn McHorter(C); Livingston Platt(S); ACK(C)

Venus at Large (1962) Donald Oenslager(S)(L); Ann Roth(C)

Venus Observed (1952) Roger Furse(S); Mildred Trebor(C); Valentina(C)

Vera Violetta (1911) Melville Ellis(C); ACK(S)

Verge, The (1921) Blanche Hays(C); Cleon Throckmorton(S)

Vermont (1929) ACK(L)

Veronica's Room (1973) John Gleason(L); Nancy Potts(C); Douglas W. Schmidt(S)

Veronique (1905) Percy Anderson(C); Joseph Harker(S); Julian Hicks(S)

Very Good Young Man, A (1918) ACK(C)(L)

Very Good, Eddie (1915) Elsie de Wolfe(S); Melville Ellis(C); ACK(L)

Very Good, Eddie (1975) Peter M. Ehrhardt(L); David Toser(C); Fred Voelpel(S)

Very Idea, The (1917) ACK(C)(L)

Very Minute, The (1917) Ernest Gros(S); Hickson(C); ACK(L)

Very Naked Boy, The (1916) ACK(L)

Very Rich Woman, A (1965) Audré(C); John Harvey(L); Oliver Smith(S)

Very Special Baby, A (1956) Howard Bay(S)(L); John Boxer(C)

Very Warm for May (1939) Vincente Minnelli(S); ACK(C)

Very Wise Virgin, A (1927) ACK(S)(L)

Via Dolorosa (1999) Rick Fisher(L); Ian MacNeil(S)(C)

Via Galactica (1972) Lloyd Burlingame(L); John Bury(S)(C)

Via Wireless (1908) Frederick W. Thompson(S)

Vickie (1942) Ernest Glover(S)

Victor/Victoria (1995) Jules Fisher(L); Willa Kim(C); Robin Wagner(S)

Victoria Regina (1935) Rex Whistler(S)(C)(L)

Victoria Regina (1936) DuWico(L); Rex Whistler(S)(C)(L)

Victoria Regina (1938) Rex Whistler(S)(C)(L)

Victory Belles (1943) Edward DeForrest(S)

Vienna Life (1901) Ernest Albert(S); D. Frank Dodge(S)

Vieux Carre (1977) Jane Greenwood(C); James Tilton(S)(L)

View from the Bridge, A (1997) David Gallo(S); Michael Krass(C); Kenneth Posner(L)

View from the Bridge, A (1955) Boris Aronson(S); Helene Pons(C); Lee Watson(L)

View from the Bridge, A (1983) Hugh Landwehr(S); Bill Walker(C); Ronald Wallace(L)

Vigil, The (1948) Nicholas Yellenti(S)(L); ACK(C)

Vik (1914) NONE

Vikings, The (1930) Thomas Wilfred(S)(C)

Village Green (1941) Raymond Sovey(S); ACK(C)

Village Lawyer, The (1908) NONE

Village Postmaster, The (1900) Homer Emens(S); Richard Francis(L)

Vincent Price in Diversions and Delights (1978) H. R. Poindexter(S)(L); Noel Taylor(C)

Vinegar Buyer, The (1903) Homer Emens(S); Gates and Morange(S)

Vinegar Tree, The (1930) Raymond Sovey(S); ACK(C)

Vintage '60 (1960) Raymond Aghayan(C); Ret Turner(C); Fred

Voelpel[S]

Violet (1944) Howard Bay[S]; Grace Houston[C]

Virgin Man, The (1927) Ack[S][L]

Virgin of Bethulia, The (1925) Watson Barratt[S]; Ack[L]

Virgin, The (1926) Ack[L]

Virginia (1937) Irene Sharaff[C]; Lee Simonson[S]

Virginia Runs Away (1923) Ack[L]

Virginian, The (1904) Ernest Albert[S]; H. L. Reid[S]

Virginius (1907) None

Virtue's Bed (1930) Ack[S][C][L]

Virtue? (1922) Ack[S][L]

Visit to a Small Planet, A (1957) A. H. Feder[L]; Oliver Smith[S]; Patricia Zipprodt[C]

Visit, The (1958) Castillo[C]; Paul Morrison[S]; Teo Otto[S][C]

Visit, The (1973) Ken Billington[L]; Edward Burbridge[S]; Carolyn Parker[C]

Visit, The (1992) Frank Krenz[C]; Thomas Lynch[S]; Roger Morgan[L]

Visitor, The (1944) Howard Bay[S]

Viva Madison Avenue (1960) William and Jean Eckart[S][L]; Frank Thompson[C]

Viva O'Brien (1941) John N. Booth, Jr.[C]; Clarke Robinson[S]

Vivat! Vivat Regina! (1972) Lloyd Burlingame[L]; Carl Toms[S][C]

Vivian's Papas (1903) None

Vogues of 1924 (1924) Watson Barratt[S]; Charles LeMaire[C]

Voice from the Midwest, The (1922) Ack[C]

Voice from the Minaret, The (1922) Joseph and Phil Harker[S]; Ack[L]

Voice in the Dark, A (1919) Henri Bendel[C]; Ack[L]

Voice of McConnell, The (1918) Ack[L]

Voice of the Turtle, The (1943) Stewart Chaney[S]; Bianca Stroock[C]

Voices (1972) Theoni V. Aldredge[C]; Jo Mielziner[S][L]

Voices in the Dark (1999) David Gallo[S]; Lauren Helpern[S]; Donald Holder[L]; David C. Woolard[C]

Volpone (1928) Lee Simonson[S][C]

Volpone (1930) Lee Simonson[S][C]; Ack[L]

Volpone (1947) Herbert Brodkin[L]; Emeline Clarke Roche[S]

Voltaire (1922) Robert Edmond Jones[S][C]; Ack[L]

Vortex, The (1925) Gladys E. Calthrop[S][C]

Votes For Women (1909) None

Wait a Minim! (1966) Heather MacDonald[C]; Frank Rembach[S][L]

Wait till We're Married (1921) Harry Collins[C]; Joseph Physioc[S]

Wait until Dark (1966) George Jenkins[S][L]; Ruth Morley[C]

Wait until Dark (1998) Brian MacDevitt[L]; Michael McGarty[S]; David C. Woolard[C]

Waiting for Godot (1956) Stanley Simmons[S][C]

Waiting for Godot (1957) Louis Kennel[S]; Stanley Simmons[C]

Waiting for Lefty (1935) Alexander Chertov[S]

Waiting in the Wings (1999) Ken Billington[L]; Alvin Colt[C]; Ray Klausen[S]

Wake of Jamie Foster, The (1982) Santo Loquasto[S]; Jennifer Tipton[L]; Jennifer von Mayrhauser[C]

Wake Up and Dream (1929) Paul Colin[S][C]; Marc Henri[S][C]; Laverdet[S][C]; Oliver Messel[S][C]; Miss Peacock[S][C]; Rex Whistler[S][C]; Norman Wilkinson[S][C]; Doris Zinkeisen[S][C]

Wake Up, Darling (1956) Ballou[S][L]; Guy Kent[C]

Wake Up, Jonathan (1921) Gates and Morange[S]

Waldies, The (1915) Ack[L]

Walk a Little Faster (1932) Boris Aronson[S]; Yetta Kiviette[C]

Walk Hard (1946) John Wenger[S][L]

Walk in the Woods, A (1988) Bill Clarke[S]; Ellen V. McCartney[C]; Richard Riddell[L]

Walk into My Parlor (1941) Paul Morrison[S][C][L]

Walk Offs, The (1918) Ack[L]

Walk Together Chillun (1936) Manuel Essman[S]

Walk with Music (1940) Watson Barratt[S]; Tom Lee[C]

Walking Gentleman (1942) A. H. Feder[L]; Harry Horner[S]

Walking Happy (1966) Robert Fletcher[C]; Robert Randolph[S][L]

Wall Street (1927) Cleon Throckmorton[S]; Ack[C]

Wall Street Girl, The (1912) Madame
Julie[C]; H. Robert Studio Law[S];
Cora MacGeachy[C]; ACK[C]

Wall Street Scene (1937) Edward
Fitzgerald[S]

Wall, The (1960) Howard Bay[S][L]; Noel
Taylor[C]

Wallflower (1944) Samuel Leve[S];
Bianca Stroock[C]

Walls of Jericho (1905) Joseph
Physioc[S]

Wally's Cafe (1981) Ken Billington[L];
Albert Wolsky[C]; Stuart Wurtzel[S]

Walrus and the Carpenter, The
(1941) Raymond Sovey[S]; ACK[C]

Waltz Dream, A (1908) F. Richards
Anderson[C]; Homer Emens[S]

Waltz in Goose Steps (1938) Norris
Houghton[S]; ACK[C]

Waltz of the Dogs (1928) Charles
Friedman[S]

Waltz of the Stork (1982) Bernard
Johnson[C]; Kert Lundell[S]; Shirley
Prendergast[L]

Waltz of the Toreadors, The (1957)
Ben Edwards[S][C][L]

Waltz of the Toreadors, The (1958)
Ben Edwards[S][C][L]

Waltz of the Toreadors, The (1973)
Joseph F. Bella[C]; Clarke Dunham[S];
Thomas Skelton[L]

Wanderer, The (1917) ACK[S][C][L]

Wandering Jew, The (1921) Kliegl
Brothers[L]; ACK[S][C]

Wandering Jew, The (1927) Frances
H. Ball[S]; T. J. Digby[L]; Ferris
Norris[C]; Herbert Norris[C]

Wang (1904) NONE

Wanted (1928) ACK[L]

War and Peace (1967) Gilbert V.
Hemsley, Jr.[L]; Nancy Potts[C]; James
Tilton[S]

War President (1944) Rose
Bogdanoff[S][C]; Jack Landau[L]

War Song, The (1928) Nicholas
Yellenti[S]

Ware Case, The (1915) H. Robert
Law[S]; Ed Sundquist[S]; ACK[L]

Warm Body, A (1967) Anna Hill
Johnstone[C]; Robert T. Williams[S][L]

Warm Peninsula, The (1959) Kenn
Barr[C]; Frederick Fox[S][L]

Warp (1973) Laura Crow[C]; Cookie
Gluck[C]; Robert Guerra[S]; Jane
Reisman[L]

Warrens of Virginia, The (1907)

Ernest Gros[S]

Warrior's Husband, The (1932)
Woodman Thompson[S][C]

Wars of the World (1914) Joseph
Elsner[L]; William Henry Matthews[C];
Arthur Voegtlin[S]; Madame Frances
Ziebarth[C]

Washington Heights (1931) ACK[S][C][L]

Washington Jitters (1938) Lawrence L.
Goldwasser[S]; ACK[C]

Washington's First Defeat (1907)
NONE

Wasp's Nest, The (1927) Sheldon K.
Viele[S]; ACK[C]

Wasp, The (1923) P. Dodd Ackerman[S];
Anna Scheer[C]; ACK[L]

Watch on the Rhine (1941) Jo
Mielziner[S][L]; Helene Pons[C]

Watch on the Rhine (1980) John
Jensen[S]; Bill Walker[C]; Ronald
Wallace[L]

Watch Your Neighbor (1918) Joseph
Physioc[S]; ACK[C][L]

Watch Your Step (1914) Helen
Dryden[S]; Lucile[C]; Robert
McQuinn[S]; ACK[C]

Watcher, The (1910) ACK[C]

Water Color/ Criss Crossing (1970)
Peter Harvey[S][C]; Richard Nelson[L]

Water Engine, The/ Mr. Happiness
(1978) John Lee Beatty[S]; Laura
Crow[C]; Dennis Parichy[L]

Watering Place, The (1969) Jeanne
Button[C]; Jules Fisher[L]; Robin
Wagner[S]

Waterloo (1899) Joseph Harker[S]

Waterloo Bridge (1930) Raymond
Sovey[S]; ACK[C][L]

Way Down East (1903) Frank
Platzer[S]; Theodore Reisig[S]

Way of the World, The (1901)
ACK[S][C]

Way of the World, The (1924) Joseph
Mullen[S][C]

Way of the World, The (1931)
Raymond Sovey[S][C][L]

Way Things Happen, The (1924)
Franklin Abbott[S]; O'Kane Conwell[C]

Wayward Saint, The (1955) Audré[C];
Frederick Fox[S][L]

Wayward Stork (1966) Will Steven
Armstrong[S]; Peter Hunt[L]; Ann
Roth[C]

We All Do (1927) Rose Clark[C];
Schaffner and Sweet Studio[S]

We Americans (1926) Nicholas

Yellenti[S]; ACK[C][L]

We Are No Longer Children (1932) Livingston Platt[S]; ACK[C]

We Are Seven (1913) NO PLAYBILL

We Bombed in New Haven (1968) John Gleason[L]; William Ritman[S]; Noel Taylor[C]

We Can't Be As Bad As All That (1910) Joseph[C]; Frank Platzer[S]

We Girls (1921) Sheldon K. Viele[S]; ACK[C]

We Have Always Lived in the Castle (1966) David Hays[S][L]; Noel Taylor[C]

We Interrupt this Program (1975) Robert Randolph[S]; Pearl Somner[C]; Marc B. Weiss[L]

We Moderns (1924) ACK[S][L]

We Never Learn (1928) Karle O. Amend[S]; ACK[C][L]

We've Got to Have Money (1923) Cleon Throckmorton[S]; ACK[C]

We, Comrades Three (1966) Gilbert V. Hemsley, Jr.[L]; Nancy Potts[C]; James Tilton[S]

We, the People (1933) Aline Bernstein[S]; ACK[C]

Weak Link, The (1940) Harry Horner[S]; ACK[C]

Weak Sisters (1925) Cleon Throckmorton[S]; ACK[L]

Weak Woman, A (1926) P. Dodd Ackerman[S]; ACK[C]

Weather Clear–Track Fast (1927) ACK[S][L]

Weather Hen, The (1900) ACK[S][C]

Weather Permitting (1935) Ed Sundquist[S]; ACK[C]

Weavers, The (1915) ACK[S][L]

Web, The (1932) Nicholas Yellenti[S]

Wedding Breakfast (1954) Edith Lutyens Bel Geddes[C]; William and Jean Eckart[S][L]

Wedding Day, The (1909) NO PLAYBILL

Wedding Trip, The (1911) H. Robert Law[S]; Cora MacGeachy[C]; James Surridge[S]

Wednesday's Child (1934) Tom Adrian Cracraft[S]; Mary Merrill[C]

Week-End (1929) Robert Edmond Jones[S]; ACK[C]

Weekend (1968) Theoni V. Aldredge[C]; Jean Rosenthal[L]; Oliver Smith[S]

Weep for the Virgins (1935) Boris Aronson[S]; ACK[C]

Weir, The (1999) Paule Constable[L];

Rae Smith[S][C]

Welcome Stranger (1920) ACK[L]

Welcome to Our City (Hobart) (1910) NONE

Welcome to the Club (1989) David Jenkins[S]; William Ivey Long[C]; Tharon Musser[L]

Welded (1924) Robert Edmond Jones[S][C][L]

Well of Romance, The (1930) Gates and Morange[S]; ACK[C][L]

Well of the Saints, The (1932) Power O'Malley[S]

Werewolf, The (1924) Watson Barratt[S]; ACK[C][L]

West Point Cadet, The (1904) NONE

West Side Story (1957) Jean Rosenthal[L]; Irene Sharaff[C]; Oliver Smith[S]

West Side Story (1960) Jean Rosenthal[L]; Irene Sharaff[C]; Oliver Smith[S]

West Side Story (1980) Jean Rosenthal[L]; Irene Sharaff[C]; Oliver Smith[S]

West Side Waltz, The (1981) Ben Edwards[S]; Jane Greenwood[C]; Thomas Skelton[L]

Western Waters (1937) Boris Aronson[S][C]

What a Life (1938) Cirker and Robbins[S]; ACK[C]

What Ails You? (1912) Ernest Gros[S]; Joseph Wilson[L]; ACK[C]

What Ann Brought Home (1927) ACK[L]

What Big Ears (1942) Horace Armistead[S]; Kenn Barr[C]

What D' You Call It/ According to Law/ etc. (1940) Edwin H. Vandernoot[S]; ACK[C]

What Did We Do Wrong? (1967) Jack Edwards[C]; Albert R. Johnson[S]; Leo B. Meyer[L]

What Do We Know? (1927) Bruck-Weiss[C]; Miriam Frazer[C]; Joseph Teichner[S]

What Every Woman Knows (1908) Unitt and Wickes[S]

What Every Woman Knows (1926) ACK[S][C][L]

What Every Woman Knows (1946) David Ffolkes[C]; Paul Morrison[S][L]

What Happened at 22 (1914) NONE

What Happened to Jones (1917) ACK[L]

What Happened to Mary (1913) P.
Dodd Ackerman Studio[S]

What Is Love? (1914) NONE

What It Means to a Woman (1914)
Callot Soeurs[C]; ACK[C]

What Makes Sammy Run? (1964)
Helen Pond[S][L]; Herbert Senn[S][L];
Noel Taylor[C]

What Never Dies (1926) Louis
Hartmann[L]; Joseph Wickes[S]; ACK[C]

What Price Glory? (1924) Woodman
Thompson[S]

What the Butler Saw (Parry and
Mouillot) (1906) ACK[C]

What the Doctor Ordered (1911) No
PLAYBILL

What the Doctor Ordered (1927)
ACK[C][L]

What the Public Wants (1922)
ACK[C][L]

What Would You Do? (1914) John L.
Arthur[S]; William Hawley[S]; Madame
Julie[C]

What's in a Name (1920) Frank
Detering[L]; Robert E. Locher[C];
James Reynolds[S][C]; Kay Turner[C]

What's the Big Idea (1926) P. Dodd
Ackerman[S]

What's the Matter with Susan?
(1903) Joseph Physioc[S]; ACK[C]

What's the Use? (1926) ACK[L]

What's Up (1943) Boris Aronson[S];
Grace Houston[C]

What's Wrong with this Picture?
(1994) Brian MacDevitt[L]; Derek
McLane[S]; Ann Roth[C]

What's Your Husband Doing?
(1917) ACK[L]

What's Your Wife Doing (1923) P.
Dodd Ackerman Studio[S]; ACK[C][L]

Whatever Goes Up (1935) G.
Bradford Ashworth[S]; ACK[C]

Whatever Possessed Her (1934)
Brymer[C]; Eugene Fitsch[S]

Wheel, The (1921) Wade Douglas[S];
ACK[C]

Wheelbarrow Closers (1976) Charles
Carmello, Jr. Jr.[S]; Leon Di Leone[L];
Jean Wallace[C]

Wheels within Wheels (1899) Mrs.
Robert Osborn[C]; Edward G. Unitt[S]

When Claudia Smiles (1914) H.
Robert Law[S]; ACK[C]

When Crummles Played (1928)
ACK[L]

When Dreams Come True (1913)

Gates and Morange[S]; ACK[C]

When in Rome (1934) Charles
Chrisdie[C]; Nicholas Yellenti[S]

When Johnny Comes Marching
Home (1902) Ernest Albert[S]; D.
Frank Dodge[S]; Homer Emens[S]; Mrs.
Caroline Siedle[C]

When Johnny Comes Marching
Home (1917) Dodge and Castle[S];
Madame Freisinger[C]; H. Robert
Law[S]

When Knighthood Was in Flower
(1901) Ernest Albert[S]; Frank E.
Gates[S]; Mrs. Charles Hone[C];
Harper Pennington[C]

When Knights Were Bold (1907)
Ernest Gros[S]

When Ladies Meet (1932) Eugene
Fitsch[S]; Mrs. Seeley Neilson[C];
Livingston Platt[L]

When Sweet Sixteen (1911) H. Robert
Law[S]; T. Bernard McDonald[S];
ACK[C]

When the Bough Breaks (1932)
Alexander Wyckoff[S]; ACK[C]

When the Young Vine Blooms
(1915) Ruth Carnegie[C]; H. P. Scenic
Studio Knight[S]

When Was In Flower (1901) Edward
Morange[S]

When We Are Married (1939) Karle
O. Amend[S]; ACK[C]

When We Are Young (1920) ACK[L]

When We Dead Awake (1905) No
PLAYBILL

When We Were Twenty-One (1900)
NONE

When We Were Twenty-One (1905)
NONE

When We Were Twenty-One (1906)
NONE

When You Smile (1925)
Pogany-Teichner Studios[S]; ACK[C][L]

Where Do We Go from Here? (1938)
Hugh Willoughby[S]

Where Ignorance Is Bliss (1913)
NONE

Where Poppies Bloom (1918) Joseph
Physioc[S]; ACK[L]

Where Stars Walk (1948) Hilton
Edwards[L]; Molly MacEwan[S]; Helene
Pons[C]

Where There's A Will (1910) No
PLAYBILL

Where There's a Will (1939) Donna
Gabriel[C]; Laura Gordon[C]; A. A.

Ostrander[S]

Where's Charley (1948) David Ffolkes[S][C]

Where's Charley (1951) David Ffolkes[S][C]

Where's Charley? (1974) Arthur Boccia[C]; Marjorie Bradley Kellogg[S]; Thomas Skelton[L]

Where's Daddy (1966) Ben Edwards[S][L]; Jane Greenwood[C]

Where's Your Husband (1927) ACK[S][L]

Where's Your Wife? (1919) ACK[L]

While Parents Sleep (1934) Robert Barnhart[S]; ACK[C]

While the Sun Shines (1944) Edward Gilbert[S]

Whip, The (1912) NONE

Whirl of New York, The (1921) Watson Barratt[S]; ACK[C]

Whirl of Society (1912) Callot Soeurs[C]; Lucile[C]; Paul Poiret[C]; ACK[S][C]

Whirl of the World, The (1914) Melville Ellis[C]

Whirl-I-Gig (1899) NONE

Whirlpool (1929) ACK[S][C][L]

Whirlwind, The (1910) ACK[C]

Whirlwind, The (1911) NONE

Whirlwind, The (1919) ACK[S][L]

Whispering Friends (1928) ACK[C][L]

Whispering Gallery, The (1929) ACK[C][L]

Whispering Wires (1922) ACK[L]

Whistler's Grandmother (1952) Leo Kerz[S][L]

Whistling in the Dark (1932) Donald Oenslager[S]; ACK[C]

White Cargo (1923) George W. Howe[S]; Mabel E. Johnston[C]

White Cargo (1926) George W. Howe[S]

White Cat, The (1905) F. Richards Anderson[C]; Mathias Armbruster[S]; Robert Caney[S]; Comelli[C]; Henry Emden[S]; R. McCleery[S]; Bruce Smith[S]

White Collars (1925) ACK[C][L]

White Desert (1923) Raymond Sovey[S]; Joseph Wilson[L]

White Eagle (1927) James Reynolds[S]

White Feather, The (1915) H. Robert Law[S]; ACK[L]

White Flame (1929) Vasser Elam[L]; Neppel and Brousseau[S]; ACK[C]

White Gold (1925) Elizabeth Stuart Close[C]; Alexander Wyckoff[S]; ACK[L]

White Hen, The (1907) Ernest Albert[S]; Arthur Voegtlin[S]

White Horse Inn (1936) Irene Sharaff[C]; Ernest Stern[S]

White House, The (1964) Jules Fisher[L]; Ed Wittstein[S][C]

White Liars & Black Comedy (1993) John Lee Beatty[S]; Jess Goldstein[C]; Craig Miller[L]

White Lights (1927) Ward and Harvey Studios[S]; ACK[L]

White Lilacs (1928) Georges Barbier[C]; Ernest Schraps[C]; Rollo Wayne[S]; ACK[L]

White Magic (1912) NONE

White Man (1936) Nat Karson[S][C]

White Oaks (1938) Norris Houghton[S]

White Peacock, The (1921) Lucile[C]; Clifford F. Pember[S]; Olga Petrova[S]

White Sister, The (1909) Gates and Morange[S]

White Steed, The (1939) Watson Barratt[S]; ACK[C]

White Villa, The (1921) Livingston Platt[S]

White Wings (1926) Aline Bernstein[C]; Woodman Thompson[S]

White-headed Boy, The (1921) NONE

Whitewashed (1924) ACK[L]

Whitewashing of Julia, The (1903) NONE

Who Cares? (1930) Cirker and Robbins[S]; ACK[C]

Who Did It (1919) ACK[L]

Who Goes There? (1905) NONE

Who Was That Lady I Saw You With? (1958) Ruth Morley[C]; Rouben Ter-Arutunian[S]

Who's Afraid of Virginia Woolf? (1962) William Ritman[S][C][L]

Who's Afraid of Virginia Woolf? (1976) Jane Greenwood[C]; William Ritman[S][L]

Who's Life Is It Anyway? (1979) Tharon Musser[L]; Pearl Somner[C]; Alan Tagg[S]

Who's Life Is It Anyway? (1980) Tharon Musser[L]; Pearl Somner[C]; Alan Tagg[S]

Who's Tommy, The (1993) John Arnone[S]; Chris Parry[L]; David C. Woolard[C]

Who's Who (1913) NONE

Who's Who (1938) Billy Livingston[C]; Mercedes[S]

Who's Who in Hell (1974) John

Gleason[L]; Nancy Potts[C]; Douglas W. Schmidt[S]

Whodunnit (1982) Martin Aronstein[L]; Andrew Jackness[S]; Patricia Zipprodt[C]

Whole Town's Talking, The (1923) ACK[C][L]

Whole World Over, The (1947) Ralph Alswang[S][C]

Whoop-Dee-Doo (1903) Mrs. Caroline Siedle[C]; John H. Young[S]

Whoop-Up (1958) Anna Hill Johnstone[C]; Jo Mielziner[S][L]

Whoopee (1928) John W. Harkrider[C]; Joseph Urban[S]; ACK[L]

Whoopee (1979) John Lee Beatty[S]; Peter M. Ehrhardt[L]; David Toser[C]

Whoopi Goldberg (1984) Jennifer Tipton[L]; Tony Walton[S][C]

Why Marry? (1917) Arthur Ebbetts[L]; Lucile[C]; Roi Cooper Megrue[L]; Joseph Physioc Studio[S]

Why Marry? (1918) Arthur Ebbetts[L]; Lucile[C]; Roi Cooper Megrue[L]; Joseph Physioc Studio[S]

Why Men Leave Home (1922) ACK[C][L]

Why Not? (1922) Woodman Thompson[S]; ACK[C][L]

Why Smith Left Home (1899) John Cunningham[S]; Henry E. Hoyt[S]

Wicked Age, The (1927) ACK[S][C][L]

Widow by Proxy (1913) Gates and Morange[S]

Widow in Green, A (1931) Cleon Throckmorton[S]; ACK[C]

Widow Jones, The (1901) St. John Lewis[S]

Widow's Might, The (1909) Oliver P. Bernard[S]; ACK[C][L]

Widower's Houses (1907) NONE

Wiener Blut (Vienna Life) (1964) Hill Rheis-Gromes[C]; Thomas Skelton[L]; Ferry Windberger[S]

Wife Decides, The (1911) NONE

Wife Hunters, The (1911) John H. Young[S]

Wife Insurance (1934) William H. Mensching[S]; ACK[C]

Wife without a Smile, A (1904) Emens and Unitt[S]

Wild and Wonderful (1972) Stephen Hendrickson[S]; Neil Peter Jampolis[L]; Frank Thompson[C]

Wild Birds (1925) Frank Carrington[L]; Joseph Mullen[S]

Wild Duck, The (1918) Robert Edmond Jones[S]

Wild Duck, The (1925) Jo Mielziner[S][L]

Wild Duck, The (1938) Harry L. Abbott[S]; Jo Mielziner[C]; Ed Sundquist[S]

Wild Duck, The (1967) Gilbert V. Hemsley, Jr.[L]; Nancy Potts[C]; James Tilton[S]

Wild Honey (1986) Martin Aronstein[L]; Deirdre Clancy[C]; John Gunter[S]

Wild Man of Borneo, The (1927) Booth-Willoughby[C]; Clemons[C]; Raymond Sovey[S]; ACK[L]

Wild Oats Lane (1922) ACK[S][L]

Wild Party, The (2000) Peggy Eisenhauer[L]; Jules Fisher[L]; Toni-Leslie James[C]; Robin Wagner[S]

Wild Rose, The (1902) D. Frank Dodge[S]; ACK[C][L]

Wild Rose, The (1926) Mark Mooring[C]; Joseph Urban[S]

Wild Waves (1932) Raymond Sovey[S][C][L]

Wild Westcotts, The (1923) ACK[S][L]

Wildcat (1960) Alvin Colt[C]; Charles Elson[L]; Peter Larkin[S]

Wilder, Wilder, Wilder (1993) Fiona Davis[C]; Miguel Lopez-Castillo[S]; Dede Pochos[C]; Steven Rust[L]

Wilderness, The (1901) Edward G. Unitt[S]

Wildfire (1908) T. Bernard McDonald[S]

Wildflower (1923) Gates and Morange[S]; Charles LeMaire[C]

Will Rogers Follies (1991) Jules Fisher[L]; Willa Kim[C]; Tony Walton[S]

Will Shakespeare (1923) Norman Bel Geddes[S][C]; ACK[L]

Will Success Spoil Rock Hunter? (1955) Peggy Clark[L]; Oliver Smith[S][C]

Will, The (1913) Unitt and Wickes[S]

Willow and I, The (1942) Lemuel Ayers[S]; Aline Bernstein[C]; Girvan Higginson[S][L]

Willow Tree, The (1917) Benrimo[S][C]

Wilson in the Promise Land (1970) Eugene Lee[S]; John Lehmeyer[C]; Roger Morgan[L]

Wind and the Rain, The (1934) Selma Alexander[C]; Philip Gelb[S]; ACK[L]

Wind in the Willows (1985) Sam Kirkpatrick[S]; Craig Miller[L]; Freddy Wittop[C]

Wind is Ninety, The (1945) John Davis[L]; Frederick Fox[S]; Natalie Barth Walker[C]

Window Panes (1927) P. Dodd Ackerman[S]

Window Shopping (1938) Tom Adrian Cracraft[S]; Ack[C]

Windows (1923) Carolyn Hancock[S]; Ack[C]

Wine of Choice (1938) Lee Simonson[S]; Ack[C]

Wine, Women and Song (1942) Frederick Fox[S]; Ack[L]

Winesburg, Ohio (1958) Dorothy Jeakins[C]; Jean Rosenthal[L]; Oliver Smith[S]

Winged Victory (1943) A. H. Feder[L]; Harry Horner[S]; Howard Shoup[C]

Wingless Victory, The (1936) Jo Mielziner[S][C][L]

Wings (1979) Jeanne Button[C]; Andrew Jackness[S]; Tom Schraeder[L]

Wings over Europe (1928) Raymond Sovey[S]

Winner, The (1954) Lester Polakov[S]; Ack[C]

Winslow Boy, The (1947) Michael Wright[S]; Ack[C][L]

Winsome Widow, A (1912) Ack[C]

Winsome Winnie (1903) None

Winter Bound (1929) Eugene Fitsch[S]

Winter Garden (1911) Ernest Albert[S]; Castle and Harvey[S]; Emens and Unitt[S]; Cora MacGeachy[C]; William Henry Matthews[C]; Arthur Voegtlin[S]

Winter Soldiers (1942) H. A. Condell[S]; Hans Sondheimer[L]; Ack[C]

Winter's Tale, The (1899) None

Winter's Tale, The (1904) Ernest Albert[S]; Castle and Harvey[S]; Homer Emens[S]; Edward G. Unitt[S]

Winter's Tale, The (1910) E. Hamilton Bell[S][C]; Meixner[S]

Winter's Tale, The (1946) Stewart Chaney[S][C]

Winterfeast, The (1908) Unitt and Wickes[S]

Winterset (1935) Jo Mielziner[S][L]; Ack[C]

Wise Child (1972) Jane Greenwood[C]; Neil Peter Jampolis[L]; Peter Larkin[S]

Wise Tomorrow (1937) Watson Barratt[S]; Ack[C]

Wise-crackers, The (1925) Cleon Throckmorton[S]; Ack[L]

Wiser They Are, The (1931) Raymond Sovey[S]

Wish Me Mazel-Tov (1980) Adina Reich[S][C]

Wish You Were Here (1952) Robert Mackintosh[C]; Jo Mielziner[S][L]

Wisteria Trees, The (1950) Lucinda Ballard[C]; Jo Mielziner[S][L]

Witch, The (1910) E. Hamilton Bell[S][C]

Witch, The (1926) Livingston Platt[S]

Witching Hour, The (1907) None

With a Silk Thread (1950) Watson Barratt[S][C][L]

With Privileges (1930) Lou Wertheim[S]; Ack[C]

Within Four Walls (1923) Joseph Physioc[S]; Ack[C][L]

Within the Gates (1934) James Reynolds[S][C]

Within the Law (1912) H. Robert Law[S]; Ack[C]

Within the Law (1928) Rollo Wayne[S]; Ack[L]

Without Love (1942) Robert Edmond Jones[S][C][L]

Without Warning (1937) A. H. Feder[L]; Cleon Throckmorton[S]; Ack[C]

Witness for the Defense, The (1911) None

Witness for the Prosecution (1954) Kathryn B. Miller[C]; Raymond Sovey[S][C][L]

Wives of Henry VIII, The (1931) Helene Pons[C]; Ack[L]

Wives of Henry VIII, The (1932) Helene Pons[C]; Ack[L]

Wiz, The (1975) Geoffrey Holder[C]; Tom John[S]; Tharon Musser[L]

Wiz, The (1984) Geoffrey Holder[C]; Paul Sullivan[L]; Peter Wolf[S]

Wizard of Oz, The (1903) Walter W. Burridge[S]; W. W. Denslow[C]; Frederick Gibson[S]; Kliegl Brothers[L]; Mrs. Caroline Siedle[C]; John H. Young[S]

Wizard of Oz, The (1997) Michael Anania[S]; Gregg Barnes[C]; Timothy Hunter[L]

Wizard of Oz, The (1998) Michael Anania[S]; Gregg Barnes[C]; Timothy Hunter[L]

Wizard of Oz, The (1999) Michael Anania[S]; Gregg Barnes[C]; Steve Cochrane[L]

Wolf, The (1908) H. Robert Law[S]

Wolves (1932) Robert Van Rosen[S];

ACK[C]

Woman and Wine (1900) Will R. Barnes[C]; D. Frank Dodge[S]; Frank Platzer[S]; John H. Young[S]

Woman Bites Dog (1946) Howard Bay[S]; Mary Grant[C]

Woman Brown, The (1939) Raymond Sovey[S][C][L]

Woman Denied, A (1931) Cirker and Robbins[S]; Margaret Pemberton[C]; James Reynolds[C]

Woman Disputed, The (1926) P. Dodd Ackerman[S]; ACK[C][L]

Woman in Room 13, The (1919) Henri Bendel[C]; ACK[L]

Woman in the Case, The (1905) NONE

Woman Is My Idea (1968) Lloyd Burlingame[S][C][L]

Woman Killed with Kindness, A (1914) ACK[S]

Woman of Bronze, The (1920) ACK[S][C][L]

Woman of Bronze, The (1927) ACK[S][C][L]

Woman of Destiny, A (1936) Cleon Throckmorton[S]

Woman of Impulse, A (1909) P. Dodd Ackerman[S]; Gates and Morange[S]; ACK[C]

Woman of Independent Means, A (1984) Martin Aronstein[L]; Roy Christopher[S]; Garland Kiddle[C]

Woman of It, The (1913) NONE

Woman of No Importance, A (1916) ACK[S][L]

Woman of the Soil, A (1935) Nicholas Yellenti[S]; ACK[C]

Woman of the Year (1981) Theoni V. Aldredge[C]; Marilyn Rennagel[L]; Tony Walton[S]

Woman on the Index, The (1918) Henri Bendel[C]; ACK[S][L]

Woman on the Jury, The (1923) ACK[L]

Woman Who Laughed, The (1922) ACK[L]

Woman's a Fool to Be Clever, A (1938) Donald Oenslager[S]

Woman's Pity, A (1905) NO PLAYBILL

Woman's Way, A (1909) H. Robert Law[S]

Woman, The (1911) Ernest Gros[S]

Woman-Haters, The (1912) Walter W. Burridge[S]; Dodge and Castle[S]; Madame Frances[C]

Women Go on Forever (1927) ACK[L]

Women Have Their Way/ The Open Door (1930) Aline Bernstein[S][C]

Women of Twilight (1952) Mary Purvis[S]; ACK[C]

Women, The (1936) Al Alloy[L]; John Hambleton[C]; Jo Mielziner[S][L]

Women, The (1973) John Gleason[L]; Ann Roth[C]; Oliver Smith[S]

Wonder Bar, The (1931) Watson Barratt[S]; Yetta Kiviette[C]; Charles LeMaire[C]

Wonder Boy (1931) Kurzman[C]; Fania Mindell[C]; Raymond Sovey[S]; ACK[L]

Wonderful Journey (1946) Raymond Sovey[S]; Bianca Stroock[C]

Wonderful Night, A (1929) Watson Barratt[S]; Herbert Moore[S]; Orry-Kelly[C]; Ernest Schraps[C]; ACK[L]

Wonderful Tennessee (1993) Mick Hughes[L]; Joe Vaněk[S][L]

Wonderful Thing, The (1920) Mrs. Lillian Trimble Bradley[S]; ACK[C][L]

Wonderful Town (1953) Peggy Clark[L]; Raoul Pène Du Bois[S][C]

Wonderful Town (1994) Michael Anania[S]; Gail Baldoni[C]; Jeff Davis[L]

Wonderful Visit, The (1924) David S. Gaither[S]; ACK[C]

Wonderland (1905) Edward G. Unitt[S]; John H. Young[S]

Wooden Dish, The (1955) John Boyt[C]; Donald Oenslager[S][L]

Wooden Kimono (1926) DuWico[L]; ACK[S][C]

Wooden Slipper, The (1934) Raymond Sovey[S]; Bianca Stroock[C]

Wooden Soldier, The (1931) Karle O. Amend Studio[S]; ACK[C]

Woodland (1904) Walter W. Burridge[S]; Archie Gunn[C]; Joseph Wilson[L]

Woof, Woof (1929) Mabel E. Johnston[C]; Clarke Robinson[S]

Wooing of Eve, The (1917) Clifford F. Pember[S]; ACK[L]

Wookey, The (1941) Jo Mielziner[S][L]; Ernest Schraps[C]

Words and Music (1917) ACK[L]

Words and Music (1974) Robert Randolph[S][C]; Marc B. Weiss[L]

Work Is for Horses (1937) Karle O. Amend Studio[S]; Frederica Bond[C]

Working (1978) Ken Billington[L]; David Mitchell[S]; Marjorie Slaiman[C]

World According to Me, The (1986) Neil Peter Jampolis[S][L]

Barratt[S]; Hallye Clogg[C]

Yesterday's Orchids (1934) P. Dodd Ackerman[S]; ACK[C]

Yip Yip Yaphank (1918) ACK[C][L]

Yokel Boy (1939) Frances Feist[C]; Walter Jagemann[S]; Veronica[C]

York State Folks (1905) NONE

Yosemite (1914) Joseph Urban[L]

Yoshe Kalb (1933) Alexander Chertov[S]

You and I (1923) Raymond Sovey[S]; ACK[C]

You Can Never Tell (1986) Thomas Lynch[S]; Richard Nelson[L]; Martin Pakledinaz[C]

You Can't Take It with You (1936) John Hambleton[C]; Donald Oenslager[S]; ACK[L]

You Can't Take It with You (1965) Nancy Potts[C]; James Tilton[S][L]

You Can't Take It with You (1967) Gilbert V. Hemsley, Jr.[L]; Nancy Potts[C]; James Tilton[S]

You Can't Take It with You (1983) Nancy Potts[C]; James Tilton[S][L]

You Can't Win (1926) ACK[L]

You Know I Can't Hear You When the Water's Running (1967) Theoni V. Aldredge[C]; Jules Fisher[L]; Ed Wittstein[S]

You Never Can Tell (1905) NONE

You Never Can Tell (1915) Charles E. Boss[S]; H. A. Vincent[S]; ACK[C][L]

You Never Can Tell (1948) Stewart Chaney[S][C]; ACK[L]

You Never Know (1938) Watson Barratt[S]; Albert R. Johnson[S]

You Said It (1931) Yetta Kiviette[C]; Donald Oenslager[S]

You Touched Me (1945) Motley[S][C]; ACK[L]

You'll See the Stars (1942) DuWico[L]; Perry Watkins[S]

You're a Good Man, Charlie Brown (1971) Jules Fisher[L]; Alan Kimmel[S][C]

You're a Good Man, Charlie Brown (1999) David Gallo[S]; Michael Krass[C]; Kenneth Posner[L]

You're in Love (1917) ACK[C][L]

Young Abe Lincoln (1961) Fred Voelpel[S][C][L]

Young Alexander (1929) Agnes Clarke[C]; Jo Mielziner[S][L]

Young America (1915) ACK[C][L]

Young and Beautiful, The (1955) Eldon Elder[S]; A. H. Feder[L];

Motley[C]

Young and the Fair, The (1948) Eleanor Goldsmith[C]; Paul Morrison[S][L]

Young Blood (1925) Clarke Robinson[S]

Young Couple Wanted (1940) Donald Oenslager[S]

Young Go First, The (1935) Mordecai Gorelik[S]; ACK[C]

Young Idea, The (1932) ACK[C][L]

Young Love (1928) Watson Barratt[S]; ACK[C]

Young Madame Conti (1937) Ernest Stern[S]

Young Man from Atlanta, The (1997) James F. Ingalls[L]; Thomas Lynch[S]; David C. Woolard[C]

Young Man's Fancy, A (1919) William Henry Matthews[C]; Joseph Urban[S]; ACK[L]

Young Man's Fancy, A (1947) Ralph Alswang[S][L]; Lou Eisele[C]

Young Mr. Disraeli (1937) David Ffolkes[S][C]

Young Sinners (1929) Rollo Wayne[S]; ACK[C]

Young Sinners (1931) Rollo Wayne[S]; ACK[C][L]

Young Sinners (1933) Rollo Wayne[S]; ACK[L]

Young Turk, The (1910) NONE

Young Visitors, The (1920) ACK[L]

Young Wife, A (1899) Joseph L. Menchen, Jr.[L]; ACK[C]

Young Wisdom (1914) NONE

Young Woodley (1925) Gladys E. Calthrop[S][C]

Younger Generation, The (1913) Ernest Albert[S]; Elizabeth Axtman[C]

Younger Mrs. Parling, The (1904) NONE

Youngest, The (1924) Livingston Platt[S]; ACK[C]

Your Arms Too Short to Box with God (1976) Gilbert V. Hemsley, Jr.[L]; William Schroder[S][C]

Your Arms Too Short to Box with God (1980) William Schroder[S][C]; Richard Winkler[L]

Your Arms Too Short to Box with God (1982) William Schroder[S][C]; Richard Winkler[L]

Your Humble Servant (1910) E. Hamilton Bell[S][C]

Your Loving Son (1941) Raymond Sovey[S]

Your Uncle Dudley (1929) Gates and Morange[S]; Anthony Greshoff[L]; Evelyn McHorter[C]

Your Woman and Mine (1922) ACK[L]

Yours Is My Heart (1946) H. A. Condell[S][C]; Milton Lowe[L]

Yours Truly (1927) Mabel E. Johnston[C]; Joseph Urban[S]

Yours Truly (1928) Mabel E. Johnston[C]; Joseph Urban[S]

Yours, A. Lincoln (1942) ACK[S][L]

Youth (1911) Avril[C]; Rollo Peters[S]; Adams T. Rice[L]

Youth (1920) Rollo Peters[S]; Adams T. Rice[L]

Yr. Obedient Husband (1938) Jo Mielziner[S][C][L]

Yvette (1904) Ernest Gros[S]

Yvette (1916) ACK[S][C][L]

Zalmen or the Madness of God (1976) Richard Nelson[L]; William Ritman[S]; Marjorie Slaiman[C]

Zander the Great (1923) ACK[L]

Zaza (1900) Ernest Gros[S]

Zaza (1904) Wilfred Buckland[S]; Louis Hartmann[L]; Madame Hermann[C]

Zebra, The (1911) Homer Emens[S]

Zelda (1969) Theoni V. Aldredge[C]; Will Steven Armstrong[S][L]

Zeno (1923) ACK[L]

Zeppelin (1929) Cirker and Robbins[S]; ACK[C]

Ziegfeld Follies (1957) Raoul Pène Du Bois[S][C]; Paul Morrison[L]

Ziegfeld Follies of 1907 (1907) Madame Freisinger[C]; Peter V. Griffin[S]; William Henry Matthews[C]; T. Bernard McDonald[S]; John H. Young[S]

Ziegfeld Follies of 1908 (1908) F. Richards Anderson[C]; Alfredo Edel[C]; Madame Freisinger[C]; Anthony Greshoff[L]; William Henry Matthews[C]; T. Bernard McDonald[S]; John H. Young[S]

Ziegfeld Follies of 1909 (1909) Hugo Baruch[C]; Alfredo Edel[C]; William Henry Matthews[C]; ACK[S]

Ziegfeld Follies of 1910 (1910) Hugo Baruch[C]; Alfredo Edel[C]; William Henry Matthews[C]; ACK[S]

Ziegfeld Follies of 1911 (1911) Ernest Albert[S]; Klaw & Erlanger[C]; William Henry Matthews[C]; Tryon[C]; Unitt and Wickes[S]

Ziegfeld Follies of 1912 (1912) Ernest Albert[S]; Callot Soeurs[C]; Anthony Greshoff[L]; ACK[C]

Ziegfeld Follies of 1913 (1913) Ernest Albert[S]; Frank Detering[L]; Gates and Morange[S]; John H. Young[S]; ACK[C]

Ziegfeld Follies of 1914 (1914) Ernest Albert[S]; Homer Emens[S]; Cora MacGeachy[C]; Unitt and Wickes[S]; John H. Young[S]

Ziegfeld Follies: 1915 (1915) Lucile[C]; Cora MacGeachy[C]; Joseph Urban[S]; ACK[L]

Ziegfeld Follies: 1916 (1916) Vyvian Donner[C]; Lucile[C]; Cora MacGeachy[C]; Alice O'Neil[C]; Joseph Urban[S]; ACK[L]

Ziegfeld Follies: 1917 (1917) Ben Beerwald[L]; Callot Soeurs[C]; Marie Cooke[C]; Lucile[C]; Cora MacGeachy[C]; Alice O'Neil[C]; Joseph Urban[S]

Ziegfeld Follies: 1918 (1918) Lucile[C]; Joseph Urban[S]; ACK[C][L]

Ziegfeld Follies: 1920 (1920) Lucile[C]; Alice O'Neil[C]; Joseph Urban[S]

Ziegfeld Follies: 1921 (1921) Henri Bendel[C]; Alfred Nelson[C]; James Reynolds[S][C]; Joseph Urban[S]

Ziegfeld Follies: 1922 (1922) Ada B. Fields[C]; Charles LeMaire[C]; Cora MacGeachy[C]; Evelyn McHorter[C]; Alice O'Neil[C]; James Reynolds[S]; Herman Rosse[S]; Joseph Urban[S]

Ziegfeld Follies: 1923 (1923) Madame Frances[C]; Evelyn McHorter[C]; Alice O'Neil[C]; James Reynolds[C]; Joseph Urban[S]

Ziegfeld Follies: 1924 (1924) Ben Ali Haggin[C]; Charles LeMaire[C]; Evelyn McHorter[C]; Alice O'Neil[C]; James Reynolds[C]; Joseph Urban[S]; John Wenger[S]

Ziegfeld Follies: 1927 (1927) John W. Harkrider[C]; Lucile[C]; Cora MacGeachy[C]; Joseph Urban[S]

Ziegfeld Follies: 1931 (1931) John W. Harkrider[C]; Joseph Urban[S]

Ziegfeld Follies: 1934 (1934) Watson Barratt[S]; Raoul Pène Du Bois[C]; Albert R. Johnson[S]; Yetta Kiviette[C]; Charles LeMaire[C]; Billy Livingston[C]; Russell Patterson[C]

Ziegfeld Follies: 1936 (1936) Raoul Pène Du Bois[C]; Vincente Minnelli[S][C]

Ziegfeld Follies: 1936-1937 (1936)

Vincente Minnelli[S][C]

Ziegfeld Follies: 1943 (1943) Watson Barratt[S]; Miles White[C]; ACK[L]

Ziegfeld Girls: 1920 (1920) Marie Cooke[C]; Alice O'Neil[C]; ACK[S][L]

Ziegfeld Midnight Follies (1921) Howard Greer[C]; Anthony Greshoff[L]; Cora MacGeachy[C]; Joseph Urban[S]

Ziegfeld Midnight Frolic (1915) Cora MacGeachy[C]; Joseph Urban[S]; ACK[L]

Ziegfeld Midnight Frolic (1919) Marie Cooke[C]; Alice O'Neil[C]; Joseph Urban[S]; ACK[L]

Ziegfeld's 9 O'clock Frolic (1921) Lucile[C]; Alice O'Neil[C]; Joseph Urban[S]

Ziegfeld's Midnight Frolics (1915) Cora MacGeachy[C]

Zira (1905) Walter B. Spong[S]

Zizi (1964) Yves Saint Laurent[C]; Thomas Skelton[L]

Zombie (1932) Anthony W. Street[S]; ACK[C]

Zoot Suit (1979) Dawn Chiang[L]; Peter J. Hall[C]; Thomas A. Walsh[S]

Zorba (1968) Boris Aronson[S]; Richard Pilbrow[L]; Patricia Zipprodt[C]

Zorba (1983) David Chapman[S]; Hal George[C]; Marc B. Weiss[L]

Zoya's Apartment (1990) Mary Jo Dondlinger[L]; Cynthia Doty[C]; Tatiana Gleboya[C]; James Morgan [active 1989-][S]; Josef Sumbatsivily[S]

Zulu and the Zayda, The (1965) William and Jean Eckart[S][L]; Frank Thompson[C]

About the Author

BOBBI OWEN is Professor of Dramatic Art at The University of North Carolina at Chapel Hill, and has published widely on drama and theater.